G. K. CHESTERTON

G. K. CHESTERTON

A BIOGRAPHY

IAN KER

OXFORD
UNIVERSITY PRESS

OXFORD
UNIVERSITY PRESS

Great Clarendon Street, Oxford OX2 6DP

Oxford University Press is a department of the University of Oxford.
It furthers the University's objective of excellence in research, scholarship,
and education by publishing worldwide in

Oxford New York

Auckland Cape Town Dar es Salaam Hong Kong Karachi
Kuala Lumpur Madrid Melbourne Mexico City Nairobi
New Delhi Shanghai Taipei Toronto

With offices in

Argentina Austria Brazil Chile Czech Republic France Greece
Guatemala Hungary Italy Japan Poland Portugal Singapore
South Korea Switzerland Thailand Turkey Ukraine Vietnam

Oxford is a registered trade mark of Oxford University Press
in the UK and in certain other countries

Published in the United States
by Oxford University Press Inc., New York

British Library Cataloguing in Publication Data
Data available

Library of Congress Cataloging in Publication Data
Library of Congress Control Number: 2010940318

Typeset by SPI Publisher Services, Pondicherry, India
Printed in Great Britain
on acid-free paper by
MPG Biddles, King's Lynn and Bodmin

ISBN 978-0-19-960128-8

3 5 7 9 10 8 6 4

In Memory of S. M. K.

PREFACE

When I began work on my book *The Catholic Revival in English Literature 1845–1961* (2003), which contains a chapter on G. K. Chesterton, I knew, of course, some of Chesterton's writings—*Orthodoxy*, *The Everlasting Man*, *The Man who was Thursday*, the Father Brown stories, and a handful of the better-known poems. But, as I read more extensively, I made several discoveries. In the first place, I realized that Chesterton was a much bigger figure than either I or the academic world that I knew was aware. Then I was struck with the parallel or parallels with John Henry Newman, a writer and thinker I had spent many years studying, and whose influence I thought I could clearly detect. Both Newman and Chesterton were converts to and apologists for Catholicism; both were pre-eminently controversialists. Chesterton was a professional journalist, but Newman edited two periodicals in his time: one of his best works from a literary point of view was his *The Tamworth Reading Room*, a collection of seven lengthy commissioned letters to *The Times*, a slim volume of fifty pages and one of his two satirical masterpieces.[1] Then again, both writers' main output lay in non-fiction prose, but both published fiction and verse, including two innovative novels and two long poems that were immensely popular in their time and that still resonate with religious believers, although neither the novels nor the poems could be called, except by uncritical enthusiasts, major or great works. Thus, just as Newman's *Loss and Gain* introduced a new kind of introspective self-questioning into the English novel, while Chesterton's nightmarish fantasy *The Man who was Thursday* anticipated the sinister world of Kafka; so, too, Newman's *The Dream of Gerontius* was the second most widely read work on death and the future life after Tennyson's

---

[1] Newman once even described himself as 'a Christian journalist'. See *The Letters and Diaries of John Henry Newman*, xviii, ed. Charles Stephen Dessain (London: Nelson, 1968), 580.

In Memoriam[2] in an age obsessed with death, as well as inspiring Elgar's great oratorio, while Chesterton's immensely popular *The Ballad of the White Horse* inspired soldiers in the trenches during the First World War, as well the famously terse leader in *The Times* during the Second World War that quoted two verses from it after the disastrous fall of Crete. But, whereas Newman is recognized as a major literary figure to be ranked with his contemporaries, Carlyle, Ruskin, and Arnold, Chesterton, naturally enough—that is, if he is principally to be remembered as the author of the *The Man who was Thursday*, *The Napoleon of Notting Hill*, *The Ballad of the White Horse*, 'Lepanto', and the Father Brown stories—is dismissed as a minor writer. However, it became increasingly clear to me as I read through Chesterton's writings that, just as Newman's great literary works are not *Loss and Gain*, *Callista*, *The Dream of Gerontius*, and 'Lead, kindly light', but *The Tamworth Reading Room*, *An Essay on the Development of Christian Doctrine*, *Lectures on the Present Position of Catholics*, *The Idea of a University*, and the *Apologia pro Vita sua*—so, too, Chesterton's great literary works are not the novels and poems but *Charles Dickens*, *Orthodoxy*, *The Victorian Age in Literature*, *St Francis of Assisi*, *The Everlasting Man*, *St Thomas Aquinas*, and the *Autobiography*. Of these seven books, it is worth noting, incidentally, in view of the common assertion that Chesterton wrote his best work as an Anglican, that four were written when he was a Catholic. Of course, one would have to add, in the case of Chesterton, that he was the author also of some of the finest nonsense and satirical verse as well as some of the most distinctive and original detective stories in the English language. In conclusion, then, I came to realize that Chesterton should be seen as the obvious successor to Newman, and indeed as a successor to the other great Victorian 'sages' (to borrow John Holloway's term from his seminal study *The Victorian Sage* (1955)), specifically the other great non-fiction prose writers, Carlyle, Ruskin, and Arnold (the critic).

The biographer of G. K. Chesterton, who is attempting to write not only a personal but an intellectual and literary life, is presented with both considerable difficulties and considerable opportunities. On the one hand, the biographical materials available leave a very great deal to be desired. Chesterton wrote few letters—of which there is still no edition—and the ones he himself wrote, as opposed to those he dictated to secretaries, are never dated. Apart from three early notebooks in which he entered his thoughts and reflections, particularly one that dates from 1894 to 1898 or

---

[2] Michael Wheeler, *Death and the Future Life in Victorian Literature and Theology* (Cambridge: Cambridge University Press, 1990), 305.

1899, a period of intense intellectual and spiritual development,[3] he kept no diaries or journals. After his mother had died, he 'threw away ... most of the contents of his father's study, including all family records', his first biographer, Maisie Ward, records; later in her book she amends this to 'half', but her informant, Dorothy Collins, Chesterton's last secretary and literary executor, has recorded that she was able to save only the last of four loads of papers, so in other words about three-quarters of the papers were destroyed.[4] Some of the papers that Dorothy Collins lent to Maisie Ward for her biography (1944) were destroyed in an air raid in the Second World War. Other papers, particularly early love letters from Chesterton to his wife, Frances, were destroyed by Dorothy Collins at Frances's behest. According to Aidan Mackey, a lifelong Chesterton enthusiast and collector of things Chestertonian, Dorothy Collins also freely gave away other papers, including two diaries that Frances Chesterton kept during 1904 and 1905 and the first American trip, the former of which she gave (inadvertently, it seems[5]) to Aidan Mackey. Mr Mackey also informs me that a particular second-hand bookseller, who obtained books for Dorothy Collins, was regularly invited to help himself from the Chesterton papers that were haphazardly stored in the damp loft of Top Meadow Cottage, built on the kitchen garden of the Chestertons' house Top Meadow, to which she moved after Frances's death.[6] The popular biographies by Dudley Barker (1973), Michael Ffinch (1986), and Michael Coren (1989), which appeared after Maisie Ward's life but during Dorothy Collins's life, clearly reveal the existence of letters and papers to which they had access but which are no longer to be found in the British Library collection of Chesterton papers that the Library purchased from the Dorothy Collins Charitable Trust after her death. Subsequent biographers, therefore, in these cases have no means of checking information and quotations, or even of knowing what the source might have been, given that only one of these three biographers, Michael Ffinch, gives any source notes, and these are scanty and vague. Along with Maisie Ward, these biographers also had the advantage of Dorothy Collins's memories. An obvious and important example of this is Ffinch's report of Chesterton's last words, which, pre-

---

[3] See Oddie, 109, 144–5.
[4] Ward, *GKC* 7, 536; Dorothy Collins's notes for talks, BL Add. MS 73477, fo. 139.
[5] Aidan Mackey, 'Diary of Frances Chesterton, 1904–1905', *CR* 25/3 (Aug. 1999), 283.
[6] Dorothy Collins's notes for talks, BL Add. MS 73477, fo. 110.

sumably, he heard from Dorothy Collins, although typically he gives no source.

The principal source for Chesterton's life for any biographer, apart from his *Autobiography*, must, therefore, remain Maisie Ward's biography, which she wrote at Frances Chesterton's request on the suggestion of Dorothy Collins,[7] and its sequel *Return to Chesterton* (1952). Maisie Ward was not only, like her parents, a friend of both the Chestertons, but she was able to consult and interview their contemporaries and friends and relations. Otherwise, the best-documented periods of Chesterton's life are the times when he was travelling abroad and when Frances recorded their experiences in diaries and letters, as did Dorothy Collins in later years. I have made much more use of these papers than any previous biographer. I have also discovered an apparently hitherto unknown correspondence file in the archives of the University of Notre Dame, Indiana, containing the letters that passed between the President of Notre Dame, Father Charles O'Donnell, CSC, the Chestertons, and Dorothy Collins in connection with the six weeks that Chesterton lectured at the University in 1930, and that reveal a relationship between American host and English visitors that grew from an awkward beginning to great warmth and friendship. In addition, I have been able to take advantage of some hitherto unused, if not unknown, letters from Chesterton to Hilaire Belloc, in the possession of the John J. Burns Library at Boston College, to throw new light on Chesterton's attitude towards his sister-in-law, 'Keith' Chesterton, who was to launch a spiteful attack on Frances Chesterton in her book *The Chestertons* (1941), which was published a few years after their deaths.

So far as this biography is a personal life, I differ from my predecessors in the emphasis I place on Chesterton's humour, a humour that was inseparable from his humility, a humility that can, I think, be suitably called heroic, particularly since a heroic humility sounds so like a Chesterton paradox. For it is one thing to retail the familiar jokes of the Market Harborough variety, but it is another to appreciate with what steadiness of humour—a steadiness that can also be called heroic in adverse circumstances—Chesterton contemplated life and the world. No doubt a lack of that appreciation is one important reason for the strange neglect by his biographers of the posthumously published *Autobiography*, which so wonderfully conveys that joyful humour. This great work, surely to be ranked with Newman's *Apologia* and Ruskin's *Praeterita*, is one invaluable resource that the biographer does have and I have not hesitated to quote

---

[7] Maisie Ward to Dorothy Collins, 7 Jan. 1943, BL Add. MS 73472, fo. 4.

generously from this vividly authentic self-portrait—although it is certainly not a book to which one would turn for chronological and documentary facts, any more than one would to any of Chesterton's critical biographies.

When I began this Preface by saying that the biographer of Chesterton was faced with considerable opportunities as well as difficulties, I had in mind the fact that the dearth of primary biographical materials is more than matched by the lack of the kind of secondary critical literature, both in terms of quantity and quality, that one would normally take for granted in the case of a writer of such importance and significance as I have claimed. In, therefore, writing what I think can claim to be the first full-length intellectual and literary life of Chesterton, I have the challenge, more than seventy years after his death, of attempting to help establish his rightful position as the successor of the great Victorian 'sages', and particularly Newman.

The unfailing humour that was so significant an aspect of Chesterton's personal life has its parallel in the enormous importance he attached in his writings to humour as a medium for comprehending and interpreting life, regarding comedy as he did as an art form at least as serious as tragedy. One can, without exaggeration, find in Chesterton a mini-philosophy, not to say mini-theology, of laughter. Chesterton's philosophy of wonder at and gratitude for existence is well known, but I have also highlighted the complementary principle of limitation that informs all his thinking about art, literature, politics, and religion. Linked, too, to his philosophy of wonder is his concept of the role of the imagination in enabling us to see the familiar afresh, as it were for the first time. Thus in his apologetic classics, *Orthodoxy* and *The Everlasting Man*, Chesterton's most effective strategy is to assail the post-Christian imagination and its stereotypes with startlingly fresh perspectives of Christianity and the figure of Christ. I have also given due weight to his specifically Catholic apologetics, which have been virtually ignored in the secondary literature, and which, at their best, recall the brilliance of Newman's satire on the English 'no Popery' tradition in his *Lectures on the Present Position of Catholics*. Perhaps the most serious way in which Chesterton has been underestimated is as a literary critic: this may be because, apart from his book on Browning, his best criticism is not of poetry but of prose. Whatever the reason, it is my hope that I have set out enough evidence to show that Chesterton is one of our great literary critics, to be mentioned in the same breath as Johnson, Coleridge, Arnold, and Eliot. I have passed more or less rapidly over Chesterton's fiction, apart from *The Man who was Thursday* and the Father Brown stories, neither of which suffers from Chesterton's admitted inability to bring alive his fictional characters as more than simply mouthpieces for ideas and points of view, since in both these exceptional cases it is essential that the characters should not reveal themselves. While I do not think, any more than Chesterton did, that he is a major poet, he did write a handful of good serious poems, as well as, as I have already pointed out, nonsense and satirical verse that have few parallels in the language and that I have freely quoted. I have also tried to do justice to Chesterton's political and social writings, emphasizing in particular the remarkable way in which he differed from contemporary intellectuals in not only defending but valuing the despised 'masses'. Finally, I should add that this book does not in any way aspire to be a chronicle of Chesterton's career as a journalist. Even to try to do so would, in my view, be at the expense of the clear and concise intellectual and literary portrait I have attempted to draw. In fact, of course, a number of Chesterton's books are collections of his journalism, and, apart from those collections on specific subjects, such as America or Ireland, in the other more general collections inevitably the same ideas and themes regularly reappear, as would be the case with any columnist having to produce regular articles to order. For, while Chesterton was an enormously prolific writer, he was not, needless to say, endlessly endowed with new ideas and themes.

ACKNOWLEDGEMENTS

In writing this book, I have incurred a number of debts. I am, first and foremost, indebted to Aidan Mackey, who has allowed me exceptionally generous access to his Chesterton collection, as well as sharing with me the unique knowledge he possesses as a result of personally knowing both Dorothy Collins and 'Keith' Chesterton. He has answered my many questions with unfailing patience, read much of my typescript, corrected my mistakes and misconceptions, and provided me with much useful information. His Chesterton collection, up to now housed in the G. K. Chesterton Study Centre at his home in Bedford, is in the process of being metamorphosed into the G. K. Chesterton Library, which, it is hoped, will eventually be housed at the Oxford Oratory. I am grateful to Stratford Caldecott, the Director of the Oxford Centre for Culture and Faith, where a number of books and papers from Aidan Mackey's collection are temporarily stored, for also kindly allowing me unrestricted access.

Geir Hasnes, who is preparing a comprehensive bibliography of Chesterton's writings that will replace John Sullivan's *G. K. Chesterton: A Bibliography* (1958) and its sequel *Chesterton Continued: A Bibliographical Supplement* (1968) as the standard bibliography, has unfailingly answered my queries and checked and corrected my bibliographical references. He has done more than that: he has read the entire typescript and saved me from a number of blunders, some minor, some major and embarrassing. I am grateful to Edward Short for testing the typescript for readability, as well as for correcting my ignorance of Irish history. I must also thank the following people who have answered specific questions or provided me with particular information I required: Dale Ahlquist, Wendy Butler, Judith Blincow, Stephen Boyd, Don and Matthew Briel, Nadia Cockayne, R. A. Christophers, Susan Faragher, Suzannah Goode, Kevin Hales, Donal and Julie Lowry, Peter J. Lysy,

Sheila Mawhood, Dan Mitchell, Maria Queenan, James Reidy, and Martin Thompson.

David Horn, Head, Archives and Manuscripts, John J. Burns Library, Boston College, Peter J. Lysy, Senior Archivist, Archives, University of Notre Dame, Ben Panciera, Rare Books Librarian and Curator for Special Collections, Hesburgh Libraries, University of Notre Dame, and Heidi Truty, Archivist, The Marion E. Wade Center, Wheaton College, Illinois, have kindly provided me with photocopies of Chesterton letters. For permission to quote from Father Charles O'Donnell's letters I am grateful to Wm. Kevin Cawley, Senior Archivist and Curator of Manuscripts, Archives, University of Notre Dame. Acknowledgements are due to A. P. Watt Ltd. on behalf of the Royal Literary Fund for permission to quote from Chesterton's unpublished letters, and to the Society of Authors on behalf of the Bernard Shaw Estate for permission to quote from Bernard Shaw's unpublished letters. For the loan of photographs used as illustrations in this book, I am indebted to Aidan Mackey, Patricia Baker-Caffidy, Martin Thompson, and Tom Sullivan.

Chesterton scholarship is hardly more advanced than Chesterton criticism, but in the last few years there have been two very significant publications that have been of enormous help to me. In 2001 the British Library published an indispensable catalogue, compiled by R. A. Christophers, of the Chesterton papers that came into its possession on the death of Dorothy Collins.[1] And then in 2008 William Oddie published his ground-breaking *Chesterton and the Romance of Orthodoxy: The Making of GKC 1874–1908*, a detailed study of Chesterton's religious development in the years up to the time that he discovered Christian 'orthodoxy', which draws on barely explored sources and unpublished papers, making it the most original and serious work of research since Maisie Ward's pioneering biography and its sequel. Readers will notice my great debt to this work of careful scholarship in the early part of this book. I am also much indebted to its author for many long conversations about Chesterton, which have been of great help in formulating my thoughts.

[1] *The British Library Catalogue of Additions to the Manuscripts. The G. K. Chesterton Papers. Additional Manuscripts 73186–73484* (London: British Library, 2001).

CONTENTS

ABBREVIATIONS   xvii
LIST OF PLATES   xxi

1. The Early Days   1
2. Publishing and Engagement   39
3. Marriage and Fame   77
4. Controversy   115
5. Dickens   159
6. *Orthodoxy*   195
7. Shaw and Beaconsfield   233
8. Father Brown and the Marconi Scandal   277
9. The Victorian Compromise and Illness   323
10. War and Travel   365
11. America and Conversion   427
12. *The Everlasting Man*   487
13. Distributism and Apologetics   539
14. Rome and America Again   605
15. The Last Years   673

INDEX   731

ABBREVIATIONS

All references are to *The Collected Works of G. K. Chesterton* (San Francisco: Ignatius Press, 1986–), with the relevant volume number following in brackets, except where otherwise stated. Where the Ignatius *Collected Works* invents a title to cover a number of writings, which were in fact never published as a book, the title is not italicized.

Chesterton's Works

A.	*Autobiography* (XVI)
ACD	*Appreciations and Criticisms of the Works of Charles Dickens* (XV)
AD	*Alarms and Discussions* (London: Methuen, 1910)
AG	*All is Grist: A Book of Essays* (London: Methuen, 1931)
AIS	*'All I Survey': A Book of Essays* (London: Methuen, 1933)
AP	'Appendix' (XXI)
AS	*As I was Saying: A Book of Essays* (London: Methuen, 1936)
AT	*The Appetite of Tyranny* (V)
ATC	All Things Considered (London: Methuen, 1908)
AV	*Avowals and Denials: A Book of Essays* (London: Methuen, 1934)
AWD	*The Apostle and the Wild Ducks and Other Essays*, ed. Dorothy L. Collins (London: Paul Elek, 1975)
B.	*Robert Browning* (London: House of Stratus, 2001)
BAC	*The Ball and the Cross* (VI)
BC	The Blatchford Controversies (I)
BH	*Basil Howe*, ed. Denis J. Conlon (London: New City, 2001)
C.	*Chaucer* (XVIII)
CCC	*The Catholic Church and Conversion* (III)
CD	*Charles Dickens* (XV)
CE	*Crimes of England* (V)
CID	*Christendom in Dublin* (XX)

CL	*The Coloured Lands*, ed. Maisie Ward (London: Sheed & Ward, 1938)
CM	*The Common Man* (London: Sheed & Ward, 1950)
COS	*Chesterton on Shakespeare*, ed. Dorothy Collins (Henley-on-Thames: Darwen Finlayson, 1971)
CP i, ii	*Collected Poetry*, i, ii (X, pts 1, 2)
CP (1933)	*Collected Poetry* (London: Methuen, 1933)
CQT	*The Club of Queer Trades* (VI)
CS	Chesterton on Shaw (XI)
CT	*Come to Think of it . . . A Book of Essays* (London: Methuen, 1930)
DD	*Divorce versus Democracy* (IV)
Def.	*The Defendant* (London: J. M. Dent, 1914)
DJ	*The Judgement of Dr Johnson* (XI)
EA	*The End of the Armistice* (V)
EM	*The Everlasting Man* (San Francisco: Ignatius Press, 1993)
EOE	*Eugenics and Other Evils* (IV)
FB i, ii	The Father Brown Stories (XII, XIII)
FFF	*Four Faultless Felons* (New York: Dover, 1989)
FI	*The Flying Inn* (VII)
FVF	*Fancies versus Fads* (London: Methuen, 1923)
GS	*Generally Speaking: A Book of Essays* (London: Methuen, 1928)
H.	*Heretics* (I)
HA	*A Handful of Authors*, ed. Dorothy Collins (London: Sheed & Ward, 1953)
II	*Irish Impressions* (XX)
ILN	*Illustrated London News* (XXVII–XXXV)
K.	*Lord Kitchener* (V)
LL	*Lunacy and Letters*, ed. Dorothy Collins (London: Sheed & Ward, 1958)
LT	*Leo Tolstoy* (XVIII)
M.	*Manalive* (VII)
MC	*G.K.C. as M.C.: Being a Collection of Thirty-Seven Introductions*, ed. J. P. de Fonseka (London: Methuen, 1929)
MKM	*The Man who Knew too Much* (VIII)
MM	*A Miscellany of Men* (London: Methuen, 1912)
MO	*The Man who was Orthodox: A Selection from the Uncollected Writings*, ed. L. Maycock (London: Dennis Dobson, 1963)
MT	*The Man who was Thursday* (VI)
NJ	*The New Jerusalem* (XX)
NNH	*The Napoleon of Notting Hill* (VI)

O.	*Orthodoxy* (I)
OS	*The Outline of Sanity* (V)
PI	'The Patriotic Idea', in Lucian Oldershaw (ed.), *England: A Nation* (London and Edinburgh: R. Brimley Johnson, 1904), 1–43
PL	*The Poet and the Lunatics* (London: Cassell, 1929)
RDQ	*The Return of Don Quixote* (VIII)
RLS	*Robert Louis Stevenson* (XVIII)
RR	*The Resurrection of Rome* (XXI)
S.	*Sidelights* (XXI)
SD	*The Superstition of Divorce* (IV)
SFA	*St Francis of Assisi* (II)
SHE	*A Short History of England* (XX)
SL	*The Spice of Life*, ed. Dorothy Collins (Beaconsfield: Darwen Finlayson, 1964)
SRBC	*Social Reform versus Birth Control* (IV)
SS	*The Superstitions of the Sceptic* (Cambridge: W. Heffer, 1925)
T.	*The Thing* (III)
TA	*St Thomas Aquinas* (II)
TC	*Thomas Carlyle* (XVIII)
TLB	*Tales of the Long Bow* (VIII)
TS	*The Surprise* (XI)
TT	*Tremendous Trifles* (London: Methuen, 1909)
TWTY	*Twelve Types* (London: Arthur L. Humphreys, 1902)
UD	*The Uses of Diversity: A Book of Essays* (London: Methuen, 1920)
UU	*Utopia of Usurers* (V)
VAL	*The Victorian Age in Literature* (XV)
W.	*G. F. Watts* (London: Duckworth, 1920)
WARL	*Where All Roads Lead* (III)
WB	*William Blake* (London: Duckworh, n.d.)
WC	*William Cobbett* (London: Hodder and Stoughton, n.d.)
WIC	*Why I am a Catholic* (III)
WISA	*What I Saw in America* (XXI)
WK	*The Wild Knight* (London: J. M. Dent, 1914)
WS	*The Well and the Shallows* (III)
WW	*What's Wrong with the World* (IV)

Other Abbreviations

Barker	Dudley Barker, *G. K. Chesterton: A Biography* (London: Constable, 1973)

Bentley	E. C. Bentley, *Those Days* (London: Constable, 1940)
BL	British Library
CC	[Cecil Chesterton], *G. K. Chesterton: A Criticism* (London: Alston Rivers, 1908)
Clemens	Cyril Clemens, *Chesterton as Seen by his Contemporaries* (New York: Haskell House, 1969)
Conlon, i	D. J. Conlon (ed.), *G. K. Chesterton: The Critical Judgments* Part I: 1900–1937 (Antwerp: Antwerp Studies in English Literature, 1976)
Conlon, ii	D. J. Conlon (ed.), *G. K. Chesterton: A Half Century of Views* (Oxford: Oxford University Press, 1987)
Coren	Michael Coren, *Gilbert: The Man who was G. K. Chesterton* (New York: Paragon House, 1990)
CR	*Chesterton Review*
Dale	Alzina Stone Dale, *The Outline of Sanity: A Biography of G. K. Chesterton* (Grand Rapids, MI: William B. Eerdmans, 1982)
Ffinch	Michael Ffinch, *G. K. Chesterton* (London: Weidenfeld and Nicolson, 1986)
GKCL	G. K. Chesterton Library (see Acknowledgements)
JJBL	John J. Burns Library, Boston College
MCC	Mrs Cecil Chesterton, *The Chestertons* (London: Chapman and Hall, 1941)
O'Connor	John O'Connor, *Father Brown on Chesterton* (London: Burns Oates & Washbourne, 1938)
Oddie	William Oddie, *Chesterton and the Romance of Orthodoxy: The Making of GKC 1874–1908* (Oxford: Oxford University Press, 2008)
Pearce	Joseph Pearce, *Wisdom and Innocence: A Life of G. K. Chesterton* (London: Hodder & Stoughton, 1996)
Sullivan	John Sullivan (ed.), *G. K. Chesterton: A Centenary Appraisal* (London: Paul Elek, 1974)
Titterton	W. R. Titterton, *G. K. Chesterton: A Portrait* (London: Douglas Organ, 1936)
UNDA	University of Notre Dame Archives
Ward, *GKC*	Maisie Ward, *Gilbert Keith Chesterton* (London: Sheed and Ward, 1944)
Ward, *RC*	Maisie Ward, *Return to Chesterton* (London: Sheed and Ward, 1952)

LIST OF PLATES

1. The young Gilbert Keith Chesterton, aged 7 or 8, with his younger brother Cecil.
2. Chesterton's childhood home, 11 Warwick Gardens, Kensington.
3. Members of the Junior Debating Club, St. Paul's School. Chesterton is on the third row on the left.
4. Chesterton and Frances Blogg before their marriage.
5. Frances Chesterton, 1901, the year of her marriage.
6. Frances Chesterton at the time of her marriage.
7. Overstrand Mansions, Battersea, where the Chestertons lived from 1901 to 1909.
8. Cecil Chesterton sometime before his death in 1914.
9. Overroads, Beaconsfield, where the Chestertons lived from 1909 to 1922.
10. Chesterton sometime before 1920.
11. Chesterton c. 1920.
12. Chesterton and Frances in 1922.
13. Studio portrait of Chesterton by Howard Coster, 1926.
14. Chesterton with his host, Fr Michael Earls, S.J., at Holy Cross College, Massachussets, when he lectured there in December 1930.
15. Top Meadow, Beaconsfield, where the Chestertons lived from 1922.
16. Chesterton and Dorothy Collins with a young friend, Manhattan Beach, California, 14 February 1931.

All images listed above appear by kind permission of the G. K. Chesterton Library Trust with the exception of images 13 and 14. Image 13 appears by kind permission of Martin Thompson and image 14 by kind permission of Thomas J. Sullivan.

1

The Early Days

G ILBERT KEITH CHESTERTON began his posthumously published *Auto-biography* (1936) with an ironic reference to himself as an apologist for dogmatic Christianity and the Church of Rome: 'Bowing down in blind credulity, as is my custom, before mere authority and the tradition of the elders, superstitiously swallowing a story I could not test at the time by experiment or private judgment, I am firmly of opinion that I was born on the 29th of May, 1874, on Campden Hill, Kensington; and baptised according to the formularies of the Church of England in the little church of St George opposite the large Waterworks Tower that dominated that ridge.'[1] Employing one of his most important strategies as an apologist, he added humorously: 'I do not allege any significance in the relation of the two buildings; and I indignantly deny that the church was chosen because it needed the whole water-power of West London to turn me into a Christian.' Whereas the Waterworks Tower was to feature later in his life, his birth was simply 'an accident which I accept, like some poor ignorant peasant, only because it has been handed down to me by oral tradition'. Not only are Catholic ideas of authority and tradition invoked, but 'common sense' agrees (another part of his apologetic strategy) that, while 'some of the sceptical methods applied to the world's origin might be applied to my origin, and a grave and earnest enquirer come to the conclusion that I was never born at all', this conclusion should be rejected.[2]

[1] He was baptized on 1 July 1874. Photocopy of parish baptismal record, GKCL.

[2] *A.* 21.

Of Chesterton's ancestry we know very little apart from what he tells us in his *Autobiography*, since on his mother's death he threw away 'without examination' all the family records preserved in his father's study. He also threw away his father's collection of press cuttings, mostly relating to his famous son, about a quarter of which, however, his secretary Dorothy Collins managed to save, rather against Chesterton's will, from the dustmen.[3] When it was once suggested to him, while lecturing in Cambridge, by the vicar of the nearby village of Chesterton that it might have been named after his ancestors, he replied that this was possible, but he thought it more likely that his father's family had taken the name from the village. Perhaps they had once lived there under a different name, but then a worthless member of the family was driven out and came to live in Cambridge, where he was given the nickname of Chesterton after the village he had come from.[4] His father enjoyed reading out to the family letters written from the debtors' prison by the head of the family at the time of the Regency who was a friend of the Prince and led a disreputable life and squandered his fortune. As a result of the loss of his inheritance, Chesterton's great-grandfather Charles had become first a poulterer, then a coal merchant, and finally an estate agent.[5]

Although we can add details to Chesterton's account of his early childhood, no biographer has ever improved on, or could improve on, the story as he tells it in the best and most strictly autobiographical part of the *Autobiography*. At the end of the first chapter, he admits that his story is 'deficient in all those unpleasant qualities that make a biography really popular. I regret that I have no gloomy and savage father to offer to the public gaze as the true cause of all my tragic heritage; no pale-faced and partially poisoned mother whose suicidal instincts have cursed me with the temptation of the artistic temperament.' He was unable to do what was expected of him 'by cursing everybody who made me whatever I am'. On the contrary, he was 'compelled to confess that I look back to that landscape of my first days with a pleasure that should doubtless be reserved for the Utopias of the Futurist'.[6] This was not mere loyalty to or even partiality for his family; as the man who was his closest boyhood friend later recalled:

Family affection, indeed, was the cradle of that immense benevolence that lived in him. I never met with such parental devotion or conjugal sympathy more strong

[3] Ward, *GKC* 7; Ffinch, 6.   [4] Clemens, 48.
[5] Ward, *GKC* 7, 8; Ffinch, 6.   [6] *A.* 38.

than they were in the exceptional woman who was his mother; or with greater kindliness—to say nothing of other sterling qualities—than that of his father, the business man whose feeling for literature and all beautiful things worked so much upon his sons in childhood. The parents made their home a place of happiness for their two boys' many friends...[7]

As Chesterton looked back on his life he found himself returning to those objects that were among the first he ever saw with his eyes—the little church and the waterworks opposite. They seemed to him now to be symbolic of life itself. For the 'notion of a tower of water' was to suggest to his imagination some 'colossal water-snake that might be the Great Sea Serpent, and had something of the nightmare nearness of a dragon in a dream'; while 'over against it, the small church rose in a spire like a spear; and I have always been pleased to remember that it was dedicated to St George'.[8]

He was born into a literally 'respectable' middle-class family, who were business people but who minded 'their own business' and were not desirous of swallowing up 'everybody else's business'. He could remember his father's father, 'a fine-looking old man with white hair and beard and manners that had something of that rounded solemnity that went with the old-fashioned customs of proposing toasts', who 'kept up the ancient Christian custom of singing at the dinner-table'. This was a middle class that truly was *middle* and separate from both the classes above and below. Its weakness was that it knew too little about the working class, not least the domestic servants who worked for it. Towards them his own family were kind, 'but in the class as a whole there was neither the coarse familiarity in work, which belongs to democracies... nor the remains of a feudal friendliness such as lingers in the real aristocracy'. Instead, there was 'a sort of silence and embarrassment'. Chesterton recalled a female member of his family who went to stay in the house of an absent friend where the attending servant liked to eat what was left over from the meals she served, but the guest, thinking nothing should be wasted, was determined to eat whatever was served, however much the servant might increase the portions—in the hope that there might be something left for her to eat—with the result that presumably the servant starved and the guest burst... There was a terror lest children might pick up the accent of the servants; but this was not so much snobbishness as the understandable fear of a class that had managed to acquire culture and education. Chesterton's own

---

[7] Bentley, 48–9.   [8] *A.* 38.

father, for example, 'knew all his English literature backwards', and
Chesterton himself 'knew a great deal of it by heart' long before he
could properly understand it. To learn poetry by heart uncomprehend-
ingly was 'perhaps the right way to begin to appreciate verse'. This
Victorian middle class was equally cut off from the upper classes. It had
a pride of its own and had no desire to get into Society.[9]

Chesterton's mother was born Marie Grosjean, one of twenty-three
children, her father belonging to a family that had originally come from
French Switzerland, while her mother was a Keith from Aberdeen—
hence Chesterton's middle name.[10] Chesterton liked his Scots ancestry,
partly because, while he never knew his maternal grandfather, his maternal grandmother 'was a very attractive personality', and partly because 'of
a certain vividness in any infusion of Scots blood or patriotism', which
'made a sort of Scottish romance in my childhood'. However, the grandfather 'had been one of the old Wesleyan lay-preachers and was thus
involved in public controversy, a characteristic which has descended to
his grandchild. He was also one of the leaders of the early Teetotal
movement; a characteristic which has not.' But Chesterton thought there
must have been much more to his grandfather than being a controversialist and teetotaller because of two casual remarks he was remembered as
making: one was that, far from fashion being merely convention, it *was*
'civilisation', and the other was that, far from life being depressing, he
would thank God for his creation even if he knew he was 'a lost soul'.[11]

One of Chesterton's father's ancestors was a Captain George Laval
Chesterton (whose letters he also used to read out to the family), a friend
of Dickens and a prison-reformer, who had served in the Peninsular War
and later saw military action in both North and South America before
becoming a prison governor in England; he published his autobiography
as well as a book about prison life.[12] Chesterton imagined that he was
himself something of a Dickens character—like the friend of his father's
father who used to go for a walk on Sundays carrying a prayer book but
without the slightest intention of attending church, a practice he defended
by 'calmly' saying 'with uplifted hand', 'I do it . . . as an example to others'.
The brazenness of such hypocrisy showed that Dickens did not invent
Dickensian characters; they already existed. The exuberance of that
expansive era, Chesterton thought, was the effect of 'that popular humour,
which is perhaps our only really popular institution, working upon the

[9] *A.* 25–6.   [10] Ward, *GKC* 9.   [11] *A.* 29–30.
[12] Ward, *GKC* 8, 555–7.

remains of the rhetoric of the eighteenth-century orators, and the almost equally rhetorical rhetoric of the nineteenth-century poets, like Byron and Moore'. The 'savour' of it then could be found in 'countless common or average people'. This was 'a race that really dealt in periods as rounded as Christmas platters and punchbowls', with whom there was even a 'pomp and ritual about jokes', just as there was 'something as stately about the cheap-jacks demanding money as the orators demanding fame'. The 'pompous geniality' and the joviality of the jeers combined 'the mock heroic' in a way that marked these Victorians. And the world, thought Chesterton, was 'less gay for losing that solemnity'.[13]

Although Chesterton came from a 'respectable' commercial middle-class family that thoroughly disapproved of a new kind of businessmen they branded as 'adventurers', nevertheless they 'were entirely of that period that believed in progress, and generally in new things, all the more because they were finding it increasingly difficult to believe in old things; and in some cases in anything at all'. They were Liberals who 'believed in progress', even if they did recognize a deterioration in commercial probity. His uncle Sidney was his father's partner in the firm of estate agents (it still exists) founded by Chesterton's great-grandfather. 'Mr Ed', as his father was known to the family, retired early from the business because of a weak heart. Since his real interest was not in selling houses but in art and literature, retirement was a blessing. Like his son, Mr Chesterton was 'one of the few men...who really listened to argument'. Like his son, too, the father was a traditionalist in spite of his liberalism: 'he loved many old things, and had especially a passion for the French cathedrals and all the Gothic architecture opened up by Ruskin at that time.' Uncle Sidney, on the other hand, was a thoroughgoing progressive typical of his age, who 'had the same scrupulous sense of the duty of accepting new things, and sympathising with the young, that older moralists may have had about preserving old things and obeying the elders'. But, while both brothers were 'indignant' at the 'swindling' that was beginning to enter business, they were 'ignorant of, or even indifferent to the sweating'—that is, to the question of 'economic exploitation'. A lingering Puritanism, Chesterton thought, was responsible for the delay of 'the full triumph of flashy finance and the mere antics of avarice'.[14]

The word 'Victorian' suggests 'solid respectability', but these Victorians were hardly Victorian in that sense, for it was 'a period of increasing strain' in which 'ethics and theology were wearing thin'. Even Victorian domesticity

---

[13] *A.* 30–3.   [14] *A.* 33–5.

was something of a misnomer, for this kind of Englishman's home 'was not half so domestic as that of the horrid foreigner; the profligate Frenchman'. After all, this was 'the age when the Englishman sent all his sons to boarding-school and sent all his servants to Coventry'. Far from the Englishman's house being his castle, 'he was one of the few Europeans who did not even own his house; and his house was avowedly a dull box of brick, of all the houses the least like a castle'. But the greatest paradox of all was that, 'so far from being stiff with orthodox religion, it was almost the first irreligious home in all human history'. This was 'the first generation that ever asked its children to worship the hearth without the altar'. It made no difference, claimed Chesterton, whether these Victorians 'went to church at eleven o'clock... or were reverently agnostic or latitudinarian, as was much of my own circle'. These Victorians were the first people 'for whom there were no household gods but only furniture'. Although 'the darker side' had been exaggerated, still it was true that the Victorian domestic tyrant did exist and he was *sui generis*, for he was 'the product of the precise moment when a middle-class man still had children and servants to control; but no longer had creeds or guilds or kings or priests or anything to control him. He was already an anarchist to those above him; but still an authoritarian to those below.' Apart from financial probity, the 'Puritanic element' showed itself in 'a rather illogical disapproval of certain forms of luxury and expenditure'. For, while the Chesterton family table would 'groan under far grander dinners than many aristocrats eat today', they 'had, for instance, a fixed feeling that there was something raffish about taking a cab. It was probably connected with their sensitive pride about not aping the aristocracy.' Chesterton could remember his grandfather,

when he was nearly eighty and able to afford any number of cabs, standing in the pouring rain while seven or eight crowded omnibuses went by; and afterwards whispering to my father (in a hushed voice lest the blasphemy be heard by the young), 'If three more omnibuses had gone by, upon my soul I think I should have taken a cab.'[15]

Chesterton was more than to make up for his forebears' scruples.

The greatest influence on the child came from his father. Apart from being bearded and not bald, he might have brought Mr Pickwick to mind; he certainly had 'all the Pickwickian evenness of temper'. What was most remarkable about him was his 'versatility both as an experimentalist and a

[15] *A* 36–7.

handy man': 'His den or study was piled high with the stratified layers of about ten or twelve creative amusements; water-colour painting and modelling and photography and stained glass and fretwork and magic lanterns and mediaeval illumination.' Watching his father at work had given Chesterton a love of 'seeing things done', and this experience had made him

profoundly sceptical of all the modern talk about the necessary dullness of domesticity; and the degrading drudgery that only has to make puddings and pies. Only to make things! There is no greater thing to be said of God Himself than that He makes things. . . . Toffee still tastes nicer to me than the most expensive chocolate which Quaker millionaires sell by the million; and mostly because we made toffee for ourselves.

All his father's hobbies were purely private pursuits that he would never have dreamed of pursuing professionally in any way. There had been an idea of his studying art in his youth, as his son was to do, but the latter was glad he had not done so: 'It might have stood in his way in becoming an amateur. It might have spoilt his career; his private career.' There was nothing more English about him than this love for hobbies. Nor was it 'a question of one hobby but a hundred hobbies, piled on top of each other'. But of all those hobbies, 'the one which has clung to my memory through life is the hobby of the toy theatre'.[16]

It was indeed a scene in his father's toy theatre that provided Chesterton with his first memory:

The very first thing I can ever remember seeing with my own eyes was a young man walking across a bridge. He had a curly moustache and an attitude of confidence verging on swagger. He carried in his hand a disproportionately large key of a shining yellow metal and wore a large golden or gilded crown. The bridge he was crossing sprang on the one side from the edge of a highly perilous mountain chasm, the peaks of the range rising fantastically in the distance; and at the other end it joined the upper part of the tower of an almost excessively castellated castle. In the castle tower there was one window, out of which a young lady was looking. I cannot remember in the least what she looked like; but I will do battle with anyone who denies her superlative good looks.

The scene was not just the first thing he could remember seeing; it was more significant than that, for it had 'a sort of aboriginal authenticity impossible to describe; something at the background of all my thoughts; like the very back-scene of the theatre of things'. He had no recollection of what the scene was meant to represent, but nevertheless 'that one scene

---

[16] *A.* 46–7, 49–50.

glows in my memory like a glimpse of some incredible paradise'. And the significance of it for Chesterton brings us to the most important theme that pervades his thought and writings: the idea of limitation, which was central to his thought on art, literature, politics, and religion. 'Why should looking through a square hole, at yellow pasteboard, lift anybody into the seventh heaven of happiness . . .' The scene was, Chesterton explained, 'a sort of symbol of all that I happen to like in imagery and ideas. All my life I have loved edges; and the boundary line that brings one thing sharply against another. All my life I have loved frames and limits; and I will maintain that the largest wilderness looks larger seen through a window.' And so in his view 'the perfect drama must strive to arise to the higher ecstasy of the peep-show'. This was why he particularly liked 'abysses and bottomless chasms and everything else that emphasises a fine shade of distinction between one thing and another; and the warm affection I have always felt for bridges is connected with the fact that the dark and dizzy arch accentuates the chasm even more than the chasm itself.' In these earliest sensations, Chesterton believed he was 'feeling the fragmentary suggestions of a philosophy I have since found to be true'.[17]

Another early memory was 'playing in the garden under the care of a girl with ropes of golden hair; to whom my mother afterwards called out from the house, "You are an angel;" which I was disposed to accept without metaphor'. But perhaps this young lady was indeed a veritable angel for the little Gilbert at this time if he had just been bereaved:

I had a little sister who died when I was a child. I have little to go on; for she was the only subject about which my father did not talk. It was the one dreadful sorrow of his abnormally happy and even merry existence; and it is strange to think that I never spoke to him about it to the day of his death. I do not remember her dying; but I remember her falling off a rocking-horse . . . the greater catastrophe must somehow have become confused and identified with the smaller one. I always felt it as a tragic memory, as if she had been thrown by a real horse and killed.

This was the problem about memory: 'we have remembered too much— for we have remembered too often.' Thus another of his earliest memories was

of a long upper room filled with light (the light that never was on sea or land) and of somebody carving or painting with white paint the deal head of a hobby-horse . . . Ever since that day my depths have been stirred by a wooden post

<hr />

[17] *A.* 39–41.

painted white; and even more so by any white horse in the street; and it was like meeting a friend in a fairy-tale to find myself under the sign of the White Horse at Ipswich on the first day of my honeymoon.

Chesterton's point was that, the more we dwell on a memory, the more 'it becomes . . . our own memory of the thing rather than the thing remembered'; the more we dwell on a memory the more we 'transform' and even 'veil' it.[18]

What was really memorable about childhood was that 'anything in it was a wonder. It was not merely a world full of miracles; it was a miraculous world.' So central to Chesterton's vision of life was this sense of wonder that he even tells us that, if he were to 'think of the backs of houses of which I saw only the fronts; the streets that stretched away behind the streets I knew; the things that remained round the corner'— they would 'still give me a thrill'. So uniquely developed was this sense in Chesterton that one of his favourite games—it would be hard to imagine anyone else playing it—all his life was 'to take a certain book with pictures of old Dutch houses, and think not of what was in the pictures but of all that was out of the pictures, the unknown corners and side-streets of the same quaint town'. But, if the child's world is full of wonders, that does not mean that a child 'is concerned only with make-believe'. On the contrary, Chesterton insists, the child 'does not confuse fact and fiction. . . . To him no two things could possibly be more totally contrary than playing at robbers and stealing sweets.' Another confusion is to suppose that a 'child dislikes a fable that has a moral' and that a child regards rewards for good actions as bribes, as a cynical adult would, rather than as their natural accompaniment.[19]

Although his mother's ancestry clearly seemed to the child more interesting than his father's, there is no question but that his father had far more influence on the young Chesterton's formative years. Indeed, in his account of his childhood his mother is only mentioned twice in connection with her ancestry. The second time is to contrast the French make-up of her family—'tough, extraordinarily tenacious, prejudiced in a humorous fashion and full of the fighting spirit'—with the 'extraordinarily English' background on his father's side—'of good nature, of good sense . . . and a certain tranquil loyalty in their personal relations'. Significantly, Chesterton adds that the last quality 'was very notable even in one, like my brother Cecil, who in his public relations was supremely pugnacious and provocative'.

[18] *A.* 42–4.   [19] *A.* 45–6, 51.

The implication is clearly that Cecil took more after his mother, whose favourite he was, whereas his elder brother was more like his father.[20] Gilbert was 5 when Cecil was born, whereupon he remarked, 'Now I shall always have an audience.'[21] In fact, it seems that the little Gilbert had not long had the power of speech at this point. For there was a family story that 'the power of language descended on him like a tongue of flame, suddenly and irresistibly' on the occasion of a children's party when a younger cousin about 4 years old was so talkative that he 'became indignant, and seizing her arms shook her to and fro, pouring out a flood of unintelligible eloquence. From that day his vocabulary increased and multiplied, ready, as his father once said, for the arrival of his brother.'[22] Gilbert's remark on the arrival of Cecil was always remembered by the family because it proved to be so totally off the mark, since as soon as Cecil could speak the two brothers began to argue incessantly, arguments that the younger brother dominated, having been, as his brother was to remark, 'born a fighter... [who] argued from his very cradle'.[23] Their longest recorded argument lasted for just over eighteen hours while they were on holiday at the seaside, beginning at breakfast and ending in the early hours of the next day. Their liberal parents refused to interfere with their freedom of speech.[24] Chesterton's wife, Frances, too recounted how once, when they were on holiday at the seaside, 'the landlady would sometimes clear away breakfast, leaving the brothers arguing, come to set lunch and later set dinner while still they argued. They had come to the seaside but they never saw the sea.'[25] Cecil was born in the new home, 11 Warwick Gardens, which was also in Kensington but south of the old house at 32 Sheffield Terrace and to which the family had moved after the death of Beatrice at the age of 8. Beatrice, or Birdie as she was called, had been five years older than Gilbert.[26] After her death the two brothers were

---

[20] *A.* 48; Ward, *GKC* 17.   [21] Ward, *GKC* 13.   [22] MCC 119.

[23] G. K. Chesterton, introduction to Cecil Chesterton, *A History of the United States* (New York: George Doran, 1919), pp. vii–viii.

[24] Barker, 38–9.   [25] Ward, *GKC* 112.

[26] According to Annie Kidd née Firmin, Birdie died of typhoid fever. Annie Kidd to Maisie Ward, 13 Aug. [1942], BL Add. MS 73481A, fo. 24. This memory may be correct, as she was intimate with the family then, but her recollection all those years later that it was Frances who persuaded Chesterton to give up the Slade School and art for publishing and writing is certainly wrong, as the two had not yet met. Annie Kidd to Maisie Ward, 16 Dec. 1941, 3 Aug. [1942], BL Add. MS 73481A, fos. 8, 22.

never allowed to see a funeral cortège pass. Their mother was told by her husband never again to mention Birdie's name, and her portrait was turned to the wall. Their father had too a horror of sickness, which was also a forbidden subject, a horror that his elder son inherited. The golden-haired angel, Annie Firmin, recalled how he would rush from the room if his younger brother gave the slightest sign of choking at meals. She also remembered how, when his father was dying, Chesterton 'only with real pain and difficulty...summoned sufficient fortitude to see the dying man'.[27]

Marie Chesterton did not do much in the way of house-training her sons; there was no attempt to insist on punctuality at meals, for example. On the other hand, Annie Firmin remembered her 'as a bit of a tyrant in her own family', in deciding, for instance, what members of the family should eat at meals. She was famous for her hospitality and the huge meals she served. Like her husband, she had a sense of humour and was known for her witty conversation. Her appearance, however, was as untidy as her house, while her 'blackened and protruding teeth which gave her a witchlike appearance' made her a somewhat forbidding figure.[28] Her sons, too, were not known for their cleanliness and tidiness. But that did not stop the Italian artist Attilio Baccani, who lived in London, from so admiring the little Gilbert's golden locks that he asked his father if he could paint his portrait when he met them out for a walk. The finished portrait was hung up in the dining-room and showed Gilbert in his sailor suit.[29]

As he looked back on his childhood, Chesterton could not agree with Robert Louis Stevenson, a writer he so admired, that there was anything 'vague' about it. Far from 'moving with his head in a cloud' or being 'in a dazed daydream', unable to 'distinguish fancy from fact', he remembered his childhood as being chiefly characterized by 'clearness': 'Mine is a memory of a sort of white light on everything, cutting things out very clearly, and rather emphasising their solidity.' Although this white light had 'a sort of wonder in it, as if the world were as new as myself',[30] nevertheless the world was nothing if not 'real'. And not only that, but he had 'never lost the sense that this was my real life; the real beginning of what should have been a more real life'—if only it had not been darkened by the grown-up 'dreams', 'self-deception', 'make-believe and pretending' of the adult with 'his head in a cloud'. Of course, as a child he was not

---

[27] Ward, *GKC* 13, 16; Ffinch, 10.   [28] Ward, *GKC* 17–18.
[29] Ffinch, 11.
[30] For the background influence of Romanticism, see Oddie, 347, 349.

explicitly 'conscious' of the distinctions he was now aware of, but he 'contained' them implicitly. Thus he knew that pretending was not the same as deceiving, and that imagination was 'almost the opposite of illusion'. Far from life seeming a dream, he seemed then 'more wide-awake' than he was now, he seemed to be 'moving in broader daylight'. Yet that did not mean that he never suffered unhappiness as a child; he did, but 'the pain did not leave on my memory the sort of stain of the intolerable or mysterious that it leaves on the mature mind'.[31]

Everything was both wonderful and real, whether it was his father's toy theatre, which he knew was not a real theatre, or a street scene, which might have been a scene in a theatre but which was in fact a real street scene. There was one street scene of which he retained a vivid memory, and with which Chesterton concludes his account of his early childhood— he had promised the reader earlier that he would drop, like a detective-story writer, some clues as to his future development.

I remember once walking with my father along Kensington High Street, and seeing a crowd of people gathered by a rather dark and narrow entry on the southern side of that thoroughfare. I had seen crowds before; and was quite prepared for their shouting or shoving. But I was not prepared for what happened next. In a flash a sort of ripple ran along the line and all these eccentrics went down on their knees on the public pavement. I had never seen people play any such antics except in church; and I stopped and stared. Then I realised that a sort of little dark cab or carriage had drawn up opposite the entry; and out of it came a ghost clad in flames. Nothing in the shilling paint-box had ever spread such a conflagration of scarlet, such lakes of lake; or seemed so splendidly likely to incarnadine the multitudinous sea. He came on with all his glowing draperies like a great crimson cloud of sunset, lifting long frail fingers over the crowd in blessing. And then I looked at his face and was startled with a contrast; for his face was dead pale like ivory and very wrinkled and old, fitted together out of naked nerve and bone and sinew; with hollow eyes in shadow; but not ugly; having in every line the ruin of great beauty. The face was so extraordinary that for a moment I even forgot such perfectly scrumptious clothes.

We passed on; and then my father said, 'Do you know who that was? That was Cardinal Manning.'[32]

It seems that Chesterton's father had actually been to hear Manning preach on one occasion, and the references to the Roman Catholic Church in his letters showed no hostility. Liberal in politics and religion, Mr Ed was comparatively tolerant of Popery.[33]

---

[31] *A.* 53, 56–8.   [32] *A.* 59.   [33] Ward, *GKC* 11.

The Chesterton family themselves were irregular attenders at church, and when they did go it was to listen to the sermons of the Revd Stopford Brooke, a well-known Unitarian preacher, who had left the Church of England's ministry because he could not believe in miracles.[34] As Chesterton was later to write in one of his early 'clerihews':

> The Rev. Stopford Brooke
> The Church forsook.
> He preached about an apple
> In Bedford Chapel.[35]

In his *Autobiography* Chesterton remembered him as a 'large-hearted and poetic orator', whose 'optimistic theism' he accepted for a long time: 'it was substantially the same as that which I had learnt since childhood under the glamorous mysticism of George Macdonald. It was full and substantial faith in the Fatherhood of God, and little could be said against it, even in theological theory, except that it rather ignored the free-will of man. Its Universalism was a sort of optimistic Calvinism.'[36]

Chesterton thought his parents 'were rather exceptional, among people so intelligent, in believing at all in a personal God or in personal immortality'.[37] But it was a liberal, un-dogmatic religion that naturally went hand-in-hand with their liberal politics. And the young Chesterton grew up knowing that he was a Roundhead and not a Cavalier—so much so that as a small boy he rewrote William Aytoun's popular *Lays of the Scottish Cavaliers*, turning the Cavalier hero Montrose into a 'false' traitor and the traitor Argyll into the hero who triumphantly 'drove right backwards | All the servants of the Pope', 'the trembling Papists'.[38]

2

The first school Chesterton attended was Colet Court, generally called 'Bewsher's' after the name of the headmaster, a day as opposed to the usual boarding preparatory school, which stood opposite St Paul's School in the Hammersmith Road, for which it was first the unofficial and later the official preparatory school. The date of his entry is unknown (he does not

---

[34] CC 8.   [35] *CP* ii. 346–7.   [36] *A*. 167.
[37] *A*. 140.   [38] Ward, *GKC* 20–2.

even refer to it in the *Autobiography*), although the fact that when he went to St Paul's his classmates were a year or two younger suggests that he went later than was normal, perhaps at the age of 9 in 1883.[39] One of his contemporaries who lived nearby remembered walking to school with him and passing 'a very entrancing toy shop'; but he had 'very little money', so on one occasion the young Gilbert, with the generosity that would be characteristic of him, offered him the ten shillings, then a very large sum of money for a small boy, that he had at home. It seems that Chesterton appeared as unpromising a pupil as he was to strike the staff at St Paul's, his form master once remarking: 'You know, Chesterton, if we could open your head, we should not find any brain but only a lump of white fat!' A fellow pupil Edmund Clerihew Bentley, who gave his name to the 'clerihew' and who became a journalist like Chesterton and the author of the prototype of the modern detective novel *Trent's Last Case* (1913), doubted if he was ever beaten, although Samuel Bewsher was a believer in caning; at St Paul's the practice had become very rare and would hardly have been provoked by Chesterton, who was, one of the masters there recalled, 'as easy to control as an old sheep'. The young Gilbert must have

[39] Oddie, 43. Dale, 18, gives the date as Jan. 1880 and Pearce, 13, as 1881; neither offers any evidence or reason for his statement. Ward, *GKC* 23, does not profess to know. But her assertion on p. 14 that Chesterton was 'in some ways a very backward child' who did not 'talk much' before he was 3 and learned to read only at 8 (according to Coren, 23, not until he was 9) should be treated with caution. Oddie, 25, argues that 'there is good evidence ... which suggests not only that he was reading well before the age of eight, but which establishes that he was writing stories at the latest by the age of six and probably sooner, and quoting poetry that he had learned by heart not long afterwards. By the age of eight, he was writing tidily in cursive script; there has survived an exercise book which belongs either to his early days at prep school or (more likely) from the period immediately before it. This contains, among other exercises, a number of neatly written passages taken down from dictation; this alone disproves the notion that he was at this age still struggling to read.' Oddie notes that this exercise book contains, inside the cover, an inscription in Dorothy Collins's handwriting, 'With Miss Seamark | eight years old.' As Oddie points out, it would not have been normal then for a preparatory school for boys to have women on the staff, and so this teacher was probably privately engaged before Chesterton went to Colet Court and was not his form mistress there (*pace* Pearce, 13). No doubt Maisie Ward herself selected the age of 8 for Chesterton's entry to Colet Court because of this exercise book.

been something of a sight at Bewsher's, still dressed in a sailor suit but as tall as the average grown man.[40]

At the age of 12 in January 1887, he graduated to St Paul's. It too was, very unusually for a public school, a day school, so Chesterton never suffered the trauma of leaving home at an early age and suffering the hardships and brutality of the typical public school with its regime of fagging and cult of games (indeed, it was only in his later years at the school that physical exercise became compulsory). Unlike generations of Englishmen of his class, Chesterton continued to enjoy the amenities of home and never endured abrupt separation from family life. A happy childhood was followed by a happy boyhood, and his innocence, especially of sex, lasted much longer than was normal for his middle-class contemporaries who encountered at the age of 13 the typical homosexual culture of the all-male boarding-school.[41] Surprisingly, perhaps, Chesterton does not allude to what he, with his enormous sense of the importance of the family, must have regarded as his huge good fortune. Instead, he speaks of the 'mysterious transformation' of the child into 'that monster the schoolboy'; whereas the pupils at St Paul's were hardly the 'monsters' that Chesterton would have encountered at the great public schools, where the discipline of the classroom was heaven compared with the discipline of the boarding houses, which was left in the hands of the largely unsupervised older boys. Many of his contemporaries would have laughed contemptuously or enviously at the 12-year-old for whom the transition to schoolboy meant chiefly encountering the Greek small letters for the first time! The large letters he had learned at home 'for fun', whereas the small he learned 'during the period of what is commonly called education; that is, the period during which I was being instructed by somebody I did not know, about something I did not want to know'. How common an experience this really is may be doubted, but Chesterton himself could give his 'own private testimony to the curious fact that . . . a boy often does pass, from an early stage when he wants to know nearly everything, to a later stage when he wants to know next to nothing'. In his view, childhood was simple compared with 'complex and incomprehensible' boyhood. The child does not pretend to be what it is not: it says, 'let's pretend'; but the boy really does pretend to be a man. 'Schoolboys in my time could be

---

[40] Ward, *RC* 12–13.

[41] Cf. Oddie, 52, on how Chesterton was saved from this 'major traumatic shock . . . which . . . might well have undermined forever his essentially warm and secure personality'.

blasted with the horrible revelation of having a sister, or even a Christian name. And the deadly nature of this blow really consisted in the fact that it cracked the whole convention of our lives; the convention that each of us was on his own; an independent gentleman living on private means.'[42]

One particular peculiarity about boyhood Chesterton singles out, 'a callousness, a carelessness, a . . . random and quite objectless energy'. This energy also curiously seemed to be exercised by boys all over the world by 'going about in threes', 'having no apparent object in going about at all', and 'suddenly attacking each other and equally suddenly desisting from the attack'. Thus, when Chesterton first met E. C. Bentley, who was to become his best friend at St Paul's, in the playground, he 'fought with him wildly for three-quarters of an hour; not scientifically and certainly not vindictively (I had never seen him before and I have been very fond of him ever since) but by a sort of inexhaustible and insatiable impulse'. The other great friend was Lucian Oldershaw, the son of an actor and Chesterton's future brother-in-law, 'who brought into our secrets the breath of ambition and the air of the great world'. In particular, 'there possessed him, almost feverishly, a vast, amazing and devastating idea, the idea of *doing* something; of doing something in the manner of grown-up people'. According to Chesterton, it was Oldershaw who 'proposed in cold blood that we should publish a magazine of our own; and have it printed at a real printer's'.[43] The first printed issue appeared in March 1891, some months after the first meeting of the Junior Debating Club in July 1890, the debating society that Chesterton and his friends founded, since the official school debating society, the 'Union', was open only to boys 'in the top form'.[44] But there is a typically undated letter of Chesterton to Bentley— Ronald Knox once remarked in amused exasperation, 'You have the habit of the Immortals—not dating your letters'[45]—in which Chesterton proposes that they start a 'periodical', 'bringing out the papers read at each meeting, with notes, essays, or even stories written by members' of the Junior Debating Club.[46] It would be typical of Chesterton to give the credit to someone else, but perhaps the truth is that, while it was originally his idea, it was Oldershaw who was 'the moving spirit'.[47] At first the *Debater*, which was edited by Oldershaw, was produced, after being typed, on a duplicating machine at one of the boys' houses, but Oldershaw was so successful in selling copies at sixpence a copy to other boys and to

[42] *A.* 61–3.   [43] *A.* 61–2, 65–6.   [44] *A.* 66.
[45] Ronald Knox to G. K. Chesterton, 29 July 1928, BL Add. MS 73195, fo. 155.
[46] BL Add. MS 73191, fo. 3.   [47] Oddie, 58.

parents—the first issue sold out on the first day—that after the first two issues it was printed as a magazine with 'pale fawn colours' and attained a circulation of between sixty and a hundred.[48] His own 'turgid poems' Chesterton dismissed as a mixture of 'bad imitations' of Swinburne and even 'worse' ones of Macaulay's *Lays of Ancient Rome*. Nevertheless, they attracted the attention of the school authorities: 'One day, to my consternation, the High Master stopped me in the street and led me along, roaring in my deafened and bewildered ears that I had a literary faculty which might come to something if somebody could give it solidity.' Later, on a prize-giving day, 'he bellowed aloud to a whole crowd of parents and other preposterous intruders . . . that our little magazine showed signs of considerable talent'.[49]

The weekly meetings of the Junior Debating Club, which had originally been intended to be the Shakespeare Club, consisted almost entirely not of political debate but of the reading and discussion of literary papers, although other topics were possible when there was no paper given. The first meeting was held in 1890, when Chesterton was 16, and Chesterton was elected chairman, with Oldershaw as secretary, although apparently it was his, Oldershaw's, initiative.[50] In the words of Bentley, Chesterton was chairman 'because we insisted on his being . . . the club centred in his personality'. They all vied with one another for his friendship and were greatly jealous of the fact that Bentley was clearly his best friend.[51] As Bentley wrote after his death, he had an 'extraordinary power—of which he always remained quite unconscious—of inspiring affection and trust in all who had to do with him'. His 'essential goodness, perfect sincerity, chivalrous generosity, boundless good temper, a total absence of self-esteem . . . and with them, even in boyhood, were united brilliant intellectual powers and an enormous gift of humor', which was combined with as great a 'sense of beauty and his sense of reverence'. Bentley emphasized his unusual 'faculty of enjoying things', especially in 'vigorous and long-sustained arguments', which were his keenest pleasure even more than his 'joy in books' and his drawing.[52] Bentley was a year younger, but his experience of the world made him seem much older than his years. The group met for tea in one another's houses before the paper and ensuing discussion. These ample teas were often extremely boisterous, when buns and slices of cake flew through the air; as chairman, Chesterton, whose

[48] Ward, *GKC* 31; Bentley, 49–50; Barker, 31; Oddie, 58.
[49] *A.* 67, 71.   [50] Bentley, 49.   [51] Ward, *GKC* 31–3; Bentley, 48–9.
[52] Clemens, p. iii; Bentley, 45–7.

'laugh was the loudest and the most infectious of all', took no part in the horseplay, which he would stop when it threatened the discussion. In this fraternity the presence of Chesterton's younger brother Cecil was not welcome to his friends. Oldershaw recalled later how he used to hate Cecil, who insisted on monopolizing the conversation; another of the circle remembered him as an 'ugly little boy creeping about'. Every issue of the *Debater* contained contributions from Chesterton, generally both verse and prose. The first number contained an essay about dragons, which began: 'The Dragon is the most cosmopolitan of impossibilities.' This struck the others as *real* literature. For the most part it is conspicuous how little of the Chestertonian humour is evident—apart from Chesterton's own scribbled caricatures and drawings on his own copies. But his literary papers are striking in their range and quality and must have astonished any of the masters who taught him.[53] The truth is that he was a voracious reader, even devouring, in his own words, 'whole volumes of *Chambers' Encyclopaedia* and of a very musty and unreliable *History of English Trade*. The thing was a mere brute pleasure of reading, a pleasure in leisurely and mechanical receptiveness. It was the sort of pleasure that a cow must have in grazing all day long.'[54]

But in the classroom he was extremely successful in concealing his ability. Only two masters, he maintained, 'managed, heaven knows how, to penetrate through my deep and desperately consolidated desire to appear stupid; and discover the horrible secret that I was, after all, endowed with the gift of reason above the brutes'. One of them 'would suddenly ask me questions a thousand miles away from the subject at hand, and surprise me into admitting that I had heard of the *Song of Roland*, or even read a play or two of Shakespeare'. This was very embarrassing, as 'perhaps the only consistent moral principle' English schoolboys then possessed was 'a horror of showing off'. Chesterton could remember 'running to school in sheer excitement repeating militant lines' of Scott's *Marmion* 'with passionate emphasis and exultation; and then going into class and repeating the same lines in the lifeless manner of a hurdy-gurdy, hoping that there was nothing whatever in my intonation to indicate that I distinguished between the sense of one word and another'.[55] But Chesterton was being slightly disingenuous, as his desire not to be noticed did not prevent him from putting in a successful entry for a prize poem in the summer term of 1892, his last term at the school, the subject set being

---

[53] Ward, *GKC* 30–3, 36, 40–2; Clemens, iii. 4–5.   [54] *MC* 228.
[55] *A.* 70–2.

St Francis Xavier. Still, in his defence, it was 'the only "regular" thing he ever did at school', according to his friend Bentley.[56] After successfully winning the Milton school prize for poetry—which he left behind on the platform 'so confused was he at his success'[57]—he was 'frozen with astonishment' to find an announcement on the notice board to the effect that he was to be given the privileges of the top form, although he was two forms below.[58] This was an edict by the formidable High Master of St Paul's, Frederick Walker, who reminded Chesterton in some ways of Dr Johnson, 'in the startling volume of his voice, in his heavy face and figure, and in a certain tendency to explode at what did not seem to be exactly the appropriate moment; he would talk with perfect good humour and rationality and rend the roof over what seemed a trifle'. The famous story told of him was that, 'when a fastidious lady wrote to ask him what was the social standing of the boys at his school, he replied, "Madam, so long as your son behaves himself and the fees are paid, no questions will be asked about his social standing." '[59]

Looking back, Chesterton thought that the chief impression he left on both the masters and his contemporaries was that he was asleep. But if he was asleep he was also dreaming, so that 'my mind was already occupied, though I myself was idle'.[60]

Lawrence Solomon, later a lecturer at University College, London, who sat next to him in class, remembered him as sleepily indifferent to what went on, but he also noticed that it was not ability he lacked but the will to apply himself. Tall, untidy, clumsy, and absent-minded, he became a spectacle of fun to the other boys when some form of physical exercise became compulsory and Chesterton would endeavour to fulfil the requirement in the gymnasium on the trapeze and parallel bars, where he was the despair of the instructor. Even if he had been so inclined, his poor eyesight would have made it impossible for him to take any part in sport. But he was a great walker, and still slim till his twenties, when he began to get fat, probably at least partly because of glandular trouble. One friend and member of the Junior Debating Club was to recall: 'I can see him now, very tall and lanky, striding untidily along Kensington High Street, smiling and sometimes scowling as he talked to himself, apparently oblivious of everything he passed, but in reality a far closer observer than most, and

[56] Clemens, 1–2.
[57] Dorothy Collins's notes for talks, BL Add. MS 73477, fo. 102.
[58] *A.* 72.   [59] Ward, *GKC* 42.   [60] *A.* 72–3.

one who not only observed but remembered what he had seen.'[61] Bentley remembered his 'serious, even brooding, expression that gave way very easily to one of laughing happiness. He was by nature the happiest boy and man I have ever known . . . laughter was never far away . . . '.[62] At the same time, however, his absent-mindedness made him an obvious target for practical jokes, as on one very cold day when the other boys, unbeknown to Chesterton, filled his pockets with snow in the playground, which began to melt in the classroom, forming pools around him, all completely unnoticed by him.[63] One friend recorded: 'He meandered his way through school like a rudderless bark. He put up a smoke-screen over his real interests.' Years later the same friend could still see him 'wandering round the corridors . . . His Greek primer all dog-eared, tattered, covered with drawings . . . all over the text as well as in the margins.' Called on to construe—that is, translate from Greek or Latin—'he would sway backwards and forwards, his head bowed over a hopelessly ragged book. He would hold it in one hand and clutch it with the other to prevent it from disintegrating. He would construe adequately enough—but he would do the minimum.' There was a much-repeated story told of him that 'he had been found wandering round the playground in school hours and gave as his excuse that he "thought it was Saturday" '.[64]

Before Chesterton had made any friends, he had been 'somewhat solitary; not sharply unpopular or in any sense persecuted, but solitary'.[65] He was never unpopular at school but nor was he a popular boy outside his small circle of friends.[66] He was too big and strong to be bullied, while 'he used to accept [teasing] with such unfailing good temper that there soon ceased to be any fun in it'.[67] His strength was useful 'in standing between a small boy and others who were badgering him'.[68] In his failure or refusal to apply himself to conventional academic work, he was unlike an unusually large number of the boys at St Paul's, which, not being a conventional boarding public school with the usual cult of sport, encouraged on the contrary those who in schoolboy slang were called 'swots'. Another reason why 'swottishness' was a feature of St Paul's was the high proportion of Jewish boys. And here, early in his *Autobiography*, Chesterton takes the opportunity to defend himself against the anti-Semitism with which he

---

[61] Clemens, 2, 8–9.   [62] Bentley, 46.   [63] *A.* 72; Ward, *GKC* 25–6.
[64] *A.* 72; Ward, *GKC* 25–6; Ward, *RC* 13–14.   [65] *A.* 73.
[66] Clemens, p. iii; Bentley, 49.   [67] Ward, *GKC*, pp. ii. 15.
[68] Clemens, 3.

has often been charged both in his lifetime and since. He points out that he had a number of Jewish friends at school, some of whom had remained lifelong friends, where he was known rather for his pro-Semitism and for protecting Jewish boys from bullying and teasing.[69] The Jewish brothers Lawrence and Maurice Solomon were both members of the Junior Debating Club, as were the D'Avigdor brothers, Digby and Waldo, who, between them, constituted no less than a third of the membership of the Junior Debating Club.[70] But a couple of letters to Bentley make it perfectly clear, however jocularly, that the other boys were very conscious of their Jewishness.[71] Both schoolboy and wider English society, says Chesterton in the *Autobiography*, regarded Jews as 'foreigners; only foreigners that were not called foreigners'.[72] But there is no evidence of anti-Semitism in the usual sense. On the contrary, he strongly condemned the pogroms of Jews in Russia and Poland, to the extent of even writing in a poem, 'Christ has borne from you more insult than from Israel he has borne | Ye have placed the scourge of murder where they placed the reed of scorn.'[73] A magazine article he read in January 1891 about the brutal ill-treatment of a Jewish girl in Russia filled him with fury, and he wrote in his diary: 'Made me feel strongly inclined to knock somebody down, but refrained.'[74] And in the *Debater* he wrote a fictional letter from an Englishman in Russia who springs to the defence of a Jewish student against an attack by Czarist troops, having previously written that the Russian persecution of the Jews had 'at least done one service to orthodoxy. It has restored my belief in the devil.'[75]

Partly because he had never in fact reached the top form because of his unwillingness to apply himself in the classroom and partly because he 'was almost wholly taken up with the idea of drawing pictures', when his time at St Paul's came to an end in the summer of 1892, Chesterton, unlike his friends, was not destined for Oxford or Cambridge but for art school.[76] Bentley remembered his 'wonderful decorative handwriting' and his 'masterly' draughtsmanship.[77] In spite of his striking literary contributions to the *Debater*, neither his parents nor his teachers appear to have seen where his real talents lay. According to Bentley, Chesterton himself had no

---

[69] *A.* 74–5.   [70] Oddie, 80.
[71] Barker, 36–7. This sense of the foreignness of Jews, which was not peculiar to Chesterton, is not the same as anti-Semitism, as Barker claims.
[72] *A.* 77.   [73] *CP* i. 28.   [74] BL Add. MS 73317A, fo. 24.
[75] Oddie, 81.   [76] *A.* 78.   [77] Clemens, 2.

literary ambitions, while his parents were more hopeful about his artistic gifts;[78] perhaps too his father was thinking of what *he* would have wanted to do at that age. At any rate, when Mrs Chesterton two years later consulted the High Master on her son's prospects in the light of his disappointing progress at the Slade School, the great man was in no doubt about one thing: 'Six foot of genius. Cherish him, Mrs. Chesterton, cherish him.'[79]

As for Chesterton's own awareness of himself, as we have already seen, failure at academic work had not meant that his mind was inactive: on the contrary, 'all this time very queer things were groping and wrestling inside my own undeveloped mind'. But, in not saying anything about them in his autobiographical account of his schooldays, he was being consistent with 'the sustained and successful effort of most of my school life to keep them to myself'.[80]

Chesterton's poems in the *Debater* give us some idea of the ways in which his mind was working during these formative two years.[81] In view of his impending crisis at the Slade School, it is striking that in the Junior Debating Club debates he strongly upheld the moral basis of literature as opposed to any pure aestheticism or art for art's sake. His religious attitudes were distinctly ambivalent. On the one hand, the theological liberalism with which he had grown up is evident enough. Half of his twelve poems in the *Debater* are overtly religious and explicitly anti-dogmatic. They specifically echo the views of the Revd Stopford Brooke, whose sermons in the Bedford Chapel the family attended, albeit inter-mittently, and for whom the gospel of Christ was 'simple' as opposed to 'complex' as the creeds made it. In these poems dogma and church authority are 'almost synonymous with intolerance and bloodshed'.[82] But there is definitely a spiritual note, which confirms Oldershaw's comment to Maisie Ward that: 'We felt that he was looking for God.'[83] Thus he would write to Bentley, apparently in the summer of 1893, when he was 19, that it was 'impossible' to '*feel*' that the world was a 'sham', ' the sum of all things being barren': 'Whatever the secret of the world may be, it must in the face of feelings that are in me, be something intelligible and satisfying. This instinct of the hidden meaning is the eternal ground of all religions... religion has always been, relatively to the time, good news.'[84] The last of

---

[78] Bentley, 67. [79] Ward, *GKC* 42. [80] *A.* 78.
[81] For the following account, see Oddie, 67–74. [82] Oddie, 69.
[83] Ward, *GKC* 26.
[84] G. K. Chesterton to E. C. Bentley, n.d. but annotated by hand (presumably Bentley's) on typewritten copy, 'Long vac 1893', BL Add. MS 73191, fo. 33.

the *Debater* poems, 'Ave Maria', begins on an anti-dogmatic note, and then continues:, 'Hail Mary, thou blessed among women, generations shall rise up to greet, | After ages of wrangle and dogma, I come with a prayer to thy feet.' And Chesterton proceeds to regret that 'the crown' has been 'reft from thy forehead' by 'stern elders'.[85] There is also a remarkable article written in 1892 when he was 18, where he defends 'the vivid democratic medieval piety which felt that there was in reality a great "communion of saints" in which they and their personal acquaintances could walk naturally with angels and archangels', as opposed to a religion 'shut up in a cupboard and exhibited on Sundays'. This was a 'real' not a 'sham' religion, and it was 'this intense reality in their religion which marks' the religion of Dante in contrast to 'the vague renaissance mythology of the great poem of Milton'.[86] In his prize poem of the same year, 'St Francis Xavier', Chesterton had been rather less flattering about the Church of Rome; there the great Jesuit missionary, while acknowledged as 'a hero of his wars', is nevertheless 'No child of truth or priest of progress he'.[87] A less ambivalent attitude to Roman Catholicism would no doubt have been more acceptable to his religious mentor, the Revd Stopford Brooke.

His later political and social views are also anticipated in these last two happy and stimulating years at St Paul's, the years of the Junior Debating Club and *The Debater*. In a 'dramatic journal' that he kept during the Christmas holidays when he was 16, his 'Conservative' friend Oldershaw accuses Chesterton of being a 'red hot raging Republican'; but Chesterton insists that 'there is real misery, physical and mental, in the low and criminal classes, and I don't believe in crying peace where there is no peace'.[88]

However, Oldershaw was not typical of the Junior Debating Club. To Lawrence Solomon Chesterton wrote that he 'cordially' assented with his Socialism; and a significant connection is made for the benefit of his Jewish friend with Christianity: 'It is almost as impracticable as Christianity.' Later Chesterton informed Solomon that 'those early Christians were the only true socialists . . . for democracy is an essentially spiritual idea, a contradiction of the modern materialism which would encourage the brute-tendency to an aristocracy of the physically "fittest"'.[89] And then in December 1892, two years later, Chesterton's first published writing in the national press appeared in the *Speaker*, a poem called 'The Song of Labour', in which the author wholly aligned himself with the workers of

---

[85] Oddie, 73.   [86] Oddie, 75–6.   [87] *CP* i. 166.
[88] Ward, *GKC* 29.   [89] Ffinch, 27–8.

the world, who have 'claimed and conquered the earth' and to whom
'work is the title of worth'.[90] In the following year he read a best-seller
called *Merrie England*, a collection of articles on Socialism originally published
in the *Clarion* newspaper by its founder and editor, Robert Blatchford. It
was a publishing sensation, with over two million copies sold, almost
doubling the *Clarion*'s circulation. Blatchford was influenced by William
Morris and 'idealised pre-industrial societies in which workers could be
artists and craftsmen'. It is quite possible that the book influenced Chesterton's
own later idealization of the Middle Ages. Be that as it may, it certainly
confirmed Chesterton in his Socialism. 'A Blatchford! A Blatchford! St
Henry George [an American socialist journalist who invented the concept
of wage slavery] for "Merrie England" and down with everything,' he
wrote excitedly to Oldershaw. The idea of Socialism leading to centralization and collectivism, which he later held to be true, is here dismissed: 'The
fact is that the dead level barrack idea of socialism is really much more true
of warehouse commercialism. Under socialism people would have peace
and time to be individuals instead of being clerks.'[91]

No doubt to mark his eighteenth year and his leaving school, as well as
his success in winning the Milton prize, Chesterton's father took him on his
first trip abroad for a holiday in France. They travelled by train round
northern France, going first to Rouen and ending up in Paris. The voluble
Latin was a new experience for English people in the nineteenth century
visiting the Continent for the first time: 'The people are most rapid,
obliging and polite, but talk too much.' Close as Normandy was to
England, it seemed to Chesterton to be another world: 'A foreign town
is a very funny sight with solemn old abbés in their broad brims and black
robes and sashes and fiery bronzed little French soldiers staring right and
left under their red caps, dotted everywhere among the blue blouses of the
labourers and the white caps of the women.'[92]

3

Chesterton entitled the fourth chapter of his *Autobiography* 'How to be a
Lunatic': 'I deal here with the darkest and most difficult part of my task;
the period of youth which is full of doubts and morbidities and temptations;

---

[90] *CP* i. 413. Bentley, 68, mistakenly thought Chesterton's first publication was
his first review published in 1895 (see below, p. 39).

[91] Oddie, 100.   [92] Barker, 44–5.

and which, though in my case mainly subjective, has left in my mind for ever a certitude upon the objective solidity of Sin.' (It is worth noting, however, lest too much is read into his words, that, according to his friend Bentley, 'even in [this] adolescent phase of morbid misery...laughter was never far away'.[93]) It was a period, he explains, when through his 'own fault' he made the 'acquaintance' of the Devil, 'and followed it up along lines which, had they been followed further, might have led me to devil-worship of the devil knows what'. On the subject of sin and the Devil he knew he was 'intellectually right only through being morally wrong'. And he knew that those who held that evil was 'only relative' and sin 'only negative' were 'talking balderdash only because they are much better men than I'. This 'period of madness coincided with a period of drifting and doing nothing; in which I could not settle down to any regular work'. Instead, he had 'dabbled in a number of things; and some of them may have had something to do with the psychology of the affair'.[94]

One of the things he 'dabbled in' was Spiritualism—although he 'would not for a moment suggest it as a cause, far less as an excuse'—but it was 'a contributory fact'. His brother and he played with planchette, although only for fun, unlike most people who played. But, while he was never seriously interested in Spiritualism, nevertheless he was sure that 'something happens which is not in the ordinary sense natural, or produced by the normal and conscious human will'. He did not profess to know whether it was 'by some subconscious or still human force, or by some powers, good, bad or indifferent, which are external to humanity'—what he did know was that the planchette 'tells lies'. For example, when asked the maiden name of an uncle's wife Chesterton had never known, the oracle replied 'Manning'. Told it was talking nonsense, it responded defiantly 'Married before'; and when asked to whom, the answer imme-diately came back, 'Cardinal Manning'. Playing with planchette 'without reason and without result' and without coming to any particular conclu-sion about it illustrated for Chesterton how during this confused period of his life he was 'merely dreaming and drifting; and often drifting onto very dangerous rocks'. But, if Spiritualism was sinister, it still had its amusing side. In his first job with a publisher who 'rather specialised in spiritualistic and theosophical literature', he remembered a distraught lady bursting into the office and demanding books suitable for her spiritual condition; but when Chesterton offered her *The Life and Letters of the Late Dr Anna Kingsford*, which they had just published, the said lady 'shrank away with

---

[93] Bentley, 46.   [94] *A*. 85–6.

something like a faint shriek', crying that Anna Kingsford had only that morning forbidden her to read the book; whereupon the young Chesterton expressed a hope that Dr Kingsford was not giving the advice to too many people, as 'it would be rather bad for business' and would suggest malice on the part of Dr Kingsford. This lady had boasted that 'she had killed a number of men merely by thinking about them' on the ground that they defended vivisection. She also boasted of 'very visionary but very intimate interviews with various eminent public men, apparently in a place of torture', including one with Gladstone, 'in which a discussion about Ireland and the Sudan was interrupted by Mr Gladsone gradually growing 'red-hot' from inside. "Feeling that he would wish to be alone," said Dr Anna Kingsford with delicacy, "I passed out."' She was obviously a lady with a 'fine tact and sense of social decorum, which told her that turning completely red-hot is what no gentleman would desire to do in the presence of a lady'. However, the 'jolliest' Spiritualist and the most sympathetic 'psychic enquirer' Chesterton met in those days was a man who had once received a successful tip for the Derby from some medium and was ever on the look-out for similar information. Chesterton therefore suggested to him that

he should purchase *The Pink-'un* and turn it into a paper combining the two interests, and sold at every bookstall under the name of *The Sporting and Spiritual Times*. This, I said, could not fail to lift bookmakers and jockeys into a loftier sphere of spiritual contemplation, not to mention owners, who probably needed it quite as much; while it would give to Spiritualism a sound, shrewd and successful business side, vastly increase its popularity, and give to some of its followers an indefinable air of contact with concrete objective matters and what is coarsely called common sense, which some of them, as I felt at the time, seemed in some fashion to lack.[95]

Years later, he told Father John O'Connor, who was to play such a significant role in his life, that he gave up playing with planchette after getting headaches, following which there 'came a horrid feeling as if one were trying to get over a very bad spree, with what I can best describe as a bad smell in the mind'.[96] Later, when he denounced Spiritualism, he did so not because he did not believe in it but because he did believe in it: 'the real objection to Spiritualism is that it calls entirely upon unknown gods—that is, upon any spirits that may be strolling about.... Spiritualists do

[95] *A.* 86–8, 91–3.   [96] O'Connor, 74.

not worship gods; they advertise for gods. They lay themselves open to evil . . .'.[97]

What else was Chesterton 'dabbling in'? The one thing he was not supposed to be 'dabbling in' and was, was art, which he was supposed to start studying seriously when in October 1893 he entered University College, London, of which the Slade School for Art was a constituent part. For the year 1892–3, the year he spent between St Paul's and University College, we have very little information, apart from what the minutes of the Junior Debating Club tell us.[98] There was a meeting on 16 December to discuss the future of the Club. It was decided to discontinue the *Debater* but not the Club, although the rule that it should be limited to twelve members was abolished. The February 1893 issue of the *Debater* announced that it was the last issue; it had been losing money and, apart from Chesterton himself, who was no longer at St Paul's, the other main contributors had to concentrate their efforts on gaining scholarships to Oxford. In fact, one further issue appeared in June to commemorate the club's demise.[99] Chesterton no longer saw his friends on a daily basis at school, but he could still see them at weekends and during school holidays. Apparently, he was attending at least for some of the time an art school in St John's Wood, called 'Calderon's' according to Lawrence Solomon.[100] In September 1893 Chesterton ended what was presumably a kind of 'gap' year between school and university by completing a series of drawings for a notebook collection of four-line verses, edited by Bentley, which later came to be known as 'clerihews' after Bentley's second name. Bentley was the principal contributor, but contributions came from the other members of the Junior Debating Club, and even Chesterton's father contributed some lines.[101] Chesterton himself contributed one of the best:

---

[97] *ILN* xxviii. 417–18.

[98] This explains why Ward, *GKC* 43, thought Chesterton started at University College in 1892.

[99] Oddie, 86–7.

[100] Ward, *GKC* 43. But, according to Ffinch, 33, Calderon's was a group of artists in St John's Wood presided over by the son of a Spanish ex-priest, called Philip Calderon, who, Oddie, 88, points out was actually Keeper of the Royal Academy.

[101] Ffinch, 34. The notebook was eventually published in facsimile as *The First Clerihews* (Oxford: Oxford University Press, 1982). About a third of the verses were published in *Biography for Beginners: Being a Collection of Miscellaneous Examples for the Use of Upper Forms*, ed. E. C. Bentley, with 40 diagrams by G. K. Chesterton (London: T. Werner Laurie, 1905).

> The Spanish people think Cervantes
> Equal to half a dozen Dantes;
> An opinion resented most bitterly
> By the people of Italy.[102]

On 6 October 1893 Chesterton entered University College to study art at its Slade School. At that time the Slade did not give even diplomas, let alone degrees; instead certificates were issued for different art subjects. The normal course of study was three years.[103] Since the Slade was a part of University College, Chesterton took the opportunity to attend lectures in other faculties. This may have been unusual, not to say irregular, for, when he returned to the College in 1927 to give a lecture, the Provost introduced him by saying: 'He was a member of the Slade School. I believe that during his period of studentship he frequented lectures in other Faculties almost as much as he frequented the Slade School. At all events, whether that was strictly according to rule or not, we know that it was a very wise proceeding.'[104] In fact, since he gave up studying fine art at the Slade after only one year, but stayed on at University College for another year, he actually ended up attending more lectures in other faculties, as even in his first year when he was supposed to be studying at the Slade, he attended lecture courses in English, French, and Latin.[105] There was no incentive or obligation to sit for examinations in these subjects, as he was officially enrolled at the Slade. At the time it was noted that when studying at the Slade he always seemed to be writing and when attending the lectures always to be drawing.[106] According to Bentley, it had been a 'quite fruitless enterprise of study at the Slade', when 'he did not learn the slightest shade of technical improvement on his natural gift for decorative and grotesque drawing'.[107] One of his teachers, the formidable and sarcastic Henry Tonks, who would become Slade Professor of Fine Art, told his parents that 'he had such a mature style of his own that they could teach him nothing without spoiling his originality, which . . . amounted to

[102] *CP* i. 344.

[103] Stephen Chaplin, 'The Slade Archive Reader', unpublished typescript, n.d., University College Library Services, Special Collections, Add. MS 400, p. 42, n. 31.

[104] G. K. Chesterton, *Culture and the Coming Peril* (London: London University Press, 1927), 5.

[105] University College, London, Records Office.   [106] Ward, *GKC* 49.

[107] Bentley, 67; Ward, *RC* 19.

genius'.[108] However, his brother Cecil thought that, while he had a 'considerable gift as a draftsman . . . it was not in that direction that his deepest impulses led. He proved this by the fact that he shrank from the technical toils of art as he [had] never shrunk from the technical toils of writing.'[109] While he was a student[110] he did, in fact, write two short stories that were eventually published in the *Quarto*, a short-lived journal that was intended to be quarterly and to publish work principally by those who had studied at the Slade, and that was published in large, hardbound volumes, the first appearing in the summer of 1896 and the fourth and last in 1898. 'A Picture of Tuesday' is the story of four young men who belong to a sketching club and who pick Tuesday as their weekly subject: one of them draws 'a huge human figure . . . driving up a load of waters, while below his feet moved upon a solemn infinite sea', with the text from the Book of Genesis written below: 'And God divided the waters . . .'. The artist demands to know, 'Why there are no rituals for every day?'—after all: 'The week is the colossal epic of creation.' Less seriously, another member of the club draws a picture of his mother's 'At-Home day' with the appended scriptural text: 'And Job lifted up his voice and cursed his day.' [111] The second story, 'A Crazy Tale', which is also on the subject of the wonder of existence, is the story of a boy 'called mad by his neighbours, who is utterly aware of the mysteries of life taken by them as commonplace' and who seems to see everything as though it were 'for the first time'.[112]

Because of the psychological and spiritual crisis that Chesterton always associated with his year at the Slade, it is often forgotten that in the event fine art was not his only or even principal subject of study. Among the professors in the arts faculty whose lectures he attended were two famous scholars. One was Professor A. E. Housman, the eminent classical scholar and also, of course, the author of *A Shropshire Lad*, published three years after Chesterton's arrival. However, after a year he dropped Latin, but continued attending lectures in English and French, as well as in history

---

[108] Dorothy Collins's notes for talks, BL Add. MS 73477, fo. 91.

[109] *CC* 16.   [110] According to Ward, *RC* 19, while he was still at the Slade.

[111] Ward, *RC* 19–20. Strangely, Maisie Ward denies that the story is 'an adumbration' of *The Man who was Thursday*, but claims it reflects Chesterton's preoccupation at this time with 'creation and existence', as if that were not also the subject of the later novel that recalls this period of his life. See also Oddie, 160–1.

[112] Ward, *RC* 19–20.

and political economy.[113] In recounting his time at University College in the *Autobiography*, Chesterton does not mention Housman, who had begun his great edition of Manilius in 1893 when he was appointed to the chair of Latin at the College, and whose *A Shropshire Lad* was published in 1896. But he does mention 'the extraordinarily lively and stimulating learning' of W. P. Ker, whose lectures on English literature he attended for two years, at one of which he had

the honour of constituting the whole of Professor Ker's audience. But he gave as thorough and thoughtful a lecture as I have ever heard given, in a slightly more colloquial style; asked me some questions about my reading; and, on my mentioning something from the poetry of Pope, said with great satisfaction, 'Ah, I see you have been well brought up.'

Unlike most of the other students, Chesterton was not studying for an examination—'I had not even that object in this objectless period of my life'—and therefore 'gained an entirely undeserved reputation for disinterested devotion to culture for its own sake'.[114] But what is important in the light of his future career is that he had the benefit of the teaching of one of the greatest literary scholars. When he returned to lecture at the College in 1927, he remarked self-deprecatingly:

It was at the Slade School that I discovered I should never be an artist; it was at the lectures of Professor A. E. Housman that I discovered that I should never be a

---

[113] See n. 104 above.

[114] *A.* 101–2. According to Ffinch, 36, the 'forms he filled in at the beginning of each academic year show a blank where students were invited to state which examinations they had in view'. But Oddie, 91, cites an unpublished letter to Oldershaw noting that Chesterton had 'discovered, much to my amusement, that I did rather well in the year's French examination at U.C.'. He had been 'awarded the Sixth Form ('A' Group) Prize for French at St Paul's School in 1891'. Aidan Mackey, *G. K. Chesterton: A Prophet for the 21st Century* (privately printed, n.d.), 30. See also Aidan Mackey, 'G. K. Chesterton among the Permanent Poets', in Andrew A. Tadie and Michael H. Macdonald (eds.), *Permanent Things: Toward the Recovery of a More Human Scale at the End of the Twentieth Century* (Grand Rapids, MI: William B. Eerdmans, 1995), 190–1, on Chesterton's verse translation of a French poem, 'Translation from du Bellay' (*CP.* i. 373–4; first published in *Occasional Papers*, 1/4 (July 1904), 130–1): 'It was printed in a little book, *Masterpieces of Lyrical Translation* [1911] ... Much later, in 1966, it was included in the prestigious *Penguin Book of Modern Verse in Translation*. The tribute paid to it by the compiler, George Steiner, is astonishing ... '.

scholar; and it was at the lectures of Professor W. P. Ker that I discovered I should never be a literary man. The warning, alas! fell on heedless ears, and I still attempted the practice of writing, which, let me tell you in the name of the whole Slade School, is very much easier than the practice of drawing and painting.[115]

Since Chesterton had come to University College principally in order to study art at the Slade School, it is ironic that he ended up by actually studying English and French literature for two years and art for only one. But, of course, it was the right outcome, as his future lay in writing not painting. Looking back, Chesterton thought: 'There is nothing harder to learn than painting and nothing which most people take less trouble about learning.' That explains why an 'art school is a place where about three people work with feverish energy and everybody else idles to a degree that I should have conceived unattainable by human nature'. The former 'do not want to be discursive and philosophical; because the trick they are trying to learn is at once incommunicable and practical; like playing the violin'. But the latter have plenty of time for 'philosophy…and it is generally a very idle philosophy'. At the time Chesterton was at the Slade 'it was also a very negative and even nihilistic philosophy'. But, although he 'never accepted it altogether, it threw a shadow over my mind and made me feel that the most profitable and worthy ideas were, as it were, on the defensive'. As one of the 'very idle', he knew only too well how 'very idle' a place such an institution can be. The dominant school of art at the time was the Impressionism of Whistler, which had 'a spiritual signifi-cance' in that it had a connection with the scepticism of the age: 'I mean that it illustrated scepticism in the sense of subjectivism. Its principle was that if all that could be seen of a cow was a white line and a purple shadow, we should only render the line and the shadow; in a sense we should only believe in the line and the shadow, rather than in the cow.' Such a theory 'naturally lends itself to the metaphysical suggestion that things only exist as we perceive them, or that things do not exist at all', for 'the philosophy of Impressionism is necessarily close to the philosophy of illusion'. It certainly 'tended to contribute, however indirectly, to a certain mood of unreality and sterile desolation that settled at this time upon' the young Chesterton. Looking back, it was surprising to Chesterton how at that youthful age he had been able so quickly to think his 'way back to thought

[115] Chesterton, *Culture and the Coming Peril*, 6.

itself. It is a very dreadful thing to do; for it may lead to thinking that there is nothing but thought.' He

did not very clearly distinguish between dreaming and waking; not only as a mood but as a metaphysical doubt, I felt as if everything might be a dream. It was as if I had myself projected the universe from within, with its trees and stars; and that is so near to the notion of being God that it is manifestly even nearer to going mad.

But, far from being mad in any medical sense, he 'was simply carrying the scepticism of my time as far as it would go'. He had outplayed the sceptics at their own game, so that, when 'dull atheists came and explained to me that there was nothing but matter, I listened with a sort of calm horror of detachment, suspecting that there was nothing but mind'. As a result, he had 'always felt that there was something thin and third-rate about materialists and materialism ever since. The atheist told me so pompously that he did not believe there was any God; and there were moments when I did not even believe there was any atheist.'[116]

But even intellectual scepticism was not as bad as the moral scepticism of the Decadents of the *fin de siècle*, chief among them Oscar Wilde. Chesterton, however, surprisingly places very little blame on them in contrast to the Impressionists in the *Autobiography*. He tells us: 'There is something truly menacing in the thought of how quickly I could imagine the maddest, when I had never committed the mildest crime.' But he then merely remarks: 'Something may have been due to the atmosphere of the Decadents, and their perpetual hints of the luxurious horrors of paganism; but I am not disposed to dwell much on that defence; I suspect I manufactured most of my morbidities for myself.' In spite of having reached a 'condition of moral anarchy', he pointedly adds that he had never 'felt the faintest temptation to the particular madness of Wilde', referring to Wilde's homosexuality, even though he 'could at this time imagine the worst and wildest disproportions and distortions of more normal passion', 'overpowered and oppressed with a sort of congestion of imagination' as he was. He had 'an overpowering impulse to record or draw horrible ideas and images; plunging in deeper and deeper as in a blind spiritual suicide'.[117] Part of the crisis was probably due to the fact that 'he was going through an unusually late puberty... his voice had barely broken', so that he was experiencing the kind of sexual awareness that would normally have come much earlier at school.[118] Contemporary ideas of 'the relativity

---

[116] *A.* 94–5.   [117] *A.* 95–6.   [118] Ward, *GKC* 43.

of evil or the unreality of sin' barely occurred to him: for he had 'dug quite low enough to discover the devil; and even in some dim way to recognise the devil'. As a result, when he eventually emerged as what 'was called an Optimist, it was because I was one of the few people in that world of diabolism who really believed in devils'.[119]

Chesterton does not mention in the *Autobiography* his encounter with a real diabolist, which clearly affected him very powerfully, a failure that suggests that in retrospect he underestimated the influence of the Decadent atmosphere of the 1890s on his mood and exaggerated the effects of adolescence aggravated by idleness and lack of purpose in his studies. In fact, in 1907, only little more than a decade later when the memory of the event and of the time was much fresher in his mind than at the end of his life, he wrote an account of this encounter in an article for the *Daily News* called 'The Diabolist'. And here he makes it very clear that his experience of moral evil was by no means uninfluenced by others. What he makes clear, unlike in the *Autobiography*, is that his own idleness at the Slade threw him into the company of other idlers 'who were very different from myself, and who were idle for reasons very different from mine'. Chesterton was idle not merely because he was drifting and dabbling in various things, but because he 'was very much occupied; I was engaged about that time in discovering, to my own extreme and lasting astonishment, that I was not an atheist'. However, there were other idlers at a loose end who were 'engaged in discovering' very different things. Chesterton remembered very vividly one of these 'blackguards', 'a man with a long, ironical face, and close and red hair; he was by class a gentleman, and could walk like one, but preferred, for some reason, to walk like a groom carrying two pails'. Similarly, he was different from his 'dirty, drunken' cronies, with whom he could 'talk a foul triviality' as easily as he 'would talk with me about Milton or Gothic architecture'. One dark wintry evening he and Chesterton were strolling on the long flight of steps in front of the College building where the Slade was housed. All that could be distinguished below was a bonfire in the grounds, from which 'from time to time the red sparks went whirling past us'; above it was just possible to make out 'the colossal façade of the Doric building, phantasmal, yet filling the sky, as if Heaven were still filled with the gigantic ghost of Paganism'. Suddenly, his companion asked Chesterton why he was becoming 'orthodox'. Because, Chesterton replied:

[119] *A.* 96.

'I have come, rightly or wrongly, after stretching my brain till it bursts, to the old belief that heresy is worse even than sin. An error is more menacing than a crime, for an error begets crimes.' 'You mean dangerous to morality,' he said in a voice of wonderful gentleness. 'I expect you are right. But why do you care about morality?'

He had thrust his head forward into the light of the bonfire, 'so that he looked like a fiend staring down into the flaming pit'. Chesterton had the 'sense of being tempted in the wilderness'. As some more sparks flew past, he asked his companion, 'Aren't those sparks splendid?' If his companion would grant that, as he did, then Chesterton declared that he could 'deduce Christian morality' from them. He himself had once thought that 'one's pleasure in a flying spark was a thing that would come and go with the spark'. Now he knew that the pleasure in fact depended on the humble gratitude that things existed at all. With 'a horrible fairness of the intellect that made me despair of his soul', the diabolist freely admitted that religion produced humility and humility joy: 'But,' he countered, 'shall I not find in evil a life of its own? Granted that for every woman I ruin one of those red sparks will go out; will not the expanding pleasure of ruin...'. 'Do you not see that fire?' Chesterton interrupted, 'If we had a real fighting democracy, some one would burn you in it; like the devil-worshipper that you are.' In his 'tired, fair way', the diabolist concluded the exchange: 'Perhaps. Only what you call evil I call good.' He descended the steps alone, 'and I felt as if I wanted the steps swept and cleaned'. Following him later into the building to collect his hat that hung in 'a low, dark passage', Chesterton heard him uttering the unforgettable words to 'one of the vilest of his associates': 'I tell you I have done everything else. If I do that I shan't know the difference between right and wrong.' Chesterton 'rushed out without daring to pause; and as I passed the fire I did not know whether it was hell or the furious love of God.'[120]

In his *Autobiography* Chesterton explains how he had come to his 'ortho-dox' position. After having been for some time in 'the darkest depths of the contemporary pessimism', he had 'a strong inward impulse to revolt; to dislodge this incubus or throw off this nightmare'. And he came, 'with little help from philosophy and no real help from religion', to invent 'a rudi-mentary and makeshift mystical theory of my own', namely, that 'even mere existence ... was extraordinary enough to be exciting. Anything was magnificent compared with nothing.' For this idea of fundamental gratitude

---

[120] *TT* 226–31.

he was to some extent indebted to such writers as Whitman, Browning, and Stevenson, even though he had his own inchoate way of understanding that 'no man knows how much he is an optimist, even when he calls himself a pessimist, because he has not really measured the depths of his debt to whatever created him and enabled him to call himself anything'. Religion and art were meant 'to dig for this submerged sunrise of wonder; so that a man sitting in a chair might suddenly understand that he was actually alive, and be happy'. When, then, he began to write, he was filled with a 'fiery' determination 'to write against the Decadents and the Pessimists who ruled the culture of the age'. He mentions as an example his poem 'By the Babe Unborn' (in *The Wild Knight*), 'which imagined the uncreated creature crying out for existence and promising every virtue if he might only have the experience of life. Another conceived the scoffer as begging God to give him eyes and lips and a tongue that he might mock the giver of them; a more angry version of the same fancy.' He also thought of the idea that would become the theme of his novel *Manalive*.[121]

Chesterton's gratitude for life itself included a special gratitude for friendship. Among his notebooks that survive, which contain both drawings and stories (finished and unfinished),[122] there is one in particular that dates from 1894 to 1896,[123] that is a kind of record of Chesterton's emerging philosophy of life, and that for convenience may be referred to as 'the Notebook'. There in 'An Idyll' he writes:

Tea is made; the red fogs shut round the house but the gas burns.
I wish I had at this moment round the table
A company of fine people.
Two of them are at Oxford and one in Scotland and two at other places.
But I wish they would all walk in now, for the tea is made.[124]

To his great friend Bentley he wrote while on holiday in North Berwick, presumably in the summer of 1894:

Inwardly speaking, I have had a funny time. A meaningless fit of depression, taking the form of certain absurd psychological worries, came upon me, and instead of dismissing it and talking to people, I had it out and went very far into

---

[121] *A*. 96–7.

[122] Some of the best drawings and completed fairy tales were published posthumously in *The Coloured Lands* (London: Sheed & Ward, 1938), with an introduction by Maisie Ward.

[123] BL Add. MS 73334.   [124] Ward, *GKC* 47.

the abysses, indeed. The result was that I found that things, when examined, necessarily *spelt* such a mystically satisfactory state of mind, that without getting back to earth, I saw lots that made me certain it is all right. The vision is fading into common day now, and I am glad. The frame of mind was the reverse of gloomy, but it would not do for long. It is embarrassing, talking with God face to face, as a man speaketh to his friend.

In another letter he wrote: 'A cosmos one day being rebuked by a pessimist, replied, "How can you, who revile me, consent to speak by my machinery? Permit me to reduce you to nothingness and then we will discuss the matter." Moral. You should not look a gift universe in the mouth.'[125] In the Notebook he noted charmingly: 'Existence is the deepest fact we can think of | And it is such a nice fact.'[126]

Lucian Oldershaw remembered reading Walt Whitman to Chesterton in his bedroom: 'The séance lasted from two to three hours, and we were intoxicated with the excitement of the discovery.'[127] And Cecil Chesterton testified to the 'profound and decisive' influence of Whitman's *Leaves of Grass* on his brother:

The effect...was electric. They [the poems] seemed to sum up the aspirations of his own youth. They gave him a faith to hold to, and a gospel to preach. He set himself to proclaim 'the whole divine democracy of things,' as he calls it in the *Wild Knight*. He idealized the remnant of the J.D.C. into the Mystical City of Friends. He embraced passionately the three great articles of Whitman's faith, the ultimate goodness of all things implying the acceptance of the basest and meanest no less than the noblest in life, the equality and solidarity of men, and the redemption of the world by comradeship. You will find Whitman's influence everywhere present in his earlier work...[128]

The idea of the 'equality and solidarity of men' is reflected in a letter Chesterton wrote to Bentley while on holiday in Scotland, in which he rejoices in the absence of 'the cursed class feeling'.[129] Above all, Whitman was a salutary antidote to the Decadents. In a novel he wrote probably either in late 1893 or early 1894, which was unpublished during his lifetime, *Basil Howe: A Story of Young Love*,[130] his hero defended 'the egalitarian vigour of the modern world against the aesthetic distaste of a young poet' in true

---

[125] Ward, *GKC* 48, with text corrected from BL Add. MS 43191, fo. 145.
[126] Oddie, 133.   [127] Ward, *GKC* 49.   [128] *CC* 24–5.
[129] G. K. Chesterton to E. C. Bentley, n.d., BL Add MS 73191, fos. 33–4.
[130] *Basil Howe: A Story of Young Love*, ed. Denis J. Conlon (London: New City, 2001). For the date, see pp. 12–13.

Whitmanian fashion.[131] Writing again, apparently in the same summer of 1894, to Bentley from Florence, Chesterton declares that Whitman, had he been an architect, would have built a tower like that of Giotto in the Piazza del Duomo, with its series of bas-reliefs celebrating the achievements of man: 'It is religion in the grandest sense, but there is not a shred of doctrine (even the Fall is omitted) about the history in stone.' Delighted to find that 'the great fresco' in Santa Maria Novella describing the communion of saints contained not only Plato and Cicero but 'best of all, Arius', he exclaimed '"Heretico!" (a word of impromptu manufacture)' to the guide, who 'nodded, smiled and was positively radiant with the latitudinarianism of the old Italian painter'. Chesterton's own reflection, which would have greatly embarrassed him later, was: 'It was interesting for it was a fresh proof that even the early Church united had a period of thought and tolerance before the dark ages closed round it.'[132]

Gratitude for existence and life implied gratitude to someone, and it seems from Chesterton's Notebook that his new-found 'orthodoxy' at first simply meant that Chesterton reverted to the Unitarian theism of the Revd Stopford Brooke. The emphasis is on the humanity of Christ, the Son of Man, who is the perfect human being, but who is only the Son of God in the sense that every man is. But a late entry towards the end of 1896 shows a distinct development away from this religion of humanity to a more orthodox Christianity. It is a brief but striking poem entitled 'Parables':

> There was a man who dwelt in the east centuries ago,
> And now I cannot look at a sheep or a sparrow,
> A lily or a cornfield, a raven or a sunset,
> A vineyard or a mountain, without thinking of him;
> If this be not to be divine, what is it?[133]

It was in the autumn of 1896 that Chesterton also first met his future wife, who was a Christian.

[131] Oddie, 138.

[132] Ward, *GKC* 51, with text corrected from BL Add. MS 73191, fo. 43.

[133] Oddie, 156. Oddie, 145–56, enlarges on and corrects the account given in Ward, *GKC* 60–4.

2

Publishing and Engagement

Aᴄᴄᴏʀᴅɪɴɢ to Chesterton's account in the *Autobiography*, it was Ernest Hodder Williams, a fellow student and friend at University College, whose family ran the publishing house of Hodder & Stoughton, who was responsible for his change of intended career from art to literature. Their literary conversations following Professor Ker's lectures persuaded Williams that Chesterton could write, 'a delusion which he retained to the day of his death'. As a result and in the light of his art studies, Williams gave him some books on art to review for the *Bookman*, 'the famous organ of his firm and family'. Having 'entirely failed to learn how to draw or paint' at the Slade, he 'tossed off easily enough some criticisms of the weaker points of Rubens or the misdirected talents of Tintoretto'. He had found his métier: 'I had discovered the easiest of all professions; which I have pursued ever since.' What struck Chesterton as he looked back was his 'extraordinary luck'. It was particularly extraordinary that 'so unbusinesslike a person should have so businesslike a friend'. And it was also 'outrageously unjust that a man should succeed in becoming a journalist merely by failing to become an artist'.[1] In actual fact, it was not until December 1899 that a review of a book on Velasquez and Poussin appeared, but without his name, in the *Bookman*. But it was not his first publication,[2] nor his first review, which appeared in the *Academy* on 22 June 1895, an unsigned review of a Ruskin reader.

---

[1] *A.* 101–2.   [2] See above, p. 23.

On the eve of his twenty-first birthday in May 1895, Chesterton had written to tell Bentley that he had been asked to write for the *Academy*. He described his interview with the 'fidgety' editor, a Mr Cotton, 'who runs round the table while he talks with you. When he agrees with you he shuts his eyes tight and shakes his head. When he means anything rather seriously he ends up with a loud nervous laugh.' Chesterton had sent him a review of a Ruskin anthology, which Cotton read in his presence, and then 'delivered himself with astonishing rapidity to the following effect: "This is very good: you've got something to say: Oh, yes: this is worth saying..."'. Cotton asked him to 'make it a little longer and then send it in'. Cotton also offered him a book of prose by Robert Bridges to review. The two reviews appeared unsigned among the shorter, unsigned reviews in the June and October issues.[3] Chesterton's journalistic career had begun. And Cotton was his 'first taskmaster'. He was 'tired of writing about what [he] liked'. 'Well,' he was told, 'you'll have no reason to complain of that in journalism'.[4]

When he later looked back on 'these first stages' in his career, Chesterton wondered at the 'element of luck, and even of accident'. For 'these opportunities were merely things that happened to me'. It was not lack of ambition:

The essential reason was that my eyes were turned inwards rather than outwards...I was still oppressed with the metaphysical nightmare of negations about mind and matter, with the morbid imagery of evil, with the burden of my own mysterious brain and body; but by this time I was in revolt against them; and trying to construct a healthier conception of cosmic life, even if it were one that should err on the side of health. I even called myself an optimist, because I was so horribly near to being a pessimist.[5]

Obviously, these small commissions—and contributors to the *Academy* were not even paid—could not support Chesterton. And so, after leaving University College in the summer of 1895, without a degree, he got a job at Redway's, a publisher of occult literature, possibly on the suggestion and

[3] Oddie, 157.

[4] Ward, *GKC* 65, with text corrected from BL Add. MS 73191, fos. 141–2. Ward is not the most accurate of transcribers, but here her text is unusually inaccurate. In particular, she fails to transcribe 'He is my first taskmaster' but prints instead 'And my joy in having begun my life is very great', words that do not appear in this undated letter to Bentley.

[5] *A*. 102–3.

even with the help of Williams.[6] The office was near the British Museum. He told Bentley that he was 'beastly busy, but there is something exciting about it'. For he would 'much rather be busy in a varied, mixed up way, with half a hundred things to attend to, than with one blank day of monotonous "study" before me'. He was writing late at night after working during the evening on the revision of his story 'A Picture of Tuesday' that would be published in the Slade's new *Quarto* journal.[7] And he contrasted this with the varied day's work:

there is no work so tiring as writing: that is, not for fun, but for publication. Other works [*sic*] has a repetition, a machinery, a reflex action about it somewhere, but to be on the stretch *inventing things*, making them out of nothing, making them as good as you can for a matter of four hours leaves me more inclined to lie down and read Dickens than I ever feel after nine hours ramp at Redway's.

He had two jobs at Redway's: reading manuscripts sent for publication and sending out review copies of published books.[8] He had begun work at Redway's at the end of September 1895 and remained there for just over a year, before moving to the much more prestigious publishing house of Fisher Unwin at 11 Paternoster Buildings at the end of October 1896.[9]

Here he was involved in editing books as well as reviewing manuscripts, some of which required expert knowledge he did not possess—but 'the more I see of the publishing world, the more I come to the conclusion that I know next to nothing, but that the vast mass of literary people know less'. One of the books he had to edit was a travel book by a sea captain whose ship was attacked off the New Guinea coast by 'shoals of canoes full of myriads of cannibals of a race who file their teeth to look like the teeth of dogs, and hang weights in their ears till the ears hang like dogs' ears, on the shoulder'. The captain had escaped, but some of his men were left dead on the shore: 'All night long he heard the horrible noise of the banqueting gongs and saw the huge fires that told his friends were being eaten.' Chesterton's job was to translate 'the honest captain into English

[6] Barker, 67.
[7] 'A Picture of Tuesday', as well as the other story, 'A Crazy Tale', that he had been working on as a student in either 1894 or more likely 1895, were published respectively in the first number of summer 1896 (pp. 19–22) and the third number of autumn 1897 (pp. 25–31) of the *Quarto*, and have been republished in *The Collected Works of G. K. Chesterton*, xiv (San Francisco: Ignatius Press, 1993), pp. 60–3, 69–75.
[8] Ward, *GKC* 66–8, with text corrected from BL Add. MS 73191, fos. 146–7.
[9] Oddie, 159, 162.

grammar, a thing which appals him much more than Papuan savages', and that meant a good deal of rewriting 'where relatives and dependent sentences have been lost past recovery'. Then there was a book of Chinese history for which he had to find illustrations—but 'I know no more of China than the man in the moon (less, for he has seen it, at any rate)'. He hoped that he would become so knowledgeable that 'people will be looking behind for my pig-tail'.[10]

Chesterton also had a practical chore to perform at Fisher Unwin. Having written up publicity blurbs for books the firm was publishing, he had to duplicate them on a cyclostyle. This was the hardest of his jobs, from which he would emerge covered with ink to the vast amusement of the rest of the office. Always untidily dressed, he would invariably carry a sword-stick, from which the rapier would slip and clatter down the steps outside the office as he fiddled with the handle, adding to the mirth of his colleagues within.[11]

At the same time Chesterton was busy with his own writing. He was polishing up a collection of nonsense verse, *Greybeards at Play*, to send to a publisher; he was also putting together a collection of his serious verse that would become *The Wild Knight*. There was also a novel that 'has become too much a part of me not to be constantly having chapters written—or rather growing out of the others'.[12]

In 1893 Chesterton had enthusiastically embraced the Socialism of Robert Blatchford's *Merrie England*, which he saw as essentially Christian: 'what the old churches felt instinctively to be the essential conflict between riches and the soul.'[13] But now he rejected the idea that a Christian must be a Socialist: no reasonable person could confuse the tone of the Sermon on the Mount with that of contemporary Socialist literature. The rich young man of the gospel asked 'What shall I do?'—whereas the modern rich young man who becomes a Socialist asks not what he should do but 'What will society do?' Humility was 'the exciting paradox of Christianity', but its absence was especially notable among Socialists, even if they were Christian Socialists. Then there was Christian joy, or what Chesterton calls 'cheerfulness', and its absence was strangely conspicuous among Socialists, who believed so optimistically in the inevitability of social progress; but it was not so surprising when one considered the difference again between predicting, however confidently, 'ultimate social perfection' and actually

[10] Ward, *GKC* 68–70.   [11] Barker, 69–70; Coren, 76.

[12] Ward, *GKC* 70.

[13] Oddie, 100, with text corrected from BL Add. MS 73197, fo. 6.

having 'something to do' that makes a human being 'cheerful', whose nature demands not 'an ultimate idea' but an 'immediate way of making for it'.[14] Whether or not Chesterton had yet met his future wife, 'Who brought the Cross to me' (according to the dedication in *The Ballad of the White Horse*[15]), when he wrote any of this, we do not know.[16]

Not long before meeting her, he had written whimsically in a notebook 'begun in 1894 and used at intervals for the next four or five years, in which [he] wrote down his philosophy step by step as he came to discover it':[17]

> About Her whom I have not yet met
>   I wonder what she is doing
>   Now, at this sunset hour,
> Working perhaps, or playing, worrying or laughing,
> Is she making tea, or singing a song, or writing,
>   or praying, or reading?
> Is she thoughtful, as I am thoughtful?
>   Is she looking now out of the window
>   As I am looking out of the window?

A little later in this notebook, however, he wrote: 'You are a very stupid person, | I don't believe you have the least idea how nice you are.' The lines are entitled 'F.B.'.[18] The couplet appears ten pages before 'Parables' in the notebook, 'with its question "If this be not divine, what is it?"' Was it possible to detect here the influence of 'F.B.'?[19]

2

Frances Blogg was the eldest daughter of a deceased diamond merchant. She was four years older than Chesterton.[20] The original Huguenot French surname 'de Blogue' had been unfortunately anglicized into 'Blogg'. The father's early death had left the family in reduced circumstances, and the three daughters had had to find jobs. Frances herself was a

---

[14] Ward, *GKC* 72–4, 76.   [15] *CP* (1933), 223.

[16] Ward, *GKC* 76, who attributes this fragmentary manuscript to the years 1895–8.

[17] Ward, *GKC* 56–7.   [18] Ward, *GKC* 77. For the poem, see also *CP* i. 62.

[19] Oddie, 156.

[20] She was born on 28 June 1869. St George's Church, Bloomsbury, baptismal register. Strangely, the date of her birth is given as 1870 in the baptismal register of St Augustine's Church, High Wycombe when she was conditionally baptised (see p. 556).

secretary at the Westminster headquarters of the Parents' National Educational Union. Chesterton first met the family in the autumn of 1896 through his friend Oldershaw, who was romantically interested in one of the three attractive daughters who was called Ethel, whom he was to marry.[21] The family lived at 6 Bath Road, Bedford Park, an outer suburb of West London, to the west of Hammersmith. Bedford Park was the first garden city in the world, built in half-timbered red brick with quaintly twisted high chimneys, and set in tree-lined avenues with spacious lawns.[22]

Chesterton's mother did not approve of arty-crafty Bedford Park, which was frequented by artists and writers. Besides, she had already chosen a wife for her son, the golden-tressed angel he had played with as a child, Annie Firmin, the daughter of a childhood friend of hers.[23] 'Very open air,' according to Lawrence Solomon, 'not booky, but good at games and practical'. No doubt Mrs Chesterton saw her as the perfect foil to her intellectual son's impracticality. As a married lady in Vancouver, Annie years later recalled that Chesterton's mother never liked either his best friend Bentley or Frances. Annie herself preferred Cecil to his brother (not that she was in the least romantically interested in him either), and thought that Cecil was the favourite of both his parents, having, as she put it, 'more heart than the brilliant Gilbert'. No doubt, it was Chesterton's realization of his mother's feelings that made him tell her by letter, while sitting in the same room ('You may possibly think this a somewhat eccentric proceeding'), of his feelings for Frances. 'I am going to tell you,' he wrote, 'the whole of a situation in which I believe I have acted rightly, though I am not absolutely certain, and to ask for your advice on it.' The approach could not have been more diplomatic or sensitive. He cleverly then quoted a remark of his mother's back at her:

About eight years ago, you made a remark.—This may show you that if we 'jeer' at your remarks, we remember them. The remark applied to the hypothetical young lady with whom I should fall in love and took the form of saying 'If she is good, I shan't mind who she is.' I don't know how many times I have said that over to myself in the last two or three days in which I have decided on this letter.

He was not married, he assured her, or even engaged. But he was sure that his mother realized that he did not go to Bedford Park every Sunday 'for the sake of the scenery'. At first, he had simply enjoyed 'a very intimate, but quite breezy and Platonic friendship with Frances Blogg,

---

[21] Ward, *GKC* 77–8; Ffinch, 49.   [22] Barker, 70–2.
[23] Ward, *GKC* 15.

reading, talking and enjoying life together, having great sympathies on all subjects'. But then he made 'the thrilling, but painfully responsible discovery that Platonism, on my side, had not the field by any means to itself'. 'That is how we stand now,' he concluded. 'Noone [*sic*] knows, except her family and yourself.' Frances herself had asked him to tell his mother 'soon': 'Tell her I am not so silly as to expect her to think me good enough, but really I will try to be.' This, from Chesterton's point of view, was an 'aspiration which . . . naturally provokes a smile'. At this his mother came up to him: 'Here you give me a cup of cocoa. Thank you.'[24] It is ironic that at this most important moment of his life Chesterton should have been offered cocoa, a drink that he was much later famously to revile.

In assuring his mother that they were not yet engaged, Chesterton presumably meant that their engagement had not been publicly announced and formalized by the wearing of engagement rings, since that could not be done until their parents had been told. Chesterton's admission to his mother that he was not 'absolutely certain' that he had 'acted rightly' presumably refers to his getting informally engaged so quickly; he does not seem to have had any doubt about his love for Frances or hers for him, but perhaps he means to acknowledge that he should possibly have talked to his mother before committing himself. As for his prospective mother-in-law, his first meeting with her after his engagement was apparently marked with great embarrassment, so, looking for a topic for conversation, she asked him how he liked the new wallpaper. He went straight over to the wall, gazed at it and drew a piece of chalk out of his pocket, with which he proceeded to draw a portrait of Frances on the new wallpaper. Mrs Blogg said nothing but had the drawing wiped off. It seems that she thought that the engagement should be kept secret, since it looked as if they would not be in a financial position to marry for a long time. But such a secret could hardly be kept—especially when Chesterton would visit Frances's office most mornings before going to work in order to write a message for her on her blotting-paper. In a letter thanking her for sending him some pressed flowers in the Victorian fashion, including a forget-me-not, he wrote: 'I must answer with proper caution. I will try not to forget you.' As for keeping their engagement secret, he assured her that she and her mother were 'the only guardians of reticence' that she needed 'to appease or satisfy':

---

[24] Ward, *GKC* 80–3, with text corrected from BL MS Add. 73193, fos. 73–9.

For my part, it is no exaggeration but the simple fact that if any fine morning you feel inclined to send the news on a postcard to Queen Victoria, I should merely be pleased at the incident. I want everybody to know: I want even the Siberian standing beside his dog-sledge to have something to rejoice his soul: I hunger for the congratulations of the Tasmanian blacks. Always tell anyone you feel inclined to and the instant you feel inclined to. For the sake of your Mother's anxieties I cheerfully put off the time when I can appear in my regalia, but it is rather rough to be timidly appealed to as if I were the mystery-mongering blackguard adventurer of 'the secret engagement', despised even by the Editress of 'Home Chats'.[25]

In his *Autobiography* Chesterton tells us that he had had a distant vision of Bedford Park before being introduced to the Blogg family. In the years after he had left school he had been accustomed to walk for miles in London. Before the advent of motor traffic it was possible to walk for most of the way from Kensington to St Paul's Cathedral, for instance, in the middle of the road. It was on one of these walks that he 'first saw as from afar, the first fantastic signal of something new and as yet far from fashionable; something like a new purple patch on that grey stretch of streets'. He had been wandering towards Kew through Hammersmith, when he 'turned for some reason, or more likely without a reason, into a side street and straggled across the dusty turf through which ran a railway, and across the railway one of those disproportionately high bridges which bestride such narrow railway-lines like stilts'. Again, for no particular reason, he climbed up to this bridge: 'it was evening and I think it was then I saw in the distance of that grey landscape, like a ragged red cloud of sunset, the queer artificial village of Bedford Park.' Its 'manufactured quaintness' was very suitable for 'a colony for artists who were almost aliens; a refuge for persecuted poets and painters hiding in their red-brick catacombs or dying behind their red-brick barricades, when the world should conquer Bedford Park'.[26]

The most famous inhabitant of Bedford Park was the Irish poet W. B. Yeats, 'perhaps the best talker I ever met, except his old father who alas will talk no more in this earthly tavern, though I hope he is still talking in Paradise'. The older Yeats was the painter John Butler Yeats, who owned the house in Bedford Park where Chesterton got to know 'the family more a less as a whole', not only the poet but his brother Jack and sisters Lily and Lolly, 'names cast backwards and forwards in a unique sort of comedy of Irish wit, gossip, satire, family quarrels and family pride'. The father 'had

---

[25] Ward, *RC* 36–7, with text corrected from BL Add. MS 73193, fo. 26.
[26] *A.* 135–6.

that rare but very real thing, entirely spontaneous style': 'That style, or swift construction of a complicated sentence, was the sign of a lucidity now largely lost.' It was to be found in 'the most spontaneous explosions of Dr Johnson'; but since then 'some muddled notion' had 'arisen that talking in that complete style is artificial; merely because the man knows what he means and means to say it'. The idea that there was something artificial about eloquence was a prejudice that Chesterton often attacked: 'I know not from what nonsense world the notion first came; that there is some connection between being sincere and being semi-articulate.' The poet son 'affected' Chesterton 'strongly, but in two opposite ways; like the positive and negative poles of a magnet'. He stood out against the 'drab background of dreary modern materialism' that he attacked with his 'concrete mysticism'. Chesterton approved of Yeats's belief in fairies, whose existence Yeats defended with an argument that Chesterton never forgot and that was bound to appeal to him—namely, that it was not 'abnormal men like artists, but normal men like peasants', who witnessed to their existence. But Yeats's belief in theosophy, on the other hand, he 'disliked', even at a time when he himself was, he says with more than a little exaggeration, 'almost entirely Pagan and Pantheist'. But perhaps it was not so much theosophy that Chesterton disliked as theosophists who were elitists who had no interest in a common man like the peasant:

they had shiny pebbly eyes and patient smiles. Their patience mostly consisted of waiting for others to rise to the spiritual plane where they themselves already stood . . . they never seemed to hope that *they* might evolve and reach the plane where their honest green-grocer already stood. They never wanted to hitch their own lumbering wagon to a soaring cabman; or see the soul of their charwoman like a star beckon to the spheres where the immortals are.

However, Yeats himself was very different from the usual theosophical lady who had Mrs Besant as her 'special spiritual prophetess', 'a dignified, ladylike, sincere, idealistic egoist'. Instead, Yeats 'sought out Madam Blavatsky, who was a coarse, witty, vigorous, scandalous old scally-wag; and I admire his taste'. But Chesterton did think that 'this particular Oriental twist led' Yeats 'a dance, when he followed the fakirs and not the fairies'. Chesterton thought that Yeats had been 'bewitched' and that 'Madam Blavatsky was the witch'. On the other hand, Yeats was 'not deceived' and 'taken in by the theosophical smile; or all that shining, or rather shiny, surface of optimism. He, having a more penetrating mind, had already penetrated to the essential pessimism that lies behind the Asiatic placidity; and it is arguable that the pessimism was not so depressing as the optimism.' Anyway, Chesterton found himself in 'this odd double attitude towards the poet, agreeing with him about the fairytales on which most people disagreed with him, and disagreeing with him about the philosophy on which most people agreed with him'.[27]

Among Bedford Park's artistic and intellectual attractions was a debating club called the 'I.D.K.'. It was there that Chesterton first tried crudely to expound his 'inchoate and half-baked philosophy' that 'where there is anything there is God'; philosophically inadequate as this proposition was, at the time he would have been 'amazed to know how near in some ways was my Anything to the *Ens* of St Thomas Aquinas'. There was 'an awful awe of secrecy' that was 'supposed to attach to the true meaning of the initials' by which the club was named. For

it was a strict rule of the club that its members should profess ignorance of the meaning of its name . . . The stranger, the mere intruder into the sacred village, would ask, 'But what does I.D.K. mean?'—and the initiate was expected to shrug his shoulders and say, 'I don't know,' in an offhand manner; in the hope that it would not be realised that, in a seeming refusal to reply, he had in fact replied.

Chesterton did not know whether the motto was indicative of the 'mysticism' and 'Celtic twilight' of the school of Yeats or 'the materialistic midnight' of religious agnosticism—'both points of view were, of course, present; and I think they pretty well divided that intellectual world between them'. As for himself, he preferred the former.[28] Frances Blogg was one of its founders, her sister Ethel the secretary, and her brother Knollys the treasurer. Chesterton wrote to 'Miss Blogg' asking if he might bring his friend Bentley to a meeting, in accordance with the rules of the I. D. K. '(which I repeat nightly before laying my head on my pillow) [where] it is written that any member may bring a visitor to a meeting provided he does not bring same visitor twice during the same Term (vol. CCXXXIX. Fol 2299183512. sect 676 ab)'. If Miss Blogg had no objection, he would bring Bentley to the next debate. However, the rules also indicated 'the desirability of letting the hostess know of the contemplated invasion. This seems slightly reasonable. But though I love, reverence and adore the hostess I do not know who she is.' Perhaps Miss Blogg would kindly tell him her name, or alternatively tell her herself if the notification ought to come from her.[29]

In his *Autobiography* Chesterton recalled how one day Ethel Blogg came home to announce with delight that Yeats had 'cast her horoscope, or

---

[27] *A.* 138–9, 144–7.   [28] *A.* 148.
[29] G. K. Chesterton to Miss Blogg, n.d., photocopy, GKCL.

performed some such occult rite, and told her that she was especially under the influence of the moon. I happened to mention this to a sister of the secretary, who had only just returned to the family circle, and she told me in the most normal and unpretentious tone that she hated the moon.' The sister was Frances. Apart from hating the moon and

all those natural forces that seemed to be sterile or aimless; she disliked loud winds that seemed to be going nowhere; she did not care much for the sea, a spectacle of which I was very fond; and by the same instinct she was up against the moon, which she said looked like an imbecile. On the other hand, she had a sort of hungry appetite for all the fruitful things like fields and gardens and anything connected with production; about which she was quite practical.

However, not only did this strange young lady 'practise gardening'—but she 'actually practised a religion'. Professing a religion, especially an oriental religion, was not uncommon in the 'fussy culture' of Bedford Park—'but that anybody could regard religion as a practical thing like gardening was something quite new to me and, to her neighbours, new and incomprehensible'. Apparently, Frances had been sent to an Anglo-Catholic convent school, where she had imbibed high Anglicanism. She struck Chesterton as 'a queer card'. He remembered the 'green velvet dress barred with grey fur' she wore; he would have told her it was 'artistic'—'but that she hated all the talk about art'. Again, Chesterton noticed that 'she had an attractive face, which I should have called elvish'—'but that she hated all the talk about elves'.[30] In 'An Encyclopaedia of Bloggs', written on sheets of foolscap when he first got to know the family, the entry for Frances (all the other entries apart from the one on Ethel were never filled in), is not inconsistent with Chesterton's later memory:

A harmony in green and brown. There is some gold somewhere in it, but cannot be located on examination. Probably the golden crown. Harp not yet arrived. Physically there is not quite enough of her to carry all that temperament: she looks slight, fiery and wasted, with a face which would be a Burne Jones if it were not brave: it has the asceticism of cheerfulness, not the easier asceticism of melancholy. Devouring appetite for sensations; very fond of the Bible; very fond of dancing. When she is enjoying herself thoroughly, one has a sense that it would be well for her to go to sleep for a hundred years. It would be jolly fine for some prince too.

[30] *A.* 148–9.

One of the few girls, with all their spiritual superiority, who have souls, i.e. intellect and emotion pulling the same way. That all women are supernatural is obvious to the meanest capacity. But she is especially so. She dresses nicely and looks all green and furry.[31]

Cecil Chesterton's widow remembered her not dissimilarly if more prosaically: 'She had a queer elusive attraction . . . with her pale face, quite devoid of powder or the least tinge of make-up, and curiously vague eyes. She looked charming in blue or green, but she rarely wore those shades, and usually affected dim browns or greys.'[32]

What really astonished Chesterton about this strange girl was not so much that she hated the culture of Bedford Park, but that she was 'entirely unaffected' by it. To her the idea of being 'under the influence' of somebody like Yeats was incomprehensible. It was not that she did not love literature; she did, and her favourite writer was none other than Stevenson, who had had a part in bringing Chesterton back to sanity. But, unlike the other inhabitants of Bedford Park, she did not therefore regard Stevenson as her teacher or master—indeed, if he had 'walked into the room and explained his personal doubts about personal immortality, she would have regretted that he should be wrong upon the point; but would otherwise have been utterly unaffected'.[33] When she and the hugely well-read Chesterton became engaged, it was only natural that she would want to extend her reading under the tutelage of her fiancé. 'So glad', he wrote to her, 'you want to read that fascinating old liar, the Father of History [Herodotus]. I don't know why he was called the Father of History, except that he didn't pay much attention to it: may be said to have cut it off with a shilling.'[34] Meredith the novelist, on the other hand, she had almost certainly read and could respond to her fiancé's view that he was the only writer who

completely realised my profoundest conviction that the discreditable secrets of human nature seemed hugely discreditable mainly because they are secrets; weaknesses and contradictions which do not fit into the severe classical outline of our external theory of ourselves. We feel them grinning in the dark, as Robinson Crusoe saw with terror the eyes gleaming in the dark cave. But it was only his goat . . . [35]

Frances like any London commuter had to spend a good deal of her day travelling, and it struck Chesterton that 'the worst of work nowadays is

---

[31] Ward, *RC* 23–4.   [32] MCC, 26.   [33] *A.* 150.

[34] Ward, *RC* 39, with text corrected from BL Add. MS 73193, fo. 45.

[35] Ward, *RC* 40, with text corrected from BL Add. MS 73193, fo. 28.

what happens to people when they cease working; the racketing of trains and trams and the slow return to remote homes'. One day 'through sheer fatigue' Frances left her parasol in a station waiting-room; it was a fortunate loss, for it provided her shy admirer with a rare opportunity. Walking home that night from Bedford Park to his parents' home in Kensington where he was still living, Chesterton chanced to notice the station in question—'and I committed my first and last crime which was burglary, and very enjoyable'. The station was apparently closed, and so he climbed up the grass embankment and then crawled under the platform on to the line, whence he could climb onto the platform and recover the missing parasol: 'as I looked back up the tilt of turf grey in the moonshine, like unearthly lunar grasses, I did not share the lady's impiety to the patroness of lunatics.' After that momentous night of chivalrous devotion, their 'next most important meeting was not under the sign of the moon but of the sun'.[36]

Frances later often used to tell him that, 'if the sun had not been shining to her complete satisfaction on that day, the issue might have been quite different'.[37] It was fortunate, then, for the suitor that it was the kind of 'glorious' day that he did not enjoy, preferring that 'grey weather', which, his 'ungrateful countrymen' complained, was 'quite as common in summer' as in winter and appeared 'to last all the year round'.[38] In the *Autobiography*, after quoting from an essay on bridges by Belloc, where he says that the bridge that least frightens you is the bridge in St James's Park, Chesterton confesses: 'I admit that I crossed that bridge in undeserved safety; and perhaps I was affected by my early romantic vision of the bridge leading to the princess's tower. But I can assure my friend the author that the bridge in St James's Park can frighten you a good deal.'[39] On the evening after Chesterton had proposed to Frances in the summer of 1898[40] on the bridge in St James's Park and had been accepted, he wrote what seems to have been his first letter to her. He had, he informed her, been 'recently appointed to the post of Emperor of Creation'. And he had 'discovered that my existence until today has been, in truth past [*sic*] in the most intense gloom'. Never, he assured her, had he known before what happiness was: 'Happiness is not at all smug: it is not peaceful or contented, as I have always been till today. Happiness brings not peace but a sword: it shakes you like rattling dice: it breaks your speech and

[36] *A.* 150–1.   [37] *A.* 151.   [38] *RR* 382.   [39] *A.* 151; Ward, *RC* 29.
[40] Ffinch, 55.

darkens your sight. Happiness is stronger than oneself and sets its palpable foot upon one's neck.' Going home that evening in the bus (he was 'pained...that it was not a winged omnibus'), for the first time since he was a small child he felt himself 'in a kind of fierce proximity to tears', 'a new weird feeling'. He had also discovered that, 'if there is such a thing as falling in love with anyone over again, I did it in St James's Park'. There was a way of testing a man's love: one 'can always tell the real love from the slight by the fact that the latter weakens at the moment of success; the former is quadrupled'. They would be seeing each other tomorrow 'of course': 'Should you then be inclined to spurn me, pray do so. I can't think why you don't, but I suppose you know your own business best.' In another love letter, probably written not long after, he turns to her beauty:

Mr Fisher Unwin's face, however lit up by sunset, I cannot accept as any substitute. Mr Nutt the publisher [Chesterton was hoping he would publish his first book, *Greybeards at Play*] may go down week after week and stand by the hedge ['the broken hedge in the little lane at Eltham' where Chesterton saw Frances's face 'lit up by the sunset'] and endeavour to look equally lovely, but I advise him to desist.

There was a beauty 'which one must be good in order to have': 'I know that there was a Cleopatra of Egypt, who, in your temporary but unavoid-able absence, attracted the male sex to a large extent.' But hers was merely 'animal regularity', whereas Frances's kind of beauty 'begins inside and works out... Any actress with a pot of rouge and a stick of grease paint could make herself like Helen of Troy. But no one *could* look like you, without having a benediction in her heart...'.[41]

The happy suitor was anxious to share his good news with friends. To Mildred Wain, who was engaged to a member of the J.D.C., Waldo d'Avigdor, he wrote:

On rising this morning, I carefully washed my boots in hot water and blacked my face. Then assuming my coat with graceful ease and with the tails in front, I descended to breakfast, where I gaily poured the coffee on the sardines and put my hat on the fire to boil. These activities will give you some idea of my frame of mind. My family, observing me leave the house by way of the chimney, and take the fender with me under one arm, thought I must have something on my mind. So I had.

---

[41] Ward, *RC* 34–5, with text corrected from BL Add. MS 73193, fo. 21.

After announcing he was engaged, the question then arose: to whom? 'I have investigated this problem with some care, and, as far as can make out, the best authorities point to Frances Blogg. There can I think be no reasonable doubt that she is the lady. It is as well to have these minor matters clear in one's mind.'[42] In a later letter, he thanked her for providing a topic of conversation on his first visit to the Blogg family, 'with which I have since formed a dark and shameful connection'.[43] To Annie Firmin he wrote to say that one of his earliest memories was of her helping him to build a house with bricks:

I am building another one now, and it would not have been complete without your going over it. It is indeed, as you say, quaint to think of me with a wife. As to the bull fights on the landing, I think of instructing my wife in that valuable pastime and think it would form a most pleasing diversion in domestic life.'

Frances was 'quite right (as she is occasionally)' about Annie's 'lovely' letter. It was 'very nice' of Annie

to say that you mean to like Frances. I think (pardon the ardour of the observation) that there are toils even more difficult. I did it myself with great neatness. As for her, she will certainly like you, which is, in my humble and perhaps partial opinion, another way of saying that she is not a born fool. Really she is not though you might think so from—well, from a recent act on her part.[44]

Frances's sister Gertrude, who was Kipling's secretary, wrote: 'of course you are quite unworthy of Frances, but the sooner you forget it the better!'[45]

The conventional love poems he wrote at the time are not nearly as effective in conveying Chesterton's feelings as his surviving love letters, some of which were destroyed or cut as being too intimate after Frances's death, at her insistence.[46] They display that *seriousness* of humour that was to be one of the most prominent themes in his writings. In one letter he signs himself as 'always your own adoring nuisance', adding as a postscript:

[42] Ward, *GKC* 84.   [43] Ward, *GKC* 83.

[44] G. K. Chesterton to Annie Firmin, n.d., BL Add. MS 73237, fo. 51. Ward, *GKC* 84, quotes the first two sentences.

[45] Barker, 87.

[46] Dorothy Collins, Chesterton's secretary and later literary executor, left three notes among the letters that Maisie Ward was allowed to see. The first reads: 'All other letters which have not been quoted [in Ward] have been destroyed according to a promise made to Frances.' The second reads: 'Cut according to a promise made to Frances,' and the third: 'Beautiful love *paragraphs*. Cut according to a

'By the way,—I love you. I thought the fact might interest you.'[47] Writing to Frances from the seaside in Suffolk, he attempts 'to reckon up the estate I have to offer you'. It includes the 'admirable relic' of a straw hat, a walking stick 'admirably fitted to break the head of any denizen of Suffolk who denies that you are the noblest of ladies, but of no other manifest use', a copy of Whitman's poems, a packet of letters from a young lady, 'containing everything good and generous and loyal and holy and wise that isn't in Whitman's poems', a pocket knife with a device to take stones out of a horse's hoof (given a horse with a lame foot, 'one stands prepared, with a defiant smile'), a 'heart . . . mislaid somewhere'. As a reminder of his financial situation, he included also 'about three pounds in gold and silver, the remains of Mr Unwin's bursts of affection: those explosions of spontaneous love for myself, which, such is the perfect order and harmony of his mind, occur at startlingly exact intervals of time'. But, as a hope of better things to come, the inventory also included 'a book of Children's Rhymes, in manuscript, called the "Weather Book" about ¾ finished, and destined for Mr Nutt', the publisher.[48] On a more solemn note in another letter, he wonders if death may not be like love, a 'transformation . . . as beautiful and dazzling'. In the presence of Frances's mother he says he feels like a 'thief'. She would have had every right to be 'worried if you had been engaged to the Archangel Michael (who, indeed, is bearing his disappointment very well): how much more when you are engaged to an aimless, tactless, reckless, unbrushed, strange-hatted, opinionated scarecrow who has suddenly walked into the vacant place'. The adjective Chesterton should have included, indeed emphasized, in this derogatory

promise made to Frances.' BL Add. MS 73193, fos. 9, 14. Dorothy Collins had been left all Chesterton's papers 'to keep or destroy as I thought fit. The only promise I was asked to give was to destroy the love-letters which he wrote to Frances. She most generously allowed me to go through these and copy the less personal parts for the use of his biographer which I did, after which I burnt them.' Free Europe Radio interview, BL Add. MS 73477, fo. 15. Maisie Ward considered that it was 'tragic indeed that the whole of this correspondence was not spared. Dorothy Collins begged Frances to let me at least read it, but she could not prevail. And deeply as I regret, I do partly understand. Gilbert shared her feeling and with both of them it arose in part from the fact that no couple ever suffered more from the impertinences of journalistic intrusion into private life' (Ward, *RC* 47).

[47] G. K. Chesterton to Frances Blogg, n.d., BL Add. MS 73193, fo. 13.
[48] Ward, *GKC* 85–6, with text corrected from BL Add. MS 73193, fos. 10–11.

catalogue was 'poor', since it was not so much his appearance as his poverty that bothered his prospective mother-in-law.[49]

In another letter, he draws a light-hearted autobiographical sketch for Frances that includes an account of his introduction to her family:

One pleasant Saturday afternoon Lucian [Oldershaw] said to me, 'I am going to take you to see the Bloggs'—'The what?' said the unhappy man. 'The Bloggs,' said the other, darkly. Naturally assuming that it was the name of a public-house he reluctantly followed his friend. He came to a small front-garden—if it was a public-house it was not a businesslike one. They raised the latch—they rang the bell (if the bell was not in its close time just then). No flower in the pots winked. No brick grinned. No sign in Heaven or earth warned him. The birds sang on in the trees. He went in.

He becomes more serious in the description of his second visit:

he was plumped down on a sofa beside a being of whom he had a vague impression that brown hair grew at intervals all down her like a caterpillar. Once in the course of conversation she looked straight at him and he said to himself as plainly as if he had read it in a book: 'If I had anything to do with this girl I should go on my knees to her: if I spoke with her she would never deceive me: if I depended on her she would never deny me: if I loved her she would never play with me: if I trusted her she would never go back on me: if I remembered her she would never forget me'...

If not love it was trust at first sight. For his part, Chesterton can promise Frances that 'he has not, with all his faults, "gone after strange women". You cannot think how a man's self-restraint is rewarded in this.' He can also promise her that 'he has tried to love everything alive: a dim preparation for loving you'. The little mini-autobiography ends with the words: 'Here ends my previous existence. Take it: it led me to you.'[50]

3

Their happiness was suddenly shattered by the death in the summer of 1899 of Gertrude, Frances's favourite sister, whom she had offered to her fiancé as his sister too. She had been knocked down and run over by a bus while she was riding her bicycle. She was engaged to a young man called R. Brimley Johnson, who had just set up as a publisher. Frances was devastated, unable to go to work or to stay in the house where she had

---

[49] Ward, *GKC* 90.
[50] Ward, *GKC* 93–4, with text corrected from BL Add. MS 73193, fos. 19–20.

grown up with Gertrude. Immediately after the funeral she went to Italy, not only grieving for her sister but inevitably tormented as a believing Christian with the problem of how to reconcile tragic loss with a loving God. Only recently Chesterton, who had been shielded from illness and death when he was growing up, had written to her about the death of an old friend, assuring her of his belief that somehow the death must be for the good:

It seems terrible to think of so much force going out of the world suddenly, to say nothing of the blacker void left to those to whom that great heart was more thoroughly known . . . Somewhere, doubtless, in the million problems of new stars and unfinished creations, in the campaigns of God, some good thing was wavering or at bay and in the dark hour that strong name was remembered. . . . But we have to lose her. Still, I like to think of this—rather to be sure of it.[51]

All the wreaths on Gertrude's coffin were white flowers except Chesterton's, which were scarlet and orange; the card on his wreath bore the words 'He that maketh His angels spirits and His ministers a flame of fire'.[52] He had 'this sense of a great power that, hidden from us for awhile, was energising in eternity'. This 'faith' Frances shared with him. He thought that 'sorrow for the dead should above all not be a matter of conventional expression, should not stifle human mirth'.[53] 'If there occurs to anyone', he wrote to Frances, 'a really good joke about the look of my coffin, I command him by all the thunders to make it. If he doesn't I'll kick the lid up and make it myself . . . No, darling, if we are picking flowers we will not hide them if a hearse goes by.'[54]

His first letter to Frances in Italy began with a joke about his appearance: 'I am black but comely at this moment: because the cyclostyle has blacked me. Fear not. I shall wash myself. But I think it my duty to render an accurate account of my physical appearance every time I write: and shall be glad of any advice and assistance . . . '. But the humour is deadly serious as Chesterton finds consolation in his 'inchoate and half-baked' philosophy of gratitude:

I like the cyclostyle ink; it is so inky. I do not think there is anyone who takes quite such a fierce pleasure in things being themselves as I do. The startling wetness of water excites and intoxicates me: the fieriness of fire, the steeliness of steel, the

[51] Ward, *RC* 42,   [52] Ward, *RC* 43.
[53] Pencilled note by an unknown hand among material gathered by Maisie Ward for *RC*. BL Add. MS 73481A, fo. 184.
[54] Ward, *RC* 43.

unutterable muddiness of mud. It is just the same with people. . . . When we call a man 'manly' or a woman 'womanly' we touch the deepest philosophy.

He refuses to apologize for his 'rambling levity': 'I have sworn that Gertrude should *not* feel, wherever she is, that the comedy has gone out of our theatre.' Whatever else, his future wife's concern about his untidy appearance was a useful source of humour in distracting her from her grief. In another letter posted next day, he boasts:

My appearance . . . is singularly exemplary. My boots are placed, after the fastidious London fashion, on the feet: the laces are done up, the watch is going, the hair is brushed, the sleeve-links are inserted, for of such is the Kingdom of Heaven. As for my straw hat, I put it on eighteen times consecutively, taking a rush and a jump to each try, till at last I hit the right angle. I have not taken it off for three days and nights lest I should disturb that exquisite poise. Ladies, princes, queens, ecclesiastical processions go by in vain: I do not remove it. That angle of the hat is something to mount guard over.

In the same letter he returns to his philosophy of gratitude, seizing on a remark by Frances that 'it is good for us to be here':

The same remark, if I remember right, was made on the mountain of the Transfiguration. It has always been one of my unclerical sermons to myself, that that remark which Peter made on seeing the vision of a single hour, ought to be made by us all, in contemplating every panoramic change in the long Vision we call life . . .

Two days later he returned to the same theme. He had made a 'discovery' or rather seen a 'vision' between two cups of black coffee in a French restaurant in Soho—'that all good things are one thing'. And this 'one thing' was merely disguised in all the good things of this world, including Gertrude. This was the great discovery of 'the savage old Hebrews', who, unlike the polytheistic Greeks and Romans, were 'thrilled . . . by the blazing idea of all being the same God: an idea worthy of a detective story'. A few days later, again writing from Felixstowe, he told Frances that he had written some verses for her about her sister's death—'but for real strength (I don't like the word "comfort") for real peace, no human words are much good except perhaps some of the unfathomable, unintelligible, unconquerable epigrams of the Bible'. One such text was 'precious in the sight of the Lord is the death of one of his saints'—except that in accord with the philosophy of gratitude he thought it was 'a miraculous remark about anybody'. That was the one word to describe Gertrude's death: it was certainly not 'happy or providential or sweet or even perhaps good'—but it *was* 'precious'. For her death awoke in one 'a passionate sense of the "*value*"' of her life, so that even her death was 'a thing of incalculable value and mysterious sweetness: it is awful, tragic, desolating, desperately hard to bear—but still "precious".'[55]

In a letter to Frances at the end of September, Chesterton acknowledged that he was not good at giving 'many practical details' about himself; when he had time to think he thought of 'the Kosmos [*sic*] first and the Ego afterwards'. However, this was not much help to Frances, he admitted, since she was not engaged to the Kosmos:

dear me! What a time the Kosmos would have! All its Comets would have their hair brushed every morning. The Whirlwind would be adjured not to walk about when it was talking. The Oceans would be warmed with hot-water pipes. Not even the lowest forms of life would escape the crusade of tidiness: you would walk round and round the jellyfish, looking for a place to put in shirt-links.

If Frances wanted to know what he did every day he could tell her in either of two ways. He could describe a day in his life in the normal way one does: get up, dress, breakfast, take the train, then work on manuscripts at the office till two o'clock, then go out to lunch—'have—(but here perhaps it would be safer to become vague), come back, work till six . . . have dinner at home, write the novel till 11, then write to you and go to bed'. But there was another, altogether different and more real way of describing his day. This was to look at everything he did with the kind of astonished wonder at 'the sacred intoxication of existence' that his philosophy of gratitude demanded. He can say that he is going to post the letter in a red pillar box; but alternatively and more really he can say that he is going to drop it into 'the mouth of a little red goblin at the corner of the street'. Because he was so completely convinced of 'the spirituality of things', in other words that the universe is '*good* or spiritual', and only of that—he did not claim to know 'on what principle the Universe is run'—he knew that Gertrude's death was 'beautiful'. The reason it did not seem beautiful to them was that 'we do not *see* it now. What we see is her absence: but her Death is not her absence, but her Presence somewhere else.'[56]

Chesterton was now anxious to hasten the date of their marriage: this was the only cure for Frances's grief. In the meantime he could only offer his love as consolation with an attempt to make her laugh: 'I love you dear—even in the British Museum. That is the climax of the triumph of romance.' But he was becoming hopeful of improving his prospects:

[55] Ward, *GKC* 97–101.   [56] Ward, *GKC* 102–4.

I think I feel myself 'getting on': I have come out of all the worrying jobs I had to do and I am having quite a lot of chances, or half-chances, opening round me. The senior reader here, for example (a novelist and a large person), urges me to collect a book of serious poems and offers to put them before another publisher of his acquaintance.[57]

The publisher's reader referred to here was Edward Garnett, who encouraged and advised some of the most prominent writers of the period, including Conrad, Lawrence, and Forster, as well as being himself a novelist, playwright, and critic. Garnett also took Chesterton out to lunch and, when he heard that Chesterton was trying his hand at fiction, asked if he could see what he had written. 'I certainly cannot complain', Chesterton gratefully acknowledged, 'of not being sympathetically treated by the literary men I know. I wonder where the jealous, spiteful, depreciating man of letters we read of in books has got to.'[58] At the beginning of October 1899 Chesterton wrote to Frances to say that he was hoping that the first number of the *Speaker*, under its new management, would shortly contain an article by him. Meanwhile his father was corresponding with Fisher Unwin about raising his son's salary. The publishers offered an immediate rise of five shillings and a further but undisclosed one in January, together with a royalty of 10 per cent for a book Chesterton had been commissioned to write about Paris, as well as expenses for a fortnight's research in Paris. Chesterton did not need his father to point out the flaw in this offer: the lack of any assurance that he would not have to write the book on Paris *outside* the working hours for which he was paid. He may have been impractical and unworldly, but even he could see that 'the net result would be that instead of gaining more liberty to rise in the literary world', he would be 'selling the small liberty of rising that I have now for five more shillings'. His father had therefore declined the offer and asked for a better one: 'The diplomacy is worrying, yet I enjoy it: I feel like Mr Chamberlain [Joseph Chamberlain the imperialist Colonial Secretary] on the eve of war.' He was prepared to stay at Fisher Unwin for nothing less than £100 a year—which probably meant that he would not be staying. In another letter he emphasized, perhaps because he knew how impractical Mrs Blogg in particular thought he was, how interested he had become in making money:

[57] Ward, *RC* 43, with text corrected from BL Add. MS 73193, fo. 40.
[58] Barker, 104.

It is hideous how systematic and mentally *mean* I am becoming under the influence of a certain mercenary intention. Once I would pour out notions like Niagara and care as little where they went as that cataract cares for its foam: now I solemnly and with feelings of unutterable disgrace, make a note of any workable fancy I think of. I cultivate ideas like so many cursed cabbages.

At the end of October he told Frances that he was 'developing into a sort of art critic, under the persistent delusion which possesses the Editor of *The Bookman*', and that his 'first experiment in art criticism' should probably be appearing in a few days' time.[59] In fact, the Velasquez and Poussin review article appeared not in the November issue but in the December one; unfortunately it was unattributed, although Hodder Williams had written to say that he thought Chesterton would like his name to appear in an issue with an apparently extended print run of 30,000.[60]

Although the matter was of crucial importance to both of them, as Chesterton could not marry on what he was earning at present—it was inconceivable then that somebody of Frances's social position would continue working after her marriage—Chesterton light-heartedly proceeded to dismiss these 'revolutions, literary, financial and political', as insignificant 'compared with the one really tremendous event of the week' that was about to take place. 'The sun will stand still upon Leicester Square and the Moon on the Valley of Wardour St', he announced. 'For then will assemble the Grand Commemorative Meeting of the Junior Debating Club.' The Club was and always would be 'one of the main strands of my life', and it had 'left its roots deep in the hearts of twelve strangely different men'. In his next letter containing the promised account of the meeting, Chesterton began by informing Frances that he was 'certainly leaving Fisher Unwin, with much mutual courtesy and good will'. There followed a detailed lengthy account of the dinner, for which illustrated menus had been provided. Chesterton himself had proposed the toast, saying merely that 'nothing could be alleged against the Queen, except the fact that she is not a member of the J.D.C. and that I thought it spoke well for the chivalry of Englishmen that with this fact she had never been publicly taunted'. The dinner ended with them singing the anthem of the J.D.C.: 'I'm a Member—I'm a Member—Member of the J.D.C. I belong to it for ever—don't you wish that you were me.'[61] When in the next year, 1900, the Junior Debating Club threw open its annual dinner to ladies, Chesterton drew a menu for each guest: Frances's menu offered 'Crocodile de Nile Rôti

[59] Ward, *GKC* 105; Ward, *RC* 46–7.   [60] Coren, 108; Ffinch, 68.
[61] Ward, *GKC* 105–6, 109.

Dhabea' and 'Poisson extraordinaire à la société naturaliste P.N.E.U. [the Parents' National Educational Union, her employer]', accompanied by a drawing of a pair of hands, one of which was brushing an unkempt head (clearly of her fiancé) and the other turning the pages of a book.[62]

4

The *Speaker*, which was a radical weekly, was bought in the autumn of 1899 by a group of young Liberals who had been together at Oxford and who included Chesterton's friends Bentley and Oldershaw. The first number appeared just before the outbreak of the Boer War in October 1899. These young radicals were united in their opposition to the war, not because they were pacifists but because they were implacably opposed to the imperialism that was so fashionable then: 'for most men about this time Imperialism, or at least patriotism, was a substitute for religion. Men believed in the British Empire precisely because they had nothing else to believe in. Those beacon-fires of an imperial insularity shot a momentary gleam over the dark landscape of the Shropshire Lad . . .'. In his *Autobiography* Chesterton tells us that, as a patriot opposed to pacifism, he had been a 'reluctant' imperialist if 'colonial adventure . . . was the only way of protecting my country', just as he had been a 'reluctant' Socialist if 'collective organisation . . . was the only way of protecting my poorer fellow-citizens'. It was when he was in this uncomfortable position that events in South Africa 'not only woke me from my dreams like a thunder-clap, but like a lightening-flash revealed me to myself'. Public opinion was far more favourable to the Boer War than it was later to the First World War, which Chesterton considered much more important and a 'much more just' cause. But he 'suddenly realised' that he 'hated it [the Boer War]', that he 'hated the whole thing' as he 'had never hated anything before'. He hated what others liked about it: that it was such a 'cheerful' war with 'its vile assurance of victory'. The assumption that the defeat of the Boers was inevitable, 'an almost automatic process like the operation of a natural law', was repugnant to him: 'I have always hated that sort of heathen notion of a natural law.' What was perhaps even more repulsive to him was the hypocrisy of the British claim to be fighting, like the Boers, for their own countrymen, 'the commercial citizens of Johannesburg, who were commonly called the Outlanders'. For these people did not look or sound very British, as was demonstrated when Chesterton and

---

[62] Ffinch, 60.

a friend called for three cheers for some of these Outlanders with foreign names (Jews like 'Beit' and 'Eckstein', as well as 'Albu', presumably a black African) in the midst of an imperialist demonstration. When the 'Jingo mob' realized it was being laughed at, a fight broke out. Chesterton found himself engaged 'in a pugilistic encounter with an Imperialist clerk, whose pugilism was no more scientific than my own. While this encounter . . . was proceeding, another Imperialist must have abstracted my watch; the last I ever troubled to possess. He at any rate believed in the policy of Annexation.' Unlike most of his compatriots who were on the side of the Boers because they were pacifists, Chesterton was pro-Boer because he thought the Boers were fully entitled to take up arms against 'a more cosmopolitan empire at the command of very cosmopolitan financiers', which was threatening their farming communities.[63] Chesterton, of course, was not interested in the fact that some of the 'Outsiders' or *uitlanders* had indeed been oppressed by the Boers and were subjects of the British Empire; he was not interested in the British Empire or even in Britain—only in England. Nor did he take account of the fanaticism of Kruger, the Boer leader, who looked to Germany for military support against the British. As for the native Africans, who had lost their land to the Boers, they too did not come into Chesterton's calculations.[64] His own view of Africa (as described in one of his notebooks) as the 'Dark Continent', where 'step by step civilization has driven that darkness into the interior', was quite unexceptional for the time.[65]

To the young Oxford Liberals who had acquired the *Speaker* Chesterton had 'a permanent gratitude', for it was they who made possible for him his 'first connected series of articles', his 'first regular job in support of a regular cause'. As well as 'many pugnacious political articles', he also contributed 'a series of casual essays afterwards republished as *The Defendant*.[66] These were his 'A Defence of . . .' articles, which first made his name as a journalist.[67] It was, of course, his old friends Bentley and Oldershaw who had encouraged him to write for the magazine: 'He did nothing for himself till we came down from Oxford and pushed him,' recalled Oldershaw.[68] Ironically, his hope that a book review by him would appear in the first number of the new *Speaker* was disappointed when Francis Yvon Eccles, who was 'largely the literary adviser', rejected his article, as well as several subsequent articles that Oldershaw had passed on to him, because 'the handwriting was that of a Jew'.[69] It was not until April of the next year

---

[63] *A.* 112–15, 141.   [64] Ward, *RC* 54.   [65] Ffinch, 83.
[66] *A.* 118–19.   [67] Ffinch, 86.   [68] Ffinch, 49.
[69] Ward, *GKC* 113.

that book reviews and articles by Chesterton began to appear, the first being a review of a life of Ruskin, which appeared on 28 April 1900.[70] It has been suggested that Oldershaw failed to inform Eccles that Chesterton was not in fact Jewish because he did not wish to 'dignify' Eccles's anti-Semitic prejudice; after all, a third of the membership of the Junior Debating Club had been Jewish.[71] But Eccles's words, as reported by Oldershaw, do not necessarily mean that Eccles was seriously contending that Chesterton was Jewish; his name alone made it extremely unlikely, to say the least. Eccles rather was simply saying that Chesterton's handwriting was *like* that of a Jew; what he was no doubt really objecting to was Chesterton's highly ornate, Gothic script writing and his flowery signature, which he *drew* rather than wrote[72] and which Eccles probably disliked as being too artistic, Jews being famously artistic. Given that handwriting and signatures *are* generally seen as indicative of character, editors and publishers before the advent of the typewriter must have often been prejudiced in favour of or against an author because of their handwriting. Bentley and Oldershaw were both very anxious to launch their admired friend on a literary career, and it is not credible to suppose that Oldershaw did not inform Eccles of Chesterton's impeccable Gentile origins, if there had really been any such idea in Eccles's mind.

Eccles had belonged with Belloc to the Republican Club at Oxford, a club that 'never consisted of more than four members, and generally of less'. A third member was John Swinnerton Phillimore, the son of an admiral, who would become Professor of Latin at Glasgow University. The Chesterton family firm was 'agent for the large Phillimore Estate' owned by the admiral and his brother Lord Justice Phillimore, who would one day sit in judgment of Cecil Chesterton and hear the evidence of his brother. Eccles and Phillimore had been Belloc's 'most intimate friends' at Oxford. Eccles, who would become a 'distinguished French scholar', looked much more like a Frenchman than Belloc, with his French surname, who looked much more like an Englishman, indeed 'exactly like what all English farmers ought to look like; and was, as it were, a better portrait of Cobbett than Cobbett was'. Chesterton recalled in his *Autobiography* 'drinking a pot of beer with a publican' in Sussex where Belloc lived and mentioning his friend's name: 'and the publican, who obviously had never heard of books or such bosh, merely said, "Farms a bit, doesn't he?" and I thought how hugely flattered Belloc would be'. As for Phillimore, with his naval background, he looked 'very much more like a sailor than a don'. This was just as well, as you needed

[70] Clemens, 19, with corrected date.   [71] Oddie, 176.
[72] Ward, *GKC* 163–4.

'some of the qualities of the quarter-deck' in order to 'conduct classes amid
the racial and religious chaos of Glasgow, full of wild Highlanders and wild
Irish, and young fanatical Communists and old fanatical Calvinists'. On one
occasion he had been known to call for silence with the words, 'Gentlemen,
gentlemen! I have not yet ceased casting my pearls'—'the gratifying irony' of
which appeal seems 'to have been instantly grasped'. Chesterton himself
notes the irony that republicans like Belloc and Eccles 'ended as strong
Monarchists': 'But there is a thin difference between good despotism and
good democracy; both imply equality, with authority; whether the authority
be impersonal or personal. What both detest is oligarchy; even in its more
human form of aristocracy, let alone its present repulsive form of plutocracy.' For Chesterton 'the most democratic thing' next to 'a genuine republic' was 'hereditary despotism' because it was 'the ordinary man enthroned';
while 'an irrational oligarchy' such as the House of Lords, the members of
which 'owed their power to accident', was preferable to a rational oligarchy
of talent.[73] After he had become a Roman Catholic, Chesterton made
exactly the same point about the papacy and the episcopate:

It is not the people who would be the heirs of a dethroned Pope; it is some synod or
bench of bishops. It is not an alternative between monarchy and democracy, but an
alternative between monarchy and oligarchy. And, being myself one of the democratic idealists, I have not the faintest hesitation in my choice between the two latter
forms of privilege. A monarch is a man; but an oligarchy is not men; it is a few men
forming a group small enough to be insolent and large enough to be irresponsible.[74]

   Chesterton came to think that Belloc was an English traditionalist and a
French revolutionist. England had not got 'a decent revolutionary song' to
its name, for the trouble with its 'popular war songs' was that 'they were
not war-songs. They never gave the faintest hint of how anybody could
ever make war on anything. They were always waiting for the Dawn;
without the least anticipation that they might be shot at dawn, or the least
intelligent preparation for shooting anybody else at dawn.' For, Chesterton
discovered, 'the Socialist idea of war was exactly like the Imperialist idea of
war', as both Socialists and Imperialists 'always assumed that they would
win the war'. But then Belloc wrote his poem 'The Rebel', 'a very violent
and bitter poem' and 'the only revolutionary poem I ever read, that
suggested that there was any plan for making an attack'.[75]
   It seems to have been Oldershaw who arranged for Chesterton to meet
Belloc. Eccles, Bentley, and Oldershaw all claimed to have made the

[73] *H.* 186–8.   [74] *T.* 326.   [75] *A.* 28–9, 277–81.

introduction; but both Chesterton and Belloc remembered that it was Oldershaw who was responsible for the meeting, 'at the end of 1900', according to Belloc,[76] but 'soon after' his reunion with his friends who came down from Oxford in 1899, according to Chesterton, which might indicate an earlier date in the summer of 1899 but for the fact that Belloc announced that he was familiar with Chesterton's writings, which would hardly have been possible before 1900, when Chesterton began writing for the *Speaker*. A summer date is suggested by the fact that Belloc was wearing a straw hat to shade his eyes. Although, according to Oldershaw, Eccles had also tried to prejudice Belloc against reading anything by Chesterton, when they met Belloc began the conversation by announcing, 'Chesterton, you wr-r-ite very well.'[77] Belloc was four years older and already an established writer, having made his mark in the late 1890s. According to Chesterton's own recollection some fifteen or sixteen years after the event, they met 'between a little Soho paper shop and a little Soho restaurant; Belloc's arms and pockets were stuffed with French Nationalist and French Atheist newspapers. He wore a straw hat shading his eyes, which are like a sailor's, and emphasizing his Napoleonic chin . . .'. The 'little' restaurant was Mont Blanc in Gerrard Street, which 'had already become a haunt for three or four of us who held strong but unfashionable views about the South African War'. What Belloc, who was no less opposed to the war, added 'was this Roman appetite for reality and for reason in action, and when he came into the door there entered with him the smell of danger'. According to Belloc, 'he was in low spirits'; but it struck Chesterton that his 'low spirits were and are much more uproarious and enlivening than anybody else's high spirits. He talked into the night, and left behind in it a glowing track of good things.'[78] Belloc himself apparently thought that the chief effect he had on Chesterton was indeed his 'appetite for reality', particularly with regard to politics: unlike the younger man, who remarkably for someone of his class had never even left the family home, Belloc had been a boarder at the Oratory School in Birmingham while Newman was still alive, had done military service in France (being half-French), had been at Oxford, and had worked his way across America to California to bring back an American bride.[79] In his account of their first meeting in the *Autobiography*, Chesterton recalled not only 'the peculiar length and

---

[76] Clemens, 24.   [77] Ward, *GKC* 113.
[78] G. K. Chesterton, introduction to C. Creighton Mandell and Edward Shanks, *Hilaire Belloc: The Man and his Work* (London: Methuen, 1916), pp. vii, ix.
[79] Ward, *GKC* 114–15.

strength' of Belloc's chin, but also his 'high-shouldered way of wearing a coat so that it looked like a heavy overcoat, and instantly reminded me of the pictures of Napoleon'. As he talked, in particular of whether King John was the best English king, 'he every now and then volleyed out very provocative parentheses on the subject of religion'.

He said that an important Californian lawyer was coming to England to call on his family, and had put up a great candle to St Christopher praying that he might be able to make the voyage. He declared that he, Belloc, was going to put up an even bigger candle in the hope that the visitor would not make the voyage. 'People say what's the good of doing that?' he observed explosively. 'I don't know what good it does. I know it's a thing that's done. Then they say it can't do any good— and there you have a Dogma at once.' All this amused me very much, but I was already conscious of a curious undercurrent of sympathy with him...

Chesterton ends his account of this first meeting with Belloc by joking that it was 'from that dingy little Soho café, as from a cave of witchcraft, that there emerged the quadruped, the twiformed monster Mr [George Bernard] Shaw has nicknamed the Chesterbelloc'.[80]

In an unfinished letter to J. L. Hammond, the editor of the *Speaker*, presumably written when Chesterton was an established contributor, he revealed his political realism or his idealism or naivety, depending on how one looks at it. His complaint was that the magazine was too much of 'a mere Party rag', albeit a moderate one, whereas he and others had 'built hopes on it as the pioneer of a younger and larger political spirit'. What he wanted and hoped the *Speaker* would do was 'to renovate Liberalism' by 'the persistent exposition of persuasive and unanswerable truths'.[81] In the years to come he was to learn a great deal about practical politics and politicians not only from Belloc but from his own experience.

At last on Good Friday 1900 Chesterton was able to write excitedly to Frances: 'I have got a really important job in reviewing—the *Life of Ruskin* for the *Speaker*. As I have precisely 73 theories about Ruskin it will be brilliant and condensed. I am also reviewing the *Life of the Kendals*, a book on the Renascence and one on Correggio for the *Bookman*.' 'Really and truly,' he continued, 'I see no reason why we should not be married in April if not before.... I have been making some money calculations... and as far as I can see we could live in the country on quite a small amount of regular literary work...'.[82] The Ruskin review duly appeared in the

[80] *A.* 116–18.   [81] Ward, *GKC* 119–20.   [82] Ward, *GKC* 123.

Speaker on 28 April, and the *Bookman* reviews (in collaboration with Hodder Williams) in June, July, and August. His first poem in the new *Speaker* appeared on 18 August[83] (although he had already published six poems in the old *Speaker*). Articles, as opposed to book reviews, appeared both in the *Speaker* and in the *Bookman* in December.

The Boer War was the main issue in the 'khaki' election campaign of 1900, which lasted from 25 September to 24 October, so-called because that was the colour of the new uniform for the British army that was adopted for the war. Chesterton had his first taste of the realities of politics when he and Oldershaw went down to Frome in Somerset to support the Liberal candidate, who was against the war. Chesterton wandered around the town inveighing against the war to whoever would listen to him. He also designed a poster attacking the Tory poster, which showed the Conservative leaders in front of the Union Jack. Chesterton's poster showed them pulling at the flag till it split, with the inscription below: 'Leave the flag alone; it wasn't made for *you* to hide behind.' In the evenings he would visit the pub where the local Conservative Party had its unofficial headquarters and hold forth and argue with anyone he could. Even the Tory canvassers would leave their canvassing to come and listen to him, much to the annoyance of the party officials. Meanwhile Oldershaw was busy working on a special edition of the *Beacon*, a radical magazine; the issue was continually held up thanks to new suggestions from Chesterton—with the result that it came out the day after the actual poll! However, their candidate won with an increased majority.[84] Chesterton had made his first attempt at election canvassing with the 'extraordinary delusion that the object of canvassing is conversion. The object of canvassing is counting' those 'likely to vote for the party candidate, or not to vote at all'. He was disillusioned in another way too: 'a curious and obscure feeling began to grow' in his mind; and when this 'cold and creeping suggestion of the unconscious . . . ultimately rose to the surface and shaped itself, long afterwards in other campaigns, into a half-articulate question, I think the question was, "Why is the candidate nearly always the worst duffer on his own platform?" ' Invariably the parliamentary candidate 'could not speak at all', but 'repeated exactly the same dull formula' at every meeting. Later experience of politics taught Chesterton what he did not understand then— namely, that 'what runs modern politics is money', and to be a candidate you had to have money.[85]

---

[83] 'The Liberal Party', *CP* i. 396.   [84] Ward, *RC* 53.   [85] *A*. 126–7.

Political disillusionment there may have been, but canvassing certainly had its amusing moments. At another election in the countryside—'I saw more of the country life than a Londoner like myself had yet imagined, and encountered not a few entertaining country types'—he met an old woman in Somerset, 'with a somewhat menacing and almost malevolent stare',

who informed me on her own doorstep that she was a Liberal and I could not see her husband, because he was still a Tory. She then informed me that she had been twice married before, and both her husbands had been Tories when they married her, but had become Liberals afterwards. She jerked her thumb over her shoulder towards the invisible Conservative within and said, 'I'll have him ready by the 'lection.' I was not permitted to penetrate further into this cavern of witchcraft, where she manufactured Liberals out of the most unpromising materials; and (it would appear) destroyed them afterwards.[86]

5

In October 1900 Chesterton published his first book, *Greybeards at Play*. The publisher was R. Brimley Johnson, who had become engaged to Frances's sister Gertrude before Chesterton and Frances became engaged, a fact that Gertrude had teasingly reminded Chesterton of when writing to congratulate him on his engagement: 'I feel just centuries older than you two!'[87] The book consists of three long nonsense poems, a dedication, and 'envoy', with accompanying illustrations by Chesterton. W. H. Auden maintained that the book, which sold very well, contained 'some of the best pure nonsense verse in English, and the author's illustrations are equally good'. Auden also thought that Chesterton was 'essentially a comic poet. Very few of his "serious" poems are as good as these.'[88] Chesterton presumably did not agree, since he neither included *Greybeards at Play* in his *Collected Poems* nor even mentioned the book, which is a little gem, in his *Autobiography*, where he says that his next book of verse, *The Wild Knight*, was his 'introduction to literature'.[89]

The best of the three poems is as clever and witty as its title, 'Of the Dangers Attending Altruism on the High Seas', suggests, and is worth quoting in full to illustrate Auden's point.

---

[86] *A.* 127–8.
[87] Barker, 56, with text corrected from BL Add. MS 73193, fos. 48–9.
[88] Sullivan, 78–9.   [89] *A.* 98.

Observe these Pirates bold and gay,
    That sail a gory sea:
Notice their bright expression:—
    The handsome one is me.

We plundered ships and harbours,
    We spoiled the Spanish main;
But Nemesis watched over us,
    For it began to rain.

Oh all well-meaning folk take heed!
    Our Captain's fate was sore;
A more well-meaning Pirate,
    Had never dripped with gore.

The rain was pouring long and loud,
    The sea was drear and dim:
A little fish was floating there:
    Our Captain pitied him.

'How sad', he said, and dropped a tear
    Splash on the cabin roof,
'That we are dry, while he is there
    Without a waterproof.

'We'll get him up on board at once;
    For Science teaches me,
He will be wet if he remains
    Much longer in the sea.'

They fished him out; the First Mate wept,
    And came with rugs and ale:
The Boatswain brought him one golosh,
    And fixed it on his tail.

But yet he never loved the ship:
    Against the mast he'd lean;
If spoken to, he coughed and smiled,
    And blushed a pallid green.

Though plied with hardbake, beef and beer,
    He showed no wish to sup:
The neatest riddles they could ask,
    He always gave them up.

They seized him and court-martialled him,
    In some excess of spleen,
For lack of social sympathy,
    (Victoria xii.18).

> They gathered every evidence
> >That might remove a doubt:
> They wrote a postcard in his name,
> >And partly scratched it out.
>
> Till, when his guilt was clear as day,
> >With all formality
> They doomed the traitor to be drowned,
> >And threw him in the sea.
>
> The flashing sunset, as he sank,
> >Made every scale a gem;
> And, turning with a gracious bow
> >He kissed his fin to them.[90]

Greybeards at Play received few reviews, although Bentley reviewed it at length on 6 October 1900 in the *Speaker*, pointing out that the verse and the drawings went together like Gilbert's librettos and Sullivan's music.[91] As Bentley put it, it was a 'feast of [Chestertons's] own peculiar sort of nonsense, rhymes and drawings full of extravagant fun'.[92] The author himself dismissed it with a somewhat curious analogy: 'To publish a book of my nonsense verses seems to me exactly like summoning the whole of the people of Kensington to see me smoke cigarettes.'[93]

A month later *The Wild Knight and Other Poems* was published. Brimley Johnson was not prepared to publish that as well but passed it on to another publisher, Grant Richards, who said that 'he could not see his way to "venturing" the book—as a refusal was in those days delicately put—but would be prepared to publish it at the author's expense'. The money was put up by Chesterton's father.[94] Letters from him to the publisher show him trying to do business on behalf of his unworldly son. He suggested that, as his son 'has now become so widely known', it ought to be possible to 'push' sales. When Grant Richards pointed out that Chesterton had failed to come and see him or write to him 'as arranged', he agreed that 'it must be admitted that he (like many of his craft) is quite unbusinesslike to his disadvantage in practical affairs'. It had therefore been decided that in future the literary agent A. P. Watt would act for him.[95] Sales had been poor.[96]

---

[90] *CP* ii. 366–71.

[91] Conlon, i. 23–4, who follows Sullivan, *G. K. Chesterton: A Bibliography*, 161, in wrongly attributing the review to Chesterton's father (who could hardly have reviewed his own son's book).

[92] Bentley, 68.   [93] Ffinch, 78.   [94] Barker, 106.

[95] Ward, *RC* 62.   [96] CC 31.

Some of the poems had already appeared in the *Speaker* and one in the *Outlook*, but the majority were appearing for the first time in print.[97] It was widely and favourably reviewed (unlike *Greybeards at Play*, which was scarcely noticed), although the poet John Davidson (to whom T. S. Eliot acknowledged a debt for his use of dingy urban images and colloquial idiom) dismissed it as 'frantic rubbish'.[98] One reviewer had, in fact, attributed the work to Davidson on the ground that the name G. K. Chesterton must be a *nom de plume*, since the poems were clearly 'not that of a novice but a successful writer'. 'This naturally brought an indignant denial from ... Davidson. That spirited poet very legitimately thanked the Lord that he had never written such nonsense; and I for one very heartily sympathised with him.'[99] Brimley Johnson sent a copy to Rudyard Kipling, who had been Johnson's intended wife's employer. In his diplomatic letter thanking the author's prospective brother-in-law, Kipling remarked that he had already read some of the poems, 'notably, *The Donkey* which stuck in my mind at the time I read it'. He thought the collection was very promising, although he had two criticisms, the first of which is very Chestertonian: 'We all begin with arrainging [*sic*] and elaborating all the Heavens and Hells and stars and tragedies we can lay our poetic hands on—Later we see folk—just common people under the heavens—'. He also noted too many uses of the word 'aureole': 'I think every one is bound in each book to employ unconsciously some pet word but that was Rossetti's', as well as too many ' "wans" and things that "catch and cling" '.[100] Kipling had picked out the best poem in the book, which contained none of the words he had objected to, and is one of a handful of Chesterton's serious, as opposed to comic or satirical, poems that are still read.

> When fishes flew and forests walked
> And figs grew upon thorn,
> Some moment when the moon was blood
> Then surely I was born;
>
> With monstrous head and sickening cry
> And ears like errant wings,
> The devil's walking parody
> On all four-footed things.
>
> The tattered outlaw of the earth,
> Of ancient crooked will;

---

97 Ffinch, 78.   98 Ward, *GKC* 125.   99 *A.* 98.
100 Ward, *GKC* 126.

Starve, scourge, deride me: I am dumb,
  I keep my secret still.

Fools! For I also had my hour;
  One far fierce hour and sweet:
There was a shout about my ears,
  And palms before my feet.[101]

The opening poem of the book, 'By the Babe Unborn', expresses Chesterton's philosophy of gratitude for life itself: 'If only I could find the door, | If only I were born.'[102] 'The Wild Knight' itself, a brief but tedious verse drama, recalls in its villain Lord Orme Chesterton's encounter with the diabolist student. But the truth is that the collection was 'an incongruous ragbag of work' that Chesterton had been 'collecting over the previous five years; it recalls the raw anti-clericalism of his schoolboy verse, and the intermittent but traumatic pessimism of his time of crisis as a student at the Slade School of Art; it also contains poems which reflect the recovery of his underlying optimism, though these do not predominate'. Worse still, Chesterton 'had fatally undermined such utterly flat and humourless writing as predominates (despite some striking exceptions) in his first volume of "serious" poetry' with his inspired comic verse of the previous volume: to go from the one to the other is indeed 'to proceed from the absurd to the would-be sublime in a way which can only make the young Chesterton's attempts at high seriousness look dangerously like self-parody:

My eyes are full of lonely mirth
  Reeling with want and worn with scars,
For pride of every stone on earth,
  I shake my spear at all the stars.'[103]

Again, curiously, one poem, 'An Alliance', was included that contained four lines that suggested not so much an early 'reluctant' imperialism as an imperialism that even Kipling, his brother Cecil pointed out, 'might have thought a trifle extravagant'.[104]

---

[101] *CP* i. 134.   [102] *CP* i. 198.

[103] Oddie, 6, 200–1. However, to be fair to Chesterton, he did himself write a sardonic critique, which he circulated among his friends, of a number of his own poems, some of which were included in *The Wild Knight*. It has been published in *P* ii. xxi–xxv, although some opening and closing pages may be missing.

[104] CC 38.

6

On Christmas Eve 1900, Chesterton went to Midnight Mass with Belloc and his wife. This was almost certainly the first time he had attended Mass in a Catholic church.[105] The death of Queen Victoria on 22 January 1901 brought the long Victorian era to a close. Like the rest of the nation Chesterton was very upset and apparently wept when he heard the news. He did not watch the funeral procession, he wrote to Frances, partly because he had an appointment with the editor of the *Speaker* and partly because 'I think I felt the matter too genuinely' and preferred to mourn alone. It was 'a great and serious hour, and it is felt so completely by all England that I cannot deny the enduring wish I have . . . to do my best for this country of mine which I love with a love passing the love of Jingoes'. He saw his mission as being 'to give her truth' ('Sometimes the hardest thing of all').[106]

On 19 February he sent a letter in a very different key to Frances:

I am, for the first time in my life, thoroughly *worried*, and I find it a rather exciting and not entirely unpleasant sensation. But everything depends just now, not only on my sticking hard to work and doing a lot of my very best, but on my thinking about it, keeping wide awake to the turn of the market, being ready to do things not in half a week, but in half an hour . . .

The reason for his nervousness was that he had an appointment next day with the editor of the *Daily News*, 'and many things may come of it':

I cannot express to you what it is to feel the grip of the great wheel of real life on you for the first time. For the first time I know what is meant by the word 'enemies'—men who deliberately dislike you and oppose your career—and the funny thing is that I don't dislike them at all myself.

Perhaps they had the same reason as himself for desperately wanting more money: 'Poor devils—very likely they want to be married in June too.' A couple of weeks later he wrote to tell Frances that 'arrangements' with the *Daily News* had been 'again put off'. However, he was optimistic that they could get married that year. Not only had the *Speaker* nearly doubled what they had been paying him, and was ready to pay him for any extra writing he did, but the editor, J. L. Hammond, had 'pushed' him 'so strongly' with the editor of the *Daily News* 'for the post of manager of the literary page' that he thought it was 'probable' he would get it. Hammond

[105] Ffinch, 81.   [106] Ward, *GKC* 127.

had assured him that the salary should be at least £200 a year, more than the £150 he hoped he could earn altogether at the *Speaker*. Even without the prospective job at the *Daily News*, he thought that he could earn £144 a year from his writing for the paper—indeed he had 'just started a set of popular fighting articles on literature'. Besides, his name was getting known and so other opportunities would arise. He promised Frances that he had calculated the minimum rather than the maximum income he could earn.[107] Writing for the *Daily News* was the 'turning-point of his journalistic fate' in Chesterton's view. Like the *Speaker*, the paper had been bought by Liberals opposed to the Boer War, who included Lloyd George and George Cadbury, the chocolate manufacturer, who provided most of the financial backing. Chesterton's first review for the paper had appeared unsigned on 6 January, the first of regular book reviews, mostly unsigned, for the Saturday issue. February saw the publication in the *Speaker* of 'In Defence of Nonsense', the first of such articles (the last appeared in August) that he would later collect in *The Defendant*.[108]

In an undated letter to his mother, which presumably was written after the one to Frances, Chesterton raised his estimated income to £470 a year, which he pointed out to her was only £30 less than the £500 which she had said was necessary to enable him to marry. Again, he assured her that his sums had been carefully done: 'I have been doing nothing but sums in my head for the last months.' He calculated that he could make £192 from the *Speaker*, at least £100 from the *Daily News* and more if he got the job of literary editor. He also now had a contract with the *Manchester Sunday Chronicle* that was worth £72 a year. 'The matter now, I think, largely depends on *Reynolds's Newspaper*. If I do, as is contemplated, weekly articles and thumbnail sketches, they cannot give me less than £100 a year.' That would bring the total close to the income considered necessary by his mother. He realized that earning one's living by journalism was more precarious than other kinds of occupation: 'But we should live a long way within this income, if we took a very cheap flat, even a workman's flat if necessary, had a woman in to do the laborious daily work and for the rest waited on ourselves, as many people I know do in cheap flats.' At any rate, even if journalism did have its 'downs', it also had its 'ups', 'and I, I can fairly say, am on the upward wave'. His name was becoming well known, and it was a 'remarkable fact' that the papers he wrote for had come to him, not the other way round. He concluded by telling his mother that it was not his financial prospects that worried him:

[107] Ward, *GKC* 128–9.   [108] Barker, 115; Ffinch, 82, 95.

But I am terribly worried for fear you should be angry or sorry about all this. I am only kept in hope by the remembrance that I had the same fear when I told you of my engagement and that you dispelled it with a directness and generosity that I shall not forget. I think, my dear Mother, that we have always understood each other really. We are neither of us very demonstrative: we come of some queer stock that can always say least when it means most.

Chesterton knew it was not only the financial aspect that bothered his mother; he knew that Frances would not have been her choice as a wife for him. But he asked her to trust him when he thought that something was 'really right', even if he could 'hardly explain why'—for that would be to 'communicate the incommunicable'. 'The most I can say is that I know Frances like the back of my hand and can tell without a word from her that she has never recovered from a wound and that there is only one kind of peace that will heal it.' Marriage was the only cure for Frances's grief for her sister Gertrude. Once again Chesterton had fallen back on writing to his mother. 'I have tried to explain myself in this letter: I can do it better in a letter, somehow, but I do not think I have done it very successfully. However, with you it does not matter and it never will matter, how my thoughts come tumbling out. You at least have always understood what I meant.' His mother might not approve, but he relied on her understanding.[109]

[109] Ward, *GKC* 131–2, text corrected from BL MS Add. 73193, fos. 80–2.

3

Marriage and Fame

THE wedding finally took place on 28 June 1901 at St Mary Abbots Church in Kensington. It was Frances's birthday: she was 31, and the bridegroom 27. Predictably, Chesterton arrived at the church without a tie. The day was saved by a brother of Rhoda Bastable, who was a bridesmaid and a cousin of Frances, and for whom Chesterton had written the best poem in *Greybeards at Play*, 'Of the Dangers Attending Altruism on the High Seas'. A tie was hastily obtained from a shop nearby, and it was round Chesterton's neck before the bride arrived. The Revd Conrad Noel, with whom Chesterton and his brother had become friends, officiated. When Chesterton's mother and Annie Firmin saw the price tag on the sole of one of his new shoes that the kneeling bridegroom had bought for the occasion, they looked at each other and laughed. Annie seemed to remember that at the reception afterwards for once in their lives Chesterton and his brother did not argue. Faced with all the wedding presents, Chesterton remarked to Annie: 'I feel like the young man in the Gospel, sorrowful, because I have great possessions.' Lucian Oldershaw went ahead to the station with the luggage for the honeymoon, which he put on the train the couple were supposed to be catching. Chesterton, however, and his wife arrived only after another train had also left the station. They took the next train, which was a slow one. On arrival at the White Horse inn in Ipswich, on their way to the Norfolk Broads, Chesterton noticed that his new wife looked tired and told her to lie down and rest after drinking a glass of wine with him. He himself took a walk in the countryside and managed to get lost. But 'in the end he found his way back to his wife under the sign of the

White Horse—that supreme symbol since his earliest childhood of romance and adventure'.[1]

In his *Autobiography*, Chesterton admitted that there were a number of
family legends surrounding 'such a highly comic wedding-day'. Apart
from missing trains and losing luggage:

It is alleged against me, and with perfect truth, that I stopped on the way to drink
a glass of milk in one shop and to buy a revolver with cartridges in another. Some
have seen these as singular wedding-presents for a bridegroom to give to himself;
and if the bride had known less of him, I suppose she might have fancied that he
was a suicide or a murderer, or, worst of all, a teetotaller. They seemed to me the
most natural things in the world. I did not buy the pistol to murder myself or my
wife; I never was really modern. I bought it because it was the great adventure of
my youth, with a general notion of protecting her from the pirates doubtless
infesting the Norfolk Broads, to which we were bound . . . I shall not be annoyed if
it is called childish; but obviously it was rather a reminiscence of boyhood, and not
of childhood.

As for the glass of milk, 'I had always drunk a glass of milk there when
walking with my mother in my infancy. And it seemed to me a fitting
ceremonial to unite the two great relations of a man's life.' There was
something else that was important symbolically for Chesterton in this visit
to the dairy: the figure of a white cow outside, 'standing', as it were, 'at the
beginning of my new journey', a journey that would end 'under the sign of
the White Horse at Ipswich', the inn where he was to spend the first night
of his honeymoon. It recalled that very early powerful childhood memory
of the white head of a hobby horse.[2]

There is no record of the newly married Chestertons being attacked by
pirates during their brief honeymoon on the Norfolk Broads. But, like his
sword-stick that had so amused his colleagues at Fisher Unwin's, the
revolver reflected that boyish love of adventure that drew Chesterton so
strongly to the romances of Stevenson and that he delighted in expressing
(rather less successfully) in his own stories. His first letter to his parents did
not mention the revolver, however, but began with the following inventory: 'I have a wife, a piece of string, a pencil and a knife: what more can
any man want on a honeymoon.'[3] The honeymoon was very brief, no
doubt because of financial considerations: 'I only stole six days,—six days |
Enough for God to make the world,' as he put it in a poem for Frances,

---

[1] Ward, *GKC* 133; Barker, 105, 109–11; Ward, *RC* 66.
[2] See above, pp. 8–9.   [3] Ward, *GKC* 133–4.

called 'Creation Day',[4] dated July 1901 and so written not long after the honeymoon.[5]

Unfortunately for the couple, creation was not to follow in their marriage. According to Ada Jones, who was to become Cecil's wife in 1917, this was because of Frances's frigidity. Ada was a hard-bitten journalist who had been a reporter since the age of 16 and who, appropriately at a time when journalism was a male preserve, used a male pseudonym, John Keith Prothero, being known to her friends as 'Keith'. A veteran of Fleet Street, who drank in its taverns like any man, she could hardly have been more unlike Frances, and indeed makes it clear in her book about the Chestertons (published long after her husband's death) that they 'did not find much mutual ground of understanding'. According to 'Keith', on the first night of their honeymoon, Frances 'shrank' from her husband's 'touch and screamed when he embraced her'. For his part, the husband 'was haunted by the fear that his brutality and lust had frightened the woman he would have died to protect'. His younger brother, to whom he went 'quivering with self-reproach and condemnation', attempted to reassure him 'and suggested that some citadels must be taken by storm, while others yield only to long siege'. At any rate there was nothing for his brother to fear— 'But the mischief had been done. Gilbert hated himself for what had happened, and Frances could not reconcile herself to the physical realities of marriage.' 'Keith' concluded bluntly that Chesterton was thus 'condemned to a pseudo-monastic life, in which he lived with a woman but never enjoyed one'.[6] It suited 'Keith', who must have resented she had been married to the much less famous brother who died tragically young, to portray their married life as less than happy. But her account is simply refuted by the fact that, after a few years of marriage, Frances underwent an operation in the hope that she might have children, whom, as 'Keith' allows, she desperately wanted to have.[7] Of course, 'Keith' was writing

---

[4] *CP* i. 344.   [5] Ward, *RC* 67.   [6] MCC 26, 171.
[7] Ward, *GKC* 210. See also Margaret Joyce to Dorothy Collins, 25 Oct. 1942, BL Add. MS 73475A, fo. 72: 'The fact that she underwent an operation in the attempt to cure her sterility shows how anxious she was to have children.' Dr Joyce was attached to the local Battersea Bridge branch of the Clapham Maternity Hospital (*The Medical Directory*, 1907), the first maternity hospital where women were treated solely by women doctors. The operation was not performed by her but by a young doctor, the then unmarried Frances Ivens, who had only recently qualified in 1900 and was to have a highly distinguished medical career. 'The operation was not performed by me,' Dr Joyce told Dorothy Collins,

some four decades after the event (her book was published in 1941), and the memory of an old woman cannot altogether be trusted, especially when it is prejudiced. What may well have happened on that first night was that the young couple, both virgins and brought up in all the proprieties of the Victorian age, found their first sexual contact very difficult: the young husband, who was as inexperienced as his wife, was no doubt clumsy, and Frances may well have shrunk away in embarrassment and panic. Such an experience would have been common to many newly married middle-class couples at that time.[8] 'Keith's' account, therefore, of what happened may be substantially true, but what was not true was what she took it upon herself to deduce from it: she claimed to be reporting what her husband had told her, but her account of what he had said did not include the claim that Cecil had also told her that her brother was thereafter condemned to a life of celibacy.[9]

'but by Mrs Ivens-Knowles the gynaecological surgeon. I forget the date.' Margaret Joyce to Dorothy Collins, n.d., BL Add. MS 73475A, fo. 74. On reading 'Keith's' book *The Chestertons* many years later, Dr Joyce remarked: 'How jealous she ['Keith'] must have been of Frances! And how fiendishly she sugars her sourest bits!' Margaret Joyce to Dorothy Collins, 11 Nov. 1942, BL Add. MS 73475A, fo. 75. In 1924 Frances was referred to a specialist at the Clinical Medical Unit at St Thomas's Hospital, London, who wrote to her general practitioner, Dr Bakewell, in Beaconsfield: 'She has apparently been putting on weight—chiefly about the hips—and getting rather easily fatigued. I think this is largely the result of the menopause. She appears to me to have been always an individual of the rather underdeveloped pituitary type—onset of menstruation late (c 17)—sterility—lack of genital development etc.' Harold Gardiner Hill to George Bakewell, 9 Dec. 1924, BL Add. MS 74370, fo. 26.

[8] Ward, *GKC* 560–1.

[9] According to Oddie, 216–17, 'Keith', as a writer of sensational romantic literature, 'either . . . imagined it all and believed her own imaginings or . . . she simply made it up, consciously or unconsciously prompted by her detestation of Frances and envy of her long and happy marriage (she had lost Cecil after only two years of her own marriage)', or else 'perhaps (much less likely) it was Cecil who imagined it or made it up'. As Oddie notes, Maisie Ward, who knew Cecil well, found it 'difficult to imagine' that he told 'Keith' that his brother never again attempted marital intimacy (Ward, *GKC* 560). But the story of what happened on that first honeymoon night needs to be separated from 'Keith's' allegation of what the consequence of that night was—an allegation she does not attribute to Cecil. It is much more likely that, as in all such stories, there is at least a grain of truth in it—in this case perhaps more than a grain, as Cecil perhaps did recount to 'Keith' what his brother had told him about that first honeymoon night. The grain or

On their return from the honeymoon, the Chestertons moved into a small house, 1 Edwardes Square, Kensington, close to his parents in Warwick Gardens, which they rented on a temporary basis from an old friend of Frances. Asked what wallpaper he would prefer, he asked for brown paper to draw on. Bentley remembered the house

with its garden of old trees and its general air of Georgian peace. I remember too the splendid flaming frescoes, done in vivid crayons, of knights and heroes and divinities with which G.K.C. embellished the outside wall at the back, beneath a sheltering portico. I have often wondered whether the landlord charged for them as dilapidations at the end of the tenancy.[10]

While the young couple were in Edwardes Square, Chesterton wrote to 8-year-old Doris Child, who had been a bridesmaid along with Rhoda Bastable at the wedding and who was living with her mother with Mrs Blogg at the time: 'I myself have become terribly good to please Frances.'[11]

I never read at meals now; the mere sight of a book near the table makes me quite ill. I brush my hair without stopping all day: I am brushing it with one hand while I write to you with the other. This is a symbolic approximation, which means something that is not true. But I cannot help feeling that I should be better still if you were here to help Frances to make me behave well. It is very funny, but I will tell you a secret—I really want to behave well now. You must come and see us and our house and show me how. I am young and strong and can behave well for 17½ minutes on end without the least fatigue.[12]

Below the letter were five drawings of a figure progressively brushing his hair down.[13]

After a few months the young couple moved to Overstrand Mansions, Battersea, where they were to remain for the rest of their life together in London. According to 'Keith', Chesterton did not like flats—certainly he had never lived in one before—but the name 'Over-Strand Mansions'

more than grain of untruth was what 'Keith' deduced from the story—what it suited her to believe was the clear implication of the story and which she believed to be true to Frances's character. As for Frances's husband, nobody has ever suggested that he was unable to consummate the marriage: indeed, his mother told Annie Kidd née Firmin that she '*knew*' it was not her son's fault that he and Frances could not have children. Annie Kidd to Maisie Ward, n.d., BL Add. MS 73481A, fo. 27.

[10] Ward, *GKC* 134.
[11] G. K. Chesterton to Doris Child, n.d., BL Add. MS 73236, fo. 31.
[12] Ward, *RC* 90.   [13] BL Add. MS 73236, fo. 32.

appealed to him.[14] The red-brick block was attractively situated beside
Battersea Park, which lies along the river. From one side of their flat they
had a view of Battersea Park, while the other side looked out on the roofs
of Battersea. Because it was the 'wrong' (south) side of the river but close
to central London, it was both affordable and convenient for a journalist
of modest means. When they could afford to have the work done, they
had the wall between the drawing-room and the dining-room knocked
down—thus anticipating a fashion that was to become popular more
than half a century later. At one end of the little study, lined with brown
paper to allow for his drawings, in which Chesterton worked, hung a
board, inscribed 'lest we forget', on which were noted 'projected articles
and pending literary and other engagements'. Hilaire Belloc added a
witty little poem:

> Frances and Gilbert have a little flat
> At eighty pounds a year and cheap at that
> Where Frances who is Gilbert's only wife
> Leads an unhappy and complaining life:
> While Gilbert who is Frances' only man
> Puts up with it as gamely as he can.[15]

Two of their immediate neighbours became close friends. One couple,
Charles Rann (always known simply as Rann) Kennedy, an actor, and his
actress wife Edith Wynne-Matthison, Ellen Terry's successor as Henry
Irving's leading lady, who would emigrate to the United States where
Rann wrote several plays about moral problems, lived in the flat below.
Chesterton used to meet Rann Kennedy on the stairs (there was no lift), as
he walked up 'very slowly, writing an article on his cuff'. One day
Chesterton remarked 'Isn't it jolly out in the park there?' Kennedy replied,
'Yes, it is lovely, have you just been there?' Next day he pointed out to
Chesterton, 'Did you notice when we saluted yesterday we both greeted
each other in choriambs and a hypermetric?' Kennedy had a large library
and was happy to lend books to Chesterton. He was struck by Chesterton's
capacity for extracting the essence of a book even without reading right
through it: 'In three hours lolling against a bookcase he would have left
aside all unnecessary, absorbed all vital elements.' He also enjoyed arguing, a trait that naturally endeared him to Chesterton. One or other of
them would often bang on the floor or ceiling of their flat to attract the
other's attention in the hope of an argument. Another neighbour, Saxon

---

[14] MCC 65.   [15] Ward, *GKC* 134; Ffinch, 99.

Mills, a Liberal imperialist who was introduced to Chesterton by Cecil, was also good for an argument. His wife remembered one argument that continued till five in the morning; next day the room was found littered 'with cigar butts, empty glasses and siphons scattered everywhere and the smell of stale smoke hanging over it like a pall'. On occasions when money was short, the Chestertons and Millses would loan each other money or even give each other food. Mrs. Mills was struck by how placidly Frances reacted to her husband's eccentricities, one of which was his habit of letting out a bloodcurdling cry in the morning for his wife to come and tie his tie. The Chestertons' maid (even an impoverished journalist could afford a servant in those days) told Mrs Mills how Chesterton would flood the bathroom floor, which required immediate mopping up; on one occasion, while waiting for him to come out, she heard a loud splash and then a groan: 'Dammit, I've been in here already.'[16] There was another much more important neighbour, not actually in the block but just across the river in more fashionable Chelsea: Hilaire Belloc, who lived at 104 Chelsea Walk. One of the Belloc children remembered Chesterton giving them 'absorbing displays of phantasy through puppets with plaster heads and appropriate gowns... They came to life by the gowns and heads being slipped on to those gifted hands... as Uncle Gilbert sat perilously on the edge of a nursery chair and rumbled off into the story of action!'[17]

2

In December 1901 Chesterton published his first book of prose, *The Defendant*. It was much more widely reviewed than the two books of verse, but not all the reviewers were pleased by his generous use of paradox, a criticism that would continue to be made about his writings. In a letter to *The Speaker* defending himself against one critic, Chesterton justified his use of paradox, not as a literary device but as a necessary tool for understanding the world. Because 'there really is a strand of contradiction running through the universe', it is impossible to avoid the use of paradox. And, he concluded, this was the reason why 'so many religions' were led to 'boast not that they had an explanation of the Universe, but that they had a pure, defiant paradox, like the Athanasian Creed'.[18] The book consisted of the 'in defence of' articles he had published in the *Speaker*. In the introduction he returned to the *fin de siècle* pessimism he had

[16] Ward, *RC* 68–70.   [17] Ffinch, 107.   [18] Oddie, 189–90.

grappled with at the Slade: 'The great sin of mankind, the sin typified by the fall of Adam, is the tendency, not towards pride, but towards this weird and horrible humility' of 'tending to undervalue their environment, to undervalue their happiness, to undervalue themselves'. The true revolutionaries were not the pessimists but the optimists who 'have been indignant not about the badness of existence, but about the slowness of men in realising its goodness'. Thus Jesus Christ was crucified 'on a charge of saying that a man could in three days pull down and rebuild the Temple'. This central theme of Chesterton's writings is touched on in more than one of the articles. Optimism depends on our ability to *wonder* at the world—a 'simple sense of wonder at the shapes of things, and at their exuberant independence of our intellectual standards and our trivial definitions'. But this leads to the kind of paradoxical assertion that so irritated some of his critics: 'This simple sense of wonder . . . is the basis of spirituality as it is the basis of nonsense.' Chesterton recognizes but insists on the paradox: 'Nonsense and faith (strange as the conjunction may seem) are the two supreme symbolic assertions of the truth that to draw out the soul of things with a syllogism is as impossible as to draw out Leviathan with a hook.' This insistence on the strict limitations of logic, combined with no less an emphasis on the importance of imagination, reminds one of Newman; but the function of the imagination for Chesterton is not to make the notional and theoretical concrete and real as for Newman, but 'to make settled things strange; not so much to make wonders facts as to make facts wonders'. In other words, the imagination is essential for that wonder at existence that underpins optimism.[19]

This is one important reason for the defence of the common man that runs through Chesterton's writings and that distinguished him so sharply from the majority of other contemporary writers. What Chesterton calls the

merely educated can scarcely ever be brought to believe that this world is itself an interesting place. When they look at a work of art, good or bad, they expect to be interested, but when they look at a newspaper advertisement or a group in the street, they do not, properly and literally speaking, expect to be interested. But to common and simple people this world is a work of art, though it is, like many great works of art, anonymous.

Their popular literature, unlike the morbidities of modern literature, contains 'a plainer and better gospel'. To them 'this planet is like a new house into which we have just moved our baggage'. The common and simple are

[19] *Def.* 13–14, 70, 84.

humble and therefore are privileged to have a 'colossal vision' of 'things as they really are'. The loss of respect for the virtue of humility had led to the revival of 'the bitterness of Greek pessimism'. The 'merely educated' have also 'lost altogether that primitive and typical taste of man—the taste for news'. And Chesterton then makes a familiar and hackneyed expression come alive in all its original sense: 'When Christianity was named the good news, it spread rapidly, not only because it was good, but also because it was news.' The dignity of the poor was always close to Chesterton's heart, a dignity he thought was more threatened in modern society than even in 'ages in which the most arrogant and elaborate ideals of power and civilisation held . . . undisputed sway', when 'the ideal of the perfect and healthy peasant did undoubtedly represent in some shape or form the conception that there was a dignity in simplicity and a dignity in labour'. Sadly, 'no such ideal exists in the case of the vast number of honourable trades and crafts on which the existence of a modern city depends'. The romance, however, of modern urban life was to be a persistent theme of Chesterton's writings, again in marked contrast to contemporary writers. And he considered that there was one art form, a popular art form, that did do justice to it, the detective story: 'it is the earliest and only form of popular literature in which is expressed some sense of the poetry of modern life.' After all, it was not until the romantic movement of the nineteenth century that mountains, for example, came to seem poetic. The detective story was not idealizing the city, because 'properly speaking' the city is 'more poetic even than a countryside, for while nature is a chaos of unconscious forces, a city is a chaos of conscious ones'. Thus, while a particular flower may or may not have a symbolic significance, 'there is no stone in the street and no brick in the wall that is not actually a deliberate symbol—a message from some man, as much as if it were a telegram or a post card'. 'A rude, popular literature of the romantic possibilities of the modern city was bound', therefore, 'to arise. It has arisen in the popular detective stories, as rough and refreshing as the ballads of Robin Hood,' which celebrate the 'romance of the police force'.[20]

But, if the modern urban world denied the dignity of the poor, there was an important way in which it also degraded the upper classes. Since the nineteenth century, the aristocracy had 'destroyed entirely their one solitary utility. It is their business to be flaunting and arrogant; but they flaunt unobtrusively, and their attempts at arrogance are depressing.' The aristocracy was meant to stand for 'the idea of variety, experiment, and colour', whereas now one had to look to the lower classes for these things:

[20] *Def.* 85, 88, 97–9, 133, 137, 158–9, 161.

'chiefly, for example, to omnibus conductors, with their rich and rococo mode of thought . . . '. Their slang was 'poetic', unlike 'the heavy, formless, lifeless slang of the man-about-town'. A barrow-boy's curse contained more 'remote metaphors' than any sonnet of Keats. The working class lived in 'a war of words': 'Any cabman has to be ready with his tongue, as any gentleman of the last century had to be ready with his sword. It is unfortunate that the poetry which is developed by this process should be purely a grotesque poetry.' But the truth is that 'all slang is metaphor, and all metaphor is poetry'.[21]

How had it come about that the lower classes preserved what the upper classes had lost? Chesterton put the blame on the spread of democratic ideas in the nineteenth century. Whereas previously the masses were certainly 'conceived as mean and commonplace, but only as comparatively mean and commonplace', 'with the Victorian era came a principle which conceived men not as comparatively, but as positively, mean and commonplace'. Instead of the democrats extending the 'pride and vivacity', the 'towering symbols and flamboyant colours' of the aristocracy to everyone as they should have done, they decreased rather than increased 'the human magnificence of the past'. The tobacconist, for instance, should have been given a 'crest' and 'the cheesemonger a war-cry'. There follows a marvellous passage of indignant Chestertonian rhetoric as he deplores the failure of democracy to uphold the dignity of the poor by upholding human dignity in general:

It began to be thought that it was ridiculous for a man to wear beautiful garments, instead of it being—as, of course, it is—ridiculous to wear deliberately ugly ones. It was considered affected for a man to speak bold and heroic words, whereas, of course, it is emotional speech which is natural, and ordinary civil speech which is affected. The whole relations of beauty and ugliness, of dignity and ignominy were turned upside down. . . . Dignity became a form of foolery and shamelessness, as if the very essence of a fool were not a lack of dignity. . . . We are forbidden to say that tradesmen should have a poetry of their own, although there is nothing so poetical as trade. A grocer should have a coat-of-arms worthy of his strange merchandise gathered from distant and fantastic lands; a postman should have a coat-of-arms capable of expressing the strange honour and responsibility of the man who carries men's souls in a bag; the chemist should have a coat-of-arms symbolising something of the mysteries of the house of healing, the cavern of a merciful witchcraft.

[21] *Def.* 141–2, 145–6.

A true belief in real democracy would soon lead to a blossoming of 'symbolic colours and shapes'. It was significant that Shakespeare's plays, for example, would never be presented on the stage in contemporary dress, unlike in the past, because of a lack of a 'conviction of the poetry of our own life and manners'.[22] These deficiencies were to be supplied in Chesterton's first published novel, *The Napoleon of Notting Hill*.

These early journalistic essays introduce other ideas that recur in Chesterton's works. The threat to the institution of marriage was in his view founded on a form of pessimism, pessimism about the self: 'this terror of one's self, of the weakness and mutability of one's self, has perilously increased, and is the real basis of the objection to vows of any kind.' 'Free' love, he argued, was a contradiction in terms: 'It is the nature of love to bind itself . . .'. The institution of marriage 'merely paid the average man the compliment of taking him at his word'. That is to say, it did not pessimistically assume the worst of man, but 'respected' him to the extent of giving him 'the liberty to sell his liberty'.[23]

The Middle Ages that Chesterton was constantly to compare favourably with the modern world are here contrasted with Greek civilization, which, with all its 'splendid work', has 'blinded us to the fact of their great and terrible sin against the variety of life' through their 'worship of one aesthetic type alone' and their 'terror . . . of size, vitality, variety, energy, ugliness'. But 'Nature intended every human face, so long as it was forcible, individual, and expressive, to be regarded as distinct from all others'. The medieval world, however, 'broke away from the Greek standard of beauty, and lifted up in adoration to heaven great towers, which seemed alive with dancing apes and devils'. Chesterton now uses a term that was to loom large in his thought: 'This branch of art is commonly dismissed as the grotesque. We have never been able to understand why it should be humiliating to be laughable, since it is giving an elevated artistic pleasure to others.' But he goes on to say that the word 'grotesque' 'is a misleading description of ugliness in art' insofar as it suggests something comical. Gothic gargoyles, for example, were not intended to be funny: 'Their extravagance was not the extravagance of satire, but simply the extravagance of vitality; and here lies the whole key to the place of ugliness in aesthetics.' The same was true of nature itself: 'We like to see a crag jut out in shameless decision from the cliff, we like to see the red pines stand up hardily upon a high cliff', because 'they are expressive of the dramatic stillness of Nature, her bold experiments, her definite departures,

[22] *Def.* 107–10, 160.   [23] *Def.* 33, 36.

her fearlessness and savage pride in her children'; but we 'do not burst with amusement' at the sight of them. As opposed to a Greek idea of 'conventional beauty', the Middle Ages knew that 'there are a million beautiful faces waiting for us everywhere'. In one of the two best-known articles in the book, 'A Defence of Skeletons', Chesterton maintains that 'man's horror of the skeleton is not horror of death at all'; but rather 'the fundamental matter which troubles him in the skeleton is the reminder that the ground-plan of his appearance is shamelessly grotesque'. And man is not tempted to laugh at the human skeleton, which is fantastic- or bizarre-looking but not comical. Again, in nature, her 'highest and most valuable quality...is not her beauty, but her generous and defiant ugliness'. The essay ends with the hardly amusing thought: 'And, however much my face clouds with sombre vanity, or vulgar vengeance, or contemptible contempt, the bones of my skull underneath it are laughing for ever.'[24]

We have already seen from his *Autobiography* how seriously Chesterton took childhood. He also made the subject of children a regular theme of his writings. What was special about children was they had that sense of wonder at existence that adults only too often lost. But that 'gravity of astonishment at the universe' that 'dwells in the eyes of a baby of three months old' was only 'transcendent common sense'. And 'their solemnity gives us more hope for all things than a thousand carnivals of optimism'. One should not conclude from this that Chesterton was generally in approval of the serious and solemn. On the contrary, children were the exception to the rule, because their seriousness and solemnity were the result of their wonder at the world. Elsewhere in the book Chesterton condemns the lack of 'belief in . . . hilarity which marks modern aesthetics'. Farce and pantomime, although 'glorified' by great writers like Aristophanes and Molière, were now despised, and yet they corresponded to human emotions that include more than 'the painful side of life only'. Indeed, in Chesterton's view, the 'literature of joy is infinitely more difficult, more rare, and more triumphant than the black and white literature of pain'.[25]

The final chapter in the book was the article that had attracted the most attention, 'A Defence of Patriotism'. Instead of 'the ancient love of country' the English were consumed with a 'lust for territory'. The failure to question the morality of the Boer War was not patriotism. ' "My country, right or wrong," is a thing that no patriot would think of saying except in a desperate case. It is like saying, "My mother, drunk or sober." ' A 'deaf and

[24] *Def.* 46, 48, 49, 114, 115, 117.   [25] *Def.* 123–4, 149, 153.

raucous Jingoism' needed to be discarded in favour of 'a renascence of the love of the native land'. To be proud of colonies was like 'a man being only proud of his legs', in other words, of his 'extremities'. Chesterton had his own explanation for this 'decay of patriotism': the fact that 'we are the only people in the world who are not taught in childhood our own literature and our own history'. This failure to teach English literature in English schools 'is, when we come to think of it, an almost amazing phenomenon'. He demanded to know: 'What have we done, and where have we wandered, we that have produced sages who could have spoken with Socrates and poets who could walk with Dante, that we should talk as if we have never done anything more intelligent than found colonies and kick niggers?'[26]

Before we leave *The Defendant*, it is important to emphasize Chesterton's defence of the common man, which so distinguishes him from most other contemporary writers.[27] The growth of population in Europe in the nineteenth century aroused panic and loathing among intellectuals. Nietzsche wrote chillingly: 'Many too many are born, and they hang on their branches much too long. I wish a storm would come and shake all this rottenness and worm-eatenness from the tree!' Nietzsche's ideas were immensely popular among early twentieth-century writers: W. B. Yeats praised him as an antidote to 'the spread of democratic vulgarity' and George Bernard Shaw hailed *Thus Spoke Zarathustra* as 'the first modern book that can be set above the Psalms of David'. The Norwegian novelist Knut Hamsun, who influenced Thomas Mann and André Gide among others, looked forward to the advent of Hitler, of whom he was to write an admiring obituary: 'I believe in the born leader, the natural despot, the master, not the man who is chosen but the man who elects himself to be ruler over the masses. I believe in and hope for one thing, and that is the return of the great terrorist, the living essence of human power, the Caesar.'[28]

On top of population explosion came educational reforms in England in the last decades of the nineteenth century that led to universal elementary education and consequently mass literacy. This in turn produced the popular newspaper, beginning with the launch of the *Daily Mail* in 1896. The masses 'vomit their bile, and call it a newspaper', snarled Nietzsche.

---

[26] *Def.* 165–8, 170–1.

[27] For the following account, I am indebted to John Carey, *The Intellectuals and the Masses: Pride and Prejudice among the Literary Intelligentsia, 1880–1939* (London: Faber and Faber, 1992).

[28] Carey, *The Intellectuals and the Masses*, 4–5.

An interesting aspect of the intellectuals' hatred for newspapers was their catering for women readers: Nietzsche, who thought women should be regarded only in an 'oriental way', notoriously advised, 'Are you visiting women? Do not forget your whip.' There were exceptions among writers. Arthur Conan Doyle's cerebral detective Sherlock Holmes has no hesitation in using newspapers extensively in his detection work, and for him members of the 'masses' are not anonymous units but individuals in their own right to whom he pays no less attention and respect than to their social superiors. Indeed, most of the stories were first published in the *Strand Magazine*, which catered for middle- and lower-middle-class readers.[29]

Other writers, on the contrary, far from being interested in individual members of the masses, simply favoured the wholesale extermination of the masses. Nietzsche thought that 'the great majority of men have no right to existence, but are a misfortune to higher men'. He looked forward to the breeding of a higher race and the consequent 'annihilation of millions of failures'. The new science of eugenics offered the possibility of more selective elimination, and Yeats joined the Eugenics Education Society founded in 1907, which Shaw also supported. If there was no possibility of abolishing universal education—as Nietzsche favoured, again in contrast to Sherlock Holmes, who hailed the new elementary schools as 'Lighthouses...Beacons of the future!'—then writers could write in such a way that at least their writings could not be understood by the masses. Thus arose the movement called Modernism. Prior to that, Thomas Hardy feared that, when the masses 'are our masters', 'the utter ruin of art and literature' could follow. The literalism of the masses, who, Shaw noted, preferred the adventure stories of Stevenson to 'serious' literature, was counteracted before Modernism by the Impressionists in art and the Symbolists in literature, who eschewed fact and realism.[30] It was, Chesterton noted, 'the first time, perhaps, in the whole history of the world in which things can be praised because they are unpopular'. Artists and writers in the past 'did not declare themselves great artists because they were unsuccessful: that is the peculiarity of our own time, which has a positive bias against the populace'.[31]

Chesterton, on the other hand, deplored 'the deep anti-popular bias of the modern intellectuals'. 'The evil', he protested, 'of our attitude to the masses is simply that we do think of them as masses'. He knew 'nothing so vulgar as that contempt for vulgarity which sneers at the clerks on a Bank

---

[29] Carey, *The Intellectuals and the Masses*, 7–8.
[30] Carey, *The Intellectuals and the Masses*, 12, 16, 24.   [31] *ILN* xxviii. 31–2.

Holiday or the Cockneys on Margate sands'.[32] In *The Defendant* he wrote explicitly, as we have seen, in defence of the poor and uneducated, of popular literature, particularly the detective story, of marriage and children. He delighted in newspapers, defending the profession of a journalist as against that of a poet in an article in a northern provincial newspaper a year later in 1902:

The poet writing his name upon a score of little pages in the silence of his study, may or may not have an intellectual right to despise the journalist: but I greatly doubt whether he would not morally be the better if he saw the great lights burning on through darkness into dawn, and heard the roar of the printing wheels weaving the destinies of another day. Here at least is a school of labour and of some rough humility, the largest work ever published anonymously since the great Christian cathedrals.[33]

On the other hand, he disliked Impressionism and Modernism, hated the idea of a Superman and loathed eugenics. He was also a solitary defender—although a forerunner of later writers like John Betjeman and Stevie Smith—of the despised suburbs where the masses lived.

The suburban clerk, the typical product of the new Board Schools, included Shaw and H. G. Wells among his favourite writers. Nevertheless Shaw, who became a highly successful journalist writing for the very newspapers that he saw as 'fearfully mischievous', as a follower of Nietzsche denigrated 'the promiscuously bred masses', asserting that 'the majority of men at present in Europe have no business to be alive' and anticipating Hitler's gas chambers: 'Extermination must be put on a scientific basis if it is ever to be carried out humanely and apologetically as well as thoroughly... If we desire a certain type of civilization and culture, we must exterminate the sort of people who do not fit into it.' Shaw believed in a 'Life Force' that was struggling to evolve the 'Superman', a struggle that required the practice of eugenics in order to 'eliminate the Yahoo'. There was certainly no possibility of a 'Superwoman': in Nietzsche's view women were not equal with men and should be treated as property, slaves, or domestics. One reason for belittling the suburbs was that they were associated with female trivialities. George Gissing, who was in fact 'the earliest English writer to formulate the intellectuals' case against mass culture', used women characters to exemplify the worst examples of bogus culture in his novels. Moreover, an interest in children and parenthood was disdained as a suburban distraction from serious culture.

---

[32] *ILN* xxviii. 198–9, 570; xxix. 108–9.   [33] Ward, *GKC* 137.

The contrast between journalists and popular writers catering for the masses and serious writers provides the theme of Gissing's best-known novel, *New Grub Street* (1891). The idea that popular writing might possess some literary value simply never occurred to Gissing. The penny weekly *Tit-Bits*, which began in 1882, is satirized there as *Chit-Chat*. And yet the paper, which had no pictures, published excerpts from selected major writers, as well as serializing Conan Doyle's novels *The Sign of the Four* and *A Study in Scarlet* in 1893. But the fact that it had a mass readership was enough to condemn it. H. G. Wells's birthplace, Bromley in Kent, was 'spoiled' by suburban development, and anger against suburbia as well as mass tourism, advertising, and popular newspapers permeates his fiction. Women he condemned not only for their fertility that was responsible for overpopulation but also for their sex appeal that forced men into marriage and consequently into the work of breadwinning that drew them from intellectual pursuits. Wells did not hesitate to advocate sterilization and poisoning of the 'vicious, helpless and pauper masses'; as for black, brown, and yellow people, genocide was the only solution.[34]

Against all this more or less evil nonsense, Chesterton was to battle almost alone in defence of the common man and against the intellectuals.[35]

3

Most of the articles that Chesterton wrote for the *Speaker* were book reviews, and it was on the strength of these reviews that he began reviewing for a much larger audience in the *Daily News*, the first review signed with his initials appearing on 21 March 1901, and the first signed with his full name on 7 June.[36] After these first two signed pieces, Chesterton's

[34] Carey, *The Intellectuals and the Masses*, 62–3, 93, 123.

[35] The hero of Carey's *The Intellectuals and the Masses* is Arnold Bennett, with Conan Doyle as a minor hero. Chesterton himself similarly had 'a great admiration' for Bennett as a writer and 'a strong liking' for his 'personality': 'I like his …contempt for contempt. I like his humanity and merciful curiosity about everything human. I like [his] essential absence of snobbishness…' (*T.* 297). This makes the conspicuous absence of Chesterton from Carey's book, apart from a mention of his sympathy with the suburbs, all the more unfortunate. However, Carey does elsewhere briefly acknowledge Chesterton's 'lifelong respect for the common man, as against intellectuals and other cranks' (Conlon ii. 346).

[36] But cf. Oddie, 203, who says that 'his first signed piece appeared on 31 May 1901'.

reviews appeared as lengthy articles and with his name at the top, unlike nearly all the reviews of the other book reviewers, which were unsigned and short. He thus become one of the three leading reviewers for the *Daily News*, only one of whom appeared more regularly, the famous literary critic Arthur Quiller-Couch, whose classic anthology the first *Oxford Book of English Verse* had appeared in 1900.[37] In March 1902 a new editor, A. G. Gardiner, took over, Cadbury having become sole owner. The paper was in financial difficulties because of its anti-imperialist, pro-Boer stance. Gardiner therefore gave the paper a new format, new features, and an expanded literary section.[38] In 1903 Chesterton was given a regular column every other Saturday on the leader page, which the following year became a weekly column.[39] It was noticeable that in time the newspaper's circulation doubled on a Saturday.[40] It amused Chesterton that he was described, 'in the phrase of the time, as having a Saturday pulpit, rather like a Sunday pulpit. Whatever were the merits of the sermons, it is probable that I had a larger congregation than I have ever had before or since.'[41]

Chesterton was becoming very well known not only as a journalist and writer but also as a personality. 'He was a striking figure in those days, upright and with a gallant carriage. His magnificent head had a thick mane of wavy chestnut hair, inevitably rumpled. His hands were beautifully shaped, with long slender fingers, but in sudden, almost painful contradistinction, his feet were very small and podgy, and never seemed to afford a stable base.'[42] He was conspicuous for three things: his dress including his sword-stick, his absent-mindedness, and his predilection for taking cabs, however unnecessarily and regardless of the cost. Abandoning the struggle to make him dress tidily, Frances replaced the usual frock-coat and top hat with a sombrero-style hat and a cloak. The hat successfully covered the uncombed thick wavy chestnut hair and was much less likely to fall off, while the cloak was especially useful as he began rapidly to put on weight. Once, when he did lose his hat (no doubt a pre-sombrero-style hat) in the street and started chasing it, a passer-by rescued it 'to his own imminent peril', only to be met with Chesterton's ungrateful comment that his wife would be sorry to see it again as she had just bought him a new one. Asked why in that case he had run after it, Chesterton replied, 'It's an old friend. I am fond of it and I wanted to be with it at the end.' He was a tall man, six foot two. As a boy he had been thin, but now he was rapidly

[37] Oddie, 203–4.   [38] Dale, 77–8.   [39] Oddie, 271.
[40] Ffinch, 83.   [41] *A.* 119–20.   [42] MCC 1.

gaining weight. 'His mere bulk is impressive,' wrote one observer, but his absent-mindedness was even more impressive.

On one occasion I saw him emerge from Shoe Lane, hurry into the middle of Fleet Street, and abruptly come to a standstill in the centre of the traffic. He stood there for some time, wrapped in thought, while 'buses, taxis and lorries eddied about him in a whirlpool and while drivers exercised to the full their gentle art of expostulation. Having come to the end of his meditations, he held up his hand, turned round, cleared a passage through the horses and vehicles and returned to Shoe Lane. It was just as though he had deliberately chosen the middle of Fleet Street as the most fruitful place for thought. Nobody else in London could have done it with his air of absolute unconsciousness, of absent-mindedness. And not even the most stalwart policeman, vested with full authority, could have dammed up London's stream of traffic more effectively.

The same astonished observer on another occasion saw him arrive at a newspaper office in a cab, the driver of which was told to wait outside. Talking to himself, Chesterton noted that he had half-an-hour to write an article. He asked for a file of back numbers of the paper and looked at some of his own articles.

Presently, he smiled. Then he laughed. Then he leaned back in his chair and roared. 'Good—oh, damned good!' exclaimed he. He turned to another article and frowned a little, but a third pleased him better. After a while, he pushed the papers from him and sat awhile in thought. And . . . he wrote his article, rapidly, calmly, drowsily. Save that his hand moved, he might have been asleep. Nothing disturbed him—neither the noise of the office nor the faint throb of his taxi-cab rapidly ticking off twopences in the street below . . . He finished his article and rolled dreamily away.

On another occasion when he had a lunch date in a restaurant at one o'clock, his host was handed a message from a cab-driver at three o'clock asking, 'Would the gentleman please pay him off now as he wanted to eat too?'[43]

The story was told of him that he would take a cab from his home in Battersea to a Fleet Street newspaper office to claim money owed to him for an article, and then spend so much time talking to journalist friends that by the time he arrived back (in the same cab) at Battersea the fare practically came to the fee for the article that he had gone to collect.[44] Lucy Masterman remembered that his 'practice was to drive in a hansom' to the

[43] Ward, *RC* 61, 72–3.   [44] Conlon, i. 530.

office of the *Daily News*, where her husband Charles, the Liberal politician, was the literary editor at the time. 'Having acquired his book for review he would climb back into the hansom and signal it to drive on until he had finished his article which he wrote on his knee. The plan had its amenities; but when he had drawn his fee and paid off the hansom there was not much left to take back to Frances and the Battersea tradesmen.' As a result, it was arranged that payment for his articles was in future to go directly to Frances—although it meant that sometimes he had to borrow the money for the fare home.[45] A waiting cab in Fleet Street as likely as not indicated the presence of Chesterton: 'He quite forgot it was there, and would chuckle delightedly when he realised it had been stationary for hours. He would pull out a handful of money and invite the cabby to take his fare and a tip . . .'. That was also his method of settling for drinks in pubs—and if his pockets were empty, 'it would not matter, every pub within the radius of Fleet Street knew the big figure, recognised the chuckling laugh and would have given credit for so long as it was wanted'.[46] Restaurants and pubs, in fact, not newspaper offices, were much more likely places to find Chesterton writing his articles. Charles Masterman remembered one such Fleet Street restaurant where Chesterton used to write articles,

mixing a terrible conjunction of drinks, while many waiters hovered about him, partly in awe, and partly in case he should leave the restaurant without paying for what he had had. One day . . . the headwaiter approached [Masterman]. 'Your friend,' he whispered, admiringly, 'he very clever man. He sit and laugh. And then he write. And then he laugh at what he write.'[47]

Lucy Masterman recalled that his 'favourite spot was a corner table . . . where he would turn back the cloth and lay his manuscript on the baize underneath'.[48] The restaurant was probably El Vino, one of his 'favourite haunts, with the George and the Bodega'. 'Under the shelter of a vast cask of sherry, on the corner of an old mahogany table', he 'would reel off hundreds of words and talk in a glowing flow of epigram and paradox. It became a custom to look in round about six in the hope of finding him.'[49] One American visitor to London met Chesterton face-to-face in Fleet Street: 'Wrapped in a cloak and standing in the doorway of a pie-shop,

[45] Lucy Masterman, 'The Private Chesterton', *Manchester Guardian*, 28 Apr. 1955.

[46] MCC 47.   [47] Ward, *GKC* 138.

[48] Masterman, 'The Private Chesterton'.   [49] MCC 44–5.

he was composing a poem, reciting it aloud as he wrote. The most striking thing about the incident was that no one took the slightest notice.'[50]

Chesterton was becoming a great London character like Dr Johnson. Unlike many eccentrics, he was well aware of his public image, but that does not necessarily mean that it was 'put on'—although he no doubt enjoyed playing up to it to a certain extent. It is true that there was at least one contemporary who knew him well, Mildred Wain, who had her doubts.[51] She used to meet Chesterton regularly in a café in Fleet Street before she got married when they were both students. Meeting another student there once, she observed Chesterton enter arguing with another man.

They sat down at a table a short distance away and Gilbert ordered two poached eggs on toast and some coffee. They were brought to him in due course and he, apparently not noticing their arrival, continued to talk and argue, and, lifting his hand to emphasize some point, brought it down with great force on the edge of the plate and tipped the eggs right into his lap. He still continued talking and when the waitress came to him all he said was: 'Will you please bring me two more poached eggs—I seem to have lost the others.'

At the party celebrating her engagement to Waldo d'Avigdor, she discovered Chesterton in a distant corner of the house talking rapidly and walking up and down. She went up to him to say good night and found her sister sound asleep behind him. She had got bored with arguing and fallen asleep, but Chesterton continued perfectly happily, answering all his own questions. 'You had to be careful not to give him an opening if you didn't want him to talk. A chance remark would set him off for half an hour.'[52] Neither of these two stories necessarily suggests anything like cultivated eccentricity. What they do show is the sheer absent-mindedness of a mind totally detached from immediate practicalities and constantly engaged in thought—what Chesterton himself called 'presence of mind on other things'[53]—that bore fruit in a phenomenal amount of writing. Nor was there anything new about Chesterton's extraordinary absent-mindedness: he had been noted for it even while still a schoolboy at St Paul's, when he could scarcely have been accused of cultivating an image for publicity purposes. His insouciance about taxis was only an aspect of his absent-mindedness. As for his dress, Frances had merely chosen a simple costume that was likely to cause the least problems, as well as to accommodate his

[50] Ward, *GKC* 139–40.   [51] Ward, *RC* 72.   [52] Ward, *RC* 20–1.
[53] Dorothy Collins's notes for talks, BL Add. MS 73477, fo. 136.

enormous size.[54] The only deliberate eccentricity was the sword-stick that symbolized adventure and romance. But it was there for its wearer's own boyish satisfaction, not to create a particular image. The charge made by Robert Blatchford, soon to be one of his most significant opponents in controversy, that Chesterton was 'an actor' who 'played a part, and dressed for a part' has been supported by one of his later biographers, who even alleges that his absent-mindedness and appearance were 'a publicity device', adopted 'at the instigation of Frances' so far as his dress was concerned.[55] But such a deliberate self-seeking strategy would have been completely repugnant to the devoutly Anglican Frances and totally inconsistent with her dislike of publicity.[56]

No one can claim that Chesterton's drinking habits were a cultivated eccentricity. Heavy drinking in the bars of Fleet Street went with the job. 'Keith' Jones herself, though a woman, joined in the drinking of her fellow male journalists. Chesterton would sit for hours in a wine bar opposite the *Daily News* with a bottle of burgundy.[57] His brother Cecil described how he would 'pour out conversation to anybody who happens be about. He talks, especially in argument, with powerful voice and gesture. He laughs at his own jokes loudly and with quite unaffected enjoyment.' The brother noticed too how he would 'take a cab halfway up a street, keep it waiting for an hour or so, and then drive halfway down the street again'. On one occasion, Cecil related, his brother met a friend in a bookshop opposite the Law Courts at one end of Fleet Street. A waiting cab then took them to a pub a few doors down, where they ordered a bottle of wine and talked for three-quarters of an hour while the cab waited. Finally, the cab took Chesterton to his destination, an office a few yards in the other direction, when the driver was probably given at least twice the proper fare.[58]

---

[54] Ward, *GKC* 138, recognizes that Frances gave up the struggle to try and make her husband tidy in conventional clothes, but then unfortunately adds, 'By a stroke of genius she decided instead to make him picturesque.' This would seem to support the charge that Frances aided and abetted Chesterton in cultivating a public image.

[55] Barker, 132–3, who quotes Chesterton on the 'faintly ostentatious' appearance of Stevenson ('such a man is not entirely averse from being looked at') who wore a hat with a long feather or an embroidered smoking cap over his long flowing hair and carried a rapier at the ready, concludes that 'the remarks apply equally to himself'. But Chesterton's costume was strictly functional and by no means so ostentatious—apart from the sword-stick.

[56] See Ward, *RC* 47.   [57] Barker, 135.   [58] *CC* 254–5.

Not surprisingly, Chesterton's absent-mindedness included forgetting engagements. One evening in El Vino, 'Keith' Jones remembered him suddenly musing, 'I oughtn't to be here, I'm supposed to be speaking to the Literary Society at Bletchley—I should be speaking *now!*' Even then there was time to order another glass of port. 'Keith' and Cecil hurried with him in a cab to Conrad Noel's, the clergyman who had married him and Frances, where he was staying. On emerging from the bedroom he was sharing with Noel, he appeared wearing an evening dress coat far too small but without the trousers; he was still wearing the brown tweed plus fours in which he had entered the bedroom. Clearly, Chesterton explained, 'some strange magic had been at work': 'Perhaps the Mesopotamian deacon staying at the flat had put a spell on him.' Certainly, he had donned or attempted to don the required evening dress laid out on the bed he was sleeping on. Refusing to change again, he left in his cab for Bletchley. The return of Conrad Noel, who also needed to change into evening dress, revealed all: the wrong evening dress had been laid on the wrong bed.[59] In his *Autobiography* Chesterton had a less bizarre version of the story: that he had merely made the excusable error of mistaking Noel's black clerical trousers for his own evening trousers.[60] Constantly writing not only in pubs with a bottle of Burgundy (his favourite drink) beside him, but also in cabs, buses, trains, and in the street, he was constantly preoccupied—'He was always working out something in his mind'[61]—with the inevitable result that appointments were not kept—'and he frequently wrote to explain why he had failed to turn up'. He was certainly capable of eccentric behaviour that was without doubt beyond the imagination and invention of man—or of his own acting capabilities: 'Once he called on a publisher at the exact hour agreed upon, but he spoilt the effect by handing the man a letter explaining elaborately why he could not keep the appointment.'[62] Indeed, his readiness to risk his life does not immediately suggest contrived eccentricity: 'I have seen the traffic of Ludgate Circus held up for him, as he strolled by in cloak and sombrero like a brigand of Adelphi drama or a

---

[59] MCC 52–3. Barker, 134, claims that 'Keith' Jones was one of those close to Chesterton who 'assisted in the legend' he and Frances had created, and that 'it is unbelievable that Ada Jones or any of the others failed to realise what had happened'. But how could 'Keith' and Cecil have realized that there was another, the right, evening dress suit lying on another, the wrong, bed? Given Chesterton's understandable anxiety to leave as soon as possible for the lecture, there was not much time for reflection anyway.

[60] *A*. 157–8.   [61] O'Connor, 44.   [62] Conlon, ii. 209.

Spanish hidalgo by Velasquez, oblivious alike of critical bus-driver and wonder-struck multitude.'[63] And yet, in spite of his being 'apparently oblivious of everything that passed before him', his future secretary Dorothy Collins noticed, 'really he was a much closer observer than most, and remembered what he had seen and what he had read'. But his memory was certainly not visual: 'He always remembered what he had seen and those with whom he had talked, not so much by their faces as by their minds—for that is how he saw people.'[64]

4

In September 1902 Chesterton became involved in a controversy in the letters column of the *Daily News*. The Balfour government's educational bill, which abolished independent school boards and replaced them with municipal local-education authorities, was before parliament. Nonconformists opposed the bill, as the new educational system would include Church of England and Roman Catholic elementary schools, which would now be subsidized by local taxes. The opposition was led by a Dr Clifford, a Baptist minister of extreme Protestant views. Liberals like Chesterton opposed the bill because it violated 'an elementary liberal principle in not equalising contribution and control'—that is to say, he did not think it fair that the ordinary tax-payer should be required to pay for exclusively church schools. Nevertheless, Chesterton vehemently opposed any opposition on religious grounds. Attacking the 'No Popery Cry' of Clifford, he urged his party to attack the bill as Liberals, 'without binding the living body of Liberalism to the slimy corpse of the Protestant Truth Society'. He wrote to Clifford to remind him how they had stood together against popular jingoism at the time of the Boer War, and now Clifford should not be exploiting the 'No Popery' cry: in this they should show their superiority to the Conservatives by not resorting to 'an old, an effectual, an infallible, and a filthy weapon'. However, he also saw that the Liberal 'compromise' of compulsory Bible teaching in all state schools was in fact 'in favour of the Protestant view of the Bible', as it implied that Christian belief is derived from the Bible rather than the Church.[65]

Chesterton's second book of selected journalism was published in October 1902. *Twelve Types* consisted of articles from the *Speaker*, the *Daily*

---

[63] Clemens, 44.   [64] Sullivan, 157, 160.
[65] Ward, *GKC* 249–50; Ffinch, 103–4; Dale, 83.

News, and one from the *Literary Gazette*, with some revisions and additions. The majority of the pieces were literary, not surprisingly, since, although the pieces collected in *The Defendant* were articles of a general nature rather than book reviews, such articles counted for considerably less than half of his contributions to the *Speaker*, and when he began writing for the *Daily News* he wrote almost entirely for the books page.[66] As in the articles collected in *The Defendant*, so too in the pieces that comprise *Twelve Types* we find already in Chesterton's early journalism many of his central ideas to which he would return time and time again in his writings. The twelve essays are about one woman and eleven men, mostly writers, who make up the 'types' referred to in the title of the book. A third of them, all writers, are Victorians, a foretaste of Chesterton's writings about Victorian literature, which ought to have won him a place among the great literary critics.

The opening essay on Charlotte Brontë states a paradox pertinent to Chesterton's gospel of wonder. The Brontë novel, we are told, stands for 'a certain most important truth about the enduring spirit of youth, the truth of the near kinship between terror and joy'. As 'the epic of the exhilaration of the shy man', it shows how fear is 'one of the eternal ingredients of joy'. For joy to be reverent, the presence of fear is necessary. The Brontë heroine 'approaches the universe . . . with real fear and delight', for she is 'shy before the multitude of the stars', so that her joyful wonder at the universe is not 'as black and barren as routine'. The Charlotte Brontë heroine was only a 'shabby and inconspicuous governess'; she was not a 'dark wild' heroine of the 'dark wild Yorkshire' of the Brontës. For her emotions were 'universal emotions, emotions of the morning of existence, the springtide joy and the springtide terror'. They were emotions, Chesterton insists, that can be felt even in the *suburbs*. Yes, he agrees with the intellectuals, 'the branches of the great city' are so 'endless' that there are 'times when we are almost stricken crazy . . . by the multiplicity of those appalling perspectives, the frantic arithmetic of that unthinkable population'. But to dismiss all these countless people as simply 'the masses' is 'nothing but a fancy'. The truth is that there is no such thing as 'the masses', Chesterton passionately insists, contrary to the dogmatic assumption of virtually every contemporary writer: 'There are no chains of houses; there are no crowds of men. The colossal diagram of streets and houses is an illusion . . . Each of these men is supremely solitary and supremely important to himself. Each of these houses stands in the centre of the world.'[67]

---

[66] Oddie, 209.   [67] *TWTY* 8, 10–11,13–14.

The 'elaborate and deliberate ugliness' of the Victorians is another regular Chestertonian theme. How was it possible 'to account for the clinging curse of ugliness which blights everything brought forth by the most prosperous of centuries'? How could a cultivated and educated man wish 'by a farcical bathos' to 'be buried in a black coat, and hidden under a chimney-pot hat'? Could 'all created nature' show 'anything so completely ugly as a pillar-box'? And there was 'no reason whatever why such hideousness should possess an object full of civic dignity, the treasure-house of a thousand secrets, the fortress of a thousand souls'. Against all this ugliness stood William Morris, who in reaction held up 'for practical imitation the costumes and handicrafts of the Middle Ages'. But literal imitation was as far as Morris went. He failed to see that the costumes and handicrafts of medieval people 'sprang honestly and naturally out of the life they led and preferred to lead'. And yet Morris should have seen the point. For—and this is another perennial theme in Chesterton—'Of all the various works he performed, none, perhaps, was so splendidly and solidly valuable as his great protest for the fables and superstitions of mankind. He has the supreme credit of showing that the fairy-tales contain the deepest truth of the earth, the real record of men's feelings for things.' And no fairy tale contained 'so vital a moral truth' as the story of Beauty and the Beast, which teaches 'the eternal and essential truth that until we love a thing in all its ugliness we cannot make it beautiful'. That was where Morris failed: 'he sought to reform modern life', but 'he hated modern life instead of loving it'. The trouble was that Morris was too close to the nineteenth century to appreciate its 'fascination'; modern London was indeed 'a beast, big enough and black enough to be the beast in Apocalypse, blazing with a million eyes, and roaring with a million voices'—but unless one loved 'this fabulous monster', one could not 'change the beast into the fairy princess'. Morris could create beautiful things, but he was incapable of making 'modern things...beautiful', for 'he had not the supreme courage to face the ugliness of things'.[68]

Turning to the previous century, Chesterton calls Pope the supreme poet of paradox, since the 'antitheses' of his poetry are 'fully in harmony with existence, which is itself a contradiction in terms'. The modern idea that 'the very antithesis of the typical line of Pope is a mark of artificiality' ignores the fact that an 'element of paradox runs through the whole of existence itself'. Physically, it was impossible to 'imagine a space that is infinite' but equally impossible to 'imagine a space that is finite'. Or, again,

[68] *TWTY* 18–20, 23–8.

all moral qualities demanded the possibility of their opposite—'we cannot imagine courage existing except in conjunction with fear'. As 'the last great poet of civilisation', Pope was 'supreme' in 'the great and civilised art' of satire. For he understood, unlike modern writers, the paradox that generosity is required for satire. An attack on somebody's weaknesses is only convincing and effective when one also recognizes their strengths. Otherwise the portrait painted is unreal and lacks conviction.[69]

Chesterton was to write a book about Francis of Assisi many years later, but in the essay here the central paradox of Francis's life, as Chesterton saw it, was that 'all true joy expresses itself in terms of asceticism'. It was 'the universe itself' that made Francis's followers 'mad with joy'—'the only thing really worthy of enjoyment.' Francis himself was 'the happiest of the sons of men', and yet he 'undoubtedly founded his whole polity on the negation of what we think the most imperious necessities'. Ultimately, people in Chesterton's view are either optimists or pessimists: either they see 'life black against white' or 'white against black'. And the Franciscans embraced sacrifice because they saw life as 'full of the blaze of an universal mercy', whereas pessimists indulge themselves because they see only 'a black curtain of incalculable night'. But Chesterton concludes: 'The revellers are old, and the monks are young. It was the monks who were the spendthrifts of happiness, and we who are its misers.'[70]

When Chesterton said that Francis 'expressed in loftier and bolder language than any earthly thinker the conception that laughter is as divine as tears',[71] he was touching on an idea that was to be one of the major themes in his writings. He complained that there was 'no tradition in English literature which would justify us in calling a comedy heroic', the hero's place being in tragedy according to the modern conception. But great comedy, like that of Shakespeare, 'not only can be, but must be, taken seriously. There is nothing to which a man must give himself up with more faith and self-abandonment than to genuine laughter.' The idea that comedy was artificial was due to 'a profound pessimism', in other words to the assumption that the world was no place for laughter.[72] Humour, Chesterton was to declare, is 'mystical; it is no more to be argued about than a religion', between which and 'real fun' 'there is an alliance', religion being 'much nearer to riotous happiness than it is to the detached and temperate types of happiness in which gentlemen and philosophers find their peace'.[73]

[69] *TWTY* 49–51.   [70] *TWTY* 65, 69, 74–6.   [71] *TWTY* 74.
[72] *TWTY* 79, 81–2.   [73] *ILN* xxvii. 153; xxviii. 24.

Chesterton's book on Robert Louis Stevenson, published a quarter of a century later, is also prefigured in a book review reprinted here. He had been an effective antidote to Chesterton's *fin de siècle* gloom because 'he took pleasure in life, in every muscular and emphatic action of life, even if it were an action that took the life of another'. He is one of Chesterton's heroes because he delights in existence itself. He had 'a positive love for inanimate objects such as had not been known since St Francis called the sun brother and the well sister'. Stylistically, his writings, Chesterton notes, were distinguished by 'a certain clean-cut angularity which make us remember that he was fond of cutting wood with an axe'—a point he would develop in the book.[74]

The essay on Stevenson introduces another Chestertonian idea—the importance of romance: 'The conception which unites the whole varied work of Stevenson was that romance, or the vision of the possibilities of things, was far more important than mere occurrences: that one was the soul of our life, the other the body, and that the soul was the precious thing.'[75] In the last essay of the book on Walter Scott, Chesterton returns to the theme. He insists again on the importance of romance as 'a state of the soul', as against 'the idea that romance is in some way a plaything with life, a figment, a conventionality, a thing upon the outside'. Far from romance being escapist or unreal, Chesterton insists that it 'lies not upon the outside of life but absolutely in the centre of it'. For the 'centre of every man's existence is a dream'—'a man's vision of himself, as swaggering and sentimental as a penny novelette', a 'vanity which is the mother of all day-dreams and adventures...'. Scott's 'spiritual adventurousness' sets him apart from Dumas, for Scott understands that romance paradoxically 'does not consist by any means so much in experiencing adventures as in being ready for them'. Action in itself is not the stuff of romantic adventure: nothing is more typical of Scott's heroes than 'their disposition to linger over their meals'. Like Stevenson, Scott is seen to have a Chestertonian love of *things* for themselves: 'he loved weapons' not just for the sake of adventure, but

with a manual materialistic love, as one loves the softness of fur or the coolness of marble. One of the profound philosophical truths which are almost confined to infants is this love of things, not for their use or origin, but for their own inherent characteristics, the child's love of the toughness of wood, the wetness of water, the magnificent soapiness of soap.

[74] *TWTY* 111–13.   [75] *TWTY* 117.

Chesterton even suggests that people were not the only 'characters' in his novels: 'Like a true child, he almost ignored the distinction between the animate and inanimate.' Similarly, Scott made no distinction between his characters in the sense that he endows them equally, whether heroes or villains, with eloquence. His 'difficulty, or rather incapacity, for despising any of his characters' means that 'every man of Scott can speak like a king'. This Scottish inability to distinguish the common man from the king Chesterton was later to contrast favourably with the class-consciousness of the English Dickens. Nor did Scott despise bombast as being 'merely superficial'. Again, Scott stood with the common man or the child against the sophisticated intellectual: 'The superficial impression of the world is by far the deepest. What we really feel, naturally and casually, about the look of skies and trees and the face of friends, that and that alone will almost certainly remain our vital philosophy to our dying day.'[76]

Where Carlyle and Ruskin, on the other hand, failed as prophets was in failing to treat 'the average man as their equal, of trusting to his reason and good feeling without fear and without condescension'. Nevertheless Carlyle did possess that indispensable Chestertonian attribute—humour about what he was most serious about: 'A man must be very full of faith to jest about his divinity.' Because he had a 'sense of the sarcasm of eternity' he could see that there was 'something elemental and eternal in a joke'. In Chesterton's view, Carlyle's main achievement was to induce people 'to study less the truth of their reasoning, and more the truth of the assumptions upon which they reasoned'. Nothing was more common than to hear people arguing quite logically but 'without troubling about the deep assumptions involved, having lost their sense, as it were, of the real colour and character' of the relevant underlying assumptions. But it was only common sense that there are truths that 'cannot be formally demonstrated or even formally named' and 'realities that we all know to be real, but which have no place in argument except as postulates'. However, Chesterton was clear about the 'evil side' of Carlyle's 'religion of hero worship', which led him to defend slavery 'from the passion for applying everywhere his paradoxical defence of aristocracy'. And he was clear too about his evil influence: 'Out of him flows most of the philosophy of Nietzsche, who is in modern times the supreme maniac of this moon-struck consistency' of applying a 'single ethical test to everything in heaven and earth'.[77]

[76] *TWTY* 183–5, 187–9, 191–3, 197–8.
[77] *TWTY* 122–4, 128–9, 131, 135, 137–8.

This kind of simplification is again the object of attack in 'Tolstoy and the Cult of Simplicity'. On the one hand, understanding leads naturally to simplification: 'The more consistently things are contemplated, the more they tend to unify themselves and therefore to simplify themselves. The simplification of anything is always sensational. Thus monotheism is the most sensational of things.' On the other hand, a 'self-conscious simplicity' that consists in 'warring on complexity' is likely to lead to even more complexity. Instead of this 'search after a false simplicity, the aim of being . . . more natural than it is natural to be', it 'would not only be more human, it would be more humble of us to be content to be complex'. Tolstoy well exemplifies for Chesterton how 'an artist teaches far more by his mere background and properties, his landscape, his costume, his idiom and technique—all the part of his work, in short, of which he is probably entirely unconscious, than by the elaborate and pompous moral dicta which he fondly imagines to be his opinions'. Thus 'the real moral of Tolstoy' emerges in his fiction, a moral 'of which he is probably unconscious, and of which it is quite likely that he would vehemently disapprove'. This moral through great art is in contrast to 'the trumpeting and tearing nonsense of the didactic Tolstoy', 'the almost venomous reformer'. As for the Tolstoyan doctrine of loving humanity, 'Christ did not love humanity; He never said He loved humanity: He loved men. Neither He nor anyone else can love humanity . . .'. But then Christ never 'wrote a word, except with his finger in the sand'. His teaching was characterized by its spontaneity: 'It was not for any pompous proclamation, it was not for any elaborate output of printed volumes; it was for a few splendid and idle words that the cross was set up on Calvary, and the earth gaped, and the sun was darkened at noonday.'[78] Here Chesterton anticipates his ability in *Orthodoxy* to make us see familiar biblical texts with new eyes.

In his essay on Savonarola, Chesterton returns to his favourite theme of grateful wonder.

He was making war against no trivial sins, but against godless and thankless quiescence, against getting used to happiness, the mystic sin by which all creation fell. . . . He was preaching that alertness, that clean agility and vigilance, which is as necessary to gain pleasure as to gain holiness, as indispensable in a lover as in a monk. . . . The fact is that this purification and austerity are even more necessary for the appreciation of life and laughter than for anything else.

[78] *TWTY* 40, 145, 147–9, 151, 164–6.

This appreciation of life itself required 'a discipline in pleasure, and an education in gratitude'. For it was the hardest of all tasks to make people 'turn back and wonder at the simplicities they had learned to ignore'. Like Chesterton, Savonarola believed in democracy because he believed in that 'most unpopular' of doctrines 'which declares the common life divine'. It was 'the hardest of gospels', since nothing so terrifies people as 'the decree that they are all kings'. For Savonarola, Christianity was 'identical with democracy' and was 'the hardest of gospels', because nothing 'so strikes men with fear as the saying that they are all the sons of God'. Chesterton thought his own time was like that of the Florence of Savonarola and the Medici, with its decadent *fin de siècle* aestheticism and the Carlylean 'hunger for the strong man which is unknown among strong men'.[79] The concept of the masses as sons of God who were kings in their own right could hardly have been further away from that of the typical intellectuals and writers of the day to whom the masses represented such a threat that autocratic rule was the only possible alternative to extermination.

5

This is a good point at which to consider how far Chesterton would have professed himself to be a Christian when he published *Twelve Types*. We have already seen how Frances's practice of Anglo-Catholicism had intrigued him. And we know that he had become friends with the Revd Conrad Noel before his marriage in June 1901. Noel's recollection was that he and his wife met Chesterton for the first time at a meeting of the Christo-Theosophic Society. This must have been after April 1900, when Chesterton's first review appeared in the *Speaker*, as Noel says: 'We had been much intrigued by the weekly contributions of an unknown writer to the *Speaker* . . . brilliant work, and my wife and I, independently, came to the conclusion when we heard this young man speak that it must be he. The style was unmistakable.' Before Noel could write to congratulate him on his speech, he received a letter from Chesterton, 'saying that he was coming to hear me . . . in a week or so; it was thus we first became acquainted, and the acquaintance ripened into a warm friendship with us both. He and his brother Cecil were in and out of our flat in Paddington Green, where I was assistant curate.'[80] Unlike his brother, who professed not even to wish to believe, Chesterton 'always retained a sort of lingering

<hr>

[79] *TWTY* 170–5.   [80] Ward, *GKC* 121.

loyalty or vague sympathy with the traditions of the past; so that, even during the period when I practically believed in nothing, I believed in what some have called "the wish to believe"'.[81]

Chesterton himself could not remember exactly when he first met Noel, but thought it was

at some strange club where somebody was lecturing on Nietzsche; and where the debaters (by typical transition) passed from the gratifying thought that Nietzsche attacked Christianity to the natural inference that he was a True Christian. And I admired the common sense of a curate, with dark curly hair and a striking face, who got up and pointed out that Nietzsche would be even more opposed to True Christianity than to False Christianity, supposing there was any True Christianity to oppose.

The curate's common sense contracted favourably with the absence of thought among the intelligentsia of that 'very strange world' of 'artistic and vaguely anarchic clubs', which 'thought a great deal about thinking' but 'did not think'. Its ideas came 'at second or third hand; from Nietzsche or Tolstoy or Ibsen or Shaw'.

Those who pontificated most pompously were often the most windy and hollow. I remember a man with a long beard and a deep booming voice who proclaimed at intervals, 'What we need is Love,' or, 'All we require is Love,' like the detonations of a heavy gun. I remember another radiant little man who spread out his fingers and said, 'Heaven is here! It is now!' which seemed a disturbing thought under the circumstances. There was an aged, aged man who seemed to live at one of these literary clubs; and who would hold up a large hand at intervals and preface some fairly ordinary observation by saying, 'A Thought.' . . . A sort of Theosophist said to me, 'Good and evil, truth and falsehood, folly and wisdom are only aspects of the same upward movement of the universe.' Even at that stage it occurred to me to ask, 'Supposing there is no difference between good and bad, or between false and true, what is the difference between up and down?'

These intellectuals, of course, who admired Ibsen and Shaw, were naturally totally contemptuous of Victorian farces, in which the curate was a stock type. And Chesterton himself had been 'quite ready to believe that a dying superstition was represented by such feeble persons'. But, in fact, in these debates what struck Chesterton was that as often as not 'it was the feeble-minded clergyman, who got up and applied to the wandering discussion at least some sort of test of some sort of truth'. 'Dreadful seeds of doubt began to be sown in my mind. . . . It seemed to me that the despised curates were rather more intelligent than anybody else; that they, alone in that world of intellectualism, were trying to use their intellects.'[82]

---

[81] *A.* 159.   [82] *A.* 152–4.

Noel was an eccentric who later became famous for flying the red flag from his church in Thaxted, Essex. But in these early days he was known as a 'Bohemian' rather than 'Bolshevist' clergyman. He specialized in wearing a combination of clerical, artistic, and working-class clothes. Chesterton remembered walking from a meeting with Noel and Dr Percy Dearmer, 'then chiefly famous as an authority on the history of ritual and of vestments'.

Dr Dearmer was in the habit of walking about in a cassock and biretta which he had carefully reconstructed as being of exactly the right pattern for an Anglican or Anglo-Catholic priest; and he was humorously grieved when its strictly traditional and national character was misunderstood by the little boys in the street. Somebody would call out, 'No Popery,' or 'To hell with the Pope,' or some other sentiment of larger and more liberal religion. And Percy Dearmer would sternly stop them and say, 'Are you aware that this is the precise costume in which Latimer went to the stake?'[83]

Such Anglo-Catholic eccentricities were the means of drawing Bohemians like Chesterton ('I had no religion except the very haziest religiosity'[84]) and his 'frankly anti-religious' brother 'towards the serious consideration of the theory of a Church'. The 'most fascinating and memorable' member of the Anglo-Catholic clergy to whom Chesterton always felt 'gratitude' was Canon Henry Scott Holland, a close friend of Canon, later Bishop, Charles Gore, the founder of Pusey House in Oxford. Holland, with his 'humorous frog's face and great stature and voice of bull-like bellowing', was the founder of the Christian Social Union which had chapters all over the country and which Chesterton was to join. Like Chesterton himself, he had a strong sense of humour that could prevent him too from being taken seriously. At a meeting in Nottingham he was urging the merits of positive rather than merely negative state intervention, when he could not repress the 'natural surge of laughter within him'—

and he said, waving his hand to the rigid and respectable Nottingham audience, 'Punishment is an exceptional instrument. After all, it is only occasionally that you and I feel that tap on the shoulder, and that gruff recommendation to "come along quietly." It is not every day of our lives that we are put in the dock and sentenced to some term of imprisonment. . . . Why, I suppose that even in this

[83] *A.* 158.

[84] *A.* 165. But cf. Oddie, 179: 'That this was an exaggeration is clear enough: "The Notebook," for instance, shows plainly that by 1894, although Chesterton's religious feelings were far from dogmatically well-defined, they amounted to something considerably more definite and powerfully experienced than can properly be described as "the very haziest religiosity".'

room there are quite half a dozen people who have never been to jail at all.' A ghastly stare was fixed on all the faces of the audience; and I have ever since seen it in my own dreams; for it has constituted a considerable part of my own problem.

On the same occasion Chesterton penned some comic verses on the reaction of one of these respectable Nottingham tradesmen to being told their 'Christian duty towards the modern problem of industrial poverty':

> The Christian Social Union here
> Was very much annoyed;
> It seems there is some duty
> Which we never should avoid,
> And so they sang a lot of hymns
> To help the Unemployed....

As he recalled 'those old exhilarating days', Chesterton, now a Roman Catholic, could not help wondering 'whither' 'those old' Anglo-Catholic Socialist friends, 'from whom I have been sundered in thought but never in sympathy', were 'marching so gallantly that you could not find the natural way?'[85]

6

Chesterton's review article on Stevenson, republished in *Twelve Types*, was especially important in establishing his reputation. On the strength of it, the leading literary critic, Sir Sidney Colvin, who had recently edited both the works and letters of Stevenson, wrote to him and subsequently invited him to his house, where Chesterton became a frequent visitor. They differed on every possible subject, apart from their mutual love of Stevenson. When Colvin became engaged in 1903 to the charming and talented Mrs Fanny Sitwell, with whom Colvin's friend Stevenson had also been deeply in love, the widow of a clergyman from whom she had been separated, Chesterton wrote to congratulate Colvin: 'I have as much right to look on your new arrangements with delight as a criminal has to admire a sunset.' However, 'congratulations upon these real things' always seemed to him 'to be quite unsuited to this nasty and elegant language in which we write letters. If we could write a page of very exquisite blank verse, it might be all right, or erect an altar and slaughter a thousand oxen.' But as 'a milder form of burnt-offering', he could only think of sending him his recently published book on Browning.[86] Even more

---

[85] *A.* 159–63, 165.
[86] G. K. Chesterton to Sidney Colvin, n.d., BL Add. MS 73236, fo. 59.

importantly, Edmund Gosse, the author of *Father and Son*, and another lover of
Stevenson, was taken by the article. Chesterton felt 'far more at home' with
him, because 'he despised all opinions and not merely my opinions'.

He had an extraordinary depth of geniality in his impartial cynicism. He had the
art of snubbing without sneering. We always felt that he had not enjoyed snubbing
but the snub itself, as a sort of art for art's sake, a million miles from any personal
malice. It was all the more artistic because of the courtly and silken manner that
he commonly assumed. I was very fond of him . . .

Chesterton also at the same time 'discovered the secret of amiability in
another person with a rather misleading reputation for acidity', the cari-
caturist Max Beerbohm, whose novel *Zuleika Dobson* would be published a
few years later.[87] Like Chesterton, his humour misled people, in his case
into thinking that he suffered from egoism as though humour could not
accompany humility, just as Chesterton's humour persuaded people that
he could not be serious. It was at any rate a humorous note that he sent to
Chesterton inviting him to lunch in May 1902.

I am quite different from my writings (and so, I daresay, are you from yours)—so
that we should not necessarily fail to hit it off.
     I, in the flesh, am modest, full of commonsense, very genial, and rather dull.
     What you are remains to be seen—or not to be seen—by me, according to your
decision.[88]

George Bernard Shaw, too, was so impressed in the summer of 1901 by

a review of Scott's *Ivanhoe* which [Chesterton] wrote for the *Daily News* . . . that I
wrote to him asking who he was and where he came from, as he was evidently a
new star in literature. He was either too shy or too lazy to answer. The next thing I
remember is his lunching with us on quite intimate terms, accompanied by Belloc.[89]

According to Lucian Oldershaw, Chesterton did not meet Shaw till five
years later while visiting Paris in April 1906 when they went to see Rodin
making a bust of Shaw.[90] It seems that quite an audience would gather
every day to watch the great French sculptor modelling the famous English
playwright, sitting 'in mesmerised silence' while Shaw 'concentrated and

<hr />

[87] *A.* 99–100.   [88] Ward, *GKC* 135.

[89] Ward, *GKC* 135–6. The reference is probably to Chesterton's article 'The
Position of Sir Walter Scott' in the *Daily News*, 10 Aug. 1901, in which he praises
Shaw and his play *Candida*. *Bernard Shaw: Collected Letters 1926–1950*, ed. Dan H.
Laurence (London: Max Reinhardt, 1988), 464.

[90] Ward, *GKC* 136; Dale, 105.

collected himself and Rodin filled the place' with violent movement and cries.[91] Rodin's secretary, who was then the German poet Rainer Maria Rilke, told them that Shaw had been trying to explain at some length what the Salvation Army was, no doubt in connection with his play *Major Barbara*. When Shaw had completed his explanation, the secretary informed him that 'The Master says you have not much French but you impose yourself'. Oldershaw thought he imposed himself too much—he 'talked Gilbert down'. As a great talker himself, Chesterton was most unusual in also being very good at listening to other people, and listening because he genuinely wanted to hear them talk.[92]

More important, however, for his literary career than the society he was now moving in was an invitation from the publisher Macmillan to write a book on Browning for its 'English Men of Letters' series. Even the self-deprecating Chesterton admitted it was 'a very flattering invitation' and 'a crown of what I can only call respectability'.[93] This was a very distinguished series: other contributors included J. A. Froude, Trollope, and Henry James. It was also a very bold move on the publisher's part, as Chesterton had not yet written a book, apart from his collections of verse and essays. The gamble more than paid off, as the resulting book was often to be reprinted and is the only volume in the series that is remembered and still read today. The invitation had just arrived when he had lunch with Beerbohm, who advised him 'in a pensive way: "A man ought to write on Browning while he is young." ' Chesterton did not understand this cryptic advice at the time, but claimed that he did when he wrote his *Autobiography*—but without explaining to his readers what it meant. In characteristic self-deprecation, Chesterton said that he did not claim to have written a book on Browning but to have written

a book on love, liberty, poetry, my own views on God and religion (highly undeveloped), and various theories of my own about optimism and pessimism and the hope of the world; a book in which the name of Browning was introduced from time to time, I might almost say with considerable art, or at any rate with some decent appearance of regularity. There were very few biographical facts in the book, and those were nearly all wrong. But there is something buried somewhere in the book; though I think it is rather my boyhood than Browning's biography.[94]

---

[91] Michael Holroyd, *Bernard* Shaw, ii. *1898–1918, The Pursuit of Power* (London: Chatto and Windus, 1989), 182.

[92] Ward, *GKC* 136.   [93] *A.* 101.   [94] *A.* 101.

In fact, Chesterton spent many long hours in the British Museum Reading Room reading up on his subject. And there is a story that once, finding himself with no money, he sketched the picture of a man shaking with hunger and wrote underneath it a request for the loan of a sixpence, which he placed in turn on the desks of anyone he knew in the Reading Room. He collected enough for a visit to the nearest pub.[95] The editor who had suggested that Chesterton should be commissioned to write the volume on Browning for the prestigious series was sent for by the senior partner in Macmillans, who was in a 'white fury' at the sight of the corrected proofs—

or rather not corrected; there were still thirteen errors uncorrected on one page; mostly in quotations from Browning. A selection from a Scottish ballad had been quoted from memory and three of the four lines were wrong. I wrote to Chesterton saying that the firm thought the book was going to 'disgrace' them. His reply was like the trumpeting of a crushed elephant. But the book was a huge success.[96]

The book was published in May 1903 and was widely and on the whole enthusiastically reviewed, although not all the reviewers appreciated the factual inaccuracies; one reviewer angrily pointed out that one line allegedly of Browning's poetry was not inaccurate but simply invented by Chesterton. The truth was that Chesterton simply quoted from his extraordinary but not infallible memory; years after leaving Fisher Unwin he could still remember all the plots and most of the characters of the 'thousands' of novels he had read for the publisher, according to Frances. He did not bother to verify his facts and thought it pedantic to worry about verbal inaccuracies. Much later, when Dorothy Collins became his secretary, he was not at all keen on her checking references.[97] A few years after publishing his book on Browning, he wrote: 'I quote from memory both by temper and on principle. That is what literature is for; it ought to be part of a man.'[98] But, whatever its shortcomings in accuracy, the book firmly established his literary reputation, so much so that a year later he was even invited to apply for the chair of English literature at Birmingham University, even though he had no degree.[99] It is arguable that his book is still the best criticism of Browning ever written.[100] On 15 July 1903 Anne Ritchie, the eldest daughter of Thackeray, wrote to Chesterton to

[95] Barker, 127–8.   [96] Clemens, 14–15.   [97] Ward, *GKC* 145–6.
[98] *Daily News*, 28 Sept. 1912. See also Barker, 128.   [99] Ward, *GKC* 146.
[100] See, e.g., Harold Bloom, *The Western Canon: The Books and Schools of the Ages* (London: Macmillan, 1995), 311.

say that she was 'much interested' by his book, 'which recalls dear Mr Browning so vividly to me', indeed 'instantaneously *more* vividly than my remembrances of him'.[101]

Browning is known as a difficult and obscure poet. But Chesterton argues that he is not obscure because he was an intellectual like his admirers. On the contrary, and the book begins with this paradox, he is difficult because 'he was a very ordinary and spontaneous man'. Had he been more self-conscious and subtle he would, Chesterton claims, have been 'immeasurably easier to understand' because he would have practised 'the art of self-analysis'. As it was, 'the mystery of the unconscious man, far deeper than any mystery of the conscious one ... existed peculiarly in Browning' precisely because he was so un-self-conscious. Again, it was not any intellectual elitism that made him 'unintelligible' but rather the opposite; nor was it because his thoughts were 'vague, but because to him they were obvious'. Unlike Matthew Arnold, who was 'an intellectual aristocrat', Browning was 'an intellectual democrat'. Unlike his followers, he was not an intellectual but simply a poet. And he 'discovered the one thing that he could really do better than any one else, the dramatic lyric'. This form of verse was 'absolutely original; he had discovered a new field of poetry'. What especially distinguished this new form of poetry was 'the fearless and most dexterous use of grotesque things in order to express sublime emotions'. This central paradox is at the heart of Chesterton's understanding of Browning: that he was the greatest of love poets because he did 'not talk about raptures and ideals and gates of heaven, but about window-panes and gloves and garden walls'. In short, his love poetry, far from dealing with 'abstractions', 'is the truest of all love poetry, because it does not speak much about love'.[102] The same could be said of Chesterton's own love letters to Frances, at least the ones that survive, although not of his love poetry.

Chesterton's fascination with the grotesque evokes his most original criticism of Browning. For what is so peculiar to Browning was 'his sense of the symbolism of material trifles', and it is 'this spirit of grotesque allegory which really characterises Browning among all other poets'. 'Enormous problems, and yet more enormous answers, about pain, prayer, destiny, liberty, and conscience are suggested by cherries, by the sun, by a melon-seller, by an eagle flying in the sky, by a man tilling a plot of ground.' Far from being incompatible with the spontaneity and naturalness of

---

[101] Anne Ritchie to G. K. Chesterton, 15 July 1903, GKCL.
[102] *B*. 1–2, 22–4, 28.

Browning's poetry, 'the element of the grotesque in art, like the element of the grotesque in nature, means...energy, the energy which takes its own forms and goes its own way. Browning's verse, in so far as it is grotesque, is not complex or artificial; it is natural...'. And just 'as these strange things meant to Browning energy in the physical world, so strange thoughts and strange images meant to him energies in the mental world'. As Chesterton had already argued in one of the articles collected in *The Defendant*, the grotesque conveys the idea of vitality. But the grotesque also has another effect that is much more significant for Chesterton: 'To present a matter in a grotesque manner does certainly tend to touch the nerve of surprise and thus to draw attention to the intrinsically miraculous character of the object itself.' So important is the grotesque for Chesterton that he can even speak of 'the philosopher of the grotesque', whose 'supreme function' is 'to make the world stand on its head that people may look at it'. As a poet, Browning wants his readers to look at the world with new eyes because he himself is 'passionately interested in and in love with existence', even with 'the poetry of mean landscapes', the 'scrubbiness' of which is 'as of a man unshaved'. But one cannot be in love with or lost in wonder at existence and the world without loving and wondering at the 'small things' of which they are made up. And this is what makes *The Ring and the Book* 'the great epic of the nineteenth century, because it is the great epic of the enormous importance of small things'. By this exaltation or 'apotheosis of the insignificant', *The Ring and the Book* 'pays to existence the highest of all possible compliments...the compliment of selecting from it almost at random'. The poem also exemplifies another key Chestertonian idea— namely, that it is impossible to live without some kind of philosophy or point of view. And this is 'the second great respect in which *The Ring and the Book* is the great epic of the age. It is the great epic of the age, because it is the expression of the belief... of the discovery, that no man ever lived upon this earth without possessing a point of view.'[103]

Ten years later in *The Victorian Age of Literature* Chesterton was to be more critical of Browning, but without repudiating the insights of the book that made his name.

---

[103] *B.* 73, 86–8, 92, 96, 98, 100, 109.

4

Controversy

I

I N March 1903, two months before the publication of *Robert Browning*, Chesterton's former hero Robert Blatchford, the author of *Merrie England*, the collection of Socialist articles first published in the *Clarion*, in the same paper challenged Christians to respond to his attack on Christianity in the course of an enthusiastic review of a reprint of an anti-Christian polemic by the zoologist Ernst Haeckel, 'who used the theory of evolution to justify racism, aggressive nationalism and social Darwinism and whose arguments were later used in Germany to justify National Socialism'.[1] Chesterton took up the challenge in the *Daily News*, thus inaugurating a controversy between the two men that lasted through to the end of 1904 and was carried on not only in the *Clarion* and the *Daily News* but also in the *Commonwealth*, the organ of the Anglo-Catholic Christian Social Union, which was edited by Henry Scott Holland. Chesterton's first article was called 'The Return of the Angels'. He wrote with 'one great hope, that of arousing controversy'. It was time to break 'the silence' about religion, as Blatchford had done. He based his own defence of religious belief on science itself. The greatest modern scientific discovery was 'the method of the hypothesis', 'the mother of innumerable facts', including that of evolution. Chesterton's own method of apologetic could hardly have been cleverer, since if there was one dogma his contemporaries believed in it was evolution. And so he now uses the methodology of hypothesis to justify religious belief—that is, of the 'method of the successful hypothesis, of the

---

[1] Oddie, 239.

theory that justifies itself', in this case the hypothesis that explains why 'so large a number of the young in this generation have returned to a certain doctrine of the spiritual'. He does not call it Christianity but the doctrine that 'the world, clearly examined, does point with an extreme suggestiveness, to the existence of a spiritual world'. He and others who had 'returned to this belief' had done so, 'not because of this argument or that argument, but because the theory, when it is adopted, works out everywhere'. Just like the hypothesis of evolution, it made sense of things.[2]

It was supremely ironic that not only had Blatchford's attack appeared in the *Clarion*, where the original articles once so admired by Chesterton that comprised *Merrie England* had also appeared, but it was in the same paper that Chesterton had published in 1895 a highly anti-clerical, not to say anti-Christian, poem called 'Easter Sunday' (which he had not included in *The Wild Knight*). Blachford briefly dismissed Chesterton's reply. But four months later Chesterton returned to the attack in six articles in the *Commonwealth*, and then in articles and letters in the *Daily News* as well as the *Clarion* over the course of the next six months. In the first of these articles, which appeared in July, Chesterton is specific that he is defending Christianity rather than simply religious belief in general. He acknowledges the failures of Christianity but attributes them to human sinfulness—arguing that the same would apply to the Socialist state that Blatchford advocated. Chesterton then challenges Blatchford's determinism, which was to be the main point of controversy between them.[3] In his *Autobiography* he claims:

It was not that I began by believing in supernormal things. It was that the unbelievers began by disbelieving even in normal things. It was the secularists who drove me to theological ethics, by themselves destroying any sane or rational possibility of secular ethics. I might myself have been a secularist, so long as it meant that I could be merely responsible to secular society. It was the Determinist who told me, at the top of his voice, that I could not be responsible at all. And as I rather like being treated as a responsible being, and not as a lunatic let out for the day, I began to look around for some spiritual asylum that was not merely a lunatic asylum.

He recalls the particular example he had used against Blatchford—an example that itself exemplifies his self-confessed inability to avoid humour even on such issues that 'strike direct at the heart of this our human life'. 'Logically,' he had pointed out to Blatchford, 'it would stop a man in the act of saying "Thank you" to somebody for passing the mustard. For how

---

[2] Oddie, 338–9.   [3] Oddie, 340–2.

could he be praised for passing the mustard, if he could not be blamed for not passing the mustard?' The reason Blatchford wanted to deny free will, Chesterton thought, was because of his 'undiluted compassion' for the 'underdog', who was to be forgiven because nothing was his fault. But this did not stop Blatchford from 'demanding justice, punishment, vengeance almost without pardon, upon . . . strong tyrants who had trampled on the weak . . . So do paper sophistries go up in a great fire.'[4]

In his first *Commonwealth* article, where he contrasts the 'Calvinism' of Blatchford with 'the free will of Catholicism' that he is defending, Chesterton is clearly writing as an Anglo-Catholic for Anglo-Catholic readers. In a later article he cites the specifically Roman Catholic doctrine of Transubstantiation to show how science and religion cannot come into conflict, for the doctrine 'does not make any assertions at all about any material things'. Moreover, science advances by testing hypotheses, but sceptics like Blatchford, 'by refusing to experience faith . . . have refused to test it'. They claim to be 'impartial', but the experts in any subject are 'obviously partial' because they have a view, unlike the ignorant who are indeed impartial.[5] Later in the controversy, Chesterton again corrects Blatchford on a point of science, when he points out that to say, for example, that 'it is a law of nature that pumpkins should remain pumpkins' only really means that no pumpkin has ever been known to change into anything else, not that there is actually 'a law of nature' that one can point to. The expression is simply a metaphor taken from human laws, just as the Christian idea that pumpkins always remain pumpkins because that is the will of a heavenly father is also a metaphor drawn from the idea of an earthly father. Far from being a 'law of nature', it was 'extraordinary that a pumpkin is always a pumpkin'. Once one understood that it was extraordinary and not determined by some law one had 'begun philosophy'.[6]

Finally, in December, Blatchford threw down the gauntlet to Chesterton, demanding to know if he was a Christian, what he meant by the word Christianity, what he himself believed, and why. Chesterton replied that he was a Christian because he believed Christ was the son of God in a unique transcendental sense. He had already in a letter to the *Clarion* defined a Christian as someone who believes in the Trinity. And he believed in the Christian creed, because it seemed to him that life was 'logical and workable with these beliefs, and illogical and unworkable without them'.

---

[4] *A.* 173–5.   [5] Oddie, 343–4, 348, 352.
[6] BC 387–8. Cf. Stanley L. Jaki, *Chesterton: A Seer of Science* (Urbana, IL: University of Illinois Press, 1986), 13–16.

That Christmas in an article in the *Daily News* he made it clear that the feast only made sense in the light of the doctrine of the Incarnation.[7]

At the end of the article of 4 December in which Blatchford posed his four questions to Chesterton, he invited proponents of Christianity to put their case in the pages of the *Clarion* without any editorial interference, against whom he would produce writers to put the opposite case; both sides would be given equal space. The pro-Christian articles began to appear in January 1904 and ended in August, when a selection was published in a book entitled *The Religious Doubts of Democracy*. The book included three articles by Chesterton, the last of which was divided into two in the book. In the first Chesterton introduces a most unusual argument in favour of Christianity, but one that was very characteristic and would always play an important part in his religious apologetics. His own flippancy in talking about serious matters is held against him, but he cannot help himself: 'Christianity is itself so jolly a thing that it fills the possessor of it with a certain silly exuberance, which sad and high-minded Rationalists might reasonably mistake for mere buffoonery and blasphemy; just as their prototypes, the sad and high-minded Stoics of old Rome, did mistake the Christian joyousness for buffoonery and blasphemy.' This contract is reflected 'in the cold Pagan architecture and the grinning gargoyles of Christendom, in the preposterous motley of the Middle Ages and the dingy dress of this rationalist century'. Indeed, Chesterton claims: 'Nowhere in history has there ever been any popular brightness and gaiety without religion.' It is clear that he is equating Christianity, not to say religion itself, with a Catholic form of Christianity, since Chesterton would scarcely have claimed that laughter and brightness were characteristic of Puritanism or Islam. Asceticism, on the other hand, is characteristic of Catholicism with its 'austere or ferocious saints who have given up home and happiness and macerated health and sex'. But why should they have done so unless 'there were really something actual and solid in the thing for which they sold themselves'? Surely, the only explanation can be: 'They gave up all pleasures for one pleasure of spiritual ecstasy.' In the same sort of way, Chesterton wickedly suggests, a man may go 'ragged and homeless in order to drink brandy'. Both examples suggested the existence of some 'terrible consolation and a lonely joy' that made such sacrifices worthwhile. Chesterton enjoys turning Blatchford's arguments against Christianity on their head. The existence

[7] Oddie, 352–4.

of pagan myths resembling Christianity is only what one would expect: if Christianity is true, 'would not the human race tend to rumours and perversions of the Christian God?' Again, the crimes committed in the name of Christians do not necessarily tell against Christianity but rather the opposite: 'For men commit crimes not only for bad things, far more often for good things. For no bad things can be desired quite so passionately and persistently as good things can be desired ... '. Again, the particularity of a historical religion like Christianity tells for rather than against it: 'if Moses had said God was an Infinity Energy, I should be certain he had seen nothing extraordinary. As he said he was a Burning Bush, I think it very likely that he did see something extraordinary.'[8]

The importance of paradox is central to Chesterton's argument. 'Christianity,' he argues, 'which is a very mystical religion, has nevertheless been the religion of the most practical section of mankind. It has far more paradoxes than the Eastern philosophies, but it also builds far better roads.' The God of Islam is free from contradictions, whereas the Trinitarian God seems a contradiction in terms. The doctrine of free will is held to be contradictory by a determinist like Blatchford because if man is created by God then man can act only as God created him to act; but then so is determinism, which denies free will in theory and yet assumes it exists in practice. The difference is that, unlike the determinist, the Christian 'puts the contradiction into his philosophy'. And yet paradoxically the 'mystery by its darkness enlightens all things'. On the other hand, the determinist 'makes the matter of the will logical and lucid: and in the light of that lucidity all things are darkened'. Chesterton insists that it is not a choice between 'mysticism and rationality' but between 'mysticism and madness. For mysticism, and mysticism alone, has kept men sane from the beginning of the world. All the straight roads of logic lead to some Bedlam ... '. Christianity as a religion of mystery 'accepts the contradictions' of this world and can therefore 'laugh and walk easily through the world'. But, if we accept pantheism, for example, we end up by either embracing all that is 'natural' or by rejecting nature as simply evil. Christianity by contrast neither worships nor rejects nature but sees it as the creation of God: 'He made Nature but He was a Man.' Or again, paradoxically, far from the Christian doctrine of the Fall and original sin being a depressing bar to progress, 'without the doctrine of the Fall all idea of progress is unmeaning.' Chesterton's satire at the expense of Blatchford's anti-Christianity, 'the most placid and perfect of all ... orthodoxies',

[8] BC 374–7, 379.

is humorous but not sarcastic: 'If you wanted to dissuade a man from drinking his tenth whisky you would slap him on the back and say, "Be a man." No one who wished to dissuade a crocodile from eating his tenth explorer would slap it on the back and say, "Be a crocodile." For we have no notion of a perfect crocodile ...'. But Chesterton can be very sharp indeed when it comes to the defence of the poor, who, according to Blatchford, are 'determined' by their poverty: 'I will not deign even to answer Mr Blatchford when he asks "how" a man born in filth and sin can live a noble life. I know so many who are doing it, within a stone's throw of my own house in Battersea ...'. Because the existence of the spiritual world 'is a part of the common sense of all mankind', Chesterton concludes his articles in defence of Christianity by wickedly imagining what would happen if Blatchford's philosophy were ever to prevail:

> Man, the machine, will stand up ... and cry aloud, 'Was there not once a thing, a church, that taught us we were free in our souls? Did it not surround itself with tortures and dungeons in order to force men to believe that their souls were free? If there was, let it return, tortures, dungeons and all. Put me in those dungeons, rack me with those tortures, if by that means I may possibly believe it again.[9]

If it was necessary to have the Inquisition to preserve the idea of free will and therefore human responsibility and to escape from the materialistic determinism of Blatchford, then so be it. The defence of free will was certainly Chesterton's main contention in his controversy with Blatchford. As he says in the *Autobiography*, he was engaged not in 'abstract theological' questions ('I was not yet so far gone in orthodoxy as to be so theological as all that') but in 'defending' what seemed to him 'a plain matter of ordinary human morals'—namely, the concept of free will and responsibility. Indeed, it was 'common sense' that was most disturbed by this kind of scepticism, which strikes 'direct at the heart of this our human life'.[10] Nevertheless, Chesterton's articles and letters against Blatchford are also a defence of Christianity, and Catholic Christianity in particular.

2

Chesterton's childhood friend Annie Firmin, whom his mother had hoped he would marry, was also now living in a flat at Overstrand Mansions. She had got married the previous year in 1903. Her engagement elicited an all

---

[9] BC 380, 382–5, 394–5.   [10] *A.* 173–4.

too rare letter from Chesterton, undated as usual and written from a restaurant. He claimed that he had often thought of her, although he had never written her a line. This failure he explained as 'part of the Mystery of the Male, and you will soon, even if you do not already, get the hang of it, by the society of an individual who while being unmistakably a much better man than I am, is nevertheless male'. Humorously, if disingenuously, he argued that men put off doing what they want to do so as they can do it as well as possible: 'I put off writing to you because I wanted to write something that had in it all that you have been, to me, to all of us. And now instead I am scrawling this nonsense in a tavern after lunch.' The male sex, he continued, 'very seldom takes real trouble', 'forgets the little necessities of time', and 'is by nature lazy'. He himself had 'never wanted really but one thing in my life and that I got'. And now he observed 'the same tendency' in another person who, also being male, 'also . . . has only wanted one thing seriously in his life. He also has got it: another male weakness which I recognise with sympathy.' His affection for Annie as an old family friend and his love for Frances are enhanced not diminished by the humour. It is the same point that he had made to Frances in his letters to her during their courtship and that he was to make so often in his writings: the comic is not the opposite of the serious. 'All my reviewers call me frivolous . . . Damn it all (excuse me), what can one be but frivolous about serious things.' Why? Because seriousness cannot cope with really serious things: 'without frivolity they are simply too tremendous.' He ended by saying that he was not going to wish her happiness because he was 'placidly certain' that her happiness was 'inevitable': 'I know it because my wife is happy with me and the wild, weird, extravagant, singular origin of this is a certain enduring fact in my psychology which you will find paralleled elsewhere.' After she had married and come to live at Overstrand Mansions, Annie recalled an evening when Chesterton came round to their flat on his way to dinner at the House of Commons with a shoe on one foot and a slipper on the other. Did it matter? Chesterton asked, when it was pointed out to him. 'I told him I was sure Frances would not like him to go out like that—the only argument to affect him!'[11]

Frances Chesterton's diary for 1904, which she began on 18 January and continued until 16 July 1905, shows how her husband's success as a critic and journalist had opened the doors of society to them, and not only literary society. She begins the diary by noting that she has no intention of writings the 'memoirs' that her husband had suggested she should

---

[11] Ward, *GKC* 150–2, with text corrected from BL Add. MS 73237, fo. 52.

write when she was feeling 'flat or tired'—'the very moments when other people's memoirs are impossible to read and one's own impossible to write'. However, she did 'mean to (weather permitting, for everything in my mental world depends on that) note down any small matters of interest to myself, try and recall occasional conversations, mention people I meet . . . remembering always that on no account is this book to be made use of in print . . .'. And now that she had enjoyed 'two fine days after weeks of grey depression', she felt 'energy in commencing this labour of Hercules'. Unlike her husband, who enjoyed rain and grey skies, Frances felt a new person 'because the sun is shining', which made her feel 'warm with the thought of all I have, warmer with the thought of all I am going to have and warmest of all with the thought that Love thought well to include me in his list of favoured persons'.[12] Reading between the lines, it seems clear that the husband, who was so totally dependent on his wife for the practical side of life, had suggested that Frances should write her memoirs to distract her from her depression and that the depressive wife depended on his love for the emotional side of life.[13] The first entry for 18 January records 'an amusing lunch at Max Beerbohm's'. On 1 February they dined at the Fisher Unwins, Chesterton's old employer. The entry for 17 February is revealing about Frances's refusal to be impressed by famous people, which Chesterton had noted with approval in his days of courtship: of an 'at home' at the house of Sir Sydney Colvin and his wife, she writes: 'It was rather jolly but too many clever people there', who included Joseph Conrad and Henry James, 'to be really nice'. A few days later Chesterton was the guest of the publisher John Lane at a literary dinner at which he and Robert Baden-Powell, the founder of the Scouts, were the speakers. On 5 March the Chestertons gave 'a little dinner party on our own account'; one of the guests was Laurence Housman the writer and dramatist, and brother of Chesterton's old teacher at University College, A. E. Housman. A week later they went to a 'grand dinner party', where the guests included the Liberal politicians Charles Masterman and Herbert Samuel, the latter

[12] 'Diary of Frances Chesterton, 1904–1905', ed. Aidan Mackey, *CR* 25/3 (August 1999), 283–4. Aidan Mackey found the diary, which is at GKCL, in a thick boarded exercise book given to him by Dorothy Collins, containing records of a local Chesterton society that she had founded in Beaconsfield.

[13] John Coates, 'Commentary on the Diary of Frances Chesterton,' *CR* 25/3 (August 1999), 295–6. But Coates, pp. 296–8, reads too much into what Frances does say and what she does not say about the famous people she met.

of whom would loom large in Chesterton's life when the Marconi scandal broke.[14]

3

March 1904 saw the publication of a new book that marked a return to the art criticism with which Chesterton had begun his career as a journalist. *G. F. Watts* was published by Duckworth in their 'Popular Library of Art' series. The painter's wife wrote 'a charming note' to say that her husband was 'really pleased with the little book'.[15] With one important exception, most of the book's interest lies not in what Chesterton has to say about Watts but in what he has to say by way of general observation. He begins the book by remarking on the extraordinary way in which 'a period can suddenly become unintelligible'. He is thinking, of course, of the Victorian period that had only ended so recently and yet already seemed a world away. Born in that era himself, Chesterton was to become its great champion and interpreter. He sees Watts as an example of the Victorians' 'attitude of devouring and concentrated interest in things which were by their own system, impossible or unknowable'. Agnostic in religion, they nevertheless were far from indifferent. When they ceased to believe in creeds, they did not, like Chesterton's contemporaries, fall back upon materialism, but 'fell in love with abstractions and became enamoured of great and desolate words'. They continued to believe in and preach 'an eternal message and destiny' with total certainty of its truth. Because they were 'ingrainedly ethical', the idea of art for art's sake was as meaningless to them as the idea of religion for religion's sake.[16]

Inevitably, Chesterton finds paradox in Watts: the paradox of a 'union of small self-esteem with a vast ambition'. It was in fact 'the great paradox of the Gospel'—although 'meek', he, Watts, claimed to 'inherit the earth'. Watts also, according to Chesterton, shared his, Chesterton's, fundamental philosophy—that 'illimitable worship and wonder directed towards the fact of existence', the optimism that believes not that 'this is the best of all possible worlds' but that it is 'the best of all possible things that a world should be possible'. It was this sense of wonder, this optimism that had led Chesterton, if not Watts, to Christianity. But Watts's Victorian seriousness, his inability not to take morality seriously, did mean that he was 'dogmatic

---

[14] 'Diary of Frances Chesterton', 284–5.
[15] 'Diary of Frances Chesterton', 286.   [16] *W.* 3, 8, 11–13, 69.

as all sane men are dogmatic'—he 'draws the line somewhere, as all men, including anarchists, draw it somewhere'. However, the necessity of dogma in the sense of drawing a line, of defining, did not mean for Chesterton that the 'meaning' of a work of art could be defined in words. This in itself presupposed 'the perfection of language', which he thought lay 'at the root of rationalism', the idea that one can express plainly in words one's meaning when 'language is not a scientific thing at all, but wholly an artistic thing'.[17] It is noticeable that, apart from the favourable references to Christianity, Chesterton himself does not hesitate to use the language of sacramental Catholicism when he says that a 'Carlylean' like Watts thought that 'the great man' or 'hero' was 'a man more human than humanity itself' and in 'worshipping him you were worshipping humanity in a sacrament'.[18]

The Victorian age may not have been an age of faith, but then, Chesterton thought, 'there never was an age of faith. Faith is always at a disadvantage; it is a perpetually defeated thing which survives all its conquerors.' This is a significant comment that shows that he did not idealize the Middle Ages without reservation. Again, he insists on the gaiety of Christianity as opposed to the sadness of paganism. Christianity was attacked for its austerity—and yet it 'invented the thing which is more intoxicating than all the wines of the world, stained glass windows'. But Christianity only exemplifies Chesterton's insistence that there is no contradiction between seriousness and hilarity, but rather the opposite: 'to enjoy life means to take it seriously. There is an eternal kinship between solemnity and high spirits . . .'. And this combination of 'exuberant seriousness' and 'uproarious gravity' was characteristic of Victorians like Watts.[19]

The most striking passage in the book, which throws light on Chesterton's best novel, *The Man who was Thursday*, and deserves to be quoted at length, concerns what he calls 'the most interesting and most supremely personal of all the elements in the painter's designs and draughtsmanship':

That is, of course, his magnificent discovery of the artistic effect of the human back. The back is the most awful and mysterious thing in the universe: it is impossible to speak about it. It is the part of man that he knows nothing of; like

[17] *W.* 63, 70, 87.

[18] *W.* 149. See Oddie, 276: 'In 1900, Chesterton [in a review] had seen Watts's attitude to his subjects as being simply allegorical; by 1904 he has enlarged Watts's vision by perceiving it as being sacramental.'

[19] *W.* 101, 130, 165–6.

an outlying province forgotten by an emperor. . . . But this mystery of the human back has again its other side in the strange impression produced on those behind: to walk behind anyone along a lane is a thing that . . . touches the oldest nerve of awe. Watts has realised this as no one in art or letters has realised it in the whole history of the world; it has made him great. There is one possible exception to his monopoly of this magnificent craze. Two thousand years before, in the dark scriptures of a nomad people, it has been said that their prophet saw the immense Creator of all things, but only saw Him from behind. I do not know whether even Watts would dare to paint that. But it reads like one of his pictures: like the most terrific of all his pictures, which he has kept veiled.[20]

However, that very same year Chesterton himself touched in print on the 'mystery of the human back': to see someone 'from the rear', he wrote in *The Napoleon of Notting Hill*, thus breaking the 'monopoly' so far enjoyed by the Book of Genesis and Watts, was 'to look into the eyes of their soul'.[21]

4

This first novel of Chesterton was also published in March 1904. Apart from *The Man who was Thursday*, it is the only one of his novels that is likely to continue to be read. He had been working on the book for a number of years—according to his brother parts of it went back to his schooldays—and certainly from 1897.[22] Chesterton later thought it 'was a book very well worth writing; but I am not sure that it was ever written'. In his considered view, his novels as stories were

more or less fresh and personal; but considered as novels, they were not only not as good as a real novelist would have made them, but they were not as good as I might have made them myself, if I had really even been trying to be a real novelist. And among many more abject reasons for not being able to be a novelist, is the fact that I always have been and presumably always shall be a journalist.

But Chesterton is quick to rebut any assumption on the part of the reader that this characteristic self-deprecation in any way implies any denigration of journalism. On the contrary, it was the 'serious or even solemn' part of him that had made him a journalist. And there is perhaps a hint of the implication that it *was*, on the other hand, 'the superficial or silly or jolly part' of him that had made him try his hand at fiction. He was not a serious novelist simply because of incapacity—indeed he says that he could have

---

[20] *W.* 136, 139.   [21] *NNH* 228.   [22] Oddie, 267.

been a better novelist had he chosen to try harder—but 'because I really like to see ideas or notions wrestling naked, as it were, and not dressed up in a masquerade as men and women'. The truth was that he was not really interested in the imaginative creation of living fictional characters that was the work of a novelist: 'But I could be a journalist because I could not help being a controversialist.'[23] It might be argued that, because modest self-disclaimers came naturally to him, we should not take too literally his disclaimer of being a real novelist,[24] but it is noticeable that he was never self-deprecatory about his journalism—nor did he denigrate the art of journalism, writing a few years later that Thackeray's *The Book of Snobs* could only be called 'ephemeral journalism', which proved 'how eternal journalism can be'.[25] Nor was Chesterton self-deprecatory regarding his biographies or his criticism or his apologetic works. But he was self-deprecating about his novels, and rightly so.

Nobody can say I am a novelist; nobody, at least, who has tried to read my novels. The novelist can do something very splendid which I cannot do at all—something that may well be much more splendid than theorising or thinking; he can call up living souls out of the void; he can make another world which is something more than a mirror of this one; he can give to fancy the positive solidity of fact.[26]

Here he does not deny that he *can* theorize and think, *nor* is he prepared to say that it is inferior to the art of creation. While talking about *The Napoleon of Notting Hill* in his *Autobiography*, he says: 'I have never taken my books seriously; but I take my opinions quite seriously.'[27] It may, then, be asked, why in that case did Chesterton write novels?[28] As has been already

---

[23] *A.* 276–7.

[24] John D. Coates, *Chesterton and the Edwardian Cultural Crisis* (Hull: Hull University Press, 1984), 85, 87, not only argues that 'to read Chesterton as an artist one has, of course, to cut through his own disclaimers and constant self-deprecation, one of the thickets of Chesterton criticism', but he claims that Chesterton 'did his subtlest thinking' in his fiction rather than in his journalism. However, Chesterton's 'self-deprecation' was not 'constant': he was self-deprecatory about his fiction but not his journalism.

[25] *MC* 77.   [26] *ILN* xxxiv. 88.   [27] *A.* 111.

[28] Ian Boyd, *The Novels of G. K. Chesterton: A Study in Art and Propaganda* (London: Paul Elek, 1975), 9–10, points out that the 'novels mediate a distinctive political and social view of life' and are therefore 'the kind of literature' that the Victorian 'sages' wrote. But he fails to recognize that Chesterton mediated his view of life much better through his non-fiction prose writings, or to ask the question why in that case he wrote novels. Boyd argues that 'in the very passage' of the

suggested, it was partly at least for the fun of the thing—he had, after all, been an avid storyteller ever since his earliest years, delighting particularly in adventure stories involving the clash of arms, hence his love for Stevenson. Again, it was partly, at least in the early years when his financial position was still precarious, for the money. But there was another, the most important reason: he was ready to use any platform to spread ideas he considered both true and important. And he recognized that 'the sage, the sayer of things', which is what he saw himself as, was 'forced', unlike in other ages, 'to pretend to be something else, a minor poet or a novelist'.[29] That passing remark tells us all we need to know about how Chesterton saw himself as a writer: he was a 'sage' (in the tradition, we might add, of the great Victorian sages) who only 'pretended' to be a minor poet or novelist—but he did not pretend to be a sage; he knew that he had 'ideas' that he thought important and true and worth propagating by any means available. But, if Chesterton was a minor novelist and 'a very minor poet', indeed 'a very much minor poet',[30] as he described himself, he did write one innovative and original novel, *The Man who was Thursday*, which will continue to be read, as well as some of the best comic and satirical verse in the language.

In his *Autobiography* Chesterton explains at some length how the central idea of *The Napoleon of Notting Hill* that he wanted to propagate developed out of childhood impressions and instincts. In that late Victorian world of developing technology when 'science was in the air', he could remember the invention of the telephone, which he first experienced when his father and uncle fitted up a miniature one at home. He was 'really impressed imaginatively' that 'a voice should sound in the room when it was really as distant as the next street'. But, once he had experienced the 'miracle' on a small scale, he was not startled that he could hear a voice from the next town or even the next continent. What this showed was that he 'admired even the large scientific things most on a small scale. So I always found that I was much more attracted by the microscope than the telescope. I was not overwhelmed in childhood, by being told of remote stars which the sun never reached, any more than in manhood by being told of an empire on

---

Autobiography 'in which he deprecates the value of the novels as works of literature he makes a claim for their serious value as journalism' (p. 6). However, Chesterton does no such thing: he simply says that he 'could not be a novelist' but that he 'could be a journalist'—not that his novels are journalism, which, of course, they are not.

[29] *MO* 163.   [30] *OS* 92; *CT* 19.

which the sun never set.' Just as he denied that childhood was a kind of dream and that children did not like moral tales, so he denied that the childish imagination reached out towards 'larger and larger horizons'. After all, 'the imagination deals with an image. And an image is in its nature a thing that has an outline and therefore a limit.' Far from being in love with the infinite, then, the child on the contrary is plainly 'in love with limits'. Chesterton's philosophy of limitations has its origins very firmly in his childhood, as he expounds in one of those brilliant and penetrating (and amusing) passages that give the *Autobiography*—a work that has been shamefully neglected by Chesterton's biographers and critics as a work in its own right—a very real claim to the kind of classic status enjoyed by the autobiographies of two of the great Victorian sages, Newman and Ruskin, the *Apologia pro Vita sua* and *Praeterita*.

He [the child] uses his imagination to invent imaginary limits. The nurse and the governess have never told him that it is his moral duty to step on alternate paving-stones. He deliberately deprives this world of half its paving-stones, in order to exult in a challenge that he has offered to himself. I played that kind of game with myself all over the mats and boards and carpets of the house; and, at the risk of being detained during His Majesty's pleasure, I will admit that I often play it still. In that sense I have constantly tried to cut down the actual space at my disposal; to divide and subdivide, into these happy prisons, the house in which I was quite free to run wild. . . . If we look at the favourite nursery romances, or at least if we have the patience to look at them twice, we shall find that they all really support this view; even when they have largely been accepted as supporting the opposite view. The charm of Robinson Crusoe is not in the fact that he could find his way to a remote island; but in the fact that he could not find any way of getting away from it. It is that fact which gives an intensive interest and excitement to all the things that he had with him on the island; the axe and the parrot and the guns and the little hoard of grain. The tale of Treasure Island is not the record of a vague desire to go on a sea voyage for one's health. It ends where it began; and it began with Stevenson drawing a map of the island, with all its bays and capes cut out as clearly as fretwork. And the eternal interest of the Noah's Ark, considered as a toy, consists in its complete suggestion of compactness and isolation; of creatures so comically remote and fantastic being all locked up in one box; as if Noah had been told to pack up the sun and moon with his luggage. In other words, it is exactly the same game that I have played myself, by piling all the things I wanted on a sofa, and imagining that the carpet around me was the surrounding sea.

Chesterton was happy if anyone 'chooses to say that I have founded all my social philosophy on the antics of a baby', given that he did believe that this 'game of self-limitation' was 'one of the secret pleasures of life'. At what point in his childhood or youth 'the idea consolidated as a sort of local patriotism' he was not sure. But there was nothing surprising in the fact that the child's instinctive sense 'of fortifying and defending things; of saying that he is the king of the castle, but of being rather glad than otherwise that it is such a small castle' turned out to correspond to 'a private idea' that subsequently was 'clinched and supported by a public idea'—namely, that of patriotism or nationalism.[31]

As a young journalist on the *Daily News*, Chesterton had been startled to discover that his 'immediate superior' was ashamed of living in a suburb like Clapham. He had never forgotten this journalist against whom he had 'marshalled the silly pantomime halberdiers of Notting Hill and all the rest'. Of course, Chesterton was not unaware of why this citizen of Clapham was not also a Clapham patriot. How could people 'be made to realise the wonder and splendour of being alive, in environments which their own daily criticism treated as dead-alive, and which their imagination had left for dead', having 'resigned themselves to being citizens of mean cities'? For 'on every side of us the mean cities stretched far away beyond the horizon; mean in architecture, mean in costume, mean even in manners; but, what was the only thing that really mattered, mean in the imaginative conception of their own inhabitants'. It was a time when 'the very dullest phase of dead Victorianism was in most of the newspapers and nearly all the walls', when that 'huge thing', London, was 'a hideous thing', its 'landscape ... a thing of flat-chested houses, blank windows, ugly iron lamp-posts and vulgar vermilion pillar-boxes ...'. As for the inhabitants, who were 'imprisoned in these inhuman outlines' of 'houses like ill-drawn diagrams of Euclid' and forced to frequent 'streets and railways like dingy sections of machinery', 'we were as ugly as the railings and lamp-posts between which we walked'. How, then, was it possible to make suburbs like Clapham 'become shrines or sacred sites'? For it was Clapham and not Clapham Junction that interested Chesterton:

What was called my dislike of imperialism was a dislike of making England an Empire, in the sense of something more like Clapham Junction. For my own visionary Clapham consisted of houses standing still; and not of trucks and trains rattling by; and I did not want England to be a sort of cloakroom or clearing-house for luggage labelled exports and imports. I wanted real English things that nobody else could import and that we enjoyed too much to export.[32]

---

[31] *A.* 108–10. [32] *A.* 132–3, 135.

It was while wandering about north Kensington, he tells us, that the idea of *The Napoleon of Notting Hill* came to him. He had been dreaming of 'stories of feudal sallies and sieges, in the manner of Walter Scott, and vaguely trying to apply them to the wilderness of bricks and mortar' around him. As a city, London seemed too large already to be a 'citadel', and indeed seemed even larger than the British Empire. And then

something irrationally arrested and pleased my eye about the look of one small block of little lighted shops, and I amused myself with the supposition that these alone were to be preserved and defended, like a hamlet in a desert. I found it quite exciting to count them and perceive that they contained the essentials of a civilisation, a chemist's shop, a bookshop, a provision merchant for food and public-house for drink. Lastly, to my great delight, there was also an old curiosity shop bristling with swords and halberds; manifestly intended to arm the guard that was to fight for the sacred street. I wondered vaguely what they would attack or whither they would advance. And looking up, I saw grey with distance but still seemingly immense in altitude, the tower of the Waterworks close to the street where I was born. It suddenly occurred to me that capturing the Waterworks might really mean the military stroke of flooding the valley . . . [33]

It was this street that he calls Pump Street in the novel, where it is romanticized by the patriotic provost of Notting Hill, who insists that its shopkeepers take pride in their wares, dress up in colourful medieval dress, and belong to the equivalent of medieval guilds.

In an interview later with an American journalist, Chesterton said that he considered that *The Napoleon of Notting Hill* was his first important book. He claimed that he had 'almost missed writing it', and that if he had not written it, he would have 'stopped writing'—presumably he meant novels, since he had to write for a living as a journalist.

I was what you Americans call 'broke'—only ten shillings in my pocket. Leaving my worried wife, I went down Fleet Street, got a shave, and then ordered for myself, at the Cheshire Cheese, an enormous luncheon of my favorite dishes and a bottle of wine. It took my all, but I could then go to my publishers fortified. I told them I wanted to write a book and outlined the story of 'Napoleon of Notting Hill.' But I must have twenty pounds, I said, before I begin.

'We will send it to you on Monday.'

'If you want the book,' I replied, 'you will have to give it to me today as I am disappearing to write it.' They gave it. [34]

[33] *A.* III.   [34] Clemens, 16–17.

According to Frances's own account, she had stayed at home, 'thinking . . . hard thoughts of his disappearance with their only remaining coin'. He had then 'dramatically . . . appeared with twenty golden sovereigns and poured them into her lap'. It was not the only time, it seems, that Chesterton refused to leave a publisher's office until he was paid: 'it was his way to let the money shortage become acute and then deal with it abruptly.'[35] Commenting later on the incident, he remarked: 'What a fool a man is, when he comes to the last ditch, not to spend the last farthing to satisfy the inner man before he goes out to fight a battle with wits.'[36] The story of the meal in the Cheshire Cheese sounds wholly authentic and in character, but Chesterton had forgotten that he had in fact already written in advance to the publisher about his novel, which seems to have been nearing completion, asking if he could call at the office with some specimens of the manuscript. However, there is a later letter to the publisher agreeing to meet a completion deadline provided he could be given an advance of '£5 or so on the book for the next twelve hours', and it is this that Chesterton had, no doubt, confused with his first visit to the publisher. Originally, the novel had been called 'either The Lion of Notting Hill or the King and the Madman', with the choice being left to the publisher.[37] The book was typed 'in rather a two-fingered way' by the Chestertons' neighbour, Mrs Saxon Mills.[38]

The philosophy of nationalism or patriotism is expressed at the beginning of the novel by the deposed President of Nicaragua, whose country has been annexed. He is not deceived by the philosophy of imperialism. To the claim, 'We moderns believe in a great cosmopolitan civilization, one which shall include all the talents of all the absorbed peoples,' he retorts, 'That is what I complain of your cosmopolitanism. When you say you want all people to unite, you really mean that you want all peoples to unite to learn the tricks of your people.' England itself in 1984, eighty years after the publication of the novel, has become a 'popular despotism' in which

---

[35] Ward, *GKC* 152–3.   [36] Clemens, 17.

[37] Ward, *RC* 76–7. According to Barker, 144, the story of the circumstances of the book's publication was a 'legend . . . just part of the image creation'. But, while Chesterton was certainly not the most accurate of people and his memory cannot always be trusted in the *Autobiography*, he did not invent stories to his own self-advantage, rather the opposite. Nor was lying part of his character, any more than it was of Frances's. The essentials of the story were true; it was just that Chesterton had muddled them.

[38] Ffinch, 126.

the 'King of England is chosen like a juryman upon an official rotation system'. When the lot falls to the whimsical, flippant Auberon Quin, he decides to give independence to the boroughs of London, intending his reign to be marked by a 'revival of the arrogance of the old medieval cities applied to our glorious suburbs'. It was a small boy calling out, 'I'm the King of the Castle', that had given him the idea. In his turn, the little boy called Adam Wayne had his 'dim patriotism' 'stirred ... into flame' by the 'ridiculous' response of King Auberon about how he should be 'ready to die for the sacred mountain' of Notting Hill. Years later Wayne becomes Provost of Notting Hill by the same random method by which the king was elected and decides to take 'the Charter of the Cities' with deadly serious-ness. As a child, he had been a patriot who knows that 'the patriot never under any circumstances boasts of the largeness of his country, but always, and of necessity, boasts of the smallness of it'. And he knew this 'not because he was a philosopher or a genius, but because he was a child. Any one who cares to walk up a side slum, can see a little Adam claiming to be king of a paving-stone. And he will always be proudest if the stone is almost too narrow for him to keep his feet inside it.' When an attempt is made to run a main road through one of its streets, Notting Hill under Wayne rallies to the defence of 'one dirty little street—Pump Street', which contains the five shops at its upper end that Wayne's 'childish fastidious-ness had first selected as the essentials of the Notting Hill campaign, the citadel of the city'. Auberon Quin at first thinks Wayne is joking, since obviously 'the valiant independence' of Pump Street is 'the deification of the ludicrous'. However, Wayne is not joking, and Quin realizes that he exemplifies his own maxim, 'seriousness sends men mad'. Victory over the other boroughs gives 'the dominion of London' to Notting Hill. But eventually a revolt by the other boroughs leads to the defeat of Notting Hill, which ignores Wayne's protest against its 'imperial envy', its desire to be 'a mere empire' instead of a 'nation'.[39]

At the end of the novel, the two voices of Quin and Wayne are heard. Quin confesses to Wayne that what Wayne had taken so seriously was meant only as a joke; what had begun as a 'farce' had ended as a 'tragedy'. In response, Wayne points out that both men had been called mad, Quin for his frivolity and Wayne for his fanaticism: 'We are mad, because we are not two men but one man. We are mad, because we are two lobes of the same brain, and that brain has been cloven in two.' As a result, Quin has been without 'the joy of gravity' and Wayne deprived of 'humour'.

[39] *NNH* 237, 239, 252, 254, 266, 272, 275, 277, 279, 288–9, 355, 364.

Although apparently the opposite of each other, in fact both men had been aiming at the same thing, the 'poetry' of a suburb like Notting Hill, which is 'romantic' because even the pillar-boxes are 'poetic' and because the 'street is really more poetical than a meadow, because a street has a secret'. Quin interposes that that does not alter the fact that he had been laughing at and Wayne adoring the same thing. But Wayne's response is that, when the two lobes of the brain come together in a balanced human being, there is 'no real antagonism between laughter and respect, [for this] human being, the common man, whom mere geniuses like you and me can only worship like a god'. This, of course, is the voice of Chesterton insisting that seriousness implies humour and humour seriousness. Quin and Wayne are two sides of what should be one and the same coin, as was the case in a 'healthy' time like the Middle Ages: 'The cathedrals, built in the ages that loved God, are full of blasphemous grotesques.' But the medieval cathedral, built to the glory of and the worship of God, is not the only serious thing to have a funny side to it—nor the only thing that has a very Catholic, not to say Roman Catholic, aspect to it. For the most startling moment in the book is when the serious Wayne suddenly informs the comical Quin that the Crucifixion itself, the most serious of all things, has a more than funny side to it:

'Crucifixion is comic. It is exquisitely diverting. It was an absurd and obscene kind of impaling reserved for people who were made to be laughed at . . . Peter was crucified, and crucified head downwards. What could be funnier than the idea of a respectable old Apostle upside down? . . . Upside down or right side up, Peter was Peter to mankind. Upside down he still hangs over Europe, and millions move and breathe only in the life of his church.'

The moral of the novel is that, if Quin had taken his joke more seriously and Wayne more humorously, then Notting Hill could have discovered a sense of local identity and pride and set an example to the other boroughs, but without its 'patriotism' degenerating into 'the monstrous absurdity' of the war and then into imperialism.[40]

In the same year, 1904, Chesterton also contributed a chapter called 'The Patriotic Idea' to *England: A Nation*, a collection of papers produced by the so-called Patriots' Club, which, according to Cecil Chesterton, was his brother's 'own idea' but which 'never did anything as far as I know except to produce the . . . volume'.[41] The book was edited by Lucian Oldershaw and published by R. Brimley Johnson. It opened with Chesterton's essay.

---

[40] *NNH* 279, 302, 356, 376, 378–9.   [41] *CC* 43.

Chesterton begins by comparing the attack on 'the idea of patriotism as interfering with the larger sentiment of love of humanity' (which he connects particularly with the name of Tolstoy, 'perhaps the greatest of living Europeans') to the idea that 'nobody should go to church, since God is omnipresent, and not to be found in churches'. In other words, for Chesterton the cause of patriotism is bound up with his key idea that there 'is one thing that is vitally essential to everything which is to be intensely enjoyed or intensely admired—limitation': 'Whenever we look through an archway, and are stricken into delight with the magnetic clarity and completeness of the landscape beyond, we are realizing the necessity of boundaries. Whenever we put a picture in a frame, we are acting upon that primeval truth...'. And it is this 'truth' that is 'the value of small nationalities', and that underlies patriotism, itself only an example of that 'devotion to particular things' that is involved in the idea of limitation.[42] He admits that empires look strong and nations comparatively weaker, 'but that is merely because all things that are eternal always look weak'. He does not deny that nationalism has its dangers, but that does not mean one should resort to what he calls 'the teetotal method': one is more likely to drink wine temperately when wine is freely available than when it is prohibited. Because of its dangers, Islam 'makes wine a poison', whereas Christianity 'makes it a sacrament'. Accordingly, 'the right way to avoid the incidental excesses of patriotism is the same as that in the cases of sex or war—it is to know something about it'. Nor should it be any objection to nationalism that it is 'the mother of wars': 'So in a sense it is, just as love and religion are. Men will always fight about the things they care for, and in many cases quite rightly.' This was to be a regular theme of Chesterton, not only against pacifism but also against the commonly held view that religion, in particular, must be a bad thing because it leads to wars.[43]

Apart from Tolstoyan love of humanity as opposed to particular human beings, the other great enemy of patriotism was, of course, imperialism, which could also be termed 'opportunist cosmopolitanism'. Chesterton contrasts the 'Little England patriotism' of Shakespeare with Kipling,

[42] PI 595, 603, 618. Oddie, 261–3, compares Conrad Noel's contribution to the volume, which defends patriotism 'by relating it specifically to Catholic sacramental theology' according to which God is present, for example, in a single piece of bread consecrated in the Mass, and suggests that this sacramental principle that Chesterton learned from Noel and his Anglo-Catholic friends lent theological force to his philosophy of limitation.

[43] PI 598–9, 606.

whose writing 'is always at its truest and most beautiful when the writer is speaking of cosmopolitanism, of the sensations of the traveller'. Kipling's work 'is very beautiful literature', Chesterton acknowledges; but, whereas 'Shakespeare's patriotism has the joy and pain of a passionate lover; Mr Kipling's has the gaiety and sadness of a philanderer among the nations'. The English, he argues, would not have to emigrate and colonize other countries rather than their own, except that the 'immense and absurd estates' of the land-owning oligarchy 'make impossible the colonization of England'. And this state of affairs is allowed to remain because the English confuse 'self-government and independence' with the parliamentary system. The Boer War, as an instance of imperialism, which 'is Asiatic', was simply 'a crime committed against the European virtue of nationalism'.[44]

5

In February 1903 Chesterton had received a letter from a Roman Catholic priest called Father John O'Connor, who at the time was a curate at St Anne's, Keighley, Yorkshire, to say that, though he might not find him 'quite orthodox in details', he thanked God 'for having gifted you with the spirituality which alone makes literature immortal'. The priest had been impressed by the poetry he had read.[45] According to O'Connor, writing many years later, they met for the first time at Keighley in Yorkshire in the spring of 1904 in the house of a fellow fan of Chesterton, after which they walked together over the moor to Ilkley, where Chesterton was 'spending a short holiday'.[46] But O'Connor's memory was at fault: he had already met Chesterton on an earlier occasion when they had taken the walk O'Connor refers to. Perhaps O'Connor confused the two events, because it was in spring 1904, when he came over by himself to Ilkley, that he met Frances for the first time. For it was in October of the same year that O'Connor first contacted him that Chesterton wrote to his Yorkshire fan to say that he was coming to lecture to the Keighley literary society in December and hoped that they might meet. 'Certainly you may come and see me,' replied O'Connor; though 'but a salaried minion of this establishment, I may be

---

[44] PI 601, 604–6, 612, 618.
[45] Ffinch, 114. John O'Connor to G. K. Chesterton, 11 Feb. 1903, BL Add. MS 73196, fo. 31.
[46] O'Connor, 1.

able to get you put up for the night', he added, unless Chesterton had already arranged to stay with another member of the society.[47] Since, according to O'Connor, they met for the first time at the house of a Herbert Hugill, 'who was a much older Chesterton fan than I was',[48] it was presumably Hugill who was Chesterton's host and to whose house probably selected members of the audience were invited to meet the speaker after the lecture. On 6 December 1903 O'Connor wrote to Frances to say, 'I think I ought to tell you how I enjoyed myself with the great big boy on Thursday–Friday'. It looks, then, as if the lecture was on a Thursday evening, when Chesterton stayed the night with his host, and it was the next day that he and O'Connor 'walked together over the moor to Ilkley, favoured', O'Connor told Frances, 'by the only two hours sunshine in three days. It was all delightful...'. In order 'to reward his faithful guide and willing slave', Chesterton had then introduced the priest to a couple, called the Steinthals, who lived in Ilkley, 'where eight hours went by like one'.[49]

At the end of March 1904 Chesterton was again staying with the Steinthals, but this time with Frances. The Steinthals' house, St John's, stood opposite the church of St Margaret's, Ilkley, which coincidentally shared the same architect with Bedford Park. The husband was a businessman of German, possibly Jewish, descent and his wife a close friend of Frances from the days when they had worked together at the Parents' National Educational Union.[50] On 31 March Frances confided to her diary her delight to be in the country and away from London: 'The country is wonderful and there is room to breathe.' A few days later she met Father O'Connor for the first time and wrote down her impressions on 5 April:

Father O'Connor came over. He is delightful. So boyish, so wise, so young, so old—There is a sort of charm about him difficult to define—He uses his hands to help out his meaning very effectively and yet never suggests affectation or theatricality. It is wonderful that he should lead that quiet life of a parish priest in Keighley when he appears so dazzling.[51]

It may have been this April that George Holbrook Jackson, the journalist, publisher, and bibliophile, who was then living in Leeds and who 'doubted

---

[47] John O'Connor to G. K. Chesterton, 4 Oct. 1903, BL Add. MS 73196, fo. 35.
[48] O'Connor, 1.
[49] John O'Connor to Frances Chesterton, 6 Dec. 1903, BL Add. MS 73196, fo. 37.
[50] Barker, 153.   [51] 'Diary of Frances Chesterton', 286.

the existence of G. K. C.', decided, since Chesterton was 'in the locality on holiday . . . to verify his existence just as one might go to the Arctic regions to verify the existence of the North Pole or the Northwest passage'. A meeting had apparently been arranged, so the explorer was not unexpected.

It was April and raining. I trudged through the damp furze and heather up to the house only to find that the object of my pilgrimage had disappeared without leaving a trace behind him. No alarm was felt, as that was one of his habits. Sometimes he would go down to the railway station, and taking a ticket to any place that had a name which appealed to him, vanish into the unknown, making his way home on foot or wheel as fancy or circumstances directed.

Taken upstairs by Frances, Holbrook Jackson 'peered into the wild' of the moor, 'half hoping that I should first behold the great form of Gilbert Chesterton looming over the bare brow of the wold, silhouetted against the grey sky . . .'. In the event, Chesterton's return was rather an anti-climax: 'For quite close to the house we espied him, hatless and negligently clad in a Norfolk suit of homespun, leaning in the rain against a budding tree, absorbed in the pages of a little red book.'[52]

Father O'Connor was not only to become a close friend of both the Chestertons but also the inspiration of the Father Brown detective stories. Not that Father Brown was *modelled* on O'Connor. As his creator explains in the *Autobiography*, a writer may take 'a hint from a human being'.

But he will not hesitate to alter the human being, especially in externals, because he is not thinking of a portrait but of a picture. In Father Brown, it was the chief feature to be featureless. The point of him was to appear pointless; and one might say that his conspicuous quality was not being conspicuous. His commonplace exterior was meant to contrast with his unsuspected vigilance and intelligence; and that being so, of course I made his appearance shabby and shapeless, his face round and expressionless, his manners clumsy, and so on. At the same time, I did take some of his inner intellectual qualities from my friend, Father O'Connor . . . who has not, as a matter of fact, any of these external qualities. He is not shabby, but rather neat; he is not clumsy, but very delicate and dexterous; he not only is but looks amusing and amused. He is a sensitive and quick-witted Irishman, with the profound irony and some of the potential irritability of his race. My Father Brown was deliberately described as a Suffolk dumpling from East Anglia. That, and the rest of his description, was a deliberate disguise for the purpose of detective fiction. But for all that, there is a very real sense in which Father O'Connor was

---

[52] Clemens, 41–3.

the intellectual inspiration of these stories; and of much more important things as well.[53]

Chesterton then proceeds to explain how he first met Father O'Connor and how he came to give him the idea of Father Brown.

Particularly just before and after Chesterton was married, he was fated 'to wander over many parts of England, delivering what were politely called lectures'. At a time when he had to make money where he could, Chesterton found, in those days before cinema or radio, let alone television, that there was 'considerable appetite for such bleak entertainments, especially in the north of England, the south of Scotland and among certain active Nonconformist centres even in the suburbs of London'. Bleakness and Nonconformity reminded him of one particular experience he had had in a chapel in 'the last featureless wastes to the north of London'. Although he had to make his way there through 'a blinding snow-storm', this was no reason why any reader should 'weep prematurely over my experience, or imagine that I am pitying myself or asking for pity'. *That* was no ground for sympathy: on the contrary, he 'enjoyed' it 'very much; because I like snowstorms. In fact, I like practically all kinds of English weather except that particular sort of weather that is called "a glorious day".' After nearly two hours in the elements walking or on the top of a bus, he arrived looking like 'the Snow Man that children make in the garden'. But now something happened that *did* call for his readers' pity. After lecturing 'God knows on what', he was about to make his journey home

when the worthy minister of the chapel, robustly rubbing his hands and slapping his chest and beaming at me with the rich hospitality of Father Christmas, said in a deep, hearty, fruity voice, 'Come, Mr. Chesterton; it's a bitter cold night! Do let me offer you an Oswego biscuit.' I assured him gratefully that I felt no such craving; it was very kind of him, for there was no possible reason, in the circumstances, for his offering me any refreshment at all. But I confess that the thought of returning through the snow and the freezing blast, for two more hours, with the glow of that one biscuit within me, and the Oswego fire running through all my veins, struck me as a little out of proportion. I fear it was with considerable pleasure that I crossed the road and entered a public-house immediately opposite the chapel, under the very eyes of the Nonconformist Conscience.[54]

Not that Chesterton had any difficulty in confronting head-on the Nonconformist Conscience. In September 1905, for example, he was to find

---

[53] *A.* 314.   [54] *A.* 314–15.

himself lecturing one Sunday afternoon in a large circus tent, to the noise of the animals enjoying their Sunday rest, on 'Religion and Liberty'. Drunkenness was, he acknowledged, an evil, but that was because

the most dangerous things and the chief evils of the world are spiritual things. It is only because drink is very nearly a spiritual pleasure that it is so highly dangerous.... If materialism were true, people would be as intemperate over ham sandwiches and pork pies as they are now over drink. It is because man has a soul that he drinks and because animals have no souls that they do not drink.[55]

Un-spiritual Oswego biscuits were all right for animals but not for human beings.

Recalling those 'distant days of vagabond lecturing', Chesterton tells against himself the famous story of how he telegraphed his wife in London: 'Am in Market Harborough. Where ought I to be?' True or not, he admits the tale sounded probable enough.[56] Invitations came not only from Nonconformists. The 'immeasurable annoyance' with which Chesterton had to decline an invitation to 'sup' with the publisher John Lane and his wife was 'increased by a bitterly ironical fact' that he was 'engaged... to lecture to a body bearing the wonderful name of THE PECKHAM ETHICAL FELLOWSHIP. Isn't it too beautiful? I'm sure they come out of a book. I only wish they'd go back into it.'[57]

It was on one of these lecturing jaunts that Chesterton found himself in the same house as Father O'Connor. He was 'struck by the tact and humour' with which this 'small man with a smooth face and a demure but elfish expression... mingled with his very Yorkshire and very Protestant company'. It was clear that he was appreciated as a 'character'. Hitherto Chesterton had consorted with English Anglo-Catholic clergy, but now he warmed to this Irish Roman Catholic priest—although, 'if you had told me that ten years afterwards I should be a Mormon Missionary in the Cannibal Islands, I should not have been more surprised than at the suggestion that, fully fifteen years afterwards, I should be making to him my General Confession and being received into the Church that he served'. The day after the lecture, when they walked over the moor to

[55] Ffinch, 132.

[56] *A.* 315. According to Aidan Mackey, whose source was Dorothy Collins, it is a true story. In those days, even in small railway stations, it was possible to ask the station master to send a telegram down the line, using his morse code signalling key.

[57] G. K. Chesterton to Mrs John Lane, n.d., JJBL.

Ilkley, the priest stayed on with the Steinthals, to whom he introduced his
new friend. The priest stayed on for lunch, tea, and dinner—and perhaps
also for the night, Chesterton thought. It was there that they were usually
to meet. And it was one of these meetings that led to the Father Brown
stories. While out for a walk, Chesterton mentioned to O'Connor an
article he was intending to write on 'some rather sordid social questions
of vice and crime'. His companion, however, thought he was ill informed,
and proceeded to tell him 'certain facts he knew about perverted practices'. Having in his own youth 'imagined' for himself 'any amount of
iniquity... it was a curious experience to find that this quiet and pleasant
celibate had plumbed those abysses far deeper'—'I had not imagined that
the world could hold such horrors.' On returning to the house, they met a
couple of Cambridge undergraduates who were on holiday. O'Connor
impressed them with his wide knowledge; but one of the undergraduates
could not help remarking when the priest had left the room that it was
wrong to shut oneself away like that from the world and all its evil.
Chesterton could hardly restrain himself from laughing out loud at this
'colossal and crushing irony': 'For I knew perfectly well that, as regards all
the solid Satanism which the priest knew and warred against with all his
life, these two Cambridge gentlemen (luckily for them) knew about as
much of real evil as two babies in the same perambulator.' It was this
incident that gave Chesterton the idea of a detective story in which the
priest would be the detective who 'should appear to know nothing and in
fact know more about crime than the criminals'. But the detective priest
would otherwise be very different from Father O'Connor: 'I permitted
myself the great liberty of taking my friend and knocking him about;
beating his hat and umbrella shapeless, untidying his clothes, punching
his intelligent countenance into a condition of pudding-faced fatuity...
The disguise...was a deliberate piece of fiction, meant to bring out or
accentuate the contrast that was the point of the comedy.' Not the least of
the flaws in the stories, Chesterton was aware, was 'the general suggestion
of Father Brown having nothing in particular to do, except to hang about
in any household where there was likely to be a murder'. He was appropriately complimented by a 'very charming' Catholic lady he knew who
said, 'I am very fond of that officious little loafer.'[58] The real Father
O'Connor thought that it was his 'miraculous' attention to the practical

---

[58] *A.* 316–18. Clemens, 139–40, has Chesterton giving a slightly different
account.

details of life—as it seemed to the utterly absent-minded Chesterton—that had inspired the meticulously minded Father Brown. Like Father Brown, he was also very given to carrying brown paper parcels.[59]

6

On 26 April 1904 Frances enjoyed a 'delightful dinner party' at John Lane's house; the publisher was in America, but 'that didn't matter' as his American wife was 'an ideal hostess'. 'How is it', Frances wondered, 'that Americans entertain so much better than we do? She behaves as if she were beautiful. Most Americans do. It is the secret of their charm.' The talk that evening was 'mostly' about Chesterton's recently published novel, *The Napoleon of Notting Hill*. Max Beerbohm took Frances into dinner and was 'really nice'; he was 'a good fellow'—although his 'costume was extraordinary'. Beerbohm 'seemed only pleased' at the way he had been identified with King Auberon, one of the two protagonists in the novel. He told Chesterton not to apologize: he and John Lane, who had published the book the month before, had 'settled it all at lunch'. Frances wondered if he was not 'a little put out' at 'finding no red carpet put down for his royal feet'. They 'had quite a discussion as to whether as a king he should not precede Frances into the dining room'. Graham Robertson, who was sitting on the other side of Frances, had done the illustrations for *The Napoleon of Notting Hill*, taking Max Beerbohm as his model for King Auberon. He 'kept on producing wonderful rings and stones out of his pockets', and said 'he wished he could go about covered in the pieces of a chandelier'. The Chestertons drove Beerbohm home, 'where he basely enticed us in' and 'made himself very entertaining'. They did not get home till 1.30 in the morning. The next day the Bellocs with the Noels came to dinner; Belloc 'recited his own poetry with great enthusiasm the whole evening'. On 9 May they attended the 'Literary Fund Dinner'—'about the greatest treat I have [ever] had in my life'. J. M. Barrie, who presided, was 'so splendid and so complimentary', telling Frances 'he thought a lot of Gilbert's work'; the speakers included Barrie and A. E. W. Mason, the author of *The Four Feathers*.[60] Another who spoke was Arthur S. Comyns Carr, the barrister and economist, who 'was not only regarded as the patriarch or oldest inhabitant' of the Bedford Park community, 'but in

---

[59] O'Connor, 36, 39. [60] 'Diary of Frances Chesterton', 284–7.

some sense as the founder and father of the republic'. Barrie was to become a great friend of Chesterton, 'of all friends the least egotistical' with his 'humorous self-effacement'.[61] Frances noted how pretty his wife was, but her accolade for beauty went to the wife of Anthony Hope, the author of *The Prisoner of Zenda*. 'It is wonderful', she wrote, 'the way in which they all accept Gilbert, and one well-known man told me he was the biggest man present'. A few days later she went to see Max Beerbohm's 'very funny' caricature of her husband on display in a gallery: 'G.K.C.—Humanist Kissing the World.' Next month Frances recorded a political 'at home' at the Fabian Mrs Sidney Webb's (who she thought was 'very handsome'), where she saw the future prime ministers Winston Churchill and David Lloyd George. She thought politics 'and nothing but politics' was 'dull work', and 'an intriguer's life must be a pretty poor affair'. Towards the end of June there was another 'at home' at the house of the poet Alice Meynell, a convert to Roman Catholicism, who Frances thought was 'nice, intelligent, but affected (I suppose unconsciously)'. 'I don't really like the "precious people". They worry me.' Her husband Wilfrid, also a writer, struck her as 'a good-hearted snob'. On 23 June there was 'a gorgeous "at home" at the Duchess of Sutherland's', where Frances was 'interested to see' the Birmingham politician Austen Chamberlain, the future Conservative foreign secretary, and 'impressed with his extraordinary eagerness and his only too apparent vulgarity'. On 30 June the illustrator Graham Robertson held an 'exceedingly select' 'at home', where Frances 'felt rather too uncultivated to talk much'.[62]

On 5 July Chesterton went by himself to visit Swinburne, who was very gratified by a review Chesterton had written of a book about his friend Tennyson. Because of the deafness of the poet, a visit was suggested for the afternoon by his companion and disciple, 'after the clatter of feeding time is over'.[63] This 'Grand Vizier' to the 'Sultan and Prophet of Putney' was the writer Theodore Watts-Dunton. For, by this time, the aged poet 'was a sort of god in a temple, who could only be approached through a high-priest'—namely, Watts-Dunton. Chesterton found Swinburne 'quite gay and skittish, though in a manner that affected me strangely as spinsterish'. His companion, or rather high priest, was on the contrary 'very serious indeed. It is said that he made the poet a religion; but what struck me as odd, even at that time, was that his religion seemed to consist largely of preserving and protecting the poet's irreligion'—although 'the prophet

[61] *A.* 136, 264.   [62] 'Diary of Frances Chesterton', 287–8.
[63] Barker, 130–1.

was not really a commander of the faithful because there was no faith'.[64] In her diary Frances wrote that she thought her husband 'found it rather hard to reconcile the idea with the man, but he was interested, though I could not gather much about the visit. He was amused at the compliments which Watts Dunton and Swinburne pay to each other unceasingly.' The Meynells' 'at home' on 22 June—'rather a dull affair'—had been enlivened by 'a nice little conversation with Watts Dunton. His walrus-y appearance which makes the bottom of his face looked [*sic*] fierce, is counteracted by the kindness of his little eyes.'[65]

On 13 November there was a supper party at Laurence Housman's; his brother A. E. Housman was also there, who Frances thought was 'much nicer'. The Impressionist painter Walter Sickert 'dropped in after supper. The talk was interesting but dilletante [*sic*] and I can't help a certain numbness creeping over me in this sort of society. It is so futile.' The 8 December diary entry records that the impresario and actor manager George Alexander 'has an idea that he wants Gilbert to write a play for him and sent for him to come and see him. He was apparently taken with the notion of a play on the Crusades . . . It may come off some day, perhaps.'[66]

7

A year after the publication of Chesterton's first novel, *The Napoleon of Notting Hill*, his second work of fiction, *The Club of Queer Trades*, appeared in March 1905. It consists of amusing, whimsical stories of detection by the members of a club whose membership depends on their practising a 'queer' trade they had invented themselves. The first story had been published in December 1903 in *Harper's Weekly* and the other stories in the middle of 1904 both in *Harper's Magazine* and the *Idler*. The latter were commissioned by the *Idler*'s editor and founder, Jerome K. Jerome, the author of *Three Men in a Boat* (1889), and with illustrations by Chesterton. Jerome was more than fulsome in his praise of the six stories: 'They form the most remarkable set of stories that any magazine has ever been privileged to print since magazines were first published. Their humour is delicious; their ingenuity is marvellous; they are unique, and will always stand alone in the literature of short stories.'[67] However, what is so striking is that Chesterton is never as funny in his fiction as he is in his non-fiction prose writings, particularly his

[64] *A.* 265–7.   [65] 'Diary of Frances Chesterton', 288.
[66] 'Diary of Frances Chesterton', 288–9.   [67] *CQT* 51.

Autobiography, or in his letters. He could be whimsically amusing in his stories and novels, but he never achieved the same level of irony and satire. It is striking, for instance, that the 'Introductory Remarks on the Art of Prophecy' that preface *The Napoleon of Notting Hill*, in which he satirizes the practice of linear prophecy—whereby 'the prophets of the twentieth century... took something or other that was certainly going on in their time, and then said it would go on more and more until something extraordinary happened'—is funnier than anything in the novel itself.[68] *The Club of Queer Trades* is the least ambitious of Chesterton's fictional works—although the stories are very readable and entertaining[69]—and there are fewer of the Chestertonian paradoxical insights. The most interesting is the observation 'how facts obscure truth... Facts point in all directions': 'The mere facts! Do you really admit—are you still so sunk in superstition, so clinging to dim and historic altars, that you believe in facts? Do you not trust an immediate impression?'[70] And it is consistent with one of Chesterton's views on biography: that it should be an accurate 'caricature' in the sense of 'something as simple as the single line that marks the sweeping curve of the sharp corner in a weather-chart'. Or, as he puts it in an essay on Boswell when condemning 'the realistic or keyhole method' of biography: 'Facts always contradict each other.' This kind of biography 'does *not* give the true portrait of a man'.[71] It certainly was not the kind of biography practised by Chesterton, on whom the facts sat lightly but for whom it was all important to get to the essence and heart of his subject.

On 16 March 1905, Frances proudly noted in her diary: 'One of the proudest days of my life. Gilbert preached at St Paul's Covent Garden for CSU [Christian Social Union]... A crammed church—he was very eloquent and restrained.' On 30 March she recorded that he preached 'even better than last week'.[72] He was the first in a series of lay preachers, and the sermons were published under the title *Preachers from the Pew*.[73] Frances's pride at her already famous husband's preaching in a city church shows how important her religion was to her and how much it meant to her that her husband now shared it.

Conrad Noel was to recall an occasion when Frances was less pleased with her husband. He had gone to their flat in Battersea to speak at a meeting, which Chesterton was to chair, to establish a local branch of the

---

[68] *NNH* 221.

[69] They are too readily dismissed by Ward, *GKC* 155, and Ffinch, 132.

[70] *CQT* 67, 88.   [71] *WC* 57; *MC* 5–6.

[72] 'Diary of Frances Chesterton', 289–90.   [73] Ward, *GKC* 141.

Christian Social Union. The two men were still talking in the dining room (still a separate room) when Frances in some agitation told Chesterton that he must get dressed as people would be arriving any moment. On finding the two men still arguing as the drawing room began to fill up, she brought his clothes into the dining room and made him change. Propelled into the drawing room, he began drawing caricatures of bishops, only to knock over the small table at which he was sitting when Frances forced him to take the chair of the meeting. It was probably a small fit of sulks rather than absent-mindedness, as he was not used to having an argument interrupted. Later in the evening he scandalized a serious young lady who asked the company's advice about her maid's evening off: 'I'm so afraid of her going to the Red Lion.' Chesterton's response was: 'Best place she could go to.'[74]

On 18 May the Chestertons called on the Duchess of Sutherland:

When I had got used to the splendour, it was jolly enough. Her Grace is a pretty, sweet woman who wears the ugliest hat I've ever seen. She was very nervous, but got better under the fire of Gilbert's chaff. She made him write in her album which he did, a most ridiculous poem of which he should be ashamed. It must be truly awful to live in the sort of way the Duchess does, and endeavour to keep sane.

On 20 May 1905 Frances Chesterton noted in her diary that words failed her when she tried 'to recall the sensation aroused by a J.D.C. dinner. It seems so odd to think of these men as boys, to realize what their school life was and what a powerful element the J.D.C. was in the lives of all.'[75]

On 24 May both Chesterton and Frances went down to see George Meredith in Surrey. 'He talks without stopping except to drink ginger-beer,' noted Frances after the visit. 'He told us many stories, mostly about society scandals of some time back. I remember he asked Gilbert, "Do you like babies?" '[76] Chesterton himself remembered him as very old but still 'magnificently vain . . . even, for instance, to the point of preferring to dazzle women rather than men; for he talked the whole time to my wife rather than to me'. He, too, was struck by how he 'talked and talked, and drank ginger-beer, which he assured us with glorious gaiety he had learned to like quite as much as champagne'. Unlike most novelists he appeared more interested in the books he had not written than in those he had.[77]

On 5 June Harley Granville Barker, the theatre director and producer, came to see Chesterton 'touching the possibility of a play'.[78] This was a

[74] Ward, *GKC* 142.   [75] 'Diary of Frances Chesterton', 290.
[76] 'Diary of Frances Chesterton', 290.   [77] *A*. 263–4.
[78] 'Diary of Frances Chesterton', 290.

very distinct sign of Chesterton's growing reputation, as the young Granville Barker began directing in 1904 with brilliant success at the Royal
Court Theatre, where for the next three years he produced not only the
classics but also contemporary plays, in particular those of George Bernard
Shaw, whose reputation he effectively established. On 27 June the Bishop
of Southwark told Frances at a garden party that A. J. Balfour, the
Conservative Prime Minister, had told him that he had been 'very impressed' by her husband's latest book.[79]

Heretics, one of Chesterton's major, if not great, works, had been
published only three weeks before. It consists of revised articles he had
already published in the *Daily News* over several years,[80] some pre-dating
the controversy with Blatchford, some written contemporaneously with it,
others after it, together with additional material added later. Some of
the book is consequently more openly and specifically Christian than
other parts.[81] The book comprises by no means therefore purely negative
critiques of 'heretics' and only by implication a work of Christian apologetics.[82] Belloc wrote to tell him that he was 'delighted' with what he had
read in the newspaper: 'Hit them again. Hurt them. . . . Give them hell.'[83]

[79] 'Diary of Frances Chesterton', 290.

[80] See David Evans, 'The Making of G. K. Chesterton's *Heretics*', *The Yearbook of
English Studies*, 5 (1975), 207–13. Evans, p. 207, points out that his journalism gave
Chesterton 'the first opportunity to formulate many of his characteristic turns of
expression and thought in print'.

[81] Oddie, 288.

[82] The failure to appreciate the explicitly Christian, and indeed Catholic, apologetic in *Heretics* is common among critics of Chesterton, beginning with his own
brother, who complained (CC 152) that he 'criticizes his opponents with much vigour
and acumen. But he does not very clearly define, much less defend, his own position.'
See also Gary Wills, *Chesterton: Man and Mask* (New York: Sheed and Ward, 1961), 87,
89, who maintains that it is not Christian apologetics but a defence of 'philosophy
itself' and that Christianity is merely seen as a 'fine code of common sense'; Adam
Schwartz, *The Third Spring: G. K. Chesterton, Graham Greene, Christopher Dawson, and David
Jones* (Washington: Catholic University of America Press, 2005), 58, who claims that
Heretics is 'the best example' of the early 'phase' when Chesterton 'continued to
define himself negatively, as against modern theology and philosophy, leaving his
affirmation of orthodox Christianity largely implied'; and David Dooley, foreword to
H. 22, who states: 'By showing what heresy implies, Chesterton illustrates what
orthodoxy implies.' Cf. Oddie, 288, 290–6.

[83] Ward, *GKC* 159.

In his 'Introductory Remarks on the Importance of Orthodoxy' (with its glance at the author of *The Importance of Being Earnest*[84]), Chesterton condemns the fundamental heresy of his time—the idea that a person's 'philosophy does not matter'. It was perfectly acceptable to talk about anything—but 'that strange object, the universe', for as soon as one did that one would 'have a religion, and be lost'. And so underlying all the contemporary heresies was the heresy that 'everything matters—except everything'. This had not been the intention of the Victorian liberals when they achieved freedom of speech in defence of religious freedom. It had once been 'bad taste' to be an atheist; now it was 'bad taste' even to discuss religion. But, in fact, 'the most practical and important thing about a man is still his view of the universe'. Chesterton's famous example of the importance of discussing 'fundamentals' is the lamp post that a number of people wish to pull down. A monk, 'who is the spirit of the Middle Ages', is consulted and promptly proceeds to suggest a preliminary discussion about the value of light itself. At this everybody else rushes forward and proceeds to pull the lamp post down, 'congratulating each other on their unmediaeval practicality'. But, unfortunately, those pulling down the lamp post have very different reasons for doing so. And eventually it becomes clear that the monk was right, that one has to be theoretical before being practical: 'Only what we might have discussed under the gas-lamp, we now must discuss in the dark.' Far from the 'absence of definite convictions' giving 'the mind freedom and agility', the opposite is true because somebody 'who believes something . . . has all his weapons about him'. The fundamental contention of the book is that 'it is a fundamental point of view, a philosophy or religion which is needed . . . The things we need most for immediate practical purposes are all abstractions. We need a right view of the human lot, a right view of the human society . . . '. But we cannot have a 'right view' unless we have 'a clear idealism', unless we have a 'definite image of good'. To be without 'ideals' is to be 'in permanent danger of fanaticism'. The 'most bigoted are the people who have no convictions at all'. And bigotry 'may be roughly defined as the anger of men who have no opinions', 'the appalling frenzy of the indifferent'. But, that said, everybody does have 'a general view of existence, whether we like it or not; it alters, or, to speak more accurately, it creates and involves everything we say or do, whether we like it or not'. In that sense, 'religion is exactly the thing which cannot be left out—because it includes everything'.

---

[84] Oddie, 286.

It is impossible to be without some kind of 'a metaphysical system'. The problem is that the 'modern world is filled with men who hold dogmas so strongly that they do not even know that they are dogmas'. The concept of 'progress' is considered to be 'progressive', but in fact it is a 'dogma'. Again, it does not strike people that it is 'dogmatic' to assume the good of collecting scientific 'facts for the sake of facts, even though they seem as useless as sticks and straws'. Consequently, while a society that does not believe in 'oracles or sacred places' sees 'the full frenzy of those who killed themselves to find the sepulchre of Christ', it cannot see 'the full frenzy of those who kill themselves to find the North Pole' because it believes in the 'dogma of facts for facts' sake'. At the end of the book, Chesterton teasingly urges his readers: 'Let us, then, go upon a long journey and enter on a dreadful search. Let us, at least, dig and seek till we have discovered our own opinions. The dogmas we really hold are far more fantastic, and, perhaps, far more beautiful than we think.' Even more teasingly, he assures the rationalists: 'There are no rationalists. We all believe fairy-tales, and live in them.' They may think they are free of undemonstrable religious dogmas, but they hold 'the equally undemonstrable dogma of the existence of the man next door'. When a truth is denied it becomes a dogma. Scepticism, then, does not destroy beliefs: 'rather it creates them; gives them their limits and their plain and defiant shape.' Rationalism denies common-sense truths that then become dogmas to be defended, and the author concludes with a wonderfully paradoxical Chestertonian peroration:

Everything will be denied. Everything will become a creed. It is a reasonable position to deny the stones in the street; it will be a religious dogma to assert them. It is a rational thesis that we are all in a dream; it will be a mystical sanity to say that we are all awake. Fires will be kindled to testify that two and two make four. Swords will be drawn to prove that leaves are green in summer. We shall be left defending, not only the incredible virtues and sanities of human life, but something more incredible still, this huge impossible universe which stares us in the face. We shall fight for visible prodigies as if they were invisible. We shall look upon the impossible grass and the skies with a strange courage. We shall be of those who have seen and yet have believed.[85]

The contemporary worship of progress is a particularly absurd heresy. How, asks Chesterton, can one talk about progress without 'being doctrinal' in the sense of having 'a definite creed and a cast-iron code of morals'?

[85] *H.* 40–1, 46, 49, 51, 65–6, 113, 201–3, 205–7.

In the despised Middle Ages, people had an idea of the 'direction' in which they wanted to go, but the contemporary age that liked to talk so much about progress but that differed so much on which 'direction' to go 'had less right to use the word "progress"' than any previous age. The cult of progress also contravened one of Chesterton's most fundamental convictions, the necessity of limitation: for it was 'always concerned with the breaking of bonds, the effacing of boundaries, the casting away of dogmas'. Chesterton enjoys brandishing dogma in the face of a culture that prided itself on the absence of dogmas that allegedly constrict but that in fact paradoxically liberate the human mind:

But if there be such a thing as mental growth, it must mean the growth into more and more definite convictions, into more and more dogmas. . . . When we hear of a man too clever to believe, we are hearing of something having almost the character of a contradiction in terms. It is like hearing of a nail that was too good to hold down a carpet; or a bolt that was too strong to keep a door shut.

That sarcastic analogy is succeeded by a provocative celebration of dogma that concludes with even more devastating analogies to show that it is dogma that makes us human and lack of dogma sub-human:

Man can be defined as an animal that makes dogmas. As he piles doctrine on doctrine and conclusion on conclusion in the formation of some tremendous scheme of philosophy and religion, he is, in the only legitimate sense of which the expression is capable, becoming more and more human. When he drops one doctrine after another in a refined scepticism, when he declines to tie himself to a system, when he says that he has outgrown definitions, when he says that he disbelieves in finality, when, in his own imagination, he sits as God, holding no form of creed but contemplating all, then he is by that very process sinking slowly backwards into the vagueness of the vagrant animals and the unconsciousness of the grass. Trees have no dogmas. Turnips are singularly broad-minded.

Intellectual progress therefore means 'the construction of a definite philosophy of life' that is 'right'. Chesterton takes two examples of contemporary writers who at least have 'a constructive and affirmative view', even if it is not one he agrees with. Kipling the imperialist and Shaw the Socialist, who were both 'moralists', showed that 'the fiercest dogmatists can make the best artists', whereas the *fin de siècle* slogan was that 'literature should be free from all causes and all ethical creeds'.[86]

---

[86] *H.* 53, 196–8.

Chesterton makes it clear in *Heretics* that his own view of life is religious and the dogmas he believes in are those of Christianity. The wonder at the very fact of existence had led him first to believe that 'where there is anything there is God'. But this 'inchoate' religion[87] had developed into a definite Christianity when Chesterton looked at the *nature* as opposed to the *fact* of existence. And what struck him most forcibly was that the *paradoxes* of Christianity are true to life. Thus the Christian virtue of hope is 'justified in life' by the fact that the more hopeless a situation is the more hopeful one has to be. Or again, the virtue of humility is 'justified in life' by the fact that pride ('which the Roman Catholic Church . . . has done her best work in singling out') 'dries up laughter . . . dries up wonder . . . dries up chivalry and energy'. Vanity, on the other hand, is 'humorous, and can enjoy the joke even of itself; pride is dull, and cannot even smile'. Chesterton's hero Stevenson 'had found that the secret of life lies in laughter and humility'. The characteristic virtues of Christianity—which, again significantly, Chesterton notes, 'the Church of Rome calls virtues of grace'—of, that is, faith, hope, and charity, are 'the gay and exuberant virtues' in contrast to the pagan virtues of, for example, justice and temperance, which are 'the sad virtues'. Even more obviously, the pagan virtues are 'reasonable', whereas the Christian virtues are 'in their essence as unreasonable as they can be', or, in other words, are inherently paradoxical. But the pre-Christian pagan world only 'discovered in its death-pang this lasting and valuable truth, a heritage for the ages, that reasonableness will not do'. This 'naked innocence of the intellect', claims Chesterton, cannot be recovered after Christianity. And here he adduces a startling example: 'The greatest tribute to Christianity in the modern world is Tennyson's "Ulysses".' For the poet 'reads into the story . . . the conception of an incurable desire to wander'. But 'the real Ulysses does not desire to wander at all. He desires to get home.' Why? Because there is 'no love of adventure for its own sake; that is a Christian product. There is no love of Penelope for her own sake; that is a Christian product.' In this reasonable, sensible pagan world, there were good men and bad men, but there was no concept of charity, since 'charity is a reverent agnosticism towards the complexity of the human soul'. Nor had they any 'idea of romance; for romance consists in thinking a thing more delightful because it is dangerous; it is a Christian idea'. The Christian virtues are paradoxes certainly, but 'they are all three practical, and they are all three paradoxical because they are practical'. That is, they

---

[87] *A.* 148.

are true to life, which is inherently paradoxical: 'It is the stress of ultimate need, and a terrible knowledge of things as they are, which led men to set up these riddles, and to die for them.'[88]

But there is another Christian virtue, Chesterton argues, which illustrates even better 'the connection between paradox and practical necessity'. The pagans had set out to enjoy themselves but in the end made 'the great psychological discovery' that 'a man cannot enjoy himself and continue to enjoy anything else', and that, 'whereas it had been supposed that the fullest possible enjoyment is to be found by extending our ego to infinity, the truth is that the fullest possible enjoyment is to be found by reducing our ego to zero'. This virtue of humility is for Chesterton what saves us from 'a tendency to be weary of wonders':

To the humble man, and to the humble man alone, the sun is really a sun; to the humble man, and to the humble man alone, the sea is really a sea. When he looks at all the faces in the street, he does not only realize that men are alive, he realizes with a dramatic pleasure that they are not dead.[89]

Chesterton once quoted to his friend Charles Masterman Kipling's lines about the doomed crew of a disabled battleship: 'it is not meet that English stock | Should bide . . . | The death they may not see,' as they 'watched the harassed crowds pouring through the passages of the Underground to the iron and symbolic Inner Circle'. He, Chesterton, had 'always retained a dim sense of something sacred in English stock, or in human stock, which separated me from the mere pessimism of the period'.[90]

A proud intellectual like Carlyle, with his philosophy of hero worship, rejected the truism that no man is a hero to his valet; whereas, in reality, the 'ultimate psychological truth, the foundation of Christianity, is that no man is a hero to himself'. Carlyle thought most men were fools, but Christianity regarded *all* men as fools. This doctrine of original sin, the 'permanent possibility of selfishness' arising 'from the mere fact of having a self'—'almost the first thing to be believed in'—could be called 'the doctrine of the equality of men'. The discovery that 'pride does not lead to enjoyment' was an important discovery in the history of the world. But another aspect of the foolish modern cult of progress was the idea that progress depended on 'independent thinking', when in reality, 'under independent or individualistic thinking, every man starts at the beginning,

---

[88] *H.* 106–7, 124–6.   [89] *H.* 127–8.   [90] *A.* 135.

and goes on, in all probability, just as far as his father before him. But if there really be anything of the nature of progress, it must mean, above all things, the careful study and assumption of the whole of the past.'[91] Chesterton might have added that a deference to tradition is itself a product of humility.

Another 'intellectual' with a contempt, like Carlyle, for the common man was George Bernard Shaw. Chesterton teases this 'heretic' with two connected paradoxes. The 'only defect' in his 'greatness', 'to his claim to be a great man', is 'that he is not easily pleased. He is an almost solitary exception to the general and essential maxim, that little things please great minds.' And from the lack of 'that most uproarious of all things, humility, comes . . . the peculiar insistence on the Superman'. Both these paradoxes were, of course, particularly offensive to the intellectuals, for whom 'little things' were obviously what pleased little not great men, and for whom the Christian virtue of humility, far from being a glorious thing, was the Christian virtue which their prophet Nietzsche held in especial contempt. Having discovered that the masses were not 'progressive', instead of deciding 'to abandon progress and remain with humanity', Shaw, 'not being easily pleased', has opted 'to throw over humanity with all its limitations and go in for progress for its own sake'. Instead of looking for 'a new kind of philosophy', Shaw wants 'a new kind of man'. What Chesterton finds 'valuable and lovable' in the common man, 'the old beer-drinking, creed-making, fighting, failing, sensual, respectable man', Shaw finds contemptible. Chesterton ends his dissection of Shaw with yet another paradox and yet another pointed reference to the Church of Rome, which of course Shaw also held in great contempt, but which for Chesterton was a glorious, or, to use his own word, 'uproarious', vindication of the common man.

When Christ at a symbolic moment was establishing His great society, He chose for its corner-stone neither the brilliant Paul nor the mystic John, but a shuffler, a snob, a coward—in a word, a man. And upon this rock He has built His Church, and the gates of Hell have not prevailed against it. All the empires and the kingdoms have failed, because of this inherent and continual weakness, that they were founded by strong men and upon strong men. But this one thing, the historic Christian Church, was founded on a weak man, and for that reason it is indestructible. For no chain is stronger than its weakest link.[92]

[91] *H.* 77, 129, 131.　　　　[92] *H.* 69–70.

What Chesterton calls 'the practical success of Christendom' is due to 'this gay humility, this holding of ourselves lightly and yet ready for an infinity of unmerited triumphs'. And one of its fruits is 'Romance, a purely Christian product', the idea that something is 'more delightful because it is dangerous'. For the most 'herculean efforts' are made for the things of which people know they are 'unworthy'. Nor can anyone 'deserve adventures; he cannot earn dragons and hippogriffs'. It was Christian 'mediaeval Europe which asserted humility' that 'gained Romance'. But the contemporary world refuses to believe in the romance of the urban street, from which it says it flees 'because it is dull', whereas in fact it flees 'because it is a great deal too exciting. It is exciting because it is exacting; it is exacting because it is alive.' And so the contemporary man 'invents modern hygiene and goes to Margate. Then he invents modern culture and goes to Florence. Then he invents modern imperialism and goes to Timbuctoo.' It is because the 'street in Brixton is too glowing and overpowering' that he has 'to soothe and quiet himself among tigers and vultures, camels and crocodiles'. But actually 'he would have a much more romantic . . . change if he jumped over the wall into his neighbour's garden'. For our neighbour 'comes to us clad in all the careless terrors of nature; he is as strange as the stars, as reckless and indifferent as the rain. He is Man, the most terrible of the beasts.' Now to shrink from 'the brutal vivacity and brutal variety of common men' is perfectly natural but it is not admirable or superior as Nietzsche, 'who represents most prominently this pretentious claim of the fastidious', thinks.

Every man has hated mankind when he was less than a man. Every man has had humanity in his eyes like a blinding fog, humanity in his nostrils like a suffocating smell. But when Nietzsche has the incredible lack of humour and lack of imagination to ask us to believe that his aristocracy is an aristocracy of strong muscles or an aristocracy of strong wills, it is necessary to point out the truth. It is an aristocracy of weak nerves.

Aversion to the masses, Chesterton dares to suggest, is really aversion to their 'energy. The misanthropes pretend that they despise humanity for its weakness. As a matter of fact, they hate it for its strength.'[93]

The same intellectuals also for the same reasons find the family an 'uncongenial' institution, whereas, like the suburban street, it is precisely its 'divergencies and varieties' that make it 'a good institution'. It is 'romantic because it is a toss-up' involving the 'element of adventure'.

[93] *H.* 71–2, 126, 138–41.

The 'supreme adventure' in life is not falling in love but being born: 'There we do walk suddenly into a splendid and startling trap. . . . Our father and mother do lie in wait for us and leap out on us, like brigands from a bush. Our uncle is a surprise. Our aunt is a bolt from the blue.' The intellectuals see the family as a dreary restricting bourgeois institution. Chesterton, on the contrary, insists that the 'colour as of a fantastic narrative ought to cling to the family and to our relations with it throughout life. Romance is the deepest thing in life; romance is deeper even than reality.' Life itself is not only a romance but 'is always a novel' or 'story' because it involves the will as well as the intellect. And the same Christian civilization that 'asserted free will in the thirteenth century, produced the thing called "fiction" in the eighteenth. When Thomas Aquinas asserted the spiritual liberty of man, he created all the bad novels in the circulating libraries.' Inevitably, for Chesterton romance and the novel involve the idea of limitation: 'The thing which keeps life romantic . . . is the existence of these great plain limitations which force all of us to meet the things we do not like or expect.' To be born is to be 'born into uncongenial surroundings, hence to be born into a romance', since, 'in order that life should be a story or romance to us, it is necessary that a great part of it, any rate, should be settled for us without our permission'. Modern intellectuals 'imagine that romance would exist most perfectly in a complete state of what they call liberty', seeking as they do 'a world where there are no limitations—that is, a world where there are no outlines'. And of all the 'great limitations and frame-works which fashion and create the poetry and variety of life, the family is the most definite and important', which is why the intellectuals so hate it.[94]

Intellectuals, on the other hand, who consider themselves superior to the ordinary man talk 'very solemnly' about art, whereas the truly great artists are 'ordinary men' who do not take themselves or their art too seriously but have a 'god-like carelessness'—unlike one of Chesterton's 'heretics' who receives the ultimate Chestertonian condemnation: 'The truth is, I believe, that Whistler never laughed at all. There was no laughter in his nature; because there was no thoughtlessness and self-abandonment, no humility.' The 'extreme ordinariness' of a great artist like Shakespeare, who could be so 'keen . . . on business transactions in a little town in Warwickshire', is incomprehensible to the 'modern artistic temperament'. Far from being 'superior to other men', Shakespeare felt himself 'equal with other men'. This, maintains Chesterton, is true also of all the really

[94] *H.* 141–5.

great teachers and leaders whose superiority to other men is shown in their belief in 'the equality of man'. The 'plainness', the 'almost prosaic camaraderie' with which Jesus Christ 'addressed any motley crowd that happened to stand about Him', 'is the note of all great minds'.[95]

Laughter is characteristic not only of men who think they are ordinary rather than superior, but also of religious believers. Neither the Salvation Army nor Roman Catholics are 'reverent', for 'reverence in the sad and delicate meaning of the term reverence is a thing only possible to infidels'. As opposed to the 'beautiful twilight' of a Matthew Arnold, the believer is characterized by 'laughter and war': 'A man cannot pay that kind of reverence to truth solid as marble': a man 'can only be reverent towards a beautiful lie'. Laughter for Chesterton goes hand-in-hand with sentimentality, which is so dreaded by modern writers, who consequently lack 'the robust and uproarious humour' that was natural to the great English writers like Dickens, who had the 'heart' not merely for sentimentalism, but a 'very silly sentimentalism'. All joking 'is in its nature profane, in the sense that it must be the sudden realization that something which thinks itself solemn is not so very solemn after all'. The 'oldest jokes' in the world are about really serious things'—like 'being married' or 'being hanged'. The Bible shows that 'funny' is not 'the opposite of serious': 'God himself overwhelms Job with a torrent of terrible levities. The same book which says that God's name must not be taken vainly, talks easily and carelessly about God laughing and God winking.' If a man is not 'in part a humorist, he is only in part a man,' since 'frivolity is a part of the nature of man'.[96]

The natural, however, depends on the supernatural: 'Take away the supernatural, and what remains is the unnatural.' Nor is the spiritual opposed to the material: 'Men only become greedily and gloriously material about something spiritualistic.' A holiday like Christmas is only a holiday because it is a 'holy day'. Merry Christmas is merry because religion produces merriment: 'If by vulgarity we mean coarseness of speech, rowdiness of behaviour, gossip, horseplay, and some heavy drinking, vulgarity there always was wherever there was joy, wherever there was faith in the gods. Wherever you have belief you will have hilarity, wherever you have hilarity you will have some dangers.' To be 'truly gay, we must believe that there is some eternal gaiety in the nature of things'. One has to be 'serious' to be 'really hilarious': 'The thing called high spirits is possible only to the spiritual. Ultimately a man cannot rejoice in anything except

---

[95] *H.* 169–73.   [96] *H.* 85, 152, 160.

the nature of things. Ultimately a man can enjoy nothing except religion.' Comte's substitute for Christianity, Positivism, is absurd, as it is 'evidently impossible to worship humanity, just as it is impossible to worship the Savile Club; both are excellent institutions to which we may happen to belong'. But Comte's new religious calendar recognized that 'men must always have the sacredness of mummery' and the 'rites and forms' of ritual that is 'much older than thought'. Daily life indeed is 'one continual and compressed catalogue of mystical mummery and flummery'.[97] The importance and inevitability of ritual were a theme to which Chesterton would often return.

8

Politicians apparently were as anxious to meet Chesterton as writers. On 5 July he dined with H. H. Asquith, the future Liberal Prime Minister, where he met the former Liberal Prime Minister Lord Roseberry. 'I think he hated it,' wrote Frances in her diary. A few days later he met A. J. Balfour, whom he found 'most interesting to talk to, but appears bored'.[98] As a Scottish Presbyterian, Balfour, Chesterton thought, 'had something in his blood which I think was the cold ferocity of Calvinism', his 'long fine head' reminding Chesterton not of English squires and castles but the manse.[99] Chesterton also met Austen Chamberlain ('stiffer than a gentleman should be'), and George Wyndham, the radical reforming Chief Secretary for Ireland, whom he found 'delightful'.[100]

Wyndham was on the opposite political side to Chesterton, but he was the politician who most attracted and impressed him. In fact, Chesterton regarded him as a Tory rather than a Conservative: indeed, 'he was capable of being a Jacobite', which greatly commended him to Chesterton, who 'always got on much better with revolutionists than with reformers; even when I entirely disagreed with the revolutions or entirely agreed with the reformers', for revolutionists 'did, in a sense, judge the world; not justly like the saints; but independently like the saints', whereas reformers were too 'much a part of the world they reformed'. Wyndham did not simply 'wish to preserve Protestantism or Free Trade, or anything grown native to the nation; he wanted to revive things older and really more international'.

---

[97] *H.* 87–8, 96.   [98] 'Diary of Frances Chesterton', 291.
[99] *A.* 253.   [100] 'Diary of Frances Chesterton', 291.

Realizing that his political opinions 'were at least of the same general colour' as his own made Chesterton see 'the falsity of the Party System'. Like Chesterton, Wyndham was at home with the poor: 'He had huge sympathy with gypsies and tramps; and collected many men of letters (including myself) who looked rather like tramps.' Remarkably, Wyndham 'had come through political life without losing his political opinions, or indeed any opinions'. He had 'a genius for friendship', and politics had not changed him: he was his own man with his own 'prejudices and private dogmas for which he would fight like a private person'. Unlike the Liberal Asquith, who 'was fully satisfied with that sort of broad idealism, that rather diluted "essence of Christianity" which is often sincere but seldom significant of any special social decision', Wyndham 'was an Anglo-Catholic as an individual, and would have practised his religion in any state of life. There was about him that edge, like the edge of a sword, which I cannot help preferring to being knocked down with a spiritual sandbag.' Chesterton, however, got 'great joy out of the hearty humours' of Asquith, who, like Chesterton himself, 'rose gloriously to flippancy. Once when he appeared in Court dress, on some superbly important occasion, an uncontrollable impulse of impertinence led me to ask whether the Court sword would really come out of its sheath. "Oh, yes," he said, shaking a shaggily frowning head at me, "Do not provoke me." ' Chesterton noticed, on the other hand, that he had a curious vagueness about fundamental issue of ethics and politics, a quality he 'found so often in men holding high responsibilities'. His experience of politicians led him to conclude, 'politicians have no politics'. He remembered, for instance, a discussion when a difficult question was raised and Churchill 'smiled the inscrutable smile of the statesman . . .'.[101]

Although it was mostly Liberal politicians, especially those sympathetic to the *Daily News*'s stance, that Chesterton met, particularly thanks to the hospitality of its owner George Cadbury, it was at one of his house parties that he first met the Labour politician Will Crooks, the only Labour leader he ever knew who 'reminded me for a single moment of the English labouring classes. His humour really was the humour of an omnibus conductor or a railway porter; and that sort of humour is a much more powerful and real thing than most modern forms of education or eloquence.' His wife also was as representative of the working class. On one occasion, 'an ethereal little lady with pale blue eyes

---

[101] *A.* 120–2; 250–1, 255.

and pale green garments, who was the wife of a well-known Anti-War journalist', on hearing another guest mention that during hectic electioneering he had just had time 'to snatch a cutlet', intervened; although normally slow to advance her ideas, when she did it was 'a very serious business indeed'.

'Do you think that was really necessary?' she said with a painful fixity, like one in a trance. 'Man is no better than a cutlet. Man does not really need cutlets.'

At this point she received hearty, one might almost say heavy, support, from what was probably an unexpected quarter.

'No, my dear,' said Mrs Crooks in resounding tones, 'A man doesn't want a cutlet! What's the good of a cutlet? What a man wants is a good chump chop or a bit of the undercut; and I'd see he got it.'

The other lady sighed; it was not quite what she had meant; and she was obviously a little alarmed to advance again against her large and solid opponent and be felled to the earth with a mutton-bone.

This scene seemed to Chesterton to be 'a perfect parable of the two kinds of Simple Life, the false and the true'. Shortly afterwards he had to take the vegetarian lady into dinner, and, on passing through the conservatory, he pointed out an insect-eating plant to his companion and asked, 'Don't you vegetarians feel remorse when you look at that? You live by devouring harmless plants; and here is a plant that actually devours animals. Surely that is a just judgment. It is the revenge of the animal world.' The lady stared at him 'with staring blue eyes that were absolutely grave and unsmiling. "Oh," she said, "But I don't approve of revenge." '[102]

Chesterton was to write an introduction to a biography of Will Crooks, called *From Workhouse to Westminster*, in 1907, in which he maintained that representative government, the democratic substitute for direct government by the people, 'may for a time represent the people, and for a time cease to represent anything'. The people's representative could be either like a shadow or like a stone—either by being like the people he represents or by being useful to the people he represents. The House of Commons, he complained, was full of stones rather than shadows, Will Crooks being the solitary exception as the one Member of Parliament who actually resembled the people he represented. Chesterton looked forward to the day when all Members of Parliament would be like him: then the people would have 'entered politics', bringing with it 'a trail of all the things that politicians detest . . . '.[103]

---

[102] *A.* 124–5.   [103] Ward, *GKC* 251–2.

5

Dickens

THE autumn of 1905 brought a welcome improvement in the Chestertons' financial position. In October the editor of the *Illustrated London
News* invited Chesterton to take over the famous 'Our Notebook' column
on the death of its previous writer: 'The article runs to about 2,000
words and takes the form of a light discussion on matters of the moment,
and it is treated without political bias.... I do not know that the remuneration is very dazzling...'. On receiving Chesterton's immediate
acceptance of the offer, the editor replied that he was 'much gratified',
feeling 'confident that as long as your hand is in it, no-one will question
the sanity of that institution, may I say, of English life'. The remuneration was later increased, but Chesterton subsequently refused to allow
his literary agent to ask for more: 'That paper gave me a regular income
when I needed it badly.' Several volumes of these columns were to sell
well, the early ones being selected by the essayist E. V. Lucas, who
suggested the titles.[1]

The general election of January 1906, in which the Liberals won a
landslide victory, found Chesterton once again canvassing on behalf of a
Liberal candidate, this time Charles Masterman, his friend from the
Christian Social Union, who was successfully elected for West Ham
North. According to Chesterton, Masterman 'used to swear with derisive
gusto that when we were canvassing together, he went all down one side of
a street and up most of the other, and found me in the first house, still

---

[1] Barker, 160–2.

arguing the philosophy of government with the first householder'.
But Chesterton thought that Masterman's memory was 'unduly darkened
by a jovial pessimism' characteristic of the man.[2] Hilaire Belloc stood for
South Salford as the Liberal candidate and won. 'This is a great day for the
British Empire, but a bad one for the little Bellocs,' he announced, on
arriving at Euston station, to Chesterton and another friend who had been
summoned to meet him.[3]

Frances acted in effect as both her husband's valet and secretary (from
1907 she took over correspondence with A. P. Watt, the literary agents,
from Chesterton's father[4]). She might even be asked to take down an
article in dictation as he early began to hate writing by hand. Her husband
was the classic mother's boy who had never lived away from home before
getting married and was used to everything practical being done for him,
never having had to fend for himself. As one of his friends remarked, he
literally passed from the care of his mother to that of his wife.[5] Frances
looked after his diary so far as she was able; if she was not there to record
the acceptance of a writing or speaking invitation, it would be forgotten.
But of course she was not present when her husband was in Fleet Street, in
whose pubs and restaurants so many of his articles were written. When
these were completed there, the necessary cab would be hired to take the
article the hundred yards or so to the *Daily News* office. When they were
written at home, invariably at the last minute, Frances would be needed to
get them to their destination in time for the deadline. A journalist who later
worked on *G.K.'s Weekly* recalled how one day Chesterton failed to show up
for a board meeting, some months after the paper had moved to a new
address. When he finally arrived, Chesterton explained that he had been
unable to remember the address to give to the cab-driver, and had made
the cab wait outside a tea shop while he turned out his pockets over a cup
of tea in the hope of finding something with the address on it. Unable to
find any clue and still unable to remember the address, he told the driver to
take him to a bookstall where he could buy a copy of his own paper, which
he managed to do at the third bookstall they visited.[6]

There were those who pitied Frances for having such a helpless and
unpractical husband. Robert Blatchford, for example, remembered with
disgust an occasion when he had to go out into the rain to hail a cab for his
wife, whereas it was Frances who had to go out into the rain to get a cab for

[2] *A.* 126.
[3] Robert Speaight, *The Life of Hilaire Belloc* (London: Hollis & Carter, 1957), 207.
[4] Oddie, 222.   [5] Ward, *GKC* 109–10.   [6] Ward, *GKC* 161–4.

her husband. The convivial drinking in Fleet Street, the late nights, the money wasted on cabs, the endless talk while the food got cold on the table, the absent-mindedness and forgetfulness, not to mention all the daily ministrations Chesterton required, all suggested the long-suffering wife and the uncaring husband. This after all was a husband who would 'suddenly say, "Where is Frances? I don't want her now, but I might want her any minute."'[7] Others saw Chesterton as henpecked by a wife who always got her own way and made all the decisions such as where they went on holiday. There were, not surprisingly, grains of truth in these different perspectives. Daily life was not easy with Chesterton, and inevitably in the circumstances Frances could come across as domineering. But, while Frances may have made all the practical decisions, when it came to something that her husband did care about, like his journalistic work, he made his own decision. Their closest friends saw them as utterly devoted to each other, and could not imagine one without the other. Chesterton himself took the Christian idea of the marriage union, whereby a man and a woman become as one, very literally. According to the Bible, he argued, they become 'one flesh . . . parts of one creature . . . the two ends of a quadruped':

an ordinary honest man is a part of his wife even when he wishes he wasn't. . . . an ordinary good woman is part of her husband even when she wishes him to the bottom of the sea. . . . They are a nation, a society, a machine. I tell you they are one flesh, even when they are not one spirit.

While marriage, Chesterton thought, 'can be, and I believe generally is, the happiest state for a man, you cannot deprive it of its power to make him the most miserable thing on earth. It is always "for better, for worse".' No doubt, as in every marriage, he and Frances experienced something of the 'worse' as well as much of the 'better'. The debt Chesterton owed to her was obvious enough, but one old friend of theirs remarked, 'She became a much nicer person after she married him.' Although Frances, of course, was not absent-minded and impractical like her husband, she was like him, a close friend from the days in Beaconsfield commented, in being 'utterly unworldly': 'Not even interested in having great people around them. She was *too* unworldly, she didn't want to spend money on her clothes. Funny old friends meant more to her than important people. She was wonderful with children, they adored her.'[8]

---

[7] Dorothy Collins's notes for talks, BL Add. MS 73477, fo. 141.
[8] Ward, *RC* 80–3, 86.

It seems that it was in 1906,[9] probably in April, that Frances underwent the operation to enable her to have children. There survives a letter dated 12 April (but no year) in which she tells Father O'Connor that she is about to go into a nursing home for a month 'to get satisfactorily through an operation'. She was then going to stay at Ilkley for 'a course of bed and massage', where she hoped O'Connor would visit her 'and leave me with your priestly blessing'. 'It's all very horrid,' she continued, 'and I hate leaving my husband, but I've been obliged at last to give in and I hope to end as an Amazon'.[10] Chesterton stayed with friends in Abercorn Place, London, while Frances convalesced in the nursing home. Freda Rivière was a close friend of Frances from her Bedford Park days, when she had also become friends with Chesterton; her husband Hugh, who was a painter, took the opportunity to paint Chesterton's portrait. Chesterton would write his articles in the evening while a messenger boy waited in the hall, sometimes on the landings between stairs. Frances's specialist, Dr Margaret Joyce, who worked at the local Battersea Bridge branch of the Clapham Maternity Hospital,[11] one day received a telephone call from the matron of the nursing home complaining that Chesterton was sitting on the stairs there too and ignoring requests to move out of the way. When the doctor arrived, he had been sitting there already for two hours, dissatisfied with the last line of a sonnet he had written to Frances on her recovery from the operation. He refused to go into Frances's room until he was satisfied with the poem.[12] He stayed five days with the Rivières and continued afterwards to come round for sittings. Not having Frances at hand, he failed to bring any luggage with him, apart from a green glass bottle-stopper and a horse-pistol that he had bought on the way. Hugh Rivière found him a delightful sitter who never stopped talking. He and his wife noted how carefully he deposited his huge frame on their antique chairs, none of which he broke. A few years later when Freda visited the

[9] Ward, *RC* 79 quotes a poem by Chesterton, 'dated by Frances May 1906', which 'belongs to this time'. Frances Ivens, the gynaecological surgeon who performed the operation (see above, Ch. 3, n. 7), worked at the Clapham Maternity Hospital from 1902 to 1907, when she went to Liverpool (*The Medical Directory*, 1908), so the operation could not have been later than 1907.

[10] Frances Chesterton to John O'Connor, 12 April [*sic*], BL Add. MS 73196, fo. 43.

[11] See above, Ch. 3, n. 7.

[12] Margaret Joyce to Dorothy Collins, 25 Oct. 1942, BL Add. MS 73475A, fos 72–3. See also Ward, *GKC* 210–11.

Chestertons in their new home at Beaconsfield, he pointed out a small window high in the wall and remarked: 'I like that window. When the light catches her hair, it gives Frances a halo and makes her look something like what she really is.'[13]

Although the operation failed to produce any children, instead of becoming bitter and jealous of other more fortunate couples, the Chestertons lavished the affection they could not lavish on their own children on those of others. Not that it came easily to Frances, as she was the first to confess to her friends. When her neighbour Mrs Saxon Mills told her she was expecting another child, it took her some days before she could bring herself to see her again. She told her sister Ethel, married to Lucian Oldershaw, that she could hardly bear it when her sister brought her first child when she visited Frances in hospital. She confided to one of Chesterton's secretaries that she had hoped 'to have seven beautiful children'.[14]

Since Chesterton was fascinated by childhood, it is not surprising that nothing delighted him more than playing with children. He had written the marvellous nonsense poem 'Of the Dangers Attending Altruism on the High Seas' in *Greybeards at Play* for Frances's young cousin Rhoda Bastable, who was to be one of her bridesmaids, as part of a conspiracy against Frances. The two of them had founded a 'Society for the Encouragement of Rain', which the sun-loving Frances hated like most people—but which Chesterton loved with a passion:

I have just been out and got soaking and dripping wet; one of my favourite dissipations. I never enjoy weather so much as when it is driving, drenching, rattling, washing rain. . . . Yes, I like rain. It means some thing, I am not sure what; some thing freshening, cleaning, washing out, taking in hand, not caring-a-damn-what-you-think, doing-its-duty, robust, noisy, moral, wet.[15]

There were membership cards: Rhoda was president, Chesterton secretary, and Miss Blogg the 'Eternal Enemy'. Meetings were to take place on Salisbury Plain under the sign of an umbrella, at which members would be served coffee and cakes under the rain. He wrote out *Greybeards* for Rhoda, with more illustrations than are in the published version, and fastened the pages together with one of her mother's hairpins. Doris Child, the other bridesmaid at their wedding, remembered what she called 'the battle of potatoes and port' that Frances fought against Chesterton's increasing obesity.

---

[13] Ward, *RC* 78–9.   [14] Ward, *RC* 87–8.
[15] Ward, *GKC* 55, with text corrected from BL Add. MS 73191, fo. 143.

Returning an autograph book to Doris, Chesterton apologized in verse for keeping it so long with a rueful reference to his former shape when he had borrowed it:

> When I was graceful, slim and strong
> And very like a Norman Knight;
> My collars did not feel so tight,
> My trousers bagged not at the knee:
> I was a lovely, lovely sight
> When first this book was lent to me.

In a *Daily News* article, after they had moved to Battersea, Chesterton did not hesitate to inform his readers: 'In the flat immediately under mine there is a Liberal Imperialist baby, on whose judgment I rely a great deal.' This was the eldest Saxon Mills boy, who enjoyed mischievously asking his father to 'make pictures for me like Uncle Gilbert', knowing that his father was incapable of drawing anything, while also asking the totally unmusical Chesterton to 'sing a song for me like Daddy does'. One of the Saxon Mills girls was to recall, 'When I was alone with him, I felt I was an important person worth talking to.'[16]

2

On 30 August 1906 *Charles Dickens*, the first of Chesterton's half-a-dozen or so great works, was published. It is his best critical study, one of the classics of English literary criticism, and a book that is widely considered the best criticism of Dickens ever written. Both realist and symbolist writers had reacted sharply against Dickens; Chesterton's unfashionable defence of him is also his finest tribute to the despised, recently departed Victorian era. Five years later in 1911, as a kind of supplementary volume to *Charles Dickens*, he published *Appreciations and Criticisms of the Works of Charles Dickens*, which consisted of introductions to Dickens's novels commissioned for the new Everyman Library edition. Both books may conveniently be considered together.

Chesterton begins *Charles Dickens* by hailing the novelist as the 'living expression' of the French Revolution's philosophy of equality and liberty. This 'happy philosophy', this 'idea that all men are equal', had the effect of producing 'very great men'. But Chesterton insists that the great man is the

[16] Ward, *RC* 89–91.

opposite of Shaw's Superman, 'who makes every man feel small', for 'the real great man is the man who makes every man feel great'. The early nineteenth century 'produced great men, because it believed that men were great. It made strong men by encouraging weak men.' Far from the common man being despised as in Chesterton's time, 'the high rapture of equality' meant that the 'best men of the Revolution were simply common men at their best'. The 'other main factory of heroes' is a religion 'which, by its nature, does not think of men as more or less valuable, but of men as all intensely and painfully valuable, a democracy of eternal danger': 'For religion all men are equal, as all pennies are equal, because the only value in any of them is that they bear the image of the King.' Religion not only 'makes the ordinary man feel extraordinary', but 'makes the extraordinary man feel ordinary'. By contrast, Carlyle had killed the heroes and the heroic 'by forcing upon each man this question: "Am I strong or weak?" What Carlyle failed to understand was that real heroes come out of 'an ecstasy of the ordinary'. The idea would have been as strange to him as it was shocking to twentieth-century intellectuals and writers with their contempt for the common man. But the democratic Chesterton believed that people are great when they feel great. The founder of Christianity found the honest man in a thief on a gibbet 'and promised him Paradise'. Democracy 'encouraged the fool to be wise'. Naturally this optimism about human potential had, in the Christian Chesterton's view, its serious limitations: it failed to understand original sin, it thought that education would make everyone good, and it believed in 'human perfectibility'.[17]

Dickens, then, was 'the voice in England of this humane intoxication and expansion, this encouraging of anybody to be anything'. No writer has ever '*encouraged* his characters so much' in books that are 'a carnival of liberty'. Indeed, they are like 'spoilt children. They shake the house like heavy and shouting schoolboys; they smash the story to pieces like so much furniture.' The fundamental democratic doctrine is that 'all men are interesting; Dickens tried to make some of his people appear dull people, but he could not keep them dull. He could not make a monotonous man. The bores in his books are brighter than the wits in other books.' Dickens is 'like life, at least in this detail, that he is alive', and his art is 'like life because like life, it is irresponsible, because, like life, it is incredible'. 'Exaggeration is the definition of art,' and the now unfashionable truth Dickens exaggerated was the

---

[17] *CD* 42–4, 46.

'old Revolution sense of infinite opportunity and boisterous brotherhood'. Writers now may 'emphasize doubts for instance, for doubts are their religion', but they are not allowed 'to emphasize dogmas'. Similarly, they 'know what it is to feel a sadness so strange and deep that only impossible characters can express it', but 'they do not know what it is to feel a joy so vital and violent that only impossible characters can express that'. Again, it was a familiar Chesterton complaint, the modern world cannot understand how humour can and should accompany seriousness: it speaks of 'the wisdom of the spiritual world' but never of 'the jokes of the patron saints', 'of a man who was so silly that he touched the supernatural, like Bottom the weaver'. But Dickens knew that 'exhilaration is … a mystical fact; that exhilaration can be infinite, like sorrow; that a joke can be so big that it breaks the roof of the stars. By simply going on being absurd, a thing can become godlike; there is but one step from the ridiculous to the sublime.' Like all writers with a very distinctive, idiosyncratic style, Chesterton hovers constantly on the verge of self-parody, always liable to abuse or overuse of paradox; but equally the use of paradox can be brilliantly illuminating and stimulating, as here. He ends his introduction to the world of Dickens with an inversion of the words Dante wrote over the gates of hell: 'abandon hopelessness, all ye who enter here.'[18]

For Chesterton, the central paradox of Dickens's life was that the hated blacking factory of his unhappy boyhood 'manufactured also the greatest optimist of the nineteenth century', so that, if (as his critics complain) 'he learnt to whitewash the universe, it was in a blacking factory that he learnt it'. He proved that 'there is no kind of connection between a man being unhappy and a man being pessimistic'. Of the 'numberless points' on which Dickens was 'spiritually at one with the poor, that is, with the great mass of mankind', on none was he 'more perfectly at one with them'. He was one of the 'higher optimists' who 'do not approve of the universe; they do not even admire the universe; they fall in love with it. They embrace life too close to criticize or even to see it. Existence to such men has the wild beauty of a woman, and those love her with most intensity who love her with least cause.' So it was with Dickens: those unhappy early years, which 'may have given him many moral and mental wounds, from which he never recovered', 'did nothing to prevent him from laying up those hilarious memories of which all his books are made'—they 'gave him the key of the street'. He may have been

---

[18] *CD* 46–51.

'desperate' at that time but he was 'delighted at the same moment': 'His soul was like a shot silk of black and crimson, a shot silk of misery and joy.'[19]

The hell of Dickens's boyhood London, the hell that would be the source of his creativity, is evoked by Chesterton in one of his greatest passages, a rhetorical triumph, rich in compelling paradox, that is also one of the most creative pieces of biographical criticism ever written of an author.

He did not go in for 'observation', a priggish habit; he did not look at Charing Cross to improve his mind or count the lamp-posts in Holborn to practise his arithmetic. But unconsciously he made all these places the scenes of the monstrous drama in his miserable little soul. He walked in darkness under the lamps of Holborn, and was crucified at Charing Cross. So for him ever afterwards these places had the beauty that only belongs to battlefields. For our memory never fixes the facts which we have merely observed. The only way to remember a place for ever is to live in the place for an hour; and the only way to live in the place for an hour is to forget the place for an hour. The undying scenes we can all see if we shut our eyes are not the scenes that we have stared at under the direction of guide-books; the scenes we see are the scenes at which we did not look at all—the scenes in which we walked when we were thinking about something else—about a sin, or a love-affair, or some childish sorrow. We can see the background now because we did not see it then. So Dickens did not stamp these scenes on his mind; he stamped his mind on these places. For him ever afterwards these streets were mortally romantic; they were dipped in the purple dyes of youth and its tragedy, and rich with irrevocable sunsets.

Herein is the whole secret of that eerie realism with which Dickens could always vitalize some dark or dull corner of London. There are details in the Dickens descriptions—a window, or a railing, or the key-hole of a door—which he endows with demoniac life. The things seem more actual than things really are. Indeed, that degree of realism does not exist in reality; it is the unbearable realism of a dream. And this kind of realism can only be gained by walking dreamily in a place; it cannot be gained by walking observantly. Dickens himself has given a perfect instance of how these nightmare minutiæ grew upon him in his trance of abstraction. He mentions among the coffee-shops into which he crept in those wretched days one in St Martin's Lane, 'of which I only recollect that it stood near the church, and that in the door there was an oval plate with "COFFEE ROOM" painted on it, addressed towards the street. If I ever find myself in a very different kind of coffee-room now, but where there is such an inscription on glass, and read it backwards on the wrong side (as I often used to do then in a dismal reverie), a

---

[19] *CD* 60–2, 66–7.

shock goes through my blood.' That wild word, 'Moor Eeffoc,' is the motto of all effective realism; it is the masterpiece of the good realistic principle—the principle that the most fantastic thing of all is often the precise fact. And that elvish kind of realism Dickens adopted everywhere. His world was alive with inanimate objects. The date on the door danced over Mr Grewgious's, the knocker grinned at Mr Scrooge, the Roman on the ceiling pointed down at Mr Tulkinghorn, the elderly armchair leered at Tom Smart—these are all moor eeffocish things. A man sees them because he does not look at them.[20]

For Dickens as for Chesterton, there was at least as much, or rather more, poetry and romance in the city as in the countryside. And when Chesterton wonders why Dickens gave the name *The Old Curiosity Shop* for no apparent reason to one of his novels, he realizes that 'this title is something in the nature of a key to the whole Dickens romance. His tales always started from some splendid hint in the streets. And shops, perhaps the most poetical of all things, often set off his fancy galloping. Every shop, in fact, was to him the door of romance.'[21] One is reminded of the street in north Kensington with its row of shops that actually included an old curiosity shop that gave Chesterton the idea of Pump Street and *The Napoleon of Notting Hill*.

The young Dickens had spent his boyhood with the poor, the masses, of London, and a central theme of Chesterton's critical study is Dickens's total empathy with them. Because he knew their life from the inside, rather than as an observer from the outside, he understood, for instance, that there were 'no pleasures like the pleasures of the poor'. Chesterton quotes an 'intellectual' in a *fin de siècle* play as complaining that Dickens was a 'vulgar optimist'. Chesterton concedes that the term could be applied negatively to Dickens when he 'threw comfort' at his characters 'like alms' and when his 'literary hospitality', whereby he 'treated his characters as if they were his guests', failed with characters 'who for one reason or another could not be cured with one good dinner'. Then he could act like the hated philanthropist with his 'careless and insolent kindness', the 'charity' that was not 'real' but 'the charity that is puffed up, and that does behave itself unseemly'. 'At the end of some of his stories,' Chesterton admits in the severest criticism he ever made of Dickens, 'he deals out his characters a kind of out-door relief'. He gives two examples. Mr Micawber in *David Copperfield* showed how 'a man can be always almost rich by constantly expecting riches'; his life could not be 'a failure, because it is always a crisis', 'he cannot despair of life, for he is too much occupied in living'.

---

[20] *CD* 64–5.   [21] *CD* 107.

How, then, could Dickens 'pension him off at the end of the story and make him a successful colonial mayor? Micawber never did succeed, never ought to succeed; his kingdom is not of this world.' Chesterton's second example from the same novel is Dora, who 'represents the infinite and divine irrationality of the human heart'; whatever, then, 'possessed Dickens to make her such a dehumanised prig as to recommend her husband to marry another woman'? And yet Chesterton also thought the term 'vulgar optimist' had a very positive sense: 'When we consider what the conditions of the vulgar really are, it is difficult to imagine a stranger or more splendid tribute to humanity than such a phrase as vulgar optimism.' It was like speaking of a 'vulgar martyrdom' or 'common crucifixion'. Dickens was talking about what he knew about: he knew from personal experience what 'a little pleasure' meant to the poor, he knew that there was no greater happiness than 'the happiness of the unhappy'. No other writer, claims Chesterton, has 'ever come so near the quick nerve of happiness as his descriptions of the rare extravagances of the poor'. When, for example, Kit Nubbles takes his family to the theatre, Dickens 'seizes on the real source of the whole pleasure; a holy fear', the fear that, when he asks the waiter for a pot of beer, the waiter may respond, as one poor man to another, with a snub. But, as Chesterton conveys with a brilliant paradox, Dickens enters fully into the immense relief of Kit, when the waiter, 'instead of saying, "Did you address that language to me," said, "Pot of beer, sir; yes, sir." That internal and quivering humility of Kit is the only way to enjoy life or banquets; and the fear of the waiter is the beginning of dining.'[22]

However, Dickens also understood only too well the privations of the poor, and hated nothing more than the patronizing attitude of intellectuals towards them—'the whole tone taken by three-quarters of the political and economic world': 'It was a vague and vulgar Benthamism with a rollicking Tory touch in it. It explained to the poor their duties with a cold and coarse philanthropy unendurable by any free man. It also had at its command a kind of brutal banter, a loud good-humour... He fell furiously on all their ideas: the cheap advice to live cheaply, the base advice to live basely, above all, the preposterous primary assumption that the rich are to advise the poor and not the poor the rich.' Dickens did not have to sympathize with the poor in the usual sense of that word, since he actually sympathized with them in the literal sense of the word—unlike the 'philanthropists':

[22] *CD* 68, 190–2.

Dickens had sympathy with the poor in the Greek and literal sense; he suffered with them mentally; for the things that irritated them were the things that irritated him. He did not pity the people, or even champion the people, or even merely love the people; in this matter he was the people. He alone in our literature is the voice not merely of the social substratum, but even of the subconsciousness of the substratum. He utters the secret anger of the humble. He says what the uneducated only think, or even only feel, about the educated. And in nothing is he so genuinely such a voice as in this fact of his fiercest mood being reserved for methods that are counted scientific and progressive. Pure and exalted atheists talk themselves into believing that the working-classes are turning with indignant scorn from the churches. The working-classes are not indignant against the churches in the least. The things the working-classes really are indignant against are the hospitals.... The things the poor hate are the modern things, the rationalistic things—doctors, inspectors, poor law guardians, professional philanthropy. They never showed any reluctance to be helped by the old and corrupt monasteries. They will often die rather than be helped by the modern and efficient workhouse. Of all this anger, good or bad, Dickens is the voice of an accusing energy.... If the barricades went up in our streets and the poor became masters, I think the priests would escape, I fear the gentlemen would; but I believe the gutters would be simply running with the blood of philanthropists.[23]

The reference to the poor in the Middle Ages and their monasteries brings us to the other central, critical rather than biographical, paradox of Chesterton's study: Dickens's attitude to the Middle Ages. No one was more contemptuous of the Middle Ages than Dickens or more enthusiastic about modern progress—and yet Dickens 'loved whatever good things the Middle Ages left behind' and loathed 'the smug and stingy philosophy' of Benthamism, the 'exclusive creation' of progressive nineteenth-century England. One of the 'good things' that the Middle Ages had left behind was the feast of Christmas, and Dickens 'was at one with the poor in this chief matter... of special festivity'. There was 'nothing on which the poor are more criticized'—not least by philanthropic intellectuals—'than on the point of spending large sums on small feasts; and... there is nothing in which they are more right'. Christmas is a recurring theme in Chesterton, and the 'Christmas sentiment' in Dickens, the 'cosiness, that is the comfort that depends upon a discomfort surrounding it', was one that was very close to Chesterton's own heart. Apart from comfort and cosiness, there were two other very Chestertonian features of Christmas: first, its 'dramatic quality' of 'limitation', such as the time for opening the presents—the

---

[23] *CD* 137–9.

'hour has come or it has not come'; and, second, the 'great Christmas element' was 'the element of the grotesque'—that is, what Chesterton elsewhere calls the 'genial grotesque', which he thought so characteristic of English literature[24]—like the ghost stories traditionally told on Christmas Eve. Nowhere in English literature, Chesterton thought, was the state known as happiness better described than in Dickens's Christmas tales.[25]

But Christmas was only one, if the most obvious, example of the medievalism of Dickens. To Chesterton the great paradox was that, for all his 'cheapest cockney utilitarianism', upon Dickens paradoxically 'descended the real tradition of "Merry England"', and not upon the pallid mediaevalists who thought they were reviving it', as he explains in one of the great passages in *Charles Dickens*:

The Pre-Raphaelites, the Gothicists, the admirers of the Middle Ages, had in their subtlety and sadness the spirit of the present day. Dickens had in his buffoonery and bravery the spirit of the Middle Ages. He was much more mediaeval in his attacks on mediaevalism than they were in their defences of it. It was he who had the things of Chaucer, the love of large jokes and long stories and brown ale and all the white roads of England. Like Chaucer he loved story within story, every man telling a tale. Like Chaucer he saw something openly comic in men's motley trades. Sam Weller would have been a great gain to the Canterbury Pilgrimage and told an admirable story. Rossetti's Damozel would have been a great bore, regarded as too fast by the Prioress and too priggish by the Wife of Bath. It is said that in the somewhat sickly Victorian revival of feudalism which was called 'Young England', a nobleman hired a hermit to live in his grounds. It is also said that the hermit struck for more beer. Whether this anecdote be true or not, it is always told as showing a collapse from the ideal of the Middle Ages to the level of the present day. But in the mere act of striking for beer the holy man was very much more 'mediaeval' than the fool who employed him.

But nothing was so medieval in Dickens as his 'defence of Christmas': 'In fighting for Christmas he was fighting for the old European festival, Pagan and Christian, for that trinity of eating, drinking and praying which to moderns appears irreverent, for the holy day which is really a holiday.' Yet in spite of all his unconscious medievalism, Dickens had no time at all for the Middle Ages: 'He had himself the most babyish ideas about the past. He supposed the Middle Ages to have consisted of tournaments and torture-chambers, he supposed himself to be a brisk man of the manufacturing age, almost a Utilitarian.' And yet there he was defending 'the

---

[24] *LL* 141.   [25] *CD* 138–40; *ACD* 313–14.

mediaeval feast which was going out against the Utilitarianism which was coming in', there he was fighting for all that was good in the medievalism, while only seeing all that was bad in it. But then, after all, he was no more interested than were the medievals themselves in medievalism:

He cared as little for mediaevalism as the mediaevals did. He cared as much as they did for lustiness and virile laughter and sad tales of good lovers and pleasant tales of good lovers. He would have been very much bored by Ruskin and Walter Pater if they had explained to him the strange sunset tints of Lippi and Botticelli. He had no pleasure in looking on the dying Middle Ages. But he looked on the living Middle Ages, on a piece of the old uproarious superstition still unbroken; and he hailed it like a new religion. The Dickens character ate pudding to an extent at which the modern mediaevalists turned pale. They would do every kind of honour to an old observance, except observing it. They would pay to a Church feast every sort of compliment except feasting.

Theologically, Dickens was hardly a Christian in any way the Middle Ages would have recognized: no doubt he did not believe in 'a personal devil', and yet paradoxically 'he certainly created a personal devil in every one of his books'. And a devil like Quilp 'is precisely the devil of the Middle Ages; he belongs to that amazingly healthy period when even the lost spirits were hilarious'. To be a devil seriously meant for Chesterton being a devil humorously.

Quilp is not in the least unhappy. His whole picturesqueness consists in the fact that he has a kind of hellish happiness, an atrocious hilarity that makes him go bounding about like an indiarubber ball. Quilp is not in the least bitter; he has an unaffected gaiety, an expansiveness, an universality. He desires to hurt people in the same hearty way that a good-natured man desires to help them. He likes to poison people with the same kind of clamorous camaraderie with which an honest man likes to stand them drink.[26]

Being medieval in spirit meant inevitably also being Catholic in spirit, although again Dickens had about as much sympathy for and understanding of the Roman Catholic Church as he had for the Middle Ages: not only did he never understand 'the mystery of the immutable Church', but when he came across it in Europe 'he simply called it an old-world superstition, and sat looking at it like a moonlit ruin'. In arguing that Dickens was unconsciously medieval and even Catholic, Chesterton was exercising the true role of the literary critic as he saw it: 'Criticism does not exist to say

---

[26] *CD* 130–2, 201.

about authors the things that they knew themselves. It exists to say the things about them which they did not know themselves.' Defending the exaggeration of Dickens's caricatures, Chesterton explains that their creator knew 'what it is to feel a joy so vital and violent that only impossible characters can express that'. For, just as Catholic Christianity says that 'any man could be a saint if he chose', so Dickens believed in the 'encouraging of any body to be any thing'—so much so that, although he 'tried to make some of his people appear dull people . . . he could not keep them dull'. Even in Scrooge Chesterton finds 'a heartiness in his inhospitable sentiments that is akin to humour and therefore to humanity', for there 'glows' through him 'the great furnace of real happiness . . . that great furnace, the heart of Dickens'. Perhaps it is not altogether fanciful to detect an allusion here to the Catholic cult of the Sacred Heart of Jesus, given that Chesterton attributes divinity to Dickens as creator: 'One of the godlike things about Dickens is his quantity, as such, the enormous output, the incredible fecundity of his invention,' so much so that his 'power' is shown even in his 'scraps', 'just as the virtue of a saint is said to be shown in fragments of his property or rags from his robe'. But like the divine Creator, Chesterton does not create cardboard characters; they have the same sort of relation to him as human creatures to God; they are dependent on him, but they are not puppets: 'He is not come, as a writer, that his creatures may copy life and copy its narrowness; he is come that they may have life, and that they may have it more abundantly.' And, like God, he loves and values even his most unattractive creatures, like Mr Toots: 'He makes us not only like, but love, not only love, but reverence this little dunce and cad. The power to do this is a power truly and literally to be called divine.' Because Dickens 'conceives an endless joy' in conceiving his immortal creations, he is 'close to popular religion, which is the ultimate and reliable religion'. That this popular religion is Catholicism is made plain a few pages later, when Chesterton speaks of how the 'fragments' and 'the wrecks of that enormous religion', the cult of Dickens, have become part of ordinary language spoken by people who may never have opened a novel by Dickens—'just as Catholics can live in a tradition of Christianity without having looked at the New Testament'. Again, the 'abnormal amount of drinking in a page of Dickens'—'If you reckon up the beers and brandies of Mr Bob Sawyer, with the care of an arithmetician and the deductions of a pathologist, they rise alarmingly like a rising tide at sea'—is only the 'celebration of social drinking as a supreme symbol of social living' that Dickens's novels 'share with almost all the great literature of mankind, including the New Testament', where wine is a 'sacrament'.

Indeed, *Charles Dickens* ends with the sentence: 'And all roads point at last to an ultimate inn, where we shall meet Dickens and all his characters; and when we drink again it shall be from the great flagons in the tavern at the end of the world.'[27]

The concept of the 'holy fool' was hardly familiar to the Protestantism with which Dickens was familiar. It is very much, though, a Catholic and even more an Eastern Orthodox idea (one has only to think of Dostoevsky). Yet again, according to Chesterton, Dickens unconsciously created characters that conform to the type. Not only that, but his 'great characters' are 'all great fools'. Thus Miss Podsnap in *Our Mutual Friend* 'is, like Toots, a holy fool'. And, just as 'Bottom the Weaver is great because he is foolish', so too 'Mr Toots is great because he is foolish'. Mr Pickwick is 'wise enough to be made a fool of', 'he will be always "taken in" '; but then literally 'to be taken in everywhere is to see the inside of everything'. Mrs Nickleby 'is one of those fools who are wiser than the world'. These holy fools, like the Misses Pecksniff in *Martin Chuzzlewit*, are certainly not treated reverently, otherwise they would be just cardboard characters, as the characters Dickens 'tried to treat unsmilingly and grandly' are the very characters who are not human: 'Dickens had to make a character humorous before he could make it human...when once he had laughed at a thing it is sacred for ever.' The secret of Dickens's 'humble characters' is that 'they are all great fools', a 'great fool' being someone 'who is above wisdom rather than below it'. And this kind of fool is defined in very Catholic terms:

The present that each man brings in hand is his own incredible personality. In the most sacred sense and in the most literal sense of the phrase, he 'gives himself away'. Now, the man who gives himself away does the last act of generosity; he is like a martyr, a lover, or a monk. But he is almost certainly what we commonly call a fool.

A character like Toots is 'turned from a small fool into a great Fool' not by being altered 'in any vital point' but by Dickens's 'enthusiasm', which 'fills us, as does the love of God, with a glorious shame; after all he has only found in Toots what we might have found for ourselves'. It is Dickens again who has properly understood the gospel 'injunction to suffer fools gladly': 'We always lay the stress on the word "suffer", and interpret the

[27] *CD* 89, 96, 128, 137, 162, 178, 187, 209; *ACD* 272, 292, 336. See also Ian Ker, *The Catholic Revival in English Literature, 1845–1961* (Notre Dame, IN: University of Notre Dame Press, 2003), 79–89.

passage as one urging resignation. It might be better, perhaps, to lay the stress upon the word "gladly", and make our familiarity with fools a delight, and almost a dissipation.' In the same way, with Dickens we can even suffer bores *gladly*: 'Almost every one of his amusing characters is in reality a great bore. The very people that we fly to in Dickens are the very people that we fly from in life.' And Chesterton even claims that Toots in *Dombey and Son*, not one of Dickens's better-known characters, is 'in some ways the masterpiece of Dickens'. The reason he gives is that in this creation, more than anywhere else, Dickens shows how essential humility is for that wonder which was the basis of Chesterton's own philosophy, and indeed his Christianity.

Nowhere else does Dickens express with such astonishing insight and truth his main contention, which is that to be good and idiotic is not a poor fate, but, on the contrary, an experience of primeval innocence, which wonders at all things. Dickens did not know, any more than any great man ever knows, what was the particular thing that he had to preach. He did not know it; he only preached it. But the particular thing that he had to preach was this: That humility is the only possible basis of enjoyment; that if one has no other way of being humble except being poor, then it is better to be poor, and to enjoy; that if one has no other way of being humble except being imbecile, then it is better to be imbecile, and to enjoy.[28]

These 'great, grotesque characters are almost entirely to be found where Dickens found them—among the poorer classes'. Public personalities (like intellectuals) have to 'prove' that they are 'clever', and are consequently 'small men'. Among them will not be found the 'rich and reeking personality', the 'truly great and gorgeous personality... who talks as no one else could talk'. Such a person is 'too large' for 'the glory of this world', which 'is a very small and priggish affair'. But, quite apart from that, Dickens 'could only get to the most solemn emotions adequately if he got to them through the grotesque', for he 'had to be ridiculous in order to begin to be true'. Toots, for example, is a ridiculous character, but it is Toots who is 'in the most serious sense, a true lover', for Dickens had revealed 'a certain grotesque greatness inside an obscure and even unattractive type'. Chesterton understands perfectly why Dickens's 'serious' characters fail, while his comic characters succeed brilliantly: 'His characters that begin solemn end futile; his characters that begin frivolous end solemn in the best sense.' The phenomenon was a particularly striking example of Chesterton's

---

[28] *CD* 94, 104,147, 184–5, 187–8; *ACD* 261, 326.

great paradoxical theme that to be serious is to be humorous: 'His foolish figures are not only more entertaining than his serious figures, they are also much more serious.' Chesterton does not deny that the later, more 'serious' Dickens achieved a human and social realism that is not there in the earlier novels—'but were not his earlier characters more like immortals?' After all, *there* was 'beatific buffoonery'. But that does not mean that Chesterton thought that Dickens's comic characters, his 'caricatures', existed only in the world of Dickens's imagination. They were real people but writ large. They were the ordinary people the intellectuals of Chesterton's day dismissed, but for the democratic Dickens they were the *real* people not those who bestride the 'defined and lighted public stage'. This is 'the last and deepest lesson of Dickens', explains Chesterton in a magnificent passage that raises literary criticism to the level of creative art:

It is in our own daily life that we are to look for the portents and the prodigies. . . . It is true of the whole stream and substance of our daily experience; every instant we reject a great fool merely because he is foolish. Every day we neglect Tootses and Swivellers, Guppys and Joblings, Simmerys and Flashers. Every day we lose the last sight of Jobbling and Chuckster, the Analytical Chemist, or the Marchioness. Every day we are missing a monster whom we might easily love, and an imbecile whom we should certainly admire. This is the real gospel of Dickens; the inexhaustible opportunities offered by the liberty and the variety of man. . . . It is the utterly unknown people, who can grow in all directions like an exuberant tree. It is in our interior lives that we find that people are too much themselves. It is in our private life that we find people intolerably individual, that we find them swelling into the enormous contours, and taking on the colours of caricatures.[29]

Because Dickens's realism lies in realizing the vividness of everyday life, there was one thing he could not depict—dullness: 'his vitality was so violent that he could not introduce into his books the genuine impression even of a moment of monotony.' This 'inability to imagine tedium' meant that he could 'splendidly describe gloomy places, but he could not describe dreary places'. He could attack any abuse except 'the soul-destroying potency of routine'. Nevertheless, by making characters like Squeers and Bumble so vivid, 'he flattered them; but he destroyed them with the flattery'. Before he could make them die, he had to make them live.[30]

For Chesterton, the novels of Dickens are really the characters of Dickens. Strictly speaking, he exaggerates, there are no novels—there are 'simply lengths cut from the flowing and mixed substance called Dickens'.

[29] *CD* 146–7, 175–6, 185–6, 188–9.　　　　[30] *CD* 199.

Characters do not necessarily particularly belong to the novel in which they appear: 'There is no reason why Sam Weller, in the course of his wanderings, should not wander into "Nicholas Nickleby". There is no reason why Major Bagstock, in his brisk way, should not walk straight out of "Dombey and Son" and straight into "Martin Chuzzlewit".' And so the 'primary elements' of Dickens's novels 'are not the stories, but the characters who affect the stories—or, more often still, the characters who do not affect the story'. Indeed, they

are at their best when they have least to do. Dickens's characters are perfect as long as he can keep them out of his stories. Bumble is divine until a dark and practical secret is entrusted to him—as if anybody but a lunatic would entrust a secret to Bumble. Micawber is noble when he is doing nothing; but he is quite unconvincing when he is spying on Uriah Heep, for obviously neither Micawber nor any one else would employ Micawber as a private detective.

Chesterton suggests that Dickens was a 'mythologist' rather than a novelist, who created 'gods' rather than men:

They live statically, in a perpetual summer of being themselves. It was not the aim of Dickens to show the effect of time and circumstances upon a character; it was not even his aim to show the effect of a character on time and circumstance. It is worth remarking ... that whenever he tried to describe change in a character, he made a mess of it ...

Critics who complain about Dickens's 'unchanging characters and recurring catch-words' as though they indicated 'a mere stiffness and lack of living movement miss the point and nature of his work'. The 'old comic writers' were not 'dull because they wished their unchanging characters to last for ever'. But the 'undying vigour' of the old comic story 'with its endless jokes', like 'popular religion, with its endless joys', is no longer fashionable in a culture that believes that 'you can have too much of a good thing—a blasphemous belief, which at one blow wrecks all the heavens that men have hoped for. The grand old defiers of God were not afraid of an eternity of torment. We have come to be afraid of an eternity of joy.'[31]

It should have become obvious by now why Chesterton is the perfect commentator on Dickens—because they had so much in common, as reviewers noted. And it is no surprise that Chesterton finds his gospel of wonder in Dickens, with his 'incomparable hunger and pleasure for the

---

[31] *CD* 84–5, 87–9, 123.

vitality and the variety, for the infinite eccentricity of existence'. Like Chesterton, he felt the strangeness of the world: 'This sentiment of the grotesqueness of the universe ran through Dickens's brain and body like the mad blood of the elves.' For Chesterton, 'its merit is that it is wild and utterly unexplained. Its merit is precisely that none of us could have conceived such a thing, that we should have rejected the bare idea of it as miracle and unreason. It is the best of all impossible worlds.' And he knew that that was how Dickens saw it too. That, for instance, was why 'the round, moon-like spectacles of Samuel Pickwick... are fixed in that grave surprise which is the only real happiness that is possible to man. Pickwick's round face is like a round and honourable mirror, in which are reflected all the fantasies of earthly existence; for surprise is, strictly speaking, the only kind of reflection.' Pickwick does not 'see things through the rosy spectacles of the modern optimist or the green-smoked spectacles of the pessimist; he sees it through the crystal glasses of his own innocence. One must see the world clearly even in order to see its wildest poetry.' Chesterton is delighted that Dickens chose an old, middle-class man as his hero for a 'romantic adventure', as it gives him the opportunity to defend the middle classes so despised by the writers and intellectuals of his day. Molière in his day had laughed at M. Jourdain for delightedly discovering that he had been talking prose all his life—but M. Jourdain 'towers above' the writer because he had 'the freshness to enjoy a fresh fact, the freshness to enjoy even an old one'. M. Jourdain was a 'true romantic', like Pickwick 'the type' of 'the romance of the middle classes'. Intellectuals like artists

profess to find the bourgeoisie dull; as if artists had any business to find anything dull. Decadents talk contemptuously of its conventions and its set tasks; it never occurs to them that conventions and set tasks are the very way to keep that greenness in the grass and that redness in the roses—which they have lost for ever. Stevenson, in his incomparable 'Lantern Bearers', describes the ecstasy of a schoolboy in the mere fact of buttoning a dark lantern under a dark great-coat. If you wish for the ecstasy of the schoolboy, you must have the boy; but you must also have the school. Strict opportunities and defined hours are the very outline of that enjoyment.

Again we touch on that key Chestertonian theme, for it is the very despised *limitations* of the bourgeoisie that he maintains are conducive to, not destructive of, the romance of wonder.[32]

---

[32] *CD* 91–3, 203; *ACD* 406.

Another paradox Chesterton enjoys highlighting is what he calls 'the conjunction of common sense with uncommon sensibility' in Dickens. His 'interests' were the same as the 'ordinary man', 'but he felt all of them more excitedly'. He had the power of expressing 'with an energy and brilliance quite uncommon the things close to the common mind'. And Chesterton has his answer to those twentieth-century intellectuals who elevated the artist and writer above the masses and praised art that was esoteric and incomprehensible to the ordinary person:

Commonness and the common mind are now generally spoken of as meaning in some manner inferiority and the inferior mind; the mind of the mere mob. But the common mind means the mind of all the artists and heroes; or else it would not be common.... and it was this that Dickens grasped and developed. In everybody there is a certain thing that loves babies, that fears death, that likes sunlight: that thing enjoys Dickens.

His closeness to the 'common mind' was shown in the two things in which he excelled as a writer: not only 'his humour', but 'his horror': he 'supped on horrors as he supped on Christmas puddings'. The same writer imagined 'the humane hospitalities of Pickwick' as well as 'the inhuman laughter of Fagin's den'. But while he knew how to 'make the flesh creep', unlike the Decadents he did not 'make the soul crawl'. This ability 'to make the flesh creep and to make the sides ache were a sort of twins of his spirit'. Both humour and horror are 'universal'. And they are the 'best expression' of Dickens's liking for 'quite ordinary things'—although he 'made an extraordinary fuss about them'. It was hardly surprising that Dickens had fallen out of favour by the time Chesterton was writing: 'he was merely a normal man' with an 'abnormal normality'. He was undeniably 'a genius and an unique writer, but he did not wish to be an unique writer'. So uninterested was he in being 'original' that he 'denied his own divine originality, and pretended that he had plagiarized from life'. Similarly, when abroad Dickens was not interested in the things intellectuals are interested in: he took 'to his heart the streets, as it were, rather than the spires of the Continent'. It was the differences from ordinary English life that struck him—'the things that do strike the traveller as extraordinary are the ordinary things, the food, the clothes, the vehicles; the strange things are cosmopolitan, the common things are national and peculiar'. The Gothic architecture of France or Germany can be seen in England—but not the German beer-garden. The differences from England that interested Dickens were the differences that 'the simple and not the subtle' see: 'he saw all his colours through the clear eyes of the poor.'[33]

A similar paradox in Chesterton's view was that, while Dickens is in an obvious sense an eccentric and extravagant writer, he himself 'detested and despised extravagance'; he was 'an immoderate jester because he was a moderate thinker'; insofar as he was a 'buffoon' he was 'laughing at buffoonery'. His own innate 'good sense' and 'sanity' made him feel 'the full insanity of all extreme tendencies'. In politics he might look like an 'almost anarchic satirist', but he was in fact 'a very moderate politician'. And so, while he created Stiggins and Chadband 'out of the quietude of his religious preference', the Barnacles and Bounderbys 'were produced in a kind of' (and Chesterton enjoys reusing a striking phrase he had already used earlier in the book) 'ecstasy of the ordinary, of the obvious in political justice'.[34]

Chesterton knew that there was what he called a 'growth of technique and probability' in the later novels, where Dickens's characters were 'more like men', and Dickens improved 'as an artist if not always as a creator'. Modern critics would regard these 'serious' novels as the best novels of Dickens; but Chesterton insists that Dickens's 'serious genius' was his 'comic genius'. Dickens for Chesterton is the supreme embodiment of his conviction not only that 'serious' is not the opposite of 'humorous', but that the most serious truths can be expressed through the medium of humour. Indeed, Chesterton had a quasi-religious conception of humour: 'A good joke is the one ultimate and sacred thing which cannot be criticized. Our relations with a good joke are direct and even divine relations. We speak of "seeing" a joke just as we speak of "seeing" a ghost or a vision.' And in the case of Dickens supremely, 'Humour was his medium; his only way of approaching emotion.' His 'pure farce' is not 'superficial' but 'goes down to the roots of the universe'. He, on the other hand, would have been 'surprised to see all the work he thought solid and responsible wasted almost utterly away, but the shortest frivolities and the most momentary jokes remaining like colossal rocks for ever'. When a Dickens character becomes emotional, 'he grows more and more into a gargoyle or grotesque'. However, it was not only emotion that Dickens expressed through humour, but also his 'serious moral ideas' that again he expressed through the 'fantastic medium' of frivolity. It is the comic not the serious characters who tell us about 'the human soul'—although Chesterton

---

[33] *CD* 100–1, 103, 111–12, 128–9, 148; *ACD* 264.   [34] *CD* 164–7.

makes an exception for 'some of the later experiments'. The 'whole superiority' of Dickens over an 'intellectual' like Gissing, in Chesterton's view, was that 'Gissing would have liked to prove that poor men could instruct themselves and could instruct others', whereas what was important for Dickens was that 'poor men could amuse themselves and could amuse him': 'He troubled little about the mere education of that life; he declared two essential things about it—that it was laughable, and that it was livable.' Intellectuals can amuse themselves with 'epigrams', but the 'humble characters' of Dickens 'amuse each other with themselves'. Even in the very last, unfinished novel, the comic genius of Dickens 'makes one splendid and staggering appearance, like a magician saying farewell to mankind'. It is as if Dickens had kept the best joke till the end. In this 'dark and secretive story', he has 'calmly inserted one entirely delightful and entirely insane passage':

I mean the frantic and inconceivable epitaph of Mrs Sapsea, that which describes her as 'the reverential wife' of Thomas Sapsea, speaks of her consistency in 'looking up to him', and ends with the words, spaced out so admirably on the tombstone, 'Stranger pause. And ask thyself this question, Canst thou do likewise? If not, with a blush retire.' Not the wildest tale in Pickwick contains such an impossibility as that; Dickens dare scarcely have introduced it, even as one of Jingle's lies. In no human churchyard will you find that invaluable tombstone; indeed, you could scarcely find it in any world where there are churchyards. You could scarcely have such an immortal folly as that in a world where there is also death. Mr Sapsea is one of the golden things stored up for us in a better world.[35]

But this wonderfully funny passage is one of 'the golden things' that Chesterton has 'stored up' for us in this world, and, if the 'wild epitaph of Mrs Sapsea should be the serious epitaph of Dickens',[36] then this passage makes a suitable epitaph for *Charles Dickens*, one of Chesterton's finest achievements, possibly his finest achievement, and one of the great works of literary criticism. Chesterton's lack of attention to and interest in the later novels makes the study certainly incomplete and one-sided, but his study of the earlier novels is criticism where the critic becomes as much a creator as the subject of his criticism.

Reviewers noted, as usual, a number of factual inaccuracies, including the statement that everything Dickens wrote was a work of art, even the very postcards he wrote. When it was pointed out that this was impossible, since postcards had not yet been invented, Chesterton's response was: 'A

---

[35] *CD* 170, 175–6, 181, 184; *ACD* 253, 276–7, 299, 387.   [36] *CD* 176.

wonderful instance of Dickens's never-varying propensity to keep ahead of his age.'[37]

More seriously, Dickens's daughter Kate Perugini wrote from 32 Victoria Rd, Kensington, a couple of months after publication on 26 October to correct him on two points of fact. But, first, she wanted to thank him for his 'very interesting' book—'nothing so interesting', including Gissing's study, which was 'delightful in many ways', had appeared since Forster's *Life*. However, she had noticed two mistakes, 'one particularly'.[38] Chesterton had said that the young Dickens had been 'suddenly thrown into the society of a whole family of girls' and had fallen 'in love with all of them', but 'by a kind of accident he got hold of the wrong sister'.[39] In fact, while her mother was aged 'between eighteen and nineteen' when she was courted by her father, the next oldest Hogarth sister, Mary, was only 'aged between fourteen and fifteen, very young and childish in appearance'. As for the two youngest sisters, they were only aged eight and three and were still in the nursery and not even able to attend their older sister's wedding! The truth was that there was 'no sister with whom it was possible to fall in love' except the one Dickens did fall in love with![40] The 'other little mistake' that Chesterton had made was to assume that his family had to listen to Dickens's 'railings' when, as was true, he was 'often unhappy'. In fact, 'when he was really sorrowful, he was very quiet, and depression with him never took the form of petulance, for in his unhappy moods he was singularly gentle, and thoughtful of those surrounding him'.[41] It seems that Chesterton and Frances called on Mrs Perugini at the end of November or early in December, for Frances wrote to the publisher Methuen on 25 November, presumably with regard to a reprint: 'Mrs Perugini and Miss Hogarth are a little agitated about a paragraph in my husband's Dickens. Until my husband has seen them, which he is going to do early next week, please do not print (if you are doing so) as some alteration may be necessary. I fancy it is only a matter of a few words.'[42] Subsequently, Kate Perugini

---

[37] Ward, *GKC* 156.

[38] Kate Perugini to G. K. Chesterton, 26 Oct. 1906, BL Add. MS 73239, fo. 64.

[39] *CD* 75–6.

[40] Kate Perugini to G. K. Chesterton, 26 Oct. 1906, BL Add. MS 73239, fo. 65; Kate Perugini to G. K. Chesterton, n.d., BL Add. MS 73239, fo. 71.

[41] Kate Perugini to G. K. Chesterton, 26 Oct. 1906, BL Add. MS 73239, fo. 65.

[42] Frances Chesterton to Mr Methuen, 25 Nov. [*sic*], BL Add. MS 73231A, fo. 4. The letter has been annotated in pencil, presumably by Dorothy Collins, '1905', but it is clear that it belongs to 1906.

wrote to Frances to say that she had been 'thinking over our interview' and felt that she did not 'adequately express all the gratitude I really feel to your husband for his extreme kindness in wishing to meet our views upon the subject of the Hogarth family'. She was 'chiefly' anxious for her mother's sake that 'this thing should be set straight'. She was sure that when engaged to her father her mother was 'a very winning and affectionate creature, and although the marriage...turned out "a dismal failure", I am also convinced that my dear father gained much from her refining influence' and that of her family and 'perhaps' otherwise 'would never have been quite what he became'.[43] In the event, Chesterton never rectified either of the mistakes to which Kate Perugini had drawn his attention.[44] Perhaps she never realized. At any rate, she kept in touch with the Chestertons, writing, for example, nearly four years later a letter to Frances in which she discusses the characters in her father's novels, and says that she was always glad to see them both.[45] Even after they moved to Beaconsfield, she used to visit, according to Dorothy Collins, and talk about the Dickens family life.[46]

Shaw also wrote to express his concern about one or two inaccuracies in *Charles Dickens*, which he had 'pounced on...and read...right slap through'.[47] He took the opportunity to point out to his bibulous friend that 'Dickens's moderation in drinking must be interpreted according to the old standard for mail coach travellers'.

In the Staplehurst railway accident...he congratulated himself on having a bottle and a half of brandy with him; and he killed several of the survivors by administering hatfuls of it as first aid. I invite you to consider the effect on the public mind if, in a railway accident today, Mr Gilbert Chesterton were reported as

[43] Kate Perugini to Frances Chesterton, n.d., BL Add. MS 73239, fo. 66.

[44] There is no obvious text that Kate Perugini was thinking of when she complained about what Chesterton had said about her father's 'railings', but since the glaring error about the sisters was never corrected, it is hardly likely that this mistake was ever corrected. She may have been thinking of this sentence: 'He was everything that we currently call a weak man; he was a man hung on wires; he was a man who might at any moment cry like a child; he was so sensitive to criticism that one may say that he lacked a skin; he was so nervous that he allowed great tragedies in his life to arise only out of nerves' (*CD* 71). Or there are the later sentences, 'Sometimes his nerve snapped; and then he was mad' (*CD* 167), and 'he had the temper of an irrational invalid' (*CD* 174).

[45] Kate Perugini to Frances Chesterton, 28 Aug. 1910, BL Add. MS 73239, fos 69–70.

[46] BL Add. MS 73477, fo. 112.   [47] Ward, *GKC* 156.

having been in the train with a bottle and a half of brandy on his person as normal refreshment.[48]

William James wrote from America: 'O Chesterton, but you are a darling! I have just read your "Dickens"—it's as good as Rabelais. Thanks!'[49] Swinburne's 'Grand Vizier', Watts-Dunton, wrote to Frances to say that the 'high priest' liked the book very much and would like to talk to him about it. An English theatre critic who had visited President Theodore Roosevelt reported that Chesterton was the only English writer he had mentioned and that he had just been reading *Charles Dickens* with great appreciation.[50] In 1927 T. S. Eliot was to write, 'there is no better critic of Dickens living than Mr Chesterton'.[51]

3

Meanwhile, Chesterton's life in Fleet Street continued as usual. Recalling it in his *Autobiography*, he pondered on the 'profound problem of how I ever managed to fall on my feet in Fleet Street'; it was 'a mystery'. His 'success' he attributed on the whole 'to having listened respectfully and rather bashfully to the very best advice, given by all the best journalists who had achieved the best sort of success in journalism; and then going away and doing the exact opposite'. Their unanimous advice was to find out what the particular paper wanted and write accordingly. On the contrary, 'partly by accident and ignorance and partly through the real rabid certainties of youth', he never 'wrote any article that was at all suitable to any paper'. On the Nonconformist *Daily News* he wrote about French cafés and Catholic cathedrals—'and they loved it, because they had never heard of them before'. On the Socialist *Clarion* he 'defended medieval theology and all the things their readers had never heard of; and their readers did not mind me a bit'. This 'old Bohemian life of Fleet Street', with its 'taverns and ragged pressmen and work and recreation coming at random at all hours of the night', had since been destroyed by 'the materialism of machinery'. And Chesterton had sadly to agree with a

[48] George Bernard Shaw to G. K. Chesterton, 6 Sept. 1906, in *Bernard Shaw: Collected Letters, 1898–1910*, ed. Dan H. Laurence (London: Max Reinhardt, 1972), 646.

[49] Ward, *GKC* 323.   [50] Barker, 163–4.

[51] T. S. Eliot, *Selected Essays* (London: Faber and Faber, 1958), 461.

newspaper proprietor who assured him that a newspaper office was now like any other office.[52]

One of the Fleet Street characters Chesterton enjoyed recalling was a Johnston Stephen, of the same Scottish family as Leslie Stephen, who told him that he would be a Roman Catholic if it was not that he did not think that he believed in God. A patriotic Scotsman, Stephen did not endear himself to his Presbyterian countrymen with such sentiments: when asked if he did not agree that a corrupt Church was crying out for a Reformation, 'he answered with disconcerting warmth, "Who can doubt it? How horrible must have been the corruption which could have tolerated for so long three Catholic priests like John Knox and John Calvin and Martin Luther." '[53]

Looking back, Chesterton thought that 'the most brilliant' of the Fleet Street journalists who 'kept their intellectual independence' was 'Keith' Jones, 'the Queen of Fleet Street', who was ever ready to try her hand at any sort of journalism, including melodramatic romances for women readers. The story was told that, 'having driven whole teams of plotters and counter-plotters successfully through a serious Scotch newspaper, she was pursuing one of the side-plots for a few chapters, when she received a telegram from the editor, "You have left your hero and heroine tied up in a cavern under the Thames for a week, and they are not married." ' Chesterton suspected that the same lady was involved with his brother in a spoof correspondence in the *Eye-Witness*, when Cecil was editor. It began, he thought, with his brother writing an article about a meeting between H. G. Wells and Brooker Washington, a black American publicist, in which Cecil suggested that Wells failed to understand the situation in the segregated South. In response, a letter from Bexley was published warning of the dangers of racial mixing and intermarriage, signed 'White Man'. Wells replied in a letter headed 'The White Man of Bexley', 'as if the man were a sort of monster' saying that 'he did not know what life was like "among the pure Whites of Bexley", but that elsewhere meeting people did not always mean marrying them; "The etiquette is calmer." ' Next there appeared a letter signed 'Black Man', and then 'a more detached query, I should guess from some Brahmin or Parsee student at some college, pointing out that the racial problem was not confined to the races of Africa; and asking what view was taken of intermarriage with the races of Asia. He signed his letter "Brown Man".' Finally, appeared a letter, 'almost every word' of which

---

[52] *A.* 176–8.   [53] *A.* 179–80.

Chesterton remembered, 'for it was short and simple and touching in its appeal to larger and more tolerant ideals':

Sir,

May I express my regret that you should continue a correspondence which causes considerable pain to many innocent persons who, by no fault of their own, but by the iron laws of nature, inherit a complexion uncommon among their fellow-creatures and attractive only to the elite. Surely we can forget all these differences; and, whatever our race or colour, work hand in hand for the broadening of the brotherhood of humanity.

Yours faithfully,
Mauve Man with Green Spots.[54]

Although no book appeared in 1907, the journalism of course continued apace. And in November Chesterton published one of his handful of good serious poems, 'The Secret People', which contains the well-known lines: 'But we are the people of England; and we have not spoken yet. | Smile at us, pay us, pass us. But do not quite forget.' The beginning of the plight of England's poor Chesterton laid squarely at the door of the Reformation that destroyed the monasteries that provided free food and lodging. Then the lords, who 'had eaten the abbey's fruits', came to be more powerful than the king, whom 'they killed' in league with 'the men of the new religion, with their bibles in their boots'.[55] The poem could hardly have been more Catholic in its view of English history. In December 1907, Chesterton also wrote two letters to the *Nation*, in the first of which he accused the paper of a 'strange irritation' with Catholicism that struck him as rather 'a tribute to its strength than as any evidence of its decline' and of 'pathetically' clinging to 'one last Protestant doctrine', having 'openly abandoned all the others'. When the editor demanded to know if he was a Roman Catholic, Chesterton replied, 'I am not. I shall not be until you have convinced me that the Church of England is really the muddle-headed provincial heresy that you make it out.' He followed these letters up with an article defending sacramental confession in the *Daily News* in January 1908.[56]

4

February 1908 saw the publication of Chesterton's most successful work of fiction apart from the Father Brown stories, as well as one of his two

---

[54] *A.* 180–1, 185.   [55] *CP* i. 408–11.   [56] Pearce, 105–6.

apologetic masterpieces. The dedication to his friend Bentley made it clear that *The Man who was Thursday* was born out of the nihilism of the 1890s:

> A cloud was on the mind of men, and wailing went the weather,
> Yea, a sick cloud upon the soul when we were boys together.
> Science announced nonentity and art admired decay . . .[57]

The novel's subtitle 'A Nightmare' is the key to understanding why this novel is more successful than the other novels. Here Chesterton's 'medium' *is* the 'message'—the nightmare of nihilism is evoked precisely in and through a fictional nightmare, a Kafkaesque surrealist nightmare, but where there is at least as much hilarity as there is terror.[58] As we have seen, Chesterton did not consider himself a real novelist, as he liked 'to see ideas or notions wrestling naked . . . and not dressed up in a masquerade as men and women'.[59] But in a nightmare the lack of characterization is not important or even relevant: 'the faces of friends may appear as the faces of fiends.' Nor is narrative a problem, as it is in the other novels, since in a dream events happen without any logic or reason. Both these points are also very relevant to the Father Brown stories, whose brevity obviously does not raise the problem of narrative,[60] and, where characterization again is not relevant, or rather not desirable, since in detective stories the reader must not be told too much about any character, except the detective, but where instead the reader expects the faces of friends will turn out to be the faces of fiends and vice versa. Or, as Chesterton himself put it, 'the detective story is . . . a drama of masks and not of faces. . . . The author cannot tell us until the last chapter any of the most interesting things about the most interesting people.'[61]

This novel of nightmare begins with Gabriel Syme appearing in the artistic colony of Saffron Park (Bedford Park) as a rival poet to Lucian Gregory. Syme, with his angelic first name, stands for law and order; he is in rebellion against his parents' rebellion against convention and stands for common sense and sanity. Lucian, with his satanic first name, is on the

---

[57] *MT* 472.

[58] C. S. Lewis, who first made the parallel with Kafka, speaks of 'the exhilaration as well as the terror'. However, Bernard Bergonzi ignores the terror when he says that 'Chesterton's story never rises above the level of a charade, or at least a prolonged and ingenious joke'. Conlon ii. 72, 182.

[59] See above, p. 126.

[60] Cf. Sullivan, 38; Wills, *Chesterton: Man and Mask*, 125.

[61] *ILN* xxxii. 432.

contrary an anarchist—but in real life quite harmless, as Syme assures his sister. However, in Syme's nightmare Gregory introduces Syme to the Central Anarchist Council, having first sworn him to secrecy. The members of the Council are called after the days of the week, the President being Sunday. There is a vacancy for the member called Thursday, for which Lucian Gregory is standing. But Syme manages to get himself elected in order to infiltrate these anarchists, who are intent not just on throwing bombs but upon abolishing 'Right and Wrong', having in his turn sworn Gregory to secrecy about his own identity as a detective 'philosophical' policeman.[62]

Syme has been recruited into this 'special corps' by its chief, 'a man of massive stature' with his 'back to him'—a significant oddity in view of the author's fascination with the human back that he had expatiated on in his book on Watts (and to which he had returned in *The Napoleon of Notting Hill*, with the curious incident at the beginning when the whimsical Auberon Quin walking behind his two friends in frock-coats suddenly sees two black dragons with evil eyes instead of two black buttons at the back of the frock coats). This corps has been formed to combat 'a crusade against the Family and the State' waged by intellectuals, compared with whom ordinary criminals like thieves were honest men. The poor, in the form of barrel-organ players (a recurrent motif) or the French peasant at the end of the book, who are not attracted by the 'intellectual fanaticism and intellectual crime' of moral anarchy, symbolize normality and sanity in this nightmare world. But it is also the modern world that says one 'must not punish heretics', who are the only people, Syme thinks, 'we have a right to punish'. Sunday had not been present at the meeting when Syme was elected on to the Council, but when Syme first sees him he sees 'the back of a great mountain of a man', a man 'abnormally tall and quite incredibly fat', 'enlarged terribly to scale'. Syme had a sense of nearing 'the headquarters of hell' as he walks across to meet the President, whose 'large face ... grew larger and larger'. Syme might have given his 'allegiance' to this 'superman', but he cannot 'sink' to the 'modern meanness' of 'weak worship of intellect and force'. In the end, all the members of the Council are revealed to be 'philosophical' policemen like Syme and Sunday himself to be the head of this corps.[63]

Who, then, is Sunday? In his own words, he is a 'riddle'—a riddle like nature, like the universe itself. Sunday's 'mockeries' remind Syme of how

---

[62] *MT* 490, 508.   [63] *MT* 508–9, 511, 518–19, 526.

'Nature was always making quite mysterious jokes. Sunday had told them that they would understand him when they had understood the stars.' But when Sunday 'offered the solid stretch of his unconscious back', they felt even more mocked. He 'seemed like the final form of matter', 'absent-minded' in the way that wild animals are 'at once innocent and pitiless'. Syme thinks of Sunday as he thinks of 'the whole world'. When he first saw him, he saw only his back, and he 'knew he was the worst man in the world', indeed 'not a man at all, but a beast dressed up in men's clothes'. But when he saw him face to face, his face 'frightened' him 'because it was so beautiful, because it was so good'. From behind he had seemed 'an animal', but from the front 'a god'. 'Pan', interposes another member of the Council, 'was a god and an animal'. Syme wonders whether 'the mystery of Sunday' is not also 'the mystery of the world': 'When I see the horrible back, I am sure the noble face is but a mask. When I see the face but for an instant, I know the back is only a jest. Bad is so bad, that we cannot but think good an accident; good is so good, that we feel certain that evil could be explained.' That, suddenly exclaims Syme, is 'the secret of the whole world', that 'we have only known the back of the world'. At the end of the book, Sunday reveals himself as 'the Sabbath, 'the peace of God' who rested on the Sabbath after the creation of the world. How then could he be both 'friend' and 'enemy'? Like God in the Book of Job, taxed with the existence of evil and pain, Sunday responds, 'I have heard your complaints . . . And here I think, comes another to complain . . . '. It is the 'real anarchist', Lucian Gregory—'when the sons of God came to present themselves before the Lord, and Satan came also among them', one of the members of the Council quotes from the Book of Job. Gregory curses 'the people in power', who have never suffered like him. Syme responds that now he understands why he had 'to be alone in the dreadful Council of the Days', so that he might 'have the glory and isolation of the anarchist' and 'be as brave and good a man as the dynamiter', in order that 'the real lie of Satan may be flung back in the face of this blasphemer', because he too has suffered. But what about Sunday himself—has he ever suffered?

the great face grew to an awful size . . . grew larger and larger, filling the whole sky; then everything went black. Only in the darkness before it entirely destroyed his brain he seemed to hear a distant voice saying a commonplace text that he had heard somewhere, 'Can ye drink of the cup that I drink of?'[64]

---

[64] *MT* 608, 613, 619, 621–2, 631–4.

Syme then wakes from his nightmare. And, because in dreams people say inconsequential, strange, unexpected things, the voice of Sunday (if it is Sunday), so far only identified with nature or the world itself, quoting Christ's words from the gospel referring to his imminent crucifixion, does not demand the kind of justification it otherwise would. Indeed, the book must be judged as a literary evocation of a nightmare and not of real life.[65] In dreams we grope at meaning and significance, and that is what the novel itself does.

As Chesterton explained in the *Autobiography*, when in the 1890s he was 'so horribly near to being a pessimist', he was 'trying to construct a healthier conception of cosmic life'. It was this stage in his development that he had attempted to fictionalize in a novel, the key to which was its subtitle, 'A Nightmare'. It had been suggested, 'and in one sense not untruly', that 'the monstrous pantomime ogre' Sunday 'was meant for a blasphemous version of the Creator'. But the point was that the story was 'a nightmare of things, not as they are, but as they seemed to the young half-pessimist of the '90s; and the ogre who appears brutal but is also

---

[65] This is why it should not be judged as though it were a realistic novel and criticized for its improbabilities and discrepancies and obscurity, as Kingsley Amis and David Lodge do (Conlon ii. 271–2, 330–1). Amis also objects to Sunday's buffoonery (Sullivan, 35–6)—but in dreams the most extraordinary and ludicrous things are said and done. However, that does not mean the book can be interpreted to mean anything, regardless of the text and Chesterton's own explanation of it, as in Adam Schwartz's bizarre misreading in *The Third Spring*, 50–4. According to Schwartz, 'Sunday's peace is unforgivable because it is peace as the world gives peace' and is a source of temptation to the detectives. Schwartz quotes the Secretary's refusal to forgive Sunday his 'peace'; but omits his reason—how in that case can Sunday be both the good chief detective and the evil President of the Council? According to Schwartz, Gregory is 'the sole sincere anarchist in the book', who 'chides Sunday and his minions for their capitulation to comfort and their consequent ignorance of, and inattention to, the sufferings of the weak'. (Actually at the beginning of the novel in real life, Syme reassures his sister that Gregory is 'insincere' as an anarchist and says more than he really means, as anyone does who, for example, 'thanks' someone for passing the salt.) Schwartz then interprets Syme's realization of why he had to suffer as being the realization of the importance of 'solidarity with the sufferings of others'—having just quoted Syme's realization that he had to suffer in order to fling Satan's lie back in the face of the blasphemer Gregory! Schwartz again misunderstands the final scene of the nightmare when Gregory appears, as in the Book of Job, before God (Sunday) as Satan (Lucifer) among the 'sons of God', the angels, that is, the detectives, who

cryptically benevolent is not so much God' as 'Nature as it appears to the pantheist, whose pantheism is struggling out of pessimism. So far as the story had any sense in it, it was meant to begin with the picture of the world at its worst and to work towards the suggestion that the picture was not so black as it was already painted.' For he was 'trying vaguely to found a new optimism, not on the maximum but the minimum of good'. He 'did not so much mind the pessimist who complained that there was so little good' as 'the pessimist who asked what was the good of good'. But he also 'even for the worst reasons ... already knew too much to pretend to get rid of evil', which was why he 'introduced at the end one figure who really does, with a full understanding, deny and defy the good'. For Lucian Gregory testifies 'to the extreme evil (which is merely the unpardonable sin of not wishing to be pardoned)' that Chesterton knew from experience: 'I had learned it from myself. I was already quite certain that I could if I chose cut myself from the whole life of the universe.'[66]

When the book was adapted for the stage in 1926 by Ralph Neale and 'Keith' Jones, by then Mrs Cecil Chesterton, Chesterton explained in an introduction that the pessimism he was opposing was 'dogmatic ... even orthodox'. This philosophy of 'narrow despair', deriving from Schopenhauer, was an imprisoning 'system' that 'really resembled a nightmare'. It was 'in the middle of a thick London fog' of 'pessimism and materialism' that he had written the novel. But he was not opposing 'the heresy of pessimism' with 'the equally morbid and diseased insanity of optimism'. The question was 'whether everything is really evil', and regarding this 'nightmare' possibility it was relevant that 'nightmares are not true; and that in them even the faces of friends may appear as the faces of fiends'. In the novel itself, there was a scene in a wood 'full of shattered sunlight and shaken shadows' where the hero could hardly see his companions 'for the patterns of sun and shade that danced upon them'; this 'chaos of chiaroscuro' seemed to symbolize the nightmare world in which he had been

---

cannot, *pace* Schwartz, be 'Job's comforters' because they obviously do not appear in the two scenes referred to in the Book of Job that take place in heaven. Finally, Schwartz quotes Christ's words 'Can ye drink ...' as being the words of Sunday—but then bizarrely accuses Sunday and the detectives of falling under Christ's condemnation of the sons of Zebedee. For Sunday can hardly be both Christ *and* one of the sons of Zebedee—any more than Gregory can be both the 'accuser' of the Book of Job, that is, Satan *and* the Christ who rebukes the 'pride' of Sunday and the detectives (according to Schwartz, the sons of Zebedee).

[66] *A.* 103–4.

moving, where he wondered 'what was a friend and what an enemy'. And Chesterton adds, in allusion to his time at the Slade: 'He had found the thing which the modern people call Impressionism, which is another name for that final scepticism which can find no floor to the universe.'[67]

In an interview in the *Observer* shortly before the play opened, Chesterton explained his motive in writing the original novel. He had thought 'it would be fun' to reverse the usual detective plot in which an apparently innocent person is revealed as the murderer by 'tearing away... menacing masks' to 'reveal benevolence'. There was also the related idea 'that there is actually a lot of good to be discovered in unlikely places, and that we who are fighting each other may be all fighting on the right side'—but that it was as well that we do not know this as 'the soul must be solitary, or there would be no place for courage'. But the novel's moral was not the pantheist message that 'there was good in everything', as was shown by 'the introduction of the one real anarchist and pessimist', the 'final Adversary... a man resolutely turned away from goodness'. He thought that Sunday could be taken 'to stand for Nature as distinguished from God. Huge, boisterous, full of vitality, dancing with a hundred legs, bright with the glare of the sun, and at first sight, somewhat regardless of us and our desires.' However, the quotation from the Gospel at the end of the book 'seems to mean that Sunday is God. That is the only serious note in the book, the face of Sunday changes, you tear off the mask of Nature and you find God.' Nevertheless, Chesterton warned his interviewer, when he wrote the novel he was 'feeling his way in matters of belief. The book, to use a monstrously incongruent parallel, is a sort of "Lead, Kindly Light."' Still, he was protesting against 'the pessimism of the nineties', and, although he did not know 'much about God', he 'was ready to stick up for him': 'It was a bad period when it was unfashionable to believe in innocence, and we were all supposed to worship Wilde and Whistler, and everything twisty and strange. I suppose it was a natural revolt.' Comparing the pessimism of *The Man who was Thursday* with that of 1926, Chesterton thought the contemporary pessimism was 'much more noble': 'The sad souls of the 'nineties lost hope because they had taken too much absinthe; our young men lost hope because a friend died with a bullet in his head.'[68]

[67] *MT* 470, 472, 583–4.
[68] *Observer*, 10 Jan. 1926, partially repr. in Ward, *GKC* 168–9.

A fortnight later Chesterton was also interviewed in the *Illustrated Sunday Herald*. What had he meant when he wrote the book? 'There you have me. It was so long ago, and I am a very forgetful person.' It was certainly meant to be a detective story, written partly to please himself and partly to please his friend E. C. Bentley. But he wanted 'to write a particular kind of detective tale'. He wanted to 'reverse' the 'usual' 'process', 'and have a number of characters who are apparently able-bodied villains who, when unmasked, prove to be decent citizens'. The 'idea behind this... standing of the ordinary detective tale on its head' was that 'we who think we are fighting for justice are often aiming tremendous blows at villainous masks which hide people who have the same aim as we have, and think of us as we do of them. Most people, in fact are on the right side, only they keep it dark.' However, he was also 'convinced then, and... convinced still, that there are people who have definitely taken sides with the devil'. And this was true of Lucian Gregory, 'who does stand for the forces of evil and despair'. It was no accident that the 'villain—the real anarchist of the story' was 'a decadent artist', who was typical of that 'poisonous period'. There was now 'a nobler sort of pessimism' born of the carnage of the First World War and not 'born of the reaction from debauch'; the contemporary 'young pessimists' were not 'merely contemptible' like Gregory. 'But there is still as great a need as ever for faith... that most of those round us are on the right side, fight as we do and must with each other in the darkness.' As for Sunday, he could be called 'Nature': 'But you will note that I hold that when the mask of Nature is lifted you find God behind. All that wild exuberance of Nature, all its strange pranks, all its seeming indifference... all that is only a mask.' Chesterton concluded by saying that 'it is well that we should not know all about those around us, that we should fight in the dark, while having the faith that most men are on the right side, for to possess courage the soul of man must be lonely until at last it knows all'.[69]

[69] *Illustrated Sunday Herald*, 24 Jan. 1926.

6

Orthodoxy

IN the summer of 1908 the Chestertons 'took a house' at Rye in Sussex, 'that wonderful inland island, crowned with a town as with a citadel, like a hill in a mediaeval picture'. It so happened that the rented house was next door to Lamb House, 'the old oak-panelled mansion which had attracted, one might almost say across the Atlantic, the fine aquiline eye of Henry James'. As an American, 'who had reacted against America; and steeped his sensitive psychology in everything that seemed most antiquatedly and aristocratically English', James had, in his 'search for the finest shades among the shadows of the past', picked out, as 'one might have guessed that he would . . . that town from all towns and that house from all houses'.

It had been the seat of a considerable patrician family of the neighbourhood, which had long ago decayed and disappeared. It had, I believe, rows of family portraits, which Henry James treated as reverently as family ghosts. I think in a way he really regarded himself as a sort of steward or custodian of the mysteries and secrets of a great house, where ghosts might have walked with all possible propriety. The legend says (I never learned for certain if it was true) that he had actually traced that dead family-tree until he found that there was far away in some manufacturing town, one unconscious descendant of the family, who was a cheerful and commonplace commercial clerk. And it is said that Henry James would ask this youth down to his dark ancestral house, and receive him with funereal hospitality, and I am sure with comments of a quite excruciating tact and delicacy. Henry James always spoke with an air which I can only call gracefully groping; that is not so much groping in the dark in blindness as groping in the light in bewilderment, through seeing too many avenues and obstacles.... feeling [his] way through a forest of facts; to us often invisible facts. It is said, I say, that these thin straws of sympathy and subtlety were duly split for the benefit of the astonished commercial gentleman, while Henry James, with his bowed dome-like head, drooped with unfathomable apologies and rendered a sort of silent account of his stewardship. It is also said that the commercial gentleman thought the visit a great bore and the ancestral home a hell of a place . . .

Whatever the truth of the legend, what was 'certain was that Henry James inhabited the house with all the gravity and loyalty of the family ghost; not without something of the oppressive delicacy of a highly cultured family butler'. This 'very stately and courteous old gentleman' was 'uniquely gracious' in his 'cult of tact', which rang true in at least one respect: 'He was serious with children. I saw a little boy gravely present him with a crushed and dirty dandelion. He bowed; but he did not smile.' However, his 'solemnity and slowness' were too much for his neighbour H. G. Wells, who had a house on the other side of Romney Marsh from Rye on the Kent coast at Sandgate, and 'who used . . . to make irreverent darts and dashes through the sombre house and the sacred garden and drop notes to me over the garden wall'.[1]

Wells was not the only guest of Henry James to misbehave over the garden wall. While the Chestertons were staying in Rye, William James, the philosopher, was staying next door with his brother. William James had been impressed by *Heretics*: 'A tremendously strong writer and true thinker, despite his mannerism of paradox.' Now William was 'immensely excited' that this 'great teller of the truth' was actually living next door.[2] Wells, who tells us the story, thought in his memoirs that Chesterton was staying at the Mermaid Inn, 'which had its garden just over the high brick wall of the garden of Lamb House'.[3] But, apart from the fact that Ches-terton tells us that they 'took a house', the inn is in Mermaid Street and Lamb House in the adjacent West Street, nor does the garden of the inn border on that of Lamb House. It is reasonable to suppose that Wells's mistake was due to the fact that the Chestertons *were* staying at a house in Mermaid *Street*. At the time there was only one house in Mermaid Street

[1] *A.* 205, 208–9.

[2] *Letters of William James*, ed. Henry James (London: Longman, Green and Co., 1926), 241, 257.

[3] H. G. Wells, *Experiments in Autobiography: Discoveries and Conclusions of a Very Ordinary Brain (since 1866)*, ii (London: Victor Gollancz and the Cresset Press, 1934), 538.

that had a garden bordering on that of Lamb House, 4 Mermaid Street, on the other side of the street from the Mermaid Inn, so it is more than probable that this was the house the Chestertons were renting that summer.[4] At any rate, Wells recalled how William 'with a scandalous directness...had put the gardener's ladder against that ripe red wall and clambered up and peeped over'! Unfortunately, Henry 'caught him at it', 'lost his calm', and 'was terribly unnerved'. 'He appealed to me, of all people, to adjudicate on what was and what was not permissible behaviour in England. William was arguing about it in an indisputably American accent, with an indecently naked reasonableness.' Sadly, he 'had none of Henry's passionate regard for the polish upon the surfaces of life'. 'It was the sort of thing that isn't done. It was most emphatically the sort of thing that isn't done...' Henry James ordered the gardener to put away the ladder. William, meanwhile, 'was looking thoroughly naughty'. To the 'manifest relief' of Henry, Wells, who had come to take his brother and niece to his house at Sandgate, 'carried William off and in the road just outside the town we ran against the Chestertons...Chesterton was heated and I think rather swollen by the sunshine; he seemed to overhang

---

[4] William James could have been trying to look into the main garden of 4 Mermaid St, or alternatively into the so-called 'secret garden' (which now belongs to 7 Mermaid St) that was then rented by James to 4 Mermaid St, which had access to it through a gate made in the wall. James had bought this 'secret garden' in 1903 from J. H. Gasson, a local tradesman who had bought 6 Mermaid St, to which the garden then belonged. On 16 Feb. 1903 James wrote to his secretary Mary Weld from London to say that he had just heard that 'Gasson the dreadful' had bought 'the house and garden in Mermaid Street, that menaces and (potentially by any building on the ground) would fatally injure the west end of my garden. I have had to buy the ground from him at an extortionate price and now have got to spend money on enclosing it...' (*Henry James Letters*, iv. *1895–1916*, ed. Leon Edel (Cambridge, MA.: Harvard University Press, 1984), 267). H. Montgomery Hyde, *The Story of Lamb House: The Home of Henry James* (Rye: Adams of Rye, 1966), 77, adds that James was afraid of being overlooked if a house was built on the plot, a fear he may have remembered when rebuking his brother for attempting to look over the wall. See Leon Edel, *Henry James: The Master, 1901–1916* (London: Rupert Hart-Davis, 1972), 178, for James's leasing the 'secret garden' to a neighbour, who must have been the occupant of 4 Mermaid St, given the existence of the gate into its garden. It is also conceivable that the Chestertons had taken a house in Watchbell St, which runs off West St, parallel with Mermaid St, the only other street that has gardens adjoining the wall of Lamb House garden.

his one-horse fly; he descended slowly but firmly; he was moist and steamy but cordial; we chatted in the road for a time and William got his coveted impression.'[5]

Subsequently, after Belloc's dramatic arrival in Rye, which unnerved Henry James at least as much as his brother's peeping, William James recorded in his diary: 'at nine to Chestertons's where we sat till midnight drinking port with Hilaire Belloc.'[6] What neither Wells nor William presumably knew was that the 'unnerved' Henry James was not above a little peeping himself—even if the peeping had to be done by somebody else rather than the Sage of Rye himself. His secretary, Theodora Bosanquet, recorded in her diary on 27 July 1908: 'In the course of the morning Mr James made me go and peep through the curtain to see "the unspeakable Chesterton" pass by[7]—a sort of elephant with a crimson face and oily curls. He [James] thinks it very tragic that his mind should be imprisoned in such a body.'[8] When he did meet Chesterton, he noticed that 'he had "an enormous little slavey" of a wife with him'. He was 'impressed by the way Chesterton used to retire into the corner of a room and just sat and wrote. It was wonderful to be able to do that, he told Theodora Bosanquet; he could not quite do it himself.'[9]

Chesterton's own memory was of Henry James calling on them 'after exactly the correct interval'. It was naturally 'a very stately call of state', and, although William James was 'breezier' than his brother when you got to know him, 'there was something finally ceremonial about this idea of the whole family on the march'.[10] Still, 'there was an almost fantastic contrast' between the older brother William, 'as breezy as the sea', 'so hearty about abstract studies generally considered dry', who 'talked about the metabolism and the involution of values with the air of a man recounting his flirtations on the steamer', and the younger brother, 'so solemn about social details often considered trivial', who 'talked about toast and teacups with the impressiveness of a family ghost'.[11] At any rate, on this particular occasion it seems that they all talked about 'the best literature of the day'. James was 'complimentary about something of mine; but represented himself as respectfully wondering how I wrote all I did. I suspect him of

---

[5] Wells, *Experiments*, 538.   [6] Edel, *James: the Master*, 374.

[7] James worked in the summer in a garden room that had a window looking into West Street.

[8] Edel, *James: the Master*, 373.

[9] H. Montgomery Hyde, *Henry James at Home* (London: Methuen, 1969), 190.

[10] *A*. 209.   [11] *CM* 31.

meaning why rather than how.' While they were 'gravely' considering the
works of Hugh Walpole, 'with many delicate degrees of appreciation and
doubt', there was 'heard from the front-garden a loud bellowing noise
resembling that of an impatient fog-horn'. Chesterton knew immediately
that it was in fact no foghorn, 'because it was roaring out, "Gilbert!
Gilbert!" and was like only one voice in the world'. It was Belloc, 'probably
shouting for bacon and beer'—but even Chesterton 'had no notion of the
form or guise under which he would present himself'. So far as Chesterton
was concerned, Belloc was on a walking tour of France with a friend from
the Foreign Office who belonged to one of the old Catholic families. It
seemed they had, by some miscalculation, run out of money. Belloc
boasted of his ability to live like a tramp, and, practically penniless, they
began thus to walk home, unshaven and dressed in workmen's clothes.
Presumably they had had just enough money to make the crossing to
Dover, whence they began walking to Rye, knowing that Chesterton was
staying there. 'They arrived, roaring for food and drink and derisively
accusing each other of having secretly washed, in violation of an implied
contract between tramps. In this fashion they burst in upon the balanced
tea-cup and tentative sentence of Mr Henry James.'[12]

The scene was too subtle even for Henry James, renowned as he was for
his subtlety, to appreciate. Chesterton was sure that he missed 'the irony of
the best comedy in which he ever played a part'.

He had left America because he loved Europe, and all that was meant by England
or France; the gentry, the gallantry, the traditions of lineage and locality, the life
that had been lived beneath old portraits in oak-panelled-rooms. And there, on
the other side of the tea-table, was Europe, was the old thing that made France
and England, the posterity of the English squires and the French soldiers; ragged,
unshaven, shouting for beer, shameless above all shades of poverty and wealth;
sprawling, indifferent, secure. And what looked across at it was still the Puritan
refinement of Boston; and the space it looked across was wider than the Atlantic.

Chesterton remained 'haunted by the contradictions of that comedy', 'the
most comic comedy of cross-purposes that ever happened in the world',
about which books could be written 'about its significance, social, national,
international and historic'. He felt that, if he could 'ever express all that
was involved in it', he would 'write a great book on international affairs'.
Still, James could be forgiven for a certain dismayed astonishment, when
even the local English inn-keeper, who knew that Belloc and his friend

[12] *A.* 209–10.

were not tramps, nevertheless found it hard to believe that one of these two disreputable companions was a Member of Parliament and the other an official of the Foreign Office. But when one of them 'insisted on having a bottle of port decanted and carrying it through the streets of Rye, like a part of a religious procession', his disbelief was dispelled.[13] As for Henry James, Chesterton may not have known that thirty years before he had published a delightful and funny novel, *The Europeans*, contrasting American and European ways—although, it has to be said, James's conception of the European hardly included the idea of Hilaire Belloc.

During this summer at Rye, Chesterton 'learnt to appreciate' what it was in Wells that 'made him rebel against the atmosphere of Henry James'. Actually, James himself 'did really appreciate that quality' and 'expressed it as well as it could be expressed by saying, "Whatever Wells writes is not only alive, but kicking" '. It seemed to Chesterton 'rather unfortunate that, after this, it should have been Henry James who was kicked'. But he could 'sympathise in some ways' with Wells's 'mutiny against the oak-panelling and the ghosts'. What he had 'always liked about Wells' was 'his vigorous and unaffected readiness for a lark. He was one of the best men in the world with whom to start a standing joke; though perhaps he did not like it to stand too long after it was started.' Together they had devised a toy-theatre pantomime about Wells's fellow Fabian Sidney Webb, as well as one about the Poor Law Commission, in which the Commissioners took Mr Bumble the Beadle to pieces, and then stewed him in a cauldron, until he jumped out, rejuvenated and much enlarged. And together they had 'invented the well-known and widespread national game of Gype', which had all sorts of variations, including 'Table Gype; a game for the little ones'. It was decided that players of the game who were too keen 'tended to suffer from Gype's ear'. Allusions to 'the fashionable sport' were introduced into articles by Chesterton and his journalist friends. 'Everything was in order and going forward; except the game itself, which has not yet been invented.' Chesterton could understand why Wells would assume that Henry James 'would show a certain frigidity towards Gype'; and 'for the sacred memory of Gype', he could 'excuse' Wells's feeling. But Wells's own reactions in Chesterton's view were not above reproach: he thought that Wells 'reacted too swiftly to everything'; indeed, to use the word that would most annoy Wells, he was a 'permanent reactionary'. Wells always 'seemed to be coming from somewhere, rather than going anywhere'.

[13] *A.* 205, 210–11.

He was 'so often nearly right' that his reactions 'irritated' Chesterton, 'like the sight of somebody's hat being perpetually washed up by the sea and never touching the shore'. It struck Chesterton that Wells 'thought that the object of opening the mind is simply opening the mind', whereas he, Chesterton, was 'incurably convinced that the object of opening the mind, as of opening the mouth, is to shut it again on something solid'.[14] Or, as he put it in an article published later in the year: 'An open mind is really a mark of foolishness, like an open mouth. Mouths and minds were made to shut; they were made to open only in order to shut.'[15]

Wells, for his part, remembered Chesterton on one memorable occasion sitting down on something quite solid without even noticing. Wells had bumped into the whole Chesterton family in a town in France and invited them to lunch. Noticing that his youngest son, then a small boy, was missing, Wells exclaimed: 'Where's Frank? Good God, Gilbert, you're sitting on him.' At this Chesterton got up and looked down apologetically at his chair and the small boy. His wife thought Wells was good for her husband because he would take him out walking. But when Frances was not present, Chesterton inquired anxiously, 'We won't go for a walk today, will we?' In Wells's view, Frances was good for Chesterton because she prevented him from becoming even more obese than he already was.[16] But he also thought that Chesterton's presence was good for any company where he found himself: 'I notice that the whole gathering is by a sort of radiation convivial.'[17]

When Chesterton compared Wells with Shaw, 'the other genius of the Fabians', he felt 'rather more in sympathy' with the latter. But Shaw's Puritan 'austerity' did not appreciate 'buffoonery', and here Chesterton felt more in tune with Wells who understood 'the glow and body of good spirits, even when they are animal spirits'. It was not that Shaw did not have 'plenty of appetite for adventure', but the adventure had to have 'a levity in some sense celestial', which meant 'skylarking' as opposed to 'larking'. In the matter of the Boer War, like most Fabians both Shaw and Wells had been imperialists, the latter holding that, while all wars were 'indefensible', this was 'the only sort of war to be defended', on the ground that 'it might be necessary, in policing the planet, to force backward peoples to open their resources to cosmopolitan commerce'. In other words, Fabians like Wells defended the one kind of war that Chesterton

[14] *A.* 211–12; Ward, *GKC* 321.   [15] *ILN* xxviii. 196.
[16] Ward, *GKC* 321–3.
[17] Dorothy Collins's notes for talk, BL Add. MS 73477, fo. 144.

considered despicable, 'the bullying of small states for their oil or gold', while condemning the only sort of war that Chesterton considered defensible—namely, 'a war of civilisations and religions, to determine the moral destiny of mankind'.[18]

When Chesterton looked back on his friendship with Shaw, he seemed to have been in one long argument with him. And yet he had 'learned to have a warmer admiration and affection out of all that argument than most people get out of agreement'. In his view, Shaw was 'at his best when he is antagonistic. I might say that he is seen at his best when he is wrong. Or rather, everything is wrong about him but himself.' He had argued on practically every subject with Shaw, as he had done with his brother, but without ever quarrelling or with any 'animosity'. He had never argued with Shaw without ending 'in a better and not a worse temper or frame of mind', such were his 'inexhaustible fountains of fairmindedness and intellectual geniality'. It seemed that Chesterton had to argue with him as much as he did in order to admire him as much as he did—'and I am proud of him as a foe even more than as a friend'. The odd thing was that, while there were few of his contemporaries he liked better, they had actually 'met more in public than in private; and generally upon platforms'—'especially upon platforms where we were put up to fight each other, like two knock-about comedians'. If not exactly a comedian, Shaw was certainly eccentric in ways that hampered 'conventional conviviality': 'Even hostesses, let alone hosts, are sometimes puzzled by a gentleman who has rather more horror of tea than of wine or beer.' In retrospect, Chesterton thought that all their differences came back to a religious difference—as 'indeed I think all differences do'. Shaw and his followers believed in 'evolution' just as imperialists believed in 'expansion'. Chesterton, on the other hand, was a believer in the philosophy of limitation:

They believe in a great growing and groping thing like a tree; but I believe in the flower and the fruit; and the flower is often small. The fruit is final and in that sense finite; it has a form and therefore a limit. There has been stamped upon it an image, which is the crown and consummation of an aim...And as applied to man, it means this; that a man has been made more sacred than any superman or super-monkey; that his very limitations have already become holy and like a home; because of that sunken chamber in the rocks, where God became very small.[19]

---

[18] *A.* 213–14, 218–19.   [19] *A.* 213–16.

Chesterton's book on Shaw would appear a year after the holiday in Rye, in the summer of 1909. In the meantime, he was about to publish one of his major works in which he would defend the religion in which God was not a limitless 'life-force' but a tiny baby born in a cave. But a month before publication tragedy again came to Frances and her family.

On 25 August 1908 Frances received another great blow, this time the death of her brother Knollys. According to the newspaper report,[20] 'the body of a well-dressed man was discovered in the [river] Cuckmere a short distance on the sea side of Exeat Bridge', near Seaford in East Sussex, where the inquest was held. The dead man's brother-in-law, Lucian Oldershaw, identified the body from previous injuries and also from a ring and other articles and writings found on the body. Oldershaw, who was described as 'a tutor, living at Fernley, Maiden-head', explained that Knollys, who was 36, had 'recently' been tutoring a pupil in Rye—which might explain why the Chestertons were spending the summer there. He added that he was a writer and had written a book. Oldershaw had been expecting his brother-in-law to come and stay at Maidenhead on 15 August, but had received a telegram to say that Knollys was feeling unwell and would come later. 'A few years ago,' Oldershaw told the inquest, 'while in business in London', the deceased 'had a nervous breakdown . . . which affected his mind, and he had to go to the Holloway Sanatorium. He had left that institution for about three years and seemed to have recovered perfectly with the exception that he was at times somewhat despondent.' At the time of his death he had been staying at nearby West Dean 'with the members of a London Working Men's Club in which he was interested, as he had done a year previously'. Oldershaw knew of nothing that could have been on the dead man's mind: 'He could always have made a home with his mother. He was not suffering from a lack of means.' Indeed, Oldershaw had 'just made arrangements' to get him 'more work next year and his prospects in life were bright'. The steward at the Hammersmith Working Men's Club, where Knollys worked as a helper, which was 'managed on temperance lines', told the court that the club organized a country holiday for

[20] *East Sussex News*, 28 Aug. 1908. Ffinch, 144, followed by Coren, 159, and Pearce, 274, dates Knollys's death to August 1906 because of a pencilled annotation, '1906?', made presumably by Dorothy Collins, on the letter (quoted below) that Frances Chesterton sent Father O'Connor about her brother's death, which is merely dated 25 Aug. She wrote from Battersea and must therefore have left Rye by then.

working men every summer. On 15 August, when the holiday ended and when the dead man was supposed to go to Maidenhead, he failed to catch the train and returned to West Dean Farm, where they had been staying, saying that 'he had had a letter and it was inconvenient for him to go that day, but he would leave on the following day'. He slept at the farm that night 'and it was arranged that he should leave Seaford about 2 p.m. on the following day', which was a Sunday. However, the steward was surprised to see him about six o'clock on Sunday evening and asked why he had not gone, but the dead man 'turned away as though he resented being asked questions'. That was the last the steward saw of him. The dead man had not complained of being unwell: 'He was naturally a very quiet man and had the appearance of being very studious. He seemed in good health and spirits, and on the Thursday previous gave several recitations at a concert which was held.' The body had been discovered in the afternoon of 21 August by a shepherd in the river about 30 yards below Exeat Bridge. The surgeon who examined the body told the court that the face was unrecognizable and that he thought the body had been in the water for five or six days before being discovered, but that death had not probably been due to drowning. 'On both sides of the neck there were clear cut wounds, leaving about an inch of healthy skin between them at the throat. The wound on the left side was the deeper and had divided the jugular vein ... Both wounds could have been self-inflicted and that on the left side would have been fatal.' The surgeon also testified that at some time in the past the dead man's right leg had been broken and his left elbow fractured. Oldershaw explained that the injuries to the leg and elbow had been self-inflicted while his brother-in-law had been in Holloway Sanatorium. The coroner's verdict was suicide resulting from depression.

In her distress, Frances Chesterton turned to Father O'Connor. She wrote on 25 August:

I have to write in great trouble. My dear brother was found drowned at Seaford a few days ago.

It is a terrible shock to us all—we were so happy about him. He seemed to have quite recovered from his terrible illness. But he sought death himself and I pray that God has given him the peace of heart and mind which we who loved him so could never give.

She was going the next day to see the Catholic priest at Newhaven about the funeral, for Knollys was a convert to Catholicism. Although the newspaper report of the inquest did not mention this, Frances had apparently discovered that her brother had been to Mass on the morning of Sunday 16 August before seemingly killing himself in the evening.[21] To Father O'Connor's letter of condolence, Frances replied: 'Thank you for your comforting words. You will remember my brother in your prayers at Mass—I know.'[22] Three years before O'Connor had told her that he had often said Mass not only for Knollys but for her and her husband.[23] And she had thanked him for writing to Knollys: 'please don't be put off by any rebuff and encourage him when you can.'[24]

So desperate was Frances that it seems she tried to find solace briefly in spiritualism, attending a couple of séances in the hope of making contact with her beloved brother,[25] much to the disapproval of her husband, who wrote a poem called 'The Crystal' in which he deplored his wife 'Staring for spirits in a lump of glass', a poem he naturally chose never to publish.[26]

As is the way with tragedies, good did come out of it for both husband and wife. According to 'Keith' Chesterton, Frances had already been agitating to leave London. And one evening after dinner at a famous London restaurant, suddenly after midnight Chesterton announced to his brother and 'Keith', 'Frances wants to leave London'. The idea seemed 'fantastic', as though it had been suggested that Dr Johnson should move to the Cotswolds. Chesterton and London seemed as inseparable. His parents, who were Londoners through and through, were horrified. The truth, according to 'Keith', was that Frances could not bear Fleet Street. It was not just the irregularity of a journalist's life that upset her; it was the 'whole atmosphere' that was 'alien to her. The bars and wine shops, the desultory meetings, queer associates, the perpetual, never-ending talk . . .'. Anyway she was not interested in newspapers and disliked the press *tout court*. But apart from all that and her husband's late nights when Frances would be alone in the flat, the truth was that her husband's life in Fleet

[21] Barker, 155, with text corrected from BL Add. MS 73196, fos 71–2.

[22] Frances Chesterton to John O'Connor, 2 Sept. [*sic*], BL Add. MS 73196, fo. 73.

[23] John O'Connor to Frances Chesterton, 8 Sept. 1905, BL Add. MS 73196, fo. 59.

[24] Barker, 155, with text corrected from BL Add. MS 73196, fo. 43.

[25] I owe this information to Aidan Mackey, who was told by Dorothy Collins of a reference to this resort to spiritualism in a part of Frances's diary that she had destroyed after Chesterton's death. This diary, if it was not all destroyed, has disappeared.

[26] It has now been published in *CP* i. 345–6.

Street affected her directly in a way that would not have appealed to many wives. As 'Keith' recounts in her memoir of the family, Chesterton's Fleet Street associates would also socialize in the flat at Overstrand Mansions, where late in the evening they would resort to the small kitchen 'where mounds of sausages were eaten and pints of beer consumed and the talk grew better and better'. Yet this was not a Fleet Street tavern but Frances's home, and perhaps to her the talk did not grow 'better and better'. As a great procrastinator, her husband might have been able to shelve the issue indefinitely. But then came the suicide of Knollys: 'She insisted that they must leave London permanently, and fearful of the effect of a refusal on her state of mind, and because he loved her with a great and unfailing devotion, he consented . . .'.[27]

What 'Keith' did not know—for she would surely have been quick to pounce on any weakness in Frances—was that Chesterton was worried about more than the shock Frances had suffered from her brother's suicide. Suicide was worse than the accidental death of Gertrude: there was bound to be guilt that his family had failed Knollys. Any sister would have felt the same. However, much more serious for her husband was the fear that she too might conceivably take the same path, given her own depressive nature, of which her husband was well aware. Certainly she had good reason to be depressed: not only was there her brother's suicide, but there was also the inability to have a baby. Then, too, she suffered a good deal of pain from rheumatism of the spine, which had long afflicted her.[28]

2

On 10 September 1908, fifteen days before the publication of *Orthodoxy*, a collection of Chesterton's essays in the *Illustrated London News*, called *All Things Considered*, together with an introductory essay, appeared. Many years later the author dedicated a different kind of collection to the writer, editor, and publisher E. V. Lucas, who had himself earlier published a couple of selected volumes of Chesterton's writings. In his dedication, Chesterton thanked him for his 'friendly advice', which had often helped him bring 'something like order into the chaos of my articles, and especially in the most thankless task of all, in providing such a nameless

[27] MCC 65–7, 69, 71.
[28] Her GP, Dr Bakewell, told Dorothy Collins that 'Frances had arthritis of the spine. (Not curvature as stated by Mrs Cecil.)' (Ward, *GKC* 563).

anarchy with a name'. He had Lucas to thank for the 'excellent' title *All Things Considered*, 'probably the only really witty words in the book', as well as for making 'the extravagant demand' for *A Shilling for my Thoughts*, another selection Lucas had made a few years later. These titles (which were 'better' than his essays), Chesterton had written earlier to Lucas, would suggest to any future biographer or bibliographer, 'if they find any trace of me at all,' that, from such 'fragments left by this now forgotten writer', there was 'reason to believe that he was not without certain fugitive mental gifts' (even though it was now 'difficult to understand the cause even of such publicity as he obtained in his own day'). In the later dedication, he confessed to Lucas: 'Somehow I always feel a fool... when I consider myself in a literary light... except when I am arguing with people. Then it is always they who are indefensible.' But he did claim some credit in the matter of titles for his own collection of articles called *Tremendous Trifles*—though even that was 'only too magniloquent and... a mournful example of that taste for alliteration which is one of my worst vices'.[29]

The introductory essay to *All Things Considered* begins with one of those Chestertonian paradoxes that are likely to irritate the reader: 'It is so easy to be solemn; it is so hard to be frivolous.' But humour, of course, is a very serious theme in Chesterton's writings, even if, without rather more explanation, the paradox here seems merely flippantly clever. Humour is an important reason why Chesterton thought the 'hilarious' masses superior to the solemn intellectuals: 'When once you have got hold of a vulgar joke, you may be certain that you have got hold of a subtle and spiritual idea,' for to see the joke is to see 'something deep', which can be expressed only 'by something silly and emphatic'. Thus silly jokes about people sitting on their hats 'refer to the primary paradox that man is superior to all the things around him and yet is at their mercy'. The 'vulgar comic papers' so despised by the intellectuals 'are so subtle and true that they are even prophetic'. And it seemed obvious to Chesterton that 'the literature which the people studies' was much more informative sociologically than the sociological 'literature which studies the people'. Even the 'best of the intellectuals of to-day' thought that the masses regarded the woman as 'the chattel of her lord, like his bath or his bed'. But in the 'comic literature' of 'the mass of the democracy' it is the lord who 'hides under the bed to escape from the wrath of his chattel'. The 'higher culture', which was

---

[29] *MC*, pp. v–vi; John Sullivan, *Chesterton Continued: A Bibliographical Supplement* (London: London University Press, 1968), 94, 97.

'worse even than philanthropy', was totally without 'democratic sympathy'. And it did not understand that 'the more serious is the discussion the more grotesque should be its terms', for if 'a thing is universal it is full of comic things'. And it was 'the test of a good philosophy whether you can defend it grotesquely. It is the test of a good religion whether you can joke about it.' We have to 'defend grotesquely what we believe seriously', since 'all grotesqueness is itself related to seriousness': 'The fall of roofs and high buildings is taken seriously. It is only when a man tumbles down that we laugh. Why do we laugh? Because it is a grave religious matter: it is the Fall of Man. Only man can be absurd: for only man can be dignified.' After all, man occupies an 'extraordinary position' in the world and 'is an exception, whatever else he is'. Man is an animal, but he is not simply an animal; he is spiritual, but he is not simply spiritual: 'His body has got too much mixed up with his soul, as we see in the supreme instance of sex.' The same is true of alcohol: when man wants an alcoholic drink, it does not necessarily mean that he wants alcohol: 'The real case against drunkenness is not that it calls up the beast, but that it calls up the Devil.' Animals do not drink, but then neither do they get drunk, and 'in sex no animal is either chivalrous or obscene'.[30]

The masses in Chesterton's view are superior to the intellectuals in common sense as well as humour: 'If there is one class of men whom history has proved especially and supremely capable of going quite wrong in all directions, it is the class of highly intellectual men. I would always prefer to go by the bulk of humanity; that is why I am a democrat.' Again, it is the despised masses that have won England its wars: 'The Battle of Waterloo was won by the stubbornness of the common soldier—that is to say, it was won by the man who had never been to Eton,' 'won on the village green' not on the playing fields of Eton. Chesterton is in no doubt that it is the dread of the masses that is responsible for the fact that 'this is the first time, perhaps, in the whole history of the world in which things can be praised because they are unpopular'. Artists in the past 'did not declare themselves great artists, because they were unsuccessful: that is the peculiarity of our own time, which has a positive bias against the populace'. Modern intellectuals were 'mystagogues', 'a new sort' of 'aristocracy'.[31]

Several favourite topics of Chesterton crop up in these selected essays. Most prominent is the question of drink, already touched upon.

---

[30] *ATC* 2, 12–13, 15–17, 104–5, 202–4, 232–4.
[31] *ATC* 61–2, 212–13, 237–8, 240.

The temperance movement, which was to achieve victory in the United States with Prohibition, is a pet target. It is, Chesterton declares, a form of 'religious persecution', since it is an attempt to coerce one's fellow citizens in accordance with one's own 'religion or philosophy' rather than the 'religion of the democracy'. It is particularly directed against the masses, as prohibitionists 'systematically act on an ethical assumption entirely unfamiliar to the mass of the people'. They were attempting 'to force upon them a Mohamedan morality which they actively deny'. Temperance reform was also against civilization, which 'merely means the full authority of the human spirit over all externals', as opposed to barbarism, which 'means the worship of those externals in their crude and unconquered state'. For temperance reform called 'the problem of human intemperance the Problem of Drink', which was 'an inverted form of fetish worship; it is no sillier to say that a bottle is a god than to say that a bottle is a devil'. It was also an example of another barbarian trait of the times, 'the disposition to talk about material substances instead of about ideas'. At least it was preferable to speak of drink to alcohol, which was, 'to judge by the sound of it, an Arabic word, like "algebra" and "Alhambra", those two other unpleasant things'. The real answer to the 'Drink Problem' was not to drive drink underground but to give it on the contrary a high profile. If a public house were a really public place like a post office or railway station, through which

all types of people passed . . . for all types of refreshment, you would have the same safeguard against a man behaving in a disgusting way in a tavern that you have at present against his behaving in a disgusting way in a post-office: simply the presence of his ordinary sensible neighbours. In such a place the kind of lunatic who wants to drink an unlimited number of whiskies would be treated with the same severity with which the post office authorities would treat an amiable lunatic who had an appetite for licking an unlimited number of stamps.

If drinking were thus made 'open and official we might be taking one step towards making it careless'. And in such a matter, 'to be careless is to be sane: for neither drunkards nor Moslems can be careless about drink'.[32]

Other familiar Chestertonian themes are only briefly touched on in this volume. It was 'incomprehensible' how 'any thinker can calmly call himself a modernist; he might as well call himself a Thursdayite'. The English 'boast' of their 'anomalies' and 'illogicality', and of their consequent practicality, is very dangerous, for anomalies and lack of

---

[32] *ATC* 5–7, 226–8, 231, 235–6.

logic in fact 'do a great deal of harm' and 'accustom the mind to the idea of unreason and untruth'. To resist injustice, for instance, requires thinking it '*absurd*', in other words contrary to reason, not merely 'unpleasant'. It is optimists not pessimists who are the 'practical reformers', because they look at a wrong 'with a startled indignation', whereas the pessimists see 'only a repetition of the infamy of existence'. The purpose of education is to 'to restore simplicity', 'to unlearn things', in order that people may 'see things as they are', a view that is clearly connected with the philosophy of wonder. Nationalism is good if only because it enables one to be 'international' as opposed to 'cosmopolitan'. England and Scotland are nations, but 'What is Britain? Where is Britain? There is no such place.' England has an aristocracy in place of a religion—'The nobility are to the English poor...the poetry of life'—and also in place of a government, since, as a political anomaly, there is a 'contradictory constitution', which the aristocracy is relied upon to interpret with 'good humour'. Science cannot disprove religion: 'How could physical science prove that man is not depraved? You do not cut a man open to find his sins. You do not boil him until he gives forth the unmistakable green fumes of depravity. How could physical science find any traces of a moral fall?' How could a scientist 'expect to find a fossil Eve with a fossil apple inside her?' How could a scientist 'suppose that the ages would have spared for him a complete skeleton of Adam attached to a slightly faded fig-leaf?' The central idea in fairy tales is that 'peace and happiness can only exist on some condition', that 'all happiness hangs on one thin veto; all positive joy depends on one negative'. This idea is 'the core of ethics', and also of Judaeo-Christianity: 'A man and woman are put in a garden on condition that they do not eat one fruit: they eat it, and lose their joy in all the fruits of the earth.'[33]

3

In the chapter of the *Autobiography* called 'The Crime of Orthodoxy', Chesterton reminds his readers that he had been 'brought up among people who were Unitarians and Universalists', such as the Revd Stopford Brooke, at whose feet he had sat. These were people who thought that,

---

[33] *ATC* 3, 42–5, 69, 73, 131, 142, 189–90, 256.

'because God was in His heaven, all must be right with the world; with this world or with the next'. But there was an opposite agnostic or atheist tendency 'in what was called the emancipation of faith from the creeds and dogmas of the past', which held that 'it was very doubtful if there was any God in any heaven, and that it was so certain to the scientific eye that all is not right with the world, that it would be nearer the truth to say that all is wrong with the world'. The first progressive tendency 'led into the glorious fairyland of George Macdonald, the other led into the stark and hollowed hills of Thomas Hardy'. The first insisted that 'God must be supremely perfect if He exists; the other that, if He exists, He must be grossly imperfect'. Now what was odd was that these two schools of thought, the one blithely optimistic and the other darkly pessimistic, were 'practically in combination', although they were 'logically in contradiction'. For a long time Chesterton could not understand why they seemed to be 'in the same camp', until he realized that they were 'only connected by the convention of unconventionality'.[34]

In the midst of all this 'scatter-brained thinking', Chesterton himself 'began to piece together the fragments of the old religious scheme; mainly by the various gaps that denoted its disappearance'.

And the more I saw of real human nature, the more I came to suspect that it was really rather bad for all these people that it had disappeared. Many of them held, and still hold, very noble and necessary truths in the social and secular area. But even these it seemed to me they held less firmly than they might have done, if there had been anything like a fundamental principle of morals and metaphysics to support them. Men who believed ardently in altruism were yet troubled by the necessity of believing with even more religious reverence in Darwinism, and even in the deductions from Darwinism about a ruthless struggle as the rule of life. Men who naturally accepted the moral equality of mankind yet did so, in a manner, shrinkingly, under the gigantic shadow of the Superman of Nietzsche and Shaw. Their hearts were in the right place; but their heads were emphatically in the wrong place, being generally poked or plunged into vast volumes of materialism and scepticism, crabbed, barren, servile and without any light of liberty or of hope.

And so Chesterton 'began to examine more exactly the general Christian theology which many execrated and few examined'. He 'soon found that it did in fact correspond to many of these experiences of life'—and, most importantly for Chesterton, 'that even its paradoxes corresponded to the paradoxes of life'.[35]

<hr />

[34] *A.* 166–8.   [35] *A.* 170.

About the same time that he discovered that 'the old theological theory seemed more or less to fit into experience, while the new and negative theories did not fit into anything, least of all into each other', he published *Heretics* about contemporary writers, 'each of whom', he felt, 'erred through an ultimate or religious error'. One reviewer challenged him to state his own beliefs.

With all the solemnity of youth, I accepted this as a challenge; and wrote an outline of my own reasons for believing that the Christian theory, as summarised in the Apostles' Creed, would be found to be a better criticism of life than any of those I had criticised. I called it *Orthodoxy*, but even at the time I was very much dissatisfied with the title. It sounded a thinnish sort of thing to be defending through thick and thin. Even then I fancy I had a dim foreshadowing that I should have to find some better name for it before I died.[36]

However, there was 'one rather vague virtue about the title': 'it was provocative.' For he began to discover that, 'in all that welter of inconsistent and incompatible heresies, the one and only really unpardonable heresy was orthodoxy'. Nearly everyone in his journalistic and literary world assumed that it was 'a pose or a paradox': 'The more generous and loyal warmly maintained that it was only a joke. It was not until long afterwards that the full horror of the truth burst upon them; the disgraceful truth that I really thought the thing was true.' This first dawned upon him at a dinner party given by the staff of the *Clarion* not long after his controversy with its editor, Robert Blatchford—'a landmark' in his life when he was 'a comparatively young though relatively rising journalist'. Sitting next to him was 'one of those very refined and rather academic gentlemen from Cambridge who seemed to form so considerable a section of the rugged stalwarts of Labour'.

There was a cloud on his brow, as if he were beginning to be puzzled about something; and he said suddenly, with abrupt civility, 'Excuse my asking, Mr Chesterton, of course I shall quite understand if you prefer not to answer, and I shan't think any the worse of it, you know, even if it's true. But I suppose I'm right in thinking you don't really *believe* in those things you're defending against Blatchford?' I informed him with adamantine gravity that I did most definitely believe in those things I was defending against Blatchford. His cold and refined face did not move a visible muscle; and yet I knew in some fashion it had completely altered. 'Oh, you *do*,' he said, 'I beg your pardon. Thank you. That's all I wanted to know.' And he went on eating his

[36] *A.* 171.

(probably vegetarian) meal. But I was sure that for the rest of the evening, despite his calm, he felt as if he was sitting next to a fabulous griffin.[37]

4

Orthodoxy, published in September 1908, is the explanation of what Chesterton believed, in answer to the challenge of the reviewer of *Heretics*, and how he had come to see that the orthodox Christianity of the Apostles' Creed, as traditionally understood, coincided with the philosophy he had come to believe in himself. It was not a theological treatise but 'a sort of slovenly autobiography'.[38] Or, as he explained in his preface to the American edition, the book was 'meant to be a companion to "Heretics", and to put the positive side in addition to the negative'. It was 'unavoidably autobiographical', because he had been 'driven back upon somewhat the same difficulty as that which beset Newman in writing his Apologia'—that is, he had been 'forced to be egotistical only in order to be sincere'. The book dealt with 'a riddle and its answer'—'the Christian theology', which the author thought was 'a convincing creed', and if it was not, it was 'at least a repeated and surprising coincidence'.[39] Chesterton had often thought of writing a story about an English yachtsman who mistook his course and 'discovered' England under the illusion that it was an island in the South Seas. He was like that man, for he was 'the man who with the utmost daring discovered what had been discovered before'.[40] But, significantly, he was not prepared to discuss 'the very fascinating but quite different question of what is the present seat of authority for the proclamation of that creed'.[41]

[37] *A.* 171–2.

[38] *O.* 215. It is only autobiographical in the loosest sense (see Oddie, 356–60).

[39] *Orthodoxy* (New York: John Lane, 1909), pp. vii–viii.

[40] For the unpublished story 'Homesick at Home', which Chesterton wrote sometime 'during the years at University College and the Slade, his time at Redway's and then at Fisher Unwin's', and which he 'extensively worked and reworked ... in his notebooks' producing 'four versions of it in various stages of development', see Oddie, 161–2, who comments that it was never published in Chesterton's lifetime 'perhaps because its real literary outcome was the first chapter of *Orthodoxy*'. Maisie Ward published the most finished version in *CL* 233–8, dating its composition to about 1896.

[41] *O.* 211, 213–15.

Philosophers might be surprised to hear that their 'main problem' and 'the main problem' to be discussed in *Orthodoxy* is: 'How can we contrive to be at once astonished at the world and yet at home in it? How can this queer cosmic town . . . give us at once the fascination of a strange town and the comfort and honour of being our own town?' The aim of the book is to show how Christianity satisfies 'this double spiritual need, the need for that mixture of the familiar and the unfamiliar which Christendom has rightly named romance'. But all arguments rest on unproven assumption—in this case the 'desirability of an active and imaginative life, picturesque and full of a poetical curiosity, a life such as western man at any rate always seems to have desired'. More prosaically, the assumption is that a life of 'variety and adventure' is better than a 'blank existence', that there is a human need for 'the combination of something that is strange with something that is secure'. In other words, Chesterton's starting point is the need for wonder at the world with which we are familiar, the basis from which he had evolved his own philosophy of life: 'We need so to view the world as to combine an idea of wonder and an idea of welcome. We need to be happy in this wonderland without once being merely comfortable.'[42]

Apologists for Christianity in the past could begin with the fact of sin, but original sin, 'the only part of Christian theology which can really be proved', was now being questioned by liberal theologians. Chesterton decides therefore to begin with the question of sanity rather than sin. And he argues that modern intellectuals show a 'combination between a logical completeness and a spiritual contraction' or a 'combination of an expansive and exhaustive reason with a contracted common sense'. Thus 'materialism has a sort of insane simplicity': one has 'at once the sense of it covering everything and the sense of it leaving everything out'. The certainty that 'history has been simply and solely a chain of causation' leads to 'a complete fatalism', which is the opposite of 'a liberating force': 'It is absurd to say that you are especially advancing freedom when you only use free thought to destroy free will.' But there is another scepticism even 'more terrible' than believing that 'everything began in matter' and that is the idealism that rejects any reality external to oneself. However, 'this panegoistic extreme of thought exhibits the same paradox as the other extreme of materialism', being 'equally complete in theory and equally crippling in practice'. Both sceptics have 'locked themselves up in two boxes', both the one 'who cannot believe his senses' and the one 'who cannot believe anything else'. Both sceptics can claim to be

---

[42] *O.* 212–13.

'infinitely reasonable' like a coin that is 'infinitely circular', but both have lost their reason. Both have begun from the wrong 'first principles', whereas what Chesterton calls 'mysticism' keeps people 'sane': 'As long as you have mystery you have health; when you destroy mystery you create morbidity.' What mysticism understands is that one 'can understand everything by the help of what' one 'does not understand': 'The morbid logician seeks to make everything lucid, and succeeds in making everything mysterious. The mystic allows one thing to be mysterious, and everything else becomes lucid.' It is like the sun: 'The one created thing which we cannot look at is the one thing in the light of which we look at everything.' Christianity allows for 'apparent contradictions' like free will, which it leaves as 'a sacred mystery'; whereas determinism 'makes the theory of causation quite clear' but leaves the determinist unable rationally to say 'please pass the mustard' to his prede-termined neighbour at the table. The Christian, on the contrary, allows for 'apparent contradictions' like free will, which it leaves 'a sacred mystery'. And here Chesterton employs imagery that he had already used for the title of his forthcoming novel *The Ball and the Cross*, which had been serialized during 1905 and 1906 in the Anglo-Catholic *Commonwealth*:

He puts the seed of dogma in a central darkness; but it branches forth in all directions with abounding natural health. As we have taken the circle as the symbol of reason and madness, we may very well take the cross as the symbol at once of mystery and health. Buddhism is centripetal, but Christianity is centrifu-gal: it breaks out. For the circle is perfect and infinite in its nature; but it is fixed for ever in its size; it can never be larger or smaller. But the cross, though it has at its heart a collision and a contradiction, can extend its four arms for ever without altering its shape. Because it has a paradox in its centre it can grow without changing. The circle returns upon itself and is bound. The cross opens its arms to the four winds; it is a signpost for free travellers.[43]

Because Christianity was shattered at the Reformation, Chesterton argues, the Christian virtues even more than the vices have been 'let loose, and they wander and do terrible damage'. One example is the way people now are humble not about themselves but about their convictions: 'At any street corner we may meet a man who utters the frantic and blasphemous statement that he may be wrong. Every day one comes across somebody who says that of course his view may not be the right one. Of course his view must be the right one, or it is not his view.' Religious authority was intended to be 'a barrier' against 'a great and possible peril to the human

---

[43] *O*. 217, 222, 225, 227, 229, 230–1.

mind: a peril as practical as burglary'. For—and remarkably Chesterton was writing before the onset of post-modernism—it is possible to 'prevent further thinking by teaching...that there is no validity in any human thought'. For to believe that there is any point in thinking is a matter of faith not reason: 'It is an act of faith to assert that our thoughts have any relation to reality at all.' Far from religion being opposed to reason, 'they are both methods of proof which cannot themselves be proved'. It was not surprising that, insofar as 'religion is gone, reason is going'. If the theory of evolution is anything more than 'an innocent scientific description of how certain earthly things came about', then it is an example of the thought that 'destroys itself', 'an attack upon thought itself'. It is one thing to believe that a personal God chose slowly to evolve man out of an ape, but, if evolution means 'a flux of everything and anything', then it is 'an attack not upon the faith, but upon the mind; you cannot think if there are no things to think about. You cannot think if you are not separate from the subject of thought.' Another attack upon thought itself is the common idea that what is right for one age is wrong for another, as 'this idea of a fundamental alteration in the standard is one of the things that make thought about the past or future simply impossible'. And, if one makes 'change itself' one's 'object or ideal', then 'change itself becomes un-changeable'. The pragmatist insists that 'there is an authoritative need to believe the things that are necessary to the human mind', but 'one of those necessities precisely is a belief in objective truth', and so it is necessary to be 'more than a pragmatist'. Seeing how 'reason destroys', Nietzsche's 'phil-osophy of Will' holds that the 'ultimate authority...is in will, not in reason'. But this philosophy of volition ends in the same cul-de-sac as 'the mere pursuit of logic': 'Exactly as complete free thought involves the doubting of thought itself, so the acceptation of mere "willing" really paralyses the will.' For, if will is all that matters, how can one choose to will one thing rather than another? 'And yet choosing one course as better than another is the very definition of the will you are praising.' To worship the will is effectively to negate the will. The philosophers of will speak of will as 'something that expands and breaks out. But it is quite the opposite. Every act of will is an act of self-limitation.' The 'anarchic will-worshippers' urge people to 'care for no laws or limits', but the 'moment you step into a world of facts, you step into a world of limits': 'If a triangle breaks out of its three sides, its life comes to a lamentable end.'[44]

---

[44] *O.* 233, 235–9, 240–4.

Chapter IV, 'The Ethics of Elfland', begins with an apparent digression, a very characteristic feature of Chesterton's writing. He explains that he has always been a Liberal (although he no longer believes in Liberal politicians), who believes in democracy in the sense of 'a self-governing humanity'. There are two principles of democracy: first, that 'the things common to all men are more important than the things peculiar to any men', that 'Ordinary things are more valuable than extraordinary things', in other words, that the 'sense of the miracle of humanity itself should always be more vivid to us than any marvels of power, intellect, art, or civilization'; and, second, that 'the political instinct or desire' is one of the things everyone has in common. Far from democracy being opposed to tradition, 'tradition is only democracy extended through time', a 'trusting to a consensus of common human voices' rather than the 'aristocracy' of talent. As always, Chesterton is on the side of the masses not the intellectuals: 'I have always been more inclined to believe the ruck of hard-working people than to believe that special and troublesome literary class to which I belong.' He prefers to trust to 'the awful authority of a mob' than to 'the authority of one expert'. And the 'mob' or masses also include the dead, as Chesterton explains in one of the most memorable passages in the book:

Tradition means giving votes to the most obscure of all classes, our ancestors. It is the democracy of the dead. Tradition refuses to submit to the small and arrogant oligarchy of those who merely happen to be walking about. All democrats object to men being disqualified by the accident of birth; tradition objects to their being disqualified by the accident of death.[45]

These prefatory remarks are intended to introduce what Chesterton wants to say about the idea of 'popular tradition', the 'earliest' of 'the three or four fundamental ideas' he has discovered for himself and that make up his 'personal philosophy or natural religion', and that he had been startled to discover had already been 'discovered by Christianity'. What he first came to believe in and what he still believes in are fairy tales. And what they taught him was that, while you cannot '*imagine* two and one not making three', you 'can easily imagine trees not bearing fruit; you can imagine them growing golden candlesticks or tigers hanging on by the tail'. Now in fairy tales 'this sharp distinction' was always observed 'between the science of mental relations, in which there really are laws, and the science of physical facts, in which there are no laws, but only weird repetitions'.

[45] *O*. 249–51.

But in the world of intellectuals, people talked of 'the actual things that happened—dawn and death and so on—as if *they* were rational and inevitable. They talked as if the fact that trees bear fruit were just as *necessary* as the fact that two and one trees make three.' In fairy tales, on the contrary, 'life was as precious as it was puzzling'. And fairy tales also included the necessity of limitation: 'The vision always hangs upon a veto. All the dizzy and colossal things conceded depend upon one small thing withheld.' Fairy tales gave Chesterton 'two convictions': 'first, that this world is a wild and startling place, which might have been quite different, but which is quite delightful; second, that before this wildness and delight one may well be modest and submit to the queerest limitations of so queer a kindness.' However, he was to discover that all the intellectuals were 'talking scientific fatalism', although they had 'really no proof' of an 'unavoidable repetition in things except the fact that the things were repeated'. 'All the towering materialism which dominates the modern mind', Chesterton protests, 'rests ultimately upon one assumption; a false assumption. It is supposed that if a thing goes on repeating itself it is probably dead; a piece of clockwork.' But suppose 'the sun rises regularly because he never gets tired of rising. His routine might be due, not to a lifelessness, but to a rush of life.' Children typically provide Chesterton with an analogy particularly shocking to the intellectuals:

A child kicks his legs rhythmically through excess, not absence, of life. Because children have abounding vitality, because they are in spirit fierce and free, therefore they want things repeated and unchanged. They always say, 'Do it again'; and the grown-up person does it again until he is nearly dead. For grown-up people are not strong enough to exult in monotony. But perhaps God is strong enough to exult in monotony. It is possible that God says every morning, 'Do it again' to the sun; and every evening, 'Do it again' to the moon. . . . The repetition in Nature may not be a mere recurrence; it may be a theatrical *encore.*

Since the world seemed magical to Chesterton rather than determined by some law, there might be a magician behind it. And if there was 'a purpose' there must be 'a person'. He had always 'felt life first as a story: and if there is a story there is a story-teller'. Again, modern intellectuals were very opposed to Chesterton's second conviction that this world involved 'strict limits and conditions' and preferred to talk about 'expansion and largeness'. But, as well as fairy tales, Chesterton had read as a boy *Robinson Crusoe*, 'which owes its eternal vivacity to the fact that it celebrates the poetry of limits': 'Crusoe is man on a small rock with a few comforts just snatched from the sea: the best thing in the book is simply the list of things saved from the wreck.' And so Chesterton, lastly, had a sense not only of the magic of the world, that it 'must have a meaning, and meaning must have some one to mean it', and that 'the proper form of thanks' for the 'pleasure' and 'privilege' of the world was 'some form of humility and restraint'—but 'last, and strangest, there had come into my mind a vague and vast impression that in some way all good was a remnant to be stored and held sacred out of some primordial ruin'. 'And all this time I had not even thought of Christian theology.'[46]

One 'belongs to this world' before one 'begins to ask if it is nice to belong to it'. But Chesterton's own 'acceptance of the universe' was not 'optimism' but 'more like patriotism. It is a matter of primary loyalty. The world is not a lodging-house at Brighton, which we are to leave because it is miserable. It is the fortress of our family, with the flag flying on the turret, and the more miserable it is the less we should leave it.' And in order to make it less miserable we need to have taken 'a cosmic oath of allegiance': 'We have to feel the universe at once as an ogre's castle, to be stormed, and yet as our own cottage, to which we can return at evening.' We need to 'hate it enough to change it, and yet love it enough to think it worth changing'. This idea that there was a 'need for a first loyalty to things, and then for a ruinous reform of things' was the point at which Chesterton felt an affinity to Christianity, for it was 'accused at one and the same time, of being too optimistic about the universe and of being too pessimistic about the world'. The reason was that Christianity was 'the answer to a riddle'. It taught that God in 'making' the world 'set it free. God had written not so much a poem, but rather a play; a play he had planned as perfect, but which had necessarily been left to human actors and stage-managers, who had since made a great mess of it.' The 'riddle' was how could one 'somehow find a way of loving the world without trusting it'. The answer was 'the dogmatic insistence that God was personal, and had made a world separate from him'. Christian optimism was 'based on the fact that we do *not* fit in to the world' and 'dwelt on the unnaturalness of everything in the light of the supernatural'. Having understood that he was 'in the *wrong* place', Chesterton's 'soul sang for joy, like a bird in spring'.[47]

Having attacked the 'imbecile habit . . . of saying that such and such a creed can be held in one age but cannot be held in another', Chesterton

---

[46] *O.* 252, 254, 258, 262–4, 267–8. Stanley L. Jaki, *Chesterton: A Seer of Science* (Michigan: Pinckney, 2001), 13, calls this chapter 'one of the most penetrating discourses on the nature of scientific reasoning that has been so far produced'.

[47] *O.* 270, 274–5, 277, 282–3.

proceeds to qualify this by arguing that 'a creed . . . can be believed more fixedly in a complex society than in a simple one'. Christianity is a complicated creed, which is why its truth can be seen more clearly in a complicated society. Far from being ashamed of the 'complexity' of Christianity, Christians should be as proud of it as scientists are 'proud of the complexity of science'. Keys and locks are 'complex' things, which is why, 'if a key fits a lock, you know it is the right key'. But the more reasons there are for believing something, the harder it is to explain this 'accumulation of truth':

It is very hard for a man to defend anything of which he is entirely convinced. It is comparatively easy when he is only partially convinced. He is partially convinced because he has found this or that proof of the thing, and he can expound it. But a man is not really convinced of a philosophic theory when he finds that something proves it. He is only really convinced when he finds that everything proves it. And the more converging reasons he finds pointing to this conviction, the more bewildered he is if asked suddenly to sum them up. Thus, if one asked an ordinary intelligent man on the spur of the moment, 'Why do you prefer civilization to savagery?' he would look wildly round at object after object, and would only be able to answer vaguely . . . The whole case for civilization is that the case for it is complex.

There is, then, 'a kind of huge helplessness' regarding 'all complete conviction': 'The belief is so big that it takes a long time to get it into action.' One does not know 'where one should begin'. And then Chesterton adds, almost as if the words applied to himself—he was after all fourteen years away from becoming a Roman Catholic: 'All roads lead to Rome; which is one reason why many people never get there.'[48]

There is, however, in Chesterton's view one very big objection to Christianity, and his admission is particularly significant a hundred years later in an age of globalization and religious pluralism: 'The one real objection to the Christian religion is simply that it is one religion.' After all, the world is a very large place, 'full of very different kinds of people'. However, Chesterton's next admission was hardly valid even a century ago: 'Christianity (it may reasonably be said) is one thing confined to one kind of people; it began in Palestine, it has practically stopped with Europe.' At any rate the objection had once impressed Chesterton, as it came to impress pluralist theologians later in the twentieth century. He too had been attracted by the idea of 'one great unconscious church of all

---

[48] *O.* 278, 286–7.

humanity founded on the omnipresence of the human conscience'. But what next struck Chesterton was that the ethical pluralists of his day 'were the very people who said that morality had changed altogether, and that what was right in one age was wrong in another'. And yet the same people who reproached Christianity for preaching a distinctive revelation to a particular people at a particular time were the same people who believed that 'science and progress were the discovery of one people, and that all other peoples had died in the dark'. But this was not their only inconsistency: they also reproached Christianity both for its asceticism *and* for its 'pomp' and 'ritualism'. But if their contradictory charges were correct, then Christianity, which they claimed was 'only one of the ordinary myths and errors of mortals', was guilty of 'exceptional corruption' that required an explanation. And it occurred to Chesterton that, 'if Jesus of Nazareth was not Christ, He must have been Antichrist'. It also struck him that these critics were guilty in their own lives of an extraordinary self-contradiction in combining 'extreme bodily luxury with an extreme absence of artistic pomp', and in being themselves 'really exceptional in history', for 'no man before ever ate such elaborate dinners in such ugly clothes'.[49]

Chesterton came to see that the problem was how 'to keep a balance', a problem that Christianity 'solved and solved in a very strange way'. Instead of saying like Greek philosophy that 'virtue was in a balance', Christianity 'declared it was in a conflict: the collision of two passions apparently opposite'. There was in fact no real inconsistency, only the difficulty of holding both 'simultaneously'. Courage, for example, 'is almost a contradiction in terms. It means a strong desire to live taking the form of a readiness to die.' The Christian precept that in order to save one's life it was necessary to lose it might have been 'a piece of everyday advice for sailors or mountaineers'. The paradox was 'the whole principle of courage'. And indeed paradox was 'the Christian key to ethics everywhere'. The Christian virtue of charity says that we must forgive the sinner, whom we must love very much, but not the sin, which we must hate very much: 'There was room for wrath and love to run wild.' Not surprisingly, with the decay of Christianity the 'heroic and monumental manner in ethics' had vanished. Unlike paganism, which was 'like a pillar of marble, upright because proportioned with symmetry',

Christianity was like a huge and ragged and romantic rock, which, though it sways on its pedestal at a touch, yet, because its exaggerated excrescences exactly

---

[49] *O.* 291–5.

balance each other, is enthroned there for a thousand years. In a Gothic cathedral the columns were all different, but they were all necessary. Every support seemed an accidental and fantastic support; every buttress was a flying buttress.

This explained the Christian care over exact theological definitions that so baffled its modern critics: 'The Church could not afford to swerve a hair's breadth on some things if she was to continue her great and daring experiment of the irregular equilibrium.' And it was 'the thrilling romance of Orthodoxy' that the Church had avoided the traps that beset her on every side:

People have fallen into a foolish habit of speaking of orthodoxy as something heavy, humdrum, and safe. There never was anything so perilous or so exciting as orthodoxy.... It was the equilibrium of a man behind madly rushing horses, seeming to stoop this way and to sway that, yet in every attitude having the grace of statuary and the accuracy of arithmetic.... She [the Church] swerved to left and right, so exactly as to avoid enormous obstacles.... The orthodox Church never took the tame course or accepted the conventions; the orthodox Church was never respectable.... It is always easy to let the age have its head; the difficult thing is to keep one's own. It is always easy to be a modernist; as it is easy to be a snob.... To have fallen into any one of the fads from Gnosticism to Christian Science would indeed have been obvious and tame. But to have avoided them all has been one whirling adventure; and in my vision the heavenly chariot flies thundering through the ages, the dull heresies sprawling and prostrate, the wild truth reeling but erect.[50]

And so Chesterton concludes this chapter on 'The Paradoxes of Christianity' with the ultimate paradox that the very word orthodoxy is the exact opposite of what the word normally suggests.

If 'some faith in our life is required even to improve it', as well as a 'necessary discontent with things as they are', it is not sufficient to have the 'equilibrium' of 'mere resignation'. Anyway, it is impossible to follow the Stoical advice 'to grin and bear' an unsatisfactory state of affairs, since, 'if you merely bear it, you do not grin'.

Greek heroes do not grin: but gargoyles do—because they are Christian. And when a Christian is pleased, he is (in the most exact sense) frightfully pleased; his pleasure is frightful. Christ prophesied the whole of Gothic architecture in that hour when nervous and respectable people (such people as now object to barrel organs) objected to the shouting of the gutter-snipes of Jerusalem. He said, 'If these were silent, the very stones would cry out.' Under the impulse of His spirit

[50] *O.* 297–8, 300–1, 303–5.

arose like a clamorous chorus, the façades of the mediaeval cathedrals, thronged with shouting faces and open mouths. The prophecy has fulfilled itself: the very stones cry out.

The grin of a Christian is alarming because, while the Christian is ready to 'bear', the Christian is not prepared to do so with 'mere resignation'. For the Christian who is sufficiently 'fond of this world, even in order to change it', is also 'fond of another world...to change it to'. But for modern intellectuals, 'the vision of heaven is always changing', which means that 'the vision of earth will be exactly the same'. For progress means 'changing the world to suit the vision', not 'always changing the vision', in which case the reality will remain the same. There will be no possibility of a revolution; whereas, to the Christian, 'there must always be a case for revolution; for in the hearts of men God has been put under the feet of Satan'. But the Christian vision is not only 'fixed', it is 'composite'—that is, it is 'a definite picture composed of...elements in their best proportion and relation'. But such a picture 'must be fixed by some mind; for only a mind can place the exact proportions of a composite happiness'. And, thirdly, 'watchfulness' is also needed for progress, which means that one must be revolutionary not conservative. Practically echoing Newman's theory of development, namely, that there has to be change precisely to preserve identity, Chesterton writes:

all conservatism is based upon the idea that if you leave things alone you leave them as they are. But you do not. If you leave a thing alone you leave it to a torrent of change. If you leave a white post alone it will soon be a black post. If you particularly want it to be white you must be always painting it again; that is, you must be always having a revolution. Briefly, if you want the old white post you must have a new white post.

Chesterton's 'theory of progress' demands, then, a constant vigilance, for it has to deal with original sin, which means that the constant danger is 'not in man's environment, but in man'. This is why the only political system Chesterton can trust is democracy, which agrees with Christianity that 'the man should rule who does *not* think he can rule'. Democracy is also

profoundly Christian in this practical sense—that it is an attempt to get at the opinion of those who would be too modest to offer it. It is a mystical adventure; it is specially trusting those who do not trust themselves. That enigma is strictly peculiar to Christendom....there is something psychologically Christian about the idea of seeking for the opinion of the obscure rather than taking the obvious course of accepting the opinion of the prominent. To say that voting is Christian may seem somewhat curious. To say that canvassing is Christian may seem quite crazy.

But canvassing is very Christian in its primary idea. It is encouraging the humble; it is saying to the modest man, 'Friend, go up higher.'

Unlike the humility of democracy, the pride of aristocracy means 'the drift or slide of men into a sort of natural pomposity and praise of the powerful'. The 'natural trend or lapse into taking one's self seriously' comes naturally to fallen men: 'For solemnity flows out of men naturally; but laughter is a leap. It is easy to be heavy: hard to be light. Satan fell by the force of gravity.' As Chesterton constructed his Utopia, he found 'as usual' that Christianity had anticipated him. But there was one final requirement that again he found in Christianity, 'the liberty for which I chiefly care, the liberty to bind myself'. Limitation, like paradox and humour, is an essential element in Chesterton's philosophy: 'Complete anarchy would not merely make it impossible to have any discipline or fidelity; it would also make it impossible to have any fun. To take an obvious example, it would not be worth while to bet if a bet were not binding.' This, then, is the last of his requirements of his 'social paradise': 'I should ask to be kept to my bargain, to have my oaths and engagements taken seriously'—above all in marriage, which 'is the great example of a real and irrevocable result; and that is why it is the chief subject and centre of all our romantic writing'.[51]

Orthodoxy is under threat from so-called liberal theologians, whose ideas are in fact 'definitely illiberal' and would 'bring tyranny into the world'. A liberal clergyman

always means a man who wishes at least to diminish the number of miracles; it never means a man who wishes to increase that number. It always means a man who is free to disbelieve that Christ came out of His grave; it never means a man who is free to believe that his own aunt came out of her grave.

It is not liberalism that permits disbelief in the Resurrection, but 'strict materialism' that forbids belief. Tennyson's dictum that there was faith in doubt was true in 'a profound and even a horrible' way: the refusal to believe in miracles represented 'faith in a fixed and godless fate; a deep and sincere faith in the incurable routine of the cosmos'. To deny 'the liberty of God' to work miracles is hardly 'a triumph of the liberal idea' but rather 'leaves nothing free in the universe'. Again, liberal theologians believe that religions teach the same things, albeit in different 'rites and forms'. The favourite example of 'this alleged identity of all human religions is the alleged spiritual identity of Buddhism and Christianity'. (It was noticeable

[51] *O.* 307, 310, 312–13, 315, 319–21, 323–8.

that these liberals were 'cautious in their praises' of Islam, 'generally confining themselves to imposing its morality only upon the refreshment of the lower classes', and even 'cold' in their attitude to its view of marriage.) In fact, the Christian saint was the diametrical opposite of the Buddhist saint who 'always has his eyes shut, while the Christian saint always has them very wide open. The Buddhist saint has a sleek and harmonious body, but his eyes are heavy and sealed with sleep. The mediaeval saint's body is wasted to its crazy bones, but his eyes are frightfully alive.' The reason is that the Buddhist 'is looking with a peculiar intentness inwards. The Christian is staring with a frantic intentness outwards.' For the Buddhist, 'personality is the fall of man, for the Christian it is the purpose of God, the whole point of his cosmic idea'. The significance of the 'almost insane happiness in the eyes' of the Christian saint, as opposed to 'the sealed eyes' of the Buddhist, is that the Christian is happy because he has been 'cut off from the world; he is separate from things and is staring at them in astonishment. But why should the Buddhist saint be astonished at things?—since there is really only one thing, and that being impersonal can hardly be astonished at itself.' In Buddhism 'God is inside man', and consequently 'man is always inside himself'; but because Christianity insists that 'God transcends man, man has transcended himself'. Again, there is nothing liberal in substituting monotheism for Trinitarian Christianity which sees God as 'a society':

The *heart* of humanity, especially of European humanity, is certainly much more satisfied by the strange hints and symbols that gather round the Trinitarian idea, the image of a council at which mercy pleads as well as justice, the conception of a sort of liberty and variety existing even in the inmost chamber of the world. For Western religion has always felt keenly the idea 'it is not well for man to be alone'.

The doctrine that 'bewilders the intellect utterly quiets the heart'. Very different is the religion of Islam: 'out of the desert, from the dry places and the dreadful suns, come the cruel children of the lonely God; the real Unitarians who with scimitar in hand have laid waste the world. For it is not well for God to be alone.' Or again, on the question of salvation, it is considered liberal to believe that salvation is 'inevitable'—but 'it is not specially favourable to activity or progress'. For the Buddhist, 'existence . . . must end up in a certain way. But to a Christian existence is a *story*, which may end up in any way.' That is why, Chesterton enjoys adding, it is very like the despised 'popular fiction' of the masses—and if 'you say that popular fiction is vulgar and tawdry, you only say what the dreary and well-informed say about the images in the Catholic churches'.[52] Indeed, life is actually 'very like a serial story in a magazine: life ends with the promise (or menace) "to be continued in our next"'. For, 'with a noble vulgarity, life imitates the serial and leaves off at the exciting moment. For death is distinctly an exciting moment.' Life is an 'exciting' story 'because it has in it so strong an element of will, of what theology calls free will'—which is why 'Christendom has excelled in the narrative romance'. As for the liberal 'attempts to diminish or explain away the divinity of Christ', what is certain is that the alleged divinity is 'terribly revolutionary'. And here paradox rises to an extraordinary theological intensity and penetration, a paradox to which he would only dare to allude briefly in *The Everlasting Man*:

That a good man may have his back to the wall is no more than we knew already; but that God could have His back to the wall is a boast for all insurgents for ever. Christianity is the only religion on earth that has felt that omnipotence made God incomplete. Christianity alone has felt that God, to be wholly God, must have been a rebel as well as a king. Alone of all creeds, Christianity has added courage to the virtues of the Creator. For the only courage worth calling courage must necessarily mean that the soul passes a breaking point—and does not break. . . . But in that terrific tale of the Passion there is a distinct emotional suggestion that the author of all things (in some unthinkable way) went not only through agony, but through doubt. It is written, 'Thou shalt not tempt the Lord thy God.' No: but the Lord thy God may tempt Himself; and it seems as if this was what happened in Gethsemane. In a garden Satan tempted man: and in a garden God tempted God. He passed in some superhuman manner through our human horror of pessimism. When the world shook and the sun was wiped out of heaven, it was not at the crucifixion, but at the cry from the cross: the cry which confessed that God was forsaken of God.

Chesterton boasts that there has never been 'another god who has himself been in revolt'; and atheists will never find another god 'who has ever uttered their desolation', for there is 'only one religion in which God seemed for an instant to be an atheist'.[53]

The reason why Chesterton believes in orthodox Christianity is the same reason why an unbeliever does not believe; and it is the same reason,

[52] 'His comment on the bad statues and fripperies which so many Catholics find a trial was: "It shows the wisdom of the Church. The whole thing is so terrific that if people did not have these let-downs they would go mad' (Ward, *GKC* 522).

[53] *O.* 330–4, 336–8, 340–3.

as Chesterton knew, that Newman gives. In both cases, the evidence lies 'in
an enormous accumulation of small but unanimous facts' that 'converge'.
But are the unbeliever's 'facts' true in fact? Above all, the stereotyped idea
of Jesus Christ does not in the least resemble the man Chesterton encoun-
ters in the Gospels, as he explains in a passage that startles the reader's
imagination into seeing a figure he has long looked at, or thought he
looked at, only to see for the first time:

Instead of looking at books and pictures about the New Testament I looked at the
New Testament. There I found an account, not in the least of a person with his
hair parted in the middle or his hands clasped in appeal, but of an extraordinary
being with lips of thunder and acts of lurid decision, flinging down tables, casting
out devils, passing with the wild secrecy of the wind from mountain isolation to a
sort of dreadful demagogy; a being who often acted like an angry god—and
always like a god.

    Christ had even a literary style of his own, not to be found, I think, elsewhere;
it consists of an almost furious use of the *a fortiori*. His 'how much more' is piled
one upon another like castle upon castle in the clouds. The diction ... used by
Christ is quite curiously gigantesque; it is full of camels leaping through needles
and mountains hurled into the sea. Morally, it is equally terrific; he called himself
a sword of slaughter, and told men to buy swords if they sold their coats for them.
That he used even wilder words on the side of non-resistance greatly increases the
mystery; but it also, if anything, rather increases the violence. We cannot even
explain it by calling such a being insane; for insanity is usually along one
consistent channel. The maniac is generally a monomaniac. Here we must
remember the difficult definition of Christianity already given; Christianity is a
superhuman paradox whereby two opposite passions may blaze beside each
other. The one explanation of the Gospel language that does explain it, is that
it is the survey of one who from some supernatural height beholds some more
startling synthesis.[54]

Among the many converging facts that convince Chesterton of the truth of
orthodox Christianity is the existence of miracles. Yet

an extraordinary idea has arisen that the disbelievers in miracles consider them
coldly and fairly, while believers in miracles accept them only in connection with
some dogma. The fact is quite the other way. The believers in miracles accept
them (rightly or wrongly) because they have evidence for them. The disbelievers
in miracles deny them (rightly or wrongly) because they have doctrine against
them.

[54] *O.* 348, 351–2.

And the democratic Chesterton who believes in the common man rather than the Superman adds: 'The open, democratic thing is to believe an old apple-woman when she bears testimony to a miracle, just as you believe an old apple-woman when she bears testimony to a murder.' Similarly, if a peasant's story about a ghost is dismissed, it is dismissed 'either because the man is a peasant or because the story is a ghost story. That is, you either deny the main principle of democracy, or you affirm the main principle of materialism—the abstract impossibility of miracles.' Another reason Chesterton has for believing in Christianity is that 'the Christian Church in its practical relation to my soul is a living teacher, not a dead one. It not only certainly taught me yesterday, but will almost certainly teach me to-morrow.' The Christ who dies on the cross still teaches:

Plato has told you a truth; but Plato is dead. Shakespeare has startled you with an image; but Shakespeare will not startle you with any more. But imagine what it would be like to live with such men still living, to know that Plato might break out with an original lecture tomorrow, or that at any moment Shakespeare might shatter everything with a single song. The man who lives in contact with what he believes to be a living Church is a man always expecting to meet Plato and Shakespeare tomorrow at breakfast.

When Chesterton gives the ideal of virginity as an example of the Church teaching him something he knows nothing about, it is hard not to believe that this living Christian Church was already for Chesterton the Roman Catholic Church. At any rate, this living Christian Church 'has revealed itself as truth-telling thing. All other philosophies say the things that plainly seem to be true; only this philosophy has again and again said the thing that does not seem to be true, but is true. Alone of all creeds it is convincing where it is not attractive . . .'. One such unattractive doctrine is the doctrine of original sin: indeed, it is the 'primary paradox of Christianity . . . that the ordinary condition of man is not his sane or sensible condition; that the normal itself is an abnormality'. And this doctrine 'has one special application to the ultimate idea of joy'. For it has to be part of the Chestertonian philosophy of wonder that 'it is not native to man' to be 'sad': 'Man is more himself, man is more manlike, when joy is the fundamental thing in him, and grief the superficial.' But the unbeliever cannot experience joy at a universe without meaning or purpose, but only pleasure in transient things. And Chesterton ends this chapter and the book with a passage as startling to the imagination as that at the end of the previous chapter, as a Christ we had never before seen we now see for the first time.

Joy...is the gigantic secret of the Christian. And as I close this chaotic volume I open again the strange small book from which all Christianity came; and I am again haunted by a kind of confirmation. The tremendous figure which fills the Gospels towers in this respect, as in every other, above all the thinkers who ever thought themselves tall. His pathos was natural, almost casual. The Stoics, ancient and modern, were proud of concealing their tears. He never concealed His tears; He showed them plainly on His open face at any daily sight, such as the far sight of His native city. Yet He concealed something. Solemn supermen and imperial diplomatists are proud of restraining their anger. He never restrained His anger. He flung furniture down the front steps of the Temple, and asked men how they expected to escape the damnation of Hell. Yet He restrained something. I say it with reverence; there was in that shattering personality a thread that must be called shyness. There was something that He hid from all men when He went up a mountain to pray. There was something that He covered constantly by abrupt silence or impetuous isolation. There was some one thing that was too great for God to show us when He walked upon our earth; and I have sometimes fancied that it was His mirth.[55]

5

The rumour had been that the Chestertons were intending to live on the Yorkshire moors, a reasonable guess in view of their fondness for the area and the fact that they would be close to their friends the Steinthals and Father O'Connor. When Chesterton eventually revealed their destination to his brother, it seemed something of an anti-climax. 'Frances wants to go to Beaconsfield,' Cecil reported to 'Keith', according to her account. '"Why—Beaconsfield?" I asked, and Fleet Street echoed the query.' 'It was, and is,' 'Keith' commented scornfully, 'a clean, bright place, inhabited by the wives and families of City men—solicitors, stockbrokers and the like, who return for bed and breakfast every evening and enjoy full board on Sundays.' It was, the ultimate insult, a suburban 'dormitory, but little more'. It was certainly not a place for intellectuals, being hardly 'a centre of mental activity or creative idea'. The proper countryside with proper peasants would have been far more acceptable:

---

[55] *O.* 355, 359–60, 362–6. Cf. 'And I knew there can be laughter | On the secret face of God.' ('The Fish', *CP* i. 212); 'But mirth is sacred: when from all his own | He sundered, going up a mount to pray | Under the terrible stars in stern array | Upon the lonely peak he laughed alone.' ('Secrecy', *CP* i. 167).

'Now,' said Cecil, 'if Frances had taken Gilbert to a village it would have been quite different. Labourers, ploughmen and poachers have a grip on fundamentals—food and marriage, God and the land; all the things that really matter. They can think, you know, and argue. How Gilbert would enjoy sitting in a jolly local, talking to the country folk and drinking country ale.'

'Keith' thought that the local pub and ale were not Frances's scene—even if less hateful than Fleet Street, which she hated 'with an ice-cold detachment, unmitigated by her husband's meteoric journalistic success or the unstinted praise which applauded his work, or even the considerable income he made by it'. Until the tragic death of Frances's brother, Chesterton had succeeded in shelving the issue of their leaving London:

He would dwell on how in ripe old age they would retire to an oak-timbered cottage on a wold or a weald—descriptively delightful but geographically vague—and once . . . they took the train to Buckinghamshire in search of such a paradise. Frances had buns and tea, Gilbert consumed bread and cheese and ale in a jolly old inn, which he always swore they found at Beaconsfield.

'Keith' and Cecil 'one irresponsible Saturday' looked for that inn, which they never found, although they searched the roads with their 'neat suburban villas many times and passed along the last remnants of the fine old village High Street, flanked by an extremely up-to-date hotel'. Nevertheless Frances, 'Keith' scornfully remarked, was apparently taken by 'the vision', and began to look for a house there.[56]

Chesterton's own recollection was that, while they were living in Kensington immediately after they were married, one day they 'strolled out . . . for a sort of second honeymoon, and went upon a journey into the void, a voyage deliberately objectless'.

I saw a passing omnibus labelled 'Hanwell' and, feeling this to be an appropriate omen, we boarded it and left it somewhere at a stray station, which I entered and asked the man in the ticket-office where the next train went to. He uttered the pedantic reply, 'Where do you want to go to?' And I uttered the profound and philosophical rejoinder, 'Wherever the next train goes to.' It seemed that it went to Slough; which may seem to be singular taste, even in a train. However, we went to Slough, and from there set out walking with even less notion of where were going. And in that fashion we passed through the large and quiet cross-roads of a sort of village, and stayed at an inn called The White Hart. We asked the name of the place and were told that it was called Beaconsfield (I mean of course that it was

---

[56] MCC, 67–70.

called Beconsfield and not Beaconsfield), and we said to each other, 'This is the sort of place where some day we will make our home.'[57]

The White Heart still stands in old Beaconsfield, the original village, and the original sixteenth-century inn has become a hotel. The Chestertons were married in 1901, and 'Keith' and Cecil obviously had no reason to visit Beaconsfield before hearing the news of the impending move in 1909, and indeed may not have made the visit till well after the move; by then the inn that Chesterton talked of may have become the 'up-to-date hotel' which 'Keith' refers to. But even if it was already a hotel when the Chestertons visited it, Chesterton was justified in referring to the old inn that still stood there.

[57] *A.* 202–3.

7

Shaw and Beaconsfield

I N April 1905 Chesterton had replied, in his weekly column in the *Daily News* on three consecutive Saturdays, to an attack by George Bernard Shaw on Shakespeare for writing for popular appeal and for money. It was the beginning of an argument mostly about politics and religion that lasted for a number of years, which they conducted not only in print but in live debates and eventually in the new medium of the wireless. It was also the beginning of a friendship between the two sharply contrasting opponents, the thin, vegetarian, teetotal Shaw and the fat, carnivorous, bibulous Chesterton.

Chesterton's first article on 15 April was headed 'The Great Shawkspear Mystery'. The problem with Shaw, Chesterton pronounced, was that he was too 'serious to enjoy Shakespeare', indeed 'too serious properly to enjoy life'. Both Shakespeare and life were 'illogical where he is logical, chaotic where he is orderly, mystical where he is clear'. Apart from failing the Chestertonian test of 'sanity' by being over serious and over logical and unmystical, Shaw also did not understand 'exuberance, an outrageous excess of words, a violent physical pleasure in mere vocabulary, an animal spirit in intellectual things'. The inevitable connection with Dickens is made—but, to a modern writer like Shaw, Shakespeare is even more incomprehensible, for Renaissance writers 'were sometimes so exuberant and exultant in their mere joy of existence that their mirth is not even obvious . . . These giants are shaken with a mysterious laughter. They seem torn by the agony of jokes as incommunicable as the wisdom of the gods.' It was 'this almost animal joy of self-expression' that Shaw fatally lacked.

Shaw could 'give a living and startling photograph of the prose of our existence' because he lacked 'an ear for its poetry'. He had 'plenty of common sense', which was 'one half of human sanity'—but he was without the other half, 'he has no common nonsense'.[1]

A week later Chesterton answered Shaw's complaint that Shakespeare wrote 'romantic nonsense' because he found it 'paid'. In fact, Shakespeare wrote romantic plays because he 'enjoyed the same romance as the ordinary man, just as he enjoyed the same beer'. Shakespeare's tastes were those of the common man because he was 'an ordinary man' as well as 'an extraordinary man'—whereas Shaw might be 'as extraordinary a man as Shakespeare; but he is only an extraordinary man'. Shakespeare, like his heroes, was both. In his third column on the subject a week later, Chesterton rejected Shaw's criticism of Shakespeare's alleged pessimism. On the contrary, Shakespeare had 'an atmosphere or spirit' that was common before the advent of the Puritans, that of 'the comic supernatural'. The modern world had 'sad mysticism' but not 'farcical mysticism'—it had no conception of 'any energies in the universe being actually merrier than we'.[2]

More than two years later on 7 December 1907, Hilaire Belloc published an article called 'Thoughts about Modern Thought' in the *New Age*, a radical Socialist journal edited by A. R. Orage. This was followed on 4 January 1908 by Chesterton's article 'Why I am not a Socialist'. He fully recognized the situation Socialism sought to remedy: 'To say that I do not like the present state of wealth and poverty is merely to say I am not a devil in human form. No one but Satan or Beelzebub could like the present state of wealth and poverty.' However, what he objected to in the typical socialist Utopia was that it made sharing rather than giving and receiving 'the highest or most human of altruistic pleasures'. For what Socialists proposed was less significant than 'the spirit in which it is proposed': 'When a great revolution is made, it is seldom the fulfilment of its own exact formula; but it is almost always in the image of its own impulse and feeling for life.' In the event of a Socialist revolution, its 'practical proposal' might not be fulfilled, but its 'ideal vision' certainly would be. But where Chesterton differed not only from Socialists but also from anarchists, Conservatives, and Liberals was in his strong belief in 'the mass of the common people': 'Caught in the trap of a terrible industrial machinery, harried by a shameful economic cruelty, surrounded with an ugliness and

[1] CS 347–9.   [2] CS 352–3, 357–8.

desolation never endured before among men, stunted by a stupid and provincial religion, or by a more stupid and more provincial irreligion, the poor are still by far the sanest, jolliest, and most reliable part of the community . . .'. And what was certain, Chesterton declared, was that they hated and despised 'the whole smell and sentiment and general ideal of Socialism'. Those things to which they were most attached, such as 'the privacy of homes, the control of one's own children, the minding of one's own business', were 'opposite to the tone of most Socialists'. They had no desire for the kind of Socialism that 'a handful of decorative artists and Oxford dons and journalists and Countesses on the Spree' wished to impose on them. Not that Chesterton had any truck with capitalism: 'It is the negation of property that the Duke of Westminster should own whole streets and squares of London; just as it would be the negation of marriage if he had all living women in one great harem.' And he ended by declaring that he was neither a Socialist nor a Tory because he had 'not lost faith in democracy'.

H. G. Wells replied to Belloc and Chesterton on 11 January. Chesterton responded on 25 January. Like Shaw, Wells had 'a contempt for mankind'—although he expressed it 'gently' rather than 'fiercely'—assuming that those who frequented 'the bar must be as dull and greasy as the bar; that mean streets must have mean emotions'. Chesterton agreed, however, that there was 'one evil' that Socialism would 'cure—starvation': 'There is one argument for Socialism—hunger.' On 15 February Shaw joined battle with the best-known article of the controversy, in which he introduced to the public the 'Chesterbelloc'—'a very amusing pantomime elephant, the front legs being that very exceptional and unEnglish individual Hilaire Belloc, and the hind legs . . . G. K. Chesterton'. It was not a well-coordinated animal: 'Chesterton and Belloc are so unlike that they get frightfully in one another's way,' and, 'in order to co-ordinate the movements of the Chesterbelloc, Chesterton has to make all the intellectual sacrifices that are demanded by Belloc'. Shaw issued this challenge to this ill-matched beast:

And now, what has the Chesterbelloc (or either of its two pairs of legs) to say in its defence? But it is from the hind legs that I particularly want to hear: because South Salford will very soon cure Hilaire Forelegs of his fancy for the ideals of the Catholic peasant proprietor. He is up against his problems in Parliament: it is in Battersea Park that a great force is in danger of being wasted.[3]

---

[3] Conlon, i. 138–9, 143.

Chesterton replied on 29 February in an article called 'The Last of the Rationalists', complaining again that Shaw and his fellow Socialists had 'no sympathy with the poor': they had 'Niagaras of pity. But they have no sympathy; they do not feel with ordinary men about ordinary things.' It was not surprising that this 'monstrous animal, the Chester-Belloc, with its horrible fore legs and its hideous hind legs', terrified them: 'it is Humanity on the move.' As for Shaw's rejection of Christianity, this was simply because of 'the positivist philosophy in which we were all brought up; but some of us have thought our way out of it'. Shaw was telling everybody 'ten times a week that what we want is not reason but life', and that 'the lust to live, to live even for oneself, to live infinitely' was 'glorious': 'Exactly: but the moment you mention life beyond the grave, Shaw's mind drops forty feet to the level of the Hall of Science, and he begins to say that it is mean and cowardly to wish to live for ever. This is manifest nonsense. It cannot be noble to desire life and mean to desire everlasting life.' Again, for the last five years Shaw had been 'preaching' the 'doctrine of the transforming power of will. But it will give him a great shock when he discovers that it is only the Christian doctrine of Miracles: then, very likely, he will drop it like a hot potato.'

The next day Shaw wrote to Chesterton, demanding to know why he had still not written a play, Shaw's own favoured medium for communicating his ideas. That should be Chesterton's medium, too, for responding to Shaw's 'Chesterbelloc' attack.

What about that play? It is no use trying to answer me in the New Age: the real answer to my article is the play. I have tried fair means: the New Age article was the inauguration of an assault below the belt. I shall deliberately destroy your credit as an essayist, as a journalist, as a critic, as a Liberal, as everything that offers your laziness a refuge, until starvation and shame drive you to serious dramatic parturition. I shall repeat my public challenge to you; vaunt my superiority; insult your corpulence; torture Belloc; if necessary, call on you and steal your wife's affections by intellectual and athletic displays, until you contribute something to the British drama. You are played out as an essayist: your ardour is soddened, your intellectual substance crumbled, by the attempt to keep up the work of your twenties in your thirties. Another five years of this and you will be the apologist of every infamy that wears a Liberal or Catholic mask.

In conclusion, Shaw insists: 'Nothing can save you now except a rebirth as a dramatist.'[4]

---

[4] *Bernard Shaw: Collected Letters 1898–1910*, ed. Dan H. Laurence (London: Max Reinhardt, 1972), 759.

Meanwhile the debate continued in the *New Age* into the next year and spread to public meetings, at one of which in November 1908 Shaw and Cecil Chesterton supported Socialism against Belloc and Chesterton.

In December Chesterton returned to the attack on Shaw in his weekly platform, the *Daily News*, demonstrating to Shaw how to be serious by being farcical. The article, a little satirical gem, typically much funnier than anything in Chesterton's fiction, was headed 'How I Found the Superman'. He had found him, he teased, in just the kind of place the intellectuals like Shaw and Wells most despised—the London dormitory suburb of South Croydon. His mother was 'Lady Hypatia Smyth-Browne (now Lady Hypatia Hagg)', whose name 'will never be forgotten in the East End, where she did such splendid social work'. Chesterton evokes the aristocratic, Socialist philanthropist (he once defined the philanthropist as 'not a brother' but 'a supercilious aunt'[5]): 'Her constant cry of "Save the children!" referred to the cruel neglect of children's eyesight involved in allowing them to play with crudely painted toys.' As a good Fabian, she could quote 'unanswerable statistics to prove that children allowed to look at violet and vermilion often suffered from failing eyesight in their extreme old age; and it was owing to her ceaseless crusade that the pestilence of the Monkey-on-the-Stick was almost swept from Hoxton.' This 'devoted worker would tramp the streets untiringly, taking away the toys from all the poor children, who were often moved to tears by her kindness'. But then, unfortunately, her 'good work was interrupted, partly by a new interest in the creed of Zoroaster, and partly by a savage blow from an umbrella'.

It was inflicted by a dissolute Irish apple-woman, who, on returning from some orgy to her ill-kept apartment, found Lady Hypatia in the bedroom taking down some oleograph, which, to say the least of it, could not really elevate the mind. At this the ignorant and partly intoxicated Celt dealt the social reformer a severe blow, adding to it an absurd accusation of theft. The lady's exquisitely balanced mind received a shock; and it was during a short mental illness that she married Dr Hagg.

At first, there seemed to be 'something like a rift, a faint, but perceptible, fissure' between the views of Dr Hagg, a practitioner of eugenics, with a 'ruthless insight into the history of religions', and 'those of his aristocratic wife':

---

[5] Ward, *GKC* 254.

For she was in favour (to use her own powerful epigram) of protecting the poor against themselves; while he declared pitilessly, in a new and striking metaphor, that the weakest must go to the wall. Eventually, however, the married pair perceived an essential union in the unmistakably modern character of both their views; and in this enlightened and comprehensible expression their souls found peace. The result is that this union of the two highest types of our civilization, the fashionable lady and the all but vulgar medical man, has been blessed by the birth of the Superman, that being whom all the labourers in Battersea are so eagerly expecting night and day.

The discoverer of the Superman finds the residence of Dr and Lady Hagg without difficulty, and boldly asks 'if the Superman was nice looking'.

'He creates his own standard, you see,' [Lady Hypatia] replied, with a slight sigh. 'Upon that plane he is more than Apollo. Seen from our lower plane, of course . . . ' And she sighed again.
   I had a horrible impulse, and said suddenly, 'Has he got any hair?'
   There was a long and painful silence, and then Dr Hagg said smoothly, 'Everything upon that plane is different; what he has got is not . . . well, not, of course, what we call hair . . . but . . . '

As a journalist, the discoverer says that he would like to be able to say that he has shaken hands with the Superman. That presents problems: 'You know he can't exactly shake hands . . . not hands, you know . . . The structure, of course . . . ' Rushing into the room where he supposes the Superman to be, the discoverer finds it to be pitch black. He hears 'a small sad yelp' from within, and behind him 'a double shriek'. 'You have let in a draught on him; and he is dead.' As he walks away from Croydon that night, he sees a coffin being carried out 'that was not of any human shape'. Above the wind whirled the poplars, 'so that they drooped and nodded like the plumes of some cosmic funeral'. ' "It is, indeed," said Dr Hagg, "the whole universe weeping over the frustration of its most magnificent birth." But I thought that there was a hoot of laughter in the high wail of the wind.'[6]
   Next year, Chesterton became engaged in controversy of a very different kind. In January 1909 he published an article in the modernist *Church Socialist Quarterly*, contrasting traditional Christianity, which 'like a tree goes on growing, and therefore goes on changing; but always in the fringes surrounding something unchangeable', with modernist Christianity, which means not 'something that produces external changes from a permanent

---

[6] CS 359–62. The article was reprinted in *AD* 129–34.

and organic centre' but 'something that changes completely and entirely in every part, at every minute, like a cloud'. In reply to a scathing attack in the April issue by Robert Dell, a Roman Catholic Modernist, Chesterton responded in the July issue by wondering why Dell could not 'become a new-fashioned Catholic without immediately becoming an old-fashioned Protestant'. Dell must know that a convert like Newman did not stop thinking when he became a Roman Catholic. And he added for good measure words that remind one of Newman's defence of the infallibility of the Roman Catholic Church in the last chapter of his *Apologia pro Vita sua*:

he must know that the whole phrase about being saved the trouble of thinking is a boyish fallacy. Euclid does not save geometricians the trouble of thinking when he insists on absolute definitions and unalterable axioms. On the contrary, he gives them the great trouble of thinking logically. The dogma of the Church limits thought about as much as the dogma of the solar system limits physical science. It is not an arrest of thought, but a fertile basis and constant provocation of thought.

Significantly, Chesterton admitted that he was 'still in some doubt' as to 'the seat of the Catholic authority', but he was in no doubt that he was closer to 'high Anglicans than the Roman Modernists'. And he had never felt closer to the Church of Rome than when he read Dell's attack on it. Unsurprisingly, Dell left the Roman Catholic Church and abandoned Christianity.[7]

In the same month in the *Hibbert Journal* Chesterton replied to an article denying the divinity of Christ. As in *Orthodoxy*, he challenged stereotyped conceptions of Jesus. Reading the Gospels does not, he protested, give us the picture of 'a recognisable Jew of the first century, with the traceable limitations of such a man'. This was 'exactly what we do not see'; rather what we see is 'an extraordinary being who would certainly have seemed as mad in one century as another, who makes a vague and vast claim to divinity'. Sometimes he seemed like a 'maniac', at other times like a 'prophet'. What he definitely was not was 'a Galilean of the time of Tiberius'; nor did he appear so to his fellow Jews, 'who lynched him, still shuddering at his earth-shaking blasphemies'. Nor was he any ordinary teacher: he was 'splendid and suggestive indeed, but full of riddles and outrageous demands'. On the other hand, if God had really become man, then 'I think we should see in such a being exactly the perplexities that we see in the central figure of the Gospels':

[7] Pearce, 148–50.

I think he would seem to us to contradict himself; because, looking down on life like a map, he would see a connection between things which to us are disconnected. I think, however, that he would always ring true to our own sense of right, but ring (so to speak) too loud and too clear. He would be too good . . . for us . . . I think there would be, in the nature of things, some tragic collision between him and the humanity he had created, culminating in something that would be at once a crime and an expiation . . . I think, in short, that he would give us a sensation that he was turning all our standards upside down, and yet also a sensation that he had undeniably put them the right way up.[8]

At the beginning of July Chesterton wrote confidentially to Father O'Connor about the state of Frances's health. They were again up north staying in Ilkley but not with the Steinthals (he wrote from 10 Crossbeck Road, where they had presumably taken lodgings). Clearly, Chesterton was or had been very worried not about Frances's physical but about her mental health, no doubt wondering if depression did not run in his wife's family. He had 'brought Frances away here she was hit so heavily with a sort of wasting fatigue'. He was anxious to discover whether 'the doctors were right in thinking it *only* fatigue or whether (by the hellish chance out of a hundred) it might be the beginning of some real illness'. But he was now 'pretty well convinced' that 'the doctors are right and it is only nervous exhaustion'.[9] He would not, he continued,

write this to anyone else, but you combine so unusually in your own single personality the characters of (1) Priest (2) human being (3) man of science (4) man of the world (5) man of the other world (6) old friend (7) new friend, not to mention Irishman and picture dealer, that I dont [*sic*] mind suggesting the truth to you.

'Frances', he explained, 'has just come out of what looked bad enough to be an illness, and is just going to plunge into one of her recurrent problems of pain and depression. The two may be just a bit too much for her and I want to be with her every night for a few days—there's an Irish Bull for you!' He ended by enlightening the priest on an aspect of the sacrament of marriage that he may not have learned in his theological studies:

One of the mysteries of Marriage (which must be a Sacrament and an extraordinary one too) is that a man evidently useless like me can yet become at certain instances indispensable. And the further oddity (which I invite you to explain on

    [8] Pearce, 150–1.
    [9] G. K. Chesterton to John O'Connor, n.d. but postmarked 3 July 1909, BL Add. MS 73196, fo. 78.

mystical grounds) is that he never feels so small as when he really knows that he is necessary.[10]

Chesterton's critical study *George Bernard Shaw* was published in August. The central focus of the book is the seriousness that comes from Puritanism. Shaw sees 'existence as an illusion and yet as an obligation'; his is 'the heroism of a morbid and almost asphyxiated age' that sees this world 'as a man-trap into which we may just have the manhood to jump', where one speaks of 'the courage to live'. His slogan is 'Let us eat, drink, and be serious'. And the reason is that he is 'the greatest of the modern Puritans and perhaps the last'. Chesterton defines the essence of Puritanism as 'a refusal to contemplate God or goodness with anything lighter or milder than the most fierce concentration of the intellect', the idea that 'God can only be praised by direct contemplation of Him' and only with the 'brain', it being 'wicked to praise Him with your passions or your physical habits or your gesture or instinct of beauty'. The English had decided 'to be hearty and humane in spite of the Puritans' and the Scots 'to be romantic in spite of the Puritans', as was reflected in a writer like Dickens who had 'picked up the tradition of Chaucer', and writers like Scott and Stevenson who had also returned to the medieval tradition. Only in Ireland did there survive 'the fierce detachment of the true Puritan' like Shaw, who 'is never frivolous... never gives his opinions a holiday... is never irresponsible even for an instant'. He therefore falls under Chesterton's greatest condemnation: 'his wit is never a weakness; therefore it is never a sense of humour.' Shaw was 'not a humorist, but a great wit'. The difference between wit and humour is that 'wit is always connected with the idea that truth is close and clear', humour 'with the idea that truth is tricky and mystical and easily mistaken'. The trouble with Shaw was that he had 'no nonsensical second self which he can get into as one gets into a dressing-gown; that ridiculous disguise which is yet more real than the real person'. He 'never said an indefensible thing; that is, he never said a thing that he was not prepared brilliantly to defend'. It is the Calvinist who 'sees the consistency in things' and is therefore a wit; but it is the Catholic who 'sees the inconsistency in things' who is the humorist. That was why there was 'nothing Gothic' about Shaw's genius: 'he could not build a mediaeval cathedral in which laughter and terror are twisted together in stone, molten by a mystical passion. He can build, by way of amusement, a Chinese pagoda; but when he is in earnest, only a Roman temple.' Even in Shaw's comedies, where the heroes 'always seem to flinch' from

[10] Ward, *GKC* 220–1, with text corrected from BL Add. MS 73196, fos. 78–9.

making fools of themselves, there was 'a certain kicking' against the 'great doom of laughter' at man who is 'absurd from the grave baby to the grinning skull', who 'is born ridiculous, as can easily be seen if you look at him soon after he is born'. Insofar as Shaw was a humorist, he was the kind of humorist who hates rather than loves to see man as 'absurd'. Shaw, however, did exhibit 'all that is purest in the Puritan; the desire to see truth face to face even if it slay us, the high impatience with irrelevant sentiment or obstructive symbol; the constant effort to keep the soul at its highest pressure and speed'. Unfortunately, Shaw also suffered from Puritan prejudices, for Puritanism had naturally 'not been able to sustain through three centuries that naked ecstasy of the direct contemplation of truth'— 'One cannot be serious for three hundred years. . . . In eternal temples you must have frivolity. You must be "at ease in Zion" unless you are only paying it a flying visit.' Puritanism had consequently degenerated, on the one hand, into a 'fatal fluency' of uplifting 'righteousness'; on this 'weak and lukewarm torrent', into which had 'melted down much of that mountainous ice which sparkled in the seventeenth century, bleak indeed but blazing', Shaw had 'made fierce and on the whole fruitful war'. On the other hand, Shaw, while abandoning 'that great and systematic philosophy of Calvinism which has much in common with modern science and strongly resembles ordinary . . . determinism', was like modern Puritans in retaining 'the savage part' of Puritanism—the 'savage negations' of its 'philosophy of taboos', to which had been added in the nineteenth century 'a mystical horror of those fermented drinks which are part of the food of civilised mankind'. It was clear that the prohibition was 'very largely a mystical one' from the fact that money, for instance, could be as socially harmful as drink but nobody shuddered at the sight of a man going to the bank as opposed to the pub. This showed that the real objection was not to the 'excess . . . but the beer' itself. It was regarded as a 'drug' rather than a 'drink', as a 'mystical substance' that could 'give monstrous pleasures or call down monstrous punishments'. Again, such was the grip of Irish Puritanism that it would never even have occurred to Shaw to 'stroll into one of the churches of his own country, and learn something of the philosophy that had satisfied Dante and Bossuet, Pascal and Descartes'. The truth was that he had 'never seen' the Catholic Church—which he 'is sure he does not like'. Puritanism was also the reason why he disliked Shakespeare, who was 'spiritually a Catholic'.[11]

[11] CS 378–84, 386, 407, 411, 437, 456, 476–7.

The greatest paradox about Shaw for Chesterton, which was consistent with his excessive seriousness, was that the 'one or two plain truths which quite stupid people learn at the beginning are exactly the one or two truths which Bernard Shaw may not even learn at the end'. He had never experienced 'the things that most of us absorb in childhood; especially the sense of the supernatural and the sense of the natural; the love of the sky with its infinity of vision, and the love of the soil with its strict hedges and solid shapes of ownership'. He was like 'a daring pilgrim' who had 'set out from the grave to find the cradle. He started from points of view which no one else was clever enough to discover, and he is at last discovering points of view which no one else was ever stupid enough to ignore.' Chesterton attributed this 'absence of the red-hot truisms of boyhood; this sense that he is not rooted' to Shaw's 'position as a member of an alien minority in Ireland'. He 'was never national enough to be domestic'. The fact that he did not celebrate his birthday was typical:

A man should always be tied to his mother's apron-strings; he should always have a hold on his childhood, and be ready at intervals to start anew from a childish standpoint. Theologically the thing is best expressed by saying, 'You must be born again.' Secularly it is best expressed by saying, 'You must keep your birthday.' Even if you will not be born again, at least remind yourself occasionally that you were born once.[12]

For birthdays for Chesterton involved the humility of laughing at oneself:

Birthdays are a glorification of the idea of life, and it exactly hits the weak point in the Shaw type of optimism . . . that it does not instinctively side with such religious celebrations of life. Mr Shaw is ready to praise the Life-force, but he is not willing to keep his birthday, which would be the best of all ways to praise it. And the reason is that the modern people will do anything whatever for their religion except play the fool for it. . . . Mr Shaw is quite clearly aware that it is a very good thing for him and for everyone else that he is alive. But to be told so in the symbolic form of brown-paper parcels containing slippers or cigarettes makes him feel a fool; which is exactly what he ought to feel. . . . A birthday does not come merely to remind a man that he has been born. It comes that he may be born again. And if a man is born again he must be as clumsy and as comic as a baby.[13]

A few years later, Chesterton wrote that he considered neglecting birthdays

a subtle form of the infernal pessimism which poisoned literature in my boyhood; and which I wish I could think I had done something to defeat. Bernard Shaw

---

[12] CS 375, 440.   [13] *ILN* xxviii. 222–3.

cannot be induced to keep his birthday, I think I shall keep it for him and so have two birthdays; which might be regarded as a less mystical method of being born again.[14]

This 'lack of roots, this remoteness from ancient instincts and traditions', was responsible for Shaw saying things that were 'not so much false as startlingly and arrestingly foolish', such as that 'Christmas Day is only a conspiracy kept up by poulterers and wine merchants from strictly business motives'. Again, Shaw could not 'grasp and enjoy the things commonly called convention and tradition; which are foods upon which all human creatures must feed frequently if they are to live'. Convention meant literally 'the coming together of men; every mob is a convention'. But then Shaw despised the masses—whereas Chesterton 'in matters of theory... would always trust the mob': 'He has no respect for collective humanity in its two great forms; either in that momentary form which we call a mob, or in that enduring form which we call a convention.' Far from being dead, conventions are 'full of accumulated emotions, the piled-up and passionate experiences of many generations asserting what they could not explain'. But Shaw had 'always made this one immense mistake (arising out of that bad progressive education of his), the mistake of treating convention as a dead thing; treating it as if it were a mere physical environment like the pavement or the rain. Whereas it is a result of will; a rain of blessings and a pavement of good intentions.' He would be worried if the evening paper disagreed with him: 'That the tradition of two thousand years contradicted him did not trouble him for an instant.' Perhaps one could say that his 'only pure paradox' was 'this almost unconscious one; that he tended to think that because something has satisfied generations of men it must be untrue'. The root trouble with Shaw was that 'he was exiled from Ireland in the very act of being born in Ireland'. In order to be a revolutionary without being a nationalist as well he had to move to England: 'But the result was that he was not really *born* in either of the two countries.' Having started from 'homelessness', he 'had no traditions'. But the truth was that he was not so much homeless as unborn: 'he still suffers, even down to his splendid old age, from the annoying omission of having never been born.'[15]

Shaw's lack of interest in and enjoyment of the ordinary things of the common man was evident in his humanitarianism, which did not mean

[14] G. K. Chesterton to 'Sir', 21 July 1915, Rare Books and Special Collections, Hesburgh Libraries, University of Notre Dame, Indiana.
[15] CS 442–3, 450–1, 454, 482, 590–1.

'the cause of humanity, but rather, if anything, the cause of everything else': 'At its noblest it meant a sort of mystical identification of our life with the whole life of nature.' Chesterton considered Shaw's greatest defect was his 'lack of democratic sentiment'. For 'there was nothing democratic either in his humanitarianism or his Socialism'. He was 'a demagogue without being a democrat'.

These new and refined faiths tended rather to make the Irishman yet more aristocratic, the Puritan yet more exclusive. To be a Socialist was to look down on all the peasant owners of the earth, especially on the peasant owners of his own island. To be a Vegetarian was to be a man with a strange and mysterious morality, a man who thought the good lord who roasted oxen for his vassals only less bad than the bad lord who roasted the vassals. None of these advanced views could the common people hear gladly; nor indeed was Shaw especially anxious to please the common people. It was his glory that he pitied animals like men; it was his defect that he pitied men only too much like animals.

Still, Shaw was at least a republican who had no time for the 'artistic individualism' of the *fin de siècle*, when the 'decay of society was praised by artists as the decay of a corpse is praised by worms'. Shaw could have been the 'wittiest' of the Decadents, 'who could have made epigrams like diamonds'. Instead, he had as a Fabian 'laboured in a mill of statistics and crammed his mind with all the most dreary and the most filthy details'. This was indeed 'a passion so implacable and so pure' that one could not but admire it. And the 'noblest', 'the greatest thing' in Shaw was 'a serious optimism—even a tragic optimism. Life is a thing too glorious to be enjoyed.' For Shaw's 'worship of life'—'Man...must follow the flag of life as fiercely from conviction as all other creatures follow it from instinct'—was 'by no means lively'. Shaw had, as it were, turned his master Schopenhauer, the great prophet of pessimism, on his head. Schopenhauer had taught that 'life is unreasonable. The intellect, if it could be impartial, would tell us to cease; but a blind partiality, an instinct quite distinct from thought, drives us on to take desperate chances in an essentially bankrupt lottery.' Shaw agreed that life was unreasonable, but 'so much the worse for reason'. For 'life is the primary thing', while 'reason is lifeless' and must therefore 'be trodden down'. The ordinary or common man, however, unlike the master of pessimism and his pupil, did not share this philosophy of misery, which was reflected in 'the ingrained grimness and even inhumanity of Shaw's art'.[16]

---

[16] CS 395, 400–2, 410, 425, 436, 455.

For all Shaw's contempt for the masses, his Socialism was 'the noblest thing in him'. He really did have 'a proper brotherly bitterness about the oppression of the poor'. However, as a disciple of Nietzsche, Shaw believed not in democracy but in the Superman, which meant the 'incredibly caddish doctrine that the strength of the strong is admirable, but not the valour of the weak':

Nietzsche might really have done some good if he had taught Bernard Shaw to draw the sword, to drink wine, or even to dance. But he only succeeded in putting into his head a new superstition, which bids fair to be the chief superstition of the dark ages which are possibly in front of us—I mean the superstition of what is called the Superman.[17]

Chesterton's foreboding, long before the rise of Hitler and the outbreak of the Second World War, was chillingly fulfilled in Shaw's later enthusiasm for Stalin, who, he thought, should be awarded the Nobel prize for peace! A few years before, Chesterton had warned Robert Blatchford in a private letter about the danger of believing that 'perfect heredity and environment make the perfect man'—namely, that it would lead to a 'political aristocracy'. Indeed, while he, Blatchford, was 'turning over the musty folios of early Victorian materialism, newer things are happening: a fresh and fierce philosophy of oligarchy and the wise few is spreading from Germany all over the world.' But the wisest oligarchy or Superman with unlimited power could not escape the consequences of the Fall: 'Selfishness is a permanent and natural danger which arises from the existence of a self.'[18]

Chesterton thought that Shaw would in the end have seen through the nonsense of the Superman—who was to 'come by natural selection' by means of 'the life-force' which 'desires above all things to make suitable marriages ... eventually to produce a Superman'—had it not been that he 'ceased to believe in progress altogether'. The disillusion was general, and helped Nietzsche establish 'the Superman on his pedestal'. Chesterton himself had never been a believer in progress for the sake of progress. Those 'two incredible figures' who had appeared towards the end of the nineteenth century, the progressive and the conservative, would have been 'overwhelmed with laughter by any other intellectual commonwealth of history. There was hardly a human generation which could not have seen the folly of merely going forward or mere standing still ... '. The modern progressive now meant, 'not a man who wanted democracy, but a man

---

[17] CS 397–8, 439, 461.
[18] G. K. Chesterton to Robert Blatchford, n.d., photocopy, GKCL.

who wanted something newer than democracy', a reformer 'a man who wanted anything that he hadn't got'. This progressive 'was so eager to be in advance of his age that he pretended to be in advance of himself'. Institutions had to be sneered at 'as old-fashioned', out of 'a servile and snobbish fear of the future'. Now, while Shaw had 'pleasantly surprised innumerable cranks and revolutionaries by finding quite rational arguments for them, he surprised them unpleasantly also by . . . revolutionising the revolutionists'. And this 'great game of dishing the anarchists continued for some time to be his most effective business', this 'great game of catching revolutionists napping, of catching the unconventional people in conventional poses, of outmarching and outmanoeuvring progressives till they felt like conservatives, of undermining the mines of Nihilists till they felt like the House of Lords'. But Shaw's 'modernity—which means, the seeking for truth in terms of time' was 'that silliest and most snobbish of all superiorities, the mere aristocracy of time': 'All works must thus become old and insipid which have ever tried to be "modern," which have consented to smell of time rather than eternity. Only those who have stooped to be in advance of their time will ever find themselves behind it.' Shaw had been 'the unhappy Progressive trying to be in front of his own religion, trying to destroy his own idol and even to desecrate his own tomb'. And Chesterton's cruellest hit was that progressivism, far from showing the strength of the Superman that Shaw now admired, was actually characteristic of 'all feeble spirits' who 'naturally live in the future, because it is featureless; it is a soft job; you can make it what you like. The next page is blank, and I can paint it freely with my favourite colour. It requires real courage to face the past, because the past is full of facts which cannot be got over . . .'.[19]

Apart from lack of humour, Shaw also lacked another essential Chestertonian attribute: he suffered from a 'blindness to paradox'. Thus he could not understand marriage because he could not understand 'the paradox of marriage; that the woman is all the more the house for not being the head of it'. Nor could he understand patriotism, because he could not understand 'the paradox of patriotism; that one is all the more human for not merely loving humanity'. Indeed, Shaw could not 'quite understand life, because he will not accept its contradictions'. One might say he could 'understand everything in life except its paradoxes, especially that ultimate paradox that the very things that we cannot comprehend are the things that we have to take for granted'.[20]

---

[19] CS 387–91, 393, 424–5, 461–2, 465, 475, 479.   [20] CS 450, 454.

Shaw had predicted that the book would 'not contain any facts; but it will be exceedingly interesting'.[21] Years later, he was to write that, although Chesterton had 'apparently never read a word of mine, or saw more than one play (which he does not remember), he makes me a peg on which to hang a very readable essay on things in general'.[22] At the time in a review article in the *Nation*, Shaw called the book 'the best work of literary art I have yet provoked. It is a fascinating portrait study; and I am proud to have been the painter's model.' It was, he thought, 'in the great tradition of literary portraiture: it gives not only the figure, but the epoch'. But for Shaw there was a paradox: 'Everything about me which Mr Chesterton had to divine he has divined miraculously. But everything that he could have ascertained easily by reading my own plain directions on the bottle, as it were, remains for him a muddled and painful problem solved by a comically wrong guess.' It was undoubtedly 'a very fine' picture. The problem was that it did not bear any resemblance to Shaw's actual 'doctrine'. As to his objectionable teetotalism: 'Have I survived the cry of Art for Art's Sake, and War for War's Sake, for which Mr Chesterton rebukes Whistler and Mr. Rudyard Kipling, to fall a victim to this maddest of all cries: the cry of Beer for Beer's Sake?'[23]

The reviews were mostly favourable, although the spectacle of Shaw reviewing Chesterton on Shaw aroused some sarcastic comment on the financial aspects of this mutual self-publicity. One reviewer wondered whether Shaw had actually invented Chesterton:

Shaw, it is said, tired of Socialism, weary of wearing Jaegers, and broken down by teetotalism and vegetarianism, sought, some years ago, an escape from them. His adoption, however, of these attitudes had a decided commercial value, which he did not think it advisable to prejudice by wholesale surrender. Therefore he, in order to taste the forbidden joys of individualistic philosophy, meat, food and strong drink, created 'Chesterton'. This mammoth myth, he decided, should enjoy all the forms of fame which Shaw had to deny himself. Outwardly, he should be Shaw's antithesis. He should be beardless, large in girth, smiling of countenance, and he should be licensed to sell paradoxes only in essay and novel form, all stage and platform rights being reserved by Shaw.

In order to carry out the impersonation, Shaw had had the idea of living near the tunnel that connects Adelphi with the Strand. Having changed

---

[21] Michael Holroyd, *Bernard Shaw*, ii. *1898–1918, The Pursuit of Power* (London: Chatto and Windus, 1989), 213.

[22] *Shaw: Collected Letters 1911–1925*, ed. Laurence, 523.

[23] Conlon, i. 201–04.

in a cellar, he would emerge on the Strand side of the tunnel, free to enjoy the life of Chesterton before returning in the evening to be Shaw in Adelphi.[24]

2

In his *Illustrated London News* column of 2 October 1909, Chesterton addressed the question of Indian nationalism. 'The test of a democracy is not whether the people vote,' he argued, 'but whether the people rule. The essence of a democracy is that the national tone and spirit of the typical citizen is apparent and striking in the actions of the state.' And he thought that the 'principal weakness' of Indian nationalists seeking independence was that their nationalism was 'not very Indian and not very national': 'There is a difference between a conquered people demanding its own institutions and the same people demanding the institutions of the conqueror.'[25] The article was read by Gandhi, who was in London at the time to press for 'freer rights of residence, travel and trade to members of the Indian diaspora in South Africa', where he was then living. He referred to the article in a dispatch he sent to the paper he had founded in Durban, *Indian Opinion*. This article for some reason did not appear until January of the following year. In the meantime, Gandhi had responded to Chesterton's criticism by completing in ten days, on board the ship that carried him back to South Africa, 'an extended defence of the virtues of ancient Indian civilization'. Written in Gandhi's mother tongue, it was published under the title *Hind Swaraj*, and also in English under the title *Indian Home Rule*, in Durban in 1910. Apart from Gandhi's two-volume autobiography and collections of articles and speeches, it was the only book qua book that Gandhi ever published.[26]

On 30 October 1909 Shaw responded to a letter (undated, of course) from Chesterton introducing a man who needed Shaw's help: 'Chesterton. | Shaw speaks. | Attention!' In his letter Chesterton had asked Shaw to excuse his 'abruptness in this letter of introduction': they were 'moving into the country and every piece of furniture I begin to write at is taken

---

[24] Ward, *GKC* 205–6.   [25] *ILN* xxviii. 400–2.

[26] Ramachandra Guha, 'A Prophet Announces Himself: Mahatma Gandhi's "Hind Swaraj" a Hundred Years on', *Times Literary Supplement*, 4 Sept. 2009. The author mistakenly dates Chesterton's article to the third week of September.

away and put in a van'.[27] Shaw again urged Chesterton to write a play. It was 'quite unendurable' that he should be 'wasting [his] time' writing about Shaw. He had, however, liked Chesterton's book, particularly since he had in no way at all influenced what Chesterton had written, which was 'evidently founded on a very hazy recollection of a five-year-old perusal of *Man and Superman*'—and 'a lot of it was fearful nonsense'. Chesterton had 'no conscience' regarding facts; and his 'punishment' was that, instead of 'dull inferences' as to Shaw's narrow Puritanism, he could have easily 'ascertained' the 'delightful and fantastic realities' of Shaw's home had Chesterton 'taken greater advantage of what is really the only thing to be said in favor of Battersea; namely, that it is within easy reach of Adelphi Terrace' where Shaw lived. He was now writing to tell Chesterton that he had been in his native Ireland the previous month, where 'one becomes a practical man', and where, instead of merely urging his friend to write for the theatre, he had actually written a 'scenario' for him. This unfinished scenario—he could 'do nothing but talk' in England—he was now sending to Chesterton as far as he had 'scribbled it'. However, experience had taught Shaw that offering help of this sort was not necessarily the best way of 'getting work' out of somebody like Chesterton. He was therefore resorting to his youthful rule of insulting 'an important man' if possible. And he thought there was one respect in which Chesterton was 'insult-able'. It could 'be plausibly held that you are a venal ruffian, pouring forth great quantities of immediately saleable stuff, but altogether declining to lay up for yourself treasures in heaven'. Well, perhaps Chesterton could not 'afford to do otherwise', and he therefore was ready to make him an attractive financial proposition, which he proceeded to outline. He would be at his 'country quarters' at Ayot St Lawrence near Welwyn in Hert-fordshire, where he had 'a motor car which could carry me on sufficient provocation as far as Beaconsfield; but I do not know how much time you spend there and how much in Fleet Street'. Was Chesterton 'only a week-ender', or had his 'wise wife' taken him 'properly in hand' and 'committed' him to 'a pastoral life'?[28]

Shaw's scenario for the proposed play, dated October 1909, begins with the Devil asking St Augustine of Canterbury who he is and what he has done. When Augustine 'innocently' replies that he has converted England to Christianity, the Devil, 'overcome by the stupendousness of the joke,

[27] Ward, *GKC* 202, with text corrected from BL Add. MS 73198, fo. 6.
[28] Ward, *GKC* 202–4, with text corrected from BL Add. MS 73198, fo. 7.

roars with laughter'. Augustine thereupon, accompanied by the Devil, comes to England to investigate. On arriving at the House of Commons, Augustine asks Balfour, the Leader of the Opposition, if there is a Christian who could show him round. Balfour professes not to know of any, but says that Mr Bellaire Hilloc claims to be one. The astonished policeman on duty exclaims, 'Fancy you a Christian, Mr Hilloc. We never thought you was anything.'[29]

From the date of Shaw's letter it seems clear that the Chestertons finally moved to Beaconsfield in October 1909. By a curious coincidence they had exchanged Overstrand Mansions for 'Overroads', the name of their new house, which they also rented. For Frances there were only advantages in the move. First and foremost, she had removed her husband from the taverns and late nights of Fleet Street. As a lover and practitioner of gardening, who 'had a sort of hungry appetite for all the fruitful things like fields and gardens and anything connected with production',[30] she now had the large garden she could scarcely have had in London, even if she had had a house rather than a gardenless flat. For Chesterton there was obviously the loss of the life of Fleet Street, but on the other hand the gain of Frances's happiness; there was also the gain of finding himself in a small community where he could rub shoulders with his beloved common man in a way in which it was not possible in London, even in the comparatively circumscribed district of Battersea. Moreover, he was by no means cut off in Beaconsfield, where there was a railway station with regular trains to London.

However, it was not only his brother, parents, and friends who deplored his leaving London, but Belloc, too, now himself living down in Sussex, lamented, 'She [Frances] has taken my Chesterton from me'—although later he admitted it was probably a wise move.[31] As for Cecil and 'Keith' Jones, they remained utterly unreconciled to the move. They even hatched a plan to charter a plane, fly to Beaconsfield, and invite Chesterton up for a spin in the air: 'Once on the wing, the plane would make for Calais, where he could be held to ransom—the renunciation of Beaconsfield or enforced liberty in France.'[32] Whatever the loss to Fleet Street, it is more than probable that, if Chesterton had not left its irregular life, with its male camaraderie and heavy drinking, his life could easily have been cut short,

---

[29] *Shaw: Collected Letters 1898–1910*, 877, 881.
[30] *A.* 149.   [31] Ward, *GKC* 212.   [32] MCC 75.

given his obesity and all the dangers to health that that presented. At Beaconsfield, there was the possibility of a routine and an ordered way of life, with Frances there to supervise as far as possible his eating and drinking. As his doctor in later years said, had he 'racketed around Fleet Street any longer' he would have died twenty years earlier than he did.[33]

Cecil Chesterton and 'Keith' Jones had mocked, as other intellectuals would have done, the move to quasi-suburban Beaconsfield as opposed to the real countryside. But Chesterton enjoyed defending the despised move in his *Daily News* column. He actually derived satisfaction from the fact that Beaconsfield was already being built over:

Within a stone's throw of my house they are building another house. I am glad they are building it and I am glad it is within a stone's throw; quite well within it, with a good catapult. Nevertheless, I have not yet cast the first stone at the new house—not being, strictly speaking, guiltless myself in the matter of new houses.

He liked having other human beings near him. But that was not then the usual attitude of intellectuals and writers like himself: 'Rival ruralists would quarrel about which had the most completely inconvenient postal service; and there were many jealous heartburnings if one friend found out any uncomfortable situation which the other friend had thoughtlessly overlooked.' He was to sound the same defiant note in his *Autobiography* at the end of his life: 'I have lived in Beaconsfield from the time when it was almost a village, to the time when, as the enemy profanely says, it is a suburb.'[34]

3

Just before the move to Beaconsfield, a selection of Chesterton's columns in the *Daily News* called *Tremendous Trifles* was published on 23 September 1909. Prolific as he was as a journalist and writer, Chesterton inevitably was not as prolific in ideas, and the familiar themes emerge in these weekly articles. First, there was the usual emphasis on seeing the wonder of existence, 'the startling facts that run across the landscape as plain as a painted fence'. In a well-known essay he celebrates a piece of chalk, telling his readers that he had once 'planned to write a book of poems entirely about the things in my pocket. But I found it would be too long; and the

---

[33] Ward, *GKC* 563.   [34] Ward, *GKC* 213; Ffinch, 177; *A.* 223.

age of the great epics is past.' 'The way to love anything', whether or not it was in one's pocket, was 'to realize that it might be lost'. The point of travel was not to see foreign countries but to see one's own country for the first time: 'it is at last to set foot on one's own country as a foreign land.'[35]

Limitation, that other central theme in Chesterton's thought, is the way to appreciate how 'awful and beautiful' this world is: 'If you wish to perceive that limitless felicity, limit yourself if only for a moment.' Indeed, to 'love anything is to love its boundaries', since 'boundaries are the most beautiful things in the world'. Art 'consists of limitation', 'is limitation'. (As he wrote elsewhere, artistic 'convention is a form of freedom': 'A dramatic convention is not a constraint on the dramatist; it is a permission to the dramatist. It is a permit allowing him to depart from the routine of external reality, in order to express a more internal and intimate reality.'[36]) One very important form of limitation for Chesterton was dogma, which becomes 'elaborate' not because it is dead but because 'it is only the live tree that grows too many branches'. Dogma was akin to architecture, which also was 'insolent' enough to claim 'permanence' and was also 'difficult to get rid of'. And the reason why there was 'no typical architecture of the modern world' was because 'we have not enough dogmas; we cannot bear to see anything in the sky that is solid and enduring . . .'. Gothic architecture, on the contrary, was based on a dogma—namely, the words of Christ in rebuke to 'certain priggish disciples' who rebuked 'the street children' for making too much noise 'in the name of good taste': 'He said: "If these were silent the very stones would cry out." With these words He called up all the wealth of artistic creation that has been founded on this creed.' For the very stones did cry out: 'The front of vast buildings is thronged with open mouths, angels praising God, or devils defying Him. Rock itself is racked and twisted, until it seems to scream.' The Greeks had 'preferred to carve their gods and heroes doing nothing', whereas mediaeval art chose to represent 'people doing something': 'the whole front of a great cathedral has the hum of a huge hive.'[37] Analogously, the 'origin and essence' of ritual lay in the fact that 'in the presence of . . . sacred riddles about which we can say nothing it is often more decent merely to do something'. Again, rhetorical energy in speaking does not betray insincerity but sincerity: contrary to the contemporary assumption, one becomes 'more rhetorical' the 'more sincere' one becomes.[38]

[35] *TT*, pp. vi, 3, 42, 204, 271.   [36] *ILN* xxxiii. 302–3.
[37] *TT* 53–4, 110–11, 183 195–6.   [38] *TT* 14, 134, 238.

Limitation is also for Chesterton the whole point of his beloved toy theatre—'you are looking through a small window': 'Has not every one noticed how sweet and startling any landscape looks when seen through an arch? This strong, square shape, this shutting off of everything else is not only an assistance to beauty; it is the essential of beauty. The most beautiful part of every picture is the frame.' The same was true of ideas like Greek philosophy, which 'could fit easier into the small city of Athens than into the immense empire of Persia' because it was only possible to 'represent very big ideas in very small spaces'. Boundaries, Chesterton was even prepared to assert, 'are the most beautiful things in the world'.[39] The reason why adults do not play with toys like toy theatres is because it 'takes so very much more time and trouble than anything else. Playing as children mean playing is the most serious thing in the world.'[40] Nor did Chesterton despise the 'popular things', such as the popular press, a particular object of the intellectuals' contempt. He thought it was preferable to the broadsheets because of its 'healthiness', its 'essential antiquity and permanence': 'Even in the crudest and most clamorous aspects of the newspaper world I still prefer the popular to the proud and fastidious.' Nobody believed in a tabloid newspaper like the *Daily Mail*, which never had any new ideas but which contained all the 'old human' things of interest to ordinary human beings, unlike the *Times*, which people did believe in. The 'new democratic journalism' had simply replaced the 'old chronicles' that also chiefly recorded 'accidents and prodigies'. The same was true of the places frequented by the masses: 'Ruskin could have found more memories of the Middle Ages in the Underground Railway than in the grand hotels outside the stations.' And it was twelve 'ordinary men' not the 'specialists' in law who determined guilt or innocence in the courts of law: 'The same was done, if I remember rightly, by the Founder of Christianity.'[41]

Chesterton made the same point the day after the publication of *Tremendous Trifles*, when he appeared before a Joint Select Committee of both Houses of Parliament inquiring into the question of stage censorship. Unlike Shaw, who was also called, Chesterton, he said, appeared on behalf of the audience not the playwright or the critic. While in favour of censorship, he thought the official censor should be replaced by a jury of 'twelve ordinary men'. There were photographs in the papers of Chesterton in the company of the Jewish author Israel Zangwill. A couple

[39] *TT* 42, 150–1, 183.   [40] *TT* 145.   [41] *TT* 68, 220–2.

of months later a weekly reported on the apparition of this successor of Dr Johnson on the streets of London:

His huge figure, enveloped in its cloak and shaded by a slouch hat, rolls through the streets unheeding his fellow beings. His eyes stare before him in a troubled dream; his lips move, muttering, composing, arguing. He is an imposing figure; of immense proportions, almost balloon-like with a fine impetuous head which rises over the surrounding crowds; his hair is properly shaggy, his countenance open and frank, wearing indeed a curious childlike unconsciousness in spite of the thought intensity that clouds his brow.[42]

4

The subject of children brings one to the huge advantage that Beaconsfield had over Battersea for both the Chestertons: the childless couple now had plenty of room to have the offspring of relatives and friends to stay. Then there was a big garden too, which Chesterton explored on his arrival. He plucked up courage to speak to the gardener, 'an enterprise of no little valour', to ask the name of 'a strange dark red rose, at once theatrical and sulky'. Unlike Frances, whose knowledge of the names of flowers he admired, Chesterton, according to another gardener who later worked for them, only knew the name of the wallflower: 'Master, he do like a bit of wallflower. It's the only flower he knows the name of.' There was also a vegetable garden.[43]

Children adored this huge giant of a man who encouraged them to call him 'uncle' or 'unclet', and who was not only a fund of stories, but could also draw whatever they wanted. Charles and Stephen Johnson, the children of one of Frances's cousins, often stayed during school holidays. Chesterton 'took immense trouble and devoted many hours of his overworked time' to a couple of magazines the boys started, to which everyone in the house was expected to contribute. Chesterton would say, 'I must just go upstairs and finish an article for the Daily News and then I can come down and do some serious work.' Teas at Overroads were memorable events, fulfilling 'all one's dreams of the perfect tea'. One child later in life recalled Chesterton founding a Seed Cake Club, from which he excluded Frances, who did not like seed cake. As a middle-aged woman, she admired how Frances was able to talk to children as though they were

---

[42] Ffinch, 174.   [43] Ward, *GKC* 214; Ffinch, 176.

her 'mental and moral equals', without at the same time losing her authority. Chesterton's study was upstairs and from its window, she remembered, he would throw out 'great birds cut out of brown paper' for the children to shoot at with home-made bows and arrows. On one occasion he threw a sea serpent down the stairs for harpooning in the hall. But Chesterton was not only seeking to amuse the children, he was also amusing himself. He would walk by himself around the garden endlessly shooting arrows with a bow or throwing a stick in the air and catching it. But he would also work while walking in the garden. Lucy Masterman remembered on one visit watching him walking up and down the lawn while he wrote a poem: 'He had the paper in one hand, a swordstick in the other, and his fountain pen in his teeth. Whenever he added a line the swordstick had to be laid down to enable him to use the pen.' When a child was about 12, Chesterton would introduce him or her to the detective story. He always gave the impression of being busy, writing on Sundays and dictating on weekdays to a secretary, while 'walking up and down and making passes at the cushions with his sword-stick. He was always in his study or wandering round talking to himself. He never seemed to relax.' But nor did he ever seem to be angry. At Christmas there was always a pantomime to be acted, and Chesterton liked to sit by the dressing-up box running through his fingers the materials of the various costumes, just as he would '*feel* the wood of a chair' or 'finger a pencil' or 'roll a walking stick between his hands'. In accordance with his philosophy of wonder at existence, he relished these insignificant things for what they were in themselves. What all the children remembered most of all was how they were treated as equals—that is, as adults; he did not come down to their level by pretending to be a small boy, but he brought children up to his own level by making them feel they were adults, whose views were important and with whom a serious conversation was possible. He was never patronizing, nor did he make children feel they were ignorant or stupid. As Ronald Knox put it, he did not 'exploit the simplicity of childhood for his own amusement. He entered, with tremendous gravity, into the tremendous gravity of the child.' On only one occasion was Chesterton known to have punished a child, when a little girl was rude to the maid and was told by him to apologize. 'She retorted "What does it matter? She's only a servant."' Chesterton angrily sent her to her room. All the children who stayed at Overroads had vivid memories of the two dogs, Winkle and Quoodle, his successor, after whom a character in Chesterton's novel *The Flying Inn* was named. Chesterton would 'surreptitiously feed them during meals until Frances called a halt'. Chesterton was particularly fond of Quoodle, whom he would allow to sit with him on the sofa, contrary to Frances's edict. When Quoodle died, one child was met by Frances in the hall with the request: 'Quoodle is dead, so *please* don't mention him to Gilbert.' He was once heard anxiously asking about a 'rather stupid little dog' they had, 'I think Dolfuss quite likes me, don't you, Frances?' There was also a cat called Perky, who was once caught eating the kippers that Chesterton loved for breakfast; but when the housemaid was about to throw out the half-eaten kippers, Chesterton stopped her: 'I don't mind eating after Perky.' Frances, of course, was the disciplinarian, but she did not always have her way: there is a story that on one occasion Chesterton demanded that some children should be allowed to stay up late and banged the table with his slipper saying, 'You see, I am putting my foot down.'[44]

There was no question of Chesterton underestimating the arduous nature of playing with children. It was, he explained in his column in the *Daily News*, totally absorbing of one's energies, as serious a business as playing with toys such as toy theatres. Playing with children was in Chesterton's view 'a glorious thing'—but hardly 'a soothing or idyllic one'. It was not like 'watering little budding flowers' but like 'wrestling for hours with gigantic angels and devils'. One was confronted constantly by moral problems 'of the most monstrous complexity'. For instance, one might have

to decide before the awful eyes of innocence, whether, when a sister has knocked down a brother's bricks, in revenge for the brother having taken two sweets out of his turn, it is endurable that the brother should retaliate by scribbling on the sister's picture-book, and whether such conduct does not justify the sister in blowing out the brother's unlawfully lit match.

But just as he was 'solving this problem upon principles of the highest morality', he would suddenly remember that he had not yet written his Saturday column for the *Daily News*, which was due in an hour's time. Barricading himself in another room with the children drumming on the door, he manages to produce 'fifteen hundred unimportant words', before turning 'his attention to the enigma of whether a brother should comman-deer a sister's necklace because the sister pinched him . . . '.[45]

---

[44] Ward, *RC* 92–8, 100–1, 111–12; Conlon, ii. 48; Sullivan, 160; Lucy Masterman, 'The Private Chesterton', *Manchester Guardian*, 28 Apr. 1955; Dorothy Collins's notes for talks, BL Add. MS 73477, fo. 141.

[45] *MM* 103–4.

Chesterton had the same sort of effect on adults as on children. When you talked with him, you did not feel 'how brilliant he was but how brilliant you were'. And he thought nothing of his own writings: 'He seemed to regard what he wrote as ephemeral, as ephemeral as speech. It was an accident that what he said, when transferred to the typewriter and delivered to the publisher, constituted a livelihood.' His attitude was that everybody had to make a living somehow and his 'trade' unfortunately happened to be 'words'. His nephew Peter Oldershaw remembered how amazed Chesterton was that his poem 'The Donkey' was constantly being reprinted, 'as if some idle jest were now being bandied about *ad nauseam*'. When he heard that someone was being given a copy of his collected poems as a wedding present, he 'cried "Good Lord! What has the poor girl done to deserve that?" in whole-hearted wonder.'[46] The Chestertons' closest Beaconsfield friends in the early days were the rector and his wife and the doctor and his wife. The doctor found him a difficult patient because of his 'detachment from his own physical circumstances. If there was anything wrong with him he usually did not notice it. "He was the most uncomplaining person. You had to hunt him all over" to find out if anything was wrong.' The doctor's wife remembered how he would come back from a dinner with Beaconsfield tradesmen, fascinated by what he had heard and anxious to share the news.[47] Chesterton's neglect of his health is well exemplified by the tiny *pince-nez* he wore (two pairs survive), both of which are virtually just plain glass; he would naturally have preferred to patronize a local high-street optician in Beaconsfield to going to the trouble of consulting a specialist in London.[48]

It was not only educated people who were made to feel on the same intellectual level as Chesterton. One of the barbers in Beaconsfield who shaved him—he was never able to shave himself—remembered how he could always bring himself down to their level and was always ready to argue with anyone. He was too shy to talk when other people were in the barber's shop, but if there was no one else there and he was asked a question, 'it was like rich cream pouring out'. The head barber's wife was an invalid, and Chesterton never came to the shop without asking after her. Abstracted as he was in thought, he would always stand and raise his hat if a woman came in. He would sit patiently in the queue waiting his turn in the shop, until, that is, Dorothy Collins had the bright idea of

[46] Ward, *RC* 102–3.   [47] Ward, *GKC* 226.
[48] I owe this point to Aidan Mackey.

getting the barber to come to the house. One day when the assistant barber was cutting Chesterton's hair at the house, Frances, who took a keen interest in its cutting, was suggesting 'a bit off here and a bit off there', when the barber 'caught hold of her hand and patted it and said: "Make up your mind, old girl." ' As Beaconsfield expanded, another barber's shop was established in what came to be known as New (as opposed to Old) Beaconsfield. Barbers and hairdressers are famous for their conversational resources, and Chesterton later thought of writing 'a massive and exhaustive sociological work, in several volumes, which was to be called "The Two Barbers of Beaconsfield" and based entirely upon the talk of the two excellent citizens to whom I went to get shaved. For these two shops do indeed belong to two different civilisations.' The hairdresser in the new town belonged to 'the new world' and had 'the spotlessness of the specialist', while the one in the old town had 'what may be called the ambidexterity of the peasant, shaving... with one hand while he stuffs squirrels or sells tobacco with the other'. 'The latter tells me from his own recollection what happened in Old Beaconsfield; the former, or his assistants, tell me from the *Daily Mail* what has not happened in a wider world.' Chesterton also had a taxi-driver, whose first arduous task was to try and get his massive frame into the car, no easy feat. The return journey from London would pose an immediate hazard, because Chesterton could never remember where the car was waiting for him. Interestingly, his driver later said that he knew that Chesterton would become a Roman Catholic one day, because he would always tell him to stop if he saw a Catholic church: 'He liked to look at RC churches and go in and stroll about. Not for services... but just at any time. There was one church where we often stopped between Waterloo and Charing Cross.'[49]

Father O'Connor, who was a frequent visitor to the house, was struck like others by the abstracted way Chesterton moved and spoke, but it was the opposite of 'mooning': 'He was always working out something in his mind, and when he drifted from his study to the garden and was seen making deadly passes with his sword-stick at the dahlias, we knew that he had got to a dead end in his composition and was getting his thoughts into order.' This abstraction could get in the way of the exquisite courtesy that 'was with him both a passion and a principle', if he was 'late in tumbling to the situation'. But it was always 'a new thrill' for O'Connor to watch 'the vast mass of G.K.C. nimbly mobilising itself to make room or place a chair

---

[49] *A.* 223–4; Ward, *GKC* 216; Ward, *RC* 106–9.

or get out of the way'. Apart from his sword-stick he liked to play with a very large knife that he had had for years, even taking it to bed with him! When they were staying at a hotel this habit required Frances to remove the offending knife from under the pillow 'for fear of complications'. He was observed once sharpening a pencil with it at a lecture to the amused astonishment of the audience. O'Connor immediately knew when a book had been read by Chesterton because it 'had gone through every indignity' a book could endure: 'He turned it inside out, dog-eared it, pencilled it, sat on it, took it to bed and rolled on it, and got up again and spilled tea on it—if he were sufficiently interested.' He remembered the sad case of a pamphlet on 'the Roman Menace' by a Dr Horton—it 'had a refuted look when I saw it'. Like Frances, O'Connor wanted Chesterton to give up the journalist treadmill for purely literary work. This made sense if, like O'Connor and other contemporary and later admirers, you thought Chesterton's greatness lay in his poetry and novels; but it did not make so much sense if Chesterton's real greatness lies in his non-fiction prose works, into which the journalism fed, not just in the books of collected articles but also in terms of working out the ideas that would go into the books. Anyway Frances knew it was hopeless: 'You will not change Gilbert, you will only fidget him. He is bent on being a jolly journalist, to paint the town red, and he does not need style to do that. All he wants is buckets and buckets of red paint.' According to O'Connor, Chesterton did his 'best work' between ten and midnight, when he would 'sip a glass of wine' and 'stroll between sips in and out of his study, brooding and jotting, and then the dictation was ready for the morning'.[50]

There was one thing that could ruffle Chesterton's geniality. His jokes about his size were at least in part defensive, for he was sensitive about it, as O'Connor discovered one evening. The 'little triangular house' that was Overroads, as Maisie Ward recalled it, did not provide enough room for 'the sort of fun the Chestertons enjoyed'; so in November 1911 they bought the field across the road and had a brick-and-timber studio built on it. The night the studio was opened, there was 'a large party at which charades were acted'. Returning to the house, O'Connor offered his arm to Chesterton, who 'refused it with a finality foreign to our friendship'. Ten yards behind O'Connor, Chesterton fell over a tree-pot and broke his arm, a few minutes before midnight; the result was six weeks in bed. Another

---

[50] O'Connor, 44, 61, 112–3, 118–19.

friend remembered 'the only time when he saw Chesterton annoyed was when he offered him an arm going upstairs'.[51]

Friends visited from London, as did Belloc from Sussex. But more often meetings would take place in London. There was a regular train service from Beaconsfield to Marylebone Station, where Chesterton became a familiar figure, with his black bag containing a bottle of wine. Train times were, unsurprisingly, beyond him, but when Frances expressed her surprise at his ignorance of the timetable, he responded, 'My dear, I couldn't earn our daily bread if I had to study timetables.' Then there were the lecture engagements, at one of which in December 1909 a lady remarked, 'You seem to know everything.' On the contrary, Chesterton retorted, 'I know nothing, Madam, I am a journalist.'[52] And there is the even more famous reply that he gave to an elderly lady after a debate at which various racial characteristics were discussed, who asked 'with something of a simper, "Mr Chesterton, I wonder if you could tell what race I belong to?" With a characteristic adjustment of his glasses he replied at once, "I should certainly say, Madam, one of the conquering races." '[53]

There were also the visits to the parental home in Kensington, where his mother laid on her usual lavish meals. According to 'Keith' Jones, these visits undermined Frances's efforts to get her husband to lose weight. Knowing better than the Edwardians the dire effects of obesity on health, a modern reader will view these efforts rather differently from 'Keith', who scornfully presents them as stemming solely from Frances's Puritanism: 'She did not like food, except cakes, chocolate and similar flim-flams, and her appreciation of liquor stopped short at tea. She was not in sympathy with Gilbert's masculine taste for succulent dishes and drink—especially drink—and would have liked it better had he consumed appreciably less of both.' She contrasted the Beaconsfield regime where Chesterton 'ate Spartan fare—or tried to eat it—washing it down with restricted claret, quite unconscious and uncritical', with the maternal table at Warwick Gardens, which 'groaned with salmon, veal cutlet, cream meringues, all the things of which Gilbert was most fond, with lashings of Burgundy and *crème de menthe*'. While his mother heaped up his plate, his wife, not surprisingly perhaps, 'looked on, concerned and really unhappy'. Interestingly, 'Keith' admitted that the battle to cut down on her husband's enormous consumption continued 'silent and unceasing' only until Frances herself became a Roman

[51] Ward, *GKC* 220; O'Connor, 78–9; Ffinch, 202.
[52] Barker, 192; Ffinch, 175–6.   [53] Clemens, 8.

Catholic: 'Then, by some miraculous intervention, she accepted food—for others if not for herself—as desirable, and though the cooking at Beaconsfield, to my mind, was execrable, salt beef appeared less frequently, and was of a milder flavour. Moreover, the supply of claret expanded.'[54] Perhaps, however, there was a less supernatural reason why the food improved: the retirement of their cook, aged 75, whom Chesterton and Frances had decided to keep on even when she reached her seventies for as long as she wanted to stay. How 'dull' the meals were, one guest remembered, 'roast and boiled, boiled and roast, with potatoes day in and day out, and usually rice pudding'.[55]

Frances may not have been able to win the dietary battle with Mrs Chesterton senior, but one battle she did win with great ease, according to 'Keith', was over the question of money. Frances naturally needed to be sure that there was money in the bank to pay for the housekeeping, and, given her husband's total lack of any money sense, she proposed that

she should take over the business of paying his cheques in and drawing them out, and be wholly responsible for the settlement of bills. Gilbert agreed like a bird, blithely signing the necessary documents for the bank and discovered that he had made over his rights to every penny of his earning and was a pensioner on his own bounty.

In fact, this is an exaggeration of what was true—namely, that Frances did take over the practical administration of cash and the paying of bills. It was agreed between them that he should handle only small sums of money, in effect pocket money. As Belloc put it, 'he spent money like water'—not least on beggars, whom he was incapable of refusing. Any expenses he had that could not be covered by his pocket money could be settled on account at places where he was likely to want to spend money. But so far as was possible Frances herself bought whatever he was likely to want, anticipating as best she could all his needs, with 'loving care' in the words of Father O'Connor.[56] But nevertheless Chesterton remained the sole signatory on his bank account, and when later he paid money into the accounts of the *New Witness* and *G.K.'s Weekly* he certainly required neither Frances's signature on the cheques nor her approval in the form of a counter-signature.[57] If 'Keith' was right that Chesterton was freed of certain

---

[54] MCC 73.   [55] Ward, *RC* 110.   [56] Ward, *GKC* 453.

[57] Examples of cheques signed by Chesterton as sole signatory are at GKCL. Ward, *GKC* 453–4, accepts 'Keith's' assertion that Frances was the account-holder who signed the cheques, although she dismisses the rest of 'Keith's' story.

practical financial responsibilities and was given the equivalent of an agreed allowance (from the money, of course, that he drew from the bank by means of cheques signed by him), then there was no doubt a drawback: what if the allowance did not cover unexpected expenses? 'Keith' remembered one particular occasion at a lunch at Chesterton's parents. Chesterton was to meet a publisher later at his club, the National Liberal, but he did not have enough money to entertain his guest. The standard allowance was apparently half-a-crown; but that was not enough, nor was the extra shilling that Frances produced. Thereupon the parents withdrew from this domestic scene, accompanied by 'Keith'. It was, she said, the only time that she remembered Mr Ed ever expressing any criticism of Frances, 'for whom he had a great affection and esteem', considering her to be 'a most desirable check on Gilbert's irresponsibility'. ' "Frances should not argue about money before us," he said gravely. "After all, it is Gilbert's money, and he has a right to what is just. I wish they would come to some sort of satisfactory arrangement." ' 'Keith' thought the half-a-crown restriction was most acutely felt by Chesterton on return visits to Fleet Street when it was his turn to buy the round— when, 'with an expansive gesture of his beautiful hand, he would look round—one could feel the words of invitation hovering on his lips—until remembering that he had no money, his hand fell, almost wounded'. But, according to 'Keith', he never complained and remained totally loyal to his wife.[58] However, the truth is that he must surely have agreed with Frances the amount of his 'allowance'.

5

In January 1910 a general election was called after the House of Lords had rejected the Liberal government's budget. Speaking on behalf of the Liberal candidate for Beaconsfield, Chesterton argued that Conservatism was self-contradictory: if you wanted to keep things as they were, the only way to do that was to change them, as, for example, in the case of wanting a white shirt it was necessary to wash or even replace the shirt from time to time. Belloc retained his seat, but Chesterton's friend Charles Masterman, who had been a Cabinet minister, lost his, partly because of the bitter attacks on his integrity by Belloc and Cecil Chesterton, who accused him

[58] MCC 78–80.

of betraying his liberal principles to become a member of the government—much to the distress of Cecil's brother, who knew that Masterman had gone into politics from 'noble bitterness on behalf of the poor'.[59]

In February another novel, *The Ball and the Cross*, was published—although the first eight chapters had in fact been published already serially between March 1905 and November 1906 in the *Commonwealth*.[60] As in *The Napoleon of Notting Hill*, there are two protagonists, both Scotsmen, the emotional Catholic Highlander Evan MacIan and the cerebral atheist Lowlander James Turnbull. Diametrically opposed in politics, too, MacIan being a monarchist and Turnbull a Socialist, they nevertheless are both democrats, believers in the individual's rights and without any of the contemporary intellectuals' contempt for the masses. They are also, more importantly, at one in taking religion seriously. Their attempt to fight a duel over an article displayed in the window of the editorial office of 'The Atheist', edited by Turnbull, which MacIan denounces as a blasphemy against the Virgin Mary, is constantly frustrated by a society that, unlike MacIan and Turnbull, is indifferent to whether religion is true or not, and that eventually confines them to a lunatic asylum. 'Religion is—a—too personal a matter to be mentioned in such a place,' the magistrate angrily informs MacIan when he is brought to court for smashing Turnbull's window. One 'peacemaker' the two protagonists encounter, who urges, 'we won't quarrel about a word,' is informed by MacIan: 'The Church and the heresies always used to fight about words, because they are the only things worth fighting about.' The 'peacemaker', who is a pacifist disciple of Tolstoy, urges the Christian 'principle of love' against the prospect of a duel, to which MacIan's harsh response is:

'Talk about love ... till the world is sick of the word. But don't you talk about Christianity. Don't you dare to say one word, white or black, about it. Christianity is, as far as you are concerned, a horrible mystery. Keep clear of it, keep silent upon it, as you would upon an abomination. It is a thing that has made men slay and torture each other; and you will never know why.'

But hearing the word 'Love' pronounced with the 'intonation' of a Tolstoyan idealist rekindles the determination of MacIan, whose friendship with the like-minded Turnbull—who agrees, unlike the modern world, that 'God is essentially important'—has been growing apace, to fight the duel: 'Give up vows and dogmas, and fixed things, and you may grow like That.'[61] As Chesterton put it, with one of his most brilliant paradoxes,

[59] Ffinch, 177–9.   [60] Oddie, 297.   [61] *BAC* 58, 90–2, 99.

many years later in one of his *Illustrated London News* columns, people who boast that they live by 'the spirit of Christianity' rather than by its dogmas in fact keep 'some of the words and terminology, words like Peace and Righteousness and Love; but they make these words stand for an atmosphere utterly alien to Christendom; they keep the letter and lose the spirit'.[62]

Father O'Connor bought a copy of the novel in London and took it to Beaconsfield to be inscribed by the author. Chesterton arrived ten minutes late for lunch, having written a lengthy inscription in verse, that begins:

> This is a book I do not like,
> Take it away to Heckmondwike,
> A lurid exile, lost and sad
> To punish it for being bad.
> You need not take it from the shelf
> (I tried to read it once myself:
> The speeches jerk, the chapters sprawl,
> The story makes no sense at all)
> Hide it your Yorkshire moors among
> Where no man speaks the English tongue.

But the verses end on a more hopeful note:

> Take then this book I do not like—
> It may improve in Heckmondwike.[63]

About the time the novel appeared, Chesterton had given a lecture at Coventry when he was seen by a couple of Roman Catholic priests at the station bookstall, who asked him if the rumour was true that he was thinking of joining the Church. He replied that it was a question that was giving him 'a great deal of agony of mind', and he asked the priests to pray for him. Father O'Connor remembered how in the late spring, he thought, of 1912, after he and Chesterton had taken part in a debate in Leeds, as they were travelling in the train to Ilkley, Chesterton suddenly interrupted him by saying out of the blue that he had made up his mind to become a Roman Catholic, but he was waiting for Frances to make the same decision, as it was she who had brought him to Christianity. He explained: 'Because I think I have known intimately by now all the best kinds of Anglicanism, and I find them only a pale imitation.' In fact, this conversation must have taken place in 1911 prior to the publication of

---

[62] *ILN* xxxiii. 686–7.   [63] O'Connor, 111–12.

Chesterton's ballad 'Lepanto', as, according to O'Connor, it was what he said on this occasion about the significance of the Battle of Lepanto that gave Chesterton the idea of writing the poem.[64] When Chesterton fell seriously ill in 1914, and O'Connor came to visit him, he was able to explain to Frances the mysterious hints her husband seemed to be dropping, of which she 'could not make head or tail', by telling her of the conversation that had taken place in the train.[65]

In March 1910 the *Daily Star* newspaper published a photograph of Chesterton with the headline, 'Mr Gilbert K. Chesterton to be a parish constable.' When interviewed by the paper, Chesterton did not know that his name had been put forward for what was only an honorary post, and thought there must have been a mistake: 'It would be a good thing for the criminal,' he joked. Other newspapers carried the story, one with a cartoon depicting Chesterton as a helmeted and truncheon-wielding constable, while another speculated that the constable would enjoy arresting Shaw for speeding through Beaconsfield. A newspaper in Montreal also picked up the story: 'The Police Station at Beaconsfield would become the thinking centre of the Empire. The lock-up system would probably be put aside in favour of a new system of street conversation. If Mr Chesterton should lock up an offender he would probably try to convince him that he was really being set at liberty.'[66]

In June 1910 Chesterton published *What's Wrong with the World*.[67] It went through six editions within two months.[68] His central argument is that to change the world does not mean ignoring the past and looking only at the future, and assuming that the past cannot be restored. On the contrary, he argues, all revolutions are really restorations, which is one reason why he is 'doubtful about the modern habit of fixing eyes on the future'—namely, because 'all the men in history who have really done anything with the future have had their eyes fixed on the past'. To see 'fate and futurity as

---

[64] O'Connor, 84–5.   [65] Ward, *GKC* 242–3.   [66] Ffinch, 184.

[67] According to Ward, *GKC* 269, Chesterton had 'originally intended to call the book *What's Wrong?* laying some emphasis on the note of interrogation'; but the publishers added to the title and dropped the question mark, which 'represented a certain loss'. But the question mark in fact was retained on both the front cover and the spine, although not on the title page. John Sullivan, *G. K. Chesterton: A Bibliography* (New York: Barnes and Noble, 1958), 33. Actually, according to Chesterton in his Dedication, he had originally called the book *What is Wrong*, without a question mark.

[68] Pearce, 155.

clear and inevitable' is to be turned to stone—like the Calvinists with their 'perfect creed of predestination' or modern eugenists, who, however, make 'amusing' rather than 'dignified' statues unlike the Calvinists. Chesterton ridicules the so-called courage of those who attack tradition: 'There is not really any courage at all in attacking hoary or antiquated things, any more than in offering to fight one's grandmother.' In fact, the 'only true free-thinker is he whose intellect is as much free from the future as from the past. He cares as little for what will be as for what has been; he cares only for what ought to be.' In particular, he has no time for 'the deep and silent modern assumption that past things have become impossible. There is one metaphor of which the moderns are very fond; they are always saying, "You can't put the clock back." The simple and obvious answer is "You can".' The trouble with modern thinkers is that they are reactionaries, 'for their thought is always a reaction from what went before'. They are 'always coming from a place, not going to it'. What Chesterton is attacking is

the huge heresy of Precedent. It is the view that because we have got into a mess we must grow messier to suit it; that because we have taken a wrong turn some time ago we must go forward and not backwards; that because we have lost our way we must lose our map also; and because we have missed our ideal, we must forget it.

An obvious example is the Christian ideal, which 'has not been tried and found wanting. It has been found difficult; and left untried.' It is not that people have 'got tired of Christianity; they have never found enough Christianity to get tired of'. Another ideal that has not been found wanting but has not been properly tried is that of democracy, which 'has in a strict and practical sense been a dream unfulfilled'. But then 'the world is full of these unfulfilled ideas, these uncompleted temples'. And Chesterton concludes: 'History does not consist of completed and crumbling ruins; rather it consists of half-built villas abandoned by a bankrupt-builder. This world is more like an unfinished suburb than a deserted cemetery.'[69]

There is the recurring insistence on the human need for limitation. The 'joy of God' is 'unlimited creation', but

the special joy of man is limited creation, the combination of creation with limits. Man's pleasure, therefore, is to possess conditions, but also to be partly possessed by them; to be half-controlled by the flute he plays or by the field he digs. The

[69] *WW* 54–5, 57, 142, 148–9, 61, 65, 63.

excitement is to get the utmost out of given conditions; the conditions will stretch, but not indefinitely.

Thus, for instance, the pleasure of owning property depends on the property being limited, for a property-owner 'cannot see the shape of his own land unless he sees the edges of his neighbour's. It is the negation of property that the Duke of Sutherland should have all the farms in one estate; just as it would be the negation of marriage if he had all our wives in one harem.' So-called free love is a contradiction in terms: 'a man cannot be a free lover; he is either a traitor or a tied man.' There have to be limitations to sexual love in view of 'the earthquake consequences that Nature has attached to sex'. Any kind of pleasure must have limitations attached to it, since 'in everything worth having... there is a point of pain or tedium that must be survived, so that the pleasure may revive and endure'. The last of the examples Chesterton gives is surprising and may well have autobiographical significance: 'The joy of battle comes after the first fear of death; the joy of reading Virgil comes after the bore of learning him; the glow of the sea-bather comes after the icy shock of the sea bath; and the success of the marriage comes after the failure of the honeymoon.' The limitation of vows, laws, and contracts are all 'ways of surviving with success this breaking point, this instant of potential surrender'. Limitation indeed comes with life itself, for we are limited by our bodies: 'Each human soul has in a sense to enact for itself the gigantic humility of the Incarnation. Every man must descend into the flesh to meet mankind.' Then again there is no such thing as limitless intellectual freedom: 'There are two things, and two things only, for the human mind, a dogma and a prejudice.' In other words, every thought depends on some conviction, whether it be a dogma or a prejudice. The idea, then, that one can have a dogma-less education is absurd: 'Dogma is actually the only thing that cannot be separated from education. It is education. A teacher who is not dogmatic is simply a teacher who is not teaching.' Chesterton thought the real object of education was to restore that Wordsworthian sense of wonder at the world with which we are born ('when we see things for the first time we feel instantly that they are creative fictions; we feel the finger of God'):

There was a time when you and I and all of us were all very close to God; so that even now the colour of a pebble (or a paint), the smell of a flower (or a firework), comes to our hearts with a kind of authority and certainty; as if they were fragments of a muddled message, or features of a forgotten face.

To pour that fiery simplicity upon the whole of life is the only real aim of education . . . [70]

The common man with his ordinary desires and pleasures is, as usual, a priority for Chesterton. He warns that, just as his 'personal land has been silently stolen ever since the sixteenth century', so now his 'personal liberty is being stolen', 'piece by piece, and quite silently'. There is a marvellously indignant, satirical passage in which Chesterton charts his descent from owning his own house and a strip of land to his confinement to the workhouse:

[He] has always desired the divinely ordinary things; he has married for love, he has chosen or built a small house that fits like a coat . . . And just as he is moving in, something goes wrong. Some tyranny, personal or political, suddenly debars him from the home; and he has to take his meals in the front garden. A passing philosopher (who is also, by a mere coincidence, the man who turned him out) pauses, and leaning elegantly on the railings, explains to him that he is now living that bold life upon the bounty of nature which will be the life of the sublime future. He finds life in the front garden more bold than bountiful, and has to move into mean lodgings in the next spring. The philosopher (who turned him out), happening to call at these lodgings, with the probable intention of raising the rent, stops to explain to him that he is now in the real life of mercantile endeavour; the economic struggle between him and the landlady is the only thing out of which, in the sublime future, the wealth of nations can come. He is defeated in the economic struggle, and goes to the workhouse. The philosopher who turned him out (happening at that very moment to be inspecting the workhouse) assures him that he is now at last in that golden republic which is the goal of mankind; he is in an equal, scientific, Socialist commonwealth, owned by the State and ruled by public officers; in fact, the commonwealth of the sublime future.

Secular Calvinism like that of the Socialist Shaw led, Chesterton thought, to 'a singular depression about what one can do with the populace'—that is, the masses—for the Calvinist sees them as predestined from eternity and 'merely filling up [their] time until the crack of doom'. Far from being 'intensely thrilling and precious', their life is seen as 'automatic and uninteresting', for, while Shaw and his followers 'admit it is a superstition that a man is judged after death, they stick to their central doctrine, that he is judged before he is born'. This explains their 'strange disembodied gaiety about what may be done with posterity' through their 'sociology and eugenics and the rest of it'.[71]

---

[70] *WW* 65–7, 69, 93–4, 48, 162, 199, 125.   [71] *WW* 209, 82–3, 153–4.

Finally, the rise of the suffragette movement leads Chesterton to some conservative but radical thoughts on women. On the one hand, he defines the absolutely crucial difference between men and women as the fact that women not men give birth:

Nothing can ever overcome that one enormous sex superiority, that even the male child is born closer to his mother than to his father. No one, staring at that frightful female privilege, can quite believe in the equality of the sexes. Here and there we read of a girl brought up like a tom-boy; but every boy is brought up like a tame girl. The flesh and spirit of femininity surround him from the first like the four walls of a house; and even the ... most brutal man has been womanized by being born. Man that is born of a woman has short days and full of misery; but nobody can picture the obscenity and bestial tragedy that would belong to such a monster as man that was born of a man.

Then again, Chesterton argues, a woman at home is at an advantage over a man at work, because she is not limited to 'one trade' but may cultivate 'twenty hobbies':

Women were not kept at home in order to keep them narrow; on the contrary, they were kept at home in order to keep them broad. The world outside the home was one mass of narrowness, a maze of cramped paths, a madhouse of mono-maniacs. It was only by partly limiting and protecting the woman that she was enabled to play at five or six professions ...

The manifold variety of tasks the wife and mother is called upon to perform 'might exhaust the mind, but I cannot imagine how it could narrow it'. The feminist, on the other hand, he defines as 'one who dislikes the chief feminine characteristics'. And one of these characteristics, Chesterton considers, is to 'regard a vote as unwomanly'.[72]

On 18 June 1910, the same month as the publication of *What's Wrong with the World*, ten thousand women marched from the Embankment to the Albert Hall, demonstrating for a vote for women and carrying a banner inscribed 'From Prison to Citizenship'. Chesterton's reaction is famous: 'Ten thousand women marched through the streets of London saying: "We will not be dictated to," and then went off to become stenographers.' Four years earlier he had admitted in an interview that the question of women's suffrage was the one question on which he was undecided: if the majority of women wanted the vote, then he thought they should have it, in spite of his reservation that women should not want to be like men.[73]

[72] *WW* 148, 143–4, 116, 118, 221.   [73] Ffinch, 180–1.

In November 1910 Chesterton published another collection of his *Daily News* articles called *Alarms and Discussions*, as well as another volume for the Popular Library of Art on William Blake. In one of these *Daily News* columns, he addresses that favourite topic of contemporary intellectuals, the growth of population and the urbanization of England. Contrary to the received wisdom, he argued that there was 'not the slightest objection, in itself, to England being built over . . . any more than there is to its being (as it is already) built over by birds, or by squirrels, or by spiders'. There was, of course, an objection to overpopulation—'If whenever I tried to walk down the road I found the whole thoroughfare one crawling carpet of spiders, closely interlocked, I should feel a distress verging on distaste.' But Chesterton explicitly rejects the intellectuals' aversion for the masses: 'It is not humanity that disgusts us in the huge cities; it is inhumanity. It is not that there are human beings; but that they are not treated as such. . . . It is not the presence of people that makes London appalling. It is merely the absence of the people.' He then rejoices in that very phenomenon of suburbia that so distressed the intellectuals:

Therefore, I dance with joy to think that my part of England is being built over, so long as it is being built over in a human way at human intervals and in a human proportion. So long, in short, as I am not myself built over . . . I do not want the nearest human house to be too distant to see; that is my objection to the wilderness. But neither do I want the nearest human house to be too close to see; that is my objection to the modern city.

The landscape of the countryside itself anyway was created by human beings: 'It is not only nonsense, but blasphemy, to say that man has spoilt the country. Man has created the country; it was his business, as the image of God.' Chesterton also tackles head-on another pet prejudice of the intellectuals, mass tourism: 'Why does the idea of a char-à-banc full of tourists going to see the birthplace of Nelson or the death-scene of Simon de Montford strike a strange chill to the soul?' Contempt for the masses always aroused his strongest indignation:

If there is one thing more dwarfish and pitiful than irreverence for the past, it is irreverence for the present, for the passionate and many-coloured procession of life, which includes the char-à-banc among its many chariots and triumphal cars. I know nothing so vulgar as that contempt for vulgarity which sneers at the clerks on a Bank Holiday or the Cockneys on Margate sands.

Far from 'commonplace crowds' and 'antiquities' not going together, Chesterton argues the opposite is true: 'For the truth is that it has been almost entirely the antiquities that have normally interested the populace; and it has been almost entirely the populace who have systematically preserved the antiquities.' Besides, antiquities like cathedrals 'were meant, not for people more cultured and self-conscious than modern tourists, but for people much rougher and more casual'. Contrary to the advice of Ruskin, the 'true way of reviving the magic of our great minsters and historic sepulchres' was 'not to be more careful' of them but 'to be more careless of them'. There was another consideration, naturally of no interest to 'modern artistic cathedral-lovers', the fact that the people went originally to cathedrals to pray: 'these two elements of sanctity and democracy have been socially connected and allied throughout history.' In one essay in the book Chesterton explicitly castigates those he calls 'Intellectuals' as 'a blight and desolation', who like to dismiss the masses' 'strange preferences' as 'prejudices and superstitions', and who despise their 'slang and rude dialect'. A country girl who saw the sea for the first time and likened it to cauliflowers may not have been talking about it in the 'appreciative', that is 'bookish', way of intellectuals, but she was talking 'pure literature'. The 'appreciative' way of looking at the sea was to stress its boundlessness and 'infinity', but the simile of the cauliflower conveyed 'the opposite impression, the impression of boundary and of barrier': 'So far from being vague and vanishing, the sea is the one hard straight line in Nature. It is the one plain limit; the only thing that God has made that really looks like a wall. . . . the one straight line; the limit of the intellect; the dark and ultimate dogma of the world.'[74]

There are other familiar themes in the essays. The medieval 'idea of a sense of humour defying and dominating hell' is praised because 'terror must be fundamentally frivolous'. And the hell of the ego is especially defied by humour, which 'is meant, in a literal sense, to make game of man; that is to dethrone him from his official dignity and hunt him like game'. It is because joking is 'undignified' that 'it is so good for one's soul'.[75] 'Hilarity,', he wrote elsewhere, 'involves humility', and being undignified is 'the essence of all real happiness'. There is, he insisted, 'an alliance between religion and real fun'; whereas Socialist like pagan utopias 'have all one horrible fault. They are all dignified.' For religion 'is much nearer to riotous happiness than it is to the detached and temperate types of happiness in which gentlemen and philosophers find their peace'. Without religion, humour is impossible anyway since it involves humility: 'No man has ever

[74] *AD* 137–9, 72–4, 76, 78–9, 147, 150, 207–8, 210–1.   [75] *AD* 17, 33, 201.

laughed at anything till he has laughed at himself.'[76] Chesterton delighted in the thought that the soul might be 'rapt out of the body in an agony of sorrow, or a trance of ecstasy; but it might also be rapt out of the body in a paroxysm of laughter': 'Laughter has something in it in common with the ancient winds of faith and inspiration; it unfreezes pride and unwinds secrecy; it makes men forget themselves in the presence of something greater than themselves...'[77] For 'laughter...is an elemental agony, shaking the jester himself....'.[78] Religion itself required laughter: 'you can be a great deal too solemn about Christianity to be a good Christian...you must have mirth. If you do not have mirth you will certainly have madness.'[79] You will also have pride, to which humour is 'the chief antidote'.[80]

Chesterton's love for that unloved thing, the English weather, is celebrated in one article in *Alarms and Discussions*. Writing in the midst of a terrible English summer, he provokes his readers by declaring:

But for my part I will praise the English climate till I die—even if I die of the English climate. There is no weather as good as English weather. Nay, in a real sense there is no weather at all anywhere but in England.... Only in our own romantic country do you have the strictly romantic thing called Weather; beautiful and changing as a woman. The great English landscape painters...have this salient characteristic: that the Weather is not the atmosphere of their pictures; it is the subject of their pictures. They paint portraits of the Weather. The Weather sat to Constable. The Weather posed for Turner...

The English weather is notoriously variable, but it was this very variability that Chesterton enjoyed so much—like the variability of women which he considered one of their virtues: 'It avoids the crude requirement of polygamy. So long as you have one good wife you are sure to have a spiritual harem.' Even the dreaded greyness of the English sky was not uniform, as it seems to its native observers, but full of exciting variability: 'One day may be grey like steel, and another grey like dove's plumage. One may seem grey like the deathly frost, and another grey like the smoke of substantial kitchens.' As a descriptive writer who was also an artist, Chesterton was particularly interested in depicting colours, especially the constantly varying colours of the English sky, and that was a reason why he liked the colour grey: 'rich colours actually look more luminous on a grey sky, because they are seen against a sombre background and seem to be burning with a lustre of their own.' Then, again, the colour that people

---

[76] *ILN* xxviii. 24; xxix. 546.   [77] *CM* 12, 158.   [78] *HA* 28.
[79] *LL* 97.   [80] *SL* 29.

referred to as 'colourless' had this advantage: 'that it suggests in some way the mixed and troubled average of existence, especially in its quality of strife and expectation and promise. Grey is a colour that always seems on the eve of changing to some other colour...So we may be perpetually reminded of the indefinite hope that is in doubt itself...'[81]

In another article about Beaconsfield being 'built over', Chesterton returned to the subject of the building that was going up around him in Beaconsfield, but this time it gave him an opportunity to celebrate 'domesticity', 'one of the wildest adventures'. The idea was obviously related to the view of woman's primary role as being primarily that of housewife, which he had expressed in *What's Wrong with the World*. The sight of the 'open staircases' of a half-built house indicates why domesticity is far from being 'tame': 'every such staircase is truly only an awful and naked ladder running up into the Infinite to a deadly height.' Householder, tiler, and roof-mender alike are each 'a sort of domestic mountaineer', climbing to 'a point from which mere idle falling will kill a man; and life is always worth living while men feel they may die'. Again, we encounter the Chestertonian philosophy of wonder as we are made to see the awful implications of a staircase: 'How sublime and, indeed, almost dizzy is the thought of these veiled ladders on which we all live, like climbing monkeys!' Back from his walk of inspection of the 'skeleton' of the half-built house, Chesterton climbs the staircase in his own house: 'I climbed the stairs stubbornly, planting each foot with savage care, as if ascending a glacier. When I got to a landing I was wildly relieved, and waved my hat.... Believe me, it is only one of the wild and wonderful things that one can learn by stopping at home.'[82]

William Blake, published in November 1910, was a companion volume to Chesterton's earlier volume in the Popular Library of Art on Watts. His philosophy of limitation, which he was also later to apply to his discussion of Stevenson's fiction, is here invoked for appreciating Blake, who 'was a fanatic on the subject of the firm line', and would no more have tolerated Impressionism, which Chesterton equates with 'scepticism', than Chesterton did. This 'decision of tint and outline' belonged, 'not only to Blake's pictures, but even to his poetry'. And when one calls Blake a mystic, insists Chesterton, one is not saying he is 'mysterious', for a mere 'verbal accident has confused the mystical with the mysterious'. Far from being 'vague', the mystic 'does not bring doubts or riddles: the doubts and riddles exist already'.

[81] *AD* 115–17, 119–20.   [82] *AD* 141–5.

After all, 'the 'mystery of life' was 'the plainest part of it'. The mystic, therefore, was not someone 'who makes mysteries' but someone 'who destroys them'. The 'explanation' offered by the mystic may be true or false, but it was '*always* comprehensible': even though it was not 'always comprehended', there was always something to 'be comprehended' and 'even when [the mystic] was himself hard to be understood, it was never through himself not understanding: it was never because he was vague or mystified or groping, that he was unintelligible'. There was 'one element always to be remarked in the true mystic, however disputed his symbolism', and that was 'its brightness of colour and clearness of shape'. For, continues Chesterton, 'the highest dogma of the spiritual is to affirm the material'.[83] It was a point he had already made in one of the essays in *Alarms and Discussions*, when he maintained that true religion was always sacramental:

it is always trying to make men feel truths as facts; always trying to make abstract things as plain and solid as concrete things; always trying to make men, not merely admit the truth, but see, smell, handle, hear, and devour the truth. All great spiritual scriptures are full of the invitation not to test, but to taste; not to examine, but to eat. Their phrases are full of living water and heavenly bread, mysterious manna and dreadful wine. Worldliness, and the polite society of the world, has despised this instinct of eating; but religion has never despised it.[84]

And so for Blake, God 'was not more and more vague and diaphanous as one came near to Him', but 'was more and more solid as one came near'. And the closer one came to God, the more it was clear that God was a 'person', a 'fact', and not the 'impersonal God of the Pantheists': 'God is merely light to the merely unenlightened. God is a man to the enlightened.' Indeed, for Blake, God was 'more solid than humanity', 'the ideal . . . not only more beautiful but more actual than the real'. Chesterton summarizes Blake's philosophy as 'primarily the assertion that the ideal is more actual than the real'. Blake set imagination against nature, which, unlike imagination, 'had no outline'. For imagination did not mean for Blake 'something shadowy or fantastic, but rather something clear-cut, definite, and unalterable'—that is, 'images; the eternal images of things'.[85]

Unfortunately, Blake was also a spiritualist in the most 'vulgar' sense. The difference between mysticism and spiritualism was the 'difference between having a real religion and having a mere curiosity about psychic marvels'. The spiritualist who invokes supernatural beings does so 'only because they are supernatural', not because they are necessarily

---

[83] *WB* 17, 137, 131–3, 135.   [84] *AD* 47.   [85] *WB* 148–9, 160, 166.

'good or wise or helpful'. Spiritualism was like spirits—it provided 'excitement' but not 'satisfaction'. Nor was Blake's mysticism always admirable— it could become 'separated from the people', thanks to 'the element of oligarchy and fastidiousness in the mystics and masonries of that epoch'. Christian mysticism, on the other hand, was of its essence democratic: 'The Christian mysteries are so far democratic that nobody understands them at all.' Chesterton distinguishes between Christian and oriental mysticism. The latter aspires to 'an insane simplicity', to perfection by 'simplification' and the eradication of individuality. Against 'all this emasculate mysticism', which holds that, 'as a man climbs higher and higher, God becomes to him more and more formless, ethereal, and even thin', Blake 'rears his colossal figure and his earthquake voice', passionately reiterating 'that the more we know of higher things the more palpable and incarnate we shall find them; that the form filling the heavens is the likeness of the appearance of a man'. This is the fundamental difference between Christian and Eastern mysticism: 'the idea that personality is the glory of the universe and not its shame.' There was, however, a third kind of mysticism, a 'healthier heathen mysticism, which did not shrink from the shapes of things or the emphatic colours of existence'. This 'solid and joyful occultism' was to be found 'at its boldest and most brilliant' in Blake. Chesterton himself, however, was convinced that ultimately there were only the two alternatives, 'utter pessimistic scepticism' or 'the Catholic creed'.[86]

[86] *WB* 100, 98–9, 180, 183, 202, 209–10.

8

---·◆·◆·◆·---

Father Brown and the
Marconi Scandal

I

T HE most important review of *Orthodoxy* had been that of Wilfrid Ward,
the son of W. G. Ward, the *enfant terrible* of the Oxford Movement and
subsequently the Ultramontane critic of Newman. The younger Ward,
however, was to publish, four years after the publication of *Orthodoxy*, a
deeply sympathetic intellectual biography of Newman, in which he did his
best to distance his hero from the Catholic Modernists who liked to claim
him as their forebear.[1] In his review, Ward appreciated Chesterton as the
successor of Newman as an apologist for Christianity, noting the similarity
with Newman's own account of reasoning in the *Grammar of Assent*. Classing
Chesterton with such thinkers as Burke, Butler, and Coleridge, he wrote:
'His pages are marked by the freshness and often by the insight of genius.'[2]
Chesterton for his part was grateful for Ward's 'most sympathetic critique
. . . at a time when many of his world must have thought it a piece of rowdy
paradox. He laid down the excellent critical test; that the critics could not
understand what he liked, but he could understand what they disliked.
"Truth can understand error; but error cannot understand Truth." '[3]

---

[1] Wilfrid Ward, *The Life of John Henry Cardinal Newman*, 2 vols. (London:
Longmans, Green, and Co., 1912).
[2] Wilfrid Ward, 'Mr Chesterton among the Prophets', *Dublin Review*, 144 (Jan.
1909), 1, 15, 29.
[3] *A.* 248.

Chesterton had as a result become a regular guest at the Wards' London and country houses. One hot summer weekend at Lotus, the Wards' home in Surrey, Chesterton was delighted to hear the comment of an aristocratic lady, who had been a disciple of the German historian Döllinger, who was excommunicated after the First Vatican Council for refusing to accept the definition of papal infallibility, that she had to have the same religion as her washerwoman and that the Modernist Father Tyrrell's religion was not the religion of her washerwoman. That was a crucial test for Chesterton, too: a religion that was not the religion of the common man was not a real religion. On this occasion, Chesterton was offered a wicker chair as they sat in the sunshine on the terrace, but he opted for the grass since otherwise 'there was grave danger he might unduly "modify" the chair'. The Wards, like their daughter Maisie Ward, Chesterton's first biographer, regarded Chesterton as 'the greatest man of the age'.[4] For his part, Chesterton admired Wilfrid Ward's life of Newman, considering that he had 'achieved something quite other and stronger than self-effacement . . . He was anything but merely receptive . . . he could . . . be strongly co-operative with another's mind. His intellectual qualities could be invisible because they were active, when they were the very virile virtues of a biographer which are those of a friend.'[5]

When the Wards were in their house in London they liked to invite their friends to meet the great Chesterton at lunch. At one of the first of these lunch parties, at which Chesterton's favourite, albeit Conservative, politician George Wyndham, himself a great admirer of Chesterton, was present, Maisie Ward remembered Chesterton ridiculing partial social reforms: to gain only half a reform was like gaining half a cow—and what use was half a cow to anyone? He commented on the paradox that, while Christianity was 'mystical and full of paradoxes', the West was much more practical than the East, which was 'so logical and clear' in its religion. When the question arose as to the nature of Englishness, Chesterton's two examples of the archetypal Englishman were, unsurprisingly, Johnson and Dickens.[6]

That lunch was probably in 1911, the year when Chesterton was elected through Ward's 'kindness' to the Synthetic Society, 'which was justly proud of its continuity with the Society in which the great Huxley could debate

[4] Ward, *GKC* 229.

[5] Maisie Ward, *The Wilfrid Wards and the Transition*, i. *The Nineteenth Century* (London: Sheed and Ward, 1934), 259.

[6] Ward, *GKC* 230.

with the equally great Ward'. Chesterton was surprised by how few 'literary men' there were in a society 'devoted to philosophy; except Wilfrid Ward himself, who was an excellent editor and expositor'. There was a loud noise heralding the late arrival of Chesterton at his first meeting—'a figure enormous and extended, a kind of walking mountain but with large rounded corners'. Depositing his coat and stick 'with a fresh crash', 'he sat, eager and attentive...filling up the whole space at the bottom of the table, drawing caricatures of the company on a sheet of foolscap, a memorable figure,' Ward reported to Wyndham, 'very welcome to me, but arousing the fury of the conventional and the "dreary and well-informed"', who were convinced that he would 'ruin the society and ought never to have been elected'. Ward thought Chesterton would be an even more suitable member of 'The Club' that Dr Johnson had founded; but here he met with less success, having only Wyndham's enthusiastic support. The fact that Chesterton rivalled its founder in his conversation failed to ensure his election to a club that had unfortunately become socially exclusive.[7]

There was an obvious bond between Wyndham and the Chestertons on account of their Anglo-Catholicism, but Wyndham's deeply spiritual wife, Lady Grosvenor, also greatly impressed them. 'She always showed a most moving curiosity about where I had picked up this passion for what is called Mariolatry in this Protestant land; and I could assure her with truth, though without any complete explanation, that I had had it in some form from boyhood.' According to Maisie Ward, the Chestertons at this time were 'much in contact with the extreme Anglo-Catholic group in the Church of England' and became friendly with Lady Grosvenor's friend, Father Philip Waggett of the Cowley Fathers, who may have become Chesterton's confessor.[8] On the Chestertons' second visit to Lotus, after *The Ballad of the White Horse* had been published, Wyndham told the company of 'his habit of "shouting" the ballad "to submissive listeners"'. The company 'hoped for the same treat. But Gilbert got the book and kicked it under his chair defying us to recover it.' On this occasion he remarked to the granddaughter of a duke: 'You and I...belong to the jolly old upper Middle Classes.' No doubt, he thought he was paying the aristocratic lady a compliment. But apart from being proud of belonging to the middle class, class distinctions meant nothing to Chesterton.[9]

---

[7] *A.* 248; Ward, *GKC* 232–4.   [8] See below, p. 547.
[9] *A.* 251–2; Ward, *GKC* 234–6.

It was also at the Wards' house, 'that great clearing-house of philoso-phies and theologies', that Chesterton first met the Conservative politician Lord Hugh Cecil. The meeting affected Chesterton both politically and religiously. His realization of how much he had in common with Wynd-ham had already made him sceptical about the party system, but when he saw how little Cecil had in common with Wyndham his scepticism was confirmed. And, secondly, it was Cecil's 'perfect and solid Protestantism' that 'fully revealed to me that I was no longer a Protestant'. Cecil, thought Chesterton, was probably the only 'real Protestant' left, which was why he startled the world he lived in every now and again by 'a stark and upstanding defence of the common Christian theology and ethics, in which all Protestants once believed. For the Protestant world in England today is a very curious and subtle thing': 'while it is naturally a little disturbed by a Protestant accepting Catholicism . . . [it] is far more terribly disturbed by any Protestant who still preserves Protestantism.'[10]

Although Chesterton was no Tory or Conservative, he no longer felt he belonged to the party opposing that of Wyndham, as he had become deeply disillusioned with the Liberals who had been returned to power at two general elections in 1910, although with greatly reduced majorities and only able to govern as a minority government. In January 1911 he wrote to the Liberal *Nation*, complaining that 'the big questions' of social reform were being 'squeezed out'. He explained: 'I say our representatives accept designs and desires almost entirely from the Cabinet class above them; and practically not at all from the constituents below them. I say the people does not wield a Parliament which wields a Cabinet. I say the Cabinet bullies a timid parliament which bullies a bewildered people.' If examples were needed, then 'I say the people do not cry out that all children whose parents lunch on cheese and beer in an inn should be left out in the rain. I say the people did not demand that a man's sentence should be settled by his jailers instead of by his judges.' The Editor replied that these two instances—about which he agreed—were 'too small to prove so large a case'. He could hardly have said anything more likely to provoke Chesterton, who had very strong views both about the licensing laws, not least as they affected children, and about the penal system, and who retorted: 'Why do you think of these things as small? They are really enormous. One alters the daily habits of millions of people; the other destroys the public law of thousands of years. What can be more funda-mental than food, drink, and children? What can be more catastrophic

---

[10] *A* 249–51.

than putting us back in the primal anarchy, in which a man was flung into a dungeon and left there "till he listened to reason?"' But Chesterton knew why such matters were considered unimportant: 'simply' because 'the Front Benches did not announce them as big. They were not "first-class measures"; they were not "full-dress debates". The governing class shot them through in the quick, quiet, secondary way in which they pass things that the people positively detests...'[11]

Belloc and Cecil Chesterton made their disillusionment with the Liberals known in their book *The Party System*, which was also published in 1911, in which they took exactly the same line as Chesterton—namely, that, far from the people or even parliament governing, it was the cabinet that ruled, the ministers chosen by the oligarchies that controlled the two parties. The two authors even alleged that these governing families not only belonged to the same social set but were actually related by birth or marriage. It was also possible to buy one's way into this oligarchy by contributing to party funds. The Liberal government was not the first— or the last—to sell honours for money, but the practice had increased notably. Belloc, who was too disillusioned with party politics to stand again in 1910, had already as the member for South Salford in the 1906 parliament proposed, without success, that at least the names of subscribers to party funds should be made public. And Chesterton himself had written an article for the *Daily News* following an attack in the House of Commons in 1907 on the then Liberal Prime Minister Campbell-Bannerman over the sale of peerages. The Editor, A. G. Gardiner, refused to publish it, although he promised to keep it 'for a later occasion when the general question is not complicated with a particularly offensive incident'. Chesterton replied in a letter to the editor, saying that, while in general he would never resent one of his articles not being published, this was a matter for his conscience ('just now the animal is awake and roaring'): it was 'a question of which is the more important, politeness or political morality'. Unless some Liberal journalists spoke out, 'the secret funds and the secret powers are safe'. His letter was published by Gardiner and was quoted, to general applause, in the House of Commons. However, this kind of corruption was not the preserve of the Liberal Party: what was special about contemporary Liberalism was that it was becoming less and less concerned for its liberal principles of freedom and liberty and more and more for the kind of Socialist legislation that interfered in the lives of the ordinary people. Several years later Chesterton was to write that 'the

[11] Ward, *GKC* 271–4.

least hint of a revolution would have caused quite as much horror' in the Liberal *Daily News* office as in that of the Conservative *Morning Post*: 'The fact is that Liberalism was in no way whatever on the side of Labour; on the contrary, it was on the side of the Labour Party...'.[12]

2

The first of the Father Brown stories, 'The Blue Cross', had been published in September 1910 in the *Storyteller* magazine. It had been written at the time of the move from London to Beaconsfield, when Chesterton was staying with Lucian Oldershaw and, unable to find a detective story he had not read, decided to write one himself.[13] It was the first of twelve stories, previously published as stories in magazines, in the first of the Father Brown volumes, *The Innocence of Father Brown*, which appeared in July 1911. There is a general view—held for example by Ronald Knox—that this is the best of the Father Brown volumes and that there is a falling-off in subsequent volumes, albeit, according to Knox, a recovery in the last volume.[14] Perhaps this view is persuasive because it is well known that some later stories were written for money.[15] It has even been suggested that the stories deteriorate in the course of each volume.[16] However, when a few years ago this writer made a selection of what seemed to him the best of the Father Brown stories,[17] the resulting selection indicated the opposite of this view: not a single story was selected from the second of the Father Brown volumes, *The Wisdom of Father Brown* (1914), which followed only three years after what is presumed to be the best of the volumes, while on the other hand six stories were selected from *The Incredulity of Father Brown* (1926), as opposed to five stories from *The Innocence of Father Brown*, four from *The Secret of Father Brown* (1927), and no less than six stories from the final volume, *The Scandal of Father Brown* (1935), published only a year before

---

[12] Ward, *GKC* 252–5, 269–70.   [13] Ward, *RC* 110.

[14] Conlon, ii. 139: 'When he wrote *The Incredulity* and *The Secret (of Father Brown)*, Chesterton had perhaps rather written himself out ... At the end of his life, he seemed to get a second wind, and *The Scandal of Father Brown* contains some of his most ingenious plots.' Cf. Conlon, i. 427; ii. 304; Sullivan, 13–14; Barker, 196; W. W. Robson, 'Introduction', in W. W. Robson (ed.), *G. K. Chesterton: Father Brown: A Selection* (Oxford: Oxford University Press, 1995), p. xvi.

[15] Sullivan, 14, 158.   [16] Barker, 196–7.

[17] *G. K. Chesterton: Father Brown*, ed. Ian Ker (London: Penguin, 2001).

Chesterton's death, when he was heavily preoccupied with editing *G.K.'s Weekly*. This selection at any rate would indicate that, with the exception of the second volume, there was no deterioration in quality but a slight improvement if anything. As for a deterioration of quality within the stories in a volume, this selection certainly did not support that allegation.

The Father Brown stories are certainly not the most important of Chesterton's writings, but they have remained the most popular and widely read.[18] Chesterton himself did not regard them as of any great importance. Dorothy Collins has recorded how some of the later ones were written for purely financial reasons, particularly to help pay for *G.K.'s Weekly*. On being informed of his precarious bank balance, Chesterton would reply: ' "Oh, well. We must write another Father Brown story," and this would be done at lightning speed a day or two later from a few notes on the back of an envelope'.[19]

The point of making Father Brown appear commonplace and inconspicuous was not only to disguise his penetrating powers of insight and observation. For the character reflects Chesterton's own love of ordinariness. Just as Father Brown's creator delights in depicting the most commonplace and familiar things with a vivid freshness as though they were entirely novel and strange, so too Father Brown is able to detect a vital significance in the most unremarkable things; what everyone else fails to notice because of its apparent insignificance, he sees.[20] Nobody noticed that somebody *did* actually enter the building: namely, the postman, or somebody who purported to be the postman, but who was ignored precisely because he looked like a postman. Or it may be, as in another story, a completely unsuspicious remark, as when the murdered admiral's solicitor is told that he has been drowned, and instead of assuming that it was at sea—as anybody else would—he asks *where* he was drowned. The identity of another murderer is spotted by Father Brown when he fails to start or look around at his victim screaming as she crashes to her death. In the story of the postman, Father Brown makes the shrewd observation that people do not answer what you ask but what they think you mean.

---

[18] The following is an adapted version of my introduction to my selection of Father Brown stories cited above.

[19] Sullivan, 158.

[20] Cf. Conlon, ii. 325: 'In the Father Brown stories ... everything depends on the seemingly casual but illuminating observation of ordinary things and ordinary language.'

Ronald Knox thought that the Father Brown stories could not really be counted among 'mystery stories'.[21] In the first place, Father Brown is neither a police nor a private detective; nor is he a detective in the sense of being someone who is an expert at solving crimes.[22] The only expertise that Father Brown possesses is his intimate knowledge of the human heart. And this knowledge he acquires from his religion, in two ways. First, there is his belief in original sin and the human capacity for evil. It is precisely because of his own sins as a human being that he can understand another's sins, as he explains in the story that gives its name to the volume called *The Secret of Father Brown*. He rejects the science of criminology because it means 'getting *outside* a man and studying him as if he were a gigantic insect: in what they would call a dry impartial light, in what I should call a dead and dehumanised light';[23] whereas he knows that criminals are friends not strangers, because they are fellow human beings. Instead of trying to observe the suspected criminal from the outside, Father Brown tries to get inside, or rather tries to *be* the criminal. He sees himself as a kind of 'understudy'[24] who will know who has committed the crime once he has really learned the part. The reformed criminal Flambeau, for example, stops stealing once Father Brown has explained to him why he was stealing. Far from seeing criminals as a race apart, Father Brown sees them as people like himself—that is, sinners. This is how he explains, with unusual passion, the source of his powers of detection:

No man's really any good till he knows how bad he is, or might be; till he's realized exactly how much right he has to all this snobbery, and sneering, and talking about 'criminals', as if they were apes in a forest ten thousand miles away; till he's got rid of all the dirty self-deception of talking about low types and deficient skulls; till he's squeezed out of his soul the last drop of the oil of the Pharisees; till his only hope is somehow or other to have captured one criminal, and kept him safe and sane under his own hat.[25]

---

[21] Conlon, ii. 133. Cf. John D. Coates, *Chesterton and the Edwardian Cultural Crisis* (Hull: Hull University Press, 1984), 12–13: 'The stories mark a sharp break with the ratiocinative methods of detection which were the staple of the detective story from . . . Poe and which reached a climax in Conan Doyle. Father Brown operates instead by intuition informed by a theological knowledge of human nature.'

[22] Robson, 'Introduction', p. xvi, comments on the fact that, while Father Brown is not a professional but an amateur detective, he is a professional priest.

[23] FB ii. 218.   [24] FB ii. 373.   [25] FB ii. 219.

The other source of his knowledge of the human heart is his priestly work of hearing confessions. He knows about evil because he hears about actual sins. On one occasion he uncovers the villain because he can tell immediately that he has made a false confession. As a priest, too, he picks up vital information that the normal detective would never gather because he does not possess that empathy that comes naturally to a good pastoral priest, used to mixing with all kinds of people.

Because it is impossible in a detective story to have normal fictional characterization, since every character has to be a suspect *except* the detective, this means that the one character who can be a character in his own right is the detective. And this is certainly true in the case of Father Brown, who *is* Chesterton in his views. As Knox observed, the sheer physical expansiveness of Chesterton was matched by the way in which he 'overflowed' every literary form he attempted, putting more of himself into it than it could contain. Even his great study of Dickens was 'really the Chestertonian philosophy as illustrated by the life of Dickens'. Similarly, the fact that Father Brown speaks with the voice of Chesterton makes him a much larger personality than he would otherwise be. The Father Brown stories, then, are 'something more' than detective stories: 'Like everything else Chesterton wrote, they are a Chestertonian manifesto.'[26]

Because Father Brown is a Roman Catholic priest, unsurprisingly much of the Chestertonian manifesto in the stories concerns Catholicism. A typical Chestertonian paradox is that Father Brown, in spite of being a Catholic priest, never employs any specifically spiritual powers. The overwhelmingly Protestant or secular readership for which Chesterton was writing would have naturally assumed that a detective priest would resort to all the tricks of 'priestcraft'. But Chesterton's Father Brown categorically repudiates special spiritual powers: 'Frankly, I don't care for spiritual powers much myself. I've got much more sympathy for spiritual weaknesses.'[27] This disclaimer contrasts with characters who do (falsely) claim miraculous powers, as in 'The Red Moon of Meru'. Nor is there ever any suggestion that Father Brown possesses any particular supernatural insights.

The reason for this insistence is not just because Chesterton wants all the emphasis to fall upon Father Brown's experience of human nature. At least as important is the idea that Catholicism and Catholic theology are entirely consonant with common sense and reason, while false religions dabble in the mysterious and occult. At the end of 'The Blue Cross', Father

[26] Sullivan, 133, 138.   [27] FB ii. 337.

Brown completes his triumph over Flambeau by telling him that he knew the disguised Flambeau was not a real priest. How could he have known? the astonished Flambeau asks. 'You attacked reason. It's bad theology.' Flambeau had speculated that there might be other worlds where reason was not rational, to which Father Brown had responded: 'Alone on earth, the Church makes reason really supreme. Alone on earth, the Church affirms that God Himself is bound by reason.'[28] In 'The Queer Feet', the author refers to the Catholic Church as 'wedded to common sense'.[29] Elsewhere Father Brown is adamant that the first effect of not believing in God is that one loses one's common sense, which leads to superstitious gullibility. Mystery (in the non-Christian sense) is regularly denounced. In 'The Arrow of Heaven', Father Brown declares: 'Real mystics don't hide mysteries, they reveal them. They set up a thing in broad daylight, and when you've seen it it's still a mystery. But the mystagogues hide a thing in darkness and secrecy, and when you find it, it's a platitude.'[30] In 'The Miracle of Moon Crescent', he goes further, saying that Satanism loves 'mysteries and initiations and secret societies and all the rest of it'.[31] In 'The Doom of the Darnaways', the priest speaks of 'nonsense' as 'the most terrible thing' known to human beings. Whether it is 'scientific superstition' or other 'magical superstition', he believes in 'daylight' not 'subterranean superstition' that ends 'in the dark'.[32] As he puts it in 'The Red Moon of Meru': 'Reason is from God, and when things are unreasonable there is something the matter.'[33]

The voice of Father Brown is often audibly the voice of Chesterton. The 'one mark of all genuine religions', Father Brown asserts, perhaps to the surprise of most readers, is 'materialism', which is why 'devil-worship is a perfectly genuine religion'. Mystery can mean two quite separate things: 'mystery in the sense of what is marvellous, and mystery in the sense of what is complicated'; and miracles, being 'startling' but 'simple', are mysterious in the first sense. Similarly, Chesterton argues through the mouth of Father Brown: 'It really is more natural to believe a preternatural story, that deals with things we don't understand, than a natural story that contradicts things we do understand.' When Father Brown asserts, 'Aristocrats live not in traditions but in fashions,' whereas it is the poor who 'preserve traditions', it is the voice of Chesterton that we hear. The Protestant doctrine of the Bible as the sole authority for Christians is answered by Father Brown with Chestertonian wit: 'When will people

[28] FB i. 45, 49.   [29] FB i. 77.   [30] FB ii. 64.   [31] FB ii. 114–15.
[32] FB ii. 179, 185.   [33] FB ii. 348.

understand that it is useless for a man to read his Bible unless he also reads everybody else's Bible? A printer reads a Bible for misprints. A Mormon reads his Bible and finds polygamy; a Christian Scientist reads his and finds we have no arms and legs.' As always in Chesterton, laughter is praised, but not 'a permanent smile', as 'cheerfulness without humour is a very trying thing'. If somebody stops believing in God he loses his 'common sense and can't see things as they are'. Just as Chesterton believed materialism was integral to real religion, so he thought that even 'hard-shelled materialists' are 'all balanced on the very edge of belief—of belief in almost anything': 'There are thousands balanced on it to-day; but it's a sharp, uncomfortable edge to sit on.' Paradox naturally comes easily to Chesterton's Father Brown's lips: 'A thing can sometimes be too close to be seen, as, for instance, a man cannot see himself.' It is the worldly man who 'will really do anything, when he is in danger of losing the whole world and saving nothing': 'It is not the revolutionary man but the respectable man who would commit any crime—to save his respectability.' Father Brown has no time for intellectuals, if only because 'you don't need any intellect to be an intellectual'. Like his creator, Father Brown has no time for the fashionable contemporary idea that all religions are the same: 'I tell you some of them are so different that the best man of one creed will be callous, where the worst of another will be sensitive.' And, again, he dislikes 'spiritual power, because the accent is on the word power'. The 'real difference between human charity and Christian charity' is that there is 'a limit to human charity'. According to Father Brown, 'the hardest thing in theology to believe' is that 'all men matter'.[34]

Chesterton's extraordinary ingenuity in the plots he constructs—he is surely the most ingenious of detective storywriters—may not exceed the bounds of possibility, but it certainly detracts from the realism of the stories.[35] The detective genre was invented by Edgar Allan Poe, for whom crime was strictly an intellectual problem. But, while his detective, Auguste Dupin, purports to investigate solely by logical deduction, in fact what Poe achieves is 'not a triumph of reason, but a conjuring trick'. And it could be said that 'many of the Father Brown stories can be regarded as ingenious variations on the theme of "The Purloined Letter"', the best known of the Dupin stories. What makes the difference between the two writers is that between 'Poe and Chesterton comes Conan Doyle'. For Sherlock Holmes is a character in a way that Dupin is not, just as Watson

[34] FB i. 127, 148, 172, 217, 226; ii. 93, 116, 137, 276, 349, 371, 374, 395, 409.
[35] Sullivan, 58; Robson, 'Introduction', p. xvi.

has a personality that Dupin's confidant totally lacks.[36] Indeed, Chesterton thought that without Dr Watson the Sherlock Homes stories were 'stale and dull': 'It is quite thrilling to realise how entirely the point of the stories [depends] on the Watsonian notes of exclamation. . . . The atmosphere of these stories [is] the glamour of Watson's inexhaustible power of wonder.'[37]

There is a further debt that Chesterton owes to Conan Doyle and that is the way in which the Sherlock Holmes stories invest the most prosaic of London scenes with romance. But then behind Conan Doyle is Dickens, 'the great master of the unfamiliarity in the familiar'.[38] Chesterton himself in his *Charles Dickens* gave a vivid example, as we have already seen, of 'that eerie realism with which Dickens could always vitalize some dark or dull corner of London', so that 'things seem more actual than things really are', when he describes the coffee shop where Dickens read the sign on the outside of the door, 'COFFEE ROOM', from inside as 'MOOR EEFOC'.[39] And Chesterton makes use of exactly the same kind of visual shock, although he chooses a public house rather than a coffee shop:

> Then his dubious eye roamed again to the white lettering on the glass front of the public-house. The young woman's eyes followed his, and rested there also, but in pure puzzledom.
>
> 'No,' said Father Brown, answering her thoughts. 'It doesn't say "Sela", like the thing in the Psalms; I read it like that myself when I was wool-gathering just now; it says "Ales".'[40]

There is a further similarity with, or influence of, Dickens, the author of the unfinished detective novel, *The Mystery of Edwin Drood*: 'The quality of Chesterton's work at its best, in the Father Brown stories, is comparable to that of *Edwin Drood* . . . full of suspense, sensation, genuine clues, red herrings, "atmosphere", real mystery and spurious mystery.'[41]

Like Dickens, moreover, especially in *Hard Times*, Chesterton does not hesitate to introduce social criticism into his stories. The fact that his protagonist, Father Brown, is himself on the fringe of society as a Roman Catholic priest rather than a clergyman of the Established Church helps to encourage the reader to look critically at the English class system. As a religious nonconformist, Father Brown sees things that an outsider would not notice or pay any attention to. In 'The Blast of the Book', for instance, Professor Openshaw 'was rather surprised to find Father Brown talking to the waiter . . . apparently about the waiter's most private affairs',

---

[36] Sullivan, 59.   [37] *ILN* xxxiv. 238–9.   [38] Sullivan, 61.
[39] See above, pp. 167–8.   [40] FB i. 321.   [41] Sullivan, 59.

for, although 'he himself dined there about five times a week', he 'was conscious that he had never thought of talking to the man'. Here, too, the priestly dimension is also relevant in Father Brown's pastoral concern, which gives him an intimate access to people that the ordinary detective would not have. At the end of the story, Father Brown explains the disappearance of Openshaw's clerk: '*because* you had never looked at him in your life ... You never found out even what a stranger strolling into your office could find out, in five minutes' chat ... '.[42]

Chesterton's social criticism extends beyond the class system. Capitalism is satirized in 'The Queer Feet', where the existence of the ridiculous select club of 'The twelve True Fishermen' is accounted for by the fact that in 'a plutocracy tradesmen become cunning enough to be more fastidious than their customers. They positively create difficulties so that their wealthy and weary clients may spend money and diplomacy in overcoming them.' In this case the owner of the hotel, where the club meets, 'made nearly a million out of it, by making it difficult to get into'. The waiter, who comes to tell the members of the club that their silver fish service has disappeared, cannot bring himself to do so:

A genuine historic aristocrat would have thrown things at the waiter, beginning with empty bottles, and very probably ending with money. A genuine democrat would have asked him, with a comrade-like clearness of speech, what the devil he was doing. But these modern plutocrats could not bear a poor man near to them, either as a slave or as a friend.[43]

But a Socialist society is no more welcome, where, for example, chimney sweeps may get properly paid, but, as Father Brown puts it, where you are not allowed 'to own your own soot'.[44]

As a graphic artist himself, Chesterton puts his visual imagination to good effect, [45] for a mystery story requires that the writer evoke the right scene and atmosphere if the necessary element of suspense is to be created.[46] He is particularly good at describing light and sky. In 'The Dagger with Wings', for example, the picture he paints produces the appropriate *frisson*:

[42] FB ii. 429, 432.   [43] FB i. 70, 80.   [44] FB i. 93.
[45] Cf. Sullivan, 69. But Knox complains that Chesterton 'occupies a good deal of his space with scene-painting', which 'takes up ... valuable room' (Conlon, ii. 136).
[46] Cf. Coates, *Chesterton and the Edwardian Cultural Crisis*, 13: 'Almost all [the stories] have striking settings which illustrate Chesterton's taste in the visual.'

The rolling country round the little town was sealed and bound with frost, and the sky was as clear and cold as steel, except in the north-east, where clouds and lurid haloes were beginning to climb up the sky. It was against these darker and more sinister colours that the house on the hill gleamed with a row of pale pillars ... [47]

Chesterton is especially interested in the colours of dawn and dusk,[48] as another instance from 'The Green Man' shows, where the briefest of pictures produces the required shudder at the beginning of the story:

The last of the sunset lay in long bars of copper and gold above the last dark strip of sea that seemed rather black than blue. But blacker still against this gleam in the west, there passed in sharp outline, like figures in a shadow pantomime, two men with three-cornered cocked hats and swords ... [49]

In the Father Brown stories, then, Chesterton makes his own very distinctive and original contribution to the genre of the detective story. They are not among his major writings, and they can hardly be called his 'masterpiece' compared with his great non-fictional prose works, let alone 'a major classic of English literature'.[50] Nevertheless, as highly readable short stories—and in general they are much more readable than the novels—they will no doubt continue to be the most popular of his writings.

3

Chesterton came to think that his travels at the beginning of the century, when he was engaged in political canvassing, over the southern country-side, 'that enormous area of noble hills and valleys which had seen so many vaster struggles in the past, reaching back to that aboriginal struggle of the Pagans and the Christians which is the genesis of all our history', had implanted in his imagination the seeds of his longest and most ambitious poem:

such primitive things were probably already working their way to the surface of my own mind; things that I afterwards attempted to throw into very inadequate but at least more elemental and universal literary form. For I remember the faint

---

[47] FB ii. 147.

[48] Cf. Kingsley Amis on Chesterton's 'fascination with the effects of light', according to whom Chesterton achieved 'some of the finest, and least regarded, descriptive writing' of the twentieth century. Sullivan, 33, 38. See also Sullivan, 69; Robson, 'Introduction', p. xvii.

[49] FB ii. 434.   [50] Robson, 'Introduction', pp. ix, xix.

and hazy inspiration that troubled me one evening on the road, as I looked beyond the little hamlet, patched so incongruously with a few election posters, and saw hung upon the hills, as if it were hung upon the heavens, remote as a pale cloud and archaic as a gigantic hieroglyph; the White Horse.[51]

In one of the essays in *Alarms and Discursions*, Chesterton mentioned how he had hired a car to go and 'visit in very rapid succession the battle-places and hiding-places of Alfred the Great'.[52]

Back in March of 1904, when Chesterton and Father O'Connor had walked over the moor from Keighley to Ilkley, Frances told the priest after lunch that Chesterton had already written a good deal of an 'Epic of Alfred', which was to become *The Ballad of the White Horse*. O'Connor could see that she 'cherished it very carefully' and that 'she was more in love with it than with anything else he had in hand'.[53] However, Frances was later to say that Chesterton 'wrote the whole thing in a fortnight; that she gathered the sheets as he threw them on the floor; and that when they went through them all there was scarcely a correction to be made'.[54] Frances must have been referring to a final draft of a poem that was already more or less written. Some stanzas had already been published in January 1911 in *A Chesterton Calendar*, which included unpublished as well as published writings; others from an early draft had been published in the *Albany* magazine in 1907. Father O'Connor remembered some stanzas being written just before dinner one evening in Yorkshire.[55]

Chesterton chose the Vale of the White Horse in Berkshire for the scene of King Alfred's victorious battle of Ethandane, both because of the importance of the symbol of a white horse for him and also because the huge white horse etched out on the side of the Berkshire valley is prehistoric, and therefore symbolizes, as it were, an eternal England; in fact, the battle took place at Edington, near Froude in Somerset, about thirty miles to the west.[56] The theme of the poem, published in August 1911, is the Christian king's heroic resistance to the pagan Danish invaders. It is not only Christian civilization but civilization itself that is threatened by the barbarian invaders. For 'The White Horse of the White Horse Vale' itself, 'cut of the grass', which 'knew England | When there was none to know', has been 'left to darken and fail' by the Danish invaders, 'because it is only Christian men | Guard even heathen things'. But Alfred warns his Christian followers that, 'If ye would have the horse of old, | Scour ye

[51] *A.* 128.   [52] *AD* 220.   [53] O'Connor, 31.   [54] Ward, *GKC* 244.
[55] Ward, *GKC* 244; O'Connor, 63; Ffinch, 197.   [56] Barker, 199–200.

the horse anew.'[57] Conservation for Chesterton meant the opposite of conservatism:

All conservatism goes upon the assumption that if you leave a thing alone, you leave a thing as it is. But you do not. If you leave a thing to itself, you are leaving it to wild and violent changes...if you want a white horse, you must not leave it white...you must continually be painting it white...if you want your old white horse, you must have a new white horse.[58]

Not dissimilarly, the battle for Christian civilization is never won. Even after repulsing the Danes, Alfred knows that the threat of pagan barbarism is always there: 'I have a vision, and I know | The heathen shall return.' But Alfred knew that victory would come through Christian humility. When, disguised as a beggar, he was offered a cake by a peasant woman if he would watch the fire, and then famously let the cake fall into the fire, the woman struck him across the face with the burnt cake. Instead of returning the blow, the king laughed the 'giant laughter of Christian men' that is the antidote to pride. His Christian humility ('For I am the first king known of Heaven | That has been struck by a slave') he knows will conquer pagan pride: 'This blow that I return not | Ten times will I return | On kings and earls of all degree...'.[59]

The *Ballad*, which many soldiers had with them in the trenches during the First World War, reached the height of its popular fame when *The Times* quoted from it at two pivotal points in the Second World War. First, the lines beginning 'I tell you naught for your comfort...' were quoted at the end of *The Times*'s briefest ever first leader on the disastrous fall of Crete in May 1941; and then in November 1942 after the first British victory of the war at El Alamein, when Winston Churchill announced 'the end of the beginning', *The Times* quoted the lines ' "The high tide!" King Alfred cried. | "The high tide and the turn!" '[60] In retrospect, critical opinion is not likely to differ from T. S. Eliot's assessment in his obituary of Chesterton, in which he noted that the obituaries in the press 'seem to me to have exaggerated Chesterton's achievements in some obvious respects, and to have ignored his achievements in some more important ones'. Thinking presumably particularly of *The Ballad of the White Horse* and 'Lepanto', Eliot

---

[57] *CP* (1933), 257, 310.

[58] *MO* 149. Cf. *ILN* xxxi. 129: 'An intelligent Conservative is not one who wishes to conserve things just as they are, for if he is intelligent he knows that, in the medium of time, they never remain just as they are.'

[59] *CP* (1933), 266–8, 311.   [60] Ward, *GKC* 245–6.

referred to Chesterton's poetry as 'first-rate journalistic balladry'. Eliot did not 'suppose that he took it more seriously than it deserved'. On the other hand, Eliot considered that Chesterton had 'reached a high imaginative level with *The Napoleon of Notting Hill* and higher with *The Man who was Thursday*, romances in which he turned the Stevensonian fantasy to more serious purposes'.[61] Chesterton would not have been too pleased with this slighting reference to Stevenson, and he may have thought more of his poetry than Eliot suggests, but he would certainly have been gratified by the obituary's high praise of his *Charles Dickens*.

The furore engendered by their book *The Party System* emboldened Belloc and Cecil Chesterton to found their own weekly magazine in June 1911, the *Eye-Witness*, with the backing of a rich friend. For the first year it was edited by Belloc. When he grew weary of editing the paper, he handed it over to Cecil Chesterton. After nearly six months its financial backer went bankrupt. Cecil secured financial backing from his father and re-named the paper the *New Witness*. He proposed that 'Keith' Jones, who supposed she was about to make his usual vain proposal of marriage, should be assistant editor, and she gladly accepted. His brother contributed first an occasional and eventually a weekly article. The paper had two aims: to fight for the individual's freedom and liberty and to fight against corruption in public life. The *Eye-Witness* consequently opposed Lloyd George's national insurance act of 1911 on the ground that it took away the liberty and personal responsibility of the poor. The welfare dependency that was to be the eventual unforeseen result of the welfare state shows that the paper had a point. G. K. Chesterton's role in the paper was at first restricted to an occasional book review and some ballades, some of which he wrote in conjunction with Belloc, Bentley, and Maurice Baring, who was a member of the Baring banking family. Baring had supported Belloc's forerunner to the *Eye-Witness*, the *North Street Gazette*—named after the street Baring lived in, where it was printed—which folded after only one issue in 1908. Baring, who was to write some highly successful novels depicting the high society of the time, was a linguist whose knowledge of Russia, where he had been the *Morning Post*'s correspondent, led to the publication in 1910 of *Landmarks in Russian Literature*; he is also credited with having introduced Chekhov to the West. He had been received into the Roman Catholic Church in 1909, having been impressed by a Mass he had been taken to in Paris when he was a diplomat attached to the embassy there. The well-known picture by Sir James Gunn, *Conversation Piece*, which

[61] Conlon, i. 531.

now hangs in the National Portrait Gallery in London, depicts Chesterton, Baring, and Belloc reputedly writing a ballade. On 21 September 1911 Chesterton's 'A Ballade of Suicide', one of the best of his nonsense poems, was published in the *Eye-Witness*.[62]

> The gallows in my garden, people say,
> Is new and neat and adequately tall.
> I tie the noose on in a knowing way
> As one that knots his necktie for a ball;
> But just as all the neighbours—on the wall—
> Are drawing a long breath to shout 'hurray!'
> The strangest whim has seized me ... After all
> I think I will not hang myself today.[63]

In the issue of 12 October Chesterton published 'Lepanto', a much shorter historical ballad than *The Ballad of the White Horse* but on the same theme, the preservation of Christian civilization. Just as Chesterton is more successful in the restricted form of the short story as opposed to the novel, so the considerably more concentrated 'Lepanto' is a more dramatic and exciting ballad than the lengthy White Horse epic, which tends to drag and frequently lapses into obscurity. With its insistent refrain (and variations on) 'Don John of Austria is going to the war', the ballad must have been much easier to recite in the trenches of the First World War than *The Ballad of the White Horse*. On 21 June 1915 Chesterton was to receive a gratifying note from John Buchan saying: 'The other day in the trenches we shouted your Lepanto.'[64] According to Father O'Connor, Chesterton got the idea of writing 'Lepanto' from the conversation in the train already referred to,[65] when they were on their way back to Ilkley from Leeds, where they had both been taking part in a debate at which Chesterton had spoken in favour of the motion that all wars are religious wars. O'Connor had told the story of how Philip II of Spain had been assembling his Armada to invade England, and could therefore spare only two ships for the Christian fleet under Don Juan of Austria that had been assembled to confront the menace of the Ottoman Empire. In the event, the outnumbered fleet of Don Juan won a decisive victory over the fleet of Ali Pasha in 1571. O'Connor had told of how the Pope spent the day in prayer, and of 'his vision of the crisis of the action at three in the afternoon, with his vision of the victory about the time of the Angelus'. The story could hardly help

---

[62] Ward, *GKC* 275, 317; MCC 85–6; Barker, 16, 210–11; Ffinch, 193–4.
[63] *CP* i. 439.   [64] Ward, *GKC* 317.   [65] See above, p. 266.

but appeal to Chesterton, and O'Connor claimed that the poem was published on 7 October, the anniversary of Lepanto, although it was actually five days later.[66]

On 29 May 1911 Shaw had addressed a Cambridge university debating society called the 'Heretics' at the Victoria Assembly Rooms in Cambridge on 'The Religion of the Future'. Invited to respond by the same society, Chesterton agreed to speak on 'The Future of Religion'. It had become a popular practice to invite the two famous speakers separately to address the same subject. Thus, for instance, in August Chesterton had been invited to speak on the subject of cremation in response to a lecture by Shaw praising the practice as opposed to the alleged superstition of burial. Chesterton's answer was that Christian burial was 'a humane and religious' recognition that 'the flesh is a sacred thing' that does not cease to be sacred when life has left it. But, if modern pagans wanted to cremate, let them at least cremate in style like the pagans of old:[67]

> If I had been a Heathen,
>   I'd have piled my pyre on high
> And in a great red whirlwind
>   Gone roaring to the sky.
> But Higgins is a heathen,
>   And a richer man than I;
> And they put him in an oven,
>   Just as if he were a pie.[68]

There was an audience of between 800 and 900 for Chesterton's November Cambridge lecture at the Guildhall, with few empty seats.[69] As usual, Chesterton was late in arriving, explaining that he had asked his cab-driver to go slowly so that he might enjoy the sights of Cambridge and also prepare what he was going to say.[70] He had been sent the pamphlet containing Shaw's lecture, and the hurriedly scribbled notes in it suggest that the lecture may well indeed have been prepared in the cab. Inside the pamphlet Chesterton wrote: 'It has taken about 1800 years to build up my religion. It will not take 18 minutes to destroy Mr Shaw's.'[71] According to the report in the *Cambridge Daily News*, Chesterton began by dismissing the complaint that Shaw had been blasphemous: one could only be blasphemous in a Christian country, which England was not. That was why it

---

[66] O'Connor, 84.   [67] Ffinch, 191–2.   [68] *CP* i. 524.
[69] *Cambridge Review*, 23 Nov. 1911.   [70] *Cambridge Daily News*, 18 Nov. 1911.
[71] Pearce, 168.

oppressed the poor, undermined marriage, and revived pagan practices such as slavery by banning strikes and infanticide by encouraging eugenics. Because Nietzsche was 'entirely off his head' he 'had that peculiar lucidity that belonged to the insane' and saw that God had died in the middle of the eighteenth century. 'That was perfectly true, only the Christian God was used to dying and rising from the dead.' Shaw had argued that 'we must have a God because we must believe in a purpose in the Universe'. But to say that we must help a God to exist who does not yet exist was like five orphaned children saying they must create a mother who did not exist—'there was a certain slip in the logic of the observation'. For there was 'no such thing as trying to exist', since one had to exist in order to try. As for the Christian religion, it was founded on the two principles of reason and liberty. Finally, if, he, Chesterton, had to choose between Shaw's religion and old-fashioned atheism, he would choose the latter. During question time, it was put to the speaker that one can know only things for which one has scientific proof. But did not the questioner know that he existed? asked Chesterton. No, he only had an intuition. 'Cherish it,' replied Chesterton to laughter. On the subject of hell, 'as he could not speak from personal experience, he regarded it as a thing to be avoided.' He admitted that the Roman Catholic Church was possibly nearer the truth than the Orthodox and Anglican Churches. He had always believed in the possibility of miracles, even before he was a Christian, as he had never been able to see 'why spirit should not alter matter'. Asked about the excommunication of the Modernist Jesuit Father George Tyrrell, Chesterton replied that he would expect to be asked to resign from the National Liberal Club if he denied Liberal principles.[72] The question and answer session lasted, very unusually, for more than an hour.[73]

Apart from his tendency to be late, even sometimes not to arrive at all, Chesterton's worst fault as a lecturer was to begin by telling his audience, which had paid to hear him, that he had not prepared his lecture. This was not literally true: what was true was that he had not prepared it as much as he might have, and that he would have put more effort into it had it been a newspaper article. Sometimes he would begin by saying that he had left his notes in the cab; this would raise a laugh, and enable him to get off the subject he was supposed to be lecturing on—not that possession of his notes ever deterred him from straying from his topic. What he was good at was the cut-and-thrust of debate and the opportunity for repartee in the question time that followed the lecture. Asked once what he would do if he

---

[72] *Cambridge Daily News*, 18 Nov. 1911.   [73] *Gownsman*, 25 Nov. 1911.

were prime minister, he responded, 'If I were Prime Minister I should resign.' On another occasion, a questioner enquired whether he had considered what the Reformation had done for Germany. The answer was terse: 'It did for Germany.' Some people could be irritated by his constant references to his weight, which, like his sense that he was not properly prepared for a lecture, indicated a certain self-consciousness. But it gave him the opportunity for some good jokes. When his late arrival was once politely greeted by the fear that he had been involved in a traffic accident, he replied: 'Had I met a tramcar, it would have been a great, and if I may say so, an equal encounter.' During the First World War he was once angrily asked, 'Mr Chesterton, why aren't you out at the front?' Quick as a flash he replied: 'Go round to the side, Madam, and you'll see that I am.' Once at a Distributist meeting he was told that he seemed to be enjoying himself: 'I always enjoy myself more than others, there's such a lot of me that's having a good time.' But he could startle as well as amuse. Debating once in Dublin, he took out the large Texan knife he always carried in his pocket with a view to sharpening his pencil—to the dismay of his opponent but to the delight of his audience, who roared their encour-agement—'Have at him!' He never lectured from a text, but would come armed with notes on scraps of paper (if he had not left them behind in the cab), which he was likely to dispense with altogether as he got into his stride.[74]

At the end of October 1911, Shaw had written to Chesterton about a proposed debate between them. A reassuring note was struck before the letter began: 'Dont [*sic*] be dismayed: this doesnt [*sic*] need a reply.' Shaw did not think there was any need to have any strict rules for the debate, involving as it did three friends, Chesterton, himself, and Belloc in the chair—who 'we both want . . . to let himself go' and who anyway would not bother about rules of procedure even if he knew what they were. Shaw ended with: 'My love to Mrs Chesterton, and my most distinguished consideration to Winkle. To hell with the Pope!'[75] Delighted with the friendly tone of Chesterton's Cambridge lecture, Shaw now invited him to lunch to make arrangements for the debate.[76]

[74] Ward, *GKC* 313–14; Ward, *RC* 114, 127, 129–30.

[75] *Bernard Shaw: Collected Letters 1911–1925*, ed. Dan H. Laurence (London: Max Reinhardt, 1985), 54–5.

[76] Michael Holroyd, *Bernard Shaw*, ii. *1898–1918, The Pursuit of Power* (London: Chatto and Windus, 1989), 218.

The debate took place at the Memorial Hall in London on 30 November. Shaw began by defining Socialism as the equal division of wealth. In reply, Chesterton said that he was a democrat, as Shaw certainly was not, and that he believed in the absolute right of personal property as opposed to state ownership. Shaw replied that he wanted property to be equally distributed in the form of money so that everyone could have some. Chesterton in turn responded that what he objected to in Shaw's Socialism was that it was remarkably like the Capitalism it sought to replace: the only difference was that the state would now dole out the wages instead of the employer. What was required in place of Capitalism was the largest possible distribution of property. Shaw objected that, as a Socialist, he believed in the equal distribution of property. But this was, of course, somewhat disingenuous, as Chesterton pointed out, since Socialism had always been understood to mean state ownership of the means of production.[77] Chesterton could not fail to be popular with an audience, whereas Shaw commanded admiration but not affection. The Cavalier Chesterton and the Puritan Shaw were certainly two sharply contrasting figures:

Chesterton's rolling good nature was obvious in his bulky swaying presence, the immense range of illustration he gave his simple ideas, his spirit of enjoyment and comic inventiveness. Shaw was less simple, more incisive, his emphatic eyebrows like two supplementary moustaches, an assured and wiry figure standing with arms folded who could speak with a force thrilling to all who heard it.[78]

That November was an important month in the domestic life of the Chestertons.[79] The event that had led to Frances entering into negotiations to buy the field behind Overroads, where first a studio would be built and then their new home, Top Meadow, was a summer mini-picnic that Chesterton had suggested: 'I want to read you something.' As Frances and Mildred Wain, who was staying with them, lay on rugs eating gooseberries, Chesterton read aloud to them one of the first Father Brown stories. Suddenly breaking off from reading, he looked across at the field opposite and said that he would like to build a house on it. Frances replied that there was no reason why he should not when he had the money. Chesterton then added that he would like to build the house round a particular tree.[80] Since the first of the Father Brown stories had been written only at the time of the move to Beaconsfield in the autumn of 1909, this conversation could have taken place in the summer of either 1910 or 1911. But, given that the first Father Brown

[77] CS 489–96.   [78] Holroyd, *The Pursuit of Power*, 219.
[79] Ffinch, 202.   [80] Ward, *RC* 110.

story was published in July 1910 and given that Chesterton clearly wanted to give his wife and guest a surprise, as well as presumably to test their reaction, the exchange must have occurred earlier in that summer of 1910.

In the event the threat of a laundry being built on the field opposite was decisive.[81] And in 1912 the Chestertons had a studio built on the field that they had bought, where Chesterton could lay on his beloved toy-theatre productions and puppet shows for children, and where parties could also be held for their older friends, at which Chesterton could enjoy dressing up and acting in the charades he so loved.[82] Although the Chestertons were saved from the laundry, they were liable to be disturbed by noise from some local film studios, in connection with which Chesterton enjoyed telling a joke about how he had sent 'several ineffectual letters of protest', but 'eventually asked his secretary to call upon the manager of the studios': 'Upon doing so, that lady made a strong protest saying emphatically, "The position is becoming impossible... Mr Chesterton can't write," to which the manager replied, "We were well aware of that." '[83]

Chesterton was also a keen participant in local amateur drama. A neighbour called Margaret Halford, who had retired from the London stage to get married, was the leading light of Beaconsfield theatricals. One year she played Puck in *A Midsummer Night's Dream*, with Chesterton as Theseus. Like Lawrence Solomon, who had been a member of the Junior Debating Club at St Paul's and was also now living in Beaconsfield, Mrs Halford was Jewish. Hearing that Chesterton was anti-Semitic, she had been wary of meeting him, although she had long been an admirer of his writings. They first met at the studio at an event to raise money for the local children's convalescent home. She had felt 'a certain constraint. But it was impossible to maintain this feeling. The benevolence and love in the air were unmistakable, and irresistible.' Together they helped to found a dramatic society called the Players Club, of which Chesterton became the president, with Margaret Halford producing as well as acting.[84]

4

In February 1912 Chesterton published another novel, *Manalive*. The hero, Innocent Smith, is a man who really is a man alive, which is why society regards him as either mad or bad. Chesterton had begun work on the book

[81] Sullivan, 156.   [82] Ward, *GKC* 454.   [83] Clemens, 28.
[84] Ward, *RC* 116–17, 121.

while he was still at University College, London,[85] and it is the most autobiographical of the novels he published. As a student at Cambridge, Smith had encountered the nihilism of Chesterton's diabolist. His reaction was to flourish

a loaded firearm in the very face of a distinguished don … driving him to climb out of the window and cling to a waterspout. He had done it solely because the poor don had professed in theory a preference for non-existence. For this very unacademic type of argument he had been sent down. Vomiting as he was with revulsion, from the pessimism that had quailed under his pistol, he made himself a kind of fanatic of the joy of life.

Not so silly as to embrace a naive optimism about life ('men flee from the embrace of a great optimist as from the embrace of a bear'), Smith nevertheless solemnly revels in existence, as Chesterton puts it: 'His eccentricities sprang from a static fact of faith, in itself mystical, and even childlike and Christian.' For his 'creed of wonder was Christian by this absolute test; that he felt it continually slipping from himself as much as from others'. He had to make extraordinary efforts 'to keep alive the mere conviction that he was alive': 'Sometimes he would, of a sudden, treat his wife with a kind of paralysed politeness, like a young stranger struck with love at first sight. Sometimes he would extend this poetic fear to the very furniture; would seem to apologize to the chair he sat on, and climb the staircase as cautiously as a cragsman, to renew in himself the sense of their skeleton of reality.' Laughter is the favourite Chestertonian weapon in the ceaseless battle: 'He lashed his soul with laughter to prevent it falling asleep.' Professing the paradox that 'going right round the world is the shortest way to where you are already', Smith is confronted with the sensible objection: 'Is it not even shorter to stop where you are?'

'No, no, no!' he cried emphatically. 'That way is very long and very weary. At the end of the world, at the back of the dawn, I shall find the wife I really married and the house that is really mine. And that house will have a greener lamp-post and a redder pillar-box. Do you,' he asked with a sudden intensity; 'do you never want to rush out of your house in order to find it?'

Like Chesterton himself, Innocent Smith is 'so young that climbing garden trees and playing silly practical jokes are still to him what they once were for all of us'. Happy in his innocence, Smith has 'the trick … of coveting

---

[85] Ffinch, 203.

his own goods' rather than his neighbour's, of enjoying 'a hundred honey-moons' just because 'he loves one wife'. Smith's secret is that 'he had distinguished between custom and creed. He has broken the conventions, but he has kept the commandments.'[86]

Chesterton's own voice is often heard in the novel. There is the inevitable idea of limitation expressed in the form of an arresting and revealing paradox:

The truth is that when people are in exceptionally high spirits, really wild with freedom and invention, they always must, and they always do, create institutions. When men are weary they fall into anarchy; but while they are gay and vigorous they invariably make rules. This, which is true of all the churches and republics of history, is also true of the most trivial parlour game or the most unsophisticated meadow romp. We are never free until some institution frees us, and liberty cannot exist till it is declared by authority.

The revolutionary is a reactionary because he is interested in the past and not the future, like modern intellectuals such as Nietzsche and Shaw: 'That is revolution—going right round. Every revolution . . . is a return.' As for evolutionary theories, 'All we know of the Missing Link is that he is missing—and he won't be missed either.'[87]

On 12 April 1912 Chesterton told a mass meeting at Church House that the trouble with England was that it had not had a civil war for so long. Looking out at his audience, though, he thought that one would be possible that night. The meeting had been organized by the Church Socialist League, with Conrad Noel presiding, during a miners' strike. A procession then headed for Lambeth Palace to present a letter to the Archbishop of Canterbury. Chesterton's well-known hymn 'O God of Earth and Altar' was sung on this occasion (it had already been published in 1905 in *The Christian Commonwealth*[88]): 'O God of earth and altar, | Bow down and hear our cry, | Our earthly rulers falter, | Our people drift and die . . .'.[89]

On 30 May 1912 Chesterton published his best-known satirical poem, 'Antichrist, or the Reunion of Christendom: An Ode', in the *Eye-Witness*. On 13 May F. E. Smith, the future Earl of Birkenhead, a Conservative backbencher on the Unionist wing of the party, had denounced in the House of Commons the bill for the disestablishment of the Anglican Church of Wales—a bill that the Liberal government had promised

---

[86] *M.* 377–80, 386, 414–15.   [87] *M.* 268, 387, 412.
[88] Ffinch, 205–6.   [89] *CP* i. 141.

Lloyd George and their Welsh Nonconformist supporters—as a bill 'which has shocked the conscience of every Christian community in Europe'. Smith must have regretted this incautious moment of pompous bombast when Chesterton used his ridiculous outburst as an epigraph to his crushing verses.

> Are they clinging to their crosses,
>   F. E. Smith,
> Where the Breton boat-fleet tosses,
>   Are they, Smith?
> Do they, fasting, trembling, bleeding,
>   Wait the news from this our city?
> Groaning 'That's the Second Reading!'
>   Hissing 'There is still Committee!'
> If the voice of Cecil falters,
>   If McKenna's point has pith,
> Do they tremble for their altars?
>   Do they, Smith?
>
> Russian peasants round their pope
>   Huddled, Smith,
> Hear about it all, I hope,
>   Don't they, Smith?
> In the mountain hamlets clothing
>   Peaks beyond Caucasian pales,
> Where Establishment means nothing
>   And they never heard of Wales,
> Do they read it all in Hansard
>   With a crib to read it with—
> 'Welsh tithes: Dr Clifford answered.'
>   Really, Smith?
>
> In the lands where Christians were,
>   F. E. Smith,
> In the little lands laid bare,
>   Smith, O Smith!
> Where the Turkish bands are busy,
>   And the Tory name is blessed
> Since they haled the Cross of Dizzy
>   On the banners from the West!
> Men don't think it half so bad if
>   Islam burns their kin and kith,
> Since a curate lives in Cardiff
>   Saved by Smith.

> It would greatly, I must own,
>   Soothe me, Smith!
> If you left this theme alone,
>   Holy Smith!
> For your legal cause or civil
>   You fight well and get your fee;
> For your God or dream or devil
>   You will answer, not to me.
> Talk about the pews and steeples
>   And the Cash that goes therewith!
> But the soul of Christian peoples...
>   Chuck it, Smith![90]

F. E. Smith would hardly have been human if he did not derive some satisfaction as a counsel for the prosecution in the trial the following year of the brother of the poet who had tormented him with some of the most deflating satirical verse in the English language.

In October Chesterton published another selection of his *Daily News* columns, *A Miscellany of Men*. In one of these he put forward a new argument for the importance of limitation in the form of a creed or dogma: 'an intellectual formula is the only thing that can create a communication that does not depend on mere blood, class, or capricious sympathy.' Without this 'liberty of dogma, you have the tyranny of taste'. Once an 'original intellectual formula' is rejected, 'not only does the individual become narrow, but he spreads narrowness across the world like a cloud; he causes narrowness to increase and multiply like a weed'. Thus Socialism means state ownership of the means of production, but, if people who call themselves Socialists refuse to be 'bound by what they call a narrow dogma' and Socialism is taken to mean 'far, far more than this', then without the limitation of this 'narrow economic formula' Socialism can mean anything. Again, Puritanism was once a creed that united Puritans, but, now that the unifying 'bond of doctrine' has been broken, Puritans have to be identified by 'certain social habits, certain common notions, both permissive and prohibitive, in connection with particular social pleasures'. When people pride themselves on 'having got beyond creeds', they end up with a paralysing 'incapacity to get beyond catchwords'. For the truth is that people must 'agree on a principle' so that 'they may differ on everything else'. Chesterton was prophetic about the rise of an intolerant 'political correctness' in a secular society inevitably 'bigoted'

[90] *CP* (1933), 152–4.

because of its lack of 'a root religion'. Limitation also implies separation, which is what distinguishes Eastern pantheism from Christian 'mysticism', which is not 'an ecstasy of unity' but one of 'creation, that is of separation'. The Eastern saint wants 'to be swallowed up', whereas a Christian saint like St George is very anxious not to be swallowed and absorbed into 'the darkness of a dragon's stomach'.[91]

Another religious theme is the significance of ritual, the 'essence' of which is a 'profound paradox': 'the concealment of the personality combined with the exaggeration of the person. The man performing a rite seeks to be at once invisible and conspicuous. It is part of that divine madness which all creatures wonder at in Man, that he alone parades this pomp of obliteration and anonymity.' The Protestant critics of Catholic ritual are right to call it 'Mummery', for that is what it is: 'it is the noble conception of making Man something other and more than himself when he stands at the limit of human beings.'[92]

Then there is that favourite Chestertonian subject of free will. Medieval Catholicism believed in free will, whereas seventeenth-century Calvinism and nineteenth-century science 'darkened this liberty with a sense of doom', with the result that modern society has 'lost the idea of repentance' and criminals are now seen as 'a separate and incurable kind of people'— quite unlike the criminals of the Father Brown stories, who share original sin with Father Brown, a sinner like them. Indeed, the Catholic Church 'can best be defined as an enormous private detective, correcting that official detective—the State', for the Church 'is the only thing that has ever attempted by system to pursue and discover crimes, not in order to avenge, but in order to forgive them', being 'the only institution that ever attempted to create a machinery of pardon'. Medieval Catholics believed that 'Man was free, not because there was no God, but because it needed a God to set him free. By authority he was free.... The mediaeval Christian insisted that God gave man a charter.' Chesterton contrasts his beloved medieval Gothic architecture with oriental art: 'Over all the exquisite ornament of Arabia and India there is the presence of something stiff and heartless, of something tortured and silent.... It is like the vision of a sneering sage, who sees the whole universe as a pattern.' Gothic architecture, by contrast, is characterized by its 'gaiety': 'They put into a Miserere seat the very scenes that we put into a music-hall song: comic domestic scenes similar to the spilling of the beer and the hanging out of the washing.' And, far from being stiff and silent, Gothic architecture 'is

---

[91] *MM* 114–20, 163, 165.   [92] *MM* 168–9.

alive, and . . . on the march. It is the Church Militant; it is the only fighting architecture.'[93]

Chestertonian political and social themes are also aired. No one should be deceived into thinking that elections equal democracy: 'We shall have real Democracy, when . . . the ordinary man will decide not only how he will vote, but what he is going to vote about.' Liberty in England was actually decreasing, Chesterton thought: 'Never before has it been so easy to slip small Bills through Parliament for the purpose of locking people up.' The satire of the absurd is powerfully enlisted in Chesterton's battle on behalf of the dispossessed and landless poor. Forced to be a tramp, the poor man has to sleep in the open: 'That retreat was perceived; and that retreat was cut off. A landless man in England can be punished for sleeping under a hedge in Surrey or on a seat on the Embankment. His sin is described (with a hideous sense of fun) as that of having no visible means of subsistence.' Just as Capitalist employers produce unemployment ('the very pivot upon which the whole process turns'), so the 'practical effect of having landlords is not having tenants'. The lack of tenants only worsened the rural situation, where the smallholding peasant was not a familiar figure as in France: 'there is no such thing as an English peasant,' Chesterton complained. Unlike France, too, England did not have 'the great gift of a revolution', which made Frenchmen 'free in the past as well as free in the future', for if you have 'cleared everything away' you can 'put back everything'. The English, on the other hand, 'who have preserved everything . . . cannot restore anything', for they 'have all the ages on top of them, and can only lie groaning under that imposing tower, without being able to take a brick out of it', so that it would be very difficult for them to decide to have a republic, whereas the French can always get rid of their republic if they want to. But Chesterton certainly did not have in mind a Marxist revolution based on its 'materialist theory of history', according to which 'all the important things in history are rooted in an economic motive'; in other words, history is the 'science of the search for food'. This would certainly be true of the cow, which is why 'the cow has no history'. But saying that human actions are based on economic considerations is like saying that human actions 'have depended on having two legs'. Chesterton, however, has no more time for British imperialism, which paradoxically borrows such ideas as it has from 'the brown and

---

[93] *MM* 163, 168, 208–9, 212, 231, 235–6, 251–2.

black people to whom it seeks to extend them', such as that of despotism and 'inevitable fate'.[94]

Other miscellaneous Chesterton topics appear in this selection of *Daily News* columns. An important distinction between animals and human beings, humbling to the latter, is that man 'is the only naked animal... He has to go outside himself for everything that he wants.' Lacking a 'hide or 'hair' to keep himself warm, he had to discover fire; similarly, having 'taken leave of his senses' as a result of the Fall, this 'need of his has lit in his dark brain the dreadful star called religion'. The limitation that consists in defining an idea in definite words is a good test of the idea: 'If the idea does not seek to be the word, the chances are that it is an evil idea. If the word is not made flesh it is a bad word.' For what is good always tends to the limitation of incarnation:

> But, on the other hand, those refined thinkers who worship the Devil... always insist upon the shapelessness, the wordlessness, the unutterable character of the abomination.... It was the Christians who gave the Devil a grotesque and energetic outline, with sharp horns and spiked tail. It was the saints who drew Satan as comic and even lively. The Satanists never drew him at all.

Anyone who has a clear rather than confused idea 'will always try to explain that idea'. Critics who are unable 'to translate beauty into words' and claim that 'it is untranslatable—that is, unutterable, indefinable, indescribable, impalpable, ineffable, and all the rest of it', give themselves away: 'They can explain nothing because they have found nothing; and they have found nothing because there is nothing to be found.' Unlike other contemporary intellectuals, Chesterton did not despise tourists *per se*; but he did think there were vulgar tourists, those, for instance, who 'admire Italian art while despising Italian religion': 'If you admire what Italians did without admiring Italians—you are a cheap tripper.' And he has an amusing and penetrating image for such tourism: 'One has no right to visit a Christian society like a diver visiting the deep-sea fishes—fed along a lengthy tube by another atmosphere, and seeing the sights without breathing the air.' It was a mystery to Chesterton, or so he claimed, why the rain that is such a prominent part of the English weather and that, as we have seen, he liked so much, should inspire in the modern English middle classes such a 'mysterious dislike', when they were 'quite fanatically fond of washing; and... often enthusiastic for teetotalism'. Besides, in a

---

[94] *MM* 30, 37–8, 60–2, 68, 80, 155, 157, 204–5, 219–20.

society where Socialism was so fashionable, rain could be commended as 'a thoroughly Socialistic institution', being 'a public and communal' shower and better than a private shower, especially 'because somebody else pulls the string'. Finally, there is the favourite Chesterton point that religious differences do not prove that no one religion can be right: 'Diversity does show that most of the views must be wrong. It does not by the faintest logic show that they must all be wrong.'[95]

In December, in an article in *Everyman* called 'A Salute to the Last Socialist', Chesterton returned to the fray with Shaw, poking fun at Shaw's argument that a peasant state must evolve into a capitalist state. Chesterton claimed he had 'two true affections—one for truth, and the other for Mr Shaw. I follow truth with reluctance.' He imagined Shaw going every year to a village in France 'to see how the evolution of Capitalism is getting on'.

I picture him every year peering eagerly along the dreary French road for the first factory chimney; and then, with a sudden sinking of the heart, seeing only the dreary French poplar. I conceive him crouching with his hand to his ear, or, perhaps, even his ear to the ground, to hear the far-off sound of the factory 'hooter' which makes men so happy in Belfast; and then bursting into tears as he hears only the confounded old cattle-call that tells him that free men are still alive.[96]

5

It is necessary now to go back to 1911 when a chain of events began that would lead up to the so-called Marconi scandal, a scandal that was profoundly to affect Chesterton.[97] It had been decided that year to build state-owned wireless stations throughout the British Empire. The project had been entrusted to the Post Office under Herbert Samuel, the Postmaster General in the Liberal government. The Marconi Wireless Telegraph Company, under its managing director Godfrey Isaacs, had its tender for the first six stations accepted on 7 March 1912. A contract to this effect was to be put before the House of Commons for its approval on 19 July, which contained a clause to the effect that royalties would cease to

---

[95] *MM* 15–16, 145–7, 151, 179–80, 190–1, 264.   [96] CS 498–9.

[97] The following account of the Marconi scandal is based on Ward, *GKC* 283–304, and Frances Donaldson, *The Marconi Scandal* (London: Rupert Hart-Davis, 1962).

be paid to Marconi if its patents ceased to be used. Nothing had been said publicly by the Postmaster General, but on 8 March, the day after its tender was accepted, the Marconi company informed its shareholders, but failed to tell them about the conditional clause—without the knowledge of the Postmaster General, he later claimed. In the same month shares in English Marconi soared in price, reaching a peak in April, after which they rapidly fell in value. Rumours began to spread. In the House of Commons it was alleged that Marconi had been especially favoured at the expense of the national interest. It was noted that the Postmaster General seemed anxious to prevent any discussion of the contract. And, inevitably, it was also noted that the Postmaster General was a Jew, as was Godfrey Isaacs, the managing director of Marconi, who was the brother of Sir Rufus Isaacs, the Attorney General. In the City it was rumoured that ministers had used their inside knowledge to gamble in Marconi shares.

In the meantime, Godfrey Isaacs had left for America, where he bought the assets of the principal rival (by now in liquidation) of the American Marconi Company on behalf of the English company that owned more than half of American Marconi's shares, which he then sold at considerable profit to the American company, of which he was a director. American Marconi, whose shares were at a discount, agreed to make an issue of 1,200,000 $5 shares, on condition that Godfrey Isaacs made himself personally responsible for selling 500,000 and English Marconi the rest. Returning to England, Godfrey Isaacs met his brothers Harry and Rufus, the latter being the Attorney General, for lunch on 9 April, when he told them about the forthcoming issue of shares, of which he offered them 100,000. Rufus Isaacs rejected the offer, he was to say later, although he was assured that American Marconi held no shares in the English company, because he did not think it ethical for him as a government minister to buy shares in a company with which the government was in negotiation. Harry Isaacs, on the other hand, bought 50,000, $5 then being worth just over a pound. On 17 April, however, Rufus Isaacs bought 10,000 of Harry Isaacs's shares for £2 each, nearly twice the price of the same shares he had refused to buy a week earlier. His argument would be that, while it was wrong to buy from the managing director of the company, it was all right to buy from Harry Isaacs, but that it was only fair to pay him a higher price than he had paid for them. Of these 10,000 shares Rufus Isaacs proceeded to sell 1,000 to the Chancellor of the Exchequer, David Lloyd George, and another 1,000 to the Liberal Chief Whip. On 18 April the American Marconi Company announced the new issue of shares, and the next day the shares were put on the market at the price of £3 5s. The same day the shares rose in value to £4. In the course of the day Rufus Isaacs sold 7,000 shares at an average price of £3 10s. This meant he had made a profit of £3,000, with 1,000 shares still unsold, which he sold at £2 13s. Rufus Isaacs later explained that some of the shares belonged to Lloyd George and the Chief Whip, who sold another 1,000 of their shares on 20 April for slightly over £3. On 22 May they bought a further 3,000 shares at just over £2. And in April and May the Chief Whip bought another 3,000 shares for the Liberal Party.

Apart from their public dealings on the stock market, the only evidence for the private transactions of the Isaacs brothers and the two Liberal politicians was their own word. Nevertheless it was clearly a flagrant instance of insider trader dealing. But it was worse than that. Ministers in the government had been offered shares at a special price in a company that had close links with the company with which the government had drawn up a contract that was awaiting parliamentary approval. It could look like a clear case of bribery. Moreover, the governing Liberal Party as a whole now had a financial interest in Parliament's approval of the contract, since a rejection of the contract with the English company would certainly lower the value of the American company's shares. What made it look even more sinister was the nature of the portfolios held by the three ministers involved, one in charge of the country's finances, another the government's legal adviser, and the third responsible for ensuring that Liberal members of parliament voted for the government.

Criticism of the proposed contract as being too favourable to the Marconi Company began to grow, as well as rumours that government ministers had been buying shares in it (in fact, of course, in the *American* Marconi Company). Questions were asked in the House of Commons. The Postmaster General and the government Chief Whip tried—in vain—to get the contract approved before the session ended. On 6 August, two days before the House was adjourned for the summer vacation, the Prime Minister promised a full discussion of the proposed contract with Marconi. He did not mention that he was not unaware that ministers had been buying Marconi shares. In fact, he had been briefed by Herbert Samuel, who had been informed by Rufus Isaacs, when rumours began to spread in June. Asquith thought that his ministers 'could not have done a more foolish thing'. He was to tell King George V in April of the next year that their conduct had been 'lamentable' and was 'difficult to defend', and that they had offered their resignations, which he had refused, as acceptance would have meant the fall of the government.[98]

[98] Donaldson, *The Marconi Scandal*, 55, 102.

On 20 July and in later successive weekly articles the contract was
attacked in the *Outlook*. Significantly, the Isaacs brothers and Herbert
Samuel were described as being of 'the same nationality', in line with the
commonly accepted notion then that Jews were foreigners. On 8 August
the *Eye-Witness* published a news story headed 'The Marconi Scandal',
which did not mention ministers buying shares but attacked the way a
monopoly was being given to Godfrey Isaacs by Herbert Samuel, with the
help of Rufus Isaacs, that involved rejecting other cheaper and more
efficient tenders. Rufus Isaacs advised Samuel not to sue, since the
paper, which had only a small circulation, was notorious for its personal
abuse of politicians. In fact, the *Eye-Witness* had a number of distinguished
contributors and an influential if small readership. Failure to sue only
increased the rumours. In September the *National Review* joined in the
criticism, while the *Morning Post* and the *Spectator* pressed for an inquiry.
The October issue of the *National Review* returned to the subject, drawing
particular attention to the stock-exchange gamble in American Marconi
shares. Later, the *New Witness* would boast of having publicized the
Marconi scandal, but in truth it had been anticipated by the *Outlook*, and
other sections of the press had been by no means silent.

On 11 October the House of Commons held the promised debate.
Three of the chief speakers against the government were Liberals. Both
Liberal and Conservative speakers dismissed any idea of corruption. Rufus
Isaacs truthfully denied the rumours that he and his colleagues had bought
shares in 'that company' with which the government proposed to enter
into a contract. He could hardly have specified the *English* Marconi
Company, as that would have raised the question of the *American* company.
Herbert Samuel, who knew of the dealings in the American company but
did not mention them either, also truthfully denied the rumours, and gave
details of the various government departments that had been involved in
the decision to give the tender to Marconi. In fact, there was a German
company that could have competed with Marconi, but the government
had ruled out any foreign company. Samuel, too, avoided referring to the
Marconi Company as the *English* company. Lloyd George also angrily
denied the rumours. The Liberal Chief Whip did not speak; he was now in
the House of Lords.

On 29 October the members of the House's committee of inquiry were
announced. The Liberal members, supported by Irish Nationalists and
Labour members, outnumbered the Conservative members. For five
months no ministers were called to give evidence, but much emerged in
the meantime about the contract with Marconi. It transpired that another

company had submitted a lower tender, the same cost as the Admiralty estimate. It was admitted that the government had made concessions to the Marconi Company, but no minutes of these conversations were available; similarly, relevant letters were found to have gone missing from the Post Office files. It turned out that Marconi had not had to undergo the same rigorous scrutiny as other companies tendering. The terms of the contract were no less unsatisfactory. Marconi had originally been offered a 3 per cent share of the gross profits, but successfully held out for 10 per cent. This was to be paid as long as any Marconi patent was being used in the wireless stations, although the Patents Act gave the government the right to take over patents after paying reasonable compensation. The Marconi Company was also, incredibly, given the right to advise the Post Office on any new inventions offered to the Post Office by their rivals! Had the Post Office consulted its own technical staff? It seemed that a technical subcommittee had advised investigating the main rival tender, but its report was shelved and the subcommittee had not met again. Early in January 1913 the committee of inquiry, against the wishes of the Postmaster General, called for a subcommittee of technical experts to advise on the various existing wireless systems and to report within three months. The *New Witness* commented that this was precisely what the Postmaster General ought to have done in the first place before entering into a contract with Marconi. The subcommittee acknowledged that, if one single wireless system was to be used, then Marconi was the best one for the government's purposes. But at the same time its view was that the technology was in such a constant process of development that it would be better for the government not to be tied to any particular system.

After investigating the contract, the committee of inquiry turned to the question of the rumours about ministers. On 12 February the editor of the *National Review* was called to give evidence. Having expressed surprise that the ministers had still not been called, he commented on the strange fact that they had not demanded to be called at the earliest possible opportunity in order to deny that they had bought shares in *any* Marconi company. Two days later *Le Matin*, a Paris daily newspaper, falsely reported that the editor of the *National Review* had alleged that Herbert Samuel and the Isaacs brothers had bought shares in the English Marconi Company for about £2 and then sold them for £8. Rufus Isaacs happened to be in Paris when the story appeared, and he and Samuel sued for libel. In response to this decision to sue a foreign newspaper for a silly libel rather than a British paper, Chesterton wrote some of his best satirical verses in the *New Witness*, entitled 'Song of Cosmopolitan Courage':

I am so swift to seize affronts,
  My spirit is so high,
Whoever has insulted me
  Some foreigner must die.

I brought a libel action,
  For *The Times* had called me 'thief',
Against a paper in Bordeaux,
  A paper called *Le Juif*.

The *Nation* called me 'cannibal'
  I could not let it pass—
I got a retractation
  From a journal in Alsace.

And when *The Morning Post* raked up
  Some murders I'd devised,
A Polish organ of finance
  At once apologised.

I know the charges varied much;
  At times, I am afraid
The *Frankfurt Frank* withdrew a charge
  The *Outlook* had not made.

And what the true injustice
  Of the *Standard*'s words had been,
Was not correctly altered
  In the *Young Turk's Magazine*.

I know it sounds confusing—
  But as Mr Lammle said,
The anger of a gentleman
  Is boiling in my head.[99]

Samuel and Isaacs, who had retained Sir Edward Carson and F. E. Smith, both Conservative backbenchers curiously enough, as counsel for the prosecution, decided to make a statement through their lawyers at the court hearing on 19 March, even though the Paris newspaper had retracted the story and apologised three days after printing it. Since the defendants were not contesting the case, there was no chance they could be cross-examined in court. Carson merely mentioned the purchase of American Marconi shares at the end of a long speech, claiming that it was strictly irrelevant to the libel case, but that the Attorney General did not wish to seem to be concealing anything. In fact, Carson's statement was

---

[99] *P.* i. 411–12.

not as full as he maintained. The court was not told from whom Rufus Isaacs had bought the 10,000 shares nor at what price nor that the shares had not yet been on the market. The sale of shares to Lloyd George and the Chief Whip was disclosed, but not their subsequent dealings. Isaacs claimed irrelevantly that, while he had gained on the shares he had sold, he had lost on the shares he had retained. But he had lost only because he had paid his brother Harry nearly twice the price he had been offered a week before by his brother Godfrey, even though Harry had offered to sell the shares for the same price he had paid for them.

A week after the court hearing Rufus Isaacs finally appeared before the parliamentary committee of inquiry. He claimed that the reason he had not mentioned the American Marconi shares was because his sole concern was to rebut the libellous rumours that did not refer to American Marconi shares. The chairman of the committee made the obvious point that, had Isaacs specified that his dealings had been in American not English Marconi shares, the confusion that had caused the rumours would have been cleared up. As to why he had not appeared before the committee earlier to clarify matters, Isaacs replied that he had not sought preferential treatment. The Conservative Lord Robert Cecil succeeded in extracting from Isaacs the admission that he had indeed bought the shares before they were put on the market and at a lower price. Isaacs also divulged the later dealings of Lloyd George and the Chief Whip that had not been revealed at the court hearing. He furthermore admitted that he had briefed two of his friends on the committee to forearm them when the journalists in question gave evidence. At earlier committee hearings these journalists had been treated very differently from Isaacs, to whom the Liberal members of the committee deferred and whom the Conservatives questioned politely if tenaciously. On 28 March Lloyd George in his turn appeared before the committee. Both ministers claimed that, so far as they were concerned, Marconi *was* wireless telegraph and that it had never occurred to them that there was any other possible company. The *New Witness* contrasted the performance of Rufus Isaacs—like 'a panther at bay, anxious to escape, but ready with tooth and claw'—with that of Lloyd George—'like a spitting, angry cat, which had got, perhaps, out of serious danger from her pursuers, but which caterwauled and spat and swore with vigour and venomousness quite surprising in that diminutive bulk'.[100] Asked why he had not originally told the House of Commons that he had bought American Marconi shares, Lloyd George replied that there

[100] Ward, *GKC* 297.

was no time on that Friday afternoon and that two ministers had already spoken.

The question was raised as to whether the American Marconi shares Godfrey Isaacs had bought really belonged to him or to his company. If he was acting as an agent for his company, then he had no right to sell some of the shares at cost price or to retain the profit he had made on the stock exchange by selling the others. His claim that he had in fact passed on £46,000 of profits to the English Marconi Company was not recorded in the Company's books. Lord Robert Cecil naturally wanted to recall him to explain why there was no record of it. But the committee voted on party lines not to recall him. On 7 May the committee concluded its hearings, but was recalled early in June to hear that a London stockbroker who had bought 3,000 American Marconi shares for the former Chief Whip for Liberal Party funds had absconded.

On 9 January the *New Witness* had listed twenty companies connected with Godfrey Isaacs that had gone bankrupt. Sandwich men had paraded outside the House of Commons and the office of the Marconi Company, bearing placards proclaiming 'Godfrey Isaacs' Ghastly Record' and selling copies of the paper.[101] Although this was not done on his instructions, Cecil Chesterton later declined to disclaim responsibility. Isaacs's solicitors wrote to warn him that Isaacs would prosecute unless he undertook not to make further libellous attacks on their client until both had given evidence to the parliamentary committee of inquiry. Cecil replied that he was happy that Isaacs intended to bring an action against him. While waiting for the trial to begin, Cecil slipped out of the office one day to be received into the Roman Catholic Church by Father Sebastian Bowden of the Brompton Oratory, the son of Newman's close undergraduate friend, J. W. Bowden, who had earlier received Maurice Baring. According to 'Keith' Jones, 'His decision had been taken swiftly and without any period of doubt. He sought a working philosophy of life, and, his reason satisfied, he accepted the Catholic fundamentals quite simply.' He had been influenced by Belloc's Californian wife, Elodie, who had had long talks with him about Catholicism.[102]

Chesterton and Belloc were there to support him on 28 February when he attended Bow Street magistrates' court to be committed for trial. Cecil made a speech that impressed Godfrey Isaacs's counsel, in which he boasted that some of the best-known writers of the day wrote for the *New Witness*, mentioning among others Wells, Shaw, and Belloc by name.

---

[101] MCC 94.   [102] MCC 97.

The *New Witness* printed the speech in full in its issue of 6 March, in which Chesterton enthusiastically reviewed his old friend E. C. Bentley's famous detective novel *Trent's Last Case*. Bentley had dedicated it to him, saying, 'I owe you a book in return for *The Man who was Thursday*.'[103]

On 27 May the trial opened at the Old Bailey, with Isaacs represented by Sir Edward Carson and F. E. Smith, the same counsel that his brother and Herbert Samuel had engaged. The judge, Mr Justice Phillimore, strangely enough, was the uncle of Belloc's old Oxford friend J. S. Phillimore, who, in 'Keith' Jones's words, was one of 'the most distinguished' contributors to the *New Witness*, to which he would send 'very brilliant, but almost indecipherable articles on classical subjects'. That week, by an extraordinary coincidence, the 'principal article' was by him, but it had 'arrived very late and was written practically in Latin, spiced with Greek'. After the printers' reader 'gave up the ghost at the sight of the proof', and with Belloc on the continent and not one of their scholarly contributors to be found, there 'was but one hope left—the prisoner'. So 'Keith' rushed to the Old Bailey and managed to persuade 'the gaoler to slip Cecil the proofs in the luncheon interval'. 'Next morning the sandwich squad announcing that the *New Witness* had an article by J. S. Phillimore circled the Old Bailey outside, while a man of the same name was trying the Editor inside.'[104] Cecil was charged with criminal libel; if found guilty he could be sent to prison. He took full responsibility as the editor for all attacks on Isaacs in the *New Witness* and refused to divulge the names of other contributors. In his opening speech Carson divided the six alleged libels into those that accused his client of corruptly persuading his corrupt brother Rufus Isaacs to persuade the corrupt Herbert Samuel into agreeing to a corrupt contract, and those that accused his client of criminal business activities for which he would have been prosecuted but for the protection of his brother, the Attorney General. Cecil's defence counsel argued that, in the case of the Marconi shares, the alleged libels were directed not against Godfrey Isaacs but against Rufus Isaacs and Herbert Samuel. But, if the Marconi contract was corrupt, then how could Godfrey Isaacs not be implicated? However, under cross-examination Cecil refused to charge Rufus Isaacs and Herbert Samuel with corruption, since they had denied it on oath, but alleged that Godfrey Isaacs had attempted to corrupt them. The case brought out into the open not only the fact that Godfrey Isaacs had concealed the clause in the contract that allowed the

---

[103] Ffinch, 212–13; Dale, 173.   [104] MCC 98, 100–1.

government to terminate it whenever it wished, but also that Isaacs had asked the Secretary to the Post Office to keep it quiet.

The judge in his summing up on 9 June allowed for the possibility that the American Marconi shares really belonged to the English company rather than Godfrey Isaacs and that he, Isaacs, had certainly been involved in a lot of company failures. But the summing up was heavily against Cecil, and the jury was out for only five minutes before pronouncing a verdict of guilty. The judge then gave Cecil a lecture but only fined him £100 with costs—although, he said, 'it is extremely difficult to refrain from sending you to prison'.[105] Writing more than a decade later, F. E. Smith explained that Cecil had not been sent to prison because he was 'completely honest' if misguided and the libel was not malicious.[106] The verdict was greeted with cheers: in the jubilant words of 'Keith' Jones, 'Against the Marconi Goliath of wealth and power David had more than held his own; he had...forced Ministers of the Crown to face public opinion.' Although Cecil had withdrawn his charges against the ministers and had failed to prove dishonesty on Godfrey Isaacs's part, his family regarded it as a moral victory—apparently because he had not been sent to prison, which, however, was a very rare sentence indeed, and because he had forced the ministers to face the bar of public opinion. Chesterton had defiantly told the judge, when giving evidence as to Cecil's character: 'I envy my brother his position.' (He subsequently admitted at a public lecture, to the vast amusement of the large audience, that, when he was asked by the judge whether his brother's character was 'respectable', he was tempted to reply: ' "Lord bless me, he was in the Fabian Society." By a violent effort I refrained from alluding to the fact. We have all gone through many paths and stages in arriving at our present political opinions.'[107])

Their mother and father had come to the Old Bailey every morning, but Mrs Chesterton could not bear to see her son in the dock, so Chesterton and his uncle Arthur took it in turns to bring them reports of the proceedings. Also present every day was Chesterton's friend the writer J. M. Barrie ('of all friends the least egotistical', whose 'humorous self-effacement' seemed 'to create round him a silence like his own'[108]), a 'small brown figure in shabby tweeds...shy and alert as a squirrel on the look-out for nuts'. Present every day, too, was Godfrey Isaacs's mother, 'a large and heavily-built woman' who 'watched

[105] Donaldson, *The Marconi Scandal*, 185.

[106] Frederick Edwin Smith Birkenhead, *Famous Trials of History* (London: Hutchinson, 1926), 286, 288.

[107] Ffinch, 217–18.   [108] *A.* 264–5.

every movement, each expression of the prisoner, as though she feared he might by some nefarious miracle be spirited from the dock and beyond human punishment'. Astonished and outraged by the cheers of the crowd, according to 'Keith' (the crowd may have been more or less restricted to Cecil's family, friends, and supporters), Mrs Isaacs found herself afterwards in the same hotel to which the Chesterton family had repaired for refreshments. While the two Chesterton brothers argued as usual over tea, Mrs Isaacs 'fixed' the Chesterton party 'with a warrior eye and drank her tea as if it were transferable poison'.[109] The *New Witness* was triumphant, its circulation boosted by the publicity the trial had received. Shortly afterwards, it announced a national 'Clean Government League', as well as publishing details of the kind of money that had to be given to a political party's funds in order to receive a peerage.[110]

On 13 June the committee of inquiry adopted a report prepared by one of the Liberal members Rufus Isaacs had briefed, which merely said that the ministers had acted in good faith. The original report prepared by the ineffectual Liberal chairman, that had mildly criticized the ministers for indiscretion in buying the shares and for lack of frankness to the House of Commons, had been completely watered down. It was a disgraceful whitewash, in which the Labour and Irish Nationalist members who supported the Liberal government were implicated. Some years later, Chesterton excused the Nationalists for agreeing 'to whitewash the tricks of Jew jobbers whom they must have despised', since their 'motive was wholly disinterested and even idealistic', acting as they did 'solely for the sake of Home Rule', albeit misguidedly in Chesterton's view.[111] The vote was 8 to 6. *The Times* called it a 'pailful of whitewash' that instead of whitening the ministers had blackened the committee. Lord Robert Cecil's minority report criticized Rufus Isaacs for acting with 'grave impropriety in making an advantageous purchase of shares ... upon advice and information not yet fully available to the public', and for failing to be open with the House of Commons to which he had been lacking in 'respect'.[112] It also said that it was 'highly inadvisable' for ministers to buy shares in American Marconi whose interests were indirectly bound up in the success of English Marconi obtaining the contract.[113] Not only was the minority Conservative report published, but also, significantly, the Chairman had his own report published. The Conservatives tabled a motion on the lines of the minority report, which was predictably defeated, but three Liberal

---

[109] MCC 99, 106, 111–12.   [110] Barker, 217–18.   [111] *II* 153.
[112] Ward, *GKC* 303; Donaldson, *The Marconi Scandal*, 203.
[113] Donaldson, *The Marconi Scandal*, 204.

members voted against the government, while Carson and Smith, who had disgusted many of their colleagues by acting as counsel for Herbert Samuel and the Isaacs brothers, were constrained from speaking in the debate and felt obliged to abstain. Even Asquith admitted that the ministers had shown lack of prudence by leaving their actions open to misinterpretation.

There was certainly no collusion between the two main parties in this affair, as Cecil Chesterton and Belloc had claimed in *The Party System* was typical of the parliamentary system. True, Arthur Balfour, the Conservative leader—who was in fact under criticism from his backbenchers for not opposing the Asquith government more effectively—utterly repudiated any suggestion that the ministers involved had been guilty of corruption, but he did severely criticize them for their lack of frankness; he also rebuked the Attorney General for apparently not carefully inquiring into a transaction that was in fact quite improper, and the Chancellor of the Exchequer for speculating on the stock market, which he called 'the very gravest indiscretion' in view of his position, as well as criticizing them both for their failure to apologize. And he demanded that the House should formally express its 'regret' that the ministers had bought the shares and then concealed from the House the fact that they had done so—although the opposition was happy for the statement to include the recognition that the ministers had not acted corruptly.[114] Not only was Balfour much more critical than Chesterton remembered more than twenty years later, but it had after all been a Conservative member who had first raised the matter in the House and it was a group of young Conservatives who had paid Cecil Chesterton's legal costs, while the Conservative minority on the committee of inquiry had done their best to establish the truth in the face of considerable obstruction on the part of the Liberal members. The Conservative *Times* in its leader of 19 June was scathing:

A man is not blamed for being splashed with mud. He is commiserated. But if he has stepped into a puddle which he might easily have avoided, we say that it is his own fault. If he protests that he did not know it was a puddle, we say that he ought to know better, but if he says that it was after all quite a clean puddle, then we judge him deficient in the sense of cleanliness. And the British public like their public men to have a very nice sense of cleanliness.[115]

L. S. Amery, the leading Conservative member of the committee along with Lord Robert Cecil, was later scathing about the committee's failure

[114] On the second day's debate, 19 June 1913. Hansard, pp. 559–71.
[115] Ward, *GKC* 308–9.

even to report on the Marconi contract, for which it had been convened in the first place: 'the resources of the whitewash pail were exhausted, and ... there would not be enough left to furbish up poor Mr Samuel.'[116] Even the Cadbury Liberal press was uneasy, an unease that was amusingly satirized in the *New Witness* by one of its contributors:

> 'Tis the voice of the Cocoa
> I hear it exclaim
> O Geordie, dear Geordie
> Don't do it again.[117]

The Liberal *Nation* observed acidly: 'Political corruption is the Achilles heel of Liberalism.'[118] The ministers had been guilty of more than gambling on the stock market, but, even if that was all they had been doing, it was particularly hypocritical of Lloyd George, who, as Chesterton was to point out in his *Autobiography*, had 'made himself the mouthpiece of the Nonconformist Conscience', and of whom 'we did make fun ... when he appeared in a transaction uncommonly like a gamble'.[119]

As for Sir Rufus Isaacs, he became Lord Chief Justice only a few months later in October 1913. It was then the custom for the attorney general to succeed the outgoing lord chief justice, and Asquith, faced with the choice of appearing to accept that Isaacs's reputation had been tarnished by the Marconi scandal or of outraging public opinion, chose the latter course. The unfortunate appointment had one good result: it inspired the scandalized Rudyard Kipling, who had followed the Marconi scandal with close interest, to write his witheringly sarcastic poem 'Gehazi', which contained this particularly damaging stanza:

> Well done, well done, Gehazi,
>   Stretch forth thy ready hand,
> Thou barely 'scaped from Judgment,
>   Take oath to judge the land.
> Unswayed by gift of money
>   Or privy bribe more base,
> Or knowledge which is profit
>   In any market place.[120]

---

[116] Donaldson, *The Marconi Scandal*, 238.   [117] Ward, *GKC* 306.
[118] MCC 93.   [119] *A.* 192.
[120] *Rudyard Kipling's Verse: Inclusive Edition 1885–1918* (London: Hodder and Stoughton, 1919), ii. 2.

Looking back, Chesterton saw the scandal as a turning point in English history: the division between the pre-Marconi and the post-Marconi days was almost as significant, he thought, as that between the pre-war and post-war periods. The Victorian public 'belief that English politics were not only free from political corruption, but almost entirely free from personal motives about money' had been destroyed for ever. What for Chesterton made the politicians' behaviour particularly disgraceful was that they had brazenly claimed to be telling the truth, even though they had conveniently and deliberately suppressed all reference to the *American* Marconi Company. This deception by 'a verbal equivocation of the double sense of "this Company"' was much worse than if they had lied out of some misguided loyalty 'and under certain conventions of parliamentary self-defence', behaviour that could possibly be excused as a 'perverted form of honour'. However, Chesterton unfortunately persisted in believing what Belloc and his brother had continued to insist during the parliamentary inquiry—namely, that the scandal proved what they had claimed about party collusion in *The Party System*. No doubt loyalty to his beloved dead brother's memory made him grossly understate the strength of the condemnation in Lord Robert Cecil's minority report, which, he most unfairly sneered, 'reported that some things were not quite so nice'. However, when he complained that Balfour had 'said that they must judge men like Lloyd George (whom they knew so well and loved so much) more leniently than they would judge a common outsider', he was rather closer to the truth. For Balfour had gone out of his way to exonerate the ministers of any possible corruption on the ground that they were honourable fellow members of Parliament whom he would not dream of suspecting of any such thing. Chesterton recognized that Cecil had 'undoubtedly used all the violent vocabulary of Cobbett' in his attacks in the *New Witness*, but, he claimed, his brother 'had not in fact the faintest grain of malice, or even irritation', but always spoke of his opponents 'with perfect good humour and charity'. He allowed for the Isaacs brothers' 'Jewish virtues of family loyalty and the rest', and even found 'excuses for the other politicians; though it is extremely typical of the real attitude of our group, which was accused of fanatical Anti-semitism, that he was always more ready to excuse the Jews than the Gentiles'. As for the myth that the Marconi scandal was used as an excuse for an attack on the Jews, Belloc had neatly refuted that when, in giving evidence in court, he had observed that 'anybody less like a Jew than... Lloyd George it would be difficult to imagine'. (When he appeared before the parliamentary committee of inquiry, Belloc maintained that he had never written against poor Jews but only the rich Jews who were so prominent in the international finance world, a world that might become largely Gentile with the growing power of America, in which case he would attack it just the same.) The story had an ironically happy ending: many years after his brother had died, fortified by the last rites of the Catholic Church, 'his old enemy, Godfrey Isaacs, died very shortly after having been converted to the same Universal Catholic Church. No one would have rejoiced more than my brother...It is the only reconciliation; and it can reconcile anybody. *Requiescant in pace.*'[121]

---

[121] *A.* 191, 195–8.

9

The Victorian Compromise and Illness

WRITING to Father O'Connor on 15 May 1913 about Cecil Chesterton's forthcoming trial and asking for his prayers, Frances added: 'Sir William Lever has taken out a writ for libel against Gilbert. But our solicitors don't think he has a case. But it is worrying and the law is tricky.'[1] In answering questions after a lecture, Chesterton had referred to Port Sunlight, home to the Lever Brothers' soap-manufacturing business, as 'a slave-compound'. With the matter still unresolved a year later, Shaw wrote on 11 June 1914, offering financial help to fight the case: 'How about money? Can I do anything? Dont [sic] spare my banker. You wont [sic] hurt me, as I have just now an unnecessarily large current balance.'[2] On the 20th he wrote again, to say that, if an employee lost his benefits and savings if he left Lever Brothers' employment, then, 'though Lever may treat him as well as Pickwick would no doubt have treated old Weller, if he had consented to take charge of *his* savings, Lever is master of his employee's fate and captain of his employee's soul, which is slavery'.[3] Chesterton wrote to apologize to the editor of the *Christian Commonwealth*, which had reported the lecture and was also threatened with legal proceedings. He was

[1] Frances Chesterton to John O'Connor, 15 May 1913, BL Add. MS 73196, fo. 92.

[2] George Bernard Shaw to G. K. Chesterton, 11 June 1914, BL Add. MS 73198, fo. 43.

[3] Ward, *GKC* 319, with text corrected from BL Add. MS 731978, fo. 44.

confident that, if a case were brought, he could offer a successful defence. After all, he had gone out of his way to say that the slaves of such a slave compound 'may be better off under slavery...physically', as had been the case in ancient Athens and the American South. On the advice of his solicitor, he wrote to H. G. Wells to ask if Wells would be prepared to testify that 'the Servile State and servile terms in connection with it' were known to him 'as parts of a current and quite unmalicious controversy'. With the approval of his solicitor ('rather to my surprise'), he wanted to fight the case 'purely as a point of the liberty of letters and public speech; and to show that the phrase "slavery"...is current in the educated controversy about the tendency of Capitalism today'.[4]

He told Belloc that he had decided to fight the case 'on the broadest and simplest lines of the freedom of political utterance...and with scarcely any details at all'. He would 'prove the semi-servile conditions, but scarcely any that are not admitted in their own pamphlets and regulations'. He would not 'spy on poor old Port Sunlight'. His solicitor approved his course of action because it would 'prove the absence of personal malice'. He proposed to conduct his own case 'and make it something of a political trial...an advertisement for the new sociology that you started'. His solicitor thought he would even be allowed to 'call witnesses to the *existence* of the Servile State controversy; and the recognised and impersonal use of the servile terminology'. And he had suggested Belloc, who had 'dealt with it as impartial economic theory'. Belloc could testify to 'the existence' of his book *The Servile State* and to the fact that the book and its 'theory' were being 'discussed apart from any individual abuse—or abuses'. Even before this action against him, he had been 'thinking a great deal' about Belloc's view that his brother Cecil had been 'unwise to fix on the technical finance of Godfrey Isaacs rather than the public position of ministers', and he had come to the conclusion that Belloc was right. This 'line of attack would have been plainer and more popular; and therefore more damaging'. What Belloc had said now confirmed him in the decision he had 'almost' already made.[5] He subsequently wrote to tell Belloc that his solicitor had telephoned to say that the other side's solicitors would not proceed against him if he was ready to sign a statement that merely stated what he had 'empowered' his solicitor 'to say a year before, and what was already in my prepared defence. That is, that my remarks were political criticism of the tendency to slavery...and did not imply that Lever was personally cruel.'

[4] Ward, *GKC* 319–21, with text corrected from BL Add. MS 73198, fo. 43.
[5] G. K. Chesterton to Hilaire Belloc, n.d., JJBL.

Chesterton insisted that his solicitor should consult his brother Cecil, who had also been served with a writ by Lever. They both agreed that the statements they had been asked to sign constituted 'an apologia, the opposite of an apology', and that therefore there was no logical reason why they should refuse to sign.[6] To Wells he attributed the climbdown to the fact that the other side knew he had people like Wells on his side.[7]

2

On 1 February 1913, when his last column appeared, Chesterton's career as a Saturday columnist on the *Daily News* had come to an end. A week before, his poem 'A Song of Strange Drinks' had appeared in the *New Witness* in the issue of 23 January. It began:

> Feast on wine and fast on water
> And your honour shall stand sure...

But if an angel from heaven offers you any other drinks, the poem advises:

> Thank him for his kind intentions,
> Go and pour them down the sink.

The second stanza is fairly disparaging about tea, but the third stanza makes it clear that tea is greatly preferable to another hot beverage:

> Tea, although an Oriental,
> Is a gentleman at least;
> Cocoa is a cad and coward,
> Cocoa is a vulgar beast,
> Cocoa is a dull, disloyal,
> Lying, crawling cad and clown,
> And may very well be grateful
> To the fool that takes him down.

The poem ends by deploring another non-alcoholic drink that has appeared on the contemporary scene:

> Heaven sent us Soda Water
> As a torment for our crimes.[8]

[6] G. K. Chesterton to Hilaire Belloc, n.d., JJBL.
[7] G. K. Chesterton to H. G. Wells, n.d., BL Add. MS 73199, fo. 23.
[8] *FI* 588; *CP* i. 475.

In one of his columns in the *Daily News* in 1909, republished in *Alarms and Discussions*, Chesterton had associated soda water with imperialism: 'You can get a whisky and soda at every outpost of the Empire: that is why so many Empire-builders go mad.'[9] But all his readers knew what cocoa was associated with and why Chesterton held it up for special opprobrium. These readers included A. G. Gardiner, the editor of the *Daily News*, the owner of which was George Cadbury, the chocolate and cocoa manufacturer. The Marconi scandal had completed Chesterton's total disillusion with the Liberal Party, of which Cadbury was a leading supporter. Cadbury and his 'Cocoa Press' were under constant attack in the *New Witness*, and Chesterton was probably relieved when, as Chesterton recalled in his *Autobiography*, Gardiner wrote him 'a very sympathetic but rather sad letter, hoping that no personal attack was meant on some of the pillars of the Party'. Chesterton was able truthfully to assure him that his 'unaffected physical recoil from cocoa was not an attack' on Cadbury, any more than his praise of wine, which 'was a traditional thing', was 'intended for an advertisement' for a well-known wine merchant.[10] For, in his book on Blake, Chesterton had already made clear his dislike of cocoa on other grounds than political: 'Modern hygienic materialism is very like cocoa; it would be impossible to express one's contempt for it in stronger terms than that.' There he had also said, 'Most modern ethical and idealistic movements might well be represented by soda-water—which is a fuss about nothing.'[11] But, of course, he knew quite well the political significance of attacking cocoa, quite apart from his own dislike of the beverage. Recalling his exchange with Gardiner in his *Autobiography*, Chesterton was confused about dates, as it was the appearance of the verses in the *New Witness* in January 1913 and not their republication in the *Flying Inn* a year later, that brought about his resignation as the *Daily News*'s immensely popular Saturday columnist. Gardiner had written to say that he had 'too much respect for your sense of decency to suppose you would stoop to so gross an outrage on those with whom you have been associated in journalism for years', and asked Chesterton to correct the unfortunate and doubtless unintended 'impression' the verse had given. Chesterton had replied that he had nothing but warm feelings personally for Cadbury, in spite of their fundamental political differences.[12] Nevertheless, he wrote, 'it is quite impossible for me to continue taking the money of a man who may think I have insulted him. *It is equally impossible for me to permit him or anyone*

[9] *AD* 60.   [10] *A*. 258–9.   [11] *WB* 99.

[12] Stephen Koss, *Fleet Street Radical* (London: Allen Lane, 1973), 116.

else to control what I choose to write in other places. Therefore I see no other course but to surrender my position on the paper quite finally.'[13] 'I hate all separations,' Gardiner replied. 'This I hate for many reasons, but I will not trouble you with them.' But Gardiner was sanguine that the separation would not be permanent: 'I think you will find the columns of the D.N. open to you in the future, as they have always been.'[14]

Meanwhile Chesterton wrote to the editor of the Socialist *Daily Herald* that the *Daily News* 'had come to stand for almost everything I disagree with; and I thought I had better resign before the next great measure of social reform made it illegal to go on strike'. Thankfully, he could no longer be sarcastically referred to as 'a flourishing property of Mr Cadbury', as Shaw had recently done in a debate with Belloc.[15] But his association with the *Daily Herald*, for which he now began to write, his first article appearing on 12 April, was to be short lived: 'I left the Liberal paper and wrote for a Labour paper, which turned ferociously Pacifist when the War came: and since then I have been the gloomy and hated outcast you behold, cut off from the joys of all the political parties,' he lamented to the readers of his *Autobiography*. But, he says, with the passing of Lloyd George's National Insurance Act of 1911, whereby insurance contributions became compulsory, he had already effectively left the Liberal Party as 'too illiberal to be endured', for he thought that the act was 'a step to the Servile State; as legally recognising two classes of citizens; fixed as masters and servants'. His 'verse of violent abuse of Cocoa' was 'a comic coincidence' that helped him on his way.[16]

Belloc's trenchant analysis of the Capitalist and Socialist systems, *The Servile State*, to which Chesterton was referring, was published in 1912 a year after Lloyd George's act, which the latter openly advocated as his answer to the German insurance system established by Bismarck—another reason for Chesterton to oppose the act.[17] According to Chesterton, Belloc's analysis of the so-called Servile State was 'as strictly scientific as a military map is military'. And, while no one could say the book was a popular success, 'the title of the book was immediately and vastly popular. There was a time when errand-boys and railway-porters said "Servile State"; they did not know what it meant; but they knew about as much as the

[13] Julia Stapleton, *Christianity, Patriotism, and Nationhood: The England of G. K. Chesterton* (Lanham, MD: Lexington Books, 2009), 112, quotes the sentence in italics omitted by Koss in his account.

[14] Barker, 219.   [15] Ward, *GKC* 255–6.   [16] *A.* 258–9.

[17] See below, p. 367.

book-reviewers and even the dons.' The thesis of the book was that Socialism does not lead to a Socialist society:

This is partly because of compromise and cowardice; but partly also because men have a dim indestructible respect for property, even in its disgusting disguise of modern monopoly. Therefore, instead of the intentional result, Socialism, we shall have the unintentional resultant: Slavery. The compromise will take the form of saying, 'We must feed the poor; we won't rob the rich; so we will tell the rich to feed the poor, handing them over to be the permanent servants of a master-class, to be maintained whether they are working or no, and in return for that complete maintenance giving a complete obedience.' All this, or the beginnings of it, can be seen in a hundred modern changes, from such things as Insurance Acts, which divide citizens by law into two classes of masters and servants, to all sorts of proposals for preventing strikes and lock-outs by compulsory arbitration. Any law that sends a man back to work, when he wants to leave it, is in plain fact a Fugitive Slave Law.[18]

3

February 1913 saw the publication of Chesterton's *The Victorian Age in Literature* in the Home University Library series. The editors of the series prefaced the book with a cautionary advice: 'this book is not put forward as an authoritative history of Victorian literature. It is a free and personal statement of views and impressions about the significance of Victorian literature ... '[19]

The first and best chapter of the book is entitled 'The Victorian Compromise and its Enemies'. For Chesterton, 'the most important event in English history was the event that never happened at all—the English Revolution on the lines of the French Revolution'. The democratic 'spirit of Cobbett' had 'burned like a beacon', but the revolution 'failed because it was foiled by another revolution; an aristocratic revolution, a victory of the rich over the poor'. This revolution of enclosures and game laws, whereby England 'became finally a land of landlords instead of common land-owners', resulted in 'the spirit of revolt' taking 'a wholly literary form'. It was a paradox that the 'practical' English became 'rebels in arts', whereas the French were 'rebels in arms'. Following on from the visionary Blake, the English Romantic poets were unequalled in giving to 'the imagination ... the sense of having broken out into the very borderlands of being'.

[18] *A.* 283–4.   [19] *VAL* 423.

Subsequently, the Victorian Carlyle's *French Revolution*, verbally speaking, 'was more revolutionary than the real French revolution'. Thus it was English literature that retained 'the romantic liberalism of Rousseau' that had inspired revolutions on the Continent. Instead of revolution, then, the newly enriched early Victorian middle class, unlike its French counterpart, decided to support 'a sort of aristocratical compromise' rather than 'a clean sweep and a clear democratic programme'. Its representative was Macaulay, who supported the great Reform Bill but condemned the Chartists: 'Cobbett was dead.' Macaulay was also quintessentially Victorian in his 'praise of Puritan politics and abandonment of Puritan theology', his 'belief in a cautious but perpetual patching up of the Constitution', his 'admiration for industrial wealth'. But above all else, 'he typifies the two things that really make the Victorian Age itself, the cheapness and narrowness of its conscious formulae; the richness and humanity of its unconscious tradition'. For there were two Macaulays, 'a rational Macaulay who was generally wrong, and a romantic Macaulay who was almost invariably right': 'His reason was entirely one-sided and fanatical. It was his imagination that was well-balanced and broad.' As a typical Victorian, he believed in the inevitability of progress: he thought politics, like technology, 'as an experimental science, must go on improving'; but unfortunately he forgot that 'unless the soul improves with time there is no guarantee that the accumulations of experience will be adequately used'. Chesterton regarded the defeat of the 'larger' by the 'smaller' Macaulay as the Victorian tragedy: 'Later men had less and less of that hot love of history he had inherited from Scott. They had more and more of that cold science of self-interests which he had learnt from Bentham.' But even the arch-Utilitarian Mill, who 'had to preach a hard rationalism in religion, a hard competition in economics, a hard egoism in ethics', still had 'a sort of embarrassment' as 'he exhibited all the wheels of his iron universe rather reluctantly, like a gentleman in trade showing ladies over his factory'.[20]

The intellectual history of the Victorian age consisted for Chesterton of the 'series of reactions against [this dominant rationalism], which came wave after wave'.

They have succeeded in shaking it, but not in dislodging it from the modern mind. The first of these was the Oxford Movement; a bow that broke when it had let loose the flashing arrow that was Newman. The second reaction was one man; without teachers or pupils—Dickens. The third reaction was a group that tried to

[20] *VAL* 427–9, 430, 434–6.

create a sort of new romantic Protestantism, to pit against both Reason and Rome—Carlyle, Ruskin, Kingsley, Maurice—perhaps Tennyson. Browning also was at once romantic and Puritan; but he belonged to no group, and worked against materialism in a manner entirely his own.[21]

The study of Victorian literature, then, for Chesterton meant the study of 'the romance of these various attacks' on the dominant rationalism of the period. Newman was the 'one great literary' figure of the Oxford Movement, which Chesterton thought 'was not so much a taste for Catholic dogma, but simply a hunger for dogma. For dogma means the serious satisfaction of the mind. Dogma does not mean the absence of thought, but the end of thought.' The Movement, therefore, was 'a revolt against the Victorian spirit in one particular aspect of it; which may roughly be called (in cosy and domestic Victorian metaphor) having your cake and eating it. It saw that the solid and serious Victorians were fundamentally frivolous—because they were fundamentally inconsistent.' The struggle of the Tractarians was, of course, the struggle of Chesterton himself in his own time to insist on the necessity of the intellectual limitation that is dogma. To make a profession of creed is to gain something but also to give up something, and that means creating something because it involves 'making an outline and a shape'. Muhammad could be said to have created 'when he forbade wine but allowed five wives'; just as the French Revolution created 'when it affirmed property and abolished peerages'. The Tractarians' 'sub-conscious thirst' for 'the exalted excitement of consistency' was something they therefore shared with Muslims and Jacobins—but not with the members of their own Church. In this sense, the Oxford Movement was 'a rational movement; almost a rationalist movement'. And in that it was very different from 'the other reactions that shook the Utilitarian compromise; the blinding mysticism of Carlyle, the mere manly emotionalism of Dickens'. Against the 'damaged Puritanism' of the Victorian middle class, this idea of the consistency of dogma 'narrowed into a sort of sharp spear, of which the spear-blade was Newman'. Chesterton had no doubt that Newman had a 'complete right to be in any book on modern English literature'. Far from Newman going over to Rome in order to 'find peace and an end of argument', he actually then had 'far more quarrels'. However, he also had 'far fewer compromises: and he was of that temper which is tortured more by compromise than by quarrel'. Long before anything practically

[21] *VAL* 438.

had been written about Newman as a writer, Chesterton's brief literary sketch is still as acute a piece of criticism as anything that has been written:

He was a man at once of abnormal energy and abnormal sensibility: nobody without that combination could have written the *Apologia*. If he sometimes seems to skin his enemies alive, it was because he himself lacked a skin. In this sense his *Apologia* is a triumph far beyond the ephemeral charge on which it was founded; in this sense he does indeed (to use his own expression) vanquish not his accusers but his judges. Many men would shrink from recording all their mere cold fits and hesitations and prolonged inconsistencies: I am sure it was the breath of life to Newman to confess them, now that he was done with them for ever.

And Newman receives the highest Chestertonian praise for his satirical masterpiece, *Lectures on the Present Position of Catholics*, 'practically' delivered 'against a raging mob' protesting at the so-called papal aggression of the re-establishment of the English Catholic hierarchy: 'there is something grander than humour, there is fun ... '. But even these lectures are 'the triumphs of a highly sensitive man: a man must feel insults before he can so insultingly and splendidly avenge them. He is a naked man who carries a naked sword.' The argumentation of his great predecessor as a controversialist is defined with beautiful precision and succinctness: 'The quality of his logic is that of a long but passionate patience, which waits until he has fixed all corners of an iron trap.' And Chesterton concludes as he began: 'But the quality of his moral comment on the age remains what I have said: a protest of the rationality of religion as against the increasing irrationality of mere Victorian comfort and compromise.'[22]

In a 1904 article in the *Speaker*, Chesterton had criticized the 'one weakness of Newman's temper and attitude as a whole': his lack of 'democratic warmth', which had 'nothing to do with his religion; for in Manning, who was a far more rigid and central Catholic than he, democracy roared like a bonfire. It had something to do with his character and something to do with his training.' But, in complete contrast to this alleged lack of democratic feeling, Newman, Chesterton went on, more than anyone else possessed that 'finest instinct of geniality' that 'is to speak of common things with some dignity and care'. Indeed, and no higher praise was possible from Chesterton, Newman had achieved 'that awful and beautiful thing which is the dream of all democracy, the seeing of all things as wonderful, the thing for which Whitman strove and which he did not

[22] *VAL* 438–41.

perfectly attain'. As a controversialist, Newman had the 'knack' of having 'the air of not being in any way in a hurry'. And it was this 'air of leisure and large-mindedness, this scrupulosity about exceptions, that gave to the final assertion its sudden fire'. Certainly, Newman 'often seemed', in his 'mildness and restraint, a long time coming to the point, but the point was deadly sharp'. This was reflected in his style, particularly in one 'rhetorical effect' that he had 'perfectly': 'the art of passing smoothly and yet suddenly from philosophical to popular language.' It was this kind of 'abrupt colloquialism' that marked 'the wonderful termination of the introduction to the *Apologia*. After describing with 'careful and melancholy phrases... how delicate and painful a matter it must necessarily be to give an account to the world of all the secret transactions of the soul', Newman exclaims: 'But I do not like to be called a knave and liar to my face, and—'. Chesterton concluded that he thought that

it was very fortunate for Newman, considered merely as a temperament and a personality, that he was forced into the insatiably fighting thing, the Catholic Church, and that he was forced into it in a deeply Protestant country. His spirit might have been too much protected by the politeness of our English temper and our modern age, but it was flayed alive by the living spirit of 'No Popery'. The frigid philosopher was called a liar and turned into a man.

Here one has to interject that Chesterton seems only to have known about the 'many tears' that he says Newman shed 'in the sweet but too refined atmosphere of the Oxford High Churchmen': 'But, like all brave men when he first saw the face of battle, he began to laugh.' This would certainly have greatly surprised the Anglican Newman's Evangelical and liberal opponents, who had been the butt of so much marvellously sarcastic satire. But all that sarcasm does no doubt pale in the face of what Chesterton calls the 'wild and exuberant satire' of the first lecture of *Lectures on the Present Position of Catholics in England*, in which Newman compares 'the English view of the Catholic church to the probable Russian view of the British Constitution': 'It is one of the great pages of fierce English humour.'[23]

From Scotland, Chesterton continues in *The Victorian Age in Literature*, had come 'so many of those harsh economists who made the first Radical philosophies of the Victorian Age', but it was Scotland that was 'to fling forth...almost...to spit forth...their fiercest and most extraordinary enemy'. Around Carlyle, as around Newman, gathered another group of

---

[23] *HA* 130–3.

'reactionaries or romantics' hostile to the spirit of the age. Chesterton thought that Carlyle's strength came mainly from his Scottish background and his weaknesses partly from the later German influences he came under. He was a Scotsman in his classless 'consideration of men as merely men' and in his 'power of seeing things suddenly . . . a grand power of guessing'. The influence of Goethe, on the other hand, was less positive, for Goethe lacked the key Chestertonian virtue of humour: 'The one civilised element that the German classicists forgot to put into their beautiful balance was a sense of humour.' Indeed, there was 'something faintly fatuous' about Goethe's 'half sceptical, half sentimental self-importance'. Carlyle, on the other hand, did have humour, not least in 'his very style; but it never got into his philosophy', which 'largely remained a heavy Teutonic idealism, absurdly unaware of the complexity of things'. But behind 'all this transcendental haze', 'there hovered . . . a certain presence of old northern paganism; he really had some sympathy with the vast vague gods of that moody but not unmanly Nature-worship which seems to have filled the darkness of the North before the coming of the Roman Eagle or the Christian Cross'. Apart from 'certain sceptical omissions', it seemed to Chesterton that Carlyle combined all this 'with the grisly Old Testament God he had heard about in the black Sabbaths of his childhood; and so promulgated (against both Rationalists and Catholics) a sort of heathen Puritanism: Protestantism purged of its evidences of Christianity.' The Carlyle, on the other hand, that Chesterton thoroughly approved of was the Carlyle who assailed Utilitarianism in *Past and Present* and in his essay on Chartism; this was his 'great and real work': 'It is his real glory that he was the first to see clearly and say plainly the great truth of our time; that the wealth of the state is not the prosperity of the people.' The truth was that 'only some of the less pleasing people' were getting richer. And what Carlyle saw he saw 'with stronger . . . humour than he showed on any other question', never rising 'to more deadly irony than in such *macabre* descriptions as that of the poor woman proving her sisterhood with the rich by giving them all typhoid fever'. But where Carlyle's influence was bad, Chesterton thought, was through his philosophy of history: 'he seems to have held the theory that the good could not be definitely defeated in this world.' This had the corollary that what happens in history 'happens for a higher purpose'. But this was tantamount to saying that 'God is on the side of the big battalions—or at least, of the victorious ones'. This 'dangerously optimist' view of history was 'the first cry of Imperialism'.[24]

[24] *VAL* 441–6.

As Carlyle's successor as the scourge of Utilitarianism, Ruskin did not, like his master, 'set up the romance of the great Puritans as a rival to the romance of the Catholic Church', but rather 'he set up and worshipped all the arts and trophies of the Catholic Church as a rival to the Church itself'. The great paradox of Ruskin was that he wanted 'to tear down the gargoyles of Amiens or the marbles of Venice, as things of which Europe is not worthy; and take them away with him to a really careful museum, situated dangerously near Clapham'. But this was a common paradox among the Victorians, who had 'a sort of divided head; an ethical headache which was literally a "splitting headache"; for there was a schism in the sympathies'. When they 'looked at some historic object, like the Catholic Church or the French revolution, they did not know whether they loved or hated it most'. Thus Ruskin had 'a strong right hand that wrote of the great mediaeval minsters in tall harmonies and traceries as splendid as their own; and also, so to speak, a weak and feverish left hand that was always fidgeting and trying to take the pen away—and write an evangelical tract about the immorality of foreigners'. Ruskin had very 'mediaeval tastes' but a 'very unmediaeval temper': 'he seemed to want all parts of the Cathedral except the altar.' This 'dark and doubtful' acceptance of 'Catholic art but not Catholic ethics' was to produce 'flagrant fruit' in Swinburne, who was to use 'mediaeval imagery to blaspheme the mediaeval religion'. Chesterton pounces on another paradox in Ruskin: his style. On the one hand, a Ruskin sentence 'branches into brackets and relative clauses as a straight strong tree branches into boughs and bifurcations', reminding us that their author 'wrote some of the best of these sentences in the attempt to show that he did understand the growth of trees, and that nobody else did—except Turner, of course'. On the other hand, 'if a Ruskin sentence (occupying one or two pages of small print) does not remind us of the growth of a tree, the only other thing it does remind us of is the triumphant passage of a railway train'—a modern invention Ruskin attacked repeatedly.[25]

In Walter Pater, Ruskin's successor as the great art critic, 'we have Ruskin', joked Chesterton, 'without the prejudices, that is, without the funny parts'. For the 'moral tone' of Pater's writings was far from being Puritan; not that it was Catholic either—it was 'strictly and splendidly Pagan'. Ruskin, like Newman, could 'let himself go'; but that was impossible for Pater, 'for the excellent reason that he wants to stay: to stay at the point where all the keenest emotions meet'. However, there is an

[25] *VAL* 447–9, 450.

'objection to being where all the keenest emotions meet'—namely, 'that you feel none of them'. Like Swinburne, Pater 'wanted to see Paganism *through* Christianity: because it involved the accidental amusement of seeing through Christianity itself'.[26]

Chesterton saw Matthew Arnold as being 'even more concentrated' on Carlyle's and Ruskin's 'main task—the task of convicting liberal *bourgeois* England of priggishness and provinciality'. For Arnold, the answer was 'culture', 'the disinterested play of the mind through the sifting of the best books and authorities'. Chesterton wickedly suggests that 'some may suspect that culture was a man, whose name was Matthew Arnold'. But nevertheless, just as Carlyle 'was a man who saw things', so Arnold 'was chiefly valuable as a man who knew things'. 'He simply happened to know certain things' that Carlyle and others did not know, such as that 'England was a part of Europe', that 'England was then (as it is now) an oligarchical State, and that many great nations are not'. He also knew that 'the Catholic Church had been in history "the Church of the multitude": he knew it was not a sect. He knew that great landlords are no more a part of the economic law than nigger-drivers: he knew that small owners could and did prosper.' He reminded the English that 'Europe was a society while Ruskin was treating it as a picture gallery'. In conclusion:

His frontal attack on the vulgar and sullen optimism of Victorian utility may be summed up in the admirable sentence, in which he asked the English what was the use of a train taking them quickly from Islington to Camberwell, if it only took them 'from a dismal and illiberal life in Islington to a dismal and illiberal life in Camberwell?'

Chesterton also brilliantly evokes Arnold's method as a critic:

The most vital thing he invented was a new style: founded on the patient unravelling of the tangled Victorian ideas, as if they were matted hair under a comb. He did not mind how elaborately long he made a sentence, so long as he made it clear. He would constantly repeat whole phrases word for word in the same sentence, rather than risk ambiguity by abbreviation. His genius showed itself in turning this method of a laborious lucidity into a peculiarly exasperating form of satire and controversy. Newman's strength was in a sort of stifled passion, a dangerous patience of logic . . . But Arnold kept a smile of heart-broken forbear-ance, as of the teacher in an idiot school, that was enormously insulting. One trick he often tried with success. If his opponent had said something foolish, like 'the

[26] *VAL* 450–1.

destiny of England is in the great heart of England', Arnold would repeat the phrase again and again until it looked more foolish than it really was.

On the other hand, the irony of Chesterton's amused dissection of Arnold's religious views is deadly.

He seems to have believed that a 'Historic Church', that is, some established organisation with ceremonies and sacred books, etc., could be perpetually preserved as a sort of vessel to contain the spiritual ideas of the age, whatever those ideas might happen to be. He clearly seems to have contemplated a melting away of the doctrines of the Church and even of the meaning of the words: but he thought a certain need in man would always be best satisfied by public worship and especially by the great religious literatures of the past. He would embalm the body that it might often be revisited by the soul—or souls. . . . But while Arnold would loosen the theological bonds of the Church, he would not loosen the official bonds of the State. You must not disestablish the Church: you must not even leave the Church: you must stop inside it and think what you choose. Enemies might say that he was simply trying to establish and endow Agnosticism. It is fairer and truer to say that unconsciously he was trying to restore Paganism: for this State Ritualism without theology, and without much belief, actually was the practice of the ancient world. Arnold may have thought that he was building an altar to the Unknown God; but he was really building it to Divus Caesar.[27]

It is significant that by far the best part of *The Victorian Age in Literature* are these pages on the Victorian 'sages', Newman, Carlyle, Ruskin, and Arnold. It is here that Chesterton is clearly himself most personally involved. And that is as it should be if Chesterton is their successor in the twentieth century. By contrast, the pages on the Victorian novelists and poets are much less interesting—with the exception, naturally, of the discussion of his beloved Dickens.

While these Victorian 'sages' were protesting against 'the cold commercial rationalism' of early Victorian England 'in the name of neglected intellect, insulted art, forgotten heroism and desecrated religion', 'already the Utilitarian citadel had been more heavily bombarded on the other side by one lonely and unlettered man of genius'. For, Chesterton explains, the 'rise of Dickens' was 'like the rising of a vast mob'—'and a mob in revolt; he fought by the light of nature; he had not a theory, but a thirst'. And his thirst was for 'things as humble, as human, as laughable as that daily bread for which we cry to God. He had no particular plan of reform; or, when he had it, it was startlingly petty and parochial compared with the deep,

---

[27] *VAL* 452–4.

confused clamour of comradeship and insurrection that fills all his narra-tive.' He 'attacked the cold Victorian compromise', but he attacked it without knowing he was doing so. He hated the Little Bethel chapel without knowing anything of religious history: 'Newman could have told him that it was hateful, because it had no root in religious history; it was not even a sapling sprung of the seed of some great human and heathen tree: it was a monstrous mushroom that grows in the moonshine and dies in the dawn.' Dickens knew none of this: 'he simply smelt fungus, and it stank.' Again, Dickens travelled on the French railways 'and noticed that this eccentric nation provided him with wine that he could drink and sandwiches he could eat, and manners he could tolerate', while 'remem-bering the ghastly sawdust-eating waiting-rooms of the North English railways'.

Matthew Arnold could have told him that this was but a part of the general thinning down of European civilisation in these islands at the edge of it; that for two or three thousand years the Latin society has learnt how to drink wine, and how not to drink too much of it. Dickens did not in the least understand the Latin society: but he did understand the wine.

For if Carlyle 'saw' and Arnold 'knew', Dickens 'tasted' and 'felt'. What makes Dickens's attack on 'the solid scientific school' seem so 'successful' to Chesterton was because it was the protest of the common man: 'because he did not attack from the standpoint of extraordinary faith, like Newman; or the standpoint of extraordinary detachment or serenity, like Arnold; but from the standpoint of quite ordinary and quite hearty dislike.' Dickens, then, 'the great romanticist', turns out to be 'truly the great realist also. For he had no abstractions: he had nothing except realities out of which to make a romance.' He was in effect Cobbett come back to life—'in this vital sense; that he is proud of being the ordinary man'. It was the triumph of the common sense of the common man:

That which had not been achieved by the fierce facts of Cobbett, the burning dreams of Carlyle, the white-hot proofs of Newman, was really or very nearly achieved by a crowd of impossible people. In the centre stood that citadel of atheist industrialism: and if indeed it has ever been taken, it was taken by the rush of that unreal army.[28]

When Chesterton turns to the other Victorian novelists and to the poets he is never dull, but he never writes with such power as in this first chapter

[28] *VAL* 454–9.

on the Victorian 'compromise', where Dickens finds himself unexpectedly classed with the great Victorian 'sages'—except in the next chapter on the novelists, where Dickens again appears. Here, inevitably, Chesterton echoes his great book on Dickens as he evokes Dickens's sheer *enjoyment* of his characters—'he enjoyed everybody in his books':

His books are full of baffled villains stalking out or cowardly bullies kicked downstairs. But the villains and the cowards are such delightful people that the reader always hopes the villain will put his head through a side window and make a last remark; or that the bully will say one thing more, even from the bottom of the stairs.

It is the same central point that Chesterton makes over and over again in *Charles Dickens* without ever boring the reader—any more than he thought Dickens's caricatures (as opposed to his serious characters) ever could bore the reader: 'He had the power of creating people, both possible and impossible, who were simply precious and priceless people ... '. The only comic villain Chesterton could remember Dickens ever killing was Quilp—but then he was made deliberately 'more villainous than comic':

There can be no serious fears for the life of Mr Wegg in the muckcart; though Mr Pecksniff fell to be a borrower of money, and Mr Mantalini to turning a mangle, the human race has the comfort of thinking they are still alive: and one might have the rapture of receiving a begging letter from Mr Pecksniff, or even of catching Mr Mantalini collecting the washing, if one always lurked about on Monday mornings. This sentiment (the true artist will be relieved to hear) is entirely unmoral. Mrs Wilfer deserved death much more than Mr Quilp, for she had succeeded in poisoning family life persistently, while he was (to say the least of it) intermittent in his domesticity. But who can honestly say he does not hope Mrs Wilfer is still talking like Mrs Wilfer ... [29]

The most famous or notorious sentence in *The Victorian Age in Literature* is Chesterton's remark that 'Hardy became a sort of village atheist brooding and blaspheming over the village idiot'.[30] In his *Autobiography* Chesterton was to speak very warmly of the pessimistic Hardy. He was, he tells us, the 'first great Victorian' he had ever met, 'though only for a brief interview'. He was then 'a quite obscure and shabby young writer awaiting an interview with a publisher'. But what struck Chesterton so forcibly was that Hardy behaved as though he were in the same situation himself, as though he were 'even a new writer awaiting his first publisher'. In actual fact, he was already a famous writer who had already written his most

[29] *VAL* 473.   [30] *VAL* 483.

famous novels. Although he had 'already the wrinkle of worry on his elfish face that might have made a man look old . . . yet, in some strange way, he seemed to me very young'. He was even ready to defend his pessimism 'somehow with the innocence of a boys' debating-club'. And so the youthful Chesterton actually 'argued with Thomas Hardy' for 'about five minutes, in a publisher's office' that the 'nonexistence' that Hardy professed to prefer to the pains and pleasures of life was 'not an experience' and that therefore it made no sense to express a preference or liking for it. Chesterton does not tell us what, if any, was Hardy's response to his logic. But what he does tell us is that he had discovered 'the rather tremendous truth about Hardy; that he had humility'. As for his observation about Hardy in *The Victorian Age in Literature*, far from intending to attack Hardy he was actually defending him: 'The whole case for him is that he had the sincerity and simplicity of the village atheist; that is, that he valued atheism as a truth and not a triumph.' For, while Hardy was 'blasphemous . . . he was not proud; and it is pride that is a sin and not blasphemy'. Chesterton's final judgement was this: 'Hardy was a well, covered with the weeds of a stagnant period of scepticism . . . but with truth at the bottom of it; or anyhow with truthfulness at the bottom of it.'[31]

In his *Autobiography* Chesterton was to contrast another pagan pessimist with Hardy, his old teacher at University College, A. E. Housman, by whom he had 'always been more intellectually impressed'. It was not that he was 'impressed by anybody with the intellectual claims of pessimism, which I always thought was piffle as well as poison'; but Housman seemed to him to possess a literary authority that Hardy did not have, 'which is all the more classic because its English is such very plain English'. Certainly, Housman seemed to him 'one of the one or two great classic poets of our time', whereas he 'could never quite digest Hardy as a poet', much as he admired him as a novelist. And he warmed to 'that high heathen genius' in the unflinching pessimism of his wonderful lines, 'The troubles of our proud and angry dust | Are from eternity and shall not fail,' by contrast with that 'official optimism' of 'the collectivist ticket-collector of the Fabian tram', with his cry, 'Next stop, Utopia'. He also cherished the story of Housman's after-dinner speech at Trinity College, Cambridge, in which he was reputed to have pronounced: 'This great College, of this ancient University, has seen some strange sights. It has seen Wordsworth drunk and Porson sober. And here am I, a better poet than Porson, and a better scholar than Wordsworth, betwixt and between.' Whether the story was

[31] *A.* 261–3.

true or not, whoever was responsible for those words had 'a superb sense of style'.[32]

At the beginning of the chapter on the Victorian poets in *The Victorian Age in Literature*, Chesterton has some harsh words about 'a certain odd provincialism' that distinguished even the great Victorian writers from their continental counterparts. While they were giants, they were also dwarfs: 'we do most frequently feel, with the Victorians, that the very vastness of the number of things they know illustrates the abrupt abyss of the things they do not know.' And he does not exclude the great 'sages' from his strictures.

There is a moment when Carlyle turns suddenly from a high creative mystic to a common Calvinist. There are moments when George Eliot turns from a prophetess into a governess.... We feel that it *is* a disgrace to a man like Ruskin when he says, with a solemn visage, that building in iron is ugly and unreal, but that the weightiest objection is that there is no mention of it in the Bible; we feel as if he had just said he could find no hair-brushes in Habakkuk. We feel that it *is* a disgrace to a man like Thackeray when he proposes that people should be forcibly prevented from being nuns, merely because he has no fixed intention of becoming a nun himself.... We feel that it *is* a disgrace to a man like Browning to make spluttering and spiteful puns about the names Newman, Wiseman, and Manning. We feel that it *is* a disgrace to a man like Newman when he confesses that for some time he felt as if he couldn't come into the Catholic Church, because of that dreadful Mr Daniel O'Connor, who had the vulgarity to fight for his own country.... Even Matthew Arnold, though he saw this peril and prided himself on escaping it, did not altogether escape it. There must be (to use an Irishism) something shallow in the depths of any man who talks about the *Zeitgeist* as if it were a living thing.

Chesterton thought that this kind of parochialism was the key to understanding what was wrong with the two great Victorian poets, Tennyson in particular but also Browning. As a disciple of Virgil, Tennyson also aimed at 'the universal balance of all the ideas at which the great Roman had aimed; but he hadn't got hold of all the ideas to balance'. He achieved rather not 'a balance of truths' but 'a balance of whims; like the British Constitution'. He was in truth a 'provincial' or 'suburban' Virgil, a believer in 'the Victorian compromise' that was 'as freakish and unphilosophic, as arbitrary and untranslatable, as a beggar's patched coat or a child's secret language'. Browning's 'eccentric style', on the other hand, was 'more suitable to the poetry of a nation of eccentrics; of people . . .

[32] *A.* 266–7.

removed far from the centre of intellectual interests'. His poetry was 'deliberately grotesque': 'But there certainly was, over and above this grotesqueness, a perversity and irrationality about the man which led him to play the fool in the middle of his own poems; to leave off carving gargoyles and simply begin throwing stones.' But at least Browning did not take himself too seriously like Tennyson: 'Browning is the Englishman taking himself wilfully, following his nose like a bulldog, going by his own likes and dislikes. We cannot help feeling that Tennyson is the Englishman taking himself seriously—an awful sight.'[33]

Chesterton does not say so in so many words, but we cannot also help feeling that he thought those great Victorians might have saved themselves, in spite of whatever limitations their insular ignorance imposed, from their lapses into narrow provincialism if they had not taken themselves quite so seriously, if they had exercised, or at least exercised more vigilantly, the Chestertonian virtue of humour—something rather different from Browning's playing the fool—which includes above all the ability to laugh at oneself, without which self-criticism is of necessity constrained. As Chesterton says, speaking of the limitations of George Eliot's novels, 'there was something by instinct unsmiling' about them, even though they were certainly not 'without humour'.[34] Chesterton underestimates her mature masterpieces, as he did the later novels of Dickens, but any reader of *Middlemarch* and *Daniel Deronda* must regret that their author lacked enough humour, if nothing else, to see what ridiculous characters Will Ladislaw and Daniel Deronda are—characters that their creator took only too seriously but who spoil these two great novels, and especially of course the latter novel.

4

Shaw had not given up trying to persuade Chesterton to write for the stage. The previous year he had written to Frances to try and draw her into a plot against her husband. He, Shaw, was going to be in the neighbourhood with his wife and would like to call on the Chestertons provided they had 'no visitors who couldn't stand us'. He wanted to read a play (*Androcles and the Lion*) to Chesterton that would take an hour and a half (it was only a sketch).

---

[33] *VAL* 489–92, 496.   [34] *VAL* 466.

I want to insult and taunt and stimulate Gilbert with it. It is the sort of thing he could write and ought to write: a religious harlequinade. In fact, he could do it better if a sufficient number of pins were stuck into him. My proposal is that I read the play to him ... and that you fall into transports of admiration of it; declare that you can never love a man who cannot write things like that; and definitely announce that if Gilbert has not finished a worthy successor to it before the end of the third week ensuing, you will go out like the lady in A Doll's House, and live your own life—whatever that dark threat may mean.

If you are at home, I count on your ready complicity; but the difficulty is that you may have visitors; and if they are pious Gilbert will be under a tacit obligation not to blaspheme, or let me blaspheme, while they are beneath his roof (my play is about the Christian Martyrs, and perfectly awful in parts); and if they are journalists, it will be necessary to administer an oath of secrecy. I dont [*sic*] object to the oath; and nothing would please Gilbert more than to make them drink blood from a skull: the difficulty is, they wouldnt [*sic*] keep it. In short, they must be the right sort of people, of whom the more the merrier.[35]

On 7 November 1913 Shaw's demand that Chesterton write a play was finally met with the production of *Magic* at the Little Theatre in London— although it was not the play that Shaw had sketched out for him. *Magic* is a dramatic and autobiographical defence of the supernatural. A conjuror, provoked by a sceptic who declares that all his tricks are explicable and that science will eventually be able to explain all so-called miracles, turns a lamp from red to blue and then back to red. Eventually, the conjuror reveals that, having once (like the playwright himself) dabbled in spiritualism in spite of the terrible headaches that followed the séances, he had come to believe in the existence of evil spirits, and these he had accordingly invoked to change the lamp's colours. But having done the trick by magic, he discovers a natural way of doing it—but once he has given his audience the natural explanation, he knows that that is how afterwards they will say the trick was done. At the end of the first performance, Shaw cried out 'bravo' and 'speech'. Chesterton came on to the stage, 'and in a delightful little speech', recalled one member of the audience,

told us he did not believe in his powers as a writer. He did not believe he could write a good play, nor a good article, nor even a picture post card, perhaps the hardest task of all. But he did believe in his own opinions, and so sure was he that they were right that he wanted his audience to believe them too.

Another spectator thought the 'best part of the whole evening' was 'the spectacle of Chesterton roaring with huge delight' at his jokes. The

---

[35] Ward, *GKC* 207–8, with text corrected from BL Add. MS 73198, fo. 39.

newspaper reviews were generally favourable next morning. George Moore, the Anglo-Irish novelist whom Chesterton had attacked in *Heretics*, praised it to the skies: 'I followed the comedy of *Magic* from the first line to the last with interest and appreciation, and I am not exaggerating when I say that I think of all modern plays I like it the best.' He considered the play to be 'practically perfect' inasmuch as the plot and dialogue perfectly fitted the idea that lay behind the drama. In Germany, where the play was also produced, reviewers compared Chesterton to Shaw, some more favourably.[36] Shaw thought the play was better than Chesterton's novels: 'the characters which seem so fantastic and even ragdolly . . . in his romances become credible and solid behind the footlights, just the opposite of what his critics expected.'[37] But Chesterton's own judgement was more to the point: 'It is a bad play, because it was a good short story.' And the kind of short story Chesterton had in mind was, predictably, the detective story, the genre in which he did excel.[38] However, as Frances wrote to Father O'Connor, 'Really "Magic" seems to have caught on, though it will only be played for a short time in London. Already two companies are getting ready to go on tour with it.'[39]

Shaw, who had also tried unsuccessfully to persuade Conrad, Kipling, and Wells to write for the theatre, was so incensed by the contract Chesterton had signed that he wrote disgustedly to Frances:

In Sweden, where the marriage laws are comparatively enlightened, I believe you could obtain a divorce on the ground that your husband threw away an important part of the provision for your old age for twenty pieces of silver. . . . In future, the moment he has finished a play and the question of disposing of it arises, lock him up and bring the agreement to me. Explanations would be thrown away on him.[40]

The contract Chesterton had signed was 'monstrous': 'I tell you these things calmly: but my feelings would prompt me to write them in blood

---

[36] Ward, *GKC* 315–16 (with text of Moore's letter to Forster Bovill, 24 Nov. 1913, corrected from BL Add. MS 73231A, fo. 18); Ffinch, 222; Patrick Braybrooke, *I Remember G. K. Chesterton* (Epsom: Dorling, n.d.), 23, 25.

[37] *New Statesman*, 13 May 1916.

[38] John Sullivan, *Chesterton Continued: A Bibliographical Supplement* (London: London University Press, 1968), 91, quoting from 'Notes on Recent Books by their Authors', *Dublin Review*, Jan. 1914.

[39] Frances Chesterton to John O'Connor, n.d., BL Add. MS 73196, fo. 101.

[40] Ward, *GKC* 208, with text corrected from BL Add. MS 73198, fo. 40.

across the heavens.'[41] There is an undated letter urging Chesterton to support the Society of Authors ('your trade union'), on one of whose 'two big committees' Shaw was

one of the unhappy slaves who . . . drudge at the heart-breaking work of defending our miserable profession against being devoured, body and soul, by the publishers— themselves a pitiful gang of literature-struck impostors who are crumpled up by the booksellers, who, though small folk, are at least in contact with reality in the shape of the book buyer.

'It is a ghastly and infuriating business, because the authors *will* go to lunch with their publishers and sell them anything for £20 over the cigarettes, but it has to be done; and I, with half a dozen others, have to do it.' Shaw, who had missed the last committee meeting, had now heard from 'the harassed secretary' that it had been 'decided to take proceedings in the case of a book of yours which you (oh Esau, Esau!) sold to John Lane (John is a—well!—no matter: when you take your turn on the committee you will find him out)'. But apparently everything was 'hung up' because Chesterton had failed to reply to letters sent to him by the Society's barrister, Herbert Thring. Shaw reminded Chesterton of his 'obligations to us wretched committee men' that were 'simply incalculable': 'We get nothing but abuse and denigration: authors weep with indignation when we put our foot on some blood-sucking, widow-cheating, orphan starving [*sic*] scoundrel and ruthlessly force him to keep to his mite of obligation under an agreement which would have revolted Shylock . . . We get nothing and spend our time like water for you.' Shaw ended his plea to Chesterton:

All we ask you to do is to answer Thring and let us get along with your work.
Look here: *will* you write to Thring
Please write to Thring
I say: have you written to Thring yet?[42]

There is also an undated letter from Chesterton, which would have infuriated Shaw, to Chesterton's agents, A. P. Watt & Son, written from the Battersea flat, in which he wonders at the 'prices' the agents had obtained for his books, 'compared with what I used weakly to demand', which 'seem to me to come out of fairyland':

---

[41] George Bernard Shaw to Frances Chesterton, 24 Feb. 1914, BL Add. MS 73198, fos. 40–1.
[42] Ward, *GKC* 206–7, with text corrected and name of publisher restored from BL Add. MS 73198, fo. 30.

It seems to me there is a genuine business problem which creates a permanent need for a literary agent. It consists in this—that our work, even when it has become entirely a duty and a worry, still remains in some vague way a pleasure. And how can we put a fair price on what is at once a worry and a pleasure?[43]

On the evening of 7 January 1914, Chesterton presided at the King's Hall, King Street, Covent Garden, as judge at the mock trial of John Jasper for the murder of Edwin Drood, after whom Dickens's unfinished novel, *The Mystery of Edwin Drood*, is named. The trial had attracted 'so much interest' that it had had to be moved to 'a more capacious place for its enactment', the *Dickensian*, the Dickens Fellowship's magazine, announced. The counsel for the defence was Cecil Chesterton and the jury included W. W. Jacobs and Hilaire Belloc, with Shaw as foreman. The unsolved mystery apparently fascinated Cecil, who believed that the hero had not really been murdered at all and who knew great chunks of the novel off by heart. The mock trial was a charity event in aid of some of the grandchildren of the great novelist who were living in poverty, organized by the Dickens Fellowship, of which both Chesterton brothers were members. The trial was given extensive publicity by the press and tickets were soon sold out. 'Keith' Jones, who played Princess Puffer, thought that Evelyn Waugh's father, who played Canon Crisparkle, was the most impressive member of the cast. There was standing room only in the King's Hall, which was filled to more than capacity, beyond what was permitted by law. But the performance ended with an anti-climax: according to 'Keith', remembering the event many years later, after the judge's witty and penetrating summing-up, as the jury was about to retire to consider their verdict, Shaw, as foreman of the jury, rose to object that nobody knew what Dickens's intention had been and that it would be presumptuous to try and second-guess him. But, according to the contemporary report in the *Dickensian*, which was disgusted with the 'outrage', Shaw, who 'was the one man in the building who was not in serious mood', with his usual 'impishness', 'spoiled' everything by jumping up before the jury could consider its verdict and announcing that the jury had decided during their lunch break and that it was one of manslaughter. However, Shaw did not have the last word, for the judge then committed everyone but himself to prison for contempt of court. It was now midnight.[44]

On 22 January 1914 Chesterton's next novel, *The Flying Inn*, was published. Humphrey Pump, the dispossessed landlord of The Old Ship,

[43] Ward, *GKC* 207.
[44] MCC 144–8; *Dickensian*, 10/1 (Jan. 1914), 10, 34, 40.

succeeds in evading Lord Ivywood's Islamic prohibition regulations by simply moving the inn's sign round the country and serving his customers wherever he parks the sign. Chesterton could hardly have predicted the mass Muslim immigration into Europe, and not least England, of the late twentieth century which makes the novel uncannily prophetic in its satire of multiculturalism and political correctness. For example, Lord Ivywood wants Muslims in Britain to be able to vote differently from the rest of the population:

If we are to give Moslem Britain representative government, we ... must not ask them to make a cross on their ballot papers; for though it seems a small thing, it may offend them. So I brought in a little bill to make it optional between the old-fashioned cross and an upward curved mark that might stand for a crescent—and as it's rather easier to make, I believe it will be generally adopted.

However, Ivywood is more than just a multiculturist, for he sees in Islam a valuable if improbable ally in the contemporary prohibition campaign, invoking the religious pluralism that was already becoming fashionable in the early part of the twentieth century:

Ours is an age when men come more and more to see that the creeds hold treasures for each other, that each religion has a secret for its neighbour, that faith unto faith uttereth speech and church unto church showeth knowledge. . . . we of the West have brought some light to Islam in the matter of preciousness of peace and of civil order, may we not say that Islam, in answer, shall give us peace in a thousand homes, and encourage us to cut down the curse that has done so much to thwart and madden the virtues of Western Christendom? . . . Already the legislature takes more and more sweeping action to deliver the populace from the bondage of the all-destroying drug.

Ivywood claims that prohibition is intended 'to protect the savings of the more humble and necessitous classes'. But of course it does not apply to the rich, who can continue to enjoy drinking champagne in their homes, while the public houses of the poor are closed. Like the intellectuals of the day, Ivywood believes in the inevitability of progress, and here too Islam is seen as an ally, for 'the principle of the Crescent' seems to him 'the principle of perpetual growth towards an implied and infinite perfection'. Indeed, he believes that 'Islam has in it the potentialities of being the most progressive of all religions'. As an admirer, too, of Nietzsche, Ivywood admires the oriental 'love of fate'. As for the Muslim view of women, that he pronounces is somehow 'too simple and solid for our paradoxical Christendom to understand', with its belief in the individual woman rather than simply 'Womanhood'. Like the typical intellectual of the time, Ivywood cares not for human beings but for Humanity, just as he cares not for dogs but 'the Cause of Dogs, of course'. And naturally, Ivywood embraces 'eastern Vegetarianism'. But Ivywood is most fundamentally oriental in believing that 'everything lives by turning into something else' as no 'limit is set upon living things', as opposed to the Western idea that the 'prime fact of identity is the limit set on all living things'.[45]

The most memorable part of *The Flying Inn* for most readers will be the verses reprinted from the *New Witness*, which had appeared there under the heading 'Songs of the Simple Life', together with three new songs. They include not only the 'Song of Strange Drinks', but also well-known poems like 'The Rolling English Road' with its famous line 'The rolling English Drunkard made the rolling English Road'—which had originally been entitled 'A Song of Temperance Reform'. In August 1915 the 'songs' were again reprinted, but with the addition of one poem that had also been originally published in the *New Witness* but not included in *The Flying Inn*, under the title of *Wine, Water and Song*.

On 28 January 1914 Chesterton and Frances travelled down to Sussex to see Elodie Belloc, who was seriously ill and died a couple of weeks later. 'Keith' Jones thought Elodie was the most attractive woman she had ever known; Cecil Chesterton adored her. According to 'Keith', after Chesterton had been exiled to Beaconsfield by Frances, Cecil was rarely able to arrange a meeting with his brother there. Telephoning was of little avail, as Chesterton hated the instrument, and the maid who answered would invariably say that 'the great man could not be disturbed, and would they ring again when he might be less busy'. Only Belloc, according to her, was able to run 'the blockade'; he would insist on speaking directly to Frances, whom he would inform at what time he proposed to call, at the same time demanding: 'Have you any beer? If not, I'll bring some with me.' Once Cecil told Elodie that he had not seen his brother for over a month:

Elodie sighed. 'Poor Gilbert!' She leaned forward with an expressive gesture of her little hands. 'I'm very sorry for Frances. It would distress her terribly if she knew how this—this ban hurt him.' . . . 'Why on earth does Gilbert stand it?' asked Cecil in an unusual burst of irritability. 'He loves her,' said Elodie with eloquent simplicity. . . . 'But really he should beat her. Hilary would beat me if I behaved like that.'

---

[45] *FI* 631, 435–6, 513, 456, 450, 474, 498, 526, 610–1.

Yes, Elodie repeated. 'Frances would be much better if Gilbert _could_ beat her.' But sadly to 'Keith', 'the thought of Gilbert laying about Frances with a stick, though impiously joyful, was incredible'.[46] Perhaps Chesterton was less unhappy in his exile than his brother and friends supposed—who after all had not chosen to marry Frances. There was, however, one respect in which Elodie, 'a very charming Californian', resembled Frances, and that was in their mutual dislike of the cold weather that so appealed to their husbands, as Chesterton recalled in his _Autobiography_. He remembered one wintry day when Belloc dragged the four of them through Sussex to find the source of the river Arun. They found the half-frozen pool set among 'a small grove of slender trees, silver with the frost': 'But I think the ladies, though both of them sensitive to scenery, looked on that cold paradise with something of a cold eye.' Nor did Belloc's 'remedy of hot rum, in large tumblers at an adjoining inn' appeal to them: 'we were puzzled by the fact that the remedy was regarded with almost as much distaste as the disease.'[47]

On the night of 2 July 1914 Chesterton attended 'a cinematograph supper in two acts' at the Savoy Theatre. The invitation came from J. M. Barrie and Harley Granville Barker. The other guests were prominent members of society and included the Prime Minister Herbert Asquith and the former Sir Rufus Isaacs, now Lord Reading, the Lord Chief Justice, as well as Edward Elgar and Yeats. Guests began arriving at 11.30 p.m. As they entered the theatre foyer, they were filmed on camera, and also while they sat for supper at small tables on the stage. After supper, the guests moved to the auditorium and the second act began. This consisted of a series of short revue sketches played by well-known actors and actresses, who were interrupted by members of the audience with obviously pre-arranged gags. The last of these came from Shaw, who rose from his seat, with the film camera pointed at him, and proceeded to deliver a series of witty remarks, while the camera filmed him and the audience. He then explained the point of the theatre supper: 'You understand, a Scotsman doesn't give you a supper for nothing.' They were, he informed them, all 'supers' in a revue that Barrie was writing for Granville Barker: 'You'll have the pleasure of seeing yourselves—and me—on the film, for I'm working tonight for a greater dramatist than myself.' Then, according to the _New York Times_ report, 'Seizing a property sword, Shaw brandished it, crying, "Who'll follow me?" Chesterton and Barker cried, "I will follow!" and charged the stage. Then the curtain fell and the

[46] MCC 76–7.   [47] A. 203–4.

cinematograph machine stopped. The guests filed out, laughing at the realization that they had been "caught".[48] The Prime Minister may have been less amused: at any rate, a stern letter was sent from 10 Downing Street forbidding his appearance on film.

Chesterton's involvement in the film experiments of Barrie, who was fascinated by the new art form, began with a visit from Shaw, who proposed 'in the heartiest spirits' that they 'should appear together, disguised as Cowboys, in a film of some sort projected by Sir James Barrie'. What the purpose of this film was nobody ever discovered—and 'even Barrie had rather the appearance of concealing his secret from himself'. All that Chesterton could discover was that 'two other well-known persons, Lord Howard de Walden and Mr William Archer, the grave Scottish critic and translator of Ibsen, had also consented to be Cowboys'. ' "Well", I said, after a somewhat blank pause of reflection, "God forbid that anyone should say I did not see a joke, if William Archer could see it." Then after a pause I asked, "But what is the joke?" Shaw replied with hilarious vagueness that nobody knew what the joke was. That was the joke.' Invited to a supper at the Savoy Theatre in order to 'talk things over' with Barrie and Granville Barker, Chesterton was expecting only a small party there, but instead he found the stage crowded with 'nearly everybody in London, as the Society papers say when they mean everybody in Society'. Barrie made himself 'almost completely invisible'. Towards the end of the supper, Elgar 'casually remarked' to Frances, 'I suppose you know you're being filmed all the time.' But, while some of the company were 'throwing bread about and showing marked relaxation from the cares of State', it was 'unlikely that she was brandishing a champagne-bottle or otherwise attracting social attention'. Meanwhile, 'the Original Four, whom destiny had selected for a wild western life', were privately given their instructions. When the company had left the stage for the auditorium, Shaw 'harangued them in a furious speech, with savage gesticulations denouncing Barker and Barrie and finally drawing an enormous sword. The other three of us rose at this signal, also brandishing swords, and stormed the stage, going out through the back scenery.' Then 'the Original Four' disappeared 'for ever from the record and reasonable understanding of mankind; for never from that day to this has the faintest light been thrown on the reasons of our remarkable behaviour'. Immediately after this memorable theatre supper Chesterton says he received 'a friendly and apologetic note' from Barrie, 'saying that the whole scheme was going to be dropped'.[49] Chesterton's account,

---

[48] *New York Times*, 4 July 1914.   [49] A. 219–21.

written a couple of decades after the event, which omits in particular Shaw's joke about the parsimony of Scotsmen, differs a little from that of the contemporary report in the *New York Times*, which was presumably more accurate.

The note from Barrie to which Chesterton refers cannot have been sent *immediately* after the supper, since 'the whole scheme' was in two parts, of which the Savoy Theatre farce was only the first part. For 'the Original Four' had an appointment to make yet another appearance, 'in a sort of abandoned brickfield somewhere in the wilds of Essex; in which spot, it was alleged, our cowpunching costumes were already concealed'. On the second of these two 'melodramatic assignments' their 'Wild West equipment' was duly found in 'the waste land in Essex'; but much indignation was felt against Archer, 'who, with true Scottish foresight, arrived there first and put on the best pair of trousers': 'They were indeed a magnificent pair of fur trousers; while the other three riders of the prairie had to be content with canvas trousers.' This 'piece of individualism' on the part of Archer aroused much comment throughout the afternoon proceedings— 'while we were being rolled in barrels, roped over faked precipices and eventually turned loose in a field to lasso wild ponies, which were so tame that they ran after us instead of our running after them, and nosed in our pockets for pieces of sugar'. Again, it was also a fact—'whatever may be the strain on credulity'—that they all got onto the same motor-bicycle, 'the wheels of which were spun round under us to produce the illusion of hurtling like a thunderbolt down the mountain-pass'.

When the rest finally vanished over the cliffs clinging to the rope, they left me behind as a necessary weight to secure it; and Granville Barker kept on calling out to me to Register Self-sacrifice and Register Resignation, which I did with such wild and sweeping gestures as occurred to me; not, I am proud to say, without general applause. And all this time Barrie, with his little figure behind his large pipe, was standing about in an impenetrable manner; and nothing could extract from him the faintest indication of why we were being put through these ordeals. . . . It was as if the smoke that rose from that pipe was a vapour not only of magic, but of black magic.[50]

Nor was even that the end of 'the whole scheme', as Barrie had promised. Two years later, on 9 June 1916, a silent film was shown as part of a matinée at the London Coliseum in aid of the War Hospital, with the title 'How Men Love', featuring the very adventures of 'the Original Four' that

[50] *A.* 219–20.

Chesterton was to describe twenty years later more or less accurately—except that in the film Chesterton was seen to drop the rope, which not even his weight could secure.[51] Shaw saw the film and wrote to William Archer on 30 December 1916: 'It wasnt [*sic*] in the least funny. Chesterton has possibilities as a comic film actor—or had before his illness spoilt his figure—but the rest of us were dismal failures as amateur Charlie Chaplins. The Savoy supper was the most interesting.'[52]

Reflecting later on these bizarre events, Chesterton wondered whether there was not another sense, 'darker than my own fancy', in which 'the secret put in Barrie's pipe had ended in smoke'. After all, there really had been a 'sort of unearthly unreality in all the levity of those last hours; like something high and shrill that might crack; and it did crack'. Certainly, Barrie's fantastic farce could hardly help but appear 'incongruous with something that happened some days later. For what happened then was that a certain Ultimatum went out from the Austrian government against Serbia.' And then on 4 August 1914 Germany rejected the British ultimatum to withdraw its forces from Belgium, which it had promised not to invade. The First World War had begun. Chesterton later heard, 'in a remote and roundabout way certain vague suggestions' that Barrie had had 'some symbolical notion of our vanishing from real life and being captured or caught up into the film world of romance', and then spending the rest of the film 'struggling to fight our way back to reality'. In the event, if the cowboys, 'the Original Four', were 'indeed struggling to find the road back to Reality they found it all right'.[53]

When Chesterton looked back years later at the causes of the First World War, he had no doubt who was responsible. He did not think the Kaiser was to blame, that simplified bogey figure of the British popular imagination—'though I am quite certain the evil originally arose with the power of Prussia'. And it certainly was not the Serbian fanatic who assassinated the Archduke Ferdinand at Sarajevo. Chesterton was convinced of the paradoxical truth that the 'fire-eater' who precipitated a war that could have been prevented, and that everyone wanted to prevent, was none other than a Quaker pacifist 'of the type of old Mr Cadbury, whom I knew and served in my youth'. For, if the Liberal government had made it absolutely clear early on that Britain would certainly intervene if France

---

[51] *New York Times*, 10 June 1916.

[52] *Bernard Shaw: Collected Letters 1911–1925*, ed. Dan H. Laurence (London: Max Reinhardt, 1985), 447–8.

[53] *A.* 221–2.

was threatened by Germany, 'Germany would never have challenged the power of such an alliance'. And millions would still be alive. Why had not Asquith's government done so? Not because they disagreed with the Tory opposition on foreign policy but because they were afraid of alienating the pacifist Quaker millionaires who were the main contributors to Liberal Party funds. This failure for Chesterton proved both the unreality of party politics, as his brother and Belloc had argued in *The Party System*, but also the fact that the country was ruled not by a democracy but by a plutocracy.[54]

A couple of weeks after the outbreak of war, on 20 August, Pope Pius X, the scourge of the Modernists, died. Writing in the *Illustrated London News*, Chesterton agreed with all those 'numberless liberal and large-minded journals' that 'pointed out, with subtle power and all proper delicacy', that the late pope had 'had all the prejudices of the peasant'. Indeed he had: 'He had a prejudice to the effect that the mystical word "Yes" should be distinguished from the equally unfathomable expression "No".'[55]

On 2 September Chesterton's old friend Charles Masterman, who had been appointed head of a new War Propaganda Bureau the previous month, invited twenty-five leading writers, including Conan Doyle, Arnold Bennett, John Masefield, Ford Madox Ford, John Galsworthy, Hardy, Kipling, Wells, and Chesterton, to discuss how they could contribute to the war effort. At the outbreak of war Chesterton's 'first thought' had been, 'what could he do for his coun-try'. Hugh Rivière remembered the Sunday after war had broken out when he was staying a few miles from Beaconsfield and walked over to see the Chestertons. Like everyone else, they shared 'the very national state of excitement and emotion'. 'I couldn't wield a sword,' Chesterton remarked ruefully, 'as I can't lift my right arm above my shoulder. I should be no use in cavalry, no horse could carry me.' Then he added hopefully: 'I might possibly form part of a barricade.'[56] However, Chesterton's contribution to the war effort would be in the field of propaganda, above all in *The Barbarism of Berlin*, published in November 1914, a collection of articles published during October and November in the *Daily Mail*. It was published the following year in America under the title *The Appetite of Tyranny* and included *Letters to an Old Garibaldian*, published in January 1915, a propaganda booklet aimed at

[54] *A*. 199–201.   [55] *ILN* xxx. 153.   [56] Clemens, 166–7.

an Italian audience. This, to the great glee of Masterman, was to go 'from Patagonia to Sweden, to the joy and conversion of many to the true faith'. According to 'many of our correspondents', he told Frances Chesterton in October 1915, 'it was the most effective piece of writing of all our work'.[57]

Chesterton was adamant that the real aggressor was not so much Germany as Prussia, the king of which was also the German emperor. His quarrel was not with Catholic Bavarians or Rhinelanders but with the Prussians who dominated them, who were simply 'barbarians', 'the enemy of civilisation by design', whose aim was 'to destroy two ideas, the twin root ideas of rational society'—namely, 'the idea of record and promise' and 'the idea of reciprocity'. For the Prussian 'had made a new discovery in international politics: that it may often be convenient to make a promise; and yet curiously inconvenient to keep it'. Long before the scandalous spectacle of cultured, music-loving Nazis, and unlike Victorians like Matthew Arnold and George Eliot but like Newman, Chesterton saw very clearly that culture and education are no guarantee of morality: 'the Berlin philosopher' was actually morally inferior to uneducated savages who respected 'obligation' and therefore had 'at least a seed of civilisation that these intellectual anarchists would kill'. For all his culture and education, the Prussian was 'a spiritual barbarian, because he is not bound by his own past, any more than a man in a dream'. The Prussian felt entitled 'to break the law' but 'also to appeal to the law'. Certainly, the Prussian did not feel bound by law in his dealings with the weaker sex and inferior nations. His attitude to women was well summed up in Nietzsche's infamous dictum: 'Thou goest with women, forget not thy whip.' Chesterton observes the significance of the whip rather than, say, poker: for a poker 'is a part of domesticity; and might be used by the wife as well as the husband'; whereas the whip is the weapon of 'a privileged cast'. But, if Prussian men believed it was their natural right to lord it over their women, so too as 'the master-race' they believed they had the same right to lord it over other nations.[58] These were the facts, but, as Chesterton was to observe, 'the modern mind can scarcely believe that men so modern, so cultivated, and so successful can also be so immoral'.[59]

[57] Charles Masterman to Frances Chesterton, 7 Oct. 1915, BL Add. MS 73454, fo. 53.
[58] *AT* 248–9, 250–2, 254–5, 258–9.   [59] *ILN* xxxi. 165.

5

On 14 November 1914 the *New Statesman* published as a war supplement Shaw's *Common Sense about the War*, a pamphlet that was widely regarded as treasonable and turned its author into a pariah. According to Shaw, no particular country was to blame for the war, which was simply the result of capitalism. Among others it shocked was Chesterton. There survive three drafts of a letter to Shaw in Frances's hand,[60] as well as a longer typed draft, undated, unfinished, and unsigned. Chesterton began: 'I think you are a great man: and I think that your first great misfortune was that you were born in a small epoch. But I think it is your last and worst misfortune that now at last the epoch is really growing greater: but you are not.' 'You are wrestling with something too romantic for you to realise,' he continued. It was '*not* nonsense' to go to war with Germany over the invasion of Belgium, which was a 'sin' requiring 'expiation', 'an outrage on the spirit'. The invasion had not been used by the British as a 'pretext'. Rather, British soldiers were dying because of the 'passion' they felt at 'Satan made flesh in the fields of Flanders'. This was a war 'involving more fundamental questions' than Shaw's 'modern drama has ever dared to raise and driven by more dynamic passions than ever' Shaw's beloved 'modern music has sought to explore and explode'. Yes, Shaw had been 'right in the old days to be always tilting at illusions; but this is *not* an illusion': 'You are out of your depth, my dear Shaw; for you jumped into this deep river to prove that it was shallow.' The trouble was that he could not 'bear to be on the democratic side'. For in this case this was a war of the British people, who were actually and unexpectedly on the side of an aristocratic government: 'the Government *represents* us.'[61]

Just before trying to write this passionate and outraged letter, Chesterton had collapsed while speaking at Oxford

to a huge packed mass of undergraduates in defence of the English Declaration of War. That night is a nightmare to me; and I remember nothing except that I spoke on the right side. Then I went home and went to bed, tried to write a reply

[60] BL Add. MS 73198, fos. 46–52.

[61] BL Add. MS 73198, fos. 55–9. On the third of the handwritten drafts Dorothy Collins has noted, 'This letter was probably not sent.' In fact, Shaw's subsequent letter to Frances of 5 May 1915 and Chesterton's letter to Shaw of 12 June 1915, as well as Chesterton's own account in the *Autobiography* that follows immediately below, make it clear that the letter was never sent or even finished.

to Bernard Shaw, of which about one paragraph may still exist, and was soon incapable of writing anything.

He was 'already very ill', he remembered, when he went to Oxford—and this was the 'last thing' he did before completely taking to his bed. It seems from Chesterton's own memory that he had been seriously unwell since September. He remembered that, when he 'first recovered full consciousness, in the final turn' of his long illness, he asked for the periodical *Land and Water*, in which Belloc 'had already begun his well-known series of War articles'. He was 'perfectly clear' in his own mind that the last of these articles by Belloc that he had 'read, or been able to understand' was about 'the news of the new hope from the Marne'. The Battle of the Marne, that finally stopped the German advance that threatened Paris itself, lasted from 6 to 12 September. And Chesterton was absolutely 'clear' that he had read none of Belloc's articles 'that had appeared since the Battle of the Marne'.[62]

On his return home from Oxford, Chesterton fell so heavily on his bed that it broke.[63] The chronology of the *Autobiography* is often confused or mistaken, but in this instance Chesterton was positive that his serious, life-threatening illness began during or just after the Battle of the Marne. According to 'Keith' Jones, it came as no surprise to those who knew him. Grossly obese, he had imbibed his father's taboo against any discussion of health (he refused, for example, to go to the dentist). He led an almost entirely sedentary life, avoiding taking any exercise as far as possible. And the old social drinking in Fleet Street taverns had been replaced, according to her, by solitary drinking.[64] Presumably, 'Keith's' reference to solitary drinking refers to the evenings after Frances had gone to bed and Chesterton would sit up late working, sipping, according to Father O'Connor, a glass of wine.[65] One glass of wine could easily become several, as 'in an absent-minded way he was always liable to drink too much of anything if it were there—even water'. This was why Dr Bakewell, his doctor from 1919 till his death, as he later told Dorothy Collins, 'did forbid alcohol at certain periods . . . simply to make liquid less attractive, as too much even of water was bad' for him; but this ban, which was always observed 'most meticulously', was rarely imposed, as for 'the greater part of the time' he had treated Chesterton he was not aware of drink in any way affecting his patient's health. And Dr Bakewell said that he had never treated Chesterton

---

[62] *A.* 233, 235.   [63] Ffinch, 229.   [64] MCC 168–9, 300–1.
[65] See above, p. 260.

for alcoholism, nor did he ever see any signs of it. Similarly, Dr Bakewell's predecessor, Dr Pocock, only occasionally advised total abstention, as he did for a few years after Chesterton's life-threatening illness of 1914–15, and then it was only to reduce Chesterton's liquid intake, which would be increased not only by the wine drunk but the thirst it created. The Wards' daughter Maisie noticed how he seemed constantly thirsty, drinking several bottles of mineral water a day. She remembered the daily routine from one visit she paid to Beaconsfield when Chesterton was hard at work on one of his major books. He would be in his study by ten, working until lunch at one. After a break of an hour and a half, he would be back in his study till tea at 4.30, after which he would again work till dinner at 7.30. Frances would go to bed at 10.30, leaving Chesterton to work well past midnight.[66] During those couple of hours Chesterton could easily have drunk a great deal without even noticing: apart from being absent-minded when eating or drinking, he had an exceptionally strong head.

Dr Pocock was called, who found him 'lying in a grotesquely awkward position, his hips higher than his head'. Asked if he was not uncomfortable lying like that, the patient acknowledged that he supposed he was. The doctor prescribed a water-bed. Before Chesterton lost consciousness, he heard Chesterton murmur, 'I wonder if this bally ship will ever get to shore.'[67] When after a week or more he momentarily recovered consciousness, Frances, hoping he knew who she was, asked, 'Who is looking after you?' He replied, 'God.'[68]

Frances wrote on 25 November to Father O'Connor asking for prayers. 'He is seriously ill and I have two nurses. It is mostly heart trouble, but there are complications. The Dr is hopeful and we can only hope and trust he will pull round. He is quite his normal self, as regards head and brain, which makes it almost impossible to realise how ill he is. He even dictates and reads a great deal.'[69] But on Christmas Eve he had 'a bad relapse' and was now 'very desperately ill'. Faced with the prospect of her husband dying, who in his moments of consciousness was rambling on about wanting to be buried in Kensal Green, a Catholic cemetery, Frances broached the subject of conversion: 'He is not often conscious, and is so

---

[66] Ward, *GKC* 328, 454–5, 562–3.   [67] Ward, *GKC* 329.

[68] Sullivan, 162.

[69] Frances Chesterton to John O'Connor, [25 Nov. 1914], BL Add. MS 73196, fo. 104. Partly printed (with errors) in O'Connor, 98, where the date, which has been pencilled in on the letter, is supplied, as in the case of the following letters where Frances failed to supply a date.

weak—I feel he might ask for you—if so I shall wire. Dr is still hopeful, but I feel in despair.'[70] She also consulted Wilfrid Ward's wife Josephine, who wrote to Father O'Connor:

if anyone could help him towards the Church it would be you. I have reason to believe that at one time he thought of becoming a Catholic. I want to make sure that you know how ill he is in case you should think it wise *and* possible, to go and see them and give him the opportunity of speaking to you.[71]

And on 2 January 1915 Mrs Ward wrote again to say, 'if you could come to London . . . for the inside of the week you could go down to Beaconsfield for a few hours without startling them. Surely they would think it natural for you to take advantage of a short holiday in London to go and see them?'[72] But the following day Frances wrote to say that she saw no point in O'Connor coming: 'If you came he would not know you and this condition may last some time. The brain is dormant and must be kept so.' But, if he regained consciousness sufficiently, she would 'ask him to let you come—or will send on my own responsibility'. In the meantime, she asked him: 'Pray for his soul and for mine.'[73] However, on 7 January she was able to write that Chesterton 'seemed decidedly clearer yesterday and though not quite so well to-day, the Doctor says he has reason to hope the mental trouble is working off. His heart is stronger and he is able to take plenty of nourishment.' She therefore hoped that he would 'soon be sufficiently himself to tell us what he wants done': 'I am dreadfully un-happy at not knowing how he would wish me to act. His parents would never forgive me if I acted only on my own authority.' She felt that God would answer her prayer and she would know what to do, even if her husband were to die. A postcard of 9 January confirmed that there had been a 'quite distinct improvement'.[74] From a letter dated 10 January from Mrs Ward to O'Connor, it appears that the priest had in fact gone down to Beaconsfield. Mrs Ward did not suppose that he had been able to see Chesterton, but at least his talk with Frances 'must have done much good'—adding: 'I hope that Frances may be nearer the Church than she knows herself.'[75] On 12 January Frances wrote again to O'Connor to say

---

[70] O'Connor, 98, with text corrected from BL Add. MS 73196, fo. 104.
[71] Josephine Ward to John O'Connor, n.d., BL Add. MS 73196, fo. 105.
[72] Josephine Ward to John O'Connor, 2 Jan. 1915, BL Add. MS 73196, fo. 106.
[73] O'Connor, 98, with text corrected from BL Add. MS 73196, fo. 107.
[74] O'Connor, 98–9.
[75] Josephine Ward to John O'Connor, 10 Jan. 1915, BL Add. MS 73196, fo. 109.

that she was convinced that her husband was 'really better' and would live: 'Physically he is stronger and the brain is beginning to work normally, and soon I trust we shall be able to ask him his wishes with regard to the Church.'[76] On 18 January she reported an improvement, although the recovery had stalled for a week: 'He *asked* for me to-day, which is a great advance. He is dreadfully weak, but the brain clouds are clearing, though the doctors won't allow him to make the slightest effort to think.'[77]

In a later undated letter to Josephine Ward, Frances wrote that Chesterton had actually '*asked*' for her and had 'hugged' her: 'I feel like Elijah (wasn't it?) and shall go on "in the strength of that hug forty days".' The doctors had told her that the recovery would be 'very slow' and that it was essential to prevent the patient 'using his brain at all, as far as possible'.[78] It was 'a dreadful time', and she felt 'so helpless'; it was difficult to 'settle to ordinary occupations', but she was reading the proofs of Chesterton's new volume of collected poems: 'they keep me both sad and happy.' She wondered whether Josephine Ward would be in London, in which case she would try and go and see her if she felt that she could leave Beaconsfield for an hour or two.[79] On 24 January she wrote again to Mrs Ward to say that Chesterton was 'much the same, in a semi-conscious condition—sleeping a great deal'. She felt 'absolutely hopeless': 'it seems impossible it can go on like this. The impossibility of reaching him is too terrible an experience and I don't know how to go through with it.'[80]

On 29 January Frances wrote again to O'Connor confirming that the recovery was continuing, although practically imperceptible from one day to the next. Nearly two months later on 15 March the news was the same: there was progress, but it was very slow: 'He has to be kept very quiet, as he is easily upset and that affects his heart.' But the patient was not only steadily regaining consciousness, but becoming aware of his situation. He asked Frances if she had thought he was going to die, and she replied that she had thought so but now she knew he would live. He then asked: 'Does Father O'Connor know [?]' After hearing that he did, he 'wandered off again into something else'. She thought the priest would 'like to know he

---

[76] O'Connor, 98–9, with text corrected from BL Add. MS 73196, fo. 114.

[77] O'Connor, 100, with text corrected from BL Add. MS 73196, fo. 111.

[78] Ward, *GKC* 330, with text corrected from BL Add. MS 73454, fo. 46.

[79] Frances Chesterton to Josephine Ward, n.d., BL Add. MS 73454, fo. 46.

[80] Ward, *GKC* 329–30. Frances Chesterton to Josephine Ward, 24 Jan. 1915, BL Add. MS 73454, fo. 47.

had and was evidently thinking of you'.[81] On Easter Saturday Frances again wrote that there was still very slow progress: Chesterton's mind was 'gradually clearing', although it was difficult for him 'to distinguish between the real and the unreal'. And she was sure that he would 'soon be able to think and act for himself, but I dare not hurry matters at all'. She had told him that she was writing regularly to O'Connor, and he said, 'that is right—I'll see him soon. I want to talk to him.' He still wandered 'at times, but the clear intervals are longer'. The night before he had actually recited the Creed. She felt now she understood 'something of the significance of the resurrection of the body', when she saw him 'just consciously laying hold of life again'.[82]

When Frances finally met Mrs Ward, she told her how one day she had 'tried to test whether Gilbert was conscious by asking him, "Who is looking after you?" He answered very gravely, "God," and I felt so small.' She also revealed to Josephine Ward that her husband had talked to her before his illness about becoming a Catholic. But on 21 March after their meeting she wrote to Mrs Ward, saying:

I think I would rather you did not tell anyone just yet of what I told you regarding my husband and the Catholic Church. Not that I doubt for a moment that he meant it and knew what he was saying and was relieved at saying it, but I don't want the world at large to be able to say that he came to this decision when he was weak and unlike himself.

He will ratify it no doubt when his complete manhood is restored. *I* know it was not weakness that made him say it, but you will understand my scruples. I know in God's good time he will make his confession of faith—and if death comes near him again I shall know how to act.

On Easter Eve she wrote again to confirm that she was 'sure it was a decision'.[83]

The last of Chesterton's weekly columns for the *Illustrated London News* had appeared in the issue of 21 November 1914. And it was not until 22 May 1915 that another article appeared, by which time he had recovered from his long and serious illness. On 12 June he wrote to apologize to Shaw for not having written earlier to thank him for the 'kind letter' he had sent on Chesterton's recovery. But he had other apologies to make: 'I am not a vegetarian; and I am only in a very comparative sense a skeleton.'

---

[81] O'Connor, 100–1, with text corrected from BL Add. MS 73196, fo. 114.

[82] O'Connor, 101–2, with text corrected from BL Add. MS 73196, fo. 116.

[83] Ward, *GKC* 330–1.

However, it was not only his eating habits and size that he feared had not changed: 'Indeed I am afraid you must reconcile yourself to the dismal prospect of my being more or less like what I was before: and any resumption of my ordinary habits must necessarily include the habit of disagreeing with you.' (As he was to put it in his *Autobiography*, 'like one resuming the normal routine of his life, I started again to answer Mr Bernard Shaw'.[84]) He was particularly anxious for information about Shaw's latest publication about the war, a sequel to his notorious *Common Sense about the War*: 'What and where and when is Uncommon Sense about the War? How can I get hold of it? I do not merely ask as one hungry for hostilities, but as one unusually hungry for good literature.' Shaw 'probably' knew that Chesterton did not agree with him about the war: 'I do not think it is going on of its own momentum; I think it is going on in accordance with that logical paradox whereby the thing that is most difficult to do is also the thing that must be done.' He had 'always thought that there was in Prussia an evil will', although he 'would not have made it a ground for going to war'.[85] Shaw had written to Frances on 5 May to say that, presuming Chesterton was 'now quite well', he pictured him 'a tall attenuated figure . . . and a confirmed vegetarian'. He himself was 'working at Uncommon Sense about the War. Compared with it, my poor old Common Sense will seem like a stale article . . .'. He needed her husband's

help . . . over this war job. The war is going on by its own horrible momentum because the imbeciles who could not prevent the Junkers from beginning it are equally unable to make them stop it; and there is absolutely nothing but mischief in it now that we have shown the Prussians that we can be just as formidable ruffians as they.[86]

Shaw replied ten days later to Chesterton's letter, saying that he was 'delighted to learn under your own hand that you have recovered all your health and powers with an unimpaired figure'. He informed Chesterton:

It is perfectly useless for you to try to differ with me about the war. NOBODY can differ with me about the war; you might as well differ from the Almighty about the orbit of the sun. I have got the war right; and to that complexion, you too, must come at last, your nature not being a fundamentally erroneous one.

[84] *A.* 236.
[85] Ward, *GKC* 332, with text corrected from BL Add. MS 73198, fo. 70.
[86] *Shaw: Collected Letters 1911–1925*, ed. Laurence, 294.

It was a pity that he and his brother had not been born in Ireland, where, he, Chesterton, would have heard Irish patriots saying 'exactly the same thing' about England that English patriots were now saying about Prussia, and where Cecil 'would have seen what the Catholic church is really like when the apostolic succession falls to the farmer's son who is cleverer with schoolbooks than with agricultural implements'. And as for the 'evil will' of Prussia, he, Shaw, had been 'fighting that evil will, in myself and others, all my life'. Finally, he was sorry to say that 'some fool has stolen my title, and issued a two page pamphlet called Uncommon Sense about the War. So I shall have to call mine More Uncommon Sense about the War. It is not yet in type: I havent [*sic*] quite settled its destination.'[87]

Apart from correcting the proofs of Chesterton's new volume of poetry, which was published in April 1915,while he was still ill, Frances had also had to deal with all the letters from well-wishers, to help with which she enlisted the services of a young lady in the neighbourhood called Freda Spencer. When Frances herself had been a secretary in London, she knew neither shorthand nor typing. And this amateur tradition had been carried on. True, Mrs Saxon Mills had typed *The Napoleon of Notting Hill*, but Chesterton's first regular secretary, Nellie Allport, was also ignorant of both shorthand and typing, taking down Chesterton's dictation in long-hand; she remained with him till the move to Beaconsfield. The next secretary was a Mrs Meredith, a friend of the Solomons, who lived very close to Overroads. She had at first protested that she did not know how to spell and that only the Post Office could read her handwriting. Chesterton's reply was: 'You seem to be the very person for me. I used to be able to spell very well when I was at St Paul's.' Punctuation was dictated by Chesterton, who was very fond of the semi-colon, which he used a great deal where other writers would have used a comma. According to Mrs Meredith, the most astonishing thing about Chesterton was that he was able to compose two articles on completely different subjects simul-taneously, writing the one while he dictated the other, although the rate of dictation was not rapid. This practice apparently stopped after his illness. The weekly crisis was on a Thursday, when his article was due for the *Illustrated London News*. Frances would remind the secretary, who would remind Chesterton, who would procrastinate saying, 'We'll do it presently, but I don't think it would matter if my worthless words didn't appear this week.' By the time the article was finished, the last post had gone, which meant that the secretary had to bicycle hastily to the station and entrust it

[87] Ward, *GKC* 333–4, with text corrected from BL Add. MS 37198, fos. 72–3, 75.

with a tip to the guard on the train, which would then have to be met at London. The agitation caused to the whole household affected even the dog; it was as though Chesterton did it on purpose every Thursday. Mrs Meredith would often stay for meals, when she remembered Chesterton talking constantly, sometimes even reciting whole chapters of Dickens by heart. He would ask Frances after a first helping whether he should have any more. He disliked jelly because he did not, as he put it, 'like a food that's afraid of me'. Totally absent-minded as he was, oblivious of what he was eating or drinking, of time and of his physical surroundings, he was nevertheless always courteous and humorous. Once Mrs Meredith was very upset about spilling the ink all over a manuscript, but Chesterton immediately reassured her that it was entirely his own fault for leaving the manuscript where he had, worthless in any case as it was. Frances she remembered as utterly devoted to Chesterton and anxious to keep herself in the background. She suffered from constant poor health and tended to worry. Not having children upset her more than Chesterton, because he could bury himself in his work.[88]

Mrs Meredith remained with them up until the war, leaving just before Chesterton was taken ill. Freda Spencer, her successor, remembered how he would dictate slowly, drawing his sword-stick and fencing with the cushions as he walked up and down. Every week he would place a box of caramels on her typewriter on his return from having his hair cut. Poems would accompany the gift, or a picture of a stout, smirking gentleman with moustaches called Juan Alvarez who was depicted on the lid of one of Chesterton's cigar boxes. Señor Alvarez was supposed to be greatly enamoured of the cold cruel Freda, to whom he addressed these lines:

> Look, girl, upon the pallid wreck you made;
> Demon, behold your work; let conscience hiss.
> Ye have reduced a substance to a shade
> A fairly solid gentleman to this.

Other neighbours, too, would inspire wonderful nonsense verse. 'We are not amused' headed these verses on a fictitious Mrs Baines:

> Puck and the woodland elves shall weep with me
> For that lost joke I made in Ledborough Lane,
> The joke that Mrs Baines declined to see
> Although I made it very loud and plain.
> I made the joke again and yet again,

[88] Ward, *RC* 133–5.

I analysed it, parsed it and explained:
I did my very best to entertain,
But Mrs Baines would not be entertained.

When Freda was asked to become a school secretary to replace a lady who had left for war duties, she asked Chesterton for a reference. She was, he told her, 'quite welcome' to use his name in any way that might be useful.

The only serious objection to your forging it is that it does not at present represent any considerable balance at the bank. I am ready to sign any testimonial to your character, capacity, courtesy, beauty, health, humour, sanity and even appetite. Essays on each of these qualities in yourself should be set as themes to your young pupils.[89]

In retrospect, Freda summed up what she saw as his great merit and his great fault. On the one hand, she marvelled at the amount of time and effort he could expend on 'giving pleasure and amusement to entirely unimportant people', endowing 'the trivialities of life' with 'a richness and importance which was essentially Christian' and enlivening the daily routine with so much 'fun and laughter'. On the other hand, what she thought 'spoilt him and made life very difficult for those who had to do with him, was his utter abhorrence of anything approaching discipline, restraint, or order'. This placed a great strain on Frances, who had to cope with all the practicalities of life. The nearest she ever saw him get to anger was 'if he detected her in any attempt to bring order and discipline into his or indeed anyone else's life'.[90] So, on the one side, there was the immense good nature, the humility, the humour. And, on the other side, a curious, unusual kind of self-indulgent selfishness that went back to his childhood and the permissive parents who had spoiled him and his brother.

[89] Ward, *RC* 139–40, 143–4.   [90] Ward, *RC* 156–7.

10

War and Travel

O N recovering from his long and potentially fatal illness, Chesterton returned to his propaganda work. His experience of the various government departments that commissioned propaganda literature threw light on 'the mystery and inconsistency of man', who was revealed as being 'capable of great virtues but not small virtues; capable of defying his torturer but not of keeping his temper'. He was 'astounded...at the small and spinsterish vanities and jealousies that seemed to divide those Departments'. He 'could understand a man being a coward and running away from a German'; but what he could not imagine was any Englishman behaving 'as if it were not a fight between an Englishman and a German, but a fight between a Foreign Office clerk and a War Office clerk': 'I daresay every one of those Government officials would have died for England without any fuss at all. But he could not have it suggested that some two-penny leaflet should pass through another little cell in the huge hive of Whitehall, without making a most frightful fuss.' However, bureaucratic rivalry had its positive side. Charles Masterman 'crowed aloud with glee' that 'his enemies were complaining that no British propaganda was being pushed in Spain or Sweden', for that 'meant that propaganda like mine was being absorbed without people even knowing it was propaganda'. Chesterton's own 'bellicose' *The Barbarism of Berlin* had actually appeared in 'a quiet Spanish philosophical study' on the concept of barbarism! Masterman's enemies 'would have published it with a Union Jack cover and a picture of the British Lion, so that hardly one Spaniard would read it, and no Spaniard would believe it'. Masterman's 'dark humour' delighted in 'this attack on his success as an intellectual smuggler'. And his 'rather subtle individuality' showed its superiority to 'his political surroundings', into which 'he suffered himself to sink too deeply' by allowing himself 'to be used as a Party hack by Party leaders who were in every way his inferiors'.[1] This gentle rebuke contrasts with the vitriolic attacks, of which Chesterton disapproved, of Cecil Chesterton and Belloc on Masterman for betraying his political principles by accepting office in a Liberal government of which he had previously been a critic.[2]

The Crimes of England was published in November 1915. Chesterton was 'rather proud' of it:

> For I was vividly convinced of the folly of England merely playing the Pharisee in this moment of intense moral reality. I therefore wrote a book actually making a list of the real sins of the British Empire in modern history; and then pointing out that in every one of them, not only was the German Empire far worse, but the worst tendencies of Britain had actually been borrowed from Germany.

But he admitted that the title was 'liable to misunderstanding', and he thought that 'in some places the book was banned like a pacifist pamphlet'.[3]

In his dedication to an imaginary German Professor Whirlwind, Chesterton provides him with a list of English crimes, all involving either the failure to resist Prussian aggression in Europe or the abject imitation of 'soulless' Prussian practices: 'Whoever we may have wronged, we have never wronged Germany. Again and again we have dragged her from under the just vengeance of her enemies...'. England had used German mercenaries to suppress the Irish—and to say that 'the German mercenary was worse than the Orangeman' was to 'say as much as human mouth can utter'. Chesterton advises his readers that he speaks of England's rather than Britain's crimes because it was not Scotland or Ireland that was responsible for them but England, whose 'populace lacked a religion... with its inevitable result of plutocracy and class contempt'. Fortunately, there was another kind of democratic, liberal England, the England of the common people, of the ruled rather than the rulers, represented above all by William Cobbett, who 'ventured to plead against certain extraordinary cruelties being inflicted on Englishmen whose hands were tied, by the whips of German superiors', for 'Teutonic mercenaries did not confine themselves solely to torturing Irishman. They were equally ready to torture Englishmen: for mercenaries are mostly unprejudiced.'

---

[1] *A*. 234–6.   [2] Ward, *GKC* 279–80; Ffinch, 179–80.   [3] *A*. 236.

The Teutonic mind did not accept the democratic concept of the citizen, whose 'individual human nature shall be constantly and creatively active in *altering* the State', an idea the Germans rightly regard as 'dangerously revolutionary':

Every Citizen is a revolution. That is, he destroys, devours and adapts his environment to the extent of his own thought and conscience. This is what separates the human social effort from the non-human; the bee creates the honey-comb, but he does not criticise it. The German ruler really does feed and train the German as carefully as a gardener waters a flower. But if the flower suddenly began to water the gardener, he would be much surprised.

To compensate for 'the iron framework of the fixed State', the German is allowed 'the Irresponsibility of Thought', whereby 'anything can be said although, or rather because, nothing can be done'. The resulting multitude of 'mad theories', however, all depend on the one assumption that 'all *important* events of history are biological'. The great advantage of this 'theory of all history as a search for food' is that it 'makes the masses content with having food and physic, but not freedom'. By 1914 England, too, had become 'the Servile State', having, for example, adopted in 1911 the German system of compulsory insurance, thanks to 'the Prussian prestige in "social reform"', at the instigation of Lloyd George, 'who had studied its operations in Germany'. And, of course, Cobbett was by 'now little more than a name', 'criticised to be underrated and not to be understood', while 'his enemy, the "efficient" foreigner', was taken as 'a model for men'. Cobbett was 'medieval' and stood for merry England—but 'I do not think that even Prussians ever boasted about "Merry Prussia"'. On the contrary, the Prussians prided themselves on their 'dehumanised seriousness' and 'earnestness', on their refusal 'to be superficial', which is why they 'cannot really be deep'. For instance, they took art too seriously: they forgot that 'Shakespeare was a man; that he had moods, that he made mistakes, and, above all, that he knew his art was an art and not an attribute of deity'. Again, Prussia '*hated* romance', which, like chivalry, 'filled the Prussian with a cold fury'. In England, on the other hand, the spirit of Cobbett who had 'sought to break' the 'bloody whip of a German bully... when it was wielded over the men of England', lived on in the masses—'the gallantry was in the gutter'. And it was these common people, the masses themselves, whose 'hate of injustice' was now rolling back the 'empire of blood and iron... towards the darkness of the northern forests'.[4]

[4] *CE* 300, 324, 330–1, 335, 337, 350, 355–6, 359, 363, 367, 373–4.

German Zeppelin air raids had begun over London on 31 May 1915. But, although Chesterton regularly went to London, it seems it was a long time before he experienced one for himself. On that occasion, according to anecdote, he and Belloc went on talking without realizing what was happening: 'I am not sure at what stage we did eventually realise it; but I am quite sure we went on talking. I cannot see quite what else there was to do.' He remembered the occasion very well, not only because it was his first air raid but because of one of the guests at the house he was visiting, a uniformed Russian who had been brought along by Maurice Baring. The said Russian 'talked French in a flowing monologue that suavely swept us all before it; and the things he said had a certain quality characteristic of his nation; a quality which many have tried to define, but which may best be simplified by saying that his nation appears to possess every human talent except common sense'. The 'practical proposal' of this aristocratic officer in 'one of the crack regiments of the Czar' was that 'poets alone should be allowed to rule the world. He was himself, as he gravely observed, a poet.' At some point during the Russian's monologue, after he had been 'so courteous and complimentary as to select me, as being also a poet, to be the absolute and autocratic governor of England' and after he had 'waved...away' Chesterton's doubts ('literary men can never quarrel'), the poet who had been selected to rule England 'began to be conscious of noises without (as they say in the stage directions) and then of the thrilling reverberations and the thunder of the war in heaven'.

We went on talking, of course, with no alteration in the arrangements, except that the lady of the house brought down her baby from an upper floor; and still the great plan unfolded itself for the poetic government of the world. Nobody in such circumstances is entirely without passing thoughts of the possible end; and much has been written about ideal or ironic circumstances in which that end might come. But I could imagine few more singular circumstances, in which to find myself at the point of death, than sitting in a big house in Mayfair and listening to a mad Russian, offering me the Crown of England.

After the Russian poet had left, Chesterton and Belloc 'walked across the Park with the last rumblings still echoing in the sky, and heard the All Clear signal' as they 'came out by Buckingham Gate, like the noise of trumpets of triumph'. They talked 'a little of the prospects of the War, which was then in the transition stage between the last peril and the last deliverance', and they 'parted, not without a certain belated emotion of excitement'.[5] The occasion

<hr>

[5] *A.* 236–8.

must have been before February 1917, when the Russian Revolution broke out and the Czar abdicated, in view of the presence of the Czarist officer. Within, then, the time frame, 'the last peril' must have been the German assault on Verdun, which began on 21 February 1916 and which was intended to wipe out the French army, while 'the last deliverance' must refer to the British Somme offensive, which began on 1 July, successfully eased the pressure on the French, and ended on 18 November, exactly a month before the final relief of Verdun.

The Zeppelin air raids, which were launched from occupied Belgium and always took place at night, inspired Ford Madox Hueffer (who would change his name to Ford Madox Ford in 1919), the son of a German father, Francis Hueffer, a music critic of *The Times*, and an English mother, the daughter of the painter Ford Madox Brown, to publish, with Violet Hunt, *Zeppelin Nights* in 1915. The book was reviewed by J. K. Prothero, 'Keith' Jones's pseudonym, in the *New Witness* of 6 January 1916. The review attacked the 'dull offensiveness' of the book, while acknowledging that Violet Hunt had provided some 'fugitive gleams of patriotism'. Hueffer's lack of patriotism in suggesting that Londoners were cowering in terror in their cellars, 'Keith' suggested, only projected 'his own fear into the minds of the nation with whom he resides', and was written 'for German consumption.' The only panic was in the 'foreign' parts of London, particularly Whitechapel, which were 'inhabited by non-Europeans'. 'It is generally supposed', 'Keith' wrote, 'that Mr Hueffer is not exactly of pure European extraction, and this book is certain to confirm such impression.' The truth was that, apart from these 'aliens', the people of London 'not only refrain from cowering by day and palpitating by night, but with their own particular sense of humour, have turned the terror that walks in darkness, as devised by Berlin and ratified by Mr Hueffer into a joke...'.

The review provoked a letter in the next issue from a certain 'J.M.', which acknowledged that the book was a dreary pot-boiler, but complained: 'That is no reason why you should go out of your way to insult Mr Hueffer by calling him a Jew and a coward.' In fact, the letter went on, Hueffer was a Catholic and, although already in his forties, had secured a commission in the army. Furthermore, he had written the 'two most brilliant' analyses of Prussianism that had been published since the beginning of the war. 'Keith' retorted in the next issue of the paper that, because Hueffer had converted to Catholicism, that did not mean that 'he ceases to be a Jew'. She was also aware that he had 'written a novel centering round a particularly brutal type of sensualist'. This sneering reference to

Hueffer's *The Good Soldier*, which was also published in 1915, was too much even for one of the directors of the *New Witness*, E. S. P. Haynes, a literary solicitor and writer, to whom Belloc had dedicated *The Servile State*. Writing in the issue of 27 January, as 'a personal friend' of Hueffer, he took exception to J. K. Prothero's 'at best eccentric' dismissal of 'one of the ten greatest novels so far published in the twentieth century'. As for the author, he was 'absent on military service'. 'Keith' replied to this rebuke in the next issue by citing in support the review the paper had published of *The Good Soldier* in the issue of 3 June 1915 by Thomas Seccombe, 'a literary critic of considerable distinction'—who had indeed trashed a novel that has a claim to be one of the ten greatest English novels of the entire twentieth century. 'Keith' was supported by a letter in the issue of 10 February by a certain 'M.F.', who complained that Ford's (adulterous) 'Good Soldier' was a slur on English soldiers fighting in the war, at which point the editor brought the correspondence to a close.

'Keith's' offensive and vicious review was also too much for H. G. Wells, who wrote privately an undated letter to Chesterton to express his outrage.

Haven't I on the whole behaved decently to you? Haven't I always shown a reasonable civility to you and your brother and Belloc? Haven't I betrayed at times a certain affection for you? Very well, then you will understand that I don't start out to pick a needless quarrel with the *New Witness* crowd. But this business of the Hueffer book in the *New Witness* makes me sick. Some disgusting little greaser named Prothero has been allowed to insult old F.M.H. in a series of letters that make me ashamed of my species. Hueffer has many faults no doubt but firstly he's poor, secondly he's notoriously unhappy and in a most miserable position, thirdly he's a better writer than any of your little crowd and fourthly, instead of pleading his age and his fat, and taking refuge from service in greasy obesity as your brother has done, he is serving his country. His book is a great book and Prothero just lies about it—I guess he's a dirty minded priest or some such unclean thing ... The whole outburst is so envious, so base, so cat-in-the-gutter-spitting-at-the-passer-by, that I will never let the *New Witness* into the house again.[6]

To a reader today, Chesterton's response (also undated) is remarkable for its forbearance on the one hand, and on the other for the lack of condemnation of 'Keith's' disgusting personal attack on Hueffer. Clearly, the Marconi affair still deeply rankled with him. He told Wells that he knew

[6] Ward, *GKC* 350, corrected from BL Add. MS 73199, fo. 26, with the deleted name 'Prothero' restored.

enough of his 'good qualities in other ways to put down everything' in his letter to 'an emotion of loyalty to another friend':

Any quarrel between us will not come from me; and I confess I am puzzled as to why it should come from you, merely because somebody else who is not I dislikes a book by somebody else who is not you, and says so in an article for which neither of us is even remotely responsible. I very often disagree with the criticisms of Prothero; who is not a priest, but a poor journalist, and I believe a Free-Thinker. But whoever he may be (and I hardly think the problem worth a row between you and me) he has a right to justice; and you must surely see that even if it were my paper, I could not either tell a man to find a book good when he found it bad, or sack him for a point of taste which has nothing in the world to do with the principles of the paper. For the rest, Haynes represents the *New Witness* much more than a reviewer does, being both on the board and the staff; and he has put your view in the paper—I cannot help thinking with a more convincing logic. Don't you sometimes find it convenient, even in my case, that your friends are less touchy than you are?

Extraordinarily conciliatory as Chesterton was in the face of Wells's furious outburst, the truth is his response was somewhat disingenuous. What Chesterton calls 'a point of taste' had unfortunately a great deal to do with the 'principles' of a paper that under his brother's editorship was violently and virulently anti-Semitic (as even Belloc acknowledged[7]). Moreover, Haynes had responded only to 'Keith's' offensive and ignorant dismissal of *The Good Soldier*, not to her personal abuse of Hueffer. The remainder of Chesterton's letter makes it clear that the political corruption, in which leading Jewish politicians had been deeply involved on one notorious occasion, that the *New Witness* was courageously attacking, justified any lapses of 'good taste'.

By all means drop any paper you dislike, though if you do it for every book review you think unfair, I fear your admirable range of modern knowledge will be narrow. Of the paper in question I will merely say this. My brother and in some degree the few who have worked with him have undertaken a task of public criticism for the sake of which they stand in permanent danger of imprisonment and personal ruin. We are incessantly reminded of this danger; and no one has ever dared to suggest that we have any motive but the best. If you should ever think it right to undertake such a venture, you will find that the number of those who will commit their journalistic fortunes to it is singularly small: and include some who have more courage and honesty than acquaintance with the hierarchy of art. It is even likely that you will come to think the latter less important.

---

[7] See below, p. 395.

Chesterton added in a postscript that, since Wells 'specially' mentioned Prothero's letters, he must surely see that not to publish Prothero's letters would mean not publishing 'Haynes' letter and others on your side', which 'could not be printed without permitting a rejoinder'.[8]

Wells could hardly refuse this olive branch and replied that he too could not quarrel with Chesterton.

> But the Hueffer business aroused my long dormant moral indignation and I let fly at the most sensitive part of the *New Witness* constellation, the only part about whose soul I care. I *hate* these attacks on rather miserable exceptional people like Hueffer and Masterman. I know these arent [*sic*] perfect men but their defects make quite sufficient hells for them without these public peltings.

He admitted that he should have written to Cecil Chesterton instead, and one of these days he would 'go and have a heart to heart talk with him'— except that he always got 'so amiable' when he met a man in the flesh. But Cecil 'needs it—I mean the talking to'.[9]

2

In January 1916 *Divorce versus Democracy* was published by The Society of SS Peter and Paul, publishers to the Church of England. In the Preface, Chesterton says that he had been 'asked to put forward in pamphlet form this rather hasty essay as it appeared in "Nash's Magazine" '. And he begins with another attack on Prussia, the fount of all evil, for having 'become the peculiar champions of that modern change which would make the State infinitely superior to the Family'. Christianity, on the contrary, 'conceives of the home as self-governing in a manner analogous to an independent state; that is, that it may include internal reform and even internal rebellion; but because of the bond, not against it. In this way it is itself a sort of standing reformer of the State; for the State is judged by whether its arrangements bear helpfully or bear hardly on the human fulness and fertility of the free family.' It was that section of the plutocracy that wanted 'the division of sex for the division of labour' that favoured 'the extension of divorce': 'The very same economic calculation which makes them encourage tyranny in the shop makes them encourage licence in the family.'[10]

---

[8] Ward, *GKC* 351–2, with text corrected from BL Add. MS 73199, fos. 27–8.
[9] Ward, *GKC* 352, with text corrected from BL Add. MS 73199, fo. 29.
[10] *DD* 421–2.

Chesterton begins his argument that divorce is essentially undemocratic by conceding that the 'difficulty of believing in democracy is that it is so hard to believe—like God and most other good things'. But there was also the difficulty of disbelieving in it, namely, that 'there is nothing else to believe in'. It was mere 'babytalk' to talk about 'Supermen' or 'Nature's Aristocracy', who 'must be either those whom others think wise—who are often fools; or those who think themselves wise—who are always fools'. But if one is a democrat, then one must regard the extension of divorce as 'the last and vilest of the insults offered by the modern rich to the modern poor', who, unlike the rich, mainly believed in marital fidelity. Even if they did not, 'the popularising of divorce' would no doubt be used against the poor by the rich for 'power goes with wealth'. It was easy to 'forget that there is a great deal of difference between what laws define and what they do': 'Marriage will be called a failure wherever it is a struggle; just as parents in modern England are sent to prison for neglecting the children whom they cannot afford to feed.' Upper-class 'sentiment' frowned on men hitting women as ungentlemanly: to a judge coming from the same social background, 'a small pat or push' could be exaggerated or invented 'to assist those faked divorces so common among the fashionable'. But in a working-class culture, 'to divorce people for a blow' would be like divorcing a rich man for 'slamming a door'. Easy divorce would mean that people could have 'a series of lives' rather than 'a life'. It would be like but worse than the 'cold creed' of reincarnation in which 'each incarnation must forget the other': for 'this short human life' would be 'broken up into yet shorter lives', each of which would be 'in its turn forgotten'.[11]

In October 1916 Cecil Chesterton was at last accepted for military service in the East Surrey regiment, having been rejected several times on medical grounds, before securing a transfer to the Highland Light Infantry by claiming Scots ancestry through his mother. Just before his brother had fallen ill, he had accompanied 'Keith' Jones to France when she was commissioned to write about the military hospitals in Boulogne. Once again he asked her to marry him, but this time there was a difference: would she marry him if he were sent to the front to fight? And this time it was impossible for her to refuse.[12]

The last issue of the *New Witness* to be edited by Cecil was that of 12 October 1916. In the next week's issue he wrote 'An Au Revoir to *The New Witness*'—it was in fact 'An Adieu', as he must have thought not unlikely at

---

[11] *DD* 423–9.   [12] MCC 164, 167, 193, 198.

the time—in which he thanked his brother, 'who, at no little personal sacrifice, has consented to undertake the editorship in my absence, and to allow his name to appear on the front page of the paper'. The name would not only bring prestige to the paper but guarantee a continuity of editorial policy.[13] In his *Autobiography* Chesterton explains that, while it 'would at any time have seemed to me about as probable or promising as that I should become a publisher or a banker or a leader-writer on *The Times*...the necessity arose' out of the fact that 'the *New Witness*...was passionately patriotic and Pro-Ally but as emphatically opposed to the Jingoism of the *Daily Mail*', as well as the fact that there were 'not too many people who could be trusted to maintain these two distinct indignations, without combining them by the disgusting expedient of being moderate'. The new editor promised readers that he would not take himself too seriously either as editor or as a contributor. There was an idea that the Christmas number should carry a picture of him, and he doubted if he would summon sufficient seriousness to resist: 'There will be given away with the paper a lock of my hair, a fragment of one of my broken bootlaces, a small piece of blotting-paper, which I have really used (and used up) and some of the shavings of a blue pencil actually used in *The New Witness* office.' 'Keith', who had looked after the paper while Cecil was in America speaking on behalf of the Allied cause and debating with supporters of Germany, was in charge of the office, since the new editor out in Beacons-field would to a large extent be an absentee editor.[14]

According to 'Keith', Chesterton was not only an absent but 'an extremely bad editor', who 'could not realise the necessity for a cohesive policy for the paper, or a close association with its staff'. Had he spent at least one 'strenuous day' a week in the office, much might have been accomplished, she thought. But his visits were 'occasional and fugitive, most of the time being occupied in the dictation of his articles'. His leading articles also, she considered, were less decisive than his brother's, although 'his amazing journalistic flair kept them succinct'. But he lacked Cecil's crusading spirit and could not 'inspire the same enthusiasm'. One aspect of his writing greatly entertained the staff, his 'ingenuousness in corporeal matters', that made him on one occasion write that whenever 'Mr George is in trouble he goes into a corner, by himself, and makes a nasty mess'. The *New Witness*, 'Keith' recalled, 'always referred to the Welsh politician by his surname only, which was bitterly resented by his fellow Liberals', in order to avoid using the 'double-barrelled name that suggests to the simple a

---

[13] Ffinch, 244.   [14] Ffinch, 244–5.

loftiness of character, an integrity of purpose that a plain surname does not contain'. When an amendment was suggested, Chesterton still did not see the point: 'Of course, if you think I've been too hard on him you might tone it down.'[15] W. R. Titterton, who was on the staff and would succeed 'Keith' as assistant editor, observed: 'Nothing bored him, but business bothered him.' At first he did not at all care for 'the rough-and-tumble hurry of the business of putting a paper to bed', although Titterton thought he came to enjoy it. However, it was obvious that Chesterton had never wanted to be an editor, but had simply taken on the editing because he felt 'it was a sacred trust'.[16] Poor an editor as Chesterton may have been, as a prolific contributor he was the most valuable asset the paper had: he was the anonymous main leader writer and author of the weekly page of comment, which he started, called 'At the Sign of the World's End', while he also contributed signed articles and verses.[17]

As an editor, he was much more open than his brother to contributions from outside the small circle of writers sympathetic to the views of the paper. Thus he was ready to publish a 'Republican article' by Shaw in February 1917,[18] to which he intended to write an answer, 'for my dis-agreement and agreement with you are equally vital'. He would not have been prepared to publish the article had he thought that the article could endanger the Allied cause, and he was sure that Shaw would have under-stood, even if he had 'violently' disagreed. He personally thought it was 'bosh to treat political theories' as though they were military secrets. He always thought that 'if a thesis is wrong enough to be suppressed it is wrong enough to be rationally answered'. However, in spite of assurances he had previously received, at the last moment he had received 'an intimation from my Press Bureau friends that they think after all it ought not to be published. I can only suppose their stupider superiors are stricken with some blithering blue funk.' But he could not risk his brother's paper being closed down 'except for its own principles' and it would be 'illogical to defy the authorities' over a 'thesis' he would anyway have to dissociate himself from.[19]

On 19 May 1917 John Buchan wrote Chesterton 'a line of warmest congratulation on your perfectly admirable article on Kitchener, which you have written for the War Office and my department'. In February

[15] MCC 190–1. [16] *A.* 240; Titterton, 119–21.
[17] Barker, 234. [18] The date '1917' has been pencilled on to the letter.
[19] G. K. Chesterton to George Bernard Shaw, 25 Feb. [1917], BL Add. MS 73198, fos. 76–7.

Lloyd George had appointed Buchan head of a new Department of Information. In June of the previous year Lord Kitchener, the Secretary of State for War, had been sent on a diplomatic mission to Russia, but his ship had been sunk by a German mine off the Orkneys. The lengthy obituary, published as a pamphlet, which Chesterton had been commissioned to write, 'could not' Buchan thought, 'be better, and will do a great deal of good in Russia'.[20]

Kitchener, as the conqueror of the Mahdi, was a public hero. But Chesterton began with the paradox that the man who was 'destined ... to be the greatest enemy of Mahomedanism ... was quite exceptionally a friend of Mahomedans'. With his 'knowledge of Arabic, and still more his knowledge of Arabs', he combined 'detailed experience and almost eccentric sympathy' with them. Chesterton follows this with another paradox, a devastating and fascinating analysis of the perpetual threat of Islam, a passage that is worth quoting in full, given the rise of modern Islamic fundamentalism.

There is in Islam a paradox which is perhaps a permanent menace. The great creed born in the desert creates a kind of ecstasy out of the very emptiness of its own land, and even, one may say, out of the emptiness of its own theology. It affirms, with no little sublimity, something that is not merely the singleness but rather the solitude of God. There is the same extreme simplification in the solitary figure of the Prophet; and yet this isolation perpetually reacts into its own opposite. A void is made in the heart of Islam which has to be filled up again and again by a mere repetition of the revolution that founded it. There are no sacraments; the only thing that can happen is a sort of apocalypse, as unique as the end of the world; so the apocalypse can only be repeated and the world end again and again. There are no priests; and yet this equality can only breed a multitude of lawless prophets almost as numerous as priests. The very dogma that there is only one Mahomet produces an endless procession of Mahomets.

Chesterton thought there was 'something truly historic' about Kitchener's 'work with the Fellaheen, or native race of Egypt', with whose aid he had crushed the Mahdi: 'For centuries they had lain as level as the slime of the Nile, and all the conquerors ... had passed over them like a pavement.' The story of the Battle of Omfurman began with 'a terrible triviality ... the new noise heard just before daybreak, revealing the nearness of the enemy: the dreadful drum of Islam, calling for prayer to an awful God—a God not to be worshipped by the changing ... notes of harp or organ, but only by

---

[20] Photocopy, GKCL.

the drum that maddens by mere repetition'. But Kitchener was to find there was something more terrible than the Mahdi, and he 'became the mouthpiece of the national horror at the German fashion of fighting, which he declared to have left a stain upon the whole profession of arms', at the same time dramatically saluting 'across the long stretch of years the comparative chivalry and nobility of his dead enemies of the Soudan' and announcing that 'in the heart of Europe, in learned academies and ordered government offices, there had appeared a lunacy so cruel and unclean that the maddest dervish dead in the desert had a right to disdain it where he lay'. A symbol of imperialism, Kitchener had been 'the supreme figure of that strange and sprawling England which lies beyond England; which carries the habits of English clubs and hotels into the solitudes of the Nile or up the passes of the Himalayas, and is infinitely ignorant of things infinitely nearer home', Cairo being 'nearer than Calais'. But Kitchener had 'passed through Imperialism and reached patriotism', opening 'again the ancient gate of Calais' and leading 'in a new and noble fashion the return of England to Europe'. Finally, he had died while 'seeking what for us his countrymen' had 'long been a dark continent':

The glory of a great people, long hidden from the English by accidents and by lies, lay before him at his journey's end. That journey was never ended.... In that waste of seas beyond the last northern isles where his ship went down one might fancy his spirit standing, a figure frustrated yet prophetic and pointing to the East, whence are the light of the world and the reunion of Christian men.[21]

Three days before leaving for the front in June 1917, Cecil Chesterton arrived after midnight at 'Keith's' flat and demanded she immediately fulfil her promise. It was agreed that they would first get married at what was then her 'church', the Registry Office, and then at Cecil's church, Corpus Christi, Maiden Lane. Just before 'Keith' and Cecil took their marriage vows at the altar, Cecil warned his prospective wife, 'they'll sprinkle you with Holy Water and you'll say my beastly religion has spoilt your hat. But don't worry, I'll buy you a new one!' Cecil's parents, brother, and sister-in-law were present at both ceremonies. So excited was Cecil to be married at last, that he invited the whole congregation after the church service to lunch at the Cheshire Cheese, to the dismay of the management who had been expecting only a few guests and whose famous lark pudding ran out. A number of speeches were made, by, among others, Belloc,

[21] *K.* 380–1, 384–5, 389–90, 397–8.

Conrad Noel, Sir Thomas Beecham, the conductor and wealthy supporter of the *New Witness*, and of course Cecil's brother.[22]

In August Shaw offered Chesterton the opportunity 'to expose a scandalous orgy in the *New Witness*', based on an account by an eyewitness, Shaw himself. The shocking scene, in which Chesterton had featured, that Shaw had witnessed took place at 'an uplifting At Home' at the Fabian Office of 'The Fabian Research Department', of which the 'moving spirit' was Mrs Sidney Webb. A 'large number of young innocent men and women' had been 'attracted to this body by promises of employment by the said Mrs S. W. in works of unlimited and inspiring uplift, such as are unceasingly denounced, along with Marconi and other matters, in your well written organ'. Having summoned 'all these young things', Mrs Webb 'prophesied unto them', as they sat in crowds at her feet, until the prophetess herself withdrew at 'the decent hour of ten o'clock'. Thinking that 'all the young things had gone home', Shaw himself was about to leave when he was 'stunned by the most infernal din . . . coming from the Fabian Hall'.

On rushing to this temple I found the young enthusiasts sprawling over tables, over radiators, over everything except chairs, in a state of scandalous abandonment, roaring at the tops of their voices and in a quite unintelligible manner a string of presumably obscene songs, accompanied on the piano with frantic gestures . . . by a man whom I had always regarded as a respectable Fabian Researcher . . . A horribly sacrilegious character was given to the proceedings by the fact that the tune they were singing when I entered was Luther's hymn *Eine Feste Burg is Unser Gott*. As they went on (for I regret to say that my presence exercised no restraint whatever) they sang their extraordinary and incomprehensible litany to every tune, however august its associations, which happened to fit it. These, if you please, are the solemn and sour neophytes whose puritanical influence has kept you in dread for so many years.

But I have not told you the worst. Before I fled from the building I did at last discover what words it was they were singing. When it first flashed on me, I really could not believe it. But at the end of the next verse no doubt or error was possible. The young maenad nearest me was concluding every strophe by shrieking that she didnt [*sic*] care where the water went if it didnt [*sic*] get into the wine. Now you know.

Shaw concluded: 'This letter needs no answer—indeed, admits of none. I leave you to your reflections.'[23] 'But I don't care where the water goes if it doesn't get into the wine' is the refrain that ends each stanza of one of

[22] MCC 202–4.
[23] Ward, *GKC* 348–9, with text corrected from BL Add. MS 73198, fos. 79–80.

1. The young Gilbert Keith Chesterton, aged 7 or 8, with his younger brother Cecil.

2. Chesterton's childhood home, 11 Warwick Gardens, Kensington.

3. Members of the Junior Debating Club, St. Paul's School. Chesterton is on the third row on the left.

4. Chesterton and Frances Blogg before their marriage.

1. The young Gilbert Keith Chesterton,
aged 7 or 8, with his younger brother Cecil.

2. Chesterton's childhood home,
11 Warwick Gardens, Kensington.

3. Members of the Junior
Debating Club, St. Paul's
School. Chesterton is on the
third row on the left.

4. Chesterton and Frances
Blogg before their marriage.

5 Frances Chesterton, 1901, the year of her marriage.

6. Frances Chesterton at the time of her marriage.

7. Overstrand Mansions, Battersea, where the Chestertons lived from 1901 to 1909.

8. Cecil Chesterton sometime before his death in 1918.

9. Overroads, Beaconsfield, where the Chestertons lived from 1909 to 1922.

10. Chesterton sometime before 1920.

11. Chesterton *c.* 1920.

12. Chesterton and Frances in 1922.

13. Studio portrait of Chesterton by Howard Coster, 1926.

14. Chesterton with his host, Fr Michael Earls, S.J., at Holy Cross College, Massachussets, when he lectured there in December 1930.

15. Top Meadow, Beaconsfield, where the Chestertons lived from 1922.

16. Chesterton and Dorothy Collins with a young friend, Manhattan Beach, California, 14 February 1931.

Chesterton's most famous nonsense poems, originally published in *The Flying Inn* and reprinted in *Wine, Water and Song* under the title 'Wine and Water', which begins with the delightful stanza:

> Old Noah he had an ostrich farm and fowls on the largest scale,
> He ate his egg with a ladle in a egg-cup big as a pail,
> And the soup he took was Elephant Soup and the fish he took was Whale,
> But they all were small to the cellar he took when he set out to sail,
> And Noah he often said to his wife when he sat down to dine,
> 'I don't care where the water goes if it doesn't get into the wine.'[24]

In October Chesterton published *A Short History of England*. He had been asked to write a history by the publishers Chatto & Windus, but had refused on the ground that he was no historian. However, later he had signed a contract for a book of essays, only to discover that he was already contracted to give this book to another publisher. On asking Chatto & Windus to cancel the contract on the condition that he would do another book for them, he was reminded to his dismay of their original proposal for a short history of England.[25]

Chesterton begins his history by stressing that Britain was originally a province of the Roman Empire. Far from its origins being Germanic, as it had become the fashion to believe, at least before the First World War with Germany, the truth was that it had been 'directly Roman for fully four hundred years'. The 'important thing' about both France and England was not 'that they have Roman remains. They are Roman remains.' Before the war, English life had been 'overshadowed by Germany'. Social reforms like Lloyd George's National Insurance Act had been 'modelled upon Germany'. Religion, too, had been affected: 'German metaphysics had thinned our theology...'. So much had German history 'simply annexed English history... that it was almost counted the duty of any patriotic Englishman to be proud of being a German'. It was partly 'the genius of Carlyle' and 'the culture of Matthew Arnold' that were responsible, partly British foreign policy that persisted, even in the face of German aggression against its European neighbours, in the traditional belief that, ever since the victory over Napoleon at Waterloo, Germany was Britain's natural ally.[26]

Inevitably, Chesterton's enthusiasm for the Middle Ages takes up commensurate space in his short history. He enjoys the paradox that the very word 'monk' 'means solitude and came to mean community—one might

---

[24] *CP* i. 490.   [25] Ward, *GKC* 355.   [26] *SHE* 429, 584–5.

call it sociality'. Far from rejecting this world, the monasteries 'kept the world's diary, faced the plagues of all flesh, taught the first technical arts, preserved the pagan literature, and above all, by a perpetual patchwork of charity, kept the poor from the most distant sight of their modern despair'. In addition, the abbots and abbesses were elected, thus introducing 'representative government'. But medieval society anyway had 'a self-government' that was 'self-made' through the guild system, of which the 'attenuated and threatened' modern trade unions were but 'a ghost'. Medieval chivalry, on the other hand, was 'an attempt to bring the justice and even the logic of the Catholic creed into a military system which already existed'. The Middle Ages were supposed to be backward, but Chesterton wondered if 'it is a self-evident step in progress that their holidays were derived from saints, while ours are dictated by bankers'. Characteristically, he resorts to the use of grotesque examples to make our imaginations grasp the revolutionary concept of the Catholic saint:

The notion of an eminence merely moral, consistent with complete stupidity or unsuccess, is a revolutionary image grown unfamiliar by its very familiarity, and needing, as do so many things of this older society, some almost preposterous modern parallel to give its original freshness and point. If we entered a foreign town and found a pillar like the Nelson Column, we should be surprised to learn that the hero on the top of it had been famous for his politeness and hilarity during a chronic toothache. If a procession came down the street with a brass band and a hero on a white horse, we should think it odd to be told that he had been very patient with a half-witted maiden aunt.

The medieval 'craving for equality' found expression not only in the guilds but also in the idea of 'communal land for peasants'. The capitalists were the Jews, and 'the real unfairness' of their position was that Christian kings, nobles, and even popes and bishops, 'used . . . the money that could only be accumulated in such mountains by a usury they inconsistently denounced as unchristian; and then, when worse times came, gave up the Jew to the fury of the poor whom that useful usury had ruined'. The Jew might well feel oppressed, but unfortunately the Christian equally felt the Jew to be the oppressor—'and that *mutual* charge of tyranny is the Semitic trouble in all times'.[27]

As for Islam, Chesterton saw it as 'following' Christianity 'like its gigantic shadow', having arisen in the same Eastern lands as Christianity about six hundred years afterwards. Its 'highest motive was a hatred of

---

[27] *SHE* 449, 469, 473, 484–5, 488, 498.

idols, and in its view Incarnation itself was an idolatry. The two things it persecuted were the idea of God being made flesh and of His being afterwards made wood or stone.' 'In this sense,' then, 'Islam was something like a Christian heresy': 'The early heresies had been full of mad reversals and evasions of the Incarnation . . .'. But there is one peculiarly Chestertonian objection to Islam: 'It was an element in this sublime and yet sinister simplicity of Islam that it knew no boundaries. Its very home was homeless. For it was born in a sandy waste among nomads, and it went everywhere because it came from nowhere.' The contrast between Islam and Christianity was entirely in the latter's favour: 'The mystery of locality, with all its hold on the human heart, was as much present in the most ethereal things of Christendom as it was absent from the most practical things of Islam.'[28]

Christmas was the one major survivor from pre-Reformation Catholic England, although only its 'remains', which had to be 'rescued from the Puritans' and later 'eventually to be rescued again by Dickens from the Utilitarians, and may yet have to be rescued by somebody from the vegetarians and teetotallers'. But there remained vestiges of Catholicism in the Church of England, whether one called the phenomenon 'the Catholic continuity of Anglicanism or merely the slow extirpation of Catholicism'. This ambiguity meant that the Church of England remained a most unusual institution, for the continuing debate about the Church of England was not what it 'ought to do' or whether it 'ought to alter', but rather 'about what that institution actually is'.[29]

At the Reformation, Henry VIII's dissolution of the monasteries led to the enrichment not of the King but of the rich, 'and especially of the new rich'. The destruction of 'the institutions of the poor' involved not only the monasteries but also the guilds. It was Chesterton's hero Cobbett who saw 'the Reformation as the root of both squirearchy and industrialism'. For Chesterton, the real threat always came not from the king but from the nobles, for 'one of the virtues of a despot is distance': 'It is "the little tyrant of the fields" that poisons human life. . . . even a bad king is a good king, for his oppression weakens the nobility and relieves the pressure on the populace.' Despotism can be justified as 'democratic': 'As a rule its cruelty to the strong is kindness to the weak.' It puts 'a limit to the ambitions of the rich'. It was significant that 'England was never so little of a democracy as during the short time when she was a republic'. The Americans forced the

---

[28] *SHE* 465–7.   [29] *SHE* 544–5, 547–8.

war of independence not simply because they wished to be separate from
the mother country but because they wished to be free: 'She was not
thinking of her wrongs as a colony, but already of her rights as a republic.'
But the one thing England was not prepared to grant to the colonists was
'equality', not equality with England but 'even with each other'. It was
impossible for the rulers of England even to conceive of 'a country not
governed by gentlemen'. As for Burke, he would have been as 'appalled'
by American democracy as he was by French democracy. The very idea of
the equality of men 'seemed startling and indecent to a society whose
whole romance and religion now consisted of the importance of a gentleman'. Nevertheless in England 'the typical aristocrat was the typical
upstart', whose family was 'founded on stealing' and whose 'family was
stealing still': 'Parliament was passing bill after bill for the enclosure, by the
great landlords, of such of the common lands as had survived out of the
great communal system of the Middle Ages. It is much more than a pun, it
is the prime political irony of our history, that the Commons were destroying the commons.' If the Commons are no longer the commons, so too 'the
Public Schools were once undoubtedly public'. But, in spite of the lack of
equality and democracy, in spite of the enrichment of the rich and the
impoverishment of the poor, England had, Chesterton thought, not lost its
sense of humour: 'An illogical laughter survives everything in the English
soul.'

That sort of liberty, that sort of humanity, and it is no mean sort, did indeed
survive all the drift and downward eddy of an evil economic system, as well as the
dragooning of a reactionary epoch and the drearier menace of materialistic social
science, as embodied in the new Puritans, who have purified themselves even of
religion. Under this long process, the worst that can be said is that the English
humourist has been slowly driven downwards in the social scale. Falstaff was a
knight, Sam Weller was a gentleman's servant, and some of our recent restrictions
seem designed to drive Sam Weller to the status of the Artful Dodger.

And so 'some such trampled tradition and dark memory of Merry
England' had survived. The English people had managed to retain 'the
laughter that had become almost the religion of the race': 'And men might
know of what nation Shakespeare was, who broke into puns and practical
jokes in the darkest passion of his tragedies, if they had only heard those
boys in France and Flanders who called out "Early doors!" themselves
in a theatrical memory, as they went so early in their youth to break
down the doors of death.' ('Early doors', now an obsolete expression,
was used of anyone who arrived long before they were expected, in this

case by the German enemy.) Who were these 'boys'? For the most part, 'the English poor, broken in every revolt, long despoiled of property, and now being despoiled of liberty', who now 'entered history with a noise of trumpets, and turned themselves in two years into one of the iron armies of the world'.[30]

The year 1917 also saw the publication in New York of *Utopia of Usurers and Other Essays*, which comprised nine articles under the general title of *Utopia of Usurers* as well as seventeen other articles originally published in the *Daily Herald* in 1913 and 1914. The 'first and fundamental fact of our time' for Chesterton is that 'the capitalists of our community are becoming quite openly the kings of it'. This was not surprising, given that the English 'system has been aristocratic: in the special sense of there being only a few actors on the stage'. And Chesterton blames 'the absence of something one may call the democratic imagination'. This helped also partly to explain English intellectuals' contempt for the masses. For the English 'find it easy to realise an individual, but very hard to realise that the great masses consist of individuals'. Now the capitalist had 'managed to create' 'a certain hazy association . . . between the idea of bigness and the idea of practicality'. There had resulted 'this queer idolatry of the enormous and elaborate', the assumption that 'anything so complicated must go like clockwork'. Every serious religion or philosophy of life, Chesterton thought, must have 'some trace of the doctrine of the equality of men', but capitalism 'really depends on some religion of inequality'. This means that the capitalist is always ready to make exceptions in his favour and cannot accept any hard and fast limitations: 'The religion of the Servile State must have no dogmas or definitions. It cannot afford to have any definitions. For definitions are very dreadful things: they do the two things that most men, especially comfortable men, cannot endure. They fight; and they fight fair.' Definitions and dogmas impose limitations, but there can be no limitations for the capitalist: 'Modern broad-mindedness benefits the rich; and benefits nobody else.' Islam is even-handed in its ban on alcohol, but the capitalist will make a distinction between the gin that the poor drink and the champagne that he drinks; Catholicism condemns usury, but the capitalist distinguishes 'more delicately between two kinds of usury; the kind he finds useful and the kind he does not find useful'. To improve the conditions of the workers would increase their output, but that would be expensive for the capitalist—so 'there one day came into his

---

[30] *SHE* 479, 506, 525, 527, 539, 552, 554, 561–3, 570, 573, 576–7, 587–8, 590.

mind a new and curious idea—one of the most strange, simple, and horrible ideas that have ever risen from the deep pit of original sin'. There would be one way 'to have some physical improvement without any moral, political, or social improvement. It might be possible to keep a supply of strong and healthy slaves without coddling them with decent conditions.' 'That is what', Chesterton concludes, 'Eugenics means; and that is all that it means'. Another means of control for the capitalist is through imprisonment, which could 'become an almost universal experience'. Prison conditions might be made 'more humane only in order to contain more of humanity'. It would no longer be 'a question of whether the law has been broken by a crime; but, now, solely a question of whether the situation could be mended by an imprisonment'. Another strategy for the capitalist would be to 'make the Servile State *look* rather like Socialism'. Such a 'Plutocracy, pretending to be a Bureaucracy', might be successfully achieved: after all, 'the rich man to-day does not only rule by using private property; he also rules by treating public property as if it were private property'. And Chesterton cannot avoid the temptation of referring to the Marconi scandal, pointing out that Lloyd George's salaries as a Member of Parliament and Minister were nothing to what 'he might at any time get . . . by speculating on State secrets that are necessarily known to him'.[31]

The 'poison' of the 'Servile State' for Chesterton is 'very largely a Prussian poison', for 'Prussia is capitalism' and 'her Servile State is complete, while ours is incomplete'. All the legislation of the Prussian Servile State is 'designed . . . to protect a man from *himself*'. This will include 'restraining' as opposed to 'punishing' a man. There is a very important distinction: 'The moral difference is that a man can be punished for a crime because he is born a citizen; while he can be constrained because he is born a slave.' Punishment assumes that 'the extent of the evil is known, and that a certain amount of expiation goes with it', whereas 'medical restraint . . . may go on as long as the authorities choose to think (or say) that it ought to go on'. In the case of punishment 'the past . . . is supposed to have been investigated', whereas 'restraint refers to the future, which his doctors, keepers, and wardens have yet to investigate'. In the 'Servile State' the 'appetite for liberty' was disappearing. The 'philanthropic' capitalist employer liked to enquire whether 'a woman who has given up all she loved to death and the fatherland has or has not shown some weakness in her seeking for self-comfort'. In his turn, Chesterton wanted to record some 'simple truths'. First,

---

[31] *UU* 409, 414–15, 421–2, 424, 428, 435–6.

beer, which is largely drunk in public-houses, is not a spirit or a grog or a cocktail or a drug. It is the common English liquid for quenching the thirst... To tell a poor woman that she must not have any until half the day is over is... like telling a dog or a child that he must not have water.

Secondly, the 'public-house is not a secret rendezvous of bad characters. It is the open and obvious place for a certain purpose.' Not least, thirdly, is this true of the poor, who 'live in houses where they cannot, without great preparation, offer hospitality', and who, fourthly, live in a climate that 'does not favour conducting long conversations with one's oldest friends on an iron bench in the park'. Fifthly, 'half-past eleven a.m. is not early in the day for a woman who gets up before six'. And, sixthly, 'the bodies and minds of these women belong to God and to themselves'.[32]

Apart from the restraints imposed upon the poor, there were the lies and misrepresentations. One thing, Chesterton thought, that was very much needed was 'A Working-Man's History of England', which would demolish the current version of English history, which held that the country had 'emerged slowly from a semi-barbarism in which all the power and wealth were in the hands of Kings and a few nobles; that the King's power was broken first and then in due time that of the nobles, that this piece-meal improvement was brought about by one class after another waking up to a sense of citizenship... until we practically became a democracy...'. Such was the official, accepted view—'and there is not one word of truth in it from beginning to end'. Apart from the fact that power and wealth were 'very much more popularly distributed in the Middle Ages than they are now', the gradual extension of the franchise was granted 'solely for the convenience of the aristocrats': 'The Great Reform Bill was passed in order to seal an alliance between the landed aristocrats and the rich manufacturers of the north,' as well as in order 'to *prevent* the English populace getting any political power in the general excitement after the French revolution'. As for 'Disraeli's further extension of the suffrage', this was 'effected by a politician who saw an opportunity to dish the Whigs, and guessed that certain orthodoxies in the more prosperous artisan might yet give him a balance against the commercial Radicals'. While all this political manœuvring was going on, 'the solid and real thing that was going on was the steady despoiling of the poor of all power or wealth, until they find themselves to-day upon the threshold of slavery'. There was also the

[32] *UU* 444–5, 479–80, 495, 499.

same kind of misinformation and misunderstanding about the so-called popular press: 'The point about the Press is that it is not what it is called. It is not the "popular Press". It is not the Public Press. It is not an organ of public opinion. It is a conspiracy of a very few millionaires...'. Again, there was 'the notion that the Press is flashy or trivial *because* it is popular. In other words, an attempt is made to discredit democracy by representing journalism as the natural literature of democracy'. In fact, it was the natural literature of the millionaire proprietors who 'are silly and vulgar'.[33]

3

On 22 March 1918 Chesterton published in the *New Witness* the first of five articles on the subject of divorce, about which there was much controversy at the time in the press. In January 1920 he republished the articles in a book called *The Superstition of Divorce*; he had found it 'very difficult to recast even in order to expand', and had 'therefore decided to reprint the original articles as they stood, save for a few introductory words; and then, at the risk of repetition, to add a few further chapters, explaining more fully any conceptions that may seem to have been too crudely assumed or dismissed'.[34] The original five articles form the first third of the book.

Chesterton begins with the obvious point that it makes no sense to talk about divorce without first talking about marriage: people say they want divorce—but do they want marriage? As an illustration he takes his own fondness for the limitation yet liberation of windows: 'there is nothing I feel to be so beautiful and wonderful as a window. All casements are magical casements, whether they open on the foam or the front-garden; they lie close to the ultimate mystery and paradox of limitation and liberty.' For a window, which is defined by the limits of its frame, offers the freedom of access to the outside world. But, if a house were made up entirely of windows there would be no walls and therefore no windows. Even more basically, if one wants windows, one has first to want a house. There is therefore no point in wanting divorce if one does not first want marriage. Now marriage, Chesterton insists, is as natural as the 'brotherhood of men'; neither is founded simply on certain texts in the Bible—although there are these texts and although it may come about that only Christians will affirm either. For upon the attraction between men and women depends 'the renewal of the race itself'. Chesterton defines marriage as a

---

[33] *UU* 450–2, 500–1.   [34] *SD* 227.

promise or rather a vow. And it is a limitation, since it is a promise or vow 'to bind oneself. For the vow is a tryst with oneself.' Being of all vows 'the vow made most freely', one would expect it to be 'the vow kept most firmly'. And the loyalty it should inspire should be stronger than, for example, patriotism, since one does not choose one's country, whereas marriage is 'a voluntary loyalty'. But the advocates of divorce 'hold that vow or violation, loyalty or disloyalty, can all be disposed of by a mysterious and magic rite, performed first in a law-court and then in a church or a registry office'. This was the rankest 'superstition', 'sheer barbarous credulity'. The Christian Middle Ages were 'the age of vows', pagan antiquity 'the age of status', and a 'sceptical modernity has been the age of contracts; or rather has tried to be, and has failed'. A slave was a slave in antiquity 'merely by status', whereas a medieval serf took a vow. Similarly, medieval tradesmen in a guild took 'something like the vow of knighthood', having made 'the free choice of a fixed estate'. This was 'the vital revolt and innovation of vows, as compared with castes or slavery'. It was 'the personal pledge, feudal or civic or monastic', which 'was the way in which the world did escape from the system of slavery'—and 'the modern breakdown of mere contract leaves it still doubtful if there be any other way of escaping it in the future'. The idea or ideal of the vow is 'to combine the fixity that goes with finality with the self-respect that only goes with freedom'; it was the only way history had found of 'combining . . . stability with any sort of freedom'. It was Henry VIII who destroyed the 'civilisation of vows' when he 'broke his own vow of marriage'. He also destroyed the monasteries 'that had been built by vows'. What had begun with 'divorce for a king' had ended in 'divorces for a whole kingdom'. Of course, vows like any valuable cause asked people 'to suffer abnegations'. The fallacy, Chesterton thought, that lay behind the desire for divorce was the 'fallacy of being universal', a 'bottomless ambition', an 'unnatural hunger' for 'the impossible, that is the universal', the desire 'to try every situation', an inability to 'refuse any' and therefore to 'resolve on any'. What, on the contrary, was 'vitally needed' in every area of modern life was 'choice; a creative power in the will as well as in the mind'. In short, the need was for that very Chestertonian power of 'self-limitation'.[35]

But marriage was also threatened by the capitalist state, which was 'at war with the family', because, while it believed in 'collectivism for itself', it believed in 'individualism for its enemies':

---

[35] *SD* 229, 231, 233, 235, 237, 253, 264–9, 279, 289–90.

If there be any bond, if there be any brotherhood, if there be any class loyalty or domestic discipline, by which the poor can help the poor, these emancipators will certainly strive to loosen that bond or lift that discipline in the most liberal fashion. If there be any brotherhood, these individualists will redistribute it in the form of individuals; or in other words smash it to atoms.

And the reason why the 'Servile State' wished to destroy marriage was because without 'the family we are helpless before the State'. It was true that Socialism attacked the family 'in theory', but it was 'far more certain that Capitalism attacks it in practice'. Capitalists recognized 'the vow as the vital antithesis to servile status; the alternative and therefore the antagonist. Marriage makes a small state within the state, which resists ... regimentation.' What the Capitalist state feared 'in the most literal sense' was 'home rule'. Not surprisingly, it was precisely those societies that 'have been conservative about the family who have been revolutionary about the state'. The truth is that 'that social pressure from below which we call freedom is vital to the health of the State; and this it is which cannot be fully exercised by individuals, but only by groups and traditions', among which there was only one 'which all human beings have a spontaneous and omnipresent inspiration to build for themselves; and this ... is the family'. But, because marriage is 'an ideal and an institution making for popular freedom', it 'has to be paid for in vigilance and pain'.[36]

The 'tremendous' consequence of marriage, this 'institution that puzzles intellectuals so much', is, of course, children—who 'are, generally speaking, younger than their parents', a fact that is 'perceptible even to intellectuals'. For children mean 'the renewal of the race itself'. And it is only common sense that 'the only people who either can or will give individual care, to each of the individual children, are their individual parents'. But common sense has been cast out of the modern 'academy of fads and fashions conducted on the lines of a luxurious madhouse'. Thus the archetypal story of the marriage at Cana had met with disapproval from that 'school of prigs who disapprove of wine; and there may now be a school of prigs who disapprove of the wedding'. The contrast between the attempts to liberalize the laws on divorce and euthanasia and the curtailment of other freedoms was striking. Socialists, Tories and Liberals alike were united in their efforts 'to destroy the independence of Englishmen': 'As all these doors were successfully shut in our faces along the chilly and cheerless corridor of progress ... the doors of death and divorce alone

---

[36] *SD* 241–2, 245–7, 260, 270, 275.

stood open, or rather opened wider and wider.' What was 'the meaning of this mysterious immunity, this special permit for adultery'? Why was a man constrained by

Labour Exchanges, Insurance cards, Welfare Work, and a hundred forms of police inspection and supervision . . . allowed to go to look for a new wife? He is more and more compelled to recognise a Moslem code about liquor; why is it made easy for him to escape from his old Christian code about sex? . . . Why must he love as he pleases; when he may not even live as he pleases?

The new proposals for divorce suffered from 'the modern and morbid weaknesses of always sacrificing the normal to the abnormal', of allowing 'the exception . . . to alter the rule'. The man who was unhappily married and had got himself 'into a hole' was 'allowed to burrow in it like a rabbit and undermine a whole countryside'. It was said, 'with a monotonous metaphor, that we cannot put the clock back'. But what if the clock had stopped? For there was nothing 'so hopeless as clockwork when it stops. A machine cannot mend itself; it requires a man to mend it; and the future lies with those who can make living laws for men and not merely dead laws for machinery.'[37] In hindsight, Chesterton can be seen to have been over-optimistic. What, of course, he was witnessing was the gradual de-Christianization and secularization of the country, whereby restrictions imposed by Christianity were being relaxed and replaced, as though by compensation, by new secular restrictions.

4

On 11 April 1918 the inaugural meeting of the New Witness League was held in London at Essex Hall, at which Chesterton announced the objectives of the League. There were five: to prosecute the war to a victorious conclusion, to fight against political corruption, to restore civil liberties curtailed by Parliament in the interests of the war effort, to support small nations, and to build up an organization to publicize the League's objectives and to expose political corruption. Chesterton was elected president. There were debates and talks at subsequent meetings.[38]

Meanwhile that spring Cecil Chesterton was discharged from active service because of a septic hand and sent to the regimental office in Scotland to recuperate, where he carried out light desk duties. 'Keith' visited him

---

[37] *SD* 237–41, 247–9, 253–4, 288.   [38] Ffinch, 248–9.

there and secured a promise that he would not volunteer again for active service. However, the news from the front grew worse and reinforcements were desperately needed, so Cecil broke his promise and once again volunteered for the front. 'Keith's' 'telegram of joy' to him on 11 November, Armistice Day, was left unanswered, although he had always written regularly to her. A few days later a delayed letter did reach her, explaining that 'he had not been feeling at all well, but had not gone sick until after the Armistice, when he felt he could be spared from the line. He wrote from a hospital at Wimereux, and there was an underlying note of pain and disappointment that gave me a queer foreboding...'. In fact, she later learned that after

reporting sick he had had to march from Ypres for twelve miles in the heavy rain, until at last the Officer Commanding, seeing how ill he was, told him to fall out. He was by then soaked through and through and when, after a long train journey and a bumpy passage in a lorry, he finally reached the base, he was seriously ill with nephritis.

A couple of days later, 'Keith' received a telegram, which had also been delayed, from the War Office to say that 'Private Chesterton was on the danger list, but regretted that owing to transport difficulties [she] could not be allowed to visit him'. Had Cecil been an officer, transport would have been arranged for her. To get a journalist's pass would take three days. Fortunately, her brother-in-law had contacted Maurice Baring, who was able to pull strings, and 'Keith' left for France. There she was confronted at the hospital by the matron, who coldly demanded to know why she had not come weeks before in response to a telegram they had sent; it had apparently gone astray. Cecil spoke 'a little wistfully' about things at home but declared he was feeling much better. During the night his condition worsened, and when dawn came he clutched 'Keith's' hand and smiling said, 'It's good-bye...'. She telegraphed her brother-in-law, who got Frances to break the news to his mother ('which added to her hurt', according to 'Keith')—he 'could not face his brother's death'. Of the family only 'Keith' was present at Cecil's burial in a military cemetery.[39]

On 13 December, exactly a week after his brother's death on 6 December, Chesterton wrote somewhat ambiguously in his editorial in the *New Witness* that his brother had 'died in France of the effects of the last days of the fighting', as though he might have died while actually in action. 'The work which he put first he did before he died. The work which he put second, but

[39] MCC 219–20, 224, 233–8.

very near to the other, he left for us to do. There are many of us who will abandon many other things, and recognise no greater duty than to do it.' In his *Autobiography* Chesterton eulogized his brother as one who 'alone of all the men of our time possessed the two kinds of courage that have nourished the nation; the courage of the forum and of the field', implying even more strongly that he had actually died in action: 'In the second case he suffered with thousands of men equally brave; in the first he suffered alone. For it is another example of the human irony that it seems easier to die in battle than to tell the truth in politics.' However, Cecil had as good as died in battle, and his brother cannot be blamed for a very excusable slight exaggeration. In the same issue of the *New Witness*, Belloc also praised Cecil's courage: 'He never in his life checked an action or a word from consideration of personal caution, and that is more than can be said of any other man of his time.'[40] As for Chesterton, in his grief, he wrote in his 'At the Sign of the World's End' column 'An Open Letter to Lord Reading', the former Sir Rufus Isaacs. Since January 1918 Reading had been acting as the ambassador-extraordinary and high commissioner in Washington, as well as being lord chief justice. He was now attending the Peace Conference in Paris with Lloyd George, who was now prime minister. At this crucial juncture when the future of Europe was to be decided, it was humiliating, Chesterton considered, that Britain should be represented by the two ministers involved in the Marconi scandal. In his well-known satirical poem 'Elegy in a Country Churchyard', Chesterton complained bitterly:

> The men that worked for England
> They have their graves at home:
> And bees and birds of England
> About the cross can roam.

> But they that fought for England,
> Following a falling star,
> Alas, alas for England
> They have their graves afar.

> And they that rule in England,
> In stately conclave met,
> Alas, alas for England
> They have no graves as yet.[41]

Ironically, before Cecil had died, Godfrey Isaacs had in effect been found guilty in court of perjury in an action he had taken against a

---

[40] *A.* 240–1; Ward, *GKC* 358; Ffinch, 250–1.   [41] *CP* i. 389.

Liberal politician. His brother, Chesterton wrote in his open letter to Lord Reading with not a little inaccuracy, had 'found death in the trenches to which he had freely gone'; while Godfrey Isaacs had 'found dismissal in those very Courts to which he had once successfully appealed': 'You are far more unhappy; for your brother is still alive.' Isaacs was, of course, he continued, 'a blot on the English landscape' and 'the political men who made you are the creeping things of the earth'. But Chesterton was willing to believe that in the Marconi scandal 'it was the mutual dependence of the members of your family' that had 'necessitated the sacrifice of the dignity and independence of my country', and that, if it was 'decreed that the English nation is to lose its public honour, it will be partly because certain men of the tribe of Isaacs kept their own strange private loyalty'. And he was willing to count this as a virtue 'as your own code may interpret virtue; but the fact would alone be enough to make me protest against any man professing your code and administering our law'. It was not, he claimed, a 'question of disliking any race' nor 'even a question of disliking any individual'. But it was a question of Jewish international financiers wanting in their own interests to protect the German states, headed by Prussia. In particular, there was the question of Poland:

Are we to lose the War which we have already won? That and nothing else is involved in losing the full satisfaction of the national claim of Poland. Is there any man who doubts that the Jewish International is unsympathetic with that full national demand? And is there any man who doubts that you will be sympathetic with the Jewish International?

To send the 'the chief Marconi Minister as our chief Foreign Minister' was to send 'a man who is a standing joke against England'. His very name in the countries he was going to have to deal with was 'a sort of pantomime proverb like Panama or the South Sea Bubble'. Did Lord Reading, Chesterton demanded, have 'the serious impudence' to call Chesterton and his friends 'Anti-Semites because we are not so extravagantly fond of one particular Jew as to endure this for him alone'? Sometimes Chesterton wondered whether Jews like Isaacs felt their position to be

unreal, a mere masquerade; as I myself might feel it if, by some fantastic luck in the old fantastic civilisation of China, I were raised from the Yellow Button to the Coral Button, or from the Coral Button to the Peacock's Feather. Precisely because these things would be grotesque, I might hardly feel them as incongruous. Precisely because they meant nothing to me I might be satisfied with them, I might enjoy them without any shame at my own impudence as an alien adventurer. Precisely because I could not feel them as dignified, I should not know what I had degraded.

He had often tried 'to imagine and allow for an alien psychology in this matter', and he recommended Lord Reading 'and Jews far worthier than you' not to 'dismiss as Anti-Semitism what may well prove the last serious attempt to sympathise with Semitism'. He, Chesterton, he insisted, allowed for Lord Reading's 'position more than most men allow for it; more, most assuredly, than most men *will* allow for it in the darker days that yet may come'. It was 'utterly false to suggest' that either he or his brother, 'a better man than I, whose work I now inherit, desired this disaster for you and yours, I wish you no such ghastly retribution. Daniel son of Isaac, Go in peace; but go.'[42] In his *Autobiography*, Chesterton claimed that he had tried to write 'with all restraint', believing that Rufus Isaacs 'had really acted against my nation, but in favour of his own blood; and that he who had talked, and doubtless despised even in talking, the tedious Parliamentary foolery about having once met his brother at a family function, had in truth acted throughout from those deep domestic loyalties that were my own tragedy in that hour'.[43] To later readers, the letter seems utterly anti-Semitic—and the question of Chesterton's alleged anti-Semitism will be discussed in due course[44]—but the fact remains that a 'ghastly retribution' would not fall upon Lord Reading but within a couple of decades upon the whole hapless Jewish people at the hands of the very nation that Rufus Isaacs had allegedly gone to Paris to protect. For Chesterton and the *New Witness*, the overwhelming priority was to ensure that a strong Prussia at the head of Germany would never again be a threat to the peace of Europe. But of hardly less importance was the strengthening of Poland and a return to its historic boundaries, which included in particular the port of Danzig, which could give Poland access to Western Europe, and East Prussia, where the majority of the population was Polish. In the event, the Treaty of Versailles (the result of the Peace Conference that had begun in January 1919), which was signed on 28 June 1919 and which humiliated but only weakened Germany in the short term, was for Chesterton and the *New Witness* a complete disaster—as, indeed, it proved to be, since it aroused great German resentment but failed to render it sufficiently weak. French public opinion had called for the crippling of Germany through massive reparations, but Britain and the United States were unwilling to lose an

---

[42] Ward, *GKC* 359–62.   [43] *A.* 241.   [44] See below, pp. 421–4.

important trading partner and feared the threat from revolutionary Communist Russia. As for the ineffectual League of Nations that was supposed to guarantee peace, it appealed to the idealistic American President Wilson, who was at least as ignorant as Lloyd George of the realities of continental European politics, to international finance, and to pacifist opinion strengthened by the horrors of the recent war.[45]

According to Titterton, Cecil Chesterton's widow was 'unable to carry on' as assistant editor for a year after her husband's death; but he saw no reason to go into 'details' as to why not.[46] At her suggestion, Titterton succeeded her. 'Keith' herself said that she 'could not have borne just then to live and breathe and have my being in the Street where Cecil and I had worked together and planned and loved together'. But she had contemplated the alternative, enduring 'familiar surroundings until time softened the sting of reiterated memory'.[47] It seems, however, as will shortly become clear, that her brother-in-law also put some pressure on her to go— Titterton's reference to 'details' suggests that 'Keith's' reason for going was not the only one. As for Chesterton himself, editing was hardly his natural avocation. Nor would politics, he wrote in the paper, ever 'have been my province, either in the highest or the lowest sense'. He had hitherto thought of himself as 'merely a stop-gap', but this had 'terribly' changed:

I must now either accept this duty entirely or abandon it entirely. I will not abandon it; for every instinct and nerve of intelligence I have tells me that this is a time when it must not be abandoned. I must accept a comparison that must be a contrast, and a crushing contrast; but though I can never be as good as my brother, I will see if I can be better than myself.

There was, however, one way in which he would be a better editor than his brother: he was much less reckless and indifferent about checking his facts. He told a contributor whose article had been held up while its accuracy was checked that, while he did not fear a lawsuit or even a fine or imprisonment, what he did dread was printing something that was untrue.[48] Nevertheless, while Chesterton was proud of being a journalist, being an editor was a very different matter: it involved responsibilities and the need to make decisions, duties that did not pertain to a newspaper columnist. Nor was his wife at all happy about it: 'It seemed to her too great a drain on his time and energy: it made the writing of his important

[45] Ward, *GKC* 362–5. [46] Titterton, 111. [47] MCC 241.
[48] Ward, *GKC* 367–8.

books more difficult.' Although she would not attempt to dissuade him, she would have been delighted if he had decided not to attempt to carry on his brother's work.[49] Apart from anything else, the *New Witness* needed constant injections of cash, most of which had to come from Chesterton himself, although Sir Thomas Beecham, who joined the editorial board, invested some capital.[50]

During the spring and summer of 1919 Chesterton and Belloc discussed the possibility of Belloc returning as editor. But there was a problem. While Belloc had liked Cecil Chesterton and sympathized with many of his ideas, he had thought him a bad editor, drawing his contributors from too small a clique. The paper was not sufficiently 'broad' and 'diversified' and 'witty', he told Maurice Baring in 1913, and, while he entirely agreed with the paper's hostility to 'Jewish financial power', it was 'essential to avoid anything like the suspicion of fanaticism': 'I think it is particularly silly to turn the one independent paper we still have into a monotonous mass of repetition upon the one single question of the hundred it should deal with.' But his advice had always been ignored and the points which he had emphasied when he was editor had been 'quite abandoned'.[51] There was, therefore, no chance that Belloc would resume editorship if 'Keith' Chesterton returned as assistant editor.

On 22 April 1919 Chesterton wrote to Belloc: 'You know the somewhat delicate personal situation with which I should have to deal first; but I brought it off once before; and I have little doubt that if necessary I could do it again.'[52] Chesterton must here be referring to his persuading 'Keith' to relinquish, at least temporarily, the assistant editorship the previous year when he took over as permanent editor. On 3 May he wrote again to say that, while he agreed with Belloc about the 'policy' the paper should pursue, 'there are certain limits to my action which I will not pass even for a good public object.'

My sister-in-law is my sister-in-law; and, apart from my sympathy for her, she is not and never has been a person I could treat like an ordinary subordinate on what was, after all, my brother's paper when he died. If it were a property, she would be the heiress. . . . This being so, I have to get her consent in a free and friendly fashion. As you know, I once got it; but the very way in which I got it

---

[49] Ward, *GKC* 381.   [50] MCC 183.

[51] Robert Speaight, *The Life of Hilaire Belloc* (London: Hollis & Carter, 1957), 362–4.

[52] G. K. Chesterton to Hilaire Belloc, 22 Apr. [1919], JJBL.

happens to make it a rather different matter to get it again; though I still have every hope of doing so. I got it by saying that you alone could get the paper financed (as you then had good hopes of doing) and that if you financed it, you would naturally want to manage it. Now of course my own real reasons for wanting you go far beyond this; but you will see the logical difficulty of insisting on you without the funds, when I had only insisted on you because of the funds. I put it thus baldly, knowing that you prefer lucidity to good taste. I must have some special reason for re-opening the matter at this time . . . I think I can manage it; but it may not be done at one stroke. Meanwhile I suggest two things, which you might possibly be able to do, and which would make it easier.

First, if you could weigh in now with some important articles on some point of policy, preferably involving particular knowledge, such as foreign policy; I could take up the point more generally in the leaders . . . I think I should be more in a position to say 'I want this vein worked thoroughly; and nobody but Belloc can work it'. I think this would be much better than your entering abruptly to edit a paper to which you did not contribute. I have known new people on the New Witness, who had the absurd idea that you would entirely alter the policy which, as a fact, you originally invented. . . .

Second, I wonder whether it would be possible for you to collect *some* money for the paper; not large sums to finance it, but small sums to help it. . . . anybody who brought any sort of marriage portion to the union, so to speak, would make it possible to use something of the same argument as before. I will let you have more details about this side of the business when I have heard from the New Witness people; but if they are in a hole, I should like to have a general reason for renewing negotiations with you.

Chesterton ended the letter by saying that he had 'never believed so strongly . . . that England needs an organ like the New Witness, as I think you and I could make it'.[53]

On 25 August he wrote again to say that there were 'really three separate things' he had to consider. There was the 'cause', regarding which he was 'sure' that it would be better if Belloc were editor, especially if he could succeed in finding money as he, Chesterton, had not been able to: 'You are the only man in the world to do it; and Cecil would have thought so as much as I.' He did not necessarily agree with all Belloc's 'criticisms', but he did 'broadly agree' that the paper would be 'better without any intervention by other influences Cecil left on it'. He obviously could not have sacked Cecil's wife while he was only 'in temporary control of Cecil's paper at Cecil's request': 'If it can be done now by agreement with her, I certainly think the ideals involved will be all right.' Personally, he

[53] G. K. Chesterton to Hilaire Belloc, 3 May [1919], JJBL.

would be 'relieved to be clear' of the paper, except as a contributor: 'Editing is about as much my job as tight-rope dancing...'. And it was 'physically impossible' for him 'really to edit the paper and also earn enough money to finance it'. 'Besides, I want to write things of my own, a lot of which I have promised.' Finally, there was the 'personal matter', which he put last but which really came first.

I can't help feeling private relations as more important than public; and I will not at any price go out in a sort of stink of having treated my present colleagues badly. The case of my sister-in-law cannot be for me even an ordinary case of treating an assistant well. Those nearest to our nearest may not happen to be the people who would have been our chief chosen friends, but they must be our friends; or memories are wounded and life made very ugly. I have not only a great respect for her real loyalty to the cause, but a great regard for her many good qualities; and I must protect not only her interests but her feelings.

He wondered whether Belloc could, for example, give her 'some dramatic criticism' to do: 'That would rule out all political intervention; and of course you would have the ordinary right to oversee or end the experiment; but it would make it rather easier for me to make the whole negotiation successful.'[54]

In the next, handwritten (and therefore undated) letter, he tells Belloc he has succeeded:

The obstacle has removed herself with a gesture of considerable generosity; I feel under an obligation to her for the tone she takes. Hence, you will understand me, I should like to provide for her contributing something, preferably dramatic criticism; not because she stipulates for it, but rather because she does not. She is a curious and in some ways a very fine character; but she is not the sub-editor for the *NW*.[55]

Towards the end of July 'Keith' had received a letter from Chesterton asking when she was returning from Poland, where she had been a special correspondent for the *Daily Express*. In her account of what happened when she arrived back in England, she draws a veil over what transpired between her and her brother-in-law. She simply recounts that she 'launched out on a new enterprise' by starting 'the Eastern European News Service', and resumed writing dramatic criticism and other articles for the *New Witness*, while Titterton continued as assistant editor.[56]

[54] G. K. Chesterton to Hilaire Belloc, 25 Aug. 1919, JJBL.
[55] G. K. Chesterton to Hilaire Belloc, n.d., JJBL.   [56] MCC 252–3.

Chesterton, too, continued as editor. Editing a paper was not Belloc's line any more than it was Chesterton's: his editorship of the *Eye-Witness* had not lasted long, nor would he last long after Chesterton's death as editor of *G.K.'s Weekly*, when he took over in the same sort of spirit of loyalty as Chesterton had done when his brother died. But if nothing came of Chesterton's attempt to make Belloc editor of the *New Witness*, the episode certainly throws light on his feelings about his 'curious' sister-in-law.

On 9 June 1919 Shaw wrote to Chesterton to say that he had been asked to review *Irish Impressions* for the first number of a new periodical, the *Irish Statesman*, and wondered whether the book would be out in time for him to do so. 'I might of course construct it imaginatively, and give quotations expressive of your amazement at the incredible reality of the race you had idealized and championed so generously; but on the whole I should prefer to have the real book.'[57] Frances replied that the book was 'almost finished' and Chesterton hoped to let Shaw have a duplicate copy in a day or two.[58] But next day Shaw wrote to say that it was 'too late' as a printers' strike had meant that the 'first number had to be sent in long ago so as to leave time for setting it up by hand'.[59] Posterity may be entitled to bear those striking printers a grudge for preventing Shaw from reviewing Chesterton on his native land.

During that summer of 1919 the *New Witness* again aroused H. G. Wells's wrath, but this time over a series of biographical articles by Edwin Pugh, the novelist, short-story writer, and critic, called 'Big Little H. G. Wells' and published between 4 July and 15 August. It was announced that the articles were due to be published in book form early in the autumn (the book never appeared). On hearing that Wells had written a letter to the paper,[60] Chesterton hastily wrote to say that the 'sudden demands of other duties' had recently prevented him from 'attending to the *New Witness*', but that he had directed the acting editor (Titterton, the assistant editor, who had accepted the articles) to publish the letter, whatever its contents. It was true that he had 'agreed to the general idea

[57] George Bernard Shaw to G. K. Chesterton, 9 June 1919, BL Add. MS 73198, fo. 81.

[58] Frances Chesterton to George Bernard Shaw, 25 June 1919, BL Add. MS 73198, fo. 83.

[59] George Bernard Shaw to Frances Chesterton, 26 June 1919, BL Add. MS 73198, fo. 84.

[60] No letter was published either during or after the publication of Pugh's articles.

of a study' of Wells's work by Pugh; indeed he had 'rather welcomed the idea of a criticism in the paper (which so often differs from you) from a modernist and collectivist standpoint more like your own. I should imagine Pugh would agree with you more than I do, and not less.'[61] Chesterton had good reason for saying what he did: as recently as in May Pugh had praised a preface by Wells to a book as a 'very fine piece of literary criticism', and even more recently in June his 'most wonderfully penetrating introduction' to another book.[62]

Chesterton also wrote to E. S. P. Haynes to say that he was glad that Wells had turned to him for advice, 'for I can think of nobody so likely to deal fairly with him and everybody else in such a case'. Wells had written 'a very temperate and reasonable letter' to him, and he had replied in substantially the same terms as he had written to Pugh. Had he personally been in charge of the paper at the time, he would 'certainly' not have published all that Pugh had written, and he hoped that Pugh would be willing to express 'regret'. However, the truth was that it was Wells himself who was 'largely responsible' for encouraging this rather 'coarse and familliar [*sic*] style of modern portraiture'. Indeed, Wells had written things about Chesterton himself that 'I could easily quarrel over, if I had been so quarrelsome'. And he had written 'things about my brother far more unpardonable than anything Pugh could say', 'practically' accusing him 'of a sort of drunken shirking of military service; though it is fair to say that he withdrew it when Cecil disproved it by going to the front'. At any rate, nothing would 'induce' him to allow Titterton, 'a man I most warmly respect and value . . . to suffer even rudeness, if I can help it'.[63] A few days later, he wrote again to say that he had a feeling that 'such writing often stretches the wrong thing; and that conversation is much better . . . it is like the difference between shooting at a man with a gun and playing on him with a hose'. He hoped to see Haynes next day when he would be in London—but 'I shall not play on you for long'.[64]

At the same time Chesterton wrote to Titterton to say that he ought to have written to Pugh to thank him for his 'most interesting sketch', which Titterton had been 'good enough' to arrange. He was especially 'glad of his kind offer', because he thought 'nobody could more ably and sincerely

[61] Ward, *GKC* 369.

[62] *New Witness*, 16 May, 27 June 1919.

[63] G. K. Chesterton to E. S. P. Haynes, 10 Aug. 1919, BL Add. MS 73237, fo. 156.

[64] G. K. Chesterton to E. S. P. Haynes, 18 Aug. 1919, BL Add. MS 73237, fo. 158.

appreciate' Wells 'in a paper where he has been so often criticized'. However, he hoped that 'this work will not turn into anything like a mere attack on Wells, especially in the rather realistic and personal modern manner'.

I do not merely feel this because I have managed to keep Wells as a friend on the whole. I feel it much more . . . because I have a sort of sense of honor [*sic*] about him as an enemy, or at least a potential enemy. We are so certain to collide in controversial warfare, that I have a horror of his thinking I would attack him with anything but fair controversial weapons. . . .

I am honestly in a very difficult position on the *New Witness*, because it is physically impossible for me really to edit it, and also do enough outside work to be able to edit it unpaid, as well as having a little over to give it from time to time. . . . I cannot oversee everything that goes into the paper . . . I cannot . . . resign, without dropping as you truly said, the work of a great man who is gone; and who, I feel, would wish me to continue it.[65]

Many years later, after Chesterton had died, Wells wrote apropos of this letter: 'From first to last he and I were very close friends and never for a moment did I consider him responsible for Pugh's pathetic and silly little outburst. I never knew anyone so steadily true to form as G.K.C.'[66]

Ever conciliatory, Chesterton also wrote to soothe Pugh in case he misunderstood a comment in the *New Witness* by its editor 'touching a possible misunderstanding of some of your phrases about Wells'. The truth was that he disliked what he called 'the unconventional method of biography', although he was sure that, in the case of Pugh, it was 'derived from the truth that the smallness of men ultimately reveals their greatness'. Still, in Chesterton's view, it was 'always misunderstood and generally refers to things that were really misunderstandings'. Nevertheless, Wells had 'less right than most to resent the more modern method; for he has applied it constantly both to others and to himself'. Even so, Chesterton could not 'allow a series of mere personal attacks on him', not that he thought that that was Pugh's intention. And he had written to Wells to assure him that Pugh's 'purpose was not mere hostility, but merely artistic sincerity': 'Wells is too much my opponent to be so treated as my enemy.'[67]

---

[65] Clemens, 81–3.   [66] Ward, *GKC* 371.
[67] G. K. Chesterton to Edwin Pugh, n.d., BL Add. MS 73481B, fo. 66.

5

Chesterton's other than editorial responsibilities had included travelling. He had already visited Ireland in the autumn of 1918 at the invitation of Yeats, who wanted both Chesterton and Shaw to give lectures as part of a series at the Abbey Theatre in Dublin. Another reason for the visit was to help recruit Irishmen for the British army. Writing on 1 October 1918, Yeats had promised his 'old Bedford Park acquaintance' that he would be able to debate with Larkinite socialists and 'might start a movement'.[68] Chesterton's lecture was on 'Poetry and Property', the theme of which was that poetry witnessed to 'a certain dignity in man's sense of private possessions'. Subsequently, at the Dublin Arts Club he spent 'a most exhilarating evening' in 'further talk about poetry and property' with Yeats, who asked him 'to open a debate at the Abbey Theatre defending property on its more political side'. His opponent was a fellow Englishman, Thomas Johnson, 'one of the ablest leaders of Liberty Hall, the famous stronghold of Labour politics in Dublin...and deservedly popular with the proletarian Irish'. Chesterton's argument in the debate was 'confined to the particular value of small property as a weapon of militant democracy, and was based on the idea that the citizen resisting injustice could find no substitute for private property'. He 'caused some amusement by cutting a pencil' in the course of the debate 'with a very large knife' that had been given to him by Father O'Connor. Chesterton himself was greatly amused by an exchange he had with Johnson, who 'had said something about the waste of property on guns, and who interrupted my remark that there would never be a good revolution without guns, by humorously calling out, "Treason." As I told him afterwards, few scenes would be more artistic than that of an Englishman, sent over to recruit for the British army, being collared and given up to justice (or injustice) by a Pacifist from Liberty Hall.'[69] At a dinner in Chesterton's honour, when a toast to the king's health was proposed, Yeats was so angered at the embarrassment caused to Irish nationalists who were present that he refused to stand up.[70] Nearly twenty years later, Yeats, asked for his memories of Chesterton, claimed that, as far as he could

[68] R. F. Foster, *W. B. Yeats: A Life*, ii. *The Arch-Poet 1915–1939* (Oxford: Oxford University Press, 2003), 131.

[69] *II* 118–22.

[70] Foster, *W. B. Yeats: A Life*, 132–3.

remember, he had met Chesterton ('a kindly and generous man of whom I constantly heard from friends') only a couple of times socially and had read very little of his work.[71]

In the weeks leading up to the Armistice, Chesterton wrote a series of articles for the *New Witness* giving his impressions of Ireland. A revised and enlarged version of them appeared in book form in November 1919. When Chesterton first saw the Emerald Isle, his first impression was not of its greenness but of its brownness. Although he knew there was a British garrison in Dublin, he had not realized how conspicuous it would be: 'I had no notion that it had been considered necessary to occupy the country in such force or with so much parade of force.' His first thought was how useful all those soldiers would have been during 'those awful days which led up to the end of the war, and seemed more like the end of the world'. It was madness to waste troops in Ireland in order to enforce 'Irish conscription'. And when he saw the devastation wrought by British troops during the Easter Rising, he felt 'bitterly distressed that such a cannonade had ever been aimed at the Irish; but even more distressed that it had not been aimed at the Germans'.[72]

Chesterton begins *Irish Impressions* with his usual insistence on the importance of *wonder*, a sense that needed to be awakened not only for 'things superficially familiar', but also for 'things superficially fresh'. But wonder does not come easily, because it depends on 'some subordination of the self to a glory existing beyond it, and even in spite of it'. He had often battled against

the stale trick of taking things for granted: all the more because it is not even taking them for granted. It is taking them without gratitude; that is, emphatically as not granted. Even one's own front door, released by one's own latchkey, should not only open inward on things familiar, but outward on things unknown. Even one's own domestic fireside should be wild as well as domesticated...

---

[71] Clemens, 145. William M. Murphy, *The Life of John Butler Yeats 1839–1922* (Ithaca, NY: Cornell University Press, 1978), 584 n. 54, suggests that the explanation of this forgetfulness is that when Yeats knew Chesterton in Bedford Park he was 'unaware of the large, insecure young man who was then a nobody'. But Yeats's invitation in 1918 clearly shows that he had not forgotten 'his old Bedford Park acquaintance', and the debate that he had arranged at the Abbey Theatre shows that, since the Bedford Park days, he had had certainly met Chesterton on more than a couple of social occasions.

[72] *II* 113–14.

After all, 'all the most dramatic things happen at home, from being born to being dead'. And so an English visitor to Ireland should look at the people 'simply and steadily, as he would look at the natives of an entirely new nation with a new name'. He would find a peasantry that did not exist in England, and discover that these peasant proprietors were successful '*because* they were on a small scale . . . It was because they were too poor to have servants that they grew rich in spite of strikers.' This unexpected fact was 'the flattest possible contradiction of all that is said in England, both by Collectivists and Capitalists, about the efficiency of the great organisation'. These Irish 'small men were still working, because they were not machines'. England might 'be moving towards a condition which some call Socialism and I call Slavery; but whatever it is, Ireland is speeding farther and farther from it'. The legislation by Liberal govern-ments in England, such as Lloyd George's National Insurance Act, was for Chesterton nothing but Socialism and 'at the expense of the independence of the family, especially of the poor family'. In Ireland, on the contrary, 'the fortress of the family . . . is the key-fortress of the whole strategy of the island'. And Irish Catholics 'may almost be said to admit an experience in the Holy Family':

Their historical experience, alas, has made it seem to them not unnatural that the Holy Family should be a homeless family. They also have found that there was no room for them at the inn, or anywhere but in the jail; they also have dragged their new-born babes out of their cradles, and trailed in despair along the road to Egypt, or at least along the road to exile. They also have heard, in the dark and the distance behind them, the noise of the horsemen of Herod.[73]

The religious problem of Ireland *is*, insists Chesterton, 'a religious ques-tion; and it will not have an irrelevant answer' by dismissing 'spiritual questions in favour of what are called social questions'. There were such things as 'universal wars of religion, not concerned with what one nation will do, but with what all nations shall be'. For 'nearly everything in history has a religious root, and especially nearly everything in Irish history'. One thing, however, Irish Catholics and Protestants did have in common, both being 'theological', was that they were likely to be 'logical': 'The Irish are as logical as the English are illogical,' Chesterton remarked elsewhere.[74] Nevertheless, there was a creedal 'chasm', well summed up in 'the Prot-estant generally saying, "I am a good Protestant," while the Catholic

[73] *II* 91–2, 96, 98, 111, 171, 183–4, 186–7.   [74] *WB* 5.

always says, "I am a bad Catholic." ' The reason for this was simple: 'The essence of Calvinism was certainty about salvation; the essence of Catholicism is uncertainty about salvation.' The Catholic tradition was that 'the highest form of faith was doubt. It was the doubt of a man about his soul.' Because of its Calvinism, Protestant Belfast and Berlin were 'on the same side in the deepest of all the spiritual issues involved in the war. And that is the simple issue of whether pride is a sin, and therefore a weakness.' Chesterton was astonished to hear 'worthy and kindly merchants' say 'there was no poverty in Belfast'; in response to which he had 'remarked mildly that the people must have a singular taste in dress. I was gravely assured that they had indeed a most singular taste in dress. I was left with the general impression that wearing shirts or trousers decorated with large holes at irregular intervals was a pardonable form of foppery or fashionable extravagance.' Kindly the merchants might seem to be, but, in Chesterton's view: 'What cuts this spirit off from Christian common sense is the fact that the delusion, like most insane delusions, is merely egotistical. It is simply the pleasure of thinking extravagantly well of oneself.' And, Chesterton adds with a pointed reference to the Puritanism of Protestant Belfast, 'unlimited indulgence in that pleasure is far more weakening than any indulgence in drink or dissipation'. If Protestant Belfast was spiritually linked with Berlin, Catholicism, being 'the most fundamental fact in Ireland, is itself a permanent communication with the Continent'. As for Protestant England, its 'ascendancy' became 'intellectually impossible . . . on the day when Newman published the first pages of the *Apologia*' and Protestantism was no longer 'self-evidently superior'.[75]

6

After the war, it was proposed that Beaconsfield, like other towns and villages, should erect a war memorial to its dead. A committee was set up consisting of the town's rector, the doctor, the bank manager and 'the respectable trades-men of the place; with a few hangers-on' like Chesterton 'of the more disreputable professions of journalism or the arts'. The initial proposal was that a cross should be erected at the town's crossroads. Underlying the committee's discussions was the question of 'the great war of religion which has never ceased to divide mankind,

[75] *II* 149, 177–9, 182–4.

especially since that sign was set up among them'. It was, Chesterton thought, characteristic of the tolerance of the modern age that, while everybody was supposed to be free to discuss religion, in practice it was practically impossible to do so. The working-class inhabitants of Old Beaconsfield displayed 'an immense intellectual superiority' in openly saying they liked the idea of a cross 'because it was Christian', or alternatively disliking it 'because it was Popish'. Their social and intellectual betters, however, were 'ashamed to talk No-Popery', and instead advocated various other monuments, in particular a club intended especially for ex-servicemen, where 'they could have refreshment (that is where the Drink Question came in)' and 'possibly even share the Club on equal terms with their wives and women-folk (that is where the Wrongs of Women came in)'. The advocates of the club called themselves inevitably 'the Practical Party', and denounced the advocates of the cross as 'dreamers and mystical visionaries'. These practical citizens inevitably ended up with the most impractical scheme for which there was not 'the remotest chance of collecting subscriptions': 'Meanwhile, the vision of the mere visionaries could be realised easily for a few hundred pounds.' Chesterton himself observed that, admirable as a club, for example, was, it was not a war memorial, quoting Jane Austen's Mr Bingley in *Pride and Prejudice*, who, when asked by his sister 'whether it would not be much more rational if conversation at a ball took the place of dancing', answered, "Much more rational, but not half so like a ball."' The local doctor, 'a sceptic of rather a schoolboy sort', voiced the opinion that traffic would collide with a cross in the dark and expressed the hope that a light would be put on it; whereupon Frances, 'who was then an ardent Anglo-Catholic, observed with an appearance of dreamy rapture, "Oh, yes! How beautiful! A lamp continually burning before the Cross." Which was not exactly what the man of science had proposed; but it could not have been more warmly seconded.' A referendum showed there was a narrow majority in favour of the club, but the club advocated by this 'practical majority' was never built. The cross, on the other hand, was erected by the town's rector, who privately raised the necessary money. Meanwhile the local chief landlord 'casually' announced that ex-servicemen were free to use a hall that belonged to him for the purpose of a club. This outcome showed how, in spite of democratic elections and referendums, England was still an 'aristocratic' society.[76]

[76] *A.* 224–7.

The cross, however, which turned out to be a crucifix, revealed the inconsistency of English Protestantism:

The sort of Evangelical who demands what he calls a Living Christ must surely find it difficult to reconcile with his religion an indifference to a Dying Christ; but anyhow one would think he would prefer it to a Dead Cross. To salute the Cross in that sense is literally to bow down to wood and stone; since it is only an image in stone of something that was made of wood. . . . If a man were ready to wreck every statue of Julius Caesar, but also ready to kiss the sword that killed him, he would be liable to be misunderstood as an ardent admirer of Caesar. If a man hated to have a portrait of Charles the First, but rubbed his hands with joy at the sight of the axe that beheaded him, he would have himself to blame if he were regarded rather as a Roundhead than a Royalist. And to permit a picture of the engine of execution, while forbidding a picture of the victim, is just as strange and sinister in the case of Christ as in that of Caesar.

But, although it was 'naturally a source of intense and somewhat ironic joy' to Chesterton that a carved crucifix now stood in the heart of Beaconsfield, the whole episode threw light on the fundamental question that was bothering him 'and initiated the next step in my life'. For there was something about the way in which it came to be erected and then tolerated that was not 'entirely acceptable' to him:

I do not want to be in a religion in which I am *allowed* to have a crucifix. I feel the same about the much more controversial question of the honour paid to the Blessed Virgin. If people do not like that cult, they are quite right not to be Catholics. But in people who are Catholics, or call themselves Catholics, I want the idea not only liked but loved and loved ardently, and above all loudly proclaimed. I want it to be what the Protestants are perfectly right in calling it; the badge and sign of a papist. I want to be allowed to be enthusiastic about the existence of the enthusiasm; not to have my chief enthusiasm coldly tolerated as an eccentricity of myself.

Still, at least there was a war memorial now 'to commemorate the fact that something had been saved out of the Great War'—Beaconsfield and Britain. True, Chesterton did not like 'the English landed system, with its absence of peasants and its predominance of squires'; nor did he like 'the formless religious compromise of Puritanism turning into Paganism'—but still he did not 'want it discredited and flattened out by Prussianism'. England had been right to enter the war to prevent 'Prussian militarism and materialism' from dominating Europe.[77]

[77] *A.* 228–33.

7

In the summer of 1919, Chesterton wrote to Maurice Baring asking 'a great favour'. He had been commissioned by a publisher to write a book about Jerusalem, 'not political but romantic and religious, so to speak; I conceive it as mostly about pilgrimages and crusades, in poetical prose . . .'. His travel expenses were being paid, but he still needed 'the political or military permissions to go there'. He had another motive (his chief one, he told Belloc[78]) for going to Jerusalem apart from 'the desire to write the book; though I do think I could do it in the right way and, what matters more, on the right side'. Frances had been told by doctors that the only way she could 'get rid of her neuritis' would be if she went abroad and missed 'part of an English winter'. As 'a man who knows everybody', did Baring 'know anybody on Allenby's staff; or know anybody who knows anybody on Allenby's staff; or know anybody who would know anybody who would know anything about it'? Field Marshal Allenby, who had captured Jerusalem in December 1917 from the Turks, whose forces he defeated decisively in September 1918, was High Commissioner for Egypt and the Sudan. Chesterton understood that arrangements could not 'be done as yet in the ordinary way by Cook's [the travel agents]; and that the oracle must be worked in some such fashion'. If Baring were to 'be so kind as to refer to any worried soldier or official', Chesterton would 'like it understood' that he was 'not nosing about touching any diplomatic or military matter' or for 'any copy for the *New Witness*': 'I only want to write semi-historical rhetoric on the spot.' Baring would be 'helping things you yourself care about; and one person, not myself, who deserves it': 'I will not say it would be killing two birds with one stone; which might seem a tragic metaphor; but bringing one bird at least to life; and allowing the other bird, who is a goose, to go on a wild goose-chase.'[79] In fact, when Chesterton's publishers suggested he should go to the Holy Land, 'it sounded to me like going to the moon'. They would have to travel through 'a country still imperilled and under arms; it involved crossing the desert at night in something like a cattle-truck; and parts even of the Promised Land had some of the qualities of a lunar landscape'.[80]

It was almost certainly Chesterton's old friend E. C. Bentley, who was on the staff of the *Daily Telegraph*, who had suggested that he be

---

[78] G. K. Chesterton to Hilaire Belloc, 13 Nov. [1919], JJBL.
[79] Ward, *GKC* 377.   [80] *A.* 299.

commissioned to write a series of articles on the Holy Land that would become the book. Allenby's victory over the Turks and his capture of Jerusalem were being hailed as a successful modern Crusade. Baring had, as Chesterton expected, a contact on Allenby's staff, and the general himself replied that he would be delighted to welcome the Chestertons in Jerusalem and afford them every facility in Palestine.[81]

On 29 December 1919 the Chestertons set off for France. From Paris they took a sleeper to Rome, where they arrived late in the evening on New Year's Eve. Next day they visited the Forum and the Colosseum, before leaving by train that night for Brindisi via Bari. There they had to wait a day for a boat to Alexandria. There was no hotel room available, so they stayed the night in a private house, in 'a good Christian room with a statue of Our Lady and a crucifix and holy water', Frances recorded in the diary she kept on this trip to the Holy Land.[82] They sailed in the late afternoon of 3 January. By the evening Frances was feeling 'very seasick'. They reached Taranto next day, sailing on in the late afternoon. On the 5th Frances still felt 'rather sick' but stayed on deck all day. After passing the coasts of Greece and Crete, they saw no land before Alexandria, where they arrived early in the morning of the 7th. A 'dignified Egyptian gentleman' took them under his 'protection', seating them in the shade while he secured their luggage, changed their money, 'settled the customs and put us into a carriage', which took them to the Grand Hotel in the centre of the city. And there on the verandah was the first chance of seeing the East: 'It is quite wonderful—arabs—Egyptians, Jordanese, black niggers, all sorts of Europeans passing every moment . . .'. They visited the Catholic cathedral, where Frances was impressed by the 'lovely crib—one of the most beautiful I have ever seen'. Next day they took the midday train. 'Ismail (of the hotel) vowed eternal fealty for the time being and took us to the station and saw us off with oriental hand kissing and salaams.' The journey to Cairo was 'most marvellous of all':

Across the Nile Delta, flat as flat, with fields of cotton, or beans, or sugar cane—little Arab mud huts all along the way—here and there a small mosque—and by the road that runs beside the railway an unending procession of camels, mules, donkeys, goats, sheep, oxen, buffaloes, men, women[,] children[.] Every scene like some picture familiar from childhood from some illustrated Bible. The palm

[81] Ffinch, 257–8.
[82] 'Diary of Visit to Jerusalem 1920', BL Add. MS 73468, fo. 5.

trees and date trees are the only things that rise any height above the ground. Then we saw the Nile and to our surprise in the distance the Pyramids![83]

They arrived in Cairo at three o'clock on the afternoon of the 8th. 'It looks like any other great cosmopolitan centre,' Frances wrote in her diary; 'though these are Eastern houses—and the vegetation is quite strange—everyone talks a little English or French'. Frances had a headache and stayed in their hotel room till dinner. Still not feeling very well next morning, she stayed in bed till eleven, as she did too the next day. On 11 January her diary records: 'Went to church at St Mary's (the chapel of the English Bishop of Jerusalem) who was there—Choral Eucharist.' After lunch they went for a drive on the road leading to the Pyramids. They 'saw all sorts of things—shepherds bringing in droves of Sudanese sheep—Mahomedans at prayers—sellers of sugar cane—water sellers, booths all along the route'. The boats on the Nile were 'quite lovely, so is the view of the city from this further side. The city stands out very majestically against the background of the desert.' On the 13th they went for 'a prowl' in the morning, and in the afternoon 'for a drive into the bazaars'. Europeans were 'not allowed into the inmost heart of the native quarter nor into the mosques but accompanied by our faithful guide we had a marvellous view of the Eastern part of this remarkable city. It is impossible to describe the sights, the smells, the noise[,] the colour-movement in the narrowest and darkest of alleys—Every craftsman at his art . . . '. Next day they drove to the Pyramids, which were 'really impressive though in a sense ugly': 'What is truly wonderful is coming on the Sphinx which you approach from behind. It is gigantic and weird—the face all hacked away . . . '. They drove home 'in the glow of a real Egyptian sunset. The desert is unlike anything else being hilly and almost mountainous.'[84]

On the evening of 16 January Chesterton lectured at general headquarters to the military stationed there on 'Sightseeing for the Blind'. Frances was the only lady present. Next day they drove in the afternoon to the Citadel, 'the fortress on the heights above the town built by the great Saladin (the enemy of our Richard Cœur de Lion)'. From its wall they could see 'a splendid panorama of the whole country for miles—Pyramids—Nile—a hundred mosques with their minarets'. They visited two of the mosques, one modern, one ancient. The former was 'like a very palatial dancing . . . hall . . . hung with glass chandeliers—built of alabaster and very magnificent'. On the 18th Chesterton donned a cassock and

[83] BL Add. MS 73468, fos. 6–9.   [84] BL Add. MS 73468, fos. 8–15.

surplice and gave what Frances considered a 'very good' address after
evensong in the Anglican bishop's chapel. Next day he again lectured at a
military barracks.[85] He had been given an official post as lecturer 'in order
to facilitate our means of getting to Jerusalem'.[86]

Setting off for Jerusalem on 20 January, they arrived at Ismailia, 'a
perfectly beautiful little place', in the afternoon. Chesterton gave a lecture
to the English Club. Next day he spoke again to a military audience. In the
afternoon the commanding general arranged for a motor launch to take
them up the Suez Canal to Kantara, where Chesterton spoke in the
theatre of the military camp ('nine miles of tents they say'). They then
left by train for Port Said, where they arrived at 11.30 at night. There was
another lecture in the evening next day. On the 23rd they took a train for
Suez, where Chesterton again lectured in the evening to a mostly military
audience. Next day they took the late afternoon train back to Ismailia,
from where they took a train after dinner back to Kantara. From there
they took 'a kind of cattle truck train' which was 'not so terrible as had
been made out', sleeping somehow by 'fits and starts'. From Ludd, where
they arrived at 6.30 in the morning, they were sent on by car to Jaffa,
where Chesterton lectured in 'the great camp outside the city'. They drove
back to Ludd on the 26th. From there they took the train to Jerusalem—'a
wonderful journey up the most perilous heights'—where they arrived at
4.30 in the afternoon. Next day Father Waggett 'called' on them.[87]

There they stayed in a suite in the Grand Hotel. It was pouring with
rain. Next day it was bitterly cold, with heavy rain again. On 28 January
they walked to 'the Zion gate near the house of Caiaphas and the scene of
the Last Supper'. The day after they visited the Holy Sepulchre and the
Christian quarter. It was a 'hopeless' city to find one's way around—'no
names or numbers anywhere'. On the 31st Frances went out by herself and
found the Via Dolorosa. On 2 February the weather was like a 'glorious'
June day in England, and they walked to where they could see the Mount
of Olives and the Garden of Gethsemane. Four days later they drove up
into the mountains and had their 'first glimpse of the Dead Sea'. Next day
they went to the Holy Sepulchre, where they had 'rather a nice' guide, a
Catholic, who talked to them as though they were 'small heathen children'.[88]

By 9 February the rain—'when it rains in Jerusalem it does rain'—was
turning to snow. Next day they woke up to 'deep snow', the first time it had

[85] BL Add. MS 73468, fos. 17–18.   [86] BL Add. MS 73468, fo. 12.
[87] BL Add. MS 73468, fos. 19–24.   [88] BL Add. MS 73468, fos. 25–32.

snowed in Jerusalem for ten years. It was impossible to get out and the city was 'quite cut off'. By the 11th the snow was 29 inches deep, a record for Jerusalem. The hotel dining room was flooded, and there was no water. Frances managed to keep warm in her fur coat. She noted that no effort was made 'to clear the snow or make a path'. Next day the snow peaked 'at a depth of about 33 inches on the level', though the 'actual snowfall was 43 inches'. But it began to thaw in the afternoon. Frances had 'a violent headache' and stayed in bed all day. On the 15th the weather turned and the sun came out in the late morning. It was 'warm and sunny like a lovely May day'. Chesterton was working, so Frances went out by herself in the morning to the Garden of Gethsemane. It was 'like a little cottage garden', she noted, 'at home'. There were 'one or two olives (one called the Tree of Agony) so old they *might* have been there in Our Lord's time'. That afternoon they both went to the English College, where Chesterton gave what Frances called 'a very effective' lecture. Speeches of thanks were made by the students in five languages. Next day it was again cold and rainy. There was again a short fall of snow on the 20th, but when the weather improved they both had 'a lovely walk', in Frances's words, to the Garden of Gethsemane. Next day they 'penetrated the interior' of the Dome of the Rock, 'supposed by Mahomedans to be the place where Mahomet ascended to Paradise and by the Jews where Abraham was told to sacrifice Isaac'. On the 22nd the Chestertons went to a service in St George's Anglican Cathedral. Next day they attended a party where 'all Jerusalem must have been present. Grand Mufti, the Greek Patriarch, Armenian Patriarch, Syrian Patriarch, Coptic, Roman C, Greek Orthodox priests, Jews, Arabs, Musulmen, British officers and their wives and a good band and a good tea.'[89]

Two days later they saw the Upper Room, 'the traditional site of the Last Supper which at any rate is just the sort of place one would expect it to be', remarked Frances. Next day after dinner Chesterton lectured to British officers and their friends on the Arthurian legend. He was 'a little embarrassed at having *Herbert Samuel* sitting opposite to him'. On the 29th they again attended church at St George's Cathedral. Father Waggett was the preacher, who after the service drove them in a 'sort of lorry car' to the Dead Sea. On 2 March Frances was taken by car to Bethlehem, where she 'just peeped inside the Church of the Nativity'—she was 'reserving it for a visit' with her husband. That afternoon Chesterton lectured at St George's Cathedral on Dickens's England. On 4 March Frances went by herself to

---

[89] BL Add. MS 73468, fos. 32–40.

the Church and Convent of Ecce Homo. Two days later the Chestertons both walked out to the Garden of Gethsemane. After lunch they were driven by Father Waggett to Bethlehem, where they visited the Church of the Nativity and 'the cave of the manger'. 'As Father Waggett was responsible for our taking over the church in the war he knows all about it and we had a truly sympathetic guide,' wrote Frances in her diary. 'At the place of the Nativity we said our collect for Christmas day.' On 7 March they were taken for a drive and picnic. On the way, they saw Jacob's Well, 'the traditional spot where Our Lord spoke with the woman of Samaria', where the priest in charge 'let down the bucket and we drank of the water'. Two days later Frances went by herself to the garden, a 'very beautiful and peaceful little spot', reputed to be the garden of Joseph of Arimathea, to see the 'perfect specimen of a Jewish tomb' that was supposed to be the 'tomb of Our Lord'. She then discovered the Jews' 'Wailing Place': 'Several were wailing all right and many beggars doing a brisk trade.'[90]

On 10 March the Chestertons were driven by a leading Zionist to see 'two of the most important of the 60 odd colonies that the Jews have founded in Judea', about fifty miles south-west of Jerusalem. It was a 'glorious' drive through the mountains on to the plain, with 'fine glimpses of the sand dunes and the Mediterranean'. Although the plain was fertile, a lot had been 'reclaimed by sheer hard labour'. The drive was not 'an unmixed joy for the road is quite broken up in many places and we had violent shakings and nerve racking scrapes'. According to their host, the chauffeur was 'a reclaimed apache'. Still, Frances thought he was 'a wonderful driver'. After sampling the wine at a vineyard, they partook of a 'very nice' lunch at a little restaurant. They then went on to visit 'one of the chief colonies . . . very like an early American township'. They eventually returned to their hotel, 'very tired but after a very wonderful day', at about 8.30 in the evening after 'many halts as the tyres had to be often attended to, and the headlights eventually gave out'. On the way back they had seen 'Arab tents pitched for the night with the camels and donkeys outside'. At the entrance to the mountain pass they had passed 'an old inn, dating from the Crusades (probably earlier) where men and beasts halt for the night'.[91]

Chesterton was to recall the trip in his *Autobiography*. Here he 'was wandering about in the wilderness in a car with a zealous little Zionist', who 'seemed at first almost monomaniac, of the sort who answers the

---

[90] BL Add. MS 73468, fos. 41–57.   [91] BL Add. MS 73468, fos. 58–60.

statement, "It's a fine day," with the eager reply, "Oh, yes, the climate is perfect for our project." ' But Chesterton 'came to sympathise with his romance; and when he said, "It's a lovely land; I should like to put the Song of Solomon in my pocket and wander about," ' Chesterton 'knew that, Jew or Gentile, mad or sane, we two were of the same sort'.

The lovely land was a wilderness of terraced rock to the horizon, and really impressive; there was not a human being in sight but ourselves and the chauffeur, who was a black-browed giant... He was an excellent driver... He had gone ahead to clear some fallen stones and I remarked on this efficiency. The swarthy little professor beside me had taken a book from his pocket, but replied dispassionately, 'Yes; I only know him slightly; between ourselves, I believe he is a murderer; but I made no indelicate enquiries.' He then continued to read the Song of Solomon, and savoured those spices that rise when the south wind blows upon the garden. The hour was full of poetry; and not without irony.[92]

On 11 March the Chestertons went to a fancy dress ball ('though not in fancy dress'): 'Everyone there. "Jews, Turks, heretics and infidels!" ' exclaimed Frances with relish. All Jerusalem had turned out and 'the dresses were very wonderful indeed'. They left at about midnight. Two days later they walked out to Bethany, about three miles outside Jerusalem on the road to Jericho. They did not have time actually to go into the 'little town', where 'nothing really remains except the reputed tomb of Lazarus'.[93]

On 14 March they were taken to an Armenian church to witness a baptism. The child was laid down on cushions and undressed, 'all of us assisting'. Frances was asked—why she does not say or speculate—'to stand godmother and gladly consented'. The naked baby was handed to the priest, who 'immersed him completely under the water three times', and then anointed him on various parts of his body with oil. The child by this time was 'crying lustily'. After being dressed, he was handed into Frances's arms, while she held two lighted candles. She then followed the priest from the font to the altar, 'where a chain and a little gold cross were bound round his head (signifying that he was now a Christian)'. 'Then the priest touched his lips with the sacramental wafer and touched his nose with myrrh.' They left the church in a procession, the godfather carrying the baby. At the entrance to his parents' home, the baby was handed to his mother, 'who was waiting for it, also holding the two candles'. The parents insisted that the Chestertons should stay for refreshments.[94]

[92] *A*. 299.   [93] BL Add. MS 73468, fos. 61–3.
[94] BL Add. MS 73468, fos. 64–6.

On 15 March Frances walked by herself to the top of the Mount of Olives, not a long walk but 'rather steep': 'I saw the little dome that covers the rock of the Ascension (with Our Lord's footprint).' Returning to the hotel, she found Chesterton's Syrian typist waiting to take them to tea in his 'pretty little home'. On 18 March Frances at last did something she had 'always meant to do' and walked all round Jerusalem, a walk of about three to four miles. Next day was a 'day of adventure'. They hired a car and set off at 8.30 for Jericho, Jordan, and the Dead Sea, taking a picnic lunch with them. 'It is impossible', Frances wrote in her diary, 'to describe the beauty of the scenery or the badness of the road'. In the intense heat, bumping continually on the road, they wound their way in and out of 'the wildest and barest mountain scenery, though the flowers everywhere are perfectly marvellous'. Their car broke down 'in the narrow ravine that leads directly on to the shore of the Dead Sea'. When it got going again, it bumped its way (there was no 'real road') 'over sand hills and hollows until it reached the edge of the sea'. They saw 'droves of goats and sheep with Arabs entirely naked'. They then drove 'on an even worse road to Jericho'—that is, the Jericho of the Crusaders rather than the biblical Jericho that was 'a little higher up'. 'We found Elisha's Font and there to the sound of running water in a plantation of palms . . . we ate our lunch.' After lunch they drove to the Jordan, 'a pretty little stream, very muddy fringed with tamarisk—not at all remarkable'. Returning to Jericho, they found the car had a puncture. After waiting at a hotel till it was repaired, they set off back to Jerusalem at about four o'clock. Just outside Jerusalem they got another puncture. While they waited for it to be repaired, they sat on a wall overlooking the city and 'had a wonderful sight of the sunset succeeded by night': 'The stars in Palestine are always extraordinarily beautiful and the city looked like a jewelled picture.' They eventually reached their hotel 'very tired and shaken' at about seven o'clock.[95]

Next morning Frances was too tired to go out and stayed in her room till after lunch. The following day she still felt 'rather seedy' and stayed in the hotel all morning. After lunch they were taken by car to their 'beloved Bethlehem again'. On 22 March they dined at the Anglican Bishop of Jerusalem's residence, signing their names in the visitors' book on 'the table where the final order for surrender of the city was written', since the house had been the headquarters of the Turkish military governor during the war. Two days later Frances held a 'very successful' tea party: 'Everyone seemed to turn up.' On 26 March the Chestertons visited in the

[95] BL Add. MS 73468, fos. 66–72.

morning the Church of the Ecce Homo, meeting on the way Lady Allenby, who was 'very nice to us both'. Next day they met Dr Weitzmann, 'the famous Zionist' at lunch. Later in the afternoon Chesterton lectured at the army headquarters. The following day was Palm Sunday, and they heard the Anglican bishop preach at Christ Church in the morning. After lunch they went to Benediction at the Ecce Homo Church, where they had a long talk with an English nun. On the 29th they were taken by Father Waggett to the Convent of the Holy Sepulchre, on the roof of which they were amazed to find a couple of camels.[96]

Next day they left Jerusalem at 5.30 in the morning. On reaching Ludd, they found there had been a train accident, and they were delayed for an hour and a half before going on to Kantara. However, they managed to catch the train to Cairo, from where they went on to Alexandria, where they arrived at 5.30 on the morning of the 31st. Next day they left by sea at three in the afternoon. They found Herbert Samuel was also on board the ship. On Easter Sunday, 4 April, they arrived at Brindisi at about seven in the morning. After breakfasting in their hotel, they went to Mass. After lunch they boarded a train for Bari, from where they went on to Rome, arriving there next morning. After lunch they bumped into Maisie Ward— it seemed 'miraculous'. Next day they visited the Capitol, the Church of Ara Coeli, and the Forum. The following day there were visits to St Peter's and the Sistine Chapel. After lunch they walked in the Pincio and saw Rome in the sunset. On the 8th they toured the Catacombs. Next day they walked to the Palazzo Venezia and climbed the steps to the Church of the Ara Coeli, visiting St John Lateran in the afternoon. On 10 April Frances went to the Vatican Museum in the morning, and after lunch they both visited the Palazzo Borghese and walked in its gardens—at which point Frances's diary ends.[97]

While they were in Alexandria, Chesterton had written to Maurice Baring to say that there was something 'important' that he wanted 'very much to discuss' with him, 'because of certain things that have been touched on between us in former times'. He went on to say that his 'train of thought, which really was one of thought and not fugitive emotion, came to an explosion in the Church of the Ecce Homo in Jerusalem'. He was afraid that it might be 'at least a month' before they could meet, as the journey from Alexandria took a fortnight and they might have to stay in Paris to see a

---

[96] BL Add. MS 73468, fos. 72–80.   [97] BL Add. MS 73468, fos. 81–4.

friend who was ill. He had to get to work 'the moment' they returned 'to keep a contract', but he hoped they could meet 'by about then'.[98]

Chesterton would one day recall how it was in that church in Brindisi, where they went to Mass on that Easter Sunday, that 'in front of a gilded and very gaudy little image' of the Blessed Virgin Mary, he 'finally saw what was nobler than my fate, the freest and the hardest of all my acts of freedom' and 'promised the thing that I would do, if I returned to my own land'. He explained the significance of the ugly little statue of the Virgin in terms of his own religious development, in which Mary had never been absent:

I mean that men need an image, single, coloured and clear in outline, an image to be called up instantly in the imagination, when what is Catholic is to be distinguished from what claims to be Christian or even what in one sense is Christian. Now I can scarcely remember a time when the image of Our Lady did not stand up in my mind quite definitely, at the mention or the thought of all these things. I was quite distant from these things, and then doubtful about these things; and then disputing with the world for them, and with myself against them; for that is the condition before conversion. But whether the figure was distant, or was dark and mysterious, or was a scandal to my contemporaries, or was a challenge to myself—I never doubted that this figure was the figure of Faith; that she embodied, as a complete human being still only human, all that this Thing had to say to humanity. The instant I remembered the Catholic Church, I remembered her; when I tried to forget the Catholic Church, I tried to forget her...[99]

It would take another two years before Chesterton at last entered the Roman Catholic Church.

The 'notes' that Chesterton made 'on the spot' during this visit to the Holy Land were published in the *Daily Telegraph*, with the exception of the last half of the last chapter on Zionism, which was not published because the newspaper took a different political line on the Jewish question. The resulting 'uncomfortably large notebook' was published as *The New Jerusalem* in November 1920.[100] Chesterton, it seems, had a low opinion of his travel books because 'he always tended to see such enormous significance in every detail'.[101]

The most interesting pages in the book are those on Islam and on Zionism. As Jerusalem is the city where three religions converge most obviously, it is not surprising that religion looms large in Chesterton's 'notes'. For Chesterton, Islam is the religion of the desert, with all the advantages and disadvantages that that entails. The 'prophet' Muhammad

[98] Ward, *GKC* 380.   [99] *WS* 462–3.   [100] *NJ* 191.
[101] Ward, *GKC* 381.

had certainly discovered 'the obvious things' in the 'red circle of the desert, in the dark and secret place', to say which was not merely to 'sneer', 'for obvious things are very easily forgotten; and indeed every high civilisation decays by forgetting obvious things'. But what was true was that 'in such a solitude men tend to take very simple ideas as if they were entirely new ideas. There is a love of concentration which comes from the lack of comparison.' Because, therefore, 'the man of the desert tends to simplify too much, and to take his first truth for the last truth', Islam is 'lacking in that humane complexity that comes from comparison'. This explains why there is 'in the Moslem character... a deep and most dangerous potentiality of fanaticism'. Nevertheless, there is in 'Moslem morality... a considerable deposit of common sense' that 'can be set over against a mountain of crimes'. But there is no contradiction between these two observations, since the 'fanatic of the desert is dangerous precisely because he does take his faith as a fact'—that is, he takes it as 'literally' as though it were a thing like a palm tree. The Jew, on the other hand, 'has far more moral imagination and sympathy with the subtler ideals of the soul'. But unfortunately, 'with all their fine apprehensions, the Jews suffer from one heavy calamity; that of being a Chosen Race'. Chesterton thought it was 'fatal' when patriotism or religion depended on race, as when English people (before the First World War, at least) prided themselves on being Anglo-Saxons. Being proud in the abstract of one's country or religion did not lead to this kind of 'arrogance', and 'the more savage man of the desert' was free of it.[102]

On the other hand, the Muslim attitude to women reflected 'the philosophy of the desert', since 'chivalry is not an obvious idea. It is not as plain as a pike-staff or as a palm tree.' A Muslim, says Chesterton, can pity weakness, but 'reverence for weakness is to him simply meaningless'. The ignorance of chivalry is responsible according to Chesterton for what is to him a fatal flaw in Islam, its lack of a sense of humour: 'Wherever there is chivalry there is courtesy; and wherever there is courtesy there is comedy. There is no comedy in the desert.' The 'very logical and consistent' creed of Islam had another 'quite logical and consistent element': vandalism. In Christianity there is a 'combination' or 'rather a complexity made up of two contrary enthusiasms; as when the Dark Ages copied out the pagan poems while denying the pagan legends; or when the popes of the Renascence imitated the Greek temples while denying the Greek gods'. But such a 'high inconsistency is inconsistent with Islam', which 'takes everything

[102] *NJ* 211–14.

literally, and does not know how to play with anything'. It was inconceivable that Mohammed should have restored 'ancient Babylon as medievalism vaguely sought to restore ancient Rome'; for Islam 'was content with the idea that it had a great truth; as indeed it had a colossal truth. It was so huge a truth that it was hard to see it was a half-truth.' As 'a reaction towards simplicity', Islam was 'a violent simplification, which turned out to be an over-simplification'. While it 'had one thought, and that a most vital one; the greatness of God which levels all men', it did not have 'one thought to rub against another' simply because it did not have another thought. Complex creeds, by contrast, 'can breed thoughts'. Islamic philosophy suffered 'from a lack of the vitality that comes from complexity, and of the complexity that comes from comparison'. The Christian philosophy of free will, by contrast, is complex, being the 'sharp combination of liberty and limitation which we call choice'. Like modern liberal Christians, Muslims thought 'they had a simpler and saner sort of Christianity': 'They thought it could be made universal merely by being made uninteresting.' And this naturally led to the intolerance that results from preaching a 'platitude' rather than a 'paradox':

It was exactly because it seemed self-evident . . . that their simple creed was suited to everybody, that they wished . . . to impose it on everybody. It was because Islam was broad that Moslems were narrow. And because it was not a hard religion it was a heavy rule. Because it was without a self-correcting complexity, it allowed of . . . simple and masculine but mostly rather dangerous appetites . . .

Similarly, humanists like H. G. Wells sneered at a dogma like the co-eternity of the Son and held up as 'a model of simplicity . . . that most mystical affirmation "God is Love"'—but the 'subtle' dogma is only a theological 'explanation of the simple statement; and it would be quite possible even to make it a popular explanation, by saying that God could not love when there was nothing to be loved'. A dogma limits because it is a 'definition'. But, far from being constricting, dogmas in religion are what Chesterton calls 'creative limits', as when he insists that the war against Germany was 'the resistance of form to formlessness' or 'chaos'. Analogously, in the context of the walled city of Jerusalem Chesterton praises the absence of suburban sprawl—as opposed apparently to the kind of limited suburb he had no objection to—with its lack of a 'boundary', an 'indefinite expansion' that is 'controlled neither by the soul of the city within, nor by the resistance of the lands round about', thus destroying 'at once the dignity of a town and the freedom of a countryside'. As for the Christians of Jerusalem, they taught the lesson of 'constancy', having survived more or less constant persecution through the centuries; but they 'would never have survived at all if they had not survived their own death, even in the sense of dying daily': 'The ideal was out of date almost from the first day; that is why it is eternal; for whatever is dated is doomed.' The Christian Crusades had succeeded in checking the advance of Islam, but it had not been 'checked enough'. And, Chesterton claims, 'three-quarters of the wars of the modern world' were 'due to the fact' that it had not been 'checked enough': 'The only thing to do with unconquerable things is to conquer them. That alone will cure them of invincibility...'. Religious wars, he thought, were at least 'more rational' than other kinds of wars, for they were 'the most philosophical sort of fighting' in the 'mere act of recognising the difference, as the deepest kind of difference'.[103]

Apart from Islam and its differences from Judaism and Christianity, the other even more interesting part of the book deals with the question of Zionism, an issue that inevitably raises the question of Chesterton's alleged anti-Semitism. Indeed, Chesterton himself is quite open about it: he and his friends (meaning, of course, the *New Witness* and Belloc and his brother) had been 'for a long period rebuked and even reviled' for so-called 'Anti-Semitism'; but it was 'always much more true to call it Zionism'. That is, the 'substance' of their 'heresy was exceedingly simple. It consisted entirely in saying that Jews are Jews; and as a logical consequence that they are not Russians or Roumanians or Italians or Frenchmen or Englishmen.' Because Jews were Jews, Chesterton and his fellow heretics thought that 'in some fashion, and as far as possible, Jews should be represented by Jews and ruled by Jews'. If that was 'Anti-Semitism', then Chesterton was an 'Anti-Semite'—but it 'would seem more rational to call it Semitism'. Of this so-called Anti-Semitism he and his friends were 'now less likely than ever to repent'. Zionism, which had been 'dismissed as a fad', was now 'discussed everywhere as a fact; and one of the most menacing facts of the age'. The same people who had accused Chesterton of 'Anti-Semitism' had now 'become far more Anti-Semitic' than he was or ever had been. Those who had once thought it 'an injustice' even to refer to Jews as Jews were now 'talking with real injustice about them'. Before the First World War, English people had been encouraged to believe that Germans were 'a sort of Englishman because they were Teutons; but it was all the worse for us when we found out what Teutons really were'. Similarly, English people were told that 'Jews were a sort of Englishman because they were British subjects. It is all the worse for us now we have to regard them, not

[103] *NJ* 195, 215–18, 229, 247, 249, 351–2, 360–1, 380, 387.

subjectively as subjects, but objectively as objects; as objects of a fierce hatred among the Moslems...'.[104] What had radically changed English attitudes to the Jews was the so-called Balfour Declaration, the letter sent on 2 November 1917 by A. J. Balfour, then the Foreign Secretary, to Lord Rothschild, a leading British Jew, for him to send on to the Zionist Federation. The letter announced the decision by the Cabinet two days earlier to favour the establishment of a Jewish national home in Palestine, without prejudice to the civil and religious rights of the non-Jewish communities in Palestine, and at the same time without prejudice to the civil and political rights of Jews living in other countries. Naturally, the Declaration alarmed both Christians and Muslims living in Palestine, although it did not fully meet the Zionist demand that Palestine should *be* the Jewish national home.

There is no reason to doubt the sincerity of Chesterton's support for Zionism, which, he pointed out, was 'on the face of it, perfectly reasonable': 'It is the theory that any abnormal qualities in the Jew are due to the abnormal position of the Jews. They are traders rather than producers because they have no land of their own from which to produce, and they are cosmopolitans rather than patriots because they have no country of their own for which to be patriotic.' Since Chesterton's alleged anti-Semitism consisted precisely of his objections to these 'abnormal qualities', for which Jews were not responsible, to object to them was not to blame the Jews themselves: 'The Zionists therefore are maintaining a perfectly reasonable proposition, both about the charge of usury and the charge of treason, if they claim that both could be cured by the return to a national soil as promised in Zionism.' Given that it is

our whole complaint against the Jew that he does not till the soil or toil with the spade; it is very hard on him to refuse him if he really says, 'Give me a soil and I will till it; give me a spade and I will use it.' It is our whole reason for distrusting him that he cannot really love any of the lands in which he wanders; it seems rather indefensible to be deaf to him if he really says, 'Give me a land and I will love it.'

Consequently, Chesterton favoured not only a home for the Jews in Palestine, but if possible an 'extension of the definition of Zionism' that would 'overcome... the difficulty of resettling a sufficient number of so large a race on so small a land': namely, by giving Jews who did not live in the national homeland 'a special position best described as a privilege;

----

[104] *NJ* 392–3.

some sort of self-governing enclave with special laws and exemptions'.[105]
The obvious objection to this 'extension' of Zionism is that this would
simply create the kind of ghetto that had facilitated the persecution of Jews;
but this cannot be said to have been Chesterton's intention, which sounds
perfectly sincere even if quite impractical—or worse.

What, then, in conclusion is to be said about the charge of anti-Semitism
against Chesterton? The first and most obvious thing to be said is that
Chesterton was innocent of what we normally mean today by anti-
Semitism—that is, racial anti-Semitism, such as that of the Nazis. No
one had more contempt for racial theories. He had rejected anti-Semitism
and embraced Zionism at an early age, writing when he was about 19: 'No
Christian ought to be an Anti-Semite. But every Christian ought to be a
Zionist.'[106] What it is true to say, and what Chesterton would have said, is
that he was anti-Jewish just as he was anti-Prussian, but only in the sense
that he associated Jews with capitalism and international finance, just as he
associated Prussia with barbarism and military aggression. Like the average Englishman of the time, he could also be said to be anti-Jewish in
seeing Jews as foreigners in a largely homogeneous society, with, in the
case of rich Jews, international family ties that transcended national
loyalties. In that sense, he was anti-Jewish, just as many Europeans today
can be said to be anti-Muslim because they see a disinclination among
Muslim immigrants to integrate and an adherence to Islam that is potentially at variance with patriotism. And, if we wince at the frequent references to 'usurers', knowing to whom Chesterton is referring, we should
remind ourselves that he excoriated Prussians even more. There was a
difference, however: the Jews were not responsible for the invidious position that they found themselves in, whereas Chesterton never makes any
such excuses for the Prussians—except insofar as it was not their fault that
they 'were not converted to Christianity at all until quite close to the
Reformation. The poor creatures hardly had time to become Catholics
before they were told to become Protestants.'[107] If Chesterton was anti-
Jewish, he was anti-Jewish in exactly the same kind of way that many
Europeans are anti-American today, or that Irish Americans are or used to
be anti-British, or that British people were anti-German and anti-Japanese

---

[105] *NJ* 405, 409, 417.

[106] Dorothy Collins (ed.), 'Extracts from Note-book (about 1893. G.K.C.
aged 19)', *Tablet*, 4 Apr. 1953. 'The original notebook appears to have been
lost . . .' (Oddie, 109, n. 55).

[107] *WW* 60.

after the Second World War. Of course, to hold unfavourable views of a nation is not to condemn all the individuals in it or to preclude the possibility of having friends among them. But whereas, Chesterton himself complained, people were 'allowed to express...general impressions' about the Irish or the Scots or Yorkshiremen—this latitude was not permitted in the case of the Jews: 'There (for some reason I have never understood), the whole natural tendency has been to stop; and anybody who says anything whatever about Jews as Jews is supposed to wish to burn them at the stake.'[108] However, when Chesterton said that he did not understand this exception, he was being somewhat disingenuous: as he must have known very well, there was a perfectly good reason—namely, that the Jews had a very long history of being persecuted and treated as scapegoats. At any rate, Chesterton ignored the ban on expressing general impressions. That there was to be a 'final solution' proposed in Nazi Germany to the Jewish 'problem' was still some years ahead, and Chesterton cannot be judged in the light of the Holocaust. He was certainly well aware that general impressions are general impressions and nothing more. He himself drew clear distinctions between Jews. Speaking to the Jewish West End Literary Society in 1911, he had told the audience that the Jewish people were a highly civilized race—but the problem was that they had no country. They were bound, therefore, to be more loyal to their race than to the particular country they lived in. Because he thought they ought to have their own country, he was an unabashed Zionist. In the report of the lecture, Chesterton was quoted as saying that the Jews were no different from other people in having rich Jews who were 'nasty' and poor Jews who were 'nice'.[109] In a letter of the same year, he wrote: 'Jews (being landless) unnaturally alternate between too much power and too little...the Jew millionaire is too safe and the Jew pedlar too harassed...I don't mind how fiercely you fight for the pedlar.'[110]

Can anything, then, be said against Chesterton? Two things, I think, can be said. First, although the Holocaust lay in the future, the truth was that there had been more or less constant persecution in Europe of the Jews—and we have already noted the youthful Chesterton's disgust at the Russian pogroms—which should have made Chesterton more cautious in what he said about the Jews. On the other hand, whatever one's judgement on Belloc and Cecil Chesterton, in G. K. Chesterton's case there is

---

[108] *WC* 193.   [109] Ward, *GKC* 227–8.

[110] G. K. Chesterton to Leslie Claude Greenberg, 26 Apr. 1911, BL Add. MS 73237, fo. 109.

the mitigating circumstance that his beloved brother had died in a patriotic war soon after being found guilty in a libel case brought by a Jewish businessman who had effectively corrupted politicians in the Marconi scandal, politicians who had then got off practically scot free, one of whom, who was one of the Jews involved, was actually presiding over English justice as lord chief justice. There is also the extenuating fact that international finance, in which Jews were very prominent, had played a not inconsiderable part in leaving Germany only partially weakened by the Treaty of Versailles. When, then, Chesterton demands that any Jew who wishes to occupy a political or social position—and the office of lord chief justice is given as an example—'must be dressed like an Arab' to make it clear that he is a foreigner living in a foreign country,[111] we need to bear those factors in mind. However, we may well think that Chesterton has gone far too far, and indeed far further than he could really have countenanced had he thought calmly about his integrated Jewish friends at St Paul's and in Beaconsfield, who would have had no desire whatever to wear Arab dress, as Chesterton would have known very well. Still, the wounds left by the Marconi scandal and his brother's death had still not healed, and the outrage at the result of the Paris Peace Conference was fresh in his mind, so some excuse may be made for Chesterton, although it is a pity that, when he came to collect the *Daily Telegraph* articles in book form, he did not excise this passage.

Second, although England was a very homogeneous society at the time, in which xenophobia was so widespread that the very word 'foreigner' (constantly used of Jews, even in public) conjured up unpleasant associations, the Jews were not the only large foreign community. Mass Irish immigration since the middle of the nineteenth century had produced ghetto communities not all that dissimilar to those of the Jews, with their own schools in which a religion that was perceived as almost as foreign by the average Protestant Englishman was taught. At military parades Roman Catholics and Jews were called to fall out when religious services took place, as though they were people who fell into the same category. No doubt Chesterton would have said that the Irish were our close neighbours living in the same British Isles, who spoke English and were Christian, whom it was much easier to assimilate. Still, the Roman Catholic Church was as international as Jewry, and it might be asked how far English Catholics in a church led by Italian popes could be assumed to be loyal

[111] *NJ* 397.

to their country, especially if they were Irish by birth or descended from Irishmen. It might well seem an anomaly and a discomforting one.[112] One can understand Chesterton's desire for a homogeneous England, quite distinct from the other countries that make up Britain, a nation he did not believe in; and one can imagine what his reaction would have been to a multicultural England. But it might well look as though he was discriminating against the Jews—which he was, of course, because of their perceived cosmopolitanism and involvement in international finance, something that could not be said of Irish Catholics. In Chesterton's own words, 'the Catholic internationalism, which bids men respect their national governments, is considerably less dangerous than the financial internationalism which may make a man betray his country...'.[113]

8

A month before the publication of *The New Jerusalem* in October 1920, Chesterton had published another collection of his articles, selected from the *Illustrated London News* and the *New Witness*, called *The Uses of Diversity*. The book begins with an essay 'On Seriousness', which Chesterton calls 'irreligious' or characteristic of 'all false religions'. To take 'everything seriously', he argues, is to make 'an idol of everything'. Man is the only animal that is not 'serious', and 'the unhealthy love of animals is serious'. The right way to view animals is 'the comic view', which is 'naturally affectionate': only thus can 'a morbid idolatry be avoided'. Both 'cruelty to animals and worship of animals... come from taking animals too seriously'. The failure to take humour seriously, on the other hand, is for Chesterton extremely serious: 'Nothing has been so senselessly underrated as wit, even when it seems to be the mere wit of words. It is dismissed as merely verbal; but, in fact, it is more solemn writing that is merely verbal, or rather merely verbose. A joke is always a thought; it is grave and formal writing that can be quite literally thoughtless.' But it is not the masses who are guilty of solemn thoughtlessness, for 'the poor live on laughter as on a fairy-tale': they can be 'more scientifically studied' in the funny stories of

---

[112] Cf. Christopher Hollis, *The Mind of Chesterton* (London: Hollis and Carter, 1970), 137–8; David Lodge, *The Novelist at the Crossroads and Other Essays on Fiction and Criticism* (London: Ark, 1986), 154; Sheridan Gilley, 'Chesterton's Politics', *CR* 21/1–2 (Feb./May 1995), 41.

[113] *WS* 466.

the humorous short story writer W. W. Jacobs than in the serious socio-logical writings of Beatrice and Sidney Webb. For Chesterton, comedy was at least as important as tragedy in speaking of the human condition, and there was no reason why comedy and tragedy should not be found together. It was the 'daring mixture' of tragedy and comedy in Shake-speare's plays that sharply distinguished them from Greek tragedy or French classical drama—a distinction that clearly made Shakespeare in Chesterton's eyes a greater and more truly serious dramatist. The same mixture was to be found in the medieval miracle play, which was 'far bolder in its burlesque' and was more 'democratic' in its 'satire'. By the nineteenth century this 'weakening of democratic satire' had grown to such an extent that there was 'a tendency to find all fun in the ignorant or criminal classes; in dialect or the dropping of aitches'. But the First World War had thankfully revived the medieval democracy of satire—the miracle play had reappeared in the spectacle of the mocking of the triumphalist German Kaiser: 'We have seen a real King Herod claiming the thunders of the throne of God, and answered by the thunder not merely of human wrath but of primitive human laughter. He has done murder by proclama-tions, and he has been answered by caricatures.' Inevitably, Chesterton reverts to his beloved Christmas in his celebration of the seriousness of humour in these essays, insisting that 'the fun of Christmas is founded on the seriousness of Christmas; and to pull away the latter support even from under a Christmas clown is to let him down through a trap-door'. Christ-mas, again inevitably, means Dickens: 'It is exactly because Christmas is not only a feast of children, but in some sense a feast of fools, that Dickens is in touch with its mystery.'[114]

The common and the ordinary as always are celebrated by Chesterton. It is, he asserts, 'the mark of the truly great man: that he sees the common man afar off, and worships him'. The difference between 'ordinary' and 'extraor-dinary' men is that the 'extraordinary men' know they are 'ordinary men'. The great and important things in life happen not on the public but the private stage: 'For the drama of the home is really very dramatic. The household is the lighted stage, on which the actors appeal literally to the gods. It is in private life that things happen.' The same was true of detective stories, for, while 'the great detective story deals with small things . . . the small or silly detective story generally deals with great things'. Compared to medieval life, modern life, 'with its vastness, its energy, its elaboration, its wealth', was 'insignificant' because nobody 'knows what we mean; we do not know

---

[114] *UD* 1–4, 6, 54, 72, 97–9, 151, 153.

ourselves'—whereas the medievals 'had a much stronger idea of crowding all possible significance into things'. Linked to Chesterton's ideal of the commonplace and the ordinary is his idea of the immense significance of *limitation*: 'it is the frame that creates the picture', such 'limitations' being 'vital to man'. Compared to the God of Pantheism, the God of Christianity is limited, but it is by virtue of that limitation that the Christian God is free: 'For [Christians], God is not bound down and limited by being merely everything; He is also at liberty to be something.'[115]

Popular scientism was a regular butt of Chesterton, for whom its poet *par excellence* was Tennyson: 'No one did more to encourage the colossal blunder that the survival of the fittest means the survival of the best.' The problem with the so-called Missing Link is simply that 'he is missing'. Popular science made him into 'a lawgiver', although he was at the same time being hunted 'like a criminal': 'They built on the foundation of him before he was found.' Turning to popular religion, on the other hand, Chesterton had no doubt that there was such a thing as spiritual healing; but his objection to Christian Science was that 'the popular religious sense of mankind has always flowed in the opposite direction'. That is, 'it has flowed from spirit to flesh, and not from flesh to spirit.' The trouble with Christian Science was that it claimed to be 'purely spiritual', but 'being purely spiritual' was paradoxically 'opposed to the very essence of religion. All religions . . . have always had one enemy, which is the purely spiritual. Faith-healing has existed from the beginning of the world; but faith-healing without a material act or sacrament—never.' This religious materialism, this 'union of flesh and spirit', Chesterton believed to be the hallmark of authentic religion, which never disowns 'sacraments'. An essential difference between religion and science is that, while the 'truths' of the former are 'unprovable', the 'facts' of the latter are 'unproved'. The modern tolerance of ' "respecting" this or that person's religion', which involves not caring 'about the creed itself, from which a person's customs, good or bad, will necessarily flow', is in fact more disrespectful to that religion than the old religious intolerance, for 'the way to respect a religion is to treat it as a religion: to ask what are its tenets and what are its consequences'. When Chesterton criticizes the failure to recognize 'two facts—first, that men act from ideas; and second, that it might, therefore, be as well to discover which ideas'—one thinks, for example, of the incomprehension of secular liberalism in the face of Islamic fundamentalism.[116]

[115] *UD* 27, 33, 42–3, 116, 130, 142–3.   [116] *UD* 21, 50, 53, 122–3, 188.

11

America and Conversion

THE Chestertons returned home in April 1920. The appointment in June of Herbert Samuel as High Commissioner in Palestine explained why they had encountered him out there. The appointment of a Jew angered Chesterton for two reasons: he thought it was obviously self-contradictory, first that a Jewish High Commissioner should have been appointed, 'the whole point of the experiment being that the Jews were to develop as a separate entity'; and, second, that a Jewish High Commissioner should have been entrusted with the task of ensuring that the non-Jewish inhabitants were treated fairly. The *New Witness*, nevertheless, continued to support the Zionist cause. But by August the paper was in a serious financial state, and Chesterton was forced to appeal to its readers for money. By Christmas just over £1,000 had been raised, but half had been given by Chesterton himself and his mother had donated £100. In fact, twice that amount was needed to secure the paper's future, but the money raised at least meant that some outstanding debts could be paid, and the rest enabled the paper to continue for the time being.[1] Chesterton's contributions included some delightful parodies of Tennyson, Browning, Swinburne, Yeats and Whitman, which appeared in the issue of 10 December 1920, with the note that they 'were originally written for the Beaconsfield Convalescent Home and were on sale at a Bazaar to raise much-needed funds'. Chesterton had been asked to impersonate Old King Cole at the bazaar, at which he had run a tobacco stall. The parodies were

---

[1] Ffinch, 266–7.

later republished in *The Collected Poems of G. K. Chesterton*, published in 1927, under the title 'Variations of an Air: Composed on Having to Appear in a Pageant as Old King Cole'.[2]

Apparently some time after their return home, Chesterton wrote in an undated letter to Maurice Baring that he had 'not forgotten the things we talked of last year; though they have had further complications', about which he would 'soon probably have more to tell' him. But what preoccupied him in this letter was Frances:

For deeper reasons than I could ever explain, my mind has to turn especially on the thought of my wife, whose life has been in many ways a very heroic tragedy; and to whom I am so much in debt of honour that I cannot bear to leave her, even psychologically, if it be possible by fact and sympathy to take her with me. We have had a very difficult time lately; but the other day she rather abruptly faced the thing herself in a new way, and spoke as if she knew where we would both end. But she asked for a little time; as a great friend of hers is also (with the approval of the priest whom she consulted) delaying for the moment till she is more certain. She and Frances want to meet and have it out, I think, and I cannot imagine any way in which Frances is more likely to be moved in that direction than by an Anglican or ex-Anglican friend of exactly that type. Fond as we are of each other, I am just a little too Bellocian already, if you understand me, to effect the precise thing I mean. I only write this to tell you the thing may look rather stationary, and yet it moves.[3]

In a later undated letter he wrote to say that he intended to call on Baring in the next few days:

I would have called on you long ago, let alone written, but for this load of belated work which really seems to bury me day after day. I never realised before that business can really block out much bigger things. As you may possibly guess, I want to consider my position about the biggest thing of all, whether I am to be inside it or outside it. I used to think one could be an Anglo-Catholic and really inside it; but if that was (to use an excellent phrase of your own) only a Porch, I do not think I want a Porch, and certainly not a Porch standing some way from the building. A Porch looks so silly, standing all by itself in a field. Since then, unfortunately, there have sprung up round it real ties and complications and difficulties; difficulties that seemed almost duties.... Sometimes one suspects the real obstacles have been the weaknesses one knows to be wrong, and not the doubts that might be relatively right, or at least rational. I suppose all this is a

---

[2] *CP* (1933), 46–9.

[3] *Tablet*, 26 Dec. 1953. Part of this letter is quoted in Ward, *GKC* 455.

common story; and I hope so; for wanting to be uncommon is really not one of my weaknesses...[4]

As he had written during the war in a notebook, using a different metaphor: 'Catholicism necessarily feels for Protestantism not the superiority a man feels over sticks and straws, but that he feels over clippings of his hair and nails. She feels Protestantism not merely as something insufficient, but something that would never have been even THAT, but for herself.'[5] He wrote again to Baring, most probably in July not long after the event took place, to say that he had 'had the other day a trying experience, and I think a hard case of casuistry; I am not sure that I was right; but also not by any means sure I was wrong'.

Long ago, before my present crisis, I had promised somebody to take part in what I took to be a small debate on labour. Too late, by my own carelessness, I found to my horror it had swelled into a huge Anglo-Catholic Congress at the Albert Hall. I tried to get out of it, but I was held to my promise. Then I reflected that I could only write (as I was already writing) to my Anglo-Catholic friends on the basis that I was one of them now in doubt about continuing such; and that their conference in some sense served the same purpose as their letters. What affected me most, however, was that by my own fault I had put them into a hole. Otherwise, I would not just now speak from or for their platform, just as I could not (as yet at any rate) speak from or for yours. So I spoke very briefly, saying something of what I think about social ethics. Whether or not my decision was right, my experience was curious and suggestive, though tragic; for I felt it like a farewell. There was no doubt about the enthusiasm of those thousands of Anglo-Catholics. But there was also no doubt, unless I am much mistaken, that many of them besides myself would be Roman Catholics rather than accept things they are quite likely to be asked to accept—for instance, by the Lambeth Conference. For though my own distress, as in most cases I suppose, has much deeper grounds than clerical decisions, yet if I cannot stay where I am, it will be a sort of useful symbol that the English Church has done something decisively Protestant or Pagan. I mean that to those to whom I cannot give my spiritual biography, I can say that the insecurity I felt in Anglicanism was typified in the Lambeth Conference....A young Anglo-Catholic curate has just told me that the crowd there cheered all references to the Pope, and laughed at every mention of the Archbishop of Canterbury. It's a queer state of things. I am concerned most, however, about somebody I value more than the Archbishop of Canterbury; Frances, to whom I owe much of my own faith, and to whom therefore (as far as I can see my way) I also owe every decent chance for the conventional defence of her faith. If her

---

[4] Ward, *GKC* 384–5, with text corrected from BL Add. MS 73189, fo. 35.
[5] Ffinch, 275. This notebook, which is not in BL, has apparently disappeared.

side can convince me, they have a right to do so; if not, I shall go hot and strong to convince her. I put it clumsily, but there is a point in my mind.

'Logically', therefore, he 'must await answers' to his questions from Father Waggett and Bishop Charles Gore, as well as from Father Ronald Knox, who had been a leading Anglo-Catholic priest before converting to Roman Catholicism in 1917, and Father Vincent McNabb, the well-known Dominican preacher.[6] This Anglo-Catholic Congress, where Chesterton was 'received with enormous enthusiasm',[7] was the first of a number that took place between the two world wars when Anglo-Catholics seemed poised to take control of the Church of England, and took place at the Albert Hall from 29 June to 1 July 1920. Along with Bishop Gore, Chesterton spoke on the Church and social and industrial problems.

At the end of the year, just before leaving for America, he wrote again to Baring 'the shortest, hastiest and worst written letter in the world' to say that he had to leave for America: 'I am glad for I shall see something of Frances, without walls of work between us.' The brief note concluded: 'I have pretty well made up my mind about the thing we talked about. Fortunately, the thing we talked about can be found all over the world.'[8] Just before leaving, Chesterton had also written one of his 'rare' letters to Father O'Connor on Christmas Eve 1920. He asked O'Connor for his prayers, telling him that they were off to America 'for a month or two'. Chesterton was 'glad of it, because I shall be at least free from the load of periodical work that has prevented me from talking properly to anybody, even to [Frances]; and I want to talk very much'. When he returned to England, he would 'probably want to talk' with O'Connor 'about very important things—the most important things there are'.

Frances has not been well, and though I think she is better, I have to do things in a considerate way, if you understand me; I feel it is only right to consult also with my Anglo-Catholic friends; but I have at present a feeling that it will be something like a farewell. Things have shaken me up a good deal lately—especially the persecution of Ireland. But of course there are even bigger things than that.[9]

O'Connor felt that Chesterton was 'longing to have it out with Frances about his conversion, but his work and her delicate health were his excuses

---

[6] Ward, *GKC* 388–9.   [7] Ward, *GKC* 389.

[8] Ward, *GKC* 384–5, 388–9.

[9] O'Connor, 124–5, with text corrected from BL Add. MS 73196, fo. 121.

for not satisfying that longing. But it was also, as she had already guessed, his congenital aversion from starting a crisis.'[10]

2

Two months before the Chestertons were due to leave for America on a lecture tour, tests showed that Frances's arthritis of the spine had seriously deteriorated. It seemed the trip would have to be cancelled. But Father O'Connor asked for prayers at a crippled children's home in Vienna, which the couple had helped support financially when Austria was starving after the Treaty of Versailles. After a fortnight Frances's condition improved, and the tour could go ahead.[11]

Before leaving for America Chesterton had to go to the American consulate in London to obtain a visa. His experience there told him a great deal about the country he was about to visit for the first time. He was given a form to fill in, a form that was 'very different from any form I had ever filled up in my life'. It was a kind of examination paper. It enquired of the applicant, for example, ' "Are you an anarchist?" to which a detached philosopher would naturally feel inclined to answer, "What the devil has that to do with you? Are you an anarchist?" . . . '. Another question was: 'Are you in favour of subverting the government of the United States by force?' To this Chesterton was inclined to respond: 'I prefer to answer that question at the end of my tour and not the beginning.' His 'inquisitor' had then enquired, 'in his more than morbid curiosity': 'Are you a polygamist?' The obvious answer to this was 'No such luck'—or else 'Not such a fool'—depending on one's 'experience of the other sex'. Among the 'many things that amused' Chesterton 'almost to the point of treating the form' with disrespect was 'the thought of the ruthless outlaw who should feel compelled to treat it respectfully'.[12]

Now it was easy to laugh at such a strange form, and there was no harm in a foreigner doing so, provided he went on to consider 'the deeper causes that make people so different from him'. The contrast with Chesterton's experience of travelling in the Middle East was certainly striking. There his papers had been examined by officials of 'governments which many worthy people in the West would vaguely identify with corsairs and assassins'; but these 'slaves of Asiatic autocracy were content, in the old liberal fashion, to judge me by my actions; they did not inquire into

---

[10] O'Connor, 125.   [11] O'Connor, 121.   [12] *A.* 38–40.

my thoughts. They held their power as limited to the limitation of practice; they did not forbid me to hold a theory.' What, then, Chesterton remembered asking himself as he stood in the consulate with the examination paper in his hand, is it 'which makes America peculiar, or which is peculiar to America'? The answer, he realized, was the key to understanding the 'ultimate idea of what America *is*—namely, that 'America is the only country in the world that is founded on a creed'—for the 'American Constitution does resemble the Spanish Inquisition in this: that it is founded on a creed'. Now a creed like the Christian creed was 'at once the broadest and the narrowest thing in the world', for it brought together the most disparate peoples, while at the same time insisting that they conform to certain beliefs: it was a 'net' that drew in all kinds of people but it was 'a net of a certain pattern, the pattern of Peter the Fisherman'. In a not dissimilar way 'the great American experiment' was 'the experiment of a democracy of diverse races which has been compared to a melting-pot'. But that melting pot was 'of a certain shape and a certain substance': 'The melting-pot must not melt.' America invited everyone to become its citizen, but this implied 'the dogma that that there is such a thing as citizenship'. Before mass immigration into Europe much later in the twentieth century, America did seem to a European 'incongruous or comic' in its 'racial admixtures', and that was why 'the American international examination paper' did seem funny to an Englishman like Chesterton. But that was because England was English and took 'certain national traditions for granted'. There was no 'inquisition' for visitors to its shores because there was no 'creed'. Where there was a 'type', there was no need for a 'test'. And where there were 'national types', the types could be 'allowed to hold any theories'. But there was no such American type, and so America had to be 'not only democratic but dogmatic', both 'inquisitive' and 'intolerant'. For America wanted to make its 'new citizens patriotic Americans'. This was 'Americanisation', 'the amazing ambition to Americanise the Kamskatkan and the Hairy Ainu'. As he stood there in the American consulate with the examination paper in his hand, Chesterton realized what it was that made America so different from Europe: 'We are not trying to Anglicise thousands of French cooks or Italian organ grinders. France is not trying to Gallicize thousands of English trippers or German prisoners of war.' The American visa application form was indeed 'abnormal', but then America was abnormal in its 'experiment of a home for the homeless'. It was indeed an 'asylum'—but, added Chesterton, writing down what he had felt that day in the consulate, it was 'only since Prohibition that it has looked a little like a lunatic asylum'.

Before leaving for America, Chesterton at least understood, unlike his fellow countrymen, that America was far from being 'a sort of Anglo-Saxon colony, knowing that it was more and more thronged with crowds of very different colonists'. In that sense, it was closer to Europe than England, and during the war Chesterton had tried to persuade his countrymen 'not to appeal to the American as if he were a rather dowdy Englishman, who had been rusticating in the provinces and had not heard the latest news about the town'.[13]

On New Year's Day 1921 the Chestertons left London's Euston Station at 8.30 in the morning for Liverpool, where they arrived at 1.45 p.m. On boarding their ship, Chesterton was interviewed by two journalists. Frances was delighted at how empty the ship was, writing in the diary she kept during their trip to North America: 'all the pleasanter'.[14] The purser gave them a better cabin than the one they had booked: 'Beautiful cabin', Frances noted, 'with a sort of sitting room attached and really quite spacious'. On Sunday 2 January they had breakfast on deck. The weather was 'wonderful outside but the indoor rooms are very overheated', a complaint that Frances was to make about American hotel rooms. They had discovered 'a lending library with plenty of the new books'. They sat at the Captain's table, where they made 'a nice little party'. That night the weather became 'rough' with wind and rain; and because they had left the porthole open, 'everything on the dressing table got soaked'. Next day Frances felt 'pretty sea-sick', but Chesterton was unaffected: 'G. perfectly well'. The Captain told Frances that the ship was 'making the long course 100 miles to the South for fear of icebergs'. On Tuesday 4 January Frances noted in her diary that the ship was not as empty as she had implied in her first entry:

We have over 1000 immigrants on board of every nationality. The poor souls look so wretched though often they are merry enough. There are only two classes of passengers on this boat 1st. and 3rd. It seems a shame that 100 first class passengers should occupy nearly the whole of the ship with a winter garden, library, smoke-room, drawing room, dining room and endless cabins and staterooms and these poor folk be confined in a very small space on the lower deck, but I hear they are very well fed most often better than ever in their lives before.

---

[13] *A.* 40–8.

[14] This diary, which is in GKCL, was given to Aidan Mackey by William Braybrooke, the son of Patrick Braybrooke, a writer and critic and a cousin of Chesterton, who presumably was given it by Dorothy Collins. Hereafter referred to as 'American Diary'.

Four days later on Sunday 8 January Chesterton presided at an evening concert and 'made an excellent speech on behalf of the Merchant Service orphanage'; according to the ship's officers, there was a record collection.[15]

On Monday 10 January, nine days after leaving Liverpool, the Chestertons arrived in New York. After lunch, 'the fun (or the horrors) began. Interviewers, photographers, film men—all seized on us and we spent our last hour on the boat in a mob of what I can only term lunatics,' recorded the dismayed Frances, while noting at the same time how good-humoured her husband remained throughout.[16] In the lengthy report in the *New York Times* next day, which noted that he spoke in 'essays' and that it was 'difficult . . . to get a direct reply to any leading question', Chesterton was quoted as saying that he had come to America 'to lose his impressions of the United States'. For he had plenty of ideas about America, but he supposed that they were 'all quite wrong'. He had come 'to give inadequate after-dinner speeches known as lectures'. He did not know what he would say till the time came: 'I am a journalist and so am vastly ignorant of many things, but because I am a journalist I write and talk about them all.' He then 'shook hands with some half dozen Customs officials who welcomed him to the city'.

The impression given by Mr Chesterton as he moved majestically along the pier or on the ship was one of huge bulk. To the ordinary sized people on the pier he seemed to blot out the liner and the river. Mrs Chesterton was busy with the luggage.

'My wife understands these things,' he said with a sweep of his stick, 'I don't.'

He did not think that anything that George Bernard Shaw said about England or the English could do any harm, as he had been out of touch with events for the last ten years.[17]

In order to get the two figures into the same picture, the photographers requested Mr Chesterton to sit in a big armchair while his wife stood beside him. When they were settled in the required pose, he exclaimed: 'I say, I don't like this; people will think that I am a German.' While Frances, who 'looked very small' beside her husband, 'attended to the luggage examination, opening trunks and bags', he 'delivered a short essay on the equality of men and women in England since the war'.[18]

---

[15] 'American Diary'.   [16] 'American Diary'.

[17] *New York Times*, 11 Jan. 1921.

[18] Ward, *GKC* 478–9. Frances kept newspaper cuttings of their American trip, now in BL Add. MS 73402, but, unlike on the later visit of 1930–1, without noting the dates and names of the newspapers.

The irony of the scene was apparently not lost on Chesterton, for six years later in his play *The Judgement of Dr Johnson* a couple arrives on a wild coast after a sea voyage, and, while the wife busies herself lighting a fire, the husband merely holds forth, observing: 'Wherever we find the manual work forced upon the weaker sex, while the man merely amuses himself in his own fashion, there we have the rude original savage state of man, before the dawn of reason.'[19]

When the Chestertons arrived at their hotel, 'another frenzied mob of newspapermen attacked us and even penetrated to our room and took photographs there'.[20] As he answered the reporters' questions, Chesterton wondered if he was not violating some amendment to the American constitution by smoking. Asked about the amendment enforcing Prohibition, he replied that he did not approve of it, hastily adding that it had not affected him when a reporter wondered if he had been suffering since landing. 'No country on earth', he declared, 'could ever force me to touch a drop of cocoa, but if any country forbad its citizens to drink cocoa ... I should immediately want to drink it ... ' As the ship approached New York harbour, he had been 'tempted to take all the liquor on board and pour it out to the Statue [of Liberty] in a final libation'. (Later, he was to note how it had 'a soothing effect on earnest Prohibitionists on the boat to urge, as a point of dignity and delicacy, that it ought to be given back to the French, a vicious race abandoned to the culture of the vine'.[21]) He offered his condolences to the reporters on the fact that their country had 'started out with the Declaration of Independence and ended up with prohibition'. (On another occasion during the lecture tour, he was to refuse to discuss Prohibition on the ground that he had promised on his visa application not to upset the American government![22]) Asked why he had come to America, he replied: 'It would be absurd for a man to go to his grave without seeing America. I'm all for the Statue of Liberty.' Inevitably, the Irish question came up, and Chesterton did not hesitate to deplore the fact that Catholic Ireland had opposed the Allied cause, with which it sympathized 'at heart', while recognizing all the wrongs it had suffered at the hands of the British. Asked if he would be going to the West Coast, he responded that he did not expect to go further west than Chicago: 'having seen both Jerusalem and Chicago, I think I shall have touched on the extremes of civilization.' He refused to give his impressions of America on his first day there: 'I am only human.'[23]

---

[19] *DJ* 16. [20] 'American Diary'. [21] *WISA* 73.
[22] BL Add. MS 73402, fo. 48. [23] BL Add. MS 73402, fo. 9.

Anyway, Chesterton did not feel that he was the sightseer, as he explained to the readers of the *New Witness* in one of the articles he wrote from America that would become the book *What I Saw in America*. On the contrary, it was his lecture audiences that were the sightseers, even if they were 'seeing a rather melancholy sight'. It was said that people came 'to see the lecturer and not to hear him—in which case it seemed 'rather a pity that he should disturb and distress their minds with a lecture': 'He might merely exhibit himself on a stand or platform for a stipulated sum; or be exhibited like a monster in a menagerie.'[24]

But, if the American public stared at Chesterton, the famous man himself stared with amazement at what he saw in the New York hotel, the Biltmore, which the Chestertons were to make their base for the lecture tour. He was to discover that the inns of Europe did not exist in America. The Prohibitionists had closed the saloons, but no one could accuse them of the 'desecration' of 'chucking Chaucer out of the Tabard and Shakespeare out of the Mermaid'. However, hotels existed such as Chesterton had never before seen—or rather 'only one hotel' existed, to be found in all parts of America. For every hotel was built on the same 'rational pattern' with every floor exactly the same. There were no 'lifts' but only 'elevators', an example Chesterton thought of the American tendency 'to linger upon long words', which was 'rather strange' considering their fondness for 'hustle and hurry'. More used to stairs than to lifts, Chesterton at first wondered whether Americans 'possessed and practised a new and secret religion, which was the cult of the elevator'. Certainly, it was noticeable that gentlemen always took off their hats to ladies in this 'tiny temple', as though they were in church, but not in the lobby of the hotel, which 'is thrown open to the public streets and treated as a public square': 'My first impression was that I was in some sort of high street or market-place during a carnival or revolution.'[25]

The day after arriving in New York, the Chestertons took the 10 a.m. train to Boston. 'The heat of the trains and hotels is indescribable—but no windows are allowed to be opened,' Frances lamented. What she saw from the window of the train was no less dismal: 'Nothing had prepared me for the utterly neglected look of these unending collections of wooden houses. There are no gardens to any of them...'. They arrived in Boston at 4 o'clock in the afternoon to the same reception as in New York: 'Again assaulted by a wailing crowd of journalists...'. Next day, after the usual interviews and photographs, Frances recorded in her diary her distinctly

---

[24] *A.* 51.   [25] *WISA* 52, 55.

unfavourable feelings about America: 'So far my feelings towards this country are entirely hostile—but it would be unfair to judge too soon.' The contrast between the temperature outside and inside continued to dismay her: 'Bitterly cold outside and the heat unbearable inside'. Still, at least the audiences were 'most appreciative' and enjoyed Chesterton's humour. He lectured in Boston on 'The Ignorance of the Educated'. His mannerisms as a lecturer inevitably attracted the attention of journalists. It was noted that he spoke 'clearly' but 'in a rather high-pitched voice', accompanying 'his remarks with many nervous little gestures': 'His hands, at times, stray into his pockets. He leans over the reading desk as if he would like to get down into the audience and make it a sort of heart-to-heart talk.' One reporter was fascinated by the movement of his right hand as it 'spent a restless and rather disturbing evening':

It would start from the reading desk at which he stood and fall to the points of that vast waistcoat which inspired the description of him as 'a fellow of infinite vest'. It would wander aimlessly a moment about his—stomach is a word that is taboo among the polite English—equator, and then shift swiftly to the rear until the thumb found the hip pocket. There the hand would rest a moment, to return again to the reading desk and to describe once more the quarter circle. Once in a while it would twist a ring upon the left hand, once in a while it would be clasped behind the broad back, but only for a moment. To the hip pocket and back again was its sentry-go, and it was a faithful soldier.[26]

Chesterton had begun his lecture by observing that he was the only person in the auditorium who could not lecture, since, no lecturer himself, he found himself in the land of lecturers. The mark of being truly educated, he declared, was that one did not believe what the newspapers say.[27]

The press was interested in Frances as well as her famous husband: 'I was interviewed to my amusement but insisted on seeing a proof so that nothing too outrageous should be printed.'[28] On 15 January, Frances, who was constantly feeling tired and ill, saw a doctor, who told her she must rest for four hours a day, refuse all invitations, and absent herself from her husband's lectures. The doctor advised a few days in a nursing home but instead agreed to give her 'a strong tonic and sleeping draught'.[29]

Back in New York, they had lunch with their old friends from Overstrand Mansions, Battersea, Rann and Edith Kennedy—'a very great joy after 10 years'. The Rann Kennedys, who were now living near Poughkeepsie in

[26] Ward, *GKC* 478–80.   [27] BL Add. MS 73402, fo. 10.
[28] 'American Diary'.   [29] 'American Diary'.

New York state, had become American citizens in 1917. In spite of the doctor's orders, Frances was 'interviewed and photographed all the afternoon'.[30] Chesterton lectured on the same subject as in Boston, this time asserting that to be truly educated was to refrain from either reading or writing for the newspapers! He began the lecture by admitting, 'Mine is the voice of the original mouse that came out of the mountain,' and apologizing to those who could not hear him—and even more to those who could hear him![31] He had been introduced as a man whose 'voice was heard on four continents. "But you will have reason, I fear," said the lecturer, "to gather that it is not heard in all theatres." '[32]

On 18 January the Chestertons left New York for Northampton, Massachusetts, where Chesterton lectured at Smith College. Their hosts welcomed them in English style—'a wood fire to welcome us—tea . . .'. After the lecture the entertainment was more American: they 'sat round the fire and made pop-corn and toasted mallows'. Next day Frances felt much better: 'Got a good night sleep at last . . .'. It seems the reporters were almost as interested in her—'I saw many interviewers'—as in her husband, the 'leading American bestseller'.[33]

Back in New York, the Chestertons had lunch again on 22 January with the Kennedys at the Women's University Club, where Chesterton 'only said a few words'. The American fascination with celebrities amazed Frances: 'Why several hundred women should come together in a hot and crowded room to see us, when there was not even a speech to be made is beyond my understanding but they like to do it it seems.' That evening, only a week after seeing the doctor who had advised her not to attend her husband's lectures, Frances was present at the Brooklyn Institute to hear him speak: 'We went by subway—a new experience, like our *tube* but not so good.' She thought New York was 'a wonderful sight at night especially the view from Brooklyn Bridge (1 mile long)'.[34] Her husband had 'looked, not without joy', at Broadway's 'long kaleidescope of coloured lights arranged in large letters and sprawling trade-marks, advertising everything, from pork to pianos, through the agency of the two most vivid and most mystical of the gifts of God: colour and fire', remarking in his 'simplicity' to his American friends (it 'seemed for some reason to amuse them'): 'What a glorious garden of wonders this would be, to any one who was lucky enough to be unable to read.'[35] Next day Frances had another bad

---

[30] 'American Diary'.   [31] BL Add. MS 73402, fo. 12.
[32] AP 642.   [33] 'American Diary'.   [34] 'American Diary'.
[35] *WISA* 62.

headache, but went for a short walk in Central Park—'a poor substitute for a park as we mean it'; but still it was 'a relief from the streets'.[36]

Four days later they left for New Haven, Connecticut, where Chesterton lectured to 'a very enthusiastic audience—hundreds of Yale boys stormed the platform afterwards for hand shakes and autographs'. Next day they left for a lecture at Bridgeport, Conn. Two days later they arrived in Philadelphia, where they were met as usual by reporters and photographers. 'What I've seen of Philadelphia', Frances recorded in her diary, 'I really like'.[37] Chesterton told the press that, because of his extensive knowledge of detective stories, he imagined he would 'be right at home with any thieves in Philadelphia, if she has any'.[38] They returned to New York next day, but were back again three days later on 2 February, when they 'lunched at a cafeteria, quite an amusing experience—you take a tray and place on it all you want to eat and then get a ticket punched'.[39] After one of the lectures in Philadelphia, a woman asked Chesterton what made women talk so much, to which he replied, briefly, 'God, Madam'.[40] On this second visit a reporter asked him whether he liked lecturing, to which he responded: 'I always feel like a quack doctor. As to nervousness, I am obsessed, before I go upon the stage, by the feeling that I shall make a fool of myself; and I always have a warm, glowing feeling, when I leave the stage, that I actually have made a fool of myself.'[41]

Two days later they were in Baltimore for a lecture. During the questions at the end, Chesterton was asked if Shaw was to some extent himself the Superman and replied: 'I do not think it is as bad as that.' Would he himself prefer to be the Superman or the Missing Link? The latter, replied Chesterton without hesitation. Interviewed by the press, Frances insisted: 'The real truth is that I care more for my dog, donkey and garden in the little English village where we live than for all the publicity in the world.' 'Thank Heaven', she continued, 'my husband is thoroughly normal and unaffected; he doesn't care for popularity any more than I do, and we are both just terribly homesick for our home in England.' Her worst duty as the wife of a famous man, she confessed, was having to 'read stupid letters from feminine admirers'.[42] The state of Maryland, Chesterton was to remind his readers in the *New Witness*, 'was the first experiment in religious freedom in human history', but the fact that 'the first religious toleration ever granted in the world was granted by Roman Catholics' was 'one of

---

[36] 'American Diary'.   [37] 'American Diary'.
[38] BL Add. MS 73402, fo. 15.   [39] 'American Diary'.
[40] Ward, *GKC* 482.   [41] AP 645–6.   [42] BL Add. MS 73402, fo. 19.

those little informing details with which our Victorian histories did not exactly teem'. Chesterton visited the first monument raised to Washington after the American Revolution, where he fell into conversation with two children 'who were clambering about the bases of the monument': 'I felt a profound and radiant peace in the thought that they at any rate were not going to my lecture. It made me happy that in that talk neither they nor I had any names. I was full of that indescribable waking vision of the strangeness of life, and especially of the strangeness of locality . . .'. Baltimore was also memorable as providing 'the only sample of the substance called "tea" ever found on the American continent'.[43] The spirit of freedom that characterized Baltimore for Chesterton reminded him of the Irish struggle for freedom. 'When you hear of an organization in England fighting for liberty,' he told an Irish American he met, 'you must find whether or not that organization contains much Irish blood.' A strike in Glasgow, for instance, meant an 'exciting' strike: 'The reason is that a mass of the Irish poor is found in that city, and the Irish will not submit meekly when any person or any group tries to trample upon them.' True, there were 'plenty of old radicals in England, who, as individuals, are sincere defenders of liberty, but they are isolated'. But the Irish 'love for liberty seems to have been created by the Catholic Church—their only corporate defender of liberty today—is the Catholic Church. Liberty means much to her—something to be protected.'[44]

Returning to New York, Chesterton gave a lecture on 6 February, which the *New York Times* reported next day. When the time for questions arrived, he was asked about the 'psychological significance' of his use of paradoxes, which elicited the grave reply: 'I never use paradox. The statements I make are wearisome and obvious common sense. I have even been driven to the tedium of reading through my own books, and have been unable to find any paradox. In fact, the thing is quite tragic, and some day I shall hope to write an epic called "Paradox Lost".'[45] Asked by the *New York Herald* about his famous love of paradox, Chesterton declared: 'I should not know a paradox if it met me on the street.'[46] The Chestertons then travelled on to Pittsburgh, where there was a collective gasp from the audience when they saw the huge expanse of the lecturer, who hastened to reassure them in his opening words at the microphone: 'At the outset I want to reassure you I am not of this size, really; dear no, I'm being

[43] *WISA* 90–1.   [44] Clemens, 88–9.
[45] *New York Times*, 7 Feb. 1921.   [46] BL Add. MS 73402, fo. 25.

amplified by the thing.'[47] After a lecture in Washington, the Chestertons left New York on Saturday 12 February for Montreal on the night train, arriving at 7.45 a.m. on Sunday morning. In the afternoon Frances went for a sleigh ride to the top of Mount Royal. Interviewed by the *Montreal Daily Star*, Chesterton said that being in New York was 'very much like being in hell—pleasantly, of course. I had a wild and whirling experience.' By contrast, a city like Baltimore gave 'a very definite impression of that fine old republican spirit, which English people have never really understood'.[48]

Apparently, Chesterton had stipulated before leaving England that he must have three days free of lectures so that he could spend some time with his relations in Ottawa. But when the time for his visit approached, there was a smallpox scare, which caused Chesterton's lecture agent, Lee Keedick, to send a telegram to say that, if there was going to be any difficulty about leaving the city, he would not be able to come. But the reply was that so long as he was vaccinated there would be no problem.[49]

Accordingly, at 5 p.m. the Chestertons left Montreal for Ottawa, arriving there at eight, where Chesterton's uncle Walter Chesterton, an architect who designed many of the public buildings in Ottawa, met the train and took them to his house at 300 Waverley Street. Unfortunately, when the Chestertons went upstairs to their bedroom, they discovered that Chesterton had the wrong suitcase. Lilian, the daughter of the house, heard 'a scream of laughter from upstairs, a door opened and both Gilbert and Frances called out, "Lil, come here."' Running upstairs, Lilian found them standing over the strange suitcase. 'What amused them most was thinking of the plight of the owner if he tried to wear Gilbert's clothes!'[50]

'Such a lovely day of snow and sunshine,' Frances wrote in her diary the next day. In the afternoon there was another sleigh drive followed by sightseeing, which 'included a glimpse' of the Duke and Duchess of Devonshire, 'who had just opened Parliament', in their 'state sleigh with outriders in scarlet against the dazzling snow'.[51] Asked by a reporter if England would ever introduce Prohibition, Chesterton replied with a chuckle that, if the governing class could be assured of its indispensable glass of champagne, then it was not impossible. They were leaving America in April, on April Fool's Day, he hoped, after failing as a lecturer.[52] On Wednesday the 16th they left Ottawa at midday, arriving back in Montreal at four o'clock. After Chesterton had given a lecture in the evening, they

[47] Clemens, 62.   [48] AP 646.   [49] AP 647.
[50] AP 648.   [51] 'American Diary'.   [52] BL Add. MS 73402, fo. 22.

'hurried off to catch the night train to Toronto', where they arrived next day at 7.30 in the morning. Frances found the King Edward Hotel 'noisy and crowded'.[53] There were the usual interviews and photographs. Chesterton gave a lecture in the evening on 'The Ignorance of the Educated'. The professor of English who was in the chair 'thought there must have been an error in the title as printed, and announced that Mr Chesterton would speak on The Ignorance of the *Un*educated'.[54] That night the Chestertons' sleep was disturbed by 'a jazz band which went on till 2 a.m.'.[55]

On Friday 18 February the Chestertons left Toronto to cross back into the United States, arriving in Albany at seven o'clock in the evening, where they found a pile of letters awaiting them. The next evening Chesterton gave a lecture. Frances informed the press when she was interviewed: 'I didn't know I was the wife of a great man till I came to America. It had never bothered me before.' While in America she had failed to encounter a single draught or Prohibitionist. On Sunday they woke up to find it had snowed heavily during the night. Unable to get a taxi, they had to borrow a car to drive to Buffalo, where they arrived at 7.30 in the evening of Sunday 20 February. Next day they were driven to see the Niagara Falls, which 'were a disappointment'. After a lecture in the evening—'a tremendous success'—they left Buffalo at midnight for Chicago, where they arrived at one o'clock next day 'very tired'. Frances went to bed and stayed there till it was time for dinner with the Rann Kennedys. It was raining heavily and what Frances saw of Chicago looked 'dreadful', although Lake Michigan looked 'rather wonderful'.[56]

Next morning Chesterton visited a bookshop in the Marshall Field building, where he encountered the English writer John Drinkwater and the American novelist Sinclair Lewis, the author of the best-selling satire on small town America, *Main Street*, which had been published the previous year. The visitors were invited into the proprietor's office. Lewis told the others that he had 'received floods of letters from people in the small towns throughout the middle west taking him to task' for implying that *Main Street* was a typical American town. An onlooker of this literary gathering suggested that the three writers should collaborate in a play, a suggestion that was 'received with delight'. The proprietor invited them to stay for lunch, which he would have sent up from the tea rooms on the floor below: 'Upon his saying that he had something rare in his safe besides books, Chesterton decided to stay.' The rest of the company immediately

---

[53] 'American Diary'.   [54] Ward, *GKC* 480–1.
[55] 'American Diary'.   [56] 'American Diary'.

followed suit. Lewis's proposal that the play should be named *Marry the Queen of Scotch* was met with approval by the others, now 'in a haze of alcohol', and it was agreed that Chesterton should write the first act, which, Chesterton announced, would feature a murder mystery: 'There is nothing like a nice murder.' The hero was to be the son of a rich English whisky distiller and the heroine the daughter of an American ex-distiller from Peoria, Illinois. An American Prohibitionist of 'international fame' would be found dead in his Paris hotel room, the weapon, a broken bottle, lying beside the body. The rooms on either side would be occupied by the hero and heroine, upon whom suspicion would naturally fasten.[57]

Meanwhile, Frances, after 'a wonderful lunch' with some 'very nice women', was taken to see 'the famous Marshal Field Store', where Self-ridge, the owner of the famous London shop named after him, used to work. Chesterton gave 'a fine lecture' in the evening in Orchestra Hall to an audience of 3,000, but 'did not seem done up after it'.[58] Interviewed in his hotel by a reporter, he insisted first of all on lighting a cigar, saying: 'Some men write with a pencil, others with a typewriter, I write with my cigar.' Asked which of his works he considered the greatest, he replied: 'I don't consider any of my works in the least great.' Slang, he told the reporter, was 'too sacred and precious to be used promiscuously. Its use should be led up to reverently for it expresses what the King's English could not.'[59]

They left Chicago on Thursday morning, arriving in Columbus, Ohio, at 8.20 in the evening. The couple they stayed with were 'very delightful people—so affectionate and warm hearted'. On Friday morning they were taken by car 'to see something of the very dull country of the Middle West'. The lecture in the evening was 'a real scrum but quite good fun'. On Saturday 26 February they left Columbus in the morning for Detroit, where they arrived over six hours later at 4.30 in the afternoon. The evening lecture next day in Orchestra Hall 'went well'.[60] Chesterton acknowledged that he spoke with an 'English axn't'—'and regretted deeply that he might never apprehend what it was like'.[61] A Detroit newspaper reported that actually seeing and hearing the man provided 'a meal for the imagination' such as no books by or about Chesterton could give. The subject of his lecture, as in Toronto, was the ignorance of the

---

[57] AP 651–2; Mark Schorer, *Sinclair Lewis: An American Life* (London: Heinemann, 1961), 304.

[58] 'American Diary'.   [59] Ward, *GKC* 480.

[60] 'American Diary'.   [61] *Detroit Saturday Night*, 5 Mar. 1921.

educated: the trouble with educated people was that they substituted theories for things, whereas the uneducated simply stated the facts as they saw them: they would say, for example, that they saw that a German was drinking beer, not that a Teuton was consuming alcohol. Another Detroit newspaper quoted from the lecture: 'There is a deeper side to such fallacies. The whole catastrophe of the Great War may be traced to the racial theory. If people had looked at peoples as nations in place of races the intolerable ambition of Prussia might have been stopped before it attained the captaincy of the South German States.'[62] In a newspaper interview next morning, Frances confessed: 'I was never interviewed in my life until I came to America.' What had most touched her was 'the genuine affection' with which her husband was greeted everywhere. When the reporter congratulated her husband on his lecture the evening before, Chesterton responded: 'You can gather what I think of my lectures from the fact that I always precipitately leave town the next day!'[63]

The Chestertons left Detroit on Monday 28 February at midday 'on a miserable day of mist and rain', arriving in the evening in Cleveland. As usual, Frances found the heat of the train unbearable, and she went to bed with a headache, lying in late next morning. Both Chestertons were interviewed before lunch. Chesterton assured the *Cleveland Press* that he was losing his impressions about America. He thought politics should be kept 'as local as possible': 'Keep the politicians near enough to kick them. The villagers who met under the village tree could also hang their politicians to the tree. It's terrible to contemplate how few politicians are hung today.' He claimed he was not troubled by his weight: 'I've never taken the trouble to weigh myself.' Anyway, his weight gave him 'something with which to start after-dinner speeches'.[64] After dinner they were invited to meet Helen Keller, the author and political activist, who was staying in the same hotel. In her diary Frances describes her as 'the blind girl who [was] also deaf and dumb'. In fact, Helen Keller was only deaf and blind as a result of an illness when she was a baby. Frances thought she was 'quite wonderful or rather... the lady [was] who taught her' sign language and became her companion. Rather 'pretty and very lively', Helen 'amused herself by making up paradoxes and retailing them' to Chesterton—'very good they were too'. The writer of paradoxes would have been less amused by the progressive views of Helen Keller, who had founded the American Civil Liberties Union the previous year, and who was a Socialist, a

[62] Ward, *GKC* 480–1.   [63] AP 655–6.
[64] *Cleveland Press*, 28 Feb.–2 March 1921.

suffragette, and an advocate of contraception. Wednesday 2 March was a 'very fine day, quite a feeling of spring'. Chesterton gave an evening lecture in the hotel ball room.

Next day they left Cleveland on the 8.30 train back to Toronto, where they arrived in the evening, whereupon Frances went to bed in the same hotel she had so disliked on their previous visit. Utterly exhausted, Frances stayed in bed till four o'clock the next afternoon and did not attend Chesterton's lecture in the evening. On Saturday 5 March she had 'to submit to an interview for the Toronto "Daily Star"', before leaving after midday for Detroit, where they arrived at 10.20 in the evening, 'very done for by that time'. The 2.30 train next day took them to Dayton, Ohio, where they arrived at 11.30 at night. The next morning was another morning in bed for Frances, but in the afternoon she was taken for 'a lovely ride round Dayton which is really very pretty'.[65] It was here in Dayton, Chesterton later recalled, that he was interviewed on the roof of the hotel where they were staying:

after answering the usual questions about Labour, the League of Nations, the length of ladies' dresses, and other great matters, I took refuge in a rhapsody of warm and well-deserved praise of American bathrooms. The editor, I understand, running a gloomy eye down the column of his contributor's 'story', and seeing nothing but metaphysical terms such as justice, freedom . . . and the like, paused at last upon the ablutionary allusion, and his eye brightened. 'That's the only copy in the whole thing,' he said, 'A Bath-tub in Every Home'. So these words appeared in enormous letters above my portrait in the paper. It will be noted that, like many things that practical men make a great point of, they miss the point. What I had commended as new and national was a bathroom in every bedroom. Even feudal and moss-grown England is not entirely ignorant of the occasional bath-tub in the home. But what gave me great joy was what followed. I discovered with delight that many people, glancing rapidly at my portrait with its prodigious legend, imagined that it was a commercial advertisement, and that I was a very self-advertising commercial traveller.

This 'charming error' Chesterton was only able regretfully to trace 'with certainty' to 'two individuals', who naturally supposed that, because there was 'a Laundry Convention going on in the same hotel', he had come to Dayton to attend the said Laundry Convention, 'and had made an eloquent speech to that senate, no doubt exhibiting my tubs'.[66] After Chesterton had given a lecture at Victory Hall, there was 'a rush' to get to the station to catch the night train for Chicago.[67]

---

[65] 'American Diary'.   [66] *WISA* 56–7.   [67] 'American Diary'.

They arrived back in Chicago at the hotel at 7.30 a.m. after 'a horrible night journey', 'the worst I've experienced', wrote Frances miserably in her diary after a sleepless night. After lunch Chesterton went off to lecture, but Frances stayed in the hotel 'too tired to move'. On Wednesday 9 March they left Chicago for Madison, a four-and-a-half-hour journey. Frances was cheered up by the 'really pretty journey through Wisconsin'. The farmhouses they saw through the train window had 'that settled and ordered look that belongs to older countries'. The hotel where they stayed was also satisfactorily 'small and countrified (comparatively)'. Chesterton lectured for an hour and a half to 'a crowded and amused audience' at the university, where the 'college yell greeted him'.[68] During questions, he asserted that, in spite of being accused of an excessive love of paradox, he could not find any paradoxes in his books, only dull monotonous good sense![69] The next day was free until they took the 9.30 p.m. train for Duluth in Minnesota, where they arrived next morning at 8.30. Frances went immediately to bed, 'very done up'. Chesterton gave a lecture in the evening, while Frances stayed in bed. On Saturday 12 March they left Duluth in the afternoon and arrived in Minneapolis in the late evening.

They had a day off here to break the journey before taking the night train to Omaha, where they arrived at 7.45 a.m. on the Monday morning after a sleepless night on a 'very shaky train'. Frances was glad that there were only four more lectures to give before returning to New York. At Omaha they were entertained to lunch by the ladies of the Fine Arts Club, who had arranged the lecture Chesterton gave in the afternoon in the hotel ball room.[70] This was the only lecture of the entire tour that met with a decidedly negative response: the lecturer told his audience at the beginning of the lecture that he was 'one of those famous Englishmen who cannot lecture—and do'. The *Omaha Daily Bee* reported that by the end of the hour 'the majority of his audience agreed with him'. However, one lady confessed that, while like the rest of the audience she did not get much from the lecture, 'I think the reason we didn't is because our own education is so superficial; he's beyond us'. The *Omaha Daily Bee* subsequently explained that the anger felt by the citizens of Omaha arose from their fear that they had 'missed the fine points' of the lecture and that it was above their heads.[71] Chesterton, for his part, told reporters that he had 'left a trail of wailing rabbis all across the continent', one of whom in Omaha he believed had warned 'every lover of his fellow man' to stay away from

[68] 'American Diary'.   [69] BL Add. MS 73402, fo. 31.
[70] 'American Diary'.   [71] AP 657–9.

his lecture. This did not worry him in the slightest, as he liked a small audience: 'Just picture to yourself a few misanthropes, sitting several chairs apart, scowling into space, and all the humanitarians staying at home.' As for his book *The New Jerusalem*, if the rabbis had 'read all the chapters on the Jews' and considered they constituted 'fanaticism, then all the fanaticism is on their side'.[72] He was 'not a little hurt and puzzled about their unreasonable attitude because in that work I have honestly tried to be objective, fair, and understanding, but they won't see that'.[73] He thought Americans took his 'work absolutely too seriously, though they make the best audience to lecture to in the world. In England a lecture is a most dry affair. It is not a national sport.' What most impressed him about America were the *en suite* hotel rooms.[74]

Next day, Tuesday 15 March, they left for Kansas City at 1.30 p.m., where they arrived at 8.30 in the evening. They then took the night train to Oklahoma City, a town that had been 'created out of the ... prairie in less than thirty years' owing to the discovery of oil, where they arrived shortly after midday on the 16th. 'The journey was so lovely,' wrote Frances, 'through little spring woods with wild cherry—almond—peach and all in flower'.[75] There was no lecture that day, but Chesterton faced the usual interviews that afternoon. He found it, he said, 'interesting and agreeable to find people who were proud of having lived in a community for only three minutes'. As for himself, he lamented that he felt 'like a race horse being hauled about in a box car, if I may be permitted to compare myself with so useful and elegant an animal'.[76] The following day they were taken for 'a lovely ride ... about this startlingly new but interesting place'. After calling on the state governor, Chesterton lectured in the evening at the Presbyterian church.[77]

While they were in Oklahoma City an accident occurred that 'could not have happened in any other country' that Chesterton had 'ever clapped eyes on'. If he could understand it, he seriously believed he would understand America. Oklahoma was what foreigners imagined wrongly was true of all American cities: it was 'proud of having no history. [It was] glowing with the sense of having a great future—and nothing else.' While strolling down the main street, Chesterton was accosted by a stranger who demanded to know what he was doing in the city. The 'most singular thing about him was that the front of his coat was covered with a multitude of

[72] BL Add. MS 73402, fo. 32.   [73] Clemens, 87–8.
[74] BL Add. MS 73402, fo. 32.   [75] 'American Diary'.
[76] BL Add. MS 73402, fo. 31.   [77] 'American Diary'.

shining metallic emblems made in the shape of stars and crescents'. To this singular stranger's question, Chesterton replied 'with restraint' that he was lecturing. To this the stranger replied 'without restraint, but with an expansive and radiant pride, "I also am lecturing. I am lecturing on astronomy."'

Expanding his starry bosom and standing astraddle, with the air of one who owned the street, the strange being continued, 'Yes, I am lecturing on astronomy, anthropology, archaeology, palaeontology, embryology, eschatology,' and so on in a thunderous roll of theoretical sciences apparently beyond the scope of any single university, let alone any single professor. Having thus introduced himself, how-ever, he got to business. He apologised with true American courtesy for having questioned me at all, and excused it on the ground of his own exacting respon-sibilities. I imagined him to mean the responsibility of simultaneously occupying the chairs of all the faculties already mentioned. But these apparently were trifles to him, and something far more serious was clouding his brow. 'I feel it to be my duty' he said, 'to acquaint myself with any stranger visiting this city; and it is an additional pleasure to welcome here a member of the Upper Ten.' I assured him earnestly that I knew nothing about the Upper Ten, except that I did not belong to them...He waved my abnegation aside and continued, 'I have a great responsibility in watching over this city. My friend the mayor and I have a great responsibility.' And then an extraordinary thing happened. Suddenly diving his hand into his beast-pocket, he flashed something before my eyes like a hand-mirror; something which disappeared again almost as soon as it appeared. In that flash I could only see that it was some sort of a polished metal plate, with some letters engraved on it like a monogram. But the reward of a studious and virtuous life, which has been spent chiefly in the reading of American detective stories, shone forth for me in that hour of trial; I received at last the prize of a profound scholarship in the matter of imaginary murders in tenth-rate magazines. I remembered who it was who in the Yankee detective yarn flashes before the eyes of Slim Jim or the Lone Hand Crook a badge of metal sometimes called a shield. Assuming all the desperate composure of Slim Jim himself, I replied, 'You mean you are connected with the police authorities here, don't you? Well, if I commit a murder here, I'll let you know.' Whereupon that astonishing man waved a hand in deprecation, bowed in farewell with the grace of a dancing master; and said, 'Oh, these are not the things we expect from the Upper Ten.' Then that moving constellation moved away, disappearing in the dark tides of humanity...

'Who and what was that man?' Chesterton wondered. 'Was he an astron-omer? Was he a detective? Was he a wandering lunatic?' Two things Chesterton did know. First, he knew that 'he had something else in his pocket besides a badge' and that 'under certain circumstances he would have...shot me dead'. Second, he knew that, confronted with 'this mysterious figure', he was 'confronted with the fullness and depth of the mystery of America. Because I understand nothing, I recognise the thing that we call a nation; and I salute the flag.'[78]

On Friday 18 March the Chestertons left Oklahoma City for St Louis, which they reached at about 8.15 next morning after travelling all night with little sleep. Still, they had 'a comfortable drawing room car' and the countryside was 'looking lovely and the weather...like a perfect English June'. Frances found her hotel room 'decorated with lovely roses a gift from the management', and a pile of letters from England awaiting her: 'I was so glad of them.' Next day was Palm Sunday: 'Oh for Jerusalem,' sighed Frances. That afternoon they received an 'urgent invitation' to call at the Convent of the Sacred Heart, where Frances was presented with 'the loveliest bouquet of roses'. 'We like St Louis—though the town itself is not much to boast of but it is older and mellower than the middle west towns such as Omaha and Oklahoma City,' Frances recorded in her diary. Chesterton's lecture took place in the hall of the Ethical Society: 'very successful and many questions were asked and delightfully answered.' On Monday they left St Louis at 8.15 in the morning and travelled all day through 'pretty country' to Nashville. Next day Frances was suffering from one of her headaches and stayed in bed till after lunch. It was pouring with rain. The lecture in the evening was 'tremendously appreciated'.[79] They stayed at the Hotel Hermitage, which had been President Andrew Jackson's home. Frances was again interviewed and again declared, 'I was never interviewed in my life until I came to America.' At the end of the interview her husband appeared and again told the press, 'You can gather what I think of my lectures from the fact that I always precipitately leave town the next day.'[80] They duly left Nashville next day, Wednesday the 23rd, on the 7.25 train and travelled all day to Indianapolis, where they arrived at 6.30 in the evening, after changing trains at Louisville. Next day in the Masonic Hall there was 'a very enthusiastic though small audience' at Chesterton's lecture—'this is the last lecture on tour—thank heaven,' recorded Frances with relief. After going to church next day, which was Good Friday, they left for New York at three o'clock in the afternoon, arriving there at about two in the afternoon next day, when they were met by Chesterton's agent Lee Keedick. On Easter Sunday, which fell that year

---

[78] *WISA* 172–5.   [79] 'American Diary'.
[80] BL Add. MS 73402, fo. 14.

on 27 March, they 'got to early celebration at the Church of St Mary the Virgin near this hotel'. That evening Frances attended her husband's 'very good' lecture 'The Revolt against Reason'.[81]

Apart from the voyage home, their travels were now ended, and Frances had time to rest, as well as to see friends, including the Rann Kennedys, although it fell to her, of course, to make the practical arrangements for their departure. Before they could leave America they had to pay 8 per cent tax on the proceeds of the lecture tour. There was also a pile of correspondence waiting to be attended to. On 3 April Chesterton lectured at the Apollo Theatre on 'Ireland and the Parallel of the Confederacy'. On the evening of 5 April they left the hotel for an apartment at 56 85th East Street that belonged to some friends. During the day they saw a friend from Bedford Park days, 'old Mr Yeats who is the same as ever—talked delightfully'. On the 9th the Chestertons went to a lunch given in their honour at the National Arts Club by the Dickens Fellowship; they were greeted with great enthusiasm, Chesterton 'made an excellent speech', and even Frances was called upon to say a few words. They 'rushed away' to catch the 3.30 train for Poughkeepsie, where they stayed the night at Millbrook with the Kennedys, who were joint heads of the drama department at Bennett School for Girls. In the evening they went to watch at the Greek theatre—which the Kennedys had had built[82]—a 'part performance' of Euripides' *Electra*. Frances thought the chorus was 'quite wonderful, and Edith splendid'. Afterwards a lot of the girls came round to the Kennedys' home—'such a happy party', Frances wrote in her diary. Next day the Chestertons visited the school, where Rann and Edith Kennedy 'gave a reading' of his one-act 1912 play *The Terrible Meek*, before returning to New York in the afternoon. On 11 April Chesterton lectured for the last time.[83]

One thing that had delighted him about lecturing in America was the American sense of time: people arrived at his lectures (he would 'heartily recommend the habit of coming too late') frequently 'three-quarters of an hour or even an hour after time . . . it gave me a sort of dizzy exaltation to find I was not the most unpunctual person . . .'. Any fears that his disapproval of Prohibition might displease his hosts were soon dispelled: 'I went to America with some notion of not discussing Prohibition. But I soon found that well-to-do Americans were only too delighted to discuss it over the nuts and wine. They were even willing, if necessary, to dispense with

---

[81] 'American Diary'.   [82] Ward, *RC* 242.   [83] 'American Diary'.

the nuts.' It was 'to some extent enforced among the poor; at any rate it was intended to be enforced among the poor', but it was 'certainly not enforced among the rich; and I doubt whether it was intended to be'.[84] Frances had felt tired or ill for much of the trip, as well as homesick. One newspaper reported that she noticeably cheered up on hearing from the current secretary back at Overroads, Kathleen Chesshire, that the crocuses were in bloom. Frances again told a reporter that she cared more for her dog, donkey, and garden back home than for 'all the publicity in the world'. Far from being an adorer of her husband, while she admired intelligence, she thought life was 'too short to put one's husband on a pedestal', apart from being 'unutterably boring'. Anyway, her husband was 'thoroughly normal and unaffected' and did not 'care for popularity' any more than she did. She claimed that, while her husband lectured, she was 'organizing a campaign for the emancipation of the wives of famous men'.[85]

On Tuesday 12 April they said goodbye to America. Asked by reporters what had most impressed him in America, Chesterton replied: 'The number of people who came to my lectures. Such an outpouring of people could hardly be possible in England!'[86] The ship sailed at 12.30. On the instructions of the Cunard shipping line they were given a better cabin than they had booked, a state room with a bathroom attached. On the 14th Frances recorded that Chesterton had had 'a long and interesting talk' with Sir Ernest Shackleton, the Antarctic explorer, who gave a 'delightful' lecture with slides the following evening. The next day Chesterton presided at a concert in aid of the Liverpool Seamen's Orphanage, in which the film star Pearl White, the so-called Stunt Queen of the silent films, participated. It was 'quite a magnificent affair', and over £100 was collected. On Sunday 17 April both Chestertons attended a religious service that the Captain held in the lounge. Next day they reached Cherbourg. And on the 19th they arrived at Southampton at daybreak, where they caught the 10.15 train to Waterloo. On arrival they found Kathleen Chesshire, together with Chesterton's mother and 'Keith', awaiting them. After lunch at Waterloo and a visit to Warwick Gardens, they caught the 5.38 train from Marylebone Station to Beaconsfield—'and so HOME once more, and as I am feeling now,' wrote Frances, 'never again'.[87]

---

[84] *WISA* 121, 144.   [85] Ffinch, 271, 275.
[86] *New York Times*, 13 Apr. 1921.   [87] 'American Diary'.

3

On 15 February 1921 Chesterton had published an article in the *Manchester Guardian* condemning British atrocities in Ireland, albeit themselves a response to outrages committed by the Irish Republican Army or IRA. He expressed more briefly the same sentiments in 'What are Reprisals?', a pamphlet published by the Peace with Ireland Council either at the end of 1920 or in early 1921.[88] Like the British press in general, Chesterton expected the British government forces to behave in an altogether different way from the IRA, which was regarded as a terrorist organization of which the worst could be expected. In December 1918, following the execution of many of the leaders of the Easter Rising of 1916 and the threat of compulsory military service, the nationalist party Sinn Féin won a majority of the Irish seats in the Westminster parliament. Refusing to sit as members of the House of Commons in January 1919, they assembled in Dublin, set up a separate parliament, and declared an independent Irish republic. War then broke out between the British and the IRA. Michael Collins, the IRA leader, who led the Sinn Fein delegation at the peace talks that led eventually to the treaty of 6 December 1921 establishing the Irish Free State, was influenced in the formation of his nationalism by *The Napoleon of Notting Hill*, which he described as his favourite book. Hearing of this, Lloyd George gave copies of the book to his Cabinet before the negotiations began for insights into the mind of the Irish nationalist leader.[89] Joseph Plunkett, one of those executed after the Easter 1916 rising, was also a passionate admirer of Chesterton.[90]

Chesterton's article, which was subsequently published as a pamphlet by the Peace with Ireland Council in London under the title 'The Danger to England', began: 'The whole world thinks that England has gone mad.' The British entertained the 'most curious idea that what is done in Ireland is done in a corner and concerns only themselves. We treat Ireland not only as if it were our own farmyard, but our own backyard. The Government and the gangs of murderers between them are rapidly turning it into something rather resembling a churchyard.' Writing from North America, Chesterton maintained that people abroad knew more about what was being done in Ireland, as the details were often suppressed in British newspapers, as had been the case in the Marconi scandal. The British

[88] Repr. in the Ignatius *Collected Works*, xx. 641–2, but wrongly dated.
[89] Pearce, 89.
[90] R. F. Foster, *Paddy and Mr Punch* (London: Allen Lane, 1993), 305.

had effectively ceased to govern in Ireland, but instead were conducting what could only be called a 'Prussian war'. That is to say, they were carrying out a war of reprisals against the southern Catholic Irish, the principle of which was 'the very opposite of law and order'. Instead of ruling, the British were raiding the country; although the British government said they would never recognize Ireland as a separate nation, they were in fact 'paying the plainest possible compliment to its independence'—they were 'invading it' exactly as the Germans had invaded Belgium in the war. And, because the British seemed to be 'snatching at something as though it were slipping' from them, it gave the impression abroad that the British Empire was breaking up. Anti-British sentiment was growing worldwide, just as it had against the Germans. But the peoples Germany had invaded were not 'scattered everywhere among all the new democracies of the earth', and Britain could afford even less than Germany to make enemies everywhere, 'for we gather our food everywhere'. What people abroad saw when they saw 'the "black-and-tan" uniform in Ireland' was 'what we saw when we saw the black and yellow flag flying over Belgium'. Patriots like Chesterton who predicted the result of British reprisals would never desert their country but would be with it to the last—'to take our share in the hatred of humanity and our portion in the wrath of God'. In another article at the time, also published by the Peace with Ireland Council under the same title as that of the earlier pamphlet, 'What are Reprisals?', Chesterton again drew the analogy with the German invasion of Belgium that had brought Britain into war with Germany. Reprisals were intended to be 'indiscriminate': 'When men in our uniform shoot a woman with a baby in her arms, or kill a little girl of eight, it is a confusion of thought to profess that it was an accident, or even to discuss whether it was an accident. The whole system is designed to produce such accidents, even if you call them accidents.' The whole point of 'terror' was that innocent people should suffer. But the policy was clearly a failure: 'The very outburst of new demands for repression proves that it does not repress.' The British had copied what the Germans had done in Belgium—'down to the very last detail of all—that they were defeated'. The truth was that the British government was 'fighting against something that may express itself in wild and wicked ways but is not in itself wicked or even wild; and which therefore draws perpetually on infinite sources of strength...'. Wise statesmen would seek 'to avoid the necessity of stemming any such main stream of the nature of mankind; fighting against the love of home or the desire of freedom or the respect for the dead'. A government that had succeeded in stirring up 'all that mass of sympathies and half-sympathies' against it had ceased to govern. The common view in Ireland was that the British were 'not only wickeder but wilder' than the republican guerrillas.

The very first of the articles that would be collected together in *What I Saw in America*, published on 18 February 1921 in the *New Witness*, pointed out that Britain in its dispute with Ireland was dealing not just with the native Irish but with the huge Irish diaspora in English-speaking countries, which included a particularly numerous and powerful community in the United States.

4

In September 1922 Chesterton published *What I Saw in America*, rather less than a third of which consists of the articles he had already published while in America in the *New Witness*. He had already broken the promise he had made before leaving England, according to the *New York Times*,[91] that 'he would not write a book of American impressions on his return, as so many other' English writers had done, with the articles he had written for the *New Witness* while still in America. The book begins with the paradoxical assertion that 'travel narrows the mind', as the traveller tends to look at 'the outside' rather than 'the inside' of what he sees. In particular, the traveller is apt to be too 'much amused . . . to be instructed'. There was nothing wrong in 'thinking a thing funny because it is foreign', only in 'thinking it wrong because it is funny'. That was the mistake of Dickens when he visited America, thinking that Americans were 'foolish because they were funny'. The traveller was 'perfectly entitled to laugh at anything' so long as he understood that he himself was 'laughable'. Chesterton himself had never lost the sense of his own 'laughable position' while he was in America. Moreover, the traveller must realize that his sense of humour was not necessarily the same as that of the foreigner. Indeed, the American and English senses of humour 'are in one way directly contrary':

The most American sort of fun involves a soaring imagination, piling one house on another in a tower like that of the sky-scraper. The most English humour consists of a sort of bathos, of a man returning to the earth his mother in a homely fashion; as when he sits down suddenly on a butter-slide. English farce describes a

---

[91] *New York Times*, 2 Jan. 1921.

man as being in a hole. American fantasy, in its more aspiring spirit, describes a man as being up a tree.

American humour made 'life more wild and impossible than it is', and English humour made 'it more flat and farcical than it is'. The 'road to international friendship', Chesterton thought, was through understanding the other nations' 'jokes'.[92]

What made America superior to England in his view was that the British constitution lacked 'the theory of equality' that is 'the chief mark of the Declaration of Independence': 'Citizenship is the American ideal; and it has never been the English ideal.' On the other hand, if England could boast of 'less equality and fraternity', it had 'certainly more liberty'. And American equality did 'tend too much to uniformity', but then that uniformity reflected the idea of the 'dignity' of every citizen rather than the 'social superiority' of England. The 'danger' of a real democracy like America was 'convention', 'a general impression of unity verging on uniformity'. For democracy was 'no respecter of persons'. The American cult of individualism was, paradoxically, 'the death of individuality', since 'individualism is the reverse of individuality': 'Where men are trying to compete with each other they are trying to copy each other.' Again, the 'worship of personality' made Americans 'almost impersonal'. Unlike 'English eccentricity', there was not enough 'unconsciousness' in America 'to produce real individuality'. American women particularly tended 'too much to this cult of impersonal personality'.[93]

The uniformity of American life, Chesterton thought, undermined its democracy. It explained why, where there was 'so genuine a sense of human dignity, there should be so much of an impossible petty tyranny'. This was a country where not only was the 'sin of drink' punished but also 'the equally shameless sin of smoking a cigarette in the open air', not to mention people 'kissing each other'. How was it possible to reconcile such tyranny with 'the genuine democratic spirit' of the masses? What made 'this great democracy so unlike all other democracies, and in this so manifestly hostile to the whole democratic idea'? The 'first historical cause' was what Chesterton called 'Progressive Puritanism'—that is, 'unlimited limitation', in which 'prohibitions are bound to progress . . . more human rights and pleasures must of necessity be taken away':

Progressives are prophets . . . anybody who chooses to prophesy and prohibit can tyrannise over the people . . . people are afraid to contradict him for the fear they should be contradicting their own great-grandchild. For their

---

[92] *WISA* 37–8, 157–8, 227, 235.   [93] *WISA* 48–9, 57–8, 159–63, 250–1.

superstition is an inversion of the ancestor-worship of China; and instead of vainly appealing to something that is dead, they appeal to something that may never be born.

Another cause of 'this strange servile disease in American democracy' was American feminism. For, though 'the aggressive feminists are a minority, they are in this atmosphere . . . in which there is a sort of sanctity about the minority'. A 'feminine fad' was surrounded by 'a curious halo of hopeful solemnity', so that, when the 'earnest lady-reformer . . . utters a warning against the social evil of beer', for example, she was 'seen to be walking clothed in light, like a prophetess'. Chesterton wondered why, if drinking and smoking were prohibited, talking, which tends to lead to these two evil practices, should not also be 'put a stop to'. Indeed, 'nine-tenths of the harm in the world' was 'done simply by talking'. So perhaps the government should issue lists of subjects suitable for talking about, perhaps 'a formal application in writing' should be compulsory for making jokes, perhaps all should have to 'wear gags' except between one and three, when English pubs were allowed to open. But Chesterton knew that, if ever 'the statutory silence of the populace' became law, an exception for the rich would be made: 'It will only be the populace that is silent. The politicians will go on talking.'[94]

The worst example of 'petty tyranny' in America was Prohibition, which simply meant that the wealthy sipped their cocktails while 'discussing how much harder labourers can be made to work if only they can be kept from festivity'. That was the argument for it: 'that employees work harder, and therefore employers get richer'. Prohibition had originally been introduced in many states to prevent blacks, whose 'enslavement and importation . . . had been the crime and catastrophe of American history', from drinking; but, once 'tried successfully on black labour', it 'could be extended to all labour'. Chesterton takes the opportunity to point out that, regarding slavery, 'the eighteenth century was *more* liberal than the nineteenth century' with its dogma of inevitable progress. But then 'the utter separation and subordination of the black like a beast was a *progress*; it was a growth of nineteenth-century enlightenment and experiment; a triumph of science over superstition'. The 'dawn' of Darwinian evolution heralded 'the break-up of our brotherhood', with its 'growing evolutionary suspicion that savages were not a part of the human race'. Another 'movement of the progressive sort' that meant a 'more brazen and brutal' slavery was that of

[94] *WISA* 150–1, 164, 166–8.

industrialization, which encouraged a 'commercial and competitive' slavery.[95]

American democracy was also threatened by capitalism, which resulted in the 'unnatural ... combination of political equality with extreme economic inequality in practice'. For 'the democratic ideal' of America was in conflict with 'another tendency, an industrial progress which is of all things on earth the most undemocratic'. Industrialism, of course, was not unique to America, but it was 'alone in emphasising the ideal' that was at odds with industrialism. In addition, America had (unlike England) a 'counterweight' to industrial urban capitalism in the shape of 'a free agriculture, a vast field of free farms dotted with small freeholders'. Unfortunately, however, the 'culture' of these Puritan smallholders of the Mid West came from the city ('the Puritan tradition was originally a tradition of the town'), which meant that they were not a 'true peasantry' in that they did not 'produce their own spiritual food, in the same sense as their own material food', and they did not 'create other kinds of culture beside the kind called agriculture'. There was no 'peasant play' in Oklahoma, only the cinema: 'And the objection to the cinema is not so much that it goes to Oklahoma as that it does not come from Oklahoma.' But it certainly was not for the English, who had allowed their land 'to be stolen by squires and then vulgarised by sham squires, to sneer at such colonists as crude and prosaic': 'They at least have really kept something of the simplicity, and, therefore, the dignity of democracy ... '. Still, it was unfortunate that their 'culture, and to some great extent their creed, do come along the railroads from the great modern urban centres ... '. Chesterton concludes with a paradox that must have given him some pleasure: 'It is that influence that alone prevents the Middle West from progressing towards the Middle Ages.'[96]

Chesterton noticed what other English visitors still notice when they visit America: 'the cold passion' for 'piling up ice', the fallacy of supposing that Americans speak 'the same' language, the wooden houses that looked 'almost as fantastic to an English eye as if they had all been made of cardboard', the fact that America exports its worst rather than its best ('the best things do not travel'), the skies 'so clear' as to make it seem that 'clouds were English products like primroses', England being blessed with 'the noble thing called weather; most other countries having to be content with climate'. But, above all, Chesterton was struck by the sheer 'restlessness' of

---

[95] *WISA* 146–7, 154–7.   [96] *WISA* 70, 102, 105–7, 130.

life, particularly in New York, 'a place of unrest' loved by its admirers for 'the romance of its restlessness'. Paradoxically, Chesterton thought that the unpunctuality he had noticed at his lectures 'had the same origin as the hustling', since Americans were 'impulsive' with 'an impulse to stay as well as an impulse to go', being possessed by 'the romance of business', which really was 'like a love-affair' in that it involved 'not only rushing but lingering'. It was customary for the English to condemn America as 'materialist' because of its 'worship of success'—but 'this very worship, like any worship', was mystical rather than materialistic. For Americans worshipped 'success in the abstract, as a sort of ideal vision', and to say that they 'worship' the dollar is 'a compliment' to their 'fine spirituality', for they adore the dollar as 'an idol', 'an image of success and not of enjoyment'. That this 'romance' of success was 'also a religion' was shown by the fact that there was 'a queer sort of morality attached to it': 'America does vaguely feel a man making good as something analogous to a man being good or a man doing good.' Doing business really was a 'romance', for it was not 'reality', since half the financial operations involved dealt with 'things that do not even exist', 'all finance' being 'in that sense ... a fairy-tale'. Success involved work, and Americans had 'a very real respect for work', for 'the dignity of labour', not being enchanted with the English ideal of the gentleman of leisure—although there was 'a good side to the Englishman's daydream of leisure, and one which the American spirit tends to miss', the concept of the 'holiday' and even more that of the 'hobby'. The restlessness of Americans could also be seen in their idea that 'enthusiasm' was 'itself ... meritorious', 'the excitement itself ... dignified'. They were 'proud' not only of their 'energy' but of their 'excitement'. They admired people for being 'impressionable', for being 'excited'. They were 'not ashamed of curiosity', which they felt to be 'consistent with ... dignity, because dignity is consistent with vivacity'. That they were like children, 'in the very best sense of childhood', the 'most childlike thing about a child' being 'his curiosity ... and his power of wonder at the world', was a great compliment coming from Chesterton. The moodiness of the English was a 'mystery' to Americans, since in America there were 'no moods' but 'only one mood', whether it was called 'hustle or uplift'. The 'ups and downs of the English temperament' were a mystery to a 'people living on such a lofty but level tableland'. Such 'subtlety' of mood was simply swept away by American 'sociability'.[97]

[97] *WISA* 65, 82, 86–8, 98, 115–17, 118–19, 121–3, 199, 236–42, 248–50.

5

On their return to England in April 1921, the Chestertons had practical problems that had to be faced. The lease on Overroads would expire in the summer of next year and could not be renewed.[98] Fortunately, the American lecture tour had brought in sufficient funds to proceed with building a house in Top Meadow around the studio that had already been built. The tree in the meadow that Chesterton had said he would like to build a house round was cut down and used for the newel of the staircase.[99]

They gladly resumed life in their beloved Beaconsfield. On 14 July Chesterton played Theseus in *A Midsummer Night's Dream*, while his Jewish friend Margaret Halford played Puck, in aid of a new engine for the local fire brigade and an extension to the Church of England school.[100] But the religious problem remained on his mind. On Christmas Day 1921, the last Christmas they spent at Overroads, he wrote to Maurice Baring to say that he had 'been troubled for some time about a particular problem in connection with the great subject (which has hardly left my mind for an hour) and I hope the decision I have come to does not sound abrupt and incoherent in this hasty note'. He would very much like to see Baring, but he would also like to see 'some priest of your acquaintance, about what is involved in a certain case'. He did not 'particularly' want the priest to be a friend of his: although he knew 'they would consider principles and not friendship', he did not want 'to burden their friendship' till it was 'necessary'. If Baring would let him know after the feast of the Epiphany on 6 January '(to preserve the twelve days of Xmas)', he would arrange an appointment at Baring's at the priest's convenience.[101] What became of this request is not known.

His doubts about Anglicanism had hardly been dispelled by news of a church congress in Birmingham in October 1921, at which a Lord Dawson pronounced that artificial contraception was not inconsistent with Christian morality, in spite of the recent Lambeth Conference's condemnation of it in 1920. The way was being paved for the reversal of this teaching at the next Lambeth Conference in 1930. In an editorial of 21 October in the *New Witness* Chesterton commented on the press's agreement that the Church of England must 'move with the times' or with the 'world': 'We

---

[98] G. K. Chesterton to R. A. Knox, incomplete draft, n.d., BL Add. MS 73195, fo. 144.

[99] I owe this information to Aidan Mackey.   [100] Ffinch, 276.

[101] *Tablet*, 26 Dec. 1956.

do not want, as the newspapers say, a Church that will move with the world. We want a Church that will move the world.' He did not mind people who simply rejected Christian morals nearly so much as so-called Christians who 'brazenly' betrayed Christianity.

In *Eugenics and Other Evils*, published in February 1922, Chesterton condemned the view that 'the spread of destitution will never be stopped until we have educated the lower classes in the methods by which the upper classes prevent procreation'. Certainly, there were 'unwanted children; but unwanted by whom?' Not by the parents, Chesterton suggested, but by the employers who did not want to pay the parents properly. At the beginning of the book, Chesterton explained to his readers that, while 'most of the conclusions, especially towards the end, were conceived with reference to recent events, the actual bulk of preliminary notes about the science of Eugenics were written before the war':

It was a time when this theme was the topic of the hour; when eugenic babies (not visibly very distinguishable from other babies) sprawled all over the illustrated papers; when the evolutionary fancy of Nietzsche was the new cry among the intellectuals; and when . . . Shaw and others were considering the idea that to breed a man like a cart-horse was the true way to attain that higher civilization, of intellectual magnanimity and sympathetic insight, which may be found in cart-horses.

But the craze for eugenics, Chesterton considered, was simply part of 'a modern craze for scientific officialism and strict social organization', in other words for Prussianism. Once 'the older culture of Christendom' had prevailed against Prussia in the war, he had assumed the notes he had made had become 'irrelevant'. But, to his astonishment, he found that 'the ruling classes in England [were] still proceeding on the assumption that Prussia [was] a pattern for the whole world'.[102]

To cry out before one is hurt seemed to Chesterton to be the 'wisest thing': 'It is no good to cry out after you are hurt; especially after you are mortally hurt.' History showed that 'most tyrannies' succeeded 'because men moved too late': 'It is often essential to resist a tyranny before it exists. It is no answer to say, with a distant optimism, that the scheme is only in the air. A blow from a hatchet can only be parried while it is in the air.' Evils like eugenics had throughout history triumphed through 'a disastrous alliance between abnormal innocence and abnormal sin'. In the case of eugenics there was 'a cloud of skirmishers, of harmless and confused

---

[102] *EOE* 293–4, 386.

modern sceptics, who ought to be cleared off or calmed down before we come to debate with the real doctors of the heresy': 'When we have answered the immediate protestation of all these good, shouting, short-sighted people, we can begin to do justice to those intelligences that are really behind the idea.' These harmless skirmishers could be divided into 'five sects; whom I will call the Euphemists, the Casuists, the Autocrats, the Precedenters, and the Endeavourers'. Most of them were 'Euphemists', who were startled by 'short words' and soothed by 'long words', and who were 'utterly incapable of translating the one into the other', 'however obviously' they meant 'the same thing'.

Say to them 'The persuasive and even coercive powers of the citizen should enable him to make sure that the burden of longevity in the previous generations does not become disproportionate and intolerable, especially to the females'; say this to them and they sway slightly to and fro like babies sent to sleep in cradles. Say to them 'Murder your mother,' and they sit up quite suddenly.... Say to them, 'It is not improbable that a period may arrive when the narrow if once useful distinction between the anthropoid *homo* and the other animals, which has been modified on so many moral points, may be modified even also in regard to the important question of the extension of human diet'; say this to them, and beauty born of murmuring sound will pass into their faces. But say to them, in a simple, manly, hearty way 'Let's eat a man!' and their surprise is quite surprising.

Then there were the 'casuists', who would respond to the complaint, 'I dislike this spread of Cannibalism in the West End restaurants,' 'Well, after all Queen Eleanor when she sucked blood from her husband's arm was a cannibal.' For the 'Autocrats', 'every modern reform will "work" all right, because they will be there to see.' As for the 'Precedenters', they were mostly 'solemn' Parliamentarians who would say, for instance, that they 'could not understand the clamour against the Feeble-Minded Bill as it only extended the "principles" of the old Lunacy Laws'—to which the only answer was, 'Quite so. It only extends the "principles" of the Lunacy Laws to persons without a trace of lunacy.' Finally, there were the 'Endea-vourers', the 'weakest' of all these 'helpless' skirmishers, the 'prize speci-men' of whom was an MP 'who defended the same Bill as "an honest attempt" to deal with a great evil: as if one had a right to dragoon and enslave one's fellow citizens as a kind of chemical experiment; in a state of reverent agnosticism about what would come of it'. But there remained 'a class of controversialists so hopeless and futile' that Chesterton could not find a name for them: they were the kind of people who would say: '*You* object to all State interference; I am in favour of State interference.

You are an Individualist; I, on the other hand," etc.' Apart from these 'controversialists', there was 'an enormous mass' of 'rather thoughtless people, whose rooted sentiment is that any deep change in our society must be in some way infinitely distant', 'a thing that, good or bad, will have to fit itself to their great-great-great-grandchild, who may be very different and may like it; and who in any case is rather a distant relative'.[103]

In fact, what Chesterton considered to be the first eugenics law, the Mental Deficiency Act, which he called 'the Feeble-Minded Bill', had already been passed in 1913 'with the applause of both parties' by the House of Commons.

It is, and quite simply and literally, a Bill for incarcerating as madmen those whom no doctor will consent to call mad. It is enough if some doctor or other may happen to call them weak-minded. Since there is scarcely any human being to whom this term has not been conversationally applied by his own friends and relatives on some occasion or another (unless his friends and relatives have been lamentably lacking in spirit), it can be clearly seen that this law, like the early Christian Church (to which, however, it presents points of dissimilarity), is a net drawing in all kinds.

It was 'openly said' that the purpose of the bill was 'to prevent any person whom these propagandists do not happen to think intelligent from having any wife or children. Every tramp who is sulky, every labourer who is shy, every rustic who is eccentric, can quite easily be brought under such conditions as were designed for homicidal maniacs.' The state had 'suddenly and quietly gone mad', not so much because it admitted the abnormal as because it could not 'recover the normal'. And 'anarchy' was that condition in which a loss of 'self-control' prevented any return to the 'normal'. As always for Chesterton, it was the lack of 'rational limits' that was to blame. This limitless anarchy could be seen in 'the vague extension of punishments like imprisonment'. In the past, the state would torture a man by stretching him on the rack—but not by stretching 'the rack out'. When the practice was to burn so-called witches, no one suggested that the practice should be extended to other supposedly unsocial characters such as 'backbiting' women. The definition of crime was becoming 'more and more indefinite', so that, for example, cruelty to children had 'come to cover almost every negligence that can occur in a needy household'. The modern age was unique in its 'highly-paid' experts' inability to offer 'some kind of logical account' for their actions:

[103] *EOE* 297, 303–7.

The lowest sophist in the Greek schools would remember enough of Socrates to force the Eugenist to tell him (at least) whether Midias was segregated because he was curable or because he was incurable. The meanest Thomist of the mediaeval monasteries would have the sense to see that you cannot discuss a madman when you have not discussed a man. The most owlish Calvinist commentator in the seventeenth century would ask the Eugenist to reconcile such Bible texts as derided fools with the other Bible texts that praised them. The dullest shopkeeper in Paris in 1790 would have asked what were the Rights of Man, if they did not include the rights of the lover, the husband, and the father.[104]

Without any idea of the exception actually proving the rule, the eugenist regards the heredity of everyone as 'doubtful', in which case the eugenist's judgement itself is 'the result of a doubtful heredity'. Eugenists wanted doctors 'to meddle with the public definition of madness' and 'to enforce a new conception of sanity'. A eugenist would say that a consumptive like Keats should never have been allowed to come into this world and to endure the suffering of consumption, but happiness unlike consumption was not 'a calculable matter': 'Keats died young; but he had more pleasure in a minute than a Eugenist gets in a month.' Atheists noticeably avoided language that implied people have souls, preferring to speak of the 'outbreak' rather than the 'waging' of war, of international 'solidarity' rather than 'sympathy' (as though nations were 'physically stuck together like dates in a grocer's shop'), of 'the relations of the sexes' rather than 'love' or 'lust' ('as if a man and a woman were two wooden objects standing in a certain angle and attitude to each other, like a table and a chair'). Similarly, eugenists were 'as passive in their statements as they are active in their experiments. Their sentences always enter tail first, and have no subject, like animals without heads.' When she wanted to disembowel, Lady Macbeth demanded a dagger, whereas the eugenist preferred to say more indirectly, 'in such cases the bowels should, etc.'. In most cases, when the eugenist announced that something 'should' be done, the 'lost subject' governing the eugenist's verb was the eugenist himself. In any case, if Chesterton were a eugenist, he would not 'personally elect' to 'waste [his] time locking up the feeble-minded': 'The people I should lock up would be the strong-minded.' He had noticed when he was at school that 'the kind of boy who likes teasing halfwits was not the sort that stood up to bullies'. The eugenists seemed to be 'actually proud of the dimness of their definitions and the incompleteness of their plans'. They were 'ready to reproduce the secrecies and cruelties of the Inquisition', but they certainly could not be

---

[104] *EOE* 308–9, 310–14.

accused of offending 'with any of that close and complicated thought, that arid and exact logic which narrowed the minds of the Middle Ages; they have discovered how to combine the hardening of the heart with a sympathetic softening of the head'. The eugenists thought that there could be experts on health and sanity, but the truth was that there could only be experts on disease and insanity 'because experts can only arise out of exceptional things'. If prosecuted for trespass, one could consult a solicitor on what constituted trespass; but, if the solicitor wanted to 'map out' one's country walks, 'then that solicitor would solicit in vain'. The eugenist argued that 'a young man about to be married should be obliged to produce his health-book as he does his bank-book', but health was not calculable like money.[105]

The real established religion of England was not the Church of England (to which disestablishment 'would do a good deal of good') but science, which 'really does use the secular arm':

And the creed that really is levying tithes and capturing schools, the creed that really is enforced by fine and imprisonment, the creed that really is proclaimed not in sermons but in statutes, and spread not by pilgrims but by policemen—that creed is the great but disputed system of thought which began with Evolution and has ended in Eugenics. Materialism is really our established Church; for the Government will really help it to persecute its heretics.

But this persecution is 'a new sort of persecution', for the old kind of persecutor 'violently enforced his creed, because it was unchangeable', whereas the new scientific persecutor persecuted on behalf of a 'hypothesis', which 'he boasts that he will always abandon'. There was another difference: 'The old persecutor was trying to *teach* the citizen, with fire and sword. The new persecutor is trying to *learn* from the citizen, with scalpel and germ-injector.' Eugenics was 'the first religion to be experimental instead of doctrinal. All other established Churches have been based on somebody having found the truth. This is the first Church that was ever based on not having found it.' This was 'an Established Church of Doubt—instead of Faith'. There was no science of eugenics all, but the eugenists promised that if people gave themselves 'up to be vivisected they [would] very probably have one some day'.[106]

In Chesterton's view, eugenics was the natural consequence of a capitalism that 'thought that a margin of men out of work was good for his business', since

[105] *EOE* 320, 322, 324–9, 330–3.   [106] *EOE* 344–7, 351.

the same inequality and insecurity that makes cheap labour may make bad labour, and at last no labour at all. It was as if a man who wanted something from an enemy, should at last reduce the enemy to come knocking at his door in the despair of winter, should keep him waiting in the snow to sharpen the bargain; and then come out to find the man dead upon the doorstep.

As a result of 'the keeping of the worker half in and half out of work . . . the degraded class was really degenerating'. For the problem was that, although it was 'right and proper enough to use a man as a tool' and therefore 'quite reasonable and respectable, of course, to fling away a man like a tool', there was a snag in the 'comparison': 'If you pick up a hammer, you do not find a whole family of nails clinging to it. If you fling away a chisel by the roadside, it does not litter and leave a lot of little chisels.' For, although 'the meanest of tools', man had a 'strange privilege which God had given him, doubtless by mistake'. Swift could hardly have bettered the savagery of Chesterton's satire: 'The time came at last when the rather reckless breeding in the abyss below ceased to be a supply, and began to be something like a wastage; ceased to be something like keeping foxhounds, and began alarmingly to resemble a necessity of shooting foxes.' And so the capitalist's 'ideas began, first darkly and unconsciously, but now more and more clearly, to drift' towards the preferred solution: 'He could alter the *marriage* in the house in such a way as to promise himself the largest possible number of the kind of children he did want, with the smallest number of the kind he did not.'[107]

As a true liberal, Chesterton deplored the loss of liberty, if nothing else, that eugenics represented. But it was not the only infringement on liberty by the state. Legislation against the consumption of alcohol was no longer based on the danger to others of drunkenness but on health: now it was said that 'the government must safeguard the health of the community', and, if alcohol was now to be regarded as 'poison', then nicotine might soon be so classified. But in that case the government might as well 'control all the habits of the citizens, and among the rest their habits in the matter of sex'. If 'personal health' was to be 'a public concern', then the 'most private acts' were '*more* public' than the 'most public acts'. And so the English people who did not have 'equality' like the French or 'a great religion' like the Irish were now losing their 'life', which was their liberty. But with whom had England gone to war so recently?

[107] *EOE* 380–1, 383.

England went to war with the Superman in his native home. She went to war with that very land of scientific culture from which the very ideal of a Superman had come.... She gave battle to the birthplace of nine-tenths of the professors who were the prophets of the new hope of humanity.... The very name of Nietzsche, who had held up this hope of something superhuman to humanity, was laughed at for all the world as if he had been touched with lunacy.

But the English who had once been led to believe that Germany was 'the model State' could be deceived again—'though all the millions who died to destroy Prussianism stood up and testified against it'.[108]

6

After he had become a Catholic, Chesterton was to write that in his 'experience the convert commonly passes through three stages or states of mind'. In the first stage, the future convert 'imagines himself to be entirely detached' and anxious 'to be fair to the Church of Rome'. The second stage was when the convert 'begins to be conscious not only of the falsehood' of the charges levelled at the Church but of its 'truth, and is enormously excited to find that there is far more of it than he would ever have expected'. This process of 'discovering the Catholic Church' was 'perhaps the most pleasant and straightforward part of the business'. It was 'like discovering a new continent full of strange flowers and fantastic animals... at once wild and hospitable'. But the third stage, when the convert 'is trying not to be converted', was 'the most terrible'. For the convert had 'come too near to the truth' and had 'forgotten that truth is a magnet, with the powers of attraction and repulsion'. Or, to change the metaphor, the convert was now threatened with 'the tragic and menacing grandeur of a great love affair'. 'I may say,' Chesterton confessed, 'that I for one was never less troubled by doubts than in the last phase, when I was troubled by fears.' And he doubted that he would ever 'again have such absolute assurance' of the truth of Catholicism than when he made his 'last effort to deny it'.[109]

The two people, according to Chesterton, who helped him most in this last stage were Maurice Baring and Father Ronald Knox, who had travelled the same road themselves.[110] Knox had admired Chesterton since he was a schoolboy, and they 'had met several times on public

---

[108] *EOE* 396–7, 400, 411, 417–18.   [109] *CCC* 89, 91–3.
[110] Ward, *GKC* 387.

occasions and had written to, and of, one another with enthusiasm', but they were not personal friends.[111] It seems that Chesterton asked to meet Knox, whose account of his conversion in *A Spiritual Aenead* had been published in 1918. In the first of a series of undated letters to Knox (whose letters have not survived), the first three of which were written from Overroads before the move to Top Meadow in the summer of 1922, Chesterton said that their meeting had 'got into every chink of [his] thoughts, even the pauses of talk on practical things'. But in the meantime, he had been 'distracted' by the financial problems of the *New Witness*, which was in 'a crisis about which shareholders etc. have to be consulted'. 'I can't let my brother's paper,' he explained, 'that stands for all he believed in, go without doing all I can; and I am trying to get it started again, with Belloc to run it if possible.' At their meeting he had not been able to 'explain' himself properly to Knox, and he wanted to try again: 'I could not explain what I mean about my wife without saying much more. I see in principle it is not on the same level as the true Church; for nothing can be on the same level as God. But it is on quite a different level from social sentiments about friends and family.' He felt a 'responsibility' about Frances, 'more serious than affection, let alone passion'. First, she had given him his 'first respect for sacramental Christianity', and, second, 'she is one of the good who mysteriously suffer; and I am partly to blame and have never been good enough for her'. So far as his own 'feelings' were concerned, he thought that he 'might rightly make application to be instructed as soon as possible'; but he did not want 'to take so serious a step without reopening the matter' with Frances, which he 'could do by the end of the week': 'I have had no opportunity before, because she has only just recovered from an illness, and is going away for a few days.' He wanted Knox to tell him how he could 'arrange matters with some priest or religious in London' who might be able to see him 'once or twice a week, or whatever is required', or else to give him 'the address of someone to write to, if that is the correct way'. There were priests in High Wycombe, the nearest large town, but he imagined they were 'very busy parochial clergy'. Chesterton concluded the letter by saying that he had meant to write about 'the convictions involved in a more abstract way', but he was afraid that he had filled his letter 'with one personal point'. When he wrote again after talking with Frances he would write 'about the

---

[111] Evelyn Waugh, *The Life of Ronald Knox* (London: Chapman & Hall, 1959), 197.

other matters'—'and as they are more intellectual and less emotional, I hope I may be a little more coherent'.[112]

In May 1922 Chesterton's father, Mr Ed, died. According to 'Keith' Chesterton, in the autumn of 1921 Mr Ed had 'developed an obstinate cold, and though there was nothing sinister or alarming in his symptoms, the condition increased his nervous apprehensions and he decided to go to bed'. At first, his hypochondria only kept him in bed till tea-time, when he would get up 'and grow quite cheerful over buttered toast and cress sandwiches; but as the days shortened he left his bed less frequently'. Recommended by the doctor to leave London for 'a change of air', he refused to move, claiming he did not have the energy. That winter 'his periods of inertia grew more frequent, and he would sometimes remain silent for quite a long time'. But when he felt better he would tell fairy tales to the devoted maid's little boy. The family were accustomed to his dread of illness and did not take his condition very seriously; he would surely be on his feet again in the warmer weather of spring. But gradually he spent longer and longer in bed till the time came when he seemed to lose the energy to get up. His mental powers began to fail and 'he drifted into lassitude and inertia'.[113]

Before his father died, Chesterton had written to Knox to apologize for not having written before. By now his father was 'very ill', but his anxiety did 'not so much turn the current of [his] thoughts as deepen it'. Chesterton was, of course, thinking of his conversion to Catholicism: 'to see a man so many million times better than I am, in every way, and one to whom I owe everything, under such a shadow makes me feel, on top of all my particular feelings, that shadow that lies on us all.' His father was 'the very best man' that he 'ever knew of that generation, that never understood the new need of a spiritual authority', living 'almost perfectly by the sort of religion men had when rationalism was rational'. 'I think', added Chesterton, 'he was always subconsciously prepared for the next generation having less theology than he has; and is rather puzzled at its having more. But I think he understood my brother's conversion better than my mother did; she is more difficult, and of course I cannot bother her just now.' However, his 'family trouble' had a 'practical' consequence so far as his reception into the Church was concerned:

[112] Ward, *GKC* 391–2, with the addition of the omitted words 'and I am partly . . . good enough for her' (BL Add. MS 73195, fo. 140).

[113] MCC 263–4.

As this may bring me to London more than I thought, it seems possible I might go there after all, instead of Wycombe, if I knew to whom to go. Also I find I stupidly destroyed your letter with the names of the priests at Wycombe to whom you referred me. Would it bother you very much to send me the names again, and any alternative London ones that occur to you; and I will let you know my course of action then.

Just when he was 'settling down' to write 'a full reply' to Knox's reply, Chesterton received a telegram calling him urgently to London, apparently because his father was not expected to live rather than that he had actually died. Since his father's death, he now wrote, he had 'been doing the little' he could for his mother—'but even that little involves a great deal of business—the least valuable sort of help'. He would not now attempt to tell Knox 'all that this involves in connection with [his] deeper feelings and intentions', but was sending 'this interim scribble as an excuse for delaying the letter [he] had already begun; and which nothing less than this catastrophe would have prevented [him] from finishing'. He hoped to 'finish it in a few days'. He was not sure whether he would by then have returned to Beaconsfield, but if he had he would be at a new address: Top Meadow.[114] In the meantime he had heard again from Maurice Baring, who wrote to send his condolences. Baring said that he had 'lately felt strangely near' to Chesterton, and had 'had (quite wrongly perhaps) the impression' that his 'buffetings were over' and that his 'ship was in calm waters, well in sight of the harbour'.[115]

It was from his new home, Top Meadow, that Chesterton next wrote to Knox, apologizing for 'the disreputable haste of [his] letter': 'my normal chaos is increased by moving into a new house, which is still like a waste-paper basket.' He had

meant to make some attempt to finish the fuller reply I had actually begun to the very kind letter you sent me, I am ashamed to think how long ago, before my recent trouble; and though the trail and tangle of those troubles will still, I fear, make this very inadequate, there were two things in your letter I feel I ought to acknowledge even so late.

First, he could not say how 'pleased and honoured' he felt 'even by the suggestion' that Knox might 'possibly' give him the necessary instruction for reception into the Church: 'It is something that I should value more vividly and personally than I can possibly express.' But, as this 'was so long ago, before so many delays and interruptions', he was afraid that Knox's

---

[114] Ward, *GKC* 392–3.   [115] Letter of 29 May 1922, *Tablet*, 26 Dec. 1953.

'margin of Sundays in London must now be very much narrowed'. But he thought that 'there must be still a Sunday or two left on [his] list', and with his 'permission' he proposed to come to London next Sunday if there was a possibility of seeing him then. He imagined that a meeting could be arranged through Maurice Baring, for example, unless Knox would prefer to make his own 'arrangements'. They could then discuss the 'possibility' of Knox instructing him or 'finally make some arrangement about another one'. In any event, he would welcome the chance of another talk with Knox if it was not inconvenient. Second, he wanted to assure Knox that there was no need for him to apologize for what he had said about 'private troubles' disqualifying a person from appearing on 'public platforms', 'for it is exactly what I am feeling most intensely myself'.

I am in a state now when I feel a monstrous charlatan, as if I wore a mask and were stuffed with cushions, whenever I see anything about the public G.K.C.; it hurts me; for though the views I express are real, the image is horribly unreal compared with the real person who needs help just now. I have as much vanity as anybody about these superficial successes while they are going on; but I never feel for a moment that they affect the reality of whether I am utterly rotten or not; so that any public comments on my religious position seem like a wind on the other side of the world; as if they are about somebody else—as indeed they are. I am not troubled about a great fat man who appears on platforms and in caricatures, even when he enjoys controversies on what I believe to be the right side. I am concerned about what has become of a little boy whose father showed him a toy theatre, and a schoolboy whom nobody ever heard of, with his brooding on doubts and dirt and daydreams of crude conscientiousness so inconsistent as to [be] near to hypocrisy; and all the morbid life of the lonely mind of a living person with whom I have lived. It is that story, that so often came near to ending badly, that I want to end well. Forgive this scrawl; I think you will understand me.

He ended the latter by saying that he was going to London next day, when he would 'try to fix something up with Maurice [Baring] or somebody'.[116]

In the end, it seems that Knox suggested that he should come and see Chesterton in Beaconsfield. This, unfortunately, was not possible, Chesterton replied:

I feel horribly guilty in not having written before, and I do most earnestly hope you have not allowed my delay to interfere with any of your own arrangements. I have had a serious and very moving talk with my wife; and she is only too delighted at the idea of your visit in itself; in fact she really wants to know you very much.

[116] Waugh, *Knox*, 207–8.

The problem was that as yet they had only one spare room at Top Meadow, which was currently occupied by a nurse who was giving Frances 'a treatment that seems to be doing her good' and that he did not want to stop if he could help it.

In our conversation my wife was all that I hope you will some day know her to be; she is incapable of wanting me to do anything but what I think right; and admits the same possibility for herself: but it is much more of a wrench for her, for she has been able to practise her religion in complete good faith; which my own doubts have prevented me from doing.

He was ashamed, he added in a postscript, that he had failed to post the letter for two days 'owing to executor business. Nobody so unbusiness-like as I am ought to be busy.' Knox apparently wrote back to say that he could visit Chesterton during the summer vacation (he was teaching at St Edmund's College, Ware). But again there was the problem of the resident nurse who was giving Frances 'a treatment of radiant heat' for her arthritic spine (which 'one would hardly think needed in this weather'), although he hoped to be able to give Knox a definite answer 'in a day or two' and 'should love to accept' his 'generous suggestion' if at all possible. In the next undated letter that survives from Chesterton, he writes ('almost stepping on to the boat') of having 'to go and lecture for a week in Holland', having only just emerged from a 'hurricane of business', no doubt to do with the ailing *New Witness*. However, he promises to write again 'more fully about the business of instruction' on his return in about ten days' time. On returning from Holland, it seems he changed his mind, writing to Knox that he ought to have told him 'long ago' what he had 'done about the most practical of business matters'. His excuse for not writing was the usual one: 'I have again been torn in pieces by the wars of the *New Witness*.' Nevertheless, he had 'managed to have another talk' with Frances, after which he had written to 'our old friend Father O'Connor and asked him to come here, as he probably can' from what Chesterton had heard. He felt 'sure' that he had made the right decision:

Frances is just at the point where Rome acts both as the positive and the negative magnet; a touch would turn her either way; almost (against her will) to hatred, but with the right touch to a faith far beyond my reach. I know Father O'Connor's would be the touch that does not startle, because she knows him and is fond of him; and the only thing she asked of me was to send for him. If he cannot come, of course I shall take other action and let you know.

On 17 July Knox wrote back: 'I'm awfully glad to hear that you've sent for Father O'Connor and that you think he's likely to be available. I must say that, in the story, Father Brown's powers of neglecting his parish always seemed to me even more admirable than Dr Watson's powers of neglecting his practice; so I hope this trait was drawn from the life.'[117]

Chesterton had written an undated letter, postmarked 11 July 1922, to Father O'Connor, in which he asked the priest if he could get away 'about the end of next week or thereabouts: and would it be possible for you to come south and see our new house—or old studio?'

This sounds a very abrupt invitation; but I write in great haste, and am troubled about many things. I want to talk to you about them; especially the most serious ones, religious and concerned with my own rather difficult position. Most of the difficulty has been my own fault, but not all; some of my difficulties would commonly be called duties; though I ought perhaps to have learned sooner to regard them as lesser duties.

He concluded by saying that O'Connor was 'the person' that he and Frances thought of 'with most affection, of all who could help in such a matter'. The priest immediately replied that he was at their disposal at any time during the next fortnight. On 23 July Frances wrote to ask how long he could stay in Beaconsfield. The only small spare bedroom—'We've got to build another room, but cannot afford it yet!'—was free for one night, but after that, presumably because the nurse would be back in residence, she would have to get him a room either with friends or at one of the inns. She was 'only too pleased' that her husband wanted to see him: 'I am sure you will now be able to give him all the advice and help he wants.' She wanted them to have all the time they needed.[118] It was agreed that Father O'Connor should come on 26 July, the day the spare room was free. But then on the morning of 24 July O'Connor received a telegram ('reply paid') from Hilaire Belloc, to whom he had written to tell of Chesterton's apparently impending conversion. Belloc wanted to meet him in London that day. O'Connor duly took the morning train to St Pancras Station, arriving some time before the appointed time of 3.30 p.m. at the appointed place, Westminster Cathedral. There he waited 'until long after 4.30' in vain. There was no sign of Belloc, although he had been seen that afternoon in London. No doubt O'Connor was so flattered to know such

[117] Ward, *GKC* 393–5.
[118] Frances Chesterton to John O'Connor, 23 July [1922], BL Add. MS. 73196, fo. 124. Partially printed in O'Connor, 127–8.

famous people that he seems not even to have complained to Belloc about his non-appearance when he saw him six weeks later, when he asked him why he had sent the telegram. The answer was, 'I wanted to keep you from going to Gilbert. I thought he would never be a Catholic.' O'Connor thought that Belloc had made some 'vain efforts' himself: 'It was easy to fluster Gilbert but impossible to hustle him.' O'Connor's impatience at having to stay two nights in London was restricted to the single exclamation, 'Alone in London from Monday to Wednesday!'[119]

When O'Connor arrived in Beaconsfield, he told Frances that there was 'only one thing troubling Gilbert about the great step' he was proposing to take—the effect it would have on her. 'Oh! I shall be infinitely relieved,' she responded. 'You cannot imagine how it fidgets Gilbert to have anything on his mind. The last three months have been exceptionally trying. I should be only too glad to come with him, if God in His mercy would show the way clear, but up to now He has not made it clear enough to me to justify such a step.' Having given Chesterton the reassurance he needed, O'Connor discussed at length with him 'such special points' as he wanted to raise, before telling him 'to read through the Penny Catechism to make sure there were no snags to a prosperous passage'. 'It was', O'Connor later recalled, 'a sight for men and angels all the Friday to see him wandering in and out of the house with his fingers in the leaves of the little book, resting it on his forearm whilst he pondered with his head on one side.' O'Connor was reminded of the story, which Chesterton 'knew well', of how J. S. Phillimore had called on the Archbishop of Glasgow and asked to be received into the Church: 'The butler brought down a Penny catechism with: His Grace says will you call again when you know all this by heart?' Phillimore retorted that he had 'come to be examined in it'. Because there was as yet no Catholic church in Beaconsfield, which was then part of the parish of St Augustine's, High Wycombe, Chesterton's reception into the Catholic Church took place on Sunday 30 July in 'a small tin shed, painted red-brick, which stood among the sculleries and outhouses'[120] of the Railway Hotel, where one Mass was then celebrated on Sundays and Holydays, by courtesy of the landlady of the hotel, a Mrs Borlase, who was an Irish Catholic, and her convert husband.[121] Dom Ignatius Rice, the

---

[119] O'Connor, 125–8.   [120] *RR* 451.

[121] This 'Mass room' later became a bar when the Railway Hotel was renamed the 'Earl of Beaconsfield'. Eventually the hotel was demolished to make way for a supermarket. St Teresa's Church, Beaconsfield, parish archives.

headmaster of Douai Abbey School, 'one of Chesterton's oldest and keenest admirers', who had offered the Abbey for the service, joined O'Connor for breakfast at the inn where he was staying, after which they walked up to Top Meadow. There they found Chesterton in an armchair perusing the Penny Catechism, 'pulling faces and making noises as he used to do when reading'. At lunch he abstained from wine and drank water. At about three o'clock they set off for the Railway Hotel. Chesterton 'had no doubts or difficulties just before' his reception into the Church—'only fears, fears of something that had the finality and simplicity of suicide'. While Chesterton made his confession to Father O'Connor, Frances, who was weeping, and Dom Ignatius Rice sat in the hotel bar. After conditional baptism had been administered, the two priests left Chesterton and Frances by themselves in the makeshift chapel. Returning to collect something he had forgotten, Rice saw them coming down the aisle, Chesterton with a comforting arm round his weeping wife (not all her tears were of grief, O'Connor thought).[122] The day after the reception O'Connor wrote to the local bishop, Bishop Cary Elwes of Northampton, to report that the famous convert had been 'very humble and fervent' and that his wife had been 'much moved, but not as much as he'. 'It all took place in the Railway Hotel, the which seems rather waggish on the part of the Powers who arrange these coincidences.'[123]

After the service, O'Connor and Chesterton went to tea with the wife of Sir Evelyn Ruggles-Brise, the prison reformer and founder of the Borstal juvenile system, 'who had refused to be put off that morning'. Since Chesterton had on his father's side a famous prison reformer, Captain Chesterton, prison reform was an obvious topic of conversation. But Lady Ruggles-Brise was the widow of the head of one of England's oldest Catholic families, the Stonors, and, since O'Connor had been ordained by an Archbishop Stonor, there was another obvious topic of conversation. It was, thought O'Connor, 'a good set-off to the tension of the early afternoon, better than going back to Top Meadow, where Frances was giving tea to Father Rice'. On their twenty-minute walk into Beaconsfield from the Railway Hotel, O'Connor recalled what he had said to Chesterton during the last couple of days:

[122] Ward, *GKC* 396; O'Connor, 129–31; F. J. Sheed, *The Church and I* (London: Sheed and Ward, 1974), 103.

[123] St Teresa's Church, Beaconsfield, parish archives, parish history, p. 92. The first seventy-five pages of this typed parish history have disappeared, which means that it is untitled.

that there never was an Anglican but minimised some point, great or small, of dogma, that is of accepted fact in religion, and that now he would be inebriated with the plenteousness of the Lord's House, and do better work than ever, even as Newman of the Parochial and Plain [Sermons] was but the try-out for Newman of Gerontius and the Second Spring sermon.[124]

That somewhat obtuse comment about Newman, about whom Chesterton knew a great deal, perhaps partly explains Chesterton's lack of response: 'He was unwontedly silent that afternoon, or so it seemed to me. I do hope *I* did not talk too much, though it would not have been the first time if I had.'[125] Father Rice, who had accompanied Frances back to Top Meadow and was not present to hear his Irish colleague's prognostications of Chesterton's brilliant future, remembered only that for the rest of the day Chesterton was 'in brilliant form . . . quoting poetry and jesting in the highest spirits'. He also wrote a poem, 'The Convert', to celebrate his new life as a convert:[126]

> After one moment when I bowed my head
> And the whole world turned over and came upright,
> And I came out where the old road shone white,
> I walked the ways and heard what all men said,
> Forests of tongues, like autumn leaves unshed,
> Being not unlovable but strange and light;
> Old riddles and new creeds, not in despite
> But softly, as men smile about the dead.
>
> The sages have a hundred maps to give
> That trace their crawling cosmos like a tree,
> They rattle reason out through many a sieve
> That stores the sand and lets the gold go free:
> And all these things are less than dust to me
> Because my name is Lazarus and I live.[127]

Chesterton was now faced with no doubt the most difficult letter he had had to write since writing to tell his mother that he was unofficially engaged to Frances.

My dearest Mother,
I write this (with the worst pen in South Bucks) to tell you something before I write about it to anyone else; something about which we shall probably be in the position of the two bosom friends at Oxford, who 'never differed except in opinion'. You have always been so wise in not judging people by their opinions,

[124] O'Connor, 131–2.   [125] O'Connor, 132.
[126] Ward, *GKC* 396.   [127] *CP* (1933), 387.

but rather the opinions by the people. It is in one sense a long story by this time; but I have come to the same conclusion that Cecil did about needs of the modern world in religion and right dealing, and I am now a Catholic in the same sense as he, having long claimed the name in its Anglo-Catholic sense. I am not going to make a foolish fuss of reassuring you about things I am sure you never doubted; these things do not hurt any relations between people as fond of each other as we are; any more than they ever made any difference to the love between Cecil and ourselves.... I have thought about you, and all that I owe to you and my father, not only in the way of affection, but of the ideals of honour and freedom and charity and all other good things you always taught me: and I am not conscious of the smallest break or difference in those ideals; but only of a new and necessary way of fighting for them. I think, as Cecil did, that the fight for the family and the free citizen and everything decent must now be waged by [the] one fighting form of Christianity.... I have thought this out for myself and not in a hurry of feeling. It is months since I saw my Catholic friends and years since I talked to them about it. I believe it is the truth.[128]

The last but one sentence of this letter could be misleading.[129] Chesterton must mean that he had not talked for a long time to his friends about 'the truth' that he refers to in the last sentence, the truth, that is, of Catholicism, which he had long come to believe was true, as opposed to the question of his actual *reception*, which of course he had discussed with both Baring and O'Connor. He wanted to assure his mother that his decision had been carefully thought through and not under the influence of Catholic friends like Belloc. Mrs Chesterton replied that she was 'not altogether surprised' to hear the news. Nor could she object to anything that her son thought 'right': 'I only pray that it will bring you happiness and peace. It was kind of you to tell me first—I know how you love me. I have no one left but you my darling, and I feel so lonely I am glad to have your love and confidence...'. She ended by expressing her 'love and sympathy' with him in his 'resolve'.[130]

---

[128] Ward, *GKC* 396–7.

[129] Pearce, 270, interprets it as 'at best, Jesuitical equivocation, inasmuch as he hadn't literally *seen* or *talked* to them, but had only *written* to them'; at 'worst, it was plainly and simply a lie, albeit a white lie to spare his mother's feelings'. Ffinch, 289, comments: 'The last part of the letter was strictly accurate only as far as Belloc and Baring were concerned, but it was those two particularly that Chesterton regarded as his "Catholic friends".'

[130] Marie Louise Chesterton to G. K. Chesterton, 7 [Aug. 1922], BL Add. MS 73193, fos. 84–5.

He wrote now to Baring to assure him that his 'abominable delay' in writing to him deserved 'every penalty conceivable, hanging, burning and boiling in oil; but really not so inconceivable an idea as that I should be offended with you at any time (let alone after all you have done in this matter) however thoroughly you might be justified in being offended with me'. The reason for his delay was that he had wanted and hoped to write a letter 'quite different from all those I have had to write to other people; a very long and intimate letter, trying to tell you all about this wonderful business, in which you have helped me so much more than anyone else'. The only other person he had 'meant to write to in the same style' was Father Knox—'and his [letter] has been delayed in the same topsy-turvy way. I am drowning in whirlpools of work and worry over the New Witness which nearly went bankrupt for good this week. But worry does not worry so much as it did before . . . '. If it was not 'adding insult to injury', he would 'send the long letter after all'. The present letter was an immediate acknowledgement of Baring's letter, which had apparently contained a stamped return envelope—which he would 'humiliate' himself by using.[131]

On receiving the news of his conversion from Chesterton, Hilaire Belloc replied on 1 August in terms of what Catholicism meant to him: 'The Catholic Church is the exponent of *Reality*. It is true. Its doctrines in matters large and small are statements of what is.' By all his 'nature of mind' he was sceptical. But this was only a 'mood: not a conclusion': 'My conclusion—and that of all men who have ever once *seen* it—is the Faith: Corporate, organised, a personality, teaching. A thing, not a theory. It.' To Chesterton, who was blessed with 'profound religious emotion', this might seem too desiccated; and indeed it did lack enthusiasm. He blamed his lack of feeling on the death of his beloved Elodie:

It is my misfortune. In youth I had it: even till lately. Grief has drawn the juices from it. I am alone and unfed. The more do I affirm the Sanctity, the Unity, the Infallibility of the Catholic Church. By my very isolation do I the more affirm it, as a man in a desert knows that water is right for man: or as a wounded dog, not able to walk, yet knows the way home.

In short: 'The Catholic Church is the natural home of the human spirit.' There was no hint of congratulation or pleasure that Chesterton was now his co-religionist. But Belloc admitted that his 'reactions' were 'abominably slow': 'I must write to you again when I have collected myself. . . '.[132]

---

[131] Ward, *GKC* 396–7, with text corrected from BL Add. MS 73189, fo. 44.
[132] Ward, *GKC* 403–4, with text corrected from BL Add. MS 73190, fo. 60.

To Father O'Connor he wrote: 'It is very great news indeed!—and you were the agent therein.' And again he wrote on the 23rd: 'I had never thought it possible!... I have written to him and shall write again—but I am a poor hand at such things.' Two days later he reiterated his astonishment: 'The more I think on Gilbert the more astonished I become!'[133] On 25 August Baring wrote again but in very different terms from Belloc:

When I wrote to you the other day I was still cramped by the possibility of the news not being true although I *knew* it was true. I *felt* it was true at once. Curiously enough I felt it had happened before I saw the news in the newspaper at all.... Nothing for years has given me so much joy. I have hardly ever entered a church without putting up a candle to Our Lady or to St Joseph or St Anthony for you.[134]

On the same day, Belloc wrote to express his astonishment to Baring:

People said that he might come in at any time because he showed such a Catholic point of view and so much affection for the Catholic Church. That always seemed to me quite the wrong end of the stick. Acceptation of the Faith is an act, not a mood. Faith is an act of will and as it seemed to me the whole of his mind was occupied in expressing his liking for and attraction towards a certain mood, not all towards the acceptation of a certain Institution as defined and representing full reality in this world. There is all the difference between enjoying military ideas and even joining the volunteers, and becoming a private soldier in a common regiment.

Belloc, however, admitted that he was 'not very much good at understanding what is going on in other people's minds...'.[135] He might have added that there were other approaches to Catholicism apart from his own very individual one.

An Irish politician, whom Chesterton had come to know when he was in Ireland, and who sent him a missal, received a remarkable letter of thanks. After acknowledging his debt to friends like Baring and Belloc, Chesterton confided that he had 'an inner certainty that there was one thing which was dragging me in that divine direction long before' he knew them—'and the name of it was Ireland'.

---

[133] O'Connor, 141, with text corrected from BL Add. MS 73187, fo. 69. O'Connor significantly capitalizes 'agent'.

[134] Ward, *GKC* 404–5.

[135] *Letters from Hilaire Belloc*, ed. Robert Speaight (London: Hollis & Carter, 1958), 119.

There mingled from the first with all the feelings of a normal patriotic Englishman a sort of supernatural fear of the sorrows of Ireland; a suspicion of what they might mean; which grew until I was certain that the policy of Castlereagh and Carson was at bottom that of Nero and Diocletian. The Irish were not faultless; nor were the early Christians: but I knew we had buffeted Christ.

It was true that he had sympathized politically with Ireland long before he felt any 'religious sympathy with her'. But the fact that he had held on to his political sympathy while 'the other Liberals seemed to be abandoning all their Liberal ideas, made me guess it was more than political'.[136]

After his reception into the Catholic Church, Chesterton went to High Wycombe to be prepared by the parish priest, Father Thomas Walker, for his first Holy Communion and Confirmation. At the morning Mass in the 'shed' at the Railway Hotel in Beaconsfield on Sunday 24 September Chesterton made his first Communion, and in the afternoon was confirmed in St Augustine's, High Wycombe, by Bishop Cary Elwes, who belonged to a well-known old Catholic family, taking the confirmation name of Francis after his favourite saint, Francis of Assisi. Afterwards he met the Bishop in the presbytery.[137] Father Walker remembered preparing Chesterton for his first Communion as 'one of the happiest duties I had ever to perform': 'It certainly did not take long to prepare him for he evidently knew as much as I could tell him. Nevertheless, he said I was to treat him as any child whom I was teaching.' Since Father Walker 'had at the time' twice 'carefully waded through' Chesterton's *Orthodoxy*, this was a somewhat daunting task.

However, I went through the catechism (he was importunate that I should use it as he said all the children made use of it), very meticulously explained all the details, to which he lent a most vigilant and unswerving attention. For instance, he wanted me to explain the reason of the drop of water being put into the wine at the preparing of the chalice for the Holy Sacrifice.

So 'aware' was Chesterton 'of the immensity of the Real Presence on the morning of his First Communion . . . that he was covered with perspiration when he actually received Our Lord. When I was congratulating him he

---

[136] Ward, *RC* 239.

[137] St Augustine's Church, High Wycombe, parish archives, diary begun by Father Augustine Peacock and continued by his successor Father Thomas Walker, p. 44. Hereafter referred to as 'parish diary'. See Sheila Mawhood, *The Gem of the Diocese: St Augustine's, High Wycombe* (privately printed, n.d.), 26, 34.

said, "I have spent the happiest hour of my life." '[138] But, at least to begin with, he found it difficult going to Holy Communion, his 'best happiness': he was 'too much frightened of that tremendous reality on the altar. I have not grown up with it and it is too much for me.' That he was 'morbid' he did not doubt—but he needed 'to be told so by authority'.[139] It was not only the Eucharist but even priests themselves who inspired 'awe and reverence' in him: 'He would carefully weigh their opinions however fatuous,' Dom Ignatius Rice remembered.[140] A 12-year old boy who used to serve Mass in the tin shed at the Station Hotel in Beaconsfield was 'always impressed at the wrapt attention with which he listened to the rather poor sermons. He obviously saw much more in them than the rest of the congregation.'[141]

The last chapter of Chesterton's *Autobiography* is entitled 'The God with the Golden Key'. The point of the title is revealed at the end of the chapter, when he recalls 'the figure of a man who crosses a bridge and carries a key; as I saw him when I first looked into fairyland through the window of my father's peep-show'. Now he 'starts up again before me, standing sharp and clear in shape as of old' and 'I know that he who is called Pontifex, the Builder of the Bridge, is called also the Claviger, the Bearer of the Key; and that such keys were given him to bind and loose when he was a poor fisher in a far province, beside a small and almost secret sea'. He had already explained that, when asked why he had become a Catholic, his 'first essential answer', even though it was 'partly an elliptical answer', was: ' "To get rid of my sins." For there is no other religious system that does *really* profess to get rid of people's sins.'[142] Presumably by italicizing the word '*really*', Chesterton (who was forgetting the Orthodox Church) was referring to the Anglican Church, where sacramental confession was practised by a party within it but not by the Church in general, which, he presumably meant, could not therefore be said '*really*' to 'profess to get rid of people's sins'. (There is in fact evidence to suggest that Chesterton himself may have received the sacrament while still an Anglican, not unnaturally, since he professed to be an Anglo-Catholic.[143]) He proceeds to explain that the Roman Catholic

[138] Ward, *GKC* 463, 530.

[139] G. K. Chesterton to Thomas Walker, n.d., BL Add. MS 73241, fo. 21. A typed copy of the letter is annotated 'never sent'. BL Add. MS 73241, fo. 22.

[140] Ward, *GKC* 522.

[141] Patrick J. Fryer to Aidan Mackey, 29 Jan. 1989, GKCL.

[142] *A.* 319.   [143] See below, pp. 547–8.

Church believes that 'sin confessed and adequately repented is actually abolished'—he forgets to add 'when absolved' —'and that the sinner does really begin again as if he had never sinned'. This doctrine brought 'sharply' back to him 'those visions or fancies' with which he had dealt in his chapter on childhood. There he had spoken of 'that strange daylight, which was something more than the light of common day, that still seems in my memory to shine on those steep roads down from Campden Hill, from which one could see the Crystal Palace from afar'. Similarly,

when a Catholic comes from Confession, he does truly, by definition, step out again into that dawn of his own beginning and look with new eyes across the world to a Crystal Palace that is really of crystal. He believes that in that dim corner, and in that brief ritual, God has really remade him in His own image. He is now a new experiment of the Creator. He is as much a new experiment as he was when he was really only five years old. He stands, as I said, in the white light at the worthy beginning of the life of a man. The accumulations of time can no longer terrify. He may be grey and gouty; but he is only five minutes old.[144]

Catholic doctrines seemed to Chesterton to 'link up' the whole of his life, 'as no other doctrines could do; and especially to settle simultaneously the two problems of [his] childish happiness and [his] boyish brooding'. In particular, they affected what he hoped it was not 'pompous' to call 'the chief idea' of his life—namely, 'the idea of taking things with gratitude, and not taking things for granted'. The sacrament of confession gave 'a new life', but the 'gift' was 'given at a price'—that is, 'facing the reality about oneself'. He had first seen 'the two sides of this single truth stated together' when he had read in the Penny Catechism: 'The two sins against Hope are presumption and despair.' From the first, he had had 'an almost violently vivid sense' of the danger of both presumption and despair. The 'aim of life' was 'appreciation', and this depended on having 'humility' and feeling 'unworthy'. Both despair and presumption, on the other hand, were inspired by 'pride'. The intellectuals who thought one had a 'right' to things, he had noticed, also believed there was 'no such thing as right and wrong'. But to be 'thankful' meant being 'thankful' to somebody. And the only person one could be grateful to for existence was God. It seemed to Chesterton that Catholic theology alone had 'not only thought, but thought of everything'. Other philosophies and religions were happy with 'one idea', 'to follow a truth ... and apply it to everything'. Catholicism was in Chesterton's experience the only 'creed that could not

---

[144] *A.* 319–20.

be satisfied with a truth, but only with the Truth, which is made of a million ... truths and yet is one'. Had he, like Shaw, made up his 'own philosophy out of [his] own precious fragment of truth', merely because he had found it out for himself, he would 'soon have found that truth distorting itself into a falsehood'. His sense of wonder 'would, if unbalanced by other truths, have become ... very unbalanced indeed'. The one idea of 'transcendental contentment' could easily have led him into solipsism and 'political Quietism'.[145]

As he comes to the end of his *Autobiography*, Chesterton sees himself as 'finishing a story' that was 'very much of a mystery-story': he was 'answering at the end only the questions' he had 'asked at the beginning'. Since childhood he had had 'a certain romance of receptiveness': he had never been 'bored': 'Existence is still a strange thing to me; and as a stranger I give it welcome.' Now he found himself 'ratified' in his 'realisation of the miracle of being alive ... in a definite dogmatic sense'. However, his 'rude and primitive religion of gratitude' had not saved him from ingratitude, the sin that was 'perhaps most horrible' to him. But precisely because 'the evil' had been 'mainly of the imagination, it could only be pierced by that conception of confession which is the end of mere solitude and secrecy'. He had found the only religion that 'dared to go down' with him 'into the depths' of himself. His early 'morbidities' had been 'mental as well as moral' and had 'sounded the most appalling depths of fundamental scepticism and solipsism'. And 'there again' he had found that 'the Church had gone before [him] and established her adamantine foundations; that she had affirmed the actuality of external things'. Again, his 'instinct' had been 'to defend liberty in small nations and poor families; that is, to defend the rights of man as including the rights of property; especially the property of the poor'. But he had not really understood what he 'meant by Liberty' until he 'heard it called by the new name of Human Dignity': 'It was a new name to me; though it was part of a creed nearly two thousand years old'—the 'one key which can unlock all doors'.[146]

The change in Chesterton that conversion had brought was noticeable to at least one observer. His old Jewish school friend Lawrence Solomon, now a neighbour in Beaconsfield, noticed 'not only how happy his conversion had made [him] but also how it seemed to bring him increased strength of character'.[147]

---

[145] *A.* 320–5, 327–8.   [146] *A.* 329–31.   [147] Ward, *GKC* 406.

Between October 1922 and April 1923 Chesterton wrote a series of brief apologetic articles under the general title *Where All Roads Lead* in the Dominican review *Blackfriars*, which were published a month later in the American periodical the *Catholic World*.[148] There were, he insisted, always only two 'fundamental reasons' for converting to Catholicism: because it was true and because it offered 'liberation from...sins'. What had changed since the nineteenth century was 'the challenge of the Church'. Up until then, the convert to the Catholic Church had to justify his conversion: 'Today a man is really expected to give reasons for not joining it.' At least subconsciously, he thought this was true for many people, who were 'conscious non-Catholics'. Certainly, that was the experience of Chesterton himself, who had never felt called upon to give reasons for not joining the Orthodox or the Quakers or Islam. It was not that these 'conscious non-Catholics' did not have 'real objections'; on the contrary, they felt obliged 'to object', 'to kick and struggle'. This 'consciousness of the challenge of the Church' was 'connected with something else', which had been 'the strongest of all the purely intellectual forces' that had 'dragged' Chesterton 'towards the truth'—and that was the 'singular nature' of 'the survival of the faith', for this 'old religion' was a religion that refused 'to grow old'. It was this 'aggressiveness of Catholicism' that had put 'intellectuals on the defensive'. Personally, Chesterton could not 'understand how this unearthly freshness in something so old' could 'possibly be explained, except on the supposition that it [was] indeed unearthly'. History showed that it was not 'orthodoxy' that had 'grown old slowly' but heresy that had 'grown old quickly'. The Reformation had grown 'old amazingly quickly', whereas 'the Counter-Reformation...was full of the fire and even of the impatience of youth'. The Church had had 'any number of opportunities of dying, and even of being respectfully interred. But the younger generation always began once again to knock at the door; and never louder than when it was knocking at the lid of the coffin, in which it had been prematurely buried.' It was the Church that 'preserved the only seed and secret of novelty'. Whenever Catholicism was 'driven out as an old thing', it always returned 'as a new thing'. It was not just 'a survival', like any 'very old thing' that managed to 'survive'. The Church was characterized not by 'endurance' but by 'recovery'. It was to

[148] The Ignatius edition, which reprints the *Catholic World* articles (with the omission of a few words), wrongly dates them all to Nov. 1922. Dorothy Collins years later published extracts in a pamphlet for the Catholic Truth Society with the same title, *Where All Roads Lead* (London: Catholic Truth Society, 1961).

the 'complexity' of its doctrines, 'of which religious reformers have so constantly complained', that it owed 'its victory over modern minds', owing 'its most recent revivals to the very fact that it is the one creed that is still not ashamed of being complicated'. It was 'the simple religions' that were 'sterile' and that became 'very rapidly stale'. A simple religion that simply said that God was Love could only elicit 'a rather feeble' response, such as 'Oh' or 'Well, well'. It was not 'complex' enough to be 'living'. It was 'too simple to be true'. But a complex religion like Catholicism had 'innumerable aspects' and was 'rich' in always having 'a number of ideas in reserve'. New Catholic 'movements' generally emphasized 'some Catholic idea that was only neglected in the sense that it was not till then specially needed'; but, when it was needed, 'nothing else' could meet the need. The Church's 'power of resurrection' depended on 'this possession of reserves', and in order to have this power it was necessary to possess 'the whole' of Catholicism and not just 'parts' of it, like Anglo-Catholics who 'took their pick in the fields of Christendom', but without possessing the fields, especially 'the fallow fields': 'They could not have all the riches, because they could not have all the reserves of the religion.' Chesterton himself in his youth had made for himself, in an age of pessimism, 'a sort of rudimentary philosophy... founded on the first principle that it is, after all, a precious and wonderful privilege to exist at all'. But this 'optimism of wonder' was only a 'half-truth' that needed to be taken into 'the culture of the Catholic Church', where it could be 'balanced by other truths'—where this optimism, which was 'an incomplete philosophy', would not degenerate into 'an orgy of anarchy or a stagnation of slavery'. The Penny Catechism's condemnation of the 'two sins against hope' 'seemed exactly to sum up and define... something that I had been trying to realize and express through all my struggles with the sects and schools of my youth', for the 'heresies that have attacked human happiness in my time, have all been variations either of presumption or despair; which, in the controversies of modern culture, are called optimism and pessimism'.[149]

Chesterton had been drawn out of 'ordinary Protestantism' by the Virgin Mary 'being beautiful', while he had been drawn out of Anglicanism by the Church. In other words, he was drawn by 'the positive attractions' of what he had 'not yet got' rather than by 'negative disparagements' of what he had 'managed to get already'. The Anglo-Catholicism he had left behind could easily be called 'a piece of English half-conscious hypocrisy'

[149] *WARL* 27–9, 34–9, 40, 44–5, 48–50.

insofar as it complained about the Protestantism of England, while at the same time 'arguing that she had remained Catholic'. And it was true that there were Anglo-Catholics who talked 'as if Catholicism had never been betrayed and oppressed' and who could be unfavourably contrasted with St Peter who 'denied his Lord; but at least . . . never denied that he had denied Him'.[150]

The Church was accused of being 'too stiff and stationary'. And it was true that she could not 'change quite so fast as the charges against her' did: 'She is sometimes caught napping and still disproving what was said about her on Monday, to the neglect of the completely contrary thing that is said about her on Tuesday.' She did 'sometimes live pathetically in the past, to the extent of innocently supposing that the modern thinker' would 'think to-day what he thought yesterday': 'Modern thought does outstrip her, in the sense that it disappears, of itself, before she has done disproving it. She is slow and belated, in the sense that she studies heresy more seriously than the heresiarch does.' Indeed, 'Catholicism was ignorant; it did not even know that Protestantism was dead'. The very things that the Church had had to defend were being 'reintroduced by the modern world, and always in a lower form': 'The Puritans rejected art and symbolism, and the decadents brought them back again, with all the old appeal to sense and an additional appeal to sensuality. . . . Protestant moralists abolished the confessional and the psychoanalysts have re-established the confessional, with every one of its alleged dangers and not one of its admitted safeguards. . . . '[151]

---

[150] *WARL* 39–40.   [151] *WARL* 41, 46.

12

The Everlasting Man

I

IN November 1922 Chesterton published *The Man who Knew too Much*. The detective stories that make up the book had been originally published in *Cassell's Magazine* and the *Storyteller*. The detective in most of the stories, 'the man who knew too much', is Horne Fisher, who is related to everyone who counts in the political establishment. He also physically resembles Maurice Baring, whom Chesterton had described as 'a man who knows everybody' when applying to him for help over the trip to Palestine: 'He was a tall, fair man, cadaverous and a little lackadaisical, with heavy eyelids and a high-bridge nose.'[1] But there the resemblance ended. As a kind of political counterpart to Father Brown,[2] who understands the criminal because he too is a sinner, Horne Fisher 'knew too much' about the world of party politics in England as Chesterton, his brother, and Belloc saw it—politics in which inevitably cosmopolitan Jewish finance makes a number of sinister appearances. But there again the resemblance ends, as the Horne Fisher stories cannot be compared in quality with the Father Brown stories. Nevertheless, Chesterton chose one of the stories, 'The Five of Swords', which did not feature Horne Fisher, as his contribution to *My Best Story: An Anthology of Stories Chosen by their own Authors* (1929), and the story also appeared in the Oxford World Classics anthology *Crime and Detection* (1930).

On 14 February 1923 Chesterton wrote to the partial model for Horne Fisher at some length about the reasons that finally persuaded him that

---

[1] *MKM* 424.   [2] Sullivan, 70.

he must leave the Church of England and join the Church of Rome. He begins with one of his 'deepest reasons', which he was afraid would give 'offence' to Anglo-Catholics—'and I am sure it is the wrong method to offend the wavering Anglo-Catholic'. But he did think that one of his 'strongest motives was mixed up with the idea of honour': 'I feel there is something mean about not making complete confession and restitution after a historic error and slander. It is not the same thing to withdraw the charges against Rome one by one, or restore the traditions to Canterbury one by one.' He offered an 'imperfect' analogy for the Anglo-Catholic who did just that.

Suppose a young prig refuses to live with his father or his friend or his wife, because wine is drunk in the house or there are Greek statues in the hall. Suppose he goes off on his own and develops broader ideas. On the day he drinks his first glass of wine, I think it is essential to his honour that he should go back to his father or his friend and say, 'You were right and I was wrong, and we will drink wine together.' It is not consonant with his honour that he should set up a house of his own with wine and statues and every parallel particular, and still treat the other as if he were in the wrong. This is mean because it is making the best of both; it is combining the advantages of being right with the advantages of having been wrong.

Chesterton thought that the analogy could be applied on the 'larger' national level:

England has really got into so wrong a state, with its plutocracy and neglected populace and materialistic and servile morality, that it must take a sharp turn that will be a sensational turn. No *evolution* into Catholicism will have that moral effect. Christianity is the religion of repentance; it stands against modern fatalism and pessimistic futurism mainly in saying that a man can go back. If we do decidedly go back it will show that religion is alive.

He was not particularly bothered about the question of apostolic succession and the validity of Anglican orders that usually preoccupied Anglo-Catholics. What did bother him was the Anglo-Catholic inconsistency in complaining that England was Protestant while at the same time claiming that it had always been Catholic. There had, it was true, always been a High Church party in the Church of England—but whether there had always been a specifically Anglo-Catholic party he was less sure. But then even Anglo-Catholics only confronted Protestantism on 'particular points', such as ritual and sacraments. Even if Anglo-Catholicism was not 'the heresy of an age', it was 'only the anti-heresy of an age'. But, since becoming a Roman Catholic, Chesterton had become conscious of being in a much vaster arsenal, full of arms against countless other potential enemies. The Church, as the Church and not merely as ordinary opinion, has something to say to philosophies which the merely High Church has never had occasion to think about. If the next movement is the very reverse of Protestantism, the Church will have something to say about it; or rather has already something to say about it.

There was another 'power' that Chesterton had been impressed by—'the power of being decisive first and being proved right afterwards'.

This is exactly the quality a supernatural power would have; and I know nothing else in modern religion that has it. For instance, there was a time when I should have thought psychical enquiry the most reasonable thing in the world, and rather favourable to religion. I was afterwards convinced, by experience and not merely faith, that Spiritualism is a practical poison. Don't people see that *when* that is found in experience, a prodigious prestige accrues to the authority which, long before the experiment, did not pretend to enquire but simply said, 'Drop it.' We feel that the authority did not discover; it knew.

There were 'a hundred things more to say', Chesterton was aware: 'indeed the greatest argument for Catholicism is exactly what makes it so hard to argue for it. It is the scale and multiplicity of the forms of truth and help that it has to offer.' But the most helpful thing that converts like him and Baring could say, as his friend had suggested, was that, as men who had 'talked to a good many men about a good many things, and seen something of the world and the philosophies of the world', they had 'not the shadow of a doubt about what was the wisest act of our lives'.[3]

In an interview with the *Toronto Daily Star*, Chesterton acknowledged that 'the chief Protestant leaders in the Church of England' were among those who had 'most helped' him to realize that the Church of England was not a branch of the Catholic Church, and therefore of 'no use' to Chesterton, who had believed in Catholic Christianity for at least twenty years: 'They have done me this good service, and I wish to express gratitude for it.' It seemed perfectly plain to Chesterton that any church that claimed to be 'authoritative' 'must be able to answer quite definitely when great questions of public morals are put'. There were those in the Church of England who could do so, but as a whole it did 'not speak strongly', it had 'no united action': 'I have no use for a Church which is not a Church militant, which cannot order battle and fall in line and march in the same direction.'[4]

---

[3] Ward, *GKC* 389–91, with text corrected from BL Add. MS 73189, fos. 49–50.
[4] O'Connor, 139–41.

Chesterton's conversion to the Church of Rome, unfortunately, did nothing to help the ailing *New Witness*. Before it finally stopped publication, Chesterton, according to 'Keith' Chesterton's account, had already once determined to close the paper down. She had been summoned to Beaconsfield, where the subject of the paper's future was broached after dinner. 'Frances sat in her fireside chair, her pale delicate face set in the curious graven expression it wore for questions of finance.' 'Keith' insisted that the paper 'must go on'. Thereupon Frances looked up, and said, with a 'finality' that 'Keith' recognized: 'It's impossible for Gilbert to find the money to continue.' 'Keith', however, urged that additional capital could be raised, expenses cut down, and that she would work as Chesterton's assistant without salary, while contributors would also write unpaid 'in sheer enthusiasm'. Finally, she prevailed; but she could see that her brother-in-law was 'not enthusiastic'. However, the circulation of the paper remained static, while advertising declined. Gradually, 'Keith' came to feel that the *New Witness* 'minus its creator... could not flourish. The mainspring had broken.' The idea of a new paper bearing Chesterton's name was, 'Keith' claimed, her idea. He was far more famous than his brother, and a review called after him would surely raise the necessary financial support. The idea seemed to appeal to Chesterton, and 'even Frances was not too discouraging'. But then nothing happened, and a year went by. Eventually, Chesterton came up to London and met 'Keith', who was full of plans for the new paper. 'After a while Gilbert explained that even yet he was not quite sure when he was starting the paper, and, in those lovely verbal undulations which flowed so easily, conveyed the impression that he was going to run *G.K.'s Weekly* by himself.' 'Keith' did not 'quite take this in for a moment', thinking only of what she had done 'to raise the necessary capital'. And then Chesterton made his meaning clear: 'As, fascinated, I watched him trace the curves of a French cavalier on the blotting pad before him, he murmured: "I think, do you know, that one Chesterton on the paper is enough."' And then, to end the matter, Chesterton gave his hurt and indignant sister-in-law 'a fraternal pat'. Later, 'Keith' came to the conclusion that the reason for his lack of enthusiasm in continuing the *New Witness* was that he no longer wished to continue to be a kind of 'caretaker' for his dead brother, and that, if 'Keith' continued to work on the new paper, it would still be Cecil's rather than his own paper.[5] Maisie Ward thought that the reason for Chesterton's dispensing with 'Keith's' services was that she was neither (as yet) a

[5] MCC 257–63.

Catholic nor a Distributist.[6] It has also been suggested that another reason for Chesterton's wanting to be rid of 'Keith' was that she was 'a regular office trouble-maker'.[7] But, as Chesterton's 1919 letters to Belloc about the possibility of removing 'Keith' from the editorial control of the *New Witness* make plain, her explanation was the correct one, as indeed Chesterton himself would soon confirm in his announcement that the new paper would be *his* paper and his alone. But, although 'Keith' would not be assistant editor of *G.K.'s Weekly*, she would nevertheless contribute regularly to the paper, particularly as drama critic.

In the *New Witness* issue of 12 January 1923 Chesterton had informed readers in his weekly column, 'At the Sign of the World's End', of the possibility of 'a new *New Witness*'. The paper had been declining since the end of the war,

crippled by the death of the only man who could really do it. It lost the one great controversialist against corruption who was materially, mentally and morally on the spot. It passed, by the tragic extension of an interregnum, to an amateur who could only help it in one way by not helping it another, and who was so placed that he could not at once contribute and control.

The paper had also lost the financial support of two wealthy backers because of its opposition to divorce and its defence of the democratic right of workers to strike. Many of those working on the paper had had to do so without remuneration. Having just survived time and again thanks to small sums contributed by readers or staff, now there was the promise of further help from one generous benefactor that seriously raised 'the possibilities of renewal'. It had been put to him that there was 'now a real chance for a new paper more boldly planned to popularise the same principles'. It would be the only paper campaigning against the sale of honours and secret party funds, and championing 'small property' against both Socialism and Communism. The hope was that enough small subscribers would come forward to put the new paper in a position where it could pay its contributors and staff. This would enable the paper to become 'more popular and less political', since at the moment people who wrote for nothing would write only what they could not write elsewhere, so that the paper became 'too narrowly concerned with corruption, or... the Distributist ideal'. Contributors naturally preferred to publish their more popular writings where they could be properly remunerated. That was true of Chesterton himself, who published his mystery

<hr>

[6] Ward, *GKC* 418–19.   [7] Barker, 263; Dale, 245.

stories, for example, elsewhere, if only to bring in money for the *New Witness*: 'My own poor little corpses might have been concealed in THE NEW WITNESS, instead of the *Story Teller*.' If that was true of writers who shared the views of the paper, it was obviously even truer of those who did not and who could not be asked to make the same financial sacrifice. That was why Shaw and Wells, for example, did not appear in its pages—although the one time they had both appeared there had been complaints about writers with views so diametrically opposed to those of the paper being allowed to appear. Chesterton, however, positively favoured debate, if only because it was 'a test of conviction to have a taste for controversy'. The full page opposite his article contained an advertisement 'Concerning a new "New Witness"' to cost sixpence. The 'business management' was convinced that such a paper with Chesterton as editor would succeed. But £10,000 was needed 'as working capital'. The hope was that 1,000 readers would subscribe £10 each, or less if they could not afford it, and that they would persuade friends to buy one or two £1 shares. Below was a form for buying shares at £1.[8] The advertisement and form appeared in subsequent issues.

In his weekly column 'At the Sign of the World's End', in the next issue of 19 January, Chesterton expressed his astonishment and admiration at the generous response of readers. And he announced that he would publish the next week details of the kind of new paper that he had in mind. His general idea was that the paper should be 'more popular' than the so-called popular press but not 'stupid' in the way that the popular press was, a stupidity that merely reflected the stupidity of the self-made millionaires who were the newspaper proprietors and who fondly imagined that their readers were even stupider than they themselves were. He also intended, as in the past, 'to use the natural language of indignation', which was 'more honourable' as well as 'better fun', and which he believed too was more popular and less hypocritical than the language of 'compromise' and evasion.[9]

In the issue of 26 January, Chesterton informed readers that the new paper would 'begin with a statement on the crisis of the moment, prominently displayed on the front page, but very short'. It would be more like a 'proclamation' than a 'leading article'. To supplement it, there would be a special authoritative article on the subject. Then he wanted there to be 'a weekly note called "A Thousand Years Hence"', not about the future but the present', as it would be seen in retrospect. He also wanted there to be a

---

[8] *New Witness*, 12 Jan. 1923.   [9] *New Witness*, 19 Jan. 1923.

column called simply 'Bad News', which would list examples of threats to liberty and small property. He hoped the new paper would publish plays and stories, including a serialized novel that he would write himself if he could not find 'a real novelist to write it'. He proposed a new kind of book review, an article on a particular subject 'using books as illustration'. He would like there to be an 'Encyclopaedia of Errors'—that is, 'fixed beliefs' that were 'quite false' and that were held by the typical educated person. In addition, he had in mind a series called, for instance, 'What They Would Have Said', that is, 'great reasoners of the past' such as Dr Johnson, concerning current ideas that were threatening both 'liberty and reason', and written in their characteristic style. What, however, he would most like to have in the paper was 'something called the Cockpit or Arena . . . which should clarify our own position by comparison and controversy'. He did not have in mind the usual correspondence column, but a column that would display more prominently the views of the paper's opponents. He proposed 'two parallel and contrary statements' that would 'appear side by side on the same page or on opposite pages', consisting of selected letters or specially commissioned contributions from opponents and replies to them. It would be 'fun', an essential Chestertonian criterion. The editorial of the same issue informed readers that, in contrast to an increasingly 'impersonal' press, it had been proposed that the new paper should become even more 'personal' than the *New Witness*, 'some even desiring that its name should be changed in favour of a personal name, or personal initials'. It was proposed that 'the precedent of John O'London and Mr T. P. O'Connor' should be followed and the paper 'be known as G.K.C.'s Weekly'. While 'instinctively' regarding the suggestion 'with a distaste amounting to dismay', Chesterton admitted that he was 'almost' moved to favour it on the ground that at least it would give a character to the paper if it was 'somebody's weekly', and would make it stand out against an increasingly 'monochrome' press.[10]

Although no readers' letters had as yet been published on the proposed new paper, the 2 February issue of the *New Witness* carried a different advertisement for it, which stated that it was 'suggested' that the new paper 'should bear the title of "G.K.C.'s WEEKLY" after the precedent of *T.P.'s Weekly* and *John O'London's Weekly* as being the most compact, convenient, and popular way of stating its identification' with the policies for which the *New Witness* stood. And a number of letters were now published strongly supporting the proposed new name for the paper, as well as Chesterton's

---

[10] *New Witness*, 26 Jan. 1923.

ideas for the contents of the new paper—although the new kind of review
he proposed was criticized as introducing 'propaganda' into book reviewing. In his weekly column, Chesterton was confident about 'the possibility
of a new sort of popular paper that has never existed before. And that is
because there does exist a definite public opinion that has never been
appealed to before.' The class of people he had in mind were people like
small shopkeepers in provincial towns, who were 'still very numerous,
but . . . not very powerful', largely because they had no organ to represent
them, having 'no economic interest in common' with the proprietors of the
so-called popular press.[11] In the next issue, Chesterton acknowledged
defeat:

In this day and hour I haul down my flag, I surrender my sword, I give up a fight I
have maintained against odds for very long. No; I do not mean the fight to
maintain the NEW WITNESS, though that was a fight against impossible odds
and has gone on for years. I mean a more horrid but hidden conflict, of which
the world knew nothing; the savage but secret war I have waged against a
proposal to call a paper by the name of 'G.K.C.'s Weekly'. When the title was
first suggested my feeling was one of wild terror, which gradually softened into
disgust.

But now he had 'come to see the case for the proposal, and that not merely
to please the crowd of friends who pressed it upon me'. It was simply a
matter of 'advertisement':

I cannot really deny, though I should very much like to, that the name would
probably be better known than any new name that could easily be taken. It is my
business to think only for the paper; and I set my teeth, or grind my teeth, and do
it. If I may be allowed to relieve my feelings by saying that I execrate, abominate
and anathematise the new name, that I renounce and abjure it, that I blast it with
lightnings and curse it with bell, book and candle, I will then admit that it is
certainly the best name we can take.

At least there could be no 'vanity touching this vulgar notoriety', for which
there were two reasons: a 'joke' about his 'being fat' and his notorious love
of paradox—'when', though, 'and where I have really written any paradoxes I do not know, and have searched my works for them in vain. . . . I
think of writing a sombre spiritual epic about it, called "Paradox Lost." '[12]
In the editorial in the next issue, Chesterton reported that of his proposals
for the new paper none had found more favour than the one about 'the

---

[11] *New Witness*, 2 Feb. 1923.   [12] *New Witness*, 9 Feb. 1923.

cock-pit or controversial arena'. Nothing, he thought, was more needed than controversy as opposed to the practice of always trying 'to take a middle course', the 'only notion of a middle course' being 'to cut a thing in two'.[13]

According to W. R. Titterton, both he and 'Keith' were firmly of the view that the new paper should be called *Chesterton's Weekly*. But Chesterton would have none of it; he would rather it were called *Tuppeny Trash* or *Sixpenny Slush*.[14] Shaw naturally had his own very decided view. He was totally opposed to the suggestion that it should be called *G.K.C.'s Weekly*, although he recognized there were successful precedents such as *T.P.'s Weekly* and *John O'London's Weekly*. He considered Chesterton's initials not to be 'euphonious', although the name Chesterton he thought was 'a noble name; but Chesterton is Weakly spoils it'. He thought it should be called simply 'CHESTERTONS' [*sic*]. 'Week' was 'a detestable snivelling word; nothing can redeem it, not even the Sermon on the Mount. . . . But Chestertons leaves no room for anything else. I am more than usually sure that I am right.'[15]

It seems that Chesterton asked his permission to publish the letter as part of the discussion about the new name. Shaw replied on 16 February that, of course, Chesterton could publish his letter if he wanted to—although it would do nothing for the circulation of the paper—'nothing but a permanent feature will do that'. However, he was insistent that Chesterton should follow the advice that he gave 'to all the people who start Labor papers (about two a week or so), which always is, "Don't open with an article to say that your paper supplies a want; don't blight your columns with "messages"; don't bewilder your readers with the family jokes of your cliques; else there will be no second number'. Chesterton should 'ponder' this 'sound' advice. He thought Chesterton's main problem was that to the rural proprietor, no longer the 'peasant' that Chesterton championed, 'art, including *belles letters*, is immorality, and people who idealize peasants, unpractical fools'. Moreover, the Roman Catholic Church, 'embarrassed by recruits of your type and born scoffers like Belloc, who cling to the Church because its desecration would take all the salt out of blasphemy,' would 'quietly' put the paper on 'the unofficial index'. The Irish would not support it because an English paper 'occasionally' waved 'a green flag far better' than they

---

[13] *New Witness*, 16 Feb. 1923.   [14] MCC 242; Titterton, 135–6.
[15] Ward, *GKC* 415, with text corrected from BL Add. MS 73198, fo. 89.

could 'wave it themselves'. As for the Jews, there were not enough of them who would buy the paper 'just to see what you say about them' to keep it going. There was, Shaw asserted roundly, 'absolutely no public' for the paper's 'policy'; and, although there was 'a select one' for Chesterton himself personally, it mostly consisted of people to whom his 'oddly assorted antipathies and pseudo-racial feuds' were 'uncongenial'. Besides, he had already said all he had to say about these 'fancies' of his 'so many thousand times over' that even his 'most faithful admirers finally (and always suddenly) discover they are fed up with the New Witness and cannot go on with it'. Either Chesterton had to 'broaden' his 'basis' or else 'have no basis at all', like Dickens in *Household Words* and *All the Year Round*. But the trouble with the second alternative was that all the articles and stories that Dickens would have published were now 'mopped up by the popular press, which in his day stuck to politics and news and nothing else'. As for the first option, Chesterton could broaden his basis if he had enough money to 'try the experiment of giving ten poor but honest men in Beaconsfield and ten more in London capital enough to start for themselves as independent farmers and shopkeepers. The result would be to ruin 18 out of the twenty, and possibly to ruin the lot.' He would then learn what Shaw could never teach him—that people needed 'not property but honourable service'. Perhaps, when confronted by either twenty ruined men or eighteen ruined and the other two capitalists, Chesterton would join the Fabian Society. Certainly, Chesterton should 'drop' the 'pseudo race feuds', simply because he could not 'compete with the Morning Post, which gives the real thing in its succulent savagery', while Chesterton could only give 'a "wouldn't hurt a fly" affectation of it'. As for religion, people wanted 'the real Catholic Church' not the 'manufactured' or 'Ideal' one of Chesterton, which did not exist, as he, Shaw, an Irishman, knew. He believed that Chesterton would not have become a Catholic had he not believed that he believed in transubstantiation—which, of course, he did not. But there were worse things than transubstantiation:

You will have to go to Confession next Easter; and I find the spectacle—the box, your portly kneeling figure, the poor devil inside wishing you had become a Fireworshipper instead of coming there to shake his soul with a sense of his ridiculousness and yours—all incredible, comic, though of course I can put a perfect literary complexion on it in a brace of shakes.

However, now he was becoming 'personal'—but how else could he be 'sincere'? Besides, he was going on too long and 'the lunch bell [was] ringing'. Chesterton should not 'bother to answer' unless he could not 'help it'.[16]

In his weekly column in the *New Witness* of 20 April, Chesterton mentioned that it had been suggested to him that the new paper should be called the *Distributist Weekly*: 'The difficulty is that the word distributism is itself a necessary evil to describe a necessary good.' There was another objection: distributism was not the only cause for which the new paper would stand, and it was impossible to find a name that would cover all that the paper would be for and against. But associating the paper with Chesterton's name would give the ordinary reader a pretty good idea of what the paper stood for. He himself personally would prefer Shaw's suggestion that the paper be called 'Chesterton's', as that would remind people of his brother and that the *New Witness* was his paper. But he had to think of what would be good for the paper not for himself, and he knew that the name of the new paper should make it clear that, while he had only been the caretaker editor of the *New Witness*, the new paper was *his* paper, in a sense in which the *New Witness* never had been, 'even in operation, let alone in origin'. But he had to be 'the real and responsible editor' of the new paper. And his initials would make it clear that readers could expect not the 'dullness' of 'pompous platitudes' but the 'fun', even 'buffoonery', of that 'pantomime elephant', 'the Chesterbelloc'. Readers would know that he would 'make a fight of it', but that he would be funny at the same time. After he had referred to his brother as 'the fighter' who had been 'the real worker' where the *New Witness* was concerned, Chesterton's implication seems clear enough: that he intends his paper to be a different kind of paper, one marked by humour above all—not the quality that readers would have first associated with the combative Cecil.[17] 'Keith' understood perfectly correctly why she was not to be assistant editor of her brother-in-law's new paper.

---

[16] Ward, *GKC* 415–17, with text corrected from BL Add. MS 73198, fo. 89. The story of Shaw offensively attacking Chesterton for converting a year later in the house of a mutual friend in Chelsea, which is recounted by Hesketh Pearson in 'G.B.S. v. G.K.C.', *Adelphi Magazine* (Sept. 1923), repr. in CS 577–83, and repeated in William B. Furlong, *Shaw and Chesterton: The Metaphysical Jesters* (University Park, PA: Pennsylvania State University Press, 1970), 121–33, is a total fabrication. For the hoax, see Hesketh Pearson, *Thinking it over: The Reminiscences of Hesketh Pearson* (London: Hamish Hamilton, 1938), 221.

[17] *New Witness*, 20 Apr. 1923.

The editorial in the last but one issue of the *New Witness* of 27 April looked back on the achievements of the paper and looked forward to what still had to be done:

We set out to state certain truths about public life that were hidden from the public; especially in the matter of political corruption and the abuses of plutocracy. Our first duty was to get them accepted as truths; but certainly our second duty is to prevent them being accepted as truisms; that is, to prevent them being accepted as necessary evils. We were not content until people agreed that politics are corrupt; but we are even less content with an agreement that they must be corrupt.

That week Chesterton's column 'At the Sign of the World's End' took the form of an open letter to Belloc, a tribute to the author of *The Servile State* and, with Cecil Chesterton, the co-founder of the paper: 'You were the father and founder of this mission; we were the converts but you were the missionary.'[18] The editorial of the last issue of 4 May had this consolation: 'That we have at least lived long enough to deprive so many famous persons of so many festive hours is alone enough to surround our ending with a certain serene and radiant satisfaction.' The correspondence column consisted of tributes to the paper, including one from H. G. Wells:

I love G.K.C. and I hate the Catholicism of Belloc and Rome so that I sit by your bedside, the Phoenix death-bed from which *G.K.C.'s Weekly* is to be born, with very mingled feelings.... You've been a decent wrong-headed old paper, full of good writing. If Catholicism is still to run about the world giving tongue, it can have no better spokesman than G.K.C. But I grudge Catholicism, G.K.C.[19]

2

September 1923 saw the publication of *Fancies versus Fads*, a collection of articles from the *New Witness*, as well as from the *Illustrated London News* and the *London Mercury*. Chesterton's volumes of collected articles show very clearly that, prolific as he was, his journalism inevitably is by no means so prolific in ideas and themes. And *Fancies versus Fads* is no exception. One familiar object of attack is what we should today call 'the nanny state', which was born in the first part of the twentieth century and whose relentless expansion into the twenty-first century would not have surprised Chesterton in the least:

---

[18] *New Witness*, 27 Apr. 1923.   [19] *New Witness*, 4 May 1923.

There must be a ceaseless and almost mechanical multiplication of things forbidden. The resolution to cure all the ills that flesh is heir to, combined with the guesswork about all possible evils that flesh and nerve and brain-cell may be heir to—these two things conducted simultaneously must inevitably spread a sort of panic of prohibition. Scientific imagination and social reform between them will quite logically and almost legitimately have made us slaves.

Chesterton accurately prophesies a society terrorized by 'health and safety' regulations, a society that 'has descended to the indescribably mental degradation of trying to abolish the abuse of things by abolishing the things themselves; which is as if it were to abolish ponds or abolish trees' for fear of what might happen to children tempted to explore them: 'Perhaps it will have a try at that before long. Thus we have all heard of savages who try a tomahawk for murder, or burn a wooden club for the damage it has done to society. To such intellectual levels may the world return.' The 'nanny state' was particularly worried about people drinking 'fermented liquor' as though it were 'an artifice and a luxury; something odd like the strange self-indulgences praised by the decadent poets'— whereas actually it was 'one of the habits that are . . . man's second nature; if indeed they are not his first nature'.[20]

However, there were more sinister infringements of liberty practised by the prohibiting state. There was a new penal theory that said that the state 'may punish people, but not blame them'. But this was nothing more than a return to 'the test of the heathen world, that of considering service to the state and not justice to the individual'. In other words, people might be punished 'for the happiness of the community' rather than because they deserved to be. The idea now was not that the punishment should 'fit the crime' but that it should 'fit the community'. And, as in the old heathen world, the people who would suffer were 'chiefly' the 'subordinate and submerged classes of society'. The same classes were also threatened by the prohibition of strikes, as though they were offences like 'breaking a window or hitting a policeman on the nose'—whereas strikers were 'not *doing* something' for they were 'doing nothing'.[21]

Marriage and the family are, as usual, defended as bulwarks against the 'Servile State', which has 'always been rather embarrassed by the institution of marriage'. For marriage, Chesterton insists, is 'an institution like any other, set up deliberately to have certain functions and limitations' and not merely as 'an individual experience'. As for the

[20] *FVF* 66, 108, 181–2.   [21] *FVF* 88, 90–1, 210–1.

family, it 'is the test of freedom; because the family is the only thing that the free man makes for himself and by himself.' It blocks 'the way to a mere social assimilation and regimentation'.[22] In 'The Secret Society of Mankind', Chesterton draws our attention to three other even more basic facts about life. The first is 'not…merely…the truth that all men will die, but…the truth that all men know it'. The second is: 'We do know of any man whatever what we do not know of any other thing whatever, that his death is what we call a tragedy.' And the third fact is just as obvious—but only Chesterton would remark upon it: the 'colossal fact, dwarfing all human differentiations…that man is the only creature who does laugh'.[23]

A month after the publication of *Fancies versus Fads*, Chesterton published *St Francis of Assisi*. He had long been fascinated by the saint, whose name he had taken as a confirmation name. To the last but one issue of the *Debater*, which came out before Christmas 1892, he had contributed a poem called simply 'St Francis of Assisi', which expressed 'most powerfully' of all his poems in the *Debater* his antipathy towards religious dogma.[24] A year later, in his letter to Lucian Oldershaw expressing his enthusiasm for Robert Blatchford's *Merrie England*, he had written about 'a curious idea' he had had of a tea party consisting of about six people, including Jesus Christ, Walt Whitman—and St Francis.[25] In a letter from Milan in 1894 to E. C. Bentley, he had listed Francis, along with Whitman, among those whom 'I happen to affect'.[26] In an article in the *Speaker* in 1900 he had spoken of the 'fascinating inconsistency' that, while St Francis 'expressed in loftier and bolder language than any earthly thinker the conception that laughter is as divine as tears' and 'he was, perhaps, the happiest of the sons of men', nevertheless he embraced a life of 'extreme asceticism'.[27] In *Orthodoxy*, he had written, 'St Francis, in praising all good, could be a more shouting optimist than Walt Whitman'.[28] Now, in his book on the saint, he wrote:

The figure in the brown habit stands above the hearth in the room where I write, and alone among many such images, at no stage of my pilgrimage has he ever seemed to me to be a stranger.… His figure stands on a sort of bridge connecting my boyhood with my conversion to many other things…[29]

---

[22] *FVF* 97, 125, 127–8, 154.   [23] *FVF* 120–2.   [24] Oddie, 67, 85.
[25] Oddie, 100.   [26] Ward, *GKC* 52–3.   [27] *Speaker*, 1 Dec. 1900.
[28] *O.* 300.   [29] *SFA* 31.

The feature of St Francis that most obviously appealed to Chesterton was his 'Praise' of creation, which Chesterton insists was in no way to be identified with 'nature-worship or pantheistic optimism'. Francis's 'great gratitude' for existence was not just a feeling or sentiment: it was 'the very rock of reality', besides which 'all facts' were 'fancies'. This was 'the fundamental fact which we cover up, as with curtains, with the illusion of ordinary life': 'He who has seen the whole world hanging on a hair of the mercy of God has seen the truth; we might almost say the cold truth.' All good things 'look better when they look like gifts'—even if it did 'seem a paradox to say that a man may be transported with joy to discover that he is in debt'. Being 'above all things a great giver', Francis 'cared chiefly for the best kind of giving which is called thanksgiving': 'If another great man wrote a grammar of assent'—Chesterton is referring to Newman's book by that title—'he may well be said to have written a grammar of acceptance; a grammar of gratitude. He understood down to its very depths the theory of thanks; and its depths are a bottomless abyss. He knew that the praise of God stands on its strongest ground when it stands on nothing.' And this, paradoxically, was the key to understanding how the joyful Francis could also be the severest of ascetics: 'It is the highest and holiest of the paradoxes that the man who really knows he cannot pay his debt will be for ever paying it. He will be for ever giving back what he cannot give back, and cannot be expected to give back.' Most people were 'not generous enough to be ascetics'. 'The whole point', explains Chesterton, 'about St Francis of Assisi is that he certainly was ascetic and he certainly was not gloomy'. His asceticism was not in the least bit 'negative . . . it was not . . . a stoical simplicity of life. It was not self-denial merely in the sense of self-control. It was as positive as a passion; it had all the air of being as positive as a pleasure. He devoured fasting as a man devours food.'[30]

For all his thanksgiving for creation, Francis, insists Chesterton, 'was not a lover of nature. Properly understood, a lover of nature was precisely what he was not.' Chesterton explains the paradox as he sees it: 'The phrase implies accepting the material universe as a vague environment, a sort of sentimental pantheism.' In the literature of the Romantic period, one could easily

imagine that a hermit in the ruins of a chapel (preferably by moonlight) might find peace and a mild pleasure in the harmony of solemn forests and silent stars, while he pondered over some scroll or illuminated volume, about the liturgical nature of

[30] *SFA* 74–8, 132.

which the author was a little vague. In short, the hermit might love nature as a background.

But for St Francis,

nothing was ever in the background. . . . He saw everything as dramatic, distinct from its setting, not all of a piece like a picture but in action like a play. A bird went by him like an arrow; something with a story and a purpose, though it was a purpose of life and not a purpose of death. A bush could stop him like a brigand; and indeed he was as ready to welcome the brigand as the bush.[31]

If Francis was not 'a lover of nature', he was most certainly not a worshipper of nature. The ancient Greeks, 'the great guides and pioneers of pagan antiquity, started out with the idea of something splendidly obvious and direct; the idea that if man walked straight ahead on the high road of reason and nature, he would come to no harm; especially if he was, as the Greek was, eminently enlightened and intelligent'. But by setting out to be 'natural . . . the most unnatural thing in the world was the very first thing they did', for 'people who worship health cannot remain healthy'. And the reason, Chesterton argues, is that the ancient Greeks did not know 'the glad good news' announced by Christianity— 'the news of original sin'. The problem with the ancient Greeks and Romans was that they lacked anything 'in the way of mysticism, except that concerned with the mystery of the nameless forces of nature, such as sex and growth and death'. In particular, by 'treating sex as only one innocent thing . . . every other innocent natural thing became soaked and sodden with sex. For sex cannot be admitted to a mere equality among elementary emotions or experiences like eating and sleeping. The moment sex ceases to be a servant it becomes a tyrant.' As for the modern idea that sex is 'free like any other sense' and that the body is 'beautiful like any flower or tree', it was 'either a description of the Garden of Eden or a piece of thoroughly bad psychology, of which the world grew weary two thousand years ago'. It was no good the ancient Greeks talking about 'a natural religion full of stars and flowers; there was not a flower or even a star that had not been stained'. Only by abolishing 'nature-worship' could human beings 'return to nature'. And 'the whole philosophy of St Francis revolved round the idea of a new supernatural light on natural things, which meant the ultimate recovery not the ultimate refusal of natural things'. The idea that he was 'a mere romantic forerunner of the Renaissance and a revival of natural pleasures for their own sake' was a complete misrepresentation:

---

[31] *SFA* 81–2.

'The whole point of him was that the secret of recovering the natural pleasures lay in regarding them in the light of a supernatural pleasure.'[32]

Secular admirers of St Francis like Matthew Arnold thought of religion as a philosophy, but philosophy is 'an impersonal thing', and

man will not roll in the snow for a stream of tendency by which all things fulfil the law of their being. He will not go without food in the name of something, not ourselves, that makes for righteousness. He will do things like this, or pretty nearly like this, under quite a different impulse. He will do these things when he is in love.

And Francis was in love: 'He was a lover of God and he was really and truly a lover of men . . .'. But a 'lover of men' is almost the opposite of 'a philanthropist', since a 'lover of men' like Francis does not 'love humanity but men', just as 'he did not love Christianity but Christ'. For Francis, Christianity was not 'a thing like a theory but a thing like a love-affair'. The trouble with his secular admirers was that they could not 'believe that a heavenly love can be as real as an earthly love', that 'divine love is a reality' just as 'romantic love is a reality'. Again, his love for his fellow human beings was entirely democratic:

To him a man was always a man and did not disappear in a dense crowd any more than in a desert. He honoured all men; that is, he not only loved but respected them all. What gave him his extraordinary personal power was this; that from the Pope to the beggar, from the sultan of Syria in his pavilion to the ragged robbers crawling out of the wood, there was never a man who looked into those brown burning eyes without being certain that Francis Bernardone was really interested in *him*; in his own inner individual life from the cradle to the grave; that he himself was being valued and taken seriously, and not merely added to the spoils of some social policy or the names in some clerical document.

This 'courtesy' of St Francis towards all, not least the common man, made him the one courtier in a court of kings: 'For he treated the whole mob of men as a mob of kings.' The 'impetuous politeness' of Francis gave back to 'a broken man' what neither alms (for 'any reveller may fling largesse in mere scorn') nor even 'time and attention' ('for any number of philanthropists and benevolent bureaucrats do such work with a scorn far more cold and horrible in their hearts'), what no 'plans or proposals or efficient rearrangements will give back': 'his self-respect and sense of speaking with an equal'. Francis's 'democratic optimism' helps to explain his asceticism, which 'was in one sense the height of optimism. He demanded a great deal

---

[32] *SFA* 38–40, 45, 59, 70.

of human nature not because he despised it but rather because he trusted it.' It is not just that Francis respected the common man, as Chesterton did, but he also, like Chesterton, loved the ordinary things that the common man loves: 'He really did love and honour ordinary men and ordinary things; indeed we may say that he only sent out the extraordinary men [his friars] to encourage men to be ordinary.'[33]

Chesterton understood quite clearly the novelty of the Franciscan spirit or charism, so different from that of monasticism. For Francis's 'revolution' was 'of the nature of an earthquake or a volcano, an explosion that drove outwards with dynamic energy the forces stored up by ten centuries in the monastic fortress or arsenal and scatted all its riches recklessly to the ends of the earth'. Indeed, 'what St. Benedict had stored St. Francis scattered; but in the world of spiritual things what had been stored into the barns like grain was scattered over the world as seed. The servants of God who had been a besieged garrison became a marching army; the ways of the world were filled as with thunder with the trampling of their feet and far ahead of that ever swelling host went a man singing . . . ' Franciscanism was the opposite of monasticism 'with its idea that the monks were to become migratory and almost nomadic instead of stationary'. By insisting that the friars were to own no possessions, Francis ensured that his friars should 'not become like ordinary men': the friar was to be different from the ordinary man in the sense that he was to be 'freer than an ordinary man': 'It was necessary that he should be free from the cloister; but it was even more important that he should be free from the world.' In a contemporary world that was 'a network of feudal and family and other forms of dependence', the friars were to be 'like little fishes who could go freely in and out of that net. They could do so precisely because they were small fishes and in that sense even slippery fishes. There was nothing that the world could hold them by; for the world catches us mostly by the fringes of our garments, the futile externals of our lives.'

A man had to be thin to pass always through the bars and out of the cage; he had to travel light in order to ride so fast and so far. It was the whole calculation, so to speak, of that innocent cunning, that the world was to be outflanked and outwitted by him, and be embarrassed about what to do with him. You could not threaten to starve a man who was ever striving to fast. You could not ruin him and reduce him to beggary, for he was already a beggar. There was a very lukewarm satisfaction even in beating him with a stick, when he only indulged in little leaps

---

[33] *SFA* 88–9, 94–5.

and cries of joy because indignity was his only dignity. You could not put his head in a halter without the risk of putting it in a halo.

For Chesterton, the Franciscan life was the diametric opposite of the monastic life: its keynote was mobility as opposed to stability, motion as opposed to stationariness. The monastic life offered 'not only an ethical but an economic repose':

The whole point of a monk was that his economic affairs were settled for good; he knew where he would get his supper, though it was a very plain supper. But the whole point of a friar was that he did not know where he would get his supper. There was always the possibility that he might get no supper. There was an element of what would be called romance, as of the gipsy or adventurer. But there was also an element of potential tragedy, as of the tramp or casual labourer.[34]

This spiritual revolution or volcano presented the Church, or more particularly the Pope, with the question as to whether it was to be

the beginning of a conflagration in which the old Christian civilisation was to be consumed. That was the point the Pope had to settle; whether Christendom should absorb Francis or Francis Christendom. And he decided rightly... [that] the Church could include all that was good in the Franciscans and the Franciscans could not include all that was good in the Church.

Had the Franciscan movement 'turned into a new religion, it would... have been a narrow religion', since, just as for Chesterton unbelief means the narrowing of the mind ('Men will not believe because they will not broaden their minds'), so too every heresy 'has been an effort to narrow the Church'. When a sect called the Fraticelli did set 'the good and glorious mood of the great St Francis' against 'the whole mind of God' and 'broke away from the compromises of Rome in favour of what they would have called the complete programme of Assisi', then the upshot was more paradoxical than the most Chestertonian of paradoxes: 'In the name of the most human of saints they declared war upon humanity.' These heretics were 'mystics and nothing else but mystics; and not Catholics; mystics and not Christians; mystics and not men. They rotted away because, in the most exact sense, they would not listen to reason.' By contrast, Francis himself, 'however wild and romantic his gyrations might appear to many, always hung on to reason by one invisible and indestructible hair'. At least as important for Chesterton was that Francis, as well as being rational and sane, possessed a 'sense of humour which salts all the

[34] *SFA* 89–90, 92–4. 97.

stories of his escapades alone' and which 'alone prevented him from ever hardening into the solemnity of sectarian self-righteousness'.[35]

If Chesterton sees movement as the distinguishing mark of Franciscans as opposed to monks, it is not least because he sees Francis's whole life as one of dramatic movement: 'As he saw all things dramatically, so he himself was always dramatic.' He was the poet 'whose whole life was a poem':

He was not so much a minstrel merely singing his own songs as a dramatist capable of acting the whole of his own play. The things he said were more imaginative than the things he wrote. The things he did were more imaginative than the things he said. His whole course through life was a series of scenes in which he had a sort of perpetual luck in bringing things to a beautiful crisis. To talk about the art of living has come to sound rather artificial than artistic. But St Francis did in a definite sense make the very act of living an art, though it was an unpremeditated art. Many of his acts will seem grotesque and puzzling to a rationalistic taste.... From the moment when he rent his robes and flung them at his father's feet to the moment when he stretched himself in death on the bare earth in the pattern of the cross, his life was made up of these unconscious attitudes and unhesitating gestures.

When Francis was going blind, the only known but uncertain remedy was to apply red-hot iron to the eyeballs: 'When they took the brand from the furnace, he rose as with an urbane gesture and spoke as to an invisible presence: "Brother Fire, God made you beautiful and strong and useful; I pray you be courteous with me."' Here Chesterton reaches the high point in his life: 'If there be any such thing as the art of life, it seems to me that such a moment was one of its masterpieces. Not to many poets has it been given to remember their own poetry at such a moment, still less to live one of their own poems.' But Chesterton does not hesitate even at this most dramatic and moving moment to introduce humour, for to him the serious and the humorous, tragedy and comedy, are but two sides of the same coin:

Even William Blake would have been disconcerted if, while he was re-reading the noble lines 'Tiger, tiger, burning bright', a real large live Bengal tiger had put his head in at the window of his cottage in Felpham, evidently with every intention of biting his head off. He might have wavered before politely saluting it, above all by calmly completing the recitation of the poem to the quadruped to whom it was dedicated. Shelley, when he wished to be a cloud or a leaf carried before the wind,

---

[35] *SFA* 36, 128, 130–1.

might have been mildly surprised to find himself turning slowly head over heels in mid air a thousand feet above the sea. Even Keats, knowing that his hold on life was a frail one, might have been disturbed to discover that the true, the blushful Hippocrene of which he has just partaken freely had indeed contained a drug, which really ensured that he should cease upon the midnight with no pain.

Being funny for Chesterton did not mean not being serious; on the contrary, being funny was a, perhaps the, way of being serious. And when he returns us to the pathos of the extraordinary scene of Francis addressing the fire just before enduring a torture that could not have been less than 'the tortures of martyrdom, which he envied in martyrology', the pathos has surely been sharpened not blunted:

For Francis there was no drug; and for Francis there was plenty of pain. But his first thought was one of his first fancies from the songs of his youth. He remembered the time when a flame was a flower, only the most glorious and gaily coloured of the flowers in the garden of God; and when that shining thing returned to him in the shape of an instrument of torture, he hailed it from afar like an old friend, calling it by the nickname which might most truly be called its Christian name.[36]

The most original and penetrating pages in the book are in the chapter called 'The Mirror of Christ'. Chesterton quotes (correctly) from Newman's satirical masterpiece, *Lectures on the Present Position of Catholics in England*, which he calls Newman's 'liveliest controversial work', a sentence that he describes as 'a model' of the 'lucidity and logical courage' that is characteristic of Catholicism: 'In speaking of the ease with which truth may be made to look like its own shadow or sham, he said, "And if Antichrist is like Christ, Christ I suppose is like Antichrist." ' Analogously, Chesterton suggests that, 'if St Francis was like Christ, Christ was to that extent like St Francis'. The point, Chesterton thought, was 'really very enlightening', because, if people found 'certain riddles and hard sayings in the story of Galilee' and if they found 'the answers to those riddles in the story of Assisi', then this 'really' did 'show that a secret' had been 'handed down in one tradition and no other'. For it showed that 'the casket that was locked in Palestine' could be 'unlocked in Umbria', which was not surprising if 'the Church is the keeper of the keys'. It was 'natural to explain St Francis in the light of Christ', but it was less obvious 'to explain Christ in the light of St Francis'. But the image of the mirror seemed a more appropriate metaphor:

[36] *SFA* 83–4, 86–7.

St Francis is the mirror of Christ rather as the moon is the mirror of the sun. The moon is much smaller than the sun, but it is also much nearer to us; and being less vivid it is more visible. Exactly in the same sense St Francis is nearer to us, and being a mere man like ourselves is in that sense more imaginable. Being necessarily less of a mystery, he does not, for us, so much open his mouth in mysteries. Yet as a matter of fact, many minor things that seem mysteries in the mouth of Christ would seem merely characteristic paradoxes in the mouth of St Francis.

Chesterton then makes a very interesting point that he modestly calls a 'truism' but that actually throws a lot of light on the interpretation of the Bible:

It is a truism to say that Christ lived before Christianity; and it follows that as an historical figure He is a figure in heathen history. I mean that the medium in which He moved was not the medium of Christendom but of the old pagan empire; and from that alone, not to mention the distance of time, it follows that His circumstances are more alien to us than those of an Italian monk such as we might meet even to-day.... This archaic setting has left many of the sayings standing like hieroglyphics and subject to many and peculiar individual interpretations. Yet it is true of almost any of them that if we simply translate them into the Umbrian dialect of the first Franciscans, they would seem like any other part of the Franciscan story; doubtless in one sense fantastic, but quite familiar.[37]

Newman, Chesterton might have pointed out, had again anticipated him by making the same point about the meaning and significance of Christ becoming clearer in the history of the Church in a much more general kind of way in his *Essay on the Development of Christian Doctrine*. There in the first chapter he had written that a religion like Christianity 'necessarily rises out of an existing state of things, and for a time savours of the soil. Its vital element needs disengaging from what is foreign and temporary...'.[38]

3

Unusually, although Chesterton was no longer engaged in editorial work, no book was published in 1924. He did, however, contribute an essay on George McDonald as an introduction to his son Greville McDonald's book, *George McDonald and his Wife*, published in May 1924. As we have already seen, he was to mention George McDonald in the *Autobiography* as

---

[37] *SFA* 103–5.

[38] John Henry Newman, *An Essay on the Development of Christian Doctrine* (London: Longmans, Green and Co., 1885), 40.

having taught him in childhood more or less the same kind of 'optimistic theism' that he was to imbibe from the sermons of the Revd Stopford Brooke.[39] In this introductory essay, he explained that McDonald's *The Princess and the Goblin*, published a couple of years before Chesterton was born, was a book that

has made a difference to my whole existence, which helped me to see things in a certain way from the start; a vision of things which even so real a revolution as a change of religious allegiance has substantially only crowned and confirmed. Of all the stories I have read . . . it remains the most real, the most realistic, in the exact sense of the phrase the most like life.

The story of a little princess in a castle in the mountains where subterranean demons come up through the cellar, forcing the princess to climb up to rooms she had never seen before and where she is consoled by a fairy godmother, 'suggests how near both the best and the worst things are to us from the first'. It also made 'all the ordinary staircases and doors and windows into magical things'. And it showed how 'the evil things besieging us . . . do not appear outside but inside'. That

simple image of a house that is our home . . . but of which we hardly know the best or the worst, and must always wait for the one and watch against the other, has always remained in my mind as something singularly solid and unanswerable; and was more corroborated than corrected when I came to give a more definite name to the lady [Chesterton means that of the Blessed Virgin Mary] watching over us from the turret, and perhaps to take a more practical view of the goblins under the floor.[40]

Early in November, Chesterton addressed the I.D.K. Club at Cambridge on 'The Superstitions of the Sceptic'. A shorthand verbatim report was published as a booklet in March 1925 by the club, together with the correspondence in the *Cambridge Review* between the speaker and a Cambridge don, G. G. Coulton, the controversialist and anti-Catholic medieval historian.[41] Chesterton argued that scepticism led to intellectual servitude, whether it was Puritanism in the sixteenth century or Utilitarianism in the nineteenth or Marxism in the twentieth century: on each occasion the sceptical mind proceeds to build an intellectual prison of iron dogmas that

[39] *A.* 167.

[40] Greville McDonald, *George McDonald and his Wife* (London: Allen and Unwin, 1924), 9–11; repr. in *MC* 163–72.

[41] Gilbert K. Chesterton, *The Superstitions of the Sceptic* (Cambridge: W. Heffer, 1925).

were much narrower than the rejected creeds and traditions. On the other hand, such of the old traditional ideas that were retained were now held without reason, the rationale for them having been lost. Coulton replied that the Catholic Church preached Puritanism long before the Reformation, forbidding dancing, for example. Chesterton's response was that, if Coulton could not distinguish Catholicism from Puritanism, then that just showed that scholars could see the details, but not the obvious things. Coulton did not understand that the balance of Catholicism consisted of teachings that corrected each other but that might appear contradictory to the outside observer. St Thomas Aquinas had certainly condemned certain kinds of dancing, but not dancing in itself like the Puritans. A medieval historian, who did not understand the nature of Catholicism, was bound to run into difficulties when writing about the Catholic Middle Ages.

In May Chesterton had told Maurice Baring that the delay in starting up the new paper was due to the fact that the 'preliminary expenses' that would have to be met were beyond anything he had 'imagined' and beyond his 'means'. He had therefore had to ask the family solicitor to raise some money on his share in the family estate. But, again, he had had no idea of the length of the legal proceedings involved. But once they were completed he would 'send out a proper prospectus' and 'see if we can get the money subscribed'.[42] Before the end of 1924 an advance specimen number of the new *G.K.'s Weekly*, dated 8 November, had been produced 'with the machinery of the [London] Mercury and the kind assistance of Jack [Sir John] Squire [the editor]. It is to serve as a sort of advertisement.'[43] In the editorial Chesterton explained that he had viewed the proposal that the new paper should bear his name with a 'horror which has since softened into loathing'. He had wanted a name that would convey what the paper stood for. But if he called it ' "The Distributist Review" ' (as has been suggested) it would produce exactly the impression' that he wanted to avoid: 'It would suggest that a Distributist is something like a Socialist; a crank, a pedant, a person with a new theory of human nature'—whereas he wanted the paper 'to stand for certain very normal and human ideas', which, however, would 'not be printed in any other paper except this one'. The problem of using any title 'defining' the paper's 'doctrine' was that it would make 'it look doctrinaire'. He wanted a title that would be 'recognized as a flag, however fantastic and ridiculous', that would 'be in some sense a challenge even if the challenge be received only

---

[42] G. K. Chesterton to Maurice Baring, 26 May 1924, *Tablet*, 26 Dec. 1953.
[43] G. K. Chesterton to Hilaire Belloc, 15 Sept. [1924], JJBL.

with genial derision'. He did not want 'a colourless name; and the nearest I can get to something like a symbol is merely to fly my own colours'. The 'natural social ideal' that the paper would stand for had been so 'ignored in England' that he thought that this 'normal ideal' was 'less known' than his own name: 'I am therefore driven to use the name as the only familiar introduction to the ideal.'[44]

The specimen issue was sent out to prospective subscribers accompanied by a printed letter, dated November 1924, and prospectus. In the letter Chesterton professed himself to be 'ready to devote' himself to the paper and 'the principles maintained in the paper' as 'the primary and practical work' of his life. The coming years, he declared, would be 'emphatically a field for an alternative to Socialism' and he believed that their 'time' had come. Politics could not simply be negatively opposed to a Socialism that had failed. The rest of the press, however, was 'antediluvian' and 'out of touch with reality'. As editor, he would act on the assumption that 'politics are corrupt', politicians 'unpopular', parliaments 'everywhere menaced by a serious reaction', and that the country was 'in very deadly peril'. According to the prospectus, Chesterton had undertaken to be editor for at least ten years. A 'special feature' of the paper would be 'an arena of debate'. Accompanying the prospectus was a form for applying for shares in the company.[45]

The sample number was sent to Shaw, who had agreed to write for the new paper, while urging Chesterton, 'You should write plays instead of editing papers. Why not do George Fox, who was released from the prison in which Protestant England was trying to murder him by the Catholic Charles II?'[46] Nor was this the last time that Shaw tried to get Chesterton to write another play. Three years after the publication of *The Judgement of Dr Johnson* in 1927 and two years before its first production, he wrote to Frances to say that a new play was needed for the Malvern Festival, but that he did not see how he could possibly find time to write it: 'A chance for Gilbert . . . He leaves everything to me nowadays.'[47]

On 16 January 1925 Shaw wrote to Chesterton from the famous Reid's Hotel in Madeira to say that the sample number had been forwarded to him: 'What a collector's treasure!' But he was 'uneasy about the prospectus' where 'you drag in anti-Prohibition'. Chesterton, he thought, risked being financially dependent on the alcohol trade, which would threaten his

[44] *MC* 265–7, 269, 271.   [45] BL Add. MS 73230, fos. 14–15, 30–1.
[46] Ward, *GKC* 418, with text corrected from BL Add. MS 73198, fo. 93.
[47] Barker, 272. For the date, see BL Add. MS 73198, fo. 99.

editorial independence. But then the paper could hardly carry on without him, since his name was in the title. Nevertheless, the trade could withdraw its money if the paper, as was most likely, did not pay. He recommended that Chesterton should keep his 'list of shareholders as various and as uncommercial' as he could: 'get Catholic money rather than beer money.' There was a further consideration. Since he, Shaw, held the patent for Distributism that was really Socialism, and since 'the Church must remain at least neutral on Prohibition', and since Prohibition was 'bound to become a commonplace of civilization', Chesterton must realize that it was 'at least possible' that one day Chesterton would 'make the paper Socialist and Dry (with a capital)'. Shaw got in another dig at Chesterton's Distributism: 'By the way, don't propose equal distribution of land. It is like equal distribution of metal, rough on those who get the lead and rather too jolly for those who get the gold.' Instead, Chesterton should advocate 'equal distribution of the national income in terms of money', in other words Socialism, as opposed to the Distributism of Belloc and Chesterton, that is, the distribution of property. Finally, Shaw threw up his hands in horror at the proposed salary Chesterton would draw as editor: 'The £500 a year is absurd. . . . You have sold yourself into slavery for ten years for £3-10-2 a week. Are you quite mad? Make it at least £1,500, plus payment for copy.'[48] Shaw would have been even more horrified if he had known that, far from merely receiving miserly remuneration, Chesterton would himself have to inject periodically large amounts of cash to keep the paper going.

On 21 March 1925 the first number of *G.K's Weekly* appeared. There may have been some small consolation for Chesterton in the fact that in the end it was not called in full *G.K.C.'s Weekly*; but nevertheless it was, Titterton recalled, 'a martyrdom' for him to see even his first two initials at the top of every page of every issue. His face also appeared on the cover of the first few issues, until he insisted: 'It's not a nice face; let's drop it.'[49] Edward Macdonald, on the other hand, who succeeded Titterton as assistant editor, remembered the occasion when the artist Thomas Derrick drew his famous cartoon of Chesterton milking a cow—like a good Distributist living off the land—but hesitated whether to give it to Macdonald for publication for fear that Chesterton would be offended. Macdonald, wishing to print it in a special number, telephoned Chesterton in Beaconsfield, who assured him that, if the cartoon was 'highly satirical, insulting and otherwise unflattering', he would be delighted to have it printed on the

[48] Ward, *GKC* 418–20.　　[49] Titterton, 136.

front page.[50] The circulation was about 5,000. To the first issue Belloc contributed a short story and Walter de la Mare part of one. Chesterton had asked De la Mare to 'assist in what amounts to a conspiracy to suggest that I have something to do with real literature' by giving 'a creative touch' to the paper's 'critical and I fear often controversial pages'.[51]

The paper was Catholic (although not exclusively) in religion, as it was Distributist in politics, just as the *New Witness* had been; in that sense it was certainly a continuation of Cecil's paper. But it was also funny in a Chestertonian way. On 11 April, for example, Chesterton brilliantly satirized the 'no popery' agitation of the authoritarian, ultra-Protestant Home Secretary, Sir William Joynson-Hicks, who was to lead successfully the opposition in parliament in 1927 to a revised version of the Book of Common Prayer. The Home Secretary was reported as having told a crowd in the Albert Hall: 'We want no priestly interference, we ask for no purgatory and we will submit to no compulsory confessional.' Chesterton confessed that the 'last clause of this declaration' was in particular 'a great relief to our minds. No longer shall we see a policeman seizing a man in the street by the scruff of the neck and dragging him to the nearest confessional-box. No longer will our love of liberty be outraged by the sinister bulk of Black Maria taking its daily gang of compulsory penitents to Westminster Cathedral.' Apparently, 'auricular confession' was no longer to be 'a part of the British Constitution': it was to be voluntary not compulsory—in other words, Chesterton remarked sarcastically, just like state education or national insurance or military service. But what particularly interested Chesterton was 'the very remarkable phrase "We ask for no purgatory"', which seemed to imply that 'when Sir William reaches the gates of another world, St Peter or some well-trained angel will say to him in a slightly lowered voice, in the manner of a well-trained butler, "Would you be requiring a purgatory?"' Apparently, it did not occur to Sir William Joynson-Hicks that 'Purgatory may exist whether he likes it or not'.

If it be true, however incredible it may seem, that the powers ruling the universe think that a politician or a lawyer can reach the point of death, without being in that perfect ecstasy of purity that can see God and live—why then there may be cosmic conditions corresponding to that paradox, and there is an end of it. It may be obvious to us that the politician is already utterly sinless, at one with the saints.

[50] Ward, *GKC* 506.

[51] G. K. Chesterton to Walter de la Mare, 4 Mar. [1925], BL Add. MS 73195, fo. 2.

It may be self-evident to us that the lawyer is already utterly selfless, filled only with God and forgetful of the very meaning of gain. But if the cosmic power holds that there are still some strange finishing touches, beyond our fancy, to put to his perfection, then certainly there will be some cosmic provision for that mysterious completion of the seemingly complete. The stars are not clean in His sight and His angels He chargeth with folly; and if He should decide that even in a Home Secretary there is room for improvement, we can but admit that omniscience can heal the defect that we cannot even see.[52]

It was not the precarious financial state of the paper that bothered Chesterton nearly so much as dissension among members of the paper's board or staff, and even more the demand that he should adjudicate. Confronting intellectual challenges was never a problem; it was personal confrontation that Chesterton hated. To begin with, there was only the skeleton staff of three, consisting of the office manager, the subeditor, Miss Dunham or Bunny, and an office boy, who had been on the *New Witness*, whose salaries had been paid by Chesterton personally during the inter- regnum. Chesterton would come up from Beaconsfield once or twice a week to dictate his articles. According to Miss Dunham, it was impossible to predict when he would come. But she always knew when he was there by the smell of his cigar. Whenever he lighted a cigar or cigarette, he would make a sign in the air with a match, a ritual that particularly impressed itself on Miss Dunham—although she apparently did not realize that Chesterton was making the sign of the cross.[53] She was also very aware of his tiny feet, which seemed so inadequate for the task of moving such a large body. Because Chesterton hated having to select the contributions that would go into the paper, the job was often left to her, to her dismay. She never saw him angry or even impatient, and he was particularly loved by the unimportant members of staff, such as typists and office boys. He left evidence of his presence all over the office in the shape of doodled drawings. He had no sense of time, and, if he said he would go out, he might stay another hour or he might go out and not come back.[54]

After a few weeks, Titterton, the former temporary assistant editor of the *New Witness*, was summoned to the office at 20 Essex Street, off the Strand. Chesterton looked delightedly surprised to see him, with the same look of surprise as when he used suddenly to appear at the office in the days of the *New Witness* with 'the air . . . of having strayed in by mistake, of being about to apologize for it, and of then finding to his glad surprise

[52] 'Found Wandering: A Politician on Purgatory', *G.K.'s Weekly*, 11 Apr. 1925.
[53] Ward, *GKC* 550.   [54] Ward, *GKC* 414, 420–1.

that it's his own office'. Chesterton explained that he and Miss Dunham had been trying to run the paper between them—'but there was a screw missing somewhere. The screw may not be actually missing, but loose, probably in [his] own head.' Perhaps, if there was a screw missing, it was the screw that the paper should pay Titterton to return to the office as assistant editor. As Chesterton explained to Titterton that he had written not only the leader but also three articles for the next issue, Titterton realized that there was indeed 'a screw loose somewhere'. It was nothing but 'sheer murder' that Chesterton should have been carrying such a load (he was in effect writing half the paper), as well as writing books and his weekly column for the *Illustrated London News*. Still, Titterton was delighted that Chesterton was now much more involved than when he was editing the *New Witness*, coming to the office more often and, even more important, also to the printers in Clerkenwell Close, where the proofs had to be read. How Chesterton ever managed to penetrate that hidden spot was a mystery to Titterton, but he was 'sure that each attempt to do so was an unexpected voyage of discovery'. More often than not, before examining the proofs, he would ask Miss Dunham if she would mind him dictating a poem to her that had come into his mind *en route*. In that small crowded office where only sideways motion was possible—and Chesterton 'had no sideways'—the sight of the great man walking a pace forward and a pace back, his hands behind his back, while dictating some serious or comic verses, remained vividly in Titterton's memory. He noticed how Chesterton's manner had changed since he had known him as editor of the *New Witness*: he seemed to be more determined and serious. It was clear that he was fighting for a cause and his weapon was *G.K.'s Weekly*.[55]

In June 1925 Chesterton published *Tales of the Long Bow*, a collection of stories that he had already published in the *Storyteller*. The first story begins by announcing the author's intention in writing the stories: 'These tales concern the doing of things recognized as impossible to do; impossible to believe; and, as the weary reader may well cry aloud, impossible to read about.' In short, they were 'tall stories', which are highly unlikely to weary readers any longer as they are highly unlikely to attract any readers any longer. But there are some good satirical moments, as in the court-room scene where the chief magistrate is 'the celebrated hygienist, Sir Horace Hunter, O.B.E., M.D.', to whom was 'largely due the logical extension of the existing precautions against infection from the pig; though he was fully supported by his fellow magistrates, one being Mr Rosenbaum Low, millionaire ... and the other the young Socialist, Mr Amyas Minns, famous for his exposition of Shaw on the Simple Life ... '. His two fellow magistrates 'concurred in the argument of Sir Horace, that just as all the difficulties and doubtful cases raised by the practice of moderate drinking had been simplified by the solution of Prohibition, so the various quarrels and evasions about swine-fever were best met by a straightforward and simple regulation against swine'. In a previous story we have been told that judges are 'progressive like Dr Hunter, and ally themselves on principle with the progressive forces of the age, especially those they are likely to meet out at dinner'.[56]

4

H. G. Wells's best-selling *The Outline of History* had been published in serial paperback form in 1919 and then as a hardback in 1920. Wells's 'outline' was quite simple: through the centuries man had evolved from a primitive animal form to the civilized man of the twentieth century who would finally establish world peace and prosperity. The book was a best-seller—although its view of history was certainly rather remarkable, given its publication only one year after the end of the horrors of the First World War and ten years before the Great Depression began with the Wall Street crash of 1929, only to be followed ten years later by the Second World War. Wells had naturally been dismissive of Christianity, attacking the Roman Catholic Church in particular. Chesterton's *The Everlasting Man*, published in September 1925, was at least in part a response to Wells.

Chesterton begins *The Everlasting Man*, one of the two or three greatest of his half-dozen or so major works, by pointing out that in a post-Christian age it is very difficult to see Christianity for what it is: post-Christians 'still live in the shadow of the faith and have lost the light of the faith'. They are in a state of 'reaction': 'They cannot be Christians and they cannot leave off being Anti-Christians.' They are not 'far enough away not to hate' Christianity, nor are they 'near enough to love it'. And so, 'while the best judge of Christianity is a Christian, the next best judge would be something more like a Confucian'. But the 'worst judge of all is the man now most ready with his judgments; the ill-educated Christian turning gradually into the ill-tempered agnostic ... '. The 'anti-clericalism' of post-Christians 'has become an atmosphere, an atmosphere of negation and hostility from

[56] *TLB* 255, 288, 311.

which they cannot escape. Compared with that, it would be better to see the whole thing as something belonging to another continent, or to another planet.' It is only when one is 'impartial' that one can 'know why people are partial to it'. And Chesterton 'seriously' recommends 'those in whom a mere reaction has thus become an obsession' to imagine the Apostles as if they were pagans, 'to try to do as much justice to Christian saints as if they were Pagan sages'. Living in a country full of churches, post-Christians need 'to walk past a church as if it were a pagoda' rather than 'to stand permanently in the porch, impotent either to go inside ... or to go outside and forget'. Chesterton is quite candid about his apologetic method: to 'invoke ... the imagination that can see what is there'. For Christianity makes very serious claims that it would be absurd to dismiss with contempt. Consequently, 'when its fundamentals are doubted, as at present, we must try to recover the candour and wonder of the child; the unspoilt realism and objectivity of innocence'. If that is not possible, then 'we must try at least to shake off the cloud of mere custom and see the thing as new, if only by seeing it as unnatural. Things that may well be familiar so long as familiarity breeds affection had much better become unfamiliar when familiarity breeds contempt.' The 'heavy bias of fatigue' made it 'almost impossible to make the facts vivid, because the facts are familiar'. If, for example, one has lost 'the sane vision' of who man is, then one 'can only get it back by something very like a mad vision; that is, by seeing man as a strange animal and realising how strange an animal he is'. In short, 'it is exactly when we do regard man as an animal that we know he is not an animal'. Only then can we recover our sense of 'wonder' at the nature of man. And so, Chesterton's avowed purpose is 'to strike wherever possible this note of what is new and strange, and for that reason the style even on so serious a subject may sometimes be deliberately grotesque and fanciful'. For his aim is 'to help the reader to see Christendom from the outside in the sense of seeing it as a whole, against the background of other historic things; just as I desire him to see humanity as a whole against the background of natural things'. When both Christianity and humanity are 'seen thus, they stand out from their background like supernatural things'.[57]

After this introduction, Chesterton does indeed begin with man himself, about whom the 'simplest truth ... is that he is a very strange being; almost

---

[57] *EM* 10–12, 14–18. The Ignatius Press *Collected Works* edition unfortunately omits a lengthy passage from the introduction to *The Everlasting Man*. References are instead to the separate Ignatius Press edition of 1993.

in the sense of being a stranger on the earth'. He is not like other animals, he is 'unique':

> he has much more of the external appearance of one bringing alien habits from another land than of a mere growth of this one. He has an unfair advantage and an unfair disadvantage. He cannot sleep in his own skin; he cannot trust his own instincts. He is at once a creator moving miraculous hands and fingers and a kind of cripple. He is wrapped in artificial bandages called clothes; he is propped on artificial crutches called furniture.

But there is one aspect of him that Chesterton characteristically emphasizes: 'Alone among the animals, he is shaken with the beautiful madness called laughter; as if he had caught sight of some secret in the very shape of the universe hidden from the universe itself.' However, there is another thing that makes man absolutely unique among the animals—namely, that he has always felt that 'certain forms were necessary to fence off and protect certain private things from contempt or coarse misunderstanding; and the keeping of those forms, whatever they were, made for dignity and mutual respect'. Now these forms 'mostly refer, more or less remotely, to the relations of the sexes', a point that 'illustrates the two facts that must be put at the very beginning of the record of the race'. The first of these is that 'original sin is really original': 'Whatever else men have believed, they have all believed that there is something the matter with mankind. This sense of sin has made it impossible to be natural and have no clothes, just as it has made it impossible to be natural and have no laws.' But this sense of sin is above all 'to be found in that other fact, which is the father and mother of all laws as it is itself founded on a father and a mother; the thing that is before all thrones and even all commonwealths'—the 'form' we call the family, round which 'gather the sanctities that separate men from ants'.[58]

Chesterton dismisses the 'fashionable' idea that 'a monkey evolved into a man and in the same way a barbarian evolved into a civilised man'. Far from there having been moral progress, 'as a matter of fact some of the very highest civilisations of the world were the very places where the horns of Satan were exalted, not only to the stars but in the face of the sun'. In politics, again, a primitive society was likely to be 'like a pure democracy', since 'simple agricultural communities are by far the purest democracies'. Far from there being necessarily progress, 'democracy is a thing which is always breaking down through the complexity of civilisation'. Such is the 'evolutionary mania' that people have become convinced 'that every great

[58] *EM* 36, 53.

thing grows from a seed, or something smaller than itself. They seem to forget that every seed comes from a tree, or from something larger than itself.' In the case of religion, it was much more likely that monotheism preceded polytheism, that 'religion did not originally come from some detail that was forgotten, because it was too small to be traced': 'Much more probably it was an idea that was abandoned because it was too large to be managed. There is very good reason to suppose many people did begin with the simple but overwhelming idea of one God who governs all; and fell away into such things as demon-worship almost as a secret dissipation.' In paganism God 'is something assumed and forgotten and remembered by accident'. He is 'the higher deity' who 'is remembered in the higher moral grades and is a sort of mystery'. What seemed clear to Chesterton was that 'there was never any such thing as the Evolution of the Idea of God. The idea was concealed, was avoided, was almost forgotten, was even explained away; but it was never evolved.' Polytheism itself seems often to have consisted of 'the combination of several monotheisms', while Confucianism seems to be 'a rather vague theism' in which 'a simple truth' seems to have 'receded, until it was remote without ceasing to be true'. The fact that there was 'a strange silence' about God certainly suggested 'the absence of God'—but not necessarily the 'non-existence' of God: there was 'a void' but not 'a negation'. There was 'an empty chair' or rather 'an empty throne'. And Chesterton invokes his favourite image of the back: 'it was as if some immeasurable presence had turned its back on the world.' There was 'in a very real sense the presence of the absence of God', which one could feel, for example, 'in the unfathomable sadness of pagan poetry'. There was the implication that the gods of the pagans were 'ultimately related to something else, even when that Unknown God has faded into a Fate'. For 'what was truly divine' seemed 'very distant, so distant that they dismissed it more and more from their minds'. But what was quite clear was that they knew there was something wrong with the world: 'These men were conscious of the Fall, if they were conscious of nothing else . . .'. Still, God 'really' had been 'sacrificed to the Gods; in a very literal sense of the flippant phrase, they have been too many for him'.[59]

Chesterton rejects any glib notion of religious pluralism: 'We are accustomed to see a table or catalogue of the world's great religions in parallel columns, until we fancy they are really parallel.' But these so-called religions—which 'we choose to lump together'—'do not really show any common character'. True, Islam followed Christianity and 'was largely an

[59] *EM* 59, 71, 87–90, 92–4, 119.

imitation of Christianity. But the other eastern religions; or what we call religions, not only do not resemble the Church but do not resemble each other.' Indeed, Confucianism was not even a religion, and could no more be compared with Christianity than 'a theist with an English squire'. Christianity was bound up with the idea of a Church, while Confucianism and Buddhism were 'great things' but could not be called 'Churches'—any more than the English and French peoples could be called 'nomads' although they were 'great peoples'. The truth was that, 'humanly speaking', 'the world owes God to the Jews'. And the world also owed it to the Jews that they refused 'to follow the enlightened course of Syncretism and the pooling of all the pagan traditions': 'It is obvious indeed that his [God's] followers were always sliding down this easy slope; and it required the almost demoniac energy of certain inspired demagogues, who testified to the divine unity in words that are still like winds of inspiration and ruin.' While the rest of the world 'melted' into a 'mass of confused mythology', this God of the Jews, 'who is called tribal and narrow, precisely because he was what is called tribal and narrow, preserved the primary religion of all mankind'. It was the Jews who had enabled the world, which 'would have been lost' otherwise, 'to return to that great original simplicity of a single authority in all things'. It was to this 'secretive and restless nomadic people' that the world owed 'the supreme and serene blessing of a jealous God'. An example of the secretiveness of the Jews, who 'stood apart and kept their tradition unshaken and unshared', was the way they had 'kept a thing like the Book of Job out of the whole intellectual world of antiquity. It is as if the Egyptians had modestly concealed the Great Pyramid.' And Chesterton cannot resist the ultimate paradox: 'He [the God of the Jews] was tribal enough to be universal. He was as narrow as the universe.'[60]

The pagan was not an unbeliever like an atheist, but neither was he a believer like a Christian. He felt 'the presence of powers' about which he could only guess. His myths were never 'a religion, in the sense that Christianity or even Islam is a religion'. Certainly, they satisfied 'some of the needs satisfied by a religion; and notably the need for doing certain things at certain dates; the need of the twin ideas of festivity and formality'. But, although myths provided the pagan with 'a calendar', they did not 'provide him with a creed'. When St Paul was in Athens, he discovered that the Greeks had 'one altar to an unknown god. But in truth all their gods were unknown gods.' It was only when St Paul told them who it was 'they had ignorantly worshipped' that 'the real break in history' came.

[60] *EM* 84–6, 95, 97–8.

Paganism, then, was 'an attempt to reach the divine reality through the imagination alone' and without the restraints of reason. For reason was 'something separate from religion, even in the most rational of these civilisations'. Mythology and philosophy ran 'parallel' and did not 'mingle till they met in the sea of Christendom'. But nevertheless the pagan 'found it natural to worship; even natural to worship unnatural things'. The pagan knew that when he worshipped he was 'doing a worthy and virile thing': he was 'doing one of the things for which a man was made'. But the fact remained that it was an 'imaginative experiment' that 'began with imagination', and therefore there was 'something of mockery in it, and especially in the object of it'. This mockery became 'the almost intolerable irony of Greek tragedy'. It was not surprising that one 'feels throughout the whole of paganism a curious double feeling of trust and distrust'. For pagan mythology was 'a *search*' that combined 'a recurrent desire with a recurrent doubt'. And yet there remained 'an indestructible instinct, in the poet as represented by the pagan, that he is not entirely wrong in localising his god'. It was all right to call these pagan myths 'foreshadowings' so long as one remembered that 'foreshadowings are shadows': 'And the metaphor of a shadow happens to hit very exactly the truth that is very vital here. For a shadow is a shape; a thing which reproduces shape but not texture. These things were something *like* the real thing; and to say that they were like is to say that they were different.' For polytheism was 'never a view of the universe satisfying all sides of life; a complete and complex truth with something to say about everything. It was only a satisfaction of one side of the soul of man, even if we call it the religious side; and I think it is truer to call it the imaginative side.' Precisely, then, because 'mythology only satisfied one mood', the pagan 'turned in other moods to something totally different'. But the mythology and the philosophy never collided and 'really destroyed the other', nor was there ever 'any combination in which one was really reconciled with the other. They certainly did not work together; if anything the philosopher was a rival of the priest.'[61]

Chesterton now begins his task of trying to make us see Christianity afresh as though for the first time, however grotesquely he has to depict it. And first of all he points out that the whole of Christianity rests on this 'single paradox'—'that the hands that had made the sun and stars were too small to reach the huge heads of the cattle'. Every Christmas proclaims an 'association...between two ideas that most of mankind must regard as remote from each other; the idea of a baby and the idea of unknown

[61] *EM* 109–14, 124, 126.

strength that sustains the stars'. And 'this combination of ideas has emphatically...altered human nature': 'It would be vain to attempt to say anything adequate, or anything new, about the change which this conception of a deity born like an outcast or even an outlaw had upon the whole conception of law and its duties to the poor and outcast.' Again, Christmas, that feast so important to Chesterton, 'is in one sense even a simple thing', but, like all the truths of Christianity, 'it is in another sense a very complex thing. Its unique note is the simultaneous striking of many notes; of humility, of gaiety, of gratitude, of mystical fear, but also of vigilance and drama.' Christmas celebrates 'the exultant explosion of that one hour in the Judean hills', when 'the rejoicings in the cavern were rejoicings in a fortress or an outlaw's den; properly understood it is not unduly flippant to say they were rejoicings in a dug-out'. The 'subterranean chamber' where Jesus was born was literally 'a hiding-place from enemies', enemies who 'were already scouring the stony plain that lay above it like a sky':

It is not only that the very horse-hoofs of Herod might in that sense have passed like thunder over the sunken head of Christ. It is also that there is in that image a true idea of an outpost, of a piercing through the rock and an entrance into an enemy territory. There is in this buried divinity an idea of *undermining* the world; of shaking the towers and palaces from below...

Jesus's followers, too, were paradoxically both 'despised and...feared':

Those who charged the Christians with burning down Rome with firebrands were slanderers; but they were at least far nearer to the nature of Christianity than those among the moderns who tell us that the Christians were a sort of ethical society, being martyred in a languid fashion for telling men they had a duty to their neighbours, and only mildly disliked because they were meek and mild.

What Chesterton calls 'the combination of ideas that make up the Christian and Catholic idea' was 'already crystallised in the first Christmas story'. The 'three distinct and commonly contrasted things...are nevertheless one thing; but this is the only thing which can make them one'.

The first is the human instinct for a heaven that shall be as literal and almost as local as a home. It is the idea pursued by all poets and pagans making myths; that a particular place must be the shrine of the god or the abode of the blest...The second element is a philosophy *larger* than that of Lucretius and infinitely larger than that of Herbert Spencer. It looks at the world through a hundred windows where the ancient stoic or the modern agnostic only looks through one....And the third point is this; that while it is local enough for poetry and larger than any other philosophy, it is also a challenge and a fight. While it is deliberately broadened to embrace every aspect of truth, it is still stiffly embattled against every mode of error.

This 'trinity of truths' was 'symbolised... by the three types in the old Christmas story; the shepherds and the kings and that other king who warred upon the children'.[62]

Chesterton now turns to the figure of Christ himself. And he begins by pointing out that there is the obvious difficulty that the New Testament is no longer the *New* Testament: 'It is not at all easy to realise the good news as new.' Challenging the usual stereotypes, Chesterton insists on us looking at the actual person we read about in the Gospels:

We have all heard people say a hundred times over, for they seem never to tire of saying it, that the Jesus of the New Testament is indeed a most merciful and humane lover of humanity, but that the Church has hidden this human character in repellent dogmas and stiffened it with ecclesiastical terrors till it has taken on an inhuman character.

This, Chesterton insists, 'is... very nearly the reverse of the truth'.

The truth is that it is the image of Christ in the churches that is almost entirely mild and merciful. It is the image of Christ in the Gospels that is a good many other things as well. The figure in the Gospels does indeed utter in words of almost heart-breaking beauty his pity for our broken hearts. But they are very far from being the only sort of words that he utters. Nevertheless they are almost the only kind of words that the Church in its popular imagery ever represents him as uttering. The popular imagery is inspired by a perfectly sound popular instinct. The mass of the poor are broken, and the mass of the people are poor, and for the mass of mankind the main thing is to carry the conviction of the incredible compassion of God.... In any case there is something appalling, something that makes the blood run cold, in the idea of having a statue of Christ in wrath.

But if we turn to the Gospels themselves, what do we find? Somebody reading them for the first time, suggests Chesterton, would find that 'part of the interest' of the story 'would consist in its leaving a good deal to be guessed at or explained': 'It is full of sudden gestures evidently significant except that we hardly know what they signify; of enigmatic silences; of ironical replies. The outbreaks of wrath, like storms above our atmosphere, do not seem to break out exactly where we should expect them, but to follow some higher weather-chart of their own.' Nor is there anything 'meek and mild' about Jesus the exorcist: 'It is much more like the tone of a

---

[62] *EM* 169–71, 173, 180–4.

very business-like lion-tamer or a strong-minded doctor dealing with a homicidal maniac.' Indeed, the real Christ of the Gospels is 'actually... more strange and terrible than the Christ of the Church'. Then there are the 'puzzles' in 'a very strange story', like 'that long stretch of silence in the life of Christ up to the age of thirty. It is of all silences the most immense and imaginatively impressive'. How is it that 'he who of all humanity needed least preparation seems to have had most'? The truth is that the Gospel story is not 'easy to get to the bottom of'. It is anything but the 'simple Gospel' that people like to contrast with the Church: 'Relatively speaking, it is the Gospel that has the mysticism and the Church that has the rationalism. As I should put it, of course, it is the Gospel that is the riddle and the Church that is the answer. But whatever be the answer, the Gospel as it stands is almost a book of riddles.' Instead of the platitudes one associates with moralists, a person reading the Gospels for the first time 'would find a number of strange claims... a number of very startling pieces of advice; a number of stunning rebukes; a number of strangely beautiful stories'. Instead of platitudes, for instance, about peace, such a reader 'would find several ideals of non-resistance, which taken as they stand would be rather too pacific for any pacifist'. But, on the other hand, our reader 'would not find a word of all that obvious rhetoric against war which has filled countless books': 'There is nothing that throws any particular light on Christ's attitude towards organised warfare, except that he seems to have been rather fond of Roman soldiers. Indeed it is another perplexity... that he seems to have got on much better with Romans than he did with Jews.' The truth is, Chesterton concludes, the Jesus of popular conception is 'a made-up figure, a piece of artificial selection, like the merely evolutionary man' and impossible to reconcile with the real Jesus of the Gospels, 'a strolling carpenter's apprentice' who 'said calmly and almost carelessly, like one looking over his shoulder: "Before Abraham was, I am." '[63]

Chesterton gives examples of how it is the Church that explains the riddles of the Gospel. The assertion, for instance, that the meek would inherit the earth was not at all 'a meek statement', but rather 'a very violent statement; in the sense of doing violence to reason and probability'. But as a prophecy it would one day be fulfilled in monasticism: 'The monasteries were the most practical and prosperous estates and experiments in reconstruction after the barbaric deluge; the meek did really inherit the earth.' Again, the story of Martha and Mary found its fulfilment

[63] *EM* 186–9, 190–1, 193, 196, 198; *NJ* 333, 335.

in 'the mystics of the Christian contemplative life'. If the Gospels could be read as though they were 'as new as newspaper reports, they would puzzle and perhaps terrify us as much *more* than the same things as developed by historical Christianity': 'For instance, Christ after a clear allusion to the eunuchs of the eastern courts, said there would be eunuchs of the kingdom of heaven. If this does not mean the voluntary enthusiasm of virginity, it could only be made to mean something much more unnatural or uncouth.'[64]

As an example of 'the originality of the Gospel', Chesterton takes the 'exaltation of childhood', as strong and as startling as any. But the literary style itself of Jesus was also highly original: 'It had among other things a singular air of piling tower upon tower by the use of the *a fortiori* . . . '. And above all, his speaking as though he were divine was absolutely unique: 'of no other prophet or philosopher of the same intellectual order, would it be even possible to pretend' that he had made such a claim. The case of Jesus Christ was unique: only a 'monomaniac' could make such a claim, but no one thought that 'the preacher of the Sermon on the Mount was a horrible half-witted imbecile'. However, in spite of the Sermon on the Mount, there was a 'quality running through all his teachings' that seemed to Chesterton 'to be neglected in most modern talk about them as teachings; and that is the persistent suggestion that he has not really to come to teach'—but rather 'to die'. And, when the moment came for him to die, it was 'the supremely supernatural act, of all his miraculous life, that he did not vanish', that he did not miraculously disappear. On that Good Friday, Chesterton notes that it is 'the best things in the world that are at their worst': 'the priests of a true monotheism and the soldiers of an international civilisation'. Although 'Rome was almost another name for responsibility', the Roman governor Pontius Pilate 'stands for ever as a sort of rocking statue of the irresponsible': 'He who is enthroned to say what is justice can only ask, "What is truth?"' And the Jewish priests who were 'proud that they alone could look upon the blinding sun of a single deity . . . did not know that they themselves had gone blind'. Of the crucifixion itself Chesterton refuses to speak—for

if there be any sound that can produce a silence, we may surely be silent about the end and the extremity; when a cry was driven out of that darkness in words dreadfully distinct and dreadfully unintelligible, which man shall never understand in all the eternity they have purchased for him; and for one annihilating

---

[64] *EM* 191–2.

instant an abyss that is not for our thoughts had opened even in the unity of the absolute; and God had been forsaken of God.[65]

Chesterton had in fact dared to speak of this terrible paradox in *Orthodoxy*.[66]

When giving Peter authority over his Church, Christ used the two symbols of rock and keys. What he meant by saying that on the rock of Peter he would build his Church was another example of something that 'could only fully expand and explain itself afterwards, and even long afterwards'. But the other image of the keys, Chesterton suggests, 'has an exactitude that has hardly been exactly noticed'. Its 'peculiar aptness' lay in the fact that the early 'Christian movement' claimed to possess a key that 'could unlock the prison of the whole world; and let in the white daylight of liberty'. The Christian creed was like a key in three ways: 'First, a key is above all things a thing with a shape. It is a thing that depends entirely upon keeping its shape. The Christian creed is above all things the philosophy of shapes and the enemy of shapelessness.' Chesterton presses home the analogy: 'A man told that his solitary latchkey had been melted down with a million others into a Buddhist unity would be annoyed. But a man told that his key was gradually growing and sprouting in his pocket, and branching into new wards or complications, would not be more gratified.' Secondly, the point about a key is that it either fits or does not fit the lock. If it fits the lock, then it is pointless to ask for 'a simpler key' that has a less 'fantastic shape'. And, thirdly, to complain about the key having the 'elaborate pattern' that is necessary to open the lock is like complaining about Christianity 'being so early complicated with theology'. If Christianity had 'faced the world only with the platitudes about peace and simplicity some moralists would confine it to, it would not have had the faintest effect on that luxurious and labyrinthine lunatic asylum'. The creed *was* complicated, because the problem with the world was 'a complicated problem'. Although it did seem 'complex' like the key, there was 'one thing about it that was simple. It opened the door.' The truth was that the 'purity' of the creed was 'preserved by dogmatic definitions and exclusions. It could not possibly have been preserved by anything else.' The enlightened modern liberals who deride the Athanasian dogma of 'the Co-Eternity of the Divine Son' as 'a dreadful example of barren dogma' are the same people who like to 'offer us as a piece of pure and simple Christianity, untroubled by doctrinal disputes ... the single sentence, "God is Love"'. But the dogma is there to protect that very sentence: 'The barren

---

[65] *EM* 199, 200, 203–4, 207–8, 210–12.
[66] See above, p. 226.

dogma is only the logical way of stating the beautiful sentiment.' Never has the vital importance of defined doctrine been more compellingly expressed:

For if there be a being without beginning, existing before all things, was He loving when there was nothing to be loved? If through that unthinkable eternity He is lonely, what is the meaning of saying He is love? The only justification of such a mystery is the mystical conception that in His own nature there was something analogous to self-expression; something of what begets and beholds what it has begotten. Without some such idea, it is really illogical to complicate the ultimate essence of deity with an idea like love.

It was 'the defiance of Athanasius to the cold compromise of the Arians' that was 'the trumpet of true Christianity':

It was emphatically he who really was fighting for a God of Love against a God of colourless and remote cosmic control; the God of the stoics and the agnostics. . . . He was fighting for that very balance of beautiful interdependence and intimacy, in the very Trinity of the Divine Nature, that draws our hearts to the Trinity of the Holy Family. His dogma, if the phrase be not misunderstood, turns even God into a Holy Family.

Islam, on the other hand, was 'a barbaric reaction against that very humane complexity . . . that idea of balance in the deity, as of balance in the family, that makes that creed a sort of sanity, and that sanity the soul of civilisation'. For Islam was 'a product of Christianity; even if it was a by-product; even if it was a bad product'.[67]

There was one thing that pagan mythology and philosophy had in common: 'both were really sad.' Christianity brought hope into the world. And it was a dogmatic Christianity that did this because of its very liberality. Modern theological liberals cannot understand that 'the only liberal part' of their theology 'is really the dogmatic part': 'If dogma is incredible, it is because it is incredibly liberal. If it is irrational, it can only be in giving us more assurance of freedom than is justified by reason.' The doctrine of free will may seem irrational, but it is hardly liberality to deny personal freedom. Without the dogmas of dogmatic Christianity, monotheism turns into monism and consequently into despotism:

It is precisely the unknown God of the scientist, with his impenetrable purpose and his inevitable and unalterable law, that reminds us of a Prussian autocrat making rigid plans in a remote tent and moving mankind like machinery. It is

---

[67] *EM* 214–15, 224, 227–9, 239.

precisely the God of miracles and of answered prayers who reminds us of a liberal and popular prince, receiving petitions . . . It is the Catholic, who has the feeling that his prayers do make a difference, when offered for the living and the dead, who also has the feeling of living like a free citizen in something almost like a constitutional commonwealth. It is the monist who lives under a single iron law who must have the feeling of living like a slave under a sultan. Indeed I believe that the original use of the word *suffragium*, which we now use in politics for a vote, was that employed in theology about a prayer. The dead in Purgatory were said to have the suffrages of the living. And in this sense, of a sort of right of petition to the supreme ruler, we may truly say that the whole of the Communion of Saints, as well as the whole of the Church Militant, is founded on universal suffrage.

What theological liberals really mean is that 'dogma is too good to be true', 'too liberal to be likely'.[68]

Christianity is a revelation, 'a vision received by faith; but it is a vision of reality'. That is why it is not a mythology. But nor is it a philosophy, 'because, being a vision, it is not a pattern but a picture'. In that sense, 'it is exactly, as the phrase goes, like life'. It does not offer, for example, 'an abstract explanation' of the problem of evil. It optimistically says that existence is good, but it also at the same time pessimistically says that there is something wrong with the world. But, if Christianity is neither a mythology nor a philosophy, it is their 'reconciliation because it is the realisation both of mythology and philosophy'. It is both 'a true story' and 'a philosophy that is like life'. 'But above all, it is a reconciliation because it is something that can only be called the philosophy of stories.' It provides a philosophical justification for the 'normal narrative instinct'. For, just as 'a man in an adventure story has to pass various tests to save his life, so the man in this philosophy has to pass several tests and save his soul'. It is 'the ordeal of the free man', and it is 'this deep and democratic and dramatic' 'story-telling instinct' that 'is derided and dismissed in all the other philosophies', whether fatalistic or detached or sceptical or materialistic or mechanical or relative. And this, Chesterton insists, is why 'the myths and the philosophers were at war until Christ came'. The philosophers were 'the more rational' certainly, but the priests were 'more popular' because they 'told the people stories', the philosophy of which the philosophers did not understand. This only 'came into the world with the story of Christ', which 'met the mythological search for romance by being a story and the philosophical search for truth by being a true story', in which 'the ideal figure' became 'the historical figure'.[69]

[68] *EM* 241–3.   [69] *EM* 243–4, 246–8.

Chesterton now turns to the history of Christianity, which 'has had a series of revolutions and in each of them Christianity has died'. But because Christianity has 'a God who knew the way out of the grave', it 'has died many times' but 'risen again'. At the end of all the European revolutions, 'the same religion has again been found on top'. 'The Faith is always converting the age, not as an old religion but as a new religion.' It has 'returned again and again in this western world of rapid change and institutions perpetually perishing'. So often 'the Faith has to all appearances gone to the dogs', but always 'it was the dog that died'. Both the Oxford Movement, for example, and the French Catholic revival in the nineteenth century were 'a surprise', 'a puzzle'. Always there have been attempts to dilute Christian doctrine, but 'again and again there has followed on that dilution, coming as out of the darkness in a crimson cataract, the strength of the red original wine'. Christianity 'has not only been often killed but it has often died a natural death' through 'old age'. Nevertheless 'it has survived its own weakness and even its own surrender'. Indeed, it seems, 'the Church grows younger as the world grows old.' The Church refuses to go along with 'the tide of apparent progress' because it is alive: 'A dead thing can go with the stream, but only a living thing can go against it.' On the other hand, 'there was many a demagogue or sophist whose wild gestures were in truth as lifeless as the movement of a dead dog's limbs wavering in the eddying water; and many a philosophy uncommonly like a paper boat, of the sort that it is not difficult to knock into a cocked hat'.[70]

In his conclusion, Chesterton makes us see Christianity afresh as though for the first time, not through making it grotesque, but through invoking the image of the popular newspaper, so despised by the intellectuals, and therefore apparently so ill-suited to his theme. The Gospel, he says, 'is nothing less than the loud assertion that this mysterious maker of the world has visited his world in person'. It was 'a piece of good news; or news that seemed too good to be true': 'It declares that really...there did walk into the world this original invisible being; about whom the thinkers make theories and the mythologists hand down myths: the Man Who Made the World.' Muslims were simply monotheists 'with the old average assumption of men—that the invisible ruler remains invisible', 'along with the customs of a certain culture'. It is 'a necessary and noble truth' but not 'a new truth'. Confucians and Buddhists again are simply 'pagans whose prophets

---

[70] *EM* 250, 252, 255–9, 269.

have given them another and rather vaguer version of the invisible power; making it not only invisible but almost impersonal'. Their 'temples and idols and priests and periodical festivals ... simply mean that this sort of heathen is enough of a human being to admit the popular element of pomp and pictures and feasts and fairy-tales', having more sense than Puritans. But their priests have no 'sensational secret like what those running messengers of the Gospel had to say. Nobody else except those messengers has any Gospel; nobody else has any good news; for the simple reason that nobody else has any news.' Ages after the first announcement of the good news, the runners are still running: 'They have not lost the speed and momentum of messengers; they have hardly lost, as it were, the wild eyes of witnesses.' And 'the last proof of the miracle' is that 'something so supernatural should have become so natural'. But he, Chesterton, has not 'minimised the scale of the miracle, as some of our milder theologians think it wise to do'. On the contrary, he has 'deliberately dwelt on that incredible interruption, as a blow that broke the very backbone of history'. He sympathized with Jews and Muslims who considered this to be 'blasphemy: a blasphemy that might shake the world. But it did not shake the world; it steadied the world.' But the mystery remained: 'how anything so startling should have remained defiant and dogmatic and yet become perfectly normal and natural.' What seemed at first 'so outrageous' was really 'so solid and sane'. If the Christian claim seemed mad, 'a tall story', still the 'madhouse' of Christianity was 'a home to which, age after age, men are continually coming back as to a home'. The 'riddle' remained: that 'anything so abrupt and abnormal should still be found a habitable and hospitable thing'. If the whole thing was a 'tall story', then how could it 'have endured for nearly two thousand years'? But it has endured, and, as a result, 'the world within it has been more lucid, more level-headed, more reasonable in its hopes, more healthy in its instincts, more humorous and cheerful in the face of fate and death, then all the world outside. For it was the soul of Christendom that came forth from the incredible Christ; and the soul of it was common sense.' And, as Chesterton had argued earlier in the book, 'Christianity is at one with common sense; but all religious history shows that this common sense perishes except where there is Christianity to preserve it'.[71]

---

[71] *EM* 135, 266–9, 270.

5

In October 1925 Chesterton was persuaded by a number of the students at Glasgow University to put himself forward as a candidate at the triennial election of a new Rector.[72] Candidates were normally prominent politicians put forward by the University's political societies, and the elections were therefore a political test. The outgoing Rector was none other than F. E. Smith, now Lord Birkenhead. E. C. Bentley spoke on behalf of his old friend at one of the election meetings, and was followed by 'Keith' Chesterton, who, expecting to be derided as a woman, had taken the precaution of bringing in her bag an apple, which she began to eat in the face of the expected howls and whistles of derision, the sight of which gradually quelled the noise until a boyish voice called out: 'Carry on, Eve—we've fallen.'[73] Ronald Knox also spoke on Chesterton's behalf and was repaid for his pains by having bags of flour hurled at him. But Chesterton's chief supporter was Hilaire Belloc, who spoke twice on his behalf in the Men's Union and once in the Women's Union, as well as contributing to *G.K.C.*, the daily newssheet produced by Chesterton's student supporters. In his first speech he told the students that all the causes he had ever supported had failed, which was why he was now urging them not to vote for Chesterton. Chesterton was a great poet and his poetry demanded thought to be understood. He was not a party politician like the other two candidates, the Conservative Sir Austen Chamberlain, the Foreign Secretary, and the Socialist Sidney Webb. If, moreover, he were elected, his Rectorial address would compel them to think, a most uncomfortable practice. Normally, they were simply invited to vote for one party or another, but if there were to be candidates like Chesterton, then again they would be forced to think. Next day Belloc gave six reasons for voting *for* Chesterton. If they failed to vote for such a great man, they would look foolish in years to come. If Chesterton were elected, then not only the students but the people of Glasgow would begin to read his books, which would do Chesterton good but also them. It would be a novelty, a change from the usual drab politician. It would add to the prestige of literature, and that would be good for his, Belloc's, sales. Finally, victory for Chesterton would strike fear into the hearts of politicians. Belloc told the women students that it was as silly to vote for a candidate because

[72] For the following account, see Gerard Slevin, 'Vote for Chesterton', *CR* 12/2 (May 1986), 153–63.
[73] MCC 280–1.

of his party label as it would be to vote for him because of his initial. In the
G.K.C. newssheet, Belloc added that, while Chesterton stood for what
universities should stand for, the other two candidates merely stood for
the absurdity of the parliamentary party system. In the event, Chesterton
lost to Chamberlain. According to 'Keith', he lost because his well-known
views on the question of feminism lost him the women's vote.[74] But,
according to J. S. Phillimore, himself a professor at the University, Chesterton lost because of the 'simple snobbery' of the women students, unable
to 'get past the top hat and frock coat and Right Honourable . . . '. Certainly, of the 374 votes by which Chesterton was beaten by Chamberlain,
only 20 were cast by men. As for Webb, he received less than a quarter of
the votes cast for Chesterton.[75]

The next month in November *William Cobbett* was published. As a
critical study, it has some of the brilliance of *Charles Dickens*; and indeed
there were, as Chesterton conceived the two writers, two important features in common—an exuberance of exaggeration and an affinity to the
Middle Ages, albeit unconscious on the novelist's part. Chesterton begins
by deploring the fact that Cobbett was praised for his style but not for his
ideas, for praising 'an extravagant and impossible England in exact and
excellent English'. Until recently there seemed to be no chance of reviving
'the things that Cobbett wished to revive. . . . such as liberty, England, the
family, the honour of the yeoman, and so forth'. Cobbett's 'bad language
that is always good' had always been admired, but not its sentiments, and
certainly it was those 'violent passages' that particularly brought out 'not
only the best capacities of Cobbett but also the best capacities of English'.
For the English language excelled in 'certain angular consonants and
abrupt terminations that [made] it extraordinarily effective for the expression of the fighting spirit and a fierce contempt'. The Victorians thought
Cobbett was 'a crank whose theories had been thrashed out long ago and
found to be quite empty and fallacious. He had been preserved only for his
style; and even that was rude and old-fashioned, especially in the quaint
Saxon archaism of calling a spade a spade.' But Cobbett's ideas were now
coming into their own:

What he saw was the perishing of the whole English power of self-support,
the growth of cities that drain and dry up the countryside, the growth of
dense dependent populations incapable of finding their own food, the toppling

---

[74] MCC 281–2.   [75] Ward, *GKC* 468–9.

triumph of machines over men, the sprawling omnipotence of financiers over patriots, the herding of humanity in nomadic masses whose very homes are homeless . . .

He saw the contemporary scene—'but he saw it when it was not there. And some cannot see it—even when it is there.' The paradox of Cobbett was that 'he loved the past, and he alone really lived in the future'. He may have been wrong in his time, but 'he is right now'. He had 'frantic and fantastic nightmares of things' as they now were. The paradox was that in his time 'he seemed like a survival and a relic of times gone by'—and yet 'he alone was in any living touch with the times that were to come'. All the then reformers and revolutionaries were 'talking hopefully of the future', but actually 'were without exception living in the past', since their 'ideal democracy' was 'what democracy would have been in a simpler age than their own'. They were 'thinking of an ancient agricultural society merely changing from inequality to equality', and had 'no notion' that the commercial interest 'would grow strong enough to swallow all the rest'. It was Cobbett alone who knew that '*there* . . . lay the peril and oppression of the times to come'.[76]

It was not Carlyle but Cobbett who was the real radical. Carlyle had merely wanted to turn 'capitalism into a sort of feudalism', calling the capitalist by the 'romantic name' of 'captain of industry'; whereas Cobbett would have called him by 'a shockingly realistic name'. Carlyle had been set against the Utilitarian Mill 'as a sort of official opposition' and permitted 'to grumble like a choleric old major much respected in the club. Cobbett has been entirely removed, like the *enfant terrible*, kicking and screaming, lest he should say something dreadful in the drawing-room.' Carlyle was merely 'the skeleton' at the capitalist feast; Cobbett was 'the skeleton in the cupboard'. Unlike most modern reformers and philanthropists, Cobbett was not 'merely concerned with what is called the welfare of the workers': 'He was very much concerned for their dignity, their good name, their honour, and even their glory. . . . His whole life was a resistance to the degradation of the poor . . .'. He watched peasants being 'rooted out like weeds instead of being rooted like trees' by landlords, who refused 'to grant the long leases that gave a status to a yeomanry', with 'the old sort of squire', 'the national gentry', being driven out by 'Stockbrokers and Jews and jobbers from the town'. Cobbett, therefore, turned to 'the natural saviours of the green countryside from this yellow fever of finance',

[76] *WC* 5, 7, 12–17, 20–2.

the leaders of the Tory party, with 'his great scheme for saving English agriculture': 'It is long before even a hint leads him to look, at first with doubt and at last with horror, at the significant and sinister smile faintly present on all those unanswering faces.' For the truth was that these Tories were 'in much closer touch with the stockbrokers than with the farmers'. And what Cobbett discovered was that the Whigs and Tories 'only offered two slightly different reasons for not giving' him 'what he wanted'. For the idea that one party stood for 'aristocracy and the land' and the other for 'democracy and machinery' was 'meaningless'. It was because Cobbett, 'by nature a traditionalist and . . . by tradition a Tory', was 'a reluctant rebel' that he was 'a furious rebel'. He had as yet no 'creed', but he had an 'instinct' that 'seemed to him a natural part of that natural order' in which he had believed but which now 'condemned him as a felon', 'creating a Jacobin out of the best anti-Jacobin of the age'. He was the one man who 'could have made an English Revolution'. And yet he was a natural Tory who 'liked old customs', 'believed in the traditions of the past and the instincts of the people', and even, like Dr Johnson, had a 'surly sympathy for the Catholic tradition'. His view of Henry VIII's Archbishop of Canterbury, Thomas Cranmer, was that 'the very thought that such a being had walked the earth on two legs was enough to make the reeling brain doubt the existence of God; but that peace and faith flowed back again into the soul when we remember that he was burned alive'. Yet for Chesterton there was nothing inhuman in such a hatred: 'There is a volume and a violence of humanity in such hatred; a hatred straight from the heart like a knock-out blow straight from the shoulder. It is a blast from a furnace. And it is only in such a furnace seven times heated that men suffer for an idea.' With Johnson, again, he shared 'the most genial and humane of all forms of hatred; their passionate and personal hatred of people they had never seen'. But Cobbett could just as passionately hate places too that he had never seen. His later writings are full of allusion to 'Old Sarum . . . the outstanding, not to say outrageous example of the anomalies of the unreformed representative system; a place that had practically ceased to exist without ceasing to send representatives to make laws for England'. For Cobbett alone was Old Sarum 'a place; and because it happened to be a high and hilly place, it stood up in his imagination with the monstrosity of a mountain. He called it the Accursed Hill.' And, because Cobbett imagined Old Sarum as an actual place, there was 'more mysticism precisely because there was more materialism' in his hatred. And Chesterton dares to say that there was 'almost in such a combination a sort of sacrament of hate'. Chesterton, too, delights in the Dickensian exuberance of Cobbett's anger. When he emerged from prison, it was 'in a towering rage':

a passion that towered above towns and villages like a water-spout, or a cyclone visible from ten counties and crossing England like the stride of the storm. The most terrible of human tongues was loosened and went through the country like a wandering bell, of incessant anger and alarum; till men must have wondered why, when it was in their power, they had not cut it out.[77]

Cobbett's Catholic sympathies were consistent with his being a natural ritualist, for 'ritual that goes beyond words like an embrace or a blow, was that part of Cobbett's character which was always reaching backwards to the medieval England that has never lost the name of Merry England': 'He was a man born out of due time, and forced to live and suffer in a world of mechanical traffic going to Manchester; when he ought to have ridden with Chaucer to Canterbury.' Now Cobbett, who not only 'could see before he could read' but also 'could believe his eyes', could see what he saw in the English countryside, unlike most modern people who 'can read before they can see', and consequently 'see what they expect to see', as what they read 'has a sort of magical power over their eyes', laying 'a spell over their eyes'.

He saw a colossal contrast; the contrast between a village that was hardly a hamlet and a village church that was almost a cathedral. It was the biggest and baldest of all the facts; and yet it was the fact that nobody else saw. The others did not see it because they had been educated not to see it; because they had been educated to see the opposite.

But Cobbett really did have the 'unearthly detachment' of being able to see what was in front of his eyes. And what he saw everywhere rising in the midst of a 'little cluster or huddle of low houses' was 'something of which the spire or tower may be seen for miles'. This spire or tower was 'an experiment in engineering more extraordinary than the Eiffel Tower. For the first Gothic arch was really a thing more original than the first flying-ship.' This 'whole plan' of the 'uplifted labyrinth', from 'the highest symbol of God tortured in stone and in silence, to the last wild gargoyle flung out into the sky as a devil cast forth with a gesture', showed 'the mastery of an ordered mind'. It was, of course, the parish church, very old and 'built in the days of darkness and savage superstition'. The 'picturesque cottages' were 'all of a much later date', belonging as they did 'to the ages of

[77] WC 22–5, 45–6, 52, 69–71, 76, 79, 88, 90, 97–8, 100–1, 138, 193, 228–9.

progress and enlightenment'. But the extraordinary thing was that only Cobbett could see this 'mountain among molehills' for what it was: 'He saw the *size*. He tells us again and again that he has found a village of which the whole present population could be put into the porch of the village church, leaving the whole vast and varied interior as empty and useless as Stonehenge.' But there was 'another very big building at some distance from the village which bulked very much larger in the minds of the villagers. Indeed, it might be said that they lived in the material shadow of the church and the moral shadow of the country house.' Now, the squire's house was not, contrary to popular belief, a Norman castle or a Tudor manor-house. And Cobbett saw it was not. It was in fact more 'like a large public building from a large city exiled in the provinces'. It did not even '*look* like a private house at all'. It was usually Georgian or earlier in style, built in the seventeenth or eighteenth century. In other words, it was the 'creation of a rationalistic age', and belonged 'as much to the Age of Reason as the books of Voltaire'. Such ornamentation as it had was 'of a curious cold exuberance of heathen nymphs and hollow temples'. Because it stood for the age of the sceptics, its gods were 'not only dead' but had 'never been alive'. Its gardens were 'full of shrines without idols or idols without idolaters'. The house as often as not had a very curious name: it was called 'so-and-so Abbey'. If it were called a cathedral or a church, the 'preposterous profanity' would be obvious. It would be as though some rich man 'had gone to live in the parish church; had breakfasted on the altar, or cleaned his teeth in the font'. Nobody but Cobbett could see the profanity. But Cobbett could see, simply by using his eyes, that 'there had once been a larger religious life which was also a popular life. Somehow or other its memorials had been taken over by a new race of men, who had become great lords in the land, and had been able to disdain alike the people and the religion.' Cobbett, in short, was 'simply a man who had discovered a crime; ancient like many crimes; concealed like all crimes. He was as one who had found in a dark wood the bones of his mother, and suddenly knew she had been murdered.' He had discovered that 'England had been secretly slain'.[78]

Now Cobbett was not simply a historian who used his eyes: 'he treated this question of the past as a question of the present.' But, because it is 'possible to speak much too plainly to be understood', the world 'could not understand' him, for he 'was not obscure enough'. People found it much easier 'to listen to the merely romantic praise of the past as uttered by Scott

[78] *WC* 124, 148–9, 153–4, 156–9, 161–4, 166, 168, 176.

than to the realistic praise of the past as uttered by Cobbett'. People could see Melrose Abbey more clearly 'by moonlight than their own parish church by daylight'. The world was certainly indebted to Scott who 'opened those high dykes of mud that cut men off from the rivers of popular romantic tradition, and irrigated the dry garden of the Age of Reason'. But Scott was 'fashionable' because he assured people that 'medievalism was only a romance'; whereas Cobbett 'was far less fashionable when he urged it as a reality'. Scott was 'merely sentimental' about the Stuarts: 'he was singing "Will ye no' come back again?" to people who would have been a horrible nuisance to him if they had come back again.' But Cobbett was not in the least 'sentimental about Mary Tudor; he did solidly believe that with her the good times went; and he did really want them to return'. Cobbett's revisionary history 'really was a revelation': he 'let the cat out of the bag' and 'it was rather a wild cat when it came out of his bag'. He could certainly be called 'a reactionary', but he was nevertheless 'a realist'; he could be accused of 'merely regretting the good old times', 'the romance of... fair and market'—but he was 'really concerned with the business of the market, and not merely with the fun of the fair'. He did not look back at medieval society 'as an old-world pageant, in the manner of Ruskin or William Morris': he saw it 'as an economic question as strictly as Ricardo or John Stuart Mill'. He 'did not start with theories but with things; with the things he saw'. In his pragmatism he was entirely English: 'In so far as he had an imaginative concept of himself... it was the concept of not being imaginative.' In actual fact, he was 'so imaginative that he imagined himself to be a merely plain man'. But, far from being merely 'practical' and 'prosaic' as he imagined himself to be, he was actually a visionary because he could see what no one else could see. Indeed, he was not really what people mean by 'a practical man' at all, since he had 'no power of illusion at all'. There was another paradox: although Cobbett was uneducated in the ordinary sense, he was in fact 'too well educated for his contemporaries', for he lived 'in a world which believed that it was broadening... [which] believed itself to be growing modern and many-sided; and he alone saw that it was growing monomaniac and mean'.[79]

Chesterton concludes his biographical study by pointing out the political paradox of Cobbett—that Tories thought he was a Radical and Radicals thought he was a Tory. But this paradox certainly did not mean that Cobbett was 'a moderate'—nobody could ever call him that.

---

[79] *WC* 177–81, 205–6, 227, 229–30, 262, 267–8.

538 G. K. Chesterton: A Biography

The contrary was true and that explained the paradox. Cobbett was 'an extremist all round. He was more Tory than most Tories, and more Radical than most Radicals.' He could be called a fanatic, but he was certainly not 'narrow': 'With all his fanaticism, he was really looking at things from too many points of view at once to be understood by those who wore the blinkers of a party or even a theory.' Although, superficially, he seemed ignorant and violent, 'his spirit was like one that had lived before and after. He was there before they were all born, in the crowded medieval churches. He was there after they were all dead, in the crowded congresses of the Trades Unions.' It was impossible for his contemporaries to understand him; he thought what he stood for was 'simple', but it was 'bewildering' to them. This was the paradox of Cobbett: 'that in a sense he quarrelled with everybody because he reconciled everything'. It was because 'so many things were unified' in him that so many were 'divided' from him. The tragedy in Chesterton's eyes was that 'the mean and meagre philosophies of his day' could never have sustained Cobbett: 'The cause he felt within him was too mighty and multiform to have been fed with anything less than the Faith.'[80]

[80] *WC* 269–70, 272–4.

13

Distributism and Apologetics

I

AFTER Chesterton's secretary, Freda Spencer, had left, it proved difficult to find a replacement. One day a neighbour called Mrs Walpole offered herself as a joke, but the offer was taken seriously, with the upshot that Frances asked her if she would take on the job as her husband would like to work with her: 'He likes someone in sympathy with his ideas.' Mrs Walpole was apparently a young widow—probably, like so many young women then, a war widow—with one child at home, Felicity, who had already made friends with Frances, and who was at school for part of the day. Mrs Walpole agreed, but stipulated that she needed a couple of weeks to learn how to type. Because Chesterton had no regular hours for dictating, he would often walk round to Mrs Walpole's house at about 9 p.m. to ask if she had eaten, and if so whether she would come and take dictation: 'Absent thee from felicity awhile.' She would accompany him back to Overroads, and he would then dictate till midnight or later. Frances would sometimes call down from upstairs, 'When are you going to let that poor girl go home?' However, it seems the peculiar hours suited Mrs Walpole. She remembered how Chesterton would drink a lot of tea in bed in the morning from an enormous pint-sized cup, while he read the papers, not going downstairs till around 10.30 or 11, after which he had 'brunch' and dictation would begin again. Chesterton enjoyed teasing her by pretending to stop 'at the exciting moment' in a detective story. There was still the same last-minute panic over getting the weekly article for the *Illustrated London News* to London in time—the hasty bicycle ride to the station and the tip to the guard on the train. Apart from that weekly irritation, Mrs Walpole found Chesterton 'very easy to manage', as she put it, 'if you knew how and didn't let him know you were managing him'. She herself as a widow worried what would become of Felicity if anything happened to her. Chesterton agreed to be Felicity's guardian in the event of her mother's death, and both and he and Frances were always ready to listen sympathetically to the mother's various problems. She remembered how Chesterton would make a point of dictating a story that would take her mind off her difficulties if he noticed she was worried, as he did instinctively. When Mrs Walpole took over as secretary, Chesterton was still weak from his near-fatal illness: 'Sometimes he looked so tired, he'd shut his eyes and look as if he could hardly get his ideas out.' An impending visit from Freda Spencer, who was afraid that it would be embarrassing for the Chestertons to have to entertain her in the midst of a wartime scarcity of food, provoked 'Lines to a Friend Apprehensive of a Shortage of Food in Beaconsfield', which began:

> Lady, you will not, when you come,
> Devour us out of house and home,
> Nor do I think you come, indeed,
> Impelled by undiluted greed,
> Or merely seek our poor abodes
> To over-eat at Overroads . . .[1]

Other part-time secretaries would be employed when there was more work than the secretary could cope with. One of these was Winifred Pierpoint, who was a close neighbour. She remembered him as 'the most courteous' of men, 'and that made his long hours of dictation shorter'. She never saw him lose his temper, although she was quite untrained as a secretary and must have tried his patience. Chesterton would nearly always dictate standing or walking up and down the minute study, 'waving some weapon in his hand, often a fierce looking African knife with which he would chip bits out of his desk.' Rarely would he alter anything. Occasionally she would be asked to read a passage out aloud that she had typed—'and he would give a deep-throated chuckle if he liked the sound of his own words.' All the time he would be smoking cigars, 'lighting one from the other, until the atmosphere was as thick as a fog'. Every week there was the last-minute rush to get the 1,500 word article off in time for the *Illustrated London News*: 'The article, when at last ready, was rushed to the station a mile away, and given to the guard of a certain train to take to

[1] Ward, *RC* 146–50.

Paddington, where a messenger from the periodical met it.' A knife was not the only weapon that Chesterton wielded, and one day he shot an arrow from his bow from the window of the study that hit a passing dog in the road; fortunately, the dog was 'more surprised than hurt'. Winifred Pierpoint's job was generally to deal with the vast correspondence, while the regular secretary typed the articles and books. Every fan letter was answered, and a supply of signatures was kept for the autograph hunters who were 'a pest'. At around four o'clock she remembered there was tea at the dining-room table, at which gingerbread, which was a special favourite of Chesterton, was invariably served. Evening parties were held in the studio, which often took the form of poetry readings, at which Chesterton excelled: 'it was a joy to hear him speak some fine lyric or sonnet.' Then there were fancy-dress dances, at one of which she danced with Chesterton and was amazed by how light-footed he was: 'His sense of enjoyment was that of a child spontaneous and unclouded.' Like others, she noted 'his gift for making the other person feel intelligent and interesting'. He did not monopolize the conversation, if only because he was genuinely interested in what other people had to say. People found Frances reserved, but she would open up to you if she liked you. Winifred Pierpoint thought that her adoring devotion to Chesterton was essential to his happiness, but that it was too uncritical when it came to his writing. She seemed to think there was no one else in the world except Chesterton: 'She revolved round him too much.' But, to be fair to Frances, she was by no means unaware of the hostile criticism her husband attracted and thought it her duty as well as that of his friends to be as supportive as possible.[2]

Kathleen Chesshire was Chesterton's secretary for four years in the 1920s. Before starting to take dictation around ten o'clock in the morning, she would ride on her bicycle into Beaconsfield, paying bills and leaving notes. One June summer's day she returned to find Frances in the garden, who exclaimed delightedly what a lovely day it was. But Chesterton, who was 'pacing the garden path, lost in thought', complained, 'Isn't it a trifle hot? Personally I always feel some ogre or other is threatening me in a heat wave.' Frances's cousin Rhoda Bastable, now grown up, often stayed at Top Meadow, and Chesterton would sometimes dictate to her, so slowly that she was able to get in a good deal of reading in-between. She remembered that he hardly ever altered a word nor would he ever dictate the title of an article. When he had finished—and he had an unerring sense of word length—he would write the title in himself.[3]

---

[2] Ward, *RC* 150–3.   [3] Ward, *RC* 154, 181.

Finally, in 1926 Dorothy Collins, the last and the first properly trained secretary arrived on the scene. She recalled a summer weekend in 1926 when she was staying with friends, Mr and Mrs Church and their daughters, who lived at Gregories Cottage next door to Top Meadow, with adjoining gardens. From staying with her friends, Dorothy Collins had got to know the Chestertons. And that weekend she heard that Chesterton was 'not happy with his secretary who struck me as excellent in every way but perhaps she was too good and efficient'. Frances asked her if she would 'consider working for her husband': 'Why not try it. You won't be any the worse off if you come for six months and decide against it in the end.' Although she was perfectly happy in London, Dorothy was persuaded— perhaps it was the attraction of working for a famous writer. However, the agreement was that she would come 'not on a permanent basis' but 'for about six months' to help Chesterton 'over a difficult period. The six months extended into ten years.'[4] On 29 August Frances Chesterton wrote to say that they both thought it would be 'very nice' if she would come at the beginning of October, 'if you felt you would really like the work'. But on 12 October she wrote again to say that there was no need to come till after 10 November. She mentioned a room Dorothy Collins could rent where her predecessor, a Miss Stevens, had been living and recommended. A week later, she wrote again asking her to come on 15 November, and invited her to stay at Top Meadow for the first week while she looked for a room. She also wondered if the prospective secretary knew of a cook, as theirs was leaving at the end of the month: 'I should not like you to come and find no satisfactory meals provided!' Finally, she wrote yet again on 25 October to say that Miss Stevens was leaving them on 13 November and to invite her to stay for the weekend before she went into lodgings. 'Miss Stevens', she added, 'comes to us about 10.30 every morning and I find that answers very well. We are terribly late in the mornings—my husband works so late at night it is impossible to get him down early.' There was 'plenty' of work to do, even though it was 'rather irregular'. She concluded: 'I do hope you will be happy. I feel sure you will find what you want about room, dog and car in due course . . . '[5] Dorothy Collins remembered arriving on a Sunday in November and finding that Frances had completely forgotten about the weekend invitation and was

    [4] Free Europe Radio interview with Dorothy Collins, BL Add. MS 73477, fos. 54, 85, 102; Sullivan, 156.
    [5] Frances Chesterton to Dorothy Collins, 25 Oct. 1936, BL Add. MS 73456, fos. 2–4.

expecting her next day. There was no room ready for her nor was there anywhere to garage her car. However, a maid soon made a room ready, and a shed was found to house the car. By supper time she was already hard at work.[6]

Dorothy Collins was 32 years old and for the previous four years had been secretary and accountant at the Educational Training College in Lincoln.[7] Although not in any way hyper-efficient, Dorothy Collins nevertheless brought some order out of chaos. Until then the vast correspondence simply piled up day after day on the desk 'above or under articles written or half-written, the book of the hour and the amusement of the moment'; one former secretary would 'always put aside the letters particularly worth answering', these being the ones as a result that were 'never answered', as Chesterton groaned in apology to a correspondent whose important letter had been left unanswered and who would understand 'if you saw the other letters, or the secretary, or me'. Frances, who only seemed practical in comparison with her husband, would search hopelessly for some important paper amidst this chaos. The new secretary put a stop to the morning errands and the late evening dictations, introducing definite working hours so that work would not continue more or less over the whole day. She knew when an article was due and made sure that Chesterton dictated it on the necessary day. It was certainly a great relief to Frances, who had had to act as a sort of informal secretary ever since their marriage. Chesterton drew pictures of Dorothy driving away unwelcome visitors and importunate publishers and repelling other demands on his time. Dorothy thought that it was because she herself was 'naturally untidy' that Chesterton, who hated being organized, allowed her to have her way: there was still confusion rather than the order Chesterton hated so much, but now there was a way through the confusion.[8] However, tidying and putting things in order had to be done discreetly. And it was only when her employer was assured that his new secretary was not intending to 'revolutionise everything' that there was perfect peace.[9]

What really cemented the relationship was that both Chestertons became extremely fond of Dorothy, especially Frances, who came to see in her the daughter that she had never had. Chesterton wrote amusing and grateful inscriptions in copies of books that Dorothy had worked on. In his *Collected Poems*, published in 1927, he wrote self-deprecatingly:

[6] Dorothy Collins's notes for talks, BL Add. MS 73477, fo. 85.
[7] Ffinch, 304. [8] Ward, *RC* 157.
[9] Dorothy Collins's notes for talks, BL Add. MS 73477, fo. 85.

Here you watch the Bard's Career,
Month by month and year by year,
Writing, writing, writing verse,
Worse and worse and worse and worse.

In a presentation copy of *The Thing* (1929), he appended the following description in parenthesis under his signature: '(Author of *Thanks Old Thing, A Thing Like You, How to Pack Your Things, Tea Things and Night Things, Something Like a Thing, Not a Thing, Thing a Thong of Thixpence*—and other things.)' *Chaucer* (1932) was dedicated 'To Dorothy Collins without whom this book would have been published upside down'. According to the dedication in *Sidelights* (1932), her 'impressions of America would have more sidelights and better headlights'. Here Chesterton was referring to her driving skills, which were somewhat unusual for a woman of that time, which she brought along with her secretarial skills to the great benefit of the Chestertons, for whom she could act as chauffeur as well as secretary. The inscription in *All I Survey* (1933) was, rather predictably, to: 'Dorothy Collins, who really does the surveying.' The best of the inscriptions was in *The Well and the Shadows* (1935): 'Dorothy Collins, | Who really bound these scattered papers into a | sort of book. | To one who binds, | From one who scatters, G. K. Chesterton.'[10]

More than thirty years after their deaths, Dorothy Collins wrote down some memories of her employer. Chesterton's physical appearance was impressive: he had 'a fine head', was six foot four inches tall, and, as she tactfully put it, 'of large proportions'. By contrast, he had 'delicate hands'. Chesterton saw his size as his good fortune: 'I always enjoy myself more than most. There's such a lot of me having a good time.' But he did not enjoy monopolizing conversations: he 'would take the smallest contribution from the youngest and the most nervous of his listeners and toss it about, add to it, embroider it and return it with a remark that this was just what he needed to illustrate his point'. He could work anywhere, provided Dorothy could set up her typewriter, and in 'the most unlikely places', when he would 'suddenly say, "I think we will do a little work, if you're sure you don't mind."' When at home he never missed a day's work. He would go to bed late and rise late, breakfasting around ten and starting work in his study by 10.30, where he would work until dinner, stopping only briefly for lunch and tea.[11] During the dictation of one book, Dorothy Collins kept a record of the number of words Chesterton dictated: generally

[10] Ward, *RC* 157–8.   [11] Sullivan, 157–8.

13,000 to 14,000 words every week, amounting to about twenty-one hours of dictation. But on top of that there were the articles for *G.K.'s Weekly* and the *Illustrated London News* that had to be typed. And then, too, there were the hours spent on editing *G.K.'s Weekly* and on preparing and delivering lectures.[12]

After dinner, he would sit at a table with his books and his cigars, either reading a detective story or making a few notes for the next day's work in a shorthand of his own invention which no one else could read. He talked about his work quite often before he started, but never when he was actually dictating, which he did straight to the machine, reading each page as it came off the typewriter. As he knew exactly what he wanted to say there was only an occasional alteration. He had a prodigious memory and could quote from readings of his youth without further reference, especially from Dickens. He would map out a book with the headings, and would dictate chapter by chapter, though not always in the final order.[13]

Chesterton may have hated efficiency and organization, but when it came to his own books they were 'so carefully planned that there was very little discarded manuscript after a book was finished'. And as 'he knew exactly what he wanted to say there was only an occasional alteration'.[14] Dorothy Collins recalled how 'as each sheet came off the machine he would read it through and make perhaps one or two alterations; but never many ... '. But, while the books were planned, Chesterton was otherwise 'very casual about his work; and after I had been with him for some time, he did not bother to read his final proofs, although he would generally read the galleys. He hated fuss and pedantic accuracy. I used to see to such details in order to avoid endless letters from pedants ... '.[15]

Although a habitual late riser, on Sundays and weekday Holydays of Obligation Chesterton would force himself to get up early, as there was then only one early morning Mass in Beaconsfield, and on one occasion he was heard to say, 'What but religion would bring us to such a pass,' and on another, 'Only the devil could have done this to me.' But he never missed a Holyday of Obligation either at home or abroad. He always dedicated the day's work to the glory of God, 'by a cross on the top of the page, and even

---

[12] Ward, *GKC* 455.　　[13] Sullivan, 158.
[14] Dorothy Collins's notes for BBC 'Woman's Hour' talk, 13 Feb. 1962, BL Add. MS 73477, fo. 55.
[15] Free Europe Radio interview with Dorothy Collins, BL Add. MS 73477, fo. 54.

on the line below his signature, and by a sign of the cross made as he entered his study'.[16] According to Dorothy Collins, he did not go often to confession, but when he did he could be heard all over the church.[17] When one of the Nicholl girls ventured to say that it would be terrible to discover after death that the Catholic faith was a 'fable', Chesterton retorted: 'You may be perfectly sure that if anything can get *me* out of bed five minutes before I need to get up, there is certainly something in it.' Once when Frances was sick and received Holy Communion at home, He said: 'I am a simple man and I am afraid when God comes to my house.'[18]

Maisie Ward was told by the Saxon Mills and the Rann Kennedys that as an Anglican Chesterton never went to church. Another informant told her that A. S. Commeline, the rector of Beaconsfield, had told him that he was 'glad' that Chesterton had gone over to Rome, 'because he had always been a very bad Anglican, and presumably he would become a good Roman Catholic'. Sir Henry Slesser, the Labour politician and a leading Anglo-Catholic, told her that Chesterton had 'a religion of his own. He never went to Mass, most certainly never to Confession. He had no apparent direct association with the Anglo-Catholic party...'.[19] But this overwhelmingly negative testimony as to Chesterton's religious practice as an Anglican needs to be treated with caution, to say the least. In the first place, we know that Chesterton definitely did have a 'direct association with the Anglo-Catholic party'. Certainly by the middle of 1904, and probably well before, he had identified himself with leading Anglo-Catholics such as Henry Scott Holland, Conrad Noel, Percy Dearmer, and Charles Gore.[20] Indeed, in 1903 in his controversy with Blatchford he had written explicitly from a 'Catholic' perspective.[21] True, Chesterton would not have referred to himself as 'Anglo-Catholic, any more than his Anglo-Catholic friends would have done, but that was because Anglo-Catholics invariably refer to themselves simply as 'Catholics'.[22] Not only is the sacramental principle clearly affirmed in his writings as an Anglican, but he regularly, as we have seen, defended the idea of ritual. And we have already noted his veneration of the Blessed Virgin Mary from his child-hood. Secondly, Frances records in her diary going to church on a number of occasions on their trip to Palestine, on one of which Chesterton had actually donned a cassock and surplice to give an address after evensong. They also both attended the service of Benediction in a Roman Catholic

[16] Sullivan, 157–8, 167; Ward, *RC* 101.   [17] Ward, *GKC* 463.
[18] Ward, *RC* 240.   [19] Ward, *RC* 236.   [20] Oddie, 236.
[21] Oddie, 245, 257.   [22] Oddie, 249.

church in Jerusalem, as well as Mass in a Roman Catholic church in Brindisi on their way home. If Chesterton never or practically never attended church as an Anglican, how does one account for all this church attendance abroad? Similarly, in the diary Frances kept during their first visit to America, there are regular references to attending church services, where it is either explicitly stated or implied that her husband went with her. We know that Frances was a practising Anglo-Catholic who had helped bring Chesterton to Christianity: is it really credible that she would have gone to church all these years of their marriage by herself, while her devoted husband stayed at home?

There is also even evidence, as one would expect if Chesterton was a 'Catholic' Anglican, that he went to sacramental confession as an Anglican. After Maisie Ward's biography had been published, she received a letter from Bernard Iddings Bell, a well-known American Episcopal clergyman and educator, whose writings on the American way of life influenced later American conservative thinkers like Russell Kirk, to whom she had written in response to his review of her book. Both in his review and now in his letter Bell complained that she had neglected Chesterton's '*Anglican friendships*'. Bell had met Chesterton on six occasions, he told Maisie Ward. Chesterton was interested in him because he had converted to 'Catholicism' (that is, Anglican Catholicism) as a result of reading *Orthodoxy*, which 'had had more than anything else to do with my becoming a Catholic'. The first meeting, which was at Beaconsfield, had lasted two hours, and the second meeting, which was at Bell's London club, for even longer. Subsequent meetings had been brief with other people present, nor had he ever corresponded with Chesterton. Bell had heard from two Anglicans, who were close to Father Waggett, that Father Waggett was Chesterton's confessor, one of his informants alleging that he had heard it from Chesterton himself and the other that he had heard it from Father Waggett.[23] The following year Bell wrote again to say that his 'only direct testimony' was that, on the occasion of his telling Chesterton that he had become a Catholic Anglican after reading *Orthodoxy*, he had mentioned that one of the greatest benefits of his conversion was being able to receive sacramental absolution. And Chesterton had responded that 'it made all the difference in the world to him as a man of thought to know that Absolution was for lazy thinking and dishonest writing as well as for

---

[23] Iddings Bernard Bell to Maisie Ward, 19 Nov. 1943, BL Add. MS 73481A, fos. 32–3.

murder and adultery'. From that Bell had '*supposed*' that Chesterton (then an Anglican) went to confession.[24]

Following Bell's first letter, Maisie Ward, who of course was a 'cradle' Roman Catholic and hardly conversant with Anglo-Catholicism, wrote to Dorothy Collins, saying: 'Of course, this may be true, but I have the very strongest impression to the contrary...I suppose he did go to Communion?' Her feeling was that, unlike Frances, 'he was not *in* the Anglo-Catholic movement in the sense that he was later in the Church, but attached to its fingers!'[25] Dorothy Collins wrote back in agreement:

From all I have heard of his church-going activities in Beaconsfield, he was not an Anglo-Catholic, but a very rare worshipper at the Parish Church, which is definitely Protestant. He used to speak on Anglo-Catholic platforms and Father Waggett was a friend, whom I believe they met in Palestine. To call him a professing Anglo-Catholic would be far in advance of the truth. If he ever went to confession I am sure it would have been a very isolated event, because Frances did not go when she was an Anglican, and I am sure he would not have thought of doing so without her example. He only went about twice a year in the Catholic Church. He may have gone to Communion in the Anglican Church, but it would only have been at Easter and Christmas.[26]

But Dorothy Collins's testimony also needs to be treated with caution. She became Chesterton's secretary after Frances had been received into the Catholic Church, and, consequently, never knew either her or Chesterton as an Anglican. His absence from the 'definitely Protestant' parish church in Beaconsfield is quite unremarkable, given that Anglo-Catholics are accustomed to travelling distances to find an Anglo-Catholic church. Her testimony that Frances never went to confession as an Anglican is stronger given her closeness to Frances and the likelihood that she would have discussed confession with her when Dorothy herself converted. The safest conclusion probably is that Chesterton, like many Anglicans, was not punctiliously regular in his Sunday church attendance, as he had to be on becoming a Roman Catholic, and that no doubt it was 'a very isolated event' if he went to confession as an Anglican.

It was at Top Meadow that Maisie Ward always remembered the Chestertons. The original studio, onto which was built the rest of the house, formed one huge room. At one end there was a stage that became

[24] Bernard Iddings Bell to Maisie Ward, 27 Mar. 1944, BL Add. MS 73481A, fos. 35–6.
[25] Maisie Ward to Dorothy Collins, 24 Nov. 1943, BL Add. MS 73472, fo. 7.
[26] Dorothy Collins to Maisie Ward, 8 Feb. 1944, BL Add. MS 73472, fo. 8.

the dining room; at the other end was Chesterton's tiny study. There was a high ceiling with huge beams, and at the study end there was a musicians' gallery. There was a large open fireplace with two rush-bottomed seats, where Frances would sit in the winter. There was no room for Chesterton in this one snug corner of the room, but being well protected by flesh he did not feel the cold. Opposite the fire was a long low window looking into the garden, where a statue of St Francis could be seen. There too could be seen a pool full of water lilies. These and the surrounding flowers provided the plentiful flower displays set against the book shelves that Frances liked to have in the large studio room. As books accumulated, new shelves had to be added, and eventually, because there was no more wall space, a protruding bookcase was made to extend from the wall near the fireplace into the middle of the room, as in a public library. But at least it provided a shelter from the worst draughts in that most draughty of rooms. Compared with it, the rest of the house looked distinctly small. There was a kitchen, servants' quarters, two medium-sized and one very small bedroom. In addition, Frances had a tiny sitting room where she kept her collection of tiny toys and ornaments—she had not, Chesterton remarked, exercised the same taste in choosing her husband.[27]

Cyril Clemens, an American, who compiled a collection of memories and appreciations, *Chesterton as Seen by his Contemporaries* (1939), which he somewhat unfortunately dedicated by 'kind permission' to Mussolini as 'a warm admirer of Chesterton and his work', left his own recollection of a visit to Top Meadow. He was struck by the way Chesterton

would make a joke with true Twainian seriousness upon his face, but unlike the great American such feigned seriousness becomes too much for him, and he bursts out in peals of Gargantuan laughter that often renders him speechless for a few seconds. At other times the idea of something funny will cause him to laugh most heartily before he has had a chance to express it in words.

Having been introduced to his 'charming' wife in a little hallway, he was taken into

the living room, a tremendous chamber fully a hundred feet long, low-ceilinged and surrounded on all sides by shelves bulging and overflowing with books of every description, a massive fire-place built of large stones that must have come from the bed of a nearby brook, and a number of what proved to be exceedingly comfortable chairs grouped round the empty fire-place; for it was midsummer.

[27] Ward, *GKC* 450.

After Clemens had put some questions to Chesterton, they proceeded to 'the small dining room which was a few steps higher than, and was separated by a heavy silk curtain from, the living room'. They sat down at 'a massive oaken table . . . to a delicious tea'. Clemens asked Frances what the national dish of England was, and she 'promptly replied' that it was without doubt roast beef and Yorkshire pudding. But Chesterton 'spoke up' to say that his favourite dish was fried eggs and bacon. Asked what book he would take to his desert island, he replied that, if he was allowed to take only one book and he was not in a particular hurry to escape, then certainly it would be *Pickwick Papers*. Chesterton explained that their 'pert little Scotch terrier' was named Quoodle after the hero of one of his early, but sadly forgotten, novels, in the hope that unwary visitors like Clemens would ask about the origin of the name and he, Chesterton, would have a good excuse to talk about his novel! When Clemens expressed his admiration for *The Resurrection of Rome* (published in 1930 after the Chestertons' visit to Rome), Chesterton 'snapped' that it was not at all a good book—but then explained that he had made the mistake of reading it too soon after it was written, as the longer the interval between his writing and reading one of his books the better it seemed. Hearing that Mussolini had found *The Man who was Thursday* 'exceedingly funny', Chesterton responded that it pleased him to hear that, for sometimes he was afraid that his humorous books were taken seriously and his serious books humorously.[28] Asked when he did most of his writing, Chesterton answered that he wrote whenever he had the opportunity, and that he did not like the typewriter very much, while he was a slow writer with pen or pencil, but that he did a great deal of dictating and could write just as well that way.[29]

One striking feature of life at Top Meadow that struck visitors was the sheer difficulty of day-to-day living for Chesterton. One of the previous secretaries told Maisie Ward how she heard Frances one day telling the cook to heat the water as Chesterton needed to take a bath. 'And "Oh, need I," came in tones of deepest depression from the study. The thought of that vast form climbing into and out of the bathtub does make one realise how a matter of easy everyday practice to the normal person became to him almost a heroic venture.' In spite of Chesterton's daily morning call to Frances to fix his tie, Maisie Ward remembered one

---

[28] Clemens, 124–5, 130–2, 134–5.   [29] Clemens, 135.

breakfast when he appeared wearing two ties and, when she noticed it, claimed 'it proved he paid too much, not too little, attention to dress'.[30]

Outside in the garden Maisie Ward remembered one gardener who was paid more and worked less than any other gardener in the world, 'an exceedingly able gardener when he chose to work'. Chesterton's charity extended beyond the garden. She remembered one man who came weekly to collect his ten shillings, no mean sum then, but why nobody knew; he would be posted his money if he failed to show up; once he was found fighting another man on the doorstep for his temerity in seeking also to beg from Chesterton![31] But there were also more worthy causes, such as the various children that he and Frances were fond of and for whose education he was paying.[32] So generous were they both with their money that, when Dorothy Collins came in 1926, she found that they had saved virtually nothing in spite of the long hours Chesterton put in every day.[33]

'Keith' Chesterton liked the approach to the house: 'Approached from the front, through a pleasant tangle of flowers and crazy pavement, the studio with its wide windows and gracious line was most attractive.' But she was less favourably impressed by the 'confusing' interior, the result of local talent—and, she added predictably, Frances's 'own ideas'. Being the former stage, the dining room was several feet above the floor, that is, the old auditorium.

It was reached from the small front hall by a narrow passage and you entered, so to speak, by the doorless wings direct on to the dining-table, almost flush with the proscenium curtains. The place was heated by an anthracite stove backstage, which could not be kept at a pressure sufficient to warm the whole, as those with their backs almost against it would have been slowly roasted.

Because one was, in effect, eating on a stage, one felt one was eating in the face of 'a hidden audience', and 'Keith' 'always had the feeling that at any moment the curtain would go up "discovering the family at dinner"'. But if, on the other hand, you had your back to this 'hidden audience', 'you had to be particularly wary for fear of moving your chair too near the edge of the stage in case you tumbled headlong into the "auditorium".' Whenever Chesterton said anything particularly brilliant, 'Keith' was disappointed there was no applause. And whenever a maid appeared from the wings, one expected her to be given 'a telling line' on her entrance. At the far end of the former studio was Chesterton's 'cubby-hole', while

---

[30] Ward, *GKC* 452–3.   [31] Ward, *GKC* 450–1.   [32] Sullivan, 158.
[33] Ward, *GKC* 453.

Frances's 'warm and cosy' nook in the vast, draughty room was the open brick fireplace 'with space for a low small chair on either side, where Frances would sit for hours, watching the logs crumble into fiery particles', logs that burned most of the year round. The huge space was partly filled near the stage by some small tables that at Christmas held Chesterton's toy theatre and a nativity crib. Beyond were larger tables holding books, plants, and even a bust of Chesterton himself. 'Oases' of comfortable chairs and sofas 'culminated in a desert of carpet'. When the room was full of people, with 'the stage curtains drawn to show a table spread with good things', it had a 'festive' aspect; but it was hardly homely, 'Keith' thought. There were no rooms above the old studio. The kitchen and garage were on the ground floor of the new wing that had been added, from which led a reasonably wide staircase to a narrow passage off which, in 'Keith's' words, were 'little monkish cells'. There was an 'unusually tiny' lavatory, that could hardly accommodate the master of the house, who 'had to contort himself unbelievably to get round the narrow door which opened inwards'. 'Keith' could barely restrain herself from laughing at her brother-in-law's 'stumbling efforts and protest noises', which were 'audible all over the house'; she wished that 'he could share the joke'. As for Frances, she 'never turned a hair during these Homeric combats'. Her sister-in-law did not 'think it ever struck her that "Top Meadow" was utterly lop-sided in design—one half being framed for a giant and the other for a gnome'. It was years before a larger bathroom and bedroom were added. 'Keith' was sure that Chesterton missed the 'more comfortable if more commonplace' Overroads, from which 'he could always escape to the big studio', so suitable for large entertainments and so unsuitable as a 'home'.[34]

In her memoirs 'Keith' did have one friendly memory of Frances. In 1925, as a journalist on the *Sunday Express*, 'Keith' got permission from her editor to go out on to the streets of London for a fortnight to experience the life of a homeless woman. The articles she wrote about her experiences for the paper came out as a book in 1926 called *In Darkest London*. Frances, she says, surprised her by her 'sympathy and indeed enthusiasm' for the cause of homeless women, reviewing *In Darkest London* 'very beautifully' in *G.K.'s Weekly*, as well as accompanying her husband to a meeting, chaired by John Galsworthy, at Wyndham's Theatre, where Chesterton spoke in aid of the charity Cecil Houses, named after his brother, the first of which was opened in 1927 for homeless women.

[34] MCC 254–6.

I have never heard him more effective than on that afternoon. He declared that he would love to disguise himself as an apple woman, that he might enjoy the ease and pleasantness, and above all the individual freedom, inseparable from Cecil Houses. G.K. as an apple woman was a gorgeous idea, and a sketch of him in that ample disguise promptly appeared all over the Press.[35]

2

On 27 April 1926 Chesterton, accompanied by Frances and Rhoda Bastable, arrived in Barcelona after visiting Madrid and Toledo. He was there at the invitation of the Catalan branch of the P.E.N.—or Poets, Essayists, and Novelists—Club, which had been founded in London in 1921 by Mrs C. A. Dawson Scott and Galsworthy to promote cooperation and friendship among writers. The Catalan poet and writer Josep M. Junoy had arranged the visit. On 5 May Chesterton lectured at Barcelona University on 'England Seen from the Outside'. Next day the P.E.N. Club gave a dinner in his honour. One of the writers present, who was sitting opposite Chesterton, wrote down his impressions of the English writer. Compared to the Spanish guests he appeared 'to take on monstrous proportions', although they were the proportions of a 'legendary and jocular giant'. He seemed to be 'drowsy',

waking up from moment to moment, first to take a sip of his drink, then to utter a few words. If those words happen to be in French he has to struggle hard with them because Chesterton, like a good Englishman, travels the world with the magnificent impertinence of his own language. He has a shock of whitish hair and the sort of bushy moustache useful for catching bits of food . . .

During his stay in Barcelona he was seen devouring English newspapers, which were full of the miners' strike, which he supported. One day Junoy took him to Sitges, a seaside town, where Chesterton and his party stayed a week. There he was welcomed by the 'Friends of Fine Arts', who presented him with a bouquet of carnations, the floral symbol of Sitges. Chesterton thanked them for their 'most charming and generous gesture of welcome. You are kind enough to refer to my deplorable habit of writing; I only wish anything I had ever written was half as beautiful as that bouquet of flowers, or likely to give anybody half as much joy and encouragement as it gave to us.' At the dinner in his honour Chesterton was offered a basket of fruits as

[35] MCC 275.

dessert; he loved, he said, 'the small things; those red cherries, the children, the small nations . . . '. Back in Barcelona, he was seen on 2 June, the eve of the feast of Corpus Christi, walking with a bundle of newspapers under his arm and caught in the midst of a parade of folk figures made out of *papier maché*, trailed by a flock of children. 'You have put Voltaire's laughter at the service of God' was Junoy's tribute to him before he returned to England.[36]

On 28 June the Chestertons celebrated their silver wedding anniversary. Eight days earlier Frances had written to Father O'Connor to say that she had decided to become a Roman Catholic in spite of all the 'difficulties'. She did *not* want to receive instruction in Beaconsfield: 'I don't want to be the talk of Beaconsfield and for people to say I've only followed Gilbert. It isn't true and I've had a hard fight not to let my love for him lead me to the truth. I knew you would not accept me for such motives.' She felt 'very tired and very worried'. And her health made 'strenuous attention a bit of a strain'. What should she do? It seems that O'Connor, in spite of her misgivings, advised her to approach the local parish priest, Father Walker. O'Connor must have thought that for a woman in her frail health to have to travel weekly for months to London for instruction, or possibly to Ware, where Knox was still on the staff of St Edmund's (although he would become Catholic chaplain at Oxford in October, when he would be much nearer to Frances), let alone to Yorkshire to be instructed by him, Father O'Connor, was quite unrealistic. Besides, the shy, reserved Frances knew Father Walker, who had prepared her husband for his first Communion. Frances wrote again on 12 July to thank the priest for the gift of spoons for their wedding anniversary. She could not at the moment see her way out of various 'responsibilities' in which she was 'enmeshed and to find time for instruction'. She felt she had 'a lot to learn' and thought that 'after all' she had 'better go quietly to Father Walker and talk to him'. Her husband was 'so involved' with *G.K.'s Weekly*, which she wished he would give up, that they had not been able 'to talk over things sensibly'. Her nephew Peter was 'very ill', which meant that she had 'to spend a lot of time' with her sister.[37] On 19 July she wrote again to say that she was 'feeling' her 'way into the Catholic fold', but that it was 'a difficult load' for her, and she asked for the priest's prayers. She also complained about the demands on her husband: 'I am always trying to get out of things for him, because I feel he is dissipating his energies and his own work gets more and more thrown

[36] Silvia Coll-Vincent, 'Chesterton's First Visit to Catalonia and its Context,' *CR* 31/1–2 Spring/Summer 2005), 104–8.
[37] Ward, *GKC* 457–8.

into the background.'[38] Four days later Father Walker received a letter from Frances asking to be received into the Catholic Church.[39]

On 20 July Bishop Cary Elwes, who had confirmed Chesterton, laid the foundation stone of a church to be built on a plot of land behind the Railway Hotel that had been bought a year previously. The Chestertons had been present at the ceremony,[40] and a few days later an article was published in the *Catholic Times*, in which Chesterton referred to the 'shed at the back of the Railway Hotel' where Mass was celebrated thanks to 'the zeal and generosity of Mr and Mrs Borlase, the Catholics who keep the inn'. (Chesterton had attended the funeral of Mr Borlase, who was also a convert, the previous August.[41]) He commented on the typical 'paradox' that, whereas old Beaconsfield was full of 'memories of Catholicism', in the names of the inns, for example, it was in new Beaconsfield where the Railway Hotel was situated that the old Faith had returned to Beaconsfield.[42]

Frances wrote to tell O'Connor that she had written to Father Walker, but had not yet seen him. In the meantime, she was kept 'on edge' by anxiety about her nephew, the paper, and 'money worries' (which, of course, was a reference to the large sums of money that Chesterton was continuing to inject into *G.K.'s Weekly*). Her husband, she told O'Connor, was spending four days a week on the paper, which meant that she had 'to attend to everything else'—'Trying to settle an income-tax dispute has nearly brought me to tears.'[43] In a subsequent undated letter she reported that she was now receiving instruction and was soon to be received—'You will understand how dreadfully I hate the idea of publicity in such a matter...'. She assured O'Connor that Chesterton wanted to write a book on Savonarola as the priest had suggested, 'but it is getting increasingly difficult for him to find a moment for his real work. I feel in despair sometimes. He is wanted at every hour, by everybody, for every purpose and the worry of the paper and the financial loss is no easy burden to carry...'.[44] On 25 October she writes again, hoping that O'Connor might be present at her reception. She complains again that Chesterton is

[38] Frances Chesterton to John O'Connor, 19 July [1926], BL Add. MS 73196, fo. 128.

[39] St Teresa's Church, Beaconsfield, parish archives, parish diary, p. 67.

[40] *Bucks Free Press*, 23 July 1926.   [41] *Bucks Free Press*, 7 Aug. 1925.

[42] *Catholic Times*, 30 July 1926.   [43] Ward, *GKC* 458.

[44] Frances Chesterton to John O'Connor, n.d., BL Add. MS 73196, fo. 130.

spending four days a week on *G. K.'s Weekly* without pay: 'We can't go on much longer.'[45]

In the end, Frances was conditionally baptized and received into the Catholic Church on All Saints' day, 1 November 1926, at St Augustine's, High Wycombe, by Father Walker; she was then confirmed on the third Sunday of the month at Westminster Cathedral, having made her first Holy Communion earlier in the morning at St Augustine's.[46] According to her husband, 'when asked who converted her to Catholicism,' she always answered, 'the devil'.[47] Maisie Ward said that she had 'never known a happier Catholic' than Frances, 'once the shivering on the bank was over and the plunge had been taken. One would say she had been in the Church all her life.'[48] To Father O'Connor she wrote two days before Christmas: 'I am very happy—though the wrench was rather terrible—it was hard to part with so many memories and traditions.'[49]

3

According to W. R. Titterton, it was his idea to found the Distributist League, as a way of saving *G. K.'s Weekly*.[50] But according to Captain H. S. D. Went, who was the first secretary of the League, it was he who suggested forming the League, in order to enable Distributists to keep in touch with each other, if, as seemed probable, *G. K.'s Weekly* failed.[51] On 17 September 1926 the Distributist League was founded at an inaugural meeting in Essex Hall, Essex Street, off the Strand. Its aim was to 'restore possession', and Chesterton quoted Francis Bacon's saying, 'Property is like muck, it is good only if it be spread.'[52] It believed, said Chesterton, that

a man felt happier, more dignified, and more like the image of God, when the hat he is wearing is his own hat ... There might be people who preferred to have their

[45] Frances Chesterton to John O'Connor, 25 Oct. [1926], BL Add. MS 73196, fo. 131.

[46] St Teresa's Church, Beaconsfield, parish archives, parish diary, pp. 68–9, parish history, p. 95.

[47] *A*. 104.   [48] Ward, *GKC* 458.

[49] Frances Chesterton to John O'Connor, 23 Dec. [1926], BL Add. MS 73196, fo. 133.

[50] Titterton, 160–1.

[51] H. S. D. Went to Maisie Ward, n.d., BL Add. MS 73481A, fo. 120.

[52] Ward, *GKC* 433.

hats leased out to them every week, or wear their neighbours' hats in rotation to express the idea of comradeship, or possibly to crowd under one very large hat to represent an even larger cosmic conception; but most of them felt that something was added to the dignity of men when they put on their own hats.

He made it clear that the League would not be putting up parliamentary candidates but would support candidates sympathetic to the aims of the League. Thanks to generous financial assistance *G.K.'s Weekly* could continue 'a little longer', but he would close it down 'if it involved economic injustice to anybody'.[53] At the first committee meeting the following week Chesterton was elected president. Other possible names for the League were discussed. Chesterton thought that 'The Cow and Acres, however suitable as the name of a public house at which we could assemble', was 'too limited as an economic statement'. Another suggestion, which came from Titterton[54] and which received strong support, was 'The League of the Little People'—but, with Chesterton as president, that seemed 'at first too suggestive of the fairies'. Chesterton himself favoured 'The Lost Property League'.[55]

Branches of the League were soon formed in Bath, Birmingham, Cambridge, Chatham, Chorley, Croydon, Glasgow, Liverpool, Manchester, Oxford, and Worthing.[56] To enable *G.K.'s Weekly* to be the voice of the League to as wide a public as possible, it was announced in the editorial of the issue of 6 November, entitled 'Twopenny Trash' (the name given to Cobbett's *Weekly Register* by his enemies), that the price of the paper would be reduced to twopence. Readers who had previously paid sixpence for the paper were asked to buy three copies and give two away free to potential subscribers: 'The League would have to make itself responsible for the success of this experiment and save the paper which gave it birth, or die of inanition, for it is certainly not yet strong enough to leave its mother.' According to Titterton, it was again his idea to reduce both the price and the size of the paper as a last desperate measure, when it was still losing money even after the founding of the League.[57]

A delighted Chesterton reported in the next issue of 13 November that sales had soared. There had also been another meeting of the League, attended by over a hundred members, many of whom spoke, as would almost all those present had time permitted: 'We were astonished, we were overwhelmed. Had we anything to do with the making of this ardent, eager, indefatigable creature?' The answer was that, 'though we had

---

[53] Titterton, 165–6.   [54] Titterton, 163.   [55] Ward, *GKC* 433.
[56] Ward, *GKC* 433–4.   [57] Titterton, 162.

something to do with the shaping of the body, we had nothing to do with the birth of the soul. That was a miracle, a miracle we had hoped for, and which yet, when it happened, overwhelmed us.' Meanwhile, the circulation of *G.K.'s Weekly* nearly doubled to over 8,000 as the local branches of the League brought the existence of the paper to the notice of newsagents. At a meeting of the central London branch it was agreed that members should try to patronize only small shops that treated their employees fairly. It was hoped soon to encourage small farmers and craftsmen to deal with the small retailers. In this way a community of self-supporting people practising Distributism might be formed. In the coming months the recurring question that would be asked in the 'Cockpit' column in *G.K.'s Weekly* was—when was the League going to do something practical? Chesterton's answer was always that the League's purpose was not action but the propagating of Distributist ideas and principles. But he was opposed to any rigidity as to the means of attaining their ideals. It would be understandable if Chesterton came to regret his idea of having a column open to controversy in his paper, for it certainly encouraged the members of the League to argue and criticize. The main argument would be about whether modern machinery should be allowed in a Distributist society, but this raised the more fundamental question as to what actually constituted Distributism. Chesterton himself thought that machinery should be limited but not abolished: the English people had lost their land and property before the arrival of industrial machinery. Anyway, he argued, those who advocated abolition were not stating a first principle but arguing from first principles, and it was these principles that needed above all to be defined: true, definition meant dogma, but there was nothing wrong in that, as shared dogma united people.[58] He could at least claim impartiality as the various Distributist factions argued with each other, since he had no time to follow closely all the details of the disputes, irritating as his ignorance might be to those better informed. For the truth was that he was too busy helping to finance *G.K.'s Weekly*, albeit he was only 'the thin and shadowy approximation to a Capitalist', by earning money 'in the open market; and more especially in that busy and happy market where corpses are sold in batches; I mean the mart of Murder and Mystery, the booth of the Detective Story'.[59] Unfortunately, not even Chesterton's good-natured humour could take the sting out of the disputes among his Distributist followers. And there was a danger, he feared, that the movement might become identified with cranks and extremists,

[58] Ward, *GKC* 435–8; Titterton, 172.   [59] *G.K.'s Weekly*, 12 Oct. 1929.

alienating ordinary people who were beginning to see that nothing could be more normal than the wide distribution of property.[60]

November saw the publication in the United States (a month later in Britain) of *The Outline of Sanity*, which consisted of much-revised articles from *G.K.'s Weekly* that had appeared in the weekly column 'Straws in the Wind', the equivalent of his 'At the Sign of the World's End' column in the *New Witness*, together with a good deal of extra material. His purpose, he states at the beginning, is to 'sketch … certain aspects of the institution of Private Property, now so completely forgotten amid the journalistic jubilations over Private Enterprise', a neglect and a jubilation that are the 'measure of the moral tone of the times. A pickpocket is obviously a champion of private enterprise. But it would perhaps be an exaggeration to say that a pickpocket is a champion of private property.' Communism was successful only in reforming 'the pickpocket by forbidding pockets'. Its opposite was not private enterprise, which nobody dreamed of practising, but capitalism, with its 'big commercial combinations, often more imperial, more impersonal, more international than many a communist commonwealth—things that are at least collective if not collectivist'. And monopoly, which was 'neither private nor enterprising', was not private enterprise. As for Socialists, they would put capital into 'the hands of even fewer people'—namely, politicians. And it was ridiculous for Socialists to complain about the Communists' suppression of 'political opposition', since a Socialist government, too, would provide 'everything; and it is absurd to ask a Government to *provide* an opposition': 'Opposition and rebellion depend on property and liberty. They can only be tolerated where other rights have been allowed to strike root, besides the central right of the ruler.' Capitalism was a consequence not of private property but rather of its absence. England had become a Capitalist country 'because it had long been an oligarchical country' that lacked 'a widely scattered ownership'. But capitalism was self-contradictory, because it dealt with the masses 'in two opposite ways at once. When most men are wage-earners, it is more and more difficult for most men to be customers. For the capitalist is always trying to cut down what his servant demands, and in doing so is cutting down what his customer can spend.' But the wage-earner who is 'a tenant and servant of the [Socialist] State' enjoys exactly the same kind of 'centralized, impersonal, and monotonous' 'unification and regimentation'.[61]

---

[60] Ward, *GKC* 440.   [61] *OS* 41–2, 44–5, 47, 51, 59, 78.

Distributists, on the contrary, did not hold that 'all land should be held in the same way; or that all property should be owned on the same conditions'. Instead, they believed that the central government needed 'lesser powers to balance and check it, and that these must be of many kinds: some individual, some communal, some official, and so on'. They were not proposing that everyone should become peasants, only that the state should have 'the general character of a peasant state; that the land was largely held in that fashion and the law generally directed in that spirit; that any other institutions stood up as recognizable exceptions, as landmarks on that high tableland of equality'. Such a society would 'not necessarily exclude every modern machine any more than we should exclude every medieval monastery'. The existence of a peasant class or class of small proprietors would mean not only 'the end of what is called the class war; in so far as its theory divides all men into employers and employed'—but also an understanding as to 'why the machine must not exist save as the servant of the man'. Moreover, it would mean that 'a traditional class' or 'a conservative class' would exist for the first time for many centuries in England. Such a class, unlike the commercial class that by its very nature seeks novelty and the aristocracy that 'goes by fashion rather than by tradition', understood that one '*can* destroy machinery' if 'machinery is hostile to happiness'. After all, 'many glorious possibilities' are given up, 'in our stern and strenuous and self-sacrificing preference for having a tolerable time. Happiness, in a sense, is a hard taskmaster. It tells us not to get entangled with many things that are much more superficially attractive than machinery.' Progress in invention was not inevitable: the rack and the thumbscrew, for instance, had been left in a relatively 'rudimentary state', and many 'a talented torturer' had been 'left in obscurity by the moral prejudices of modern society': 'Our own strong sentimental bias against torture represses his noble rage and freezes the genial current of his soul. But we reconcile ourselves to this; though it be undoubtedly the loss of a whole science . . . '. But some modern machinery was liberating: the invention of the motor car signalled the return of the 'free and solitary traveller' after the 'combination and concentration' of the 'collective' railway.[62]

Ultimately, Chesterton believed that Distributism was based on a Christian view of 'the nature of man', of 'Man standing on two legs and requiring two boots . . . his own boots'. Instead of the modern 'doubt about Man', Christianity 'believed that ordinary men were clothed with

[62] *OS* 80–1, 103, 120–1, 145–7, 167.

powers and privileges', including 'the right of property'. But 'the new philosophy utterly distrusts a man', and if there is 'a very rare sort of man' who has such rights, then 'he has the right to rule others even more than himself'. A 'profound scepticism about the common man' was 'the common point in the most contradictory elements of modern thought'. That was why the common man was not to be given 'a house, or a wife, or a child, or a dog or a cow, or a piece of land, because these things really do give him power'.[63]

4

November 1926 also saw the first publication in the United States of *The Catholic Church and Conversion* (it was published a couple of months later in England), part of a series edited by Belloc, all the volumes being entitled *The Catholic Church and*... The previous year Chesterton had contributed a brief chapter to *Twelve Modern Apostles and their Creeds*, entitled 'Why I am a Catholic', which began with the assertion that there were ten thousand reasons, 'all amounting to one reason: that Catholicism is true'. The Catholic Church simply was 'catholic'—'not only larger than me, but larger than anything in the world...indeed larger than the world'. It was the only 'corporate mind in the world' that was 'on the watch to prevent minds from going wrong'. The Church, 'looking out in all directions at once', was 'not merely armed against the heresies of the past or even of the present, but equally against those of the future, that may be the exact opposite of those of the present'. She carried 'a sort of map of the mind which looks like the map of a maze, but which is in fact a guide to the maze'. Uniquely, she constituted 'one continuous intelligent institution that has been thinking about thinking for two thousand years'. The resulting map marked clearly 'all the blind alleys and bad roads'.[64]

The Catholic Church and Conversion begins with the paradox that, while Catholicism used to be regarded as an old religion, it now seemed to be a positively new religion, as the children of Protestant parents were 'breaking away' from the 'more or less Christian compromise (regarded as normal in the nineteenth century)'—one becoming a Communist, another a Catholic. Conversion to Catholicism was seen as 'a form of revolt'. No parent feared their children would become Calvinists or Lutherans: these were 'old religions', if not 'dead religions'; not 'new religions' like Roman

---

[63] *OS* 207–9.   [64] *WIC* 127, 129–30, 132.

Catholicism, which was 'the only old religion that is...new'. What it was now to the Protestant parent it had been to the pagan parent: 'a nuisance and a new and dangerous thing'. The 'old creed', on the other hand, of a typical Protestant body was held merely on 'tradition and nothing else' and had 'ceased to function as a fresh and stimulating idea'. In the past, it was the Catholic Church that had 'defended tradition in a time which stupidly denied and despised tradition'. Now it was emerging as 'the only champion of reason'.[65]

Coming from a background that was 'if not agnostic at least pantheistic or unitarian', Chesterton himself had never imbibed the usual Protestant prejudices against Popery. He had 'had all the difficulties that a heathen would have had in becoming a Catholic in the fourth century', but 'very few of the difficulties that a Protestant had, from the seventeenth to the nineteenth'. Even if he had not inherited 'a fully civilised faith', neither had he inherited 'a barbarian feud': 'The people I was born amongst wished to be just to Catholics if they did not always understand them...'. Brought up among liberal Unitarians, he had never imbibed the usual Protestant patriotism of British imperialists who 'assumed that they were the salt of the earth, and especially that they were the salt of the sea', and who thought that 'the Church first rose in the middle of the British Empire, and not of the Roman Empire'. Before his conversion, he had called himself an Anglican in the sense of being an Anglo-Catholic. But, again, he was not one of those patriotic High Anglicans 'who are concerned first and last to save the Church of England...by calling it Catholic, or making it Catholic, or believing that it is Catholic'. For whereas '*that*' was what they wanted to save, Chesterton was intent on 'finding the Catholic Church'.[66]

As for specific Protestant objections to Rome, in the world in which he grew up, 'Protestants, who had just proved that Rome did not believe the Bible, were excitedly discovering that they did not believe the Bible themselves'. His own family and friends 'were more concerned with the opening of the book of Darwin than the book of Daniel; and most of them regarded the Hebrew Scriptures as if they were Hittite sculptures'. He had never been able to understand 'the everlasting cry' of the Protestants 'that Catholic traditions are condemned by the Bible', when it had 'always belonged' to the Catholics 'and been a part of their hocus-pocus, if it was hocus-pocus'. As for the alleged wickedness of the Catholic priest, it seemed odd to Chesterton that such an evil man should 'encumber himself

---

[65] *CCC* 64–6, 68.   [66] *CCC* 72, 78–9, 81.

with special and elaborate promises to be good': 'There are many more lucrative walks of life in which a person with such shining talents for vice and villainy might have made a brighter use of his gifts.' Nor could he understand why Protestants

were so afraid of Papists; why a priest in somebody's house was a peril or an Irish servant the beginning of a pestilence. I asked them why they could not simply disagree with Papists and say so... They seemed at once pleased and shocked with my daring, as if I had undertaken to convert a burglar or tame a mad dog. Perhaps their alarm was really wiser than my bravado. Anyhow I had not then the most shadowy notion that the burglar would convert me.

A 'more plausible' objection was that, if Popish priests were 'not sensual', they were 'always sly'. The Jesuits in particular were notorious for their verbal equivocations—but the 'only difference' between them and ordinary Protestants was that they 'had been worried enough about the matter to try to make rules and limitations saving as much verbal veracity as possible; whereas the happy Protestants were not worried about it at all, but told lies from morning to night as merrily and innocently as the birds sing in the trees'. There was no avoiding casuistry, but the 'lawful casuistry' of the Jesuits was preferable to the 'utterly lawless casuistry' of the world.[67]

The 'liberal modern attack upon the Church' was quite different from 'the old doctrinal attack' of the Reformation. The modern 'no Popery' cry of Protestants included the most contradictory complaints—but 'who are we that we should set narrow dogmatic limits to the various ways in which various temperaments may desire to blame' the Church of Rome?

Why should we allow a cold difficulty of the logician, technically called a contradiction in terms, to stand between us and the warm and broadening human brotherhood of all who are full of sincere and unaffected dislike of their neighbours? Religion is of the heart, not of the head; and as long as all our hearts are full of a hatred for everything that our fathers loved, we can go on flatly contradicting each other for ever about what there is to be hated.

Similarly, the real difficulties faced by converts to Catholicism were 'almost the direct contrary of those which were alleged by the more ancient Protestants'. The modern convert, for example, had 'forgotten all about the old nonsense of the cunning lies of the confessional, in his lively and legitimate alarm of the truthfulness of the confessional'. In fact, the convert will discover 'what gigantic generosity, and even geniality, can be locked

[67] *CCC* 72–5.

up in a box . . . It is a satisfaction, and almost a joke, that it is only in a dark corner and a cramped space that any man can discover that mountain of magnanimity.' Far from pestering priests proselytizing, the prospective convert will find the 'apparent inaction of the priest' to be 'something like the statuesque stillness of the angler; and such an attitude is not unnatural in the functions of a fisher of men'. It is not 'the Protestant picture of Catholicism' that ever deters the convert, but 'the Catholic picture of Catholicism' that he may receive from 'the militant layman', 'the ecclesiastical layman' who 'is much more ecclesiastical than is good for his health, and certainly much more ecclesiastical than the ecclesiastics'.[68]

If, Chesterton claimed, the Catholic Church is not the true Church of Christ, then it 'probably is Antichrist'. Certainly, it 'really is like Antichrist in the sense that it is as unique as Christ'. The 'principle of life' in the various Protestant churches 'consists of what remained in them of Catholic Christendom; and to Catholic Christendom they have always returned to be recharged with vitality', whether it was through the Romantic movement's rediscovery of medievalism, or through 'the instinctive reaction of old-fashioned people' like Johnson or Scott or Cobbett 'wishing to save old elements that had originally been Catholic', or through the Pre-Raphaelites or 'the opening of continental art and culture by Matthew Arnold and Morris and Ruskin'. Protestants were simply 'Catholics gone wrong', who had 'exaggerated' a Catholic dogma 'into an error; and then generally reacted against and rejected as an error, bringing the individual in question a few steps back again on the homeward road'. The 'mark' of the heretic was 'wildly' to 'question' any Catholic dogma apart from 'his own favourite Catholic dogma', which 'he never dreams of questioning'. Christian Scientists, for example, were 'simply people with one idea, which they have never learnt to balance and combine with all the other ideas'— whereas 'the Catholic Church is used to living with ideas and walks among all those very dangerous beasts with the poise and the lifted head of a lion-tamer'. And so the convert will 'find nearly everything some-where' in the Church. Far from the convert finding 'peace' in the Church 'in the sense of mental inaction', to 'become a Catholic is not to leave off thinking, but to learn how to think', having 'for the first time a starting-point for straight and strenuous thinking'. So-called free thought was not really 'free thought' but 'freedom from thought . . . free thoughtlessness'. Outsiders 'see, or think they see, the convert entering with bowed head a sort of small temple which they are convinced is fitted up inside like a

---

[68] *CCC* 85–88.

prison, if not a torture-chamber'. In fact, the convert feels they have gone out 'into the broad daylight', living as they now are 'in a world with two orders, the supernatural and the natural', 'a larger world' from which they feel no 'temptation to crawl back into a smaller one'. If Chesterton were to leave the Church, it would not be for one of the 'sects which only express one idea at a time, because that idea happens to be fashionable for the moment', but for paganism, which is 'better than pantheism, for paganism is free to imagine divinities, while pantheism is forced to pretend, in a priggish way, that all things are equally divine'. Before Christianity, paganism was 'the largest thing in the world', but Christianity was 'larger; and everything else has been comparatively small'. As for Catholicism, it was 'too large' for him, and he had 'not yet explored its beautiful or terrible truths'.[69]

Having argued that Catholicism has 'all the freshness of a new religion', Chesterton now claims that its perennial newness is due to its 'antiquity': 'it has all the richness of an old religion; it has especially all the reserves of an old religion . . . for purposes of renovation and youth.' Thanks to its age, the Catholic Church 'has an accumulated armoury and treasury to choose from; it can pick and choose among the centuries and brings one age to the rescue of another'. Unlike the new religions, which 'are only suited to . . . new conditions', 'the Catholic Church is the only thing which saves a man from the degrading slavery of being a child of his age'. The 'most damning defect' of new religions like Socialism or Spiritualism is that they 'are suited to the new world', being 'produced by contemporary causes that can be clearly pointed out'. But a religion 'that binds men to their morality when it is not identical with their mood' would be 'right where we are wrong'. Thus Catholicism 'teaches us more by the words we reject than by the words we receive', and the convert is 'profoundly affected by the fact that, even when he did not see the reason, he lived to see that it was reasonable'. In spite of his own earliest Distributist instincts, Chesterton himself had in his youth been persuaded that the only escape from 'Capitalist captivity' was through 'Collectivism', that the 'only escape from our dark and filthy cells of industrial slavery' was through 'melting all our private latchkeys into one gigantic latchkey as large as a battering ram. We did not really like giving up our little private keys or local attachments or love of our own possessions; but we were quite convinced that social justice must be done somehow and could only be done socialistically.' But about the same time Pope Leo XIII taught in his encyclical *Rerum Novarum* (1891) that ownership of property should be as widespread as possible. However, 'nobody in our really

[69] *CCC* 95, 101–7, 120.

well-informed world took much notice' of the teaching of 'the poor old gentleman' who represented 'the dregs of a dead religion, essentially a superstition'. In fact, the real 'superstition is the fashion of this world that passes away'. In the same way, Chesterton's earliest feeling was one of 'repugnance' for Spiritualism, but again there was a time when he was persuaded that 'it was *the only way* into the promised land', in this case 'of a future life'. Once again, the Catholic Church was 'right when I was wrong'.[70]

In February *Social Reform versus Birth Control*, an abstract of two articles Chesterton had written for *Lansbury's Labour Weekly* in December 1926 and January 1927, was published as a six-page pamphlet for The League of National Life. Far from birth control being a progressive social reform, Chesterton argued, it was scarcely 'a provision for our descendants to say that the destruction of our descendants will render it unnecessary to provide them with anything'. Nor did 'Birth-Controllers' like the anti-Catholic Dean of St Paul's, W. R. Inge, 'say that the fashionable throng at Ascot wants thinning, or that it is desirable to decimate the people dining at the Ritz or the Savoy'. No, the 'gloomy Dean' was 'not gloomy about there being too many Dukes; and naturally not about there being too many Deans', as this progressive reform was directed at the masses not the rich. Besides, the issue was not birth control, which more or less everybody practised in the sense of exercising 'some control over the conditions of birth': 'the normal and real birth control is called self control.' What the capitalist press called 'birth control' was 'not control at all', but rather 'the idea that people should be, in one respect, completely and utterly uncontrolled' in order that they might 'filch the pleasure belonging to a natural process while violently and unnaturally thwarting the process itself'. It was intended apparently to help the woman who preferred 'the right to be a wage-slave' outside her home to 'companionship with the man she has herself freely accepted'. Since this meant that other women should have to look after their children while they were out at work, Chesterton wondered about a 'world in which women cannot manage their own children but can manage each other's'.[71]

5

On Sunday 6 February 1927, Bishop Cary Elwes blessed the new half-built church in Beaconsfield, following the last Mass to be celebrated in the Railway Station Hotel 'shed'. The Bishop then preached at a sung Mass,

[70] *CCC* 110–12, 114–17.   [71] *SRBC* 435, 437, 440–2.

before being entertained to lunch by the Chestertons. In the afternoon there was a reception at the Railway Hotel attended by the Chestertons, who presented a statue of the Virgin to the new church.[72] They had hoped that the church would be named after the English Martyrs,[73] but the recent canonization of St Térèse of Lisieux, 'the little flower', meant that the church would almost inevitably bear her name, 'St Teresa of the Child Jesus'. But the Chestertons' wish would be granted after their deaths, when, following the canonization of the two most famous English martyrs, the names St John Fisher and St Thomas More were added to that of St Teresa on the completion of the church in 1939. Shortly after the blessing of the church in 1927, Chesterton signed a petition to the bishop for a resident priest in Beaconsfield.[74]

On Tuesday April 1927 the Chestertons, accompanied by Dorothy Collins, left Liverpool Street Station, where a member of the Polish Embassy saw them off, on a train bound for Harwich.[75] Next day they were in Berlin, which they left the following day on a train for Warsaw, where they arrived at 8.30 in the evening. Dorothy had been worried about the expense of their taking her with them, and was relieved when Frances said to her, as the train left Liverpool Street: 'I can't tell you how

---

[72] *Bucks Free Press*, 11 Feb. 1927.   [73] Ward, *GKC* 463.

[74] St Teresa's Church, Beaconsfield, parish archives.

[75] The following account is based on the circular letters Frances Chesterton dictated to Dorothy Collins, duplicates of which were sent to family and friends (BL Add. MS 73456, fos. 29–35), on the diary Dorothy Collins kept (BL Add. MS 4378C), and on the letters she sent to her mother, Edith Collins (photocopies, GKCL). The duplicates of the circular letters that survive are addressed in hand to 'Nan' (not to Blanche Blogg, as *The British Library Catalogue of Additions to the Manuscripts. The G. K. Chesterton Papers* (London: British Library, 2001), 154, wrongly asserts), who is clearly Nancy Mansfield, an 'intimate friend' who 'lived very close' to Top Meadow (Ward, *RC* 86) at West Buttlands, Woodside Road. On the first of these duplicates, of a letter dated 4 May 1927, Frances has written in hand: 'This copy is for Beaconsfield. It will keep our friends au courant with what we are doin.' (fo. 29). There is a handwritten note on one of the duplicates (fo. 34) asking 'Nan' to go to Top Meadow to look up an address in Frances's address book, as well as handwritten notes on two other duplicates of circular letters (fos. 31, 33), which show that she had been asked to look after things at Top Meadow. The identification of 'Nan' with Nancy Mansfield is firmly established by a postcard dated 31 May 1927 and addressed to the latter at Top Meadow from Eric Gill (BL Add. MS 73195, fo. 93), asking her not to send back some engravings that Gill intended Chesterton to keep.

glad I am you are coming.' A couple of weeks later Dorothy noted with satisfaction how well she was getting on with them. In fact, the visit would be important for cementing the bond between her and her employers. Although she would become very much part of the family, up to this point Dorothy had not been resident at Top Meadow but had lived in her own flat nearby.[76]

Chesterton had been 'honoured by an invitation from the Government; but all the hospitality I received was far too much alive to remind me of anything official'.[77] He had been invited to see for himself what had been accomplished in the decade since Poland had won its freedom in 1917.[78] He was enormously popular in Poland because of his outspoken defence of its national sovereignty, which was constantly under threat from neighbouring Austria, Germany, and Russia. There were hundreds of people to greet the English visitors at the railway station, including the president of the local P.E.N. Club. The Club had been asked by the government to make the necessary arrangements for the visit. In his *Illustrated London News* column in the issue of 2 July 1927, Chesterton described their reception at Warsaw railway station, a reception that he thought was redolent of a 'particular sort of romance', even a 'particular sort of swagger' that made people either love or hate Poland:

Within ten minutes of my stepping from the train on to Polish territory I had heard two phrases—phrases which struck the precise note which thus inspires one-half of the world and infuriates the other half. We were received by a sort of escort of Polish cavalry, and one of the officers made a speech in French—a very fine speech in very good French. In the course of it he used the first of these two typical expressions: 'I will not say [you are] the chief friend of Poland. God is the chief friend of Poland.' And he afterwards said, in a more playful and conversational moment: 'After all, there are only two trades for a man—a poet and a soldier of cavalry.' He said it humorously, and with the delicate implication, 'You are a poet and I am a soldier of cavalry. So there we are!' I said that, allowing for the difficulty of anybody having anything to eat if this were literally true, I entirely accepted the sentiment, and heartily agreed with it.[79]

Apparently, unknown to Chesterton, the officer in question was a notorious drunkard and womanizer who had simply pushed himself forward with some other cavalry officers, ignoring the reception committee of the P.E.N. Club; but nobody dared to stop him because he was the favourite of Marshal

[76] Giles Darvill, 'With the Chestertons in Poland, 1927: Dorothy Collins's Portfolio of the Visit', *CR* 22/4 (Nov. 1996), 476.

[77] *A.* 306.   [78] Sullivan, 162.

[79] *ILN* xxxiv. 334; repr. in *GS* 42–3. See also Sullivan, 162.

Pilsudski, the hero of the struggle for independence and virtual dictator of the country since a military coup the previous year. According to the student who acted as Chesterton's interpreter, the offending officer gave quite a witty speech, 'welcoming Chesterton, not as a famous writer, not even as a friend of Poland, but as a born cavalry officer who had just missed his profession. Chesterton was very amused and laughed his head off, but the representatives of the P.E.N. Club were understandably not amused.'[80] They were then taken with a cavalry escort to the hotel where they were to stay. The Chestertons had a suite of rooms, including a large sitting room, bedroom, dressing room, and bathroom. Dorothy Collins had to make do with a single room opposite. The hotel manager soon had to beg Chesterton not to give money to beggars, as they were besieging the entrance to the hotel.[81]

The next day the P.E.N. Club entertained them to an enormous and lengthy lunch at the hotel, at which Chesterton made a speech. In the afternoon they were shown round the city; and in the evening went to a play at the National Theatre, which Frances told her friends in Beaconsfield 'we both enjoyed very much . . . and though we could not understand a single word, the acting was good enough to make a lot of it quite comprehensible'.[82] The following day there was another tour of the city followed by dinner at the British Embassy. On Sunday they were driven by a young Polish barrister in heavy rain over appalling roads covered with mud at about 45 miles an hour, at what seemed like breakneck speed to Dorothy Collins, to Lowicz, about forty miles from Warsaw. On the way they stopped at a village church full of peasants wearing brightly coloured traditional costumes. After that Chesterton must have been even more delighted to visit an agricultural school where young peasants studied for a year, having been democratically selected by the votes of the village commune. At Borowo they enjoyed at three o'clock a typical Polish dinner, including the national dish of 'bigos', a stew consisting of cabbage, sausages, and meat, at the estate of Wladyslaw Grabski, who had twice been prime minister. After a huge meal, followed by coffee and cakes, and then about an hour later by Russian tea and lemon and yet more cakes, they visited the spotless home of a small peasant farmer.

On Monday Chesterton had an audience with the Polish President; and in the evening there was a dinner at the P.E.N. Club. It was, Frances wrote home, 'a little embarrassing to have to eat hot kidneys and mushrooms

[80]   Adam Harasowski, News and Comments. *CR* 3/2 (Spring/Summer 1977), 301.
[81]   Sullivan, 162.   [82]   BL Add. MS 73456, fo. 29.

standing about with hundreds of guests, and this was only the preliminary to a long dinner that followed and refreshments that apparently continued until two o'clock in the morning'. The speeches were delivered in 'quite colloquial and very witty' English. They showed 'a detailed knowledge' of her husband's works 'which no Englishman of my acquaintance possesses'. Chesterton's speech in reply 'drew forth thunders of applause'. The Chestertons and Dorothy Collins left half an hour after midnight.[83] Next day, Tuesday 3 May, was Polish Independence Day, and the Chestertons and Dorothy Collins watched a military parade. Later they attended a reception at the royal palace given by the Polish President, at which Chesterton had quite a long conversation with Marshal Pilsudski. The following day they had lunch at the British Embassy.

After dinner that evening Chesterton and Dorothy Collins (Frances was too tired to go) were taken to a wine cellar—or, in the words of Chesterton, 'a sort of underground tavern'[84]—dating from the beginning of the seventeenth century. Pieces of bread and butter with cheese and slices of ham were passed around on huge silver trays, washed down by Tokay and a wine made from honey. Most of the members of the P.E.N. Club were there, as well as other visitors. Peasant songs were sung round the piano, as well as Polish army songs commemorating the various uprisings against foreign rule. At the end they sang a song wishing Chesterton a hundred years of life. It was now half an hour past midnight, but before leaving Chesterton and Dorothy were taken down to the storage cellars where they were shown by candlelight 400-year-old bottles of Tokay covered with black fungus.

On Thursday 5 May the Chestertons lunched with the foreign minister; and in the evening Chesterton gave a lecture to the P.E.N. Club that reduced many of the Poles present to tears; Dorothy had never heard a more inspiring talk. After the lecture, there was an informal supper with members of the P.E.N. Club, the British consul, and others. Next day Chesterton lunched with some Catholic students. In the afternoon Dorothy Collins went for a walk with the same 'nice' young barrister who had driven them at breakneck speed to Lowicz on their first Sunday in the country, and who had taken a great fancy to Dorothy.[85] That evening Chesterton had an audience with 'the great' Marshal Pilsudski.

---

[83] Ward, *GKC* 488–9.   [84] *A.* 306.

[85] According to Judith Lea, who became Dorothy Collins's companion in later years, he had fallen in love with Dorothy and visited her several times in England up to the late 1950s. Darvill, 'With the Chestertons in Poland, 1927', 484.

This 'grand and rather grim old soldier of fortune practically told' Chesterton that '*of the two*, he preferred Germany to Russia'. Faced with the 'choice of evils', 'his rival Dmowski' had 'clearly decided that, *of the two*, he preferred Russia to Germany'. Chesterton had already met Roman Dmowski, the leader of the Polish National Democratic Party, in England when he heard him taunted for his well-known anti-Semitism— 'After all, your religion came from the Jews'—to which Dmowski had rejoined: 'My religion came from Jesus Christ, who was murdered by the Jews.'[86]

On the Saturday they suffered a sleepless night journey to Poznan; the train was very noisy and their compartment was just over an axle. They attended a crowded Sunday midday Mass in Poznan. This part of Poland had been under German occupation and was therefore much more formal than the free and easy atmosphere of Warsaw, which had been under Russian occupation. On the Monday they had lunch with the provincial governor. Dorothy Collins was impressed (and ashamed) by how practically all the educated Poles they met could speak English (in addition to French and German), as well as knowing more about English literature and history than most English people did. Indeed, she had never met foreigners who were so English in their attitudes and even appearance, being, for example, like the English very fond of sport. They exemplified the old adage that imitation is the highest form of flattery, so intense apparently was their admiration of England. Next day the English visitors travelled into the country for lunch with a famous surgeon, whose mother was English. They had met several such Anglo-Polish families. Not surprisingly, the Poles did not mix much with Germans or Russians, from whom they were entirely different, in spite of or because of the fact that their country had been divided for 300 years between Austria, Germany, and Russia. But the long occupation had not stopped them from preserving their national culture and language. On Wednesday they visited Dmowski, who had visited them a few years before at Top Meadow, at his country house outside Poznan. They left Poznan next morning by train (they preferred to travel by day if possible, if only so that they could see as much of the country as possible), and arrived at Cracow in the evening of Thursday 12 May.

Next day they explored Cracow. Wawel Castle they found had been terribly damaged by Austrian troops who had occupied it for a century, but was in the process of being restored. In the evening they went to a play at

---

[86] *A.* 306.

the national theatre about the destiny of Poland; it had been specially put on for Chesterton, and before the performance began a speech was made from the stage about all that he had done for Poland, causing the audience to rise in his honour. On the Saturday they had tea with the Rector of the University, after which Chesterton gave a lecture. In the evening there was a dinner with the provincial governor. On Sunday they had tea with Catholic students, and Chesterton gave a speech that was interpreted sentence by sentence. On Monday they travelled to Zakopane; on the way back they encountered a car accident and took a man to hospital.

They then left Cracow on the night train for Lwow, where they arrived next morning. At their hotel they were waited on by bare-footed peasant women dressed in their national costume.[87] Next day they went to a tea party given by the American wife of one of the professors at the University; since she taught a number of the students English, Dorothy Collins hoped that the students did not think her accent was English! On Thursday the general commanding Lwow arranged for one of his soldiers to drive them into the countryside, where they passed through villages where everybody turned out to watch them and where they saw women washing clothes in the river by beating them on stones. They also saw a church belonging to the Uniate or Eastern rite Catholic Church, which was strong in the Eastern part of the country that bordered on Orthodox Russia. They returned to Warsaw on the Saturday. On Sunday they attended Mass in Chopin's church, and in the evening Chesterton gave a lecture to a Catholic study circle on Catholicism in England. They met Joseph Conrad's niece, who was a member of the P.E.N. Club and who lent them some books in English, including three of her uncle's, just when they were despairing of finding any books in English.[88] A few years later, Frances received a letter from Conrad's widow to say that her husband, who had died in 1924, had 'always' been a 'great admirer' of Chesterton and that it had been 'of no little regret' to him that he had not known Chesterton personally.[89]

On Monday 23 May they took the late night train to Wilno, where they arrived the next morning. Dorothy Collins had to share her compartment with a Russian woman; on the question of whether she should take the

[87] Sullivan, 163.

[88] Dorothy Collins's notes for a BBC 'Woman's Hour' talk, BL Add. MS 73477, fo. 60.

[89] Jessica Conrad to Frances Chesterton, 26 Jan. 1933, BL Add. MS 73236, fos. 84–5.

lower or upper berth Chesterton had advised: 'What you have to consider is whether you prefer to be stabbed through the front or the back.' Dorothy opted for the back and took the upper berth: 'My companion turned out to be charming...'.[90] It was bitterly cold. Above the archway entrance to the town, which seemed the most devoutly Catholic town of all the towns they had visited, was a Marian chapel, where daily Mass was celebrated. Since one side of the chapel was open to the road, passers-by kneeled during the Mass and nobody, including Jews, passed through the arch without taking their hat off. No wheeled vehicles were allowed through the arch, and the English visitors were deeply impressed by the sight of people kneeling in the narrow little street regardless of the weather. Chesterton was to recall how the voice of the lady who was driving them changed as they stopped outside the archway. As they passed through the archway she said 'in the same colourless tone: "You take off your hat here."'

And then I saw the open street. It was filled with a vast crowd, all facing me; and all on their knees on the ground.... I faced round, and saw in the centre of the arch great windows standing open, unsealing a chamber full of gold and colours; there was a picture behind; but parts of the whole picture were moving like a puppet-show, stirring strange double memories like a dream of the bridge in the puppet-show of my childhood; and then I realised that from those shifting groups there shone and sounded the ancient magnificence of the Mass.[91]

On Wednesday they visited the cathedral, where they saw an old priest with St Vitus's Dance; in the evening there was a meeting of the local P.E.N. Club, at which there were speeches and songs.

On Thursday they went out into the countryside, where they visited the home of Count Tyszkiewicz, who had been educated in England at Downside. Chesterton remembered the visit vividly in his *Autobiography*. Tyszkiewicz was

a young count whose huge and costly palace of a country house...had been burned and wrecked and left in ruins by the retreat of the Red Army...Looking at such a mountain of shattered marbles and black and blasted tapestries, one of our party said, 'It must be a terrible thing for you to see your old family home destroyed like this.' But the young man, who was very young in all his gestures, shrugged his shoulders and laughed, at the same time looking a little sad. 'Oh, I do not blame them for that,' he said. 'I have been a soldier myself, and in the same

---

[90] Sullivan, 163; Dorothy Collins's notes for talks, BL Add. MS 73477, fo. 89.
[91] *A.* 307.

campaign; and I know the temptations. I know what a fellow feels, dropping with fatigue and freezing with cold, when he asks himself what some other fellow's armchairs and curtains can matter, if he can only have fuel for the night. On the one side or the other, we were all soldiers; and it is a hard and horrible life. I don't at all resent what they did here. There is only one thing that I really resent. I will show it to you.'

And he led us out into a long avenue lined with poplars; and at the end of it was a statue of the Blessed Virgin; with the head and the hands shot off. But the hands had been lifted; and it is a strange thing that the very mutilation seemed to give more meaning to the attitude of intercession; asking mercy for the merciless race of men.[92]

They had lunch overlooking a lake with the Count's aunt and tea with another aunt. Their mansions, too, like those of almost every landed family in Poland, had been practically destroyed, first by the Germans and then by the Russian Communists, who were much worse than the Germans, and not only because they desecrated sacred images like those of the Virgin, which were so common by the roadside as well on people's property. Those families who had escaped with their lives considered themselves lucky and had terrible tales to tell of the consequences of resisting Communist propaganda—men hung upside down on trees and slowly burned to death, women shot with their children bound to them by barbed wire.

The day's expedition included a visit to a village where there was a settlement of 400 Karaim Jews, an ancient Jewish sect 2,000 years old, who did not accept the Talmud and were only to be found there and in the Crimea and in Egypt. They visited their synagogue, where a rabbi dressed in a yellow cloak or cope and a black and white velvet hat was taking a service, at which a blessing was asked for the visitors, who were mentioned by name. On the Friday they visited the Jewish ghetto in Wilno and were told of the legend that the Jews killed a Christian child 'once a year to get the blood for mixing their cake'. The Italian-looking town reminded Dorothy Collins of Florence, apart from the domed Russian Orthodox churches. There was a crowd at the station that night when they took the train back to Warsaw, where they arrived early next morning.

On Tuesday 31 May their memorable visit to Poland came to an end when they left Warsaw at 8.30 in the evening. There was again a large crowd to see them off. Twelve hours later they arrived in Berlin. They left Berlin next morning, bound as they thought for Cologne, but found that

---

[92] *A.* 307.

they were sitting in the wrong part of the train and ended up at Aachen. Next day they took an afternoon train to Bruges, where they visited the famous beguinage after Mass on Sunday. After a week in Belgium, which included a visit to Antwerp, they returned to England at the beginning of the second week of June. A month later, on 7 July, Chesterton addressed a crowded Essex Hall in the Strand on the subject of Poland. The Polish ambassador chaired the meeting, Cardinal Bourne, the Archbishop of Westminster, was on the platform, and Belloc moved the vote of thanks. Chesterton spoke with great passion about Poland as a historic nation that had continued to exist as a nation even while under foreign domination before regaining its freedom.[93]

6

The Return of Don Quixote had been published in book form on 6 May 1927, having been serialized in *G.K.'s Weekly* from 12 December 1925 to 11 November 1926, the remainder of the novel being summarized in the issue of 20 November after serialization stopped because of the reduction in the size of the paper. The novel, which is a considerable revision of the original serial instalments, reflects Chesterton's conversion to Catholicism. Seawood Abbey, the home of the industrial magnate Lord Seawood, has 'a curse' on it precisely because it has 'a blessing' on it. His daughter Rosamund learns the bitter truth: 'The curse is in the name of the house.' Rosamund fails to understand: 'You've seen it at the top of your note-paper a thousand times and taken it for granted; and you have never seen that *that* is the falsehood. It doesn't matter whether your father's position is false or not; it doesn't matter whether it's old or new.' It is not the usual class question of the aristocratic as opposed to the *nouveau riche* family; there is something much more important than that: 'This place doesn't belong to the old families any more than the new families. It belongs to God.' At the end of the novel, Seawood Abbey 'has become an Abbey' after the death of Lord Seawood and the conversion of his mistress to Catholicism. But the return of monks will also mean the return of marriage: 'Whenever monks come back, marriages will come back.' And monks really do mean the Middle Ages and not merely romantic medievalism: '*if* we want the flower of chivalry, we must go right away back to the root of chivalry. We must go back if we find it in a thorny place

---

[93] Clemens, 148–9.

people call theology.' The trouble with romantic medievalists was that they 'never began at the beginning', 'never went back to the Thing itself. The Thing that produced everything else . . .'. Romantic medievalists never conceived of romance in the urban landscape; but Chesterton knew that one could perfectly well imagine oneself to be 'a fairy prince' and one's 'clumsy walking-stick . . . a sword' as one ventured not into 'forests and valleys but into the labyrinth of commonplace and cockney towns'. Here, too, was possible that 'astonishment' of wonder that was 'lost in Eden and will return with the Beatific Vision, an astonishment so strong that it will last for ever'. The politics of the novel are those of *G.K.'s Weekly*. Strikes do not mean 'unrest' in the language of the capitalist press but 'a great deal of rest', for 'striking simply means resting'. As for trade unions, the capitalist press had ensured that 'that huge historical change had happened . . . behind a curtain; and the curtain was literally a sheet of paper; a sheet of newspaper'. The politicians' refusal to rearm in the dangerous international situation arose from their 'mixing up their Utopia that never comes with their old Victorian security that's already gone'.[94]

In June another volume of *Collected Poems* was published, consisting of poems first published in the *New Witness* and *G.K.'s Weekly* and now published for the first time in book form, as well as all the earlier volumes of poetry, with two exceptions, one being, astonishingly, *Greybeards at Play*. A further volume would be published in 1933, with certain additions, alterations, and omissions.

On 28 June Chesterton gave a lecture called 'Culture and the Coming Peril' at University College, London, as the seventh in a series of centenary lectures. In the chair was the Provost, Sir Gregory Foster, who referred, as we have seen, in his introduction to Chesterton's time at the College.[95] Chesterton's theme was that the threat to culture came from 'a certain familiarity with things that are the materials of Culture, and, at the same time, an insensibility to them'. As an example of what he called 'standardisation by a low standard', Chesterton cited the modern advertising of capitalism ('the rich asking for more money'[96]) in which a huge space on a wall would be filled with 'trivialities'. The result was 'the gradual debasing of the artistic sense and the imagination'.[97] In an article in *G.K.'s Weekly* the following year, Chesterton offered an unpromising scriptural anticipation of modern advertising: the 'salesmanship' of the Serpent in the Garden of Eden:

---

[94] *RDQ* 83, 117, 149, 216, 240–1, 248, 251.   [95] See above, p. 28.
[96] *NJ* 246.   [97] *Culture and the Coming Peril*, 11, 17–18.

he seems to have undertaken to deliver the goods with exactly the right prelim-
inaries of promise and praise. He knew all about advertisement: we may say he
knew all about publicity, though not at the moment addressing a very large public.
He not only took up the slogan of Eat More Fruit, but he distinctly declared that
any customers purchasing his particular brand of fruit would instantly become as
gods.

The ancient account ended with 'some extraordinary remarks' ('probably
the result of a malicious interpolation by priests at a later date') 'to the
effect that one thus pursuing the bright career of Salesmanship is condemned to crawl on his stomach and eat a great deal of dirt'.[98]

In June Chesterton was again invited to stand for the rectorship of a
Scottish university. In his reply to the invitation from Edinburgh University, he warned that he was only a Liberal 'in a rather independent
sense'—he found it 'difficult to imagine any real sort of Liberal who is
not really an independent Liberal'—but he was 'quite certain' that he was
not a Tory or a Socialist. He was defeated in the election by Winston
Churchill, who received 864 votes to his 593, with Mrs Sidney Webb in
third place with 332 votes.[99]

That summer of 1927 Dorothy Collins drove the Chestertons down to
the West Country for a holiday. The trip was to include two days at Lyme
Regis in Dorset, a stay that in the event lengthened to two weeks and that
was to be repeated in the following summers.[100] In the high street that runs
down to the sea they came across two little girls gazing longingly at a toy in
a shop window, their noses pressed to the glass. On calculating their
financial resources, the girls turned sadly away from the glass. Chesterton
thought of offering to supplement their insufficient resources, but it was felt
that their mother might not like it. Meanwhile the two little girls had
recognized their huge potential benefactor, and ran home to tell their elder
sister, Clare, that they had seen the writer she admired so much and whom
she had just been reading when her sisters burst in. The three sisters
promptly rushed to the Three Cups Hotel, where they assumed Chesterton was staying, telling their mother that they were going to ask him to tea.

---

[98] *G.K.'s Weekly*, 23 Mar. 1929.   [99] Ward, *GKC* 470.
[100] According to Maisie Ward (*RC* 161), the visit took place a year after the
Chestertons' silver wedding in 1926, i.e. 1927. Yet later she quotes a letter written by
Chesterton the 'third summer' they visited Lyme Regis (p. 172), but postmarked 19
August 1930 (p. 174). But the first visit was definitely in 1927. See notes headed '*G.K.C.
or The Family Circle*' by Clare Nicholl, who says that her family met the Chestertons
'for the first time in 1927 in Lyme Regis' (BL Add. MS 73481A, fo. 152).

On entering the hotel they saw Chesterton sitting in the lounge, but their courage failed them, and, instead of going up to him, they went to the desk pretending that they were enquiring about rooms for friends. On being shown round, they told the hotel that their friends were 'rather fussy' but they would let the hotel know their requirements. Although—or perhaps because—Chesterton rose with his usual gallantry to women, however tender in years, to open the hotel door for them as they left, they failed to pluck up enough courage to speak to him. But on returning home, Clare summoned up enough courage to send him a note, informing him that he was the reincarnation of Shakespeare but assuring him that they were not tourists or autograph-hunters—and begging him to come to tea. Back again at the hotel, they delivered the note at reception and waited for an answer. On reading the note, Chesterton wondered hopefully if these were the same girls whom they had seen in the high street and more recently in the hotel. When they saw Chesterton's legs descending the stairs, they thought they looked 'like the front quarters of a particularly large and friendly elephant'. Chesterton enquired: 'Am I really the ghost of Shakespeare? And may we come to tea?' A few days later, when they had become firm friends, Chesterton asked Clare 'casually, without the flicker of a wink, "By the way, those friends of yours who wanted rooms . . . did they—er—find anything suitable?"' Clare replied no less 'blandly, "As a matter of fact, they didn't . . . I believe they went elsewhere."' 'A pity,' murmured Chesterton, 'a great pity . . .' Clare was again at The Three Cups Hotel when this conversation took place in the lounge. All of a sudden an American journalist burst into the room and bowed to Chesterton: 'Mr G. K. Chesterton, I believe!' Turning to Clare and practically kissing her hand, he added, '*And* Mrs G. K. Chesterton!' After the journalist had disappeared as suddenly as he had appeared, Chesterton apologized to Clare: 'My dear, please forgive my extreme dilatoriness in waiting to be thrust upon you. I really should have proposed first.' She responded, 'Don't mention it, Mr Chesterton, I accepted you years ago.'[101]

It was decided that the children should call Chesterton by the diminutive 'Unclet' in view of his size and Frances 'Auntlet'. Apart from the three girls who were at Lyme Regis that summer, there were two other girls and a boy; the mother, Mrs Nicholl, was widowed. So close did this large family of children come to the childless Chestertons that eventually they moved to Beaconsfield, to a house called Christmas Cottage in the same road as Top Meadow. One or other of the Nicholl children would call almost every day

---

[101] Ward, *RC* 161–3.

at Top Meadow, and Chesterton, sometimes accompanied by Frances, would regularly go to supper on Saturday or Sunday evening at Christmas Cottage. These suppers were likely to be extremely lengthy, as the task of combining talking with eating was beyond Chesterton. If it was macaroni cheese, a favourite of his, he would pick up a forkful but the fork would not reach his mouth as he suddenly remembered something else he wanted to say. Down would come the fork, and when he had finished saying what he wanted to say, again the fork would gather another mouthful of macaroni cheese—and again the same process would be repeated. The family soon learned not to wait but simply to carry on with supper without his noticing, so that coffee would be served while Chesterton was still only halfway through his first course. Mrs Nicholl's strategy of pointing out that his plate must have got cold and needed replenishing had no effect: the hint was lost on Chesterton, who would simply agree with alacrity to another helping while the first remained half-eaten. Getting him out of the dining room so that the table could be cleared was a major problem. At home Frances would resort to a bell to get him out of his study to bed; but at Christmas Cottage, if Frances was not there, he was liable to stay on into the early hours. But Frances was not a late night person, and Mrs Nicholl would worry about her waiting for her husband to return. As had been his London practice, Chesterton would sometimes actually take a taxi to carry him barely fifty yards to Christmas Cottage! Fully intending an early departure, he would ask the taxi to wait—but then gave as little thought to the taxi as he did to the time. While he did not monopolize the conversation, he would easily launch into a lengthy monologue, especially if he were asked a question. However, that did not preclude his great ability to enter into somebody else's mind and find more there than the person ever suspected. In the last months of his life, it was noticeable that he listened more to others and would even interrupt his monologue if he thought someone wanted to ask a question or make a point. The Nicholl family, in fact, were great arguers—just like Chesterton himself and his brother had been.[102]

Unlike Frances, who loved children but felt ill at ease with adolescents, especially confused adolescents, her husband was able to relate to both. When Barbara Nicholl had measles as a child and he was suffering from jaundice, he wrote to apologize to her for failing to complete 'a long letter full of love, devotion and affectionate counsel, including advice on the Correct Deportment of a Young Lady when entertaining a Measle (to a German Measle the etiquette is more formal)'. He had begun it, when 'in

---

[102] Ward, *RC* 176, 195, 259–62.

an evil hour' he was 'tempted by a Devil assuming his favourite disguise of a Duty', having been told that he had fifteen articles to write in five days. 'The remnant left by Jaundice, the wretched scribe writing this in bed—he is now commonly known as the Yellow Dwarf—offers this as a Warning. Never, never, do your Duty first and put off your pleasure till after. I have never done it before myself. When I did this Doom fell upon me.' Now he knew it was too late:

> Never will you regard me as a friend and Measle Adviser. You will forget the Jaundiced Journalist: and dance your own way to fame and glory, amid crowds of applauding critics—till you dance before all the Crowned Heads of Europe and King George offers you the half of his Kingdom: and you will ask for the Head of Dean Inge on a soup-plate.

Coming from a Catholic family, Barbara Nicholl would have enjoyed the thought of asking for the head of the 'gloomy', anti-Catholic Dean of St Paul's—just as King Herod's daughter had asked for the head of the less than convivial John the Baptist.[103]

The key, of course, to Chesterton's rapport with not only children and adolescents but also young adults was an enormous sense of fun and humour that guaranteed instant empathy. But apart from that he had a natural sympathy with the young and their difficulties in growing up, making them, in the words of Clare Nicholl, 'not only feel at their ease but somehow comforted and made much of'. He advised a self-absorbed Rhoda Bastable 'to think actively and vividly' about things other than herself: 'Especially about *people* who are quite comically different from ourselves... One sees even oneself more plainly in other things—especially in things one has done. Every one of us has done some good; and it is a monument, as if we were already dead.' When, he, Chesterton, had had 'morbid nightmares', when he had doubted if he believed in anything, he had found an antidote in asking himself whether, if he had not '*really*' believed, he would ever have 'done this work, or resisted that temptation—or even tried to resist it'. As for himself, who had entertained every possible doubt, the more he saw of 'human experience' the more he believed in Christianity.[104]

Even when he was being serious, he could not resist humour—not, of course, that he saw humour and seriousness as being in any way opposed. To Felicity Walpole, who was engaged to be married and wanted help in finding a job for her fiancé, he wrote: 'I am already exploring cracks and crannies in the rather blank wall which I know is presented to intelligent

[103] Ward, *RC* 176–7.   [104] Ward, *RC* 198, 201–2.

young men looking for a job today. I think there is a crack or two in the wall opposite me in which I might get the blade of a pen-knife . . . '. When the 21-year-old Clare Nicholl sent some of her verses to Chesterton, who unfortunately mislaid them, he wrote: 'I simply could not clear a large enough space in which to grovel. When I grovel it is a huge and horrid sight and there are geological disturbances miles away. But, really and truly, I do want to grovel. I wish I could feel confident that, even when the local earthquakes were over, you would *really* forgive me.' His advice to an enthusiastic young lady contemplating a religious vocation was deadly serious despite being amusing, while its humour disarmed any resentment at the warning expressed:

If you are really For It (I use, not without justice, the jovial phrase commonly used about people going to be jailed or flogged or hanged)—If you are For IT, it is the grandest and most glorious and deific thing that any human being can be for. It is far beyond my imagination. But never, for one instant, among all my sins, have I doubted that it was *above* my imagination.'

He had no more doubt that a monk or nun was 'walking on a crystal floor' over his head than that Quoodle the dog had 'a larger equipment of legs' than he had—'and (with all respect to his many virtues) a rather simpler intellectual plan of life'.

If this is your Way Out, then everybody must stand out of your Way, as out of the way of a Celestial Fire-Engine. If one of my friends is caught up to Heaven in a fiery chariot—you will not think me capable of being a stout and solid speed-Cop or Traffic Policeman to hold her up for enquiries. No: that is unanswerable. If that is so, nobody has a right to say anything except—'God will love you even more than we do.'

But—there is still one little worrying thought left in the dregs of what I call my mind. You will be generous enough to forgive if the hesitation sounds personal. [My friend] I have often hailed as she rushed by: but I have met her rushing *from* places as well as to places. If you must rush, this is a place you must rush to and cannot rush from. I don't mean any material nonsense of the Walled-up Nun—I mean that you yourself could not go from something greater to anything less great. Now you do have black fits, don't you? Reactions—scruples and the rest. What I want you to be quite clear about (I expect you are and grovel again) is that if you have one of those black reactions *after* this, it may do you what Professor Bobsky would call psychological harm, and those who talk English would call spiritual harm. It doesn't matter if you get tired of working for the Middlesex Mummies Exploration Fund and rush to the East Ealing Ethical Dance Movement—because we all live in that world and laugh at it and earn our living in it. But if you have a reaction from this greater thing—you will feel quite differently.

You may be in danger of religious melancholia: for you will say 'I have had the Best and it did not help.' Anyhow you may be hurt . . . and I hate your being hurt.

Reassure me on this one point and I am absolutely with you—if I am worthy to say so. Let me know (by a wink or any recognised ritual) that you see what I mean, and have allowed for it, and I am at once a Trappist.[105]

Nor could the young easily offend Chesterton. When the secretary of the St Paul's School debating society invited Chesterton to their annual dinner, the sixth former received an invitation to Top Meadow, where he found himself, as a budding historian, holding forth on the glories of the Reformation, only suddenly to remember to his embarrassment that his host was a Roman Catholic. On his apologizing for dropping such a brick, Chesterton 'leant forward, tapped him on the knee, and said, "My boy, never drop bricks: always throw them."'[106]

Clare Nicholl did remember two things that made Chesterton angry: unkindness or uncharitable gossip and specious cleverness. Since he hardly ever openly found fault, one would feel his disapproval in his 'silence and sudden lack of response'. The one fault she also remembered was an occasional flash of irritability. One night while she was having supper at Top Meadow, Chesterton asked her whether she would like red or white wine. And when she answered that she would have either if Frances was also having some, Chesterton banged the bottle he was holding on the table, glared at her, and exploded: 'Look here, Clare, if you want wine, say so: if you don't want wine, say so: but for goodness' sake *don't* make your having wine or not having wine dependent on what other people do.'[107] His annoyance, it has to be said, was somewhat inconsistent given the fact that his own inability to make up his mind on such matters was a source of irritation to his wife. Dorothy Collins remembered how Frances would say, ' "Will you have some more, Gilbert?" and he would either pass his plate to her in an absent-minded way, or would say, "Oh, I will if you like." To which she would reply, "Well, make up your mind."'[108] If the occasional irascibility surprised Clare, she was also struck like other people by Chesterton's genuine modesty. One day she was visiting Top Meadow and noticed among the books that were always piled besides Frances's flowers a copy of Chesterton's new book *The Return of Don Quixote*. Asked if she might

[105] Ward, *RC* 186, 191, 198, 201–2, 204, 206–7.

[106] Edmund Esdaile to Maisie Ward, 8 Aug. 1949, BL Add. MS 73481A, fo. 69.

[107] Ward, *RC* 196–7.

[108] Dorothy Collins's notes for a BBC 'Woman's Hour' talk, BL Add. MS 73477, fo. 66.

borrow it, Chesterton looked genuinely surprised and replied that if she really wanted to read it—and he was loath to thrust his books on her—she was welcome to *have* it.[109]

Once, after the Nicholl girls had grown up, when all the other members of the family were abroad, Chesterton wrote a delightful note to one of the girls who remained at home in Beaconsfield.

When you rashly showed a momentary interest in the hotel accommodation of the Three Cups...you little knew how unscrupulous and pertinacious a Sleuth you were letting loose upon your own track. How often you must have cursed the day when that vast and shapeless shadow blotted out so large a part of the landscape of Lyme. We have been so cluttered up with visitors...that I have not been able to fix up one of those conferences between us, upon which the fate of Christendom so obviously depends...[110]

7

In October 1927 Chesterton published *The Judgement of Dr Johnson: A Comedy in Three Acts*. The previous year he had mentioned the play in the interview he gave to the *Observer*,[111] in which he had discussed *The Man who was Thursday*. He had confirmed that it was true that he had written a play called 'Doctor Johnson'. 'There are two ideas in it,' he told the interviewer.

Doctor Johnson meets a young American revolutionary who has come to England as a half-spy, and I try to show that we sympathise with American Republicanism as something frustrated, while the old Toryism of Doctor Johnson is very much alive. The other idea is that if you want to find a man bullying a woman into subjection, you must look out for a superman with his series of love-adventures.

When asked why he had not written more plays—as was Shaw's constant refrain—Chesterton replied that frankly he did not know: 'I do naturally find myself writing in dialogue form. But I have been always busy with journalism, apart from which I was put to writing novels at an early age...'. Moreover, he knew next to nothing about how to get a play on to the stage, whereas he did know 'the good old route to the good old publisher'. One theatre manager had told him that, unless he attended the theatre and seemed to take an interest in his play, he might not produce it;

[109] Ward, *RC* 198–9.
[110] G. K. Chesterton to one of the Nicholl girls, n.d., BL Add. MS 73481A, fo. 162.
[111] *Observer*, 10 Jan. 1926. See above, p. 192.

he could not imagine a publisher refusing to publish a book if he failed to show up in the bookshop. However, he understood from his literary agent that Sir Barry Jackson (the founder and director of the Birmingham Repertory Theatre) had agreed to stage his 'Doctor Johnson'. In fact, the play was not performed until 20 January 1932, when it had a very short run at the Arts Theatre Club in London, 'for 6 performances' only, Frances told Father O'Connor—but it was 'a lovely production—we are still hoping it may lead to a West End Show'.[112]

On 28 October 1927 Chesterton and Shaw debated publicly for the last time in the Kingsway Hall. W. R. Titterton had suggested to Chesterton that Shaw should be challenged to a debate after Shaw had refused to write for *G.K.'s Weekly* on the ground that 'Chesterton was wasting his time...trying to establish a false antithesis between Distributism and Socialism', when the two were really the same thing. Chesterton then wrote to Shaw to propose that they should debate on the question 'Do we agree?' Shaw agreed, but insisted that the fledgling BBC, which wanted to broadcast the debate, should pay Chesterton and him a substantial fee.[113] Organization was left to the Distributist League—much to Shaw's unease, who wrote to Chesterton on 20 October: 'Will you see to it that the meeting...is properly organized? It is evident from enquiries made about tickets that your people have not the least notion of what they are up against.' If the Distributist League was not up to it, then 'a paid manager and staff must be hired': 'Nothing must be left to well-intentioned Godforsaken idiots who have no experience or organizing power, and who believe that public meetings are natural phenomena that look after themselves.' He added that he had noticed that, without consulting him, Chesterton's Distributists had 'calmly' announced that 'part of the proceeds' were to be given to the King Edward Hospital fund: 'As if every successful commercial brigand were not buying Indulgences and pardons by pouring money into the hospitals, whilst your blessed league and its paper and the Fabian Society can hardly keep alive! I had rather pay Belloc's debts with it.'[114]

[112] Frances Chesterton to John O'Connor, 28 Feb. [1932], BL Add. MS 73196, fo. 145.

[113] Titterton, 182–3.

[114] George Bernard Shaw to G. K. Chesterton, 20 Oct. 1927, BL Add. MS 73198, fo. 96, partly quoted in Barker, 276.

Although there had been insufficient funds to do much advertising, the hall was 'packed long before the debate began'.[115] Because so many people had come without tickets, many with tickets had been unable to get in before the debate began. Belloc, who was presiding, predicted 'every prospect of a very pretty fight', a prophecy that was fulfilled when, after Shaw had been speaking for about five minutes, there was a loud banging on the doors at the back of the hall. Shaw remarked that the audience were getting more entertainment than they had paid for as they were 'having a row thrown in'. The chairman appealed for quiet, pointing out that the debate was being broadcast, and a similar plea was made by Shaw. Introducing the debate, Belloc announced that he had 'vaguely' gathered that Shaw and Chesterton were going to debate whether a man should be independent through the possession of private means as Shaw and Chesterton were, or whether they should be impoverished like he, Belloc. The debate, he said, would settle nothing, but it was 'the next best thing to a fight'.[116]

According to a 'less than . . . verbatim report' that was published the following year, Chesterton insisted that the whole question turned on what Shaw meant by saying that in a Socialist state the whole community would own all the means of production. If this meant simply that the state would own all the means of production, then the people themselves would not own them. What Shaw was really proposing was the distribution of wealth, whereas the Distributists were proposing the distribution of power. Shaw replied that Chesterton was assuming that the means of production meant machines, whereas he meant by means of production men and women. Chesterton admitted that in a Distributist state some things would have to be owned by the state. Shaw retorted that there were many more exceptions than the nationalization of the coal mines, which Chesterton had cited. It was all very well talking about the distribution of land, but the fact was that there was worthless land and immensely valuable land. Chesterton concluded by saying that Shaw's objection to private property was as negative as his desire to ban alcohol because a few people drank too much. He, Chesterton, was not advocating a society that would contain only agricultural peasants, which was absurd. He had merely given the ownership of land as an obvious example of the natural human desire for property. And when Shaw said that by means of production he meant men and women, he meant that the state should own the men and women

---

[115] Titterton, 184.
[116] *Daily Telegraph*, 29 Oct. 1927; *Manchester Guardian*, 29 Oct. 1927.

as slaves. At the end Belloc refused to sum up, predicting that the debate would soon be out of date, as either industrial civilization would break down or the masses would become content to be the slaves of a plutocracy.[117]

In November Chesterton published a slim critical study of his youthful hero Stevenson, to whom he had already devoted a chapter in *Twelve Types*. Biographies of Savonarola and Napoleon that had been advertised as 'In Preparation' in *William Cobbett* were again announced as forthcoming; they would never appear. Chesterton begins the book by laying down that 'the one really great and important work' that Stevenson 'did for the world was done quite unconsciously'. Chesterton did not mean 'the thing which he preached' so much as 'the thing which he taught': 'Or, to put it another way the thing which he could teach was not quite so large as the thing which we can learn.' It would take time for Stevenson's true 'significance' to be understood 'in relation to larger problems', which were beginning to be appreciated but of which people were 'almost entirely unaware' in his own time. Indeed, the truth to which he testified was 'a truth he did not understand'.[118]

As in the earlier essay in *Twelve Types*, Stevenson's love of sharp edges, which he shared with Chesterton, is especially emphasized, and its relevance to the 'truth he did not understand': 'The first fact about the imagery of Stevenson is that all his images stand out in very sharp outline; and are, as it were, all edges.' It was noticeable that his Highland stories had 'everything Scotch except Scotch mist', for there was 'no Celtic twilight about his Celts'. Stevenson's 'love of sharp edges and cutting or piercing action' came from exactly the same source as Chesterton's: the toy theatre of his childhood. It was because Stevenson 'loved to see . . . and to think' in terms of the toy theatre's 'definite outlines' that 'all his instinctive images are clear and not cloudy; that he liked a gay patchwork of colour combined with zigzag energy of action, as quick as the crooked lightening. He loved things to stand out; we might say he loved them to stick out . . . '. Unfortunately, there was also a downside to this angularity—namely, that 'he simplified so much that he lost some of the comfortable complexity of real life. He treated everything with an economy of detail and a suppression of irrelevance which had at last something about it stark and unnatural.' Both the strength and weakness of this brevity could be best appreciated by comparing him with 'the great Victorian novelists in whose vast shadow he grew up'. For, while it was true that their novels

---

[117] CS 539, 546–51, 554, 557, 560.	[118] *RLS* 50–1.

were full of 'padding', this did 'in a curious fashion confirm the reality of the characters' and 'made the reader feel at home with the characters'. The 'hospitality' of the great Victorian novels certainly led to their being 'a little more formless than Stevenson', but the latter's 'verbal economy' made his characters 'almost thin', 'flat figures' who 'could only be seen from one side'—like the puppets of the toy theatre.[119]

But there was another important influence: the rejected Calvinism of his upbringing. The English had 'generally' adopted 'a sentimental religiosity' in place of a 'dogmatic religion'; whereas in Presbyterian Scotland, where 'the taste for theology remained' even if 'the religion was dead', the opposite had happened. Now, theology was 'at least a form of thought' and it had survived Stevenson's loss of belief. The Scotch atheists of the eighteenth and nineteenth centuries were 'unmistakeable children of the Kirk', who might seem 'absurdly detached and dehumanised' but at least were not suffering from a lack of 'dull lucidity'—of which the world was now in such need. For 'by being theological they had at least learnt to be logical'. And it was 'this sort of clarity' that enabled Stevenson instinctively to 'draw lines that were as hard and clear as those of a mathematical diagram'. That 'certain almost arid decision in the strokes of Stevenson's style' Chesterton thought was 'due in no small degree to that inheritance of definition, that goes with an inheritance of dogma'. As Stevenson himself had put it, he did not write 'in sand with a salt-spoon' but 'in the tradition of scriptures cut with steel into stone'. The mark of his style was that he 'used the word because it was the right word': 'He does pick the words that make that picture that he particularly wants to make. They do fix a particular thing, and not some general thing of the same sort . . . '. Such was his 'beautiful and piercing sense of the clarity of form' that, even though 'he may seem to describe his subject in detail, he describes it to be done with it; and he does not return to the subject'. Even the best novelists did not have Stevenson's 'particular knack of putting a whole human figure together with a few unforgettable words'. Because of the 'sharpness' of Stevenson's 'verbal gestures' his descriptions of characters were 'seldom static but rather dynamic descriptions'. Indeed, there was nothing that he touched that 'he did not animate'. And Chesterton alludes to another aspect of Stevenson's importance and significance in this concluding passage of the chapter on his style.

[119] *RLS* 97–8, 100–02, 117.

I find everywhere, even in his mere diction and syntax, that theme that is the whole philosophy of fairy-tales, of the old romances and even of the absurd libretto of the little theatre—the conception that man is born with hope and courage indeed, but born outside that which he was meant to attain; that there is a quest, a test, a trial by combat or pilgrimage of discovery; or, in other words, that whatever else man is he is not sufficient to himself... The very movement of the sentence is the movement of a man going somewhere and generally fighting something...[120]

If Calvinistic Presbyterianism had one beneficial influence on Stevenson, it had another baleful influence. For there was a part of Stevenson's mind that was positively unhealthy owing to 'that ancient heathen fatalism, which in the seventeenth century had taken the hardly less heathen form of Calvinism'. And this took the particular form of believing that 'what is victorious is always good'. Presbyterians spoke of 'the Lord' rather than 'our Lord', implying fear rather than affection and 'the idea of glorifying God for His greatness rather than His goodness'. Like Muslims, Puritans cried, 'God is great', with the implication that greatness *is* God. Now this feeling was present in Stevenson, who 'grew too familiar in his later works with... [a] swaggering cult of fear'. Chesterton thought that this 'secret idolatry' was 'the only lesion in Stevenson's perfect sanity, the only running sore in the normal health of his soul'.[121]

The problem that Stevenson faced in his youth was the

sharp... contrast between the shelter and delicate fancies of his childhood and the sort of world which met him like the wind on the front doorstep. It was not merely the contrast between poetry and Puritanism; it was also the contrast between poetry and prose; and prose that was almost repulsively prosaic. He did not believe enough in Puritanism to cling to it; but he did believe very much in a potential poetry of life, and he was bewildered by its apparently impossible position in the world of real living.

Even if he had believed in 'his national religion' as he did in his nation, he 'would never have met that particular point at issue'. There was nothing in Presbyterianism that 'could in any way *carry on* the childish enthusiasm for simple things': there was 'no cult of the Holy Child, no feast of the Holy Innocents, no tradition of the Little Brothers of St Francis...' Puritanism had its virtues, but one it lacked: 'purity'. It lacked 'images of positive innocence'. And so, when Stevenson left home, 'he shut the door on a house lined with fairy gold, but he came out on a frightful contrast'.

---

[120] *RLS* 97–8, 100–2, 117.   [121] *RLS* 88, 91–3.

Chesterton suspected that 'it was originally out of this chasm of ugly division that there arose that two-headed monster, the mystery of Jekyll and Hyde'. The action of the story was seemingly in London, but it was 'all the time very unmistakably happening in Edinburgh'. 'The peculiar tone' of Dr Jekyll's 'respectability, and the horror of mixing his reputation with moral frailty' was redolent of 'the upper middle classes in solid Puritan communities'. But Puritanism was even more evident in Mr Hyde, in the 'sense of the sudden stink of evil, the immediate invitation to step into stark filth, the abruptness of the alternative between that prim and proper pavement and that black and reeking gutter'. The story's 'atmosphere and setting' were those of 'some tale of stiff hypocrisy in a rigid sect' with 'a system which saw no difference between the worst and the moderately bad'. Stevenson abandoned Calvinism and became 'a highly honourable, responsible and chivalrous Pagan'. And although he 'often used the old national creed as a subject', he actually used it as 'an object' upon which he 'worked ... and not with it', for he had 'left behind him a dead religion'. Neither he nor 'the inheritors of his admirable tradition, like Barrie and Buchan' would have 'treated that national secret genially and even tenderly' had it not been that 'their very tenderness was the first soft signal that the thing was dead'. For they would never have 'so fondled the tiger-cat of Calvinism until, for them, its teeth were drawn':

Indeed this was the irony and the pathos of ... Scottish Calvinism: to be rammed down people's throats for three hundred years as an unanswerable argument and then to be inherited at the last as an almost indefensible affection; to be expounded to boys with a scowl and remembered by men with a smile ... All that long agony of lucidity and masterful logic ended at last suddenly with a laugh; and the laugh was Robert Louis Stevenson.

But, having been 'emptied of all the ethics and metaphysics' of Calvinism, Stevenson became exposed to 'all the views and vices of a rationalistic civilisation'. As for 'the deeper lessons of his early life', they 'must have seemed to him to be dead within him; nor did he himself know what thing within him was yet alive'.[122]

But what was so 'individual and interesting' about Stevenson's reaction to his new surroundings was the way in which 'he refused to run with the crowd or follow the fashion' but instead rebelled into 'respectability', shaking himself 'with a sort of impatient sanity; a shrug of scepticism about scepticism'. His 'real distinction' was that he had 'the sense to see

---

[122] *RLS* 64–6, 69, 71–2.

that there is nothing to be done with Nothing'. Instead, unlike other contemporary artists, he deserted 'art for life'. In particular, he proposed the 'disturbing paradox that we should learn morality from little boys'—the 'remarkable outcome' being *Treasure Island*. If human beings were merely 'puppets of destiny' and 'as futile as puppets', was there anything to stop them from being 'as entertaining as Punch'? Such a reaction was not 'superficial' compared to so-called realism, which, 'so long as it was materialistic . . . could not really be realistic', but 'more fundamental', as it took into account the 'psychological' truth that 'happiness is not a trifle and certainly cannot be a trick'. Against *fin de siècle* pessimism, Stevenson 'appealed to his own childhood': 'Its pleasures had been as solid as the taste of sweets; and it was nonsense to say that there had been nothing in them worth living for. . . . Therefore he appealed across the void or valley of his somewhat sterile youth to that garden of childhood, which he had once known and which was his nearest notion of paradise,' 'that square of garden' on which, amidst 'all that waste of Scottish moorland, the sun still glowed'. What had 'moved' Wordsworth now 'moved' Stevenson: 'the unanswerable fact of that first vividness in the vision of life'—even though it was 'hardly the vision of meadow, grove and stream', but rather 'the vision of coffin, gallows and gory sabre that were apparelled in celestial light, the glory and the freshness of a dream'. In Stevenson's 'growing sense of the need of some escape from the suffocating cynicisms of the mass of men and artists in his time', he wanted 'to go back to that nonsense; for it seemed, by comparison, quite sensible'. By 'reviving the adventure story', he was 'escaping from an exceedingly unhealthy climate'. It represented 'a sort of dash for liberty; and especially a dash for happiness', 'the escape of a prisoner as he was led in chains from the prison of Puritanism to the prison of Pessimism'. Hardly had he emerged 'from the shadow of Calvin' when he 'came into the shadow of Schopenhauer'. Determined to escape from both, he 'took refuge in his old home' and 'barricaded himself in the nursery'. In Chesterton's view, it was this 'sharp return to simplicity, as the expression of the fiery thirst for happiness' that gave Stevenson an important place in the history of literature.[123]

Finally, as we would expect, Chesterton finds more than one paradox in Stevenson. First, while, unlike Wordsworth, Stevenson found 'it difficult to get any intimations of immortality' even 'in the vivid pleasures of childhood', he was in fact 'continually bearing witness to the Fall' by his 'constant tribute . . . to the poetry of early childhood', for this made no

---

[123] *RLS* 72, 74–6, 78, 81–2, 84, 135, 145.

sense unless it is true that 'the world of sin comes between us and something more beautiful or, as Wordsworth, says, that we came first from God who is our home'. Probably it was because Stevenson had been taught 'the doctrine of depravity' by the Calvinists rather than 'the true doctrine of the Fall' that he did not realize how orthodox a Christian he was. Then, too, there was the paradox that, partly because of the influence of Scott, Stevenson was 'intellectually on the side of the Whigs and morally on the side of the Jacobites', which resulted in the 'curious and sometimes inconsistent mingling of... grey Whiggery with... purple Jacobite romance'. Again, it was paradoxical that death was much closer to Stevenson than to the hated pessimists, 'who cowered under the shadow of death', as he knew only too well 'whenever he coughed and found blood on his handkerchief': 'He was not pretending to defy it half so much as they were pretending to seek it. It is no very unreasonable claim for him that he made a better use of his bad health than Oscar Wilde made of his good health...'.[124]

T. S. Eliot reviewed the book in *The Nation and Athenaeum*. He complained that he found Chesterton's 'style exasperating to the last point of endurance' and that Chesterton had wasted 'a good deal of time' in a 'diffuse, dissipated, but not at all stupid book' in 'attacking misconceptions which we had not heard of and in which we are not interested'. Chesterton had assumed 'a misunderstanding that we are not likely to labour under' by 'protesting' that Stevenson stood for 'health and happiness' as opposed to the decadence of the *fin de siècle*. He, Eliot, confessed to finding Chesterton's 'own cheerfulness... depressing': 'He appears less like a saint radiating spiritual vision than like a 'busman slapping himself on a frosty day.' Chesterton, he thought, had only 'partially' shown why Stevenson was 'a writer of permanent importance', although he had written concisely and to the point in defence of Stevenson's style. His 'Roman Catholic point of view' concerning *Dr Jekyll and Mr Hyde* was 'extremely interesting': 'And how illuminating his observation that though this story is nominally set in London, it is really taking place in Edinburgh!'[125]

In *The Victorian Age in Literature* Chesterton had already paid tribute to *Dr Jekyll and Mr Hyde* as 'a double triumph; it has the outside excitement that belongs to Conan Doyle with the inside excitement that belongs to Henry James'. But it was generally supposed that the story was about 'two personalities' who were 'equal, neither caring for the other' and that the moral was that 'man can be cloven into two creatures, good and evil'. But

---

[124] *RLS* 79, 87–8, 140.   [125] Conlon, i. 444–6.

the whole stab of the story' was that 'man *can't*: because while evil does not care for good, good must care for evil. Or, in other words, man cannot escape from God, because good is the God in man; and insists on omniscience. This point which is good psychology and also good theology and also good art, has missed its main intention merely because it was also good story-telling.[126]

8

In the 24 February 1928 issue of *G.K.'s Weekly*, Chesterton was forced to make a financial appeal to readers. He feared that the paper might have to close, and, if it did, that would be 'the beginning of the end ... of independent journalism', as 'a millionaire monopoly of the press' was looking more and more likely. All that Chesterton could promise was that the paper would not be 'sold', would not 'pass ... into a plutocratic combine'. Now that they were 'near the end of [their] resources', they had no alternative but to appeal to readers. Four days later he warned potential donors and subscribers that it looked 'the beginning of ... the end of independent journalism' as the 'movement towards a millionaire monopoly of the press' now appeared 'inevitable'. One of the 'few exceptions' to the general trend was *G. K.'s Weekly*, although 'hampered from the first by lack of capital, and especially by the lack of steady support from any single capitalist'. But 'no single capitalist', Chesterton promised, 'will ever count us among his numerous possessions. This organ of opinion may be smashed, but it will not be sold; it may be annihilated, but it will not be amalgamated.' In inviting supporters to buy shares in the paper, he could at least point to 'certain definite signs of the general turning of the tide in favour of own protest' against 'modern monopoly', against which, admittedly, there were 'few signs of the general turning of the tide'. Although 'prevented from making' the paper 'as good as it might be under more normal conditions', they had nonetheless 'succeeded already in changing the tone of all talk about property and freedom. Capitalists and Socialists, in the thick of their own recognised and public quarrel, are conscious of a third thing which they are forced either to allow for or to answer or to deride.' He could offer 'no certain profit' to financial backers, 'except that of playing a part in history'—whether it would be an 'effective part' rested with them. Otherwise history would 'take that turn which we regard as the tragedy of civilisation; the restoration of order in its old and heathen form

[126] *VAL* 528.

of slavery'. He would not now be 'making such an appeal' if he were 'attempting to pretend' that the paper was 'in the ordinary sense profitable': 'We are near the end of our resources; and we do not promise that such resources as we may gain can do anything but sustain the effort for its own sake. But there is a reasonable and practical chance of doing more; and if we save ourselves we may even perhaps save our country.'[127]

It was not only the financial problems of *G.K.'s Weekly* that Chesterton had to contend with: there were also the fights among the various Distributist factions. At the annual meeting of the League in October 1928, Chesterton complained: 'I can never understand how people I like so much can possibly dislike each other.' There were roughly two kinds of dispute: those about the nature of true Distributism and those about *G.K.'s Weekly*—although as the years went by the main dispute became the question whether one could be a true Distributist without also being a Catholic.[128]

His brother had been an active and professional editor, but Chesterton's editorial competence was limited to writing (or rather dictating) editorials: he lacked 'the capacity to preside over a paper, to pilot it through a crisis, "put it to bed" or do any of those ordinary things done by ordinary editors'. It was his name that had been useful to the *New Witness*. By the end of the war that paper was feeling the absence of an active editor on the spot, and subscriptions were falling. Another problem was that the *Eye-Witness* and its successor were primarily investigative papers that aimed to uncover corruption, without any very positive policy. *G.K.'s Weekly*, on the other hand, was intended to put forward Distributism as a positive political alternative to Capitalism and Socialism. And it was important personally for Chesterton to have his own paper where he could air his views, since he no longer had any access to the press, apart from his column in the *Illustrated London News*, which had to steer clear largely of politics and religion. But the fact that there had been a delay in launching the new paper, even after sufficient funds had been secured and a certain amount of publicity had greeted the new venture, including an interview with Chesterton in the *Observer*, was characteristic of both Chesterton brothers' lack of business sense. Cecil's attitude had been that the manager not the editor was responsible for the business side of the paper. But, since the war the economic conditions had worsened, so it was even more difficult to

---

[127] G. K. Chesterton to 'Sir', 24 Feb. 1928, BL Add. MS 73230, fos. 63–4. The same letter (not a photocopy) is in JJBL.

[128] Ward, *RC* 211–12, 229.

keep a paper going that had an editor so uninterested in the business side and a management that was as incompetent as that of the *New Witness*. The London or Central branch of the Distributist League used to meet at a tavern called 'The Devereux', only a few yards from the offices of *G.K.'s Weekly*. Its members were naturally therefore very alive to the paper's problems and decided that certain actions should be taken to ensure its survival. Expenses should be cut and the direction and management of the paper reorganized. When they heard about the proposed reorganization and retrenchment, the current office staff were outraged at this interference by alleged amateurs, who in fact included experienced if younger journalists, such as Edward MacDonald, who would succeed Titterton as assistant editor. Titterton, who had been mischievously misinformed that the plan was that he was to be dismissed and that a committee should run the paper, was furious. In fact, the idea was that the only way to ensure the paper was managed in a businesslike way was for a committee to have full control—a committee that Titterton would chair in the absence of the editor. There followed a public meeting at 'The Devereux' at which Chesterton took the chair. Expecting Chesterton to take his side, Titterton was confounded when he took the side of the young reformers. When the committee was formed, it was discovered that there was a large financial deficit, which the manager had concealed, no doubt for fear the paper would close before he could get new advertisers and make good the deficit. As Titterton had predicted, the committee eventually melted away, but, as he came generously to recognize, it had fulfilled its purpose by appointing Edward Macdonald as assistant editor, 'a man born for the job', who greatly improved the paper: 'read in England by most of the people who count; and abroad...quoted as an authority.' The paper still had to be run on a shoestring, but at least its existence was no longer threatened, and such subsidies as had to come from Chesterton were affordable.[129]

In May Chesterton received a letter from Sigrid Undset, the Norwegian Catholic novelist, who had converted four years earlier and become a lay Dominican. She wrote from the Wilton Hotel in Victoria:

I take the liberty to beg an interview with you, as the dominican [*sic*] fathers of Oslo want me to call on you. I am a Catholic from Norway, over here principally to see something of the work the English catholics [*sic*] do and see if I can learn something that might come in usefully for our work at home.[130]

---

[129] Ward, *RC* 213–16, 218–20, 222; Titterton, 197, 199.
[130] Sigrid Undset to G. K. Chesterton, 7 May 1928, BL Add. MS 73240, fo. 125.

The letter was acknowledged with the promise that Chesterton would write later. It seems they must have met and kept in touch, for there survives a very brief note of thanks, 'with thanks from yours truly Sigrid Undset', which the Norwegian sent from her home in Lillehammer, dated 25 November 1931.[131] Her greatest work, *Kristin Lavransdatter* (1920–2), had been published a few years before she first wrote to Chesterton in 1928, the year in which later in December she was awarded the Nobel Prize for Literature.

On 9 July 1928 Chesterton chaired a meeting in the Railway Hotel in Beaconsfield, at which a presentation was made to Father Walker, who was leaving the parish. A year previously Chesterton had been on the organizing committee for the celebration of the parish priest's silver jubilee. In his speech Chesterton thanked Father Walker for his help in problems connected with his own 'most disreputable profession' by means of 'a coherent and sane philosophy'.[132] There would not be a resident parish priest in Beaconsfield until 1931, when Monsignor Charles Smith, an ex-army chaplain, arrived and a presbytery was built.[133] Three years later Chesterton would present Monsignor Smith on his silver jubilee with a cheque and an illuminated address composed by himself; the parish priest was doubly honoured, as Ronald Knox came to preach.[134]

In October Chesterton published a selection of his *Illustrated London News* columns, *Generally Speaking: A Book of Essays*. In a piece on the detective story he lays down the excellent principle: 'The whole point of a sensational story is that the secret should be simple. The whole story exists for the moment of surprise; and it should be a moment. It should not be something that it takes twenty minutes to explain, and twenty-four hours to learn by heart, for fear of forgetting it.' Otherwise, more or less familiar themes reappear. Everyone cannot help but be a dogmatist, and there are two kinds: 'the conscious dogmatists and the unconscious dogmatists'. But the latter are 'by far the most dogmatic'. Asia had 'borrowed all the wrong things from Europe', such as 'the costume . . . of the industrial nineteenth century in the big towns', and Europe also 'very largely . . . all the wrong things from Asia', such as its 'despair'. The 'dangerous lack of an intensive national feeling' in imperialist England had led to 'a much too supine

---

[131] Sigrid Undset to G. K. Chesterton, 25 Nov. 1931, BL Add. MS 73240, fo. 127.

[132] *Free Bucks Press*, 29 July 1927; 13 July 1928.

[133] St Teresa's Church, Beaconsfield, parish archives.

[134] *Bucks Free Press*, 6 July 1934.

surrender to other feelings', especially from America. Predicting the future had to involve 'a sort of fatalism', as it was impossible to 'foresee the free part of human action'. We can see what people 'freely chose to do' in the past, whereas it was impossible to foresee what people in the future would choose to do, only what 'they must do'. It was impossible to 'predict new things, because . . . we can only calculate them logically from old things' by projecting 'its lines further into the future'. There were 'three ways of writing history'. There was the 'old Victorian way', which was 'picturesque and largely false'; there was the later academic way, which assumed one could continue to write false history so long as one avoided being 'pictur-esque' on the ground that a lie that was 'dull' would sound as if it was 'true'; and there was a third way, which was 'to use the picturesque (which is a perfectly natural instinct of man for what is memorable), but to make it a symbol of truth and not a symbol of falsehood'. It was 'natural to man to be artificial' in the sense of wearing clothes, for example, unlike the animals who did not need them—but then man had 'everywhere founded his superiorities on his inferiorities'.[135]

The beginning of 1929 saw another controversy with G. G. Coulton, who attacked an article by Chesterton in which he had argued that Catholicism encouraged humility. On 3 January the *Daily Telegraph* pub-lished a letter from Chesterton, in which he 'regretted' that, for all his scholarship and literary gifts, Coulton had 'seen fit to neglect the nature of the thing we call thought. When in his wanderings he meets anything resembling a thought he calls it a merry paradox.' Since Coulton was a medieval scholar, this was especially unfortunate, as the thing the medie-vals were most good at was thinking, and therefore the critic of their thought should possess 'an appetite for abstract thought and a certain freedom from provincial prejudices'. If the Catholic acceptance of Church authority was considered 'abject', then surely this suggested humility rather than arrogance and pride. As for persecution of heretics in the Middle Ages, this again did not indicate pride but belief in the truth of Catholicism. Again, if Catholic pomp and ritual were 'childish', then Catholics must be humble rather than proud. In reply to Coulton's complaint that Chesterton had not dealt with his charges against Catholi-cism, Chesterton rejoined in a letter in the issue of 9 January that these charges were 'irrelevant' to the question of humility. Coulton called for a collaborative work of controversy: 'But what shall we call it? "Stray Thoughts by G. G. Coulton, While not Listening to a Sermon on

---

[135] *GS* 3, 20–2, 40, 132–4, 154, 204–5.

Pride"; or "Pride, by G. K. Chesterton, with Notes on Other Subjects by Dr G. G. Coulton, of St John's College, Cambridge"?' Anyway Chesterton's original article was not for the benefit of Coulton, who still believed in the virtue of humility, but for a new generation 'who think the Victorian respectability of Mr Coulton much more dead and buried than the religion of St Thomas'.

In July Chesterton brought out another collection of short stories that had already been published in *Nash's Magazine* and the *Story Teller*. The poet in *The Poet and the Lunatics*, Gabriel Gale, stands out as a figure of Chestertonian sanity in a mad world. It is Gale who grasps the principle of limitation, that, for example, 'being oneself...is itself limitation. We are limited by our brains and bodies; and if we break out, we cease to be ourselves...'. But, in fact, 'illimitable liberty is itself a limit. It is like the circle, which is at once an eternity and a prison.' It is Gale who sees 'a small thing' as 'a large thing', for it is only by 'looking at some little thing' that he 'can ever learn anything'. According to his philosophy of wonder, 'the main object of a man's life was to see a thing as if he had never seen it before'. And human happiness consists in seeing life as 'a gift or present', a 'surprise', surprise implying that 'a thing came from outside ourselves; and gratitude that it comes from someone other than ourselves'. And it is these 'limits' that 'are the lines of the very plan of human pleasure'. For him as for Chesterton, 'everything has a halo...which makes it sacred'. In practical life, it is not practical but 'unpractical' people who are needed, who can 'see the part that theories play in practical life', for 'most men are what their theories make them'. To deny that 'there are any mysteries', to be merely 'rational', leads to madness. Materialists who 'are at least near enough to heaven to accept the earth and not imagine they made it' are infinitely preferable to Idealists, with their 'dreadful doubts...deadly and damnable doubts', who doubt 'matter and the minds of others and everything except [their] own ego'. Finally, Gale, like Father Brown, who can empathize with criminals because he too is a sinner, has 'a sympathy with lunatics—including literary men' because he too 'has a streak...of the moonshine that leads such men astray'.[136]

In October a collection of articles first published in various magazines and papers appeared entitled *The Thing* (in America it would be published under the title *The Thing: Why I am a Catholic*). As in *The Everlasting Man*, Chesterton emphasizes what he calls the 'balance' of Catholicism.

---

[136] *PL* 17, 51–3, 63–4, 94–5, 97, 122–3, 128–9, 197, 240–1.

Before and after the Reformation the 'revolts' against the Church 'told the same strange story':

Every great heretic . . . always exhibited three remarkable characteristics in combination. First, he picked out some mystical idea from the Church's bundle or balance of mystical ideas. Second, he used that one mystical idea against all the other mystical ideas. Third (and most singular), he seems generally to have had no notion that his own favourite mystical idea was a mystical idea, at least in the sense of a mysterious or dubious or dogmatic idea.

The most obvious example was the Bible. To the impartial observer it had to be the 'strangest' thing in the world that 'men rushing in to wreck a temple, overturning the altar and driving out the priest, found there certain sacred volumes . . . and (instead of throwing them on the fire with the rest) began to use them as infallible oracles rebuking all the other arrangements'. Calvinists had seized on 'the Catholic idea of the absolute knowledge and power of God', Wesleyan Evangelicals in reaction 'seized on the very Catholic idea that mankind has a sense of sin; and they wandered about offering everybody release from his mysterious burden of sin'. Then they in turn were 'quite surprised when the result of Rousseau and the revolutionary optimism began to express itself in men claiming a purely human happiness and dignity'—but the latter had simply 'taken out of the old Catholic tradition . . . the idea that there is a spiritual dignity in man as man, and a universal duty to love men as men'. In each case, out of the Catholic 'sanity and . . . balance' of 'a mind surviving a hundred moods', one idea was extracted as though it were 'absolutely self-evident' and 'nobody could ever destroy that, though in the name of it they destroyed everything else'. The new liberal version of Christianity had also seized upon one idea, that the 'message of Christ was perfectly "simple": that the cure of everything is Love', and that for some strange reason Christ had been 'killed . . . for making this remark', while, ever since his death, 'horrid people called priests' had been obsessed with useless dogmas. This was like objecting to a science of medicine when nothing 'could be simpler than the beautiful gift of Health'.[137]

It was striking that this new religion, which wanted 'a religion without dogma', believed that, while 'it is wrong to be dogmatic, it is essential to be dogmatically Protestant'. This in fact meant that it was essential to be anti-Catholic, for Protestants had not only 'lost faith' in Protestantism but had 'mostly forgotten what it was'. The average Englishman, who assumed one

---

[137] *T.* 152–3, 189–90.

is saved by leading a good life, would be very surprised to hear that 'for three hundred years, the faith in faith alone was the badge of a Protestant, the faith in good works the rather shameful badge of a disreputable Papist'. He would be immediately on the side of Catholicism against Calvinism in preferring 'a God who has made all men for joy, and desires to save them all, to a God who deliberately made some for involuntary sin and immortal misery'. Not only would he not share, but he would not understand, 'the unnatural aversion of the Puritans to all art and beauty in relation to religion'. Wherever 'the Reformation actually put Rome in the dock, Rome has since been acquitted by the jury of the whole world'. As for the real corruptions in the Church prior to the Reformation, none of them was in fact 'reformed' by the Reformation but 'made worse'. For example,

it was an abominable abuse that the corruption of the monasteries sometimes permitted a rich noble to play the patron and even play at being the Abbot, or draw on the revenues supposed to belong to a brotherhood of poverty and charity. But all that the Reformation did was to allow the same rich noble to take over *all* the revenue, to seize the whole house and turn it into a palace or a pig-sty, and utterly stamp out the last legend of the poor brotherhood.

Meanwhile, in the modern world Catholic practices were being 'copied... often caricatured': 'Psycho-analysis is the Confessional without the safeguards of the Confessional; Communism is the Franciscan movement without the moderating balance of the Church; and American sects, having howled for three centuries at the Popish theatricality and mere appeal to the senses, now "brighten" their services by super-theatrical films and rays of rose-red light falling on the head of the minister.' Protestantism really meant little more than a protest against Rome, and, since the 'charges' kept changing, it was 'only in continuity because it is still against Rome': 'In other words, the legend that Rome is wrong anyhow, is still a living thing, though all the features of the monster are now entirely altered in the caricature.' But what sort of a 'tradition' was this that told 'a different story every day or every decade... What sort of holy cause is it to inherit from our ancestors, that we should go on hating something and being consistent only in hatred...?' Chesterton himself had been 'brought up a sort of Universalist and Unitarian; at the feet of that admirable man, Stopford Brooke'. But it was hardly Protestantism 'save in a very negative sense'. The Universalist believed in heaven but not in hell, but he recognized that there must be 'a progress after death, at once punishment and enlightenment', in other words purgatory, in flat contradiction to the old Protestant belief in hell but denial of purgatory, on which Protestantism 'had waged ceaseless war'. What Chesterton, however, discovered to his astonishment was that, although the liberal Christianity of Stopford Brooke rejected 'the Protestant faith', it was 'eager to go on with the Protestant feud'. And this seemed to him 'like a rather ugly breach of honour. To find out that you have been slandering somebody about something, to refuse to apologize, and to make up another more plausible story against him, so that you can carry on the spirit of the slander, seemed to [him] at the start a rather poor way of behaving.' Why were these liberal Christians 'so very illiberal' about the Church of Rome? The 'only logical answer', which 'every fact of life' had confirmed, was that it was so 'hated, as nothing else is hated, simply because it is, in the exact sense of the popular phrase, like nothing on earth'.[138]

Chesterton's satire of Protestant anti-Popery, especially its sheer ignorance of Catholicism, recalls the brilliance of Newman's own satire on Protestant anti-Popery in his *Lectures on the Present Position of Catholics*, a work, as we have seen, that Chesterton greatly admired. Delighted to find in a well-informed paper a report that Rome tolerated 'strange heresies and even bearded and wedded clergy' among Russian-rite Uniate Catholics, he exclaims: 'Only a wild unreason... could thus make even the joints and hinges of that rickety statement rattle and creak with laughter.'

There is in the world, they would tell us, a powerful and persecuting superstition, intoxicated with the impious idea of having a monopoly of divine truth, and therefore cruelly crushing and exterminating everything else as error. It burns thinkers for thinking, discoverers for discovering, philosophers and theologians who differ by a hair's breadth from its dogmas; it will tolerate no tiny change or shadow of variety even among its friends and followers; it sweeps the whole world with one encyclical cyclone of uniformity; it would destroy nations and empires for a word, so wedded is it to its fixed idea that its own word is the Word of God. When it is thus sweeping the world, it comes to a remote and rather barbarous region somewhere on the borders of Russia; where it stops suddenly; smiles broadly; and tells the people there that they can have the strangest heresies they like.... 'By all means worship Baphomet and Beelzebub; say the Lord's Prayer backwards; continue to drink the blood of infants—nay, even,' and here her voice falters, till she rallies with an effort of generous resolution, 'yes, even, if you really must, grow a beard'.

Why 'these particular Eastern Europeans should be regarded with so much favour, or why a number of long hairs on the chin should be regarded with so much disfavour', was 'presumably a question on which

---

[138] *T.* 179–81, 184–9.

this intolerant spiritual tyranny' would 'suffer no question to be asked'. But what the report in the paper did indicate was that something that had been 'left for dead' and dismissed with 'confident contempt' had 'rather incredibly come to life' and aroused an 'irritated', 'rather restless curiosity'. This curiosity Chesterton encountered on another occasion when he heard 'a lady of educated and even elegant pretensions…mention a certain small West Country town', adding 'with a sort of hiss that it contained "a nest of Roman Catholics". This apparently referred to a family [presumably the Nicholls of Lyme Regis] with which I happen to be acquainted. The lady then said, her voice changing to a deep note of doom, "God alone knows what is said and done behind those closed doors." ' Chesterton did not know 'why a Catholic's doors should be any more closed than anybody else's doors; the habit is not unusual in persons of all philosophical beliefs when retiring for the night; and on other occasions depends on the weather and the individual taste.' He supposed the explanation was that there lingered 'the stale savour of a sort of sensational romance about us; as if we were all foreign counts and con-spirators': 'The world still pays us this wild and imaginative compliment of imagining that we are much less ordinary than we really are.' And since Catholic crimes were 'not plotted in public', it stood to reason that 'they must be plotted in private'. It was obviously 'unreasonable' to expect their fellow countrymen 'to suggest anything so fanciful' as that they were 'not plotted anywhere'. Chesterton dreaded to think what would be said if Catholics really did have secret societies like the Freemasons and the Ku Klux Klan. But it was interesting that it was those very people who 'accused us of mummery and mystery who surrounded all their secularis-ing activities with far more fantastic mysteries and mummeries'. The 'mystic materialism' of Catholicism displeased a Protestant like Dean Inge—but could he not see that 'the Incarnation is as much a part of that idea as the Mass; and that the Mass is as much a part of that idea as the Incarnation'. Chesterton simply could not understand 'why a man should accept a Creator who was a carpenter, and then worry about holy water…why he should accept the first and most stupendous part of the story of Heaven on Earth, and then furiously deny a few small but obvious deductions from it…'. This hostility to the sacramental was rooted in a 'horror of matter'. People like Dean Inge wanted worship to be 'wholly spiritual, or even wholly intellectual' out of 'a disgust at the idea of spiritual things having a body and a solid form'. The Dean shrank from the sacramental because he could not 'bear to think how natural is the craving for the supernatural'. It was nothing else but a Manichean 'horror of matter'. That was really why the Dean was opposed to the sacramental—not because '*science* could forbid men to believe in something which science does not profess to investigate'.[139]

Elsewhere Chesterton imagined the Dean's response to the news of 'the recently discovered traces of an actual historical Flood: a discovery which has shaken the Christian world to its foundations by its apparent agreement with the Book of Genesis'. 'I do not see', the Dean declared,

that there is any cause for alarm. Protestantism is still founded on an impregnable rock: on that deep and strong foundation of disbelief in the Bible which supports the spiritual and intellectual life of all true Christians today. Even if dark doubts should arise, and it should seem for the moment as if certain passages in the Scripture story were true, we must not lose heart; the cloud will pass: and we have still the priceless possession of the Open Bible, with all its inexhaustible supply or errors and inconsistencies: a continual source of interest to scholars and a permanent bulwark against Rome . . .

H. G. Wells was imagined as simply exclaiming: 'I am interested in the Flood of the future: not in any of these little local floods that may have taken place in the past.'[140]

The Catholic Church was reproached for its 'superstitions' and 'the deadness of [its] tradition', but the modern world itself had 'reached a curious condition of ritual or routine' and was 'living entirely on the life of tradition'. When it was right about something, it was 'right by prejudice' or 'instinct', whereas the Catholic Church was 'right by principle'. Thus the modern world continued 'to entertain a healthy prejudice against Cannibalism' and the 'next step' in its 'ethical evolution' seemed 'as yet far distant': 'But the notion that there is not very much difference between the bodies of men and animals—that is not by any means far distant, but exceedingly near.' Catholicism was 'the most rational of all religions', 'even, in a sense, the most rationalistic of all religions'. Unfortunately, though, there was 'a very urgent need for a verbal paraphrase of many of the fundamental doctrines, simply because people have ceased to understand them as they were traditionally stated'. Chesterton is thinking of English Catholicism when he says that these doctrines 'need to be stated afresh, and not left in language that is intrinsically correct but practically misleading'. There was one example Chesterton felt very strongly about and wished that 'somebody with better authority' would 'announce in a voice of thunder or with a salute of big guns, the vital and very much

[139] *T.* 191–2, 195, 240, 243, 258–9, 295–6.   [140] Ward, *GKC* 430.

needed truth that "dulcis" is not the Latin for "sweet" '. The word 'sweet' in English had been 'rendered hopelessly sticky by the accident of the word "sweets" '. Besides, the word suggested 'something much more intense and even pungent in sweetness like . . . concentrated sugar'. The problem was that 'English Catholicism, having in the great calamity of our history gone into exile in the sixteenth and seventeenth centuries (at the very moment when our modern language was being finally made), naturally had to seek for its own finest enthusiasms in foreign languages'. Chesterton's wish has never been granted: for example, in one of the most popular Catholic prayers, the 'Salve Regina', the Virgin Mary is addressed in the English version as 'our sweetness' and 'O sweet Virgin Mary'. His own dire verdict was that 'this incongruous and inaccurate repetition of the word "sweet" has kept more Englishmen out of the Catholic Church than all the poison of the Borgias or all the poisonous lies of the people who have written about them'. And it was this 'muddle about words' that 'terribly perpetuated' the 'old slander' of 'a slimy sentimentalism' of which English Catholics were accused.[141]

The so-called slavery of the mind of Catholics consisted merely in 'thinking a certain authority reliable; which is entirely reasonable'. Real 'slavery of the mind' consisted in the inability to 'think of certain things at all', not to be able to state another point of view—or even one's own, to assume 'certain things, in the sense of not even imagining the opposite things'. It was this that was both intellectual and 'imaginative bondage'. Conversion to Catholicism, Chesterton had found, was 'the beginning of an active, fruitful, progressive and even adventurous life of the intellect'. The 'great mysteries' were 'starting-points for trains of thought far more stimulating [and] subtle' than the 'sceptical scratching' of the Modernists. The Catholic Mass opened up 'a magnificent world of metaphysical ideas, illuminating all the relations of matter and mind, of flesh and spirit . . . '. It was the dogmas of Catholicism that were 'living . . . inspiring . . . intellectually interesting'. Far from being 'dull'. the Catholic dogmas were 'living ideas'.[142]

---

[141] *T.* 278, 283–6.   [142] *T.* 289–91, 299–300, 303.

14

Rome and America Again

THE Chestertons and Dorothy Collins were in Rome when *The Thing* was published in October 1929. They spent three months there staying in the Hotel Hassler overlooking the Spanish Steps. Here in a first floor room Chesterton wrote *The Resurrection of Rome*, which would be published the following year.[1] He warned the reader at the beginning of the book that he was 'a bad reporter because everything seems... worth reporting', and he never found 'anything dull'. Indeed, it seemed 'hardly worth while to travel' when everywhere the world seemed to him 'so amusing'. The result was that he lacked 'proportion'. And he proved his point by proceeding to 'mention first the first thing' he 'really noticed' in Rome, which perhaps nobody else had ever noticed and which probably most people would not think 'worth noticing'. It was not something a guidebook or even a book of 'impressions' of Rome would mention. Nevertheless, it was 'an event' in Chesterton's life—'in that inner, infantile and fanciful life which begins with seeing the first Punch and Judy...'. Soon after his arrival he had walked across the road from his hotel, 'filled with no particular aspiration beyond a strong appetite for lunch; and just round the corner of the small street opposite I found a whole huge gateway carved like the face of a gigantic goblin with open jaws'.

It was rather like the Mouth of Hell in the mediaeval pictures and plays. The worthy householder, who lived behind this pleasing façade, had presumably grown accustomed to popping in and out of the monster in the most prim and

---

[1] Sullivan, 163.

respectable way. Whenever he went into his house he was devoured by a giant like the princesses in the fairy-tales. Whenever he came out of his house he was vomited forth by a hideous leviathan . . .[2]

In view of the letters from all over the world inviting Chesterton to lecture, the English College, the Scots College, the North American College, the Beda College, and the Holy Child convent were fortunate to hear him speak.[3] At the dinner that preceded the lecture at the North American College, the Rector instructed the Italian waiter to keep Chesterton's plate full, presumably on the assumption that their huge guest had a huge appetite, whereas Chesterton was usually so busy talking that little eating actually took place. After some time had passed the Rector felt his cassock pulled and 'heard an agitated whisper, "It is now five times I fill him, do I go on?"' Given the leisurely pace of Italian meals, it is quite possible that Chesterton's plate was filled up five times without his ever noticing, absorbed in conversation as he would have been.[4] That peculiarly English meal, afternoon tea, as strange to Chesterton's American host as to the Italian waiter, was presumably made available for English visitors at the Hotel Hassler, as one day the Chestertons invited three small children to join them for tea. When their parents came to collect them, they found Chesterton 'tilted back in a chair, with a large white towel tucked under his collar, being lathered and shaved with a pretended razor by the four-year old visitor'.[5]

At an audience with Mussolini, Chesterton found himself doing most of the talking, being interviewed rather than interviewing. Taken into a large room, he saw at the other end 'a small table . . . from which an alert, square-shouldered man in black got up very rapidly and walked equally rapidly right across the room, till we met not far from the door'. Mussolini shook hands with him and asked in French if he 'minded talking in that language'. Chesterton replied that he spoke 'badly' but would do his best. He found there was a lot of 'fun' in the dictator, who 'laughed readily'. The 'very first thing' he did was to 'dump' Chesterton in a chair and ask about the disestablishment of the Church of England! He put to Chesterton 'a rapid succession of questions covering a wide field', but mostly about England rather than Italy.[6] He wanted Chesterton to explain the Church of England to him, a phenomenon the Englishman 'felt quite unable to

[2] *RR* 283–5.   [3] Ward, *GKC* 489–91.   [4] Ward, *RC* 251.
[5] Dorothy Collins's notes for talks, BL Add. MS 73477, fo. 135.
[6] Sullivan, 163.

make clear to a logical Latin mind'.[7] He astonished Chesterton by asking him about 'the debate on the Revised Prayer-Book'. Something Chesterton said about imperialism 'seemed to arrest his attention sharply and he said, "Ah, that is very interesting. Do you think it possible to give a different turn to the development of England?"' Chesterton replied 'in increasingly halting French' that it was 'very difficult, or perhaps nearly impossible', but that he hoped that England would be 'more self-supporting and less dependent on the ends of the earth', for 'such dependence had become very perilous'. Before he knew where he was, he was holding forth to Mussolini about his 'own fad of Distributism'; at which he became so embarrassed and excited that his 'French went all to pieces'. God only knew in what language he expressed himself in this last part of the conversation, 'or to what wild barbaric tongue, older than Babel, its gasps and nasal noises might be supposed to belong'. Thinking that Mussolini probably thought he was mad, he rose as though to bow himself out. 'He rose also and said, with what was probably irony but was none the less most polished courtesy, "Well, I will go and reflect on what you have told me."' It was, Chesterton thought, this 'self-possession' that made the Italians 'a nation of gentlemen'. As they parted, Chesterton asked to be forgiven for his bad French, at which Mussolini laughed and told him that he, Chesterton, spoke French like he, Mussolini, spoke English. Chesterton realized that as an interviewer he had failed miserably, having, for instance, 'nothing to report about the great Fascist's views on Fascism'.[8] Perhaps the dictator had been as reticent about his views as he was about his command of English, since a friend of Dorothy Collins, who had been teaching him for some months, told her that 'he was so intelligent that he was reading and appreciating Bernard Shaw's play *The Apple Cart* within a few months of instruction'.[9]

Chesterton saw Pope Pius XI three times while he was in Rome. The first time was at a private audience, when the rector of one of the colleges offered to introduce him—'and I have seldom been more grateful for human companionship'. Chesterton had felt nervous on meeting Mussolini, chiefly because *Il Duce* spoke French much better than he did. But it was 'altogether inadequate' to say that he felt nervous on meeting the Pope: in *his* presence he found he could not speak English—'or talk at all'. The Pope had come suddenly out of his study, 'a sturdy figure in a cape, with a square face and spectacles', and began speaking to Chesterton

---

[7] Dorothy Collins's notes for talks, BL Add. MS 73477, fos. 99–100.
[8] *RR* 404–7.   [9] Sullivan, 163.

about his writings, 'saying some very generous things about a sketch I wrote of St Francis of Assisi'. The Pope asked him if he wrote 'a great deal', and Chesterton 'answered in fragmentary French phrases that it was only too true, or words to that effect'. His accompanying 'clerical dignitary nobly struck in' in his support by saying it was his 'modesty', whereas in fact his 'head was in a whirl and it might have been anything'. The Pope then 'made a motion' and they all knelt—and, listening to the words of blessing that followed, Chesterton 'understood for the first time something that was once meant by the ceremonial use of the plural': 'in a flash I saw the sense of something that had always seemed to me a senseless custom of kings.' As the Pope began the blessing with 'a new strong voice, that was hardly even like his own', Chesterton 'knew that something stood there infinitely greater than an individual . . . that it was indeed "We"; We, Peter and Gregory and Hildebrand and all the dynasty that does not die'. As they left the Vatican, he said to 'the clerical dignitary, "That frightened me more than anything I have known in my life." The clerical dignitary laughed heartily.' When one of the party discovered the loss of an umbrella, someone else remarked that this pope of the foreign missions would 'certainly give it to the niggers'. And Chesterton realized that the Pope's 'enthusiasm for the missions' was 'in fact a very strong antagonism to the contempt for the aboriginal races and a gigantic faith in the fraternity of all tribes in the light of the Faith'. When later Chesterton met a 'distinguished Scandinavian' who said 'with shining eyes as one who beholds a vision, "We may yet have a black Pope,"' he responded in 'a spirit of disgraceful compromise' that he 'should be delighted to see a black Cardinal': 'Then I remembered the great King who came to Bethlehem, heavy with purple and crimson and with a face like night; and I was ashamed.' The second time Chesterton saw the Pope was at the beatification of the English martyrs on 15 December, when he heard 'the very long list of those English heroes, who resisted the despotic destruction of the national religion' read out. The third time was when the Pope celebrated Benediction to conclude the process of beatification.[10] According to Dorothy Collins, Chesterton was so excited by meeting the Pope that he could not work for two days after. She also remembered vividly how distressed he was when he lost a medal of the Blessed Virgin Mary that he always wore. The lift boy who eventually found it was richly rewarded for his pains.[11]

On their way home to England the Chestertons and Dorothy Collins visited Max Beerbohm and his wife in a villa overlooking the bay

---

[10] *RR* 451–3.   [11] Ward, *GKC* 493.

of Rapallo. They saw a fresco Beerbohm had drawn over the dining-room door depicting a number of his friends going in to a meal led by Chesterton. They also met Ezra Pound and his wife, who were living in Rapallo. Pound was full of a financial scheme that was to save the world, a scheme, he told Dorothy, that had the active support of Beerbohm. On being told of this, Beerbohm commented: 'Am I? One has only to smile, look pleasant and avoid an argument, to be accused of supporting something one knows nothing about.'[12]

2

On 31 October 1929 *G.K.C. as M.C.*, a selection of the introductions that Chesterton had written for books published between 1903 and 1929, had been published in England. In the opening essay on Boswell Chesterton justified selections (not that he had himself edited this selection): the universe itself cannot be seen in its 'unity' but only 'in selections'. If there was no justification for dipping into a book, then there was no 'justification for dipping into existence'. Everyone is born in 'the middle of something'. If all things 'fragmentary' are 'useless', then the whole of life is useless.[13]

But the chief interest of this essay is what Chesterton has to say about the art of biography. So-called realistic biography, which 'exhibits the things of which a man is ashamed', 'does *not* give the true portrait of a man' for 'the very fact that he is ashamed of them shows that they are not typical of the man'. Boswell had not had to resort to 'privacies' in order successfully to give 'a most intimate and powerful picture of a human being'. He had only described Johnson as he was 'on the surface', but he had read 'that surface like a man of genius': 'He paints him in the street, but sees his soul walking there in the sunlight.' Boswell's success provided 'an almost inexhaustible evidence of the falsehood of the realistic or keyhole method'. Unlike Carlyle, about whom we know 'all the parlour and bedroom details' and yet the man remained 'a mystery', Johnson had been 'painted by a genius' and there was 'no more mystery about him'. Far from being 'an unsavoury gossiper and detailer of private things', Boswell had 'achieved a greater triumph of psychological analysis without using one private fact or one indiscreet word'. This did not mean that Boswell had suppressed Johnson's faults, for 'he was the

[12] Sullivan, 163–4.   [13] *MC* 3.

first who discovered that in biography the suppression of a man's faults did not merely wreck truth, but wrecked his virtues'. He had 'discovered that it was not necessary to praise a man in order to admire him'. Nevertheless Boswell's 'victory' was 'proved by his defeat': 'so real' had he made Johnson's 'daily and conversational life' that people had taken it too seriously, admiring Johnson's conversation not simply 'as conversation' but as literature. This 'over-solemn treatment' ran the danger of losing 'the humorous atmosphere' of his circle, 'the peculiar uproar and frivolity of the table at Johnson's Club'. And, of course, for Chesterton there was no simple antithesis between seriousness and frivolity: 'Frivolity is, in a sense, far more sacred than seriousness.' People were less disinclined to speak of 'a family tragedy' than a 'family joke'. Chesterton thought that Johnson's *Lives of the Poets*, 'with their excellent thumb-nail sketches and rule-of-thumb criticisms', came 'nearer than anything else he wrote to the almost rollicking sagacity of his conversation'. And yet the truth was that Johnson was 'more vivid to us' in Boswell's life than in any of the books he wrote. After all, in his books he was 'all alone, and Johnson had a great dislike of being all alone'. In his books we can 'overhear Johnson in soliloquy', but for the 'comedy' we have to go to Boswell's descriptions of 'his clash with other characters'. The 'essential comedy' of Johnson lay in an 'unconscious and even agreeable' contradiction in his character: 'a strenuous and sincere belief in convention, combined with a huge natural inaptitude for observing it'. But Johnson was 'immortal' because of his 'gigantic and detached good sense'—not least in seeing the 'fallacy' in the modern idea of 'progress'—namely, 'that as human history really goes one had only to be old-fashioned long enough to be in the very newest fashion. . . . that by lagging behind the times one can generally get in front of them'. But the ultimate Chestertonian accolade is that 'he touched nothing that he did not touch with a certain mighty strength of controlled laughter', a laughter that was paradoxically 'perhaps least present when he was deliberately and consciously at play', there being 'a sort of humorous atmosphere round much of his work that was then counted most serious', while 'a more melancholy atmosphere clings to everything that could be counted more light'. However, Johnson did have one serious fault: the 'absence of the pleasures of religion', perhaps 'the only gap in the mind of that great religious genius'; but it was a lack that characterized the eighteenth century, which lacked 'colour', seeing 'everything in black and white', with the result that its religion had 'not enough positive joy'. As for Boswell's life, it was a great biography because it was a book 'in which the book vanishes and the man remains; not the man who wrote the book but the man about whom it was written'.[14] It was the same compliment that Chesterton had paid Wilfrid Ward's life of Newman: in a good biography the biographer disappears so that the subject may appear.

The same was true, though to a lesser extent, of Forster's *Life of Dickens*, where the biographer's triumph was 'to draw Dickens out' just as it had been 'the genius of Dickens to draw everybody out'. Yet this 'drawing out' was not 'of that triumphant and almost faultless kind which exists in the great model of biography'. For Forster had not been able to 'draw Dickens out as Boswell could draw Johnson out'. Still, his 'success was of the same essential sort; though he generally achieved it more by reporting correspondence than conversation'. Because the subject of his study was not only a 'creator' but a 'character', indeed 'a Dickens character', he 'must be encouraged to give himself away; as it is the essence of every Dickens character to give himself away'. And Forster had succeeded in creating 'a very vivid impression of a very vivacious person; we do feel that he is walking briskly about the street and not that he is lying in a coffin helpless under funeral orations; and that is victory in the arduous art of biography'.[15]

Turning to religion and politics, Chesterton thought that the right religion goes hand in hand with the right politics in 'the close kinship between Christianity and the democratic sentiment'. On the other hand, he detected a 'tendency of all fine naturalistic thought towards oligarchy', whose thinkers are unable to 'understand the divine vulgarity of the Christian religion'. In Protestant northern Europe the feast of Christmas had been 'kept up ... by a dull democratic tenacity', even 'through the madness of Calvinism'. The real 'hero' of Christmas, of course, for Chesterton is Dickens, who 'came just in time to save the embers of the Yule Log from being trampled out': 'Dickens struck in time, and saved a popular institution while it was still popular. A hundred aesthetes are always ready to revive it as soon as it has become unpopular.' But it was 'precisely because he was a man of the people that he was able to perpetuate the popular hold upon one of the customs that had only begun to slip from the popular grasp'. In defending Christmas in *The Christmas Carol*, Dickens waged war on 'an old miser named Scrooge', just as he was to do battle with 'a new miser named Gradgrind' in *Hard Times*. Not only did the new miser have 'the old avarice' but the old miser had

[14] *MC* 5–10, 65–7, 73–4, 197, 200–1.   [15] *MC* 238–41.

'the new arguments', for Scrooge was 'a utilitarian and an individualist', uttering 'all the sophistries' by which 'the age of machinery' had 'tried to turn the virtue of charity into a vice'. But this was 'something of an understatement', for Scrooge was 'more modern than Gradgrind', belonging 'not only to the hard times of the middle of the nineteenth century, but to the harder times of the beginning of the twentieth century; the yet harder times in which we live': 'Many amiable sociologists will say, as he said, "Let them die and decrease the surplus population." The improved proposal is that they should die before they are born.' But even Scrooge did not seek to bully the despised masses like the intellectuals of Chesterton's day. After all, he believed 'at least in the negative liberty of the Utilitarians':

He partook of gruel while his nephew partook of punch; but it never occurred to him that he could forcibly forbid a grown man like his nephew to consume punch, or coerce him into consuming gruel. In that he was far behind the ferocity and tyranny of the social reformers of our own day. If he refused to subscribe to a scheme for giving people Christmas dinners, at least he did not subscribe (as the reformers do) to a scheme for taking away the Christmas dinners they have already got.

No, to do such things 'he would need to be the more enlightened employee of a more progressive age': 'These antics were far beyond the activities of poor Scrooge, whose figure shines by comparison with something of humour and humanity.'[16]

Chesterton's essay on Matthew Arnold is one of the two most interesting pieces in this collection. On the one hand, Chesterton has no time for Arnold's lack of any 'feeling of familiarity with the loves and hungers of the common man, which is the essence of the egalitarian sentiment'. His contempt for the masses disgusts Chesterton: 'He contemptuously dismissed the wage-earning, beer-drinking, ordinary labourers of England as "merely populace". They are not populace; they are merely mankind. If you do not like them you do not like mankind.' Arnold may have been a republican, 'but he was not a democrat'. There was a certain 'pride' that was 'natural to him and prevented him...from having an adequate degree of popular sympathy'. On the other hand, he did have 'a cold humility'—as opposed to 'that hot humility which is the fascination of saints and good men'—'which he had discovered to be a mere essential of the intelligence': 'To see things clearly, he said, you must "get yourself out of the way".' Windows, he understood, needed to be washed not painted

---

[16] *MC* 15, 17, 92, 150–2, 154–5.

if one was to see out of them, but he 'found the window of the English soul opaque with its own purple'; 'so gorgeously' had 'the Englishman... painted his own image' on it that 'it had no opening on the world without':

The Englishman could not see (for instance) that the French revolution was a far-reaching, fundamental and most practical and successful change in the whole structure of Europe.... The Englishman could not see that the Catholic Church was (at the very least) an immense and enduring Latin civilization, linking us to the lost civilizations of the Mediterranean. He really thought it was a sort of sect.

Again, Chesterton thoroughly approves of one aspect of Arnold's pride as opposed to his humility: 'He prided himself not upon telling the truth but upon telling the unpopular half-truth.' Thus he criticized contemporaries like Carlyle 'not for telling falsehoods but simply for telling popular truths'. Far from being the 'Jeremiah' he 'professed to be', Carlyle was 'really a demagogue, and, in one sense, even a flatterer': 'He told Englishmen that they were Teutons, that they were Vikings, that they were practical politicians—all the things they like to be told they are, all the things that they are not.' Arnold, in contrast, reminded the English of 'the vital fact that we are Europeans': 'He had a consciousness of Europe much fuller and firmer than that of any of the great men of his great epoch.' Arnold certainly wanted, 'as every sane European wishes, that the nations that make up Europe should continue to be individual'—but at the same time 'he did wish that the contributions should be contributions, parts, that is, of a common cause and unity, the cause and unity of European civilization'. However, because Arnold prided himself upon telling only 'the half-truth that was neglected', he 'reached at times a fanaticism that was all the more extraordinary because it was a fanaticism of moderation, an intemperance of temperance'. Thus he understood and rightly pointed out 'the fault of the Mid-Victorian English was that they did not have any sense of definite excellence'; but he failed to notice that his own 'celebration of excellence when carried past a certain point might become a very considerable madness', as mad as that 'extreme... vulgar and indiscriminate acceptance' that he condemned: 'It is true that a man is in some danger of becoming a lunatic if he builds a stucco house and says it is as fine as the Parthenon. But surely a man is equally near to a lunatic if he refuses to live in any house except the Parthenon.' Similarly, Arnold's 'definition of Culture which he thought so comprehensive, knowing the best that has been said and thought on this or that subject', was 'a good definition within the field of literature; but the field of culture is much wider than the field of literature'. For culture was 'not only knowing the best that has been said' but 'also knowing the best that has been done, and even doing our best to do it'. Arnold's definition of culture was unashamedly elitist, but Chesterton's definition is characteristically democratic and more comprehensive, including as it does the creative achievements of the despised masses: 'the agricultural labourer does make a hedge with a bill-hook as much as a sculptor makes a statue of Hercules with a chisel.'[17]

The ruling class of Chesterton's day assumed that the masses made good colonists but that it was 'no good' to ask them to 'colonize' their own country. According to their 'creed', 'the common Englishman can get on anywhere' but 'the common Englishman cannot get on in England'. It was thought 'amusing' that the common Englishman 'might live in his own house as in his own hat', that 'a farm should belong to a farmer', that 'private property is proper to every private citizen'. Chesterton noticed how contemporary satirists made 'fun of common life' but lacked the early Victorians' 'firm, fresh, and unaffected conviction that the great ones of this earth are comic also'. On the other hand, Chesterton deplored in 'the Victorians' conception of success ... a certain conception of the elect who were above temptation'. As for the Comtean religion of humanity, by contrast, 'the paradox of taking an irreligious humanity as a religion', which appealed to a Victorian like George Eliot, it seemed strange to Chesterton 'to worship a humanity that is not worshipping': 'So much of what is best in our race is bound up with its religious emotions and traditions, that to worship it without those intimations of the best would come very near to worshipping it at its worst. ... A self-contained and self-centred humanity would chill us in the same way as a self-contained and self-centred human being. For the spiritual hungers of humanity are never merely hungers for humanity.' The only way of loving all human beings was to look at them 'in a certain light'—'and the most agnostic of us know that it is not exactly identical with the light of common day'.[18]

The other most interesting essay in the book is an introduction to The Book of Job, published significantly in 1907, the year before the publication of *The Man who was Thursday*. Chesterton prefaces the introduction by arguing that to attempt to understand the Old Testament one has to realize the essential fact that it has 'a quite perceptible unity', its 'main idea' being 'the idea of all men being the instruments of a higher power': 'The central idea of the great part of the Old Testament may be called the loneliness of God. God is not only the chief character of the Old Testament; God is

[17] *MC* 19–20, 23–6, 233–4.   [18] *MC* 54, 79, 118, 157–8, 161, 192, 272.

properly the only character in the Old Testament. . . . All the patriarchs and prophets are merely His tools or weapons . . .'. In the Book of Job God employs 'the logical weapon of the true mystic', 'a higher scepticism' than the scepticism of the sceptics, when he deals with 'the arrogant asserter of doubt', not by telling him 'to stop doubting' but by telling him 'to go on doubting, to doubt a little more, to doubt every day newer and wilder things in the universe, until at last, by some strange enlightenment, he may begin to doubt himself'. God's 'refusal . . . to explain His design is itself a burning hint of His design. The riddles of God are more satisfying than the solutions of man.' For Job is 'comforted' by 'the enigmas of Jehovah', although they 'seem darker and more desolate than the enigmas of Job': 'He has been told nothing, but he feels the terrible and tingling atmosphere of something which is too good to be told.' One of 'the splendid strokes' of this 'religious' rather than 'philosophical' work is that 'God rebukes alike the man who accused, and the man who defended Him', that 'He knocks down pessimists and optimists with the same hammer': 'God says, in effect, that if there is one fine thing about the world, as far as men are concerned, it is that it cannot be explained.' God is determined to make Job 'see a startling universe if He can only do it by making Job see an idiotic universe. To startle man God becomes for an instant a blasphemer; one might almost say that God becomes for an instant an atheist.' God's description of creation 'is a sort of psalm or rhapsody of the sense of wonder. The maker of all things is astonished at the things He has Himself made.' Far from proving to Job that 'it is an explicable world', God 'insists that it is a much stranger world than Job ever thought it was'. But God contrives 'to let fall here and there in the metaphors, in the parenthetical imagery, sudden and splendid suggestions that the secret of God is a bright and not a sad one—semi-accidental suggestions, like light seen for an instant through the cracks of a closed door'. The 'lesson' of the Book of Job is that 'man is most comforted by paradoxes'.[19]

2

In 1930 Chesterton became the first president or 'Ruler' of the Detection Club, the brainwave of Anthony Berkeley Cox, the mystery writer, one of whose three pseudonyms was Anthony Berkeley, who had written to

---

[19] *MC* 37–9, 45–9, 51.

Chesterton in 1929 saying that the club he wished to found 'would be quite incomplete without the creator of Father Brown'. Chesterton wrote an article in the May 1933 issue of the *Strand Magazine* about the Club that he called 'a very small and quiet conspiracy, to which I am proud to belong'. Meetings took place in various restaurants, at which members discussed 'various plots and schemes of crimes'. In the article Chesterton divulged details of the initiation ceremony, which was held once a year for new members, who had to have written two mysteries and to have been sponsored by two members, 'thereby setting a good example to the Mafia, the Ku Klux Klan, the Illuminati...and all the other secret societies which now conduct the greater part of public life, in the age of Publicity and Public Opinion'. As Chesterton

sat waiting in total darkness, enthroned on a dais, ceremonially robed in a scarlet-and-black Mandarin coat, and wearing a tiny pillbox hat...The doors were flung open and the members entered in a procession, the first carrying [a] skull on a black cushion, flanked by torch bearers; then came the other wardens with the implements of their trade—daggers, guns, vials of poison, and blunt instruments. The Ruler (Chesterton) called out in a great voice, 'What mean these lights, these ceremonies, and this reminder of our mortality?'

The new member had to promise that his or her detectives would 'well and truly detect the crimes presented to them using those wits which it may please you to bestow upon them and not placing reliance on nor making use of Divine Revelation, feminine Intuition, Mumbo Jumbo, Jiggery-Pokery, Coincidence or Act of God'. 'Do you solemnly swear', the candidate was asked, 'never to conceal a vital clue from the reader?' 'Do you promise to observe a seemly moderation in the use of Gangs, Conspiracies, Death-rays, Ghosts, Hypnotism, Trap-Doors, Chinamen, Super-Criminals and Lunatics; and utterly and for ever to forswear Mysterious Poisons unknown to Science?' And finally: 'Do you, as you hope to increase your Sales, swear to observe faithfully all these promises which you have made, so long as you are a member of the Club?' If the new member fails to keep their promises, then, the Ruler pronounces: 'May other writers anticipate your plots, may your publishers do you down in your contracts, may strangers sue you for libel, may your pages swarm with misprints and may your sales continually diminish. Amen!'[20] One could easily see the hand of Chesterton in these oaths or promises of initiation, but according to Evelyn Waugh they were adapted from a

[20] Ward, *GKC* 466–7; Dale, 272.

code of rules set out in Ronald Knox's introduction to *The Best Detective Stories of the Year*, published in 1928, a year before the founding of the Club.[21] If so, it was Dorothy Sayers who was responsible for the adaptation, since it was she who drew up, in the words of Anthony Berkeley, the 'most ceremonious ritual' used for admitting new members.[22]

According to Chesterton, perhaps 'the most characteristic thing that the Detection Club ever did was to publish a detective story, which was quite a good detective story, but the best things in which could not possibly be understood by anybody except the gang of criminals that had produced it'. *The Floating Admiral: A Detective Novel of all the Talents* by 'Certain Members of the Detection Club' was published in 1931 by Hodder and Stoughton, with an introduction by Dorothy Sayers and a prologue by Chesterton, and with contributions from among others Agatha Christie, Dorothy Sayers, Ronald Knox, and Freeman Wills Crofts.[23] It was

written somewhat uproariously in the manner of one of those 'paper games' in which each writer in turn continues a story of which he knows neither head nor tail. It turned out remarkably readable, but the joke of it will never be discovered by the ordinary reader; for the truth is that almost every chapter thus contributed by an amateur detective is a satire on the personal peculiarities of the last amateur detective.

The book sold reasonably well, and out of the proceeds 'a sort of garret' (in Gerrard Street in Soho), according to Knox, was rented to serve as 'Club Rooms; and on the night after we all received our keys the premises were burglariously entered; why or by whom it is still a mystery, but it was a good joke that it should happen to the Detective Club'.[24] Dorothy Sayers wrote to tell Chesterton how 'delighted' she was to learn from his remarks about the book in his column in the *Illustrated London News* that he did not think 'too badly' of the book: it was 'especially gratifying to find that you—alone of our critics—had appreciated our little digs at one another'.[25]

[21] Evelyn Waugh, *The Life of Ronald Knox* (London: Chapman & Hall, 1959), 189 n. 1.

[22] Anthony Berkeley to Dorothy Collins, 1 May 1931, BL Add. MS 73481B, fo. 102. See also James Brabazon, *Dorothy L. Sayers: The Life of a Courageous Woman* (London: Victor Gollancz, 1981), 144; Barbara Reynolds, *Dorothy L. Sayers: Her Life and Soul* (London: Hodder & Stoughton, 1993), 242.

[23] Ward, *GKC* 468, wrongly attributes the introduction to Chesterton.

[24] Ward, *GKC* 468.

[25] Dorothy L. Sayers to G. K. Chesterton, 12 Jan. 1932, BL Add. MS 73481B, fo. 68.

On 27 July 1930 one of 'the most amusing events' in Chesterton's life took place when he took the chair at a dinner to celebrate Belloc's sixtieth birthday. There were about forty guests, 'nearly all of them were what is called important in the public sense, and the rest were even more important in the private sense, as being his nearest intimates and connections'. It seemed to Chesterton 'something between the Day of Judgment and a dream, in which men of many groups known to me at many times, all appeared together as a sort of resurrection'. It was 'specially impressed' on Chesterton that there were to be no speeches; that only he, as the chairman, 'was to be permitted to say a few words in presenting Belloc with a golden goblet modelled on certain phrases in his heroic poem in praise of wine, which ends by asking that such a golden cup should be the stirrup-cup of his farewell to friends'. Accordingly, Chesterton 'merely said a few words to the effect that such a ceremony might have been as fitting thousands of years ago, at the festival of a great Greek poet', and that he was 'confident that Belloc's sonnets and strong verse would remain like the cups and the carved epics of the Greeks'.

He acknowledged it briefly, with a sad good humour, saying he found that, by the age of sixty, he did not care very much whether his verse remained or not. 'But I am told,' he added with suddenly reviving emphasis, 'I am told that you begin to care again frightfully when you are seventy. In which case, I hope I shall die at sixty-nine.' And then we settled down to the feast of old friends, which was to be so happy because there were no speeches.[26]

Towards the end of the dinner somebody whispered to Chesterton that 'it would perhaps be better if a word were said in acknowledgement of the efforts of somebody else' whose name Chesterton had forgotten, 'who was supposed to have arranged the affair'. Chesterton therefore 'briefly thanked' the supposed benefactor, who in his turn denied that he had been responsible because 'the real author of the scheme' was his right-hand neighbour, who 'rose solemnly to acknowledge the abruptly transferred applause; glanced to his own right, and warmly thanked whoever happened to be sitting there . . . for having inspired him with this grand conception of a banquet for Belloc'. His neighbour on the right in his turn 'explained that the gentleman on his own right . . . had been the true and deep and ultimate inspiration of this great idea; and that it was only fitting that the secret of his initiative should be now revealed'. By now 'the logic of the jest was in full gallop and could not be restrained', even if Chesterton

[26] *A.* 288–9.

had 'wished to restrain it'. When it was E. C. Bentley's turn, he 'gave one glance to his own right, and rose with exactly that supercilious gravity' that Chesterton remembered so vividly from the days of the Junior Debating Club, responding with his 'bland solemnity' and in his 'precise enunciation' that

he had himself followed through life one simple and sufficient rule. In all problems that arose, he had been content to consult exclusively the opinion of Professor Eccles. In every detail of daily life, in his choice of a wife, of a profession, of a house, of a dinner, he had done no more than carry out whatever Professor Eccles might direct. On the present occasion any appearance he might have had of arranging the Belloc dinner was in fact a mask for Professor Eccles' influence.

In the end, every single guest ended up making an after-dinner speech at a dinner 'at which there were to be no speeches'.[27] The most lasting effect of the dinner was Sir James Gunn's *Conversation Piece*, the idea of which came to the painter during the dinner, and which was to be exhibited in the Royal Academy's summer exhibition of 1932.[28]

Douglas Woodruff, the future editor of the Catholic periodical the *Tablet* and at the time a young journalist on *The Times*, had been detailed to bring Chesterton safely to the dinner and on time. He therefore accompanied Chesterton in 'the high old-fashioned car' the Chestertons used to hire in Beaconsfield. On arriving in London, they went first to *The Times*, where Woodruff had to correct some proofs. Chesterton was 'seized with the idea that it would be very good fun for him to enter Printing House Square and have it announced that it was Mr Chesterton come to write the leaders, having brought the thunder [*The Times* was known as *The Thunderer*] with him under his cloak'. Early in the drive to London Chesterton had been 'speculating about who would be at the party, and when he had suggested various figures who were certainly not going to be there he said with a mixture of regret and acceptance, "There is always such a *sundering* quality about Belloc's quarrels." ' However, when it came to propose the toast, 'he said at once that if he or anybody else in the room was remembered at all in the future it would be because they had been associated with the guest of the evening. He meant that.'[29]

Woodruff knew of no one who 'more naturally distinguished between a man and his views, or found easier the theological injunction to hate the sin but love the sinner'. One of the few occasions he remembered Chesterton as being 'hurt' himself was when he met Stanley Baldwin, three

[27] *A*. 289–91.   [28] See above, pp. 293–4.   [29] Ward, *GKC* 472.

times Conservative prime minister, 'and had not been welcomed as a fellow Englishman sharing immense things like the love of the English country or English letters, but with a cold correctitude from a politician who seemed chiefly conscious he was meeting in G.K. a man who week by week sought to bring political life into hatred, ridicule and contempt'. In fact, Woodruff did not think that the polemical journalism of Belloc and Cecil came naturally to Chesterton, and it was only his 'loyal affection for them' that made him follow in their steps. Woodruff remembered him as happiest of all when he was prosecuting in one of the mock trials that were held every summer during the last ten years of his life at the London School of Economics in aid of the King Edward VII Hospital. He loved these 'trials' of well-known personalities because they gave him the opportunity to indulge in two of his favourite pastimes, debating and amateur theatricals. Other celebrities who agreed to take part in these charitable events and who 'rarely unbent like that in public . . . were wholly facetious and trivial'. Chesterton, on the contrary, saw nothing incongruous in both acting for the fun of it and seriously debating. Once when he had been prosecuting leading headmasters of public schools, Woodruff 'found they were volubly nettled at the drastic and serious case he had made inside the stage setting of burlesque, and seemed to think he had not been playing the game when he wrapped up so much meaning in his speech and examinations'. But, of course, Chesterton never made any such rigid distinction between the serious and the comic: 'It had come perfectly naturally to make wholly real and material points even in a mock trial and with a wealth of fun.' Like Chesterton's neighbour at Overstrand Mansions, Rann Kennedy, Woodruff was fascinated by the way in which he would stand reading a book

here and there, not a process which could be called dipping, but a kind of sucking out of the printed contents, as though he were a vacuum cleaner and you could see the lines of type leaving the page and being absorbed. When he put it down it was to discuss . . . the book as a man fully possessed of its whole standpoint.

Woodruff noted his extensive knowledge of Newman's writings—' "You cannot catch me out about Newman," he said, with a joy of battle' to some Oxford dons when he was addressing a Catholic dining society. In general, though, Woodruff was struck by how 'he was curiously content to read what happened to come his way and to rely upon his friends for references and facts, remembering what they might tell him, but not ordering the books which would have greatly strengthened him in the sort of newspaper arguments in which he was so often employed'. His library at Top Meadow 'gave the impression' that the books 'had assembled themselves'. He was not, Woodruff recalled, the only well-known journalist living in Beaconsfield, since J. L. Garvin, the famous editor of the *Observer*, was a neighbour—not that Chesterton saw him 'very much' but he, Chesterton, liked 'to think that that great factory' was 'steaming night and day'.[30]

In August 1930 Chesterton published *Four Faultless Felons*, a collection of stories that had first appeared in *Cassell's Magazine* and the *Storyteller*. The four alleged felons, who belong to the Club of Men Misunderstood and tell their stories to an American journalist, are in fact heroes. But as would-be felons, they face a judicial system, which, in Chesterton's view, would be more effective if it had a sense of humour:

I think the world is much too solemn and severe about punishments; it would be far better if it were ruled like a nursery. People don't want penal servitude and execution and all the rest. What most people want is to have their ears boxed or be sent to bed. What fun it would be to take an unscrupulous millionaire and make him stand in the corner! Such an appropriate penalty.

Not only criminal offences need to be punished with humour, but also moral defects like the pomposity of a politician: 'What is needed in such a case?...A few healthful weeks standing on one leg and meditating on that fine shade of distinction between oneself and God Almighty, which is so easily overlooked.' But in a so-called civilized country like England, it is the poor man who is treated as a criminal, 'actually *punished* for being in want', 'called a criminal for *asking* for sympathy'. Fortunately, there are good as well as bad paradoxes, and Chesterton uses one in 'The Honest Quack' to illustrate his principle of limitation: 'But I say to you, always have in your garden a Forbidden Tree. Always have in your life something that you may not touch. That is the secret of being young and happy for ever. There was never a story as true as that story you call a fable.' Limitation is also essential for religious people who believe such fables and who 'have...wild visions...who want to expiate and to pray for this wicked world', for they 'can't really do it anyhow and all over the place. They have to live by rule. They have to go into monasteries...'.[31]

---

[30] Ward, *GKC* 472–3, 475–6.   [31] *FFF* 40, 47, 101, 124–5, 150.

3

In September 1930 Chesterton left for a second lecture tour of America. It was an invitation from the President of the Catholic University of Notre Dame in Indiana that occasioned this second trip. On 5 April 1929 Father Charles L. O'Donnell had written a memorandum for Robert Sencourt, an English writer of biography, criticism, and history, who was apparently on a visit to Notre Dame (no doubt lecturing) and whom the President had asked if he would make an approach to Chesterton with a view to his lecturing at Notre Dame. The idea was that Chesterton should give a six-week course of lectures, which would be 'part of the regular curriculum for which students...would receive credit toward their degree'. The President wanted the lectures to be given during either 'the spring term or the fall term', which would mean during either the last two weeks of April and the whole month of May or during October and the first two weeks of November. But the University would 'much prefer' that the lectures should be given during the spring term. There would be one lecture a day during 'the six class days of the week'. The 'lecture period' would be fifty minutes long. But if Chesterton preferred that 'certain days should be entirely free from lectures it could be arranged that two lectures a day would be given'. The subject of the lectures would be left to Chesterton, but Father O'Donnell suggested that there should be two courses on English literature and English history, with three lectures in each course given each week. The President could offer 'a flat fee of $5,000.00, plus expenses from England direct to Notre Dame and return'. If Chesterton could come in the spring term, then the University would like to confer on him an honorary degree at 'the Commencement exercises'. On 23 May Sencourt wrote from France to say that he had heard that day that Chesterton was ready to accept the invitation provided his wife's health permitted. Chesterton's secretary had asked Sencourt to make it plain that Chesterton would not go to Notre Dame without his wife and so his acceptance was conditional on her being 'really strong enough to take the journey'. Sencourt thought there was plenty of time for Frances to recuperate from an operation for appendicitis that she had recently undergone. He advised the President now to write directly to Chesterton and tell him what his 'plans and hopes' were. He warned him that his wife's accommodation at Notre Dame would be 'uppermost in his mind' and the President should reassure him on that point. He ended by thanking the President for a copy of a book of his poems, which he was pleased to tell him he was arranging to review in the *Times Literary Supplement*.[32]

Accordingly, Father O'Donnell wrote to Chesterton on 7 June to assure him that the University would be 'most happy to welcome Mrs Chesterton' and that arrangements would be made in due course for him and his wife 'to live in the neighborhood of the University'. He was sure that 'comfortable quarters' could be found. He assumed that Chesterton would be coming in the spring term. He asked Chesterton to leave it to the University to announce that he would be coming to Notre Dame when all the arrangements had been made. To 'refresh' Chesterton's memory of the terms of the invitation, he was copying into the letter the memorandum he had given to Sencourt. On the same day O'Donnell wrote to Sencourt to say that it would 'complicate arrangements a little bit but provide no insuperable obstacle' if Mrs Chesterton came too. He doubted if accommodation could be found on the University campus, but was sure that 'delightful quarters at reasonable rates' could be found in 'the near neighborhood'. He asked Sencourt to send him a copy of the *Times Literary Supplement* in which his review would appear. On 21 June Dorothy Collins wrote to confirm that, provided they were both well, the Chestertons planned to come to Notre Dame in April next year. She emphasized that there was no question of Chesterton coming if Frances was unable to accompany him, but she had made 'a splendid recovery' from her operation and the doctors saw no reason why she should not be well enough to accompany Chesterton next spring. She assumed that the President knew that the Chestertons enjoyed 'a very quiet life and would much prefer that there should be as few public functions and publicity during their visit to America as possible'.[33]

On 16 January 1930 Father O'Donnell wrote again to Chesterton asking him to confirm that he would be coming in April; on receiving confirmation, he would send an advance payment to cover the travelling expenses. On 23 January Dorothy Collins wrote to confirm that Chesterton would begin lecturing on Monday 14 April and conclude on Saturday 24 May. She now informed the President that she herself would be accompanying the Chestertons. They understood that there should be no difficulty about accommodation as they had heard that there was 'a quiet and comfortable hotel' at Notre Dame. She would write again but in the meantime she informed him that they would be probably be in America for a week or two before coming to Notre Dame

[32] UNDA, UPCO 1/80.   [33] UNDA, UPCO 1/80.

as Chesterton had been asked to give some public lectures. The Notre Dame publicity director accordingly announced that 'the famous British journalist and author' had accepted an invitation to come to the University to give two courses of lectures from April to June, when he would give the commencement address and receive an honorary doctorate. The announcement, somewhat curiously, described Chesterton as being, 'if not one of the really great men of contemporary literature, certainly... one of the most discussed and caricatured'. He was following in the footsteps of his brother Cecil, 'who lectured at the University more than twenty years ago'.[34]

It was presumably after this announcement that Lee Keedick, 'the leading American lecture agent', who had arranged the previous American lecture tour, travelled to Top Meadow to try and persuade Chesterton to give 'a few lectures throughout the States before returning to England'. Both the Chestertons, in the words of Dorothy Collins, had been 'very doubtful whether they could face the rush of American life again', and Keedick's proposal would involve even more 'travelling, press interviews, photographs, and a vast amount of hospitality and hotel'. But eventually, given the constant need to raise money for *G.K.'s Weekly*, Chesterton agreed on the basis of a promise that 'everything would be very easy and that only a few lectures would be arranged'. In retrospect, Dorothy Collins was to wonder how many a lot of lectures would have meant.[35] There was the usual financial arrangement: one half of the fees earned would go to Keedick, who had to pay the travelling expenses, and the other half to Chesterton, out of which he would pay 10 per cent to the London agent who had introduced him to Keedick, the expenses of his wife and secretary, as well as a substantial present to the latter.[36]

Then the blow fell. On 18 February Dorothy cabled O'Donnell that Chesterton was ill and that the doctor forbad a visit to America before the autumn. She had in fact written a letter four days before, which had not yet reached America when the telegram arrived. In the letter she explained that Chesterton had been ill since Christmas, and that when he had seemed to be recovering he had had a relapse that had turned to pleurisy and he had been in bed ever since. The specialist who had seen him that day advised that he should do nothing for at least three months, as the

---

[34] UNDA, UPCO 1/80, 85.

[35] Dorothy Collins, 'notes for a talk to a womens meeting in Beaconsfield' [*sic*], dated 1932. BL Add. MS 73478C, fo. 47. Hereafter referred to as 'American Notes'.

[36] Ward, *GKC* 500.

strain on his heart would be too great, but that as things stood there was no reason why he should not be well enough in the autumn to visit America. The reason why O'Donnell had not been told earlier about the illness was that, but for the relapse, Chesterton would probably have been well enough to go to America. On 10 March O'Donnell replied that the University could 'readily adjust' to the change of plan, and he hoped that by the autumn Chesterton would be 'so fully restored to health that the work he is undertaking in America will be rather a relaxation than a strain'. On 24 March Dorothy Collins confirmed that the doctor thought Chesterton would be 'quite well enough to visit America in the autumn'. She asked the President to confirm that the starting date for his lectures would be 6 October. On 9 April O'Donnell wrote to confirm that the lectures would begin on 6 October and end on 15 November.[37]

Then there came a difficulty. On 11 June Dorothy Collins wrote again to remind the President of what he had said in the memorandum he had given Sencourt about his willingness that on certain days Chesterton could give two lectures in order to have a free day. Chesterton, she said, was 'most grateful for this suggestion as it will enable him to fit in a few public lectures in the neighbourhood of the University for which there have been certain demands'. Accordingly, she hoped that Chesterton's lecture agent, Lee Keedick, might approach the President concerning these public lectures. Keedick had told Chesterton that, if he could give one public lecture a week, 'it would be a great help in working out the programme and granting the numerous requests which have been received'. They were writing to tell Keedick that it was impossible for them to make the necessary arrangements with the President, knowing nothing about the distances involved. She asked O'Donnell to let Keedick know what was 'possible from your point of view without disorganising your University time-table of lectures'. On 27 June she wrote again to ask if the students who attended Chesterton's lectures would be 'working to a prescribed syllabus' or was he 'free to lecture on his own syllabus'? Since it was understood that the lectures were to be 'part of the students' degree course', Chesterton wanted to know 'full details of the periods' in English history and literature that the President wanted him to lecture on. Having had no reply to her previous letter, Dorothy Collins wrote again on 30 June to say that they had had two telegrams from Lee Keedick saying that he had been unable to get an answer from the President, which was making it very difficult for him to arrange dates for the lectures Chesterton had been

[37] UNDA, UPCO 1/80.

asked to give. On 4 July O'Donnell wrote to say that, while he was happy for Keedick to get in touch with him about the possibility of Chesterton lecturing elsewhere during Chesterton's stay at Notre Dame, he thought it 'only fair that the University should share in the proceeds of any lectures', given that the University was paying Chesterton's travelling expenses as well as 'a rather handsome honorarium'. O'Donnell was not exaggerating: the sum of $5,000 was then equivalent to more than a full professor's annual salary. On 7 July Chesterton himself anxiously cabled to say that he had not received a syllabus and wondered whether everything was 'in order'. O'Donnell cabled the same day to assure him that there was no need for anxiety and he was writing. This he did two days later when he enclosed the University's description of Chesterton's forthcoming lectures, all of which were to be delivered in the evening apart from the Friday history lecture which would be in the afternoon. He added that he had told Lee Keedick of his stipulation regarding the external lectures Chesterton would give while at Notre Dame. And on the 11th he wrote to Keedick to confirm that he had made it 'plain' to Keedick's 'representative', when he had called on him two or three weeks previously, that the University would expect a percentage of any fees earned from lectures arranged by Keedick. He was writing, he said, at Chesterton's own request, 'since it would seem, from communications I have had from him, that your representative failed to make any report of his interview with me'. On 8 August Chesterton's literary agent in London, A. P. Watt, wrote to O'Donnell to say that Chesterton had handed him the whole correspondence, thinking that in future it would save time and trouble if his agent handled the matter. But in the meantime, he wanted to respond to the President's letter of 4 July, in which, for the first time as far as he could see, it had been suggested that Chesterton should give the University a share of his external lecture fees while at Notre Dame. This Chesterton was not prepared to contemplate, since, had he known of this condition at the beginning, he would not have accepted the President's invitation. The fee Notre Dame was offering would not be sufficient remuneration for the time Chesterton would have to spend in the United States and for his journey to and from America. On 18 August O'Donnell replied that it was impossible at that late date to cancel Chesterton's advertised lectures, and therefore he withdrew his stipulation about external lectures. However, he could not refrain from pointing out that this was the first time that he had heard that the fee he had offered was insufficient, which included travel expenses, a point Watt seemed to have overlooked. He acknowledged that there had been no 'express understanding' regarding external lectures, but that seemed to him implicit in their 'agreement'. He had after all made it clear that the lectures were to be 'regular lectures in course, which students will follow for credits towards their degrees. In the nature of things, a university professor can hardly follow a set program of lectures distributed over the school week and expect at the same time to lecture elsewhere.' The University, therefore, had been 'put in a difficult position' but had no choice but to accept Chesterton's understanding of their agreement.[38]

On 15 September Chesterton wrote in great distress to O'Donnell to say that he had heard from his literary agent, 'after an avoidable delay', that there had been some kind of misunderstanding about his Notre Dame lectures. He was anxious to make it clear that he had never in any way intended to question 'the justice, or rather the generosity', of the President's original proposition. However, Sencourt had gone 'out of his way' to assure him that the University would raise no objection to his giving lectures elsewhere—Chesterton was presumably referring to Sencourt's point that arrangements could be made to leave him with some free days from his duties at Notre Dame, a consideration that had affected his decision. He assured O'Donnell that he considered his invitation to be 'most generous, I might almost say incautious, since you know so little of my lecturing and I, alas, know only too much'. Nevertheless, munificent as the invitation was, he would not have accepted it had there not been a number of other things he wanted to do in North America—'to lecture in Canada and see my relations there; to see something of the general democratic discussion in the States; to have some debate there; to promote certain ideals expressed in my own little paper and to get some support for it; for it is constantly in need of money'. It would pain him very much if anything said in his name had given the appearance of 'disrespect or unfriendly bargaining', but it did seem there had been some misunderstanding. He did not wish to comment on the impression of his 'agents' (Chesterton is referring to his lecture agent in America rather than his literary agent in London) that O'Donnell had been incommunicative, as he was sure there had been a misunderstanding. On 30 September the President wrote to Chesterton at the address in Ottawa that Dorothy Collins had given him in a letter of 13 September, in which she pointed out that he had not told them where they would be staying at Notre Dame. He was 'pleased and relieved' by Chesterton's letter, he said: 'Naturally we should not wish your visit to Notre Dame marred by even the slightest misunderstanding. I am satisfied that arrangements for outside lectures

[38] UNDA UPCO 1/80, 1/81.

can be made without prejudice to the work which you are to undertake here.' It is hard to see how O'Donnell could ever have supposed that external lecturing must necessarily interfere with Chesterton's duties at Notre Dame. On the other hand, although free days had been mentioned, Chesterton had never specifically said that he wanted to use them to lecture elsewhere. Peace restored, O'Donnell ended by inviting Chesterton and his wife to be his guests at a football match in 'our new Stadium' on the afternoon of 4 October, the opening game of 'the intercollegiate football season', since he understood they would be arriving at Notre Dame in the first week of October. Chesterton may have wondered at the invitation, not then knowing that Notre Dame was nationally famous for its prowess at football. A day before writing, however, to Chesterton, O'Donnell had allowed himself to give vent to his feelings to Edgar J. Goodspeed, a prominent biblical scholar at the University of Chicago, who was requesting a lecture from Chesterton. Chesterton, he informed Dr Goodspeed, was 'under the management of Mr Lee Keedick of New York', adding: 'I might go so far as to say, if no one else is listening, it is my experience that English lecturers do not come to the United States for a change of climate.'[39]

On the same day that he wrote to Chesterton in Ottawa, O'Donnell also wrote to Dorothy Collins to say that he regretted that 'satisfactory arrangements for living at hotels in South Bend can hardly be made'. This somewhat evasive reply is explained by the fact that there was in fact then a hotel in South Bend, the Pick Hotel. But, presumably, O'Donnell was not prepared to pay for hotel accommodation for three people for six weeks. However, he assured Dorothy Collins that it ought to be possible to find accommodation either in a rented apartment or with a private family. Those possibilities were being investigated, but the University would be able to take care of them for a few days if there was a delay in finding lodgings for them.[40]

On 5 September Frances Chesterton had written to Father O'Connor to say that she was looking forward to being at the University of Notre Dame from a spiritual point of view. Father Walker had left the parish for a new appointment on 11 July 1928 and had been succeeded by a Father Thomas Fitzgerald, who would remain at High Wycombe for the next ten years,[41] although Beaconsfield fortunately would become a separate parish

---

[39] UNDA, UPCO 1/80, 1/81.   [40] UNDA, UPCO 1/81.

[41] Sheila Mawhood, *The Gem of the Diocese: St Augustine's, High Wycombe* (privately printed, n.d.), 42, 48.

in 1931. 'Things ecclesiastical here are horrible,' Frances lamented. 'Everyone tries to go somewhere else for Mass—and Father Fitzgerald is quite impossible to deal with. It has been a great sorrow to me—I have felt cut off and I hate going outside the parish if it can be avoided. I am almost glad to leave and go to U.S.A. where at Notre Dame Univ. I suppose we shall get all spiritual opportunities.'[42]

On 19 September the English party set sail for North America from Liverpool. They travelled, Dorothy Collins recalled, on 'one of the smaller P.&O. boats which were able to sail up the St Lawrence to Quebec and Montreal'.[43] As on the previous trip, the ship was not crowded, and the Chestertons had a suite, paid for by the University of Notre Dame. They had a twin-bedded bedroom, a bathroom, and sitting room. Dorothy's cabin was conveniently close at hand. They were 'fed like fighting cocks', as was always the way on 'these great liners', Frances wrote to her mother-in-law in a letter that, like all the succeeding ones to her, was to be sent on to Frances's mother, who was now in a nursing home in Beaconsfield, as well as to her sister Ethel Oldershaw.[44]

On 24 September Frances wrote home again to say that they had attended Mass at 7 a.m. on Sunday but that they only had 'the beginning' as the priest became sea-sick, 'a great disappointment to the nuns who are on board'. The purser, 'a rather remarkable man very full of good animal spirits and very amusing', had, with Chesterton, just organized a treasure-hunt, for which Chesterton had written 'some amusing clues in rhymed verse'. (These verses, accompanied by drawings in coloured chalk on brown paper, were later found by Dorothy Collins to have all been picked up, no doubt as collectors' items.[45]) Even as Frances wrote, the lounge was 'filled by a crowd of seekers eagerly grovelling on the floor under the grand piano in search of a further clue to the mystery'. There had already been

---

[42] Frances Chesterton to John O'Connor, 5 Sept. [1930], BL Add. MS 73196, fo. 142.

[43] Sullivan, 164.

[44] Frances Chesterton to Marie Louise Chesterton, 20 Sept. 1930, BL Add. MS 73456, fos. 37–8. *The British Library Catalogue of Additions to the Manuscripts. The G. K. Chesterton Papers. Additional Manuscripts 73186–73484* (London: British Library, 2001), 154, incorrectly says that the letters written by Frances Chesterton on this visit to North America were addressed to her mother, Blanche Blogg. Some of the letters were addressed to her but others to 'Dearest people', for whom those addressed to 'Dearest Mater' (Marie Louise Chesterton) were also intended.

[45] Sullivan, 164.

'games and competitions of all sorts'. That night at dinner they found the saloon 'decorated with streamers and balloons and we were all provided with the most beautiful head dresses', apart from the captain. There followed a 'remarkable evening entertainment'. The purser, dressed as a bookie, had held a horse-racing course on the top deck lounge—'wonderful were the races and the names of the horses . . .'. The horses were 'wooden ones on stands with numbers and jockeys complete', made to move by the 'numbers thrown by dice'. Frances, who had 'a winning horse' called 'Safety Match', found 'the entertainment . . . quite thrilling'. Continuing her letter the next day, Frances reported after lunch that they had just seen the coast of Canada. There was more excitement later when they passed an iceberg, 'like a white tower in an almost black sea'. On the night of the 26th there was a grand concert. Chesterton 'made an excellent Chinaman and his speech asking for subscriptions to sailors' charities was admirable', wrote his proud wife, 'just right—a little serious—and humorous too'. The evening ended with the singing of national songs, and they did not get to bed till after one in the morning. There was no problem about sleeping, as the St Laurence River down which they were now sailing was 'as smooth as a lake'.[46]

Before arriving at Quebec on 27 September,[47] Chesterton was told by a fellow passenger of the obelisk on the Heights of Abraham commemorating both the victorious British General Wolfe and the vanquished French general Montcalm, 'with a fine Latin inscription saying that fate gave to them the same death and the same honour'.[48] Unfortunately, the boat stopped only briefly at Quebec, so the mother of a lady who used to live in

[46] Frances Chesterton to 'Dearest People', 24 Sept. 1930, BL Add. MS 73456, fos. 38–43.

[47] The following account of this second lecture tour of North America is based not only on the letters of Frances Chesterton to her mother-in-law and family (BL Add. MS 73456, fos. 36–68) and on the letters of Dorothy Collins to her mother (BL Add. MS 73471), but also on Dorothy Collins's 'American Notes', some typed notes headed 'Trip to Canada & America. 1930' and covering the period from 19 Sept. to 6 Nov. 1930 (BL Add. MS 43748 C, fos. 12–15), another set of typed notes headed simply '1930' and covering the period from 28 Sept. 1930 to 17 April 1931 (BL Add. MS 43748C, fos. 20–2), a typed itinerary (BL Add. MS 73456, fos. 44–5), a handwritten list of dates and places (BL Add. MS 73478C, fo. 18), and a handwritten diary for 1831 (BL Add. MS 73478B).

[48] *AG* 181–2.

Overroads, who had come to meet them, only had time to drive them round the city. Still, Chesterton 'enjoyed' seeing the obelisk for himself.[49]

From Quebec the ship sailed on to Montreal, where they landed on 28 September and were met by Lee Keedick. Frances's initial impressions of Canada were as unfavourable as her first impressions of the United Sates a decade earlier. The hotels were 'dreadful…noisy, efficient and in-human—and very very expensive'. The country was just 'the same' as America. Chesterton was 'seized on by the press' the evening they arrived; 'a very nice interview', Frances wrote home, appeared next day in the papers. She would try and keep all the newspaper cuttings together and send them home in 'batches' so that 'eventually' they could be 'placed in one book and indexed and arranged', as she had done on their 'last tour'.[50] On the evening of 29 September Chesterton gave a lecture on 'The New Enslavement of Women', which, Frances reported, was 'a very great success': 'The hall was packed and very enthusiastic.'[51]

On 30 September they left for Ottawa, where they stayed for a couple of nights at 300 Waverley Street with Chesterton's uncle Walter, with whom they had stayed in 1921, and his daughter, Lilian. Uncle Walter was 'obviously frail', wrote Frances, and Lilian had 'a very hard time as a general rule, and of course our visit makes a great deal of difference to her'. They were about to go out and see 'the wonderful autumn trees in the woods around': 'certainly the Fall is the time of year for this country.' They were going on to Toronto, from where they planned to go to South Bend, Indiana, and make the University of Notre Dame their 'pied-a-terre for 6 weeks'. Frances could not believe that it was 'less than a fortnight' since they had 'left home'.[52] On 1 October Chesterton cabled Father O'Donnell from Ottawa to say that they hoped to arrive in South Bend on the following Saturday at three minutes past six in the evening and to ask him to notify them of the address of the accommodation he recommended. Next day O'Donnell cabled back: 'I recommend you remain at the

---

[49] BL Add. MS 73456, fos. 44–5.

[50] These newspaper cuttings (BL Add. MS 73403) were arranged more or less chronologically but never mounted in an album like the cuttings on the previous visit.

[51] Frances Chesterton to 'Dearest people', 30 Sept. 1930, BL Add. MS 73456, fo. 46.

[52] Frances Chesterton to undisclosed recipient, n.d., BL Add. MS 73456, fo. 60 (where it has been misplaced, as it clearly relates to this first visit and not to the later Christmas visit).

University Saturday night. Shall meet your train.' In reply, Dorothy Collins wrote a note from the hotel to say that Chesterton thanked the President for his 'kind suggestion that we should spend Saturday night at the University'.[53]

They arrived in Toronto on 2 October. After lunching next day with the Catholic Archbishop, Chesterton gave the lecture that he had already given in 1927 at University College, London, on 'Culture and the Coming Peril'. There were about 2,500 people in the audience at St Michael's College, a Catholic college in the University of Toronto. During questions, in reply to a woman's query as to his height and weight, he replied, 'about six foot two, but my weight has never been successfully calculated'.[54] Before the lecture Chesterton admitted to reporters that he did not at all like lecturing—he always felt nervous when he got up in front of an audience—and travelling even less. He felt it was presumptuous imposing his ideas and thought half an hour was quite long enough for a lecture. As for his famous paradoxes, he swore that he would not know one even if he met one 'socially'.[55] On another occasion, when asked how he felt before lecturing, he replied: 'I always think that this time they'll find me out.'[56] Chesterton explained in his lecture that by the coming peril he did not mean Communism, which had been tried and failed, nor did he mean another great war—which, Chesterton presciently predicted, would break out when Germany violated Polish sovereignty. Rather, he meant by the coming peril the threat to civilization from intellectual and economic 'overproduction', which was deadening people, leaving them no time for creativity and thought of their own. During questions Chesterton was asked why Dean Inge was so 'gloomy', to which he replied: 'Because of the advance of the Catholic Church. Next question, please.' Was George Bernard Shaw a coming peril? He was asked. 'Heavens, no. He is a disappearing pleasure.'[57] Frances could not attend the lecture because she had an attack of lumbago, but heard that it was 'a great success'.[58]

The Chestertons and Dorothy Collins left Toronto at eight on the morning of Saturday 4 October. There was 'a good deal of fuss at the customs at the American border' because of 'a great deal of liquor smuggling', but their

[53] UNDA, UPCO 1/81.   [54] BL Add. MS 73403, fo. 7.
[55] BL Add. MS 73403, fo. 9.   [56] Ward, *RC* 211.
[57] Ward, *GKC* 500–1.
[58] Frances Chesterton to Marie Louise Chesterton, 6 Oct. 1930, BL Add. MS 73456, fo. 47.

'one flask of brandy was undetected'.[59] They arrived at South Bend just after six in the evening. They were met at the station by the President, Father O'Donnell. Chesterton told the waiting reporters that he did not know why the University of Notre Dame thought that he was an educator, or even that he was educated, just because he had written a few books.[60] After dining with the President, Chesterton stayed the night at the all-male university, while Frances and Dorothy stayed in the University's infirmary under the care of the nuns who looked after it.

Writing home, Frances reported that 'rooms had been taken' for them at 209 E. Pokagon Street, 'near the University'.[61] This was not quite true. It seems that Father O'Donnell had been true to his word in looking for suitable accommodation for his English visitors but had not taken it upon himself to make the final choice. So after the eleven o'clock Mass the next day, which was a Sunday, Frances and Dorothy Collins set out with a list of possible houses nearby. The first house they went to, about a mile from the University, was 'a wooden building, rather like a bungalow but with two rooms on top'. 'It was quite small,' Dorothy recollected.

When we arrived there we saw a mother and a little girl of 4 and thought that with the father that was the extent of the family. But when we had fixed everything up and arrived with Mr Chesterton and our luggage, we suddenly saw in a cradle under the piano a baby of six months old; a little later in the day an old grandfather appeared, and later still another lodger. How we all packed in was a mystery.[62]

The day after moving in with the Bixlers, Frances wrote home to give her impressions of living with a 'real typical homely' American family. It was certainly 'an amusing experience'. The family were 'kindness itself', but they were 'so utterly unlike people of the same position at home': 'Here we have the true democracy at work and we shall all lead the family life.' As she wrote, Dorothy Collins was already nursing the baby, while Chesterton was 'conversing with the grandfather about the Civil War and Lincoln', and she, Frances, must go and help their hostess clear the table. Frances had discovered not only democracy at work, but a democracy in which men were expected to do household chores: 'father, mother, and grandfather all

[59] Frances Chesterton to Marie Louise Chesterton, 6 Oct. 1930, BL Add. MS 73456, fo. 47.

[60] BL Add. MS 73403, fo. 11.

[61] Frances Chesterton to Marie Louise Chesterton, 6 Oct. 1930, BL Add. MS 73456, fos. 47–8.

[62] 'American Notes', BL Add. MS 73478C, fo. 48.

help with the housework.' Chesterton's help, one suspects, would not have been very helpful, and Frances does not record his helping. The rooms, she reported, were 'small', but fortunately like all American houses there was 'a large porch for sitting out', as Frances feared that they would 'get a bit congested'. There were in fact only four bedrooms, with a box room that another lodger, a secretary, occupied. As for the University of Notre Dame, it was 'a perfectly enormous place with over 3000 students'. There was 'a large and beautiful church', but 'the glory of the place, to the students anyhow', was a football stadium that could hold 53,000 people: 'The university holds the record for unbeaten football and thousands come from all parts to witness matches.'[63]

Dellhard Bixler, a real-estate agent, and his wife Anna,[64] who had been a secretary before marrying, were in their thirties; they had been 'persuaded' by Father O'Donnell, according to Mrs Bixler, to offer to put the English visitors up at their home. As the son of an estate agent, Chesterton was able 'to talk about houses and prices' with his host.[65] As for Frances, she was delighted to be in the company of children and would go for walks with little 4-year-old Delphine, who 'seldom went to bed till midnight and got up in the morning when she felt inclined'.[66] Mrs. Bixler recalled many years later how Chesterton would rise usually around 9.30 or 10, occasionally having gone to bed the night before as late as 12.30 or 1, and then dictate to Dorothy between breakfast and lunch and again between lunch and tea, unless they had to go out. In the evening the Chestertons and Dorothy would go to the University from Monday to Friday at 7, returning around 9.30, although occasionally Chesterton would stay on. Every night Mrs Bixler would put a thermos flask of cold water and a plate of crackers by his bed. Originally, the idea was that the English visitors would have meals at the University, but after about two days Frances asked if they could eat at the Bixlers. Breakfast and lunch were eaten in the kitchen with the family and dinner by themselves in the living-room, according to Mrs Bixler.[67] But here her memory seems to have been at fault. The actual arrangement for meals was not quite so democratic, but only a little less so: writing to her mother, Dorothy Collins reported that she and the Chestertons ate alone in the dining room—but with the whole family trooping in

[63] Frances Chesterton to Marie Louise Chesterton, 6 Oct. 1930, BL Add. MS 73456, fos. 47–8.

[64] South Bend 1930 City Directory.   [65] Ward, *RC* 252.

[66] 'American Notes', BL Add. MS 73478C, fo. 49.

[67] Ward, *RC* 252–3.

and out[68]—while the Bixlers ate in the kitchen.[69] Mrs Bixler remembered how Chesterton would relax after his lectures by reading detective stories in a huge rocking-chair. Frances, to whom Chesterton was clearly devoted, would get impatient with her husband occasionally, especially when he left bits of the biscuits in bed or was particularly sloppy at the table or when she asked him to do things and he failed to do them. As always, she had to tie his tie and lace up his shoes. Mrs Bixler noted how the Chestertons liked roast beef and potatoes, but were not interested in salads or vegetables.[70] At least in America Chesterton would have been spared the sight of that old-fashioned English pudding the jelly, which he disliked: 'I don't like a food that's afraid of me.'[71] Chesterton kept Mr Bixler busy making home-brew in those days of Prohibition. Mrs Bixler was struck by Chesterton's admiration for the efficiency of Dorothy, of whom he and Frances were obviously as fond as if she were their daughter. Their hostess was delighted when they soon began talking about the house in South Bend as 'home'. Neither was fond of having to go out to big dinners; they preferred to be at 'home', returning with relief from the lectures in the evening. They were constantly buying presents for the 4-year-old, Delphine, of whom they were both extremely fond. But Mrs Bixler was dumbfounded when Frances insisted that the older girl should come and stay with them in England when she was a little older.[72]

While he was at Notre Dame, Chesterton gave two lecture courses, thirty-six lectures in all, one on Victorian literature and the other on Victorian history, to audiences averaging five hundred. After just over a fortnight of lectures, Frances told the family at home that Chesterton was enjoying the 'University work very much' and that Father O'Donnell informed them that the students 'particularly' liked his lectures because they were 'so original and unacademic'. She lamented that there was 'little of interest' in South Bend except the University: 'It is pure and unadulterated Middle West...'. Still, the Bixler family was 'most amusing' and provided them with 'a glimpse of the real middle class American life'. The children were 'delightful and not spoilt and grown up as American children are'. Mrs Bixler did all the housework, but she was 'always bright and

---

[68] Dorothy Collins to Edith Collins, n.d., BL Add. MS 73471, fo. 18.

[69] Dorothy Collins to Edith Collins, 7 Nov. 1930, BL Add. MS 73471, fo. 44.

[70] Ward, *RC* 252–3.

[71] Dorothy Collins's notes for talks, BL Add. MS 73477, fo. 170.

[72] Ward, *RC* 252–4.

performs miracles of labour without a murmur. It seems impossible to get servants and hired help here.'[73] But Dorothy Collins reported to her mother that the Bixlers had 'everything in the way of conveniences you can imagine'.[74] She observed, perhaps slightly snobbishly, that they knew 'all the local trades people to whom we are introduced on every possible occasion'.[75]

Chesterton gave the first of the lectures on Victorian literature on Monday 6 October. Next day he lunched with Cardinal Hayes, the Archbishop of New York, who had come to bless the new Law School. On Saturday 11 October the Chestertons, without Dorothy Collins, took the afternoon train to Chicago, where Chesterton lectured again on 'The New Enslavement of Women' in the Orchestra Hall. Several of his audience in the gallery called out that they could not hear, to which he responded: 'Good brother, don't worry, you're not missing a thing.'[76] Contrasting the restricted life of a modern typist with the freedom of an old-fashioned housewife as part of an attack on the modern tendency towards 'a complete codification of life', Chesterton coined such epigrams as 'There are moralists who propose to prevent wife-beating by prohibiting pokers' and 'An Englishman is never so fond of his friends as when they are not there'. He gave an interview to several newspapers on the Sunday afternoon. He claimed that the Catholic Church was 'everywhere winning by the collapse of its opponents', although more slowly in England, where it was only advancing 'at a trot', whereas in America it was advancing 'more at the charge'. Asked which of his books was his favourite, he replied that 'he hadn't read them all', but that *The Flying Inn* had been 'the most fun to write', while *Orthodoxy* had been 'most satisfactory, in the sense that it said what it set out to say'. He thought Notre Dame was more like Oxford and Cambridge than other American universities, since both the former were more like boarding schools, although discipline was more efficient at Notre Dame than Oxford and Cambridge. The students, he said, put up with his lectures with the same fortitude that they displayed on the football field. The Catholic newspaper reporter, however, pointed out to its readers that in fact 650 students had signed up for Chesterton's courses, and that his classes were the only ones in the University that no student would think of missing.

[73] Frances Chesterton to Marie Louise Chesterton, 23 Oct. 1930, BL Add. MS 73456, fo. 49.

[74] Dorothy Collins to Edith Collins, 7 Nov. 1930, BL Add. MS 73471, fo. 45.

[75] Dorothy Collins to Edith Collins, 18 Oct. 1930, BL Add. MS 73471, fo. 28.

[76] Clemens, 71.

Reminded that on the last occasion he had lectured at Orchestra Hall the lecture had been on 'Literature as Luggage', when he discussed what books he would take to a desert island, he was asked what books he might now add to the list. He replied that, much as he liked detective stories, he would not take them to his desert island: they were like 'returned empties', which could not be read over and again. (Chesterton was once asked, perhaps on the previous visit, what book he would take to a desert island if he could only take one and replied that he would take a guide to shipbuilding.[77]) He thought that having children was 'quite the most amazing thing the human race can do, the most miraculous'. At home women were like artists, whereas in the office they were like machines. By going out to work women had lost much of their influence, and he had noted a decline in chivalry among men. After the reporters from the daily papers had left, the Catholic newspaper reporter asked for a special message for its readers. Chesterton then spoke of his 'wonderful experience' at Notre Dame. Remarking how English visitors felt alarmed at the size of America, whose inhabitants seemed as foreign as, say, the French, on this visit he had felt very differently: 'The name of Notre Dame makes all the difference.'[78] In another interview with a newspaper, he confessed that he had 'spoiled many great ideas under the compulsion to finish a book, I needed money. Publishers pressed me. I rarely was able to give to a book all the time it needed. Books, like children, need a long period of gestation and undisturbed growth.'[79]

On Sunday the 19th the Chestertons were again in Chicago, when Chesterton debated the subject 'Is the New Woman Enslaved?' with Dr Bridges, the head of the Chicago Ethical Society, with whom he had debated a decade before. Yet again the next Saturday, 25 October, Chesterton was back in Chicago to debate with Dr Bridges in the Orchestra Hall, this time on the motion 'That Psychology is a Curse', Chesterton as on the previous occasion moving the motion. Afterwards he had lunch with Dr Bridges and the Episcopalian bishop. He told reporters that, thanks to being at Notre Dame, he now knew more about American football than psychology.[80] Four days later he was in Detroit to lecture at a crowded Orchestra Hall on 'The Curse of Psychology'.

While he was in Chicago, Chesterton wrote to Clare Nichol in coloured chalks, with the words in capitals chalked in the appropriate colour. He was writing from his hotel, 'quite near the ground, only fifteen floors up', from where he could watch 'cabs crawling like insects'. He reported with

[77] Ward, *GKC* 178.   [78] *New World*, 17 Oct. 1930.
[79] BL Add. MS 74303, fo. 19.   [80] BL Add. MS 73403, fo. 24.

amusement that he was 'constantly greeted as "Lord Chesterton" and "Sir Chesterton", but often (more strangely still) as "Professor" (the idea being that all English writers possess all English titles and they can be used according to taste and fancy)'. Everybody, he told her, was now 'complaining that "Prohibition is too wet", and nobody supports the law against drinking except the bootleggers who sell the drink'. He did not apologize that he had 'nothing to write with but a box of coloured chalks', for 'the wildness of this country... would demand all the colours of the rainbow'.

A lady was 'featured' in a paper here, posing in smiling pride, who had left her husband because he wore ORANGE NECK-TIES. I read an article of popular psychology about a man who had 'probably' dreamed in infancy of murdering his brother, because that alone could explain his dislike of A RED HAT-BAND. Quackery rules this country to a degree beyond belief: and the people are a GREEN PASTURE for every greedy charlatan in the world.

However, at least Americans were not snobs: 'They admire a Professor like me *more* than they do a millionaire: if not so much as another Professor who tells them that VIOLET RAYS are a substitute for food—or morals. Above all, by the supreme paradox, because they do care for ideas in their own mad way, and because they have kept simplicity of a sort...'.[81]

Notre Dame provided Chesterton with a driver, Johnnie Mangan, who found it very hard getting his famous passenger into the car, and even harder getting him out. Once when Chesterton got stuck in the car, he said it reminded him of an old Irishwoman, who, to a suggestion that she should get out sideways, retorted: 'I have no sideways.' Frances would entrust Johnnie Mangan with the money if, for instance, he had to take Chesterton to have his hair cut, as otherwise there might not be any change. While driving, Chesterton was very chatty. But above all he enjoyed talking to small children: 'He liked to ask them things and then if they gave a good answer he could get a good laugh at it.' One of the professors remembered how he would 'sit around consuming home-made ale by the quart', saying that the best brew was made by the head of the philosophy department. When some professors wanted to meet him, they mentioned they had

[81] G. K. Chesterton to Clare Nichol, 28 Oct. 1930, BL Add. MS 73481A, fos. 159–60. Since Chesterton's letters are never dated (unless a copy was made or they were dictated to a secretary who would type in the date) and since he was no longer in Chicago on 28 Oct., presumably Clare Nichol dated the letter by the postmark when she typed out this copy that she gave to Maisie Ward, in which she omitted to capitalize 'green pasture', an omission I have silently corrected.

some Canadian beer, to which he replied: 'The ales have it.' Once one of the professors met the invariably genial lecturer but only got a grunt in reply to his greeting; when his lack of cheerfulness was commented on, Chesterton responded: 'One should be given the luxury of a little private grouch once in a while.' When lecturing, he would climb on to the stage, searching through his pockets for his notes until he found some dirty scrap of paper, which he only occasionally consulted. He was heard once remarking that what he liked about notes was that they could be disregarded once the lecture began. He would quote at length from memory without the slightest hesitation. He stood for the first lecture; afterwards he sat at a table, constantly shifting his huge body and fiddling with his glasses. He began his first lecture by saying that until quite recently he had not been at all certain that he would be able to be there—in which case, 'you would now be gazing upon a great yawning void instead of myself'.[82] After the lectures had been delivered, Macmillans the publisher asked for the text, but unfortunately 'not a word' had been 'recorded, nor were there any notes'.[83]

On 5 November Chesterton received an honorary doctorate from the University. In his opening speech the President began by saying that it was a year since it had been agreed that Chesterton should give a series of lectures in the spring and then give the 'Commencement Address' to graduating students before receiving 'the honorary degree of Doctor of Laws'. Unfortunately for the graduating class of 1930, he had fallen ill, and the lectures had had to be postponed. And so 'it happens that, for the first time in the history of Notre Dame, there is a special convocation of the Faculty, and an honorary degree is conferred outside of a regular Commencement', an 'exception' being made for 'an altogether exceptional man'. Looking back on Chesterton's stay at Notre Dame, the President singled out 'with the greatest possible satisfaction . . . that note of confident and triumphant Catholicity' that had 'rung' through his lectures. Although he did not expect Chesterton to deliver a 'Commencement Address', he did ask him to say whatever he found it in his heart to say to the students of the 'Senior Class'.[84] After receiving the honorary doctorate, Chesterton protested not only that he was unworthy of the honour but that he was in something of a false position, as he was simply a journalist and could claim

[82] Clemens, 99; Ward, *GKC* 493–6.
[83] Dorothy Collins's notes for talks, BL Add. MS 73477, fo. 93.
[84] BL Add. MS 73403, fo. 28.

only that he had tried to show that it was possible to be an honest journalist.

I have only once before gone through a ceremony of this kind and that was at the highly Protestant University of Edinburgh, where I found that part of the ceremony consisted of being lightly touched on the head with the cap of John Knox. I was very much relieved to find that it was not part of the ceremony on the present occasion that I should, let us say, wear the hat of Senator Heflin!

(Heflin was a notoriously anti-Catholic senator from Alabama.) On his first visit to America, his first sensation had been one of terror; this second time he had felt quite differently: 'If you want to know why I felt different, the reason is in the name of your University.'[85]

Towards the end of his time at Notre Dame, a party was held in Chesterton's honour after his lecture. A keg of beer was obtained without too great a trouble. The twenty or so people present were mostly from the teaching staff. Chesterton held forth for three hours from 9.30 p.m. to 12.30 a.m., his mug never empty. The party broke up only after the amused but somewhat indignant Chesterton was firmly told that his wife had been promised that he would be returned home by midnight.[86] Three or four days before the last lecture, Chesterton invited students to bring books to the Bixlers' house to be autographed. Altogether he ended up autographing 600 or 700 books.[87] On 15 November the Chestertons and Dorothy Collins left South Bend. As they parted from the Bixler children, both Chestertons had tears in their eyes,[88] while 'the whole Bixler family' was 'in floods of tears'.[89]

The Chestertons' first stop after leaving South Bend was Ann Arbor, Michigan, where Chesterton lectured on 'The Age of Unreason' at the university there. Two days later, on Monday 17 November, they were in Cincinnati. From there Frances again wrote home. They were 'very sad' at leaving Notre Dame, where everyone had been 'so nice and the lectures so successful' and Chesterton 'so beloved by the students', who, 'poor boys', were now being examined on the lectures. On arriving at their hotel, they had found 'a large Union Jack on the walls of the hotel entrance, with

---

[85] Clemens, 105–6.

[86] Richard Baker, John R. Connolly, and Ronald Zudeck, 'Notes on Chesterton's Notre Dame Lectures on Victorian Literature', *CR* 3/2 (Spring–Summer 1977), 168–9, 172.

[87] Ward, *RC* 253.   [88] Ward, *RC* 254.

[89] 'American Notes', BL Add. MS 73478C, fo. 49.

"Welcome to G. K. Chesterton" in electric lights at the top'. That evening the hotel management had presented them with 'a huge cake, something like this—'. Below Frances drew a picture of the cake, on the white icing of which was written in gold letters the name of Chesterton's latest book, *The Resurrection of Rome*, of which the cake was 'an exact replica'. Fortunately, there was a local Chesterton Club and they had invited some of its members to tea that afternoon, who would help them to eat it.[90] Chesterton's lecture to the Club was on 'The Curse of Psychology'. The Club presented Chesterton with 'a large etching', which only added to their luggage; the English visitors already required two taxis to get anywhere. Having got it as far as New York, Chesterton sat on it in a taxi in New York, smashing the glass.[91]

From their hotel in Cincinnati Frances wrote to the President of Notre Dame on 17 November to say that she felt 'somehow' that they had never thanked him properly for all his 'goodness' to them while they had been at Notre Dame: 'It must have been a bit of a nuisance to you to think for a man's wife and his secretary—but you will have realised how impossible it would have been for him without us.' She continued, perhaps with a certain resignation: 'No man was ever so dependent on his belongings— no man was ever more compelled to carry his home with him—wherever he might go.' But they had all had 'a very happy time and for us there are nothing but loving memories—of Notre Dame and all she stands for'. Her husband wanted her to thank Notre Dame 'very warmly' for its 'generosity in the matter of payment for his lectures'. The money was 'badly needed' if he was 'to keep the flag flying' at *G.K.'s Weekly*. It was difficult to keep a paper going that lacked both capital and subsidy. For over twenty years her husband had 'tried to preach sanity ever since he could run a paper at all', without making a penny's profit and with heavy debts, which he had always paid. On 19 November O'Donnell replied to Frances's 'thank you' letter. He said they had all felt 'very lonesome' after the English visitors' departure. And, far from deserving any thanks, he felt he had 'grossly neglected' them; it was unfortunate that they had had to come in the autumn, the busiest time of the year. However, he was counting on them returning for a visit on their way back East from the West Coast. Notre Dame was 'the logical' and 'the psychological place to break that long

---

[90] Frances Chesterton to Marie Louise Chesterton, 17 Nov. 1930, BL Add. MS 73456, fos. 50–1; 'American Notes', BL Add. MS 73478C, fo. 47.
[91] 'American Notes', BL Add. MS 73478C, fo. 47.

journey'. The University would 'take care' of them 'very nicely for as many days as you will have the kindness and courage to grant us'. He understood about the paper and was glad to have been able to contribute 'even a little to keep the flag flying'.[92]

Next stop was Pittsburg, where Chesterton lectured on 'The Inhumanity of Humanism' on 18 November. The following day he was at Canisius College, Buffalo, New York, lecturing on 'Culture and the Coming Peril'. Back in his hotel in New York, he gave an interview to the *New York Sun*, in which he admitted that he did not understand why Sinclair Lewis had received the Nobel Prize for Literature for satirizing America's Main Street. 'I don't know when I have enjoyed an experience more,' he declared in reference to his stay with the Bixlers. 'They are my kind of people... fine and sincere; kindly and considerate... most Americans habitually are courteous and considerate, especially of their inferiors.' But he also struck a more critical note: 'It has long been recognized that America was an asylum, but it is only since prohibition that it has resembled a lunatic asylum.'[93]

There followed lectures in New York City on 'The Inhumanity of Humanity' on 21 November, and on 'The Age of Unreason' at Trinity College, Washington, on 22 November. On Sunday 23 November Chesterton opposed the motion 'Divorce as a Social Asset' at a debate in New York City with the English playwright and novelist Cosmo Hamilton, who wrote a number of Broadway shows. This was followed by another debate with him two days later, when Chesterton again opposed the motion 'That Immorality in Modern Books is Justified'. On 26 November they stayed for a day and a half with the Rann Kennedys in Millbrook, near Poughkeepsie, as they had done on their previous visit. A special performance was put on in Chesterton's honour at the Greek theatre the Kennedys had had built and that had become well known all over America among teachers of classical Greek. Thursday 27 November was Thanksgiving Day. 'The students carried in the turkey high in the air, and a prize was offered for the best song—to be written on the spot and handed in anonymously.' Unsurprisingly, Chesterton won the prize—'but he certainly seemed surprised and was quite obviously delighted'. When he was asked to make a speech, he suggested that he should stay on at the school and play in their next performance. The play he suggested was *The Tempest*: 'Rann Kennedy would play Prospero and he himself would be a "natural" for Caliban.' In this same speech he delighted some of his audience and infuriated others

by explaining that England too should have a Thanksgiving Day 'to celebrate the departure of those dour Puritans, the Pilgrim Fathers'.[94]

While he was staying with the Kennedys, Chesterton met Regina
Cody, who taught English at the school and was a Catholic from Ver-
mont. She remembered talking to Chesterton about the Church, and
particularly about confession. He made no bones about how difficult he
found confession; but, while he knew 'it shouldn't be easy... it was
harder for him than for many. For one reason even his being a little
oversize—naturally there was no confessional box big enough to house
him.' 'Wedged' in the confessional, 'all thought ceased, all that was left
was a sense of something that had to be got through with. Devotion
departed, even if he's had it before.' Unable to remember what he was
intending to say, 'He thanked God for the formula, "Bless me, Father, for
I have sinned," with which Confession opens.' He never felt so grateful
for ritual—about which 'the truest thing was said by Yeats... that ceremony goes with innocence'—without which in this case 'he would often
have left. If he did leave he would probably take the confessional with
him.' Coming downstairs on a Saturday morning, Frances 'wouldn't say
a word but the look in her eyes said: we are both going to Confession.'
And go they did. While Frances would use her prayer book to make a
scrupulous examination of conscience, Chesterton would get carried
away with speculations about sins... His own two chief sins, he felt,
were 'laziness... and certain kinds of anger'. The act of contrition—
'Oh my God, I am so sorry...'—after confessing his sins seemed to him
to go perfectly with the prayer before Communion—'Lord, I am not
worthy...'. The two prayers expressed his inadequacy for both sacraments. As he left the confessional he would see 'people turning to look at
him as he came out', as he had said the words of contrition 'much louder
than he realized'. He felt he followed the Latin Mass poorly compared
with Frances, and the prayer before Communion gave him the necessary
courage to receive. He spoke of his great happiness after receiving
Communion—'and yet the next time it's just the same again: the same
dread...'.[95]

Although 27 November was Thanksgiving Day, nevertheless Chesterton had to give a lecture in the evening at the Hotel Commodore in New
York. From there Frances wrote home to report that Chesterton was
'really enjoying himself'. The weather continued to be 'lovely'—'such

---

[94] Ward, *RC* 242.   [95] Ward, *RC* 242, 244–5.

glorious sunshine'.[96] Then there was a respite of a few days from lecturing, in the course of which, however, Chesterton gave an interview that
was published in the 30 November issue of the *New York Times Magazine*.
The interviewer was struck not only by his charm and humour but also
by his 'kindliness and sweetness' and his 'perpetual wonder at the universe that is almost childlike in its earnestness'. True, any reader of his
books would know that he could be 'caustic', but it was 'a causticity that
does not leave a scar, a causticity that burns with its wit rather than with
its scorn'. The interviewer wanted to know what Chesterton, after six
weeks in South Bend, thought of Main Street America. A couple of weeks
before he had met and talked with Sinclair Lewis, whose famous book by
the same name had 'made Main Street a name that stands for commonplace drabness and dulness'. Chesterton replied with a chuckle that, since
he knew very little about Main Street, he supposed that he was a good
person to discuss it! He had found Main Street to be 'most charming and
entertaining'. There were certainly things that struck an English visitor as
'rather peculiar', not that he found fault with them. He was pleasantly
surprised by a 'friendliness' that one would not find in an English small
town. He was also struck by the classlessness: he was astonished, for
example, by the familiarity with which a grocer would greet a professor
from the university. On the other hand, he missed the 'privacy' that was
valued in England. The 'almost universal hospitality' seemed to him to
make the American's home not a castle but a hotel. But he would not
want to change the 'simplicity' of the people. He had read Sinclair
Lewis's book before going to South Bend, and, while he could recognize
some of the 'characteristics' described in the book, there were others that
had been completely ignored. Any street had two sides to it, a sunny side
and a shadowy side, and both had to be taken into account. Small town
America, unlike small town England, was 'the outgrowth of Puritanism'.
American pioneers had travelled westwards in 'covered wagons with
closed minds'. Puritans believed in 'the simplicity of human nature'
and failed to realize its 'complexity'. Thus, on deciding that drink is the
cause of much misery, the Puritan 'promptly adopts prohibition as a
panacea for all ills'. The Puritanic American was 'by nature a professional reformer … constantly looking for ways to improve the world'.
Sinclair Lewis himself, Chesterton remarked with a chuckle, was just
such a reformer, as he 'tried to delve behind the scenes on Main Street',

---

[96] Frances Chesterton to Marie Louise Chesterton, BL Add. MS 73456,
fos. 52–3.

finding only 'ulcers on potatoes'. 'The real motives, the simple but full
lives of these people' had 'escaped him', or at any rate he had tried 'to
improve and reform them'. But Chesterton did not think that the people
he knew in South Bend, whatever their 'peculiarities', could be 'changed
to advantage'. The room by now was getting 'quite warm' and Chesterton tried with difficulty to open the 'new-fangled' window, a product, he
remarked, of 'the machine age and the reformer'. As he mopped his brow
with a huge handkerchief, he announced that he had changed his mind
about Prohibition: 'You know I am not so sure prohibition is not a good
thing for this country. The rooms are kept so warm here that the desire to
drink is constant.' As the interviewer left him, he was standing in front of
the opened window, 'and all that he was gulping down were great
draughts of air'.

On 30 November the Chestertons and Dorothy Collins left New York,
where they had stayed at the St Moritz Hotel in West 59th Street.[97] On 1
December the famous lecturer was back in the Mid West lecturing on 'What
I Saw at Rome' in Cleveland, Ohio. Back in New York State he lectured on 3
December in the capital Albany on 'The Age of Unreason'. Chesterton
warned his audience against the American religion of activity for its own
sake, a passion that he supposed came from the pioneering spirit and the
energy of Puritanism, which had turned from religion to business. However,
the worship of activity was no worse than the English worship of idleness
among the rich.[98] Back again at the St Moritz Hotel in New York City on 7
December, Chesterton was again visited by the Irish American who had
visited him in his hotel in Baltimore on his previous visit in 1921, when
Chesterton had praised the Irish love of freedom and attributed it to the
influence of the Catholic Church.[99] Then he had not been a Catholic, now he
was. But even before he believed in Christ, he explained to his visitor that he
had believed in Christmas. Indeed, he had 'believed in the spirit of Christmas', even when he was a boy and thought he was an atheist. Not only that,
but he had actually written a poem in honour of the Blessed Virgin:

From my earliest years I had an affection for the Blessed Virgin and for the Holy
Family. The story of Bethlehem and the story of Nazareth appealed to me deeply
when I was a boy. Long before I joined the Catholic Church the Immaculate
Conception had my allegiance . . . the thought that there was in all the ages one
creature, and that creature a woman, who was preserved from the slightest taint of
sin, won my heart.[100]

[97] UNDA, UPCO 1/83. [98] Ffinch, 324. [99] See p. 440.
[100] Clemens, 89–90.

Between 4 and 16 December Chesterton lectured at Syracuse, Philadelphia, Boston, Providence, Worcester, Newark, and Hartford, on the usual subjects: 'The Curse of Psychology', 'The New Enslavement of Women', 'Culture and the Coming Peril'. In Boston Chesterton informed reporters that he had discovered that you cannot get murdered in gangster-famous Chicago unless you belong to 'an exclusive circle'.[101] The Worcester, Massachusetts, lecture was at the invitation of Holy Cross College, where the English visitors were greeted by 'students dressed up as Homer, Virgil, Dante, Chaucer, and Shakespeare'. Chesterton commented that the pageant had made him think that 'they were the culture and he was the Peril'.[102] Dorothy Collins was less kind: she could not imagine English students behaving like that; it was a 'pantomime of a day'.[103] After a reception, a message from Paul Claudel, the dramatist and poet, who was then French ambassador to the United States, was read out. Claudel said Chesterton's books over the past twenty years had never failed to bring him 'joy and refreshment'.[104] The visit was filmed, and Dorothy Collins urged her mother to try and see it: 'They told us it will go all over the world.'[105] On 16 December Chesterton lectured on a new subject, 'Puritanism and Paganism', in Baltimore. On 7 December Frances wrote home to say that they had decided to stay on in America, so that Chesterton could give 'a second course of lectures', which he was 'very keen to do', even though this meant being away from home at Christmas and they were both feeling 'pretty homesick': 'But it seemed too good a chance to be missed.' She was very anxious for Chesterton to be 'a bit relieved of the financial anxiety of the paper—the debt on it is always so heavy, and he would hate to give it up'. They were off to Canada next week for 'a little holiday'.[106] Before leaving New York Chesterton gave another interview to the *New York Sun*, in which he praised Prohibition for encouraging people to make their own home-brew, thus reviving 'the old pride of the craftsman'.[107] On a later occasion he told reporters that he had found Americans 'invariably eager' to discuss Prohibition, 'especially over the nuts and the wine'— although they were often 'willing to dispense with the nuts'.[108]

[101] BL Add. MS 73403, fo. 57.   [102] BL Add. MS 73403, fo. 69.

[103] Dorothy Collins to Edith Collins, 15 Dec. 1930, BL Add. MS 73471, fo. 80.

[104] BL Add. MS 73403, fo. 71.

[105] Dorothy Collins to Edith Collins, 19 Dec. 1930, BL Add. MS 73471, fo. 86.

[106] Frances Chesterton to Marie Louise Chesterton, BL Add. MS 73456, fo. 54.

[107] BL Add. MS 73403, fo. 57.   [108] BL Add. MS 73403, fo. 80.

On 18 December the Chestertons left for Canada to spend Christmas and the New Year with Uncle Walter and Lilian in Ottawa. Dorothy Collins remained in New York, very happy to have time on her own, dealing with correspondence. Frances, she told her mother, departed for the arctic Canadian winter 'very reluctantly', adding that Chesterton was 'a selfish creature like all men when it comes to big things and she gives him his own way in everything. It makes me furious.' In the same letter, she offers an insight into the Chestertons' marriage: 'I tell her she makes him more helpless than he need be. Like so many women I think she likes to feel that he is dependent on her.' In an earlier letter, Dorothy had complained about her employer's 'vagueness', which was 'simply appalling'. But, she added, 'nothing is worse than when he thinks he ought to be businesslike—the fussing that then ensues cannot be described. Luckily it only happens once a week for a short time!! Mrs. C. does not encourage it.' As an example of Chesterton's 'vagueness', Dorothy mentions in passing that he was far too absent-minded even to notice the huge helpings in restaurants—an aspect of American life that visitors still comment on—to which she and Frances objected, who, when 'feeling very brave', would order one portion between them, to the contempt of the waiters. Chesterton, on the other hand, did not 'mind' whether he had 'a little or a lot' on his plate: 'he is quite oblivious either way and just munches through it.'[109] But, all things being equal, Chesterton was naturally, she recorded, 'a small eater'.[110]

Predictably, Frances developed such a bad cold in Ottawa, which she blamed on the 'hot' North American rooms, that Lilian had to send for a doctor. This upset Lilian's Christmas preparations, which 'vexed' Frances, since the 'poor girl' had 'a very hard time as her health is very undermined and Uncle Walter is a very difficult patient'. Chesterton himself was 'enjoying a real "do nothing whatever" time here', Frances informed the family at home. 'He just wanders to the bookcases and takes out books and puts them back and then has a smoke—and then a meal—and then a look at some new toy or detective story.'[111] Meanwhile Dorothy Collins, who had remained behind in New York, was invited to Christmas dinner by the

[109] Dorothy Collins to Edith Collins, 11, 19 Dec. 1930, BL Add. MS 73471, fos. 74, 85, 87.
[110] Dorothy Collins's notes for a BBC 'Woman's Hour' talk, BL Add. MS 73477, fo. 66.
[111] Frances Chesterton to Marie Louise Chesterton, 28 Dec. 1930, BL Add. MS 73456, fos. 56–9.

Rann Kennedys. New Year's Eve in New York was 'like hell let loose', she recalled, with ships' sirens blowing and taxi horns blaring. At the English Speaking Union Club she listened nostalgically to 'a relay of Big Ben striking midnight'.[112]

Back in the United States, Chesterton began lecturing again on 6 January. After lectures on the usual subjects in New York and in New Jersey at the College of St Elizabeth, Chesterton introduced a new subject, St Francis of Assisi, in a second lecture in New York. On the 11th there was another debate with Cosmo Hamilton in Boston on the subject 'Is Divorce a Social Asset?' The hall was only half-full because of the rain, which, Dorothy Collins noted, 'thoroughly disorganises things', being a comparatively rare event compared with England.[113] Two days later in Washington Chesterton first lectured on 'The Curse of Psychology' and then debated again with Cosmo Hamilton on 'Is Psychology a Curse?' From there Frances again wrote home to report that Chesterton was keeping 'wonderfully well' and that the 'drier climate' suited him 'better than the damp and fogs of home'. As always, she—if not Chesterton—rejoiced in the 'wonderful sunshine'. She could, however, assure the family at home that they would not be returning to America, as after California they would 'have seen all there is to be seen'.[114]

On 16 January and again on the 18th Chesterton debated the motion 'Will the World return to Religion?' first in New Haven and then in New York with the famous American lawyer Clarence Darrow, who had defended the Tennessee schoolteacher John Scopes, prosecuted for breaking state law by teaching evolution, in the notorious 1925 'Monkey Trial'. Chesterton was to recall that, when he had 'tried to talk about Greek cults or Asiatic asceticism', Darrow had 'appeared to be unable to think of anything except Jonah and the Whale'.[115] During his speech in New Haven, the loudspeakers had crackled and rumbled, causing Chesterton to remark that 'it seemed as if the devil was rehearsing applause for Mr Darrow'.[116] In the Mecca Temple, New York, Chesterton teased Darrow by saying that he felt he was arguing with a fundamentalist aunt; and when something again went wrong with the sound system, he jumped up and cried, 'Science you see is not infallible.' The audience

[112] 'American Notes', BL Add. MS 73478C, fo. 50.
[113] Dorothy Collins to Edith Collins, 12 Jan. 1931, BL Add. MS 73471, fo. 99.
[114] Frances Chesterton to Marie Louise Chesterton, 14 Jan. 1931, BL Add. MS 73456, fos. 63–4.
[115] A. 300–1; Sullivan, 165. [116] BL Add. MS 73403, fo. 85.

voted that Chesterton had won the debate.[117] In retrospect, Chesterton thought that it was 'the curse' of the 'comic career of lecturing' that it seemed 'to bring on the lighted stage nothing except comedies'.[118]

The English visitors left the East Coast on 20 January bound for California after lectures in the South. The following day they arrived at night at Chattanooga, Tennessee. Frances was already running a temperature, which next day was over 103. A doctor was called, who diagnosed 'an attack of "grip" which the doctors here', Dorothy Collins told her mother, 'call a disease which is like 'flu but much quicker'.[119] Meanwhile Chesterton was persuaded to carry out his lecturing engagements in St Louis and Nashville, equipped with 'pages of instructions' provided by Dorothy.[120] In St Louis he told reporters that, while he had been at Notre Dame he had soon given up pronouncing the name in the French way.[121] On 25 January Dorothy was able to report to her mother that Frances was 'better but frightfully depressed and lugubrious'.[122] On the 28th she wrote that Frances had got over the 'flu but was now ill with 'gastritis or its equivalent'. A nurse had had to be hired to help Dorothy with the nursing. On the same day Chesterton returned 'looking like *nothing* on *earth*': 'His hair had not been brushed for a week—he has slept in the train in his day clothes and his nails were filthy (as usual) and he needed a shave—He can't go about alone and I am at my wits' end what to decide.'[123] It was imperative financially that Chesterton should continue the lecture tour, but, if so, she, Dorothy, would have to accompany him. In any case, Chesterton absolutely refused to go by himself. On the other hand, Frances would be devastated if she were left alone in Chattanooga. Next day she wrote again to say that Frances had been taken to hospital in an ambulance. The doctor thought Chesterton should cancel the remaining lectures.[124] By the following day Frances was 'dangerously ill': 'in fact I have never seen anyone so ill.' She was in a private room and now had two nurses in attendance, as well as two doctors, and the night before a specialist had been called in. She hardly recognized her husband and Dorothy. She was constantly vomiting and had to be artificially fed. Dorothy and Chesterton

[117] Clemens, 67.   [118] *A.* 301.

[119] Dorothy Collins to Edith Collins, 24 Jan. 1931, BL Add. MS73471, fo. 106.

[120] Dorothy Collins to Edith Collins, 24 Jan. 1931, BL Add. MS 73471, fo. 106.

[121] BL Add. MS 73403, fo. 87.

[122] Dorothy Collins to Edith Collins, 25 Jan. 1931, BL Add. MS 73471, fo. 109.

[123] Dorothy Collins to Edith Collins, 28 Jan. 1931, BL Add. MS 73471, fo. 110.

[124] Dorothy Collins to Edith Collins, 29 Jan. 1931, BL Add. MS 73471, fo. 112.

took turns to sit with her. Chesterton was 'very anxious': 'He is marvellous though and kindness and consideration itself to me.'[125]

By 31 January Frances was 'off the danger list'. Dorothy told her mother that the papers in St Louis had made much of Chesterton's 'untidy appearance'. She herself had to take him back to his bedroom when he appeared at breakfast to dress him properly, comb his hair, and do up his shoe-laces.[126] Now that Frances was so much better, the lecture tour could continue, and Chesterton, accompanied by Dorothy, very reluctantly left Chattanooga on 7 February on the evening train bound for Los Angeles via New Orleans. The cancellation of five lectures in the South had cost over £700, and the medical bills were coming to £40 a week, while the hotel accommodation was costing another £6 or so. The day after leaving Dorothy reported to her mother: 'I drag G.K. round like a good-tempered sack of potatoes. I pay everything and give him his pocket money. He seems to get rid of about £1 a day on detective stories and magazines and getting shaved and that is all he pays. I can't think what he does with it.'[127]

On 8 February *en route* to Los Angeles, Dorothy Collins wrote to Father O'Donnell enclosing a poem Chesterton had written especially for the University, which he had composed 'a long time ago', but, as he had still not written an accompanying letter and as there would be no 'spare time in the immediate future for him' to do so, she was sending it herself. She told O'Donnell that Frances had had 'a very bad time with influenza' and that they had been 'held up for over a fortnight in Chattanooga' and that they had had to cancel 'all the Southern lectures'. They hoped that Frances, accompanied by a nurse, would be able to join them in California 'this day next week'.[128]

After travelling by train for three days and nights, Chesterton and his secretary reached Los Angeles on 10 February, where he gave a lecture on the 11th. Back in Chattanooga, Frances received a telegram from her husband to say that the lecture had been 'a tremendous success'.[129] On 12 February Chesterton lectured at Santa Barbara, where his uncle Cyril

[125] Dorothy Collins to Edith Collins, 30 Jan. 1931, BL Add. MS 73471, fos. 113, 115.

[126] Dorothy Collins to Edith Collins, 31 Jan. 1931, BL Add. MS 73471, fo. 116.

[127] Dorothy Collins to Edith Collins, 8 Feb. 1931, BL Add. MS 73471, fo. 120.

[128] UNDA, UPCO 1/82.

[129] Frances Chesterton to Marie Louise Chesterton, 12 Feb. 1931, BL Add. MS 73456, fo. 66.

Chesterton, an accountant, lived, who had invited him to make his 'headquarters' at his home and 'allow' him to drive him round to his various engagements in California.[130] There followed lectures at San Diego, Long Beach, and Pasadena on 13, 14, and 16 February.

Meanwhile Dorothy Collins found and booked 'a delightful little place which had only three bedrooms' in the hills outside Los Angeles at Palos Verdes, now a suburb of the city, called La Venta.[131] She described the inn to her mother as being 'on the top of a hill overlooking the Pacific Ocean'. It seemed quite European and quite unlike the ostentatious American hotels they were used to. Frances, accompanied by a nurse, arrived in Los Angeles on 17 February. She was 'dreadfully upset' by the long journey to Los Angeles.[132] They all moved to the La Venta Inn on the 18th, where Frances and the nurse would remain till 22 March. Their third day at La Venta was the first day Frances was without a temperature. There was now a respite from lectures until the 27th, when Chesterton had to lecture in Los Angeles, during which they—that is, Frances and Dorothy if not Chesterton—could bask in the Californian sunshine and Dorothy could bathe in the warm sea. Dorothy, however, was also able to do some business for her employer. Invited to spend a night in Hollywood with a friend of hers who worked there and his family, she was shown over the Fox Film Studio. During the visit she 'did some good business for G.K.', she proudly informed her mother, 'which he would never have done for himself. I got into touch with an honest Hollywood agent and he is negotiating for the sale of film rights in *Magic* and some of the Father Brown stories.' Chesterton could earn as much as £4,000 for the *Magic* film rights as opposed to a mere £100 for a single lecture. She herself had been offered 'tempting' secretarial jobs but felt she could not abandon the Chestertons.[133] Three weeks later she mentions to her mother a 'good job' she was offered in Hollywood, which 'might be worth it later on'.[134]

While they were at Palos Verdes, Chesterton wrote to Clare Nicholl, using again a variety of coloured crayons: 'If you only knew how we long to

[130] C. A. Chesterton to G. K. Chesterton, 25 Jan. 1931, BL Add. MS 73193, fo. 62.
[131] 'American Notes', BL Add. MS 73478 C, fo. 52.
[132] Dorothy Collins to Edith Collins, 20 Feb. 1931, BL Add. MS 73471, fo. 140.
[133] Dorothy Collins to Edith Collins, 27 Feb. 1931, BL Add. MS 73471, fo. 143.
[134] Dorothy Collins to Edith Collins, 19 Mar. 1931, BL Add. MS 73471, fo. 158.

be home in England you would not accuse us of wandering wilfully.' He reported that Frances had fallen ill suddenly and was taking time to recover. As an exile, he, Chesterton, was learning 'to hate time' and to 'see a new and savage sense in the figure of killing Time': 'I handle the large knife in my pocket.' He was certainly able to kill time by dramatizing for the benefit of Clare 'a real scene, farce, comedy or miracle play'. It had 'occurred in Chattanooga in the State of Tennessee (which is Puritan and very Dry). Near Dayton of the Monkey Trial. Frances in bed. To her enter a perfectly gigantic Popish Priest, swarthy as a Spaniard but bearing the reassuring name of Dillon.'

Priest (after a boisterous greeting) I was told ye were ill: but I didn't know how ill. I've brought the Holy Oils.

Frances (somewhat tartly) Then you can take 'em away again. I don't want *them* just yet. But I wish you'd give me your blessing, Father.

Priest I'll give ye some whiskey first. (Produces an enormous bottle of Bootleg Whisky and flourishes it like a club). Don't ye believe all that yer told about the stuff we get—you've only got to know your Bootlegger. This is perfectly sound mellow Canadian stuff and the nurse says ye need a little stimulant. (Administers a little stimulant with a convivial air.) You drink that down and ye'll be all the better.

Frances (rather faintly)... and the Blessing?

Priest (straightens himself and gabbles in a strong guttural voice) *Benedicat te Omnipotens Deus*, etc. etc., or whatever is the form for sickbeds.

Chesterton then told Clare that he would 'like to have that actual dialogue printed as a little Catholic leaflet':

It would tell people more about the Soul of the Church than ten thousand chippy chats between *A* (Anglican Enquirer) and *C* (Catholic Instructor)—about its fearlessness of the facts of life and the Fact of Death, its ease and healthy conscience, its contempt for fads and false laws, its buoyancy that comes from balance: its naturalness with the natural body as with the supernatural soul: its freedom from sniffing and snuffling embarrassment: its presence of the Priest: its utter absence of the Parson. Clare dear, Never let go of the Faith. At unlucky moments, in unworthy people, it may sometimes turn on us a face that is harsh or features that are irritant: but in moments like that, when Reality is only too close you suddenly see it quite plain: the face of your best friend: and in the sick-room that wind from beyond the world is only something fresher than fresh air.

But the note on which he ended the letter was one of gratitude to Clare and her sisters: 'You and your little sisters... came into my life about the time one fancies one's purely personal circle is closing or closed: and showed me a vista.'[135] The actual scene that Chesterton recreates for Clare's amusement is a perfect example of Chesterton's conception of the seriousness of humour and of how he saw comedy as just as serious a medium as tragedy.

Chesterton also wrote a 'hurried line' in 'chalk pencil' to his mother to say that Frances was 'ever so much better, as this Land of Sun agrees with her: and we shall soon resume the march home.' Apart from Frances's illness, the lecture tour had been 'very successful'.[136]

On 3 March Chesterton gave a lecture in San Francisco. While he was in the city, Chesterton was taken by a journalist to a 'bootleg joint', where he asked for 'some speciality of the house' and was offered a 'Mule'. 'Six of these babies will put you on your ear,' the barman remarked. What had he said about his ear? Chesterton enquired. After he had knocked back three of the special cocktails, the barman commented, 'He can take it,' a slang expression apparently unfamiliar to Chesterton. It seems that Chesterton was either just being polite or somewhat inconsistent, given his disapproval of cocktails as the product of Prohibition—'perhaps the only practical product of Prohibition':

The reason why the American millionaire does not drink wine or beer with his meals, like all poorer and better Christians, is simple if not dignified. . . . He prefers to be a Prohibitionist on public occasions; especially those highly important public occasions when he meets his wife. Hence arose, originally, the habit of the males of the party consuming hurried, secret and very potent drinks before they assembled at table. It was necessary that the sort of drink should be one that could be gulped down quickly; it was necessary that it should be very strong for its size . . .

This was what 'determined the novelty and nature of this remarkable sort of refreshment. It was, quite simply, a tippling husband hiding from a nagging wife.' But in any case, whatever its origins, Chesterton considered that cocktails were a deplorable form of drink quite simply because 'it was a worse way of drinking', it being 'rudimentary human nature' to be 'more natural to sit still and talk, and even drink, after dinner, than to stand up

---

[135] Ward, *RC* 246–8, with text corrected from BL Add. MS 73481A, fos. 160–1 and the deleted name of the Irish priest supplied. It has to be said, though, that Maisie Ward was apparently transcribing a larger version than the typewritten copy in BL.

[136] G. K. Chesterton to Marie Louise Chesterton, n.d., BL MS Add. 73193, fo. 87.

and gulp before dinner'. But, in defence of his drinking the despised cocktails, perhaps Chesterton was being more than merely polite: enjoying as he did the company of ordinary people, as he informed his host in San Francisco, on this occasion the pleasure would necessarily have entailed the drinking of the house speciality, the creation of which by a 'creative' craftsman would have seemed to Chesterton to deserve 'legitimate praise'.[137]

His stated wish to meet ordinary people emboldened a request to him to give a talk at a Catholic girls' school that could not possibly pay his normal fee. When he had given the talk and signed autographs, a large chauffeur-driven car arrived at the school. Informed that he had missed an important engagement, Chesterton replied, 'I have filled an important engagement, lecturing to the daughters of the poor.'[138]

On the same day that Chesterton was lecturing in San Francisco, Father O'Donnell wrote to Dorothy to say that he had returned home only the previous day to find her letter of 8 February enclosing Chesterton's poem. The poem would 'shortly appear in the University publications', while they planned to have Chesterton's manuscript framed and hung in the University library. Considering the amount of travelling and the various engagements, he was surprised that all three had not fallen sick. It seemed their plans had changed, as he had understood that after the Christmas holiday in Ottawa they were going directly to the West Coast 'to take it easy there for the rest of the winter'. He hoped that they would be able to stay a few days at Notre Dame on their way back to the East Coast. In her reply Dorothy Collins explained that it did seem that there had been more lectures than originally envisaged, but at least 'it has made it possible to stay out here for the winter, so we do not grumble. It has been a glorious experience to spend the winter months in such lovely surroundings.' Unfortunately, because of a lecture in Toledo and engagements in New York they would be unable to accept his kind invitation to stop off at Notre Dame, but they hoped he could join them for lunch or dinner on 26 March in Chicago before they left for Toledo. Father O'Donnell also wrote by the same post to Chesterton, thanking him for 'an immortal poem': 'We do feel that you have somehow divined the spirit of the school which moves in and around the amplitude of Our Lady's blessings.' He hoped that Frances was now fully recovered, although it was his 'private opinion that a few more days at Notre Dame [would] be needed to make her completely

---

[137] *S.* 493–4, 529.   [138] Ward, *GKC* 499.

forget the rigors of American life'. He ended the letter with his 'affectionate regards' to them both.[139]

Working his way up the West Coast with Dorothy Collins in attendance, Chesterton lectured on 5 March at Oakland, California, where he told reporters that he hardly thought that George Bernard Shaw would visit America, because he would be afraid to witness the Prohibition that he so vigorously advocated in action. He also thought that Shaw prided himself on being that rare English author who had never done a lecture tour there.[140] On 8 March he gave a lecture on a new subject, 'Shall we Abolish the Inevitable?', in Portland, Oregon. Outside their hotel there was a hold-up and killing, a common enough crime in those days of Prohibition, which, Dorothy Collins remembered, 'much to the distress of our taxi-driver, we just missed by minutes'.[141] Crossing into Canada, Chesterton lectured on 10 March in Vancouver, where he stayed with Annie Firmin, the angelic 'girl with ropes of golden hair'[142] of his childhood, now Mrs Robert Kidd. Next day he gave a lecture at neighbouring Victoria.

Meanwhile Frances wrote home from 'lovely' Palos Verdes to say that the doctor had forbidden her to 'go north into the cold after such a bad attack', so she had remained behind, although she 'hated the separation'. The Holywood studios were 'not far off' and 'some of the managers there are anxious to get hold of some Father Brown stories for filming'. She thought that Chesterton would 'try and arrange something . . . It would be splendid financially . . . and a great help, as naturally my illness has been a bit expensive. Every thing out here is about 4 times as much as in England.'[143]

On the 13th Dorothy Collins and Chesterton were back in the United States for a lecture in Seattle, where they stayed with some of Frances's relations. They all left Palos Verdes on the 22nd on their way back to New York. They arrived at the Grand Canyon at 8 a.m. the next day, where they spent the night. The following morning they left for Chicago, which they reached on the morning of 26 March, when Chesterton spoke in favour of the motion that 'Psychology is a Curse' in another debate with Dr Bridges. On the way they dropped off Frances's nurse at Kansas City. 'She was a dear', recalled Dorothy Collins, 'and said it was the happiest two months of her nursing career'.[144] On the 24th Father O'Donnell wrote to

---

[139] UNDA, UPCO 1/82.   [140] BL Add. MS 73403, fo. 114.
[141] Sullivan, 165.   [142] *A.* 42.
[143] Frances Chesterton to Marie Louise Chesterton, n.d., BL Add. MS 73456, fos. 67–8.
[144] 'American Notes', BL Add. MS 73478 C, fo. 53.

Dorothy Collins at the hotel in Chicago where they were to stay, suggesting that, unless they had engagements in Chicago on the night of the 26th, they could spend the 26th and most of the 27th at Notre Dame before leaving for the lecture in Toledo on the 28th. He was 'moved to these desperate calculations because at this moment it looks impossible for me to come to Chicago'. On the 25th he wrote again to Dorothy to confirm that he was unable to meet them in Chicago, but suggested again that, provided they had no engagements on the evening of the 26th they should leave Chicago in the afternoon, buying train 'tickets through to Toledo, arranging at the ticket window for stop-over privilege at South Bend', which they would have to pass through anyway. If this was impossible, he would like to know what train they would be leaving Chicago by on the morning of the 27th as he could 'board the train in South Bend and ride with you as far as the next station East'. When the English visitors' train stopped at South Bend, they found the platform was 'crowded with our friends from the University and the town, including the Bixlers and the two children'. One assumes that Father O'Donnell was there, but whether he accompanied them on the train as far as Chicago is not recorded.[145]

Next day, the 28th, they were in Toledo, where Chesterton lectured on 'The Age of Unreason'. The following day they were back in New York, where they stayed for three weeks as there were a few more lectures to be given if only to compensate Lee Keedick for the cancellation of the lectures in the South and to enable Chesterton, who was 'very behind' with his journalism, to catch up.[146] However, on Good Friday Dorothy Collins went on strike and insisted on the day off. 'G.K. has developed a writing craze and wants to be at it morning, noon and night,' she wrote to her mother.[147] On the Wednesday of Holy Week Frances had written from the St Moritz Hotel to thank Father O'Donnell for some chocolates and cigars he had sent them.[148] On 15 April they were back again in New Jersey, where Chesterton gave another lecture at the College of St Elizabeth entitled 'Dickens at the Present Time'.

Two days later their ship sailed from New York. What with all Frances's medical expenses, on top of the agent's fees and taxes, the trip had not been 'very remunerative in the end'.[149] On arriving at Southampton,

---

[145] 'American Notes', BL Add. MS 73478C, fo. 53.

[146] 'American Notes', BL Add. MS 73478C, fo. 53.

[147] Dorothy Collins to Edith Collins, n.d., BL Add. MS 73471, fo. 163.

[148] UNDA, UPCO 1/82.

[149] Dorothy Collins's notes for talks, BL Add. MS 73477, fo. 94.

Dorothy Collins sent Father O'Donnell a postcard, postmarked 24 April, depicting 'the altar for Mass' on the White Star liner 'Majestic'. They had had 'a splendid crossing' on what claimed to be the world's largest liner, but she had 'left America with regrets'.[150]

In his *Autobiography* Chesterton calculated that he had been guilty of 'inflicting no less than ninety-nine lectures on people who never did me any harm'. In retrospect, the American 'adventure, which was very enjoyable', broke up 'like a dream into isolated incidents'. There was the 'aged Negro porter, with a face like a walnut, whom I discouraged from brushing my hat, and who rebuked me saying, "Ho, young man. Yo's losing yo dignity before yo time. Yo've got to look nice for de girls." '[151] The 'porter' was, Dorothy Collins recalled in her old age, a 'fatherly old Negro car-attendant' who reproved Chesterton in these words: 'Ho, ho, young man, you'se getting old afore yer time. You must keep yerself nice for the gals.' Chesterton's 'day was made'.[152] But some handwritten notes, which she must have made for a talk not long after the event, give a little more detail. 'Even on the short journeys', she explained, the

coloured porters who are most fatherly... like to brush you up, polish yr. shoes and see that that you are a credit to them when you leave the train. One of these porters... descended on Mr Chesterton with his brush and polish. Mr C gave him a tip and said no no. I'm all right.

But on being admonished that he must keep himself 'smart for the gals', 'Mrs C. drily remarked that she wished he wd.'[153] Then, too, Chesterton remembered, there was the 'grave messenger' who came to Chesterton in a Los Angeles hotel, 'from a leading film magnate, wishing to arrange for my being photographed with the Twenty-Four Bathing-Beauties; Leviathan among the Nereids; an offer which was declined amid general surprise'. Or there was the memory of an 'agonising effort to be fair to the subtleties of the evolutionary controversy' in a lecture at Notre Dame, 'of which no record remained except that one student wrote in the middle of his blank notebook, "Darwin did a lot of harm." ' The student may have been right, 'but it was something of a simplification of my reasons for being agnostic about the agnostic deductions' drawn by evolutionists.[154]

---

[150] UNDA, UPCO 1/83.　　[151] *A*. 300.　　[152] Sullivan, 165.
[153] 'America', BL Add. MS 73487 C, fo. 33. These notes are an expanded version of another set of handwritten notes, also headed 'America', in which there is just a brief reference to 'Story of GK and Porter' (fo. 26).
[154] *A*. 300.

4

While Chesterton was in America, he published two new books, both on 2 October 1930, *The Resurrection of Rome* and *Come to Think of it...A Book of Essays*. The two main topics of *The Resurrection of Rome* are Catholicism and the papacy and Italian Fascism. Chesterton returns to his favourite theme of the foolishness of sneering at 'minute disputes about doctrine'. It was like sneering at 'minute disputes about medicine': 'It is the fact that many a man would be dead to-day, if his doctors had not debated fine shades about doctoring. It is also the fact that European civilization would be dead to-day, if its doctors of divinity had not debated fine points about doctrine.' Unlike 'the great international treaties, which are generally made the pivotal dates of history' and which are founded on compromises, the great councils of the Church, 'those vast and yet subtle collaborations for thrashing out a thousand thoughts to find the true thought of the Church', which were 'far more practical and important', were founded on 'subtle distinctions'. Thus, when 'certain metaphysical disputations about Fate and Freedom' had been decided, 'it was decided whether Austria should be like Arabia; or whether travelling in Spain should be the same as travelling in Morocco'. The same 'subtle distinctions' were also made by the papacy: 'It was the Pope alone, for all practical purposes, who stood out upon the fine distinction between imagery and idolatry. It was the Pope alone, therefore, who prevented the whole artistic area of Europe, and even the whole map of the modern world, from being as flat and featureless as a Turkey carpet.' It was because the Pope had 'stood firm in Rome' that 'the great David stands gigantic over Florence and the little Della Robbias have crept like scraps of sky and cloud into the palace of Perugia and the cells of Assisi'. St Peter's was 'built to assert rather the firmness and authority and even audacity' of the popes rather than 'their softness or simplicity or sympathy as holy men'. As in the case of the Iconoclasts, the same thing had 'happened again and again': 'in the awful silence after some shattering question, one voice has spoken and one signal has saved the world.' This was 'not the place where we come nearest to the charity and burning tenderness of the Heart of Christ; we can come far nearer on the gaunt and arid rocks of Assisi'. Nor was this the place 'specially designed to express that element of twilight and reverent doubt, the spirit which at once accepts the mystery and gives up the riddle. This is far better conveyed in many grey vistas of the Gothic, following in their very tracery the...uncertain skies of the north.' Nor were the popes 'here laid prostrate with folded hands, in the more pious mediaeval manner, because religious art...is not thinking of them as men now peacefully dead, but as men who on this or that occasion were terribly alive'. No, St Peter's 'is the particular place where is to be asserted...the certitude of a certain person or persons that they do in deadly fact possess a special warrant...'. It stands for 'the intolerant and intolerable notion that something is really true; true in every aspect and from every angle; true from the four quarters of the sky...'. As well as its authority, Chesterton emphasizes the papacy's power of renewal, as when it 'attempted the paradox of a new orientation away from the orient', when it turned its 'back upon the sun; upon the sunrise and all the light and learning that was associated with the sunny lands; now in the possession of some mad Manichaean aristocracy', and when the Pope 'appealed to the uncivilized against the overcivilized', even appealing 'to the unconverted against the relapsed', and 'began to make a new Roman Empire' in the West. Again, the Counter-Reformation was another example of this 'energy of resur- rection'. And it seemed to Chesterton 'something strangely right' about the loss of the Temporal Power of the papacy, about the fact that the popes now claimed 'the smallest possible political power with the largest possible pontifical power': 'I think there is something both subtle and magnificent in the idea of claiming a foothold, but only a foothold, for the foot of St Peter.' It fitted in perfectly with Chesterton's belief in 'the value of little states and local liberties, and the necessity of a general moral philosophy big enough to defend such little things'. It gave him a 'thrill' to 'accept the largest of all the religions' but 'to salute it also as the smallest of the small nationalities'.[155]

Chesterton also, albeit with reservations, was delighted by the renewal, or literally resurrection, of political Rome—by 'the same almost spectral revivification' whereby 'modern madness and treason and anarchy' had 'brought forth...ancient Romans':

> I have seen men climbing the steep stones of the Capitol carrying the eagles and the *libellum* that were carried before Marius and Pompey, and it did not look like a fancy-dress ball. I have seen a forest of human hands lifted in a salute that is three thousand years older than all the military salutes of modern armies; and it seemed a natural gesture and not a masquerade.

Here was the recovery of 'an ancient human passion forgotten for many centuries; the passion of order'. Certainly, Mussolini, like the Irish repub- lican Michael Collins, had done 'a number of things that nobody would

---

[155] *RR* 320‒4, 326‒7, 379, 443‒4.

think of defending except on the ultimate theory of national self-defence; that is, the theory that society was in dissolution and the fatherland at the point of death'. But Italy had recovered 'a thing sometimes known in the ancient world, but very nearly unknown in the whole of the modern world'—that is, 'a government, which is not merely a governing Class'. Such a government might well be tyrannical, but 'it was not necessarily the same as the tyranny of the richest class', to which it 'often made itself quite unpleasant'. True, Mussolini was no 'ideal republican', but at least he had 'reverted to the original ideal that public life should be public'. Nor were the Italians subject to 'that network of nonsensical regulations and restrictions, about eating and drinking and buying and selling' by which those living in a so-called democracy like England were enslaved: 'Prohibition would seem insane slavery in Rome.' The truth was that Mussolini did 'openly what enlightened, liberal and democratic governments' did 'secretly', which, unlike Mussolini, were 'acting against their principles'. And Chesterton 'personally' preferred 'to live in a world of reality', where freedom of speech was openly prohibited rather than secretly prevented, where the choice of candidates for parliament was openly rather than secretly limited. The criticism of Fascism was that it appealed to 'an appetite for authority, without very clearly giving the authority for the appetite': it had 'brought order into the State', but this would not be 'lasting' unless it also 'brought back order into the Mind'. Mussolini talked of 'the mistake of ruling by the Majority; and the superiority of an intense and intelligent minority', but the problem was that, while 'after all there is only one majority...there are a great many minorities'. In this sense Fascism invited rebels 'in principle', since any minority could 'claim the same superiority to Fascism which Fascism claimed to Communism'. Mussolini himself had reacted 'too much against the Liberalism of the nineteenth century', for what was wrong with Liberalism was not Liberalism but 'Liberals who were not even true to Liberalism'. In conclusion, Chesterton assured his readers that he was 'very far from being what is usually understood as a British Fascist'—but he did understand that 'the whole political and financial world...has been goading Fascism into revolt for the last fifty years'.[156]

Come to Think of it consisted of essays mostly republished from the *Illustrated London News* and selected by J. P. de Fonseka, who, Chesterton noted in the introduction, had reminded him that it was 'exactly twenty-five years ago' that he had begun writing the 'Note-Book' for the magazine. More or less

---

[156] *RR* 400–1, 412, 414, 422, 426, 428–30, 435–7, 466.

familiar themes reappear. The 'simple' Whig idea of history as progress Chesterton had accepted as a boy, but he now believed in history as 'change' and in 'the necessity of novelty': 'it is sometimes hygienic to have a change, even when it is not an improvement.' He noted the conservatism of the young who had not experienced change like their elders and 'did not really believe that the fashion of this world could pass away'. But each age was blinded by its own preconceptions: 'What is interesting about each generation of men is the things they never thought of.' The danger of basing legislation on the basis of the hard case is satirized in the example of the seasick lady who unsuccessfully begs the steward to throw her over board, and happily so, for 'she lived afterwards to a happy and serene old age; and I think she was glad he had not carried out her instructions . . .'. The argument from 'hard cases' that would be used in a later age to justify the relaxation of laws against abortion and euthanasia was already familiar to Chesterton. The rare habit of thinking—'We might almost call it the habit of secret thinking, a dark consolation like that of secret drinking'—is defined in terms of limitation: 'real thinking . . . means knowing exactly where to draw the line . . .'. Fortunately for sceptics, 'who are praised as daring and audacious', it is not their practice to 'carry a destructive idea through to its logical consequences'. Evolutionists, on the other hand, like to wrap up their 'tautological' truisms 'in clouds of mythology', with their talk of nature, 'a mythical being', selecting certain individuals for survival, when all they mean is that 'some individuals do emerge when other individuals are extinguished', or in other words that 'the successful succeed'. Preachers are only 'tolerable' insofar as they expound 'creed and dogma', a 'system of thought' that 'can be explained by any reasonably thinking man': 'To tell the priest to throw away theology and impress us with his personality, is exactly like telling the doctor to throw away physiology and merely hypnotize us with his glittering eye.' Heretics like to 'introduce their . . . heresies under new and carefully complimentary names', 'these respectable disguises' being 'adopted by those who are always railing against respectability'. For example, in looking round one's 'social circle' one can easily spy 'some chatty person or energetic social character whose disappearance, without undue fuss or farewell, would be a bright event for us all', a disappearance that might be justified by calling it 'Social Subtraction' or 'Life-Control' or 'Free Death'. For 'the very first thing' to do is to 'find some artificial term that shall sound relatively decent' when one 'wishes to wage a social war against what all normal people have regarded as a social decency'. The later employment of the euphemisms euthanasia and gay for suicide and homosexual would not have surprised Chesterton in the least.

Finally, no book of Chesterton would really be complete without the gospel of wonder and thanksgiving: 'men need thrills to produce thanks, and have to be surprised into surprise. It is the whole aim of religion, of imagination, of poetry and the arts, to awaken that sense of something saved from nothing.'[157]

5

The American lecture tour for a man of Chesterton's age and health had been gruelling enough without the weekly chore of his articles for the *London Illustrated News* and *G.K.'s Weekly*. Not surprisingly, no books appeared in 1931, apart from another collection of his *Illustrated London News* columns, entitled *All is Grist: A Book of Essays*. On returning home, the exhausted Chesterton was forced to curtail his lecturing—or at least Dorothy Collins forced him to. Even a request from Father Ronald Knox to speak to the Newman Society at Oxford, where Knox was now Catholic chaplain, was refused. On 1 July Knox wrote: 'Now it seems your secretary refuses to let you lecture for the next few months, because you've got so bored with it in America.' It was 'maddening', Knox complained, that 'after five years of being told you wouldn't come because you were lecturing so much, to be told now that you won't come because you're lecturing so little. I shall begin to believe you have a down on me, or Newman, or something.'[158] Later, Knox admitted that by now Chesterton's health was beginning to decline, 'and he was overworked, partly through our fault'—that is, because of the constant requests from Catholics for articles and talks.[159]

Chesterton was also involved in the local life of Beaconsfield. In July he was asked by the honorary secretary of the local branch of the Council for the Preservation of Rural England to attend a meeting to oppose the proposed widening of the road in the neighbouring village of Jordans, which in the seventeenth century had become a Quaker centre, with one of the oldest Quaker meeting houses in the country, in the cemetery of which William Penn is buried. What should 'remain sacred in such a place', Chesterton replied, 'that has contrived to remain a place, and has not been turned into a totally different sort of place' but remained 'a shrine

[157] *CT* pp. ix, 10–12, 39–40, 110–13, 124, 126, 131–2, 167–8, 213, 235.
[158] Ffinch, 326, with text corrected from BL Add. MS 73195, fo. 161.
[159] Ward, *GKC* 460.

of pilgrimage which does still to some extent exist for pilgrims, and not only for touts and trippers', was 'the place; the approach, the surroundings, the background; not detached and dead objects that might be put in a museum'. 'The effect of Stonehenge is the effect of Salisbury Plain. If you wire in Stonehenge like a beast at the Zoo, you are really making it into a fetish, and idolatrously worshipping the mere stones; instead of seeing the large vision of the beginnings of Britain.' But, whereas Stonehenge represented 'a dead religion', 'the other is historic in the living sense that its history is not ended, for no one knows what may come at last of that revival of a purer mysticism in spite of the storms of Puritanism; of the beginnings of a Reformation of the Reformation, and of the greatness of William Penn.'[160]

On 18 August 1931 Chesterton returned to the subject of George Bernard Shaw, recalling in *G.K.'s Weekly*: 'Wherever I wandered in the United States people leapt out upon me from holes and hedges with the question pointed like a gun: "How is Bernard Shaw?" ' Unlike Chesterton, Shaw refused to go to America, and Chesterton thought that was 'rather a good thing' for Shaw, if not America. After all, 'the awful truth' was 'how large a part' of America shared his ideas, which, 'when seen on so large a scale', seemed 'very common, not to say vulgar'. What in aristocratic England seemed 'like the rather distinguished oddities of a sage' seemed in democratic America to be nothing but 'the dull prejudices of a society': 'Total abstinence in a man like Shaw is an almost elegant eccentricity; but there is nothing elegant about Prohibition, and it is not an eccentricity but a convention. Shaw would find thousands of Americans to take quite seriously his prejudice against tea or tobacco; but their seriousness would only serve to make him absurd.' Shaw would be 'horrified if he knew how much of America follows his fads; for these things when they really begin to exist, are not fads but fanaticism'.[161]

In 1934 Chesterton would give the readers of the *New York Herald Tribune* the benefit of his 'Second Thoughts on Shaw'; the article was added as a final chapter called 'The Later Phases' to the 1935 and subsequent editions of his book on Shaw. The trouble with Shaw, he explained, was that 'the *first* things that counted with [him] were negative and anarchic things; where for most men the first things at least are positive'. Shaw lacked 'piety'— that is, not religion but 'the cult of the land, the cult of the dead,

---

[160] G. K. Chesterton to G. Langley Taylor, 15 July 1931, BL Add. MS 73240, fo. 99.
[161] CS 571–2.

the cult of that most living memory by which the dead are alive, the permanence of all that has made us...'. Shaw had 'started with the Prejudices of Progress' that were 'so much more cramping than the prejudices of memory, because memory is mixed of a thousand things': 'The past is infinitely varied; and if we would not draw from one old inspiration, we can draw from another. But the future is always atrociously simple. We can only *predict* along lines of mathematical fate...'. One form of piety, patriotism, simply bewildered Shaw, who had assumed it was outmoded, having 'a less direct vision of the Future for having no direct tradition of the Past'. As for Shaw's evolutionism, it was 'rooted in a despair about Man. That is what is picturesquely symbolised by a rather vague and evasive enthusiasm about the Superman.' The Shavian evolutionist really did 'want to cast the whole body of man into Chaos...into the melting-pot, and boil it to nothing, that a new and superior something may at last emerge'. Christianity, on the other hand, 'was 'the one and only philosophy that has refused to despair of Man'.[162]

All is Grist was published in October 1931. Travelling in America had led Chesterton to reflect on the nature of travel. The trouble with travel books, he thought, was that their authors had travelled too much in the country they were describing, as a result of which they tended 'to forget its strangeness', so that 'the real monument of landscape...was something stranger and more striking' than the travel book suggested. Mere sightseeing was certainly not the way to see a country: 'No man will ever forget the sights he really saw when he was not a sightseer.' The pilgrim, for instance, 'does not feel, as the tourist does often quite naturally feel, that he has had his tour interrupted by something that does not happen to interest him.' Unfortunately, the traveller to the monument had been replaced by the sightseer in the museum:

When the traveller saw the statue of the hero, he did not see written on the pedestal: 'This way to the Collection of Tropical Fungi', in which he possibly felt no interest at all. When the pilgrim found his way to the shrine, he did not find that the priest was eagerly waving him on to a glass case filled with the specimens of the local earthworms.

But the museum was not 'meant either for the wanderer to see by accident or for the pilgrim to see with awe': 'It is meant for the mere slave of a routine of self-education to stuff himself with every sort of incongruous intellectual food in one indigestible meal. It is meant for the

[162] CS 592, 594, 602.

mere Sightseer, the man who must see all the sights.' However, Chesterton was sure that this kind of 'cold and compulsory culture' would never be 'popular': 'It is not a product of popular imagination, but of what is called popular education ...'[163]

Other familiar Chestertonian themes are touched on in these essays. Ritual, far from being something artificial, was perfectly natural and normal:

The old ceremonial gestures of the human body are necessary to the health of the human soul ... a man actually can think with his muscles; he can pray with his muscles; he can love with his muscles and lament with his muscles. All religion that is without that gesture, all Puritan or purely Intellectualist religion that rages at ritual, is raging at human nature.

In 'On the Thrills of Boredom', Chesterton recalled from his childhood 'the continuous excitement of long days in which nothing happened; and an indescribable sense of fullness in large and empty rooms'. He still felt

a very strong and positive pleasure in being stranded in queer quiet places, in neglected corners where nothing happens and anything may happen; in unfashionable hotels, in empty waiting rooms, or in watering-places out of the season. It seems as if we needed such places, and sufficient solitude in them, to let certain nameless suggestions soak into us and make a richer soil of the subconsciousness.

But in order 'to get the fun out of' 'solitude and stagnation' it was necessary 'to be rather young and strong'—just as the monastic 'career' required 'very great vigour and vivacity'. As for childhood itself, Chesterton insists, first, that far from the child's imagination being 'a sort of dream', he remembers it 'rather as a man dreaming might remember the world where he was awake'. Secondly, he denies that children 'have suffered under a tyranny of moral tales'. And, thirdly, he claims that, far from 'the first dreams of life' being a 'mere longing for larger and larger horizons', the child is 'positively in love with limits', enjoying the 'game of self-limitation ... one of the secret pleasures of life', using 'his imagination to invent imaginary limits' like the 'moral duty to step on alternate paving-stones'. For the 'charm' of a story like that of Robinson Crusoe lay 'not in the fact that he could find his way to a remote island, but in the fact that he could not find any way of getting away from it'. The faults of historians are another favourite subject: 'historians seldom see the simple things, or even the obvious things, because they are too simple and obvious', while they

---

[163] *AG* 27, 164–7.

are 'paid to tell lies', being 'academic officials of a certain academic system' and lacking the 'disinterestedness or detachment' of popular traditions which are much more reliable.[164]

On Christmas Day 1931 Chesterton made his first radio broadcast on the BBC. It was to listeners in the United States and lasted a quarter of an hour. Chesterton explained that he had been asked to speak about Dickens and Christmas—or, as he would prefer to say, on Christmas and Dickens. He wondered why he had been asked. Perhaps the BBC did not know him very well, perhaps they had 'a grudge' against him. Why should he work on Christmas Day, and why should his listeners be made to suffer? 'Like everything connected with the mystery of suffering, it is profoundly mysterious.' Maybe as he spoke 'the mystery will grow darker and deeper'. But the question as to why the BBC wanted a talk on this subject was much easier to answer. The answer was that no other day had 'been able to do what Christmas does; and there is no writer... who has been able to do what Dickens did'. The old pagans '*could* make things... could make festivals and festive days', whereas the modern pagans who 'are merely atheists... worship nothing, and therefore create nothing'. Dickens was the only writer who 'exaggerates happiness', who 'talked about Christmas as if it was Christmas; as if it was even more Christmas than it is'. Even the most 'horrible' villains in Dickens 'make you happy'. No other writer had 'discovered Dickens's secret of getting joy out of these things'. Dickens 'exaggerated, in the sense of making things more laughable than they were; more enjoyable than they were'. Just as there was 'nothing in history so living as that little life that began in the cave at Bethlehem and now visibly lives for ever', so there was 'nothing in all literature so utterly alive' as Dickens.[165]

Frances Chesterton had sent a Christmas letter and a 'little carol' to Father O'Donnell at Notre Dame. They had 'felt quite sad', she said, on reading about the defeat of the University football team in the *New York Times*, but they did not imagine that he was 'unduly depressed'. Her husband had been very busy working on a book on Chaucer, which he had just completed and she hoped it would meet with his approval. She hoped that he would be coming to the Eucharistic Congress in Ireland, as it would be 'very delightful to meet'. On 22 January 1932 O'Donnell wrote to thank her for her Christmas letter and 'lovely poem'. He, too, hoped

[164] *AG* 41, 91–3, 125–7, 130, 150–1.
[165] John Sullivan, *Chesterton Continued: A Bibliographical Supplement* (London: London University Press, 1968), 98–103.

they could meet if by any chance he went to the Eucharistic Congress or came to England that year. Nothing in her letter, he said, had pleased him more than her 'remark about the football season':

It shows how truly you became one of us, really understanding how that sport fits into the academic and spiritual life of Notre Dame. I often recall with amused satisfaction the inquiry which you made upon your arrival in South Bend. It was the day of our encounter with Southern Methodist University. All three of you seemed to feel that somehow the honor of the Church was at stake, and almost the first question you asked was how the match came out.

He was very interested by her reference to her husband's forthcoming book on the Catholic Chaucer—'He belongs to us and we should be proud of him.'[166]

Chesterton's *Chaucer* appeared in April, the last of his critical studies. The book was not his idea but that of the son of Walter de la Mare, Richard, who originally wanted Chesterton to contribute to a collection of essays to be called 'Poets on Poets', but who subsequently encouraged him to write a full-length literary biography.[167] The best pages in the book are on the humour of Chaucer and his affinity to Dickens. Matthew Arnold had famously accused Chaucer of lacking 'high seriousness'; but not only did Chaucer in Chesterton's view display high seriousness in Arnold's sense, but also in another sense altogether, because 'there are other things that can be high as well as high seriousness'. For example, he teases Arnold, 'there can be such things as high spirits'—and 'these also can be spiritual'. For, even if one only thinks of Chaucer as a comic poet, nevertheless there can be 'grandeur in a joke'. And Chesterton claims that Chaucer displays 'laughter in the grand style'—unlike Arnold, who, 'for all his merits, did not laugh but only smiled—not to say smirked'—and that he is a 'great' poet not least because he was 'a great... humorist'. Around everything Chaucer wrote there was 'a sort of penumbra of playfulness... a halo of humour'. For humour, being 'a very Christian thing', is a very sacred thing. It is also a characteristic of Catholics ('A frivolous Puritan was not a Puritan at all'), whose external 'frivolity' is completely compatible with an internal faith, 'puzzling' as this is to those who do not realize that it is 'the Catholic philosophy' that satisfies the true philosopher who in Chesterton's philosophy must be 'a laughing philosopher'. *Pace* Arnold, Chesterton insists that 'the comic' can sometimes seem 'almost more tremendous than the tragic'. He admits that, compared with

---

[166] UNDA, UPCO 1/82, 83.   [167] Ward, *GKC* 523.

'the fun of Dickens', there was 'certainly something shrewd, sensible and solid about the humour of Chaucer'—nevertheless 'a frontier' had been 'crossed, and there is already in Chaucer an element of irrational humour, which is not the same as the old rational humour' that had been 'a form of satire'. For, while Chaucer can sound satirical in the old sense, 'he already inhabits a world of comicality that is not a world of controversy': 'He makes fun of people, in the exact sense of getting fun out of them for himself... he is already on the road to the Dickensian lunatic-asylum of laughter; because he is valuing his fools and knaves and almost wishing (as it were) to preserve them in spirits—in high spirits.' Like Dickens, no one has 'suffered fools more gladly; getting any amount of gladness or gaiety out of his private observations of their folly'. So for Chesterton Chaucer was 'a true trustee' of 'the great national heritage of humour', that 'great national contribution to the culture of Christendom', comparable to 'the Spanish sense of honour or the French sense of right reason'. It was more than 'wit', 'more even than humour': 'It is not merely a critical quality; in a sense it is even a creative quality; a sort of crooked creation that is called the fantastic or the topsy-turvy', 'full of wild images... upheld by an invisible power and lifted without support upon the wings of laughter; by a power more unanswerable and more irresponsible than pure beauty'. And it is this 'cry of pure folly' that 'can be heard, perhaps for the first time in human history', in the 'Father of English Poetry': 'He had somehow got into his head and into his note-book a certain national quality, centuries before the nation attempted to understand or describe its own quality.' The English humour first found in Chaucer can be 'compared to art for art's sake' but is more accurately 'described as adventure for adventure's sake'.[168]

If, as in Dickens, the comical in Chaucer, far from lacking in high seriousness, is felt to be as serious as the tragic—so too he shares in Dickens's (and Chesterton's) relish for the ordinary. Like the greatest poets, he had not 'bothered to invent a small philosophy', having 'inherited a large philosophy', which invariably is shared by 'very great men... with very ordinary men'. The great poet 'only professes to express the thought that everybody has always had', simply helping ordinary men to realize 'how great are the emotions which they, in a smaller way, have already experienced', showing 'the small man how great he is'. Like any great poet, Chaucer 'breathes... gratitude, or the theory of thanks', grateful for 'actuality... existence... the fact that things truly are', for 'the fundamental fact

[168] *C.* 159, 161–2, 165, 217, 245, 260, 309–11, 313, 371–2.

of being, as against not being'. Although Chesterton sees this 'primary wonder at the very existence of the world' as belonging to all great writers, he claims that Chaucer possessed 'a certain appetite for things as they actually are, and because they actually are', 'a gusto' or 'zest' that a modern and 'rather wearier' culture associates with childhood. It included 'an impulsive movement to applaud what he does not approve. It is as if their impudence gave him so much pleasure, that he could not withhold a sort of affection based on gratitude.'[169]

Chaucer's love of the ordinary is a part of what Chesterton calls his 'spiritual sanity', his 'balanced . . . habit of mind', a 'cheerfulness or sanity' that came from his Catholic theology, 'which aimed at a certain equilibrium, achieved by giving so much weight to one thing and so much less or more to another', which did not narrow but 'broadened his mind'. For Catholicism was not 'a single idea', 'a simple creed' like Calvinism— 'Nothing could be simpler than saying that men go to Hell because God made them on purpose to send them to Hell'—but 'a complicated creed'. It was not a 'theology shrivelled to a single thought; its very thunders of indignation all on one note; or the whole great Christian philosophy hardened into one harsh doctrine'. Because Chesterton saw Catholicism as the key that unlocked the meaning of this world, it had to be complex and complicated, which is why here as elsewhere he vigorously condemns the speciously attractive demand 'to *simplify* Catholicism':

That notion, in its essence a very negative notion, has never wrought anything but ill to Christendom; and is always returning with a plausibility and a false simplicity to tempt and to betray Christians. Mahomet, centuries before, had tried to create a simplified Christianity, and had created a world of fatalism and stagnation. Calvin, centuries afterwards, tried to create a simplified Christianity, and created a world of pessimism and devil-worship.

By contrast, in Catholicism 'there was a perpetual and centripetal tendency towards the discovery of a just balance of all these ideas. All those who broke away were centrifugal and not centripetal; they went away into deserts to develop a solitary doctrine. But medieval philosophy and culture . . . was always *seeking* equilibrium,' the Church being 'the balance of many movements and moods'. It was this 'tradition of a Church which had condemned heresies on the right hand and the left; and always claimed to stand for the truth as a whole and not for concentration on a part' that Chaucer inherited. Indeed, he was the 'living embodiment' of

---

[169] *C.* 166–9, 172–3, 275, 357.

that tradition: for he was full of 'common sense' in the literal sense of the original Latin phrase *communis sentential*, which meant the opposite of common sense in the modern sense of an individual's 'private judgment'. And this communal sense did not 'believe that the truth was to be found by going to extremes'.[170]

It was this *communis sentential* that made possible Chaucer's greatest work, *The Canterbury Tales*. For without it there could have been no pilgrimage to Canterbury in the first place, or at least no pilgrimage that cut across social barriers and was not that of a 'narrow clique'. For it is not a 'broad religion' but a 'religion of dogmas ... that creates a broader brotherhood and brings men of all kinds together'. It is a religion that embraces both the masses and the intellectuals, as Chesterton explains in a wryly ironic passage:

> All men share in a fact, if they believe it to be a fact. Only a few men commonly share a feeling, when it is only a feeling. If there is a deep and delicate and intangible feeling, detached from all statements, but reaching to a wordless worship of beauty, wafted in a sweet savour from the woods of Kent or the spires of Canterbury, then we may be tolerably certain that the Miller will not have it. The Miller can only become the Pilgrim, if he recognizes that God is in the heavens as he recognizes that the sun is in the sky. If he does recognize it, he can share the dogma just as he can share the day-light. But he cannot be expected to share all the shades of fine intellectual mysticism that might exist in the mind of the Prioress or the Parson. I can understand that argument being turned in an anti-democratic as well as an anti-dogmatic direction; but anyhow the individualistic mystics must either do without the mysticism or without the Miller. To some refined persons the loss of the latter would be no very insupportable laceration of the feelings. But I am not a refined person and I am not merely thinking about feelings. I am even so antiquated as to be thinking about rights; about the rights of men, which are extended even to millers. Among those rights is a certain rough working respect and consideration, which is at the basis of comradeship. And I say that if the comradeship is to include the Miller at all, it must be based on the recognition of something as really true, and not merely as ideally beautiful.

It was a dogmatic religion of 'solid fact' that had 'turned all this crowd of incongruous people into one company': 'A religion of moods would never have brought them together at the tavern, far less sent them trotting laboriously to the tomb.' It was 'an objective religion, worshipped as an object by the whole people'. But when religion becomes

---

[170] *C.* 330–1, 341, 359–60, 362, 366, 368–70, 374.

a wholly subjective thing, then the Miller, 'with his appetite for more vulgar noises', would refuse to go to Canterbury and insist on Ramsgate as his destination, while the Merchant would absolutely refuse 'to ride beyond Chatham, because all his interests are limited to the progressive industry of that wealthy and dirty town'. But that is not the worst.

Darker days will come, when the Prioress, not content with pitying mice, will withdraw to a Vegetarian Hostel . . . while the now aged Knight, swearing that the Service is going to the dogs, and that these damned pacifists haven't a damned patriotic instinct left, shall devote himself furiously to the fortifications of Dover. As their counterparts stand to-day, it is easier to imagine the Wife of Bath wanting to go sunbathing at Margate, or the Clerk instantly returning, with refined disgust, to Oxford, than to imagine either of them wanting to toil on together to a particular tomb in Canterbury.[171]

A month after the publication of *Chaucer* another collection of Chesterton's articles appeared, collected from a number of papers and periodicals. *Sidelights on New London and Newer York and Other Essays* is chiefly of interest for what it has to say about America and Americans. Chesterton begins the part of the book entitled 'Newer York' with a paradox: 'There is nothing the matter with Americans except their ideals. The real American is all right; it is the ideal American who is all wrong. . . . They have been deliberately and dogmatically taught to be conceited. They have been systematically educated in a theory of enthusiasm, which degrades it into mere egotism.' For he did not think they were 'naturally boomsters or business bullies', but that they were the victims of an 'egotistic heresy' that had 'taught them against all their Christian instincts that boasting is better than courtesy and pride better than humility'. In Chesterton's view: 'What has happened to America is that a number of people who were meant to be heroic and fighting farmers, at once peasants and pioneers, have been swept by the pestilence of a particular fad or false doctrine; the ideal which has and deserves the detestable title of Making Good.' By 'one mean twist of words' they had contrived 'to combine the notion of making money with the entirely opposite notion of being good'. They had indeed 'made good', as could be seen in 'the bumptious and purse-proud swagger of some Yankee globe-trotters in Europe'—not that they were any different from their English Victorian predecessors 'when England had the same mercantile supremacy and the same materialistic mood'. Americans not only had to be boasters but also 'optimists,—because they live in a world that

[171] *C.* 285–8.

can easily go wrong': 'Hence we find that in America, the home of...
colossal commerce and combination, practically all their strange sects
agree about this strange philosophy of Optimism. Everybody is educated
in a sort of permanent ethic of unmeaning hopefulness...'. Indeed,
Chesterton thought that, likeable as Americans were, their 'cheerfulness'
was 'the most dismal thing about them', enslaved as they were by 'the
horrible slavery of smiling'. But ultimately England was to blame, having
exported both industrialism and Puritanism to America. In fact, 'pure
Puritanism' had long expired in America, but there remained 'the only
practical product of Puritanism', which 'might be called, in the more
general sense, Prohibitionism'. This 'Puritan mood' was essentially 'the
misdirection of moral anger' into 'righteous indignation about the wrong
thing', such as 'the vice of beer drinking'. However, since 'most Americans'
were 'born drunk', they required

a little wine or beer to sober them. They have a sort of permanent intoxication
from within; a sort of invisible champagne which needs to be weighted and
soothed and supplemented by something corresponding to the glass of port with
which the English were accustomed to conclude and settle their dinner. Americans do not need drink to inspire them to do anything; though they do
sometimes ... need a little for the deeper and more delicate purpose of teaching
them how to do nothing.

Still, Chesterton did find in these American Puritans an 'unconscious
Christianity' in their 'curious careering energy', which contained 'a sort
of simplicity', a 'touch of innocence; the absence of the paralysis of pride'.
Any Englishman arriving in America felt 'a certain kind of fresh air, from
which a certain kind of smell has departed, and the thing that has vanished
is snobbishness'. Instead, he now 'instantly' felt 'equality and fraternity'.
Americans were 'democrats' and felt 'equal', having 'that sort of self-
respect which is no respecter of persons'. Unfortunately, although America
had 'a great political idea ... it had a small religious idea'. This 'individualism in religion' explained why Americans were not proper republicans in
the sense of every man having 'a direct relation to the realm or common-
weal, more direct than he has to any masters or patrons in private life': in
America the individual made 'good in trade, because it was originally the
individual making good in goodness; that is, in salvation of the soul'.[172]

---

[172] S. 523, 525, 550–3, 555, 563–4, 566–7, 572, 585–8, 590.

15

The Last Years

IN June 1932 the Chestertons went to Dublin for the 31st International Eucharistic Congress, where they stayed at the Viceroy's Lodge. Maisie Ward and her husband Frank Sheed were also in Dublin for the Congress, which lasted from 21 to 26 June. Maisie Ward remembered Chesterton being regaled with praise of his writings by an Eastern-rite Catholic priest, who asked to be photographed with him. Shocked by what seemed to him the immense smallness of himself compared with the events he was witnessing, Chesterton consoled himself by reflecting that he had heard in the East that an idiot was supposed to bring luck. Maisie Ward recalled that his favourite story was of the old woman who said on the last day when rain threatened: 'Well, if it rains now He will have brought it on Himself.'[1]

Chesterton wrote some articles for the English Catholic weekly newspaper the *Universe* and one for the Jesuit periodical *Studies: An Irish Quarterly Review*, which were subsequently published in book form in November as *Christendom in Dublin*, giving his impressions of the Congress. What most impressed him was the faith of the people, especially the poor. The festivities of this celebration of the Eucharist were not more or less confined to 'festive highways' as one would expect: 'Instead of the main stream of colour flowing down the main streets of commerce, and overflowing into the crooked and neglected slums, it was exactly the other way; it was the slums that were the springs. *There* were the furnaces of colour; *there* were the fountains of light...'. Then, too, in the countryside one could find 'a

---

[1] Ward, *GKC* 521–2.

last lonely homestead, seemingly a hundred miles from anywhere; and flying the papal Flag'. To this 'wayside home' the flag was 'so homely... that they hung it out like so much washing'. It seemed almost like an 'enchanted castle': 'There was something unearthly, as of a place on which the ends of the earth were come, about that low neglected roof and that remote blazonry of Rome.' And as the 'great flag began to flap and crackle in the freshening evening wind... those who had been toiling on the little farm, those whose fathers had been hunted like vermin, those whose religion should have been burnt out like witchcraft, came back slowly through the twilight; walking like lords on their own land...'. It gave an Englishman 'a glimpse of another history and a new slant or angle upon Europe'.[2]

As he gazed at the faith of the Irish, Chesterton reflected that Lenin had said that religion was the opium of the people; but he had got it the wrong way round. Irreligion was the opium of the people: 'Wherever the people do not believe in something beyond the world, they will worship the world. But, above all, they will worship the strongest thing in the world.' Opium could make people 'contented': 'But if you are to have anything like divine discontent, then it really must be divine.' For the abolition of God meant that 'the Government becomes the God'. The truth was that 'all those whose theories are merely human soon forget their humanity'.[3]

In the copy of *Christendom in Dublin* that he gave Dorothy Collins, Chesterton wrote an inscription that celebrated the fact that she had recently become a Catholic: now they were united not only by 'friendship' but by the 'Truth' which 'has made us free'.[4] Dorothy had been received into the Church and conditionally baptized (with the Chestertons as her godparents) on 8 October 1932 by Monsignor Charles Smith, who had become the first parish priest of Beaconsfield, which was no longer part of the parish of High Wycombe, the previous year. She was 38 years old.[5] Fortunately, the Chestertons had only had to endure the impossible Father Fitzgerald for a few more months on their return from America. A relieved Frances wrote to Father O'Connor on 21 August 1931: 'You will rejoice to hear that our Parish Priest M. [Monsignor] Smith has taken up residence and seems delightful.'[6]

In August Chesterton received a letter from the BBC inviting him to contribute to 'our commentaries upon current literature'. He would, he

[2] *CID* 40, 42–5.   [3] *CID* 55, 57–8.   [4] Ward, *RC* 158–9.
[5] St Teresa's Church, Beaconsfield, baptismal register.
[6] Frances Chesterton to John O'Connor, 21 Aug. 1931, BL Add. MS 73196, fo. 144.

was told, 'be a tremendous success at the microphone'. The idea was that he would broadcast fortnightly beginning in October 'for a trial period of six months'.[7] Chesterton accepted the invitation but asked for a three-month trial period, and stipulated that the talks would be of a general nature rather than detailed reviews of the books he was sent. It was agreed that the talks would start in the second half of October. The BBC was sorry but it could not offer a fee comparable to 'journalistic rates', but suggested that their fees were 'not unreasonable' when compared with those paid by weekly and monthly periodicals.[8] The talks eventually began on 31 October.[9] Chesterton was told he did not have to stick rigidly to the text he was asked to submit beforehand, as he was encouraged to be spontaneous. Each talk reviewed anything from four to ten books. The BBC was delighted by the talks: Chesterton had brought 'something very rare to the microphone', and he would have 'a vast public by Christmas'.[10] He agreed to give 'another series of book talks' the following autumn.[11]

But in spite of his success as a practitioner of the new medium, 'he was always very nervous beforehand', Dorothy Collins remembered, 'and he would not undertake the series without a promise that his wife or I or both of us should sit in the studio with him'. However, 'after an agonised glance at us he would begin, and immediately be oblivious to all his surroundings as he read, and improvised his text as he went along'. The advantage of having his wife and secretary sitting there in the studio with him—'a privilege which was quite out of order'—was that he was able to talk 'direct to us, which gave his talks the intimate character which the public so much enjoyed'. Even the most diehard opponents of the new medium began to acquire wireless sets in order just to listen to Chesterton.[12] In January 1934 it was arranged that he would contribute to a new series of talks, 'personal, informal, and, as far as possible, humorous commentaries on the events of the past week'.[13] Dorothy Collins years later thought his

[7] C. A. Siepmann to G. K. Chesterton, 2 Aug. 1932, BL Add. MS 73234A, fo. 4.
[8] Kathleen Houlihan to Dorothy Collins, 5 Aug. 1932, BL Add. MS 73234A, fo. 5; Dorothy Collins to C. A. Siepmann, 9 Aug. 1932, BL Add. MS 73234A, fo. 6; Kathleen Houlihan to Dorothy Collins, 10 Aug. 1932, BL Add. MS 73234A, fo. 7.
[9] Dorothy Collins to Kathleen Houlihan, 16 Aug. 1932, BL Add. MS 73234A, fo. 9.
[10] Ward, *GKC* 541.
[11] Lionel Fielden to G. K. Chesterton, 4 May 1933, BL Add. MS 73234A, fo. 46.
[12] Dorothy Collins's notes for talks, BL Add. MS 73477, fos. 93, 116.
[13] Peter Fleming to G. K. Chesterton, 3 Jan. 1934, BL Add. MS 73234A, fo. 73; Dorothy Collins to Peter Fleming, 6 Jan. 1934, BL Add. MS 73234A, fo. 75.

last broadcast was in March 1936, when he gave a talk entitled 'We will End with a Bang' in a series called 'The Spice of Life'[14] on the theme 'what you really like doing in life';[15] but in fact there was one more talk broadcast at the end of the month, 'What the Middle Ages Meant to Europe'.[16]

The year 1933 saw the deaths of Chesterton's mother in February and Frances's mother in August.[17] Marie Chesterton was still living in Warwick Gardens, but Mrs Blogg was now in a nursing home in Beaconsfield. Maisie Ward remembered driving Frances to visit the two old ladies and her saying how difficult she found it helping two agnostics facing death. During the drive Frances confided in her that she knew her mother-in-law had not liked her, but that lately she had made her very happy by telling her that she realized now that she had been the right wife for her son. A cousin of Marie Chesterton told Maisie Ward that Frances had also told her that mother-in-law and daughter-in-law had come closer together at the end and that Frances was not unaware that no mother ever thought any woman was good enough for her son. However, the older Mrs Chesterton had always acknowledged to the cousin that she respected Frances for keeping her son out of debt. The house in Warwick Gardens contained the nearest thing to a family archive; but, taking one look at the mass of papers, Chesterton consigned them to the dustbin.[18] Dorothy Collins managed to save the last of four loads that had not already gone to the rubbish dump,[19] and brought it in her car to Beaconsfield, while Chesterton grumbled about 'the hoarding habits of women'.[20] However, when they arrived back at Top Meadow, Frances was 'no more pleased' at the sight of the rescued papers, the house being already overcrowded with books and papers.[21] The money that Chesterton inherited on the death of his mother enabled him and Frances to plan legacies not only for relatives

[14] Dorothy Collins's notes for talks, BL Add. MS 73477, fo. 139. Published in the *Listener*, 18 Mar. 1936, and repr. in G. K. Chesterton, *The Spice of Life and Other Essays*, ed. Dorothy Collins (Beaconsfield: Darwen Finlayson, 1964), 161–71.

[15] Moray McLaren to G. K. Chesterton, 28 Feb. 1936, BL Add. MS 73477, fo. 126.

[16] *Listener*, 1 Apr. 1936.

[17] Frances Chesterton to Charles O'Donnell, 8 Dec. 1933, UNDA, UPCO 1/83.

[18] Ward, *GKC* 535–6.

[19] According to Ward, *GKC* 536, half was saved, but Dorothy Collins recorded that she had been able to save only a quarter (Dorothy Collins's notes for talks, BL Add. MS 73477, fo. 139).

[20] Ward, *GKC* 536.

[21] Dorothy Collins's notes for talks, BL Add. MS 73477, fo. 139.

but also for friends and the church in Beaconsfield. Top Meadow itself was to be left to the diocese of Northampton in the hope that it might become a convent school.[22]

In March 1933 Chesterton published another collection of his columns from the *Illustrated London News*, called *All I Survey: A Book of Essays*. A sense of history is a prominent feature of the articles. There is the usual complaint that the contemporary age was 'the only period in all history when people were proud of being modern': 'We are the only men in all history who fell back upon bragging about the mere fact that to-day is not yesterday.' In the Middle Ages people were not conscious of 'being medieval'; whereas Chesterton's contemporaries automatically assumed that to call something 'a relic of medievalism' was to throw 'mud' at it—although people might hesitate to blow up Westminster Abbey or to burn 'all existing copies of Dante's *Divine Comedy* and Chaucer's *Canterbury Tales*' as 'relics of medievalism'. Why, the very journalists, for whom 'medieval only means old, and old only means bad', themselves worked for 'a relic of medievalism'—namely, the printing press. The slightest knowledge of history showed the ignorance of assuming that war is always bad when wars were essential to 'preserve civilization'—at that very time Hitler seemed intent upon 'setting all Christendom aflame by a raid on Poland'. As for rebellions, they were usually rebellions 'against rebels' rather than 'reactionaries': 'Those who were, in fact, doomed to dethronement in the future were generally the futurists of the past.' Historical theories, like the 'Teutonic Theory', under whose 'gigantic shadow' Chesterton himself had grown up, affected 'the truthfulness of historians, and more often in the direction of falsehood than of truth'. And he had noticed with amusement how these theories 'pursue each other, and how the last almost always devours and destroys the last but one'. The inevitability of history was one of the 'Victorian conventions', that 'all was for the best, or at any rate that all was as it had to be'; but for Chesterton 'all the past' was 'alive with alternatives, and nobody can show, nobody has really attempted to show, that they were not real alternatives'. Ignorance of the past meant ignorance of the present: 'History is a hill or high point of vantage, from which alone men see the town in which they live or the age in which they are living.' The mind of the so-called progressive thinker 'remains fixed, in a posture that is called progressive. It never looks back, even for remembrance; it never looks the other way, even for experiment; it never looks at

---

[22] Ward, *GKC* 535–6.

the other side, even for a paradox; it never winks the other eye. It simply knows all there is; and there does not seem much to know.'[23]

The usual social questions concern Chesterton. He saw most modern 'educational and philanthropic reform' as simply 'kidnapping on a large scale': 'That is, it has shown an increasing disregard for the privacy of the private citizen, considered as a parent. I have called it a revolution; and at bottom it is really a Bolshevist revolution. For what could be more purely and perfectly Communist than to say that you regard other people's children as if they were your own?' In this 'supremely... educational age', in which 'earnest philosophers are really doubting whether it is right to teach anybody anything', this meant that 'the government's right to teach everybody's children is for the first time established', while 'the father's right to teach his own children is for the first time denied'. Indeed, in 'respectable circles', the family was now 'never mentioned'. On the other hand, the modern woman had ceased to be 'a Communist in the home', which was 'the only truly and legitimately Communist institution'—' "With all my worldly goods I thee endow" is the only satisfactory Bolshevist proclamation that has ever been made about property'—and had become 'a proletarian in the shop'. Because 'the sanctity and pride of private property' had been 'enormously exaggerated' in the early nineteenth century, there had been 'a race for wealth' that had paradoxically resulted in property becoming 'much less private', as the modern capitalist had become 'more of a communist' in no longer having 'a horror of centralization'. When Belloc and Chesterton had said that they 'really did believe that private property should be private', they were 'mildly chaffed', as though they were 'seeking solitude like hermits, or hoarding halfpence like misers'. Politically, Chesterton had considered himself a Liberal—only to discover that 'Liberals never did really believe in popular government, any more than in anything else that was popular, such as public-houses or the Dublin sweepstake'.[24]

Chesterton sees culture as inextricably connected with religion. Christian culture, like the mysteries of Christianity, was 'woven of many strands, of many fabrics and colours, and twisted into the single knot, the knot that holds the world together, but the knot that is of all knots the most difficult to trace out or untie'. Compared with that, there was 'something simple and smooth and all of a piece about the ancient silks of China or the peasant weaving of India', where Hinduism sought 'to unite all things', as

---

[23] *AIS* 11–14, 29–30, 367, 48–9, 103–5, 131–2.
[24] *AIS* 5, 44, 117–18, 160–2, 164.

opposed to Christianity, which sought 'not merely to unite all things, but to unite union with disunion'. Like Hindu India, the modern world seemed to have 'no notion of preserving different things side by side, of allowing its proper and proportionate place to each, of saving the whole varied heritage of culture'. It had 'no notion except that of simplifying something by destroying nearly everything':

> I myself value very highly the great nineteenth-century illumination of romantic love, just as I value the great eighteenth-century ideal of right reason and human dignity, or the seventeenth-century intensity, or the sixteenth-century expansion, or the divine logic and dedicated valour of the Middle Ages. I do not see why any of these cultural conquests should be lost or despised, or why it is necessary for every fashion to wash away all that is best in every other.

What had certainly also been washed away was the Christian basis of culture. The 'gods', for instance, of the republican romantics were love and liberty, which were 'both simply fragments of Christian mysticism, and even of Christian theology, torn out of their proper place, flung loosely about and finally hurled forward into an age of hard materialism which instantly destroyed them'. As soon as they ceased being 'religious ideas' they ceased being 'rational ideas': 'One of them was a hazy human exaggeration of the sacramental idea of marriage. The other was a hazy human exaggeration of the brotherhood of men in God.' The romantic lover ultimately both drew on 'the Christian capital of the old ideas of immortality and sanctity' and appealed to 'the old tradition of the martyr and ascetic, who lost the world to save his soul'. But unfortunately the Romantics held up romance in 'a sort of indeterminate pre-eminence; a dizzy and toppling idolatry' without 'making it secure' on the 'solid pedestal' of 'a religious idea'. Similarly, when 'the divine ground from under Democracy' was cut away, then 'Democracy was left to stand by itself', or, in other words, to 'fall by itself'.[25]

Chesterton's cultural criticism in these selected articles includes some striking literary criticism. The 'fragments' of Stevenson's unfinished masterpiece, *Weir of Hermiston*, are likened to 'the fragments of a colossal god lying broken in the desert'. And Stevenson's 'sharpness of *focus*' (what elsewhere Chesterton called his 'deadly precision'[26]), especially in depicting the 'ugly figures' that he 'most' enjoyed, ensured that, even they had 'a definite form', so that he turned 'everything to beauty, even to the terrible beauty that is made out of a harmony of ugly things'. But an 'odd style',

---

[25] *AIS* 87, 99, 166–8, 187–8.   [26] *HA* 9.

such as that of Carlyle, Browning, or Meredith, was not of any 'advantage' to the author's future reputation. On the other hand, it was when a poet was 'moving most smoothly on the butter-slide of praise and progress and the prevailing fashion' that he 'generally came a cropper'. In poetry, sense and sound were inseparable: 'the sense depends on the sound and the sound depends on the sense.' The trouble with contemporary satirists like Aldous Huxley was that, while they saw 'with extraordinary vividness the humbug or the impudence or intellectual cruelty of this or that social type, in this or that social situation', they really thought that things were 'too complex for anybody to do the right thing', with the result that there was 'a hollow in the heart of their whirlwind of destructive criticism, as there is a hollow in the heart of the whirlpool'. Chaucer was 'our one medieval poet', and yet he flatly contradicted all that people meant by 'medieval'. He belonged to 'that fairly large and very happy band of artists'—like Chesterton himself, we might add—'who are not troubled with the artistic temperament'. The 'extreme antithesis of the aesthete', Chaucer was blessed with an 'essentially merry' mood. Paradoxically, he was 'wide enough to be narrow; that is, he could bring a broad experience of life to the enjoyment of local or even accidental things', because he had 'a scheme of spiritual values in their right order' and because he had 'seen the great world of human beings'. Walter Scott is considered a Romantic writer, but it was not for nothing that he was born in the eighteenth century: 'He was, almost as much as he was anything, a great orator.' So much so that Chesterton thought that it would be 'well worth while to make an anthology' of his speeches. While Scott romanticized the Middle Ages, he 'knew nothing' of its religion: 'But he had extracted from his feudal traditions something on which his spirit freely fed; something without which the modern world is starving. He found the idea of Honour, which is the true energy in all militant eloquence.'[27]

2

In July 1933 Chesterton attended a lunch at Claridge's Hotel in London given by the Royal Society of Literature for the Canadian Authors' Association. Kipling proposed the toast and Chesterton seconded him. He began by acknowledging that his listeners would be 'much puzzled at my occupying any space—so much space—in this august assembly', and

---

[27] *AIS* 9–10, 55, 62, 67–8, 86, 174–5, 177–8, 221–2.

must be wondering what he could add to what Kipling, a 'great literary genius', had already said. He could hardly 'pose as a newspaperman'— 'one reads of newspaper men slipping in through half-closed doors'—and 'no one could possibly think of me as slipping through a half-closed door'! He had travelled in Canada 'in the miserable capacity of one giving lectures'—but he hesitated to call himself a lecturer for 'fear some of you may have attended my lectures'. In fact, he had twice visited Canada and enjoyed the 'overwhelming' hospitality of the Canadian Authors' Association: 'The Canadian Literature Society rushed out to welcome any stray traveller, and in the confusion I was mistaken for a literary man. I tried to explain I was merely a lecturer, and one of the first things for a lecturer to do is talk about things he does not understand, such as Canada.'[28]

In September Chesterton published the last of his half-dozen or so major works, *St Thomas Aquinas*. Even Shaw was enthusiastic about the project. 'Great news this', he wrote to Frances, 'about the Divine Doctor. I have been preaching for years that intellect is a passion that will finally become the most ecstatic of all the passions; and I have cherished Thomas as a most praiseworthy creature for being my forerunner on this point.'[29] The previous year he had sent Chesterton a copy of his irreverent, not to say blasphemous, latest book, *The Adventures of the Black Girl in her Search for God*, with the flippant message: 'Tell the Vatican that something must be done about the Bible. It is like the burden on [*Pilgrim's Progress*'s] Christian's back at present; only it won't come off.'[30] After rapidly dictating about half the book to Dorothy Collins, and without consulting any authorities, Chesterton suddenly asked her to go to London and buy some books about the Divine Doctor. When she asked what books, he replied, '*I* don't know.' Father O'Connor came to the rescue, supplying her with the names of standard and recent works on the subject. Chesterton 'flipped them rapidly through', the only way Dorothy Collins had ever see him read a book. He then dictated the rest of the book to her, without consulting any of the secondary works, which remained unmarked except for one little sketch of Thomas in the margin of one of the books. However, Étienne Gilson, the French Thomist philosopher and historian of medieval philosophy, and the pioneer of the twentieth-century Thomist revival along with Jacques Maritain, said ruefully on its publication, 'Chesterton makes one despair. I have been studying St Thomas all my life and I could

---

[28] Clemens, 76–8.   [29] Ward, *GKC* 525.
[30] George Bernard Shaw to G. K. Chesterton, 3 Dec. 1931, in *Bernard Shaw: Collected Letters 1926–1950*, ed. Dan H. Laurence (London: Max Reinhardt, 1988), 318.

never have written such a book.'[31] After Chesterton's death, he wrote that he considered the book as being 'without possible comparison the best book ever written on St Thomas': 'Nothing short of genius can account for such an achievement.' Chesterton's 'so-called "wit"' had put the scholars to 'shame'. He had 'guessed' all that they had 'tried to demonstrate' and that they had tried 'more or less clumsily... to express in academic formulas'. In Gilson's view he was 'one of the deepest thinkers who ever existed'.[32] To Father Kevin Scannell, who had been O'Connor's curate and who inherited his Chesterton collection, Gilson wrote: 'My reason for admiring his "Thomas Aquinas" as I do, precisely is that I find him *always right* in his conclusions about the man and the doctrine even though in fact, *he knew so little about him.*' He always felt that Chesterton was 'nearer the real Thomas' than he was even 'after reading and teaching the Angelic Doctor for sixty years'.[33] Of course, Chesterton's knowledge was very limited compared to Gilson's, but it would be a mistake to conclude that his portrait of Thomas was some kind of purely inspired stroke of genius. For, Dorothy Collins tells us, 'he had read the Summa in his youth'.[34]

S. Thomas Aquinas begins with an extended contrast between Thomas and Francis of Assisi. Physically, they were opposites. Francis was 'a lean and lively little man; thin as a thread and vibrant as a bow-string; and in his motions like an arrow from the bow': 'In appearance he must have been like a thin brown skeleton autumn leaf dancing eternally before the wind; but in truth it was he that was the wind.' Thomas, on the other hand, was 'a huge heavy bull of a man, fat and slow and quiet'. Unlike the 'fiery and even fidgety' Francis, Thomas was 'so solid that the scholars, in the schools which he attended regularly, thought he was a dunce'. As the son of a middle-class shopkeeper, Francis spent his 'whole life' in 'revolt against the mercantile life of his father': 'he retained none the less, something of the quickness... which makes the market hum like a hive. In the common phrase, fond as he was of green fields, he did not let the grass grow under his feet.' In American slang, Francis was 'a live wire'—or rather, since 'there is no such thing as a live wire' (a typically modern 'mechanical metaphor from a dead thing'), he was 'a live worm', indeed 'a very live worm': 'Greatest of all foes to the go-getting ideal, he had certainly abandoned getting, but he was still going.' By contrast, Thomas came from the leisured class, and his work always had 'something of the placidity

---

[31] Ward, *GKC* 525.   [32] Clemens, 150.

[33] Étienne Gilson to Kevin Scannell, 7 Jan. 1966, BL Add. MS 73472, fo. 105.

[34] Dorothy Collins's notes for talks, BL Add. MS 73477, fo. 147.

of leisure': 'He was a hard worker, but nobody could possibly mistake him for a hustler.' Chesterton had to admit that, 'while the romantic glory of St Francis has lost nothing of its glamour for me', he had 'in later years grown to feel almost as much affection, or in some aspects even more, for this man who unconsciously inhabited a large heart and a large head, like one inheriting a large house, and exercised there an equally generous if rather more absent-minded hospitality': 'There are moments when St Francis, the most unworldly man who ever walked the world, is almost too efficient for me.' Just as Chesterton had assaulted the post-Christian imagination with images of a startlingly unfamiliar Christ, so too he makes sure that we understand what Thomas did when he 'calmly announced' to his aristocratic family that he was becoming a Dominican friar, a 'new order founded by Dominic the Spaniard'—'much as the eldest son of the squire might go home and airily inform the family that he had married a gypsy; or the heir of a Tory Duke state that he was walking tomorrow with the Hunger Marchers organised by alleged Communists'. There was no objection to his becoming a monk —monasticism had become established and respectable —but when he said 'he wished to be a Friar... his brothers flew at him like wild beasts'. The paradox was that Thomas, unlike Francis, had nothing of the beggar or vagabond about him—and yet he insisted on being 'established and appointed to be a Beggar'.[35]

But, 'while the two men were thus a contrast in almost every feature, they were really doing the same thing. One of them was doing it in the world of the mind and the other in the world of the worldly.' Yet it was 'the same great medieval movement... it was more important than the Reformation.... it was the Reformation'. For, Chesterton explains, the Protestant Reformation was merely 'a belated revolt of the thirteenth-century pessimists. It was a back-wash of the old Augustinian Puritanism against the Aristotelian liberality.' But neither Francis nor Thomas was 'a backwash'. Both were uniquely suited for a new age: 'The Saint is a medicine because he is an antidote. Indeed, that is why the saint is often a martyr; he is mistaken for a poison because he is an antidote. He will generally be found restoring the world to sanity by exaggerating whatever the world neglects, which is by no means always the same element in every age.' Each generation instinctively sought its saint: 'not what the people want, but rather what the people need.' Thus it was 'the paradox of history that each generation is converted by the saint who contradicts it most'. The 'popular poetry of St Francis and the almost rationalistic prose of

[35] *TA* 422–3, 450–1.

St Thomas' both contributed to 'the development of the supreme doctrine, which was also the dogma of all dogmas'. They were 'both great growths of Catholic development, depending upon external things only as every living and growing thing depends on them; that is, it digests and transforms them, but continues in its own image and not in theirs'. Both saints were 'doing the same great work; one in the study and the other in the street':

They were not bringing something new into Christianity, in the sense of something heathen or heretical into Christianity; on the contrary, they were bringing Christianity into Christendom. But they were bringing it back against the pressure of certain historic tendencies, which had hardened into habits in many great schools and authorities in the Christian Church; and they were using tools and weapons which seemed to many people to be associated with heresy or heathenry. St Francis used Nature much as St Thomas used Aristotle; and to some they seemed to be using a Pagan goddess and a Pagan sage.... Perhaps it would sound too paradoxical to say that these two saints saved us from Spirituality; a dreadful doom. Perhaps it may be misunderstood if I say that St Francis, for all his love of animals, saved us from being Buddhists; and that St Thomas, for all his love of Greek philosophy, saved us from being Platonists. But it is best to say the truth in its simplest form; that they both reaffirmed the Incarnation, by bringing God back to earth.

For 'the historical Catholic Church began by being Platonist; by being rather too Platonist', with the result that unfortunately 'the purely spiritual or mystical side of Catholicism had very much got the upper hand in the first Catholic centuries', with the consequence that various 'things weighed down what we should now roughly call the Western element; though it has as good a right to be called the Christian element; since its common sense is but the holy familiarity of the word made flesh'. After all, a Christian, as opposed to a Jew or a Muslim or a Buddhist, '*means* a man who believes that deity or sanctity has attached to matter or entered the world of the senses'. Francis's 'readiness ... to learn from the flowers or the birds', far from anticipating 'the Pagan renaissance', instead pointed back to the New Testament and forward to 'the Aristotelian realism of the *Summa* of St Thomas Aquinas'. By 'humanising divinity', Francis was not 'paganising divinity', since 'the humanising of divinity is actually the strongest and starkest and most incredible dogma in the Creed':

St Francis was becoming more like Christ, and not merely more like Buddha, when he considered the lilies of the field or the fowls of the air; and St Thomas was becoming more of a Christian, and not merely more of an Aristotelian, when he insisted that God and the image of God had come in contact through matter with a material world.

These two saints were 'in the most exact sense of the term, Humanists; because they were insisting on the immense importance of the human being', because they were 'strengthening that staggering doctrine of Incarnation'. The more 'rational or natural' they became, the more 'orthodox' they became. Both 'the Thomist movement in metaphysics'—with its recovery, thanks to Aristotle, whom Thomas had 'baptised' and miraculously 'raised...from the dead', of 'the most defiant of all dogmas, the wedding of God with Man and therefore with Matter'—and also 'the Franciscan movement in morals and manners' were 'an enlargement and a liberation', both were 'emphatically a growth of Christian theology from within' and 'emphatically *not* a shrinking of Christian theology under heathen or even human influences'. Both Francis and Thomas 'felt subconsciously' that the 'hold' of Christians was 'slipping on the solid Catholic doctrine and discipline, worn smooth by more than a thousand years of routine; and that the Faith needed to be shown under a new light and dealt with from another angle'. It had become 'too Platonist to be popular. It needed something like the shrewd and homely touch of Aristotle to turn it again into a religion of common sense.' Christian theology 'tended more and more to be a sort of dried up Platonism; a thing of diagrams and abstractions...not sufficiently touched by that great thing that is by definition almost the opposite of abstraction: Incarnation'. The Platonic influence was definitely tending towards a Manichaean philosophy, which existed outside the Church in the 'fiercer' form of the Albigensian heresy and inside the Church in the 'subtler' form of an Augustinianism that 'derived partly from Plato'.[36]

Thomas's 'Optimism' was in direct opposition to all this pessimism about the body and the material: 'He did, with a most solid and colossal conviction, believe in Life...'. Against 'the morbid Renaissance intellectual' who wondered 'To be or not to be—that is the question', the 'massive medieval doctor' would 'most certainly have replied 'in a voice of thunder': 'To be—that is the answer.' He was 'vitally and vividly alone in declaring that life is a living story, with a great beginning and a great end'. The whole Thomist system rested on 'one huge and simple idea', that of what Thomas called in Latin *Ens*, unfortunately translated by the English word 'being', which, Chesterton complained, 'has a wild and woolly sort of sound', whereas *Ens* 'has a sound like the English word *End*': 'It is final and even abrupt; it is nothing except itself.' And it was upon 'this sharp

[36] *TA* 419, 424, 426–9, 432–3, 436–7, 464, 466–7, 485–6, 492.

pin-point of reality' that 'There *is* an is', that Thomas had reared 'the whole cosmic system of Christendom'.[37]

Thomas was not 'ashamed' to say that his reason was 'fed' by his senses, and that as far as his reason was concerned he felt 'obliged to treat all this reality as real'. For him there was 'this primary idea of a central common sense that is nourished by the five senses'. As 'one of the great liberators of the human intellect', he 'reconciled religion with reason... expanded it towards experimental science... insisted that the senses were the windows of the soul and that the reason had a divine right to feed upon facts, and that it was the business of the Faith to digest the strong meat of the toughest and most practical of pagan philosophies'. It was Thomas who was the real 'Reformer', while the later Protestants like Luther, for whom the reason was 'utterly untrustworthy', were 'by comparison reactionaries'. Now because Thomas 'stood up stoutly for the fact that a man's body is his body as his mind is his mind; and that *he* can only be a balance and union of the two', this did not in the least mean he was a materialist in the modern sense, for this conviction was 'specially connected with the most startling sort of dogma, which the Modernist can least accept; the Resurrection of the Body'. But, although Thomas's argument for revelation was 'quite rationalistic', it was also 'decidedly democratic and popular': for he thought that 'the souls of all the ordinary hard-working and simple-minded people' were 'quite as important as the souls of thinkers and truth-seekers', and he wondered how the masses as opposed to the intellectuals could 'find time for the amount of reasoning that is needed to find truth'. He believed in 'scientific enquiry' but he also had 'a strong sympathy with the average man', concluding that Revelation was necessary, since 'men must receive the highest moral truths in a miraculous manner; or most men would not receive them at all'. In a similar way, because he had a 'strong sense of human dignity and liberty', he insisted on free will: 'Upon this sublime and perilous liberty hang heaven and hell, and all the mysterious drama of the soul.'[38]

The 'materialism' of Aquinas was nothing other than 'Christian humility', for he was 'willing to begin by recording the facts and sensations of the material world, just as he would have been willing to begin by washing up the plates and dishes in the monastery'. Anyway, Christianity had brought about a revolution in the human attitude towards the senses, towards 'the sensations of the body and the experiences of the common man', which could now be regarded 'with a reverence at which great Aristotle would

---

[37] *TA* 489, 491, 517–18, 529.   [38] *TA* 429–30, 434–5.

have stared, and no man in the ancient world could have begun to understand':

The Body was no longer what it was when Plato and Porphyry and the old mystics had left it for dead. It had hung upon a gibbet. It had risen from a tomb. It was no longer possible for the soul to despise the senses, which had been the organs of something that was more than man. Plato might despise the flesh; but God had not despised it.

Since 'there was in Plato a sort of idea that people would be better without their bodies; that their heads might fly off and meet in the sky in merely intellectual marriage, like cherubs in a picture', it was not surprising that there was in the pre-Thomist Augustinian world 'an emotional mood to abandon the body in despair'. Yet, once 'the Incarnation had become the idea that is central in our civilisation, it was inevitable that there should be a return to materialism, in the sense of the serious value of matter and the making of the body'. And indeed there was in Thomas an unmistakably '*positive*' attitude to creation, a mind 'which is filled and soaked as with sunshine with the warmth of the wonder of created things'. He was positively 'avid in his acceptance of Things; in his hunger and thirst for Things':

It was his special spiritual thesis that there really are things; and not only the Thing; that the Many existed as well as the One. I do not mean things to eat or drink or wear, though he never denied to these their place in the noble hierarchy of Being; but rather things to think about, and especially things to prove, to experience and to know.

Aquinas passionately believed in the reason, but he also thought that 'everything that is in the intellect has been in the senses'. And he was a philosopher who remained 'faithful to his first love', which was 'love at first sight': 'I mean that he immediately recognised a real quality in things; and afterwards resisted all the disintegrating doubts arising from the nature of those things.' Underlying this philosophical realism was 'a sort of purely Christian humility and fidelity', which ensured that he remained 'true to the first truth' and refused 'the first treason', unlike the many philosophers who 'dissolve the stick or the stone in chemical solutions of scepticism; either in the medium of mere time and change; or in the difficulties of classification of unique units; or in the difficulty of recognising variety while admitting unity'. But Thomas remained 'stubborn in the same obstinate objective fidelity. He has seen grass and gravel; and he is not disobedient to the heavenly vision.' Even 'the doubts and difficulties about reality' drove him 'to believe in more reality rather than less': 'If things deceive us, it is by being more real than they seem.' If things seemed 'to have a relative unreality', it was because they were 'potential and not actual', 'unfulfilled, like packets of seeds or boxes of fireworks'. No other thinker, Chesterton asserts, was 'so unmistakably thinking about things and not being misled by the indirect influence of words'. There was an 'elemental and primitive poetry that shines through all his thoughts; and especially through the thought with which all his thinking begins. It is the intense rightness of his sense of the relation between the mind and the real thing outside the mind.' The 'light in all poetry, and indeed in all art' was the '*strangeness* of things'—that is, their 'otherness; or what is called their objectivity'. For Aquinas, 'the energy of the mind forces the imagination outwards' not 'inwards', because 'the images it seeks are real things'. Their 'romance and glamour' lay in the fact that they were 'real things; things *not* to be found by staring inwards at the mind'. Far from the mind being 'sufficient to itself', it was 'insufficient for itself': 'For this feeding upon fact *is* itself; as an organ it has an object which is objective; this eating of the strange strong meat of reality.' Aquinas understood that the mind was 'not merely receptive, in the sense that it absorbs sensations like so much blotting-paper; on that sort of softness has been based all that cowardly materialism, which conceives man as wholly servile to his environment'. But neither did he think that the mind was 'purely creative, in the sense that it paints pictures on the windows and then mistakes them for a landscape outside': 'In other words, the essence of the Thomist common sense is that two agencies are at work; reality and the recognition of reality; and their meeting is a sort of marriage.'[39]

It was in fact 'a matter of common sense' that Thomism was 'the philosophy of common sense'. For Thomas did not 'deal at all with what many now think the main metaphysical question; whether we can prove that the primary act of recognition of any reality is real'. And that was because he 'recognised instantly... that a man must either answer that question in the affirmative, or else never answer any question, never ask any question, never even exist intellectually, to answer or to ask'. It was true in a sense that one could be 'a fundamental sceptic'—but then one could not be 'anything else', and certainly not 'a defender of fundamental scepticism'. In his robust rejection of scepticism, Chesterton is anxious to emphasize, Aquinas supported 'the ordinary man's acceptance of ordinary truisms'. Unlike contemporary intellectuals who despised the masses,

[39] *TA* 487, 492–4, 505, 525, 536–42.

Thomas, 'the one real Rationalist' who was given to 'the unusual hobby of thinking', was 'arguing for a common sense which would... commend itself to most of the common people'.[40]

Chesterton concludes his remarkable evocation of the mind of St Thomas Aquinas—a mind, as perceived by him, so highly congenial to his own in its insistence on the fact of being, in its commitment not only to reason but also to common sense (with its consequent affinity to the common man), in its love of the limitation of definitions—on a dark and sinister note. For there came a day when, 'in one sense, perhaps, the Augustinian tradition was avenged after all'—not that either Augustine or the medieval Augustinians 'would have desired' to see that day. Nevertheless it was an Augustinian friar who took his revenge on Thomism three centuries after Thomas: 'For there was one particular monk in that Augustinian monastery in the German forests, who may be said to have had a single and special talent for emphasis; for emphasis and nothing except emphasis; for emphasis with the quality of earthquake.' And that emphasis was on the Augustinian emphasis on 'the impotence of man before God, the omniscience of God about the destiny of man, the need for holy fear and the humiliation of intellectual pride, more than the opposite and corresponding truths of free will or human dignity or good works'. It was this tradition that

came out of its cell again, in the day of storm and ruin, and cried out with a new and mighty voice for an elemental and emotional religion, and for the destruction of all philosophies. It had a peculiar horror and loathing of the great Greek philosophies, and of the scholasticism that had been founded on these philosophies. It had one theory that was the destruction of all theories; in fact it had its own theology which was itself the death of theology. Man could say nothing to God, nothing from God, nothing about God, except an almost inarticulate cry for mercy and for the supernatural help of Christ, in a world where all natural things were useless. Reason was useless. Man could not move himself an inch any more than a stone. Man could not trust what was in his head any more than a turnip. Nothing remained in earth of heaven, but the name of Christ lifted in that lonely imprecation; awful as the cry of a beast in pain.

Chesterton's searing indictment of Martin Luther is as striking as Newman's own great, extended denunciation in the last of his *Lectures on the Doctrine of Justification* (1838) of Luther's alleged religion of feelings. Chesterton insists that nothing 'trivial' had 'transformed the world'. One

---

[40] *TA* 478, 513, 517, 519, 522.

of the 'huge . . . hinges of history', Luther's 'broad and burly figure' was 'big enough to blot out for four centuries the distant human mountain of Aquinas'. Not that Luther's pessimistic theology of 'the hopelessness of all human virtue' was a theology that modern Protestants would be 'seen dead in a field with; or if the phrase be too flippant, would be specially anxious to touch with a barge-pole'. All that Lutheranism was 'now quite unreal'—yet 'Luther was not unreal': 'He was one of those great elemental barbarians, to whom it is indeed given to change the world.' Although, on 'a great map like the mind of Aquinas, the mind of Luther would be almost invisible', it was 'not altogether untrue to say . . . that Luther opened an epoch; and began the modern world'. It was said that Luther 'publicly burned the *Summa Theologica* and the works of Aquinas':

All the close-packed definitions that excluded so many errors and extremes; all the broad and balanced judgments upon the clash of loyalties or the choice of evils; all the liberal speculations upon the limits of government or the proper conditions of justice; all the distinctions between the use and abuse of private property; all the rules and exceptions about the great evil of war; all the allowances for human weakness and all the provisions for human health; all this mass of medieval humanism shrivelled and curled up in smoke before the eyes of its enemy; and that great passionate peasant rejoiced darkly, because the day of the intellect was over.[41]

3

After recovering from an attack of jaundice, Chesterton set off on 20 March 1934 for a lengthy holiday with Frances and Dorothy Collins.[42] They crossed the Channel at Calais and arrived in Rome by train three days later. They left Rome for Naples, from where they sailed two days later for Sicily, which they reached on the 7th. Arriving at Taormina on the 9th, they spent the night there before leaving next afternoon for Syracuse. There Chesterton became ill with inflammation of the nerves in the neck and shoulders. By the 22nd the inflammation was so bad that he had to spend two weeks in bed. Plans to revisit Egypt and Palestine had to be abandoned. On 13 May they sailed for Malta, where they arrived late that night. Chesterton still felt too ill to take up an invitation to dinner at

[41] *TA* 548–51.

[42] The following account is based on Dorothy Collins's travel notes headed '1934', BL Add. MS 73478C, fos. 60–4.

Admiralty House. His would-be hostess visited him in his hotel, where she found him sitting on a rickety basket chair, suffering from the cold, and evidently in pain, for all his attempts to talk as if there was nothing wrong. When she expressed her sympathy, he replied: 'You must never pity me, for I can always turn every chair into a story.'[43] The Archbishop of Malta called on the evening of 21 May. Two days later the English travellers took a boat for Marseilles. The French novelist André Maurois was also on board with his wife. And Dorothy Collins noted that on the 24th they spent 'a very pleasant evening' with them. Next day they arrived early in the morning at Marseilles, leaving early next morning for Gibraltar, which the boat reached two days later early in the morning. They then sailed on at midday to Tangier, where they arrived two and a half hours later. On the morning of 1 June they arrived back in England at Tilbury.

Unless letters had been forwarded, they would have found awaiting them a letter dated 27 March from Cardinal Francis Bourne, the Archbishop of Westminster, informing Chesterton that Pope Pius XI had conferred on him and Belloc 'the Knight Commandership with star of the Order of St Gregory the Great in recognition of the services which you have rendered to the Church by your writings'. As soon as 'the briefs' arrived he would 'have much pleasure in presenting them to you both'. Accordingly, the Cardinal's secretary had written on 22 May to invite Chesterton to come to Archbishop's House with Belloc to receive the 'document which has just arrived from Rome conferring upon [him] the honour'.[44]

At the end of August Chesterton wrote somewhat late in the day to congratulate Annie Firmin's daughter Molly on her engagement. Mollie had looked after him when he visited Vancouver and her mother had been ill. Now he apologized for not writing earlier:

I am afraid that chronologically, or by the clock, I am relatively late in sending you my most warm congratulations—and yet I do assure you that I write as one still thrilled and almost throbbing with good news. It would take pages to tell you all I feel about it: beginning with my first memory of your mother, when she was astonishingly like you, except that she had yellow plaits of hair down her back. I do not absolutely insist that you should now imitate her in this: but you would not be far wrong if you imitate her in anything.

Eventually in such a lengthy letter he would 'come to the superb rhetorical passage about You and the right fulfilment of Youth. It would take pages:

---

[43] Ward, *GKC* 543–4.   [44] Copies of letters, GKCL.

and that is why the pages are never written'. But 'bad correspondents' like
Chesterton, 'vile non-writers of letters', had 'a sort of secret excuse, that no
one will ever listen to till the Day of Judgment, when all infinite patience
will have to listen to so much', and that was that it was because they
thought so much about their friends that they did not write to them: 'the
letters would be too long.' Again, 'wretched writing men' like Chesterton
felt that to have to write 'in their spare time' was 'loathsome', as opposed to
the pleasure of 'thinking about our friends'.

In the course of turning out about ten articles, on Hitler, on Humanism, on
Determinism, on Distributism, on Dolfuss and Darwin and the Devil knows what,
there really are thoughts about real people that cross my mind suddenly and make
me really happy in a real way: and one of them is the news of your engagement.
Please believe, dear Mollie, that I am writing the truth, though I am a journalist:
and give my congratulations to everyone involved.[45]

4

Among the subjects mentioned by Chesterton as demanding articles from
him, two names stand out: Hitler and Dolfuss. Perhaps Chesterton chose
not to spoil a happy occasion by emphasizing them. Adolf Hitler had
become chancellor of Germany in January 1933. In July 1934 the Austrian
chancellor Dolfuss, who had banned the Austrian National Socialist or
Nazi party in June the year before, was murdered by a group of Austrian
Nazis who burst into the chancellery building in an unsuccessful coup
d'état. Hitler's ambition to create a 'Greater Germany' consisting of all the
German-speaking peoples, however, began to be realized four years later
when Germany invaded Austria in March 1938 and the so-called An-
schluss incorporated Austria into Nazi Germany. Dolfuss's hapless successor, Chancellor Schuschnigg, was arrested and imprisoned in Dachau
concentration camp.

Ever since the armistice at the end of the First World War, Chesterton
had been warning of the threat posed to Europe by a resentful Germany,
which had been wounded but not fatally wounded, and he would continue
to do so until his death in 1936. Since 1925 he had had his own platform in
the form of *G.K.'s Weekly* to sound the alarm and to try to arouse his
isolationist, pacifist countrymen, who thought they could stand aside
from the developing tragedy in Europe. In 1940 Maisie Ward's husband

---

[45] Ward, *GKC* 536–7, with text corrected from BL Add. MS 73237, fo. 53.

Frank Sheed edited a selection of articles, mostly taken from *G.K.'s Weekly* but also from elsewhere, in a book called *The End of the Armistice*, with the intention of showing just how prophetic a voice Chesterton's had been. It was, Sheed pointed out, 'scarcely too much' to say that Chesterton had taken the Second World War 'for granted as a simple fact of future history': 'That is to say he saw it not as possible, nor as probable, but as a thing already on the way and humanly speaking certain to arrive. He saw how it would arrive—Germany would attack Poland; he saw closer still, that Germany would do so in agreement with Russia.'[46]

The first thing that needed to be said, in Chesterton's view, was that there was an *armistice* and not peace between Germany and the allies. He himself had favoured fighting in the First World War because of 'a fountain of poison' in northern Europe, the Prussian 'heresy' of 'Pride', 'something alien to Europe, which Europe cannot digest and did not destroy'. This 'unnatural thing' had been allowed to 'grow stronger and stronger in Europe throughout the nineteenth century', in fact, 'to grow so enormously strong that it took the strength of four nations to inflict on it a belated and badly-managed defeat'. Unfortunately, however, the victors did not realize that they had been fighting not against a 'nation' but against 'a notion that was a nightmare'. Perhaps the pacifists were right: these 'perverted Pagans' could only be converted not conquered—like 'the barbarian chiefs of the Dark Ages'. It was this 'unconverted and unconquered . . . force' that was alien to Christendom that now was again threatening war.[47]

The present so-called peace reminded Chesterton of 'that great social occasion when Pilate and Herod shook hands', having previously 'hardly been on speaking terms'. Just as Christian history began with 'this happy reconciliation', so modern history began with 'that strange friendship which ended in a quarrel' between Frederick the Great of Prussia and the French Voltaire, that 'spiritual marriage' in the 'mid-winter of eighteenth-century scepticism' that had 'brought forth the modern world'. It was a 'monstrous and evil' birth since 'true friendship and love are not evil'. And it had created not 'one united thing, but two conflicting things, which between them were to shake the world to pieces': 'From Voltaire the Latins were to learn a raging scepticism. From Frederick the Teutons were to learn a raging pride.' Both Frederick and Voltaire were 'cosmopolitans' who were 'not in any sense patriots', and as cosmopolitans they did not

---

[46] *EA* 525.   [47] *EA* 530–3, 535.

care for the cosmos as patriots care for their country. Both men embraced 'the cold humanitarianism' of the age, although Voltaire was 'the more really humane'. But 'even at his best', he 'really began that modern mood that has blighted all the humanitarianism he honestly supported': 'He started the horrible habit of helping human beings only through pitying them and never through respecting them. Through him the oppression of the poor became a sort of cruelty to animals; and the loss of all that mystical sense that to wrong the image of God is to insult the ambassador of a King.' Still, Voltaire 'had a heart', whereas Frederick was 'most heartless when he was most humane'. At any rate, 'these two great sceptics' were agreed that 'there is no God, or no God who is concerned with men any more than with mites in cheese'. It was on this common basis that they agreed but also that they disagreed: Voltaire argued that 'the sneers of a sceptic' could produce revolution, whereas Frederick held that 'this same sneering scepticism can be used as easily to resist reform, let alone Revolution; that scepticism can be the basis of support for the most tyrannical of thrones, for the bare brute domination of a master over his slaves'. It was this 'cold cosmopolitan', with his 'atheist irresponsibility', who had 'heated seven times a hell of narrow national and tribal fury, which at this moment menaces mankind with a war that may be the end of the world'. But the Voltairean 'intellectual unrest of the Latins', as well as 'the very unintellectual unrest of the Teutons', was also contributing to 'the instability of international relations': 'The spiritual zero of Christendom was at that freezing instant when those two dry thin hatchet-faced men looked in each other's hollow eyes, and saw the sneer that was as eternal as the smile of a skull.'[48]

In Chesterton's view, 'the stupidest thing done' not simply in 1933 but 'in the last two or three centuries, was the acceptance by the Germans of the Dictatorship of Hitler—to say nothing of Goering'. Unlike Mussolini, Hitler had not risen to power 'by enunciating a certain theory of the State' but by 'appealing to racial pride'. It was indeed 'staggering' that 'a whole huge people should base its whole historical tradition on something that is not so much a legend as a lie'. The 'Teutonic Theory' was the invention of 'professors and imposed by schoolmasters'. The 'strange staleness' of this 'racial religion' stank with 'the odours of decay, and of something dug up when it was dead and buried'. It was the 'sudden reappearance of all that was bad and barbarous and stupid and ignorant

[48] *EA* 539–42.

in Carlyle, without a touch of what was really quaint and humorous in him. The real Carlyle, who was a Scotchman and therefore understood a joke, has been entirely replaced by the theoretical Carlyle, who was a Prussian and not allowed to see a joke.' This 'theory of a Teutonic root of all the real greatness of Europe' ignored 'the part really played, not by the Germanic chaos, but by the Roman order and the Catholic faith, in the making of anything civilised or half-civilised, including Germany'. Chesterton had no love for British imperialism, but he had even less for Prussian imperialism: 'I entirely agree that an English officer may be an insolent noodle, with a narrow contempt for everybody else and a class-arrogance that cries to God for vengeance. But he does not elbow ladies into the gutter.' The Nazi murder of Dolfuss was 'quite simply a movement to barbarise Austria; to unbaptise Austria'. For Vienna was 'a place of culture and tradition, like Paris and like Rome': 'The thought that any Germans anywhere could have condescended to common courtesy, to humanity, nay (more horrible still) to humility, filled the half-heathen Teutons of the north with that sort of furious and hungry hatred, with which the inferior always regards the superior.'[49]

Chesterton taunted the Nazis with the paradox that 'Hitlerism is almost entirely of Jewish origin'. For the idea of 'a Chosen Race' was a Jewish idea, a 'mystical idea, which came through Protestantism':

When the Reformation had rent away the more Nordic sort of German from the old idea of human fellowship in a Faith open to all, they obviously needed some other idea that would at least look equally large and towering and transcendental. They began to get it through the passionate devotion of historical Protestants to the Old Testament. . . . By concentrating on the ancient story of the Covenant with Israel, and losing the counterweight of the idea of the universal Church of Christendom, they grew more and more into the mood of seeing their religion as a mystical religion of Race.

This was 'the great Prussian illusion of pride, for which thousands of Jews have recently been rabbled or ruined or driven from their homes'. And this 'wild worship of Race' was 'far worse' than the kind of nationalism that had no respect for other nations' nationality. There were 'two peculiar perils inherent in the cult of Race': the first danger was that 'this cult . . . tends more than any other to the nourishment of Pride', and the second was 'something which can almost be more spiritually perilous than pride: something that such visionaries call The Infinite; and those who have to

---

[49] *EA* 559, 562–3, 567, 570, 574.

deal with it call The Indefinite'. The first 'more obvious' danger of 'the
curse of race religion' was that it made 'each separate man the sacred
image which he worships', for it was 'a creed in which every man is his own
incarnate god'. The second less obvious danger was that 'the essence of
Nazi Nationalism' was 'to preserve the purity of a race in a continent
where all races are impure': 'but if you merely follow race wanderings, you
follow one tribe through a complexity of tribes, which you will always be
trying to simplify... You will find German populations in the heart of
Lorraine and may at any time find them in the heart of Lincolnshire.'[50]

Some wondered how Chesterton had picked up 'the strange fancy that
Hitler and his colleagues are as warlike as they say they are'. His prophetic
reply was: if Hitler moved 'one inch towards infringing on the present
ancient frontiers of the Polish realm', then he would know that he had
been right. The infamous pact between Nazi Germany and the Soviet
Union was a 'vital or very deadly fact; that the *Nazi is ready to dally with
Communists*'. In particular, both the Nazis and the Communists would be in
agreement about Poland, for 'in hatred of the Christian civilisation they
are truly international'. Indeed, Poland was the only country in Eastern
Europe that Western Europe could rely on as a bulwark against Communism, 'a power to be permanently counted on for the protection of
the old culture of Christendom'. But unfortunately this crucial fact was
ignored in England, where there was 'a pretty large amount of Pacifism'
in reaction to the First World War: 'They are always talking about the old
men who blundered into war; have the young men done anything to avoid
blundering into war?' These pacifists, who would no doubt 'succeed in
dragging us all into war', were an exact 'fit' with the Nazis: 'they are the
active and passive mood of the same verb.' 'Their common ground is that
neither has any real idea of courage; neither has any notion of chivalry
in war... They are in fact the ancient complex of the bully and the
coward...'. The appeasement not only of Germany but of Japan meant
that 'anybody may be a land-grabber when he feels hungry for more land',
that 'the teeming Teutonic populations must find an outlet; and
must pillage Europe as the Japs will pillage Asia'. As for the totally
ineffectual League of Nations, 'impotent of action', it had 'devoted itself
principally... to the intensive development of a pacifist propaganda campaign'. After the First World War, 'at a critical period of the history of
Western civilization the direction of its destinies fell into the hands'

----

[50] *EA* 579–81, 585, 591–3.

of President Wilson, 'an American college professor, of excellent intention, but entirely devoid of human sympathy', and Lloyd George,

a Welsh demagogue. The one was concerned to devise a paper scheme for the orderly regulation of international relations, a scheme perfect in its parts, and eminently suitable for the government of angel-races and dream-people; the other showed a fine, careless disregard for what was done, so long as it was productive of noise and notoriety and the front-page 'splash'. Between them they concentrated and established in a club-house at Geneva all the richest of the world's resources of amorphous idealism, a tribunal by constitution without authority and by composition without dignity.

It was true that war was, 'in the main, a dirty, mean, inglorious business', but it was 'not the direst calamity that can befall a people. There is one worse state, at least: the state of slavery.' A 'diseased and half-witted fallacy' had arisen, according to which 'the horror of the suffering contradicts the heroism of the sufferers. We are not to admire heroes because they endured horrors which only heroes could endure. We are not to honour martyrs; because martyrdom hurts very much; which was the only reason for anybody honouring martyrs at all.'[51]

Christendom was now confronted with 'exactly the same problem which confronted it in its first days'—namely, the pride of paganism. Most of the Christian virtues had also been heathen virtues: the Christian claim was only that 'Christianity could alone really inspire a heathen to observe the heathen virtues'. But 'the whole point of the mightiest revolution in the story of Man' was that upon 'one point and one point only' there really was 'a moral revolution that broke the back of human history. And that was upon the point of Humility.' The 'stupendous truth that man does not know anything, until he can not only know himself but ignore himself', was 'the greatest psychological discovery that man has made, since man has sought to know himself'. For pride, 'which is the falsification of fact, by the introduction of self, is the enduring blunder of mankind. Christianity would be justified if it had done nothing but begin by detecting that blunder.' It might seem hopeless for Christian humility to set itself against the pagan pride that was threatening to engulf the world in war; but Christianity refused to acknowledge that there were 'any lost causes': 'It is this splendour of the hopeless hope; sometimes called the forlorn hope, which has made the peculiar chivalry of Christendom, which has given to us alone the true idea of romance: for the real romance was a

---

[51] *EA* 594–5, 608, 611, 622, 626–7, 635, 646–7, 651.

combination of fidelity to the quest as a task, with perpetual and enormous inequality to the task.'[52]

There are several references to the threat to world peace in *Avowals and Denials*, another collection of his columns in the *Illustrated London News* that Chesterton published in November 1934. His warning could hardly have been more explicit: 'ever since Herr Hitler began to turn the beer-garden into a bear-garden, there has been an increasing impression on sensitive and intelligent minds that something very dangerous has occurred. A particular sort of civilization has turned back towards barbarism.' What was 'really disquieting about this new note of narrow nationalism or tribalism in the north' was that there was 'something shrill and wild about it', the characteristic note of the 'destructive crises of history'. The 'racial mass' of the 'tribes' who were called Germans had been recently 'solidified by a staggering sense of triumph, and a hypnotic faith, that it is all one people'. Chesterton noted the ambivalence of Hitler: on the one hand, he seemed genuinely concerned about the family, but, on the other hand, he favoured the 'barbaric' science of eugenics, which was nothing but 'a violent assault' on the family. However, Chesterton was clear that the danger to peace came not only from Germany. He was as clear then, as he had been in the days when he wrote for the *Daily News* and horrified his Liberal friends by saying so, that 'there were two forces in the world threatening its peace, because of their history, their philosophy and their externality to the ethics of Christendom; and they were Prussia and Japan'. The doctrines of Prussian Protestantism had 'long been dissolving in the acids of . . . scepticism; in the laboratories of the Prussian professors': 'And the more they evaporated and left a void, the more the void was filled up with new and boiling elements; with tribalism, with militarism, with imperialism and (in short) with that very narrow type of patriotism that we call Prussianism.' Indeed, all this 'new and naked nationalism had come to many modern men as a substitute for their dead religion'. American Puritans, for example, had 'lost their religion and retained their morality': 'The severe theological credo was replaced by a severe social veto. . . . America tolerated Prohibition, not because America was Puritan, but because America had been Puritan.' Why, an original Puritan like Oliver Cromwell had actually himself been a brewer![53]

Chesterton's early denunciations of Hitler and the Nazis were acclaimed by one 'warm admirer' in the United States, Rabbi Stephen S. Wise, a

---

[52] *EA* 655–6, 661.   [53] *AV* 37, 40–2, 54, 124–7, 134–5, 208.

leading Zionist who led resistance in America to the Nazi persecution of Jews and who was instrumental in the formation of the World Jewish Congress, which was formed to create a broad representative body to fight Nazism. 'When Hitlerism came,' Rabbi Wise declared, 'he [Chesterton] was one of the first to speak out with all the directness and frankness of a great and unabashed spirit.'[54]

5

In March 1935 *G.K.'s Weekly* celebrated its tenth anniversary. Chesterton asked Shaw to contribute to a special issue of his 'own funny paper' celebrating the occasion:

I remember you told me I was selling myself into slavery for ten years; and enquired if I was quite mad. Would you care to congratulate me in print on my escape from slavery; I do not venture to say my restoration to sanity... I shall be vastly pleased if you would write even a few words such as could go on a telegram; or even refuse to write in words which would certainly be equally invigorating.[55]

Shaw obliged, sending a contribution that was 'much more than you bargained for; but you can (a) run it through half a dozen numbers as a serial, (b) invite Wells, Russell and Belloc to discuss it and publish the whole darned symposium... or (c) send it back to me with imprecations...'.[56] Among writers asked to contribute to the anniversary issue was Walter de la Mare, to whom Chesterton wrote asking him for 'any odd scrap of verse, or even curse (in the way of criticism of us)' for his 'little rag of a paper... on which I and a few other fanatics wear themselves more or less to rags'. The payment was 'next to nothing, and for most of us nothing'.[57]

On 9 April 1935 the Chestertons, accompanied by Dorothy Collins, 'who', in Chesterton's words, 'acted as secretary, courier, chauffeuse, guide, philosopher and above all friend',[58] set off for a holiday in France

[54] Clemens, 122–3.

[55] G. K. Chesterton to George Bernard Shaw, 25 Jan. 1935, BL Add. MS 73198, fo. 107.

[56] George Bernard Shaw to G. K. Chesterton, 23 Feb. 1935, BL Add. MS 73198, fo. 109.

[57] G. K. Chesterton to Walter de la Mare, 25 Jan. 1935, BL Add. MS 73195, fo. 19.

[58] *A.* 304.

and Spain.[59] They left Beaconsfield in pouring rain and arrived in Dover in the evening. Next day Dorothy took the car ferry, while the Chestertons took a later passenger ferry. They met on the quay in Calais. They arrived in Amiens on the evening of the 10th. Next day they left for Rouen, where they had lunch before going on to Chartres, where they stayed till the afternoon of the following day. After spending the night in Blois, they drove on to Brive. Next day was Palm Sunday, and they spent another night in Brive, before driving on to Rocamadour, where they had lunch. They spent the night at Montaubon, where the hotel was decayed and there were rats. After lunching in Toulouse, they drove via Carcassonne, where they spent the night, and Narbonne, arriving in Perpignon in time for lunch.

They drove through lovely mountainous scenery to the Spanish frontier. But Dorothy's Rover car was not going well, owing to dirt in the carburettor. As soon as they reached Gerona, they took it straight to a garage, where they spent two hours with a large audience watching. On the 20th they left Gerona for Barcelona, where they got very lost. After lunch they drove to Tarragona, where they attended Pontifical High Mass in the cathedral on Easter Sunday. They arrived in Sitges from Barcelona on the 24th. The roads to Montserrat, which they visited on the 27th, were bad, although the mountain scenery was lovely, and they got rather lost. They stayed in Sitges, where Chesterton and Dorothy Collins caught up with work, until the morning of 3 May, when they left for Narbonne, lunching at Gerona on the way.

Next day they left for Aix-en-Provence, lunching *en route* at Montpellier, where they spent a couple of nights before leaving for Mentone on the 6th, where they also spent two nights. They then crossed into Italy and drove through beautiful scenery to Santa Margharita. They arrived in Rapallo on the 9th. Next day Ezra Pound and his wife came to tea, and they dined with the Beerbohms in the evening. Two days later they were in Portofino, going on to Pisa in the afternoon. On the 13th they left for Florence, where Chesterton lectured next day at the Palazzo Vecchio on 'English Literature and the Latin Tradition'. Three days later they left for Como, where they spent three nights. From there they drove to Airolo, where the car was put on the train. Passing through the St Gotthard tunnel, they reached Lucerne in the evening. On the 21st they left for Langes, lunching in Basle on the way. Next day they left for Rheims, where they spent the night

---

[59] The following account is based on Dorothy Collins's travel notes headed '1935. France–Spain–Italy[–]Switzerland'. BL Add. MS 73478C, fos. 65–75.

before going on to Calais, where they caught the boat next morning. They arrived home at Top Meadow in time for a late supper. They had travelled altogether over 3,000 miles.

In his *Autobiography*, Chesterton boasted that he was a traveller rather than a tourist, a distinction he felt he owed to his father, who had first taken him to France as a boy: 'The traveller sees what he sees; the tripper sees what he has come to see.' He was glad that he had first seen France when he was young: 'For if an Englishman has understood a Frenchman, he has understood the most foreign of foreigners.' It was paradoxical that the two countries closest to England, Ireland and France, were the two countries 'we never understand'. Chesterton did not think that the Spanish were 'in a difficult sense different' from the English,

but only that a stupid Puritanism had forbidden the English to show the hearty and healthy emotions the Spanish are allowed to show. The most manifest emotion, as it struck me, was the pride of fathers in their little boys. I have seen a little boy run the whole length of the tree-lined avenues in the great streets, in order to leap into the arms of a ragged workman, who hugged him with more than maternal ecstasy.

The workman had the good fortune not to have been to a public school, where he would have acquired that 'paralysis' of a Puritanism that 'stiffens into Stoicism when it loses religion'. As for sights in Spain that he saw: 'Yes, thank you I visited Toledo; it is glorious, but I remember it best by a more glorious peasant woman who poured out wine by the gallon and talked all the time.' Outside Barcelona he had encountered the proprietor of a café who was 'an authentic American gangster, who had actually written a book of confessions about his own organised robbing and racketeering'.

Modest, like all great men, about the ability he had shown in making big business out of burglary and highway robbery, he was very proud of his literary experiment, and especially of his book; but, like some other literary men, he was dissatisfied with his publishers. He said he had rushed across just in time to find that they had stolen nearly all his royalties. 'It was a shame,' I said sympathetically, 'why it was simply robbery.' 'I'll say it was,' he said with an indignant blow on the table. 'It was just plain robbery.'[60]

Dorothy Collins well recalled in her old age that arrival in the centre of Barcelona at midday on Saturday, 20 April 1935, when they got lost. The traffic was heavy, and Dorothy did not understand the traffic lights, which

[60] *A.* 301, 303, 304–5.

were unknown in England then. They also had no idea where they wanted to go—'characteristically' and in accordance with Chesterton's idea of a holiday.

With traffic to the right and to left of us, police whistles blowing, lights flashing, G.K. sat in the back of the car, quite oblivious, reading a detective story. Having driven into a back street, I got out and went on foot to find Cook's office, our letters and an hotel. As we sat over a very late lunch, I said, 'You weren't much help to me in my hour of need!' 'Ah, my dear Dorothy,' he said, 'You don't realize how much more helpful I was than I should have been if I had been shouting directions from the back seat.'

But otherwise Dorothy thought the Chestertons were 'wonderful passengers'—although Chesterton did once 'remark rather plaintively, "Frances, I wish you wouldn't keep telling Dorothy to admire the view when we are hanging over precipices.' She had driven them through the south of France and over the Alps—'like Napoleon (or like Hannibal accompanied by an elephant)', as Chesterton put it.[61]

In June Chesterton contributed to a series of talks on the BBC, which were also relayed to American listeners, on the question of freedom. He knew, he said, that millions of his hearers would expect him, as a Catholic, to be 'a little doubtful or apologetic' on such a subject. On the contrary, he wanted 'to point out that Catholicism created English liberty; that the freedom has remained exactly in so far as the Faith has remained . . . '. The jury system, the House of Commons, common law, 'were all of Catholic origin': 'They laid the foundations of the fundamental conception of *Liber et Legalis Homo*; the Free and Lawful Man.' But now this concept was being lost:

If I steal an umbrella, knowing that the penalty is a week or a month, I am a free man even in prison. I have entered prison freely. But if you call it 'curative' I am not free anywhere. I am in prison till certain total strangers choose to say I am cured of my inordinate appetite for umbrellas. I am not only not at liberty, but I am not under law.

Protestant countries were less free than Catholic countries—'even those that have fallen under the dictatorships that openly deny freedom'. Certainly, he hated Hitler's regime, and most Catholics were even more doubtful about Mussolini than he was. But at least an Italian was allowed 'a little freedom in his ordinary affairs', and would be 'amazed' to find that

---

[61] Sullivan, 166; *A.* 305.

'there were no peasants and that next to nobody in a London street owned his little shop'.

If Mussolini were to forbid all lotteries, as we forbid the Irish Sweepstake, the Italians would think Mussolini was mad; not metaphorically, but materially, medically mad. For more than ten years the great modern American democracy declared that drinking wine was wicked; that the wine which Christ made out of water is a poison . . . The English Parliament, being famous for compromise, has decided that wine is not a poison at five minutes to three, but becomes a poison at five minutes past three.

The truth was that the freedom that was supposed to have been achieved by the Reformation was a 'limited freedom, because it was only a literary liberty': 'The Protestant world concentrated entirely on liberty of opinion; it forgot everything else . . . '. It had sacrificed the 'common rights and needs' of 'the common people, the general mass of men' to 'the special need of a few people to air their opinions. You have committed a crime for which you still suffer, even at this very moment. You have left liberty to nobody except to people like me.' But, while freedom of expression was guaranteed, 'about five millionaires own all the organs of expression'.[62]

There was some truth in Chesterton's argument, but by 1935 there must have been many Italians, not to say Germans, who would have preferred to live even in a Prohibitionist America than under their totalitarian government. But in a country where it was an accepted dogma that the Protestant Reformation had freed it from clerical tyranny, Chesterton's provocative talk had some point. The outrage it caused was quite predictable, and for weeks letters poured in attacking Chesterton in the *Listener*. But some outraged listeners wrote personally to Chesterton. One incensed Protestant provoked an unusually passionate response from him.

When you say that penitents pay for absolution, or that money can annul any marriage, it is merely as if you said that Margate is in Scotland, or that elephants lay eggs. It does not happen to be the fact, as you would discover if you investigated the facts. But when you suggest that there hangs on the fringe of the Catholic Church a vast horde of outcasts, criminals, prostitutes, etc.—you refer to a real fact; and a very interesting and remarkable fact it is. They cannot get the Church's Sacraments or solid assurances, except by changing their whole way of life; but they do actually love the faith they cannot live by . . . which would be a fascinating psychological problem to anyone whose mind was free to consider it fairly. If you explain it by supposing that the Church, though bound to refuse

---

[62] *Listener*, 19 June 1935.

them Absolution where there is no Amendment, keeps in touch with them and treats their human dignity rather more sympathetically than does the world, Puritan or Pagan—that also probably refers to a real fact. It is one of the facts that convince me most strongly that Catholicism is what it claims to be. After two thousand years of compromises and concordats with every sort of social system, the Catholic Church has never yet become quite respectable. He still eats and drinks with publicans and sinners.[63]

To a lady who wondered whether Catholics were 'allowed to use their intelligence on questions of doctrine', or whether they had to swallow them 'whole', Chesterton replied:

If you mean swallow them without thinking about them, Catholics think about them much more than anybody else does in the muddled modern world; but they think about them logically; and recognise what things go together or must be given up together. If I accept the doctrine that twice one are two, do I swallow whole the doctrine that twice thirty-two is sixty-four? I suppose I do... But... I think it is sixty-four and not sixty-five because I cannot think anything else. Not because the Senior Wrangler at Cambridge tells me I must think so. It is precisely because most non-Catholics now do *not* think, that they can hold a chaos of contrary notions at once as that Jesus was good and humble; but falsely boasted of being God; or that God became Man to guide men till the end of time; and then died without giving them a hint of how they were to discover His decision in the first quarrel that might arise; or, alternatively, that he was not God, but only a Galilean peasant, but we are bound to submit to His most startling paradoxes about peace, but not to His plainest words about marriage. Thinking means thinking connectedly. If I thought the Catholic creed untrue, I should cease to be a Catholic. But as the more I think about it, the truer I think it is, the dilemma does not arise; there is no connection in my mind between thinking about it and doubting it.

He concluded the letter by insisting that Catholicism 'makes us respect or desire freedom' precisely because it believes in free will.[64]

Foremost, naturally, among the correspondents in the *Listener* was his old adversary, the Cambridge historian and professional controversialist G. G. Coulton. In a letter of 28 August to the *Listener*, Coulton demanded to know how Chesterton could possibly claim there was more freedom in a

---

[63] Pearce, 461, with text corrected and some additional words from BL Add. MS 73481B, fo. 90.

[64] G. K. Chesterton to 'Madam', 16 June 1935, BL Add. MS 73481B, fos. 92–3, partly in Pearce, 461–2, who wrongly dates the letter to 17 June and whose text is defective.

Catholic than a Protestant country, when Catholics were notoriously subject to the Index and forbidden to worship with Protestants. Responding in a letter of 11 September, Chesterton admitted that there had been 'repressions' in the course of Catholic history, 'but never with that special note of Utopian finality, marking Prohibition'. As for the Index, it permitted 'more freedom than modern plutocracy'. In his next letter in the next week's issue, Coulton challenged Chesterton to an 'exchange of open letters' on the subject of freedom with a view to a book, the royalties of which could go to the unemployed. In his reply of 2 October in the *Listener*, Chesterton ignored the challenge but compared the Index, which allowed of 'exceptions', with 'the fanaticism' of Prohibition, which did not, as he knew from personal experience, since his wife had nearly died in Tennessee because it was impossible to obtain the champagne prescribed by the doctor. In the following issue, Coulton pointed out that the Index was still in force, while Prohibition had ended. He repeated the challenge he had issued in his previous letter. In the *Listener* of 23 October, Chesterton pointed out in his turn that Prohibition had affected the whole American 'populace', whereas the Index affected only the 'professors': 'If such popular sympathies shame me, I accept the shame.' In 'an old organised tradition of truth', he claimed, there was 'limited limitation and some liberty' as opposed to 'unlimited limitations and no liberty'. In response to Coulton's challenge, he suggested that he, Coulton, should publish the correspondence 'at his own expense'. The following week Coulton replied that he would publish not only the correspondence but also Chesterton's original broadcast talk. As regards the Index, English Roman Catholics might be able to take a relaxed view of it, but in Italy this ban on 'free reading' was far more onerous than the restrictions on drinking and betting in England. To this sally, Chesterton retorted on 15 November that the newspaper monopolies prevented free reading in England. Coulton's response in the next issue was that there was free competition in England and therefore there was a free press as it was open to anyone to start a newspaper. To this the obvious answer was that you had to be an exceedingly rich person to start a newspaper, Chesterton wrote on 15 November. Finally, on 4 December Chesterton proposed that next year he and Coulton should collaborate in a book that would begin with 'a full explanation' of the thesis of his broadcast talk, to which Coulton would respond at similar length, followed by 'shorter rejoinders'. But he insisted on his own 'full explanation coming first'. In the following week's issue, Coulton accepted Chesterton's proposal, while for his part reminding Chesterton that he, Chesterton, had already agreed that the correspondence in the *Listener* should be published together with the text of Chesterton's talk as a 'fitting introduction'.

Meanwhile in September the Catholic publishing house Sheed & Ward, founded by Maisie Ward and her husband Frank Sheed, had published another collection of Chesterton's articles, *The Well and the Shallows*, originally published in a variety of places: the *Catholic Herald*, the *Daily Mail*, the *Fortnightly Review*, *G.K.'s Weekly*, the *London Mercury*, the *Universe*, and *Liverpool Cathedral: Souvenir Programme*. The book begins with an introductory note, in which Chesterton apologised to T. S. Eliot for 'some errors that occurred' in the opening article. Since writing it, he had 'come to appreciate much more warmly [his] admirable work'. He, Chesterton, had confused Eliot with another critic who had accused Chesterton of using too much alliteration.[65] Eliot had written privately on 2 July 1928 to Chesterton to point out the error, and also to complain about his poetry being misquoted: 'And may I add, as a humble versifier, that I *prefer* my verse to be quoted correctly, if at all.' Chesterton had replied that he certainly had had the impression from what the other critic had said that Eliot disapproved of his alliteration. But he agreed that, 'on the strictest principles, all quotations should be verified; and I should certainly have done so if I had in any way resented anything you said, or been myself writing in a spirit of resentment'. He had offered to write a letter of correction to the *Mercury*, where the offending article had appeared.[66] Eliot had answered that the matter was too trivial and that a letter was unnecessary. Far from being snobbish about alliteration, as Eliot thought Chesterton had implied, he was rather fond of it himself. He also recognized that Chesterton had acknowledged he was quoting from memory. The last time he, Eliot, had done so in print, a reader had written in to say that he had made a dozen mistakes in familiar passages from Shakespeare. He hoped that Chesterton would see his way to write for the *Criterion* (of which Eliot was the editor).[67] Later that year in October, Eliot had written again urging Chesterton to contribute an article to the *Criterion* on humanism as a substitute for religion.[68] Chesterton ended the introductory note to *The Well and the Shallows* with this tribute: 'It would be adding impudence to injury to dedicate a book to an author merely on the claim of having misquoted him; but I should be proud to dedicate this book to T. S. Eliot, and the return of true logic and a luminous tradition to the world.'[69]

---

[65] *WS* 340.   [66] Ward, *GKC* 509.
[67] T. S. Eliot to G. K. Chesterton, 6 July 1928, BL Add. MS 73195, fo. 61.
[68] T. S. Eliot to G. K. Chesterton, 21 Oct. 1928, BL Add. MS 73195, fo. 63.
[69] *WS* 340.

Given the Catholic nature of four out of the seven original places of publication, it is not surprising that religion is the principal subject of the essays that comprise the book. At least six times during the previous few years Chesterton says he would have converted to the Catholic Church—but for the fact that he had been 'restrained from that rash step by the fortunate accident' that he was one already. It was generally expected that the convert would 'suffer some sort of reaction, ending in disappointment and perhaps desertion'. The most that would be conceded was that the convert had 'found peace by the surrender of reason'. But in Chesterton's experience the opposite was true: 'The strongest sort of confirmation often comes to the convert after he has received enough to establish conviction.' It was not the Catholic Church but the Protestant Churches that were obsolete, or rather 'fossils'—that is to say, not 'dead' or 'decayed' or 'antiquated' but fossilized: 'The whole point of a fossil is that it is the *form* of an animal or organism, from which all its own animal or organic substance has entirely disappeared; but which has kept its shape, because it has been filled up by some totally different substance by some process of distillation or secretion ... '. (As Chesterton had remarked pithily in *Orthodoxy*: 'Let beliefs fade fast and frequently, if you wish institutions to remain the same.'[70]) The Churches of the Reformation were clearly dying: 'But in a much deeper sense, they have long been dead.' Indeed, they had 'really died almost as soon as they were born'. For 'the incredible clumsiness of the Reformers' had miserably failed, in spite of all that was 'deservedly unpopular' about the Catholic Church, which they had 'swept out of their way', to 'set up something that would at least look a little more popular':

They waged an insane war against everything in the old faith that is most normal and sympathetic to human nature; such as prayers for the dead or the gracious image of a Mother of Men. They hardened and fixed themselves upon fads which anybody could see would pass like fashions ... Calvin was logical, but used his logic for a scheme which humanity manifestly would not long find endurable.

Unkindly, Chesterton suggests that perhaps 'the most successful' of the Reformers were the founders of the Church of England, 'who really had no ideas to offer at all': 'They at least did not exasperate human nature; but even they showed the same blindness, in binding themselves instantly to the Divine Right of Kings, which was almost immediately to break down.' The 'heresy' of Islam had not died, but then its founder was 'a far shrewder person'. After 'the theological and theoretical part' of the

[70] *O.* 311.

reformers' 'work withered with extraordinary rapidity... the void that was left was almost as rapidly filled with other things'—such as 'the Race Religion of the Germans'. Islam had 'stood by being stagnant': 'But Protestantism could not stand in the staggering rush of the West; it could only maintain itself by ceasing to be itself, and announcing its readiness to turn into anything else.' But Chesterton could only 'shudder to imagine into what sort of epileptic convulsion' Luther would have 'fallen if anybody had told him to tear out the Epistles of St Paul, because St Paul was not an Aryan'—not that he, Luther, had hesitated to tear out, in one of his 'irrational convulsions of rage', the Epistle of St James from the Bible, because 'St James exalts the importance of good works'. Luther's insistence on justification by faith alone was an example of Chesterton's definition of heresy: 'A heresy is a truth that hides all the other truths.'[71]

Nor was it possible for a church to remain Catholic, like the Church of England under Henry VIII, without Rome:

the moment when Religion lost touch with Rome, it changed instantly and internally, from top to bottom, in its very substance and the stuff of which it was made. It changed in substance; it did not necessarily change in form or features or externals. It might do the same things; but it was not the same thing that was saying them.

At the beginning of the English Reformation Henry VIII was 'a Catholic in everything except that he was not a Catholic... And in that instant of refusal, his religion became a different religion... In that instant it began to change; and it has not stopped changing yet.' True, 'Modern Churchmen' called such continuous change 'progress'—but it was only progress in the sense that 'a corpse crawling with worms has an increased vitality; or... a snow-man, slowly turning into a puddle, is purifying itself of its accretions'.[72]

It was the Prayer Book controversy of 1927 and 1928, when the House of Commons led by the Home Secretary, the ultra-Protestant William Joynson-Hicks, rejected two versions of a revised Prayer Book for the Church of England, which introduced some moderate Catholic elements, that had revealed to Chesterton 'a reality' he had not hitherto realized:

There really was a Church of England; or rather there really was an England which largely imagined that it possessed and controlled the Church. But this Church was not the Church I thought I had belonged to; the keen, cultivated and sincere group of men who claimed to be Catholic. It was a much vaster and

---

[71] *WS* 357, 259–61, 505.   [72] *WS* 367–8.

vaguer background of men; who did not believe in anything in particular, but who claimed to be Protestant.

Whether or not they were Protestant, 'they all seemed to have this fixed idea; that they owned the Church of England; and could turn it into a Mormon temple if they wished'. After 'a mob of politicians, atheists, agnostics, dissenters, Parsees; avowed enemies of the Church or of any Church' had rejected the revised Prayer Book, a Protestant body

presented all the atheists, etc., who had voted Protestant, with a big black Bible or Prayer-Book, or both, decorated outside with a picture of the Houses of Parliament. . . . It would be very idolatrous to put a cross or crucifix outside a book; but a picture of Parliament where the Party Funds are kept, and the peerages sold—. That is the temple where dwell the gods of Israel.

Actually, the Prayer Book or Book of Common Prayer was 'the masterpiece of Protestantism', its 'one positive possession and attraction'. And 'the only thing that can produce any sort of nostalgia or romantic regret, any shadow of homesickness in one who has in truth come home, is the rhythm of Cranmer's prose'. After all, it was written by 'apostate Catholics': 'It is strong, not in so far as it is the first Protestant book, but in so far as it was the last Catholic book.' Its 'most moving passages' were 'moving, or indeed thrilling, precisely because they say the things which Protestants have long left off saying; and which only Catholics still say'. The 'very finest passages' were 'concerned specially with spiritual thoughts and themes that now seem strange and terrible', such as the hour of death and the day of judgment: 'But did you ever hear the curate fresh from the cricket-field, or the vicar smiling under the Union Jacks of the Conservative Rally, dwell upon that penultimate peril; of the danger of falling from God amid the pains of death? Very morbid. Just like those Dago devotional books. So very *Roman*.'[73]

Chesterton had never attacked Anglo-Catholicism—which he knew could be 'honestly held; for I held it myself for many years'—as there were 'many things much more in need of being disputed', and, as he himself knew from experience, it often did more harm than good. But the Church of England was a different matter. It was a state church, in which illogically 'God holds his authority from Caesar; instead of Caesar holding it from God'. If Chesterton had not already left it, he would have done so after 'the shilly-shallying and sham liberality' of the 1930 Lambeth Conference of Anglican bishops, which approved artificial contraception

[73] *WS* 372–5.

under certain circumstances: 'But this particular case was only the culmination of a long process of compromise and cowardice about the problem of sex; the final surrender after a continuous retreat.' He was thankful now to be free of 'the nervous compromises of Anglicanism', which, having accepted the possibility of divorce in exceptional circumstances, had now come out with a 'weak and inconclusive pronouncement upon Birth-Prevention', which was 'only the culmination' of a 'long intellectual corruption'. The acceptance of divorce as an exception to the normal rule of marriage had inevitably led to a change in 'the whole social substance of marriage', since people were now getting married, 'thinking already that they may be divorced', as though marriage was 'a question of Mood' rather than a 'contract'. The exception had become the rule, and the same would happen with so-called 'Birth-Control', which in fact did not control but prevented birth and which was a 'hypocritical' euphemism for 'Birth-Prevention'. That anyway was a 'stale and timid compromise' compared with infanticide, which was 'real and even reasonable Eugenics', as it would ensure that only the 'healthiest' babies survived, whereas contraception only discouraged 'the early parentage of young and vigorous people' who would produce the healthiest and best babies. The 'unnatural separation' of sex from fruitfulness would have been regarded even by pre-Christian pagans as 'a perversion'. It was analogous to thinking of property only in the sense of money, 'in the sense of something which is immediately consumed, enjoyed and expended; something which gives momentary pleasure and disappears'.[74]

Chesterton was clear that he could not abandon Catholicism without 'falling back on something more shallow', without 'becoming something more narrow than a Catholic'. Hence the title of the book: 'We have come out of the shallows and the dry places to the one deep well; and the Truth is at the bottom of it.' It was ironic, considering that Darwinism in the nineteenth century was supposed to herald the end of religion, that the modern revival of Catholicism was a perfect example of what Darwin meant by 'the Survival of the Fittest': 'It is surviving because nothing else can survive.' Popular Darwinism had understood the survival of the fittest to mean that 'the Struggle for Existence was of necessity an actual struggle between the candidates for survival', in which 'the strongest creature violently crushed the others', an idea that 'came everywhere as good news to bad men'. Science, 'that nameless being', now apparently 'declared that the weakest must go to the wall', with the result that there was

[74] *WS* 397, 439–40, 502, 510, 528.

'a rapid decline and degradation in the sense of responsibility in the rich': 'The profiteer . . . was satisfied with himself; knowing that nature is unjust.' But, far from going to the wall, the Catholic Church was only said 'to be behind the times' because it was 'always in advance of the world'. What was called 'free thought' had finally come 'to threaten everything that is free', whether it was 'personal freedom' by 'denying free will' or 'civic freedom' by spreading 'a plague of hygienic and psychological quackeries'. Indeed, it was 'quite likely' to remove religious freedom.[75]

The Englishman's fear of Catholicism was usually thought of as 'a sort of claustrophobia', a fear of being 'walled up' in a confessional box, which in his Protestant 'nightmare' seemed to be 'a sort of mantrap', or in a monastic 'cell', which suggested a prison cell. But actually it was 'a sort of agoraphobia'—that is, 'a fear of something larger than himself and his tribal traditions', of an international as opposed to national Church. Chesterton himself had been brought up in a liberal Protestant atmosphere, where the Virgin Mary was referred to as the Madonna, not of course because she was literally seen as 'my Lady', but partly because of that 'queer Victorian evasion' of 'translating dangerous or improper words into foreign languages' and partly because of 'a certain sincere though vague respect for the part that Madonnas had played in the actual cultural and artistic history of our civilisation'. But Chesterton had never experienced that 'strange mania against Mariology; that mad vigilance that watches for the first signs of the cult of Mary as for the spots of a plague'. On the contrary, he had 'always had a curious longing for the remains of this particular tradition, even in a world where it was regarded as a legend'. Not only had he been 'haunted by the idea while stuck in the ordinary stage of schoolboy scepticism', but he had been 'affected by it before that', before he had 'shed the ordinary nursery religion in which the Mother of God had no fit or adequate place':

I found not long ago, scrawled in very bad handwriting, screeds of an exceedingly bad imitation of Swinburne, which was, nevertheless, apparently addressed to what I should have called a picture of the Madonna. And I can distinctly remember reciting the lines of the 'Hymn to Proserpine' . . . but deliberately directing them away from Swinburne's intention, and supposing them addressed to the new Christian Queen of Life, rather than to the fallen Pagan Queen of death.[76]

But, while England was 'solidly Protestant' in the nineteenth century in its hatred of Mariolatry, in its belief in justification by faith and the inerrancy

---

[75] *WS* 370, 384, 391–3, 395.   [76] *WS* 451, 460, 462.

of Scripture, all that now remained was anti-Catholicism: Protestantism was simply a name now for an anti-Catholicism that was 'even more against Calvinism than against Catholicism... even more insistent on works than were the Catholics...'. It attacked Protestantism to attack Catholicism. And a hundred years later, Chesterton prophetically remarked, the Church would 'look to her enemies something utterly different from what she looked like a hundred years ago': 'She will look different because she will be the same.' She would be 'facing once more her first and most formidable enemy', paganism, 'a thing more attractive because more human than any of the heresies'. For Pagans looked for their 'pleasures to the natural forces of this world', but these 'natural forces, when they are turned into gods, betray mankind by something that is in the very nature of nature-worship': 'We can already see men becoming unhealthy by the worship of health; becoming hateful by the worship of love; becoming paradoxically solemn and overstrained by the idolatry of sport; and in some cases strangely morbid and infected with horrors by the perversion of a just sympathy with animals.' The 'emergence of new issues' would 'reveal... aspects of Catholic doctrine and tradition, hidden by historical accident and the special quarrels of recent times... to the world when it begins to address new questions to the Church'. Chesterton's words are extraordinarily prophetic when one considers the contemporary world's hostility to the Catholic Church because of its protection of human life from the womb to the grave, a hostility that would have astonished nineteenth-century Protestants. Chesterton's non-Catholic contemporaries would have been hardly less astonished at the emergence of the Catholic Church in the twentieth century as the champion of human rights and freedom. His fellow Liberals, when he began to write, had 'inherited a huge legend that all persecution had come from the Church', and some still mumbled 'old memories about the Spanish Inquisition (a thing started strictly by the state)'. But the idea that 'superstition was somehow the mother of persecution' was flatly contradicted by the contemporary tyrannies of secular Communism and Fascism. In Protestant countries 'ancient universal popular liberties', taken for granted in Catholic countries, were prohibited, Protestantism or Puritanism being 'in its nature prone to what may be called Prohibitionism'—that is, 'to prohibit, rather than to curtail or control' and to apply an 'absolute idea of amputation to all parts of problematical human nature'. Thus there was 'a fanatical quality, sweeping, final, almost suicidal, in Protestant reforms'. But the modern secular—literally from the Latin *saeculi* or 'of the age', in other words 'dated'—mind also generally favoured prohibition, whether it was pacifists prohibiting war or Communists prohibiting private property, since having to decide whether it was a just war or lawful property was too much of 'a strain on the Modern Mind', not being 'at all accustomed to making up its mind'.[77]

Communism, Chesterton thought, was a very Victorian phenomenon in its 'mad optimism about the advantages of machinery'. Marx indeed had 'launched his world religion from something more British than the British Empire: the British Museum'. The late Victorian period was a time when Jews, especially German Jews, were 'at the very top of their power and influence', both 'imperial and immune'. Now the situation was very different, with Jews being 'jumped on very unjustly in Germany itself'. Chesterton and Belloc, 'who began in the days of Jewish omnipotence by attacking the Jews, will now probably die defending them'. Capitalism had destroyed the family, had 'broken up households, and encourages divorces, and treated the old domestic virtues with more and more open contempt', had 'forced a moral feud and a commercial competition between the sexes', had 'destroyed the influence of the parent in favour of the influence of the employer', had 'driven men from their homes to look for jobs', had 'forced them to live near their factories or their firms instead of near their families', and above all had 'encouraged for commercial reasons, a parade of publicity and garish novelty, which is in its nature the death of all that was called dignity and modesty by our mothers and fathers'. Communism did exactly the same, but Chesterton thought that if he had to choose between the two he would choose Communism: 'Better Bolshevist battles and the Brave New World than the ancient house of man rotted away silently by such worms of secret sensuality and individual appetite.'[78]

But even worse than 'the Communist attacking the family or the Capitalist betraying the family' was the spectacle of 'the Hitlerite defending the family' by making 'every family dependent' on Hitler and his 'semi-Socialist state'. And, if contraception and sterilization led 'the march of human progress through abortion to infanticide', then Chesterton could see the Nazis hailing infanticide 'with howls of barbaric joy, as one of the sacred commands of the Race Religion; the proceedings very probably terminating (by that time) with a little human sacrifice'. However, Chesterton, prophetic though he was, certainly underrated Hitler and the Nazis when he described them as 'simply the tail-end, we might say the rag-tag-and-bobtail of the nineteenth-century Prussianism; the camp followers of the far better disciplined army of Bismarck'—although he did

[77] *WS* 388–9, 466, 470, 473–4, 512, 521, 525–6.   [78] *WS* 427, 443–4.

qualify that rather dismissive description by adding, 'in its present practical form'. Its 'rowdy revivalism' had to be understood as 'merely a revival':

The movement that has actually abolished Bavaria, and left no State alive except the Bismarckian Empire, is but the last phase of the Bismarckian plan to Prussianise Germany, by crushing and outnumbering the Catholics of the Rhine; and stealing the old Imperial Crown from the other Catholics of the Danube. In short, he set up a new Protestant Empire, to dwarf and depose the old Catholic Empire; and Hitler is his heir and his executor.

What Chesterton does not add is that the Hitler who was soon to annexe Austria into a Greater Germany was himself an Austrian Catholic by birth. Instead, he insists that 'Prussianism came from Protestantism', was its 'historical fruit'.

The racial pride of Hitlerism is of the Reformation by twenty tests; because it divides Christendom and makes all such divisions deeper; because it is fatalistic, like Calvinism, and makes superiority depend not upon choice but only on being of the chosen; because it is Caesaro-Papist, putting the State above the Church, as in the claim of Henry VIII; because it is immoral, being an innovator of morals touching things like Eugenics and Sterility; because it is subjective, in suiting the primal fact to the personal fancy, as in asking for a German God, or saying that the Catholic revelation does not suit the German temper; as if I were to say that the Solar System does not suit the Chestertonian taste. I do not apologise, therefore, for saying that this catastrophe in history has been due to heresy...[79]

6

On 19 September 1935 Chesterton wrote to Maurice Reckitt, a leading Distributist and a member of the board of *G.K.'s Weekly*, begging him not to resign from the board. Reckitt had written to Chesterton to say that he thought he must leave the board in protest at the failure of the paper sufficiently to condemn the aggressive Italian military build-up that had begun in February in the Italian colonies of Eritrea and Italian Somaliland on the border with Abyssinia, a build-up that would eventually lead to full-scale invasion in October. Chesterton asked him to defer his decision until he saw what the editor would be saying in the next number. He, Chesterton, had been away on holiday and privately agreed with Reckitt that there 'ought to have been a more definite condemnation of the attack

---

[79] *WS* 444, 530–2.

on Abyssinia'. The truth was that the staff and readers of *G.K.'s Weekly* were even more divided over the Abyssinian crisis than over Distributism itself.[80]

There had, in fact, been no editorial comment in May and June as the crisis intensified, but the editorial in the 18 July issue had condemned colonial imperialism in Africa. However, it argued that there was one mitigating factor in Italy's favour and that was that it was not intent on 'crude exploitation' but on an 'outlet for emigration'. However, to seize somebody else's land as a solution of one's population problem was 'an assertion of the doctrine of force in its ugliest form'. Unfortunately, Britain, with its much bigger empire 'acquired by methods which the most hard-boiled fascist would repudiate with disgust', was hardly in a position 'to administer a moral rebuke'. In his 'Straws in the Wind' column of 29 August, Chesterton commented that the worst that could be said against Italy was that it had only adhered to the 'cynical colonial tradition' of other European nations. As for Fascism in Italy, it was no worse than a corrupt parliamentary system and a Capitalist press—not that he was advocating Fascism. He apologized that the paper had not dealt at greater length with Abyssinia, but he had been away for 'a short holiday', 'a thing at this time of the year not uncommon'. In his column in the next week's issue, he complained that, while Italian aggression was condemned on all sides, nothing was said about Protestant violence against Catholics in Belfast. Besides, Mussolini was only doing for his country what countries like England and France had done. The editorial in the same issue pointed out that Britain was 'not virtuously intent upon defending the honour of small nations' like Abyssinia, but was actually concerned only about the threat to British interests if Italy, with its superior power in the Mediterranean, got possession of the raw materials of Abyssinia. In his 'Straws in the Wind' column of 19 September, Chesterton claimed that British imperialism was always alleged to be 'for the protection of the oppressed', and he particularly cited the case of the Boer War. As for Italian imperialism, the Capitalist newspapers were already full of denunciation. But the main purpose of *G.K.'s Weekly* was to attack plutocracy. Certainly, he, Chesterton, detested Italian imperialism, but he also detested the spectacle of 'an English capitalist, acting for an American company, secretly buying up Abyssinia in bits without fighting for it'. The 'Straws in the Wind' column in the next issue of 26 September categorically condemned the

---

[80] Ward, *GKC* 549–50.

Italian aggression, while pointing out that it was 'hypocrisy' to suggest that Mussolini had 'discovered a new sin'.

On 16 November Chesterton and Bertrand Russell took part in an 'unrehearsed debate', broadcast by the BBC, on the subject 'Who Should Bring up our Children?' Russell, the BBC told Chesterton, had agreed to participate in a broadcast debate—'but only with you as an opponent!'[81] Russell began by asserting that parents were 'unfitted by nature' to bring up their children, not that anybody else was so fitted, he admitted. The most important thing was that children should live not die, and the huge reduction in the infant mortality rate was due to scientists and other experts not to mothers, let alone to fathers, whom Russell dismissed as obviously totally unfit to bring up children. The education of children was best left to qualified educators, while health and safety were bound to be better in a nursery school than at home. The problem with mothers of large families was that they tended to get irritable, whereas in small families mothers became excessively attentive. Russell conceded that the best people to give children affection were their parents, which was another reason why they should not be burdened with educating and looking after them. In reply, Chesterton pounced on the phrase 'unfitted by nature'. 'Who is nature?' he demanded. This goddess was purely mythological. All animals were looked after by their mothers, and human beings were no different. It was true that some people were especially good with children, but they were few in number. Russell was in favour of 'cutting off a natural force that exists and deliberately paying out money... to supply it by an artificial machinery'. But in the nursery school that Russell advocated, one teacher had to look after not one child, like a mother, but many children. As for mothers getting irritable, were teachers never irritable? The fact was that teachers were far more likely to get tired of a child than its own mother. Russell responded by again insisting that in a school environment a child was safer than at home. True, the classes were too big, but then they were too small at home. Russell also objected to the fact that in small, well-to-do families mothers expected a return for their sacrifice, an emotional pressure that interfered with the development particularly of boys. Chesterton agreed that those paid to bring up children did not have the kind of feelings that Russell objected to in mothers—but then they did not have any feelings.[82]

[81] Mary Adams to G. K. Chesterton, 29 Aug. 1935, BL Add. MS 73234A, fo. 113.

[82] *Listener*, 27 Nov. 1935.

Early in January 1936 Chesterton wrote, or rather dictated, a letter to his old friend J. M. Barrie. The letter, which was nothing more than a begging letter, is a reminder of what a wonderful letter-writer he was and what a loss it is that he had so little time for correspondence. He was writing to ask Barrie for 'a bald, banal, blatant favour'. And, since Chesterton was 'sure' that Barrie's 'generosity' must lead to his being 'pestered with millions of such requests', 'the only decent modification' he could think of was 'to make it as bald and banal and blatant as possible': 'Then at least you will not have to read through a long letter, full of fine shades of diplomacy; I receive a good many such letters, and I prefer them short if crude.' He was writing about 'a sort of niece and protegée' of Frances, who was 'normally on the stage and therefore (as things are) off the stage'. He had heard that Barrie's new play was about David and Goliath, which might suggest an opening for her: 'she is kept out of most modern feminine parts because she is (accidentally) statuesque and (unintentionally) stately; and so is better fitted to be a part of the pageantry—I might say of the scenery...'. And he wonders if she might be 'a leader of the chorus of the Daughters of the Philistines who rejoiced; or what not. Do not be alarmed. She will not want to act Goliath.'[83] The letter is a perfect example of Chesterton's extraordinary combination of courtesy, tact, and humour. Unfortunately, Barrie had to write back to say that all the parts in the new play were already filled, but he would let Chesterton know if he heard 'of a part to suit the stately lady, whom you describe very attractively'.[84]

On 23 January Chesterton wrote to Coulton suggesting that their opening statements in the proposed work of controversy should be 7,000 words in length.[85] But unfortunately he then fell ill. Because of Chesterton's inability to produce his statement within the agreed timeframe, Coulton proposed, since he was going abroad, that they should first publish the original broadcast talk together with the ensuing correspondence in the *Listener*, postponing 'the fuller and more formal discussion' for a subsequent book.[86] Chesterton agreed, but wondered if Coulton would prefer to postpone the whole thing.[87] Subsequently Coulton wrote to say

[83] G. K. Chesterton to J. M. Barrie, 3 Jan. 1936, BL Add. MS 73235, fo. 66.
[84] J. M. Barrie to G. K. Chesterton, 6 Jan. 1936, BL Add. MS 73235, fo. 67.
[85] G. K. Chesterton to G. G. Coulton, 23 Jan. 1936, BL Add. MS 73194, fo. 193.
[86] G. G. Coulton to G. K. Chesterton, 30 Jan. 1936, BL Add. MS 73194, fo. 197.
[87] G. K. Chesterton to G. G. Coulton, 6 Feb. 1936, BL Add. MS 73194, fo. 201.

that the publisher he had approached had advised against separate publication of the *Listener* 'stuff'. He presumed that by June or July Chesterton would be able to complete his 7,000-word essay.[88]

Chesterton's wife thought the controversy was 'useless' and just another obstacle to her husband doing, as she put it, 'his own job properly'. 'Poor Gilbert', she wrote to Father O'Connor, 'gets so overwhelmed with all the questions and letters he is supposed to answer...' But work had at least now become easier—at any rate for Dorothy Collins. 'Did you know', Frances asked O'Connor, 'we had built a new study?' It was 'a great success'. Her husband had remarked that, whereas previously 'he had not room to swing a cat', now he had 'room to swing a tiger'! But at least the new room was 'warm anyhow and Dorothy rejoices'.[89] Chesterton himself had not looked forward to the new study. The previous September Frances had written to O'Connor: 'we are building on to the house—a nice large study for him and he's not a bit pleased about it!'[90]

Early in 1936 Chesterton completed his *Autobiography*, a book that should be included among his half-a-dozen or so major works. According to Dorothy Collins, he had written the beginning some years before but had then laid it aside. She had feared urging him to complete it, as if finishing the account of his life would mean the end of his life. But, at Maisie Ward's urging, she did in 1935 retrieve the manuscript and put it on Chesterton's desk, whereupon he read what he had already written and then proceeded to dictate the rest of the book to her. Apart from a collection of essays published three days before his death, it was to be Chesterton's last book; the books he planned to write on Shakespeare and Napoleon would never be written.[91] On telling some friends that the autobiography was complete, one of them ominously remarked, 'Nunc dimittis', words that seemed 'chilling' to Edward Macdonald, 'though he seemed to be in fairly good health. But certainly he was tired...'.[92]

Another holiday on the Continent seemed the obvious remedy. And so in the spring Dorothy Collins drove the Chestertons through France. They

---

[88] G. G. Coulton to G. K. Chesterton, 20 Feb. 1936, BL Add. MS 73194, fo. 207.

[89] Frances Chesterton to John O'Connor, 10 Feb. [1936], BL Add. MS 73196, fos. 153–4.

[90] Frances Chesterton to John O'Connor, 11 Sept. [1935], BL Add. MS 73196, fo. 152.

[91] Dorothy Collins's notes for talks, BL Add. MS 73477, fo. 141.

[92] Ward, *GKC* 548.

left Beaconsfield on the afternoon of 27 April 1936.[93] On arriving at Dover, they took a walk on the front; it was a fine, sunny evening. Next day they lunched in Calais and arrived in Rouen that evening, after getting a puncture at Abbeville. The following day they visited the cathedral, where they saw some English visitors behaving badly. Next day they were in Lisieux in time for lunch. They attended Mass at the Carmel on the morning of 30 April, before leaving for Caen; on the way they saw the birthplace of St Thérèse of Lisieux at Alençon. Chesterton, who had hoped the church in Beaconsfield would be dedicated to the English martyrs rather than the 'Little Flower', told Dorothy Collins, who had a great devotion to St Thérèse, that he could not feel the same, 'with all apologies to you, Dorothy'.[94] They arrived in Tours in time for dinner via Le Mans. Next day, the first of May, they went on to Poitiers for lunch, arriving at Perigeux in the evening. They reached their second place of pilgrimage, Lourdes, the following evening. After dinner there was a torchlight procession. The next day, 3 May, was a Sunday, and they went to an early Mass in the famous Grotto. They were back at the Grotto two days later for Mass; in the afternoon there was a procession of the Blessed Sacrament and a blessing of the sick, followed by a huge torchlight procession in the evening. After one more visit to the Grotto on 7 May, they left Lourdes in the late morning *en route* to Montpellier via Toulouse. The following day they left Montpellier for Arles, where they spent the night before leaving for Menton, where they arrived late that evening. From there they drove one day to Nice, which they did not care for. After nine nights in Menton, they travelled on to Digne, which they reached in time for dinner, having lunched at Grasse. They arrived the following evening at Le Puy, where they spent the night. Next stop was Clermont Ferrand, where they attended Mass the following day, Ascension Day, in the cathedral, when Chesterton felt unwell. After lunch they left for Bourges, where they spent the night. Next day, 22 May, they had a long drive to Beauvais; they lunched at Orleans, reaching Beauvais in time for dinner, having visited Chartres Cathedral on the way. Two days later they left for Calais after Mass in the cathedral. Next day they took the afternoon boat back to Dover; there was fog in the Channel and the sea was choppy. They got back to Beaconsfield at about 8.30 in the evening.

---

[93] The following account is based on Dorothy Collins's travel notes headed 'France. 1936', BL Add. MS 73478C, fos. 75–8.

[94] Ward, *GKC* 463.

As they drove through the French countryside, Dorothy Collins had asked Chesterton to ' "sing us something" '. For the whole way he sang all he knew, repeated verses and cracked jokes at the top of his form.'[95] According to Dorothy, the songs from Gilbert and Sullivan were sung 'with much gusto and less tune'.[96]

A fortnight after returning home at the end of May, Chesterton began to fall asleep while dictating, something he had never done before. He also began repeating himself, as though he were losing his powers of concentration.[97] When first sent for, the doctor had not been worried, although Chesterton had been: he was always nervous at the thought of illness. But as his condition rapidly worsened, he grew calm. At first he could not lie down but sat up in his large armchair. But eventually he had to go to bed.[98]

Edward Macdonald, who had failed to receive a message saying Chesterton was too ill to be visited, called, but Chesterton had not lost his wonderful sense of humour, promising a poem on St Martin of Tours for the paper: 'The point is that he was a true Distributist. He gave *half* his cloak to the beggar.' After apparently dozing off, he woke up and remarked: 'The issue is now quite clear. It is between light and darkness and every one must choose his side.'[99] According to Dorothy Collins, this saying had become habitual with him as he saw 'the future which was coming to Europe'. But he had remained 'spiritually happy and serene in his faith in God, to the glory of Whom his daily work was always dedicated—by a cross on the top of the page, and even on the line below his signature, and by a sign of the cross made as he entered his study'.[100]

That work had now come to an end. And on 11 June his last book to be published in his lifetime came out, *As I was Saying: A Book of Essays*, more of his columns collected from the *Illustrated London News*. All that he wrote, he says at the outset, he wrote in the conviction that 'the only way to say anything definite is to define it, and all definition is by limitation and exclusion'. Another favourite topic reappears, that new kind of arrogance and superiority about the contemporary age that appears in the nineteenth century, epitomized by the 'nineteenth-century sceptics' who were sceptical about 'the other world' but 'dupes about this world': 'They accepted everything that was fashionable as if it was final; and the revolutionary romantics, who thought they would see the end of religion, never thought they would see the end of romance.' Again, the 'Victorian evolutionists' were not wrong 'because they opened the evolutionary question, but

---

[95] O'Connor, 151.   [96] Sullivan, 166.   [97] O'Connor, 151.

[98] Ward, *RC* 269–70.   [99] Ward, *GKC* 551.   [100] Sullivan, 166–7.

because they closed it': 'They were so fond of having convictions that they came prematurely to conclusions.' Then there is the usual condemnation of the intellectuals who talk about the 'masses', whether capitalist or communist in their politics:

in both cases I think that habit of dealing with men in the mass, not merely on abnormal occasions, as in a war or a strike, but in normal circumstances and as a part of ordinary social speech, is a very bad way of trying to understand the human animal. There are only a few animals, and they are not human animals, who can be best judged or best employed in packs or herds.

Even if communism, 'the child and heir of Capitalism', were to bring about 'the Dictatorship of the Proletariat, there would be the same mechanical monotony in dealing with the mob of Dictators as in dealing with the mob of wage-slaves. There would be, in practice, exactly the same sense of swarms of featureless human beings, swarms of human beings who were hardly human, swarms coming out of a hive...'. For human beings were not 'fundamentally happier for being finally lost in a crowd, even if it is called a crowd of comrades'. Finally, Chesterton turned his guns on the intellectuals who embraced eugenics. Pagan sacrifices were 'infinitely more decent and dignified': 'the pagan altar at least treated a man's life as something valuable, while the lethal chamber treats a man's life as something valueless'. But eugenists who did not believe in 'the existence of gods' ended by not believing 'even in the existence of men': 'Being scientific evolutionists, they cannot tell the difference between a man and a sheep.' Compared with the intellectuals' talk of 'eliminating the unfit, getting rid of the surplus population, segregating the feeble-minded, or destroying the hopeless', 'in the very vilest blood-rites of barbarians, there may have been cruelty, but there was not contempt. To have your throat cut before an ugly stone idol was a compliment; though perhaps a compliment that you would have politely disclaimed and waved away.' A human sacrifice, after all, meant in the literal Latin meaning 'to make a thing sacred; or, in this case, to make a man sacred'. But love of eugenics was bound up with hatred of the masses and 'the tendency to deal with men in herds; to treat them like sheep; and not only to class them with the beasts that perish but to take particular care that they do perish'. Chesterton ends this essay, the best in the book, by warning, against the 'progressive' historians, who were 'no longer very obviously progressing', that 'complex civilization' was no 'safeguard against unnatural creeds or cruel ceremonies'. Those Victorian intellectuals who so admired Germany as the most civilized and cultured country in Europe would have done well to read Chesterton's grimly prophetic words: 'Culture, like science, is no protection against demons'[101]—demons like Hitler and the Nazis.

The day before the book's publication Dorothy Collins wrote to Coulton to warn him that Chesterton was 'very ill'. He had completed about three-quarters of the essay for their book, but still had some research to do in the British Museum.[102] The Protestant idea of liberty, Chesterton had argued before he ceased dictating to Dorothy Collins, 'rests on one enormous blunder; a mere muddle in the mind. It muddles up two totally different things: the notion of opinions being spoken freely; and the notion of opinions being favourable to freedom.' The private opinion, for example, that the Pope is the Antichrist 'could not remain a *private* opinion, in the sense of needing no public action'. It obviously meant the persecution of Catholics, since the original Protestants did not believe, any more than their Catholic contemporaries, in religious freedom. However, this muddled Protestant idea of liberty began to be rejected in the nineteenth century, first of all by Carlyle, 'who put mastery above liberty'. He was followed by Nietzsche, who 'put mastery even above morality'. Subsequently, Trotsky's contempt for democracy 'began in the British Museum, where Marx exercised private judgment'. And now there was Hitler's 'frenzy about Race', which had been anticipated by Carlyle and Nietzsche 'and other nineteenth-century enemies of Catholicism'. In a Protestant country like England liberty had come to mean 'not democracy but plutocracy' and the slavery of the Servile State. Unlike Catholic France, Protestant England had become 'less a land of yeomen and more of a land of squires'. Even trade unions in 'proletarian' England 'accepted proletarianism'. The individualistic competition of nineteenth-century industrialism in England had assumed that there would be 'a free fight' and therefore 'a fair fight', but the result was the monopoly of the big Trust. At this point Chesterton's argument became repetitive before petering out altogether.[103]

Both Chesterton and Frances had thought his recovery twenty years before had been a miracle, and now Frances 'did not dare to pray for another miracle'.[104] On 12 June she wrote to tell Father O'Connor that Chesterton was 'very seriously ill. The main trouble is heart and kidney and an amount of fluid in the body that sets up a dropsical condition. I have had a specialist to see him, who says that though he is desperately ill

[101] *AS* 18,172–4, 197, 199, 217–8, 220, 222.
[102] Dorothy Collins to G. G. Coulton, 10 June 1936, BL Add. MS 73194, fo. 211.
[103] BL Add. MS 73194, fos. 234–58.   [104] Ward, *GKC* 551.

there is a fighting chance. I think possibly he is a little better today.'[105] He had been given the last rites by the parish priest, Monsignor Smith, that morning. In response to a message from Frances, his friend Father Vincent McNabb, the famous Dominican preacher and a leading Distributist, came to see him for the last time. He sang the 'Salve Regina', the hymn to the Blessed Virgin Mary that is always sung over a dying Dominican, at Chesterton's bedside, and kissed his pen that lay on a table beside his bed.[106] Next day Frances was in his room when he regained consciousness. 'Hello, my darling,' he said, and then, seeing Dorothy Collins was also in the room, 'Hello, my dear.'[107] They were his last words before again losing consciousness.

On Sunday 14 June Frances wrote to inform O'Connor that their 'beloved Gilbert passed away this morning at 10.15. He was unconscious for some time before but had received the Last Sacraments and Extreme Unction while he was still in possession of his understanding . . . '.[108] One of the two male nurses who were looking after Chesterton had been called out of morning Mass by Dorothy Collins, who suspected there 'must have been a local press agent in the congregation, for before lunch, the press from London were at the door'.[109] The death certificate listed three causes of death, which had essentially resulted from heart failure.[110]

The 'introit' or opening antiphon of the Mass of that Sunday, 14 June, began: 'The Lord became my protector and he brought me forth into a large place.' Dom Ignatius Rice noted that even Chesterton's memorial card, on which was printed the introit, thus contained a joke: the good Lord had made allowance for his size when he came for him. To the words of the 'introit' Frances added some lines written by Walter de la Mare in support of Chesterton's candidature for the rectorship of Edinburgh University.[111]

---

[105] Ward, *RC* 270.   [106] Ward, *GKC* 551–2.

[107] Ffinch, 343–4, whose source presumably was Dorothy Collins.

[108] Ward, *RC* 270.   [109] Sullivan, 167.   [110] Photocopy, GKCL.

[111] De la Mere wrote to Dorothy Collins on 18 June that he was 'fairly certain' that the original verses, as opposed to the copy he had obtained, began 'Knight of the Holy Ghost' not 'Knight of the Holy Grail'. He had written to the Edinburgh University Students' Union asking for a copy of the 'review' in which they had originally appeared. He wished 'the lines were a hundred times better', but he would 'indeed be delighted if Mrs Chesterton would make any use of them she cares to' (BL Add. MS 73195, fo. 24). According to Ward, *GKC* 552, who heard it from Dom Ignatius Rice, who heard it from a nun, the lines had been written 'for

Knight of the Holy Ghost, he goes his way
Wisdom his motley, Truth his loving jest;
The mills of Satan keep his lance in play,
Pity and innocence his heart at rest.[112]

The funeral took place ten days later on 24 June. The Mass was celebrated by Monsignor Smith, in the presence of Archbishop Hinsley of Westminster and Bishop Youens of Northampton, at the parish church.[113] It was a 'glorious day', the kind of weather Frances so liked and Chesterton so little cared for. In response to popular demand, the funeral cortege did not take the direct route to the cemetery in Shepherd's Lane but did a detour to pass through the old town.[114] The policeman at the gate to the cemetery told Edward Macdonald: 'Most of the lads are on duty, else they would all have been here.'[115]

Father, now Monsignor, O'Connor was unable to attend, as he was ill in bed with bronchitis.[116] Maurice Baring also was too ill to attend, but wrote to Frances: 'There is nothing to be said, is there, except that our loss, and especially yours, is his gain.'[117] Ronald Knox, too, was unable to attend, but wrote to Frances that Chesterton had been his 'idol' ever since reading as a schoolboy *The Napoleon of Notting Hill*. That he, Knox, had retained 'the Faith' when so many of his friends had lost it 'was due, I think, under God to him . . . I don't think he can be long for Purgatory'.[118] For Belloc, it had been 'a great benediction to know him'.[119]

Afterwards at Top Meadow Frances remained in her room, where Maisie Ward and a few others saw her for a little while. To 'Keith' Chesterton, with what Maisie Ward called 'that utter self-forgetfulness that was hers', Frances said: 'It was so much worse for you. You had

a paper run by [Chesterton's] supporters for the Lord Rectorship of Glasgow University'.

[112] Ward, *GKC* 551–2.

[113] St Teresa's Church, Beaconsfield, parish archives, parish diary, p. 96.

[114] Ward, *GKC* 552.

[115] Titterton, 234.

[116] John O'Connor to Frances Chesterton, 15 June 1936, BL Add. MS 73196, fo. 159.

[117] Maurice Baring to Frances Chesterton, 16 June 1936, BL Add. MS 73189, fo. 123.

[118] Ronald Knox to Frances Chesterton, 15 June [1936], BL Add. MS 73195, fo. 163.

[119] Dorothy Collins's notes for talks, BL Add. MS 73477, fo. 146.

Cecil for such a short time.'[120] Unsurprisingly, 'Keith' was much less sympathetic in her account. She thought Frances should not have refused to let the press know how ill Chesterton was—he was after all a public figure and a journalist himself. But Dorothy Collins took Frances's side, and when a reporter from a daily newspaper did call he was told nothing.[121] Dorothy Collins's version is rather different. According to her, two days before Chesterton died, E. C. Bentley came to visit him, but his old friend was too ill to see him. That afternoon the *Daily Mail* rang to say that they had heard he was ill. Dorothy admitted he was, but persuaded them not to release the news, as Chesterton had to be 'kept very quiet and we must not have telephones and doorbells'. Bentley, who was himself a journalist, could not believe that the paper would keep its promise, but it did.[122] The news of Chesterton's death therefore came as a great shock to many people. 'Keith' considered Frances's refusal to cooperate in any way with the press 'the final expression of the long, long struggle she waged against those forces which drew her husband ever so little from his home'. Frances told 'Keith' how 'ridiculous' she had found it in America when women would telephone her to ask what it felt like to be the wife of a genius: 'I told them that Gilbert's genius was not the important thing to me; what really mattered was the sort of husband he was . . .'. After the funeral, 'Keith' complained, little had been done to provide refreshments for the guests. Frances had retired to her room, leaving the guests in the studio: 'A few ladylike sandwiches, with sherry, spread on a long table, disappeared with the first arrivals. Forlorn little groups stood about the garden, others crowded the hall and inner rooms, and I was sorry for Belloc, who tired and hungry was looking vainly for refreshment.' When it became clear that no more food would be forthcoming, the guests departed without being able to express their condolences to Frances. 'Keith', of course, made no allowances for Frances's grief and the fact that she was a very private person at the best of times. Nor did Eric Gill's gravestone meet with her approval: 'Personally I do not think this memorial to Gilbert suggests either the poet's flaming spirit or that combination of faith and fantasy which made him unique.'[123] In her sustained attack on Frances in her book *The Chestertons* (1941), 'Keith' makes no mention of the fact that, when she died, Frances left £500 to her Cecil Houses and £1,000 to herself, the same sums that Chesterton had left her, no small sums in those days.[124]

[120] Ward, *GKC* 553.   [121] MCC 302.   [122] Sullivan, 166.
[123] MCC 303–5.   [124] Ward, *GKC* 564.

But if, predictably, nothing done by poor Frances in despised Beaconsfield met with 'Keith's' approval, the requiem Mass that was celebrated in
Westminster Cathedral on Saturday 27 June delighted her. 'The pageantry, the tumult, the trumpetings of his genius were made manifest,'
and Ronald Knox 'preached one of the most eloquent valedictories
the building can have heard'.[125] Having been unable to attend the funeral
because of illness, Monsignor O'Connor was invited by Archbishop
Hinsley to celebrate the Mass,[126] assisted by Father Vincent McNabb
and Dom Ignatius Rice, who had been present when O'Connor received
Chesterton into the Catholic Church in a very different kind of building.
The day after Chesterton's death, Rice had written to O'Connor, grateful
to him for having invited him to be present at the reception. 'It is
extraordinary', he wrote, 'how much love G.K.C. drew to himself.'[127]

In his sermon Knox began by calling Chesterton 'a prophet, in an age of
false prophets'. Not the least of his prophecies had been that 'human
liberties were threatened'. But on this occasion it was appropriate to
emphasize Chesterton's religious beliefs. He had been the 'spear-head' of
the religious reaction against nineteenth-century evolutionary materialism, even though this reaction was 'decimated' by the First World War.
Famed for his 'absent-mindedness', Chesterton was reputed to have asked:
'Am in Liverpool; where ought I to be?' It had taken him fourteen years
after the publication of *Orthodoxy* 'to find out that he ought to be in Rome'.
Chesterton had once written: 'If you look at a thing nine hundred and
ninety times, you are perfectly safe; if you look at it the thousandth time,
you are in frightful danger of seeing it for the first time.' Well, Chesterton
had 'looked for the thousandth time at the Catholic Faith, and for the first
time he saw it'. Knox ended by speaking of Chesterton's 'unbelievable
humility', which had been 'a more effective document of Catholic verity
than any word even he wrote'.[128] Afterwards he wrote to Frances to say
that he felt that he had been 'horribly impersonal and inhuman, as if
at such a moment what a man did mattered to his friends more than what
he was'.[129]

[125] MCC 306.

[126] John O'Connor to Frances Chesterton, 18 June 1936, BL Add. MS 73196,
fo. 162.

[127] Edmund Rice to John O'Connor, 15 June 1936, BL Add. MS 73196, fo. 158.

[128] *G.K.'s Weekly*, 2 July 1936.

[129] Ronald Knox to Frances Chesterton, 7 Aug. [1936], BL Add. MS 73195,
fo. 165.

On the day of the requiem Mass, O'Connor heard the story that H. G. Wells had said: 'If ever I get to heaven, presuming there *is* a Heaven, it will be by the intervention of Gilbert Chesterton.'[130] A couple of years earlier, he had told Chesterton: 'If after all my Atheology turns out wrong and your Theology right I feel I shall always be able to pass into Heaven (if I want to) as a friend of G.K.C.' In reply, Chesterton assured Wells that, if he, Chesterton, turned out to be 'right', than Wells would 'triumph, not by being a friend of mine, but by being a friend of Man...'. He did have one complaint, though: he wished that those who embraced 'the old Agnosticism of my boyhood' would remember that people like Chesterton also 'began as free-thinkers...and there was no earthly power but thinking to drive us on the way we went'.[131]

As for G. G. Coulton, he had already sent his condolences to Dorothy Collins, saying that he had 'admired' Chesterton for 'the sincerity of his conversion...a conversion from which he can have hoped for no worldly advantage but, on the contrary, an addition to his work and a certain cloud over his popularity'.[132] Dorothy replied that Chesterton had 'never made an enemy in all his controversies; as differences of opinion never influenced his personal feelings for anyone'.[133] In the end, without the extra material, Coulton was unable to publish the correspondence in the *Listener*, and decided not to publish at his own expense what he called a 'cold controversy'.[134]

Telegrams from Cardinal Pacelli, the Vatican Secretary of State and the future Pope Pius XII, on behalf of Pope Pius XI, were sent to both Frances and Archbishop Hinsley. The telegram to Hinsley, which was read out in Westminster Cathedral, referred to Chesterton as a 'gifted Defender of the Catholic Faith'. No one would have been more amused than Chesterton to be thus associated in death with Henry VIII, who, before his break with Rome, had been given the title of 'Defender of the Faith' (the initials of the Latin title 'Fidei defensor' are still on British coins alongside the name of the reigning monarch) by the then Pope for his defence of the seven sacraments against Luther. Because the Pope had conferred what was

---

[130] O'Connor, 152.   [131] Ward, *GKC* 513–14.

[132] G. G. Coulton to Dorothy Collins, 21 June 1936, BL Add. MS 73194, fo. 212.

[133] Dorothy Collins to G. G. Coulton, 22 June 1936, BL Add. MS 73194, fo. 214.

[134] G. G. Coulton to Dorothy Collins, 24 June 1936, BL Add. MS 73194, fo. 224; 10 Oct. 1936, BL Add. MS 73194, fo. 229.

traditionally a royal title on a subject, the secular press did not print the telegram in full.[135]

Among the letters of condolence that Frances received was one from Shaw, written the day after Chesterton's death:

> It seems the most ridiculous thing in the world that I, *18* years older than Gilbert, should be heartlessly surviving him.
>
> However, this is only to say that if you have any temporal bothers that I can remove, a line on a postcard (or three figures) will be sufficient.
>
> The trumpets are sounding for him; and the slightest interruption must be intolerable.[136]

Frances was 'very moved at the generous offer', according to Dorothy Collins, but she did not take it up, as she was 'adequately provided for'.[137] When the *Autobiography* was published in November, Shaw wrote again to Frances: 'It is really an ANGELIC book. I can't find any other word for it; and it has never occurred to me to apply it to any book before.'[138] According to T. E. Lawrence of Arabia, Shaw 'always' called Chesterton 'a man of colossal genius'.[139]

On 21 July Frances wrote to O'Connor: 'I find it increasingly difficult to keep going. The feeling that he needs me no longer is almost unbearable. How do lovers love without each other? We were always lovers.' She was having a weekly Mass said for him at the parish church—'but I feel it is more for the repose of my soul than for his'.[140] Her sense of loss grew rather than lessened. On 25 October she wrote again to O'Connor: 'I seem to feel his loss more and more. It does not get easier to bear as time goes on.'[141]

On the gravestone that 'Keith' felt unworthy of Chesterton, Frances had inscribed the last words of the last verse of St Thomas Aquinas's hymn 'Verbum supernum', the penultimate verse of which, beginning 'O salutaris hostia', is traditionally sung at the service of Benediction.

---

[135] Ward, *GKC* 553.

[136] George Bernard Shaw to Frances Chesterton, 15 June 1936, *Shaw: Collected Letters 1926–1950*, ed. Laurence, 433.

[137] *Shaw: Collected Letters 1926–1950*, ed. Laurence, 433.

[138] George Bernard Shaw to Frances Chesterton, 6 Dec. 1936, BL Add. MS 73198, fo. 116.

[139] Ward, *GKC* 313.   [140] Ward, *RC* 270.

[141] Frances Chesterton to John O'Connor, 25 Oct. [1936], BL Add. MS 73196, fo. 168.

... vitam sine
Termino
Nobis donet in patria.

'May He grant us life without end in our native land.' As a definition of Heaven, Chesterton had often quoted the two Latin words 'in patria': 'It tells you everything: "our native land".'[142]

Two and a half years after Chesterton's death, Frances herself died of cancer on 12 December 1938. Her last days were spent in the nursing home run by the sisters of Bon Secours in Candlemas Lane, Beaconsfield. Her husband's last public function, immediately on his return from France at the end of May 1936, had been to open a garden fête in aid of an extension to the nursing home.[143]

[142] Ward, *RC* 267.
[143] St Teresa's Church, Beaconsfield, parish archives, parish history, pp. 187–9.

INDEX

Alexander, George 143
Allenby, Edmund 407–8
Allenby, Lady 415
Allport, Nellie 361
Amery, L. S. 318–19
Amis, Kingsley 190 n.65
Aquinas, St Thomas 48, 154, 681–90, 728–9
Archer, William 349–51
Arians 527
Aristophanes 88
Aristotle 683–6
Arnold, Matthew 155, 335–7, 340, 353, 379, 503, 564, 612–14, 667
Asquith, H. H. 156–7, 309, 318–19, 348, 351
Athanasius, St 526–7
Auden, W. H. 68
Augustine, St 689
Augustine of Canterbury, St 250–1
Austen, Jane 405
Aytoun, William 13

Baccani, Attilio 11
Baden-Powell, Robert 122
Bakewell, George 79 n.7, 206 n.28, 355–6
Baldwin, Stanley 619–20
Balfour, A. J. 99, 146, 156, 251, 318, 320, 420
Baring, Maurice 293–4, 368, 390, 395, 407–8, 415, 428–30, 460, 466, 469–70, 477–8, 487, 489, 510, 724

Barker, Dudley 97 n.55, 98 n.59, 131 n.37
Barker, Harley Granville 145–6, 348–50
Barrie, J. M. 141–2, 348–51, 717
Bastable, Rhoda 77, 81, 163, 541, 553, 580
Beecham, Thomas 378, 395
Beerbohm, Max 110–11,122, 141–2, 608–9, 700
Bell, Bernard Iddings 547–8
Belloc, Elodie 65, 73, 110, 141, 314, 347–8, 477
Belloc, Hilaire 51, 63–6, 73, 82–3, 141, 146, 160, 198–200 234–7, 251, 261–3, 281, 293–4, 297, 314, 318, 320–1, 324, 327, 345, 347–8, 352, 355, 366, 368, 370–1, 377, 391, 394–8, 407, 419, 422, 467, 472–3, 476–8, 491, 495, 498, 512, 531–2, 561, 575, 584–6, 618–20, 678, 691, 699, 724–5
Benedict, St 504
Bennett, Arnold 92 n.35, 352
Bentham, Jeremy 329
Bentley, Edmund Clerihew 14, 16–17, 19–21, 21–2, 27–8, 35, 37, 40–1, 44, 48, 61–4,70, 81, 187, 192, 315, 407, 500, 531, 619, 725
Berkeley, Anthony see Anthony Berkeley Cox

Betjeman, John 91
Bewsher, Samuel 13–14
Bismarck, Otto von 327, 713–14
Bixler, Anna 633–6, 640, 642
Bixler, Delhard 633–6, 640, 642
Bixler, Delphine 634–5, 640, 642
Blake, William 271, 274–6, 328, 506
Blatchford, Robert 24, 42, 97, 115–20, 146, 160, 212, 246, 500, 546
Blogg, Blanche 45–6, 59, 81, 676
Blogg, Ethel 44, 48–9, 163
Blogg, Frances *see* Chesterton, Frances
Blogg, Gertrude 53, 55–7, 68, 75
Blogg, Knollys 48, 203–6, 230
Borlase, Mr and Mrs 473, 555
Bosanquet, Theodora 198
Boswell, James 144, 609–11
Bourne, Francis 575, 691
Bowden, J. W. 314
Bowden, Sebastian 314
Boyd, Ian 126 n.28
Bridges, Horace J. 637, 655
Bridges, Robert 40
Brontë, Charlotte 100
Brooke, Stopford 13, 22–3, 37, 210, 509, 599–600
Brown, Ford Madox 369
Browning, Robert 35, 330, 340–1, 427, 680
Buchan, John 294, 375–6
Burke, Edmund 382

Cadbury, George 74, 93, 157, 326–7, 351
Calvin, John 590, 707, 714
Campbell-Bannerman, Henry 281
Carey, John 92 n.35
Carlyle, Thomas 104, 106, 151–2, 165, 329–30, 332–7, 340, 379, 533, 609, 613, 695, 722
Carson, Edward 312–13, 315, 318
Cary Elwes, Dudley 474, 479, 555, 566–7
Cecil, Hugh 280

Cecil, Robert 313–14, 317, 320
Chamberlain, Austen 142, 156, 531–2
Chamberlain, Joseph 59
Chaucer, Geoffrey 171, 241, 436, 535, 677, 680
Chekhov, Anton 293
Chesshire, Kathleen 451, 541
Chesterton (née Jones), Ada or 'Keith' 50, 79–80, 97–8, 185, 191, 205–6, 229–30, 251–2, 261–3, 293, 314–17, 345, 347–8, 355, 369–72, 373–5, 377, 389–90, 394–8, 451, 468, 490–1, 495, 497, 531–2, 551–3, 724–6
Chesterton, Beatrice ('Birdie') 8, 10
Chesterton, Cecil 9–11, 18, 29, 36, 44, 63, 72, 77, 79, 82, 97–8, 106, 108, 125, 133, 185, 205, 229–30, 237, 251–2, 263–4, 281, 293, 303, 314–18, 320–1, 323–5, 345, 347, 366, 370–4, 377–8, 389–92, 394, 400, 419, 422–3, 467, 476, 490, 497–8, 513, 552, 593, 620, 624, 725
Chesterton, Charles 2
Chesterton, Cyril 650–1
Chesterton, Edward 2–7, 9–13, 24, 27, 70, 205, 251, 263, 316, 468–9, 476, 701
Chesterton (née Blogg), Frances:
  Anglo-Catholicism of 49, 405, 409, 429–30, 471
  childlessness of 79–80, 162–3
  and children 161, 255–7
  and confession 548
  courtship of 43–5, 49–50
  depression of 122, 206, 240
  engagement of 51–5
  and fame 50, 122, 161, 439, 442, 451, 725
  and Fleet Street 205–6, 230, 251, 725

and gardening 251
generosity of 551
honeymoon of 77–80
ill-health of 206, 240, 407, 409, 414,
    431, 437–9, 449, 451, 467, 471,
    622, 632, 649–51
married life of 83, 144–5, 160–1,
    201, 261–3, 347–8, 467, 635,
    641, 647
and John O'Connor 136, 204–5,
    259–60
and publicity 53 n.46, 97
religious influence of 43, 106, 265,
    429, 467
reserve of 541
Roman Catholic Church,
    conversion of to 261–2, 265,
    357, 428, 471, 473, 554–6
as secretary 160, 543
and spiritualism 205
tragedies of 55–8, 75, 203–6, 467
and weather 122, 163, 541
wedding of 77–8
Chesterton, George Laval 4,
    475
Chesterton, Gilbert Keith:
on abortion 713
absent-mindedness of 19–20, 93–8,
    141, 145, 160, 255, 258–9, 362,
    582, 647, 726
on the Abyssinian crisis 714–16
on the 'accumulation of truth' 220,
    226–7
as actor 299
on advertising 438, 576–7, 713
on alcohol 139, 208–9, 280, 465
on America 382, 431–4, 436, 441,
    447–9, 450–1, 454–8, 637–8,
    644–5, 671–2
anger of 582
and Anglo-Catholicism 107–9, 117,
    124, 279, 406, 409, 428–9, 476,
    480, 488–9, 546, 562, 708–9

on animals 424, 596
on anti-Catholicism 598–603
anti-dogmatic liberalism of,
    early 22–5, 37
anti-Semitism of, alleged 20–1, 299,
    320–1, 371, 380, 392–3, 419,
    420–4, 496, 695, 698–9, 713
as apologist 1, 118, 517
appearance of 15, 19, 93, 544, 553
on appeasement 696
on architecture 253
and argument 10,17, 82–3, 258
on aristocracy 210, 224, 381, 383,
    560
on the back 124–5, 188–9, 519
at Bewsher's School, 13–15
on the Bible 99, 286–7
on biography 144, 609–11
on birthdays 243–4
and Blessed Virgin Mary 23, 279,
    416, 484, 509, 546, 574, 608,
    645, 707, 711
on the Boer War 61–2, 65, 67, 88,
    135, 715
on Book of Common Prayer 709
on boredom 665
on boyhood 15–16, 18
as broadcaster 666, 674–6, 702, 716
on Buddhism 215, 224–5, 520,
    529–30
on burial and cremation 295
and cabs 6, 93–7, 160
on Calvinism 241–2, 267, 269, 304,
    404, 587–9, 598–9, 611, 669
on Capitalism 235, 289, 298, 305,
    383–4, 387–8, 403, 457, 464–5,
    559, 565, 576, 592, 678, 713, 715,
    721–2
on censorship 254
and childhood 9, 11–12, 15, 88, 128,
    132, 163, 255, 481, 665
and children 88, 91, 163–4, 218,
    254–7, 280, 458, 479, 716

Chesterton, Gilbert Keith: (*cont.*)
  on chivalry 417
  on Christ *see* Jesus Christ
  and Christianity 43, 107, 117–18,
    124, 503, 522, 580, 664
    balance of 221–2, 527
    complexity of 220, 522, 526–7
    creed of 432
    crimes of 119
    culture of 678–9
    and democracy 106, 223–4, 287,
      560–1, 611
    on difficulty of 267
    as good *news* 85, 523, 525, 529–30
    and heathen virtues 697
    humility of 151, 153, 175, 292, 697
    humour of 124, 273, 304, 667
    joy of 118, 124, 150, 153, 225, 229
    letter of 265
    liberality of 527–8
    and life 117; true to 211–12, 528
    and limitation 210, 224, 426,
      526
    and mystery 119, 215, 278, 304
    and mythology and
      philosophy 528
    and pagan myths 119
    paradoxes of 119, 150–1, 211,
      221–2, 226–8, 278
    particularity of 119, 522
    and post-Christians 516–17
    practicality of 278
    and reason 296
    and romance 150, 153, 226,
      697–8
    sanity of 530
    and Trinity 225
    and virginity 228
    vitality of 529–30
    and wine as sacrament 134
  on Christian Science 426
  and Christian Social Union 108–9,
    115, 144–5, 159

  on Christmas 170–2, 244, 381, 425,
    521–3, 611, 645, 666
  on Church of England 381, 429–30,
    459–60, 464, 489, 606–7,
    707–10
  churchgoing of 546–8
  on church schools, 99
  on the city 85–6, 129–30, 133, 153,
    168, 288, 576
  on class consciousness 36, 104,
    288–9, 366, 644, 672, 695
  'clerihews' of 13, 27–8
  on clothes 86–7, 101, 221
  on cocktails 653–4
  on cocoa 45, 325–7, 435
  on comedy 88, 102, 425, 653, 667–8
  and the common man 84–5, 89,
    133, 152–4, 165, 179, 228, 234,
    236, 244–5, 251, 269, 278, 337,
    367, 425, 503–4, 560–1, 612,
    689
  on common sense 88, 120, 179, 208,
    234, 285–7, 368, 388, 404, 530,
    670, 685, 688–9
  on Communism 491, 559, 632, 678,
    696, 712–13, 721
  and confession 480–3, 546–8,
    563–4, 643
  on Confucianism 519–20, 529–30
  on conservatism 223, 246–7, 263,
    291–2, 661
  on Conservatives 234–5, 577
  on contraception 459–60, 566,
    709–10, 713
  as controversialist 727
  on convention *see* on tradition
  on countryside 271
  courtesy of 540, 578, 717
  on culture 353, 613–14, 678–9,
    721–2
  and *The Daily News* 73–4, 92–3, 99,
    184, 325–7
  on death 54, 56–8

and *The Debater* 16–18, 21–3, 27
demands on 554–5, 662, 718
on democracy 64, 86–7, 105, 165,
 208–9, 217, 223, 228, 245–7,
 249, 267, 272, 305, 331, 367, 373,
 380–3, 401, 518, 528, 679
as descriptive writer 273–4, 289–90
and the Detection Club 615–17
and detective stories 85, 91, 187,
 192–3, 256, 343, 425, 482, 595
as detective story writer 283–7, 290
on determinism 116–17, 119–20,
 214–15, 242, 306
on development 223
disorganization of 363, 539–40,
 543, 545, 647
and Distributism 298, 491, 512–13,
 556–61, 565, 585, 592–3, 607,
 614, 678, 720
and Distributist League 556–8, 584,
 593–4
on divorce 372–3, 386–9, 713
on dogma 124, 148–9, 166, 253, 268,
 303, 330, 418, 426, 526–8, 558,
 587, 595, 658, 670–1
as dramatist 143, 145, 236, 250,
 341–3, 511, 583
eating habits of 606, 647
eccentricity of 96–8
as editor 374–5, 394, 397–8, 400,
 514–15, 593–4
on education 210, 268–9, 353,
 437–8, 444, 716
and electioneering 67–8, 159–60,
 290
on eloquence 47, 86, 104, 253, 680
empathy of 540–1, 579
engagement of 44–5, 51, 53
on England 377, 379, 383, 405, 613
on English history 385, 439–40
on English humour 382, 668
on English literature in
 education 89

on English religion 366, 382
on the English Revolution 238–9
on equality 382–3, 455, 457, 465
on eugenics 91, 237, 267, 269, 296,
 384, 460–5, 612, 698, 710, 714,
 721
on euphemisms 661
on euthanasia 388–9
on Evangelicals 598
on evolution and evolutionists 202,
 216, 301, 518–19, 657, 661, 664,
 710–11, 720–1
and fairy tales 46–7, 101, 210,
 217–18, 588
on the Fall 119, 246, 306, 519
on the family 153–4, 372, 387–8,
 403, 499–500, 518, 678, 698,
 713
on Fascism 659–60, 712, 715
on feminism 270, 405, 456
figure of 93–4
on *fin de siècle* Decadents 32–5,
 178–9, 187, 193, 245
at Fisher Unwin 41–2, 59–60
on France 24, 701
and Frances 121, 160–1, 198, 201
On Franciscanism 504–6
on 'free love' 268
on free will 119–20, 154, 215, 226,
 304, 418, 686, 689, 704, 711
on the French Revolution 613
on the future 266–7
generosity of 551
and *G. K.'s Weekly* 283, 490–8,
 510–15, 554–8, 592–4, 624, 627,
 641, 646, 699, 715
God, on abolition of 674
goodness of 17, 514, 726
on Gothic architecture 87, 222–3,
 241, 253, 304–5, 535
and gratitude 34–7, 56–8, 72,
 105–6, 219, 402, 481, 482, 501,
 597, 668

Chesterton, Gilbert Keith: (*cont.*)
  on Greek civilization 87–8
  and the grotesque 87–8, 113–14, 171,
    175, 178, 208, 380, 517, 521
  hard cases, on legislating from 661
  on hatred 534
  and health 258, 502
  on Heaven 729
  on heresy 505, 564, 598, 661, 708
  on Hinduism 678–9
  on historians 510, 596, 665–6, 677,
    721
  on holidays 702
  and Holy Communion 479–80, 643
  honeymoon of 77–80, 268
  on humanitarianism 105, 244–5,
    247, 347, 503, 694
  and humility 42, 85, 150–4, 175, 215,
    219, 224, 258, 272–3, 362–3,
    402, 443, 481, 582–3
  humour of 17–18, 20, 25, 108, 110,
    116, 143, 296–7, 299, 342, 362,
    374, 497, 513, 581, 644, 717, 720
  on humour 53, 88, 102, 104, 121,
    124, 133, 150, 154–5, 157, 166,
    172, 174, 176, 179–80, 207–8,
    224, 233–4, 237, 241–3, 247,
    272–3, 287, 300, 331–2, 333, 341,
    367, 417, 424–5, 454–5, 500,
    505–7, 518, 610, 614, 620–1,
    652, 667–8
  on idealists 597, 688
  and I. D. K. Club 48
  and illness 11, 720
  and *Illustrated London News* 159,
    361–2, 539–41, 593
  and imagination 84, 380, 517, 521,
    662, 683, 688
  on imperialism 61–2, 64, 72–3, 88–9,
    127–9, 131–5, 153, 201–2,
    305–6, 326, 333, 377, 595–6,
    607, 614, 695, 715
  on Impressionism 31–2, 192, 274

  inaccuracy of 112, 181–3, 545, 706
  inconsiderateness of 362–3
  on the Index 705
  on industrialism 456–7
  on infanticide 710, 713
  on intellectuals 90, 100, 104, 106,
    152–4, 165, 169–70, 175–6,
    178–9, 181, 188, 207–8, 214,
    217–18, 223–4, 271–2, 287, 301,
    306, 346–7, 383, 388, 481, 483,
    612, 670, 686, 688, 721
  on the Irish 366, 402–4, 430, 435,
    440, 452–4, 478–9, 481, 645,
    673–4
  irritability of 145, 260–1, 582, 639,
    643
  on Islam 119, 134, 209, 225, 330,
    346, 376–7, 380–1, 383, 416–18,
    519–20, 527, 529–30, 588,
    707–8
  on Jesus Christ
    anger of 229
    and Antichrist 221, 507
    Apostles of 'ordinary men' 254
    authority of 525
    crucifixion of 133, 226, 525–6
    enigma of 524
    as God incarnate 239–40
    in Gospels and Church 523–5
    humour of 229
    incarnation of 684–5, 687
    literary style of 227, 239, 525
    love of men not humanity 105
    passion of 226
    as speaker 105, 155
    stereotyped image of 227–8, 239,
      522–5, 683
    as teacher 239, 525
    tears of 229
  on Jews *see* on anti-Semitism
Job, on Book of 155, 189, 190 n.65,
    614–15
  on journalism 91, 125

as journalist 125–6, 184–5, 260, 374–5, 394, 434, 583
and joy 42–3, 201, 228, 233
on Judaism 417, 520, 530
and the Junior Debating Club 16–17, 21–3, 27, 36, 60, 145, 619
laziness of 643
on the League of Nations 696–7
as lecturer 296–7, 437–9, 441, 444, 446, 632, 639, 649, 681
as letter-writer 692, 717
and Liberalism 99, 217, 234, 280–2, 326–7, 577, 660, 678, 712
on liberal theologians and Modernists 214, 224–6, 238–9, 598, 600, 603, 708
on liberty 455, 465, 482
on limitation 8, 124, 127–9, 132, 134, 149, 154, 170, 178, 202, 210, 216, 218, 224, 253–4, 267–8, 272, 274–5, 301, 303–4, 306, 330, 347, 381, 383, 386–7, 418, 426, 462, 586–7, 597, 621, 661, 689, 705, 720
on linear prediction 144, 596, 664
as listener 111, 258
on literary criticism 172–3
on logic 119
on the Marconi scandal 320–1, 326, 370, 384, 391–2, 423, 452
on marriage 87, 91, 167, 224, 240–1, 247, 296, 373, 386–7, 499
on Marxism 305
and Mary *see* Blessed Virgin Mary
on the masses, 89–91, 100, 106, 152–3, 179, 207–9, 217, 225, 234–5, 244, 246, 254, 271–2, 367, 383, 424, 566, 612, 614, 670, 686, 688–9, 721
on materialism 155, 275, 286–7, 426, 534, 601–3, 684, 686–8
on materialists 597

memory of 99, 112, 545
on memory 8–9
on the Middle Ages 24, 87–8, 101, 124, 133, 149, 153, 170–2, 184, 367, 379–80, 385, 387, 425–6, 457, 464, 575–6, 677, 679–80
on the middle class 178, 279
on miracles 224, 227–8, 236, 286, 296
on the Missing Link 426, 439
in mock trials 620
on Modernism in literature and art 90–1, 179, 208
modernity, on pride in 677, 720
on monarchy 381
on monasticism 379–80, 387, 504–6, 524, 621, 665
and money 262–3
on monotheism 519–20, 527–8
on multiculturism 346, 424
on museums 664–5
on mysticism 119, 215, 233–4, 241–2, 244–5, 274–6, 286, 597, 615
on mythology 521
on the 'nanny state' 498–9, 516, 612, 660, 678
on nationalism 131, 595, 695, 698
on nature 117, 217–18, 502–3
on the Nazis 695–6, 698–9, 713–14
on newspapers 91
and the *New Witness* 371, 374–5, 378, 394–8, 427, 467, 471, 477, 490–4, 497–8, 593–4
and the New Witness League 389
on nihilism 187, 247, 300
as novelist 125–7, 143, 187, 237, 493
obesity of 19, 163–4, 252, 260–1, 297, 444
observation of 19–20, 99
on the Old Testament 614–15

Chesterton, Gilbert Keith: (*cont.*)

and optimism 84, 88, 102, 123, 191, 210, 219, 243, 245, 300, 339, 484, 509, 598, 615, 671–2, 685, 713

and the ordinary 503, 654, 668–9

on oriental religion 276, 278, 304

on original sin 151, 165, 214, 223, 228, 283, 518

and orthodoxy 33–4, 37, 40, 212, 222, 224, 276

on pacifism 696

on paganism 519–21, 527, 565, 712

on pantheism 119, 565

on the papacy 64, 608, 658–9

and paradox 83–4, 100–02, 113, 119, 123, 144, 148–52, 166, 169–71, 176, 179–80, 196, 207, 243–4, 247, 264, 278, 285, 287, 300–1, 304, 328, 334, 501, 520–1, 526, 533, 537–8, 590, 615, 621, 632

on parliamentary party politics 67, 135, 157–8, 280–1, 305, 320, 352, 511

past, on revocability of 266–7, 389

patience of 540

and patriotism 88–9, 129, 131–5, 219, 247, 377, 387, 417, 664

on peasants 245, 305, 307, 380, 403, 457, 533, 560, 674, 703

peerages, on sale of 281

on the penal system 280–1, 384, 462, 499, 621, 702

on pessimism 83–5, 87, 102, 191–2, 210, 219, 243, 245, 339, 484, 615, 685

on philanthropists 169–70, 208, 237

a philosophy or view of life, on inevitability of 114, 147–8, 597

as poet 68, 71–2, 127, 379

on poetry 680

and Poland 392, 568, 572, 575, 693, 696

on politicians 157, 444

on political correctness 303–4, 346

on polytheism 519, 521

and the poor 85–6, 91, 120, 168–70, 188, 234–6, 246, 286, 296, 305, 373, 380–3, 385, 388, 424–5, 533, 654, 694

on popular literature 84, 91, 207, 225–6

on the popular press 207, 254, 386

on practicality 209–10, 405, 597

on pragmatism 216

as preacher 144

on preaching 661

on Pre-Raphaelites 171

on pride 404, 481

on progress 148–9, 151–2, 223, 244, 246–7, 329, 346, 380, 388, 455–6, 518, 560, 610, 661, 664, 677–8, 721

on Prohibition 209, 242, 346, 381, 432, 435–6, 441, 450–1, 456, 516, 642, 645–6, 653, 660, 672, 698, 703, 705

on 'prohibitionism' 712–13

on property 401, 482, 678

on Protestantism 403–4, 406, 428, 695, 703, 707–9, 711–12, 713, 722

on Prussianism 351, 353, 360, 366–7, 372, 384, 393, 404, 406, 421, 444, 453, 460, 466, 527, 693, 695, 698, 713–14

on public houses 385

on public schools 382, 701

on Puritanism 241–2, 245, 303, 381, 404, 406, 599, 667, 672, 698, 701

on race 417, 421, 444, 608, 694–6, 698, 708, 713–14, 722

as reader 82, 620, 681

on reason 521, 686, 689

at Redway's 40–1
on the Reformation 381, 683
on relativism 216, 219, 221
on religion 216, 275, 405
religious background of 12–13, 562
on religious pluralism 220–1, 224,
    287, 307, 346, 519–20
on revolution 266, 301, 305, 677
on ritual 155, 253, 304, 535, 546,
    643, 665
on *Robinson Crusoe* 128, 218–19, 665
and Roman Catholicism *see also*
    Christianity 150, 152, 155,
    172–4, 226, 242
  advance of 636
  apologetics for 483–5, 561–6,
    597–603, 652, 703–4, 707–12
  balance of 669–70
  and civilization 613
  and common sense 285, 670
  complexity of 669
  conversion to 186, 220, 228, 239,
    259, 265–6, 296, 356–7, 359,
    406, 415–16, 428–31, 459,
    466–82, 487–9, 575, 707, 726–7
  and forgiveness 304
  and freedom 702–5, 712
  humour of 667
  and liberty 440
  omniscience of 489
  and reason 285–6, 380
  and saints 380
  and salvation 404
  and usury 383
on romance 103, 150, 153–4, 178,
    214, 234, 367, 588, 679, 697–8
routine of, daily 356, 539–41, 543–5
on the sacramental 601–2 *see also* on
    materialism
as 'sage' 127, 336
at St Paul's School 15–24
on saints 380, 683
on satire 102, 425, 680

and scepticism 31–2, 40, 120, 148–9,
    192, 214–16, 276, 482, 509–10,
    615, 661, 687, 694
on science 210, 426, 464,722
on scientism 426
on selections 609
selfishness of 363
on seriousness 424–5
on the 'Servile State' 324, 327–8,
    367, 383–4, 388, 499, 722
on sex 208, 268, 502, 518
sexuality of 32, 80 n.9
on Sherlock Holmes stories 287–8
and sickness 11, 720
simplicity, on cult of 104–5, 158
on simplification 418, 679
at Slade School 28–34
on slang 443
on slavery 324, 328, 456–7
and Socialism 23–4, 42–3, 61, 64,
    234–7, 245–6, 269, 272, 281,
    289, 298, 303, 307, 328, 384,
    388, 403, 491, 511, 559, 565, 577,
    585–6, 592
and *The Speaker* 23, 61–2, 66–7,
    73–4, 83, 92, 106
and Spiritualism 25–7, 205, 275–6,
    342, 565–6
on spirituality 684
on a 'spiritual world' 115–17
on the status quo 267
on sterilization 713–14
on strikes 296, 327–8, 499, 553, 576
on suburbia 91, 92 n.35, 100, 252,
    271
on the Superman 91, 152, 165, 188,
    228, 237–8, 246–7, 373, 439,
    466, 582, 664
on the 'Teutonic Theory' 694–5
on Thanksgiving Day 643
on theosophy 47–8
on things 56–7, 103, 256, 687–8
on tourism 90–1, 271–2, 306, 701

Chesterton, Gilbert Keith: (*cont.*)
  and the toy theatre 7–8, 586–8, 605
  on trade unions 380, 576, 722
  on tradition 217, 244, 267, 286
  on travel 454, 605, 664, 701
  as travel writer 416
  at University College,
    London 28–31
  at the University of Notre
    Dame 622–8, 633–40, 667
  on urbanization 271
  on usury 383
  on Utilitarianism 381, 612
  on vegetarianism 158, 245
  on Victorian literature 100, 164,
    328–41
  on the Victorians 5–6, 101, 123–4,
    329–30
  on virginity 228, 525
  on vows 387
  on war 134, 294, 403, 404, 419, 677,
    697, 713
  on weather 122, 138, 163, 273, 306,
    541, 724
  wedding of 77–8
  white horse, and symbol of 8–9, 77–8
  will, on philosophy of 216, 236
  on wit 241
  on women 270, 273–4, 636–7
  and wonder 9, 29, 34–5, 58, 84,
    88, 100, 105–6, 114, 123, 150–1,
    175, 177–8, 214, 228, 252, 268,
    274, 283, 300, 331–2, 402,
    482, 484, 517, 576, 597, 615,
    644, 662
  on World War II 692–3, 696, 698,
    720
  and Zionism 416, 419–22
WORKS:
  Alarms and Discussions 271–5, 291
  'An Alliance' 72
  All is Grist: A Book of Essays 662,
    664–6

All I Survey: A Book of Essays
    677–80
All Things Considered 206–10
'Antichrist, or the Reunion of
    Christendom: An Ode' 301–3
The Appetite of Tyranny 352–3
*Appreciations and Criticisms of the Works
    of Charles Dickens* 164,171, 174–5,
    178, 181
*As I was Saying: A Book of
    Essays* 720–2
Autobiography 1, 128, 144, 355, 480,
    482, 718
*Avowals and Denials: A Book of
    Essays* 698
'By The Babe Unborn' 35, 72
The Ballad of the White Horse 43, 279,
    290–4
'A Ballade of Suicide' 294
The Ball and the Cross 215, 264–5
The Barbarism of Berlin 352, 365
William Blake 274–6, 326
Robert Browning 109, 111–14
*The Catholic Church and
    Conversion* 561–6
Chaucer 666–71
A Chesterton Calendar 291
Christendom in Dublin 673–4
The Club of Queer Trades 143–4
William Cobbett 532–8, 586
Collected Poems 358, 361, 428, 543,
    576
*Come to Think of it . . . A Book of
    Essays* 658, 660–2
'The Convert' 475
'A Crazy Tale' 29, 41 n.7
The Crimes of England 366
'The Crystal' 205
'Culture and the Coming Peril' 576,
    632
'Of the Dangers Attending Altruism
    on the High Seas' 68–70, 77,
    163

The Defendant 62, 74, 83–9, 91
'The Diabolist' 33–4
Charles Dickens 164–84, 285, 288,
    293, 532
Divorce versus Democracy 372–3
'The Donkey' 71–2, 258
'Easter Sunday' 116
'Elegy in a Country
    Churchyard' 391
The End of the Armistice 693–8
Eugenics and Other Evils 460–6
The Everlasting Man 516–30, 597
Fancies versus Fads 498–500
Father Brown stories 137–8, 140,
    187, 282–90, 298–9, 304, 651,
    655
The Flying Inn 256, 326, 345–7, 378,
    636
Four Faultless Felons 621
St Francis of Assisi 500–8, 608
*Generally Speaking: A book of
    Essays* 595–6
G.K.C as M.C. 609–15
'O God of Earth and Altar' 301
Greybeards at Play 42, 68–71, 163, 576
Heretics 146–56, 212–13, 343
The Incredulity of Father Brown 282
The Innocence of Father Brown 282
Irish Impressions 398, 402–4
The Judgement of Dr Johnson 435, 511,
    583–4
'Lepanto' 266, 292, 294–5
Letters to an Old Garibaldian 352
Magic 342–3, 651
Manalive 35, 299–301
The Man Who knew Too Much 487
The Man who was Thursday 124–5,
    127, 186–93, 293, 614
A Miscellany of Men 303–7
The Napoleon of Notting Hill 87, 125–7,
    129–33, 141, 144, 168, 264, 293,
    452, 724
The New Jerusalem 416–21, 447

Orthodoxy 213–29, 239, 277, 526, 547,
    636, 707, 726
The Outline of Sanity 559–61
'A Picture of Tuesday' 29, 41
The Poet and the Lunatics 597
The Resurrection of Rome 550, 605, 641,
    658–60
The Return of Don Quixote 575–6, 582
The Scandal of Father Brown 282
The Secret of Father Brown 282, 284
'The Secret People' 186
George Bernard Shaw 241–8, 250
A Short History of England 379–83
*Sidelights on New London and Newer York
    and Other Essays* 671–2
Social Reform versus Birth Control 566
'A Song of Cosmopolitan
    Courage' 311–12
'The Song of Labour' 23
'A Song of Strange Drinks' 325
Robert Louis Stevenson 586–91
The Superstition of Divorce 386–9
'The Superstitions of the
    Sceptic' 509–10
Tales of the Long Bow 515–16
The Thing 597–603
St Thomas Aquinas 681–90
Tremendous Trifles 207, 252–4
Twelve Types 99–106, 586
*The Uses of Diversity; A Book of
    Essays* 424–6
*Utopia of Usurers and Other
    Essays* 383–6
'Variations of an Air: Composed on
    Having to Appear in a Pageant
    as Old King Cole' 428
The Victorian Age in Literature 114,
    328–41, 591
G. F. Watts 123–5
The Well and the Shallows 706–14
What I Saw in America 436, 454–8
*What's Wrong with the
    World* 266–70, 274

WORKS (*cont.*)
'Why I am a Catholic' 561
The Wild Knight 35–6, 42, 68, 70–2
'The Wild Knight' 72
'Wine and Water', 379
Wine, Water and Song 347, 379
Chesterton, Lilian 441, 631, 647
Chesterton (née Grosjean), Marie
3–4, 9–11, 13, 44–5, 74–5, 77–8,
205, 251, 261, 263, 373, 390, 427,
451, 468, 475–6, 676
Chesterton, Sidney 5
Chesterton, Walter 441, 631, 647
Child, Doris 81, 163–4
Chopin, Fryderyk 572
Christian Science 564
Church family 542
Churchill, Winston 142, 157, 292, 577
Claudel, Paul 646
Clemens, Cyril 549–50
Clifford, Dr 99
Coates, John D. 126 n.24
Cobbett, William 63, 328–9, 337,
366–7, 381, 532–8, 564
Coeur de Lion, Richard 409
Collins, Dorothy 2, 53 n.46, 99,
122 n.12, 183, 258, 283,
542–6, 548, 567–74, 582, 605,
607–9, 622–5, 628–9, 631–6,
646–51, 654–7, 674–6, 681,
690–1, 699–702, 718–20,
722–3
Collins, Michael 452, 659
Colvin, Sidney 109, 122
Commeline, A. S. 546
Comte, Auguste 156, 614
Comyns Carr, Arthur S. 141–2
Conrad, Joseph 59, 122, 343, 572
Constable, John 273
Correggio, Antonio 66
Cotton, Mr 40
Coulton, G. G. 509–10, 596–7, 704–6,
717–18, 727

Cox, Anthony Berkeley 615–17
Cranmer, Thomas 534, 709
Cromwell, Oliver 698
Crooks, Will 157–8
Crooks, Mrs 157–8

Dante Alighieri 23, 677
Darrow, Clarence 648
Darwin, Charles 211, 562, 692
Davidson, John 71
D'Avigdor, Digby 21
D'Avigdor, Waldo 21, 52, 96
Dawson, Lord 459
Dearmer, Percy 108, 546
Dell, Robert 139
Derrick, Thomas 512
Dickens, Charles 4, 104, 155, 164–83,
233, 241, 278, 288, 329–30,
336–8, 341, 345, 381, 425,
454, 496, 545, 550, 611–12,
666–8
Disraeli, Benjamin 385
Dmowski, Roman 571
Dolfuss, Engelbert 692
Döllinger, Johann Joseph Ignaz
von 278
Dooley, David 146 n.82
Doyle, Arthur Conan 90, 92, 287–8,
352, 591
Drinkwater, John 442
Dumas, Alexandre 103
Dunham, 'Bunny' 514–15

Eccles, Francis Yvon 62–5, 619
Elgar, Edward 348
Eliot, George 340–1, 353, 614
Eliot, T. S. 71, 184, 292–3, 591, 706
Evans, David 146 n.80

Ferdinand, Archduke Franz 351
Ffinch, Michael 30 n.114
Firmin, Annie, *see* Kidd, Annie
Fisher, St John 567

Fitzgerald, Thomas 628–9, 674
Fonseka, J. P. de 660
Ford, Ford Madox 352, 369–72
Forster, E.M. 59
Forster, John 182, 611
Foster, Sir Gregory 576
Francis of Assisi, St, 102, 479, 500–8, 682–5
Frederick the Great 693–4
Froude, J. A. 111

Galsworthy, John 352, 552–3
Gandhi, Mahatma 249
Gardiner, A. G. 93, 281, 326–7
Garnett, Edward 59
Garvin, J. L. 621
George V, King 309
Gide, André 89
Gill, Eric 567 n.75, 725
Gilson, Étienne 681–2
Gissing, George 91–2, 181–2
Gladstone, William 26
Goering, Hermann 694
Goethe, Johann Wolfgang von 333
Goodspeed, Edgar J. 628
Gore, Charles 108, 430, 546
Gosse, Edmund 109–10
Grabski, Wladyslaw 569
Gunn, James 293–4, 619

Haeckel, Ernst 115
Halford, Margaret 299, 459
Hamilton, Cosmo 642, 648
Hammond, J. L. 66, 73–4
Hamsun, Knit 89
Hardy, Thomas 90, 210, 338–9
Hayes, Patrick Joseph 636
Haynes, E. S. P. 370–2, 399
Heflin, Howell Thomas 640
Henry VIII, King 381, 387, 534, 708, 714, 727
Herod, King 693

Herodotus 50
Hill, Harold Gardiner 79 n.7
Hinsley, Arthur 724, 726–7
Hitler, Adolf 89, 91, 246, 677, 692, 694–6, 698–9, 702, 713–14, 722
Hogarth, Mary 182
Holland, Henry Scott 108, 546
Holmes, Sherlock 90
Hope, Anthony 142
Horton, Dr 260
Housman, A. E. 29–30, 122, 143, 339–40
Housman, Laurence 122, 143
Hueffer, Ford Madox *see* Ford Madox Ford
Hueffer, Francis 369
Hugill, Herbert 136
Hunt, Violet 369
Huxley, Aldous 680
Huxley, Thomas 278

Ibsen, Henrik 107, 349
Inge, W. R. 566, 580, 601–2, 632
Irving, Henry 82
Isaacs, Godfrey 307–8, 311, 313–16, 321, 324, 391–2
Isaacs, Harry 308, 311, 313
Isaacs, Mrs 317
Isaacs, Rufus, Lord Reading 308–13, 315, 317, 319, 348, 391–3, 423
Ivens-Knowles (née Ivens), Frances 79 n.7, 162 n.9

Jackson, Andrew 449
Jackson, Barry 584
Jackson, George Holbrook 136–7
Jacobs, W. W. 345, 425
James, Henry 111, 122, 195–200, 591
James, William 184, 196–8
Jerome, Jerome K. 143
Johnson, Charles and Stephen 255

Johnson, R. Brimley 55, 68, 70–1, 133
Johnson, Samuel 19, 47, 96, 205, 255,
    278–9, 493, 534, 564, 583, 609–11
Johnson, Thomas 401
Jones, Ada or 'Keith *see* Chesterton,
    Ada or 'Keith'
Joyce, Margaret 79 n.7, 162
Joynson-Hicks, William 513–14, 708
Junoy, Josep M. 553–4

Kafka, Franz 187
Keats, John 86, 463, 507
Keedick, Lee 441, 449, 624–8, 631,
    656
Keller, Helen 444–5
Kennedy, (Charles) Rann 82, 437–8,
    450, 546, 620, 642–3, 647–8
Kennedy, Edith (née Wynne-
    Matthison) 82, 437–8, 450,
    546, 642–3, 647–8
Ker, W. P. 30, 39
Kidd (née Firmin), Annie 8, 11, 44, 53,
    77, 120–1, 655, 691
Kidd, Molly 691–2
Kingsley, Charles 330
Kipling, Rudyard 53, 71–2, 134–5,
    149, 151, 247, 319, 343, 352,
    680–1
Kirk, Russell 547
Kitchener, Herbert 375–7
Knox, John 640
Knox, Ronald 16, 256, 282–3, 284,
    430, 466–72, 477, 531, 554, 595,
    617, 662, 724, 726
Kruger, Paul 62

Lane, John 122, 139, 141, 343
Lawrence, D. H. 59
Lawrence, T. E. 728
Lea, Judith 570 n.85
Leo XIII, Pope 565–6
Lever, William 323–5
Lewis, Sinclair 442–3, 642, 644–5

Lloyd George, David 74, 142, 302,
    308–10, 313–14, 318–20, 327,
    367, 374–6, 379, 391, 394, 452,
    697
Lodge, David 190 n.65
Lucas, E. V. 159, 206–7
Luther, Martin 686, 689–90, 727

Macaulay, Thomas 17, 329
Macdonald, Edward 512, 594, 718,
    720, 724
Macdonald, George 13, 210, 508–9
Mackey, Aidan 30 n.114, 122 n.12, 139
    n.56
Macmillans 639
McNabb, Vincent 430, 723, 726
Mahomet 376
Mangan, Johnnie 638
Mann, Thomas 89
Manning, Henry Edward 12, 25, 340
Mansfield, Nancy 567 n.75
Mare, Richard de la 667
Mare, Walter de la 513, 699, 723–4
Maritain, Jacques 681
Martin of Tours, St. 720
Marx, Karl 713, 722
Masefield, John 352
Mason, A. E. W. 141
Masterman, Charles 95, 122, 151,
    159–60, 263–4, 352, 365–6, 372
Masterman, Lucy 94–5, 256
Maurice, F. D. 330
Maurois, André 691
Meredith, George 50, 145, 680
Meredith, Mrs 361–2
Meynell, Alice 142–3
Meynell, Wilfrid 142–3
Mill, John Stuart 329, 533, 537
Mills, Saxon 82–3, 546
Mills, Mrs 83, 131, 163, 361, 546
Milton, John 23
Molière 88, 178
Montcalm, Louis-Joseph de 630

Moore, George 343
More, St Thomas 567
Morris, William 24, 101, 537, 564
Muhammad 330, 416–18, 669
Mussolini, Benito 549–50, 606–7,
 659–60, 694, 702–3, 715–16

Napoleon, Bonaparte 586, 718
Neale, Ralph 191
Newman, Blessed John Henry 65, 84,
 213, 223, 227, 239, 277–8,
 329–32, 334–7, 340, 353, 404,
 475, 501, 507–8, 600, 620, 689
Nicholl, Barbara 579–80
Nicholl, Clare 577–8, 580–2, 637–8,
 651–3
Nicholl, Mrs 577–9
Nietzsche, Friedrich 89–91, 104, 107,
 152–3, 211, 216, 246, 296, 301,
 346, 460, 466, 722
Noel, Conrad 77, 98, 106–8, 141, 144,
 301, 546

O'Connor, Daniel 340
O'Connor, John 26, 135–41, 162,
 204–05, 229, 240, 259–60, 262,
 265, 294, 323, 343, 355–9, 401,
 430–1, 471–5, 478, 554–6, 584,
 628, 674, 681, 718, 722, 724,
 726–8
Oddie, William 14 n.39, 30 n.114, 37
 n.133, 72, 80 n.9, 108 n.84, 124
 n.18
O'Donnell, Charles L. 622–8, 631–5,
 639, 641–2, 650, 654–7, 666–7
Oldershaw, Lucian 16–17, 22–4, 36,
 44, 55, 61–5, 67, 77, 110–01, 133,
 163, 203, 282, 500
Oldershaw, Peter 258
Orage, A. R. 234

Pater, Walter 172, 334–5
Pearson, Hesketh 497 n.16

Penn, William 662–3
Perugini, Kate 182–3
Phillimore, John Swinnerton 63–4,
 315, 474, 532
Phillimore, Walter 63, 315–16
Pierpoint, Winifred 540–1
Pilsudski, Jozef 569–71
Pius X, Pope St 352
Pius XI, Pope 607–8, 691, 727
Pius XII, Pope 727
Plato 684–5, 687
Plunkett, Joseph 452
Pocock, Dr 356
Poe, Edgar Allan 287
Pontius Pilate 525
Pope, Alexander 101–2
Pound, Ezra 609, 700
Poussin, Nicolas 39, 60
Pre-Raphaelites 564
Pugh, Edwin 398–9

Quiller-Couch, Arthur 93

Reading, Lord *see* Isaacs, Rufus
Reckitt, Maurice 714
Ricardo, Ricardo 537
Rice, Ignatius 473–5, 480, 723, 726
Richards, Grant 70
Rilke, Rainer Maria 111
Ritchie, Anne 112–13
Rivière, Freda 162–3
Rivière, Hugh 162, 352
Robertson, Graham 141–2
Rodin, Auguste 110–11
Roosevelt, Theodore 184
Roseberry, Archibald 156
Rousseau, Jean-Jacques 329, 598
Ruggles-Brice, Evelyn 474
Ruggles-Brice, Lady 474
Ruskin, John 39, 63, 66, 104, 172,
 254, 272, 330, 334–6, 340, 537,
 564
Russell, Bertrand 699, 716

Saladin 409

Samuel, Herbert 122–3, 307–12, 315, 319, 411, 415, 427

Savonarola, Girolamo 105–6, 555, 586

Sayers, Dorothy L. 617

Scannell, Kevin 682

Schopenhauer, Arthur 191, 245, 590

Schuschnigg, Kurt von 692

Schwartz, Adam 146 n.82, 190 n.65

Scopes, John 648

Scott, Mrs C. A. Dawson 553

Scott, Walter 103–4, 110, 130, 241, 329, 536–7, 564, 591, 680

Seccombe, Thomas 370

Selfridge, Harry 443

Sencourt, Robert 622–3, 627

Shackleton, Ernest 451

Shakespeare, William 134–5, 154, 233–4, 242, 367, 425, 436, 706, 718

Shaw, George Bernard 66, 89–91, 107, 110–11, 146, 149, 152, 165, 183–4, 201–03, 211, 233–8, 241–51, 266, 269, 295–8, 301, 307, 314, 323, 341–5, 348–51, 353, 355, 359–61, 375, 378, 398, 401, 434, 460, 482, 492. 495–7, 511–12, 516, 583–5, 607, 632, 663–4, 681, 699, 728

Sheed, Frank 673, 692–3, 706

Shelley, Percy Bysshe 506

Sickert, Walter 143

Sitwell, Mrs Fanny 109

Slesser, Sir Henry 546

Smith, Charles 595, 674, 723–4

Smith, F. E., Earl of Birkenhead 301–3, 312, 315–16, 531

Smith, Stevie 91

Solomon, Lawrence 19, 23, 27, 44, 299, 361, 482

Solomon, Maurice 21

Spencer, Freda 361–3, 539–40

Squire, John 510

Stalin, Joseph 246

Steinthal, Mr and Mrs 136, 140, 229, 240

Stephen, Johnston 185

Stephen, Leslie 185

Stevens, Miss 542

Stevenson, Robert Louis 11, 35, 50, 78, 90, 103, 109, 127–8, 150, 178, 241, 274, 293, 586–91, 679

Stonor, Edmund 474

Sutherland, Duchess of 142, 145

Swift, Jonathan 465

Swinburne, Algernon 17, 142–3, 184, 334–5, 427, 711

Tennyson, Alfred 142, 150, 224, 330, 340–1, 426–7

Térèse of Lisieux, St 567, 719

Terry, Ellen 82

Thackeray, William 112, 340

Thring, Herbert 344

Titterton, W. R. 375, 394, 398–400, 495, 512, 514–15, 556–7, 584, 594

Tolstoy, Leo 105, 107, 134, 264

Tonks, Henry 28

Trollope, Anthony 111

Turner, J. M. W. 273

Twain, Mark 549

Tyrrell, George 278, 296

Tyszkiewicz, Count 573–4

Undset, Sigrid 594–5

Unwin, Fisher 52, 54, 122

Velasquez, Diego 39, 60

Victoria, Queen 73

Virgil 268, 340

Voltaire 536, 554, 693–4

Waggett, Philip 279, 410–12, 415, 430, 547–8

Wain, Mildred 51, 96, 298

Walden, Howard de 349
Walker, Frederick 17, 19, 22
Walker, Thomas 479–80, 554–6, 595, 628
Walpole, Felicity 539–40, 580
Walpole, Hugh 199
Walpole, Mrs 539–40
Ward, Josephine 278, 280, 357–9
Ward, Maisie 14 n.39, 22, 29 n.111, 40 n.4, 53 n.46, 97 n.54, 278–9, 356, 415, 490, 546–8, 550–1, 556, 577 n.100, 673, 692, 706, 718
Ward, Wilfrid 277–80
Ward, W. G. 277, 279
Washington, Brooker 185
Watt, A. P. 70, 159–60, 344, 626–7
Watts, G. F. 123–5
Watts-Dunton, Theodore 142–3, 184
Waugh, Evelyn 345, 616
Webb, Sidney 200, 425, 531–2
Webb, Mrs Sidney 142, 378, 425, 577
Weitzmann, Dr 415
Wells, H. G. 91–2, 185, 196–7, 200–01, 235, 237, 314, 324–5, 343, 352, 370–2, 398–400, 418, 492, 516, 602, 699, 727

Went, H. S. D. 556
Whistler, James 31, 154, 192, 247
White, Pearl 451
Whitman, Walt 35–7, 54, 331–2, 427, 500
Wilde, Oscar 32, 192, 591
Wilhelm II, Kaiser 351
Williams, Ernest Hodder 39, 41
Wills, Gary 146 n.82
Wilson, Woodrow 394, 697
Wise, Stephen S. 698–9
Wiseman, Nicholas 340
Wolfe, James 630
Woodruff, Douglas 619–21
Wordsworth, William 268, 590–1
Wyndham, George 156–7, 278–80
Wyndham, Lady Grosvenor 279

Xavier, St Francis 23

Yeats, John Butler 46–7, 450
Yeats, W. B. 46–50, 89–90, 348, 401–2, 427
Youens, Laurence 724

Zangwill, Israel 254